MODERN AGE

D0163813

MODERN AGE

THE FIRST TWENTY-FIVE YEARS

A SELECTION

edited by
George A. Panichas

LibertyPress

INDIANAPOLIS

Liberty*Press* is a publishing imprint of Libery Fund, Inc., a foundation established to encourage study of the ideal of a society of free and responsible individuals.

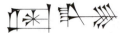

The cuneiform inscription that serves as the design motif for our endpapers is the earliest-known written appearance of the word "freedom" (*ama-gi*), or "liberty." It is taken from a clay document written about 2300 B.C. in the Sumerian city-state of Lagash.

Foreword © 1988 by George A. Panichas. All rights reserved. All inquiries should be addressed to Liberty Fund, Inc., 7440 North Shadeland Avenue, Indianapolis, IN 46250. This book was manufactured in the United States of America.

ACKNOWLEDGMENT
The publisher thanks the Intercollegiate Studies Institute, Inc. (14 S. Bryn Mawr Avenue, Bryn Mawr, PA 19010), which publishes MODERN AGE, and the author of each essay for permission to reprint the material in this volume.

Library of Congress Cataloging-in-Publication Data

Modern age, the first twenty-five years: a selection / edited by
　George A. Panichas.
　　p.　cm.
　　ISBN 0-86597-061-0.　ISBN 0-86597-062-9 (pbk.)
　　I. Panichas, George Andrew.　II. Modern age (Chicago, Ill.)
　　AC5.M712　1988　　　　　　　　　　　　　　　　88-8600
　　081—dc19　　　　　　　　　　　　　　　　　　　　CIP

10　9　8　7　6　5　4　3　2　1

To

RICHARD M. WEAVER
(1910–1963)

J. M. LALLEY
(1896–1980)

DAVID S. COLLIER
(1923–1983)

———

"One short sleep past, we wake eternally,
And death shall be no more; Death, thou shalt die."
—JOHN DONNE, *Holy Sonnets*, X

CONTENTS

II

Conservative Thinkers

III

Roots of American Order

IV

Law, Legislation, and Liberty

VII

The Anatomy of Terror

VIII

The Realm of Education

IX

Art and Criticism

Epilogue

FOREWORD

IN *The Conservative Intellectual Movement in America: Since 1945,* George H. Nash has this to say about *Modern Age*:

> . . . it immediately became the principal—indeed, the only—scholarly medium deliberately designed to publish conservative thought in the United States. . . . [It] was primarily oriented toward the traditionalist or new conservative segment of the conservative revival. . . . *Modern Age* . . . filled a desperate need . . . [as] the principal quarterly of the intellectual right.

The first issue appeared in the summer of 1957; its founding editor was Russell Kirk, the author of *The Conservative Mind,* which, since its publication in 1953, has become a classic. Henry Regnery, an independent Chicago publisher, and David S. Collier, a political scientist trained at Northwestern University, assisted Kirk. When Kirk resigned in 1959, as Nash observes, "he had established what he wanted: a dignified forum for reflective, traditionalist conservatism."

The editorial continuity of *Modern Age,* no less than the original graphic design and format, remains unbroken, despite changes in editorship. Eugene Davidson, formerly an editor and then a director of the Yale University Press, succeeded Kirk and served as editor from 1960 to 1970; in turn he was succeeded by Collier, who remained as editor until his death on November 19, 1983. The literary editors of *Modern Age* have been, successively, Richard M. Weaver (1910–1963), a professor of English at the University of Chicago and the author of the celebrated book *Ideas Have Consequences* (1948); J. M. Lalley (1896–1980), a journalist and for many years an editorial writer and book review editor for *The Washington Post*; and George A. Panichas, a moralist critic and since 1962 a professor of English at the University of Maryland. Upon Collier's death, Panichas assumed the editorship.

Bearing the subtitle "A Conservative Review," *Modern Age* was first sponsored by The Foundation for Foreign Affairs, in Chicago, which brought out the first nine issues (Volume I, number 1, Summer 1957 through Volume III, number 3,

Summer 1959). The Institute for Philosophical and Historical Studies, also in Chicago, then took over publication and brought out the next thirteen issues, up to Volume VII, number 1, Winter 1962–63, when sponsorship reverted to The Foundation for Foreign Affairs and the subtitle was changed to "A Quarterly Review." Starting with the Fall 1976 issue (Volume XX, number 4), The Intercollegiate Studies Institute, in Bryn Mawr, Pennsylvania, became the publisher.

For twenty years Chicago was the editorial base of the journal. Both Kirk and Regnery had hoped that *Modern Age* would serve as an intellectual forum for "the culture of the Middle West, and the heart of the United States generally." This hope did not materialize, for in content and outlook *Modern Age* transcended any regional identity or parochial affiliation. From the beginning, as Anthony Harrigan has observed, "*Modern Age* introduced a wider, more comprehensive intellectual tradition than existed in New York or Boston."

No statement more definitively announces the aims of *Modern Age* than does its first editorial, "Apology for a New Review." That the journal is called, in the very first sentence, "a journal of controversy" is especially pertinent, given the conditions inciting its publication, for liberal journals of opinion predominated at the time, and positions advanced by "creative sceptics in defense of the liberal temper" (as one apologist described the task of his liberal allies) identified strong tendencies in American life. That *Modern Age* was not in the mainstream of American social-political and intellectual thought points to a situation crying for the publication of "a conservative review":

By "conservative," we mean a journal dedicated to conserving the best elements in our civilization; and those best elements are in peril nowadays. We confess to a prejudice against doctrinaire radical alteration, and to a preference for the wisdom of our ancestors. Beyond this, we have no party line. Our purpose is to stimulate discussion of the great moral and social and political and economic and literary questions of the hour, and to search for means by which the legacy of our civilization may be kept safe.

As "Apology for a New Review" expresses it, "*Modern Age* intends to pursue a conservative policy for the sake of a liberal understanding." The axiological constituents of this conservative policy, in their standards of discrimination, differentiate the editorial orientation of *Modern Age* from that of other journals of opinion in America. There is a dearth of serious reading in the nation, admittedly, and therefore a serious conservative quarterly is not likely to exert great national influence or noticeably affect conditions of life and civilization. "But for all that," the editorial goes on to say, "modern society cannot endure—and its survival is immediately in question—without discussion among thinking men." These words illuminate the aspiration of "a new review" that purposes "to reach the minds of men who think of something more than the appetites of the hour," as well as "to revive the best in the old journalism and to mold it to the temper of our time."

By encouraging critical discussion of moral, social, and literary issues, *Modern Age* has unremittingly defended the idea of value as it relates to the necessity of *humanitas* and to the concept of the *honnête homme*. Virtues and values that resist a majoritarian leveling in culture and society: these are what inspire the viewpoints delineated in the journal and at the same time provide such reminding evidence of the force of truth as Paul Elmer More's contention: "We are intellectually incompetent and morally responsible: that would appear to be the last lesson of life." In registering the ramifications of More's words, *Modern Age* has exercised its conservative articles of faith on both a diagnostic and a corrective plane.

Concerned though it is with the state of American civilization, *Modern Age* is not restricted to American issues. Its perspective—generalist and universal, catholic and critical—is rooted in the larger world. And though it has also been faithful to "the idea of diversity in conservative thought," it has refused to succumb to any form of compromise bordering on the centrifugal allegiances and the imperatives of techniques that identify a mass consciousness. Its conservative principles have been absolute in their rejection of a "morality of drifting." The principles of a critical conservatism and of a "principled conservatism" that *Modern Age* seeks to preserve are planted in a fusion of moral effort and disciplinary virtues forming the bedrock of tradition, which, in Austin Warren's words, "emphasizes the shared inheritance as embodied in institutions—all organized, continuous, and more or less coherent expressions of values and ideals."

Although many of its writers are academics, *Modern Age* rejects narrow academic specializations. Its approach is interdisciplinary and transdisciplinary. The journal does not speak exclusively to or for the academy but rather to "man thinking." Indeed, even as one can discern a deepening state of social and cultural decline, one can also discern increased social and moral disarray, which many in the intellectual community have willingly tolerated, even as they have also been willing, as Wilhelm Röpke asserts, to allow "incidentals [to] recede behind the essential, the variables behind the constants, the ephemeral behind the permanent, the

fluctuating behind the durable, the fleeting moment behind the era." Disarray is a failure to locate a center of values, which in turn becomes the rejection of "paradigmatic" history, that is, of spiritual history and community. As Father Stanley Parry observes: "Civilization itself—tradition—falls out of existence when the human spirit itself becomes confused." No words could better define an initial, central concern of *Modern Age*.

In placing and evaluating the organic interconnections between the economic, the political, the philosophical, the educational, the literary, and the religious essences that embrace social and cultural qualities of existence, *Modern Age* supports the axioms of restraint and control implicit in Edmund Burke's statement: "There is no qualification for government but virtue or wisdom, actual or presumptive." But how are those two sacred concepts of virtue and wisdom, dedicated to the law of measure and the life of reverence, to be preserved when other sacred concepts, encouraging both inspiration and aspiration—loyalty, honor, nobility, honesty—have been weakened by forces hostile to the idea of value? *Modern Age* has grappled with this troubling question.

That the crisis of modernity is essentially a crisis of disorder is a phenomenon that *Modern Age* views with deep apprehension. In rejecting the presuppositions and prepossessions that instill "the faith of a liberal," the journal accepts the belief that the order of the soul is inextricably tied to order in the republic. Likewise, in going beyond political and socioeconomic arrangements of an inherently mechanico-material cast, *Modern Age* affirms metaphysical concepts and spiritual beliefs. This is not to say that it discards temporal considerations, but rather that it looks for guidance in the light of eternal values and permanent truths. With uncommon unanimity, its contributors insist that moral effort and moral conversion precede programmatic and material experiments; that principles, not possibilities, are priorities that govern the human prospect.

If no single religious viewpoint prevails either in its editorial policy or among its contributors, the Judaeo-Christian heritage has had the largest shaping influence in the perspectives enunciated in the journal. *Modern Age* exemplifies precisely the religious assumption of T. S. Eliot that "morality rests upon religious sanction, and ... the social organization of the world rests upon moral sanction." At a time that has seen an overwhelming crisis of faith, *Modern Age* has defended religious traditions, siding with the supernatural against the natural, with permanence against relativism, with the idea of cultural probity in religion against secular or pagan utopias. Clearly what can be termed a metaphysics of transcendence impels and defines the spiritual cares and the theoretical unity of the journal.

Along with the terror and revolution that are emblematic of the modern world, there are two other closely related processes that are inescapable in their consequences: the fragmentation of science through specialization and the deculturation of society. Their consequences have been anxiously monitored in *Modern Age* by writers opposed to the glorification of social egalitarianism and the diminution of the nature of man. Both the classical ideal and the biblical view, foundations of the human spirit that they are, retreat before these phenomena. The moral meaning of man, society, and history deteriorates as "enemies of the permanent things" annul the covenantal concept of existence that Eric Voegelin singles out: "Every society is burdened with the task, under its concrete conditions, of creating an order that will endow the fact of its existence with meaning in terms of ends divine and human." In essence, the mission of *Modern Age* resides in Voegelin's concept of order.

A surrender to the demands of "historical necessity," as *Modern Age* has tried to show, typifies the fate of large sectors of modern society. It further underlines retreat from the moral framework of political philosophy emphasizing what Leo Strauss calls "the character of ascent." In this connection, the anti-Marxist position of *Modern Age* has been unyielding: both Marxist politics and Marxist philosophy have been closely examined in the pages of the journal. As modern gnosticism and leftist-horizontalism have gained ground, the mission of the journal has become more urgent. And where pluralistic, pragmatic, and collectivist palliatives have tended to leaven the thinking of the American intelligentsia and political leadership, *Modern Age* has chosen to focus on the higher and ever demanding "task of intellectual and moral preparation and restoration."

Conservatism, Kirk reminds us, is a way of looking at the human condition. Such a conservatism is predicated on an equitable understanding of the relation between philosophy and practical politics, between theory and practice, between idea and reality. *Modern Age* has striven to attain this understanding; thus, what one finds in inspecting the journal as a whole is a comprehensive conservatism attuned to the total human condition. Behind its valuations lies an endemic preoccupation with the disciplines of continuity that Walter Bagehot has in mind when he declares: "The first duty of society is the preservation of society." Honoring that duty is unusually difficult in an age disposed to the doctrines of positivism, progress, reform, and much that comes under the heading of "open society." Clearly, when the scale of values and the meaning of value have been altered, the conservative's task is immeasurably complicated. The intrinsic nature of this complexity has been fully recognized in *Modern Age*.

"For a conservatism of ignorance, like a liberalism of ignorance, is a curse to society; while a conservatism of reflection is a counterbalance to a liberalism of reflection." Thus Kirk wrote back in 1955 in *Commonweal*. Two years later, with the founding of *Modern Age*, that counterbalance was to emerge as the most conspicuous goal of the journal. For its contributors the journal was to become, in Marion Montgomery's words, "a house where we gather periodically in complementary encounters." In *Modern Age* the conservative voice has been animated, as Kirk observes, by a "love of right reason" and a "desire to inform and persuade, rather than to indoctrinate in secular dogmas."

The following essays come from the pages of *Modern Age* during its first twenty-five years—1957 to 1982. In selecting the essays, I have sought to represent and chart the major ideas, themes, and problems assayed in *Modern Age*. In particular, I have sought to include essays that distinguish the genus of scholarship arising from a conservative sensibility as it evolved in the United States after World War II and as it responded, often with inquietude, to protean conditions of society and culture.

A selection in itself cannot achieve comprehensiveness, but it can capture critical discriminations. For readers who might investigate the consecutive unfolding of the subjects that *Modern Age* has confronted, a volume-by-volume examination will disclose that the journal's parts constitute a whole stamped by the critical unity that this selection endeavors to convey.

Above all, this selection seeks to show a manifold conservative outlook that goes beyond place and time to exhibit a permanence of principles. To see things in large perspective and in vital interrelationship, beyond the local and temporal, has always been a chief aim of *Modern Age*. To assess consequences, as well as to measure cause and effect, has been another aim. To impart paradigms of conservative theory and thought enabling one to become more aware of modern conservative intellect responsive to both immediate and long-range aspects of American and Western civilization has been still another aim. These aims have also guided the selection and the arrangement of the essays reprinted here.

Inevitably, one must reflect on how *Modern Age*, without an academic base, without munificent foundation grants, without popular support, and without a heavily financed visibility, has survived. Formidable privations have not deterred an entire generation of conservative scholars from speaking out on fundamental issues in *Modern Age*. That some of these issues have in more recent years received forceful national attention helps to justify the function of "a conservative review." That, also, there are now new journals that patently emulate this function accentuates the influence of *Modern Age*. It is hoped, then, that this selection shows the workings, the order and movement, of the conservative mind: its assimilative concerns and affirmations, its style and character, its critical and cultural standards, its social-political dissent and loyalties, its tradition and decorum, its veneration for universals and moral constants, its relation to the total symmetry of life—in short, its vision.

GEORGE A. PANICHAS
College Park, Maryland

EDITOR'S NOTE

EACH ESSAY IN *Modern Age: The First Twenty-Five Years* has been reprinted as it appeared in its original version. Enclosed in brackets at the end of each essay are cited the volume number in Roman numerals, the issue number (*e.g.,* Spring), the year, and the page numbers in Arabic numerals of the particular issue of *Modern Age* in which the essay first appeared.

Some slight variances in editorial style will appear from essay to essay, reflecting the decision not to tamper but to reproduce what originally appeared; points of style do change over a quarter of a century. Some corrections, of course, have been quietly incorporated when and where needed, and typographical errors have been removed. In a very few instances, ellipses indicate the omission of perfunctory transitional material within an essay.

In 1983, Earhart Foundation, in Ann Arbor, Michigan, awarded me a grant that permitted me to be released from my teaching duties in order to devote an entire academic year to the initial prepa- ration of the manuscript. I am indebted to Earhart Foundation for its help and patient confidence in my ability to complete this project in its published form.

It should not go unnoted that, in 1957, Earhart Foundation had provided an initial subvention "to publish one or more issues of *Modern Age*." Without this assistance, the journal would have been unable to embark upon its mission. In particular, the sage counsel given to *Modern Age* through the years by Richard A. Ware, now President Emeritus of Earhart Foundation, deserves thanks. I am also happy for the occasion to thank Dr. Antony T. Sullivan, Secretary of Earhart Foundation, for his kindnesses and friendly concern.

During the past ten years, the Intercollegiate Studies Institute, under the dedicated leadership of its president E. Victor Milione, has contributed both financial and moral aid to *Modern Age*. This aid has been forthcoming even when the Institute's own position and obliga-

...ions have at times been under severe economic strain. The publication of this anthology thus pays tribute to the Intercollegiate Studies Institute for its steadfast commitment to conservative scholarship. Neither the quarterly journal nor this selection would now exist without the Institute's support. Since 1979, John F. Lulves, Jr., Executive Vice President of the Intercollegiate Studies Institute, also has served as our faithful publisher.

Throughout the three years that I worked on the manuscript, I was assisted by Mary E. Slayton. There is no aspect of the manuscript and no phase of its preparation that has not had the benefit of her competence and, indeed, of her craftsmanship.

I also thank Elizabeth Dunlap, Ann Wendig and Elizabeth Manly, production editor of *Modern Age*, for their many contributions to this work.

These acknowledgments would be incomplete without an expression of deep gratitude to the "Founding Fatherhood" of *Modern Age*: to Russell Kirk, who first defined and shaped the editorial character and conscience of the journal, and to Henry Regnery, whose many generosities have helped to build the enduring principles and foundations of *Modern Age*.

For their thoughtful comments on early drafts of the foreword, I am indebted to Henry Regnery, Martha Seabrook, and William C. Dennis. Their criticisms prompted extensive and valuable changes concerning economy, orientation, and style. The foreword, it is hoped, pays tribute in its own way to all those who, whether named or unnamed, living or dead, have in any manner of word or work contributed to the continuity of *Modern Age* as "an inheritance incorruptible, and undefiled."

G.A.P.

MODERN AGE

The scholar then is unfurnished who has only literary weapons. He ought to have as many talents as he can; memory, arithmetic, practical power, manners, temper, lion-heart, are all good things, and if he has none of them he can still manage, if he have the main-mast,—if he is anything. But he must have the resource of resources, and be planted on necessity. For the sure months are bringing him to an examination-day in which nothing is remitted or excused, and for which no tutor, no book, no lectures, and almost no preparation can be of the least avail. He will have to answer certain questions, which, I must plainly tell you, cannot be staved off. For all men, all women, Time, your country, your condition, the invisible world, are the interrogators.

—RALPH WALDO EMERSON, "The Scholar" (1876)

Prologue

[1]

Apology for a New Review

WE PROPOSE TO PUBLISH a journal of controversy, *Modern Age*. For the time being, our numbers will appear quarterly; later, if your interest appears to justify more frequent publications, we may make the review monthly. This present issue is our prospectus.

More people are literate in America than in any other country; we have several times as many college graduates as we had at the beginning of this century; yet probably there is less serious reading, per head of population, than in any other great nation. Every age has its own means for informing, amusing, and governing, so that we would be naïve to expect the printed word and the journal of opinion to exert today precisely the same influence that they enjoyed during the nineteenth century.

But for all that, modern society cannot endure—and its survival is immediately in question—without discussion among thinking men. It will not do to leave the making of considered judgments, moral and social and imaginative, to radio commentators and newspaper editors, even though some men of intellectual power are to be found among them. Henry Adams remarked that the *North American Review*, under his editorship, exercised merely a trifling direct influence; but its indirect influence, because it was read by editorial-writers and men of position throughout the United States, was profound. The best medium for expressing considered judgments still is the serious journal. And by serious journal we do not mean a dull and pompous review, but rather a magazine which endeavors to reach the minds of men who think of something more than the appetites of the hour.

This is not a time in which serious reviews prosper; and of such journals as are left to us in America, the majority are professedly liberal or radical. There is room in America for many liberal and radical journals in opinion; we hope there is also room for some conservative journals. *Modern Age* intends to pursue a conservative policy for the sake of a liberal understanding.

By "conservative," we mean a journal dedicated to conserving the best elements in our civilization; and those best elements are in peril nowadays. We confess to a prejudice against doctrinaire radical alteration, and to a preference for the wisdom of our ancestors. Beyond this, we have no party line. Our purpose is to stimulate discussion of the great moral and social and political and economic and literary questions of the hour, and to search for means by which the legacy of our civilization may be kept safe.

We are not ideologists: we do not believe we have all the remedies for all the ills to which flesh is heir. With Burke, we take our stand against abstract doctrine and theoretic dogma. But, still with Burke, we are in favor of principle.

In the realm of foreign affairs especially, we believe, there is an urgent necessity for a return to principle. A considerable part of each issue of our journal will be devoted to the discussion of international questions and of American policy abroad. Foreign contributors will be welcome in our pages, and we shall endeavor to offer some intelligent account of life and thought outside America. The articles by Mr. Felix Morley, Mr. Erik von Kuehnelt-Leddihn, Mr. Béla Menczer, and Mr. J. M. Reid, in this present issue, will suggest the sort of discussion we hope to encourage. We feel that Mr. Morley's essay, in particular, may stir up a healthy controversy over the American role in this century. Our section on the work of Ortega y Gasset, including two essays of his never before published in English, is intended to bring to Americans a reminder of the importance of recent Spanish thought; and we intend to deal similarly with the work of other European philosophers and men of letters.

And we shall have space for some examination of the mind and conscience of America. Perhaps we may succeed in attracting the interest of readers abroad to American points of view inadequately presented at present. We intend particularly to emphasize humane learning in the United States: religious and ethical matters, historical problems, and the foundations of politics. Published in Chicago, our journal may also serve to represent opinion in the heart of America, and to link the Middle West and South and West with the Eastern United States and with the world overseas.

We are endeavoring to publish a journal which will make it possible for contributors to write and think as well as they possibly can. We shall not try to be popular, and we shall try not to be didactic. We shall not be afraid of the long essay, or the long review-article, or of wit. We hope to publish a few distinguished short stories, and some good verse. We shall encourage the debate and the symposium. Sometimes we may undertake a review of reviews, surveying American journalistic opinion on questions of the hour. We shall be leisurely, and we shall not always be sober-sided. We shall try not to depend solely upon "current awareness" to attract readers; we shall seek, rather, to encourage and express considered judgments more important than this week's or this month's headlines. We shall not pretend to be able to predict next fall's election or next year's revolution. We do not aim to force our editorial opinions upon our readers. Our object is not to pick quarrels, but to bring about a meeting of men's minds. Old Alfred Yule, in *The New Grub Street*, upon the prospect of founding a new critical review, growls, "How I shall scarify!" We, however, have no intention of scarifying; we think the American mind and the American heart, in this hour, require something more generous.

"The quality of civilization," Miss Freya Stark writes, "depends on the calling of things by their proper names as far as we can know them." We are going to try to call things by their right names: the essay by Mr. Wilhelmsen in this issue is a model in that endeavor. Among the articles we have scheduled for early publication are Mr. W. T. Couch's "The Word and the Rope"; Mr. Willmoore Kendall's "The Layman-Expert Dilemma"; some autobiographical pieces, commencing with Dr. Wilhelm Röpke's autobiography of a political economist; "Differences Between American and European Conservatism," by Mr. Ludwig Freund; a long critical essay by Mr. Eliseo Vivas; "Some Reflections on the Problem of Universal Style," by Mr. Rudolf Allers; "Republicans as Conservatives," by Mr. Helmut Schoeck; "Toward a Christian Approach in Judging Economic Systems," by Mr. David McCord Wright; "Matthew Arnold, the Dandy Isaiah," by the Reverend B. A. Smith; an article on rural life by Father Leo R. Ward. And there are others as good in our bank.

We shall have a symposium on American education.

This magazine needs contributors, and subscribers, and good counsel. We invite readers to send us their criticisms of this number, and we propose to publish a number of letters in each issue. We are fortunate in our board of editorial advisors, scholars who serve without payment. They are drawn from various occupations, hold various religious and ethical persuasions, and differ in their private opinions and political associations; but they share the conviction that there are elements in our American society worth conserving. Granted a kindly providence, and the support of thinking men and women, we hope to revive the best in the old journalism and to mold it to the temper of our time. With Burke, we attest the rising generation; and we think that our voices may be heard not merely by the generation that is passing, but also by the young men and women who are seeking some certitudes in this age oppressed by Dinos.

[I, Summer 1957, 2–3]

[I]

Concepts of Conservatism

[2]

Life Without Prejudice

RICHARD M. WEAVER

Richard M(alcolm) Weaver (1910–1963), whose "Life Without Prejudice" was the first article in the first issue of Modern Age, *remained closely connected with the journal until his death. His* Ideas Have Consequences (1948) *is a seminal work of conservative theory; his many articles and books assure his position as a leading figure in the history of American conservative thought. A student of John Crowe Ransom at Vanderbilt University when it dominated the Southern Agrarian school of philosophy and criticism, he later taught English for almost two decades at the University of Chicago, where he also lectured on the history of Western civilization. Synthesizing his study of rhetoric and history, and in reaction to World War II, he became a "rhetorical theorist" for whom order was of primary importance.*

WHEN ONE SETS OUT to discover how "prejudice" became a fighting word, some interesting political history comes to light. Everybody is aware that this term is no longer used in its innocent sense of "pre-judgment." It is used, instead, as a flail to beat enemies. Today the air resounds with charges of "prejudice," and the shrill note given it by the "liberals" and radicals suggests a considerable reservoir of feeling and purpose behind its invocation. This appears all the more striking when one recalls that in the controversial literature of a hundred years ago—or even of a couple of generations ago—you do not encounter the sort of waving of the bloody shirt of prejudice that greets you on all sides now. Men did not profess such indignation that other men had differing convictions and viewpoints. They rather expected to encounter these, and to argue with them as best they could. You do not find the tricky maneuvers and the air of

what might be called ultraism that we are familiar with today.

What has changed the atmosphere? I would point to the world-wide revolutionary movement which has manifested itself in almost every land. The indictment for prejudice has been one of the most potent weapons in the armory of its agents. There is need to realize what this indictment masks and how it operates, both politically and logically.

It is getting to be a bore to bring communism into every article that deals with a topic of public concern, but here the connection is so close that one finds no option. For the doctrines of Moscow are the *fons et origo* of the great pressure to eradicate "prejudice." A prime object of militant communism is to produce a general social skepticism. Not that the communists are skeptics themselves. They are the world's leading dogmatists and authoritarians. But in order to bring about

11

their dogmatic reconstruction of the world they need to produce this skepticism among the traditional believers. They need to make people question the supports of whatever social order they enjoy, to encourage a growing dissatisfaction and a feeling that they have inherited a bad article. The more subtle of them realize, no doubt, that people can be made to forget how well a system is working right under their noses if they can be allured and distracted with "pie in the sky." The communist version of pie in the sky shall be dealt with in a moment when the logical method is considered. Just now I emphasize this unfixing of faith as one of the steps in a large-scale and—it must be confessed—cunning plan. This world-wide revolutionary movement, openly conducted in some countries, operating from hiding in others, wants first of all to clear the ground.

To this end, what it knows that it must overcome is the binding element, or the cohesive force that holds a society together. For as long as this integrative power remains strong, the radical attack stands refuted and hopeless. This will explain the peculiar virulence with which communists attack those transcendental unifiers like religion, patriotism, familial relationship, and the like. It will also explain, if one penetrates the matter shrewdly, why they are so insistent upon their own programs of conformity, levelling, and de-individualization.

However paradoxical it may appear at first sight, we find when we examine actual cases that communities create a shared sentiment, a oneness, and a loyalty through selective differentiation of the persons who make them up. A society is a structure with many levels, offices, and roles, and the reason we feel grateful to the idea of society is that one man's filling his role makes it possible for another to fill his role, and so on. Because the policeman is

doing his policeman's job, the owner of the bakery can sleep well at night. Because plumbers and electricians are performing their functions, doctors and lawyers are free to perform theirs, and the reverse. This is a truistic observation, no doubt, but too little attention is given to the fact that society exists in and through its variegation and multiplicity, and when we speak of a society's "breaking down," we mean exactly a confusing of these roles, a loss of differentiation, and a consequent waning of the feeling of loyalty. Society makes possible the idea of vocation, which is the primary source of distinctions. The ceaseless campaign of the communists to make every people a mass has as its object the erasing of those distinctions which are the expression of this idea. In the communist Utopia Comrade Jones would work in the mines, and Comrade Smith would write political articles for the party organ, or perhaps he would be assigned the task of proving the non-existence of metaphysics. Their "comradeship" would be of far greater importance than their vocations, but to what end? The answer to this lies in some Messianic idea derived from the prophecies of Marx, Lenin, and Stalin.

The point is that their hostility to distinctions of all kinds as we know them in our society conceals a desire to dissolve that society altogether. And we see that practically all traditional distinctions, whether economic, moral, social, or aesthetic, are today under assault as founded on a prejudice. This shows itself in everything from the more absurd theorems of "democratic action" to the ideal of "noncompetitive education," by which teachers who ought to be on the dunce's stool themselves have been led half the distance to Moscow.

Although the aim is this general social skepticism, the communists and their helpers are sufficiently experienced in ideological warfare to know that it is often bad policy to attack everything at once. To do this may cast doubt upon your own motives and cause people to suspect that something is wrong with you. Often the best tactic is to single out some special object and concentrate your force upon this, while feigning a benevolent attitude toward the rest of the order. This enables you to appear a critic and a patriot at the same time. It is a guiltless-looking role because most of us object to and would like to reform one or more of our country's institutions, even though we have a profound attachment to it as a whole.

The difference with the communist is that this is part of a plan to discredit and do away with the whole. And this is why it is important to note the political method by which he proceeds.

He knows that if you can weaken one after another of the supporting pillars, the structure must eventually collapse. He works, then, like a termite, except that he selects and directs his effort. First things first and one thing at a time. He chooses some feature of an order where there is a potential of resentment, or he may choose some feature about which people are simply soft-headed—that is to say, confused or uncertain. It may be the existence of rich men; it may be the right to acquire and use property privately; it may be the idea of discipline and reward in education; it may be some system of preferential advancement which produces envy in the less successful. His most common maneuver, as previously suggested, is to vilify this as founded upon "prejudice." The burden of his argument usually is that since these do not have perfectly rationalized bases, they have no right to exist. You will find especially that he pours his scorn—and this seems a most important clue to his mentality—upon those things for which people have a natural (and in his sense irrational) affec-

tion. The modern communist, looking upon this world with its interesting distinctions and its prolific rewards and pleasures, may be compared to Satan peering into the Garden. Milton tells us that the arch-fiend

Saw undelighted all delight.

The more he sees people attached to their theoretically impossible happiness, the more determined he is to bring on the fall.

Just as the marshals of the communist movement have worked politically with more cleverness than many people give them credit for, so they have often been better logicians than those in the opposite camp. The fact will partly explain the sense of frustration felt by defenders of our traditional structural Western society. In their polemic use of the term "prejudice," however, they have been better logicians in the shyster's way; they have confused the other side with a boldly maintained fallacy.

The fallacy contained in the charge "prejudice," as it is usually employed to impeach somebody's judgment, has long been familiar to logicians, by whom it was given the name *argumentum ad ignorantiam*. This signifies an argument addressed to ignorance. The reason for the appellation will appear in an analysis of how the fallacy operates. Those who are guilty of the *argumentum ad ignorantiam* profess belief in something because its opposite cannot be proved, or they assert the existence of something because the something possibly may exist. It is possible that life exists on Mars; therefore life does exist on Mars. In the realm where "prejudice" is now most an issue, it normally takes a form like this: you cannot prove—by the method of statistics and quantitative measurement—that men are not equal. Therefore men are equal. You cannot prove that human beings are naturally wicked. Therefore they are naturally good, and the contrary opinion is a prejudice. You cannot prove—again by the methods of science—that one culture is higher than another. Therefore the culture of the Digger Indians is just as good as that of Muncie, Indiana, or thirteenth-century France.

Generally speaking, this type of fallacious reasoning seeks to take advantage of an opponent by confusing what is abstractly possible with what is really possible or what really exists. Expressed in another way, it would substitute what is possible in theory for that which we have some grounds, even though not decisive ones, for believing. It is possible in some abstract sense that all men are equal. But according to the Bible, Aristotle, and most considerate observers, men are not equal in natural capacity, aptitude for learning, moral education, and so on. If you can get the first belief substituted for the second, on the claim that the second cannot be proved, you have removed a "prejudice." And along with it, you have removed such perception as you have of reality.

The "pie in the sky" appeal of the communists consequently comes in this guise: you cannot prove the unworkability of the communist or statist Utopia; therefore it is workable. I say "cannot prove," although there are multitudinous evidences that it has never worked along the lines and with the motivations that are always suggested in its favor. One might indeed borrow a famous apothegm and say that all theory is for it and all experience is against it. However, since the appeal is to the dislocated, the resentful, the restless, and the malcontented, it has won its followers. We have seen how they charge the rest of us with being prejudiced in favor of the present order, or whatever feature of it they have singled out for attack. Often they manage to conceal the fallacy underlying their position by a vocabulary and a tone which intimidate the conservative into feeling ignorant.

A critical examination of their logic therefore deserves priority. But after we have seen the worst that can be said against the type of ideas which they condemn as prejudices, we ought to inquire whether such ideas are capable of positive good.

A number of years ago John Grier Hibben, a professor of logic at Princeton and later president of that university, wrote a temperate essay entitled "A Defense of Prejudice." Professor Hibben demonstrated in some detail why it is a mistake to classify all those notions which people denominate prejudices as illogical. A prejudice may be an unreasoned judgment, he pointed out, but an unreasoned judgment is not necessarily an illogical judgment. He went on to list three types of beliefs for which we cannot furnish immediate logical proof, but which may nevertheless be quite in line with truth.

First, there are those judgments whose verification has simply dropped out of memory. At one time they were reached in the same way as our "logical" conclusions, but the details of the process have simply been forgotten. It is necessary to the "economy of thought" that we retire from consciousness many of the facts that were once used to support our judgments. The judgments themselves remain as a kind of deposit of thought. They are not without foundation, though the foundation is no longer present to the mind with any particularity; and the very fact that we employ these judgments successfully from day to day is fair evidence that proof would be available if needed. The judgments are part of the learning we have assimilated in the process of developing a mind.

The second type of unreasoned judgments we hold are the opinions we adopt from others—our betters in some field of learning or experience. There is no need to labor the truth that we all appropriate such opinions on a considerable scale, and if we could not do so, books and institutions of learning would lose their utility. No man in a civilized society proves more than a small percentage of the judgments he operates on, and the more advanced or complex civilization grows, the smaller this proportion must become. If every man found it necessary to verify each judgment he proceeds on, we would all be virtual paupers in knowledge. It is well for everyone to know something concerning the *methods* of verification, but this indeed differs from having to verify all over again the hard-won and accumulated wisdom of our society. Happily there *is* such a thing as authority.

The third class of judgments in Professor Hibben's list comprises those which have subconscious origin. The material that furnishes their support does not reach the focal point of consciousness, but psychology insists upon its existence. The intuitions, innuendoes, and shadowy suggestions which combine to form our opinion about say, a character, could never be made public and formal in any convincing way. Yet only the most absurd doctrinaire would hold that they are therefore founded upon error. In some situations the mind uses a sort of oracular touchstone for testing what cannot be tested in any other way. My judgment that Mr. Blank, though a well-spoken and plausible gentleman, will one day betray his office is a conclusion I cannot afford to put aside, even though at the present moment I have no publicly verifiable facts from the space-time continuum which would prove it to another. It may be true that only those minds which are habituated to think logically can safely trust their intuitive conclusions, on the theory that the subconscious level will do its kind of work as

faithfully as the conscious does its kind. This still leaves room for what may be termed paralogical inference.

When one thinks about these well accepted and perfectly utilitarian forms of "prejudice," the objections of the rationalists seem narrow and intolerant. There is, indeed, a good deal of empirical evidence for saying that rationalistic men are more intolerant than "prejudiced" men. The latter take the position that their judgments are reasoned conclusions, and why should one swerve or deflect from what can be proved to all reasonable men? Such are often the authors of persecutions, massacres, and liquidations. The man who frankly confesses to his prejudices is usually more human and more humane. He adjusts amicably to the idea of his limitations. A limitation once admitted is a kind of monition not to try acting like something superhuman. The person who admits his prejudices, which is to say his unreasoned judgments, has a perspective on himself.

Let me instance two cases in support of this point. When H. L. Mencken wrote his brilliant series of essays on men, life, and letters, he gave them a title as illuminating as it was honest—*Prejudices*. What he meant, if such a dull addition as a gloss may be permitted with Mencken, was that these were views based on such part of experience as had passed under his observation. There was no apology because some figures were praised and others were roundly damned, and there was no canting claim to "objectivity." Mencken knew that life and action turn largely on convictions which rest upon imperfect inductions, or samplings of evidence, and he knew that feeling is often a positive factor. The result was a tonic criticism unrivalled in its time. Did his "unfairness" leave him unread and without influence? He castigates religion in many ways, and I have known churchmen who admire him and quote him. He thought nothing sillier than the vaporizing of most of our radicals, yet numbers of these looked to him as a mentor in writing and as a leader in every libertarian crusade. In brief, they found in him a *man*, whose prejudices had more of reality than the slogans and catchwords on political banners.

The same lesson, it seems to me, can be read in the career of Dr. Samuel Johnson. Johnson lives in considerable measure through the vitality of his prejudices. When he says to an interlocutor, "Sir, I perceive you are a vile Whig," you know that he is speaking from a context of reality. It is not necessary that you "agree" with him. How many people do we ever "agree" with in any unreserved sense? That he hated Whigs, Scotsmen, and Americans we accept as a sign of character; it is a kind of signature. The heartiness of his likes and dislikes constitutes an ethical proof of all he puts forward. And so it is with any formed personality. A hundred popinjays can be found to discuss brilliantly; but you will not find on every corner a man whose opinions bear a kind of witness to the man himself.

Mencken, like Johnson, is, in his more abstract political thinking, a Tory. But both men—and this is a continuation of the story—proved kind in their personal relations, and both of them were essentially modest. Upon one occasion when Boswell confessed to Johnson that he feared some things he was entering in his journal were too small, the latter advised him that nothing is too small for so small a creature as man. This is good evidence that Johnson had achieved what I referred to as perspective, which carries with it a necessary humility. And while some may be startled to hear Mencken called a modest man, I can infer nothing but a real candor and humility from those bombastic and ironical allusions to himself which

comprise much of the humor of his writings. The tone he adopted was a rhetorical instrument; he had faced his limitations.

I have given some space to these examples because I feel they show that the man of frank and strong prejudices, far from being a political and social menace and an obstacle in the path of progress, is often a benign character and a helpful citizen. The chance is far greater, furthermore, that he will be more creative than the man who can never come to more than a few gingerly held conclusions, or who thinks that all ideas should be received with equal hospitality. There is such a thing as being so broad you are flat.

Life without prejudice, were it ever to be tried, would soon reveal itself to be a life without principle. For prejudices, as we have seen earlier, are often built-in principles. They are the extract which the mind has made of experience. Try to imagine a man setting out for the day without a single prejudice. Let us suppose that he has "confessed" his prejudices in the manner of confessing sins and has decided to start next morning with a fresh mind as the sinner would start a new soul. The analogy is false. Inevitably he would be in a state of paralysis. He could not get up in the morning, or choose his necktie, or make his way to the office, or conduct his business affairs, or, to come right down to the essence of the thing, even maintain his identity. What he does in actuality is arise at his arbitrary 7:15, select the necktie which he is prejudiced in favor of, set off relatively happy with his head full of unreasoned judgments, conduct a successful day's business and return home the same man he was, with perhaps a mite or two added to his store of wisdom.

When Mark Twain wrote, "I know that I am prejudiced in this matter, but I would be ashamed of myself if I were not," he was giving a therapeutic insight into the phenomenon of prejudice. There is a kind of willful narrowness which should be called presumption and rebuked. But prejudice in the sense I have tried to outline here is often necessary to our personal rectitude, to our loyalty to our whole vision. It is time, then, for the whole matter of prejudice in relation to society and conduct to be reexamined and revalued. When this is done, it will be seen that the cry of "prejudice" which has been used to frighten so many people in recent years is often no more than caterwauling. It has a scary sound, and it has been employed by the illiberal to terrify the liberal. And since the "liberal," or the man who has not made up his mind about much of anything, is today perhaps the majority type, it has added a great deal to the world's trepidation and confusion. The conservative realizes that many orthodox positions, once abandoned in panic because they were thought to be indefensible, are quite defensible if only one gives a little thought to basic issues. Surely one of these positions is the right of an individual or a society to hold a belief which, though unreasoned, is uncontradicted. When that position is secured, we shall be in better shape to fight the battle against the forces of planned disintegration. [I, Summer 1957, 4–9]

[3]

The Restoration of Tradition

STANLEY PARRY

Stanley Parry (1918–1972), author of The Conservative Alternative *(1973), received his Ph.D. in 1953 from Yale, where he studied under Willmoore Kendall and influenced the latter's conversion to Roman Catholicism. Chairman of the Department of Political Science at Notre Dame from 1953, Parry was an active scholar in the 1950s and 1960s, publishing essays in* National Review *and* Modern Age, *editing two political science texts in the same year (1956), and contributing to one of the major conservative anthologies of the 1960s, Frank S. Meyer's* What Is Conservatism? *(1964).*

THE POSITION THIS PAPER will attempt to illustrate, if not demonstrate, is that once lost or weakened the tradition of a society can be restored only by a creative and even radical reconstruction of the tradition itself. The problem to which we address ourselves is as complex as it is profound. And clear thought about it is inhibited by the corroded vocabulary and the stylized modes of conception that distort the very formulation of the problem. In a society where the substance of tradition is already thin and unpersuasive, the term tradition is taken to indicate habitual modes of behavior normally concerned with the periphery of life, reaching at most the dignity of a campus "tradition" when they rise above the level of etiquette. More obfuscating still is the conception of tradition as the element of sameness within a world of change, so that the changing and the traditional are viewed as antithetic. To be "progressive" is to be anti-traditional. The truth is that tradition itself changes in the sense of unfolds; it

undergoes permutations; the disruption of tradition is encompassed not simply by change but by certain kinds of change. Once "bad" change eviscerates tradition, it can be brought back to life only by vigorous and even radical "good" change. To make this point we must first refurbish the idea of tradition.

First, since social change constitutes history, we must advert to the consideration that there are two kinds of history. There is the history related in books, what Voegelin[1] calls pragmatic history, or in Pieper's words (*The End of Time*, p. 22) "the empirically apprehensible element of historical reality." This type is concerned with chronology. The intellectual problem it raises is that of determining the causal relations in the unfolding of events through time. This type of history is present to man in the sense that man's current condition is always the end result of a series of prior causal acts and decisions. This type of history, it is interesting to note, is not susceptible to a "break" in

18

its continuity or an erosion of its substance. Each age is coherently related to prior ages even though the events from age to age mark the rise and fall of civilizations.

There is, however, a second type of history, spiritual history, what Voegelin calls "paradigmatic" history. It is with this type that we are concerned, for it and tradition are identical. Tradition or spiritual history also has its progressive unfolding. But this occurs in a context totally different from that of pragmatic history. For the measurement of its development is not chronology and cause but the integrity of the original compact experience of truth whose differentiation constitutes the stages of the history. In this light, let us consider the nature of tradition more closely.

For any community, tradition is nothing more than the concrete experience of truth carried distributively and in common by a multitude whom the experience unites and structures for action in pragmatic history. Tradition, therefore, is the spiritual substance that completes the distinctively human in man and constitutes the distinctively human in society. It exists as the concrete completion of human nature in a particular society. When truth is experienced within this continuum of social existence and when the experience begets a sense of communion that truth is called tradition. For above all, tradition exists as the experience of truth, as that experience has been progressively developed during the past of a people and carried forward as true to the present, where it is really experienced as true in the soul of each individual member of the community.

It follows from this approach that between tradition and community there is a real relation of identity: the community is constituted by a multitude holding the same tradition. We define society abstractly as a multitude united in pursuit of a common good. Tradition is nothing more than the concrete historical specification of the common good which is the object of common effort.

It is essential to underscore the idea that the specification is not a single *hic et nunc* determination deriving solely from contemporary and abstract speculation. For the community, as distinct from the theorists, it is a product of the experience of the truth through time. This addendum stresses the important factor that tradition is not a static force in society; it unfolds in the course of human experience revealing ever new dimensions of the basic experience of truth on which the community rests. Newman has analyzed the general process of this development in his *Development of Christian Doctrine*. Voegelin, more relevantly, has developed the concept with regard to the historical community. His theory of the "differentiation of a compact experience" admirably accounts for the phenomenon of continuity and identity within the process of social development. The problem proposed, therefore, is not one of man confronted with the tensions resulting from the contrariety between change and unvarying sameness. Such a dilemma is unreal. The real problem emerges when we regard it as the problem of the man confronted with spurious differentiations of tradition. What is a man's relation to tradition when the contemporary developments in his society replace the real experience of truth with unreal images of it? To put it in Platonic terms: What is a man to do when he finds his community returning to the cave, finds it beginning to dream?

We are confronted, therefore, with the task of distinguishing between "good" and "bad" changes in the paradigmatic history of a community. This is no small task, for social change runs a wide spectrum. It is doubtful whether any type of change is completely unrelated to the spiritual history of a people. But we can move most easily to the center of our problem by distinguishing three types. Although not mutually exclusive in themselves, they are still identifiably different in the type of response they invoke. First there is the change characteristic of any developing society, the type of change that normally involves shifts in the area of private interests of men. In economics these are common: changes from silk to nylon, from railroads to trucks. These divide the men involved into two groups according as their interests are advanced or injured. Such changes and their response are of little theoretical interest for our problem and scarcely deserve an attempt to name the responses. A second type of change reaches more deeply into the life of the community. It can be most easily identified in terms of the response it evokes, for with regard to the change itself, it normally follows from an accumulation of private interest changes. This is the type of change we call revolution, as in the term "industrial revolution." The significant thing here is that unlike the private interest response evoked by the first type of change, this type evokes a direct competition for possession of political authority. A new group rooted in the emerging economic or social forces competes with the older group rooted in the prior conditions. This change, consequently, touches upon the question of the common good in circumstances where policy changes can be achieved only by changes in the ruling class. Different conceptions of common good are involved, and so in a real sense the substance of consensus or spiritual continuity is involved. In the fortunate case, this change evokes what may be called a Whig–Tory split, the essence of which is that an adjustment of views has been reached and violent discontinuity in consensus avoided. The differ-

ence between the French and the English–American Revolution is precisely that the French never achieved a Whig–Tory adjustment. Rather, it left the community permanently divided into irreconcilable factions. It was this perception of difference that motivated Burke's efforts to distinguish the English from the French situation.

The second type of change does not necessarily involve a breach in tradition. As shown by the French experience, however, it can. And because of this, it is difficult to distinguish the French experience from the third type of change. This third type involves a change in the very structure of the community's experience of truth in history. It involves a diminution in the intensity of communally experienced truth—in consensus—and a falling out of the area of experience large segments of previously held truth. It is only in this third type of change that the liberal-conservative response is evoked. For this change is not a change from one positive position to another, but a change from order and truth to disorder and negation. The liberal-conservative division, we might observe in passing, is not of itself directly involved in a private interest conflict nor even in struggle between ruling groups. Rather it is rooted in a difference of response to the threat of social disintegration. The division is not between those who wish to preserve what they have and those who want change. Rather it is a division established by two absolutely different ways of thought with regard to man's life in society. These ways are absolutely irreconcilable because they offer two different recipes for man's redemption from chaos.[2]

The civilizational crisis, the third type of change, raises the question "what are we to do?" on the most primitive level. For the answer cannot be derived from any socially cohesive element in the disrupting community. There is no socially existential answer to the question. For the truth formerly experienced by the community no longer has existential status in the community, nor does any answer elaborated by philosophers or theoreticians. In this phase of change, no idea has social acceptance and so none has ontological status in the community. An interregnum ensues in which not men but ideas compete for existence.

If we examine the three types of change from the point of view of their internal structure we find an additional profound difference between the third and the first two, one that accounts for the notable difference between the responses they evoke. The first two types of change occur within the inward and immanent structure of the society. The first involves a simple shift of interests in the society. The second involves something deeper, but in its characteristic form focuses on a shift in policy for the community, not in the truth on which the community rests. Thus in both types attention is focused on the community itself, and its phenomenological life. The third type, however, wrenches attention from the life of action and interests in the community and focuses it on the ground of being on which the community depends for its existence. Voegelin has analyzed this experience in the case of the stable, healthy community. There the community, faced with the need to formulate policy on the level of absolute justice, can find the answer to its problem in the absolute truth which it holds as partially experienced.[3] This, however, cannot be done by a community whose very experience of truth is confused and incoherent: it has no absolute standard, and consequently cannot distinguish the absolute from the contingent. It has lost its ground of being and floats in a mist of appearances. Relativism and equality are its characteristic diseases. Pre-

cisely at the moment when it has lost its vision the mind of the community turns out from itself in a search for the ontological standard whereby it can measure itself. For paradigmatic history "breaks" rather than unfolds precisely when the movement is from order to disorder, and not from one order to a new order. The liberal–conservative split, to define it further, derives from a basic difference concerning the existential status of standard sought and about the spiritual experience that leads to its identification.

When disruptive change has penetrated to the third level of social order, the process of disruption rapidly reaches a point of no return. Indeed, it is probable that this point is reached the moment the third level of change begins. At that point we reach the "closed" historical situation: the situation in which man is no longer free to return to a *status quo ante*. At that point men become aware of the mystery of history called variously "fate," or "destiny," or "providence," and feel themselves caught helplessly in the writhing of a disrupted society. The reasons for this experience are rooted in the metaphysical characteristics of such a change.

Of all forms of being, society, or community, has the greatest element of determinability. Its ontological status is itself most tenuous because apart from individual men, who are its "matter," tradition, the "form" of society, exists only as a shared perception of truth. The ontological status of society thus is constituted by the psychological-intellectual-volitional status of society's members. The content of that psychological status determines, ultimately, the content of civilization. Those social, civilizational factors not rooted in the human spirit of the group ultimately cease to exist. Civilization itself—tradition—falls out of existence when the human spirit itself becomes confused. Civilization is what man has made of himself. Its massive contours are rooted in the simple need of man, since he is always incomplete, to complete himself.

It is not enough for man to be an ontological "esse." He needs existential completion, he needs, that is, to move in the direction of completion. And the direction of that movement is determined by his perception of the truth about himself. He must, consequently, exist as a self-perceived substantive, developing agent, or he does not exist as man. Thus, it is no mystical intuition, but an analyzable conception to say that man and his tradition can "fall out of existence." This happens at the moment man loses the perception of moral substance in himself, of a nature that, in Maritain's words, is perceived as a "locus of intelligible necessities."[4] An existentialist is a man who perceives himself only as "esse," as existence without substance.

Thus human perception and human volition is the immanent cause of all social change and this most truly when the change reaches the civilizational level. Thus with regard to the loss of tradition, in the change from order to disorder the metaphysics of change works itself out as a disruption of the individual soul, a change in which man continues as an objective ontological existent, but no longer as a man.

Further, change is a form of motion, it occurs as the act of a being in potency insofar as it is in potency and has not yet reached the terminus of the change. With regard to the change we are examining, the question is, at what point does the change become irreversible? A number of considerations suggest that this occurs early in the process. Change involves the displacement of form. This means that the inception of change itself can begin only when the factors conducive to change have already become more powerful than those anchoring the existent form in being.

If the existent form is to be retained new factors that reinforce it must be introduced into the situation. In the case of social decay, form is displaced simply by the process of dissolution with no form at the terminus of the process. Now in the mere fact of the beginning of such displacement we have prima-facie evidence of the ontological weakness of the fading form. And when we consider the tenuous hold tradition has on existence, any weakening of that hold constitutes a crisis of existence. The retention of a tradition confronted with such a crisis necessitates the introduction of new spiritual forces into the situation. However, the crisis occurs precisely as a weakening of spiritual forces. It would seem, therefore, that in a civilizational crisis man cannot save himself. The emergence of the crisis itself would seem to constitute a warranty for the victory of disorder. And it would seem that history is a witness to this truth.

As a further characterization of the liberal–conservative split we may observe that it involves differences in the formula for escaping inevitabilities in history. These differences, in turn, derive from prior differences concerning the friendly or hostile character of change.

Unanalyzed Responses

Anxiety and deep insecurity are the characteristic responses evoked by the crisis in tradition. To experience them, it is not necessary for a people to be actively aware of what is happening to it. The process of erosion need only undermine the tradition and a series of consequences begin unfolding within the individual, while in institutions a quiet but deep transformation of processes occurs. Within the individual the reaction has been called various names, all, however, pointing to the same basic experience. Weil identifies it as being "rootless,"[5] Guardini as being "placeless,"[6] Riesman as being "lonely."[7] Others call it "alienation,"[8] and mean by that no simple economic experience (as Marx does) but a deep spiritual sense of dislocation. Within institutions there is a marked decline of the process of persuasion and the substitution of a force-fear process which masquerades as the earlier one of persuasion.[9] We note the use of rhetoric as a weapon, the manipulation of the masses by propaganda, the "mobilization" of effort and resources.

Within this context of spontaneous and unanalyzed responses to the experience of civilizational crisis, two basic organizations of response are observable: reaction and ideological progressivism. These responses are explicable in terms of characteristics inherent in the crisis. Both are predictably destined to fail.

The response of reaction is dominated by a concern for what is vanishing. Its essence lies in its attempt to recover previous order through the repression of disruptive forces. To this end political authority is called upon to exercise its negative and coercive powers. The implicit assumption of this response is that history is reversible. Seemingly, order is perceived as a kind of subsistent entity now covered by adventitious accretions. The problem is to remove the accretions and thereby uncover the order that was always there. Such a response, of course, misses the point that in crisis order is going out of existence. Moreover its posture of stubborn but simple resistance is doomed to failure because of the metaphysical weakness of the existent form of order, once the activation of change has reached visible proportions. The most reaction can achieve is stasis, and a stasis that can be maintained only by the expenditure of an effort which ultimately exhausts itself.

Despite the hopelessness of the response, it is explicable in terms of the crisis of tradition itself. Since a civilizational crisis involves also a crisis in private interests and in the ruling class, reaction is normally found among those who feel themselves to be among the ruling class. Their great error is to mingle the responses typical of each of the three types of change. Since civilizational change is the most difficult to perceive and analyze, it seldom is given adequate attention. And the anxiety it generates is misinterpreted as anxiety over private interest and threatened social status.

The basic truth in the reactionary response is to be found in its realistic assumption of the primacy of the real over the ideational. But this truth is distorted by its extreme application: the assumption of the separate existence of tradition. The reactionary misses the point that tradition exists ontologically only in the form of psychological-intellectual relations. Reactionary theories, for this reason, usually assume some form of organismic theory. In its defensive formulations, the theory will attack conscious change on the grounds of the independent existence of the community. In its dynamic form, it visualizes the community as the embodiment of an ontological force—the race, for instance, which unfolds in history. In both cases the individual tends to be treated as an instrument of the organic reality.

When the reactionary response is thus bolstered by an intellectual defense, the characteristics of that defense are explicable only in terms of the basic attitudes of unanalyzed reaction. Reaction is rooted in a perception of tradition as a whole. It is a total situation that is defended: the "good old days." There is no selectivity; even the questionable features of the past are defended. The point is that the reactionary, for whatever motive, perceives himself to have been part or a partner of something that extended beyond himself, something which, consequently, he was not able to accept or reject on the basis of subjective preference. The reactionary is confused about the existential status of a decaying tradition, but he does perceive the unity tradition had when it was healthy.

The second unanalyzed response to civilizational crisis we call ideological progressivism.[10] With regard to the civilizational crisis itself, the ideological mind interprets the social disruption as a good. What the reactionary calls chaos, the ideologist calls the "open society," interpreting it as a victory for individual freedom. What the reactionary calls loss of order, the ideologist calls the disappearance of old evils, the beginning of a new rationality. The ideological progressive connives with the erosion of tradition in the name of progress. His characteristic orientation is toward the future where he discerns a new order that man will create for himself. The ideological progressive, therefore, proposes a conception of progress that involves an existential discontinuity; progress without organic evolution.

The fact of discontinuity is frequently overlooked because the order of the future is validated as the order men have always striven for. Yet the discontinuity is not only present but derives from the basic orientation of the ideologist toward social reality. Civilizational crisis, it must be remembered, is constituted by a unique type of change: existing form is not displaced by emerging form, but by emerging formlessness; the change is from order to disorder. Since the ideological mind, insofar as it seeks social order, looks to the present and the future, it finds only an ontological void. It is a matter of attitude rather than science that this void, constituted by the disruption of interpersonal relations among men, is interpreted as the good of freedom. But given the void and the attitude, the ideologist cannot conceive of himself as co-operating with an objective evolution of form. His commitment to the process of becoming consequently involves commitment not to reality but to ideas. The becoming central to his attention is a process whereby mind informs reality, a process that involves the movement from the abstract and the ideational to the real. The ideologist thinks in terms of creative action, informing action, not in terms of cooperation with an objectively emerging form. What "ought to be" is achieved by a break in being, not by an evolution of being.

The true discontinuity occurs, moreover, in the content of what "ought to be." For when tradition begins to "fall out of existence," the essence of the "fall" lies in the withdrawal of ideas from the concrete historical integration called society into the isolation of an ideational existence in the minds of unrelated individuals. Thus the ontological disruption of society is concealed by the perdurance of ideas in the minds of men. But even here in the realm of thought there is a further discontinuity. For in their movement from the real to the ideational, the substantive ideas undergo a sea change, a metamorphosis of meaning. When the ideas had ontological status in historical society their meaning was determined by their position as part of a complex of ideas polarized into a world view. In their ideational existence they become merely the debris of the earlier tradition and their meaning changes, for the ideas lose their coherence. They become individual absolutes. Where they once were the form of the society, they now become the goals of creative action.

In pursuit of these goals, the ideologist, like the reactionary, depends on political authority in its coercive form. The end of authority, however, is not to repress change, to recover form, but to create and impose form. Government thus is conceived of as having a creative role among men. And its action is validated by the goals which, in seeking to realize, it represents. The claim is that the new order is what the people want. Therefore, by the principle of consent, the government, in imposing order, represents the people who are the recipients of that order. Involved in this way of thinking is a profound confusion concerning the ontological status of ideas. The people, unformed because they need to be informed, are considered the source of the form to be imposed. This way of thinking, of course, can be sustained only by virtue of a confusion between the ideational and the real. However, once the confusion is achieved, the ideas which are the prototype of the new societal form may be imposed politically without prior debate in the democratic process. Nor need they be sustained by theoretical argumentation. For they are, as the Declaration of Independence tells us, self-evident. Those who oppose them are obviously corrupt and can be handled only by coercive repression. Thus by a curious development, the proponents of the open society become the champions of the closed idea. The chief evidence for this development may be found in the substitution of propaganda for discussion in the *conversatio civilis*. Men become the matter to be informed. It is claimed that they want to receive the form possessed by the ideological mind. Propaganda, which imposes forms in the human intellect without the process of persuasion, becomes a kind of divine praeveniant action whereby the ideologists enable men to act freely.

Thus the essence of the ideological progressive response is to be found in the primacy of mind over reality and in a utilitarian test of truth. Both these premises necessarily follow from the ideological conception of the problem of order. The ideologist finds himself with a set of ideas that seemingly by their very essence call for ontological existence among men. In this posture there is no *universale in rem*, for social reality is "open." Nor is there a *universale post rem*, for the idea in the mind was not derived from reality but acquired by virtue of the transubstantiation of ideas during their depolarization. There is only a *universale ante rem*: the ideas that exist in the ideologist's mind as the unmeasured measure of reality. From this it follows that the only standard of truth in human action can be that of the utility of the action for implementing the model ideas. If something is necessary, it is legitimate by that very fact. This standard is not applied universally. Where the central model ideas are not involved the ordinary standards of morality are retained. But when they are involved, the model in its capacity as ultimate standard becomes the source of a new morality.

Thus both unanalyzed responses come to the same general authoritative conclusion by different routes, one by demanding submission to an ontological necessity, the other to a self-imposing ideational entity. Both, moreover, feel in a blind, groping fashion for something to assuage the deep anxiety evoked by civilizational crisis.

Analyzed Partial Responses

Two other responses to crisis can be identified: economic individualism and spiritual individualism. Here we can give only a simplified characterization of each position.[11] For unlike the unanalyzed responses, these are based on a conscious and thoughtful analysis of social problems. Consequently, the proponents of each position vary, and sometimes notably, in the particular development of their ideas. They all have certain features in common, however, which distinguish them from reactionary and ideological thought.

Both define problems that are real in contemporary society. Both are rooted in individualistic premises. However, they also have a defect in common. In selecting problems for definition they both focus on social conditions evoked by the un-analyzed responses to disruption. Thus they are conscious responses to blind response. To be sure they rightly analyze basic consequences of reactionary and collectivistic policy. They propose remedies for these, remedies, let it be added, that must be involved in a total remedy. But, because they miss the crucial issue in the crisis, when accepted as adequate responses, they permit the crisis in paradigmatic history to gain momentum. We call them partial to stress the contention that they neither confront nor respond to the central problem of civilizational crisis.

Economic individualism is rooted in a radical call for the liberation of individual energy. Its concern is not so much for economics as it is for freedom.[12] One of its root propositions is that economic freedom—private property and a free market—are essential prerequisites for human freedom. Following on this, its second root proposition is that social reconstruction is possible only given the intelligent and spontaneous action of vigorous individuals. The argumentation in support of these propositions is varied, erudite, and persuasive. In its most thoughtful formulations it is enhanced by a theory of social order that gives the position a positive character. Nevertheless the position is motivated by opposition to the collectivism that results from unanalyzed responses. In its essence it is ordered to breaking down the massive legal and bureaucratic controls that substitute for the missing order inherent in healthy and integrated societies. As its crucial point, however, it relies on freedom to produce basic societal order. We hold exactly the opposite to be true. Given fundamental

order, freedom is the source of the variegated fullness of life that constitutes high civilization, but freedom itself is a product of a prior substantial order. A civilizational crisis is not a crisis about human freedom but about human order. The collectivism of blind response sometimes conceals this basic factor.

Therefore, despite the nobility of the appeal to liberty, to courage, the conclusion is inescapable that this position does not appreciate the nature of the spiritual crisis we face. Man cannot bear to be insecure about his own existence as man. When insecurity touches the very meaning of his existence he abandons all else in an attempt to recover the roots of that existence. If the attempt is enlightened he has hope of success, if it is unenlightened, then it becomes frantic and blind. But enlightened or not, this search takes priority over all else. Not even liberty has meaning when meaning threatens to drain out of human life entirely. Therefore, to approach the problem of paradigmatic crisis as though it were a crisis about liberty gravely misinterprets the problem.

It is clear that a true response to crisis is less likely, and, if discovered, will be less able to win general acceptance in proportion as unanalyzed responses pre-empt social policy. Consequently, the challenge to collectivism contained in economic individualism is a necessary preliminary to the development of a total response to crisis. But of itself economic individualism offers no such total response to the threat of anxiety. If accepted as adequate, therefore, there is a danger that the truth to be found in the position may be lost. For if, in the crisis of meaning, liberty is defended on inadequate grounds, there is danger that the true defense of liberty will be compromised.

Spiritual individualism seems, at first glance, to differ radically from the position of economic individualism. The issue between the two centers around the nature of the problem of liberty. The spiritual interpretation argues that the issue of the spirit of man is prior to that of his economic condition. Between the two there is a grave division on the issue whether a human freedom rooted solely in economic freedom can solve any problems. The spiritual position insists that freedom enables problems to be solved only when the free man is also virtuous. The economic position does not say virtue is not necessary. But it does not cope directly with the issue, being satisfied to rest in the faith that men, if left alone, will solve the problem of order.

But if the position of spiritual individualism is examined closely, it becomes apparent that it formulates its problem in much the same way as economic individualism. The difference is to be found in the objective situation on which each focuses its attention. Spiritual individualism is preoccupied with the "objectification" of society. By that is meant, the position is acutely aware of the increasingly nonhuman character of the relations among men, of the predominance of things in human relations including economic things. Now this awareness is precisely a critical awareness of the substitution of legal for human relations, and the displacement of a government of men by an administration of things. And this awareness of the social fact is dramatically intensified by the realization that the most influential policy preferences tend to increase the "dehumanization of societal relations." By doing so, they further reduce the distinctly human element in man, contribute to his "falling out of existence." This in turn reduces man's capacity for freedom. In response to these insights, the spiritual individualist formulates his solutions in terms of the defense of freedom against the objectification of society. In this defense of freedom

he rejects the contemporary society, because of its ontological inadequacy as a human system. Along with this, however, he frequently rejects also the idea that society is a necessary context for human life. Consequently, the spiritual individualist neglects the problem of right social order and in doing so, neglects the central problem of civilizational crisis. The spiritual individualist tends to suspect society as the villain of the piece. And solutions are sought finally in the realm of the individual's return to truth by paths sometimes solitary and stern.

Both analyzed partial responses follow the same method in formulating the problem of crisis: an examination of the objective condition of man, followed by the defense of some aspect of man from the dehumanizing processes emerging from the loss of societal coherence. This sameness of method leads us to the ultimate similarity in both positions, their individualism. Neither position will commit itself, as a position, on questions of substantive truth. Neither, consequently, will commit themselves to the restoration of tradition. Both defend only process truth about man, his need for freedom. For both fear that an assertion of substantive truth would become the occasion for further political control over man in the name of that truth. This fear, seemingly, arises from the policy oriented point of view from which both positions develop. While neglecting the problem of society as an ordered whole, both positions seek to discover the policies society should adopt to solve its problems. Since the objective societal situation is characterized by a progressive loss of truth, these policies can only be identified as procedures, and the basic value can only be liberty which is the mode of action, not its substance. The consequences of this preoccupation with policy suggests that the real issue in a civilizational crisis is not political at all but meta-political. We can learn from these positions their explicit teaching, that state action can only hinder problem solving. For totalitarian rule inevitably follows when a disrupted society attempts to reconstruct itself by political means. It follows, that is, if the crisis occurs on the level of substantive meaning itself.

The refusal to consider the issue of substantive truth, then, follows from a difference of interpretation on the issue of the nature of the crisis. But this difference in turn, is rooted, (at least in the two positions now under discussion) in an ultimate premise common to both, individualism. Let us immediately specify that neither position is rooted in philosophical individualism. Both of them have taken their positions in response to the collectivism that follows upon the blind attempt of an evading society to pull itself together. Nevertheless, this response makes it inevitable that the problem of civilizational crisis as described in our opening pages will be rejected as the basis of a search for solutions. For, as the interpretation offered there implicitly suggests, the real problem in the restoration of tradition is precisely that of recovering the social experience of truth. Freedom follows on this, it does not precede it.

The Prophetic Response

The true response to the civilizational crisis of our day has not yet been elaborated. The work of identifying the substantive elements in a restoration of tradition has only just begun. And this work cannot be completed in a short essay. My purpose is simply to point a finger toward the truth in this matter. Fortunately the crisis in our age is not unique in Western history, at least as regards its form. At least twice before in that history the unfolding of tradition has reached periods

of crisis. And the crisis in each case has evoked a response that seemed to be adequate: the response of Plato to the collapse of the Greek City State, and the response of Augustine to the collapse of the Roman Empire. Behind both these responses there stands as a model and paradigm, the response of the Israelitic Prophets to the crises of Jewish life under God. Therefore, we borrow from Voegelin the term, and we hope the meaning, "Prophetic Response." From these precedents we cannot, it is true, discover the substantive content of an adequate response to our own crisis. But we can, by studying previous crises and responses discover the nature and form of both crisis and response. For in each crisis the form of the response is dictated by the general nature of the problem while the substantive content is dictated by the content of the threatened tradition and the experience of losing that tradition.

Since the erosion of tradition consists in its "falling out" of social existence, the true and adequate response to the crisis must be found in the attempt to restore tradition to its ontological status as the form of society. From our opening analysis of crisis, it is clear that such restoration can be achieved only through a corporate re-experience of the tradition, a re-experiencing, that is, which begets that agreement which turns a multitude into a society. The defects of the reactionary response make it clear that this cannot be achieved by a return to a *status quo ante*. The excesses of ideology stress the need for a reintegration of truth within the context of social experience. For the restoration of tradition involves the reconstruction of community, but this can be achieved only by the communal experience of truth. In this context, the essence of the prophetic response lies in its attempt to evoke a common awareness of a truth that had been lost. In a real sense the prophet calls truth from the limbo of memory back into the dynamism of knowledge and re-establishes it as the form of interpersonal union.

This return of truth to social existence is complicated by one basic factor. The truth to which men return cannot be the identical truth that was lost. As innocence once lost cannot be regained but must be replaced by virtue, so truth once lost can only be regained in a new and more sophisticated version. The newness in this case will be found in the character of the polarization, the integration, through which individual truths are experienced as the truth about man. When paradigmatic history breaks down all that is left socially is the experience of the breakdown itself. The social reconstruction must begin with this experience, and, under the guidance of the prophet, build up again its experience of truth. The prophet is that man or men in whose souls the order of the society has survived, but survived in a critically purified manner due to the challenge of its social decay.

The first stage in the re-integration of truth shattered by civilizational crisis demands criticism. Two stages of critical thought can be identified. The first centers upon an examination of the unacceptable responses described earlier. From this we learn that the proper response must be meta-political, for truth cannot be given ontological status in society by sheer command. We learn also, from the partial responses, that the problem is social rather than individual, and so cannot be solved by withdrawal from society. The second critical stage centers upon a totally different object: the distorted society itself in its condition of decay. What was wrong with that society? What weakness or imbalance in its integration was responsible for its disruption? No society is perfect. Every one has the seeds of its own destruction planted in its way of life.

When these grow to the point where they cause disruption, thoughtful men become aware of them. Such awareness is not easy to achieve because it involves not only self-awareness but, in addition, a grasp of the relation of the defective principle to the general integration of the socially held truth. The problem here is to level the profoundest sort of criticism against the corrupting principle without rejecting the rest of the tradition. For the principle in which dissolution originates is itself part of the tradition.

Granted the critical operation, one finds himself at that stage faced, at least intellectually, with a completely dismantled tradition. The ontological collapse of the tradition leaves its component ideas scattered through the multitude without social existence. The intellectual critique results in a further theoretical disturbance of the integration. For the polarization of ideas into a coherent unity is destroyed by the subtraction of even one basic element. And at this point the prophetic response is confronted with the task of discovering the new principle on the basis of which the old truths may once again come together to give a coherent and persuasive account of the order proper to man.

The order sought at this point is not the order of politics, but the order of society. Between this order and the order appropriate to the inner life of each individual there can be no difference. For the order of society comes into existence precisely when a multitude agrees about the hierarchic structure of the goods proper to human life. Social order is nothing more than the extension into the area of interpersonal relations of the order present to or desired by the individual members of a multitude. The attempt to reconstruct a community, therefore, necessarily involves the attempt to reconstruct man.

This relation between inner and social life determines the strategy of reconstruction. The new order, derived from a new integration of a truth must above all be persuasive. The basis for its persuasive quality must be found in its appeal to the truths still recognized by the individual although no longer enjoying social status due to their depolarization. What is sought is the description of a new way of life that presents itself to the multitude as a way superior to the old, but a way that achieves its superiority through reform and critical purification rather than through creative innovation.

The idea of reform leads us to the final characteristic of the prophetic response. Reform is a temporal concept: it involves the idea of good change within a continuum of historical experience. And this is precisely what is sought objectively once a break in paradigmatic history occurs. The experience of a break must be experienced ultimately as an enlightenment if the break is to be repaired. But since the break is basically irreparable, the prophetic response must ultimately express itself as a new interpretation of history itself in which the break, the dissolution, becomes part of a larger pattern of purpose. All human order is essentially the organization of purpose in human life. Imperfect man is cursed with an ontological inability to rest and enjoy himself in his earthly existence, for whatever the goods a man may possess, the good is not yet his.[13] Life in time, therefore, has meaning only when man experiences an ordering of action which promises movement toward this good. Every socially persuasive way of life, therefore, must express itself as a philosophy of history in which each individual in the society is ordered to the achievement of a good in which he can rest. The theories of progress so characteristic of ideological thought are rooted in a basic hopelessness

with regard to this ultimate good. To each generation they offer, not personal achievement, but submission to a collectivity. And they find their response in man's desperate need to achieve significance through union, if not union with the ultimate good, at least union with destiny. And they call upon man to empty himself since he cannot achieve fulfillment. Against this, the truly prophetic response must see the loss and recovery of meaning in life to be part of the historical experience through which men perceive new and more brilliant facets of that good which is the good for man.

NOTES

[1] Those familiar with Eric Voegelin's work will recognize that my indebtedness to him is so pervasive that, to avoid a clutter of footnotes, I simply note the fact at this first explicit citation. I have drawn chiefly on his *New Science of Politics* (Univ. of Chicago Press, 1952), and his three volumes, *Order and History* (Louisiana State Univ. Press, 1956–57).

[2] The liberal-conservative division according to this interpretation has occurred not more than four and most probably three times in Western history; at the collapse of Greek City-State order, at the collapse of the Roman order, and in contemporary times. Whether or not the 16th–17th century saw the same division is debatable.

[3] E. Voegelin, *Order and History*, Vol. II, "The World of the Polis," pp. 243–253.

[4] Maritain, *Man and the State* (Univ. of Chicago Press, 1951), p. 86.

[5] S. Weil, *The Need For Roots* (1952).

[6] R. Guardini, *The End of the Modern World* (1956).

[7] D. Riesman, *The Lonely Crowd* (1953).

[8] J. Ortega y Gasset, *The Revolt of the Masses* (1932).

[9] Richard Weaver in *The Ethics of Rhetoric* studies this phenomenon. Cf. also Voegelin's analysis of the Gorgias, *Order and History*, Vol. III, 24 ff.

[10] In this analysis, in addition to Voegelin, I owe a debt to a brilliant essay by William Oliver Martin, *Metaphysics and Ideology* (Marquette Univ. Press, 1959). The vast majority of books on "policy" are examples of this position.

[11] The writings in these responses, because reflective, vary a good deal from man to man. Since I treat the position selectively here, I would not care to identify particular writers.

[12] Therefore I include here only those writers with a philosophical concern for the problem. The pure economist of the classical tradition is concerned with a different problem.

[13] I have restricted the discussion to the restoration of tradition to its world immanent aspects. One must at least note that there are other aspects equally important. [V, Spring 1961, 125–138]

[4]

Cogitations in a Roman Theatre

JOHN DOS PASSOS

John Dos Passos (1896–1970) was an American novelist best known for his massive trilogy, U.S.A. *(1930–1936; 1938) and for his experimentation with such narrative devices as the "camera eye" and the "newsreel" technique. Among a group of Harvard writers who were graduated just prior to World War I, Dos Passos and e. e. cummings, served in the Norton-Harjes Ambulance Service, along with Ernest Hemingway, during the war. As a newspaperman and free-lance author, his social and political views became increasingly conservative in the years following World War II. At the time this essay was first published in* Modern Age, *he was speaking in Rome under the auspices of the Incontro Romano della Cultura.*

IT WAS EXCITING to speak in Rome, where I read the original version of this paper in a tiny theatre a stone's throw from the column of the Antonines. Exciting but also sobering. In Rome, more than any other city in the world, one feels the weight of history. Crushing and exhilarating, history stands manifest at every streetcorner. Man can, I think, be most aptly described as an institution-building animal. At least during the few thousand years that we know anything very definite about his activities the building of institutions seems to have been his chief concern. Rome has been the pivot and hub of some of the most awesome and majestic institutions men have ever constructed. The very name connotes empire.

These connotations are particularly sobering to an American. We Americans were brought up to believe that history didn't exist. For a number of generations we thought the Declaration of Independence had repealed history. During the last fifty years the American people have gone through a painful and costly education in the realities of history. As a nation perhaps we haven't made as much progress as we might have in our education, but as individuals, here and there, a few of us may be learning.

One of the teachings of history is that whole nations and tribes of men can be crushed under the imperial weight of institutions of their own devising. History further teaches that, through all sorts of terrors and despotisms, a divine something in the human spirit has managed to keep alive and to leaven and permeate the institutions that channel men's destinies.

The working of that divine leaven is what I mean by civilization. Civilization in the abstract remains one of man's eternal aims; but civilizations, in the concrete, are subject to growth and decay, like living organisms. We are here today, I said, to exchange ideas about what can be done to defend our own peculiar type of Western Christian civilization against its own decay, and against the inroads of brutal and arbitrary institutions that grew out of the national and ideological wars that have devastated the century we live in.

It would seem a staggering assignment if it weren't one of the laws of human behavior, well expressed in Toynbee's useful catchword, that it takes challenge to provoke response.

It is my belief that at last Western civilization is beginning to show response to the challenge of the monolithic Communist state that allows no liberties at all and of its corollary, the bureaucratic socialist state, where a few loopholes of freedom still survive. We can call one type the illfare state and the other the welfare state. Young people throughout the Western world and even under the Communist regimes are beginning to question the socialist slogans. Our problem today is to ask what can a few scattered men of letters do to cherish and stimulate that response.

Before we go any further I think we need to examine our own capabilities somewhat searchingly. How well are we equipped to cope with this titanic assignment?

SOMEWHERE IN THE MIDDLE twenties a Frenchman named Julien Benda wrote a book called *La Trahison des Clercs* that made a great impression on me. As I look back on it, it was a somewhat superficial work, but its title summed up for me my disillusion with most of the men of letters I had considered great figures in my youth. This was during the period of the war of 1914–18. I was studying at Harvard up to the spring of 1916 and followed with growing astonishment the process by which the professors, most of them ra-

tional New Englanders brought up in the broadminded pragmatism of William James or in the lyric idealism of Ralph Waldo Emerson, allowed their mental processes to be so transformed by their conviction of the rightness of the Allied cause and the wickedness of the German enemy, that many of them remained narrow bigots for the rest of their lives. In joining in the war dance the American intellectuals were merely following in the footsteps of their European colleagues. Their almost joyful throwing off of the trammels of reason and ethics is now generally admitted to have been a real transgression against the cause of civilization. I can still remember the sense of relief I felt in taking refuge from the obsessions of the propagandists of hate, in the realities of war as it really was. The feeling was almost universal among the men of my generation who saw service in the field.

Benda analyzed this state of mind with pain and amazement. For two thousand years he saw the people we now tend to describe as intellectuals, whom he described as *les clercs*, as having been on the side of reason and truth. As he put it, although helpless to keep the rest of mankind from making history hideous with hatreds and massacres, they did manage to keep men from making a religion of evil. *"L'humanité faissit le mal mais honorait le bien."* Surveying the racial hatreds, the national hatreds, the class hatreds that rose from the wreck of civilization in that most crucial of the worldwide wars, he concluded *"On peut dire que l'Europe moderne fait le mal et honore le mal."*

Western civilization is only just now beginning to recover from the carnival of unreason that went along with the military massacres of the First World War. The hideously implemented creeds of the Marxists and the Nazis and the Fascists of various hues were rooted in this denial of humane and Christian values. The task before us is somehow to restore these values to primacy in men's minds and hearts.

It has been my experience through a pretty long life that the plain men and women who do the work of the world and cope with the realities of life respond almost automatically to these values. It is largely when you reach a certain intellectual sophistication that you find minds that have lost the ability to distinguish between right and wrong.

To be of use in the world the man of letters has to be continually on his guard against the professional deformations of his calling. The man who lives behind a desk or on the lecture platform has to seek daily confrontations with reality to keep his mind clear of the delusions and obsessions of the current verbiage.

In other words, he has to find every day some new way of telling the truth.

Language from its very beginnings has served two purposes: one purpose is to deceive and the other is to convey truth. One has to reach a fairly ripe age before one comes to a full understanding of how hard this is to do. Lies come easier.

The truth is hard to come by and when you do manage, by hook or crook, to come up with some fragment of it you are likely to find it as dangerous as strontium 90.

Socrates liked to call the search for truth "the examined life," and we all know what happened to Socrates. Perhaps we can take some comfort from the fact that the Athenians let Socrates live till he was seventy years old before they handed him the hemlock.

Ever since man began, the pursuit of truth has been an activity beset by many occupational hazards. The institutions through which, in almost any society, the bosstype men impose their will on the workers and the producers and the build-

ers are invariably founded on lies. Even a tiny fragment of truth tends to produce an infringement of public order. The automatic reaction of the bossmen who hold the police power is to stamp it out. The tremor runs through the whole hierarchy of time-servers and lickspittles whose lives and careers depend upon the bossmen. In any human society that you care to study you'll find that the bossmen's hangers-on have equipped themselves with the most delicate sensibilities to enable them to feel the pain in their own corns when somebody steps on the bossman's foot. Truth is by its very nature painful to authority.

History is full of examples of the dangers of truth telling, but it was not until we reached the epoch of masseducation and masscommunication that we came to the full understanding of the difficulty of discovering the truth in order to tell it. Your uneducated and illiterate man in the old days would hardly have been likely, if you showed him a pig, to have called it a goat. Today, with our minds continually indoctrinated with whatever fallacies the authorities in charge of radio and television feel it to their interest to promulgate, you can't be too sure. Your college educated intellectual is likely to explain to you that it may be on account of your own psychological disabilities that the creature in the pen looks to you like a pig. He won't go so far—everything is relative you know—as to claim that the creature is a goat; but he may well point out that treatises have been written to the effect that epistemologically speaking, the creature may be described as having goat-like characteristics.

The man of letters finds it particularly hard—as the old saying went—to tell the truth and shame the devil, because he is, by the nature of his calling, an intellectual. The intellectual's mind deals in concepts rather than in things. That's what they teach you to do in college. Of course abstract concepts are useful in the processes of thought, just as poker chips are useful when you play poker, but you have to remember that it is what they represent that counts. In the painful search for the words needed truthfully to describe an event, every word has to represent some real thing. In spite of his larger vocabulary the intellectual is sometimes more at a loss when it comes to that than the ignorant wayfaring man.

The intellectual is always taking the poker chips for real money. This flaw in his way of thinking, usually combined with an arrogant disinterest in the thought processes of the average man, shuts him into a conceptual universe divorced from life as it is really lived.

Truth is always a discovery. The discoverers are people who see the thing before they name it. For the intellectuals everything is already named.

In modern bureaucratic societies intellectuals are becoming a dominant class through their furnishing the bossmen with the slogans and delusions by which they control the general public. The twentieth century may possibly end by being known as the century of the intellectual. As they become giddy with power the usefulness of the intellectuals as a class to the cause of civilization becomes more and more doubtful.

I have been a good deal in South America during the last few years. There, as I suppose in most Latin countries, you find a much greater cleavage between the man who does the work and the man who sits behind the desk than you would find in Englishspeaking America, in Canada or the United States. The educated and the uneducated live in different worlds. The universities are full of half educated young men who out of sheer ignorance of plain workaday human behavior snap up all the slogans fed to them by Marxist agitators. Since little in their schooling fits them for engineering or dentistry or veterinary work, and they have been taught to scorn buying and selling over the counter, and would rather die than work with their hands, they have no career open to them except politics. The Communist party offers to these young men who have no intention of soiling their hands a magnificent prospect of bossing their fellows and attaining, through revolution, the use of the automobiles, airplanes, hotels and restaurants that in their countries are reserved for the very wealthy. The success of the Communists in those countries stems from their appeal to the disoriented intellectual.

Of course their careerism is veiled in idealistic verbiage. Benda's *Trahison des Clercs* in modern form. It's all for the good of the workers and peasants. This is the basis of what you might call the Fidel Castro mentality.

In our own universities you find a parallel mentality, except that outside of a few indoctrinated Marxists, the aims are less drastic. Young men who dread the risks of the competitive world of business look forward to more placid careers "in government" as it is called.

Willy nilly the world over the man of letters belongs to the class that staffs the bureaucracies. Before he can perform his duty to tell the truth about the society he lives in he must clear his mind of the ideological trappings which are part of the equipment for worldly success of the class to which he belongs. In his renunciation of the commonplace taken for granted by his class he will find himself faced with the question that comes resounding through the centuries: Pilate's anguished question: What is the truth?

It is a question to which humanity has found many answers. It has been involved in all the casuistries and sophistications and the proliferations of verbiage the human mind is capable of. I believe it can be best answered in the form of a creed. I believe that there are certain simple realities which are universal to all men, no matter how diverse their backgrounds or their environments or their social customs. The man who humbly seeks out these realities is on the firm path which will lead him to the truthful observation of the world about him. When I think of the search for truth my mind turns to the painstaking investigations of the early naturalists, to the attitude of mind reflected in Charles Darwin's *Voyage of the Beagle* or Harvey's *Circulation of the Blood*.

Man's great achievements come when he examines reality without preconceived ideas. The man of letters who will be useful to humanity in our day will examine the social conflicts with the cool and eager eye of young Darwin examining a cuttlefish or an insect. Lies and delusions are an inevitable part of the human mentality so that truth can never entirely prevail, but a tiny flash of truth is seen a long way. Small illuminations have farreaching consequences.

When I say that the man of letters must avoid preconceptions I do not mean that he must be without standards. The human mind can no more function without the conviction of right and wrong than a mammal can exist without a skeleton. Without firm belief that good is good and evil is evil where can we find the inner fortitude needed to explain to the masses of men, whose minds have been befogged by endless selfserving propaganda, what we mean by civilization?

The terms we have to use have been so mutilated in the mouths of politicians that one can hardly pronounce grand old words like liberty and democracy without an apologetic blush. The ideas behind these terms have lost all urgency for the populations that benefit most from them. It sometimes seems as if the only people who had any understanding of civil liberty were the people in the Communist states who are deprived of it.

In fact the best description I have seen in some time of the sort of thing we want to defend came from an escaped Russian sailor. It is the man who jumped overboard from a Soviet freighter anchored in the bay off Calcutta. He swam to another ship and finally made his way to the shore. The Russian authorities tried to snatch him back by claiming he'd stolen some money, but the Indian law court wouldn't give him up, and he finally made his way to the United States. On being asked why he risked his life to escape to the free world, he answered that, first, he was tired of being ordered around by stupid people who knew nothing about navigating a ship and, next, that he thought people, in America at least, really were equal before the law, and that there "each person is able to build his own life without directive from above, and that each citizen through his own development brings good to society."

FOR ME AT LEAST the story of that Russian sailor makes the problem concrete. The question before us is what can we do to preserve and improve the sort of society all these refugees from the Communist slave-camps hope for when they risk their lives to escape to freedom.

I do not believe that the values the conservatives want to conserve can be furthered by a static resistance to change. The problem is to find ways of adapting the institutions of modern industrial society so that they will serve the purposes of civilization. That this sort of adaptation is no philosopher's dream is proved by the success of United Europe. Those nearest to it probably see more defects in the foundations than we do from the other side of the Atlantic but the fact remains that in a short fifteen years extraordinary progress has been made in uniting the peoples of Europe whose wars first put our civilization in deadly jeopardy.

Turning for a moment to my own country the tasks which I would urge on the conservatives are equally arduous, but success would be equally rewarding. At home in the United States the same sort of shrewd and patient work which produced the framework of a new Europe is needed to resolve two great mass conflicts. Methods must be found to keep the agitation for Negro rights from degenerating into racial warfare. That is a very special situation that demands tact, forbearance and social inventiveness on both sides instead of the fanning up of hatreds by politicians and professional troublemakers.

The other mass conflict we don't hear so much about. The rise to power of empirebuilders among the labor unions has brought about a sort of schizophrenia in American industry. Management and labor have become two warring camps, with government, in the hands of vote-happy politicians, usually on the side of the labor leaders. While the financial gains of the workers have been so immense as to throw large sectors of the economy off balance, very little has been done to carry out the original aims of the old nineteenth century labor movement. The original impulse came from the need factory-workers felt to assert their human dignity. In modern industry the wageworker is starved for a feeling of participation in work well done. As the situation stands today the worker in the massproduction industries can have no feeling of participation in the productive enterprise that affords him his livelihood and very little in the labor union that takes such a large slice of his pay. Although useful solutions have been tried out and some with great success our politicians can only see in the labor unions a means for delivering reg-

imented blocks of votes at the polls. The social engineer who talks directly to both the man at the bench and to the man at the desk and manages to bring about a rational integration of management and labor in harmonious co-operation will have deserved well of his country.

One of the tasks of the conservatives as their influence grows will be to suggest reasonable solutions for social problems. Ideas don't depend on victory at the polls. Politicians are notorious for snatching at ideas proposed by the opposition. Practical measures that tend to humanize industrial society are in my opinion more important than neat ideological statements or victories at the polls. The trend towards a totalitarian society can only be stemmed little by little by practical measures that change the alignment of institutions. There is no way of saving civilization by a formula like the Communist Manifesto which has done so much to destroy it. The great political slogans of the past have tended to come out of the application of general ideas to specific situations, so now the vocabulary of a new conservatism will come into being gradually out of the workaday struggle to remedy specific abuses.

One of the weaknesses of conservative theorists has been that their diagnoses of social and political trends have been so pat and plausible that they have tended to stick to them too long. Some of the diagnoses applied marvelously five years ago, but they don't apply today. Even under the rigid shell of Communist dogma changes have occurred. Many free world positions have been so badly defended that for the time being at least they have become indefensible. It is time to look at social and political phenomena with a fresh eye. Only after the naturalist's calm and dispassionate evaluation will it be possible to use your humane standards as a measuring stick and to decide which trends you want to back and which you want to discourage or oppose.

The field is certainly open to fresh ideas. In spite of their successes against the loose-lipped liberals of the free world the Communists are still struggling in the straitjacket of Marxist dogma. Among the crowd of little Stalins and ersatz fuehrers and spurious duces that have climbed to power out of the debris of the European colonial system, the socialist ideology has become a cloak for the most aboriginal forms of personal dictatorship.

In Western Europe there have certainly been developments, some hopeful and some discouraging. At least there the effort to apply brains to the situation has had tangible results. In the Englishspeaking countries, after some brilliant early successes for the cause of civilization, such as the generous treatment of Germany and Japan and the aid the Marshall plan gave to the rebuilding of Europe, we have had very little to offer. The chief strategy of our leaders in the ideological war has been a refusal to face facts, and a strange inability, once the facts were admitted, to take the action the facts demanded. The world is waiting for a renovation of its political and social theories.

The conservatives must come up with invigorating new ideas. The other ideologies have come to a dead stop. It's a time of stalemate in a number of directions. A sort of calm has descended on the world. The peoples under Marxist rule seem to have run out of enthusiasm for ideological warfare. One is reminded of the sudden calm that descended on Europe when the wars of religion began to peter out. Perhaps fresh voices can make themselves heard. They must speak up fast because the calm can't last very long.

On the whole it is an interesting time to be alive. Five years ago the triumph of Communist dictatorship seemed almost certain. Now, in spite of the threat of nuclear extermination and the equally fearsome prospects consequent on the population explosion, it looks as if civilization might still have a fighting chance. It makes me wish I were a great deal younger.   [VIII, Winter, 1963–64, 77–83]

[5]

A Place To Live In

BERTRAND DE JOUVENEL

Bertrand de Jouvenel (des Ursins, baron) (1903–1987) was born in Paris, the son of a distinguished French ambassador who was also a minister and senator. A political economist and man of letters, he studied at the Lycée Hoche à Versailles and the Facultés des sciences et de droit de Paris and taught at the University of California, Berkeley, at Yale, Oxford, Cambridge, and Manchester. He was an international reporter, président-directeur general de la Société d'études et de documentation économique (Sedeis) from 1954 to 1974, and professeur associé près la faculté de droit de Paris (1966–1972). The recipient of honorary degrees from the universities of Glasgow, Bucharest, and Manchester, he was awarded a number of other honors and prizes. He was the author of numerous works, including La Crise du capitalisme américain *(1933),* Marx et Engels: la longue marche *(1983), and* La fidélité difficile *(1919), published when he was only sixteen years old.*

WE ARE THE FIRST of mankind to see and sense the Earth as a small place. I can now hang upon my wall, just as easily as a picture of my own house, a photograph of our terrestrial ball taken from outer space. But the essential reason for our new assessment of our planet is our recent ability to move to almost any point of the sphere within a day or two. Distances have been contracted by a miraculous increase in our speed of displacement. It is a common saying that thought is quicker than action: this holds true in the case of imagination, not so in the case of more reflective use of the intellect. Our popular fiction now, boldly over-stepping our powers, sets its adventures in "The Galaxy"; in the meantime, however, our approach to our here-and-now problems is still weighted down by our age-old habits of slow movement. Our views lag far behind the change in our circumstances: this change deserves to be stressed.

The Revolution of Speed

For many centuries, the fastest means of land transport was the horse. Given roads or tracks, a horseman can cover seventy-five miles in a day; across country, the cavalry of Alexander the Great is said to have covered the same distance in thirty-six hours: two thousand years later this was still accounted a remarkable performance. Cruising speeds maintained over a long journey were of course a good deal lower: an average of forty-five miles was very fair. Horse-drawn wagons, when loaded, could under the most favorable circumstances equal the achievement of a walker. Thus, during the long-lasting Age of the Horse, there was a low "ceiling" on the speed of human displacement. This can be illustrated by an anecdote involving that exceptionally dynamic figure, Napoleon. In September 1805, he proposed to "fall upon the Austrians like a bolt," and for that purpose he transported himself in his specially equipped car from St. Cloud to Strasbourg in three days: this amounts to one hundred fifty miles a day, and involved the frequent change of the best horses available to the Emperor.

Not only was the horse slow according to our modern reckoning, but moreover the diffusion of its employment was slow. The horse was domesticated more than five thousand years ago in the great plains of Central Asia. But within classical Greece it was a scarce asset and its ownership a badge of class; the same situation obtained in the Roman Empire and in feudal Europe, which was all but overwhelmed on several occasions by an avalanche of Asiatic horsemen. Even though our children associate "Red Indians" with horses, we know that horses were introduced on the American continent only by Cortés, who owed his conquest of Mexico in no small part to the impression made upon the Aztecs by this hitherto unknown animal.

Turning our attention to sea transport, we find that the transatlantic clippers, soon after the Napoleonic wars, held an average cruising speed of over one hundred fifty nautical miles per day on their westward journey, a performance which was halved on the eastward passage. Strangely enough, a Viking ship is said to have done as well a thousand years earlier, crossing from Norway to Iceland in four days and nights at an average of one hundred fifty sea miles per day—or so a saga bids us believe. We have more solid authority, that of Thucydides and Xenophon, for the achievements of Athenian triremes twenty-five centuries ago: we are told of one such ship covering one hundred sixty miles in twenty-four hours, and of another

covering six hundred twenty miles in four and a half days—of course impelled by a combination of sail and oar. It seems then that the great gain in navigation which had been achieved over the years was not mainly one of speed: it was an enormous improvement in seaworthiness and manageability, the major step of which was made in the construction of the Portuguese caravels in the fifteenth century, thanks to which Columbus reached the New World.

It is indeed fascinating to think that an improvement in the design of the sailing ship, and mainly of its rudder, allowed the hub of the modern world to be transferred from the Mediterranean to the Atlantic: it would surely be wrong to say that this technical factor was the cause of the event, but it was its precondition. And if an alteration of means, relatively so small, has been followed by so major an alteration of circumstances, what can we not expect to follow now that man has made a prodigious break through the long-lasting ceiling on his speed?

The gain in speed achieved over the Age of the Horse ranges from ten to one in the case of the motorcar to as much as a hundred to one in the case of the jet airplane. The change seems even more sensational when we associate with the increase of speeds the increase of weights which can be moved. By far the most striking progress of human technique is that which affects transportation of persons and goods. The economic benefits derived therefrom are too well known to need any stressing. Instead, I should like to draw attention to some of the political consequences.

Political Consequences of Speed

Let us compare the desks of Augustus, Jefferson, and Eisenhower. To all three desks comes news "from all over the world."

There is a great difference between the desk of Jefferson and that of Augustus; since a far smaller fraction of the world was known to the Roman Emperor than to the American President, news came in from fewer points, and the geographic coverage of information was very much narrower. But there is a no less important difference between the desk of Jefferson and that of Eisenhower. News reaching Jefferson were affected with time lags which distance and difficulty of communication often made considerable. Therefore the picture of the world pieced together by Jefferson from all items of information was a picture made up of non-simultaneous events and situations, even as is the case today with our picture of the heavens. Many "facts" he took into account had ceased to be "facts" by the time they had become "information" available to him. It is otherwise with Eisenhower: in his overall picture of the world there are no outdated elements; all the "facts" of which he is informed are "live facts," facts in being.

It is a novelty that information should be instantaneous. But it is an even more important novelty that action at a distance should be near-instantaneous. The "Berlin air-lift" in 1948 was a striking demonstration in this respect, intervention in Korea another; the French air-lift to Madagascar offers a recent illustration: a century and a half ago, relief would have reached the island at best four months after the disaster, whereas in this case the delay was only three days.

Any increase in man's power involves greater possibilities not only for good but also for harm: while it is unhealthy to concentrate upon the latter, it is unwise to ignore them. In past ages mere distance afforded a protective cushion to local autonomy and national security. Slow and costly communications opposed a physical obstacle to the centralization of decisions in a country's capital. As all incoming information had to be borne by messengers, and all outgoing orders to be conveyed in the same manner, no central government could bear the costs involved in keeping sufficiently informed about local conditions to make decisions concerning them. Further, in the case of any rapidly changing local situation, the time-lag between composing a report and receiving the corresponding instructions was apt to stultify the latter. Therefore it was in the very nature of things for local problems to be coped with by local authorities. And even if local dispositions ran counter to the will of the central government, it was such a complex and lengthy operation to bring agents of enforcement to bear that it was practical to let the local people settle their own affairs except in extreme cases. When such physical circumstances are kept in mind, it becomes clear that the opportunities for far-reaching dictation were insignificant compared to what they are today. Political despotism as we know it is a novel phenomenon. Not only were the kings of Western European States quite bereft of formal despotic authority; even the tsars and sultans and other Asiatic rulers, to whom despotic authority did belong, lacked the means to exercise this despotism throughout their vast empires.

It was an old Asiatic tag that if you wished to be safe from the will of the ruler you should stay away from his Court: but now this is not enough; the ruler's eye and hand are everywhere. In the same manner it was an old European tag that if you wished to be safe from a surprise inroad of foreigners you had to stay away from the seashore. This latter idea dates back to the snatch raids of the Vikings. Seapower was always the power to surprise. But even in the heyday of England's mastery of the seas, the sharpest blows which England could deal at an enemy without warning were to pounce upon its merchant ships on the high seas and to bombard its naval forces in port. The more vital threat of invasion was one of which the intended victim inevitably obtained ample warning. It took a great deal of time to assemble infantry forces, which lumbered forward at a slow pace. It followed that the threatened nation was always at leisure to muster its own forces. Although it could be swamped by a great superiority of forces, it could not be struck down by surprise.

I clearly remember the discussions on the prevention of aggression which were initiated at the League of Nations thirty-five years ago; we then worked on time-tables involving two assumptions. One was that quite some time would elapse during which the preparations of the aggressor would make his intentions manifest, and that this afforded a period for diplomatic intervention by the Council. The second assumption was that if the aggressor did indeed strike, the actual progress of his operations would be sluggish enough to allow the rescue of his victim by means of a long-drawn-out procedure comprising three stages: the formal decision by the Council to call upon member States, the mustering of forces by these States, and their combination on the field. It was stoutly maintained by British and Scandinavian representatives that the prior availability of some forces of intervention was unnecessary. All this implied a leisureliness which now seems quaint. Such procedures are clearly inadequate to the danger of a missile attack, where there is no pre-aggression period during which visible preparations invite diplomatic action, and no post-aggression period during which the victim is still unharmed enough to be rescued by hastily joined international forces.

Thus we find that our gains in speed place the subject more in the hand of the ruler, and the nation more at the mercy of a foreign power than was the case until

our time. This conclusion can be used to depress us or to fortify our spirit. It can fortify our spirit if we perceive these chances for evil as a challenge to mankind. By our own material achievement we are driven so to educate ourselves that we shall forbear from harmful uses of our powers.

Social Consequences of Speed

The population of the Earth has increased more since the beginning of our century than it had done in the preceding two hundred fifty years. Furthermore, the rate of growth is increasing: two hundred years ago it required a good one hundred fifty years for the doubling of the population; by a century ago, this duplication period had fallen to about one hundred ten years; on the basis of current trends, which may of course change, the duplicating period has shrunk to forty years. Demographers worry over this and foresee an overcrowded planet, but any difficulty due to mere numbers stands a long way in the future and can be coped with in ample time. Speed, however, is a much more effective and immediate cause of overcrowding. A simple comparison will show how this is so.

We all know that if we heat a gas, it seems to demand more space, and if we deny it that space it bursts the receptacle in which it was formerly held without difficulty. Chemists tells us that heating is nothing but speeding up the movements of the atoms composing the gas so that each travels faster and collides more frequently and violently with others: here we find overcrowding arising from speed, not numbers. We enjoy over atoms the fortunate superiority of being able to control our movements (and that of our vehicles) in order to avoid collisions; but to do this we must submit to traffic regulations, which extend downwards even to pedestrians. The importance of traffic problems, and the status of traffic authorities, is sure to rise beyond present recognition.

We have compared our gains in speed to what occurs as the result of heating; and indeed the comparison is justified, since heating is an input of energy, and we do increase, continuously and sharply, the input of energy into transportation, some of this energy going into the increase of the weights carried and a greater proportion into the increase of speeds. The comparison with heating can be used also to stress the point that speed, like heating, facilitates the mixing and combining of various substances. Difficulties of transport have in the past held back geographic movements of populations. In the nineteenth century the westward trek of the Americans and the northward trek of the Boers were regarded as epic, although in terms of "logistics" there was little difference between these migrations and the southward treks of the Germanic tribes which overran the Roman Empire, and historians have made it clear that these invaders were not at all numerous. Now, however, vast movements of population are physically feasible. As a consequence we must expect that the uneven distribution of world population over the surface of the planet will become an issue.

Reducing inequalities *within the nation* was the great theme of the last few generations in the various countries of the West, since people naturally compared their condition only with that of their neighbors. But we have invited the other nations of the world to take cognizance of our living standards. And while at present they are concerned to rival these standards on their own ground, should this hope prove fallacious (in part because of the unequal distribution of natural resources), the pressure to emigrate to countries which have achieved great success will be renewed, and it will pose moral and political problems.

One World

Two thousand years ago, enlightened Romans were wont to repeat a saying learnt from their Greek tutors: "Though mankind lies dispersed in many cities, yet it forms but one great City." This saying has become imbedded in Western education through Cicero, who repeatedly referred to the Society of Mankind. Thus when Wendell Willkie spoke of "One World," it seemed that the statesman was at last acknowledging what philosophers had stressed for a long time. But the world today is "One" in a sense quite opposite to that which the Greek Stoics had in mind. The purpose of their saying was to contrast physical distance with moral proximity: moral nature made it as easy for men to get on together as physical nature made it difficult for them to come together. Now the situation with which we are faced is utterly different: it is one of physical proximity and moral distance.

Progress in transport has flung down the walls of distance which insulated the many human communities; but men have not rushed over these toppled walls to greet each other as long-lost brothers now enabled to merge in one great community. In North America and Australia the advent of Western man has led to the near-extinction of the natives rather than to their combining with the newcomers in one society. The prolonged presence of Western man in Arab, African, and Asian countries has quickened a feeling of kinship, not with him but against him. Clearly nationalism is the great political force in our age of No-Distance. Nationalism made Hitler, and unmade him when he ran foul of Russian nationalism, which alone saved

Stalin's regime. Nor is the will to nationhood dependent upon actual oppression: men now define oppression as the denial of recognition as a separate and distinct sovereign community.

There seems to be no basis in fact for the idea that men are naturally prone to treat each other as brethren and have been artificially weaned by institutions from this original propensity. The only evidence which can be adduced in favor of this natural brotherhood is that all men seem to have a deep-seated reluctance to kill another man, a reluctance which is overcome only under the stress of fear or extreme excitement: hence the war dances required to put them in that unnatural mood. But "not killing" and "regarding as a brother" are very different attitudes, the second far richer in content. And the second is developed by institutions. It is quite impossible for us to estimate the number of distinct political communities which have arisen on our planet since the appearance of man. All but an infinitesimal fraction of these have disappeared; and, for want of any other means of picturing them, we pay a great deal of attention to the minute communities which have subsisted long enough to allow our anthropologists to examine them.

The feature common to all of these communities is an intense but narrowly restricted sense of fellowship. This makes us aware that the building of political societies which have mattered in history involved an enlargement, coupled with a weakening, of the sense of fellowship: our bond with a compatriot is nothing like the bond between members of a tribe; still it is a bond. And we may then think of the art of building large societies as the art of stretching bonds of fellowship as far as possible without snapping. The diffusion of a religion, of a language, of a legal system is here of far greater importance than the diffusion of tools and skills, though the importance of the latter is not negligible.

It would be mere wishful thinking, than which there is nothing more dangerous in the management of human affairs, to assert that mankind now forms One Great Society. This poses a problem because, and only because, mankind must increasingly be thought of as gathered in One Place. While it is certainly an obstacle to the achievement of human excellence that a society should be too small, it is far from clear that such excellence is fostered by increasing bigness. Greek society which has afforded us models in arts and philosophy was small: a constellation of towns of which the largest did not count a hundred thousand inhabitants. Even smaller was Jewish society, wherein was kindled the Light of this World. It is readily believable that the advocacy of the all-embracing society by the late Greek philosophers was in no small measure a means of consoling themselves for their absorption in the vast Roman Empire, which never got near to the achievement of Athens alone.

But if it can be doubted that the hugeness of society is desirable, there is little doubt that the mixing together of distinct societies retaining their distinctive traits is a cause of trouble: it was long illustrated in the Ottoman Empire. Contrary to the dreams of those who see in World Government a cure-all, experience proves that the unity of government by no means solves the problems raised by the distinctiveness of the communities over which it presides. Incidentally, in that event, the nature of things forbids that government should be of a representative character: if men attempted to make it such, it would be at worst representative of the dominant society and at best representative of the coalition of certain component societies against others. Representative government assumes that what is to be represented is a dominant opinion or feeling within one society.

Tensions between societies are not amenable to the remedy of a common government, unless it be a very authoritarian one. But on the other hand, when societies have distinct political existence, their conflicts are far more disastrous than those which occur between different States belonging to one and the same society. Burke explained the mildness of eighteenth-century wars in Europe by the fact that the nations involved belonged to some system of manners and could therefore contend only about some specific interest, which was not worth any great fury or havoc. It takes great folly to drive war to the extreme under such circumstances, and history offers but two such examples, the Peloponnesian War and the War of 1914. On the contrary war between societies is by nature absolute since it is not a squabble occurring within the same frame of values, but rather one in which neither camp recognizes the values of the other: this is potentially a war of destruction. Such were the wars waged by the Mongols and the Turks against Europe—wars between societies.

At present the combination of strong diversity between societies and of effective physical proximity poses a political problem of major dimensions. It is just not good enough to think of it in terms borrowed from the experience of diplomacy between States belonging to the same society.

Our Home

Underlying this paper is a feeling which it is perhaps time to express, an affection for the Earth similar in kind to that which our home and garden inspire, an awareness that our inheritance is precious and vulnerable. In most pre-Christian religions figured a cult of Mother-Earth, the

Bountiful. She was the primeval giantess on which short-lived men scrabbled punily; from her flanks sprang all things necessary to the sustenance and enjoyment of life; her power was adored. The Earth is still our abode and provider, but the giantess now seems far smaller and the majestic processes of her life are not immune to interference. We know that we live upon a few feet of soil, with a few miles of atmosphere above us; we know that we can blight the soil and corrupt the air, that we can produce smog and dust-bowls; we could poison the sea; we could melt the ice-caps at the poles; we might kill off bacteria on which we depend, or propagate viruses mortal to us.

Therefore the juvenile pride which we have understandably taken in our fantastically increased ability to "exploit the Earth" should now give way to a more mature thoughtfulness in "husbanding the Earth." Man, impatient with the weakness of his hands, has transformed his weakness to strength: now his handling must become more discriminating and delicate. We are like children who, as they acquire vigor, must be made aware of their new capacity to injure. Many of us no doubt have had the experience of nursing with love in our maturity a small garden through which we had blundered brutally as small children, then deeming its riches unlimited: such is the experience which mankind is now repeating.

Now that we have reached the limits of the Earth, we understand: this is the land of promise, the land beyond Jordan, a land of milk and honey, to be enjoyed, and cherished, and tended.

The Capacity To Harm

I have traveled enough not to fall into the easy accusation that modern industry is responsible for defacing the Earth. I know that shepherds, so favored by poets, can with their lambs and sheep cause the soil to become barren; I know that noble savages will burn down a forest to raise a crop, and move on to cause another desolation; I have seen the squalor of the Arab *medina* and of the Asiatic large town. Man is careless; and if our factories pour filth into our rivers, this is just in line with age-old behavior. Yet the combination of education and wealth always fosters in men the will to live in graceful surroundings, and if this is an attitude of individuals it may also be an attitude of communities. It was the attitude of Athenians, of Florentines. Surely, if they were wealthy enough to build themselves beautiful towns, so are we. The preoccupation with urban beauty seems to me to be rising in the United States; I find it to a lesser degree in Europe. Also it is an attitude of mature minds to be provident, to think of improving the home, the farm, or the plant. Certainly we cannot blame our contemporaries for any lack of investment-consciousness, but this preoccupation has not yet, or at least not adequately, extended to the conservation of the very basis upon which our structures are reared: we do not realize that the natural resources themselves are requiring upkeep. This basic capital of mankind is entered in our account books at zero, and so taken for granted that it receives no attention.

The time has come for a new spirit of "stewardship of the Earth." Every animal, however humble, provides for its offspring. As one ascends the chain of beings up to man, the period during which the young are protected by the parents stretches, allowing for more complete development. But man is unique in his determination to hand down to his adult successor some asset he has built up, to be enjoyed and improved by his son, and handed to the grandson for further improvement. As this propensity is peculiar

to man and has obviously served the progress of our species, I doubt whether the legislative fashion against it, however plausible on other grounds, is well founded. But we must at least transfer this fortunate propensity to the asset on which the children and grandchildren of all of us shall be dependent, our Earth itself.

In towns where we have no animal company other than that of an occasional cat or dog, and see no plant other than an occasional tree, we are apt to forget that Life, with a capital L, depends upon a complex combination of an immense variety of forms of life, between which the balance must be maintained. We may have air-conditioning, but should be aware that the availability of breathable air depends upon a complex cycle of operations turning upon green plants. All our devised processes in which we take justifiable pride are, as it were, derivations installed on natural circuits; and our increasing understanding of the latter not only conveys a greater power to exploit them but also implies a greater awareness of a duty to preserve them.

Cleverness and Thoughtfulness

Throughout the history of mankind, as we know it today, new procedures have been devised, new tools forged and new ways of life have been adopted. It is a truism that the pace of such change has undergone a formidable acceleration; but truisms are the best starting points for meditation. When a new procedure or new tool arose in the distant past, its use was only slowly generalized in the immediate environment and its geographic diffusion was even much slower. Inventions, far between in time and spreading sluggishly, slowly affected ways of life but did not revolutionize them: for instance, I deem it quite misleading to refer to the adoption of tilling as "the Agricultural Revolution"—a phrase which implies a turbulence of events which was lacking.

For many thousands of years men lived in a world where new practices were a rarity and old practices made up the bulk of their existence. While the impact of successive new practices successively altered the environment, this alteration was so leisurely that sons were, on the whole, adjusted to their world if only they acquired the skills of their fathers and were guided by the experience of their elders. But now discoveries so press upon one another, are so rapidly accepted and so widely put into operation, that a human generation lives in a world utterly different from that into which it was born; for instance, I was born in the year when the Wright brothers first succeeded in flying a few hundred yards, and flying has become my normal mode of transporting myself to and fro.

I marvel at the rapidity of human adjustment. Man, living in a sort of symbiosis with an ever-changing population of machines, reveals a flexibility of behavior which could hardly have been forecast. Moreover, while great individual inequalities are revealed in this capacity as in every other, they bear little apparent relation to hereditary background: given favorable early opportunities, the knack of handling complex machinery can be acquired quite rapidly by men born in the most primitive conditions. We are only beginning to discover man's cleverness.

It is again a truism to say that our thoughtfulness by no means keeps pace with this development. Prudence consists in picking out the good under the actual circumstances: faults against prudence are committed either if one fails to take full cognizance of the circumstances or if one despairs of picking out the good: such indeed are the two trends of contemporary thinking about our fast-changing world.

Certainly the stress upon our minds arising from the pace of change is unprecedented: no man in his right senses can help feeling that he is unequal to the challenge. Yet we must humbly dare to meet it. [IV, Winter 1959–60, 5–13]

[6]

Freedom, Tradition, Conservatism

FRANK S. MEYER

Frank S(traus) Meyer (1909–1972) was a key figure in the theoretical development of American conservative thought in the post-World War II era. A native of New Jersey, he was educated at Princeton and at Oxford's Balliol College. After over a decade of membership in the Communist party, at the close of World War II Meyer broke intellectually and politically with communism and devoted the balance of his life to the American conservative movement. A senior editor of National Review, *his principal works are* The Molding of Communists *(1961),* In Defense of Freedom: A Conservative Credo *(1962), and* The Conservative Mainstream *(1969).*

THE LAST HALF-DOZEN years have seen a development of conservative thought in the United States unparalleled in a century. It is ironic, although not historically unprecedented, that such a burst of creative energy on the intellectual level should occur simultaneously with a continuing spread of the influence of liberalism in the practical political sphere, to the point where it has now captured the decisive positions of power in the Republican as well as in the Democratic party. But ironic or not, it is the fact. For the first time in modern America a whole school has arisen that consciously challenges the very foundations of collectivist liberalism; two intellectually serious journals, *Modern Age* and *National Review*, have established themselves integrally in the life of the nation; and an increasing number of the newer generation of undergraduates, graduate students and young instructors in the universities openly proclaim themselves conservatives. Most important, perhaps, an intense and far-ranging dis-

cussion has been taking place among conservatives on the meaning and matter of conservatism in the circumstances of mid-twentieth-century America.

It is to this discussion that I want to address myself. In the course of it there have developed doctrines apparently sharply opposed to each other, and sometimes presented as mutually incompatible, but which I believe can in reality be united within a single broader conservative political theory, since they have their roots in a common tradition and are arrayed against a common enemy. Their opposition, which takes many forms, is essentially a division between those who abstract from the corpus of Western belief its stress upon freedom and upon the innate importance of the individual person (what we may call the libertarian position) and those who—drawing upon the same source—stress value and virtue and order (what we may call the traditionalist position).

But the source from which both draw,

the continuing consciousness of Western civilization, has been specifically distinguished by its ability to hold these apparently opposed ends in balance and tension; and in fact the two positions which confront each other today in American conservative discourse both implicitly accept, to a large degree, the ends of the other. Without the implicit acceptance of an absolute ground of value, the preeminence of the person as criterion of political and social thought and action has no philosophical foundation; and freedom would be only a meaningless excitation and could never become the serious goal of a serious politics. On the other hand, the belief in virtue as the end of men's being implicitly recognizes the necessity of freedom to choose that end; otherwise, virtue could be no more than a conditioned tropism. And the raising of order to the rank of an end overshadowing and subordinating the individual person would make of order not what the traditionalist conservative means by it, but the rule of totalitarian authority, inhuman and subhuman.

On neither side is there a purposeful, philosophically founded rejection of the ends the other side proclaims. Rather, each side emphasizes so strongly the aspect of the great tradition of the West which it sees as decisive, that distortion sets in. The place of its goals in the total tradition of the West is lost sight of, and the complementary interdependence of freedom and virtue, of the individual person and political order, is forgotten.

Nevertheless, although these contrary emphases in conservative thought can and do pull away from each other when the proponents of either forsake one side of their common heritage of belief in virtue as man's proper end *and* his freedom under God as the condition of the achievement of that end, their opposition is not irreconcilable, precisely because they do in fact jointly possess that very heritage.

Extremists on one side may be undisturbed by the danger of the recrudescence of authoritarian status society if only it would enforce the doctrines in which they believe. Extremists on the other side may care little what becomes of ultimate values if only political and economic individualism prevails. But both extremes are self-defeating: truth withers when freedom dies, however righteous the authority that kills it; and free individualism uninformed by moral value rots at its core and soon brings about conditions that pave the way for surrender to tyranny.

Such extremes, however, are not the necessary outcome of a dialectic between doctrines which emphasize opposite sides of the same truth. Indeed, a dialectic between different emphases based upon the same fundamental understanding is the mode by which finite men have achieved much of the wisdom contained in tradition. Such a dialectic is in the highest degree necessary today between the libertarians and the traditionalists among conservatives. It cannot fail to achieve results of the greatest significance, if only the protagonists, in pressing that aspect of the truth which each regards as decisive, keep constantly in their consciousness other and complementary aspects of the same truth.

THE TENDENCY TO ESTABLISH false antitheses obstructing fruitful confrontation arises in part from an inherent dilemma of conservatism in a revolutionary era, such as ours. There is a real contradiction between the deep piety of the conservative spirit towards tradition, prescription, the preservation of the fibre of society (what has been called "natural conservatism") and the more reasoned, consciously principled, militant conservatism which becomes necessary when the fibres of society have been rudely torn apart, when deleterious revolutionary principles ride high, and restoration, not preservation, is the order of the day. For what the conservative is committed to conserve is not simply whatever happens to be the established conditions of a few years or a few decades, but the consensus of his civilization, of his country, as that consensus over the centuries has reflected truth derived from the very constitution of being. We are today historically in a situation created by thirty years of slow and insidious revolution at home and a half-century of violent open revolution abroad. To conserve the true and the good under these circumstances is to restore an understanding (and a social structure reflecting that understanding) which has been all but buried, not to preserve the transient customs and prescriptions of the present.

It is here that the dilemma of conservatism affects our present doctrinal discussion. The need in our circumstances for the most vigorous use of reason to combat the collectivist, scientistic, amoral wave of the present tends to induce in the libertarian an apotheosis of reason and the neglect of tradition and prescription (which he identifies with the prevailing prescriptions of the present). The traditionalist, suspecting that he sees in this libertarian tendency the same fever to impose upon men an abstract speculative ideology that has characterized the revolution of our time—as well as the French Revolution and its spiritual forbears—tends to recoil, and in his turn to press a one-sided position. Too often he confounds reason and principle with "demon ideology." Rather than justly insisting upon the limits of reason—the finite bounds of the purview of any one man or any one generation, and the responsibility to employ reason in the context of continuing tradition—he seems sometimes to turn his back on reason altogether and to place the claims of custom and prescription in irreconcilable opposition to it.

Both attitudes obscure the truth; both

vitiate the value of the dialectic. The history of the West has been a history of reason operating within tradition. The balance has been tenuous, the tension at times has tightened till it was spiritually almost unbearable; but out of this balance and tension the glory of the West has been created. To claim exclusive sovereignty for either component—reason or tradition—is to smirch that glory and cripple the potentialities of conservatism in its struggle against the liberal collectivist Leviathan.

Abstract reason, functioning in a vacuum of tradition, can indeed give birth to an arid and distorting ideology. But, in a revolutionary age, the qualities of natural conservatism by themselves can lead only to the enthronement of the prevailing power of the revolution. Natural conservatism is a legitimate human characteristic and in settled times it is conducive to good. It represents the universal human tendency to hold by the accustomed, to maintain existing modes of life. In settled times it can exist in healthy tension with the other equally natural human characteristic, the impulse to break beyond accepted limits in the deepening of truth and the heightening of value. But this is only possible before the fibres of society have been loosened, before the "cake of custom" has been broken. Then these two human tendencies can be held in just proportion, since men of all conditions believe, each at the level of his understanding, in the same transcendent Ground of truth and value, eternal and dynamic. But when, through whatever cause, this unity in tension is riven, when the dynamic takes off into thin air, breaking its tension with the perpetual rhythms of life—in short, when a revolutionary force shatters the unity and balance of civilization—then conservatism must be of another sort if it is to fulfill its responsibility. It is not and cannot be limited to that uncritical acceptance, that uncomplicated reverence, which is the essence of natural conservatism. The world of idea and symbol and image has been turned topsy-turvy; the life-stream of civilization has been cut off and dispersed.

This is our situation. What is required of us is a *conscious* conservatism—a clearly principled restatement in new circumstances of philosophical and political truth. This conscious conservatism cannot be a simple piety—although in a deep sense it must have piety towards the constitution of being. Nevertheless in its consciousness it necessarily reflects a reaction to the rude break the revolution has made in the continuity of human wisdom. It is called forth by a sense of the loss which that cutting off has created. It cannot now be identical with the natural conservatism towards which it yearns. The world in which it exists is the revolutionary world. To accept that, to conserve that, would be to accept and conserve the very denial of man's long-developed understanding, the very destruction of achieved truth, which are the essence of the revolution.

Nor can the conscious conservatism required of us appeal simply and uncomplicatedly to the past. The past has had many aspects, all held in measured suspension. But the revolution has destroyed that suspension, that tradition; the delicate fabric can never be re-created in the same identical form; its integral character has been destroyed. The conscious conservatism of a revolutionary or post-revolutionary era faces problems inconceivable to the natural conservatism of a pre-revolutionary time. The modes of thought of natural conservatism are not by themselves adequate to the tasks of a time like this. Today's conservatism cannot simply affirm. It must select and adjudge. It is conservative because in its selection and in its judgment it bases itself

upon the accumulated wisdom of mankind over millennia, because it accepts the limits upon the irresponsible play of untrammeled reason which the unchanging values exhibited by that wisdom dictate. But it is, it has to be, not acceptance of what lies before it in the contemporary world, but challenge. In an era like ours the existing regime in philosophical thought, as in political and social actuality, is fundamentally wrong. To accept is to be, not conservative, but acquiescent to revolution.

Situations of this nature have arisen again and again in the history of civilization; and each time the great renewers have been those who were able to recover true principle out of the wreck of their heritage. They were guided by reason—reason mediated, it is true, by prudence, but in the first instance reason. Like Socrates, Plato, Aristotle, confronting the chaos in the body politic and in the minds of men created by the overweening pride of the Athenian *demos*, we do not live in the happy age of a natural conservatism. We cannot simply revere; we cannot uncritically follow tradition, for the tradition presented to us is rapidly becoming—thanks to the prevailing intellectual climate, thanks to the schools, thanks to the outpourings of all the agencies that mould opinion and belief—the tradition of a positivism scornful of truth and virtue, the tradition of the collective, the tradition of the untrammeled state.

The conservative today, like the conscious conservative of all revolutionary eras, cannot escape the necessity and the duty to bring reason to bear upon the problems that confront him. He has to separate the true from the false, applying basic principle to the task of cutting through the tangled mass of confusion and falsehood; he has the responsibility of establishing in new circumstances forms of thought and institutional arrangements which will express the truth of the great tradition of the West. Respectful though he is of the wisdom of the past and reverent though he be toward precedent and prescription, the tasks he faces can only be carried out with the aid of reason, the faculty which enables us to distinguish principle and thus to separate the true from the false.

The projection of a sharp antithesis between reason and tradition distorts the true harmony which exists between them and blocks the development of conservative thought. There is no real antagonism. Conservatism, to continue to develop today, must embrace both: reason operating within tradition: neither ideological *hubris* abstractly creating Utopian blueprints, ignoring the accumulated wisdom of mankind, nor blind dependence upon that wisdom to answer automatically the questions posed to our generation and demanding our own expenditure of our own mind and spirit.

CLOSELY RELATED to the false antithesis between reason and tradition that distorts the dialogue between the libertarian emphasis and the traditionalist emphasis among conservatives is our historical inheritance of the nineteenth-century European struggle between classical liberalism and a conservatism that was too often rigidly authoritarian. Granted there is much in classical liberalism that conservatives must reject—its philosophical foundations, its tendency towards Utopian constructions, its disregard (explicitly, though by no means implicitly) of tradition; granted that it is the source of much that is responsible for the plight of the twentieth century: but its championship of freedom and its development of political and economic theories directed towards the assurance of freedom have contributed to our heritage concepts which we need to conserve and develop as surely as we need

to reject the utilitarian ethics and the secular progressivism that classical liberalism has also passed on to us.

Nineteenth-century conservatism, with all its understanding of the pre-eminence of virtue and value, for all its piety towards the continuing tradition of mankind, was far too cavalier to the claims of freedom, far too ready to subordinate the individual person to the authority of state or society.

The conservative today is the inheritor of the best in both of these tragically bifurcated branches of the Western tradition. But the division lingers on and adds to the difficulties of conservative discourse. The traditionalist, although in practice he fights alongside the libertarian against the collectivist Leviathan state of the twentieth century, tends to reject the political and economic theories of freedom which flow from classical liberalism, in his reaction against its unsound metaphysics. He discards the true with the false, creating unnecessary obstacles to the mutual dialogue in which he is engaged with his libertarian *alter ego*. The libertarian, suffering from the mixed heritage of the nineteenth-century champions of liberty, reacts against the traditionalist's emphasis upon precedent and continuity out of antipathy to the authoritarianism with which that emphasis has been associated—although in actuality he stands firmly for continuity and tradition against the rising revolutionary wave of collectivism and statism.

We are victims here of an inherent tragedy in the history of classical liberalism. As it developed the economic and political doctrines of limited state power, the free-market economy and the freedom of the individual person, it sapped, by its utilitarianism, the foundations of belief in an organic moral order. But the only possible basis of respect for the integrity of the individual person and for the overriding value of his freedom is belief in an organic moral order. Without such a belief, no doctrine of political and economic liberty can stand.

Furthermore, when such a belief is not universally accepted, a free society, even if it could exist, would become a licentious war of all against all. Political freedom, failing a broad acceptance of the personal obligation to duty and to charity, is never viable. Deprived of an understanding of the philosophical foundations of freedom, and exposed to the ravening of conscienceless marauders, men forget that they are fully men only to the degree that they are free to choose their destiny, and they turn to whatever fallacy promises them welfare and order.

The classical liberal as philosopher dug away the foundations of the economic and political doctrines of classical liberalism. But however much he may thereby have contributed to our misfortunes, he himself continued to live on the inherited moral capital of centuries of Christendom. His philosophical doctrines attacked the foundations of conscience, but he himself was still a man of conscience. As Christopher Dawson has said: "The old liberalism, with all its shortcomings, had its roots deep in the soul of Western and Christian culture." With those roots as yet unsevered, the classical liberal was able to develop the theories of political and economic freedom which are part of the conservative heritage today.

The misunderstandings between libertarian and traditionalist are to a considerable degree the result of a failure to understand the differing levels on which classical liberal doctrines are valid and invalid. Although the classical liberal forgot—and the contemporary libertarian conservative sometimes tends to forget—that in the *moral* realm freedom is only a means whereby men can pursue their proper end, which is virtue, he did understand that in the *political* realm freedom is the primary end. If, with Acton, we "take the establishment of liberty for the realization of moral duties to be the end of civil society," the traditionalist conservative of today, living in an age when liberty is the last thought of our political mentors, has little cause to reject the contributions to the understanding of liberty of the classical liberals, however corrupted their understanding of the ends of liberty. Their error lay largely in the confusion of the temporal with the transcendent. They could not distinguish between the *authoritarianism* with which men and institutions suppress the freedom of men, and the *authority* of God and truth.

On the other hand, the same error in reverse vitiated the thought of nineteenth-century conservatives. They respected the authority of God and of truth as conveyed in tradition, but too often they imbued the authoritarianism of men and institutions with the sacred aura of divine authority. They gave way to the temptation to make of tradition, which in its rightful role serves as a guide to the operation of reason, a weapon with which to suppress reason.

It is true that from their understanding of the basis of men's moral existence, from their reverence for the continuity and precedent that ties the present to the past, contemporary conservatism has inherited elements vital to its very existence. Yet we can no more make of the great conservative minds of the nineteenth century unerring guides to be blindly followed than we can condemn out of hand their classical liberal opponents. Sound though they were on the essentials of man's being, on his destiny to virtue and his responsibility to seek it, on his duty in the moral order, they failed too often to realize that the *political* condition of moral fulfillment is freedom from coercion. Signally they failed to recognize the decisive danger in a union of political and economic power—a danger becoming daily greater before their eyes as science and technology created apace immense aggregates of economic energy. Aware, as the classical liberals were not, of the reality of original sin, they forgot that its effects are never more virulent than when men wield unlimited power. Looking to the state to promote virtue, they forgot that the power of the state rests in the hands of men as subject to the effects of original sin as those they govern. They could not, or would not, see a truth the classical liberals understood: if to the power naturally inherent in the state, to defend its citizens from violence, domestic and foreign, and to administer justice, there is added a positive power over economic and social energy, the temptation to tyranny becomes irresistible, and the political conditions of freedom wither.

The tendency of the traditionalist conservative to insist that the crystallization of a conservative outlook today requires only that we carry on the principles of those who called themselves conservatives in the nineteenth century oversimplifies and confuses the problem. That the conservative is one who preserves tradition does not mean that his task is arid imitation and repetition of what others have done before. It is true that in ultimate terms, upon the basic issue of human destiny, truths have been given us that we cannot improve upon, that we can only convey and make real in the context of our time. Here indeed the conservatives of the nineteenth century played a heroic part in preserving in the teeth of the overwhelming tendency of the era the age-old image of man as a creature of transcendent destiny.

In the political and economic realm, however, these truths establish only the foundation for an understanding of the end of civil society and the function of the state. That end, to guarantee freedom,

so that men may uncoercedly pursue virtue, can be achieved in different circumstances by different means. To the clarification of what these means are in specific circumstances, the conservative must apply his reason. The technological circumstances of the twentieth century demand above all the breaking up of power and the separation of centers of power—both within the economy itself, within the state itself, and between the state and the economy. Power of a magnitude never before dreamed of by men has been brought into being. While separation of power has always been essential to a good society, if those who possess it are to be preserved from corruption and those who do not are to be safeguarded from coercion, this has become a fateful necessity under the conditions of modern technology. To the analysis of this decisive problem and to the development of political and economic solutions of it, classical liberalism contributed mightily. If we reject that heritage, we should be casting away some of the most powerful among our weapons against socialism, Communism, and collectivist liberalism. The traditionalist who would have us do so because of the philosophical errors of classical liberalism, like the libertarian who rejects tradition because it has sometimes been associated with authoritarianism, seriously weakens the development of conservative doctrine.

The historical fact is—and it adds to the complexity of our problems—that the great tradition of the West has come to us through the nineteenth century, split, bifurcated, so that we must draw not only upon those who called themselves conservatives in that century but also upon those who called themselves liberals. The economists of the liberal British tradition, from Adam Smith through and beyond the vilified Manchesterians, like the Austrian economists from Menger and Böhm-Bawerk to Mises and Hayek, analyzed the conditions of industrial society and established the principles upon which the colossal power that it produces can be developed for the use of man without nurturing a monstrous Leviathan. Without their mighty intellectual endeavor, we should be disarmed before the collectivist economics of Marx, Keynes, and Galbraith. And in the sphere of political theory, who has surpassed the nineteenth-century liberals in their prophetic understanding of the looming dangers of the all-powerful state? Conservatives today can reject neither side of their nineteenth-century heritage; they must draw upon both.

Differences of emphasis between libertarian and traditionalist cannot be avoided and should not be regretted. Conservatism has no monolithic party line. Our task is to overcome the nineteenth century bifurcation of the Western tradition in fruitful dialogue, not to perpetuate it by refusing to understand the breadth and complexity of our heritage, out of a narrow historicism that unearths outworn party emblems.

I AM WELL AWARE that what I have been saying can be criticized as eclecticism and attacked as an effort to smother principle. But it is not the laying aside of clear belief, either by the libertarian conservative or by the traditionalist conservative, in order to present a front against contemporary collectivist liberalism, that is here conceived. Rather, it is the deepening of the beliefs which each holds through the development of their implications in a dialectic free of distorting narrowness. That deepening—and the development of a common conservative doctrine, comprehending both emphases—cannot be achieved in a surface manner by blinking differences or blurring intellectual distinctions with grandiose phraseology. It can only be achieved by a hard-fought dialectic—but a dialectic in which both sides recognize not only that they have a common enemy, but also that, despite all differences, they hold a common heritage.

As Americans indeed we have a great tradition to draw upon, in which the division, the bifurcation, of European thought between the emphasis on virtue and value and order and the emphasis on freedom and the integrity of the individual person was overcome, and a harmonious unity of the tensed poles of Western thought was achieved in political theory and practice, as never before or since. The men who created the republic, who framed the Constitution and produced that monument of political wisdom, *The Federalist Papers*, represented among them as great a conflict of emphasis as any in contemporary American conservatism. Washington, Franklin, Jefferson, Hamilton, Adams, Jay, Mason, Madison—among them there existed immense differences on the claims of the individual person and the claims of order, on the relation of virtue to freedom. But their dialectic was conducted within a continuing awareness of their joint heritage. Out of that dialectic they created a political theory and a political structure based upon the understanding that, while truth and virtue are metaphysical and moral ends, the freedom to seek them is the political condition of those ends—and that a social structure which keeps power divided is the indispensable means to this political end. The debate from which our American institutions arose is a fitting model for our debate.   [IV, Fall 1960, 355–363]

[7]

The Age of Liberalism

HENRY REGNERY

Henry Regnery (1912–   ) received his B.S. degree from Massachusetts Institute of Technology in 1934 and an M.A. degree from Harvard in 1938. Between 1934 and 1936 he studied at the University of Bonn in Germany. He was the founder in 1947 of the Henry Regnery Company (president, 1947–1966; chairman of the board, 1967–1977); in 1977 he founded Gateway Editions, Ltd., Book Publishers, now Regnery/Gateway, Inc., of which he is president. He is the author of Memoirs of a Dissident Publisher *(1979). To read about his publication of Russell Kirk's* The Conservative Mind *(1953) is to see the commitment of an independent publisher of serious literature and his "thoroughly admirable dissent"—dissent that also led him, with Russell Kirk and David S. Collier, to help found* Modern Age.

WE LIVE IN A TIME dominated by words: the printed word in the form of books, magazines and newspapers, the spoken word brought to us by radio and television. From the morning newspaper to the commentator on evening TV, from the first-grade primer, or basal reader, to use the ugly contemporary description, to the latest work of Arthur Schlesinger, Jr., or Kenneth Galbraith, we are subjected to a constant flood of words, not of the *word*, which, as the embodiment of truth and the primal order of being was *In the beginning*, but of words, words intended to implant opinions, to make us do or believe something we would not have done or believed otherwise. It is this fact of words which characterizes our time, which differentiates it from all others, and which has made those who, in one way or another, control the dissemination of words the real rulers of our society.

The lords of the media, as was demonstrated as long ago as the Spanish-American War, can start wars, or, with the black art of public relations, can make an unknown utility lawyer who makes the proper superficial impression into a great statesman, as was done with Wendell Willkie, or an amiable Illinois lawyer in the person of Adlai Stevenson, who had been a mediocre governor, but was a polished speaker, had a great facility for phrase making, and, as John Dos Passos put it, "held all the fashionable views,"[1] into a world figure. We are told that the president of the United States is the most powerful man in the world, but as the fate of Richard Nixon demonstrated, the media are more powerful still. Nixon was the first man for generations to become president in defiance of the media, but they were able—admittedly with his help—to destroy him. Without the enormous barrage of publicity the combined forces of press, TV and radio were able to concentrate on Watergate, it would have made no greater impact on public opinion than, say, the Bobby Baker case during the administration of Lyndon Johnson. Those who control press, TV and radio have become the fourth branch of government, and in many ways have the greater influence and power.

There is, then, the fact of this great instrument which modern technology and business organization have created, and the further fact that the viewpoint and general position of those who have controlled it since the 1930's has been predominantly liberal, a combination of circumstances, we must face it, which is the most striking feature of the landscape of our time. During the fight over intervention in the war that had broken out in Europe in 1939 the America First Committee and those of similar persuasion without doubt had the bulk of the American people behind them, but the press that counted, the *New York Times*, the *New York Herald-Tribune*, the *Washington Post, Harper's*, the *Atlantic, The Nation, The New Republic, Time*, were on the other side, and, needless to say, carried the day. It was possible to win the Republican nomination in 1940 for Wendell Willkie, who three months before was virtually unknown, in preference to Robert Taft, who was a national figure, because that is what those who controlled the press wanted. It was not because Willkie was a stronger candidate or a better man than Taft, but because his views were more acceptable to the rather small but powerful group that was in a position to pull the strings of public opinion, which is not, of course, the opinion of the public, but of those able to make themselves heard.

Writing of American participation in World War I, Albert J. Nock remarked, "We cannot help remembering that this was a liberal's war and a liberal's peace." World War II and the peace that followed it represented the final triumph of modern liberalism. With a four-term president in the White House, almost complete control of the means of communication, and the colleges and universities largely under their influence, the liberals had the world at their feet. But, one may well ask, Who are the liberals? What do they want? What do they stand for? As for who they are, Mrs. Roosevelt and Justice Warren were liberals, as were Adlai Stevenson and President Kennedy; Arthur Schlesinger, Jr., is a liberal, so are Kenneth Galbraith and Clark Kerr. Justice William O. Douglas and Hugh Hefner are liberals, and it is only in a time dominated by the values of liberalism that such a man as Hefner could have made his way, with his "Playboy philosophy," to fame and fortune. The Civil Liberties Union is a liberal organization, the Ford Foundation shows a strong preference for liberal causes, the *New York Times* and the *Washington Post* are liberal newspapers, *The Nation* is a liberal magazine, and Americans for Democratic Action a liberal political pressure group. What the liberals want, what they stand for, is more difficult to describe precisely, all the more so because their position often changes, is not consistent within itself, and not every liberal spokesman agrees with every other, but certain basic ideas and principles can be discerned.

The liberal, to begin with an important aspect of his position, takes a benign view of man, at least in the abstract; the idea of original sin he regards as medieval and with abhorrence. Man, he believes, whatever the theologians may say, is basically good; what tendency toward evil he may show is a result of social influences, not of any innate human flaw. Where the evil influences in society came from if man is basically good he does not explain. The liberal believes that all human and social problems are capable of solution, and in spite of his tendency to blame society for criminal or malicious behavior instead of the perpetrator, he has an almost mystical faith in the power of government and an equally strong distrust of private power. "The diversity of private power, its independence, its actual popularity in the culture at large seems to the left to be subversive of true order. Public power is endowed by the liberal-rationalist with natural superiority and with a kind of immaculateness that has theistic reverberations."[2] With public power, the liberal believes, anything is possible: the age-old problem of race relations can be solved by forcibly integrating schools and neighborhoods, the problem of poverty by a government program, of ignorance by requiring everyone to go to school, of health by socialized medicine. Even the secondary differences between the sexes can seemingly be abolished by government action.

In his Message to Congress on January 24, 1944, President Roosevelt announced a "Second Bill of Rights" which would guarantee the "right" of everyone not only to a useful and remunerative job, a decent home, a good education, protection from fear of old age and unemployment, but to good health. Such promises, ridiculous as they may sound—to whom does one go to claim one's "right" to good health?—are not at all inconsistent with the liberal position as it has been represented over the years. It is no more absurd to guarantee everyone the "right" to good health than to guarantee the freedom from fear, which was one of the "Four Freedoms" we were assured we fought World War II to attain, and which the liberal intelligentsia accepted without a qualm or murmur of protest.

Roy Campbell, with the poet's facility for getting at the substance of things, once remarked that if a dog bites a man, the liberal automatically takes the side of the dog; he equally automatically, Campbell went on to say, takes the side of the criminal against the policeman, of the striker against the employer, of the black man against the white. Mrs. Roosevelt, by way of example, said that she would never cross a picket line; when Cesar Chavez announces a boycott of table grapes, the liberal intelligentsia, whether they know anything or not of the facts of the case, dutifully stop eating grapes. If a boycott of lettuce is demanded, as one man they stop eating lettuce. Any revolutionary adventurer, whether Castro, Llumumba, Nkrumah, Sukarno, Allende, is greeted with uncritical acclaim as the saviour of his people so long as he invokes the proper anti-imperialist, democratic, class-struggle incantations; when one after another turns out to be the usual self-serving, power-seeking opportunist, it makes no difference, the next to appear evokes the same uncritical enthusiasm.

His political heroes—Adlai Stevenson, John F. Kennedy, Eugene McCarthy, George McGovern—appear to the liberal not as ordinary men seeking votes, but trailing clouds of glory, endowed with the gift of prophecy, and especially with that gift the liberal seems to regard with special favor, charisma. The liberal's capacity for self-delusion is almost unlimited, and experience seems to have little or no effect on him. He came back from Russia in the twenties and thirties with tales of having "seen the future and it works"; now he comes back from Communist China with the same breathless enthusiasm.[3]

The Nuremberg Trials, we were assured, were going to introduce the reign of law between the nations, in spite of the rather obvious fact that at least one of the judges came into court with unclean hands and that one of the basic principles of Western justice, the prohibition of *ex post facto* law, had been ignored. The United Nations Charter was greeted as the herald of a new era of peace and freedom, although one of the chartering nations, at the time, was in the process of depriving its smaller Western neighbors, with the usual methods of military occupation, mass arrests and deportations, of their freedom and national existence. The causes are endless—industrial democracy, progressive education, school rooms without walls, civil rights demonstrations, freedom marches, open housing, one man–one vote, integration—whatever it is promises the millennium, and the failure of one cause merely whets the liberal's appetite for the next.

But why should otherwise intelligent, normal people who are probably endowed with more than the usual share of good will and the spirit of generosity be so singularly lacking in the ability to see things as they are, to accept the human condition for what it is? It is an old and well established principle of logic that a false premise leads to a false conclusion— admit that the moon is made of green cheese, Norbert Wiener used to say, and it is possible to prove that Murphy is the pope. The liberal begins with the premise of the innate goodness of man and his ultimate perfectibility, all human experience notwithstanding, and finds himself, unwittingly, defending a system of government which engages in mass terror and slave labor camps, and depends for its very existence on a vast system of secret police.

There is more, however, than his inadequate conception of the nature of man that limits the liberal's grasp of reality: the basis of his system of values is faulty. The dominant philosophical position in this country for the past two generations at least has been the naturalism of, among others, John Dewey. Not all naturalists are liberals, although Dewey himself was,

and not all liberals are naturalists, but there is certainly justification for the assertion that modern American liberalism has been strongly influenced by the philosophy of naturalism, that naturalism is, in fact, the philosophy of liberalism. Values, according to naturalistic philosophy, are determined by desires; there is no such thing as good or evil in itself, values have no reality outside experience. "There was much argument among naturalistic moralists about which desires could be satisfied and how they could be satisfied to produce value. But they agreed on the basic notion that it was desires that constituted value and therefore each in and by itself was neither good nor bad."[4] Margaret Mead's *Coming of Age in Samoa*, for example, described the habits and customs of a primitive people. What right do we have, the author implied, to say that the traditional attitudes of Western civilization toward sexual relations and morality are better? It is all a matter of custom, of what people actually do, not of what they ought to do, which was also the underlying assumption of the Kinsey Report. Values, therefore, are not normative, but merely reflect a given state of affairs. The ultimate consequence of all this is the "Pleasure Principle" of the student revolutionaries, from which emanated such pearls as the following: "In SDS, f . . . . . g is a statement of community, and there's a lot of inter-f . . . . . g, but it's not casual. Sex comes out of a relationship, and is used to build a relationship stronger."[5] From John Dewey to Margaret Mead, thence to the student revolutionaries and the SDS was a perfectly logical development, although not one that Dewey himself would in any way have wanted or welcomed.

From all this derives the liberal attitude toward evil: for the liberal, evil is not an existential fact, but a social problem, which is doubtless one of the reasons liberals found it so difficult, if not impossible, to recognize Stalin and Soviet Russia for what they were. So long as the Communists arrayed themselves in the garments the liberals approved of—anti-colonialism, equality, a democratic constitution, the abolition of exploitation—the liberals were quite willing to overlook, or to forgive, what they actually did, if they were able to perceive it at all. One of the most flagrant examples of such myopia and self-delusion, but one that is by no means unique, is Joseph E. Davies' *Mission to Moscow*, and particularly the acclaim it received from the liberal press. George F. Kennan has described the indignation of the professional staff of the U.S. Embassy in Moscow when Davies arrived in 1936 as ambassador—they all seriously considered resigning in protest.[6] The quality of the book itself, and of Davies' competence as an observer, may be judged by his comments concerning the great purge trials of the old Bolsheviks, which he witnessed:

On the face of the record in this case it would be difficult for me to conceive of any court, in any jurisdiction, doing other than adjudging the defendants guilty of violations of the law as set forth in the indictments and as defined by the statutes.[7]

As if that was not enough: "The prosecutor [Vyshinsky] conducted the case calmly and generally with admirable moderation."[8] George Kennan, on the other hand, who attended the trials as Ambassador Davies' interpreter, speaks of "Vyshinsky's thundering brutalities."[9] Davies saw him differently: "The Attorney General is a man of about 60 and is much like Homer Cummings; calm, dispassionate, intellectual, and able and wise. He conducted the treason trial in a manner that won my respect and admiration as a lawyer."[10] One more quotation will probably be suf-

ficient to put *Mission to Moscow* and its author in proper perspective:

Stalin is a simple man, everyone says, but a man of tremendous singleness of purpose and capacity for work. He holds the situation in hand. He is decent and clean-living and is apparently devoted to the purpose of the projection of the socialist state and ultimate communism, with sufficient resiliency in his make-up to stamp him as a politician as well as a great leader.[11]

The book was bad enough, but Davies, let us not forget, was an ambitious, superficial man whose single claim to distinction was a very rich wife, and in his reports to Washington and in his book was only serving the purpose for which President Roosevelt had sent him to Moscow; much worse than the book was its utterly irresponsible reception by the liberal claque. *Foreign Affairs* commended it as ". . . one of the best informed books to appear in recent years on Soviet Russia";[12] *Pacific Affairs* described it as ". . . a book of exceptional importance";[13] The *Saturday Review of Literature* as ". . . one of the most significant books of our time";[14] and Walter Duranty, who for many years had been the Moscow correspondent of the *New York Times* proclaimed: "To me the charm of this book is first of all its acuteness. How well Davies understood, and how accurately he judged!"[15] (How accurately Duranty was in the habit of judging may be surmised from the following, quoted in *Time*, February 15, 1943: "I see Mr. Stalin as the clear-minded statesman who looks at East and West—both ways at once.") Perhaps the most significant and revealing comment about the book is the following, which appeared on the jacket: "The most important contribution to the literature on the Soviet Union," and came from no less an objective authority than Maxim Litvinov, Commissar for Foreign Affairs. Finally, to make the story more or less complete, it should be mentioned that *Mission to Moscow* was a selection of the Book-of-the-Month Club and was made into a much publicized movie.

It would be no problem to give many examples of such self-delusion, but one more may be sufficient to illustrate the point I am trying to make and one aspect of the general temper of the time. In its account of the Yalta Conference *Time* found itself able to say (February 19, 1945): "By any standards, the Crimean Conference was a great achievement." Now this was the conference, it seems scarcely necessary to mention, where the basic decisions, which were later ratified at Potsdam, were made which resulted in all of Eastern Europe coming under the domination of Communist Russia—the three Baltic countries, Poland, Eastern Germany, Czechoslovakia, Hungary, Roumania and Bulgaria—and by that time there could not, or need not, have been any doubt about what this meant. In addition, it was agreed that Eastern Poland would be ceded to Russia, with the Polish population of the area to be moved westward, and that all German territory East of the Oder-Neisse would go to Poland with the exception of the northern half of East Prussia, which went to Russia—this included such historically German cities as Königsberg, Breslau, Stettin and Danzig—and that the German population of over seven million would be driven out. The Yalta Conference, without doubt, resulted in one of the most monstrous international agreements in history.[16] How, then, could *Time* describe it as "a great achievement"? Because, to quote *Time* again, "there was a special recognition of certain precepts which Americans have always held dear, and which would reassure many a citizen that World War II was not being fought in

vain," namely, "free and unfettered elections by universal suffrage and secret ballot," and "the principle of collective security." So long as the verbal garment was beyond reproach—free and unfettered elections, collective security—the substance could be ignored.

By the end of World War II, liberalism had become an orthodoxy, an orthodoxy "so profoundly self-righteous," as John Dos Passos, speaking from direct experience described it, "that any critic became an untouchable."[17] While the liberals constantly affirmed their devotion to tolerance and to the idea of what they called "the open society," their tolerance did not, as a rule, include criticism of the truth, and liberalism was the embodiment of truth. The response to two books which appeared during this period which questioned the very basis of the liberal position will give an impression of some of the obstacles ideas which did not fit the prevailing and accepted thought patterns had to overcome to gain attention.

In 1944 the University of Chicago Press published an unassuming looking scholarly book without fanfare of any kind and in a very small first printing, which soon became the center of discussion and shook the liberal position to its foundations. This was F. A. Hayek's *Road to Serfdom*. It had first been published in England—Hayek at the time was professor of economics at the University of London—and had been rejected by several American trade publishers, in one case on the basis of the report of a reader who stated that, although he thought the book would enjoy a good sale, it was "unfit for publication by a reputable house."[18] The thesis of the book, simply stated, was that centralized economic planning—socialism, in other words—must inevitably lead to complete collectivism and the loss of personal freedom. The book was quite obviously the work of a serious scholar whose interest was not indulgence in ideological polemics but the preservation of the free society. The *New York Times*, to its everlasting credit and the astonishment of many, gave the book an excellent and favorable review in a prominent place by Henry Hazlitt, and the *Reader's Digest* made its ideas widely available by means of a skillful condensation. Such attention quickly mobilized a counterattack. Alvin H. Hansen, then much quoted as a "leading authority" on economic questions, pronounced categorically in the pages of the *New Republic:* "Hayek's book will not be long lived. There is no substance in it to make it long lived."[19] The *Library Journal* spoke of its "abstract presentation and poor organization,"[20] but the major attack came from Professor Herman Finer of the University of Chicago in a polemical, abusive book called *The Road to Reaction,* which is of much less interest now, except as a period piece, than the acclaim it inspired. The Kirkus Book Review Service, which was then, and still is, widely used by libraries in the selection of books, described the Finer book as "An exciting book—and a much needed one—the atomic bomb to explode the thesis of the reactionaries' Mein Kampf, Hayek's *Road to Serfdom.*"[21] In the *New York Times*, S. E. Harris of the Harvard faculty of economics welcomed Finer's polemic with the words, "This brilliant, persuasive volume . . . exposes his [Hayek's] fallacies and errors of fact." Finer, of course, was "a world authority," and his book one "no reader can afford to disregard."[22]

The American success of *Road to Serfdom* came to no one as a greater surprise than to its author, who had written it with the English situation and a scholarly audience in mind, and publication by a university press in a very small first printing would in any case ordinarily almost have guar-

anteed a limited sale. The force of its argument and the coherence of its presentation, plus the fortunate circumstance of the Hazlitt review in the *New York Times* and the condensation in the *Reader's Digest* made it an enormously influential book, and one which, in spite of Alvin Hansen's confident prediction, has become a classic in the literature of economic and political theory.

My second example was also published by the University of Chicago Press, Richard Weaver's *Ideas Have Consequences.* Weaver, when the book was published in 1948, was a rather obscure professor of English in the college of the University of Chicago; the fact that the Director of the Press, W. T. Couch, chose to publish the book and to put all the resources of the press behind it was not, in my opinion, unrelated to his rude dismissal several years later. It was Weaver's purpose to try to discover why it was, as he put it, that

> . . . in the first half of the twentieth century, we look about us to see hecatombs of slaughter; we behold entire nations desolated by war and turned into penal camps by their conquerors; we find half of mankind looking upon the other half as criminal. Everywhere occur symptoms of mass psychosis. Most portentous of all, there appear diverging bases of value, so that our single planetary globe is mocked by worlds of different understanding.[23]

The thesis of the book was that Western civilization had taken a wrong turn in the fourteenth century with William of Occam's questioning of universals; from this beginning came a gradual erosion of belief in objective truth and in the reality of transcendental values which brought us to our present predicament, a thesis which the author developed with great skill and care and in a style appropriate to his subject.

Ideas Have Consequences was a book, therefore, concerned with an enormously significant problem, and offered a serious, well-grounded analysis of its nature. How, then, did the liberal reviewers respond? Exactly as one might have expected. Howard Mumford Jones, for example, reviewing the book in the *New York Times*[24] accused Weaver of "irresponsibility," to which Weaver replied:

The way for a writer to show responsibility is to make perfectly clear the premises from which he starts. His statements can then be judged with reference to those principles. I proceeded at some length to make explicit the grounds of my argument, and I have no reason to feel that they are left unclear. I maintain, as Jones correctly infers, that form is prior to substance, and that ideas are determinants.[25]

Charles Frankel, in a review as condescending as it was superficial, found Weaver's thesis "trivial, if not self-contradictory,"[26] and the reviewer for the *Annals of the American Academy,* J. D. Hertzler, while conceding that there were a "number of things one definitely applauds," concluded with the remark, "the nostalgia for and flight to the ideas and 'conditions' of the Middle Ages leaves one cold."[27]

The book is not without faults—there are exaggerations, for example, which Howard Mumford Jones took great delight in pointing out—but it was written under the cloud of Auschwitz, Yalta, Hiroshima, the mass air raids, unconditional surrender, when civilization seemed bent on destroying itself, a situation which would incline a man as sensitive to the world around him as Weaver was to take a rather apocalyptic view. Anyone, however, who uses such words as "irresponsible" or "trivial" to describe this book says more about himself than the book, and whatever the liberal reviewers may have said, *Ideas Have Consequences,* nearly thirty years after its publication, is still in print, is still being read, and still has much to say to us, as the following sentence from the last chapter will indicate:

And, before we can bring harmony back into a world where everything seems to meet "in mere oppugnancy," we shall have to regard with the spirit of piety three things: nature, our neighbors—by which I mean all other people—and the past.[28]

While my primary purpose in this paper is to describe the temper of the period immediately following World War II, one cannot help but pose the question, How did it happen? Why was it that a substantial part of those who dominated the communication of ideas should have been, in their basic attitudes and values, in opposition to the attitudes and values which had been regarded and accepted as a traditional and basic element of American society? Jefferson had taught, and Americans believed, that "The government is best which governs least"; now the group that set the patterns of thought were telling us that social justice required more and more government supervision of every aspect of life; what came to be called, derisively, the "Puritan ethic"—faith, prudence, temperance, self-reliance, the drive to "get ahead," to improve one's self—was represented as anti-social and detrimental to the public good. How could it have happened that in a matter of only a few years such an attitude toward morality, taste and behavior as represented by Hugh Hefner's "Playboy philosophy" or the "pleasure principle" of the revolutionary students could not only have won general acceptance, but become almost an integral part of American life? Pornography, once "the last resort of those disqualified from social life," as Ronald Berman put it, had won the sanction of some of the leading people of society—can one imagine Justice Hughes or Justice Taft writing for a pornographic magazine, as Justice Douglas has seen fit to do?

Joseph Schumpeter and F. A. Hayek agree on the term "intellectuals" to describe the people who presume to speak for us, who mold opinion and tell us what to think and believe, and this, no doubt, is as good a description as any. Hayek defines intellectuals as "secondhand dealers in ideas,"[29] and Schumpeter as "people who wield the power of the spoken and written word, and one of the touches that distinguishes them from other people who do the same is the absence of direct responsibility for practical affairs."[30] Schumpeter gives a witty, interesting and convincing explanation of why so many intellectuals have become socialist (he uses socialist and liberal interchangeably), which includes the following two observations:

> . . . the intellectual group cannot help nibbling, because it lives on criticism and its whole position depends on criticism that stings; and criticism of persons and current events will, in a situation in which nothing is sacrosanct, fatally issue in criticism of classes and institutions.[31]

and the fact that mass education has made a large number of people psychologically incapable of working on the level of their talents, but has trained them for nothing else, thus creating a large group of dissatisfied people who feel themselves outside normal society.

Having described the intellectual as a "secondhand dealer in ideas," Hayek makes the important point that intellectuals are inclined "to judge all particular issues in the light of certain general ideas,"[32] and that such general ideas usually consist of a rather confused, ill-digested conglomerate of concepts which have been current and fashionable, which may derive from new truths, but which are often incorrectly applied and only partially understood. As examples of such intellectual fashions he mentions the theory of evolution, the idea of the predominant influence of environment over heredity, the theory of relativity, the power of the unconscious, equality, the superiority of planning over the results of spontaneous development, and since the intellectual is the means by which ideas and opinions reach the public, "the 'climate of opinion' of any period," Hayek goes on to say, "is thus essentially a set of very general preconceptions by which the intellectual judges the importance of new facts and opinions."[33]

Hayek further points out that the intellectual's preference for generalizations also contributes to his preference for socialism, for public power as opposed to private power. He prefers "broad visions, the specious comprehension of the social order as a whole which a planned system promises"[34] to the tiresome comprehension of technical details and practical problems which the proper understanding of the workings of a free society requires.

Granted the intellectuals are as they have been described, how was it possible for them to attain the dominant role in our society that has been ascribed to them? Why is it, for example, that the propertied class, which supports the universities, has not only permitted them to be largely taken over by a group that teaches an orthodoxy completely antithetical to its own, but goes right on supporting the universities even after this has been pointed out? Why is it, as Schumpeter put it, that "the bourgeoisie," as he calls the propertied class, "besides educating its own enemies, allows itself in turn to be educated by them?" Schumpeter's explanation is that "the bourgeois order no longer makes any sense to the bourgeoisie itself and that, when all is said and nothing is done, it does not really care."[35] This may be true, but it is only a part of the explanation, and perhaps a small part.

The infection started and was propagated in the colleges and universities. Eliseo Vivas was the assistant during the thirties, when the process was just getting underway, of a very well known and influential professor at one of the great Midwestern universities. This man was head of the department of philosophy, a friend of a powerful political family of the state, and had played an influential part in the ousting of a president of the university and in the selection of his successor. He was a man of no scholarly distinction, but a superb speaker who, as Vivas describes it, ". . . employed his superior rhetorical powers in dishing out the thin gruel that he took to be philosophic wisdom—relativism and atheism. He was at his best before large audiences, especially when the audience was not altogether with him: the voice became softer and deeper, the attitude more gentle, the manner more appealing, expressing a generous desire to lead his students to a better life than their conservative parents had led, if they accepted his reasonable views. His appeal was to the unconventional and critical resentment of the students to the *status quo*. He addressed the students in a humor they could not miss and in a quasi-poetical language that was as corny as it was middle-to-low brow. He suggested to them, clearly but never explicitly, that he and they were victims of an irrational system, hedging them around with absolutes and false theology. The students loved him and his message."[36]

Vivas was then a teaching assistant, and like many other young academics of that time deeply involved in a flirtation with Marxism, which in his case, however, did not lead to a commitment. In speaking of his own teaching in those far-off days, the early thirties, he remarks: "Viewed from outside, his teaching was quite successful. Students crowded his courses and their reactions to his teaching were always strong. . . . But was he really a teacher at all? He was not teaching philosophy; he was carrying on a relentless job of propaganda for his own views."[37] Because he and many of his colleagues at the time, he goes on to say, ". . . put more effort into getting their own ideas accepted than they did in training students to judge for themselves, they could not be called teachers. They were indoctrinators."[38]

The great question, of course, is how all this affected the students. Many of them, as Vivas said, came to the university, especially in those days, filled with political, religious, moral and social views which, as he put it, "were not merely naive but absurd." It was the teacher's duty to "lead them to think, since all they did was to parrot the nonsense they had learned at home. . . . But how far to crack their ignorance? Above all, how to crack it? It was all too easy for a teacher with his dialectical hammer to split open the student's mind and spill his beliefs on the ground, leaving him feeling total devastation, emptiness, acute and angry pain. Furthermore, neither he nor his friends," Vivas goes on to say, speaking of his own teaching, "distinguished between the millennial, fragrant, respectable orthodoxies that had sustained the civilization they claimed to champion, and the smelly little ones. For him and his friends all orthodoxies except their own were little and smelly. Their own views, they complacently believed, were not an orthodoxy, they were the truth. . . . Stripped roughly of the coverage of his beliefs, the student's personality underwent a shock from which sometimes he never successfully recovered. The upshot was that the 'smelly little orthodoxies' that were discarded from students were displaced by devastating cynicism, and since the need to believe was not eradicated when his beliefs were shown up, the student was often ready to fall for the strong dogmatism that was at hand, Marxism."[39] The process Vivas describes was going on, to a greater or less degree, in every college and university in the country, and grew in intensity as time went on, with the SDS and the student revolutionaries of the 1960's one of its more spectacular, but by no means most significant results. It was through this process that liberalism in its modern form became the reigning orthodoxy of the country.

But I have still not answered the question, Why did the propertied classes, who supply the money, permit it to happen? If Schumpeter's explanation, that they do not care, is not sufficient, what is the reason? On the face of it, it would seem that the non-university community should have no difficulty eliminating what Schumpeter calls its "enemies" from the educational institutions—it supplies the money, and the trustees, who are largely from outside the university, in theory, at least, control the institution itself. But how are such people to know what really goes on, and even if they know, what can they do about it? Such a professor of philosophy as Vivas described without doubt had a thoroughly corrupting influence, but how could a member of the legislature, let us say, or a trustee, prove it, and even if he could, what could he do? We live, we are told, in an "open society," where nothing is sacred, in which all questions are "open questions." If nothing is sacred, if all questions are open questions, what is subversive? The universities have made themselves, to a large degree, autonomous by their insistence on tenure, on academic freedom—which is interpreted as academic license—and on the principle that faculty is to be appointed on the basis of scholarly competence alone, without regard to background, point of view, or moral values, all of which has made the professor impregnable and disarmed the university itself. Much of the same thing has happened, on a modified scale, in the public high schools.

One of the principal reasons that the situation has developed which Schumpeter describes as "the bourgeoisie permitting itself to be educated by its enemies" is that what he calls the bourgeoisie has little or no understanding of the influence and importance of ideas. There are many reasons for this, one of which is doubtless inadequate education. As Eric Voegelin put it:

> It will be sufficient to state that the students have good reason to revolt; and if the reasons they actually advance are bad, one should remember that the educational institutions have cut them off from the life of reason so effectively that they cannot even articulate the causes of their legitimate unrest.[40]

Furthermore, a man who has spent his life in practical pursuits, as most of us do, whose judgments are necessarily made on the basis of everyday considerations, finds it difficult not only to think in terms of abstractions, but to attach much importance to them. Then there is the attitude of the successful businessman toward the intellectual: for rather obvious reasons, but unfortunate in their consequences for the businessman, he is inclined not to take the intellectual seriously, and considering the general impression made by intellectuals as a group, this is not difficult to understand. Why should a man who has successfully run a substantial business, which means dealing with numerous and constantly changing situations and confronting antagonists of every kind, from labor union officials to government bureaucrats, take a man seriously who chases after one half-understood idea after another and probably cannot even balance his own checkbook, to say nothing of giving another man a job or showing a profit at the end of the year and keeping the ship afloat in every kind of weather? The businessman may be justified in considering himself a better man than the intellectual, but it is the intellectual who has the last word. The intellectual is in a position to undermine the basis of order in society without the businessman, or society as a whole, for that matter, even being aware of what is going on. It is the man of business and affairs who has given the intellectual the source of his power and influence—the vast, elaborate communications network and the enormous system of mass education—but because he has little or no understanding of the role of ideas in the life of society, he has lost all control and influence over what he has created.

There is a further consideration in all this which should also not be forgotten: in any encounter between a professor or academic administrator and an ordinary citizen, the latter is almost invariably at a hopeless disadvantage. The professor enters the fray with the great prestige, whether deserved or not, associated with learning and a life devoted to the higher things, while the ordinary citizen, who pays for it all, appears as the man who has spent his life grubbing for money. In addition, the professor, by the nature of his training and the practice of his profession, is far more skillful in expressing himself, in the use of words, than the average citizen. Some years ago, to give an example, a member of the state legislature of Illinois became concerned about what was going on in the universities, and, as we should know by now, with good reason. He made some speeches about Communism, which were probably wide of the mark, and instituted an investigation. One of the first witnesses to be called was the president of the University of Chicago, who, needless to say, was far better equipped for such an encounter than any member of the legislature. When the question of communist influence in the universities came up, which was probably a rather insignificant factor in the problem, the university president innocently remarked that he didn't know much about Communism, would the chairman of the committee kindly explain it to him, give him a precise definition? None of the committee were able to make a satisfactory answer, even if they knew. The president of the university quickly made fools of the committee, the press was amused, and the world of intellectuals congratulated itself on having won another battle against the common man, but had it? The president of a university occupies a position of great honor and prestige, also of responsibility. Would it not have been better, and more in keeping with his position as the head of an educational institution the rest of the community supports, to have tried to help the members of the committee instead of making them appear foolish? There *was* something wrong with the universities, which the state legislator instinctively realized, even if he put his finger on the wrong place. Our whole situation, and that of the universities also, would be far better now if the universities, instead of contemptuously rejecting any form of criticism or questioning had taken an honest look at themselves from the standpoint of their true purpose and responsibility to society as a whole, but members of the academy are not, as a rule, characterized by the virtue of humility.

Perhaps the two words that best characterize the climate of opinion in our country in the period immediately following World War II are arrogance and its concomitant, self-delusion. We had played the decisive part in a great victory; our economic and military power were without equal. Hitler had ignominiously taken his own life, his Thousand-Year Reich was in ruins and had surrendered unconditionally. What was left of Germany was completely at our mercy. The situation of Japan was similar, but not quite so drastic. Rather than ascribing victory to our vastly greater industrial and human resources, it was easy to believe, and we succumbed to the temptation, that it had come about because we were morally better.

In the war crimes trials following the war we set out not only to demonstrate the crimes of our enemies, but to establish a new concept of international law which would institute the reign of order between the nations, an order, based on law, which would be maintained by the United Nations under the benign influence and care of the two remaining great powers, the United States and Soviet Russia. To make it all seem plausible, certain facts had to be overlooked—war crimes, for example, and crimes against humanity were tacitly assumed to have been committed by the Axis powers alone, the Hitler-Stalin Pact of 1939, which had paved the way for the outbreak of the war, and the support of the Axis powers by World Communism until Hitler's attack on Russia in 1941 were conveniently forgotten. Since the only morally admissible form of government was democracy, it was necessary to picture Soviet Russia as at least an incipient democracy—there was much talk of its "democratic" constitution, and of Stalin as a kindly father-figure: "Good old Uncle Joe."

We provided Japan with a new, democratic constitution, and set out to "reeducate" the Germans; we were going to convert them from autocratic, goose-stepping Prussians into peace-loving demo-

crats, in our image. Our democratic institutions, our free press, our system of education, had proven their superiority by our victory, and should be the model for the whole world, and certainly for the countries we had defeated in the war which were now, it seemed, as putty in our hands.

Stability of international monetary relations was assured by the Bretton Woods Agreement. We would henceforth be masters of our own fate in monetary matters also; no longer would we be slaves to the vagaries of the gold standard. Gold, we were told on the highest authority, was a "barbarous relic," and would henceforth be used only for filling teeth, wedding rings and other forms of jewelry.

In domestic matters it was assumed that we were equally successful in having found answers to the problems that had beset mankind for generations. A "full-employment" act was passed by the federal government which would banish the specter of unemployment. Since a college education had demonstrably helped some to obtain a better position in life, it would be made available to all—as a somewhat sceptical editorial writer put it at the time, the government was not only going to guarantee a college education for everyone, but that everyone would graduate at the head of his class. There were still a few problems, of course—"pockets of poverty" here and there, segregation in the South, inadequate education and medical care for some, but it was confidently believed that all these things could be taken care of by passing laws, by supreme court decisions, and new, imaginative government programs.

When all these things are taken into account, the reader will perhaps agree that I was not greatly overstating the case when I said: "World War II and the peace that followed it represented the final triumph of liberalism."

NOTES

[1] John Dos Passos, *Occasions and Protests* (Chicago: Henry Regnery Co., 1964), p. 175.

[2] Ronald Berman, *America in the Sixties* (New York: The Free Press, 1968), p. 20.

[3] For a detailed discussion of this phenomenon, with many examples, see Paul Hollander, "The Ideological Pilgrim," *Encounter*, November 1973.

[4] Eliseo Vivas, *Two Roads to Ignorance* (Unpublished manuscript), Chapter VII, page 25.

[5] Quoted by Ronald Berman, *op. cit.*, p. 176.

[6] George F. Kennan, *Memoirs 1925–1950* (Boston: Little, Brown & Co., 1967), p. 82.

[7] Joseph E. Davies, *Mission to Moscow*, (New York: Simon & Schuster, 1942), p. 44.

[8] *Ibid.*

[9] Kennan, *op. cit.*, p. 83.

[10] Davies, *op. cit.*, p. 67.

[11] *Ibid.*

[12] *Foreign Affairs*, April 1942.

[13] *Pacific Affairs*, March 1942.

[14] *The Saturday Review of Literature*, January 10, 1942.

[15] *The New Republic*, January 12, 1942.

[16] "These territorial changes seemed to me to be doubly pernicious, and the casual American acquiescence in them all the less forgivable, because of the fact that they served, like other territorial concessions to the Russians, simply to extract great productive areas from the economy of Europe and to permit the Russians, for reasons of their own military and political convenience, to deny these areas and their resources to the general purposes of European reconstruction . . . . The disaster that befell this area [East Prussia] with the entry of Soviet forces has no parallel in modern European experience. There were considerable sections of it where, to judge by all existing evidence, scarcely a man, woman, or child of the indigenous population was left alive after the initial passage of Soviet forces." Kennan, *op. cit.*, pp. 264–265.

[17] Dos Passos, *op. cit.*, p. 175.

[18] From a letter to W. T. Couch from William Miller, quoted in "The Sainted Book Burners," *The Freeman*, April 1955, p. 423.

[19] *The New Republic*, January 1, 1945.

[20] *The Library Journal*, September 15, 1944.

[21] *Kirkus Book Review Service*, September 15, 1945.

[22] *New York Times*, December 9, 1945.

[23] Richard M. Weaver, *Ideas Have Consequences* (Chicago: University of Chicago Press, 1948), p. 2.

[24] *New York Times*, February 22, 1948.

[25] *Ibid.*, March 22, 1948.

[26] *The Nation*, May 29, 1948.

[27] *Annals of the American Academy*, July 1948.

[28] Weaver, *op. cit.*, p. 172.

[29] F. A. Hayek, "The Intellectuals and Socialism," *The University of Chicago Law Review*, Spring 1949, reprinted in *Studies in Philosophy, Politics and Economics* (Chicago: University of Chicago Press, 1967), p. 178.

[30] Joseph Schumpeter, *Capitalism, Socialism and Democracy* (New York: Harper and Row, 1942), p. 147.

[31] *Ibid.*, p. 151.

[32] Hayek, *op. cit.*, p. 184.

[33] *Ibid.*, p. 185.

[34] *Ibid.*, p. 189.

[35] Schumpeter, p. 161.

[36] Vivas, *op. cit.*, Chapter IV, p. 7.

[37] *Ibid.*, p. 26.

[38] *Ibid.*, p. 30.

[39] *Ibid.*, pp. 30–31.

[40] Eric Voegelin, "On Classical Studies," *Modern Age*, Winter 1973.

[XIX, Spring 1975, 114–126]

[8]

The Divine Right of Minorities

OTTO VON HABSBURG

Otto von Habsburg (1912–   ), head of the imperial house of Habsburg-Lothringen and son of the Emperor Karl, at present resides in Bavaria, where he is a member of the European Parliament. In 1961 he renounced his claim to the throne; in 1973 he became president of the international Paneuropa Union; and in 1979 he assumed his present position. A writer as well as a politician who frequently travels in America, he has contributed to scholarly journals in this country and abroad, listing among his publications Politik für das Jahr 2000 *(1968),* Rudolph v. Habsburg *(1973),* Ein europäischer Friedensfürst *(1978), along with twenty-four books in seven languages on history, politics, and political science. He has been awarded the Bavarian Order of Merit, the Ordre du Lion d'Or, the Europäischer Karlspreis der Sudetendeutschen Landsmannschaft, and the Adenauer Prize (1977).*

ONE IMPEDIMENT to the meeting of conservative minds from both sides of the Atlantic I have found illustrated, time and again, during lecture tours I have made in the United States in the past few years. It occurs in questions concerning the difference in traditional American and European political institutions. Many Americans, with whom I find myself agreeing on political principles and goals, are happily convinced that the American form of government is the one objective form of political wisdom and has a universal claim; and any European attempt to solve political problems in another way seems to them the result of either wrongheadedness or ignorance. To the objection that what is right under American conditions may not be expedient in other worlds, they answer that Europeans persist in defending outmoded forms because they are the victims of environment, the creatures of traditions that do not include the one of liberty. The European is a prisoner of his past, especially if he falls into that vague category called "royalty" or "nobility." While the European "common man" may, given time and dollars enough, be won from his ignorance, the "upper classes" are forever set in their wrongheadedness, too steeped in notions of the divine ordainment of privilege ever to think for themselves or to conceive of valid systems outside of the ones in which they have been brought up.

It would be too easy to answer that the argument from environment cuts both ways, though it might be worth noting in passing that the European privileged classes of the last thirty-five troubled years have been neither noble nor royal. It would be too easy because the argument is not entirely an irrelevant one. Being faced with it, directly or implicitly, so often, I have tried to assess it objectively against the background of my own experience, and it seems to me to contain both truth and falsehood, as all "simple" explanations do.

Certainly, tradition and family environment predispose one to particular activities and attitudes. In a relatively stable society, the ruling class is drawn from ruling families, and the United States illustrates this as much as any other country with sons of presidents, senators, and justices who have followed in the footsteps of their fathers. To choose only very prominent contemporary examples, there are the Lodges, the Roosevelts, the Tafts, and the Longs. Persons raised in a political atmosphere, and from their earliest years accustomed to hearing affairs of state talked over in the relaxed candidness of the family circle, naturally enough develop a taste and, if there is really such a thing as education, an aptitude for public service. If the Adamses could produce another Adams or the Pendergasts another Pendergast, the same process must have been at work among the European dynasties—with, all other things being equal, similarly various results. But I think we can suppose an even greater pressure in the European case, for the son of a long line of rulers has not only the political training of his parental house, but also his own awareness of the heritage of many centuries.

Is this training and awareness always ossifying? I know of no reason why it necessarily should be, nor of any instance in history that shows it: what monarch slavishly followed the policies of his father? An interest in politics is still a long way from an unconditional acceptance of the political doctrines of one's forebears, and the broad indication of human experience is that young men, whatever their education, tend to take a view opposite to their parents'. Youth's ambition is generally large enough to demand revolutionary changes so that it questions the wisdom of its elders, when it doesn't flatly declare their folly. Because it is in the young man's nature to be impatient with life and conditions as they meet him, Clemenceau's remark that a person at twenty who is not a socialist has no heart will, any particular political formulations aside, always remain true. And the fervor and enthusiasm it recognizes is not likely to be any less present in the descendant of a well-known political family, trained in some measure in public affairs, than in a child of the great anonymous masses, for whom politics must often seem merely to happen rather than to be made.

My own concern with political matters was greatly sharpened during my years at Louvain. I speak here less of my formal studies in political and social science than of the atmosphere of fervid debate and discussion in which those of us who had an inclination for politics moved. My years at Louvain were those of the great economic crisis, when the outlook was bleak for student youth and the political life even of staid Belgium was agitated by violent undercurrents. At the University every view the diverse intellectual life of Europe retained or could newly throw up was held. In my time we had with us the man who would one day become the leader of the Belgian fascists and later the Quisling of his country: Léon Degrelle. A brilliant, erratic character, a poet of real talent, he stimulated all the discussions in which he joined without ever offering a profound view on anything. There were many others who went on into public life in every sort of office from parliamentarian to publisher; and it is a commentary on our Europe that more than one because of the views he held ended before a firing-squad or on the gallows. Drawn into the big debate that was going on all over Europe, I yet could ponder it in a kind of solitude, often enough a rainy one since this was Belgium, as I biked the fifteen miles to and the fifteen miles from Louvain. In this daily transit I could not only think over the views of such brilliant professors as Paul Van Zeeland, now Belgium's Foreign Minister, and A. E. Jansen, of League of Nations fame, but also devise ways to confront my teachers with the violent arguments of those who were my comrades as students.

The heart may dictate the political beliefs of youth; the head must make a later re-appraisal for any lasting conviction. It is one of the ironies of the human lot that we often see most clearly and come to our deepest belief in moments of adversity; our enemies are sometimes our best teachers.

In Europe the men of my generation— those around forty today—arrived at their time of decision in a world molded by the rise and numerous triumphs of totalitarianism. Whether or not we were directly engaged in politics, we could not escape the tremendous changes the new type of dictator had brought into our world: he was, after all, *totalitarian*. The idea of total war, which, spawned by the French Revolution, had germinated in the brain of that half-genius, half-madman, General Ludendorff, had begot on the civil plane the idea of total politics—something not less murderous or wicked than its monstrous military parent.

The choice each of us had to make was not so easy as hindsight may now pretend. There was a time, let us admit, when amongst totalitarianisms Hitler's indeed looked like "the wave of the future." Doubts stilled by his apparent miracles, British, French, and other statesmen made their now-forgotten pilgrimages to the false prophet of Berchtesgaden, and Lloyd George, the great Liberal leader and one of the architects of the Europe that had made Hitler's rise to power possible, could return from a call on the Fuehrer in 1936 to announce that Hitler was "one of the greatest among the very great men I have known" and the Germans were "the happiest people on earth." Forgotten, too, are the actions of those in London who encouraged Hitler's lawless expansion and his invasion of Vienna, the first step of World War II. Covering up this historical record is a necessary step in creating the schizophrenic notion of the collective guilt of the German people. Similar journeys have been more recently undertaken, to make even greater offerings to naked power, to Teheran, Yalta, and Potsdam, but they are still fresh in most memories despite the efforts of the artificers of these latter-day Munich Agreements to have their deeds forgotten and, in some cases, to have history falsified. These things must be remembered in judging those who guessed wrong in choosing between powers and in comparing them with those who sat in court on them, and often still do.

For me the choice was made quickly enough. Hitler had several times tried to lure me over to his side, but his main effort came during a visit I made to Berlin in the first weeks of 1933 to work at the Agrarian Institute of Professor Sering to finish the thesis for my doctorate. While in the German capital, I called on a number of German statesmen, President von Hindenburg amongst them, and on members of the former ruling dynasty. Most of the Hohenzollerns were men of great integrity, but unfortunately one of the sons of William II, Prince August Wilhelm, had joined the National Socialist movement and even become a member of the Reichstag. When I called on him— something I intended solely as a courtesy—he delivered himself of a message from his Fuehrer, saying Hitler and Goering would like to have a private talk with me. He added that the talk would be of great advantage to the cause I represent, for Hitler, who was shortly to become Chancellor (this was in the last days of January 1933), was willing to support me in Austria if I would outwardly accept the National Socialist tenets and rule in my country as a National Socialist ruler. To make the conversation more informal, August Wilhelm suggested that Goering, as Speaker of the Reichstag, should invite Hitler and me to dinner at the same time. It was not easy to convince him that I had no interest in such a political conversation since there was a fundamental disagreement between Hitler and myself, and that this disagreement followed directly on our agreement that there could be no peaceful co-existence of religion and totalitarianism—National Socialist or Communist. Then as now, the Christian faith was the great bulwark against totalitarianism's promise of immediate success.

We know how many were deceived by that promise in the years leading up to World War II, and again in the "love-Russia" period of the War, when it often looked as though the forces of totalitarianism might prevail. We still have no absolute assurance against the triumph of these forces, but we are now better armed to meet them in seeing one reason for their past successes: the totalitarians have a clear program and they fight for a definite world order, while we who are their opponents lack a consistent approach and must fight them with piecemeal measures. That the anti-totalitarians needed some coherent program I began to see more and more clearly in the early 1930's. After I had publicly come out against National Socialism, more than a thousand municipalities and towns in Austria in the period from 1933 to 1938 gave me their honorary citizenship, and

in my letters of acceptance I addressed myself in each case to some particular complex of the moral, political, social, and economic questions that troubled the heart of Europe. Along with this occasion to study specific problems, went consultations with thousands of my countrymen and with the leaders of Western Europe. In pursuing the fight against the Hitlerite menace, I called frequently on the statesmen of France, Great Britain, Belgium, and Holland, and I kept in touch with those persons in Italy who condemned the course of Mussolini's policy. The House of Savoy was especially a center of realism and the understanding that the Rome–Berlin Axis was a direct route to catastrophe. The experiences resulting from these meetings were sometimes encouraging, more often discouraging, but in all their complexity they seemed to reduce to the single lesson that if Europe was to be conserved, it could only be done by opposing a concrete program to the enemy.

Announcing a common dislike of the excesses of totalitarianism was not enough. The cure of our condition had to come from a knowledge of its causes. The tragic situation in which Europe has found itself since 1914—roughly for forty years now—has engaged many minds. Some, especially numerous outside of Europe, find our decadence absolute and see no hope of European resuscitation. Others find reason for hope in what has been called the dismal science, economics; the causes of Europe's decay, they insist, are remediable economic ones—economic nationalism and the disparity of wealth. The first has prevented the development of Europe's potential wealth and led to wars; the second has bred the resentment that gives rise to extremist movements, since given a fairly equitable distribution of wealth, people are always open to the persuasion of reason. Whatever truth there is in this—and I have no intention of saying that the economic organization of Europe has been ideal, technically or morally—it is still far from the whole explanation of recent European history. Without for a moment proposing that his existence was good, we can say that the German proletarian of the 1930's, who as the voting records show supported Hitler, was better off in the terms of economic statistics than the peasants of the "backward" countries of Eastern Europe, where Communism imposed its rule only by force. Again, in the more advanced nations of the West such as France and Italy—where the benefits of industrialism, with all their really great inequality of distribution, are still greater than Russia can promise for generations—there has been an alarming growth of Communism. If the exclusively economic and social explanations, despite their being contradicted by reality, are maintained by too many people and too many publications, it is only because the abandonment of the materialist approach to our problems would mean facing up to facts that people would rather ignore.

If we look at these facts dispassionately, we shall have to admit that the present state of affairs has justified a man whose great mental ability must be recognized beyond his colossal political blunders: Charles Maurras. Maurras was the dean of that group of outstanding men—amongst them the Socialist Léon Blum, the Radical Herriot, the Right Winger Tardieu—who were at once intellectuals and practical politicians and whose brilliance in political thinking in the years between the wars insured France's primacy in the field of political theory, even as it perhaps obscured the weakness of France's actual position. During the many long evenings in Paris when I had the chance to witness their Gallic agility in debate, Maurras would appear only rarely, for at night he wrote the editorials for his

newspaper—an extraordinary journal in its combination of the highbrow and the vulgarly vituperative; but when he did appear, he would, despite his total deafness, dominate the scene through his depth of insight and precision of mind. Though he was a materialist and verged on atheism—an error that led him to the wrong side in World War II and brought discredit on his name—Maurras saw clearly what was at issue in the modern world. His phrase "politique d'abord" summed up his thought. Since "politique" was for him not day-to-day party policy but public service in the best sense, his meaning was to give primacy to the moral and juridical issues over the material and economic ones. He saw that there was no genuine progress on the shifting sands of expedience and improvization, and that only a state based firmly on ethics and morals can advance toward the goal of its people's true happiness. A state whose one principle is survival through aggrandizement, at the expense of other people or its own, whose politics are not *d'abord,* may give—as Hitler's did—a momentary impression of prosperity and social well-being, but in the end that state leads the nation to catastrophe. The statesman who would achieve for his people the comparatively obvious goals of economic and social justice must start from the moral ground in which grows the enduring strength of any social entity.

Our plight was thus primarily due to the tragic betrayal of the moral principles on which Europe once stood. Without this, we should never have entered our present crisis. With our spiritual values intact, we should never have seen the rise of totalitarianism. Had we not failed in the moral field, had we not abandoned our ethical standards in the quest of an illusory economic prosperity, we should never have ended with concentration camps for people because of their ancestry, incendiary bombs for children because of their parents' error, and the life of slaves for those whose descendants are to escape the kingdom of necessity.

The truth of this was borne in on me in two conversations I had with Communists. The first was with Willy Muenzenberg, the celebrated and dreaded Comintern agent. Muenzenberg, despite his dark record, was an idealist whose heart was broken by the Hitler-Stalin pact—I am convinced that his subsequent suicide marked the despair of a man who had given his life to an idea and seen it fail. Our talk was soon after the pact. Muenzenberg did not criticize Russia, but suddenly, quite spontaneously, he burst out: "If only I could believe in God, many things would be different!" It was rather like a cry from the pit, not the one in which Muenzenberg was privately lost, but the one which was the ambience of a whole generation. The second conversation, a more recent one, was with a South American Communist leader whose name I do not mention because he is still a Party member in good standing. We met in a smoky restaurant of a Latin American seaside resort, and when at three in the morning we left to drive back to the big city, all our talk had got us nowhere. The road led along the sea and past an old Spanish fort, surrounded by palms, where we stopped for a short stroll to breathe the salty but balmy air. All at once, turning to the fort, the Communist said: "You know, we have been discussing long and hard. This much I admit: if you Christians would really be what you say, and if there were even a dim hope of returning to the glories of ancient Spain, I would gladly drop everything and follow your way. But, alas, I just can't believe it is possible!"

There was another occasion when, in even more dramatic circumstances, I heard the same thought voiced, though this time its direction was hope rather than despair.

It was said by a great friend of mine, George Mandel, in one of the most critical moments of his life. Mandel was France's iron-willed Minister of the Interior in 1940, a Jew without formal religious ties, and a great French patriot who was to die for his country before a Nazi firing-squad. It was on the night Paul Reynaud's cabinet fell. The French government had withdrawn in defeat to Bordeaux, the Battle of France was in its last hours. The Ministry of the Interior was lodged in the building of the Prefecture of the Department of Gironde, where, met with the flicker of a few weak candles, the failure of electric power betokened the gloom of a people expecting defeat. Mandel, though unbroken, knew that he was losing, and for several minutes of utter discouragement he told me of his realization of the rottenness of the Third Republic, which was beyond his worst fears. A world and a set of ideals he had served were falling down. Yet, he added, France had one last reserve: despite its atheism, regardless of its cynicism, the country could never fail to remain Christian, the eldest daughter of the Church. He was not, he explained, taking a stand in a denominational way. He was speaking of the power of the Christian force emanating from the French soil. This moral force would be, some time in the far future, the reason why the country would come back into its own.

The same Christian character invests the whole of Europe, where almost every village has at its center a church, almost every city a cathedral. It is this Christian heritage, a capital that in each individual heart can be made to yield further riches, that makes talk of returning to principles more than a pleasant-sounding and lofty generalization. What Christianity enjoins us to in our daily lives is clear enough; the standards of right and wrong it lays down are not subject to essential debate. While these injunctions and standards plainly show how wide capitalism and socialism, democracy and dictatorship are of what is required of man, they admittedly do not provide us with any ready-made program for immediate or future action. Such a program is the product of the human intelligence, of much thought and some trial and error, and the difficult task of making it falls squarely on the shoulders of an intellectual elite. We have no warrant to expect the appearance of a new St. Francis who will sway the mass of men into paths that those who have the talents to lead and instruct are too timorous or indolent to discover. Where social or economic justice can be at once redressed, it should be done—as the charity to which we are bidden shows—but we must be on guard against the error of supposing that a Christian economic and social policy can be erected on a political system that is not Christian in its orientation. Here again we have to accept Maurras' "politique d'abord" and recognize a hierarchy of urgencies, with the prime urgency a fundamental change in the political structure.

But it must be remembered that there is no Christian political orthodoxy. If past ages erred in too closely identifying Church and state, the great error of our time is to identify Christian policy with this or that political party and try to force an all-embracing idea into the straitjacket of a short-lived and necessarily faulty human construction. This applies both to Christian Conservative and Christian Democratic parties. Christianity can never be the province of a party, for a party, as the name indicates, is factional, a part, while Christianity, whose claims are universal, cannot accept such limitation. It is obvious that in different contexts religiously inspired politics will take different expressions, but what will be unchanging in any Christian policy is the public service of the natural law and the striving for the practical application in the life of the community of the eternal principles laid down by God in the soul of every man.

The concern of Christian politics is with the human person, and the criterion of whether or not a state is Christian, that is to say moral, is its attitude toward human rights. Everybody in free countries from time to time makes his libations to human rights, but by and large he assumes them as much as the air he breathes. Though I had long realized that the end of government was to insure man the maximum freedom for the working out of his own happiness, I did not see human rights as the paramount issue of our times until those evil days of March 1938, when the Nazis occupied Austria and my best and closest friends were sent to concentration camps. Those with whom I had worked day in and day out were now at the mercy of professional evil-doers, and each time news of them came it told of savagery and death. There can be few things more terrible to hear than that the men one has known are no longer being treated as men. Only a few years later, the same bestiality came again, on what may have been even a greater scale, to the Danube Valley with the advance of the Red Army. The dead and tortured are witnesses to the importance of this issue.

Yet even here our times are confused. Attempts at the codification of human rights cannot succeed without a basic philosophy of human freedom. I would even go a step further and say that without admitting the existence of God, there can be no admission of human rights, since any right has to derive from a higher source. It would be destructive of society to say that human rights have their final origin in the individual, for the source of the rights could not then be subjected to any higher authority, and we should end in anarchy. And we end in mass rather than in atomistic anarchy if, following the theory of Rousseau's social contract, we make human rights the gift of a collective will, since an accidental plurality could in all logic take away what a previous majority had given. As soon as we admit that human rights are dependent on a majority decision, that very moment we deny their existence.

If, on the other hand, we recognize that human rights have their exclusive source in God, then it is our duty to defend them against any force. The admission of God-given human rights means the primacy of the individual and his natural collectivities—family, religious community, and even professional group—over the state. The existence of inalienable human rights denies unlimited power to the state or to any other collectivity. We are under an obligation, both practical and moral, to refuse the state, whether led by a majority or by a dictator, the right to violate the basic freedoms of man. And the corollary of this is recognizing a hierarchy of freedoms, rights, and even privileges that belong to certain groups and cannot be interfered with. Once this is seen, it is evident enough that the test of a truly Christian freedom-loving state is not the rule of the majority, but the defense that state gives to the rights of minorities. It is much more important for us as individuals that these rights be safeguarded than that the will of the majority be carried out, just as it is more difficult for the state to do the first than the second. When Hitler exterminated the Jews and the Gypsies, he did so in the name of the majority, as did the Big Three when they decided to deport the German minorities from Eastern Europe. In neither case was the right with the majority, but with the abused minority, and it is a shameful commentary on our recent history that almost nobody stood up against either Hitler at the right time or against the signers of Yalta and Potsdam until their

immoral acts proved a mistake in the game of power politics.

In most cases it is not the majority that needs protection; it is the minorities. And since the role of the state is to insure order, the rule of law that protects the individual against the arbitrary and the unjust, the state's structure must in the first place be designed to protect the rights of minorities. Shocking as this may sound to the believer in unqualified majority rule, he will find on reflection that he, like all of us, is a member of a minority in one function of his life or another, and that most often one where his deepest interests are involved. Man as such, as an individual, is a minority compared to the community, and the good community is one designed to allow him to lead a full life in his minority status.

When we consider in this light the functions of the state, we find that safeguarding fundamental rights and the moral order is primarily the duty of the Judiciary Power. Both the Legislative and, in most instances, the Executive are servants of the majority. Despite the checks and balances that, in theory, are intended to keep the three powers evenly matched, in practice a state of balance is unfortunately rare. It can be achieved only under very favorable circumstances and is easily upset in times of crisis. Looking at the European republics, we see in general the supremacy of the Legislative, and in France, an outstanding example of government by assembly, the country has been deprived of its stability. Where the Executive is supreme, we have dictatorship, and both the popular will and law are told what they shall be. As for the Judiciary, its supremacy is only secured—astounding as this may be to many—in the few remaining Continental monarchies.

The reason for this is not difficult to discover if we look at what monarchy has been in historical fact. The mediaeval king stood at the summit of a system of inter-active rights and duties, with his own powers quite sharply limited by customary usage and written law; he ruled "by the grace of God," not in the absurd sense of his being someone essentially better than his fellow nationals, but in virtue of his and his subjects' acknowledging God as the ultimate source of authority and in their understanding that his powers were circumscribed by the rights and liberties God had given to each individual and each natural group. The respect accorded the king's person was not different in kind from the respect that requires everyone in an American courtroom to stand when the lowest magistrate enters. Once a Su-preme Being and His commands to justice are recognized, each legitimate authority in the state is seen to exist by His grace, which secures the humblest citizen equally in his freedom and in his share of the majesty in the name of which he is gov-erned. The notion of the ruler himself as the source of right is entirely un-Christian, and the theory of the all-powerful king, the absolute ruler, that became current in Europe with the Renaissance was de-rived from Roman ideas of the emperor's divinity. Great as was the damage done by the absolute monarchies of the sev-enteenth century to the concept of Chris-tian kingship, in plain fact none of them was absolute, and the enduringly Chris-tian fabric of society always stood in the way of their absolute rule, so that the unlimited and arbitrary ruler has only become a reality in our own day, when self-appointed or elected dictators re-peatedly violate God's law in the name of the popular will.

The highest function of the monarch is judicial, and the judge does not create the law, he administers it. The theory of hereditary monarchy is that the person who occupies the highest position in the state and succeeds to it, so to speak, in

the natural course of events, is likely above all others to have the disinterestedness, and enjoy the freedom from pressure, necessary in the Chief Justice. His unique position enables him to be independent of parties and factions, to stand outside of any groups of special interest, and to turn down all short-term measures that merely cater to popularity. At the same time, disinterest is not remoteness from common concerns; the king is not the cold oracle of the law, but is there to see that particular laws are made for men as they are; and this part of his role is expressed in the simple answer that the Emperor Francis Joseph gave to Theo-dore Roosevelt when the American asked him how he saw his place in modern times: "To protect my people from their government." I well remember that my father never permitted anyone in his house to make derogatory remarks about reli-gious communities, political parties, or social groups. If someone said something of the kind in the presence of us children, my father, usually a very mild man, would energetically reprimand him, thus teach-ing us by example that a king has no right to personal preferences or dislikes. For him everybody must be truly equal. The king is there to represent the people in his own person and character. The peo-ple's elected delegates have a similar task in any modern monarchy, and the task of each is highly necessary in today's com-plex societies, but the elected legislator represents party or region, either of which is sometimes identical with social group, and his office cannot have the same ju-diciary and dedicated nature as the king's.

Some of the import of this dedication was perhaps conveyed to me in my earliest childhood, when I saw the coronation of my father in Budapest. I was only four at the time, and the scene is of course now dim in my mind, but I still recall the solemnity of the occasion, the earnestness of my father, and the emotion of those who took part in the rite. During the ceremonies, I sat by the side of old King Ferdinand of Bulgaria, a brilliant man much learned in history, who tried to explain to the child I was the profound significance of the day. I cannot say that I remember much more than his effort to do this, but to the colorful fragments that remain in memory I have since been able to attach the deeper meaning of coronation, that sacramental which, as the Church tells us, puts on the ruler the "duty to protect the weak, the widow, and the orphan" and calls on him to give his oath to defend the liberties that derive not from the shifting will of an individual or an assembly but from the Transcendental Power that, by the principle of its own eternity, can never change.

I am aware that in making this argument I may seem to open myself to the charge of coupling a nostalgia for the past with personal ambition. Neither particular, I think, is justified. If ours is an era largely governed by republics and dictatorships, that does not mean the monarchical form is irrelevant to it, any more than health is irrelevant to a sick man: I have tried to show how monarchy might meet some of our most pressing needs. History shows monarchies and republics alternating in fairly regular cycles, and dictatorship as an aberration endemic throughout. Of these cycles, the monarchical one in almost every case is the longer and takes place in a more mature society. To say that some institutions remain entirely viable today is hardly to express an impossible wish to return to the past, for there can be no human progress unless what is good in the past can be revived or prolonged.

The Emperor Joseph is said once to have remarked: "Mon métier à moi c'est d'être royaliste"; and the assumption continues today that the member of a once-reigning family will be a professional monarchist. Yet a little reflection should show that nothing offers less opportunity for a personal career than the role "pretender," even where there is the greatest likelihood of a restoration. The machinery of political action in the modern world is almost exclusively the party and, except where dictatorship prevails, the idea of majority rule has ironically led to an increase of factionalism; but the claimant to kingship, as I have said, must above all remain outside of parties. It should be obvious that the pretender's role, in direct proportion to his interest in politics, is personally thwarting. I doubt very much that pride in and a sense of obligation to the family name alone are enough to make a man persevere in such a course. The service of a particular dynasty is not the substance of the monarchical idea, however much the notion of loyalty that is bound up with it is also bound up with monarchy. A country is not the property of a family: history reveals changes of dynasty in every state, and the claims of the institution in this case have precedence over those of its representatives. The hereditary accession of kings is not intended to magnify a single family, but to insure the stability in which all families of a nation can best flourish, and the wholehearted advocate of legitimist monarchy is far less working in the service of a family than he is making an act of faith in a determined political program. If at the same time he makes his own claims to kingship, he does this in the knowledge that success will be had at the expense of personal preferences and by binding himself over without reservations to the community that he must serve not for applause but after the demands of conscience and law.

The moral basis laid, what is to be the superstructure, the house in which the people of Europe will dwell? From a continent that was a fair unity before World War I, in which people could travel without passports and trade with few if any restrictions, Europe has been transformed in the last thirty-five years into a maze of small states, surrounded by tariff and currency barriers like walled mediaeval towns. Behind these bulwarks, as each state has tried more and more to form itself on a common megalopolitan-industrial pattern, there has been a coincident growth of nationalism, for it is one of the peculiarities of the modern world that the harder borders are to cross, the less aware we are of having crossed them. In this stifling atmosphere have occurred the suicidal outbreaks that have decimated our peoples.

Among younger persons, the benefits to be had from large areas not fragmented by customs lines are known only to those who have had the opportunity of travelling outside of Europe. My own travels in the United States—where by the end of 1942 I had visited all forty-eight states—have convinced me that America's openness not only explains its extraordinary prosperity, but also much of the American character, whose generousness, hospitality, and entire absence of suspicion seems to me a reflection of the country's broadness. It is this last quality of the American that gives him the easy assumption of intimacy that some Europeans find disconcerting. Though in the past twenty years there has been a considerable tendency toward governmental centralization in the United States, the foundations of America's wealth were laid in the days when the states exercised a high degree of local autonomy; and even today the American system remains essentially a federal one, with many differences in the administration of the different states. However, dreams of American superabundance mustn't make us forget that any unity Europe attains will have to allow for

a far greater diversity: there are borders that can be reduced in importance but not forgotten; historic facts that cannot be undone; and, while there plainly exists a common European culture recognizable from Lisbon to Warsaw, from Istanbul to Brussels, there are a difference of languages and a wide divergence in ways of life we must respect.

The economic unification of Europe is so obvious a need of the hour that no one dares to take a public stand against it, and the selfish interests that oppose it have to do so by devious means. Whatever immediate measures can be taken to strengthen the economic position of Western Europe and to satisfy the legitimate demands of our people for a higher living standard should be entered on without delay; but there is no use in overlooking the fact that the European economy was ruined at Yalta when one hundred and twenty-one million producers and consumers were removed from it. The nature of the injury is very clearly illustrated in the fact that the annual sums of Marshall Aid almost exactly corresponded to the yearly volume of trade between Eastern and Western Europe before the partition. If Western Europe, with a population greater than either the U.S.S.R. or the U.S.A., stands trembling before one and begging help from the other, that is because it finds itself in the plight in which the United States would be were the Middle West handed over to some non-American power for exploitation. The European plight begins not so much with economics as with politics, and if Europeans are to realize the economic potential of their continent, in which diffusion of skill will make use of variety of natural resources, they will at the same time have to recover their political genius and put it to the work of making a European unity whose embrace is not fatal to Europe's diversity.

The worst enemies of European unity outside of the U.S.S.R. are the professional Europeans who make their living, politically and economically, from the European idea. Most of them are politicians who were swept into power in 1945 on the coattails of the advancing Allied forces and now, turned out of their jobs by their own people, are found at every congress and signing every manifesto in the hopes of creating a Europe in their own image in which they can once more find a place for themselves. Though the survival of Europe and America is only to be had by their both standing together, the requisite of this is not an uninspired remaking of Europe on the American pattern: indeed, saving Europe in this fashion, supposing it really were possible, would mean the loss of anything that Europe still has to offer to the world. Equally, there can be no world in which the emergent influence of America is not granted, for it is that influence which secures such of the world as remains free. Any approach to a universal rule of law and order (and, of course, so long as the world endures we shall be making the approach rather than enjoying the accomplishment) that meets the rational condition of dealing with what actually is will have to proceed with a truly liberal spirit. This will mean recognizing the lessons of Europe's past history, which point, beyond the individual, to naturally grown communities, each of which has its inalienable rights. Their rightful demands require a decentralized structure, within which each national community can exercise its autonomy. Common interests and geographical proximity can then be the motives for regional federations that are the final divisions of the larger European unity. The attempt to create a unified Europe by a sort of fiat authority that makes no allowance for the ponderable and imponderable elements of the European complex will carry with it the danger of a lack of balance that must result in conflicts. Men fight not only for markets and at the behest of aggressive ideologies, but also out of the wish to conserve for the future what they feel the long lives of their communities have made them, and this is a just and valid wish that no planning from above has the right to deny. In politics impatience is one of the most frequent and one of the most fatal errors. History is full of good intentions made bad through haste and the reformer's blind insistence on violating human nature.

This haste is the great weakness of present-day politics. We have no time. The West in its dealings with the East is handicapped because it must produce results before the next election. We are forced to short-term projects that will mature in a single legislative session. Anything that cannot promise immediate results is by that token not worth undertaking. And with our eyes directed toward tomorrow's results, we too often overlook how similar maneuvers in the past had no results at all, or bad ones. But this is not alone a matter of our political habits and structures; it is the symptom of something deeper. It is characteristic of a generation that has lost its sense of historical perspective and become so self-centered that it no longer sees the continuity of which it is a part. In rejecting its past, it has renounced its future, and sometimes its erratic and futile measures in the present convince one that these are the desperate activities of those who truly anticipate annihilation. The perspective of history has been lost because history gives up its meaning only in the perspective of eternity. All that can be worked toward on earth in the span of a single human life takes on meaning and value only when seen under the aspect of eternity, man's participation in which sets the final seal on all his actions. Against the assurances that eternity holds, man discovers his own dimensions and is guarded against making the over- or under-estimation of himself that leads to destruction in the world. Those who think they have but one life to live can do little good that will outlast it. Man is distinguished from the animal by his reason, and the distinction of man's reasoning is that it can discover and work toward goals that are beyond the brief extent of his own animal life.

The perception of this is not everywhere lost. I came upon an example of it during the Spanish Civil War. The various military units in Spain were recruiting volunteers with posters. One of these was put up by the Requetes, those traditionalists who might be called the Jacobites of Spain. The poster offered no pleasures of travel, no bonuses, no benefits of an incidental education. It simply showed a dead Requete hanging on barbed wire, and over him glowed a star under which was written: "Remember—before God there is no unknown soldier." Death here was not a sentimental symbol with no reference to what dying in battle is really like, for in a civil war like the Spanish no one escapes a close knowledge of death; yet the Requetes continued to volunteer, knowing that for many of them worse deaths awaited than a clean shot on the barbed wire. Even those who will argue that their deaths were Quixotic (and I am not one who would) cannot deny that these men entered into the decisive moment of their existence certain their lives had not been in vain: their sacrifice would be acknowledged in eternity. Let us hope that the future will not make the same demand on any of us; but whatever coming years may hold in store for us we must recover the understanding that what we do is done in God's sight. It will be the source of our courage and our assurance that our works, so far as men's can, will endure.   [II, Summer 1958, 273–284]

[9]

Majority Rule Revisited

GEORGE W. CAREY

George W(escott) Carey *(1933–   ) is professor of government at Georgetown University. An associate editor of* Modern Age *since 1981, he is also editor of* The Political Science Reviewer, *an annual volume founded in 1971 that features important scholarly articles by and about conservative intellectuals. He has published widely, including a definitive study of the impact of* The Federalist *on American political theory and practice, and has edited such works as* Liberalism Versus Conservatism *(1966) and* Freedom and Virtue: The Conservative/Libertarian Debate *(1984).* Carey's The Basic Symbols of the American Political Tradition *(1970), coauthored with Willmoore Kendall, is considered "a major reassessment of the traditional American concepts of self-government."*

IN RECENT YEARS majority rule and the problems associated with both its realization and operation have been explored in great detail.[1] Concomitant with this a majoritarian *ethic* has evolved, an ethic which holds that the essential element of democratic (= just and good) government is the extent to which the majorities are able to rule (save, of course, in such areas as "civil" or "minority" "rights").[2] One has only to read our textbooks in the American field to see this. The majority rule standard is one by which we measure the democratic character of our institutions, be they formal, such as the Supreme Court, the Congress, the Electoral College, or informal, such as our political party structures and operations. Equally impressive evidence to this effect are the decisions of the Warren Court which followed Baker v. Carr.[3] "One man, one vote" is a direct derivative of the majoritarian ethic which provides proponents

for "reform" of our institutions with a very powerful argument, if only because it throws the opponents of this principle on the defensive. Who would, given our present morality and faith, cherish the task of defending a contrary proposition? Besides which, the "one man, one vote" formula enjoys inherent advantages: it is simple, relatively easy to apply, and does conform with the prevailing ethic which proclaims that all men are created equal.

What is remarkable about this is that no political theorist of the first order has ever advanced the majoritarian ethic, as, say, embodied in the formula "one man, one vote." To put the matter in some perspective, we certainly do not find democracy and the principle of majority rule exalted in our classical literature.[4] At best, this literature tells us such a decision-making system would survive only under the most propitious circumstances, or when certain barriers or mechanisms are intro-

83

duced to check or thwart majorities, at least in critical areas of decision-making. What is more, traditional theory on the whole treats the introduction of democracy and majority rule as a prelude to disaster for the political system and society.

I

The development is the more intriguing because there are a host of ethical and prudential considerations which pertain to the majority rule models that have not been fully explored. Our purpose here is to examine some of these considerations in detail. We can most conveniently proceed as follows: there is, indeed, a justification for majority rule—a justification which in our judgment is best and most fully seen when we deal with *model* situations, *i.e.*, not real situations but abstract ones wherein we are forced to face head-on the choices and the ethics involved without extraneous variables clouding our perception. Put otherwise, in such model situations we can discern more clearly and in greater depth the moral and ethical foundations of the majority principle. And such foundations, as we will attempt to show, are as appealing, if not more so, to the generally accepted ethical standards of the Western world than those which buttress nondemocratic decision-making theories or models. However, and this to our way of thinking is a crucial problem, when we move from the model situation to, say, the "real" world (as it is fashionably called), we are compelled to ask whether the justifications for the majority principle are still applicable; that is, whether the application of majority rule can still be defended on precisely the same grounds derived from the model situation or whether (and this has yet to occur) a new justification must be offered, or new ethical principles brought forth. And we must go beyond this to ask a question that will

seem relevant in light of our subsequent analysis: Does the application of the majority rule principle in non-model situations actually run counter to or even violate the ethical and moral principles which undergird majority rule in the abstract?

Let us take up this matter one point at a time.

1. What is meant by the model situation? As we have said, it is a condition or situation postulated so as to remove extraneous variables. To construct such a situation is a very difficult undertaking and no one to our knowledge has probed into the matter very systematically and in such great detail so that all conceivable variables are removed. We know various devices have been used with the end in mind of asking what principle of decision-making is most ethical without regard to the social structure, economic structure, background or intelligence of the participants, and even the historical context of any given nation. To do this one must postulate a setting in which the question of *who* should decide *what* should be done is highlighted. Such postulations run a wide gamut, from stalled elevators to stockades under Indian attack, from ships at sea in distress to "paradise islands" of one form or another. One illustration should suffice to indicate the nature of such constructions and why they are so difficult to build. We offer it because it is extremely important for our subsequent discussion of the majority principle.

Imagine five men on a raft, equipped with sail, in the middle of the Atlantic Ocean. They are the sole survivors of a shipwreck. They have enough food and water aboard for five days of survival. After collecting themselves, both mentally and physically, the question arises in which direction ought they to sail in order to maximize their chances of rescue. What emerges from their discussion is the following:

(a) They cannot stay where they are because the ship on which they were traveling was traversing a seldom-used route and the chances of another ship happening by are very remote.

(b) Chances of being rescued by going east or west are even worse than staying in place.

(c) In order to survive they must go either north or south.

The issue soon becomes whether they should go north or south, for they can do either given the prevailing wind conditions.

How should (=ought) the decision be made? Should, to get to our problem, the majority rule in this context? As a matter of ethics and plain common sense it would seem to depend on a number of considerations. We shall deal with some of them.

(A) What if one among the survivors is extremely knowledgeable about the trade routes across the Atlantic? We can imagine that the other four will listen to his words and that he ought to be able to convince them concerning the proper course of action. This, of course, is a gratuitous assumption, provided by proponents of the "open" society, and one which frequently creeps into our discussion about such matters without so much as a "by your leave." In any event, we must say as detached observers that his opinion should prevail, which would of course lead us away from the majority principle. So it is best for our purposes to assume that all five survivors are equally knowledgeable about trade routes and other relevant information which bears upon the matter of survival. Better yet, we should assume that all of them are possessed of the fullest information conceivable.

(B) Even assuming the fullest possible information and, let us add, equal intelligence, we still must ask whether each vote should count equally? It may be that one of the men is 75 and in very poor health, whereas another is 21, quite vigorous, for whom the correct decision obviously has enormous consequences. Should not the vote of the 21-year-old count more? And we must face the consequences if we say "yes" to this proposition. The vote of a 12-year-old should perhaps count more than that of a 21-year-old.[5] Indeed, and we can't go into this matter here, the logic of our thinking about these matters would dictate that anyone who understands how to vote *should* vote and be accorded that privilege. In any event, such considerations certainly do lead us away from the majority rule principle. Similarly, we can also imagine the possibility that one or more of the men might be committed to make the "wrong" decision, that is to vote for a movement in a direction that seems least likely to effect rescue. In our model, this poses no problems because the proper direction (*i.e.,* the one that increases the probability of rescue) might as well be determined by a flip of a coin. However, we can easily see that when we turn to the real world this does constitute a problem of immense proportions for supporters of the majority rule doctrine.

We can remove all of these difficulties by again postulating that all five are of the same age, that their goal is to maximize the possibilities of rescue, and that, moreover, each possesses the same potential and bears the same responsibilities in the more general society.

(C) We are still left with other difficulties.[6] One or more of the survivors might well resort to a form of bribery to win votes. He may, for example, have in his possession some extra food which he has managed to secure. He may use this food as a bribe; or, he may hold out the promise of future rewards of one kind or another.

In such a case, we see at once that the majority rule ethic as it has been set forth in our literature is prostituted. Perhaps our ethic ought to be that only those who can resist such temptations ought to be able to cast votes in the particular situation. Beyond this, again to return for a moment to the real world, we see that this is an important problem because we have been told by our highest authorities that all of politics is essentially "bribery" of sorts. And this certainly has ramifications for the majority rule principle, at least in its purest form.[7]

We can, of course, because we are dealing with a model situation, dispense with these difficulties. Indeed, we can go on and on dealing with these and similar problems simply through this dispensation process. Is one individual among the survivors a gifted orator who can use his forensic endowments to deceive the others? Well, again, we can stipulate *no*—we can stipulate that all have the same abilities in this respect. But having noted these difficulties, or at least a few of those that would arise before one would endorse the majority principle as an ethical or prudent decision-making rule, let us proceed to the essence of such model-building enterprises.

2. We must first note that we have been free in our dispensations in an effort, as we have said, to reach a condition wherein the basic ethical and moral arguments for majority rule are put in their best light. However, we should be quick to note, such dispensations cannot be granted in a real world context. We shall return to this matter shortly for it does have an important bearing on the application of the majority rule principle. Nor have we granted all the dispensations necessary to do away with all conceivable difficulties. But we can say that all dispensations have one end in mind, which we can put as follows: The impact and consequences of the decision, whether good or ill, should affect all of the participants equally. Put otherwise: *All should suffer equally or benefit equally from the decision.* And when this condition is postulated we find the strongest defense, morally and ethically, for the majority principle.

To put this another way and bring to bear one of the oldest arguments for democratic government, we can surmise that the people can best tell when the shoe pinches, where, and how much. There is, of course, a good deal of merit in this position. But we know that the shoe does not always pinch all of the people with the same degree of intensity in the same place or at the same time. When, that is, we leave the conditions stipulated in the model, we soon come to the realization that any policy decision or, for that matter, any lack of policy, program, or law in areas where it is sought, affects individuals and groups differently and unequally. We may call this the law of *differential impact,* a law which has a bearing upon the imposition or implementation of majority rule. The fact is that politics in the modern national state system in so many ways resembles what in legal terms is considered an equity proceeding. And this inevitably means that we must take into consideration a complex of factors, not the least of which is whose shoes ought to be fixed so that they don't pinch any more. For instance, there are few individuals or groups within a viable society whose shoes do not pinch and we are faced with the immediate question of priorities—whose shoes pinch the most and what the costs will be to alleviate the pain. And a host of relevant considerations, quite apart from the majority principle, enter into our deliberations. How large is the group affected or involved? How intense is the pinching pain when compared with other groups seeking relief or action of some sort? Can we devise a feasible program to alleviate their problems? What will the costs be for other segments of the community? And we ask such questions in a context that so much as tells us that if we fix one batch of shoes, we increase the pinch in another batch so that we are always dealing at the level of marginality. That certainly seems to be the way the world is constructed, which, of course, is not one in which the majority rule principle seems appropriate by any ethical standards known to the Western world. We repeat, it is only when we have model conditions such as these set forth above, wherein there is no differential impact, that we can justify majority rule without violating more sacred principles associated with our traditional conceptions of justice. There is no avoiding these problems and the theory of majority rule gives us no tools with which to deal with them.[8]

The point here is an important one, the more so as majoritarians in the social sciences have taken on a distinctly behavioral orientation, placing emphasis upon analysis of quantitative data without, it seems, a sufficient concern for the very considerations which we have mentioned. We talk of the internal inconsistency of the average citizen; he will subscribe to the maxims or principles of majority rule but he seems reluctant to practice them. For example, most individuals will say that each vote should count equally, that they do share the value of political equality as embodied in the formula "one man, one vote." But when faced with special circumstances, numerous studies have shown they will seemingly disavow their belief in political equality.[9] Our point is that, rather than trying to explain away or deplore this discrepancy, one ought to hail it. It signifies that more basic ethical considerations, along the lines we have suggested, are accorded more weight than the majority rule principle. And we would

suggest that the behavioralist, the next time he ventures forth from Ann Arbor, New York, or Chicago, should take into account the fact that respondents, when answering questions of this nature, are being placed in a very unrealistic, if not unfair, position. In the abstract (= our model situation), we venture to suggest that most would subscribe to the equality principle and thus majority rule. But in a real situation, one which almost invariably introduces complexities that lead to significant deviations from model conditions, other considerations obviously play a more dominant role in the valuational processes. We shall return to this matter shortly.

3. We can forcefully emphasize the points we have brought forth by presenting the following possibility which is now within the realm of our technological capability: Suppose we construct a device (perhaps we could attach it to television sets) that would instantaneously register the will of the people on matters of public policy. Suppose, moreover, that the alternatives could be structured such that a majority was able to express its will through these electronic devices. We could then have direct majority rule or, more simply, plebiscitary democracy.

Those committed to the majority principle, we would submit, are obliged to support and advance such a system. If they do not, they are obliged to tell us why. (We leave here to one side the "technical" complications which could easily be handled by "experts.") But most of us would be inclined to say that we are committing collective suicide and for the very reasons we have pointed out. Yet, we do find in our midst those who support the majority rule system as we have pictured it. And we ask: Could it be that they cling to the notion that there will be a collective cancellation of the difficulties presented in our model situation; that, in other words, all will come out clean from the wash? This is a fair presumption for we seldom find any introspection on the part of those who are the strongest advocates of majority rule. For instance, the notion of differential impact is usually ignored on grounds, we would suspect, that either this should not be taken into account or that the pluses and minuses will cancel out; that is, that the affected parties will divide in the same proportion as the majority. This observation is reinforced when we look at the majoritarians' criticisms of our existing institutions and procedures which are in many cases directed to the proposition that because we do not have majority rule certain groups are permanently deprived, whereas other groups (those with more representation than their numbers would seem to entitle them) are benefited. With such criticisms we find the implicit recognition of differential impact without, however, any suggested remedy other than the stricter adherence to the majority principle. The same would seem to hold true with the question of the relative intelligence of individuals; the assumption is that on any given issue the brightest among us will divide in roughly the same fashion as the dullest. These are, we submit, gratuitous assumptions on behalf of the majority ethic *in the sense we are speaking of it* at this point.

II

We can approach the ethical and moral underpinnings of majority rule from still other angles which do eventually bring us back to the questions or problems that we have posed. First, we must admit the possibility that there are those who believe that the majority principle is the equivalent of justice or the good life. We must recognize that for them, at least, majority rule is an end in itself. It is not as most

would put it an "instrumental" value but an end value. And just as those who believe free speech is our highest value and will admit of no exception to its practice, so, too, we find the majoritarian with his ends which, incidentally, also include free speech. There is no conceivable way to reason with such individuals beyond pointing out the extent of their commitment. From their point of view the matter is closed and there is nothing more to be said about it.

Second, our model situation tells us that there is abundant room for inquiry concerning the majoritarian ethic. We can simply ask what would we have to do in the real world to realize a condition in which that ethic would seem appropriate, given only *its* single end that all men ought to count equally in the political process. What do we do given the facts as set forth by virtually every social scientist from time immemorial, namely, we live in a hierarchical structure or society, and this by necessity; that, moreover, some individuals amongst us, whether due to their governmental or social position, will exercise more power and influence than others? Our problem here is not unlike that we confronted in our model situation, though this time around we are going to have to somehow strip away real, not imaginary variables. Surprisingly enough, given the empirical and behaviorist orientation of our profession, this job has not been done either.

We can illustrate this in the following terms: X is the son of a very prominent physician in Detroit. His father is an Anglo-Saxon Protestant named White. We can readily imagine Y, the son of a factory worker in Detroit named Black, and we can surmise that he is not as well off as Dr. White's son. That, at least, would be our expectation. Now these two boys are over the years going to develop preferences about what the society ought and ought not do. And we can readily envision that their preferences will be different, clashing, and even antagonistic. Who, we might ask, will most likely exercise more influence in the political process, even conceiving of it in model terms? We would probably answer: the more articulate, the more knowledgeable, the person with the greater amount of wealth, that individual best trained to present his position to the leadership of our society, etc. And we know, way down deep in our hearts, that Dr. White's son has by far the better opportunity to make his will prevail. Indeed, one of the chief preoccupations of social engineers in our age is to emphasize this very fact—the differences among us are environmental, largely due to our early training and the opportunities presented to us by the "accident" of birth.

Three observations are in order. First, unless he assumes that all will "cancel" in the sense we have mentioned above, the majoritarian must be concerned with at least those conditions which produce such inequalities. And there is more than just family status involved. Consider only the question of whether all individuals have access to the media in order to present their position or to persuade other voters to adopt their policy preferences. As we have said, we think it is a gratuitous assumption that the "pluses" and "minuses" will cancel out; that is, more precisely, that those possessed of greater influence and power within the society will nullify each other because their preferences and feelings will be the same as the general population and consequently the resources at their disposal, whether through education, inheritance, erudition, etc., are of no concern. And, it seems equally clear to us, that lacking any such assumption the majoritarian is going to have to turn his attention to rather severe readjustments of the social order—any social order of which we are aware—in

order to produce what we can term the prerequisites for majority rule.

This point is a simple one but it deserves our attention because it drives to the heart of so many theoretical questions which wrench our society. A majoritarian cannot, for the reasons we have set forth above, simply confine himself to the techniques or methods of making decisions. That is, he cannot regard democracy solely as a method or means of decision-making. He must concern himself both with the existing structure of society (elements which produce political inequality) but also the content or the ends of decision-making which could conceivably produce a state of affairs in which political inequality might result. Beyond this, the majoritarian has shown great fastidiousness about adhering to the "one man, one vote" doctrine. He has done so in the face of overwhelming evidence that this, for a variety of reasons, might lead to conditions antithetical to the majoritarian ethic. The direct primary system, for example, hailed as a "democratic" innovation along majoritarian lines, probably has resulted in a further concentration of political power in the hands of the more affluent few within society. Similarly, by failing to take into account social realities, the majoritarian ethic which has led to the reappointment of our state legislatures (under edicts of judiciary, no less) may well have served to advantage those who were already advantaged within our society. Thus, oddly enough, the outward realization of the majority principle may well serve to entrench the control of already existing minorities.

Our second observation is this: Is it possible to reduce man to the state or condition wherein the majoritarian model would be realized? This question, we think, can be answered without any equivocation, "no." Suppose, however, that we were to try. Again, nobody to my knowledge has fully explored this question. Madison, aside from saying that this would be impossible (a position which human experience would seem to verify), also tells us that the attempt to reduce a society to such a condition would involve the sacrifice of more highly held values, namely, liberty and individuality. And one must certainly see that efforts to produce the uniformity necessary for the majoritarian system would involve us with totalitarianism in its purest form. More, it would involve the imposition of a rule which runs counter to human nature. Of course, for one who holds that majority rule is the highest of all values such sacrifices may well seem a small price. But he should at least be aware of the fact, which many are not, that sacrifices of a high order will have to be made and that, in fact, even this might not produce the ideal conditions for political equality and majority control.

A third and closely related but highly important observation is that, off at the end, majoritarianism, theoretically speaking, chokes on itself simply because it is predicated on political equality which can only come about through the readjustment of society along the lines we have suggested. But please note that such readjustments involve policies, practices, and beliefs of the most fundamental concern to human beings. Granted a commitment to political equality with the end in mind of securing true majority rule, and granted, also, that all the adjustments necessary for this end have been made, we ask: What is left for the majority to decide? What range of decision-making discretion can be entrusted to a majority without fear that the majority will adopt a policy which leads to political inequality and thereby destroys the majority rule system? Put otherwise, has not the commitment to majority rule really been a commitment to a system wherein there is nothing left

for the majority to decide? Once, that is, you have decided upon social policies (whether the family structure should exist or not and, if so, under what regulations and circumstances; what provisions should be made for the education and training of the young, etc.), economic policy (*e.g.*, what is an acceptable range of income distribution, if any; how are businesses to be controlled and run in such a fashion that executives do not wield power beyond that allowed by the majoritarian model, etc.), or distinctly political concerns (what individuals or groups are to receive the dispensations of government; how are we to insure that governmental officials do not exercise a preponderant amount of power in our political determinations, etc.), there is little to talk about in the political arena.

III

The following observations would seem to be in order:

1. Man is a social being, molded and conditioned by his surroundings. Some are more introspective than others, and each in his own way brings particular insight and talents to bear to the social condition into which he was born. The contributions individuals make are of a different order (not equal); their contributions may be for good or ill (not as the relativist would have it of indeterminate value). That is our traditional teaching. The majoritarian ethic would have us believe otherwise. That ethic tells us that all men are equal in their capacity to make not only prudential but moral decisions. But we have learned enough from our behavioralist friends in the last three decades to see that this is not so. We know very well that existence within society conduces to choice or preference wherein there is no resort to the innate capacities of reason; that, moreover, we are social

beings who must somehow, each and every one of us, suffer from this same limitation. The model conditions of which we have spoken earlier cannot be achieved no matter how hard we try. We cannot for this reason "unchain" ourselves. Perhaps for that reason to make an attempt to do so would violate any ethic known to civilized man.

So much for the majoritarian ethic: It is as Kendall tells us based on a proposition that we were at one time free and equal individuals, living by ourselves, who entered into a contractual arrangement designed to secure our individual sovereignty. But these are obviously false premises. One might as well believe in Peter Pan. Yet, we remind you, they are the only "traditional" premises upon which the majority doctrine rests. And we further remind you that these premises seem to have been tacitly accepted by not only our highest court but certain of our leading political scientists whose chief preoccupation is to "improve" our form of government. The falsity of premises is of little concern. It is the results that flow from them with which we should be concerned.

2. The majoritarian ethic does make sense when model conditions such as those postulated above are *closely* approximated. Short of this it makes no sense at all for a rational and ethical people. And from this we can make certain observations which are important in considering just how far and under what circumstances we can safely employ the majority principle.

First, the fact that society is pluralistic means that decisions will always have a high differential impact. We are, of course, always dealing with *degrees* of differential impact. On any scale which attempts to measure differential impact, for instance, the American society certainly would rank very high: that is, specifically, any decision at the national, state, and local levels will be marked by a very high degree of differential impact.

Second, it follows from this that we will never be able in any given decision-making circumstance to approach the model conditions such as those set forth above, which, of course, would tend to eliminate certain serious ethical problems associated with the majority principle. Put otherwise, if all decisions affected all equally, then the majority rule formula, in our view at least, would be preferable to any other decision-making principle. We would, of course, be back on our raft. But this is not the case, nor can it be the case no matter how hard we try. And with this in mind we are obliged to ask: How can we allow for majority rule, at least a significant degree of it, without having to suffer the consequences which might flow from it? To phrase this in terms of what we have said to this point: How can we take the world as it is, the diversity which we find within it, and still employ the majority principle in a manner which is not ethically obnoxious?

We can offer here two thoughts on this which are worthy of some consideration:

(a) We should minimize as far as possible the substantive result of elections which are general in nature. We know that there are stakes involved in any election where there is political competition. Our point is that the more general the election (*i.e.*, the greater the number of voters), the less desirable it is that such elections settle substantive issues of public policy. The reasons for this are clear from our comments above, and we suspect that this is one reason why most individuals are "cool" to the notion of allowing the American people to sit down by their television sets every evening (or once a month for that matter) and push buttons to record their will.

In large measure, it seems to us, the relative success of the American system is due to the fact that our national presidential elections do, for whatever reason, conform with the rule we have just set down. The differences between major candidates have usually been very narrow, and, other than proclaiming one candidate victor over another, no matter how hard our political columnists might try to squeeze a "mandate" out of our presidential elections, this they cannot do. This is a small price to pay in order to avoid the dangers inherent in a plebiscitary system.

(b) We should try to "localize" substantive issue settlement. By this we do not necessarily mean localization on the basis of geography, though this can in some circumstances serve to allow for the implementation of majority rule without the ethical difficulties to which we have referred. What we mean by localization is confinement of the majority principle as a rule of decision-making to involved parties, whether they be geographical or functional. (Perhaps "decentralization" is a better word.) To recur to our raft model: we should seek, insofar as possible, to insure that those who participate equally will be affected equally by the decision made. Each of the participants, in other words, should, theoretically speaking, stand to benefit or suffer in equal proportions from the decision to be made. Only those within these confines should, in our view, have an equal voice.

We are quite aware that such a restriction to the application of majority rule poses many problems. But this, of course, involves the essence of politics itself. Perhaps the best we can do in general elections is to elect those who seem to hold out the best hope for making such approximations as we would ourselves.

Beyond this, we live in a welfare state where the issues transcend settling disputes between involved parties. Because, it seems, we have come to believe in an active government, one that will act as guardian for and promoter of various conceptions of social "justice" which hold currency in our contemporary world, the difficulty of confining disputes to the involved parties is extremely complicated. Certainly any such notion as we have advanced will not be well received. There are, in short, groups which are making demands upon government which involve collective sacrifices wherein the problem of determining the affected parties becomes extremely difficult, the more so as the demands by their nature involve the contention that the whole of society owes something to a minority portion of it. We can content ourselves with noting that such claims have nothing essentially to do with the majoritarian ethic, nor would the implementation of majority rule necessarily lead to the realization of the ends sought by such minorities. The claims on the part of such groups, whether they be the Blacks, Chicanos, Catholics, Protestants, businessmen, the rich, or the poor, are based on theories or conceptions of the good society that are in some cases inimical to the majority rule principle, but in no case can be supported by it.

We conclude as follows: If majority rule and its fundamental ethical principle, political equality, mean anything (anything by which we can live in peace) it must be that each of us can claim a "right" to an equal voice and equal consideration with others who will be equally affected by a given decision. There are, then, quite obviously, times when we should not be taken into account; there are other times, relating to other policy matters, when we should be listened to with the greatest of interest and concern. As trite as this might sound, and this because what we have said conforms with the Western ethics quite natural to us, it is a far cry from the theory and morality adopted and advanced by the modern proponents of majority rule.

NOTES

[1] The writings of Sartori, Dahl, Thorson, and Mayo and the reception they have received are sufficient to illustrate this point.

[2] For a revealing exchange on the matter of majority rule and rights, see Herbert McClosky's "The Fallacy of Absolute Majority Rule," *Journal of Politics*, Vol. XI (1949), and Willmoore Kendall's response, "Prolegomena to Any Future Work on Majority Rule," *Journal of Politics*, Vol. XII (1950). One should also read, for a brilliant refutation of the accepted proposition that majority rule equals just and good government, James Burnham's *Congress and the American Tradition*.

[3] A casual reading of the majority decisions in Wesberry *v.* Sanders and Reynolds *v.* Sims should serve to convince those doubtful about this statement.

[4] Nobody to my knowledge would contest this statement after a reading of the classical literature. We do find substantial disagreement about whether those in the classical tradition in repudiating this principle, save under the most propitious circumstances (*e.g.*, Aristotle), would disagree with this contention. The argument for strict majority rule is a relatively recent development. Whether one who deviates from the majority principle or ethic should be classified as totalitarian (=bad) or democratic (=good) has been a matter of dispute. I think these dichotomies false and of no real theoretical significance. On this point, I believe, I would be supported by Professors Voegelin and Strauss. If true, this would mean I stand on extremely solid grounds.

Even the philosophy of John Stuart Mill which seems to fuel the modern majoritarian ethic does not support this. Mill was no advocate of majority rule.

[5] Perhaps the "age of reason" as defined by lawyers and theologians should be used. If we were to do so we would lower the age to either 11 or 7. Lucky numbers, to be sure. But the ethic seems to require so much. Those of the age of reason *should* vote.

[6] One recalls in this connection Hubert Humphrey's observation at the 1969 national meeting of the American Political Scientists regarding Mayor Daley: "I don't know where he got them [votes], but he got them."

[7] And let us never forget we do have communists in our midst.

[8] See Kendall and Carey, "The 'Intensity' Problem and Democratic Theory," *American Political Science Review* (1968).

[9] The works of Lane, Stauffer, and a host of others will substantiate this point. See, in particular, the work of Prothro and Griggs, "Fundamental Principles of Democracy: Bases of Agreement and Disagreement," *Journal of Politics* (1960).

[XVI, Summer 1972, 226–236]

[10]

On Equality and Inequality

LUDWIG VON MISES

Ludwig von Mises (1881–1972), one of Europe's most eminent economists and the "Dean of the Austrian School," in works from The Theory of Money and Credit *(originally published in 1912 as* Theorie des Geldes und der Umlaufsmittel) *to* Planning for Freedom *(1962) profoundly affected American conservative thought. Born in Lemburg, Austria (now Lvov, U.S.S.R.), he worked from 1909 to 1934 for the Austrian Chamber of Commerce and, after 1913, taught economics at the University of Vienna. In 1934 he was appointed professor of international economic relations at the Graduate Institute of International Studies in Geneva; in 1940, wishing not to be an embarrassment to the neutral Swiss government, he emigrated to the United States. From 1945 until near the end of his life, he taught as an unsalaried visiting professor at the New York University Graduate School of Business Administration, supported by the William Volker Fund and earnings from his publications.*

THE DOCTRINE OF natural law that inspired the 18th-century declarations of the rights of man did not imply the obviously fallacious proposition that all men are biologically equal. It proclaimed that all men are born equal in rights and that this equality cannot be abrogated by any man-made law, that it is inalienable or, more precisely, imprescriptible. Only the deadly foes of individual liberty and self-determination, the champions of totalitarianism, interpreted the principle of equality before the law as derived from an alleged psychical and physiological equality of all men. The French declaration of the rights of the man and the citizen of November 3, 1789, had pronounced that all men are born and remain equal in rights. But, on the eve of the inauguration of the régime of terror, the new declaration that preceded the Constitution of June 24, 1793, proclaimed that all men are equal *"par la nature."* From then on this thesis, although manifestly contradicting biological experience, remained one of the dogmas of "leftism." Thus we read in the *Encyclopedia of the Social Sciences* that "at birth human infants, regardless of their heredity, are as equal as Fords."[1]

However, the fact that men are born unequal in regard to physical and mental capacities cannot be argued away. Some surpass their fellow men in health and vigor, in brain and aptitudes, in energy and resolution and are therefore better fitted for the pursuit of earthly affairs than the rest of mankind—a fact that has also been admitted by Marx. He spoke of "the inequality of individual endowment and therefore productive capacity (*Leistungsfähigkeit*)" as "natural privileges" and of "the unequal individuals (and they would not be different individuals if they were not unequal)."[2] In terms of popular psychological teaching we can say that some have the ability to adjust themselves better than others to the conditions of the struggle for survival. We may therefore—without indulging in any judgment of value—distinguish from this point of view between superior men and inferior men.

History shows that from time immemorial superior men took advantage of their superiority by seizing power and subjugating the masses of inferior men. In the status society there is a hierarchy of castes. On the one hand are the lords who have appropriated to themselves all the land and on the other hand their servants, the liegemen, serfs, and slaves, landless and penniless underlings. The inferiors' duty is to drudge for their masters. The institutions of the society aim at the sole benefit of the ruling minority, the princes, and their retinue, the aristocrats.

Such was by and large the state of affairs in all parts of the world before, as both Marxians and conservatives tell us, "the acquisitiveness of the bourgeoisie," in a process that went on for centuries and is still going on in many parts of the world, undermined the political, social, and economic system of the "good old days." The market economy—capitalism—radically transformed the economic and political organization of mankind.

Permit me to recapitulate some well-known facts. While under precapitalistic conditions superior men were the masters on whom the masses of the inferior had to attend, under capitalism the more gifted and more able have no means to profit from their superiority other than to serve to the best of their abilities the wishes of the majority of the less gifted. In the market, economic power is vested in the consumers. They ultimately determine, by their buying or abstention from buying, what should be produced, by whom and how, of what quality and in what quantity. The entrepreneurs, capitalists, and land-owners who fail to satisfy in the best possible and cheapest way the most urgent of the not yet satisfied wishes of the consumers are forced to go out of business and forfeit their preferred position. In business offices and in laboratories the keenest minds are busy fructifying the most complex achievements of scientific research for the production of ever better implements and gadgets for people who have no inkling of the theories that make the fabrication of such things possible. The bigger an enterprise is, the more is it forced to adjust its production to the changing whims and fancies of the masses, its masters. The fundamental principle of capitalism is mass production to supply the masses. It is the patronage of the masses that makes enterprises grow big. The common man is supreme in the market economy. He is the customer who "is always right."

In the political sphere, representative government is the corollary of the supremacy of the consumers in the market. Office-holders depend on the voters as entrepreneurs and investors depend on the consumers. The same historical process that substituted the capitalistic mode of production for precapitalistic methods substituted popular government—democracy—for royal absolutism and other forms of government by the few. And wherever the market economy is superseded by socialism, autocracy makes a comeback. It does not matter whether the socialist or communist despotism is camouflaged by the use of aliases like "dictatorship of the proletariat" or "people's democracy" or "*Führer* principle." It always amounts to a subjection of the many to the few.

It is hardly possible to misconstrue more thoroughly the state of affairs prevailing in capitalistic society than by calling the capitalists and entrepreneurs a "ruling" class intent upon "exploiting" the masses of decent men. We will not raise the question of how the men who under capitalism are in business would have tried to take advantage of their superior talents in any other thinkable organization of production. Under capitalism they are vying with one another in serving the masses of less gifted men. All their thoughts aim at perfecting the methods of supplying the consumers. Every year, every month, every week something unheard of before appears on the market and is soon made accessible to the many.

What has multiplied the "productivity of labor" is not some degree of effort on the part of manual workers, but the accumulation of capital by the savers and its reasonable employment by the entrepreneurs. Technological inventions would have remained useless trivia if the capital required for their utilization had not been previously accumulated by thrift. Man could not survive as a human being without manual labor. However, what elevates him above the beasts is not manual labor and the performance of routine jobs, but speculation, foresight that provides for the needs of the—always uncertain—future. The characteristic mark of production is that it is behavior directed by the mind. This fact cannot be conjured away by a semantics for which the word "labor" signifies only manual labor.

II

To acquiesce in a philosophy stressing the inborn inequality of men runs counter to many people's feelings. More or less reluctantly, people admit that they do not

equal the celebrities of art, literature, and science, at least in their specialties, and that they are no match for athletic champions. But they are not prepared to concede their own inferiority in other human matters and concerns. As they see it, those who outstripped them in the market, the successful entrepreneurs and businessmen, owe their ascendancy exclusively to villainy. They themselves are, thank God, too honest and conscientious to resort to those dishonest methods of conduct that, as they say, alone make a man prosper in a capitalistic environment.

Yet, there is a daily growing branch of literature that blatantly depicts the common man as an inferior type: the books on the behavior of consumers and the alleged evils of advertising. Of course, neither the authors nor the public that acclaims their writings openly state or believe that that is the real meaning of the facts they report.

As these books tell us, the typical American is constitutionally unfit for the performance of the simplest tasks of a householder's daily life. He or she does not buy what is needed for the appropriate conduct of the family's affairs. In their inwrought stupidity they are easily induced by the tricks and wiles of business to buy useless or quite worthless things. For the main concern of business is not to profit by providing the customers with the goods they need, but by unloading on them merchandise they would never take if they could resist the psychological artifices of "Madison Avenue." The innate incurable weakness of the average man's will and intellect makes the shoppers behave like "babes."[3] They are easy prey to the knavery of the hucksters.

Neither the authors nor the readers of these passionate diatribes are aware that their doctrine implies that the majority of the nation are morons, unfit to take care of their own affairs and badly in need of a paternal guardian. They are preoccupied to such an extent with their envy and hatred of successful businessmen that they fail to see how their description of consumers' behavior contradicts all that the "classical" socialist literature used to say about the eminence of the proletarians. These older socialists ascribed to the "people," to the "working and toiling masses," to the "manual workers" all the perfections of intellect and character. In their eyes, the people were not "babes" but the originators of what is great and good in the world, and the builders of a better future for mankind.

It is certainly true that the average common man is in many regards inferior to the average businessman. But this inferiority manifests itself first of all in his limited ability to think, to work, and thereby to contribute more to the joint productive effort of mankind. Most people who satisfactorily operate in routine jobs would be found wanting in any performance requiring a modicum of initiative and reflection. But they are not too dull to manage their family affairs properly. The husbands who are sent by their wives to the supermarket "for a loaf of bread and depart with their arms loaded with their favorite snack items"[4] are certainly not typical. Neither is the housewife who buys regardless of content, because she "likes the package."[5]

It is generally admitted that the average man displays poor taste. Consequently business, entirely dependent on the patronage of the masses of such men, is forced to bring to the market inferior literature and art. (One of the great problems of capitalistic civilization is how to make high-quality achievements possible in a social environment in which the "regular fellow" is supreme.) It is furthermore well known that many people indulge in habits that result in undesired effects. As the instigators of the great anticapitalistic campaign see it, the bad taste and the unsafe consumption habits of people and the other evils of our age are simply generated by the public relations or sales activities of the various branches of "capital"—wars are made by the munitions industries, the "merchants of death"; dipsomania by alcohol capital, the fabulous "whiskey trust," and the breweries.

This philosophy is not only based on the doctrine depicting the common people as guileless suckers who can easily be taken in by the ruses of a race of crafty hucksters. It implies in addition the nonsensical theorem that the sale of articles which the consumer really needs and would buy if not hypnotized by the wiles of the sellers is unprofitable for business and that on the other hand only the sale of articles which are of little or no use for the buyer or are even downright detrimental to him yields large profits. For if one were not to assume this, there would be no reason to conclude that in the competition of the market the sellers of bad articles outstrip those of better articles. The same sophisticated tricks by means of which slick traders are said to convince the buying public can also be used by those offering good and valuable merchandise on the market. But then good and poor articles compete under equal conditions and there is no reason to make a pessimistic judgment on the chances of the better merchandise. While both articles—the good and the bad— would be equally aided by the alleged trickery of the sellers, only the better one enjoys the advantage of being better.

We need not consider all the problems raised by the ample literature on the alleged stupidity of the consumers and their need for protection by a paternal government. What is important here is the fact that, notwithstanding the popular dogma of the equality of all men, the thesis that the common man is unfit to handle the ordinary affairs of his daily life is supported by a great part of popular "leftist" literature.

III

The doctrine of the inborn physiological and mental equality of men logically explains differences between human beings as caused by postnatal influences. It emphasizes especially the role played by education. In the capitalistic society, it is said, higher education is a privilege accessible only to the children of the "bourgeoisie." What is needed is to grant every child access to every school and thus educate everyone.

Guided by this principle, the United States embarked upon the noble experiment of making every boy and girl an educated person. All young men and women were to spend the years from six to eighteen in school, and as many as possible of them were to enter college. Then the intellectual and social division between an educated minority and a majority of people whose education was insufficient was to disappear. Education would no longer be a privilege; it would be the heritage of every citizen.

Statistics show that this program has been put into practice. The number of high schools, of teachers and students multiplied. If the present trend goes on for a few years more, the goal of the reform will be fully attained; every American will graduate from high school.

But the success of this plan is merely apparent. It was made possible only by a policy that, while retaining the name "high school," has entirely destroyed its scholarly and scientific value. The old high school conferred its diplomas only on students who had at least acquired a definite minimum of knowledge in some disciplines considered as basic. It elimi-

nated in the lower grades those who lacked the abilities and the disposition to comply with these requirements. But in the new régime of the high school the opportunity to choose the subjects he wished to study was badly misused by stupid or lazy pupils. Not only are fundamental subjects such as elementary arithmetic, geometry, physics, history, and foreign languages avoided by the majority of high school students, but every year boys and girls receive high school diplomas yet are deficient in reading and spelling English. It is a very characteristic fact that some universities found it necessary to provide special courses to improve the reading skill of their students. The often passionate debates concerning the high school curriculum that have now been going on for several years prove clearly that only a limited number of teenagers are intellectually and morally fit to profit from school attendance. For the rest of the high school population the years spent in classrooms are simply wasted. If one lowers the scholastic standard of high schools and colleges in order to make it possible for the majority of less gifted and less industrious youths to get diplomas, one merely hurts the minority of those who have the capacity to make use of the teaching.

The experience of the last decades in American education bears out the fact that there are inborn differences in man's intellectual capacities that cannot be eradicated by any effort of education.

IV

The desperate, but hopeless attempts to salvage, in spite of indisputable proofs to the contrary, the thesis of the inborn equality of all men are motivated by a faulty and untenable doctrine concerning popular government and majority rule.

This doctrine tries to justify popular government by referring to the supposed natural equality of all men. Since all men are equal, every individual participates in the genius that enlightened and stimulated the greatest heroes of mankind's intellectual, artistic, and political history. Only adverse postnatal influences prevented the proletarians from equaling the brilliance and the exploits of the greatest men. Therefore, as Trotsky told us,[6] once this abominable system of capitalism will have given way to socialism, "the average human being will rise to the heights of an Aristotle, a Goethe, or a Marx." The voice of the people is the voice of God, it is always right. If dissent arises among men, one must, of course, assume that some of them are mistaken. It is difficult to avoid the inference that it is more likely that the minority errs than the majority. The majority is right, because it is the majority and as such is borne by the "wave of the future."

The supporters of this doctrine must consider any doubt of the intellectual and moral eminence of the masses as an attempt to substitute despotism for representative government.

However, the arguments advanced in favor of representative government by the liberals of the 19th century—the much maligned Manchestermen and champions of laissez faire—have nothing in common with the doctrines of the natural inborn equality of men and the superhuman inspiration of majorities. They are based upon the fact, most lucidly exposed by David Hume, that those at the helm are always a small minority as against the vast majority of those subject to their orders. In this sense every system of government is minority rule and as such can last only as long as it is supported by the belief of those ruled that it is better for themselves to be loyal to the men in office than to try to supplant them by others ready to apply different methods of administration. If this opinion vanishes, the many

will rise in rebellion and replace by force the unpopular office-holders and their system by other men and another system. But the complicated industrial apparatus of modern society could not be preserved under a state of affairs in which the majority's only means of enforcing its will is revolution. The objective of representative government is to avoid the reappearance of such a violent disturbance of the peace and its detrimental effects upon morale, culture, and material well-being. Government by the people, *i.e.*, by elected representatives, makes peaceful change possible. It warrants the agreement of public opinion and the principles according to which the affairs of state are conducted. Majority rule is for those who believe in liberty not as a metaphysical principle, derived from an untenable distortion of biological facts, but as a means of securing the uninterrupted peaceful development of mankind's civilizing effort.

V

The doctrine of the inborn biological equality of all men begot in the nineteenth century a quasi-religious mysticism of the "people" that finally converted it into the dogma of the "common man's" superiority. All men are born equal. But the members of the upper classes have unfortunately been corrupted by the temptation of power and by indulgence in the luxuries they secured for themselves. The evils plaguing mankind are caused by the misdeeds of this foul minority. Once these mischief-makers are dispossessed, the inbred nobility of the common man will control human affairs. It will be a delight to live in a world in which the infinite goodness and the congenital genius of the people will be supreme. Never-dreamt-of happiness for everyone is in store for mankind.

For the Russian Social-Revolutionaries

this mystique was a substitute for the devotional practices of Russian Orthodoxy. The Marxians felt uneasy about the enthusiastic vagaries of their most dangerous rivals. But Marx's own description of the blissful conditions of the "higher phase of Communist Society"[7] was even more sanguine. After the extermination of the Social-Revolutionaries the Bolsheviks themselves adopted the cult of the common man as the main ideological disguise of their unlimited despotism of a small clique of party bosses.

The characteristic difference between socialism (communism, planning, state capitalism, or whatever other synonym one may prefer) and the market economy (capitalism, private enterprise system, economic freedom) is this: in the market economy the individuals *qua* consumers are supreme and determine by their buying or not buying what should be produced, while in the socialist economy these matters are fixed by the government. Under capitalism the customer is the man for whose patronage the suppliers are striving and to whom after the sale they say "thank you" and "please come again." Under socialism the "comrade" gets what "big brother" deigns to give him and he is to be thankful for whatever he gets. In the capitalistic West the average standard of living is incomparably higher than in the communistic East. But it is a fact that a daily increasing number of people in the capitalistic countries—among them also most of the so-called intellectuals—long for the alleged blessings of government control.

It is vain to explain to these men what the condition of the common man both in his capacity as a producer and in that of a consumer is under a socialist system. An intellectual inferiority of the masses would manifest itself most evidently in their aiming at the abolition of the system in which they themselves are supreme

and are served by the elite of the most talented men and in their yearning for the return to a system in which the elite would tread them down.

Let us not fool ourselves. It is not the progress of socialism among the backward nations, those that never surpassed the stage of primitive barbarism and those whose civilizations were arrested many centuries ago, that shows the triumphant advance of the totalitarian creed. It is in our Western circuit that socialism makes the greatest strides. Every project to narrow down what is called the "private sector" of the economic organization is considered as highly beneficial, as progress, and is, if at all, only timidly and bashfully opposed for a short time. We are marching "forward" to the realization of socialism.

VI

The classical liberals of the eighteenth and nineteenth centuries based their optimistic appreciation of mankind's future upon the assumption that the minority of eminent and honest men would always be able to guide by persuasion the majority of inferior people along the way leading to peace and prosperity. They were confident that the elite would always be in a position to prevent the masses from following the pied pipers and demagogues and adopting policies that must end in disaster. We may leave it undecided whether the error of these optimists consisted in overrating the elite or the masses or both. At any rate it is a fact that the immense majority of our contemporaries is fanatically committed to policies that ultimately aim at abolishing the social order in which the most ingenious citizens are impelled to serve the masses in the best possible way. The masses—including those called the intellectuals—passionately advocate a system in which they no longer will be the customers who give the orders but wards of an omnipotent authority. It does not matter that this economic system is sold to the common man under the label "to each according to his needs" and its political and constitutional corollary, unlimited autocracy of self-appointed office-holders, under the label "people's democracy."

In the past, the fanatical propaganda of the socialists and their abettors, the interventionists of all shades of opinion, was still opposed by a few economists, statesmen and businessmen. But even this often lame and inept defense of the market economy has almost petered out. The strongholds of American snobbism and "patricianship," fashionable, lavishly endowed universities and rich foundations, are today nurseries of "social" radicalism. Millionaires, not "proletarians," were the most efficient instigators of the New Deal and the "progressive" policies it engendered. It is well known that the Russian dictator was welcomed on his first visit to the United States with more cordiality by bankers and presidents of big corporations than by other Americans.

The tenor of the arguments of such "progressive" businessmen runs this way: "I owe the eminent position I occupy in my branch of business to my own efficiency and application. My innate talents, my ardor in acquiring the knowledge needed for the conduct of a big enterprise, my diligence raised me to the top. These personal merits would have secured a leading position for me under any economic system. As the head of an important branch of production I would also have enjoyed an enviable position in a socialist commonwealth. But my daily job under socialism would be much less exhausting and irritating. I would no longer have to live under the fear that a competitor can supersede me by offering something better or cheaper on the market. I would no longer be forced to comply with the whimsical and unreasonable wishes of the consumers. I would give them what I— the expert—think they ought to get. I would exchange the hectic and nerve-wracking job of a businessman for the dignified and smooth functioning of a public servant. The style of my life and work would resemble much more the seignorial deportment of a grandee of the past than that of an ulcer-plagued executive of a modern corporation. Let philosophers bother about the true or alleged defects of socialism. I, from my personal point of view, cannot see any reason why I should oppose it. Administrators of nationalized enterprises in all parts of the world and visiting Russian officials fully agree with my point of view."

There is, of course, no more sense in the self-deception of these capitalists and entrepreneurs than in the daydreams of the socialists and communists of all varieties.

VII

As ideological trends are today, one has to expect that in a few decades, perhaps even before the ominous year 1984, every country will have adopted the socialist system. The common man will be freed from the tedious job of directing the course of his own life. He will be told by the authorities what to do and what not to do, he will be fed, housed, clothed, educated and entertained by them. But, first of all, they will release him from the necessity of using his own brains. Everybody will receive "according to his needs." But what the needs of an individual are will be determined by the authority. As was the case in earlier periods, the superior men will no longer serve the masses, but dominate and rule them.

Yet, this outcome is not inevitable. It is the goal to which the prevailing trends in our contemporary world are leading. But trends can change and hitherto they always have changed. The trend toward socialism too may be replaced by a different one. To accomplish such a change is the task of the rising generation.

NOTES

[1] H. Kallen, "Behaviorism," *Encyclopedia of the Social Sciences,* vol. II, p. 498.

[2] Critique of the Social Democratic Program of Gotha (Letter to Bracke, May 5, 1875).

[3] V. Packard, "Babes in Consumerland," *The Hidden Persuaders* (Cardinal Editions, 1957), pp. 90–97.

[4] Packard, *op. cit.,* p. 95.

[5] Packard, *op. cit.,* p. 93.

[6] L. Trotsky, *Literature and Revolution,* tr. by R. Strunsky (London, 1925), p. 256.

[7] Letter to Bracke, May 5, 1875, as referred to above.   [V, Spring 1961, 139–147]

[11]

Freedom, Inequality, Primitivism, and the Division of Labor

MURRAY N. ROTHBARD

Murray N(ewton) Rothbard *(1926–   ), a noted economist, is the S. J. Hall Distinguished Professor of Economics at the University of Nevada, Las Vegas, and is editor of* Journal of Libertarian Studies. *A Washington columnist for* Faith and Freedom *from 1954 to 1956, he received his Ph.D. from Columbia University in 1956 and became a consulting economist for the Princeton Panel from 1957 to 1961. In 1962 he published* Man, Economy, and State *(in two volumes), heralded by Henry Hazlitt as "the most important general treatise on economic principles since Ludwig von Mises'* Human Action *in 1949." He is also the author of* America's Great Depression *(1963),* Power and Market *(1970), and* Conceived in Liberty *(1975–1979) and has made significant contributions to serious journals in his field.*

I

If men were like ants, there would be no interest in human freedom. If individual men, like ants, were uniform, interchangeable, devoid of specific personality traits of their own, then who would care whether they were free or not? Who, indeed, would care if they lived or died? The glory of the human race is the uniqueness of each individual, the fact that every person, though similar in many ways to others, possesses a completely individuated personality of his own. It is the fact of each person's uniqueness—the fact that no two people can be wholly interchangeable—that makes each and every man irreplaceable, and that makes us care whether he lives or dies, whether he is happy or oppressed. And, finally, it is the fact that these unique personalities need freedom for their full development that constitutes one of the major arguments for a free society.

Perhaps a world exists somewhere where intelligent beings are fully formed in some sort of externally determined cages, with no need for internal learning or choices by the individual beings themselves. But man is necessarily in a different situation. Individual human beings are not born or fashioned with fully formed knowledge, values, goals, or personalities; they must each form their own values and goals, develop their personalities, and learn about themselves and the world around them. Every man must have freedom, must have the scope to form, test, and act upon his

103

own choices, for any sort of development of his own personality to take place. He must, in short, be free in order that he may be fully human. In a sense, even the most frozen and totalitarian civilizations and societies have allowed at least a modicum of scope for individual choice and development. Even the most monolithic of despotisms have had to allow at least a bit of "space" for freedom of choice, if only within the interstices of societal rules. The freer the society, of course, the less has been the interference with individual actions, and the greater the scope for the development of each individual. The freer the society, then, the greater will be the variety and the diversity among men, for the more fully developed will be every man's uniquely individual personality. On the other hand, the more despotic the society, the more restrictions on the freedom of the individual, the more uniformity there will be among men and the less the diversity, and the less developed will be the unique personality of each and every man. In a profound sense, then, a despotic society prevents its members from being fully human.[1]

If freedom is a necessary condition for the full development of the individual, it is by no means the only requirement. Society itself must be sufficiently developed. No one, for example, can become a creative physicist on a desert island or in a primitive society. For, as an economy grows, the range of choice open to the producer and to the consumer proceeds to multiply greatly.[2] Furthermore, only a society with a standard of living considerably higher than subsistence can afford to devote much of its resources to improving knowledge, and to developing myriad goods and services above the level of brute subsistence. But there is another reason that full development of the creative powers of each individual cannot occur in a primitive or undeveloped society: and that is the necessity for a wide-ranging division of labor.

No one can fully develop his powers in any direction without engaging in *specialization*. The primitive tribesman or peasant, bound to an endless round of different tasks in order to maintain himself, could have no time or resources available to pursue any particular interest to the full. He had no room to specialize, to develop whatever field he was best at or in which he was most interested. Two hundred years ago, Adam Smith pointed out that the developing division of labor is a key to the advance of any economy above the most primitive level. A necessary condition for any sort of developed economy, the division of labor is also requisite to the development of any sort of civilized society. The philosopher, the scientist, the builder, the merchant—none could develop these skills or functions if he had had no scope for specialization. Furthermore, no individual who does not live in a society enjoying a wide range of division of labor can possibly employ his powers to the fullest. He cannot concentrate his powers in a field or discipline and advance that discipline and his own mental faculties. Without the opportunity to specialize in whatever he can do best, no person can develop his powers to the full; no man, then, could be fully human.

While a continuing and advancing division of labor is needed for a developed economy and society, the extent of such development at any given time limits the degree of specialization that any given economy can have. There is, therefore, no room for a physicist or a computer engineer on a primitive island; these skills would be premature within the context of that existing economy. As Adam Smith put it, "the division of labor is limited by the extent of the market." Economic and social development is therefore a mutually reinforcing process: the development of the market permits a wider division of labor, which in turn enables a further extension of the market.[3]

If the scope of the market and the extent of the division of labor are mutually reinforcing, so too are the division of labor and the diversity of individual interests and abilities among men. For just as an ever greater division of labor is needed to give full scope to the abilities and powers of each individual, so does the existence of that very division depend upon the innate diversity of men. For there would be no scope at all for a division of labor if every person were uniform and interchangeable. (A further condition of the emergence of a division of labor is the variety of natural resources; specific land areas on the earth are also not interchangeable.) Furthermore, it soon became evident in the history of man that the market economy based on a division of labor was profoundly *cooperative*, and that such division enormously multiplied the productivity and hence the wealth of every person participating in the society. The economist Ludwig von Mises put the matter very clearly:

> Historically division of labour originates in two facts of nature: the inequality of human abilities and the variety of the external conditions of human life on the earth. These two facts are really one: the diversity of Nature, which does not repeat itself but creates the universe in infinite, inexhaustible variety. . . .
>
> These two conditions . . . are indeed such as almost to force the division of labour on mankind. Old and young, men and women cooperate by making appropriate use of their various abilities. Here also is the germ of the geographical division of labour; man goes to the hunt and woman to the spring to fetch water. Had the strength and abilities of all individuals and the external conditions

> of production been everywhere equal the idea of division of labour could never have arisen. . . . No social life could have arisen among men of equal natural capacity in a world which was geographically uniform. . . .
>
> Once labour has been divided, the division itself exercises a differentiating influence. The fact that labour is divided makes possible further cultivation of individual talent and thus cooperation becomes more and more productive. Through cooperation men are able to achieve what would have been beyond them as individuals. . . .
>
> The greater productivity of work under the division of labour is a unifying influence. It leads men to regard each other as comrades in a joint struggle for welfare, rather than as competitors in a struggle for existence.[4]

Freedom, then, is needed for the development of the individual, and such development also depends upon the extent of the division of labor and the height of the standard of living. The developed economy makes room for, and encourages, an enormously greater specialization and flowering of the powers of the individual than can a primitive economy, and the greater the degree of such development, the greater the scope for each individual.

If freedom and the growth of the market are each important for the development of each individual and, therefore, to the flowering of diversity and individual differences, then so is there a causal connection between freedom and economic growth. For it is precisely freedom, the absence or limitation of interpersonal restrictions or interference, that sets the stage for economic growth and hence of the market economy and the developed division of labor. The Industrial Revolution and the corollary and consequent economic growth of the West were a product of its relative freedom for enterprise, for secure property and capital investment, for invention and innovation, for mobility and the advancement of labor. Compared to societies in other times and places, eighteenth- and nineteenth-century Western Europe and the United States were marked by a far greater social and economic freedom—a freedom to move, invest, work, and produce—secure from much harassment and interference by government. Compared to the role of government elsewhere, its role in these centuries in the West was remarkably minimal.[5]

By allowing full scope for investment, mobility, the division of labor, creativity and entrepreneurship, the free economy thereby creates the conditions for rapid economic development. It is freedom and the free market, as Adam Smith well pointed out, that develop the "wealth of nations." Thus, freedom leads to economic development, and both of these conditions in turn multiply individual development and the unfolding of the powers of the individual man. In two crucial ways, then, freedom is the root; only the free man can be fully individuated and, therefore, can be fully human.

If freedom leads to a widening division of labor, and the full scope of individual development, it leads also to a growing population. For just as the division of labor is limited by the extent of the market, so is total population limited by total production. One of the striking facts about the Industrial Revolution has been not only a great rise in the standard of living for everyone, but also the viability of such ample living standards for an enormously larger population. The land area of North America was able to support only a million or so Indians five hundred years ago, and that at a barely subsistence level. Even if we wished to eliminate the division of labor, we could not do so without literally wiping out the vast majority of the current world population.

II

We conclude that freedom and its concomitant, the widening division of labor are vital for the flowering of each individual, as well as for the literal survival of the vast bulk of the world's population. It must give us great concern, then, that over the past two centuries mighty social movements have sprung up which have been dedicated, at their heart, to the stamping out of all human differences, of all individuality.

It has become apparent in recent years, for example, that the heart of the complex social philosophy of Marxism does not lie, as it seemed to in the 1930's and '40's, in Marxian economic doctrines: in the labor theory of value, in the familiar proposal for socialist state ownership of the means of production, and in the central planning of the economy and society. The economic theories and programs of Marxism are, to use a Marxian term, merely the elaborate "superstructure" erected on the inner core of Marxian aspiration. Consequently, many Marxists have, in recent decades, been willing to abandon the labor theory of value and even centralized socialist planning, as the Marxian economic theory has been increasingly abandoned and the practice of socialist planning shown to be unworkable. Similarly, the Marxists of the "New Left" in the United States and abroad, have been willing to jettison socialist economic theory and practice. What they have *not* been willing to abandon is the philosophic heart of the Marxian ideal—not socialism or socialist planning, concerned anyway with what is supposed to be a temporary "stage" of development, but *communism* itself. It is the communist ideal, the ultimate goal of Marxism, that excites the contemporary Marxist, that engages his most fervent passions. The New Left Marxist has no use for Soviet Russia because the Soviets have clearly relegated the communist ideal to the remotest possible future. The New Leftist admires Ché, Fidel, and Mao not simply because of their role as revolutionaries and guerrilla leaders, but more because of their repeated attempts to leap into communism as rapidly as possible.[6]

Karl Marx was vague and cloudy in describing the communist ideal, let alone the specific path for attaining it. But one essential feature is the eradication of the division of labor. Contrary to current belief, Marx's now popular concept of "alienation" had little to do with a psychological sense of apartness or discontent. The heart of the concept was the individual's "alienation" from the product of labor. A worker, for example, works in a steel mill. Obviously, he himself will consume little or none of the steel he produces; he earns the value of his product in the shape of a money-commodity, and then he happily uses that money to buy whatever he chooses from the products of other people. Thus, A produces steel, B eggs, C shoes, etc., and then each exchanges them for products of the others through the use of money. To Marx this phenomenon of the market and the division of labor was a radical evil, for it meant that no one consumed any of *his own* product. The steelworker thus became "alienated" from his steel, the shoemaker from his shoes, etc.

The proper response to this "problem," it seems to me, is: "So what?" Why should anyone care about this sort of "alienation"? Surely the farmer, shoemaker, and steelworker are very happy to sell their product and exchange it for whatever products they desire; deprive them of this "alienation" and they would be most unhappy, as well as dying from starvation. For if the farmer were not allowed to produce more wheat or eggs than he himself consumes, or the shoemaker more shoes than he can wear, or the steelworker

more steel than he can use, it is clear that the great bulk of the population would rapidly starve and the rest be reduced to a primitive subsistence, with life "nasty, brutish, and short."[7] But to Marx this condition was the evil result of individualism and capitalism and had to be eradicated.

Furthermore, Marx was completely ignorant of the fact that each participant in the division of labor cooperates through the market economy, exchanging for each other's products and increasing the productivity and living standards of everyone. To Marx, any *differences* between men and, therefore, any specialization in the division of labor, is a "contradiction," and the communist goal is to replace that "contradiction" with harmony among all. This means that to the Marxist any individual differences, any diversity among men, are "contradictions" to be stamped out and replaced by the uniformity of the antheap. Friedrich Engels maintained that the emergence of the division of labor shattered the alleged classless harmony and uniformity of primitive society, and was responsible for the cleavage of society into separate and conflicting classes. Hence, for Marx and Engels, the division of labor must be eradicated in order to abolish class conflict and to usher in the ideal harmony of the "classless society," the society of total uniformity.[8]

Thus, Marx foresees his communist ideal only "after the enslaving subordination of individuals under division of labor, and therewith also the antithesis between mental and physical labor, has vanished."[9] To Marx the ideal communist society is one where, as Professor Gray puts it, "everyone must do everything." According to Marx in *The German Ideology*:

In communist society, where nobody has one exclusive sphere of activity but each can become accomplished in any branch he wishes, society regulates the general production and thus makes it possible for me to do one thing today and another tomorrow, to hunt in the morning, fish in the afternoon, rear cattle in the evening, criticize after dinner, just as I have a mind, without ever becoming hunter, fisherman, shepherd or critic.[10]

And the Marxist, August Bebel, consistently applied this dilettantish notion to the role of women:

> At one moment a practical worker in some industry she is in the next hour educator, teacher, nurse; in the third part of the day she exercises some art or cultivates a science; and in the fourth part she fulfills some administrative function.[11]

The concept of the *commune* in socialist thought takes on its central importance precisely as a means of eradicating individual differences. It is not just that the commune owns all the means of production among its members. Crucial to the communal ideal is that every man takes on every function, either all at once or in rapid rotation. Obviously, the commune has to subsist on no more than a primitive level, with only a few common tasks, for this ideal to be achieved. Hence the New Left commune, where every person is supposed to take turns equally at every task; again, specialization is eradicated, and no one can develop his powers to the full. Hence the current admiration for Cuba, which has attempted to stress "moral" rather than economic incentives in production, and which has established communes on the Isle of Pines. Hence the admiration for Mao, who has attempted to establish uniform urban and rural communes, and who recently sent several million students into permanent exile into the frontier agricultural areas, in order to eliminate the "contradiction between intellectual and physical labor."[12] Indeed, at the heart of the split between Russia and China is Russia's virtual abandonment of the communist ideal in the face of China's "fundamentalist" devotion to the original creed. The shared devotion to the commune also accounts for the similarities between the New Left, the Utopian socialists of the nineteenth century,[13] and the communist anarchists, a wing of anarchism that has always shared the communal ideal with the Marxists.[14]

The communist would deny that his ideal society would suppress the personality of every man. On the contrary, freed from the confines of the division of labor, each person would fully develop *all* of his powers in every direction. Every man would be fully rounded in all spheres of life and work. As Engels put it in his *Anti-Dühring*, communism would give "each individual the opportunity to develop and exercise all his faculties, physical and mental, in all directions. . ."[15] And Lenin wrote in 1920 of the "abolition of the division of labor among people . . . the education, schooling and training of people with *an all-round development* and *an all-round training*, people *able to do everything*. Communism is marching and must march toward this goal, and *will reach it. . ."[16]

This absurd ideal—of the man "able to do everything"—is only viable if (a) everyone does everything very badly, or (b) there are only a very few things to do, or (c) everyone is miraculously transformed into a superman. Professor Mises aptly notes that the ideal communist man is the dilettante, the man who knows a little of everything and does nothing well. For how can he develop *any* of his powers and faculties if he is prevented from developing any one of them to any sustained extent? As Mises says of Bebel's Utopia,

> Art and science are relegated to leisure hours. In this way, thinks Bebel, the society of the future "will possess scientists and artists of all kinds in countless numbers." These, according to their several inclinations, will pursue their studies and their arts

in their spare time. . . . All mental work he regards as mere dilettantism. . . . But nevertheless we must inquire whether under these conditions the mind would be able to create that freedom without which it cannot exist.

Obviously all artistic and scientific work which demands time, travel, technical education and great material expenditure, would be quite out of the question.[17]

Every person's time and energy on the earth are necessarily limited; hence, in order to develop *any* of his faculties to the full, he must specialize and concentrate on some rather than others. As Gray writes,

That each individual should have the opportunity of developing *all* his faculties, physical *and* mental, in *all* directions, is a dream which will cheer the vision only of the simple-minded, oblivious of the restrictions imposed by the narrow limits of human life. For life is a series of acts of choice, and each choice is at the same time a renunciation. . . .

Even the inhabitant of Engels' future fairyland will have to decide sooner or later whether he wishes to be Archbishop of Canterbury or First Sea Lord, whether he should seek to excel as a violinist or as a pugilist, whether he should elect to know all about Chinese literature or about the hidden pages in the life of the mackerel.[18]

Of course, one way to resolve this dilemma is to fantasize that the New Communist Man will be a superman. The Marxist, Karl Kautsky, asserted that in the future society "a new type of man will arise . . . a superman . . . an exalted man." Leon Trotsky prophesied that under communism

man will become incomparably stronger, wiser, finer. His body more harmonious, his movements more rhythmical, his voice more musical. . . . The human average will rise to the level of an Aristotle, a Goethe, a Marx. Above these other heights new peaks will arise.[19]

In recent years, communists have intensified their efforts to end the division of labor and reduce all individuals to uniformity. Fidel Castro's attempts to "build Communism" in the Isle of Pines, and Mao's Cultural Revolution, have been echoed in miniature by the American New Left in numerous attempts to form hippie communes and to create organizational "collectives" in which everyone does everything without benefit of specialization.[20] In contrast, Yugoslavia has been the quiet despair of the communist movement by moving rapidly in the opposite direction—toward ever-increasing freedom, individuality, and free-market operations—and has proved influential in leading the other "communist" countries of Eastern Europe (notably, Hungary and Czechoslovakia) in the same direction.[21]

III

One way of gauging the extent of "harmonious" development of all of the individual's powers in the absence of specialization is to consider what actually happened during primitive or preindustrial eras. And, indeed, many socialists and other opponents of the Industrial Revolution exalt the primitive and preindustrial periods as a golden age of harmony, community and social belonging— a peaceful and happy society destroyed by the development of individualism, the Industrial Revolution, and the market economy. In their exaltation of the primitive and the preindustrial, the socialists were perfectly anticipated by the reactionaries of the Romantic movement, those men who longed to roll back the tide of progress, individualism, and industry, and return to the supposed golden age of the preindustrial era. The New Left, in particular, also emphasizes a condemnation of technology and the division of labor, as well as a desire to "return to the earth" and an exaltation of the commune and the "tribe." As John W. Aldridge perceptively points out, the current New Left virtually constitutes a generational tribe that exhibits all the characteristics of a uniform and interchangeable herd, with little or no individuality among its members.[22]

Similarly, the early nineteenth-century German reactionary, Adam Müller, denounced the

> vicious tendency to divide labour in all branches of private industry.... [The] division of labour in large cities or industrial or mining provinces cuts up man, the completely free man, into wheels, rollers, spokes, shafts, etc., forces on him an utterly one-sided scope in the already one-sided field of the provisioning of one single want....[23]

The leading French conservatives of the early nineteenth century, Bonald and de Maistre, who idealized the feudal order, denounced the disruption by individualism of the pre-existing social order and social cohesion.[24] The contemporary French reactionary, Jacques Ellul, in *The Technological Society*, a book much in favor on the New Left, condemns "our dehumanized factories, our unsatisfied senses . . . our estrangement from nature." In the Middle Ages, in contrast, claims Ellul, "Man sought open spaces . . . the possibility of moving about . . . of not constantly colliding with other people."[25] In the meanwhile, on the socialist side, the economic historian Karl Polanyi's influential *The Great Transformation* makes this thesis of the disruption of a previous social harmony by individualism, the market economy, and the division of labor the central theme of the book.

For its part, the worship of the primitive is a logical extension of the worship of the preindustrial. This worship by modern sophisticated intellectuals ranges from Rousseau's "noble savage" and the lionizing of that creature by the Romantic

movement, all the way to the adoration of the Black Panthers by white intellectuals.[26] Whatever other pathology the worship of the primitive reflects, a basic part of it is a deep-seated hatred of individual diversity. Obviously, the more primitive and the less civilized a society, the less diverse and individuated it can be.[27] Also part of this primitivism reflects a hatred for the intellect and its works, since the flowering of reason and intellection leads to diversity and inequality of individual achievement.

For the individual to advance and develop, reason and the intellect must be *active*, it must embody the individual's mind working upon and transforming the materials of reality. From the time of Aristotle, the classical philosophy presented man as only fulfilling himself, his nature, and his personality through purposive action upon the world. It is from such rational and purposive action that the works of civilization have developed. In contrast, the Romantic movement has always exalted the passivity of the child who, necessarily ignorant and immature, only reacts passively to his environment rather than acts to change it. This tendency to exalt passivity and the young, and to denigrate intellect, has reached its present embodiment in the New Left, which worships both youth *per se* and a passive attitude of ignorant and purposeless spontaneity. The passivity of the New Left, its wish to live simply and in "harmony" with "the earth" and the alleged rhythms of nature, harks back completely to the Rousseauist Romantic movement. Like the Romantic movement, it is a conscious rejection of civilization and differentiated men on behalf of the primitive, the ignorant, the herd-like "tribe."[28]

If reason, purpose, and action are to be spurned, then what replace them in the Romantic pantheon are unanalyzed, spontaneous "feelings." And since the range of feelings is relatively small compared to intellectual achievements, and in any case is not objectively known to another person, the emphasis on feelings is another way to iron out diversity and inequality among individuals.

Irving Babbitt, a keen critic of Romanticism, wrote about the Romantic movement:

> The whole movement is filled with the praise of ignorance and of those who still enjoy its inappreciable advantages—the savage, the peasant and above all the child. The Rousseauist may indeed be said to have discovered the poetry of childhood . . . but at what would seem at times a rather heavy sacrifice of rationality. Rather than consent to have the bloom taken off things by analysis one should, as Coleridge tells us, *sink back* to the devout state of childlike wonder. However, to grow ethically is not to sink back but to struggle painfully forward. To affirm the contrary is to proclaim one's inability to mature. . . . [The Romantic] is ready to assert that what comes to the child spontaneously is superior to the deliberate moral effort of the mature man. The speeches of all the sages are, according to Maeterlinck, outweighed by the unconscious wisdom of the passing child.[29]

Another perceptive critique of Romanticism and primitivism was written by Ludwig von Mises. He notes that "the whole tribe of romantics" have denounced specialization and the division of labor. "For them the man of the past who developed his powers 'harmoniously' is the ideal: an ideal which alas no longer inspires our degenerate age. They recommend retrogression in the division of labour . . ." with the socialists surpassing their fellow Romantics in this regard.[30] But are primitives or preindustrial men privileged to develop themselves freely and harmoniously? Mises answers:

> It is futile to look for the harmoniously developed man at the outset of economic evolution. The almost self-sufficient economic subject as we know him in the solitary peasant of remote valleys shows none of that noble, harmonious development of body, mind, and feeling which the romantics ascribe to him. Civilization is a product of leisure and the peace of mind that only the division of labour can make possible. Nothing is more false than to assume that man first appeared in history with an independent individuality and that only during the evolution [of society] . . . did he lose . . . his spiritual independence. All history, evidence and observation of the lives of primitive peoples is directly contrary to this view. Primitive man lacks all individuality in our sense. Two South Sea Islanders resemble each other far more closely than two twentieth-century Londoners. Personality was not bestowed upon man at the outset. It has been acquired in the course of the evolution of society.[31]

Or we may note Charles Silberman's critique of Jacques Ellul's rhapsodies on the "traditional rhythms of life and nature" lived by preindustrial man, as compared to "dehumanized factories . . . our estrangement from nature." Silberman asks:

> But with what shall we contrast this dehumanized world? The beautiful, harmonious life being lived by, say, the Chinese or Vietnamese peasant woman, who works in the fields close to nature, for twelve hours a day—roughly the conditions under which the great bulk of women (and men) have worked . . . through all of human history? For this is the condition that Ellul idealizes.

And, as for Ellul's paean to the Middle Ages as being mobile, spacious and uncrowded:

> This would have been startling news to the medieval peasant, who lived with his wife and children, other relatives, and probably animals as well in a one-room thatched cottage. And even for the nobility, was there really more possibility of "moving about" in the Middle Ages, when travel was by foot or hoof, than today, when steelworkers spend sabbaticals in Europe?[32]

The savage is supposed not only to be "noble" but also supremely happy. From the Rousseauians to what Erich Fromm has called "the infantile Paradise" of Norman O. Brown and Herbert Marcuse, the Romantics have extolled the happiness yielded by the spontaneous and the child-like. To Aristotle and the classic philosophers, happiness was *acting* in accordance with man's unique and rational nature. To Marcuse, any purposive, rational action is by definition "repressive," to which he contrasts the "liberated" state of spontaneous play. Aside from the universal destitution that the proposed abolition of work would bring, the result would be a profound *un*happiness, for no individual would be able to fulfill himself, his individuality, or his rational faculties. Diversity and individuality would largely disappear, for in a world of "polymorphous" play everyone would be virtually alike.

If we consider the supposed happiness of primitive man, we must also consider that his life was, in the famous phrase of Hobbes, "nasty, brutish, and short." There were few medical aids against disease; there were none against famine, for in a world cut off from interregional markets and barely above subsistence any check to the local food supply will decimate the population. Fulfilling the dreams of Romantics, the primitive tribe is a passive creature of its given environment, and has no means for acting to overcome and transform it. Hence, when the local food supply within an area is depleted, the "happy-go-lucky" tribe dies *en masse*.

Furthermore, we must realize that the primitive faces a world which he cannot understand, since he has not engaged in much of a rational, scientific inquiry into its workings. *We* know what a thunderstorm is, and therefore take rational measures against it; but the savage does not know, and therefore surmises that the God of Thunder is displeased with him,

and must be propitiated with sacrifices and votive offerings. Since the savage has only a limited concept of a world knit together by natural law (a concept which employs reason and science) he believes that the world is governed by a host of capricious spirits and demons, each of which can only be propitiated by ritual or magic, and by a priestcraft of witch doctors who specialize in their propitiation.[33] The renaissance of astrology and similar mystic creeds on the New Left marks a reversion to such primitive forms of magic. So fearful is the savage, so bound is he by irrational taboo and by the custom of his tribe, that he cannot develop his individuality.

If tribal custom crippled and repressed the development of each individual, then so too did the various caste systems and networks of restriction and coercion in preindustrial societies that forced everyone to follow the hereditary footsteps of his father's occupation. Each child knew from birth that he was doomed to tread where his ancestors had gone before him, regardless of ability or inclination to the contrary. The "social harmony," the "sense of belonging," supplied by mercantilism, by the guilds, or by the caste system, provided such contentment that its members left the throes of the system when given an opportunity. Given the freedom to choose, the tribesmen abandon the bosom of their tribe to come to the freer, "atomistic" cities looking for jobs and opportunity. It is curious, in fact, that those Romantics who yearn to restore the mythical golden age of caste and status refuse to allow each individual the freedom to choose between market on the one hand, or caste and tribal commune on the other. Invariably, the new golden age has to be imposed by coercion.

Is it, indeed, a coincidence that the natives of undeveloped countries, when given a chance, invariably abandon their "folk culture" on behalf of Western ways, living standards, and "Coca-Colaization"? Within a few years, for example, the people of Japan were delighted to abandon their centuries-old traditional culture and folkways, and turn to the material achievements and market economy of the West. Primitive tribes, too, given a chance, are eager to differentiate and develop a market economy, to shed their stagnant "harmony" and replace their magic by knowledge of discovered law. The eminent anthropologist Bronislaw Malinowski pointed out that primitives use magic only to cover those areas of nature of which they are ignorant; in those areas where they have come to understand the natural processes at work, magic is, quite sensibly, not employed.[34]

A particularly striking example of the eager development of a pervasive market economy among primitive tribesmen is the largely unheralded case of West Africa.[35] And Bernard Siegel has pointed out that when, as among the Panajachel of Guatemala, a primitive society becomes large and technologically and societally complex, a market economy inevitably accompanies this growth, replete with specialization, competition, cash purchases, demand and supply, prices and costs, etc.[36]

There is thus ample evidence that even primitive tribesmen themselves are not fond of their primitivism, and take the earliest opportunity to escape from it; the main stronghold of love for primitivism seems to rest among the decidedly non-primitive Romantic intellectuals.

Another primitivistic institution that has been hailed by many social scientists is the system of the "extended family," a harmony and status supposedly ruptured by the individualistic "nuclear family" of the modern West. Yet the extended family system has been responsible for crippling the creative and productive individual as well as repressing economic development. Thus, West African development has been impeded by the extended family concept that, if one man prospers, he is duty bound to share this bounty with a host of relatives, thus draining off the reward for his productivity and crippling his incentive to succeed, while encouraging the relatives to live idly on the family dole. And neither do the productive members of the tribe seem very happy about this supposedly harmonious societal bond. Professor Bauer points out that

> many admit in private discussion that they dread these extensive obligations. . . . The fear of the obligations of the family system is partly responsible for the widespread use of textiles and trinkets as outlets for savings, in preference to more productive forms of investment which are more likely to attract the attention of relatives.

And many Africans distrust banks, "fearing that they may disclose the size of their accounts to members of their families. They, therefore, prefer to keep their savings under the fireplace or buried in the ground."[37]

In fact, the primitive community, far from being happy, harmonious, and idyllic, is much more likely to be ridden by mutual suspicion and envy of the more successful or better-favored, an envy so pervasive as to cripple, by the fear of its presence, all personal or general economic development. The German sociologist Helmut Schoeck, in his important recent work *Envy*, cites numerous studies of this pervasive crippling effect. Thus the anthropologist Clyde Kluckhohn found among the Navaho the absence of any concept of "personal success" or "personal achievement"; any such success was automatically attributed to exploitation of others, and, therefore, the more prosperous Navaho Indian feels himself under constant social pressure to give his money away. Allan Holmberg found that the

Siriono Indian of Bolivia eats alone and at night because, if he eats by day, a crowd gathers around him to stare in envious hatred. The result among the Siriono is that, in reaction to this pervasive pressure, no one will voluntarily share food with anybody. Sol Tax found that envy and fear of envy in "a small community where all neighbors watch and where all are neighbors" accounted for the unprogressiveness, the slowness of change toward a productive economy among the Indians of Guatemala. And when a tribe of Pueblo Indians showed the beginnings of specialization and the division of labor, the envy of their fellow tribesmen impelled them to take measures to end this process, including physical destruction of the property of those who seemed in any way better off than their fellows.

Oscar Lewis discovered an extremely pervasive fear of the envy of others in a Mexican Indian village, a fear producing intense secretiveness. Wrote Lewis:

> The man who speaks little, keeps his affairs to himself, and maintains some distance between himself and others has less chance of creating enemies or of being criticized or envied. A man does not generally discuss his plans to buy or sell or take a trip.[38]

Professor Schoeck comments:

> . . . it is difficult to envisage what it means for the economic and technical development of a community when, almost automatically and as a matter of principle, the future dimension is banned from human intercourse and conversation, when it cannot even be discussed. Ubiquitous envy, fear of it and those who harbour it, cuts off such people from any kind of communal action directed towards the future. . . . All striving, all preparation and planning for the future can be undertaken only by socially fragmented, secretive beings.[39]

Furthermore, in this Mexican village no one will warn or tell anyone else of imminent danger to the other's property; there is no sense of human social solidarity whatsoever.

Among the Indians of Aritama in Colombia, the Reichel-Dolmatoffs reported:

> Every individual lives in constant fear of the magical aggression of others, and the general social atmosphere in the village is one of mutual suspicion, of latent danger, and hidden hostility, which pervade every aspect of life. The most immediate reason for magical aggression is envy. Anything that might be interpreted as a personal advantage over others is envied: good health, economic assets, good physical appearance, popularity, a harmonious family life, a new dress. All these and other aspects imply prestige, and with it power and authority over others. Aggressive magic is, therefore, intended to prevent or to destroy this power and to act as a leveling force.[40]

The Reichel-Dolmatoffs also noted that if one member of a group in Aritama should work faster or better than his fellows, his place of work is marked with a cross before he arrives the next morning, and his envious colleagues pray to God to make this more able worker slow and tired.

Finally, Watson and Samora (*American Sociological Review*, 1954) found that the major reason for the failure of a group of lower-class Spanish-speaking citizens of a mountain township in southern Colorado to rise into parity with the upper-class Anglo community was the bitter envy of the Spanish group toward any of their number who managed to rise. Anyone who works his way upward is regarded as a man "who has sold himself to the Anglos," "who has climbed on the backs of his people."

The anthropologist Eric Wolf (*American Anthropologist*, 1955) has even coined the term "institutionalized envy" to describe such pervasive institutions, including the practice and fear of black magic in these primitive societies. Schoeck notes:

Institutionalized envy . . . or the ubiquitous fear of it, means that there is little possibility of individual economic advancement and no contact with the outside world through which the community might hope to progress. No one dares to show anything that might lead people to think he was better off. Innovations are unlikely. Agricultural methods remain traditional and primitive, to the detriment of the whole village, because every deviation from previous practice comes up against the limitations set by envy.[41]

And Schoeck aptly concludes:

There is nothing to be seen here of the close community which allegedly exists among primitive peoples in pre-affluent times—the poorer, it is held, the greater the sense of community. Sociological theory would have avoided many errors if those phenomena had been properly observed and evaluated a century ago. The myth of a golden age, when social harmony prevailed because each man had about as little as the next one, the warm and generous community spirit of simple societies, was indeed for the most part just a myth, and social scientists should have known better than to fashion out of it a set of utopian standards with which to criticize their own societies.[42]

In sum, Ludwig von Mises' strictures against Romanticism do not seem to be overdrawn:

Romanticism is man's revolt against reason, as well as against the condition under which nature has compelled him to live. The romantic is a daydreamer; he easily manages in imagination to disregard the laws of logic and nature. The thinking and rationally acting man tries to rid himself of the discomfort of unsatisfied wants by economic action and work; he produces in order to improve his position. The romantic . . . imagines the pleasures of success but he does nothing to achieve them. He does not remove the obstacles; he merely removes them in imagination. . . . He hates work, economy, and reason.

The romantic takes all the gifts of a social civilization for granted and desires, in ad-

dition, everything fine and beautiful that, as he thinks, distant times and creatures had or have to offer. Surrounded by the comforts of European town life he longs to be an Indian rajah, bedouin, corsair, or troubadour. But he sees only that portion of these people's lives which seems pleasant to him. . . . The perilous nature of their existence, the comparative poverty of their circumstances, their miseries and their toil—these things his imagination tactfully overlooks: all transfigured by a rosy gleam. Compared with this dream ideal, reality appears arid and shallow. There are obstacles to overcome which do not exist in the dream. . . . Here there is work to do, ceaselessly, assiduously. . . . Here one must plough and sow if one wishes to reap. The romantic does not choose to admit all this. Obstinate as a child, he refuses to recognize it. He mocks and jeers; he despises and loathes the bourgeois.[43]

The Romantic, or primitivist, attitude was also brilliantly criticized by the Spanish philosopher Ortega y Gasset:

. . . it is possible to have peoples who are perennially primitive . . . those who have remained in the motionless, frozen twilight, which never progresses towards midday.

This is what happens in the world which is mere Nature. But it does not happen in the world of civilisation which is ours. Civilisation is not "just there," it is not self-supporting. It is artificial. . . . If you want to make use of the advantages of civilisation, but are not prepared to concern yourself with the upholding of civilisation—you are done. In a trice you find yourself left without civilisation. . . . The primitive forest appears in its native state. . . . The jungle is always primitive and, vice versa, everything primitive is mere jungle.[44]

Ortega adds that the type of man he sees rising to the fore, the modern "mass-man," "believes that the civilization into which he was born and which he makes use of, is as spontaneous and self-producing as Nature. . . ." But the mass-man, the herd-man, is also characterized by his desire to stamp out those individuals who differ from the mass: "The mass . . . does not wish to share life with those who are not of it. It has a deadly hatred of all that is not itself."[45]

IV

The Left, of course, does not couch its demands in terms of stamping out diversity; what it seeks to achieve sounds semantically far more pleasant: *equality*. It is in the name of equality that the Left seeks all manner of measures, from progressive taxation to the ultimate stage of communism.

But what, philosophically, *is* "equality"? The term must not be left unanalyzed and accepted at face value. Let us take three entities: A, B, and C. A, B, and C are said to be "equal" to each other (*i.e.*, A = B = C) *if* a particular characteristic is found in which the three entities are uniform or identical. In short, here are three individual men: A, B, and C. Each may be similar in some respects but different in others. If each of them is precisely 5'10" in height they are then *equal* to each other *in height*. It follows from our discussion of the concept of equality that A, B, and C can be *completely* "equal" to each other only if they are identical or uniform in *all* characteristics—in short, if all of them are, like the same size of nut or bolt, completely interchangeable. We see, then, that the ideal of human equality *can only* imply total uniformity and the utter stamping out of individuality.

It is high time, then, for those who cherish freedom, individuality, the division of labor, and economic prosperity and survival, to stop conceding the supposed nobility of the ideal of equality. Too often have "conservatives" conceded the ideal of equality only to cavil at its "impracticality." Philosophically, there can

be no divorce between theory and practice. Egalitarian measures do not "work" because they violate the basic nature of man, of what it means for the individual man to be truly human. The call of "equality" is a siren song that can only mean the destruction of all that we cherish as being human.

It is ironic that the term "equality" brings its favorable connotation to us from a past usage that was radically different. For the concept of "equality" achieved its widespread popularity during the classical liberal movements of the eighteenth century, when it meant, *not* uniformity of status or income, but freedom for each and every man, without exception. In short, "equality" in those days meant the libertarian and individualist concept of full liberty for all persons. Thus, the biochemist Roger Williams correctly points out that the " 'free and equal' phrase in the Declaration of Independence was an unfortunate paraphrase of a better statement contained in the Virginia Bill of Rights . . . 'all men are by nature equally free and independent.' In other words, men can be *equally free* without being *uniform*."[46]

This libertarian credo was formulated with particular cogency by Herbert Spencer in his "Law of Equal Liberty" as the suggested fundamental core of his social philosophy:

> . . . man's happiness can be obtained only by the exercise of his faculties. . . . But the fulfillment of this duty necessarily presupposes freedom of action. Man cannot exercise his faculties without certain scope. He must have liberty to go and to come, to see, to feel, to speak, to work; to get food, raiment, shelter, and to provide for each and all of the needs of his nature. . . . To exercise his faculties he must have liberty to do all that his faculties actually impel him to do. . . . Therefore, he has a *right* to that

liberty. This, however, is not the right of one but of all. All are endowed with faculties. All are bound to . . . [exercise] them. All, therefore, must be free to do those things in which the exercise of them consists. That is, all must have rights to liberty of action.

And hence there necessarily arises a limitation. For if men have like claims to that freedom which is needful for the exercise of their faculties, then must the freedom of each be bounded by the similar freedom of all. . . . Wherefore we arrive at the general proposition, that every man may claim the fullest liberty to exercise his faculties compatible with the possession of like liberty by every other man.[47]

Thus, only the specific case of equality of *liberty*—the older view of human equality—is compatible with the basic nature of man. Equality of *condition* would reduce humanity to an antheap existence. Fortunately, the individuated nature of man, allied to the geographical diversity on the earth, makes the ideal of total equality unattainable. But an enormous amount of damage—the crippling of individuality, as well as economic and social destruction—could be generated in the attempt.

Let us turn from equality to the concept of inequality, the condition that exists when every man is *not* identical to every other in all characteristics. It is evident that inequality flows inevitably out of specialization and the division of labor. Therefore, a free economy will lead not only to diversity of occupation, with one man a baker, another an actor, a third a civil engineer, etc., but specific *in*equalities will also emerge in monetary income and in status and scope of control within each occupation. Each person will, in the free-market economy, tend to earn a monetary income equal to the value placed upon his productive contribution in satisfying the desires and demands of the consumers. In economic terminology each man will tend to earn an income equal to

his "marginal productivity," to his particular productivity in satisfying consumer demands. Clearly, in a world of developed individual diversity, some men will be more intelligent, others more alert and farsighted, than the remainder of the population. Still others, meanwhile, will be more interested in those areas reaping greater monetary gain; those who succeed at wildcatting of crude oil will reap greater monetary rewards than those who remain in secretarial jobs.

Many intellectuals are wont to denounce the "unfairness" of the market in granting a far higher monetary income to a movie star than, say, a social worker, in that way rewarding "material" far more than "spiritual" values, and treating "better" people unfairly. Without going into the peculiar usage of such terms as "spiritual" and "material," it strikes one that if the social worker's alleged "goodness" indeed resides in her "spirituality," then it is surely inappropriate and inconsistent to demand that she receive more of the "material" amenities (money) *vis à vis* the movie star. In the free society, those who are capable of providing goods and services that the consumers value and are willing to purchase, will receive precisely what the consumers are willing to spend. Those who persist in entering lower-priced occupations, either because they prefer the work or because they are not sufficiently capable in the higher-paid fields, can scarcely complain when they earn a lower salary.

If, then, *in*equality of income is the inevitable corollary of freedom, then so too is inequality of control. In *any* organization, whether it be a business firm, a lodge, or a bridge club, there will always be a minority of people who will rise to the position of leaders and others who will remain as followers in the rank and file. Robert Michels discovered this as one of the great laws of sociology, "The Iron Law of Oligarchy." In every organized activity, no matter the sphere, a small number will become the "oligarchical" leaders and the others will follow.

In the market economy, the leaders, being more productive in satisfying the consumers, will inevitably earn more money than the rank and file. Within other organizations, the difference will only be that of control. But, in either case, ability and interest will select those who rise to the top. The best and most dedicated steel producer will rise to the leadership of the steel corporation; the ablest and most energetic will tend to rise to leadership in the local bridge club; and so on.

This process of ability and dedication finding its own level works best and most smoothly, it is true, in institutions such as business firms in the market economy. For here every firm places itself under the discipline of monetary profits and income earned by selling a suitable product to the consumers. If managers or workers fall down on the job, a loss of profits provides a very rapid signal that something is wrong and that these producers must mend their ways. In non-market organizations, where profit does not provide a test of efficiency, it is far easier for other qualities extraneous to the actual activity to play a role in selecting the members of the oligarchy. Thus, a local bridge club may select its leaders, not only for ability and dedication to the activities of the club, but also for extraneous racial or physical characteristics preferred by the membership. This situation is far less likely where monetary losses will be incurred by yielding to such external factors.

We need only look around us at every human activity or organization, large or small, political, economic, philanthropic, or recreational, to see the universality of the Iron Law of Oligarchy. Take a bridge club of fifty members and, regardless of legal formalities, half-a-dozen or so will really be running the show. Michels, in fact, discovered the Iron Law by observing the rigid, bureaucratic, oligarchic rule that pervaded the Social Democratic parties in Europe in the late nineteenth century, even though these parties were supposedly dedicated to equality and the abolition of the division of labor.[48] And it is precisely the obviously frozen inequality of income and power, and the rule by oligarchy, that has totally disillusioned the equality-seeking New Left in the Soviet Union. No one lionizes Brezhnev or Kosygin.

It is the egalitarian attempt by the New Left to escape the Iron Law of inequality and oligarchy that accounts for its desperate efforts to end elite leadership within its own organizations. (Certainly there has been no indication of any disappearance of the power elite in oft-heralded Cuba or China.) The early drive toward egalitarianism in the New Left emerged in the concept of "participatory democracy." Instead of the members of an organization electing an elite leadership, so the theory ran, each person would participate equally in all of the organization's decision-making. It was, by the way, probably this *sense* of direct and intense participation by each individual that accounted for the heady enthusiasm of the masses in the very early stages of the revolutionary regimes in Soviet Russia and Cuba—an enthusiasm that quickly waned as the inevitable oligarchy began to take control and mass participation to die.

While the would-be participatory democrats have made keen criticisms of bureaucratic rule in our society, the concept itself, when applied, runs rapidly against the Iron Law. Thus, anyone who has sat through sessions of any organization engaged in participatory democracy knows the intense boredom and inefficiency that develop rapidly. For if each person must participate equally in all decisions, the time devoted to decision-making must become almost endless, and the processes of the organization *become* life itself for the participants. This is one of the reasons why many New Left organizations quickly begin to insist that their members live in communes and dedicate their entire lives to the organization—in effect, to merge their lives with the organization. For if they truly live and pursue participatory democracy, they can hardly do anything else. But despite this attempt to salvage the concept, the inevitable gross inefficiency and aggravated boredom ensure that all but the most intensely dedicated will abandon the organization. In short, if it can work at all, participatory democracy can work only in groups so tiny that they are, in effect, the "leaders" shorn of their following.

We conclude that, to succeed, any organization must eventually fall into the hands of specialized "professionals," of a minority of persons dedicated to its tasks and able to carry them out. Oddly enough, it was Lenin who, despite his lip service to the ultimate ideal of egalitarian communism, recognized that a revolution, too, in order to succeed, must be led by a minority, a "vanguard," of dedicated professionals.

It is the intense egalitarian drive of the New Left that accounts, furthermore, for its curious theory of education—a theory that has made such an enormous impact on the contemporary student movement in American universities in recent years. The theory holds that, in contrast to "old-fashioned" concepts of education, the teacher knows *no more* than any of his students. All, then, are "equal" in condition; one is no better in any sense than any other. Since only an imbecile would actually proclaim that the student knows as much about the *content* of any given

discipline as his professor, this claim of equality is sustained by arguing for the abolition of content in the classroom. This content, asserts the New Left, is "irrelevant" to the student and hence not a proper part of the educational process. The only proper subject for the classroom is not a body of truths, not assigned readings or topics, but open-ended, free-floating, participatory discussion of the student's feelings, since only his feelings are truly "relevant" to the student. And since the lecture method implies, of course, that the lecturing professor knows more than the students to whom he imparts knowledge, the lecture too must go. Such is the caricature of "education" propounded by the New Left.

One question that this doctrine calls to mind, and one that the New Left has never really answered, of course, is *why* the students should then be in college to begin with. Why couldn't they just as well achieve these open-ended discussions of their feelings at home or at the neighborhood candy store? Indeed, in this educational theory, the school as such has no particular function; it *becomes*, in effect, the local candy store, and it, too, merges with life itself. But then, again, why have a school at all? And why, in fact, should the students pay tuition and the faculty receive a salary for their nonexistent services? If all are to be truly equal, why is the faculty alone to be paid?

In any case, the emphasis on feelings rather than rational content in courses again insures an egalitarian school; or rather, the school as such may disappear, but the "courses" would surely be egalitarian, for if only "feelings" are to be discussed, then surely everyone's feelings are approximately "equal" to everyone else's. Once allow reason, intellect, and achievement full sway, and the demon of inequality will quickly raise its ugly head.

If, then, the natural inequality of ability

and of interest among men must make elites inevitable, the only sensible course is to abandon the chimera of equality and accept the universal necessity of leaders and followers. The task of the libertarian, the person dedicated to the idea of the free society, is not to inveigh against elites which, like the need for freedom, flow directly from the nature of man. The goal of the libertarian is rather to establish a free society, a society in which each man is free to find his best level. In such a free society, everyone will be "equal" only in liberty, while diverse and unequal in all other respects. In this society the elites, like everyone else, will be free to rise to their best level. In Jeffersonian terminology, we will discover "natural aristocracies" who will rise to prominence and leadership in every field. The point is to allow the rise of these natural aristocracies, but not the rule of "artificial aristocracies"—those who rule by means of coercion. The artificial aristocrats, the *coercive* oligarchs, are the men who rise to power by invading the liberties of their fellowmen, by denying them their freedom. On the contrary, the natural aristocrats live in freedom and harmony with their fellows, and rise by exercising their individuality and their highest abilities in the service of their fellows, either in an organization or by producing efficiently for the consumers. In fact, the coercive oligarchs invariably rise to power by suppressing the natural elites, along with other men; the two kinds of leadership are antithetical.

Let us take a hypothetical example of a possible case of such conflict between different kinds of elites. A large group of people voluntarily engage in professional football, selling their services to an eager consuming public. Quickly rising to the top is a natural elite of the best—the most able and dedicated—football players, coaches, and organizers of the game. Here

we have an example of the rise of a natural elite in a free society. Then, the power elite in control of the government decides in its wisdom that all professional athletics, and especially football, are evil. The government then decrees that pro football is outlawed and orders everyone to take part instead in a local eurythmics club as a mass-participatory substitute. Here the rulers of the government are clearly a coercive oligarchy, an "artificial elite," using force to repress a voluntary or natural elite (as well as the rest of the population).

The libertarian view of freedom, government, individuality, envy, and coercive *versus* natural elites has never been put more concisely or with greater verve than by H. L. Mencken:

> All government, in its essence, is a conspiracy against the superior man: its one permanent object is to oppress him and cripple him. If it be aristocratic in organization, then it seeks to protect the man who is superior only in law against the man who is superior in fact; if it be democratic, then it seeks to protect the man who is inferior in every way against both. One of its primary functions is to regiment men by force, to make them as much alike as possible and as dependent upon one another as possible, to search out and combat originality among them. All it can see in an original idea is potential change, and hence an invasion of its prerogatives. The most dangerous man to any government is the man who is able to think things out for himself, without regard to the prevailing superstitions and taboos.[49]

NOTES

[1] On the interrelations between freedom, diversity, and the development of each individual, see the classic work of Wilhelm von Humboldt, *The Limits of State Action* (Cambridge: Cambridge University Press, 1969). On freedom as necessary for the development of individuality, see also Josiah Warren, *Equitable Commerce* (New York, 1852) and Stephen Pearl Andrews, *The Science of Society* (New York, 1851).

[2] The economists Bauer and Yamey cogently define economic development as "the widening of the range of alternatives open to people as consumers and as producers." Peter T. Bauer and Basil S. Yamey, *The Economics of Underdeveloped Countries* (Cambridge: Cambridge University Press, 1957), p. 151.

[3] See George J. Stigler, "The Division of Labor is Limited by the Extent of the Market," *Journal of Political Economy* (June, 1951), p. 193.

[4] Ludwig von Mises, *Socialism* (New Haven: Yale University Press, 1951), pp. 292–295. Also *ibid.*, p. 303.

[5] Historians have been reminding us in recent decades that neither in England nor in the United States did government confine itself strictly to the ideal of *laissez-faire*. True enough; but we must compare this era to the role of government in earlier—and later—days to see the significance of the difference. Thus, cf. Karl Wittfogel, *Oriental Despotism* (New Haven: Yale University Press, 1957).

[6] The New Left, for example, ignores and scorns Marshal Tito despite his equally prominent role as Marxian revolutionary, guerrilla leader, and rebel against Soviet Russian dictation. The reason, as will be seen further below, is because Tito has pioneered in shifting from Marxism toward an individualistic philosophy and a market economy.

[7] It is difficult, of course, to see how intangible *services* could be produced at all without "alienation." How can a teacher teach, for example, if he is not allowed to "alienate" his teaching services by providing them to his students?

[8] Thus, see Alexander Gray, *The Socialist Tradition* (London: Longmans, Green & Co., 1947), pp. 306, 328.

[9] Karl Marx, *Critique of the Gotha Programme* (New York: International Publishers, 1938), p. 10.

[10] Quoted in Gray, *op.cit.*, p. 328. Gray amusingly adds: "A short week-end on a farm might have convinced Marx that the cattle themselves might have some objection to being reared in this casual manner, in the evening."

[11] August Bebel, in *Women and Socialism*. Quoted in Mises, *op.cit.*, p. 190*n*.

[12] A recent news report disclosed that China has now softened its assault on intellectual labor. The policy of interchanging students and workers seems to have worked badly, and it has been found that "a lack of teachers and of technical training has hampered industrial development and production in recent years." Furthermore, "workers appear often to have been not tempered but softened by their exposure to a more sedentary life as many students, rather than finding life on the farm rewarding, fled China or killed themselves." Lee Lescase, "China Softens Attitude on Profs, School Policy," *The Washington Post* (July 23, 1970), p. A12.

[13] On the Utopian socialists, see Mises, *op.cit.*, p. 168.

[14] It is probable that Mao's particular devotion to the communist ideal was influenced by his having been an anarchist before becoming a Marxist.

[15] Quoted in Gray, *op.cit.*, p. 328.

[16] Italics are Lenin's. V. I. Lenin, *Left-Wing Communism; An Infantile Disorder* (New York: International Publishers, 1940), p. 34.

[17] Mises, *op.cit.*, p. 190.

[18] Gray, *op.cit.*, p. 328.

[19] Quoted in Mises, *op.cit.*, p. 164.

[20] Thus, one of the major criticisms of the New Left journal, *The Guardian*, by its rebellious split-off, *The Liberated Guardian*, was that the former functioned in the same way as any "bourgeois" magazine, with specialized editors, typists, copyreaders, business staff, etc. The latter is run by a "collective" in which, assertedly, everyone does every task without specialization. The same criticism, along with the same solution, was applied by the women's caucus which confiscated the New Left weekly, *Rat*. Some of the "Women's Liberation" groups have been so extreme in the drive to extirpate individuality as to refuse to identify the names of individual members, writers, or spokesmen.

[21] Thus, a shock to orthodox communists throughout the world was the 1958 Program of the League of Communists of Yugoslavia, which declared that the individual's "personal interest . . . is the moving force of our social development. . . . The objectivity of the category of personal interest lies in the fact that [Yugoslav] socialism . . . cannot subject the personal happiness of man to any ulterior 'goals' or 'higher aims,' for the highest aim of socialism is the personal happiness of man." From *Kommunist* (Belgrade), August 8, 1963. Quoted in R. V. Burks, "Yugoslavia: Has Tito Gone Bourgeois?" *East Europe* (August, 1965), pp. 2–14. Also see T. Peter Svennevig, "The Ideology of the Yugoslav Heretics," *Social Research* (Spring, 1960), pp. 39–48. For attacks by orthodox communists, see Shih Tung-Hsiang, "The Degeneration of the Yugoslav Economy Owned by the Whole People," *Peking Review* (June 12, 1964), pp. 11–16; and "Peaceful Transition from Socialism to Capitalism?" *Monthly Review* (March, 1964), pp. 569–590.

[22] John W. Aldridge, *In the Country of the Young* (New York: Harper & Row, 1970).

[23] Quoted in Mises, *op.cit.*, p. 304.

[24] On the strong influence of these reactionary thinkers on the anti-individualism of nineteenth-century Marxists and socialists, see in particular

Leon Bramson, *The Political Context of Sociology* (Princeton: Princeton University Press, 1961), pp. 12–16 and *passim*.

[25] See the critique of Ellul in Charles Silberman, *The Myths of Automation* (New York: Harper & Row, 1966), pp. 104–105.

[26] Thus, see the perceptively satiric article by Tom Wolfe, "Radical Chic: That Party at Lenny's," *New York* (June 8, 1970).

[27] This worship of the primitive permeates Polanyi's book, which at one point seriously applies the term "noble savage" to the Kaffirs of South Africa. Karl Polanyi, *The Great Transformation* (Boston: Beacon Press, 1957), p. 157.

[28] Both the passive and the tribal aspects of New Left culture were embodied in its ideal of the "Woodstock Nation," in which hundreds of thousands of herd-like, undifferentiated youth wallowed passively in the mud listening to their tribal ritual music.

[29] Irving Babbitt, *Rousseau and Romanticism* (New York: Meridian Books, 1955), pp. 53–54. The New Left's emphasis on passivity, primitivism, the irrational, and the dissolution of individuality may account for the current popularity of Taoist and Buddhist philosophy. See *ibid.*, pp. 297ff.

[30] Mises, *op.cit.*, p. 304.

[31] *Ibid.*, p. 305.

[32] Silberman, *op.cit.*, pp. 104–105.

[33] Neither is the magic used by primitive tribes any evidence of superior, "idealistic," as opposed to this-worldly, "materialistic," ends. On the contrary, the magic rites were unsound and erroneous means *by which* the tribes hoped to attain such materialistic ends as a good harvest, rainfall, etc. Thus, the Cargo Cult of New Guinea, on observing Europeans obtaining food from overseas by sending away scraps of paper, imitated the Europeans by writing ritualistic phrases on slips of paper and sending them out to sea, after which they waited for cargoes from overseas. Cf. Ludwig von Mises, *Epistemological Problems of Economics* (Princeton: D. Van Nostrand, 1960), pp. 62–66, 102–105.

[34] Bronislaw Malinowski, *Magic, Science, Religion and Other Essays* (New York: Doubleday Anchor Books, 1955), pp. 27–31. Also see Mises, *Epistemological Problems, loc.cit.*

[35] See the inspiring discussion in Peter T. Bauer, *West African Trade* (Cambridge: Cambridge University Press, 1954).

[36] Bernard J. Siegel, "Review of Melville J. Herskovits, *Economic Anthropology*," *American Economic Review* (June, 1953), p. 402. On developing individualism among the Pondo of South Africa, see Bauer and Yamey, *op.cit.*, p. 67n. Also see Raymond Firth, *Human Types* (New York: Mentor Books, 1958),

p. 122; Sol Tax, *Penny Capitalism: A Guatemalan Indian Economy* (Washington, D. C., 1953); and Raymond Firth and Basil S. Yamey, eds., *Capital, Saving and Credit in Peasant Societies* (Chicago: Aldine Pub. Co., 1963).

On the responsiveness of African natives to market economic incentives, see (in addition to Bauer, *West African Trade*) Peter Kilby, "African Labour Productivity Reconsidered," *Economic Journal* (June, 1961), pp. 273–91.

[37] Bauer, *West African Trade*, p. 8. Also see Bauer and Yamey, *op.cit.*, pp. 64–67. Similarly, Professor S. Herbert Frankel reports on how West Africans habitually wait at entrances of banks to fall upon their relatives to demand money as they leave. Any man who accumulates money must go to great lengths to deceive his relatives on his actual status. Cited in Helmut Schoeck, *Envy: A Theory of Social Behaviour* (New York: Harcourt, Brace & World, 1970), pp. 59–60.

[38] The works cited are Clyde Kluckhohn, *The Navaho* (Cambridge, Mass., 1946) and *Navaho Witchcraft* (Cambridge, 1944); Allan R. Holmberg, *Nomads of the Long Bow: The Siriono of Eastern Bolivia* (Washington, D.C., 1950); Sol Tax, "Changing Consumption in Indian Guatemala," *Economic Development and Cultural Change* (1957); and Oscar Lewis, *Life in a Mexican Village: Tepoztlan Restudied* (Urbana, Ill., 1951). See Schoeck, *op.cit.*, pp. 26–61.

[39] *Ibid.*, p. 50.

[40] From Gerardo and Alicia Reichel-Dolmatoff, *The People of Aritama: The Cultural Personality of a Colombian Mestizo Village* (Chicago, 1961), p. 396. Quoted in Schoeck, *op.cit.*, pp. 51–52.

[41] *Ibid.*, p. 47.

[42] *Ibid.*, p. 31.

[43] Mises, *Socialism*, pp. 463–464. See also José Ortega y Gasset, *The Revolt of the Masses* (New York: W. W. Norton and Co., 1932), pp. 63–65.

[44] *Ibid.*, p. 97.

[45] *Ibid.*, pp. 98, 84. For Ortega, the great looming danger is that the mass-man will increasingly use the State "to crush beneath it any creative minority which disturbs it—disturbs it in any order of things: in politics, in ideas, in industry." *Ibid.*, p. 133.

[46] Roger J. Williams, *Free and Unequal: The Biological Basis of Individual Liberty* (Austin, Tex.: University of Texas Press, 1953), pp. 4–5. Williams adds: "Does not our love of liberty, which seems to be inherent in all of us, rest squarely upon our *inequalities*? If at birth we all possessed the same potential tastes ... would we care about being free to pursue them as we individually desire? ... It seems to me clear that the idea of freedom arose directly out of this human variability. If we were all alike there would seem to be no reason for wanting freedom; 'living

my own life' would be an empty, meaningless expression." *Ibid.,* pp. 5, 12.

[47] Herbert Spencer, *Social Statics* (London: John Chapman, 1851), pp. 76–78. In the remainder of the book, Spencer spins out the concrete implications of his basic principle. For a critique of the Law of Equal Liberty, see Murray N. Rothbard, *Power and Market* (Menlo Park, Calif.: Institute for Humane Studies, 1970), pp. 159–160.

[48] Robert Michels, *Political Parties* (Glencoe, Ill.: Free Press, 1949). See also the brilliant work by Gaetano Mosca, *The Ruling Class* (New York: Mc-Graw-Hill, 1939), which focuses on the inevitability of a minority "ruling class" wielding power in government.

[49] H. L. Mencken, *A Mencken Crestomathy* (New York: Alfred A. Knopf, 1949), p. 145. Similarly, the libertarian writer Albert Jay Nock saw in the political conflicts between Left and Right "simply a tussle between two groups of mass-men, one large and poor, the other small and rich. . . . The object of the tussle was the material gains accruing from control of the State's machinery. It is easier to seize wealth (from the producers) than to produce it; and as long as the State makes the seizure of wealth a matter of legalized privilege, so long will the squabble for that privilege go on." Albert Jay Nock, *Memoirs of a Superfluous Man* (New York: Harper & Bros., 1943), p. 121.

Helmut Schoeck's *Envy* makes a powerful case for the view that the modern egalitarian drive for socialism and similar doctrines is a pandering to envy of the different and the unequal, but that the socialist attempt to eliminate envy through egalitarianism can never hope to succeed. For there will always be personal differences, such as looks, ability, health, and good or bad fortune, which no egalitarian program, however rigorous, can stamp out, and on which envy will be able to fasten its concerns.

[XV, Summer 1971, 226–245]

[12]

Conservatives and Libertarians: Uneasy Cousins

ROBERT NISBET

Robert (A.) Nisbet (1913–   ) is Albert Schweitzer professor emeritus at Columbia University and, since 1978, resident scholar of the American Enterprise Institute in Washington, D.C. His distinguished career as a historical sociologist included teaching at the University of California at Berkeley (from which he received the Berkeley citation in 1970) and at Riverside, as well as other famous universities in this country and abroad. He has written more than fifteen books, such as The Quest for Community *(1953),* The Degradation of the Academic Dogma *(1971), and* Twilight of Authority *(1975), including several on the French sociologist Emile Durkheim (1858–1917), and he has served in an advisory capacity to such periodicals as* The American Journal of Sociology, The Public Interest, *and* The American Scholar. *Nisbet has been the recipient of many awards and citations.*

BY COMMON ASSENT modern conservatism, as political philosophy, springs from Edmund Burke: chiefly from his *Reflections on the Revolution in France*, published in 1790. That book is of course more than a brilliantly prescient analysis of the Revolution and its new and fateful modes of power over individual lives; the *Reflections* is also, through its running asides and *obiter dicta*, one of the profoundest treatments of the nature of political legitimacy ever written. Modern political conservatism, as we find it in a European philosophical tradition from about 1800 on, takes its origin in Burke's insistence upon the rights of society and its historically formed groups such as family, neighborhood, guild and church against the "ar-

bitrary power" of a political government. Individual liberty, Burke argued—and it remains the conservative thesis to this day—is only possible within the context of a plurality of social authorities, of moral codes, and of historical traditions, all of which, in organic articulation, serve at one and the same time as "the inns and resting places" of the human spirit and intermediary barriers to the power of the state over the individual. The influence of Burke's *Reflections* was immediate, and all the major works of European philosophical conservatism—those of Bonald, de Maistre, the young Lamennais, Hegel, Haller, Donoso y Cortes, Southey and Coleridge, among others—in the early nineteenth century are rooted, as their

124

authors without exception acknowledged, in Burke's seminal volume.

Burke, it might be stressed here, had a political-ideological record leading up to his famous *Reflections* that was not regarded in his time, and would not be ordinarily thought of today, as quintessentially conservative. He had been from boyhood an ardent admirer of the glorious revolution of 1688 which had taken place four decades before his birth. When troubles with the American colonies broke out in the 1760's, Burke threw himself without reserve on the side of the colonists, and his parliamentary speeches on the Americans and on what he regarded as the hateful practices of the British government are of course classics. He may not have endorsed the colonies' decision to go to war, to seek a complete break with England, but his sympathies lay nonetheless with those Englishmen who had created the New World of America. It is worth recalling that, as with respect to the Americans, some of Burke's most powerful speeches in Parliament were delivered in behalf of India and its traditional culture and in fierce opposition to Warren Hastings, whom Burke sought unsuccessfully to indict, and the British East India Company for its depredations in India. And finally, Burke, for all his love of England and English ways, was unrelenting in his criticisms of the government for its treatment of Ireland, where Burke had been born. In sum, with good reason Burke's close friend, that essential Tory, Dr. Johnson, could worry over Burke's Whiggism.

Turning now to the foundations of contemporary libertarianism, of classical liberalism, we can go back at least as far as John Locke's *Second Treatise* if we choose, to the writings of Montesquieu in France in the eighteenth century, those of Jefferson in America, and Adam Smith in England. But the securest and most vivid source of libertarianism seems to me to lie in J. S. Mill's *On Liberty*, published in 1859, the same year in which Darwin's *Origin of Species* appeared (which has its own relation to classical liberalism and thus contemporary libertarianism, through its central thesis of natural selection, the biological version of what the classical liberals called the free market, using the phrase in its widest sense).

It is in *On Liberty* that Mill expresses at the beginning of the essay the famous "one very simple principle." Mill writes: "The sole end for which mankind are warranted, individually and collectively, in interfering with the liberty of action of any of their number is self-protection. . . . His own good, either physical or moral, is not a sufficient warrant." I suggest that Mill's "one very simple principle" is the core of contemporary libertarianism. It is necessary, though, to note Mill's immediate qualifications to the principle, qualifications which may or may not be acceptable to the majority of libertarians in our own day. Thus we learn that the principle does not apply to those below their legal majority, an abridgement that large numbers of high school and college students today would ridicule and reject. Nor does the principle hold for those Mill rather cryptically identifies as being "in a state to require being taken care of by others," a state that must include all those on any form of welfare in our society as well as those whom Mill probably had chiefly in mind, the chronically ill and the mentally deficient. Mill categorically excludes from this principle of liberty all peoples on earth who are in what he calls "backward states of society." For them, he declares, despotism remains necessary, albeit as enlightened as possible, until through social evolution these peoples reach the level of the modern West in civilization.

Later in the essay Mill goes so far as to

deny the principle of liberty to those around us who are, in his word, "nuisances" to others. And, he continues, "no one pretends that actions should be as free as opinions." In its bald statement Mill's one very simple principle would most certainly give legitimacy to contemporary pornography in all spheres as well as to noisy, order-disrupting, potentially violent street demonstrations. But with the qualifications just cited, it is far from evident that Mill's view of legitimate freedom would give sanction to contemporary license—moral, political, religious, whatever. It is impossible not to believe that even in bald, abstract statement, Mill's single, simple principle was intended to apply only to people formed intellectually and morally as Mill himself was. But such observations do not affect the sheer power that has been exerted, especially during the past half-century, by Mill's principle—in philosophy, the social sciences, theology, law, and most recently in popular morality. (Looking at the scene around us, who can seriously doubt that the counterculture won the important battles in its war against traditional American morality, commencing in the 1950's and reaching its high-point in the late 1960's? And in essence these battles were waged in the spirit of Mill's one very simple principle. Mill may have taken seriously the checks and limits he prescribed, but others, looking at the principle in the discrete, abstract, and categorically imperative form in which Mill set it down, have felt no similar obligation.)

II

So much for the roots of conservatism and libertarianism. What I shall now do is turn to the more important growths from these roots which lie around us at the present time. What are they, what are their likenesses, and what are the differences, assessed by the criteria of the conservative and the libertarian mind respectively? For the sake of clarity I shall begin with what the two minds would appear to have in common.

First is common dislike of the intervention of government, especially national, centralized government, in the economic, social, political, and intellectual lives of citizens. Edmund Burke was quite as adamant in this regard (see his strictures on French centralization and nationalization in the *Reflections*) as Mill or any other classical liberal was or would be, and that position has been maintained to the present day. Doubtless conservatives are more willing than libertarians to see the occasional necessity of suspension or abrogation of this position toward national government—as with respect to national defense, which I shall come back to later, but in general, over a substantial period of time, conservatism may be seen quite as clearly as libertarianism as a philosophy anchored in opposition to statism. Certainly by comparison with what today passes for liberalism, progressivism, populism, and social democracy or socialism, there is very little difference to be found between libertarians and conservatives in respect to attitudes toward the political state.

Second, and again by comparison with the other groups I have just cited, there is a great deal of consensus among conservatives and libertarians as to what legitimate equality in society should consist of. Such equality is, in a word, *legal*. Again we may hark back to Burke and Mill on this matter. For one as much as the other, equality before the law was vital to the flourishing of individual freedom. I see nothing in the contemporary writings of libertarians and conservatives to suggest that anything more than an occasional nuance or emphasis separates the two groups when it comes to equality. There is equal condemnation of what has come to be called equality of result, of social condition, or income or wealth.

Third, there is a common belief in the necessity of *freedom*, and most notably, *economic* freedom. Again, on the record, there appear to be more conservatives than libertarians who on occasion are prepared to endorse occasional infringements upon individual economic freedom through laws and regulatory agencies designed to protect or lift up one or another disadvantaged group. One thinks of British Toryism in the nineteenth century or of Senator Robert Taft on public housing in the late 1940's. Inasmuch as few if any all-out libertarians have yet faced the kinds of pressure in high public office which come from groups demanding one or another entitlement or exemption, it is not possible to compare libertarians and conservatives in terms of demonstrated adherence to philosophical principles when political practicalities and long-range ends are involved.

Fourth, there is a common dislike of war and, more especially, of war-society, the kind of society this country knew in 1917 and 1918 under Woodrow Wilson and again under FDR in World War II. Libertarians may protest this, and with some ground. For, the complete libertarian is certainly more likely to resist in overt fashion than is the conservative—for whom respect for nation and for patriotism is likely to be decisive even when it is a war he opposes. Even so, I think there is enough common ground, at least with respect to principle, to put conservatives and libertarians together. And let us remember that beginning with the Spanish-American War, which the conservative McKinley opposed strongly, and coming down through each of the wars this century in which the United States became involved, the principal opposition to American entry came from

those elements of the economy and social order which were generally identifiable as conservative—whether "middle western isolationist," traditional Republican, central European ethnic, small business, or however we wish to designate such opposition. I am certainly not unmindful of the libertarian opposition to war that could come from a Max Eastman and a Eugene Debs and from generally libertarian conscientious objectors in considerable number in both world wars, but the solid and really formidable opposition against American entry came from those closely linked to business, church, local community, family, and traditional morality. (Tocqueville correctly identified this class in America as reluctant to engage in any foreign war because of its predictable impact upon business and commerce chiefly, but other, social and moral activities as well.) *This* was the element in American life, not the miniscule libertarian element, that both Woodrow Wilson and FDR had to woo, persuade, propagandize, convert and, in some instances, virtually terrorize, in order to pave the way for eventual entry by U.S. military forces in Europe and Asia.

As some of the foregoing has already suggested, there is shared dislike by libertarians and conservatives of what today passes for liberalism: the kind that is so widely evident in the schools, the established churches, the universities, and, above all, the media, most spectacularly the electronic media. In passing, I would like to suggest that conservatism, on the historical record, has done more to oppose, circumvent, or defeat specific manifestations of this so-called liberalism than has libertarianism. I can recall many a conservative in the 1930's speaking out against Social Security, the AAA, the NRA, and the free-wheeling, increasingly arrogant National Education Association with its canonization of progressive libertarianism for tots in kindergarten. Perhaps there were some libertarians then also active, but I don't recall. However, I'm not cavilling. History decides these things. There were far more conservatives than libertarians in the America of that day, or at least identified, politically active conservatives. In the next decade or two, things may well become reversed in this sphere.

III

Now to the differences, or some of them, at any rate. These are important, very important! For everything at the moment suggests that the *differences* between conservatism, all-out or neo-, and libertarianism, anarcho- or constitutional, are going to loom increasingly large and divisive. By and by, it will be impossible, I would guess, for the phrases "libertarian-conservative" and "conservative-libertarian" to be other than oxymoronic: like referring to a mournful optimist or a cruel kindness. Here too I shall avoid cases and cling to principles and perspectives.

First is the contrasting way in which the two groups perceive the population. Conservatives, from Burke on, have tended to see the population much in the manner medieval legists and philosophical realists (in contrast to nominalists) saw it: as composed of, not individuals directly, but the natural groups within which individuals invariably live: family, locality, church, region, social class, nation, and so on. Individuals exist, of course, but they cannot be seen or comprehended save in terms of social identities which are inseparable from groups and associations. If modern conservatism came into existence essentially through such a work as Burke's attack on the French Revolution, it is because the Revolution, so often in the name of the individual and his natural rights, destroyed or diminished the traditional groups—guild, aristocracy, pa-

triarchal family, church, school, province, etc.—which Burke declared to be the irreducible and constitutive molecules of society. Such early conservatives as Burke, Bonald, Haller, and Hegel (of *The Philosophy of Right*) and such conservative liberals as the mature Lamennais and of course Tocqueville, saw individualism—that is, the absolute doctrine of individualism, as being as much of a menace to social order and true freedom as the absolute doctrine of nationalism. Indeed, they argued, it is the pulverizing of society into a sandheap of individual particles, each claiming natural rights, that makes the arrival of collectivist nationalism inevitable.

Libertarians are not blind to the existence of groups and associations, nor to the traditions and customs which are their cement, and it would be absurd to characterize libertarians as undiscriminating enemies of all forms of association. They do not propose return to the Enlightenment's vaunted state of nature. Only rarely does a libertarian sound like a clone of Max Stirner. They are as devoted to the principle of voluntary association as any conservative. And we should not forget that the libertarian anarchism of a Proudhon or Kropotkin was based upon a social order of groups, not abstract, Godwinian individuals. Even so, reading the libertarian journals and reviews of the last several years, I am convinced that there is a much larger egoist-hormone in libertarian physiology than there is in conservative. More and more, one has the impression that for libertarians today, as for natural law theorists in the seventeenth century, individuals are alone real; institutions are but their shadows. I believe a state of mind is developing among libertarians in which the coercions of family, church, local community, and school will seem almost as inimical to freedom as those of the political government. If so, this will most certainly widen the gulf between libertarians and conservatives.

Which leads me to a second major difference between the two groups. The conservative philosophy of liberty proceeds from the conservative philosophy of *authority*. It is the existence of authority in the *social* order that staves off encroachments of power from the political sphere. Conservatism, from Burke on, has perceived society as a plurality of authorities. There is the authority of parent over the small child, of the priest over the communicant, the teacher over the pupil, the master over the apprentice, and so on. Society as we actually observe it, is a network or tissue of such authorities; they are really numberless when we think of the kinds of authority which lie within even the smallest of human groups and relationships. Such authority may be loose, gentle, protective, and designed to produce individuality, but it is authority nevertheless. For the conservative, individual freedom lies in the interstices of social and moral authority. Only because of the restraining and guiding efforts of such authority does it become possible for human beings to sustain so liberal a political government as that which the Founding Fathers designed in this country and which flourished in England from the late seventeenth century on. Remove the social bonds, as the more zealous and uncompromising of libertarian individualists have proposed ever since William Godwin, and you emerge with, not a free but a chaotic people, not with creative but impotent individuals. Human nature, Balzac correctly wrote, cannot endure a moral vacuum.

To argue, as some libertarians have, that a solid, strong body of authority in society is incompatible with individual creativity is to ignore or misread cultural history. Think of the great cultural efflorescences of the 5th century B.C. in Athens, of 1st century, Augustan Rome, of the 13th century in Europe, of the Age of Louis XIV, and Elizabethan England. One and all these were ages of social and moral order, powerfully supported by moral codes and political statutes. But the Aeschyluses, Senecas, Roger Bacons, Molières, and Shakespeares flourished nonetheless. Far from feeling oppressed by the hierarchical authority all around him, Shakespeare—about whose copious individuality there surely cannot be the slightest question—is the author of the memorable passage that begins with "Take but degree away, untune that string, and hark! what discord follows; each thing meets in mere oppugnancy." As A. L. Rowse has emphasized and documented in detail, the social structure of Shakespeare's England was not only solid, its authority ever evident, but nothing threw such fear into the people as the thought that authority—especially that designed to repulse foreign enemies and to ferret out traitors—might be made too loose and tenuous. Of course such authority could become too insistent at times, and ingenious ways were found by the dramatists and essayists to outwit the government and its censors. After all, it was strong social and moral authority the creative minds were living under— not the oppressive, political-bureaucratic, limitless, invasive, totalitarian governments of the twentieth century.

It might be noted finally that the greatest literary presences thus far to appear in the twentieth century Western culture have nearly all been votaries of tradition and cultural authority. Eliot, Pound, Joyce, Yeats, and others all gave testimony to authority in poem, essay and novel, and all, without exception, saw the eventual death of Western culture proceeding from annihilation of this authority in the names of individualism and of freedom.

To be sure there is—and this is recognized fully by the conservative—a degree of liberty below which nothing of creative significance can be accomplished. Without at least that degree of freedom, no Shakespeare, no Marlowe, no Newton. But what is less often realized, conservatives would say, is that there is a degree of freedom *above which* nothing of creative significance can be, or is likely to be, accomplished. Writers in the late twentieth century do their work in the freest air writers have ever breathed, while composing their literary works. But it is apparent from the wretched mess of narcissism, self-abuse, self-titillation, and juvenile, regressive craving for the scatological and obscene that the atmosphere has become so rarefied as to have lost its oxygen.

On balance, I would hazard the guess that for libertarians individual freedom, in almost every conceivable domain, is the *highest of all social values*—irrespective of what forms and levels of moral, aesthetic, and spiritual debasement may prove to be the unintended consequences of such freedom. For the conservative, on the other hand, freedom, while important, is but *one of several necessary values* in the good or just society, and not only may but should be restricted when such freedom shows signs of weakening or endangering national security, of doing violence to the moral order and the social fabric. The enemy common to libertarians and to conservatives is what Burke called arbitrary power, but from the conservative viewpoint this kind of power becomes almost inevitable when a population comes to resemble that of Rome during the decades leading up to the accession of Augustus in 31 B.C.; of London in the period prior to Puritan and then Cromwellian rule; of Paris prior to the accession of Napoleon as ruler of France; of Berlin during most of Weimar; and, some would say, New York City of the 1970's. It is not liberty but chaos and license which, conservatives would and do say, come to

dominate when moral and social authorities—those of family, neighborhood, local community, job, and religion—have lost their appeal to human beings. Is it likely that the present age, that of, say, the last forty years and, so far as we can now see, the next couple of decades at the very minimum, will ever be pronounced by later historians as a major age of culture? Hardly. And can it seriously be thought in this age of *Naked Lunch, Oh! Calcutta!, Hustler,* and "Broadway Sex Live" and "Explicit" that our decadent mediocrity as a culture will ever be accounted for in terms of excessive social and moral authority?

Libertarians on the other hand appear to see social and moral authority and despotic political power as elements of a single spectrum, as an unbroken continuity. If, their argument goes, we are to be spared Leviathan we must challenge any and all forms of authority, including those which are inseparable from the social bond. Libertarians seem to me to give less and less recognition to the very substantial difference between the coercions of, say, family, school, and local community and those of the centralized bureaucratic state. For me it is a generalization proved countless times in history that the onset of ever more extreme political-military power has for its necessary prelude the erosion and collapse of the authorities within the social bond which serve to give the individual a sense of identity and security, whose very diversity and lack of *unconditional* power prevents any escape-proof monopoly, and which in the aggregate are the indispensable bulwarks against the invasion of centralized political power—which of course is unconditional. But I do not often find among libertarians these days any clear recognition of the point I have just made.

There is a final area in which the difference between conservatives and libertarians is likely to grow steadily: the nation. I stand by everything I have said in support of social authority, diversity and pluralism, and in opposition to concentration of national power. I do not have to be instructed on the number of times war, and mobilization for and prosecution of war have led to "temporary" centralizations and nationalizations which, alas, proved to be permanent. War is, above any other force in history, the basis of centralization and collectivization of the social and economic orders. No conservative can relish, much less seek, war and its attendant militarization of social and civil spheres of society.

Unfortunately we do not live in a clement world so far as conservative and libertarian ideals are concerned. It is a world in which despotisms as huge and powerful as the Soviet Union and China survive and prosper—at least in political and diplomatic respects. For the United States to ignore or to profess indifference to the aggressive acts of these and many other military, aggressive despotisms would be in time suicidal. As Montesquieu wrote in a different context: it takes a power to check a power. Nothing short of a strong, well armed, alert and active American nation can possibly check the Soviet or Chinese or Cuban nation.

No conservative to my knowledge has ever renounced or reviled the nation, conceived as a cultural and spiritual, as well as political entity. Burke adored the nation. He merely insisted upon seeing it—in vivid contrast to the Jacobins in his day—as a community of communities, as one built upon a diversity of what he called "the smaller patriotisms" such as family and neighborhood. So have conservatives, or the great majority of them, ever since chosen to see the nation. But what conservatives also see in our time, and with a sharpness of perception lacking among libertarians, is the tenuous con-

dition of the American nation—and the English and French as well. There is good nationalism and bad. But even good nationalism has become an object of either nostalgia or revulsion in our time. Patriotism, the cement of the nation, has come to be an almost shameful thing. The weakness of American government right now in the world of nations, a weakness that increasingly draws contempt and distrust from nations we desire close cooperation with, and the dearth of leadership in America in whatever sphere, are rooted in a nation that shows increasing signs of moribundity.

Libertarians, whom I herewith stipulate to be as patriotic and loyal Americans as any conservatives, do not, in my judgment, see the national and world picture as I have just drawn it. For them the essential picture is not that of a weakened, softened, and endangered nation in a world of Soviet Unions and Chinas and their satellites, but, rather, an American nation swollen from the juices of nationalism, interventionism and militarism that really has little to fear from abroad. Conservatives remain by and large devoted to the smaller patriotisms of family, church, locality, job and voluntary association, but they tend to see these as perishable, as destined to destruction, unless the nation in which they exist can recover a degree of eminence and international authority it has not had since the 1950's. To libertarians on the other hand, judging from many of their writings and speeches, it is as though the steps necessary to recovery of this eminence and international authority are more dangerous to Americans and their liberties than any aggressive, imperialist totalitarianisms in the world.

Conservatives will, or certainly should, also be alert to these dangers and seek with every possible strength to reduce them, all the while the American nation is recovering its lost leadership, in do-

mestic as well as international affairs. But
for conservatives the overriding, the supreme danger will be, I imagine, and
personally hope, the danger posed by
current American weakness in a world of
dangerously aggressive military despotisms. Nothing at the moment suggests

that this consideration will be overriding
for libertarians. And it is on this rock
above all others I have mentioned that
conservatives and libertarians will surely
break off altogether what has been at least
from the start an uneasy relationship.

[XXIV, Winter 1980, 2–8]

[II]

Conservative Thinkers

[13]

Edmund Burke, the Perennial Political Philosopher

PETER J. STANLIS

Peter J. Stanlis *(1920–   ), distinguished professor of humanities at Rockford College, is a member of the National Council for the Humanities. A leading authority on Edmund Burke, he has worked during the past forty years in the areas of eighteenth-century English literature and the history of ideas. He is the author of numerous books, including the widely known* Edmund Burke and the Natural Law *(1958); he is also the editor of* Edmund Burke: Selected Writings and Speeches *(1963). Between 1959 and 1967 he served as editor of* The Burke Newsletter.

IN 1896, IN HIS ESSAY "The Interpreter of English Liberty," Woodrow Wilson praised Edmund Burke's political principles and noted that they "have emerged from the mass of political writings . . . in their time with their freshness untouched, their significance unobscured, their splendid vigor unabated." Since few things are more dead than the dead politics of past ages, there must be something uniquely vital in Burke's political writings that they should retain their luster and significance a century after his death in 1797, and even down to the present. What is Burke's perennial appeal as a political writer? In response to this and on the occasion of the silver jubilee of *Modern Age* I should like to describe three basic ingredients in his thought and expression which may explain his enduring significance: (1) his conception of society and appeal to history; (2) his basic political principles and methods in practical politics; and (3) his literary genius and supreme mastery of English prose.

Lord Acton wrote that "History . . . hails from Burke, as Education from Helvetius, or Emancipation from the Quakers." Acton correctly perceived that Burke's political writings gave to modern man a true and organic sense of historical continuity between the ancient pagan classical civilization of Rome and the Christian civilization of the Middle Ages which is modern man's inheritance. Within the narrower context of English nationalism Sir Herbert Butterfield noted much the same point as Acton: "It was Edmund Burke who—having recovered contact with the historical achievements of Restoration Eng-

135

land—exerted the presiding influence over the historical movement of the nineteenth century." All of Burke's political writings are infused by his profound sense of history, and permeated with a conscious awareness of the enduring power of all the elements which were compounded into the foundations of European civilization.

At age twenty-eight Burke wrote *An Essay towards an Abridgment of the English History* (1757), in which he defined the chief elements that comprised the basis of European civilization—Roman civil law, embodied in the code of Justinian; Christian morality; and Teutonic customs and manners. In various combinations in different provinces and nations of Europe, these three basic ingredients provided the organized structure of society in all its legal, political, religious, moral, social, economic, and personal institutions. They gave to Europe its common distinguishing character as a civilization, distinct from the Moslem and Oriental civilizations. Burke referred to this complex of nations as the "Christian commonwealth of Europe," a concept which always commanded his veneration and respect. Burke was acutely aware that such corporate bodies as the family, church, and state, together with all the subordinate institutions of society, provided each European with a deep sense of personal identity, community, provincial loyalty, and nationality. A sense of historical continuity fostered a sense of national identity, and vice versa. The unfolding order of European society, from Classical times to the eighteenth century, was for Burke a complex and delicate historical inheritance which he felt in his bones in the well-ordered civil and religious life of Britain, anchored by legal prescriptions and moral and social norms, and ultimately sanctified by revealed religion. Burke viewed society against the cosmic order of creation, with awe and humility. As the late Ross J. S. Hoffman once remarked, Burke answered the most important questions about the origin, nature, and destiny of man from the Church of England's catechism.

Religion was for Burke the foundation of civil society, because it provided mankind with its ethical norms and values, and it was "the chain that connects the ages of a nation." It made men conscious of "the great mysterious incorporation of the human race." Throughout Europe, Christianity was "the foundation upon which all our laws and institutions stand as upon their base." Apart from religion, in secular life the remnants of Roman civil law were fused with Teutonic manners to provide the structure of the state and government. In 1757 Burke perceived that Roman *municipia*, provinces, and colonies in England were "dissimilar," yet "far from being discordant." These Roman corporate bodies "united to make a firm and compact body, the motion of any member of which could only serve to confirm and establish the whole; and when time was given to this structure to coalesce and settle, it was found impossible to break any part of it from the empire." Thus did historical continuity create a conception of civil society which was essentially organic, in which "the several parts blended and softened into one another." Thus also in England there developed from Roman law transformed into English common law, and from feudal Anglo-Saxon customs, a complex political and social constitutional system which at once preserved the character and integrity of free local provinces and established a sovereign order for the nation.

Burke's writings are filled with passages which celebrate the civil diversity and unity of England preserved in her mixed constitution. Two passages will have to suffice as examples: the first was written in 1774, the second in 1790:

Nothing is more beautiful in the theory of parliaments, than that principle of renovation, and union of permanence and change, that are happily mixed in their constitution:—That in all our changes we are never either wholly old or wholly new:—that there are enough of the old to preserve unbroken the traditionary chain of the maxims and policy of our ancestors, and the law and custom of parliament; and enough of the new to invigorate us and bring us to our true character, by being taken fresh from the mass of the people; and the whole, though mostly composed of old members, have, notwithstanding, a new character and may have the advantage of change without the imputation of inconstancy.

Our political system is placed in a just correspondence and symmetry with the order of the world . . . wherein, by the disposition of a stupendous wisdom, moulding together the great mysterious incorporation of the human race, the whole, at one time, is never old, or middleaged, or young, but, in a condition of unchangeable constancy, moves on through the varied tenor of perpetual decay, fall, renovation, and progression. Thus, by preserving the method of nature in the conduct of the state, in what we improve, we are never wholly new; in what we retain, we are never wholly obsolete.

For Burke civil society is organic, not in any evolutionary sense that it follows laws of mechanical necessity, but as a creation of man's corporate reason and will, or wisdom and power, working analogically through precedents and historical continuity to fulfill the unchangeable principles and spirit of moral natural law. Civil society, patterned upon nature as an ethical norm, upon man as a corporate social animal, and upon historical continuity and change, has a rich and vast diversity of conditions and circumstances to shape its character.

Therefore, nations cannot be governed by any abstract principles projected by speculative philosophy. As Burke said: "I never govern myself, no rational man ever did govern himself, by abstractions and universals." Burke distinguished between abstractions and principles, and noted that ". . . the statesman has a number of circumstances to combine with those general ideas. . . . Circumstances are infinite, are infinitely combined; are variable and transient; he who does not take them into consideration is not erroneous, but stark mad . . . he is metaphysically mad. A statesman, never losing sight of principles, is to be guided by circumstances. . . ." Clearly, to preserve and fulfill the diversity and unity of civil life under constitutional law required statesmanship of a high order.

Burke believed that legislators learned from historical experience because "history is a preceptor of prudence, not of principles." He considered prudence to be "in all things a virtue, in politics the first of virtues." For Burke, political philosophy provided the basic principles of politics, such as natural law, but the practical art of governing man in civil society, which required the statesman, "the philosopher in action," was based upon prudence. Since the common nature of man is infinitely modified by climate, geography, history, religion, nationality, race, institutions, laws, customs, manners and habits, and by all the circumstances of time, place, and occasions, in contingent matters and details there are no general laws to guide politicians. Here prudence reigned supreme. Prudence was for Burke not an intellectual but a moral virtue. To Burke, "no moral questions are ever abstract questions," and therefore prudence, which taught that "the situation of man is the preceptor of his duty," was the most essential practical principle in politics, and the best means of avoiding abstract rational ideology:

Nothing universal can be rationally affirmed on any moral or political subject. Pure metaphysical abstraction does not belong to these matters. The lines of morality are not like ideal lines of mathematics. They are broad and deep as well as long. They admit of exceptions; they demand modifications. These exceptions and modifications are not made by the process of logic, but by the rules of prudence. Prudence is not only the first in rank of the virtues political and moral, but she is the director, the regulator, the standard of them all.

In short, prudence is not merely a matter of empirical observation and rational analysis, but a moral imperative to take all circumstances into strict account, so that the principles of constitutional law and natural law may be fulfilled in practice in civil society.

Because of the complexity of Burke's political philosophy, and the skill in method required in practical politics, both in his own political career and in his thought there has been a great range of interpretations. During much of the nineteenth century Burke was categorized as a liberal. Since 1949, in the scholarship of Ross J. S. Hoffman, Russell Kirk, and many others, Burke has come to be regarded as the fountainhead of modern conservatism. He has been called both a Whig and a Tory; a neo-classicist and a romantic; a severe critic of Rousseau and an adherent of Rousseau's political philosophy; a skeptic like David Hume, and a Christian statesman; an expedient utilitarian and pragmatic party politician, and a principled natural law statesman; and in religion both a Catholic and a Protestant. Recently, revisionist Marxian scholars have put in a claim to Burke. Burke's thought is so complex and unsystematic that some critics, such as F. L. Lucas, have dismissed him as "vague," or "inconsistent," or both. But although Burke never provided a golden key to his scriptures, he is neither vague nor inconsistent. As Morley said, "He changed his front but he never changed his ground." Burke's political thought is many-mansioned, and his *ad hoc* statements of principle, buried amidst the rich array of empirical evidence he always provided in speaking and writing, cannot be reduced to any abstract system, like the closet philosophies of Hobbes, Locke, or Bentham. Undoubtedly, this has led some scholars into serious errors of interpretation. But it is also a chief source of Burke's perennial appeal as a political writer.

Burke's method in practical political problems was extremely hard-headed, thoroughly empirical, historical, prescriptive in law and normative in ethics, and in every way and spirit the opposite of ideological, speculative, conjectural, or abstract. In examining the genesis of a problem he showed profound respect for historical facts and past experience. He revered due process in law and the need to compromise and reconcile conflicting interests without sacrificing essential constitutional principles or moral norms. He combined old common sense with new knowledge to produce equitable and acceptable social results. His aim was to serve the public good, not to establish or apply abstract theoretical "truth." History provided the genesis of political problems and analogies with similar past problems, by which insight and perspective could make prudence prevail in practical solutions. Burke expressed his method very clearly in *Thoughts and Details on Scarcity* (1795). A legislator, he wrote, should seek "the exactest detail of circumstances, guided by the surest general principles that are necessary to direct experiment and inquiry, in order again from those details to elicit principles, firm and luminous general principles, to direct a practical legislative proceeding." Burke's method was directed by his acute awareness of the delicate complexity of society as an organic whole, which obliged legislators to harmonize its conflicting interests through practical remedies, adjusting changing circumstances to accommodate present needs, while preserving unimpaired the greatest number of contrary legitimate interests, and the organic structure of society.

To a very great extent Burke's perennial appeal as a political thinker rests upon his literary genius and supreme mastery of English prose. He had perhaps the most powerful rhetoric and style of any prose nonfiction writer in English. Gerald W. Chapman has shown at length in *Edmund Burke: The Practical Imagination* (1967), the intense fusion of Burke's unique literary imagination with an ethical awareness which permeated all of his practical political concerns. Burke was master of an enormous erudition in minute facts and details, which enabled him to function well in daily party politics, and on the broad stage of the world, in the affairs of America, Ireland, England, India, and France. When Burke's pen touched paper, no matter how mundane his subject, something magical happened. Whole anthologies have been compiled of his maxims on government and on man as a social animal. Every paragraph carries some evidence of the strong perceptive power of his thought, captured in the brilliance of his expression. In the literature of enduring power, Burke has been called the foremost writer of English prose by such eminent writers as William Hazlitt, Thomas de Quincey, Edward Bulwer-Lytton, Matthew Arnold, Sir Leslie Stephen, John Morley, and James Russell Lowell, among others. Morley wrote that Burke "imprints himself upon us with a magnificence and elevation of expression that places him among the highest masters in one of its highest and most commanding senses." Hazlitt was perhaps the first critic to refute the common error that Burke was an ornate writer: "Burke was

so far from being a gaudy or flowery writer that he was one of the severest writers we have." This judgment on Burke's complex but concisely disciplined prose style was reaffirmed by W. Somerset Maugham in "After Reading Burke" (1941).

Another characteristic of Burke's prose was that he always adapted his style to his subject and the circumstances of his writing. Conor Cruise O'Brien, in the introduction to his edition of Burke's *Reflections* (1968), distinguished five different prose styles in his writings. Burke's prose styles appeal to the total nature of man, and comprehend the whole reality of his subject. This is the main point in Edward Dowden's summary of what distinguishes Burke's prose style from that of most other good writers:

> In a well-known canon of style Burke lays it down that the master sentence of every paragraph should involve, first, a thought, second an image, and thirdly, a sentiment. A thought, an image, a sentiment, and all bearing upon action—it gives us an intimation that the writer who set forth such a canon was a complete nature, no fragment of a man . . . and that when he came to write or speak, he put his total manhood into his utterance. This is . . . Burke's first and highest distinction.

Burke did indeed appeal to his reader's reason, senses, and emotions, but the mere presence of these ingredients in his speeches and writings did not, in themselves, make his style powerful. His imaginative fusion of all these elements, his skill in converting an image into a state of mind and feeling, combined with his moral imagination, intuition, and erudition, enabled his readers to leap from sight to insight, from the physical sense to the metaphysical essence of his subject and theme, so that at once they saw, understood, and felt profoundly the whole point of Burke's argument. Burke was a great phrase maker, and even his most mundane writings are marked with sudden illuminating flashes of insight.

But above all, Burke was a poet in prose: he thought in metaphor. Goldsmith once remarked that Burke "wound into his subject like a serpent," and Samuel Johnson characterized his oral and written style as showing "copiousness and fertility of allusion, a power of diversifying his matter by placing it in various relations." Johnson admired Burke's enormous erudition in many subjects, his readiness and ability to talk well on almost every subject, and "the ebullition of his mind." Johnson once noted that "his stream of mind is perpetual. He talks not from a desire to excel, but because his mind is full." The power to think in metaphor was intuitive and spontaneous in Burke. After hearing Burke speak in the House of Commons, James Boswell wrote: "It was astonishing how all kinds of figures of speech crowded upon him. He was like a man in an orchard where boughs loaded with fruit hung around him, and he pulled apples as fast as he pleased and pelted the ministry." Gibbon, Reynolds, Malone, Mackintosh, and many others of Burke's contemporaries have attested to his remarkable eloquence and metaphorical habits of speech. His ability to reason in metaphor was the hallmark of his political thought. He used language as a civilizing force, as though he were engaged in a political dramatic monologue between himself and the listening world. In that sense his political writings may be regarded as a vast epical metaphor in defense of civilization. If Jonathan Swift is the greatest master in English of the simple concise style, Burke can be considered the most polished writer in the complex concise style.

Burke's continued relevance from generation to generation is in part the result of his having said so many wise things about the perennial problems of war, empire, and revolution, of constitutional parliamentary government, of justice, order, and freedom, of rights and duties in society—subjects which never leave the center stage of public events. His wisdom in these subjects is such that even writers who disagree with his political positions often find much to admire in him.

But Burke's greatest relevance in the twentieth century—a period criminally insane with socialistic and anarchical ideologies—lies in his criticism of the respective crimes and follies of totalitarian tyranny in all its modern forms, and of the anarchy of selfish egoists who think they can live in society as though they existed as isolated, atomized individuals in a pre-civil state of nature. Burke expounds perhaps the strongest case possible against the theory, put forth by Tom Paine, that society is merely a voluntary association of isolated individuals. Those who think that their relationship to society is privately voluntaristic sooner or later believe they can live without institutions, without community, without norms not of their private will, without any historical inheritance of laws, religion, and civility. Contemporary so-called "libertarians" who attribute to themselves as individuals rights and achievements which are made possible only by their having been born and brought up in corporate society have much to learn from Burke. His criticism of voluntaristic, revocable social contract theories applies perfectly to them. Burke knew that legally organized society, due process, and constitutional government, cannot exist on the theory that each individual can of his arbitrary will separate himself from his country for any reason he sees fit, or even, as Tom Paine argued, for no reason at all. Such theories sound like defenses of freedom when directed against gross abuses of power in government, but in fact they are destructive of the very existence of organized society, including societies essentially free and just. Such anarchical ideologues, with the best of intentions, walk in darkness and know not whither they go. Burke's writings on the French Revolution contain the best correctives to their follies; he knew that anarchy prepared the way for the very leviathan state or Napoleonic military collectivism they most despised. More than any other political writer of the past, Burke addresses himself to the great problems which plague the twentieth century, with a wisdom that is more appreciated the more he is read. In the nineteenth century William Lecky wrote of Burke's writings: "The time will never come when men would not grow wiser by reading them." Lecky was merely extending Morley's remark in 1879 that Burke was the "largest master of civil wisdom in our language." By any realistic judgment, Burke deserves to be considered one of the world's outstanding thinkers in politics.   [XXVI, Summer/Fall 1982, 325–329]

Disraeli and Modern Conservatism

KLAUS EPSTEIN

Klaus (Werner) Epstein *(1927–1967), while on sabbatical leave as chairman of the history department of Brown University, finished this review article just before his untimely death as a result of an automobile accident in West Germany in the summer of 1967. Born in Hamburg, Germany, he served in the United States Navy in 1945 and completed his education at Harvard (B.A., 1948; Ph.D., 1953). Fulbright lecturer at Hamburg from 1955 to 1956, Epstein was the author of many articles and book reviews that attracted a wide audience of scholars and serious readers. His shattering review of William L. Shirer's* The Rise and Fall of the Third Reich *(1960) had the distinction of being translated in full by one of the foremost West German historical publications after it had appeared in the United States. His last book,* The Genesis of German Conservatism *(1966), was published shortly before his death by Princeton University Press.*

BLAKE'S BIOGRAPHY of Benjamin Disraeli is a brilliant and a solid book which does full justice to its great subject. It succeeds in the difficult task of weaving Disraeli's personal life, political achievement, and literary activity into a remarkably well-integrated narrative; moreover, it far transcends the task of mere biography in portraying this in many ways "un-Victorian Victorian" against the general background of the Victorian age. The book incorporates all the most recent scholarship—no mean achievement in a field where important new publications appear almost every month—but the author has also reexamined Disraeli's papers used by previous biographers; he has found that they omitted discussion of some critical problems and published important documents with significant omissions which they considered "embarrassing" to Disraeli's memory. Though Blake is basically sympathetic to Disraeli, he is free of any kind of squeamishness; above all, he breaks with the "Tory Myth" which too long hero-worshipped Disraeli in a completely uncritical manner. Blake is not concerned with promoting the somewhat Protean legacy of Disraeli, but only with discovering what he was and what he did. To conventional Disraeli worshippers, his book will appear more iconoclastic, to Disraeli detesters more favorable than is really the case; Blake has simply applied ordinary, hard-headed common sense to a figure too long distorted by friend and foe alike. The best proof of his impartiality lies in his very balanced portrait of Disraeli's great foe Gladstone.

Though Blake has written a long book there are nonetheless several gaps and disproportions in his story. The account of Disraeli's ideas is inadequate since Blake refuses to take them seriously; so important a study of Disraeli's ideas as Professor Graubard's *The Politics of Perseverance* is omitted from the bibliography. Blake's emphasis upon Disraeli as a practical politician no doubt is a salutary corrective to those who have elevated him to the role of a Tory philosopher, but like most revisions it goes a bit too far. The book terminates too abruptly with Disraeli's death in 1881, a questionable stopping point in a statesman whose legacy—however variegated and manipulated by different people for different ends—was as influential and controversial as anything he did in his lifetime. Finally, Blake gives very short shrift to the nineteen years which Disraeli spent as Leader of the Opposition in the House of Commons in the years 1852–58, 1859–66, and 1868–74. The reader learns too little about the difficult problems which confronted Disraeli in the almost equally embarrassing situations when the Opposition differed from the government too little (when Palmerston was Prime Minister in 1859–65) and when it differed too much (during Gladstone's "radical" ministry in 1868–74). Relative neglect of the years out of office also prevents any thorough analysis of the evolution of Disraeli's views on foreign policy—there is much too little information on Disraeli's attitudes toward the Crimean War of 1853–56, the Italian question in 1859, the American Civil War, the Schleswig-Holstein crisis of 1864, and the Franco-Prussian War of 1870. In general it may be said that Blake's greatest strength lies in the narration of the course of British domestic politics—indeed, a certain insularity is the only significant flaw of his book. His frequent introduction of illuminating comparisons is nearly always to English statesmen and situations; he evidently finds foreign comparisons unhelpful in understanding English

ways, though—to give only one example—his intrinsically excellent analysis of the working of the British parliamentary system in the multi-party 1850's—with its Conservatives, Peelites, Liberals, Radicals, and Irish parties—could have benefitted by comparison with the multi-party problems of France and Germany in later periods of their history. The discussion of foreign policy problems is usually based almost exclusively on English sources and does scant justice to Disraeli's foreign antagonists.

Such minor flaws and disproportions do not, however, significantly diminish Blake's scholarly achievement. His book is by all odds the best biography of Disraeli ever written. It provides much material for answering the following key questions: how could a man like Disraeli, burdened with so many handicaps on the road to success, rise to the head of the British Conservative Party and make so great an impact upon his age? What were his contributions to English history, and specifically to the Conservative cause? And what light does his career throw on the problems of modern conservatism? Our discussion will be centered on these three problems.

I

Of the numerous obstacles confronting Disraeli on the road to success, some were inherent in his circumstances but most were self-created by his personality and his own avoidable follies. He could not help being born a Jew and encountered much anti-Semitism in all stages of his career; fortunately his father's decision to have him baptized—when he was only fourteen, before his pride could prevent him from rejecting a step so necessary to his career—at least removed the legal bar to his entry into parliament. (As a religious Jew he would have been excluded until 1858, obviously too late for him to have risen to the front rank of politics.) The anti-Semitism he provoked often had a special sharpness because it was a reaction to his own aggressive and rather tiresome pride, whether in conversation or in his novels; it is much to Disraeli's credit that he championed Jewish emancipation at all times—even in 1848 when he was desperately seeking respectability in the eyes of the Tory squirearchy to qualify for leadership in the Commons—and never disowned his fellow Jews in the manner of many assimilationists.

Disraeli's middle-class origins inevitably stamped him as a parvenu as he tried to force his way into aristocratic politics and society. Blake correctly points out that his family background was "neither obscure, undistinguished, nor poor"; his father was a conspicuous man of letters with a large inherited fortune, lived as a country squire in Buckinghamshire, and sent Benjamin's younger brothers to Winchester. Nonetheless, it was a breath-taking and seemingly utopian ambition for a man of Disraeli's origins to aspire to a leading position in Conservative politics. To pin-point the obstacles in his way, it should be remembered that even Sir Robert Peel, the son of a prosperous manufacturer and MP, with Eton and Christ Church in his background, encountered a good deal of social prejudice among traditional Tory families. Disraeli's difficulties were not, however, limited to his being a Jewish parvenu; they were compounded by the recklessness of his early life. Some stock-exchange speculations while still in his twenties saddled him with debts for most of the rest of his life, debts increased by his habitual extravagance and made manageable only by a prudent marriage, a number of unforeseeable windfalls, and his great earnings as an author while at the zenith of his political career. His connection with an ill-starred newspaper enterprise, *The Representative*, in 1826 (when

he was only 21) antagonized important people like John Murray, the publisher, and J. G. Lockhart, the editor of the *Quarterly Review*. His characterization of these and others in his first novel, *Vivian Grey* (1826), gave Disraeli the reputation of an impertinent young man who unscrupulously "used" all his "experiences" irrespective of the hurt done to the people he had come into contact with. Generally speaking, all his novels proved a liability, for they showed him cynical, flamboyant, and playful with ideas—this at a time when most Englishmen expected their political leaders to be sincere, staid, and above all grave. Disraeli's social conduct also antagonized when it did not amuse the leaders of London society. The scandal connected with his celebrated affair with Henrietta Sykes (wife of a prosperous Berkshire baronet with a large town house in London) in 1833–36 took decades to die down. His affected dandyism with its garish clothes and pompous speech made him a favorite target for ridicule; it is not surprising that Disraeli made an unfavorable impression upon many important people, such as Sir Robert Peel (later his main political foe) and Edward Stanley (later as Lord Derby his political chief for twenty years). Disraeli's only prominent political patron was the somewhat disreputable ex-Lord Chancellor Lyndhurst, who, incidentally, appears to have shared Henrietta Sykes' favors with Disraeli.

To all these handicaps must be added Disraeli's well-deserved reputation for political opportunism as he tried to enter parliament between 1832 and 1837. His friends sought Whig support for him unsuccessfully in his first election, and he is supposed to have exclaimed: "The Whigs have cast me off, and they shall repent it." Thereafter he oscillated between Toryism and Radicalism, depending upon whether he wooed a rural or an urban constituency, while calling for a National

Party to overcome the petty bickering of parties. Disraeli finally settled for Conservatism in 1837, but this did not silence doubts concerning his "sincerity." Disraeli's close friend and ally Lord John Manners wrote as late as 1842: "Could I only satisfy myself that Disraeli believed all he said, I should be more happy; his historical views are quite mine, but does he believe them?" The absurd nostalgia for the past set forth in the "Young England" novels of the 1840's and the grotesque remedies proposed for modern evils—an independent crown, public-spirited aristocracy, etc., made it difficult for men either to take Disraeli seriously or to believe him to be serious.

It is a tribute to Disraeli's remarkable qualities that he was able to overcome all these handicaps. He possessed above all extraordinary intellectual gifts, which showed both in his oratory and in his pamphleteering. He could generally charm people when he made the effort and always aroused attention even when he did not evoke admiration. He was motivated by a driving ambition which Blake believes was fueled by a deep "psychological wound" going back to his school days when he felt "different" and was not "accepted" by his school fellows—perhaps because of a simple matter like his "dark Jewish complexion"; at any rate he was determined to *dominate* what he felt was an alien and hostile world. His wonderful persistence was demonstrated by his continued effort to get into parliament even after four failures—he finally succeeded on his fifth try. He was undiscouraged when howled down during his maiden speech, ending with the famous "I will sit down now, but the time will come when you will hear me!"

In explaining his success it must also be remembered that his vices did not have the inevitably ruinous effect upon his career which they would have had in the later Victorian period. At a time but a decade removed from the Regency, sexual liaisons were not considered shocking for a budding man of the world, and financial difficulties were not uncommon. Open bankruptcy probably would have left a fatal stigma, but Disraeli was able to avoid this by his wealthy father coming to the rescue on two occasions. Dandyism was more likely to amuse the few than to shock the many. His checkered career and multifarious jobs as solicitor's clerk, stock market speculator, and journalist also had the advantage of giving him a broader experience of life than fell to the lot of many of his favored competitors. Finally, his excellent marriage in 1839 to a woman twelve years his senior, while not lacking in ludicrous and mercenary elements, met his emotional needs, gave him a stable domestic life, and lessened his financial harassments.

Disraeli's great gifts were likely to lead to a successful career once he had outlived his youthful follies; it required, however, a most remarkable combination of circumstances, to make it a spectacular career. The foundation of his later leadership was laid by what appeared at the time as a heavy setback—his exclusion from Sir Robert Peel's ministry in 1841 despite importunate pleading by himself and his wife. This exclusion was apparently not due to any special hostility on Peel's part— the Conservative leader simply had too many other claims from men with longer party service than Disraeli's to consider. The exclusion threw Disraeli into despair at the time, but it allowed him four years later to lead a successful party revolt against Peel and to become the ablest man in what remained of the party after Peel and all his able supporters (most notably Gladstone) had seceded. The opportunity for revolt was created by the widening gap between Peel's essentially middle-class outlook and that of the squirearchical

MPs who constituted the bulk of the Conservative Party in parliament; the gap was made unbridgeable by Peel's incredible mishandling of his followers, and the doctrinaire and pharisaical character of his newly acquired hostility to the Corn Laws. Disraeli could make his mark as the "conscience" of the Conservative Party in a series of tremendous philippics against Peel—philippics which made Disraeli one of the most prominent members of the House though one of the most hated as well.

In the absence of able competitors he became the intellectual leader of the "gentlemen of England," though cumulative distrust prevented him from formally securing the party leadership in the Commons until 1849. Disraeli's ally and nominal chief Lord George Bentinck, who had given respectability to the revolt of 1846 by his great name, screened him against attacks when he needed it most. Bentinck's early death in 1848 removed the last real obstacle to Disraeli's leadership, though the farcical attempts to prevent his becoming in name what he was already in substance are interesting only in showing the continued prejudice against him. Lord Derby, the Tory leader in the Lords who was also the generally acknowledged party leader, loyally resisted several attempts to "ditch" Disraeli. In short, Disraeli had tremendous luck in the opportunity which offered itself in 1846; but only a man of great ambition would have seized the opportunity, and only one of great abilities could have made it the foundation of a spectacularly successful career.

It must not be thought that Disraeli's difficulties were over when he won the party's leadership in the Commons in 1849, a post he was to hold for 27 years until his elevation to the peerage. Disraeli wanted above all to exercise political power, yet he was destined to spend most of his life in opposition. The brief minority governments of 1852, 1858–59, and 1866–68 were exercises in "holding on" rather than occasions for great achievements in legislation or foreign policy. It was only in 1874 that he finally obtained a reliable majority, in the House of Commons, and by that time he was an old man of seventy, so plagued by illness that he could govern only by the exercise of his indomitable will.

The tragedy and irony of Disraeli's career are that the events of 1846, which skyrocketed him into the top leadership of the Conservative Party, also placed that party in a minority position for a generation. An essentially "squirearchical" party was contrary to the spirit of the age and the dominant interests of the British community. It had been formed as a rally of the Protectionists, though Disraeli soon abandoned this electoral liability—not without giving new fuel to those who viewed him as a pure opportunist. What was the sense in smashing Peel's government over protection only to abandon protection immediately thereafter, they asked. The obvious road to a renewed majority was rapprochement with the Peelites, yet Disraeli—who was detested by the Peelites more than any other man—stood as an insuperable obstacle in the path of such a rapprochement. The Conservatives would not ditch Disraeli with honor, yet for many years they could not secure a parliamentary majority while he was at their head—not a pleasant position for either the party or Disraeli. To compound Disraeli's frustrations, frequent friction with the party leader, Lord Derby, was inevitable. The latter's power to decide whether the Conservatives should form a government—when invited to do so by the Queen—was not always exercised wisely. Disraeli believed, for example, that Derby should have formed a government in 1855—after Aberdeen's fall—to carry the Crimean War to a victorious conclusion; Palmerston did so instead. It is uncertain, of course, whether a Derby-Disraeli government "could have done the job" in 1855; but it was galling to Disraeli that Derby's decision—not his own—deprived him of any chance to try.

Even after he had arrived at the front bench, Disraeli continued to suffer from certain personal handicaps in the pursuit and holding of power. A cumulative reputation for cynicism, opportunism, and selfish ambition was very hard to live down—although he gradually won some "respectability" through his purchase of a country estate (Hughenden Manor) in 1848, the conferral of an Oxford DCL upon Derby's nomination in 1853, the favor of the court, and the election to some clubs from which he had been blackballed in his rakish days. His total lack of humbug, and real or apparent blindness to moral issues in politics, proved a permanent liability in a pharisaical and sanctimonious age; Disraeli never achieved the solemnity, and never pretended the earnestness, which many Victorians expected from their statesmen. His detachment—as in occasional remarks about "you English"—did not help. Disraeli's aloofness, inscrutability, and unwillingness to give his confidence—except, says Blake, to young men and old women were handicaps in an age in which personal friendships still played a large role in politics; though his fault was neutralized in some degree by his ability to manage men and to conciliate able opponents like Lord Salisbury (who turned from trenchant foe into reluctant admirer and close collaborator). His absorption in the whirl of London society sometimes placed him out of touch with powerful currents of public opinion like the North Country "Nonconformist conscience" to which Gladstone was to appeal with such success in his campaign against the "Bulgarian horrors"

of 1876. All in all, it remains remarkable that a man with so many strikes against him could play so conspicuous a role on so large a stage over more than a third of a century.

II

Disraeli has three major political achievements to his credit. He provided Britain with a great administration for six years between 1874 and 1880, great both in its domestic legislation and in its conduct of foreign affairs. He did much to define conceptions of party loyalty and the constructive role of partisanship in the operation of the parliamentary system. Finally, he transformed the character of Britain's Conservative Party and thereby contributed to its ascendancy for several decades after his death. A few observations may be ventured on each of these points.

Blake rather belittles the legislative achievements of Disraeli's "great Ministry," or at least insists that the Prime Minister took little interest in the work of his domestic ministers. While it is no doubt true that Disraeli was more concerned about foreign affairs than about housing, public health, municipal waterworks, and the picketing rights of trade unionists, it must be emphasized that he picked the ministers responsible for these "humble" fields—the most important, Richard Cross, was his "personal" discovery and received the Home Office to everyone's surprise; that he gave them free rein to work out legislation; and that he used the government majority to put their proposed bills through parliament. Blake denies any connection between the social measures propagated by Disraeli in his novels in the 1840's and those put on the statute book during his Prime Ministership in the 1870's; it seems unnecessary, however, to postulate such an unnecessary discontinuity. The social legislation of the 1870's shows that Disraeli—in this respect far superior to his rival Gladstone—had considerable understanding of the social problems posed by industrialism, and believed they must be approached through massive state intervention in violation of *laissez-faire* canons. No doubt he gave preference to measures of state intervention which did not cost any money—Blake cites many instances throughout his book of Disraeli's adherence to the "Treasury point of view." No doubt he was hesitant to challenge powerful economic interests at a time when his electoral appeal was based upon opposition to Gladstonean radicalism; no doubt his legislation was too frequently permissive rather than compulsory because he suffered from an obsessive fear that bureaucratic centralization imperiled the traditional liberties of England. After all this has been admitted it remains true nonetheless that Disraeli established a fruitful tradition of Conservative legislation on behalf of the working class through a Public Health Act, an Artisans Dwellings Act, an Agricultural Holdings Act, a Factory Act, a Sale of Food and Drugs Act, and two important Trade Union Acts. "Social Reform" became an honored plank in the platform of the Conservative Party, and when combined with Imperialism and a "Strong Foreign Policy" it gave the Conservative Party a considerable appeal to sections of the working class from Disraeli's day to our own.

Disraeli gave a great impetus to Imperialism although he personally took remarkably little interest in the self-governing empire and described the colonies on one occasion as "millstones around our necks." His personal interest in Imperialism was largely confined to India, and he readily risked a political storm to please his royal mistress by securing for her the Indian Imperial title against much unreasonable Liberal opposition. Concern for the security of India was a primary factor in his foreign policy during the Eastern crisis of 1876–78. Blake's rather unsatisfactory account of this policy deals at disproportionate length with Gladstone's campaign of moral indignation against Foreign Secretary Derby's disloyal relations with the Russian Ambassador Shuvalov and the small mistakes made by Disraeli throughout the crisis. Blake fails to appreciate sufficiently the greatness of Disraeli's achievement and the mastery of diplomatic processes which it revealed— a mastery from which much can be learned even in today's changed world.

Disraeli was clear in his own mind on his objectives: reasserting Britain's prestige shaken by Gladstone's policy of abdication and moral homilies; disrupting the *Dreikaiserbund*; preventing a Russian occupation of Constantinople; and buttressing the Turkish Empire. A believer in *Realpolitik*, he considered Turkish atrocities against Bulgarians no doubt regrettable, but he considered them irrelevant to a statesmanship charged with protecting the tangible political interests of England. (It is clear that he erred in the belief that moral considerations could and should be eliminated completely from *Realpolitik*, and he created needless difficulties for himself by airily dismissing well-authenticated atrocity stories as "coffee-house babble.") He insisted that the requirements of the European balance of power necessitated the revision of the Treaty of San Stefano, which the Russians had unilaterally imposed upon the hapless Turks, at a European Congress. While willing to accept some Russian aggrandizement, he insisted that this must be balanced by the British annexation of Cyprus. Disraeli knew that decisions at international congresses are shaped less by arguments than by the power situation (of which the credible will to utilize power is always a crucial element); hence he called out the reserves, and summoned Indian troops to Malta, on the eve of the congress, even as he had earlier sent the fleet to Besika Bay, and later to Constantinople itself, to add weight to Britain's diplomatic notes. Knowing that Britain was too weak to prevail alone, he worked closely with the Habsburg monarchy whose Balkan interests paralleled Britain's. Recognizing, moreover, that "summit meetings" were bad places for the successful transaction of difficult diplomatic business, he insisted upon settling the core of Anglo-Russian disagreements through conventional secret diplomacy prior to the opening of the congress of Berlin.

There can be little question that from a technical point of view Disraeli's performance was nearly flawless; any criticism must be directed at the validity of his objectives and at his understanding of some of the elements of the Eastern Question. He probably exaggerated the aggressiveness and the extent of Russia's designs, though in such cases it is best to be prepared for contingencies by putting the worst construction on your foe's motives (even at the risk of this becoming a self-fulfilling prophecy). He certainly exaggerated the "reformability" of Turkey, though it can be argued that the integrity of even an unreformed Turkey was very much a British interest. He never understood the nature of Balkan nationalism and Gladstone's profound conception of a "wall of free nationalities" standing between Constantinople and the Russians; such a wall could assure Britain's political interests better than the effete and brutal Turk, and would conform to the higher interests of humanity. After all this has been said it remains nevertheless true that Disraeli was entirely successful in achieving the objectives he had set out to achieve and in resolving—however temporarily—the Eastern question within the terms in which he understood that question.

In party affairs Disraeli made important contributions to the question of a leader's obligation to his party. His campaign against Peel in 1846 was only partly on behalf of the protectionist principles which Peel had abandoned; it was also—in Disraeli's view—a campaign on behalf of the principle of political honesty. Peel had been elected by the voters of Great Britain in 1841 on a straightforward protectionist program dear to the hearts and pocketbooks of members of his Conservative Party. By reversing his program in midterm he betrayed the party which had elected him leader and laid himself open to the charge of having deceived the electorate. Under these circumstances he had no right to count upon the loyalty of his followers, and in fact he courted a party split. Peel's reply to the charges was, of course, that he had—and would always—place his country above his party; he believed in the traditional view—held before parties became really "respectable"—that the Queen's ministers must govern in accordance with their best judgment of what constituted the national interest under the specific circumstances of the moment—even if this meant antagonizing their staunchest followers and repudiating party pledges made in a different situation. The problem of what a leader owes respectively to the country, the party, and the electorate is still an open one, as witness President Johnson's conduct of the Vietnamese War in complete violation of his pledges during the 1964 presidential campaign. Suffice it to say that Disraeli established the point that a leader owes *some* special obligation to his party and that political honesty requires that electoral pledges *ought not* to be lightly repudiated. This point must, of course, like all general political maxims, always be interpreted in the light of any given situation.

Disraeli was Leader of the Opposition

in the House for a longer period than any English statesman since Charles James Fox. He coined the famous saying, "The duty of the opposition is to oppose," and he practiced the general rule that government measures must be opposed, or at least criticized, unless there are very special circumstances to justify what today is called bipartisanship. He believed that all measures benefit by criticism (or at least the threat of criticism) because all are capable of improvement; and he was of course by temperament a partisan fighter. On occasion he was willing to help Gladstone pass a measure disliked by the Liberal Left wing, like the famous Education Act of 1870 (left unmentioned by Blake); but his usual policy was to oppose for opposition's sake even when he agreed with the principles of a proposed measure. Moreover, he definitely did not believe that partisanship must stop at the water's edge.[1] He criticized Gladstone's foreign at least as much as his domestic policy— and his great antagonist paid him back with double interest during the Eastern crisis of 1876–78. In judging the extreme partisanship of both men in foreign affairs one must, of course, remember that this was a luxury which powerful, secure Victorian England could more readily afford than less favorably placed countries. Whatever the excesses on both sides, there can be no question that the Victorian period—and more especially Disraeli as long-time Opposition Leader—made an important contribution to the view that tough and unremitting opposition—fueled by partisanship and the desire for office— is a useful and reputable aspect of parliamentary government.

Disraeli's far-reaching opportunism of outlook, which proved in no way incompatible with sharp partisanship, played a great role in his greatest achievement— the "education" of the Conservative Party into a party capable of coping with the problems of the modern age. Blake is no doubt right in ascribing to expediency what more worshipful biographers have seen as the product of long-range design; but motives are of no great importance in evaluating Disraeli's achievement. He gave Britain the precious possession of a responsible Conservatism which did not hanker after the restoration of an earlier "golden age" and was in fact willing to take the lead in promoting necessary and timely reforms. He explicitly avowed his Reform Conservative outlook on several occasions, while always stressing the deep difference between the Conservative and Radical spirit of reform:

> In a progressive country change is constant; and the great question is not whether you should resist change which is inevitable, but whether that change should be carried out in deference to the manners, the customs, the laws, and the traditions of a people, or whether it should be carried out in deference to abstract principles, and arbitrary and general doctrines (p. 432, speech at Edinburgh on Oct. 29, 1867).

It must not be thought that Disraeli consistently adhered to this view, or that he considered the education of the Conservative Party to be his primary political objective. As Conservative party leader he frequently opposed changes—however beneficial and ultimately necessary—because they were disliked by his followers or contrary to his own prejudices; moreover, he had assumed the leadership of the party in the Commons as a result of leading a reaction against Peel's progressive or reform Conservatism. To turn the party back into a purely agrarian party, and to antagonize the middle-class elements which Peel had wooed so successfully was certainly a retrograde step; before one over-praises Disraeli's educational efforts one must remember that he was responsible for much of the retardation of his child.

Nonetheless, Disraeli did achieve two major "educational" objectives in reconciling the party to a democratic franchise (which he did not pretend to like but considered inevitable) and to social reform (which could be justified both as a tactical necessity and in terms of the *noblesse oblige* of the squirearchy). He went so far as to carry a large extension of the suffrage himself in the celebrated Reform Bill of 1867. Blake belittles the latter achievement by stating that it makes Disraeli deserve "to go down in history as a politician of genius, a superb improviser, and a parliamentarian of unrivalled skill, but not as a far-sighted statesman, a Tory democrat, or the educator of his party" (p. 477). This is one of several instances where Blake's revisionism goes too far. Whether or not Disraeli was a Tory democrat, he certainly acted like one; whether or not he intended to educate his party, he certainly committed the party to this and subsequent extensions of the franchise; whether or not he was a farsighted statesman, the effect was to reconcile the party to an inevitable development which many of its members (including himself) rather disliked, but which it would have been suicidal in the long run to oppose. The same can be said of his outlook toward social reform, where he set his party on the right track, whatever the inadequacies of the specific measures which he introduced.

The proof is surely to be found in his party's ascendancy after his death—in the next twenty-five years (1881–1906) it was in power for seventeen. More important still is the "legacy" which he left to his official successors like Lord Salisbury and his self-proclaimed successors like Lord Randolph Churchill—not to speak of later successors like R. A. Butler and Harold Macmillan, who proudly proclaimed themselves as standing in the Disraelian tradition. Their slogans and electoral appeal have included "Trust the People"—an affirmation of democracy unusual among Europe's Conservatives; "Social Reform"—an important legacy which remained alive even when the party was largely taken over by industrial interests very well satisfied with the *status quo*; "The Empire"—a highly popular slogan for several decades, and in the purified form of "The British Commonwealth" very attractive until the mid-1950's; and a "Strong Foreign Policy"—something which appealed to British nationalism and the belief that Britain had a constructive role to play in world affairs. These slogans were re-enforced, moreover, by a profound conception of human nature which understood the claims of the irrational, the colorful, and the authoritarian in politics. These needs received institutional satisfaction in the organization of the Primrose League, named after his favorite flower and devoted to propagating his legacy.

III

Disraeli's legacy, as is the case with that of many great political figures, represents only part of the man's outlook. It amounts in fact to a selection which at times approaches a falsification. The "real" Disraeli had many beliefs quite incompatible with his forward-looking legacy—beliefs which were anachronisms, and hence liabilities, and would have proved suicidal if the Conservative Party had been so ill-advised as to adhere to them. Blake rightly insists that Disraeli—contrary to the view of many of his contemporaries—did consistently believe in certain broad principles, though his conduct was often that of an ambitious careerist, and his curious mixture of cynicism and romanticism aroused distrust among friends and hostility among foes. He believed in what he called the "greatness of England," and the need of a strong foreign policy to maintain her rightful place in Europe and the world (this became part of the legacy); but he also adhered to a strictly Machiavellian conception of foreign policy which was frankly indifferent to purely moral considerations (a hard-boiled *Realpolitik* which no democratic community, and least of all one leavened by puritanism, will ever accept). In domestic affairs Disraeli identified the "greatness of England" with the ascendancy of the landed class standing at the apex of a hierarchic and pluralistic order of society; he combined this view with a hatred of the centralizing, rationalizing bureaucracy championed by Jeremy Bentham and his followers in the Liberal party and the Radical movement. (Both his love and his hatred became anachronistic in the course of his life and did not become part of the Disraelian legacy.) In his novels (and to a lesser, but still significant, degree in his life) Disraeli worshipped an independent crown; this contributed to his notorious flattery of Queen Victoria; of a public-spirited aristocracy which had little resemblance to England's real, tough, rack-renting aristocracy; and of a national Church solicitous of the people—which had no resemblance to either High Church ritualism or Broad Church rationalism, and only a limited realization in the Low Church evangelicism which he rather clumsily sought to mobilize on behalf of Tory party interests. (This part of Disraeli's outlook has become an "honorific" rather than a "functional" element in the Disraelian legacy, though affirmation of Crown, Lords, and Church has remained the stock-in-trade of every Conservative Party conference.)

Disraeli's advocacy of social reform was strongest in the 1840's when he wrote *Sybil*; it progressively diminished—though never became extinct—as he wooed middle-class elements for his party, forswore utopian dreams for practical realities, sought to benefit from the reaction against "Gladstonian radicalism," and became preoccupied with foreign affairs. (The Conservative advocacy of social reform became disproportionately inflated in the legacy.) Disraeli took a completely opportunistic view on the franchise. (This was distorted into "Trust the People" in the legacy.) Over and above all these specific views stands Disraeli's basic belief that life is an exciting adventure which must be savored but never taken too seriously, and which can never be comprehended by any single philosophy, least of all the rationalist, philistine utilitarianism he encountered in his youth. (This point of view has been shared by most of the leaders of "Tory democracy," though it is scarcely suited for propagation among the masses inevitably destined to lead humdrum lives.)

Apart from his eternal zest for life, Disraeli's "real" principles have practically no relevance today, and the political "potency" of his "legacy" has virtually diminished to the vanishing point. What then survives in his career to justify its perennial fascination for modern Conservatives? The answer lies not in his principles but rather in his conduct—or perhaps it should be said in his conduct as governed by principles so general as to become commonplace. Foremost in this connection is his practicing of a basically Reform Conservative outlook: a Conservatism which recognizes the inevitability of changes in the modern world and sees its primary function as one of anticipating, guiding, and "civilizing" changes in such a way as to maximize continuity with the past and to minimize injury to old institutions and values which still retain their vitality. Reform Conservatism—unlike the Conservatism lampooned by John Stuart Mill as the "stupid party"—requires the continuous exercise of intelligence in order to understand historical development; to distinguish between what is incorrigibly rotten (hence to be eliminated) and what can still be saved or even strengthened, through timely reform; and what specific steps are needed in a specific constellation of political forces in order to achieve the best kind of society attainable. It combines the conception of leadership by an elite with consent by the masses, though it is (alas!) necessary for democratic public relations to minimize the former and maximize the latter. It views politics as a wooing of circumstances to achieve the possible and will always be condemned by both Reactionaries and Radicals as characterized by an opportunist lack of principle. It condemns the Radical conception of politics as the translation of abstract principles into coherent policies, because it distrusts all abstractions and knows that life is not necessarily coherent.

Disraeli is perhaps not the most successful but certainly the most dazzling of modern Reform Conservatives. His improbable career in overcoming fantastic objective and self-created obstacles; his major impact upon British politics for thirty-five years of his life, and at least a half century after his death; and the irresistible vitality of his personality all guarantee that men will long continue to be interested in his career. Blake has succeeded in writing a biography of this complicated man which fulfills nearly every need of the contemporary leader, and will no doubt become and remain the "standard work" for decades to come.

NOTE

[1] It is worth noting briefly that Disraeli's secret practice was even more remarkable than his open principles. Blake—following the important study of G. B. Henderson (1947)—shows that Disraeli planted a disreputable character, Ralph Earle (soon to become his private secretary), as a spy in Britain's Paris embassy in 1854 and that he regularly received confidential documents from him which he used in his parliamentary opposition to the government; it is highly possible, moreover, that he also received regular reports from a Foreign Office official who had received rapid promotion in the dying days of the Derby-Disraeli administration of 1852. Worse still, Disraeli believed that the best chance of toppling Palmerston—since there was little difference on domestic affairs between Whigs and Tories—was to be found on a foreign policy issue, as had happened once before in the Orsini case (when Palmerston had been defeated because he had "truckled to France" in introducing a bill to prevent assassination plots against Napoleon III—like that just attempted by Felice Orsini—from being hatched on British soil). Disraeli's sharp partisanship led him into highly questionable conduct when he sent his friend Earle in April 1860 on a mission to Napoleon to encourage the French Emperor to offer resistance to some demands made by Palmerston. "In effect he was inciting Napoleon to pursue an anti-British policy in the hope that the resulting fracas would bring down Palmerston as it had in 1858" (p. 373). The case shows that there were some curious blind spots in Disraeli's much advertised patriotism.

[XII, Winter 1967–68, 66–76]. Review of *Disraeli* by Robert Blake. New York: St. Martin's Press, 1967.

[15]

"Liberty by Taste": Tocqueville's Search for Freedom

DAVID BRUDNOY

David Brudnoy (1940–   ) has been a professor at Merrimack College and at Harvard's Institute of Politics, an associate or contributing editor of various journals, a television commentator, film critic, newspaper columnist, and lecturer. The editor of The Conservative Alternative *(1973), he has also published in* National Review, Human Events, The New Republic, *and scholarly journals in Japan and Europe. Brudnoy currently lives in Boston.*

I am an aristocrat by instinct—that is to say, I despise and fear the mob. I have a passionate love for liberty, law, and respect for rights—but not for democracy. . . . I am neither of the revolutionary party nor of the conservative. Nevertheless, when all is said, I hold more by the latter than the former . . . . Liberty is my foremost passion.[1]

ALEXIS DE TOCQUEVILLE is usually lauded, often quoted, and seldom read. When Part I of *Democracy in America* was first noticed in the United States in the mid-1830's, Edward Everett wrote of the emergence of an "original thinker, an acute observer, and an eloquent writer [whose work was] by far the most philosophical, ingenious and instructive, which has been produced in Europe on the subject of America." Jared Sparks sent Everett's review to Tocqueville, greatly pleasing the young writer. The remaining portions of *Democracy* (1840) were greeted in this country, in the words of an im-

portant journal, as "the ablest view that has ever appeared."[2]

Not until a generation after Tocqueville's death did the most serious doubts appear as to the brilliance of *Democracy*. An excess of prophet-baiting, especially in the 1890's, was occasioned by various errors in the French theorist's predictions, especially as to the outcome of any conflict between the Union and, as Tocqueville put it, the "states." Even then, however, in the full sheen of America's tarnished Gilded Age, Henry Adams, who practically venerated Tocqueville, and various European scholars upheld his worth. But the resuscitation of Tocqueville's reputation, if such it be, is a phenomenon of the present century, as a new generation of scholars fell all over each other striving to lavish praise on the author of *Democracy in America*, this reaching its height in the book's centenary decade, the 1930's.

In the post-World War II period, both

154

wings of the political spectrum in the United States have found occasion to adopt Tocqueville. Harold Laski found *Democracy* the "greatest work ever written on one country by the citizen of another," while Russell Kirk and Peter Viereck fit Tocqueville into a category shared by Burke and the Adamses, *père et fils*.[3] For the "old" left and the "new" right, the popular and the scholarly, as well as for those called by the late President Kennedy men who enjoy the comfort of opinion without the discomfort of thought, Tocqueville has become a subject of respect and of almost requisite quotation. Among our contemporaries, however, as before, Tocqueville has suffered his share of disapprobation, even of curious omission from the works of scholars, like Daniel Boorstin and Arthur M. Schlesinger, Jr., whose major books have dealt with Tocqueville's period without seriously considering Tocqueville's thought. The purpose of the present study is not to examine Tocqueville's critics or adulators but, rather, to consider him anew, not so much to reinterpret his opinions as to reexamine them.

A Liberal of a New Type

On one occasion Tocqueville expressed the hope that he would be seen "to be a liberal of a new kind; not to be confounded with our ordinary modern democrats."[4] At least the first phrase is well known; the remainder is usually ignored. It is in this sense, that he must not be confounded with our ordinary democrats, that he has been seen as a "conservative." Professor Marvin Meyers wrote that Tocqueville discovered in America the "soul of an archconservative: the steady citizen, the meek thinker, the pillar of property and propriety." Meyers' approach helps us alter a simplistic view of

America as seen through Tocqueville's eyes and also aids us in delineating what Tocqueville clearly was not: he did not stand for hard-crusted, unmovable conservatism in his own France, nor did he much like it elsewhere.[5]

With all conservatives, Tocqueville defended property. This is seen frequently in his writings, as in a speech on January 27, 1848, in the Chamber of Deputies:

> As long as the right of property was the origin and groundwork of many other rights it was easily defended—or rather it was not attacked; it was then the citadel of society.... But today, when the right of property is regarded as the last undestroyed remnant of the aristocratic world ... it is a very different matter. Do you not see that, little by little, ideas and opinions are spreading amongst them which aim not merely at removing such and such laws ... but at breaking up the very foundation of society itself?[6]

But such defense of property was not a pandering to the prejudices of the bourgeoisie, which class, he felt, did not represent the whole French nation nor the natural ruling element of the human race. Often Tocqueville derided the boorish tendencies of the bourgeoisie.

Indeed, Tocqueville was in many ways a conservative critic of capitalism, conservative because his critique of bourgeois society and its capitalist system had "as its yardstick the value attitudes of a past political society, and because the critique comes from an aristocratic political class, not from an economic proletariat."[7] Tocqueville feared the loss of liberty through untrammeled *laissez-faire*; he further feared the loss of liberty through guaranteeing welfare to all by an increasingly omnipotent state. This question confronted him in 1848 and earlier as well.

Burkean thoughts run through Tocqueville's writings almost like a *basso ostinato*. The man whose motto was "government by prescription" diverged most sharply from Tocqueville not in matters of fundamental conservative attitude, but rather in their interpretations of the nature of the French Revolution. Still, this does not dislodge Tocqueville from his place as a Burkean. Viereck groups Tocqueville, Adams, and Churchill among the Burkeans, and Kirk remarks that Tocqueville's works are "shot through with Burke's ideas." Tocqueville, says Kirk, was "perhaps the only social thinker of the first. rank since the end of the eighteenth century [who] endeavors to reconcile with the inevitable tendency of society those surviving ancient values which Burke had ringingly attested." But the waters of Russell Kirk's river are muddied by his insistence both that "Tocqueville applied the wisdom of Burke to his own liberal ends," and that "Burke was liberal because he was conservative."[8] This requires explication.

As is by now well known, the "new" conservatives, of whom Kirk is in the front rank, see true nineteenth-century "liberalism" metamorphosed in our day as "conservatism." But to others, the term "libertarianism" more accurately fits, although Tocqueville was not and should not be seen as a "libertarian" in the contemporary sense either. Finding liberty and complete equality incompatible, and constantly at pains to disassociate himself from the lionized "republican" Marquis de La Fayette, Tocqueville meant by that "usual type of democrat" with whom he eschewed identity, those whose tendency it was to prefer equality to liberty. Tocqueville resignedly accepted the French Revolution, which Burke so loathed, seeing in it, as J. P. Mayer puts it, the "new commandments for the nineteenth and twentieth centuries."[9] Between Burke and Tocqueville there was what we might today call a generation gap.

Another crucial "conservative" element is religion, which Tocqueville stressed as a fundamental of freedom. It is debatable how deeply Tocqueville's Catholicism ran, but religion in a larger sense was a constant pole on which he saw freedom depending. Religion taught men the "doctrine of the immortality of the soul."[10] As much for Tocqueville a social good as an individual matter, religion meant a consciousness of man's place in the human order, the "social order," we might also say.

Yet he opposed a state religion. Separation of church and state, he saw as essential to democracy. He wanted a democracy respecting religious beliefs, not one dominated by them. In *Democracy* he made the explicit connection between the value of religion and the maintenance of freedom—the "conservative" connection:

> Despotism may govern without faith, but liberty cannot. Religion . . . is more needed in democratic republics than in any other. How is it possible that society should escape destruction if the moral tie is not strengthened in proportion as the political tie is relaxed? And what can be done with a people who are their own masters if they are not submissive to the Deity?[11]

"Do what you may," he wrote earlier in the book; "there is no true power among men except in the free union of their will; and patriotism and religion are the only two motives in the world that can long urge all the people toward the same end."[12]

It was Tocqueville's concern to see how to tame the excesses and exclusive taste for well-being that men feel in periods of equality. For him, as for conservatives then and now, the "chief concern of religion is to purify, to regulate, and to restrain" those excesses: "The more the conditions of men are equalized and assimilated to each other, the more important is it for religion . . . not needlessly to run counter to the ideas that generally prevail. . . ."[13]

In further opposition to the democrats of his day, Tocqueville disabused his readers of whatever faith they might have in individualism. In fact, he coined the word *individualisme* whence our English term comes. Tocqueville meant by that term, as Max Lerner concisely puts it,

> more than anything else, the loneliness of the individual and the atomization of the society, while we use the term to stress the self-reliant assertion of individual differences in talent and character. Today we see individualism as opposed to the leveling emphasis of egalitarianism; Tocqueville saw it as one of the consequences of egalitarianism.[14]

The conservative claim to Tocqueville stresses these interlocking dicta: the potential danger of *individualisme*, and the saving grace of religion.

Moreover, the "aristocratic" element may be educed as evidence of his conservatism, although dangers lurk. "I am an aristocrat by instinct," he wrote, but he could not have "any natural affection for it, since that aristocracy had ceased to exist, and one can be strongly attached only to the living."[15] Aristocracy in France was finished, buried forever, or so he believed. But as for England, "while you preserve your aristocracy, you will preserve your freedom. If that goes, you are in danger of falling into the worst of tyrannies—that of a despot appointed and controlled, if controlled at all, by a mob."[16] Louis Napoleon, for example.

Democracy, or rather, *equality*, was inevitable:

> The nations of our time cannot prevent the conditions of men from becoming equal, but it depends upon themselves whether the principle of equality is to lead them to servitude or freedom, to knowledge or barbarism, to prosperity or wretchedness.[17]

Thus Tocqueville concluded *Democracy*. Tocqueville the aristocrat observed that aristocratic conditions "cannot exist without laying down the inequality of man as a fundamental principle, legalizing it beforehand and introducing it into the family as well as into society; but these are things so repugnant to natural equity that they can only be extorted from men by force." As for America, "a state of equality is perhaps less elevated, but it is more just; and its justice constitutes its greatness and its beauty." The people, he observed sadly, "will endure poverty, servitude, barbarism, but they will not endure aristocracy."[18]

This brings us to the best known of Tocqueville's "conservative" tendencies: his fear of "tyranny of the majority," a fear surely derived from his reading of the history of France during the Terror. Tocqueville saw the greatest danger in America arising from the omnipotence of the majority, that tyranny of which the mass was capable, especially through the "formidable barrier" of public opinion.

> The omnipotence of the majority appears to me to be so full of peril to the American republics that the dangerous means used to bridge it seem to be more advantageous than prejudicial.[19]

It was in an excess of *individualisme* that Tocqueville saw the seeds of majority tyranny, for when man grew indifferent to his fellows at just that moment when they became socially indistinguishable, the individual became confined "entirely within the solitude of his own heart" and, in joining together into majorities, would be as disregarding of the rights, hopes, and aspirations of others *en masse* as of another *en soi*. In America he noted that white majority tyranny enslaved Negro minorities, keeping them from voting even in Philadelphia.

Hence Tocqueville's antagonism to "socialism." That "moral depravity" he observed in "mob rule," so peculiar to democratic, égalitarian societies, frightened him. In socialism he found a "profound defiance of liberty, or human reason"—it was to him a "new form of servitude."[20] And so, his disinclination to socialism and social welfare, a disinclination which extended almost to a general disinterest in questions of poverty. "If we give this right [a guarantee against starvation], we must, of course, make this relief disagreeable; we must separate families, make the workhouse a prison, and our charity repulsive."[21] It is difficult to find in Tocqueville's writings a more frankly antisocial welfaristic statement, or one more typical of a facet of nineteenth-century liberalism.

Tocqueville wanted private, voluntaristic charity for those in need. For those who paid no taxes, Tocqueville could see only an incapability of intelligent political activity, and from such people the vote should be withheld. If social welfarism implied excessive state intervention, then it was for him repugnant, leading to a strong dependency by individuals on the state, which could then be oppressively totalitarian as a consequence. He dwelt at length on his belief that a government whose aim it was to provide any permanent system to aid the poor would breed more misery than it could cure, would benumb human industry and activity, would bring about a violent revolution in the state, when "the number of those who receive alms will have become as large as those who give it, and the indigent, no longer being able to take from the impoverished rich the means of providing for his needs, will find it easier to plunder them of all their property at one stroke than to ask for their help."[22] Tocqueville lacked a clear, confident, systematic position on the problems of poverty, doubting the efficacy of private charity alone but fearing state paternalism, wanting charity for the aged and children and a

public education system, but perplexed by the dangerous tendencies such expenditures would incite. It was for him a problem that has confounded conservatives then, as now.

With his central concern being liberty, the problem of poverty, by default, was of less consequence. He feared the state and rejected collectivist notions. And in the last decade of his life, but also earlier, his confidence in the ineluctable trend toward democracy waned.

The final element in Tocqueville's conservatism was his fear of power. He wanted to limit government, not to expand its powers. While seeing centralization as a major tendency in France for seven centuries, and in America as he knew it, he was a "federalist" in the sense of favoring coordinate spheres of government, and an admirer of the English system of balanced powers. The state needed authority, without which anarchy ensues; but the type of rule he advocated—and he was far more concerned with this than with the type of ruler—was one which checked absolute power of any sort. In this he anticipated Lord Acton.

Governmental centralization, which Tocqueville praised, meant the effective control and coordination of national affairs, foreign policy, and so forth. Centralized administration, which he opposed, meant national control over local affairs. A decentralized administration was conducive to freedom since it mitigated the tyranny of the majority; thus his praise for it in America. The contrary situation, with local control surrendered to central powers, was deleterious. "The only nations which deny the utility of provincial liberties are those which have fewest of them; in other words, only those censure the institution who do not know it." He believed that little is gained when a

vigilant authority always protects the tranquility of my pleasures and constantly averts all dangers from my path ... if this same authority is absolute master of my liberty and my life, and if it so monopolizes movement and life that when it languishes everything languishes around it, that when it sleeps everything must sleep, and that when it dies the state itself must perish.[23]

As with John Stuart Mill's imprecise distinction between self-regarding and other-regarding acts, which are suggestive of Tocqueville's distinctions here, there are many loose ends. Yet, with this, a fairly rounded picture of the "conservative" Tocqueville is limned: property-respecting, religion-upholding, aristocratical, anticollectivist, and suspicious of excessive centralized powers.

Reluctant Democrat

But we come back to the naked statement: *"Je suis un libéral d'une espèce nouvelle."* The portrait of Tocqueville as conservative does not go unchallenged; the weight of opinion, if not of evidence, falls on the side of those who have seen him as a liberal. Some, who may be the sagacious ones among us; wash away the problem by hyphenating the seemingly opposing descriptions, making of Tocqueville a "liberal-conservative" or a "conservative-liberal" or a hybrid of some likely sort. Adding to our frustration is the realization that even those whom we had previously found committed to the "conservative" interpretation, also place themselves in this terminological limbo: Russell Kirk speaks of Tocqueville's great achievement as "theorist, sociologist, liberal, and conservative," and of his cause, "liberal-conservatism," as not "forlorn ... yet." J. P. Mayer stands Tocqueville above "parties, a Liberal of a new kind, a Conservative who perceived with glowing clarity the appropriate order of society in the mod-

ern Western world."[24] The literature is replete with such awkwardness. Surely he represented aspects of both great traditions, and wrote so voluminously that contradictions in his own views are to be expected.

What emerges clearly is the realization that in nineteenth-century terms he was both conservative and liberal at the same time; yet we must sharpen the focus, not take refuge in hybrid terms, if we are to comprehend him. When Harold Laski says, "Who does not know Tocqueville cannot understand liberalism,"[25] he might better have said, *cannot understand the passion for liberty.* Democratic forms of government were to Tocqueville just that, *forms,* not necessarily better than aristocratic forms, nor necessarily worse. The American voyage confirmed his belief that there were few absolute principles, perhaps *no* absolute principles—but freedom; certainly if there were any, "Democracy" was not one.

Tocqueville's views about the advantages America derives from democracy are well known: flexibility in government, broad tolerance for minority religions, limited government, a vast arena for positive growth and change. However much partisans squabble among themselves about the reason why this group or that champions Tocqueville; however much we are reminded that the aristocratic Tocqueville disdained the use of his title of viscount; however much we are told into which camp Tocqueville strode, or, alternatively, from which camp he galloped away; we still find ourselves against a wall emblazoned with some such phrase as Peter Viereck's: that Tocqueville is considered by many today as "the most perceptive blender of the best of liberalism with the best of conservatism."[26] At which point we would do well to move on, perhaps recalling how Franklin Roosevelt resolved the problem in his own case: I am that kind of liberal, Roosevelt said, because I am that kind of conservative.

An Enthusiasm for Liberty

> My critics insist on calling me a one-party man; but I am not that. Passions are attributed to me where I have only opinions, or rather I have but one opinion, an enthusiasm for liberty and for the dignity of the human race. I consider all forms of government only as so many more or less perfect means of satisfying this holy and legitimate craving.[27]

And so we have it. Liberty was his "foremost passion," he said elsewhere; freedom was sacred to him; freedom even with inequality is preferable to any form of slavery under equality. In any case, liberty was more difficult to attain than equality, the latter being more highly thought of by the people than the former. The whole of *Democracy in America* is an examination of the reality and meaning of equality, counterpoised with the author's own conviction that equality alone, without liberty, was (to say the least) undesirable. Men, he wrote, manifest a "depraved taste for equality." In democracies,

> liberty is not the chief and constant object of [men's] desires; equality is their idol: they make rapid and sudden efforts to obtain liberty and, if they miss their aim, resign themselves to their disappointment; but nothing can satisfy them without equality, and they would rather perish than lose it.[28]

This is the heart of Tocqueville's thought. The choices were, and are: free or slave, liberty or bondage; never simply equal or unequal. Tocqueville favored whatever system of government was most conducive to liberty, regardless of the precise admixtures of "equality" or "inequality" within that system; though he never gave up his belief that a general tendency to equality was salubrious. From the very first words of *Democracy*—"Among the novel objects that attracted my attention during my stay in the United States, nothing struck me more forcibly than the general equality of condition among the people"—Tocqueville seemed of two minds on the matter of equality, at once seeing it as the common thread of democracy's weave *and* as inferior to liberty.

"Social equality is at once the past and the future" of man's history, Tocqueville continued in his introduction. Meaning "democracy" here as "equality," he went on: "To attempt to check democracy would be in that case to resist the will of God." But liberty was not guaranteed by God or history; "indeed," he wrote at the start of *L'Ancien régime et la Révolution*, "it is no exaggeration to say that a man's admiration of absolute government is proportionate to the contempt that he feels for those around him." Men are free to choose freedom or to lapse into slavery; the best source for a desire to remain free is a taste of freedom.

Tocqueville wrote much about equality; the second part of *Democracy* is devoted to studying the influences of equality in American life (though he used the word "democracy"), and the reader may feel swallowed up in the concept when pursuing an exact understanding of its meaning. Tocqueville could write in *Democracy* both that "Americans are so enamored of equality they would rather be equal in slavery than unequal in freedom," and also that "the principal instrument of America is freedom; of Russia, slavery." He favored republican government, yet said of the European demagogues who praise republics:

> Until our time it had been supposed that despotism was odious, under whatever form it appeared. But it is a discovery of modern days that there are such things as legitimate tyranny and holy injustice, provided they are exercised in the name of the people.[29]

"Liberty is, in truth, a holy thing," he wrote, meaning religious, individual, and political liberty all at once—and maybe more, since he never fully defined either "democracy" or "liberty." Man, developing himself to the highest possible level, reaches toward liberty, which requires a social environment conducive to freedom. This climate is hampered by majority tyranny and by that dull sameness and uniformity which constrains variety, diversity, nonconformity. Aristocracy, he knew, was most conducive to this variety, but it was gone, finished. To preserve the highest value he had to work within the new social and political order.

Equality was a necessary but insufficient condition for complete liberty. Where equality helped check power, it aided liberty; where it produced merely another sort of power, it hindered liberty. Tocqueville denounced American slavery and slavery in the French colonies, not because the institution denied Negroes a recognition of equality, but because it denied them freedom. He bitterly denounced the imperial pretensions of Louis Napoleon[30] and retired from politics to complete his *Souvenirs,* not because of changes in the status of equality in France, but because the prince-president *cum* emperor was, in Tocqueville's eyes, a tyrant.

Tyranny was the enemy not of equality particularly but specifically of liberty. "In Massachusetts the blacks have citizens rights. They can vote at elections . . . but the prejudice is so strong against them that their children cannot be received in the schools." That was tyranny of the majority.[31] He trusted neither mankind in the abstract nor status-quoism for its own sake, nor abrupt change for the sake of change. In his *Souvenirs,* he dictated three fundamentals of liberty: protection of tradition; rejection of majority dictatorship; and rejection of *a priori* blueprints of socialistic utopias. Democracy would

work, he believed, if rooted in some ancient traditional framework. England was strong enough not to be touched by the revolution of 1848, because of her ancient customs, which protected her from the "revolutionary sickness." He felt that America's "natural aristocrats," the lawyers, would build on old traditions through the educated classes; they would work within what he called "forms," which would canalize inevitable changes in healthy ways.

Though Americans were advantaged by having arrived at a state of democracy without having to endure a democratic revolution, by being "born equal instead of becoming so," they have many evils to fear from their equality, for which "there is only one effectual remedy: namely, political freedom." Thus he thought the free press was a protector of liberty, and religion a counter to materialism. "If men are to remain civilized or to become so, the art of associating together must grow and improve in the same ratio in which the equality of conditions is increased."[32] Tocqueville was out of tune with the historical movement of nineteenth-century liberalism. He was out of step with its march; the drummer he heard tapped out "liberty, liberty."

Mill and Tocqueville

Tocqueville considered John Stuart Mill "the only one [of my reviewers] who has thoroughly understood me; who has taken a general bird's eye view of my ideas; who sees their ulterior aim, and yet has preserved a clear perception of the details."[33] The relationship between Mill and Tocqueville is interesting not only as illustration of the personal and intellectual affections of which Tocqueville was capable, but also, and more so, as an example of the depth of his intellectual influence on his most brilliant contemporary and friend. Continuing his letter to Mill, Tocqueville wrote of the Englishman's criticisms: "The friend may always be seen through the critic. They instruct, therefore, and never wound me." But the influence, intellectually, was primarily one way: Tocqueville to Mill. Tocqueville had few successors, as he had few true predecessors. Of the latter, Montesquieu, Burke, Pierre Paul Royer-Collard stood out; of the former, Mill, the "genius of nineteenth century liberalism" first and foremost.

Both men tried to assimilate democracy while maintaining freedom. Both glorified what Acton, a "liberal" Catholic like Tocqueville, later called the *idea of commonwealth*. Both were "constitutionalists" who accepted the democratic revolutions and yet recognized the new orders' dangers; both were sophisticated contributors to the advance of nineteenth-century liberalism, the one basically an outsider, the other at times its foremost exponent. Both knew that democracy in its extreme form exercised a stultifying effect on culture.

After reading Tocqueville, Mill wrote in his *Autobiography,* "my thoughts moved more and more in the same channel." From *Democracy* Mill learned more about the dangers and excesses of democracy,

> [the] weak points of popular government, the defenses by which it needs to be guarded, and the correctives which must be added to it in order that while full play is given to its beneficial tendencies, those which are of a different nature may be neutralized or mitigated.
> . . . had it not been for the lessons of Tocqueville, I do not know that I might not . . . have been hurried into excess opposite to that [anti-centralization prejudice] which, being the one prevalent in my own country, it was generally my business to combat.[34]

In his first review of Part I of *Democracy in America* in the *London (and Westminster) Review* in 1835, Mill wrote that Tocqueville was overly pessimistic about the disadvantages of democracy. Mill focused on

Tocqueville's "brilliant" method, his taste, scrupulous care, and the value of his admonitions about majority tyranny. After which review, the correspondence began in earnest, with Mill badgering Tocqueville to write for the *London Review,* and the two refining their views by virtue of the serious points each made in his letters to the other. A few Mill scholars, most insightfully Gertrude Himmelfarb, have noted the ways in which Tocqueville reshaped some of Mill's thoughts away from his father's utilitarianism. Though still editing the Radicals' *London Review* when he first wrote on Tocqueville's *Democracy,* Mill was considerably confused at the time, publicly associating himself with the Radical criticism of portions of Tocqueville's book but privately expressing himself as much more sympathetic to and enthusiastic about it. He urged Tocqueville to join the *Review* as a "counterbalance to the influence of the Radicals who were sadly lacking in general ideas. . . ." Especially useful is Himmelfarb's differentiation of the "later" Mill (in the 1840's and 1850's) and the "earlier" Mill (in the 1830's and, superficially odd as the distinction may be, after the publication of *On Liberty* in 1859). The "earlier" Mill is Mill under the influence of Tocqueville, and then again nearly two decades later than that.[35]

Tocqueville's reservations about democracy had stirred Mill. Tocqueville did not join the *Review*; Mill sold it, severing his ties with the Radicals, coming by 1840 to edit the Whig *Edinburgh Review,* in which his notice of the remaining portions of *Democracy* appeared in October, 1840. Mill, who had once referred to conservatives as "the stupid party," came to have a few second thoughts. He came to see Tocqueville as the greatest interpreter of *English* political and social constitutional practices since Burke. The Mill of whom, at a later date, the criticism could justly be made that he erred in thinking society could be ruled by *discussion*, was, under Tocqueville's influence, far less sanguine.

As Edward Everett said then, and as Russell Kirk and others said later, Tocqueville was the best friend democracy ever had, and also "democracy's most candid and judicious critic."[36] Between Mill's first and second reviews, his correspondence with Tocqueville flourished; Mill practically begged Tocqueville to send him advance sheets of the second volume—piecemeal, anything. Copies of Tocqueville's official reports, such as his 1839 report for the Chamber of Deputies advocating the abolishment of slavery, quickly found their way to Mill's desk. If Mill was not yet as ardently opposed to slavery as was Tocqueville, he was nonetheless its enemy. In this area as in others, Mill learned from Tocqueville. Nothing would do, however, until Mill had seen the rest of *Democracy*. After five years ruminating about Tocqueville's thoughts, and with only a few days in which to study the new book, Mill produced a review in 1840 which largely superseded his first. Among the foremost of Mill's political writings, the long second review was a central statement of his views in the "earlier" period. Tocqueville's views had also altered in the interval; the second parts of *Democracy* were even more reserved in praise of "democracy" than the first had been.

Liberty, Mill saw with Tocqueville, was valuable not just for its usefulness, but for its priceless merit in itself. Mill's thoughts had been led by *Democracy* into a profound modification, one representing a "more serious break with the tenets of the philosophical radicals than even Mill seemed prepared to acknowledge."[37] Mill noted that it was read by everyone

because luckily Sir R[obert] Peel praised it & made the Tories fancy it was a Tory book: but I believe they have found out their error. It could only have been written in France or in England, & if written in Eng-

land it would probably never have been known beyond a small circle.[38]

Mill stressed his agreement with Tocqueville that a democracy which fostered the egoism of individuals to the exclusion of the public interest, increased the possibilities that democracy would degenerate into despotism. Democracy's consequences were complex; one must, he wrote in his 1840 review, "hesitate long before finally pronouncing whether the good or evil of its influence on the whole predominates." Never again did Mill forget that democracy alone was no guarantee of freedom. With Tocqueville, Mill came to favor a maximum of democratic local government, as much as the needs of the state would bear, so that men might learn to manage their own affairs.

With Tocqueville, Mill's review opposed "democratic radicalism, which would admit at once to the highest of political franchises, untaught masses. . . ." Mill agreed that "equality may be equal freedom or equal servitude. America is the type of the first, France, [Tocqueville] thinks, is in danger of falling into the second." Tocqueville, Mill wrote, opposed an absolute democracy because there was no way to "retard its course [or] force it to moderate its own vehemence." And, strikingly, quoting Tocqueville exactly: "The principle of enlightened self-interest appears to me the best suited of all philosophical theories to the wants of the men of our time, and . . . I regard it as their chief remaining security against themselves." For Mill, Tocqueville's work was the first properly "scientific" study of democracy and, notably, went beyond and bettered his own father's treatment.[39]

This essay on Tocqueville ended an epoch in Mill's life, after which he reverted to a modified utilitarianism in philosophy, a modified radicalism in economics, and an unmodified, unqualified individualism in social affairs, culminating in *On Liberty*, which resulted partly from his collaboration with (and eventual marriage to) Harriet Taylor. Whatever similarities we might find between *On Liberty* and *Democracy in America*, the following, in the former, an almost perfect expression of the views of his beloved Harriet, could not have been penned by Tocqueville: the "sole end for which mankind are warranted, individually or collectively, in interfering with the liberty of action of any of their number is self-protection."[40]

After Harriet Taylor Mill's death in 1859, Mill returned in a sense to the stance of the "earlier" period, even growing religious before his death. In his 1860 "Thoughts on Parliamentary Reform," Mill wrote:

> It is the fact that one person is *not* as good as another, and it is reversing all the rules of rational conduct to attempt to raise a political fabric on a supposition which is at variance with the facts.

To Tocqueville, "the Montesquieu of our times," Mill sent *Liberty*. By that time, Tocqueville was too ill to study carefully the work of his old friend, with whom, significantly, he had not corresponded from 1844 to 1856.

The Taste . . . for Liberty

In the mid-nineteenth century, "liberalism" took a more "conservative" position than what we think it to be today, when "liberalism" is rightly equated with "leftist" encouragement of extensive governmental intervention, at least in America. Tocqueville, especially as he experienced the tyranny of Louis Napoleon, but also as he earlier expressed it in *Democracy*, moved to the "right." What Mill's England lacked—the jolt of 1848—Tocqueville's France suffered in the fullest. Whereas Mill (or, for that matter, Jefferson before him) might be seen sometimes in the tradition of Rousseau, Tocqueville is better seen as Montesquieu's heir: balances,

checks on arbitrary power, specifically defined liberties historically descended from feudal privileges, an emphasis on plurality and liberty.

Tocqueville saw "equality" (which he often, confusingly, called "democracy") operating in America to allow individual development, and in France to stifle valid individualism and institutions threatening the power of the nation-state. In one case it served as a floor, in the other as a ceiling. Tocqueville thus opposed the concept of equality when dealing with France but supported it often when America was the focus of his attention. In the long run, of course, he saw its spread as an inevitability.

The "égalité" of the French Revolution was to Tocqueville essentially a leveling movement which made a centralized, authoritarian government possible by such actions as destroying feudal rights and liberties, and replacing the provinces, with their historical privileges and traditions, with "rational," equal administrative units (the departments) controlled by prefects, who had more power than the old intendants. In America, on the other hand, he saw a flourishing federalism with vigorous state and municipal governments, a strong government in Washington but a decentralized administration.

> I admire [equality] because it lodges in the very depths of each man's mind and heart that indefinable feeling, the instinctive inclination for political independence, and thus prepares the remedy for the ill which it engenders.

The great question was "how to make liberty proceed out of that democratic state of society in which God has placed us." Despotism "appears to me peculiarly to be dreaded in democratic times. I should have loved freedom, I believe, at all times, but in the time in which we live, I am ready to worship it."[41]

Tocqueville's critique of the French

Revolution seems to place him in the Burkean tradition, but he stood in opposition to the Englishman in believing that the French Revolution was inevitable, that Burke's "ancient liberties" wouldn't do in the modern world. Tocqueville was neither a complete child of eighteenth-century liberalism nor in the mainstream of contemporary French liberalism, nor part of the opportunistic, Anglophilic liberalism of the Doctrinaires, who could scarcely see beyond the horizon of their own narrow class interests. Despite their rhetoric, few liberals of the nineteenth century believed in absolute equality; neither did Tocqueville. Louis Philippe's reign, after all, sent "liberalism" sliding off *not* toward "socialism" but toward "conservatism."[42]

"The taste which men have for liberty and that which they feel for equality are, in fact, two different things; and I am not afraid to add that among democratic nations they are two unequal things. . . ." Persons in democratic nations feel for equality a passion that is "ardent, insatiable, invincible; they call for equality in freedom; and if they cannot obtain that they still call for equality in slavery."[43]

Even looking at the finished work together with his notes on America and his letters relating to the voyage, one still finds it a study full of paradox. Alone of the sections of America (and he erroneously saw the rest of the country as culturally homogenous), the South had preserved its unique social ways, founded on the "glaring anomaly, within a democratic order," of Negro slavery. But this too was doomed, eventually. Strongest in two tendencies, toward equality and toward centralization, modern democratic nations were ever at a crossroads: either toward greater or lesser freedom. Above mere party, Tocqueville stood always for one goal: liberty. "He who seeks in liberty anything more than liberty itself is destined for servitude." From this flowed all his concerns and questions about government.

Democracy was no protector in itself. In the greatest model of democracy before his eyes, the United States, Negro slavery flourished. An evil in itself, an abomination before God and man, slavery contained a further terror: that if the Negroes were unable to become the equal of the whites, they would, he believed, show themselves to be the white's enemies, after which a horrifying bloodbath would occur.

Like Jefferson before him, Tocqueville had grave doubts about the restoration of a "natural order" in America, free of the artificial inequalities that slavery had imbedded. With his colleague and beloved friend Beaumont, Tocqueville wondered if the fate of modern society was to be both democracy and despotism. Manifestly, there was always that "dim spot which the eye of the understanding cannot penetrate" in the future of America's greatest blight, her race relations. Where men were fettered they were at the mercy of forces beyond control, at the beck and call of tyrants.

Unlike the socialists, whose doctrine he called "a form of slavery, directing its efforts toward the force of equalization of conditions and at the suppression . . . of the personality and human independence . . . exaggerating the principle of authority against which we have so much fought . . . immoderate to the material passions of man,"[44] Tocqueville felt no theoretical love of the so-called efficiency of administration. Efficiency without liberty, stagnancy without a future, as in China at that point, and now, was evil.

No fatalist, and no lover of general ideas, he would have little to do with considerations which seemed to limit man's potential for freedom. He gloried in his lack of a complete historical philosophy. His impatience with considerations of climate, or the "general march of civilization," or of race, was severe. Distrustful also of second-hand material, and consequently remiss on rare occasions in his homework, he found contact with the ideas of others "disturbing." It was not documentation he sought, but insight. He *knew* that liberty was the sole worthwhile goal. Independence "rightly understood" was his starting-point; freedom, his quest. Never possessed of the essence of the leader's art, he was not the man to capture the hearts of the masses, despite repeated election to the Chamber by his neighbors. His creed was one for which even the "liberals" had little patience; he made his mark on Mill, not on Mill's radical and liberal fellows.

While appreciative of the arts and literature, while occasionally wryly humorous in his writings, while never above a little tartness, in general Tocqueville was sober, occasionally glum, if not so grim as to deserve the sobriquet applied to him by George Sand: stuffed shirt. He could not look with pleasure at the "rabble" he found in Philadelphia, nor sanguinely at the degraded Negroes of America. He could be saddened and chilled by uniformity and disillusioned by man's tendency to bury his own liberties.

In 1910, Marcel noted of Tocqueville that *"malgré ses rare mérites,* Tocqueville *est presque abandonné."* And Laski wrote in 1930 that interest in Tocqueville was then slight, "partly, no doubt, the reason for this oblivion [lying] in the mental climate of our epoch . . . a period of insecurity."[45] Might we not ask, despite the revival of Tocqueville scholarship, if there is nonetheless a similar disinclination in our time to read Tocqueville for guidance and to take his lessons seriously? We might well reread Tocqueville on slavery, for example, and see the wisdom of his remarks about the struggle in which we currently find ourselves, noting that he accurately foresaw the agony but missed only its

timing. Tocqueville told us that the whites could not accept the Negroes as equals. But whites have changed, and more importantly, Negroes have changed, having become "blacks," having become willing to "show themselves [the whites'] enemies if they are not accepted as their equals."

Occasionally Tocqueville was elliptical, even contradictory. But his works are perspicuous as well as perspicacious. He still offers us an illuminating critique of our civilization and one of the foremost guidebooks for survival within it.

NOTES

[1] The title quotation reads "I love liberty by taste, equality by instinct and reason." Tocqueville to J. S. Mill, June 15, 1835. The lengthier quotation is Tocqueville's 1841 "Memorandum," discovered and published by A. Redier, *Comme disait M. de Tocqueville* (Paris, 1925).

[2] *North American Review* (July, 1836), p. 179; *New York Review*, VIII, 15 (July, 1840).

[3] Laski's foreword, in Phillips Bradley, ed., and intro., *Democracy in America* (New York, 1945), p. v; Russell Kirk, *The Conservative Mind* (Chicago, 1953); Peter Viereck, *Conservatism, From John Adams to Churchill* (New York, 1956).

[4] Tocqueville to Eugène Stoffels, in *Memoir, Letters and Remains of Alexis de Tocqueville* (London, 1861), pp. 380–381. Tocqueville observed that although he loved liberty, that love was tempered by a great respect for justice and for law and order; hence he might pass for a liberal of a new sort.

[5] Marvin Meyers, *The Jacksonian Persuasion* (Stanford, 1957), p. 51.

[6] Quoted in J. P. Mayer, *Political Thought in France* (London, 1943), pp. 45–46, and in his *Alexis de Tocqueville: A Biographical Essay in Political Science*, translated by M. Bozman and C. Hahn (New York, 1940).

[7] Albert Salomon, "Tocqueville," *Social Research*, XXVI, 4 (Winter, 1959), p. 317.

[8] Kirk, *Conservative Mind*, pp. 186, 29.

[9] Mayer, *Tocqueville*, p. 184.

[10] *Democracy in America*, II, p. 154.

[11] *Ibid.*, II, p. 318.

[12] *Ibid.*, I, p. 97.

[13] *Ibid.*, II, pp. 27–28. See also Jack Lively, *Social and Political Thought of Alexis de Tocqueville* (Oxford, 1962), p. 183.

[14] Max Lerner, *Tocqueville and American Civilization* (New York, 1969), p. 70.

[15] The first quotation is cited in Redier, *Comme disait*, p. 48; see also pp. 69–70.

[16] From a conversation with the English economist Nassau William Senior, on occasion of the Reform Bill of 1854, quoted in Kirk, *Conservative Mind*, p. 211, and elsewhere.

[17] *Democracy in America*, II, p. 352.

[18] *Ibid.*, I, p. 438; II, p. 351; II, pp. 102–103.

[19] *Ibid.*, I., p. 202.

[20] Quoted in Seymour Drescher, *Tocqueville and Beaumont on Social Reform* (New York, 1968), p. 144.

[21] Tocqueville to Senior, 1851, from *Tocqueville: Correspondence and Conversations*, I, pp. 204–205, quoted in Edward Gargan, "Some Problems in Tocqueville Scholarship," *Mid-America*, XLI, 1 (January, 1959), p. 14.

[22] Drescher, *op.cit.*, p. 30.

[23] *Democracy in America*, I, pp. 101, 96. See also II, pp. 314, 320, 331–333.

[24] Kirk, "The Prescience of Tocqueville," *University of Toronto Quarterly*, XXII, 4 (July, 1953), pp. 343 and 352; Mayer, *Tocqueville*, pp. 53–54. See also Paul Lucas, "From Aristocracy to Democracy: A Study of Alexis de Tocqueville," unpubl. B.A. thesis (Brandeis University, 1965), pp. 2–3.

[25] Laski, "Alexis de Tocqueville," *op. cit.*, p. 111.

[26] Viereck, *Conservatism*, p. 58. And: "His mind was totally independent. Its lonely truths upset liberal and conservative clichés equally." p. 56.

[27] Tocqueville to Henry Reeve, March 22, 1837, quoted in *Memoir, Letters and Remains*, pp. 39–40.

[28] *Democracy in America*, I, p. 56.

[29] *Ibid.*, I, p. 434.

[30] Tocqueville wrote a letter on that subject to the *Times* (London), December 11, 1851, which was printed anonymously to protect him.

[31] Tocqueville, in Alphabetic notebook 2, September 27, 1831, quoted in *Journey to America*, trans. by Geo. Lawrence, ed. by J. P. Mayer (New Haven, 1960), p. 224. The French is in tome V, Vol. I, *Oeuvres Complètes* (Paris, 1957), and quoted in several other sources.

[32] *Democracy in America*, II, pp. 108, 113, 343, 118.

[33] Tocqueville to Mill, December 3, 1835, one of the earliest of their letters. The letters of Mill to Tocqueville are available in *The Collected Works of John Stuart Mill*, Vol. XIII: *The Earlier Letters of John Stuart Mill 1812–1848*, ed. by F. E. Mineka (Toronto, 1963) and in Tocqueville, *Oeuvres Complètes*, tome VI (Paris, 1954). Some are in *Memoir, Letters and Remains*, and a few appeared in the *Times Literary Supplement*, Sept. 1, 8, and 15, 1950. The letters of Tocqueville to Mill appear in *Memoir, Letters and Remains*, and in tome VI, *Oeuvres Complètes*.

[34] The first quotation is repeated in T. H. Qualter, "John Stuart Mill, Disciple of Tocqueville," *Western Political Quarterly*, XIII (December, 1960), p. 884. The remainder are in Mill's *Autobiography* (published from the original ms. in the Columbia University Library, 1924, reissued 1944), pp. 134–36.

[35] Gertrude Himmelfarb, introduction to *John Stuart Mill: Essays on Politics and Culture* (Garden City, N.Y., 1962), pp. xiii–xix, *et passim*.

[36] Kirk, *Conservative Mind*, p. 195.

[37] Qualter, "Mill," pp. 888–889.

[38] Mill to Tocqueville, May 11, 1840, quoted in *Earlier Letters*, p. 434.

[39] *Edinburgh Review*, LXXVII (October, 1840).

[40] Mill, *On Liberty* (London, 1859).

[41] *Democracy in America*, II, pp. 305, 340–341.

[42] Richard M. Fletcher, of the Massachusetts Institute of Technology Library, has aided me in coming to grips with some of these matters, and shown me an unpublished paper of his (1969), "Quelques Pensées sur Alexis de Tocqueville."

[43] *Democracy in America*, II, pp. 100, 102.

[44] Translated from R. Marcel, *Essai politique sur Alexis de Tocqueville* (Paris, 1910), p. 169, quoting Tocqueville.

[45] *Ibid.*, p. 457; Laski, "Alexis de Tocqueville," p. 112.   [XX, Spring 1976, 164–176]

[16]

William Graham Sumner and the Old Republic

JOHN CHAMBERLAIN

John (Rensselaer) Chamberlain (1903–   ), a recognized authority on conservatism, now lives in Cheshire, Connecticut, not far from New Haven, where he was born. In the course of a distinguished career, he has been an editor of and written for many famous magazines; for example, during his tenure at Fortune, *his colleagues included James Agee, James Gould Cozzens, and Archibald MacLeish. A former dean of the School of Journalism, Troy State University in Troy, Alabama (1972–1977), he has written regularly for the* These Days *column of King Features Syndicate and has authored a number of books, including his recent autobiography,* A Life with the Printed Word *(1982).*

WILLIAM GRAHAM SUMNER, who once dominated his university (Yale) and his subject (sociology), was born in 1840, the year of the log cabin and hard cider campaign, and lived to see "hell-vahgens," his name for automobiles, snorting on city streets. He never managed to reconcile himself to this most characteristic product of the enterprise system he defended, but when he came upon a "dirty little boy" (Deane Keller, the son of his disciple and successor, Albert Galloway Keller) sitting on a curbstone and counting automobiles he approved the sight as somehow characteristic of the spirit of science, which must reckon unflinchingly with things pleasant and unpleasant. ("That's right, Deane," he said, "get the facts.") He died in 1910, believing that the "facts" of American development indicated a long-term pessimism. He had anticipated Frederick Jackson Turner in proclaiming that the closing of the frontier would make democracy more difficult. The great days of the Republic, he thought, were behind him and he was glad he was passing to another shore in whose existence he still hesitantly believed. ("We think so; we hope so," he said to his daughter-in-law in 1910 when she remarked to the supposedly implacable old skeptic that "love reaches over to the other side.")

In between the dates that bound his life, Sumner had changed himself from clergyman to political and social scientist, he had changed Yale College (and with it many another American university), and he had founded the first American school of sociology (though partisans of Columbia University's Professor Giddings might dispute the point). He was a moralist whose great pioneer work on the relativity

168

of customs (*Folkways*) undid much of his work by making any and all moralism seem dubious. He was indisputably a great man in his own time; hundreds of his former students proclaimed "Sumnerology" as their guiding philosophy throughout life and maintained membership in a Sumner Club for at least thirty years after his death. Whether he is a great man for the ages is currently moot.

Indeed, Sumner's reputation has fallen on evil days. He figures in recent polemical literature as a whipping boy, the alleged defender of a rapaciously plutocratic order, a putative philosopher for rich people who have gained their wealth by shifty means. He was a "prime minister in the empire of plutocratic education" (Upton Sinclair). "A preacher of force in a world of fate," he had a voice which "fired like a howitzer" (Van Wyck Brooks). He was Yale's "Spencerian sociologist" (historian William Miller)—and Spencer, as is well (though fallaciously) known, was an exponent of the jungle philosophy of tooth-and-claw survival. He offered a "vision of society in which beauty, charity and brotherhood could find no place, in which wealth and self-interest were the ruling norms" (Robert Green McCloskey, professor of government at Harvard). Finally, he was a "social Darwinist," the adapter of biological evolution to the thesis that just as man was the naturally selected heir to creation, so J. P. Morgan and his ilk were the naturally selected heirs to everything created by man (see historians Richard Hofstadter and Henry Steele Commager).

Since stereotypes have more lives than cats, it will probably always be believed that twentieth-century America was brought into being by a group that is collectively denominated the Robber Barons. According to this theory, it was the likes of Jay Gould and Jim Fisk (two anomalous stock market operators) who spanned America with railroads. (Actually, all Fisk managed to do was to wreck one railroad, the Erie.) The Robber Barons cliché, while it undoubtedly covers some of the commercial practices of the General Grant era, conveniently ignores the creative achievements of thousands of adventurous enterprisers, from James J. Hill (who really built a railroad) to Henry Ford (who really built a car for the millions and sold it at a price the millions could pay).

Just why a period should live in history for its excrescences is a sociological mystery which needs further exploration. Pertinent at this point is the fact that stereotypes, which have the lives of cats, also spawn like cats. The cliché of the Robber Barons has called forth another cliché—that of the dedicated academic ideologue who stands sponsor for the coldhearted Calvinist of wealth. It is not enough that John D. Rockefeller, Senior, said: "The good Lord gave me my money." An academic figure must be made to stand behind him as broker of God's revelation, and William Graham Sumner has been tapped for the dubious honor.

What the scornful historian forgets is the occasion of John D. Rockefeller's statement, which was a mere innocent pleasantry in its setting. Having attributed to God (who made the oil) the creation of the Rockefeller fortune, John D. graciously went on to say that he would be very ungrateful if he were to withhold a portion of that from President William Rainey Harper's new Baptist University of Chicago. The scornful historian forgets, too, that William Graham Sumner spent most of the more polemical moments of his life attacking plutocrats. He thought they were the biggest "jobbers" of all, and his essays on "Democracy and Plutocracy," written at the end of the 1880's, are pregnant with a fear that plutocratic jobbers will ultimately do the old Republic in. Almost alone among twentieth-century men of letters, Thomas Beer has put Sumner in his proper place as a conservative who was radical enough to believe that no class has the moral right to use the State as a weapon with which to deprive any less fortunate group of its rights and dues.

Sumner liked to think of himself as a universalist; when he was still an Episcopalian rector he remarked that the "true Catholic church is ahead of us." But as a "universalist" he made common cause with the middle class, particularly that wing of it which had not succumbed to the delusion that it had earned a snob's title to being "lower upper." The middle class, to him, was devoted to the honest universalization of all rights as a condition of the "upward mobility" (a phrase invented by a subsequent generation of sociologists) of talented individuals. The aristocracy, as Sumner saw it, was not interested in rights but in the maintenance of privileges. The plutocracy was interested in any political racket that could be devised to transfer the people's wealth into its own pockets. The proletariat wanted pap or special treatment, and was willing to toss away its long-run stake in freedom for quick attention in the here-and-now. Alone among the classes, the middle—particularly those members of it that might be graded lower- to middle-middle—seemed to Sumner to be the carrier of a sound theory of society.

IN ALL OF Sumner's social theorizing one detects the accent, not of a complacent anti-Marxist *haute bourgeoisie,* but of a radical Jacksonian adherent to the "old Jeffersonian party." When Sumner was growing up in Hartford, Connecticut, the Jacksonians and the Whigs were the contenders for power in the still young Republic. Sumner had no admiration for Old Hickory's habit of making every issue in politics a personal matter. Moreover,

he had a sense of decorum that was fully in accord with his habitat in Federalist Connecticut, the "land of steady habits." But, looking back on the political wars of his childhood days, Sumner was contemptuous of Daniel Webster's Whiggish "apostasy" on the tariff issue and he thought of Henry Clay's "American System"—of federally financed "internal improvements"—as the granddaddy of the pork barrel.

Looking for a proper political ancestry, Sumner saw fit (in his biography of Andrew Jackson) to praise the loco-focos—the working men and small traders who made up the Eastern city wing of the Jackson party—as the creators of the Democratic party he admired. The loco-focos, he wrote, had seen the value of free trade and hard money and equality before the law in the matter of such things as the right to incorporate a business. They were against special hand-outs, the "rigging" of governmental institutions in favor of anyone who was clever enough or rich enough to promote a steal. As a post-Civil War "Old Party Democrat," Sumner voted in 1876 for Samuel Tilden on the issue of getting the federal troops out of the conquered South. In 1884 he voted as a Mugwump for Grover Cleveland, and in 1888 he repeated his Cleveland vote on the tariff issue. Naturally he could not stomach Bryan in 1896—Bryan was not an "honest money" Democrat.

Since Sumner never supported the Republicanism of James G. Blaine, that charming man who lived strangely well on a small political salary, it must remain a mystery that modern historians can see in him an apologist for capitalists who depended on political power for their tickets to the "great barbeque" (Vernon Parrington's loaded phrase). The truth is that, in Sumner, the old pre-Civil War Republic lived on. He always reacted to events in a Madisonian character, opposing the tyranny of the few or the tyranny of the many, as the case might be. Some of his greatest essays celebrate representative political institutions as they have been wrested from oligarchs and defended against mobs.

Civil liberty, he said, is the great end for which modern States exist. To the end of maintaining civil liberty he counselled his students to an "extraordinary independence . . . and patient reflection," lest democracy be allowed to degenerate into the "government by interests" which "produces no statesmen but only attorneys." These words date back to 1876; they were delivered to a Chicago audience in the very midst of the "gilded age" whose "attorney" politicos were supposedly taking their cue from Sumner's "social Darwinism." At a later date Sumner denounced the rather absent-minded imperialism of our war with Spain as a sin against the tradition of the Old Republic. "The conquest of the United States by Spain," he called it in a speech that might have served as a model for Felix Morley's more extensive writings on the incompatibility of republican institutions with overseas proconsulships, even those that are most "benevolently" undertaken.

Faithful to his origins, Sumner never lowered his flag. He was a child of the upheaval that had changed Britain's Lancashire from an obscure, ill-cultivated swamp (Friedrich Engels' view of it) to a humming, overcrowded industrial warren within the space of a single generation. Sumner's grandfather, who lived on a small farm at Walton-le-Dale just across the river from the locality that was destined to become the great cotton center of Preston, watched his own cottage industry go down into ruin as new methods of factory production grew. Finding Lancashire hard scratching in the depressed post-Napoleonic times, Sumner's father Thomas, a self-educated mechanic, left for America in 1836. Thomas tried the new textile center of Paterson, New Jer-

sey, for a time, but the depression of the late 1830's drove him out (not, however, before he had married Sarah Graham, the daughter of another Lancashire emigrant). A long prospecting trip through Pennsylvania and New York to the Ohio frontier convinced Thomas Sumner that he could do better for the education of his children (William Graham and a younger brother and sister came in quick succession in the early 1840's) if he were to settle down in the East. Accordingly he picked Connecticut, getting a job in the wheel-repairing shops of the new railroad at Hartford.

This Lancashire mechanic who patronized the libraries of workingmen's institutes was always William Graham Sumner's lower-middle-class-on-the-rise hero. "His knowledge," said William Graham, "was wide, his judgment excellent. He belonged to the class of men, of whom Caleb Garth in *Middlemarch* is the type."

In time to come William Graham "generalized" his father into the Forgotten Man, who "works and votes—generally he prays—but his chief business in life is to pay." Sometimes that Forgotten Man was the average savings bank depositor; sometimes he was a workingman who scraped together enough capital to build a small two-family house whose second story he rented to meet the mortgage payments. In all cases the Forgotten Man was the C whom A and B (the professional do-good politicians) forcibly levied upon to support D. The vice of such a formula, so Sumner sardonically observed, was that C had practically no voice in the matter. And so, though he might have preferred to support E (maybe a deserving nephew who wanted to go to college), he had little left for the private charities that do so much to make the giver a sympathetic human being.

Fifty years after Sumner first paid homage to the Forgotten Man in a speech delivered to a Brooklyn audience, Franklin D. Roosevelt adapted the phrase to his own uses. But, as many surviving "Sumnerologists" were quick to note, Roosevelt got the reference exactly backward. Roosevelt's Forgotten Man was the appleseller on the corner, the man from the Hooverville shack singing "Brother, can you spare a dime?" He was the potential object of State-compelled charity. No doubt he needed charity—and lots of it— in the circumstances of 1932. But, with every politician in the land, Herbert Hoover included, paying attention to his predicament, Roosevelt's "forgotten man" was hardly in danger of being overlooked. Sumner would have appreciated the irony: it was his own Forgotten Man who would be called upon to pay the cost (in steadily mounting taxes and in a progressively debauched dollar) of caring for Roosevelt's Unforgotten Man throughout the 1930's—and (who knows?) practically forever.

The middle class, which picks up the tab for the mistakes of A and B and more or less cheerfully carries D on its back, has never had a conscious philosopher. No Marx, no Lenin has ever hymned its destiny. Ever since the middle classes came into their own the artists, the Bohemians, have spoken contemptuously of "Philistines" and "bourgeoisie." Our Sinclair Lewises and John Marquands have affectionately maligned the middle class man as Babbitt or, "sincerely," Willis Wayde. But the reason why the middle class has never had a conscious philosopher is a tribute to its own superiority. Its best brains—James Madison and John Adams are examples—have always tried to speak for the whole. And so it was with Sumner: as we have indicated, he, too, spoke for the whole. There is always the possibility that any spokesman for the whole may be motivated by selfish needs. But the self-serving interest of the middle classes in an Open Society is quite beside the point.

Rights are not rights unless they are universal, with everybody sharing in the freedom conferred by the guarantee of rights in law. The gag about General Motors holds when adapted to the case of the middle class man: what's good for him is good for the country, and vice versa.

The proof? In Sumner's own century the English middle classes, in pursuit of their own best interests, were forced to seek all their ameliorations in terms of generalities. Under the harsh British penal code, which decreed the death penalty for simple shoplifting, juries were often erratic about convicting petty thieves. The result was that nobody was safe from robbery. To protect their own shops, the middle classes had to abolish the so-called "bloody code" which bore most harshly on the indigent. At the very time when Marx and Engels were spitefully writing off the "bourgeoisie" as incredibly stupid and narrow, the English middle classes abolished imprisonment for debt, removed the religious penalties against Jews, Quakers, and Catholics, sanctioned trade unions, went far toward the universalization of the franchise, did away with the slave trade, freed the press, and repealed monopolistic restrictions on joint-stock banks, on imports, and on the trade in bullion. As Herbert Spencer has said, the State, in this middle class century, ceased to aggress against the citizen. Instead, it offered him greater protection than ever before. And this went for everybody, not only the members of the middle class.

True enough, Sumner was a "Darwinist," which kept him from looking for middle class—or Open Society—sanctions in either religious revelation or the "categorical imperative" of God-given moral instinct. The need to explain customs and institutions as well as biological phyla in terms of the relativity of origins and unfoldings had a tremendous hold on all those whose mental coming-of-age was more or less coeval with the publication, in 1859, of *The Origin of Species*. Once Sumner had pondered on Professor Othniel C. Marsh's collection of prehistoric horses, featuring the three- and four-toed eohippus, or dawn-horse, in the Peabody Museum at Yale, he capitulated to the idea of "natural selection" as the agent which resulted in the "survival of the fittest."

Sumner never did catch on to the essential emptiness of the "survival of the fittest" phrase, which provides one of those beautiful "logical circles" that can be used to justify anything that happens to exist. The beggar has survival value no less than the industrious man provided he is gay and plausible as a moocher—and if C, the Forgotten Man, is so foolish as to permit A and B to rob him in the name of D, why, what becomes of the Darwinian survival value of honesty? As for a cripple (see Alexander Pope), or an opium addict (see De Quincey), if such as these can distill meaningful literature out of their afflictions, they will live as the "fit" writers of their time. So will a trimmer like Talleyrand or a vengeful illegalist like Lenin prove "fit" to breast the waves of an anti-Sumnerian revolution. Quite apart from its use in circular reasoning, the phrase "survival of the fittest" lends itself all too easily to sloganeering; and Sumner, though distinctly anti-slogan, did help the sloganeers along by his overweening trust in the idea that "natural selection" could be counted on to purge the race of its worst qualities.

But if Sumner, on occasion, talked all too glibly in Darwinian terms, it is not true at all that his belief in evolution committed him to a "social Darwinian" advocacy of tooth-and-claw industrialism. To begin with, his view of evolution included a vast trust in the value of the voluntary association. The family offered one mode of voluntary cooperation—indeed, the family was basic to the "mutual aid" that gives man a superiority over the animals in the struggle for existence. By extension of the blood unit, the family, in the course of generations, becomes the village community; the community develops traditions of helpfulness; and lo! the cooperativeness of communalism (which Sumner regarded as quite distinct from communism) comes to abide with individualism as one of man's social aids in keeping himself "fit" to survive.

At this point a detour into the works of Herbert Spencer is in order. Though Sumner was by no means a whole-hog Spencerian, he shared with Spencer certain views about the usefulness of voluntary industrial associations in the struggle for economic survival. Sumner never liked the social habits of the *nouveaux riches,* but he thought a little vulgarity a cheap price to pay for the organizing ability of the newer industrialists. Every millionaire, he noted, carried scores of lesser people up with him; and the chances for the multitudes were vastly increased with the proliferation of big capitalists precisely because they were adept at building associations which required the cooperation of many men.

In 1873 Herbert Spencer visited America and was lionized by industrialists at a big public dinner in New York. Our modern historians, from the Beards to William Miller, Thomas Cochran, and Richard Hofstadter, have not allowed us to forget this "breaking of bread" between the great "social Darwinist" and the tariff and special-racket-seeking plutocracy of the Gilded Age. Through an analogy with "Darwinian biology," says historian William Miller, Spencer sought to justify "a Calvinism conveniently bereft of conscience, a philosophy of success without the saving grace of stewardship."

Of course, Spencer never sought to

justify anything of the kind; he merely noted that man had improved his lot by deserting a "military" organization of society for an "industrial," and he feared a relapse into the "military" would result in a worse "tooth-and-claw" barbarism than anything currently observable in Manchester, Paris, or Chicago. Far from providing a green light for anti-labor industrialists, Spencer praised trade unions for their usefulness in preventing employers "from doing unfair things which they would else do." "Conscious that trade unions are ever ready to act," said Spencer, the employers are "more prompt to raise wages when trade is flourishing than they would otherwise be; and when there come times of depression, they lower wages only when they cannot otherwise carry on their businesses." And along with his cool commendation of trade unions, Spencer endorsed both the Rochdale consumer cooperative movement and the "gain-sharing" (he thought this a more apposite description than "profit-sharing") formulae pioneered by certain progressive manufacturing companies in England and America.

Taking off from Spencer's idea that "social life at large is a progress in fitness for living and working together," Sumner said: "We are led by scientific knowledge to combine our efforts by cooperation so that we can make them more efficient." He was speaking, of course, of voluntary cooperation. As for trade unions, Sumner doubted that most strikes paid off; the worker might get more by pressing his claims in other ways. But he observed that strikes were sometimes useful and necessary in that they "tested the market," and he saw no reason to crack down on labor for demanding a right to associate even though association sometimes led to misguided and often useless violence.

Since the human race had been building institutions for "combining" their efforts since time out of mind, Sumner thought of society as a complex inheritance that belongs to everybody, including our children. That is why he objected to heated efforts to alter institutions overnight in accordance with ideological preconceptions. No less than Edmund Burke, he believed that society was an organic product (though he resisted the temptation to view it as an organism, which would imply that it had a centrally directed nervous system). An organic product, he said, is very different from an idealized system, and it cannot be changed drastically by blueprinting or "engineering" its future. This was the "absurd effort to make the world over." Though he never had any objection to criticizing prescriptive rights if they seemed unfair or illogical, Sumner, like Burke, considered it dangerous suddenly to rip prescription out by the roots. Thus, though he was a Jacksonian hard-money man, Sumner always considered Jackson's precipitate war on the Bank of the United States a most unfortunate thing. Sudden abolition of the bank plunged the country headlong into depression; moreover, far from leading to sound credit practices, the disappearance of the bank let local state banks go wild in their emissions of wild-cat paper.

Sumner, who never lost an opportunity to attack "gush," is celebrated for his caustic remark that the proper place for a confirmed drunkard is the gutter, where "nature" can go about its business of eliminating him from the scene. But if Sumner lived before the days of Alcoholics Anonymous, he nonetheless believed in the Law of Sympathy (see the final pages of his *What Social Classes Owe to Each Other*, which few anti-Sumnerians seem ever to have read). "We are all careless," Sumner wrote. "In the midst of a common peril which gives us a kind of solidarity of interest to rescue the one for whom the chances of life have turned out badly . . .

a lecture on blame would be out of place. ... Men ... owe to men, in the chances and perils of this life, aid and sympathy, on account of the common participation in human frailty and folly."

To which Sumner, who had the Christian view of charity as something that must spring voluntarily from the heart, felt constrained to add: "This observation, however, puts aid and sympathy in the field of private and personal relations, under the regulation of reason and conscience, and gives no ground for mechanical and impersonal schemes." In any good society, so Sumner felt, "reason and conscience" must be operative. For, as Sumner said, though society can do without patricians, it cannot do without the practice of the patrician virtues.

Sumner's exposition of the Law of Sympathy might be said to contradict his more "Darwinian" utterances, specifically those which deny there is any such thing as a "banquet of life" or a "boon of nature" (see his collected *Essays: Volume I* published by the Yale University Press). Actually, however, Sumner was no hard-and-fast Malthusian; the earth, he felt, could support decent populations. He felt that the progress of the arts and sciences in his own century had inured "most of all to the benefit of non-capitalists and that the social agitation which we are now witnessing is a proof of the strength, not of the weakness, of that class." In "outstripping the growth of population," the accumulation of capital had made it easier for all classes to exist in comparative comfort. And comfort, he felt, could yield a margin for decency. In a foreword to a book on lynch law, Sumner remarked that one of the reasons for frowning on the "summary" justice of lynching is not that "the victim is not bad enough, but because we are too good." "It would be a disgrace to us if amongst us men should burn a rattlesnake or a mad dog," he said. He

thought of civilization "broadening down from precedent to precedent" provided the human race continued to respect all the precedents that made for the idea that governments existed to preserve and extend civil liberty.

True enough, the "land-man ratio" must turn against the human race as frontier countries filled up. But in "Earth Hunger," an essay that was posthumously published in 1913, Sumner remarked that "the amount of land ... is not a simple arithmetical quantity." "As we make improvements in the arts," he said, "a single acre is multiplied by a new factor and is able to support more people." And the "standard of living"—an "ethical" as well as a "material" product—operates on the population-to-land ratio when it consciously refrains from over-producing children.

THE IMAGE OF Sumner as a "preacher of force in a world of fate," then, is entirely unhistorical. Though the causes for a long-term pessimism weighed upon him more heavily as he grew older, he considered it his duty to continue his fight for the Old Republic. There was the fight against the Devil from Above—*i.e.*, the plutocracy. And there was the fight against the Devil from Below—the mob that would dispense with constitutionalism, as described in his *jeu d'esprit* about the seizure of New York and Philadelphia and other American cities by a Commune run by such characters as Marx Jones and Lassalle Smith.

Written to amuse himself sometime after the time of the Paris Commune, "The Cooperative Commonwealth," Sumner's sole excursion into fictional prophecy, is a sort of crude blueprint for George Orwell's *1984*. The prophecy is far from being good drama. Nonetheless, it serves to amplify the import of Sumner's terse admonition: "If you live in a country that is run by a committee, be on the committee."

The battle against the Devil from Above—the plutocracy—was Sumner's consuming extracurricular activity of the 1880's. In 1884 he told his students that all the "rings" and "jobbers" in the land were behind the candidacy of James G. Blaine, who had won the Republican nomination for the Presidency. To fight the "jobbers" he turned to the journalism of opinion. In essay after essay in the eighties (they are now concentrated in his *Essays: Volume II*) he centered on his target. In 1886, writing in *The Independent* ("What is the 'Proletariat'?"), we find him saying "the bourgeois government has threatened, and threatens now more than ever, to degenerate into a plutocracy." This is the leitmotif of a score of essays, and there would be little point in spinning the subject out if it were not for the fact that virtually every modern "liberal" opponent of Sumner has chosen to transform him into the patron saint of everything he hated to the depths of his being.

The plutocracy, said Sumner out of the depths of his revulsion, "invented the lobby." And its first use of the "lobby" was to put over the "steal" of the protective tariff. In his campaign against protectionism Sumner scorned the use of "neutral" scientific prose. The tariff, he said, "arouses my moral indignation. It is a subtle, cruel, and unjust invasion of one man's right by another." Inasmuch as the tariff could hardly operate for long with any force upon the general price level in a continental nation whose genius for competition was shortly to create the phenomenon of mass production at popular prices, it might seem that Sumner devoted a disproportionate amount of energy to the subject. How, after all, did the tariff keep the American farmer from getting a cheap automobile or tractor?

But it was not merely the dollars-and-cents aspects of the protective tariff that brought Sumner's blood to the boil; it was its hypocrisy. He saw it as the great entering wedge for interventionism. A believer in an ethically oriented *laissez faire*, he considered it unforgivable for capitalists to pay lip service to a creed which, in practice, they were prepared to jettison in order to make a fast buck. The tariff was the one rotten apple that would eventually spoil the whole barrelful. It would lead to a "democratic" counter-lobby in favor of bringing "protection" to every last pressure group—farmers, shippers, labor unions. This might seem rough justice, but Sumner doubted that the "democracy" could win in the game of grab. "Capital," he said, would resort to "all the vices of plutocracy" to defend itself. "Thus," he noted with ominous finality, "the issue of democracy and plutocracy, numbers against capital, is made up." The fight, if inexorably joined, would destroy the Old Republic by universalizing the idea that the various groups in society had "all rights and no duties."

If there was no hope that the Old Republican virtues might survive a plutocracy-vs.-democracy free-for-all, there was even less balm in contemplating a victory for socialism. Try to "socialize" wealth, said Sumner, and it would ooze away. The reason for this is that wealth, in an advanced technological age, does not consist of a "store." It is, on the other hand, a matter of extremely complicated organization brought to a high pitch of perfection. To keep a modern industrial organization in high gear, mankind must be able to call on the continuing services of very able men. The brain-power and the genius for leadership exhibited by such men constitute a "natural monopoly" which must not be discouraged. Under socialism the "natural monopoly" of uncommon industrial ability must either take over as a dictatorship or simply quit. Thus socialism portends either a loss of civil liberty for the masses or starvation for everybody.

IN WAGING HIS lifelong campaign to maintain the Old Republic, with its traditional guarantees that no one shall be deprived of life, liberty, or property—the old inalienable right—without due process of law, Sumner was gallantry personified. Two things, however, combined to militate against his chances for success. The first was a defective understanding of the nature of rights. And the second was a shortsighted addiction to the "practical" in education. In each case Sumner was betrayed by the resolutely concrete cast of his mind. In revolting against his divinity-school training he came to disdain "metaphysics," and as he grew older he took an increasingly sardonic view of "culture" as the province of "dilettantes." A genius for Mencken-like denunciation led him inevitably into taking stands that were destructive of his own most cherished ends.

In the great struggle over the college curriculum of the eighties, Sumner was forced into making himself a battering ram merely to get houseroom for his own specialities of political and social science. But in waging his fight for his own subjects, Sumner overreached himself. He turned against Latin and Greek; he tried to rid Yale even of its elective courses in philosophy. In all of this he lost sight of the fact that both his economics and his sociology continued to make rich use of what he had learned by long exposure to the literatures of classic antiquity and to the stern training in ethical judgment he had derived from his theological background.

In his later life Sumner, for his own pleasure, learned Polish, Spanish, Portuguese, Russian, and other languages, which he added to the Latin, Greek, Hebrew, French, and German of his youth. It did not seem to dawn on him that his linguistic facility had been immensely sharpened by the fact that he had grown up in an age that had made Greek (and even Hebrew) mandatory. And when his disciple and successor, Professor Keller, wrote his thesis on the subject of *Homeric Society*, the value of an undergraduate training in Greek to the understanding of emergent social anthropology still eluded him.

Because of the magnitude of his victory in transforming the curriculum, Sumner helped rob his own subject of its longer perspectives. And, in his animus against "metaphysics," he tended to discourage that preoccupation with the Good Life that makes the attempt to determine natural economic and sociological law worthwhile.

Toward the end of his long career Sumner reached the conclusion that ethics and morals are grounded in mores; hence they are relative to their time and their place. In brief, there are no "natural rights"; "might"—whether of the conqueror or of the majority consensus—makes "right." But if "might" makes "right," what becomes of the validity of the "moral indignation" that resents the protective tariff as "a subtle, cruel, and unjust invasion of one man's rights by another"? Sumner never really faced up to this question, and in most of his essays on "rights" there is an unadmitted ambivalence in the approach to the subject.

In one thing Sumner was correct: there are no "natural rights" in the sense that man can present a draft upon nature and expect it to be honored automatically. Rights are not to be understood in that sense. The fundamental right to life merely means that one man must accord it to another if he wishes to preserve it for himself. That is the law of life. It is an induction from observable circumstances, a Golden Rule proposition. The rights to liberty and property are part of the same right. They come within the realm of means, for they are necessary to the support of the right to life in all its savor. Incidentally, they are also necessary to the pursuit of happiness.

Where the right to life and the right to the means of life are disregarded, the annals of the race become, in Hobbesian language, a record of the nasty, the brutish, and the short. There is nothing "relative" about this; one can study culture after culture without coming to divergent conclusions. One suspects that Sumner knew as much, even when he was stressing the relativity of customs in his last book, the jampacked and knotty *Folkways*. The reason for the confusion in Sumner's many passages on rights is that he uses the same word for different things. Some-

times he is talking about a universal induction, sometimes about a subjective desire, sometimes about "legal" law. And a generation deprived of the ancient training in grammar, rhetoric, and logic has never had the wit to perceive the opaque quality of Sumner's semantics.

In his fight to change the college curriculum of his day and in his pioneering study of the relativity of customs, Sumner threw away two prime supports of the Old Republic which he loved. The moralist in Sumner was defeated by the short-run scientist who was not truly scientific. It is the moralist in Sumner that we must recover by bringing his science into accord with certain long-run truths about human nature which he forgot in the heat of the forums and the jousting pits of his day.

[IV, Winter 1959–60, 52–62]

[17]

Josiah Royce and American Conservatism

MICHAEL D. CLARK

Michael D(orsey) Clark *(1937–   ) is professor of history at the University of New Orleans, where he has taught since 1970, concentrating on late nineteenth-century American thought and American intellectual and religious history. Educated at Yale (B.A., 1959) and the University of North Carolina (M.A., 1962; Ph.D., 1965), he is the author of* Coherent Variety: The Idea of Diversity in British and American Conservative Thought *(1983) and an important study,* Worldly Theologians: The Persistence of Religion in Nineteenth-Century American Thought *(1981). He has also contributed scholarly articles in his field of interest to a number of journals.*

CONSERVATIVE THOUGHT in the United States has suffered from the suspicion of illegitimacy. America possessed neither the social hierarchy nor the web of tradition, critics have argued, which framed the insights of Edmund Burke; the nation was too new, and its citizens too horizontally and vertically mobile, to foster a genuine conservatism. Louis B. Hartz maintained plausibly that American conservatives had only eighteenth-century liberalism to conserve. Any attempt to break out of this "Lockean" mold was self-defeating, Hartz pointed out, since it cut conservatives off from historical reality, as in the attempt of ante-bellum Southerners like George Fitzhugh to interpret the South as a feudal and manorial society.[1] Such aberrations aside, in this view, American "conservatism" is actually the bastard offspring of the American liberal consensus, with the paternity of economic advantage strongly suspected. Marvin Meyers discovered in Jacksonian America the "venturous conservative," the man on the make who retained a nostalgic devotion to the Jeffersonian ideal of a yeoman republic, while his practical energies were absorbed by the un-Jeffersonian exigencies of capitalistic risk and gain.[2] Meyers' type becomes by extrapolation the modern businessman who is anxious to conserve the rules of the economic game, while his factories and computers revolutionize the lives of millions.

These are one-sided interpretations that are open to debate on various levels. But they do help to delineate an embarrassment of which conservative thought in this country has not entirely divested itself. There has remained a need for conservative formulations which will do ad-

179

equate justice both to the American experience and to the profound values that gave to European conservatism a secure and independent stance. To this end, it is surprising that more attention has not been paid to Josiah Royce.

I

Long overshadowed by his contemporaries William James and John Dewey, Royce has in recent years received a recognition more commensurate with his intellectual achievement. A contemporary critic does not seem greatly extravagant in his estimation of Royce, with Charles S. Peirce and Jonathan Edwards, as one of the three foremost American philosophers.[3] Royce did not especially associate himself with the political causes which were thought of as conservative in the late nineteenth and early twentieth centuries, but his major ideas are nonetheless significant for American conservatives. Indeed, just as the pragmatism of James and Dewey has been appropriated by modern Liberals, it is quite conceivable that a realistic and constructive avenue of conservative thought could be opened by due attention to Royce's philosophy of loyalty, community, and provincialism.

This philosophy was more impressive for being rooted in the philosopher's own experience. Josiah Royce was born in a mining camp in California in 1855, and was sufficiently close to Mexican War and gold-rush days to appreciate frontier conditions in the state. He later published a carefully researched history of the early days of California, which he subtitled "A Study of American Character." Royce's interpretation of the frontier was not that of Frederick Jackson Turner or of popular American mythology. The frontier was not the seedbed of democracy, or even of any form of individualism which was not merely a stunted manifestation of irresponsibility and greed. To the Californian, the frontier meant outrages perpetrated upon the native Mexicans, vigilante justice, and all the "devils of anarchy."[4] Order was the product not of any tidy social contract, but of an extended and difficult social process, hindered always by "the struggle of the individual man . . . to escape, like a fool, from his moral obligations to society."[5] "Anarchy," Royce noted, "is a thing of degrees, and its lesser degrees often coexist even with the constitutions that are well-conceived and popular."[6]

The lesson of this moral history, to Royce, was poles removed from the Jeffersonian and Thoreauvian distrust of government. "It is the State," he concluded, "the Social Order, that is divine. We are all but dust, save as this social order gives us life."[7] Vile as the social order might seem to those who reduced it to an instrument of private gain, it was to those who truly served it the embodiment of their highest spiritual destiny. This indiscriminating exaltation of the state and the social order, like Royce's later endorsement of "a religion of patriotism,"[8] may seem sinister when taken out of the context of his intellectual system. Royce meant not to cloak any particular government with an unassailable divine right, but to find a sanction for social order in the very nature of things. He expressed the moral meaning of California history more clearly as "a lesson in reverence for the relations of life."[9] It was these relations that the frontiersmen had forgotten, and it was only by recalling them that the community was saved. This concern for the "relations of life" was fundamental to Royce's system of thought. It was articulated on two main levels. It involved a conservative sense of social relations which denied both anarchic individualism and political absolutism, and it animated a philosophy of idealism which struggled to present the finite individual as both a free agent and as part of the infinite "Absolute."

Royce's "relational" point of view was grounded in a psychology which emphasized that the individual could define himself only in the social context. Indeed, thought Royce, so basic a thing as self-consciousness could not exist apart from social consciousness; there could be no "Ego" without an "Alter." Royce believed, therefore, that the conventional nineteenth-century opposition between a natural egoism and a socially derived altruism was profoundly a misconception. One could not act in one's own interests without acting for a social end. To be sure, the altruistic end could be evil; even the deliberate murderer, Royce pointed out, killed for honor, property, power, or some other ultimately social goal.[10] In this highly realistic conception, the facile temptation to play off "individual" and "society" against each other, as abstractions labelled "good" or "bad," was avoided. "The ethical problem is not," Royce concluded, "Shall I aim to preserve social relations? but: What social relations shall I aim to preserve?"[11]

It was by focusing on relationship, moreover, that Royce developed his distinctive version of philosophic idealism. William James might reject the monistic structure of Royce's universe as comprising just another "closed system," but Royce himself was exceedingly anxious to maintain the relevance of the ideal to the real world. His "Absolute" was not the sole principle of reality, over against which all temporal phenomena were illusory or insignificant. Rather, the Absolute had "the unity of a social organism; it is the complete integration of a complexity and variety of purposes, wills, and ideals;"[12] it was "an individual whole of mutually contingent parts."[13] "Of all the neo-Kantian idealists," James Harry Cotton notes,

"Royce was the most careful to preserve variety and plurality in his system. He depended on experience, sought facts, and insisted that his was a more concrete interpretation of the world than was that of the pragmatists."[14]

Royce himself maintained that he was a pragmatist as well as an absolutist, as each of those doctrines necessarily involved the other. One could make no significant practical decision, he pointed out, without irrevocable consequences which became the property of absolute experience.[15] "If idealism means anything," Royce emphasized, "it means a theory of the universe which simply must not be divorced from empirical considerations, or from the business life. . . . It is, and in its historical representatives always has been, an effort to interpret the facts of life."[16]

II

An idealism thus conceived seems at once peculiarly American and eminently compatible with the concreteness upon which conservative thought traditionally has insisted. The American mind, insofar as one can speak of such a generalized phenomenon, has been a peculiar mixture of the practical and the abstract. Alexis de Tocqueville observed that Americans are disposed to think either in the most minute or in the most general terms,[17] and Royce had observed these very tendencies in the clash of frontier idealism and avarice. Priding themselves on their attention to the "business of life," vaunting pragmatism as the quintessential American philosophy, Americans have found nonetheless that their mobility, their "bootless chase of that complete felicity which forever escapes [them],"[18] has given to life in this country a detached and abstract quality far removed from the sort of traditional life which accretes with the centuries a sense of having a place in the universe.

Traditionalism is not manufactured overnight, and would not solve modern problems if it were, but Josiah Royce did derive from his idealistic philosophy a scheme of relationship which bridged Tocqueville's American chasm between petty ingenuity and windy generality. This scheme was Royce's philosophy of loyalty, and he was aware that it filled an American need. "We as a nation," he feared, ". . . have been forgetting loyalty. We have been neglecting to cultivate it in our social order."[19]

Royce meant by loyalty, of course, something more than simple adherence to a cause or a political authority, a habit which had not generally been lacking in the United States. Loyalty was the very relational principle of life, "the heart of all the virtues, the central duty amongst all duties."[20] As abstract as such a concept might seem, Royce took pains to emphasize its concrete and human qualities. One could not be loyal, in his definition, either to an impersonal abstraction or to a mere collection of individuals.[21] Loyalty was a far more complete involvement. It is indicative of Royce's meaning that he found in Christianity the highest expression of loyalty. St. Paul, he noted, had seen that "a community, when unified by an active indwelling purpose, is an entity more concrete and, in fact, less mysterious than is any individual man, and that such a community can love and be loved as a husband and wife love; or as a father or mother love." "In sum," Royce concluded, "Christian love, as Paul conceives it, takes on the form of Loyalty."[22]

Loyalty so conceived, for Royce, united the rational to the instinctive aspect of life. The appeal of loyalty was "elemental"; it engaged the "whole organism"; yet authentic loyalty demanded too a free and rational consent. Indeed, thought Royce,

"Loyalty is a perfect synthesis of certain natural desires, of some range of social conformity, and of your own deliberate choice."[23] Loyalty alone offered fulfillment of the "reasonable purposes" of individualism. "If you want true freedom, seek it in loyalty. If you want self-expression, spirituality, moral autonomy, loyalty alone can give you these goods."[24] Royce could make so sweeping an assertion because he defined the individual self as "a human life lived according to a plan," and this could only mean devotion to a transcendent cause, a cause at once personal and superpersonal, outside the self, yet constituting a larger self. Treason, therefore, was the fundamental, unpardonable sin; it amounted to the suicide of the moral personality.[25]

Royce faced the obvious objection that the philosophy of loyalty did not prescribe that to which one was to be loyal. But it was not his intention to provide more than a general principle. He was too much of a pluralist to propose any monolithic structure of authority; he assumed that the application of his principle would vary endlessly, with each individual serving his own personal system of causes.[26] But at the heart of Royce's morality lay a precept to keep the world from becoming an anarchy of conflicting petty loyalties. The loyal individual must above all be loyal to loyalty; he must act so that "there shall be more of this common good of loyalty in the world than there would have been, had . . . [he] . . . not lived and acted."[27] This stretched the principle of loyalty to the breaking point of abstraction—it is not invariably clear how to be loyal to loyalty—but to the idealist it was indispensable as a unifying concept.

The philosophy of loyalty, for Royce, offered the best solution to the basic problem of politics: the inevitable conflict of individual will with the will of society. The question was one, of course, which had long absorbed conservative as well as other thinkers, but it had taken a peculiar turn in the United States, where an individualistic tradition, based on an extraordinary degree of personal mobility, had joined with *laissez faire* and social Darwinist ideas to produce, in the second half of the nineteenth century, a "conservative" defense of very loose social and economic arrangements. American conservatism was thus drained of the sense of social cohesion which belonged to the larger conservative tradition. The principle of loyalty, however, suggested a new concept of cohesion, capable, Royce thought, of guiding individual liberty between blind submission and incoherent rebellion, between regimentation and a selfish detachment.[28]

The question of individual liberty ran to the roots of Royce's philosophical system. On one level a social and political question, on another plane it involved the relationship of man and the Absolute, and the whole perennial metaphysical problem of free will. His concept of loyalty, however, kept the philosopher's vision constant, and his individual stood to society much as he stood to the Absolute. The Absolute was simply a vastly greater, and perfect, community. On any level, Royce saw, the problem of freedom was equivalent to the problem of individuality: "If I am I and nobody else, and if I am I as an expression of purpose, then I am in so far free just because, as an individual, I express by my existence no will except my own."[29]

Royce anchored his manifold belief in individual freedom both in psychology and philosophy. Unwilling to consign the human mind to automatism, he attempted to make room in his limited psychological work for "mental initiative" and spontaneity. Mental attentiveness, he believed, offered a key to a phenomenon which could be defined as free choice; thus,

"... *attentive preference of one course of conduct, or of one tendency or desire, as against all others present to our minds at any time, is called a voluntary act.*"[30] As a "post-Kantian idealist," too, Royce found sufficient ground to regard individuals as ethically free and morally responsible for their deliberate acts.[31] He yielded so far to determinism as to admit that the physical world, the "world of description," was governed by law and causation, and therefore by necessity. But he insisted that physical laws were only symbols of a deeper truth, or Logos, which was lodged in a "world of appreciation" transcending the time-sequences to which attribution of causation and necessity were essential. In a profound sense, for Royce, this provided a dimension of moral freedom: "The Self, we say, regards its world in a twofold way: (1) As a time series of events in which the earlier events fatally cause the later; (2) As an externally complete world total whose significance it ideally estimates and chooses."[32]

Freedom so conceived was by its nature limited, but Royce was careful to underscore the point. If he had left the door open to free will in his psychological studies, he nevertheless acknowledged that the aspect of humanity which was of valid concern to the empirical psychologist must be regarded as subject to the ordinary rules of causation and necessity.[33] But even moral freedom, outside the empirical realm, was distinctly limited. Royce's idealism did not allow him to accept romantic notions of absolute individual freedom. "A world of so-called 'infinite' free moral agents is, at best," he thought, "a polytheistic world. At worse, it threatens ... to prove no 'City of God,' but something much more diabolical."[34] He saw no value and much danger in freedom as "limitless eccentricity, individuality without other aim than to be peculiar. ..."[35] At the same time, Royce distrusted the use of freedom as a shibboleth of mass political movements. "Human freedom," he emphasized, "is a personal affair. Man cannot be free; men must be."[36] Whether on the individual or the social plane, the desire for freedom was doomed to disappointments. Demanding freedom from restraint, the personal will demanded equally its expression in a social life full of restraints. The will to be free "asserts itself in all sorts of self-surrendering, self-entangling, self-disappointing ways," as when "the will of the people seeks freedom, and therefore accepts ere long the rule of despots or, in our age and land, the rule of the 'bosses.' "[37]

III

Royce's free individual, then, was a being considerably more complex than the model of classical economists or social Darwinists. The individual was unique, but dependent on the ideal world for his individuality. Individuality itself must always remain mysterious and elusive, for "an individual is a being that no finite search can find." Who could conceive of himself "in his uniqueness except as the remote goal of some ideal process of coming to himself and of awakening to the truth about his own life? Only an infinite process can show me who I am."[38] Seen in the social context, individuality seemed to Royce at once the most reasonable and unreasonable aspect of human existence—reasonable because it gave scope to the most valued of human qualities; unreasonable because individual caprice and waywardness involved rebellion against order, and intrusion upon the will of others.[39]

From this vantage point, Royce could gauge the limitations of the brand of "individualism" which Herbert Spencer did so much to make intellectually fashionable. The glaring contradiction in the Spencerian school of thought, Royce found, lay in the English philosopher's attempt to weld an old-fashioned British liberalism onto a social Darwinism which subjected the individual to biological determinism. "This particular synthesis of organic evolution with individual independence," he thought, "remains one of the most paradoxical, and consequently most instructive, features of Spencer's teaching."[40] Spencer himself impressed Royce as an individualist of a singularly narrow sort— a lover of humanity in the abstract who was incapable of any deep sympathy with actual men, a generalizer who recognized only one significant sort of individual— "viz, an individual of the intellectual and moral temperament of Herbert Spencer."[41] Spencer's enshrinement in society of the principle of "survival of the fittest" seemed correspondingly inadequate to one familiar with frontier days in California. "Individualistic communities," Royce observed, "are almost universally, and paradoxically enough, communities that are extremely cruel to individuals."[42]

Royce proposed a mode of individual freedom which was far different from the "moral hell" of anarchy or atomistic detachment.[43] Not only in the Spencerian dispensation did he find a threat to genuine individuality; he was aware of other, and equally menacing, centrifugal forces which have outlasted Spencer to vex modern life. To Royce, always himself loyal to loyalty, individualism could never escape a "strongly negative" aspect. At best, however, as in early nineteenth century romanticism, it had been also constructive, enthusiastic, and capable of faith. The sort of "restlessly intolerant and muscular individualism" represented by Friedrich Nietzsche, however, seemed to Royce mainly destructive, amounting to "an idealism without any ideal world of truth, a religion without a faith, a martyrdom without prospect of a paradise. . . ."

The drastic and iconoclastic individualists of his own day, he suggested, were largely absorbed in making "pyramids of the skulls of their enemies."[44] As if to furnish a counterpoise to this modern style, Royce sought to equate the ideal of freedom with the ideal of social harmony.[45] He expressed this equation in his concept of community.

Community complemented loyalty; it was both itself the object of loyalty, and the field within which the diverse loyalties of individuals were fulfilled. "Community" is a vague (and currently popular) idea, but it was an integral part of Royce's philosophy, and he took pains to make it clear. Emphasizing that the community is not a mere collection of individuals, Royce depicted it explicitly as an organism, which grows and decays, "as much a live creature" as the lone man or woman. The social mind, Royce thought, was as real as the individual, for language, custom, and religion, all genuine mental products, were possible only in a community.[46] Yet Royce did not intend to reduce the individual to a mere cell. "A community immediately presents itself to our minds both as one and as many," he explained, "and unless it is both one and many, it is no community at all."[47] The interests of the community were paramount, as Royce made clear in his history of California, but only because it represented the "ideally extended life" of every person in it.[48] Human individuality, indeed, was absolutely dependent on community. "The detached individual is essentially a lost being."[49]

Community, for Royce, existed on many levels, from the smallest social unit to the universal community to which, ideally, all men belonged. "To act as if one were a member of such a community," Royce believed, "is to win in the highest measure the goal of individual life. It is to win what religion calls salvation."[50] An ultramun-

dane web embraced all communal relationships, and knit the social to the divine order, for only he who was in love with the universe could be truly in love with the community.[51] Royce therefore could speak of "the sacredness of a true public spirit," and draw from Dostoevski's *Crime and Punishment* the lesson that "salvation involves a reconciliation both with the social and with the divine order, a reconciliation through love and suffering—an escape from the wilderness of lonely guilt to the realm where men can understand one another."[52]

IV

Royce's advocacy of provincialism as an expression of community is of especial interest to conservative thought. The trend in the philosopher's thinking, as Cotton writes, was "away from a more abstract unity towards a more sharply defined pluralism."[53] He came increasingly to distrust large political and economic units, "the great industrial forces, the aggregations of capital, the combinations of enormous physical power. . . . These vast social forces," he thought, "are like the forces of nature. They excite our loyalty as little as do the trade-winds or the blizzard. . . ."[54] In mass society, he was aware, individualism and collectivism fed upon and intensified each other in a not always healthy way. Socialism, for instance, he noted in 1912, preached solidarity, brotherhood, and love, yet it gained the adherence of those who saw it as the means to advance their own fortunes, "and to become, as Nietzsche's Superman, 'beyond good and evil,'—masters in the coming world of triumphant democracy."[55]

Royce suggested provincial loyalty as the best "mediator" between the individual and national patriotism or other larger allegiances.[56] Provincialism denoted the customs and ideals held in common by members of a relatively small social group, and especially "the love and pride which leads the inhabitants of a province to cherish as their own these traditions, beliefs and aspirations."[57] It was, he thought, "an essential basis of true civilization," and at a time when social trends ran against it, all the more "a saving power to which the world in the near future will need more and more to appeal."[58] Royce's indictment of mass society was very modern in tone. The ease of communication, spread of popular education, and consolidation in business and government, he noted, had had a homogenizing effect; all read the same news, shared the same general ideas, and submitted to the same overwhelming social forces. The result was "to approach a dead level of harassed mediocrity. . . . The vast corporation succeeds and displaces the individual. Ingenuity and initiative become subordinated to the discipline of an impersonal social order."[59] Royce proposed a partial retreat from the arena of abstract leviathans to the "real life" of locality:

> Freedom, I should say, dwells now in the small social group, and has its securest home in the provincial life. The nation by itself, apart from the influence of the province, is in danger of becoming an incomprehensible monster, in whose presence the individual loses his right, his self-consciousness, and his dignity. The province must save the individual.[60]

Loyalty, community, and provincialism composed a structure of thought which, if not inherently conservative, amply housed conservative views on man and history. Royce's idealism was not of the Utopian sort. The triumph of the good, he knew, was always uncertain, and he saw no reason for confidence that "good will ever triumph over evil in more than a very restricted sense. . . ."[61] Sin, indeed, as Vincent Buranelli points out, functioned in Royce's system as a bond be-

tween human beings.[62] Although a personal responsibility (guilt was not to be projected on society), sin violated the purposes of the Absolute, and therefore in some measure the purposes of all men. Royce achieved an uncommon balance in remaining alive both to "the lonely and darkened depths of . . . personal finitude"[63] and to the social ties that eternally mitigated this isolation.

Belief in the persistence of sin allowed Royce a truly historical perspective on the world. While his system was teleological in that it involved ideal purposes and left room for moral progress, Royce did not expect that the sequence of events would end in perfection; the ideal goal was never to be reached at a given point in time. Royce thus escaped the predicament of many American "historians against history,"[64] whose understanding of the past was vitiated by their millennial belief that America offered an escape from the evils and disharmonies that had been the customary lot of humanity. For Royce, rather, "the pursuit, the search for the goal, the new interpretation which every new event requires—this endless sequence of new acts of interpretation—this constitutes the world. This *is* the order of time. This pursuit of the goal," he acknowledged, "this bondage of the whole creation to the pursuit of that which it never reaches, this naturally tragic estrangement of this world from its goal, this constitutes the problem of the universe."[65]

Although he was himself the physical product of the frontier, and was therefore unlikely as a spokesman for tradition, Royce evinced an almost Burkean sense of the community as a partnership between generations. He emphasized that the true community is the product of time, and that history "is a part of its very essence." Indeed, he thought, "a community requires for its existence a history and is greatly aided in its consciousness by a memory."[66] Past and future are parts of the same whole, and each moment makes its unique contribution to the "symphony" of history. The "equal 'ideality' of past and future . . . logically forbids conduct to act with reference to a limited portion of time or to a limited being or group of beings. . . ."[67]

Within this vision of history, Royce suggested a more explicitly conservative attitude toward change. His thinking here was by no means original or startling, but it did help to draw his idealism into more mundane spheres. He assumed that change was an ineluctable fact of modern life; possibly as much as later generations, he was aware in 1880 that the times were revolutionary. Yet he did not believe that this made conservatism irrelevant, because he saw an ultimate bond between the conservative and the revolutionary spirit. For the sincere revolutionary, destruction was only a prelude to reconstruction, and thence to the conservation of that which was reconstructed.[68] But Royce was no apologist for revolution; he was seeking common ground on the question of innovation. "Our thesis," he emphasized, "is that conservatism and radicalism are examples of a single tendency of voluntary progress, the tendency, namely, to satisfy changing needs with the least possible change of plan, to gain as much new experience as possible with the least alteration of the ways of gaining it."[69]

Although Royce was well aware that conservatives and radicals by their nature did not agree on the application of this "single tendency" of progress, he was temperamentally disposed to seek the evolutionary path which he theoretically indicated. He had little sympathy with zealots; while acknowledging the moral values of the Transcendental abolitionists, for instance, he found the abstract God that they invoked a *Deus absconditus . . .* as remote from the imperfections and absurdities of the individual laws and processes of human society, as he was near to the hearts of his chosen worshippers." Nor did Royce have any use for the "Higher Law," which for some had condemned a constitution that condoned slavery as a covenant with hell. If that "upon which our sinful national existence depended, and upon which our only hope of better things also depended," was set at nought, he remarked sarcastically, then the individual was left to provide for himself, "and he and the Infinite might carry on a government of their own."[70] Royce's idealism was of a different stripe, which realized the value as well as the intractability of practical concerns. "In the night we deal, if we like, with the world, the universe, and God," he summed it up; "In the morning we have to deal with such things as the Sheriff, the Mayor, and the writs of the County Court. . . ."[71]

V

This mixture of idealism and practicality, integrated in Royce as it often seems schizophrenic in the general American consciousness, offers a more authentic conservative framework than the narrow precepts of Meyers' "venturous conservatism." The Roycean sense of social cohesion is at once within the tradition of Western conservatism, and distinctively American. It does not on this account avoid an abstract quality, since American communities, even American provinces, are more shifting and unstable than the groupings of the old society of Europe. Yet if American mobility has been prophetic of the character of modern society in general, Royce's concept of loyalty as a moral cement may be more durable than the ancient appeal of farm and village. While the familiar nostalgia-producing versions of provincialism would certainly appear doomed in modern society, moreover, Royce's increasingly pluralistic philosophy of loyalty and community necessarily suggested that some types of provincialism might still be possible. At least Royce meets the contemporary consciousness in seeking to elude the clutch of gigantic economic and political units.

The pluralistic system of loyalties seems also impeccably grounded in American tradition. *E pluribus unum* applies not only to the federal system, but to the myriad ethnic and religious allegiances which never succumbed to the "melting pot." Royce's rationale avoids the difficulties into which many of the previous defenses of American pluralism fell; it is not tainted by connection to special and sometimes ignoble interests, as John C. Calhoun's concept of concurrent majority and George Fitzhugh's pro-slavery sociology were, for example, and as many more recent defenses of states' rights have been. Nor is Royce so open to the charge of being divorced from American reality as the ante-bellum champions of the "reactionary Enlightenment."[72]

A conservatism drawing sustenance from the Roycean ideas of loyalty, community, and provincialism largely escapes the strictures of critics like Louis B. Hartz. Such a philosophy is by no means dependent on an aristocratic class, the lack of which, as Hartz pointed out, gave a peculiar cast to American conservatism. Indeed, it does not rest on class at all. The larger dilemma of American conservatism—that it can conserve only a fundamentally liberal tradition—is also at least partially resolved. It cannot be said that defense of local liberties and privileges was the property of either Left or Right in the eighteenth century; it was invoked in Europe by nobles and Girondins, and in this country by Jeffersonians and ultraconservative antifederalists. As liberals in the nineteenth century moved generally to ally themselves with nationalism and to discountenance strong local loyalties, however, political pluralism seems a valid enough starting point for American conservatives.

Royce is also surprisingly contemporary in his concern with decentralization and the importance of the community in nurturing individuality, as well as in his almost existentialist sense of the contingency of the individual. Appropriately for one who saw an ultimate bond between conservatism and radicalism, he here suggests points at which present conservative and radical criticisms of mass society meet. At the same time, his brand of idealism offers a corrective to political "pragmatism" which has ceased to resemble the philosophy of William James as it has become increasingly a synonym for opportunism. Although "loyalty" is susceptible to a similar devaluation—it has frequently been used to denote intolerance and conformity—it offers a profound corrective to anarchism, racial separatism, and other centrifugal ideas of present currency. The principle of "loyalty to loyalty," as difficult as it is of practical application, suggests an attitude of mutual respect which is now in short supply. In the largest view, Josiah Royce belongs to American philosophy, and can be fully claimed by no sect or party, but conservative thought in this country can draw from him both a confidence in its own legitimacy and a sense of greater relevance to the searing issues of the day.

NOTES

[1] Louis B. Hartz, *The Liberal Tradition in America: An Interpretation of American Political Thought Since the Revolution* (New York: Harcourt, Brace & World, 1955), *passim*.

[2] Marvin Meyers, *The Jacksonian Persuasion: Politics and Belief* (New York: Vintage Books, 1960), *passim*.

[3] Vincent Buranelli, *Josiah Royce* (New York: Twayne Publishers, 1964), p. 147. Buranelli suggests, in fact, that Royce should rank second, after Peirce.

[4] Josiah Royce, *California from the Conquest in 1846 to the Second Vigilance Committee in San Francisco: A Study of American Character* (Boston and New York: Houghton Mifflin and Company, 1886), p. 225 and *passim*.

[5] *Ibid.*, p. 273.

[6] *Ibid.*, p. 271.

[7] *Ibid.*, p. 501.

[8] Josiah Royce, *The Sources of Religious Insight: Lectures Delivered Before Lake Forest College on the Foundation of the Late William Bross* (Edinburgh: T. & T. Clark, 1912), p. 275.

[9] Royce, *California*, p. 500.

[10] Josiah Royce, *Studies of Good and Evil: A Series of Essays Upon Problems of Philosophy and of Life* (Hamden, Connecticut: Archon Books, 1964), pp. 201–203.

[11] *Ibid.*, p. 203.

[12] J. Loewenberg, introduction to Josiah Royce, *Fugitive Essays* (Cambridge: Harvard University Press, 1920), p. 12.

[13] Josiah Royce, Joseph Le Conte, G. H. Howison, and Sidney Edward Mezes, *The Conception of God: A Philosophical Discussion Concerning the Nature of the Divine as a Demonstrable Reality* (New York: The Macmillan Company, 1898), p. 306. This statement, as all others cited from this work, is Royce's.

[14] James Harry Cotton, *Royce on the Human Self* (Cambridge: Harvard University Press, 1954), p. 147.

[15] Josiah Royce, *Lectures on Modern Idealism* (New Haven: Yale University Press, 1923), p. 258; Josiah Royce, *William James and Other Essays on the Philosophy of Life* (New York: The Macmillan Company, 1912), p. 41. Royce was convinced that William James "himself was in spirit an ethical idealist to the core" (Royce, *William James*, p. 43).

[16] Royce, *Studies of Good and Evil*, pp. iii–iv.

[17] Alexis de Tocqueville, *Democracy in America*, 2 volumes (New York: Vintage Books, 1959), II, p. 82; Royce, *Studies of Good and Evil*, pp. 298–299. "The Transcendentalist," Royce noted, "—a being who is, in one form, a characteristic American— imagines himself called upon to lead his fellows in a struggle for property and for bread. The idealist gets into conflict with the sheriff. . . ."

[18] Tocqueville, *Democracy in America*, II, p. 145.

[19] Josiah Royce, *The Philosophy of Loyalty* (New York: The Macmillan Company, 1908), p. 114.

[20] *Ibid.*, p. vii.

[21] *Ibid.*, p. 52.

[22] Josiah Royce, *The Problem of Christianity: Lectures Delivered at the Lowell Institute in Boston, and at Manchester College, Oxford*, 2 volumes (New York: The Macmillan Company, 1913), I, pp. 95, 98.

[23] Royce, *Philosophy of Loyalty*, pp. 130–131.

[24] *Ibid.*, p. 199.

[25] *Ibid.*, pp. 168, 225; Josiah Royce, *Race Questions, Provincialism, and Other American Problems* (New York: The Macmillan Company, 1908), pp. 237–238; Royce, *Problem of Christianity*, I, pp. 263–264.

[26] Royce, *Philosophy of Loyalty*, pp. 200–201.

[27] Royce, *Race Questions*, pp. 248–249.

[28] Royce, *Philosophy of Loyalty*, pp. 39, 84.

[29] Josiah Royce, *The World and the Individual*, 2 volumes (New York: The Macmillan Company, 1900–1901), II, pp. 330–331.

[30] Josiah Royce, *Outlines of Psychology: An Elementary Treatise with Some Practical Applications* (New York: The Macmillan Company, 1908), p. 368 and *passim*.

[31] Royce, *World and the Individual*, I, p. 42; Royce, *Conception of God*, p. 318.

[32] Josiah Royce, *The Spirit of Modern Philosophy* (Boston and New York: Houghton Mifflin Company, 1892), p. 432 and *passim*.

[33] Royce, *Conception of God*, pp. 319–320.

[34] *Ibid.*, p. 321.

[35] Royce, *Fugitive Essays*, p. 128.

[36] *Ibid.*

[37] Royce, *Modern Idealism*, pp. 88–89.

[38] Josiah Royce, *The Conception of Immortality* (New York: Greenwood Press, 1968), pp. 5, 28.

[39] Royce, *Modern Idealism*, pp. 246–247.

[40] Josiah Royce, *Herbert Spencer: An Estimate and Review; Together with a Chapter of Personal Reminiscences by James Collier* (New York: Fox, Duffield & Company, 1904), pp. 63–64.

[41] *Ibid.*, pp. 153–154, 175–177.

[42] Royce, *Race Questions*, p. 128.

[43] Royce, *Conception of God*, p. 275.

[44] Royce, *Modern Idealism*, pp. 68–69.

[45] Royce, *Fugitive Essays*, p. 129.

[46] Royce, *Problem of Christianity*, I, 62.

[47] *Ibid.*, II, p. 17.

[48] Royce, *California*, p. viii; Royce, *Problem of Christianity*, II, p. 90.

[49] Josiah Royce, *The Hope of the Great Community* (New York: The Macmillan Company, 1916), p. 46.

[50] Royce, *Problem of Christianity*, I, p. 73.

[51] *Ibid.*, II, p. 102.

[52] Royce, *California*, p. 465; Royce, *Sources of Religious Insight*, pp. 70–71.

[53] Cotton, *Royce on the Human Self*, p. 263. "It is not fair to Royce's intent," Cotton notes, "to make him a champion of increasing federal power as the late President Roosevelt once tried to do." (*Ibid.*)

[54] Royce, *Philosophy of Loyalty*, p. 242.

[55] Royce, *Sources of Religious Insight*, p. 61.

[56] Royce, *Philosophy of Loyalty*, p. 248.

[57] Royce, *Race Questions*, p. 61.

[58] *Ibid.*, pp. 62, 67.

⁵⁹ *Ibid.*, pp. 74–75.

⁶⁰ *Ibid.*, p. 98.

⁶¹ Royce, *Fugitive Essays*, p. 131.

⁶² Buranelli, *Josiah Royce*, pp. 136–137.

⁶³ Royce, *Sources of Religious Insight*, p. 210.

⁶⁴ See David W. Noble, *Historians Against History: The Frontier Thesis and the National Covenant in American Historical Writing since* 1830 (University of Minnesota Press, 1965).

⁶⁵ Royce, *Problem of Christianity*, II, p. 375.

⁶⁶ *Ibid.*, II, p. 37.

⁶⁷ Royce, *Spirit of Modern Philosophy*, p. 431; J. Loewenberg, introduction to Royce, *Fugitive Essays*, p. 25.

⁶⁸ Royce, *Fugitive Essays*, pp. 81, 94.

⁶⁹ *Ibid.*, p. 104.

⁷⁰ Royce, *Studies of Good and Evil*, pp. 324–325.

⁷¹ *Ibid.*, p. 336.

⁷² The phrase is Louis B. Hartz's, in *Liberal Tradition in America*, in reference to the Southern intellectual defense of slavery.

[XIII, Fall 1969, 342–352]

[18]

The Humanism of Irving Babbitt Revisited

CLAES G. RYN

Claes G. Ryn (1943–   ), a member of the editorial advisory board of Modern Age, *was born in Norrköping, Sweden. Former chairman and now professor of the Department of Politics at the Catholic University of America, he has written books on* Nykonservatismen i USA *(1971),* Democracy and the Ethical Life *(1973), and* Will, Imagination, and Reason: Irving Babbitt and the Problem of Knowledge *(1986), as well as* Irving Babbitt in Our Time *(1986), coedited with George A. Panichas. Ryn has taught at Uppsala University in Sweden and at the University of Virginia. He is chairman of the National Humanities Institute in Washington, D.C.*

NO INTELLECTUAL TASK could be more urgent today than refuting the pseudo-scientific distinction between "facts" and "values" and restoring to the humanities and social sciences a sense of transcendent moral purpose.[1] In this effort we would be well-advised to reconsider the work of a great American whose ideas have yet to be fully comprehended and appreciated, Irving Babbitt (1865–1933). His is a contribution toward the revitalization and renewal of the classical Greek and Judaeo-Christian traditions which is not only original but highly relevant to present intellectual circumstances. Formally a professor of French and comparative literature at Harvard but also a man of formidable range, Irving Babbitt was the leading figure in the movement of ideas known as the New Humanism, which divided American academic opinion in the twen-ties and thirties. Unfortunately, his books are known today primarily through secondary sources. These do not for the most part deal in depth with his central ideas, and they are frequently unreliable. (See our discussion below.) For complex reasons, Babbitt encountered intense opposition as well as admiration among his contemporaries. Many of the available interpretations of his position were formulated in the heat of controversy and reflect an impatient and even intemperate wish to be rid of an uncomfortable opponent. There are also the misinterpretations of sympathetic commentators who have simply failed to grasp his meaning. Part of the blame must be borne by Babbitt himself. He did not always develop his ideas systematically, and he sometimes expressed them in an ambiguous manner. Although most certainly a leading philos-

191

opher by the criteria of insight, depth, and comprehensiveness, he was not a professional, "technical" philosopher.

We propose to contribute to the badly needed reinterpretation and assimilation of Babbitt's work by analyzing his notion of humanism as it relates to his central philosophical concept, "the inner check."[2] Speaking respectfully of Babbitt is not without its dangers. Even today the emotional momentum of the adverse reactions he met during his life has not been exhausted. One can only hope that the time has come when Babbitt's work can finally be examined with a degree of scholarly detachment.

I

One of the main controversies surrounding Babbitt concerned his idea of humanism as a moral and intellectual discipline arriving at its values independently of religion. He was criticized on this point both by naturalists and secularists, who rejected his affirmation of a universal principle of good, and by Christians. It was argued against him by the latter that all moral norms must finally be sanctioned by religious faith.

Babbitt does not deny that the moral life may be strengthened by religion, but he insists that the genuine values of civilization do not depend for their justification on religious faith. There is a humanistic level of life with its own intrinsic standard of perfection above the pursuit of pleasure and all other kinds of private advantage, but still distinct from religion. The primary concern of humanism is to establish the existence of a certain quality of will in man which defines his true humanity. Insofar as this will is exercised in social life, Babbitt contends, civilization is realized. Genuine civilization requires no justification apart from the values immanent in it by virtue of its ordering

principle. This self-justifying will in man is nothing other than Babbitt's much-debated, but poorly understood, "inner check." Its existence can be verified, he argues, without recourse to revelation. It is a datum of common human experience. In truth, it is the most immediate fact of human consciousness, concealed from view only by faulty moral theories.

Babbitt's idea of humanism is not intended to deny the claims of religion in its own sphere. What he disputes is the necessity for deriving the norms of justice from revelation. Humanism and religion are mutually supportive and yet separate orders of life.

> Though humanism and religion both lie on the same ascending path from the naturalistic flux, one must insist that each has its separate domain. It is an error to hold that humanism can take the place of religion. Religion indeed may more readily dispense with humanism than humanism with religion. Humanism gains greatly by having a religious background . . . whereas religion, for the man who has actually renounced the world, may very conceivably be all in all. On the other hand, the man who sets out to live religiously in the secular order without having recourse to the wisdom of the humanist is likely to fall into vicious confusions—notably, into a confusion between the things of God and the things of Caesar. The Catholic Church has therefore been well inspired in rounding out its religious doctrine with the teaching of Aristotle and other masters of the law of measure.[3]

Drawing in part on Plato, Babbitt develops a dualistic view of human nature. Life presents us with the mystery of the One and the Many. Our most immediate awareness of reality, Babbitt argues, is of a universal tension between opposites which cuts right through our inner life. What we find in the world is simultaneous order and disorder. Life is not a mere chaos of events, a flux of unrelated impressions; it is an ordered flux. "Life does not give here an element of oneness and there an element of change. It gives a *oneness that is always changing*. The oneness and the change are inseparable."[4] Change and diversity are inseparable from life, but so are their opposites. At work in the flux of events is a principle of order which introduces coherence and harmony into the stream. There is in the world beauty as well as ugliness, truth as well as falsehood, good as well as evil. Set apart from the flux, and yet also in it, is a power which orders life to a purpose. Human nature is dual in the sense that man is a unity of opposing inclinations. He is, in Babbitt's terminology, a lower and a higher self. He is drawn, on the one hand, into impulses destructive of individual and social harmony, but able, on the other hand, to structure his impulses toward the opposite goal. Of primary importance to Babbitt, as to Plato, is the moral aspect of this tension at the core of existence. Standing against the human desires in their endless diversity is an unvarying sense of higher purpose which transcends all particular impulses. The same in all men, it harmonizes the individual circumstances of each. By restraining the merely partisan, particularistic wishes present in human society, it brings men together at a common center of value. It is this moral ordering of life, in its aspect as a civilizing force, that Babbitt calls humanistic self-control.

How is it that man is not just swept along by the stream of desires? How is it that he is presented with an opportunity to interfere with his own impulses and create new behavior in consonance with a higher goal? The appearance of the inner check, Babbitt maintains, is finally a mystery, but it is an indisputable fact nevertheless. Although our finite intellect cannot fathom the "ultimate nature" of this ordering principle, it is known to us

in immediate experience. "The higher will must simply be accepted as a mystery that may be studied in its practical effects. . . ."[5] Those effects are described by Babbitt as follows: ". . . I do not hesitate to affirm that what is specifically human in man and ultimately divine is a certain quality of will, a will that is felt in its relation to his ordinary self as a will to refrain."[6] The "ordinary" self is Babbitt's term for man's impulsive life as unordered by moral considerations. The tendency to act without regard for the good of the whole he also calls, depending on the context, the "lower," "natural," or "temperamental" self. To the extent that man rises above his ordinary self by acting from inside the inner check, the latter becomes more firmly established, not only as an irrefutable fact of experience, but as the very center of meaningful life.

Babbitt's theory of "the inner check" has led to vast misunderstanding. Does he mean that morality is a completely negative act, some sort of ascetic self-denial? One of the reasons why this concept has caused so much confusion is that Babbitt's readers have frequently failed to put it in the proper context. The term is employed by him in opposition to all of those who would forget the duality of human nature and identify the moral good with particular human intentions. He is sharply critical, for instance, of the moral-sense school of thought associated with Shaftesbury. Another of his main opponents is Jean-Jacques Rousseau, whose morality of the heart vests the good in unrestrained impulse. Our moral will, Babbitt asserts repeatedly, must not be confused with gushes of "sympathy" or "pity." It is better described as an inhibition on our outgoing impulses. "As against the expansionists of every kind,"[7] he separates the ordering principle from that which is ordered. Not only is the urge of the moment frequently in conflict with the good, so that morality requires an act of self-restraint; but in those cases when our impulses do harmonize with the moral end and are thus not censured by the inner check, they are still transcended by that principle itself. There is nothing more certain, Babbitt believes, than that morality is a creation of will, an overcoming of obstacles. It is through spiritual activity, not through some easy yielding to the impulse of the moment, that good is brought into the world.

> Civilization is something that must be deliberately willed; it is not something that gushes up spontaneously from the depths of the unconscious. Furthermore, it is something that must be willed first of all by the individual in his own heart.[8]

There are no shortcuts to the genuine values of social life. Tradition and social reform can aid, but never replace, individual moral effort.

In spite of Babbitt's emphasis on civilization as the fruit of humanistic exercise of the higher will, it has been alleged again and again that he has a purely negative conception of the good. The following comment by Edmund Wilson is typical of this strangely unperceptive reading of Babbitt: ". . . how can one take seriously a philosophy which enjoins nothing but negative behavior?"[9] In a similar vein, Allen Tate believes that he has exposed "the negative basis of Professor Babbitt's morality. The good man is he who 'refrains from doing' what the 'lower nature dictates,' and he need do nothing positive."[10] Henry Hazlitt writes: "The insistence, you will notice, is always on the purely *negative* virtues."[11] Babbitt's real theory is that morality has two aspects, renunciation and affirmation of impulse. These acts are two dimensions of one and the same effort to realize good. In its relation to what is destructive of our spiritual unity, the higher will is felt as a

restraint. The moral end is advanced by censuring what is opposed to it. That Babbitt pays much attention to this "negative" side of morality is due to his assessment of what truths our time needs to hear the most. The main threat to the values of civilization today is not an excess of renunciation of the world, but an excessive release of the "expansive desires." What modern Western man needs to hear the most is not that the good is achieved through affirmation of impulse, although that is a part of the truth, but that man's true humanity lies in his ability to put checks on his desires. In the Middle Ages, with its strong emphasis on otherworldliness, the point that good can be advanced by positive human acts would have deserved more attention.

Babbitt's frequent, indeed, too frequent, use of a certain term, "the inner check," to denote moral effort should not conceal the fact that in one aspect man's higher will is not just experienced as a negation. In the person who has followed Aristotle's admonition to develop sound habits and a taste for moral values, the impulsive life tends to merge with the higher will. The sense of purpose which is experienced as a "check" on morally destructive impulse becomes a feeling of acting in consonance with one's own true humanity. The result of thus having brought one's character into harmony with a transcendent principle, Babbitt and Aristotle agree, is happiness. This is the affirmative, "positive" side of the moral life. Even here, however, there is justification for using the term "the inner check" to describe man's higher will, for human acts are never identical to what gives them ethical direction. Higher than particular instances of moral behavior, higher even than man's most noble acts, is the ultimate standard of perfection itself. The tension between immanent and transcendent is never completely removed.[12]

II

Granted that self-discipline of some kind is necessary if man is not to get lost in complete chaos, must not that discipline be tied to some outside standard, external to man himself? The principle of moral order, Babbitt contends, is found within the human self. But without an external image of perfection, does not that self-discipline have to be exercised at random? Throwing up his arms in puzzlement, T. S. Eliot exclaims, "What is the higher will to *will*. . . ? If this will is to have anything on which to operate, it must be in relation to external objects and to objective values."[13] Eliot is familiar with Babbitt's view that in its humanistic dimension the inner check is "a will to civilization," but he has great difficulty finding any definite meaning in this idea. Babbitt's "civilization" appears to leave the goal of life an empty form.

> It seems, on the face of it, to mean something definite; it is, in fact, merely a frame to be filled with definite objects, not a definite object itself. I do not believe that I can sit down for three minutes to will civilization without my mind's wandering to something else. I do not mean that civilization is a mere word; the word means something quite real. But the minds of the individuals who can be said to "have willed civilization" are minds filled with a great variety of objects of will, according to place, time, and individual constitution; what they have in common is rather a habit in the same direction than a will to civilization.[14]

This passage is clear evidence that Eliot has not grasped the meaning of Babbitt's "inner check." Ironically, Babbitt would agree almost completely with these sentences, which Eliot believes to be a refutation of his position. Babbitt wholeheartedly agrees that civilization is marked by the diversity of emphasis and perspective of those who contribute to it. What

joins those who will civilization is indeed "a habit in the same direction." Babbitt would say that it is a habit which brings unity into a multiplicity of activity. Eliot's mistake is in opposing to this "habit" what Babbitt calls "the will to civilization." What he does not see is that civilization as Babbitt understands it is defined by the quality of will which brings it into existence, namely, "the inner check." This unifying ethical activity is equally well described as "a habit in the same direction."

Perhaps we may best explain "the inner check" as a certain spirit in which men can act. Ethically speaking, there are two ways of structuring conduct. The immoral one is to insist on one's own private advantage or the advantage of one's own group to the detriment of everybody else. A special case of the same basic category of action is to seek one's own advantage in an enlightened manner. The intelligent egotist is willing to compromise with others as a means of securing his own maximum satisfaction over time. The other way to act, the moral way, is to seek to rise above mere personal or group advantage and bias. We are referring to the genuine wish (in the sense of a "divine discontent") to transcend all partisanship. The two ways of human action are thus defined in contradistinction to each other. There is action that is motivated by the self in man which puts individuals and groups in conflict with each other, and there is action inspired by that other self which tends to bring men into harmony with all who are similarly motivated. It is the spirit of the latter, supra-individual self that Babbitt gives the name "the inner check."

It should perhaps be added that in viewing the inner check as the spiritually unifying principle of civilization Babbitt is not denying that there are other aspects of the civilizing effort than the purely moral. His point is that the final measure of the success of this effort is the extent to which the various pursuits of the good society, such as science, literature, art, and politics, advance the moral end.

The goal of civilization stays forever indefinite or "open" in the sense that the higher will is manifested in the unique circumstances of emerging situations. In another sense, however, the end is *not* indefinite. All truly moral acts are performed in one and the same spirit. Man's higher self wills the special quality of life which can be created when selfishness is restrained. Civilization refers to something quite definite: the good life of community. But the particulars of that quality of life depend on the circumstances out of which the higher will is trying to shape good. It does not work in the abstract, but on the concrete material of given situations. The nobility of its creations is likely to be enhanced by its being able to work in the context of sound tradition. Although the individual is never saved from moral perplexity by such favorable conditions, but has to create his own moral synthesis out of the unique situation facing him, that synthesis is helped along by the general directives contained in the inherited norms of his society. His attempt to articulate ethical intuition can draw on previous attempts to give definite human form to man's sense of higher purpose. In a genuinely civilized society, tradition enriches the individual's moral imagination.[15] Eliot has not understood that the will to civilization is actually a transcendent spirit in which man creates new behavior. It is itself the "external" standard for which he sees a need. It is "external" in that it transcends all individual circumstances and in that it is never exhausted by human action.

One particularly misleading rendering of Babbitt's thought, which has been reprinted several times, has been offered by Allen Tate. Babbitt's morality, Tate alleges, "is only an arbitrarily individualistic *check upon itself.* . . ."[16] This interpretation does nothing less than turn Babbitt's ideas upside down. T. S. Eliot, too, although reading Babbitt in a more sympathetic frame of mind, is suspicious of his view that the human has its own intrinsic standard of perfection which can be ascertained without relying on "outer" authority, such as Church doctrine. This, Eliot argues, is an invitation to arbitrariness. The source of order must be outside the individual:

> The sum of a population of individuals, all ideally and efficiently checking and controlling themselves, will never make a whole. And if you distinguish so sharply between "outer" and "inner" checks as Mr. Babbitt does, then there is nothing left for the individual to check himself by but his own private notions and his judgment, which is pretty precarious.[17]

Babbitt would agree completely that there is always a tendency in man to act according to his own "private notions" and thus with an egocentrical bias. What Eliot does not see is that *it is on precisely this inclination that the higher will is a check.* To the extent that it is exercised, therefore, it does have the effect of turning "a population of individuals" into "a whole." ". . . the individual who is practising humanistic control is really subordinating to the part of himself which he possesses in common with other men, that part of himself which is driving him apart from them."[18] Those who take on that discipline are harmonizing their lives with reference to the same center of value and moving toward communion.

III

The main reason why it is difficult for Eliot and some other Christians to understand Babbitt's idea of the inner check is that they are accustomed to thinking of the ultimate principle of good as the will of a personal God set apart from the human. Babbitt is perfectly willing to grant that this ultimate standard is external to man in the sense of his "ordinary" or "natural" self. He ranges himself "unhesitatingly on the side of the supernaturalists."[19] But the human, Babbitt argues, is *not* just man's "ordinary" self. To be a man is to be able to impose order on the flux, most importantly to give moral structure to life. Traditional Christianity maintains, and Protestantism with particular emphasis, that it is by God's grace that man is able to rise out of sin. No one could insist more than Babbitt that within the context of Christianity the doctrine of grace is indispensable to the moral life. When speaking within that framework he even equates his own notion of the higher will with grace.[20] But he is also interested in the religions of the Far East and trying to find a common denominator. For that reason he usually prefers to speak about the higher will without emphasizing the Christian interpretation of it. His ambition is to establish the reality of the fact itself without referring to dogmatic formulations based in part on revelation. Whether it is by the grace of a personal God or some other factor that man is able to temper his egocentrical inclinations, his having that ability is an irrefutable fact. If the ethical will were not in some sense *in* man, it would be nonsensical to speak of him as a moral being. Whatever else the capacity for self-discipline may be, it is part of man's knowledge of himself. It helps to define the human.

Some Christians have been disturbed by Babbitt's philosophy of humanism because it seems to build up man at the expense of God. And yet Babbitt repeatedly argues that humanistic self-discipline is grounded in the very opposite of spiritual arrogance. Man's higher will, he argues, transcends the individual and humbles him by holding out the image of his own perfection. If the two Christians, Eliot and Tate,[21] had really understood his moral philosophy, one may doubt that they would have regarded it as a threat to religion. They failed to grasp that Babbitt's "inner check" refers to the same intuition of higher destiny which Christianity has given a certain theological formulation calling it "the will of God" or "the Holy Spirit." Babbitt differs from many Christians, firstly, in that he is primarily interested in the manifestations of this higher will insofar as it relates to the good life on this earth, and, secondly, in that he wants to establish its existence and compelling nature without having recourse to revelation. A person may reject Christian dogma, but there is no way, short of obscurantism, to deny the spiritual reality itself for which dogma offers an interpretation. "The Holy Spirit" is something known by man in immediate experience. It is because it is in a sense *in* man, that he can act in its spirit.

It should be carefully noted that in emphasizing the humanistic dimension of the inner check Babbitt is not playing down the importance of religion. He always seeks to relate humanism to what is above it. Much of his writing is devoted to defining the level of religion.[22] His reason for giving most of his attention to outlining the elements of humanistic discipline is his belief that "the world would have been a better place if more persons had made sure they were human before setting out to be superhuman."[23] To be civilized is difficult enough, indeed, frequently has proved too difficult even for those who have had at their disposal the guidance of sound tradition.

I differ from the Christian ... in that my interest in the higher will and the power of veto it exercises over man's expansive desires is humanistic rather than religious. I am concerned, in other words, less with the meditation in which true religion always culminates, than in the mediation or observance of the law of measure that should govern man in his secular relations.[24]

As humanistic discipline, the inner check establishes the rule of justice, *i.e.,* those conditions which make for social and individual harmony, "but it may be carried much further until it amounts to a turning away from the desires of the natural man altogether—the 'dying to the world' of the Christian."[25] The first concern of religion is otherworldliness. "My kingdom is not of this world." As we have indicated, Babbitt regards these two aspirations as mutually supportive. The values of humanistic discipline and religion "are after all only different stages in the same ascending 'path' and should not be arbitrarily separated."[26] The law of charity in which religion culminates is the highest manifestation of the inner check. The law of justice applies only to the creation and maintenance of the good life on this earth. Given the flawed nature of man this means something much less than turning the other cheek or walking the extra mile.

IV

Those who have not with sufficient intensity experienced the sense of higher purpose which is known to most men in some degree will forever dispute its final reality, claiming that there are only subjective standards of good. For those, on the other hand, who seek to exercise that special quality of will, life is a steady growth in the hold on life and in happiness. To them, the denial of the reality of the higher self becomes the height of unreality. According to a central tenet in Babbitt's thought, all moral theories will ultimately have to be judged by the fruits they bring forth. Sound principles are validated by the spiritual harmony they afford the individuals who follow them. Spurious moral theories are revealed as such by not keeping what they promise when put to practice. To those who doubt the intrinsic value of civilization Babbitt would say: If you are not willing to accept on authority the superiority of certain principles of life, which would save you much time and disillusionment, then judge for yourself the fruits of the programme of private advantage and the programme of ethical self-control.

Against the modern positivist who is preoccupied with studying the world of physical objects and trying to reduce man to the same level of explanation, Babbitt urges "a more complete positivism." Let us indeed be true to the facts, but not just some partial array of evidence. One dimension of experience is man's "inner life," including moral experience. This aspect of life is arbitrarily ignored by many modern scholars. According to Babbitt, "the proper procedure in refuting these incomplete positivists is not to appeal to some dogma or outer authority but rather to turn against them their own principles."[27]

The modernists have broken with tradition partly because it is not sufficiently immediate, partly because it is not sufficiently experimental. Why not meet them on their own ground and, having got rid of every ounce of unnecessary metaphysical and theological baggage, oppose to them something that is both immediate and experimental— namely the presence in man of a higher will or power of control? I use the word experimental deliberately by way of protest against the undue narrowing of this word by the scientific naturalists to observation of the phenomenal order and of man only in so far as he comes under this order.[28]

Our "inner life" warrants attention even more than physical nature, for its reality is more securely established in experience than anything else. It is more immediately known to us than the subject-matter of physical science.

> According to Mr. Walter Lippmann, the conviction the modern man has lost is that "there is an immortal essence presiding like a king over his appetites." But why abandon the affirmation of such an "essence," or higher will, to the mere traditionalist? Why not affirm it first of all as a psychological fact, one of the immediate data of consciousness, a perception so primordial that, compared with it, the deterministic denials of man's moral freedom are only a metaphysical dream? One would thus be in a position to perform a swift flanking movement on the behaviourists and other naturalistic psychologists who are to be regarded at present as among the chief enemies of human nature.[29]

Babbitt wants to retain the modern emphasis on referring questions of truth and falsehood to practical verification, but only after having broadened it to take in the specifically human type of experience. "The supreme maxim of the ethical positivist is: By their fruits shall ye know them."[30] The existence of the higher will as a self-justifying principle of conduct is conclusively demonstrated by acting on it.

Babbitt would like to be as "experimental" as possible also when dealing with the divine. As against those who would associate religion very closely with dogma, he wonders "whether one's religiousness is to be measured by the degree to which one brings forth the 'fruits of the spirit' or by one's theological affirmations."

> If one maintains that the theological affirmations are a necessary preliminary to bringing forth the fruits, early Buddhism (not to speak of other non-Christian faiths) supplies evidence to the contrary. If I had indeed to give an opinion, I should say . . . that Buddhism has had as many saints as Christianity and that it has, moreover, been less marred than Christianity by intolerance and fanaticism.[31]

Babbitt's point of view in regard to religion may be summed up in these words: "Knowledge in matters religious waits upon will."[32]

It would be a mistake to regard Babbitt's view of religion as anti-dogmatic. He is quite willing to admit that more can be true in spiritual matters than can be positively verified in general human experience. His ambition is to articulate what the great religious and ethical systems have in common. They have all emerged, he argues, in response to one and the same intuition of transcendent purpose. In the West, one of the most pressing tasks is to find the bond between men of different religious denominations and those who, while friendly to religion, have not found it possible to embrace a particular theology. They can be joined ecumenically against the forces destructive of civilization. If Christianity is losing its hold in the West, it may still be possible to save many of the values it has articulated and supported. For those who are ultimately concerned about reviving religion, the first step ought to be to promote the kind of elementary spiritual discipline without which all spiritual values are threatened. There is no pressing need for the humanist to take sides decisively between competing theological claims. For his purposes, Babbitt prefers to leave open the question of the theological rendering of that divine reality into which the ascending path of morality tends to bring the individual.

V

Irving Babbitt's call for "a more complete positivism" that encompasses man's "inner" life offers a challenge to those who pride themselves on accepting as true what can be verified in concrete experience. Since Babbitt is broadening the meaning of the term "experience" in relation to how it is used by modern empiricists, there is no guarantee that his approach will make a dent in the positivistic armor. But it would seem that the time is ripe for a fundamental questioning of the modern tendency to submerge the human in the world of objects postulated by natural science. Babbitt is suggesting a way out of scientism. He proposes a new sensitivity to the nature of specifically human experience while trying to take over what is valid in the modern commitment to critical inquiry.

Although Babbitt's attempt to focus attention on the facts of man's inner life merits careful study, it also suffers from some weaknesses which need to be remedied. We may refer briefly to his shortcomings in the field of logic. In spite of the fact that Babbitt's outlook is centered in a dualistic interpretation of life, he never comes very close to discovering the existence of the dialectical philosophical reason which alone is adequate for dealing with the paradox of self-experience.

The person who is familiar only with modern symbolic logic or the old schoolbook logic of Aristotle is likely to object that in Babbitt's moral theory the assumption that man is a unity of two selves is a case of blatant self-contradiction. How could man be at once a higher and a lower self? He would have to be either one and the same or some sort of split personality, living now in the one self and then in the other, which is nonsense. What can be said against this objection is that Babbitt's view of human nature develops a theme as old as human self-knowledge. Among the philosophers, Plato emphasizes the tension inside the soul. Among the religious sages, St. Paul espouses a similar dualistic view: "For the good that I would I do not: but the evil which I would not, that I do. Now if I do that I

would not, it is no more I that do it, but sin that dwelleth in me."[33] This paradoxical use of the word "I" has forced itself on men in all ages. What it indicates is that man *is* a tension between incompatible wills. The recognition of this fact is reflected in our everyday way of speaking about ourselves. "I am not myself." "I did not want to do it." What appears to the formalistic modern logicians to be a contradictory use of the word "I" is still a statement of fact. The objection by symbolic logic to dualistic moral philosophy is dispelled by reality itself. Apparently its type of reason is not equipped to handle the facts of self-experience. It may be well-suited to dealing pragmatically with a world of objects, but about the world of the specifically human it can say nothing. What is needed in order to give a faithful account of immediate experience is a dialectical logic, one that does not deny the paradox of the human self, but simply *thinks* it. Babbitt does use such a logic when he develops his ethical theory, but this fact is never brought to full philosophical awareness. "Reason" for Babbitt connotes reifying, pragmatic rationality, that is, the kind of logic which cuts up reality into separate objects. This explains his dissatisfaction with it as a means of ethical inquiry. It also explains why he feels a need to give another name to the knowledge by which we grasp the paradox of our being. He calls it "intuition."

In a certain sense, Babbitt is quite justified in regarding our perception of moral reality as something other than rational knowledge. Before we can formulate a philosophical concept of "the ethical" we must somehow know its referent in concrete experience. To act morally is not to philosophize, but to create new reality. The role of philosophy is to examine the nature of what has been willed. But in another sense Babbitt is not correct when he looks at ethical insight as a non-rational process. Reason does have a role to play beyond the one he assigns to it. Babbitt's own examination of the moral life is an attempt to give a theoretical account of the facts. Although his various arguments seek verification by an appeal to our actual moral experience, he is also developing *concepts*, such as "the inner check," "the lower self," "humanistic discipline," etc. By what theoretical process does he formulate these concepts? Their source is not reifying reason. They are based on a type of thought which does not treat the subject-matter of self-experience as a collection of "things," but as what it is, an irreducible paradox. Although not fully aware of it, Babbitt is using the reason of philosophy.

It is not possible here to outline the elements of a dialectical logic and show how it is appropriate to the duality of life. Our purpose is only to indicate one area in which Babbitt's thought is deficient. It would be unfair to blame him for not having explicitly incorporated into his moral theory the kind of logic which is its natural supplement. Very few thinkers in the twentieth century, even among the professional philosophers, have discovered it. Babbitt does deserve credit for seeing that reason, as understood by his contemporaries, cannot accommodate the facts of self-experience. His rejection of pragmatic rationality as a tool of spiritual insight is an important step toward a sound ethical philosophy. Still, his legitimate reaction against the exaggerated claims of reifying reason, because not balanced by recognition of another, genuinely philosophical kind of thought, pushes him further in the direction of "intuitionism" than is necessitated by the truths he is trying to convey. If Babbitt had seen that philosophy has the means of bridging, although not closing, the gap between theory and practice, he would not have felt quite the same need to reduce

the pretensions of the intellect. He would have been in a position to rest his case for the higher will, not just on "affirmation," but on philosophic-scientific *reasoning*. Discovery of dialectical logic might have transformed Babbitt from a philosophically very important literary scholar to a philosopher in the full sense of the word. As coupled with a new logic, his position offers a powerful challenge to morally relativistic or nihilistic pseudo-science in the humanities and social sciences.[34]

VI

Our analysis of Babbitt's idea of humanism has left important questions unanswered. What may be hoped is that our remarks will help to dispel some awkward interpretations of his thought which have probably been an obstacle to renewed scholarly interest in his work. It would be unfortunate indeed if analysis of Babbitt's ideas did not move beyond the rather sterile debate about humanism which took place in the twenties and thirties. That debate somehow never got down to a careful examination of his real position. Much of the time it revolved around what he was mistakenly *supposed* to have said. In addition, most of his critics *asserted* the invalidity of his ideas rather than *argued* against them.

There is a right way and a wrong way to deal with Babbitt's work as with that of any serious thinker. The proper question for scholars to ask would appear to be: Do Babbitt's various concepts faithfully account for the facts of human experience? In other words: Is he providing a scientific analysis of life? The wrong way of dealing with Babbitt's ideas, so much in evidence in the twenties and thirties, would be to judge them on the basis of whether they happen to conform to one's own favorite preconception of truth. If there is any point in studying him, it would have to be that he might have something original to offer. It does not advance philosophical scholarship for positivists, for instance, to attack him because his notion of a "fact" is different from the empirico-quantitative. It must be shown instead exactly how he fails to do justice to the facts of the human. It would be equally fruitless to complain that Babbitt fails to endorse some particular religious dogma, unless that complaint can be stated in the form of a philosophical challenge. It is incumbent on the critic to show just how he violates the available evidence. The pertinent question is if he can be refuted *on scientific grounds*. Revelation and philosophical proof, it should be remembered, are different things.

NOTES

[1] This statement of scholarly need should not be confused with the proposal, much in vogue at the present time, to infuse the various disciplines with so-called "value-preferences" in order to make up for scientific indifference to burning moral questions. A cacophony of subjectively derived "value-commitments" is precisely what is not needed.

[2] Among those who should be commended for trying to draw attention to Babbitt as a social thinker in the last decades are Russell Kirk and Peter Viereck. See, for instance, Kirk's *The Conservative Mind* (New York: Avon Books, 1968), pp. 399–411, and Viereck's *Conservatism* (New York: Van Nostrand, 1956), pp. 104–105. There are many others who have been deeply influenced by Babbitt but who have chosen not to acknowledge formally their intellectual debt. Among the most distinguished are Richard Weaver and Walter Lippmann. Weaver's master's thesis, "The Revolt Against Humanism," was accepted by Vanderbilt University in 1933. His various books, for instance, *Ideas Have Consequences* (Chicago: The University of Chicago Press, 1948), show the unmistakable traces of Babbitt's ideas. Babbitt's influence on Lippmann, a former student of his at Harvard, is discernible, for instance, in *The Public Philosophy* (New York: Mentor Books, 1955), especially chapters 7–11.

[3] Irving Babbitt, "Humanism: An Essay at Definition," in Norman Foerster, ed., *Humanism and America* (Port Washington, N.Y.: Kennikat Press, 1967; first published 1930), pp. 43–44. This essay suffers from some of the weaknesses of Babbitt's writing, but it is still useful in understanding his position.

[4] Irving Babbitt, *Rousseau and Romanticism* (New York: The World Publishing Company, 1955; originally published in 1919), p. 7 (emphasis in original).

[5] Babbitt, "Humanism: An Essay at Definition," p. 40.

[6] Irving Babbitt, *Democracy and Leadership* (New York: Houghton Mifflin Company, 1952; originally published in 1924), p. 6.

[7] *Ibid.*, p. 6.

[8] *Ibid.*, p. 229.

[9] Edmund Wilson, "Notes on Babbitt and More," in C. Hartley Grattan, ed., *The Critique of Humanism* (New York: Brewer and Warren, 1930), p. 46.

[10] Allen Tate, "The Fallacy of Humanism," in *ibid.*, p. 141.

[11] Henry Hazlitt, "Humanism and Value," in *ibid.*, p. 95 (emphasis in original).

[12] A more extensive analysis of "the inner check" as happiness is given in my own forthcoming, *Democracy and the Ethical Life* (LSU Press).

[13] T. S. Eliot, *Selected Essays* (New York: Harcourt, Brace, 1960), p. 425 (emphasis in original). Eliot's various criticisms of Babbitt should not conceal that he was also profoundly impressed and influenced by Babbitt as a thinker and as a person. A former student of his at Harvard, Eliot has commented as follows on Babbitt's forceful, idea-oriented instruction and work as a whole: "I do not believe that any pupil who was ever deeply impressed by Babbitt can ever speak of him with that mild tenderness one feels towards something one has outgrown or grown out of. If one has once had that relationship with Babbitt, he remains permanently an active influence; his ideas are permanently with one, as a measurement and test of one's own." From a memoir by T. S. Eliot in Frederick Manchester and Odell Shepard, eds., *Irving Babbitt, Man and Teacher* (New York: Greenwood Press, 1969), p. 104.

[14] T. S. Eliot, *Selected Essays*, p. 426.

[15] The moral imagination is a central and original concept in Babbitt's thought which would deserve separate treatment. Praising Edmund Burke, Babbitt writes: "He saw how much of the wisdom of life consists in an imaginative assumption of the experience of the past in such fashion as to bring it to bear as a living force upon the present. The very model that one looks up to and imitates is an imaginative creation. A man's imagination may realize in his ancestors a standard of virtue and wisdom beyond the vulgar practice of the hour; so that he may be enabled to rise with the example to whose

imitation he has aspired." Babbitt, *Democracy and Leadership*, pp. 103–104.

[16] Allen Tate, "The Fallacy of Humanism," p. 145 (emphasis in original). This essay cannot be considered one of Tate's better efforts. It compares unfavorably with interpretations of Babbitt offered by other Catholic writers.

[17] Eliot, *Selected Essays*, p. 424.

[18] Babbitt, "Humanism: An Essay at Definition," p. 49.

[19] *Ibid.*, p. 39.

[20] See the introduction to Irving Babbitt, *On Being Creative* (New York: Biblo and Tannen, 1968; first published in 1932).

[21] Ironically, although Tate attacked Babbitt in the name of Christianity, he was only nominally a Christian when he wrote what has been quoted. On the subject of Tate's religious development, see Monroe Spear, "The Criticism of Allen Tate," in Radcliffe Squires, ed., *Allen Tate and His Work* (Minneapolis: University of Minnesota Press, 1972).

[22] Babbitt has even contributed an English translation from Pāli of one of the original Buddhist holy texts, *The Dhammapada*, translated and with an *Essay on Buddha and the Occident* by Irving Babbitt (New York: New Directions Books, 1965; originally published in 1936).

[23] Babbitt, "Humanism: An Essay at Definition," pp. 28–29.

[24] Babbitt, *Democracy and Leadership*, p. 6.

[25] Babbitt, "Humanism: An Essay at Definition," p. 47.

[26] *Ibid.*, p. 41.

[27] Babbitt, *Rousseau and Romanticism*, p. 5.

[28] Babbitt, "Humanism: An Essay at Definition," pp. 44–45.

[29] *Ibid.*, p. 39.

[30] Babbitt, *Rousseau and Romanticism*, p. 9.

[31] Babbitt, *On Being Creative*, pp. xxxiii–xxxiv.

[32] Babbitt, *The Dhammapada*, p. 109.

[33] *Romans*, 7:19–20.

[34] The most sophisticated attempt to develop the logic of self-knowledge would seem to be the work of Benedetto Croce, especially *Logic as the Science of the Pure Concept* (London: Macmillan, 1917). Croce avoids most of the extravagant and highly dubious metaphysical extrapolations in Hegel. It should also be stressed that Croce's dialectical logic can be divorced from his questionable monistic assumptions which amount to a denial of the reality of evil. For a perceptive attempt to apply Crocean logic to ethical dualism, see Folke Leander, *The Inner Check* (London: Edward Wright, 1974).

[XXI, Summer 1977, 251–262]

[19]

Paul Elmer More and the Redemption of History

BYRON C. LAMBERT

Byron C(ecil) Lambert (1923–   ) is professor of philosophy at Fairleigh Dickinson University and an ordained minister. Cofounder of the C. S. Lewis Society, he is a member of a large number of professional associations and has contributed many articles and reviews to serious and scholarly publications. He is the author of The Essential Paul Elmer More *(1972),* The Rise of the Anti-Mission Baptists *(1980), and* The Recovery of Reality *(1980).*

PAUL ELMER MORE is forgotten today. In spite of one or two recent studies,[1] one seldom sees a sentence or even a footnote devoted to this greatest of conservative and classical critics of the early twentieth century.

It would not matter very much to him. As T. S. Eliot said of him, here was "the concentrated mind seeking God . . . analyzing the disease and aberrations of humanity, but too intent ever to care to display mere intellectual brilliance, and too patient ever to feel any petty irritation and impatience with a mischievous and inattentive world."[2]

From the earliest essays in the eleven volumes of the *Shelburne Essays* to the last chapters of *The Greek Tradition*, More sought to establish those permanent principles upon which literature and civilization could rest.[3] As the years went by, More found his Platonism being transformed into Christian faith; for him the ancient Hellenic experience was as much a *preparatio evangelica* as was the Hebraic.

Two themes dominate More's thought. One is *dualism*, the central conception from which all his thinking starts and the theme which controls all of his critical work, social philosophy, and historical writing. This dualism is candidly Platonic, in which the two polar elements of being are the *One* (felt in the personal sense of identity and continuity), and the *Many* (felt as a sense of multiplicity and discontinuity). The other controlling conception is that of *teleologism*, the idea that the universe is based upon *purpose* and that there is an end, or "telos," toward which both nature and history tend. The second theme appears later in More's writings and grows in importance as his thought matures, although it has been implicit in his dualism all along. More reduces knowledge to "what we possess in the form of immediate affections."[4] The "affections" are of two kinds: (a) the "objective" sensations we have when looking at or touching an object, and (b) the "subjective" feelings, like pleasure, grief, love, or self-approval. Both kinds of knowing, More holds, are irreducible. They are the ultimate data of experience beyond which knowledge cannot go. The ability to distinguish knowledge from thoughts about knowledge, or theory, is for More the mark of the finished mind, or as he would say, the complete sceptic.[5]

Knowledge itself, however, is divisible into that of the affections themselves and the other, a scarcely distinguishable "check," or inhibition, which inserts itself between an affection and the impulsive response. This subtle concentration of the self, this "Inner Check," as More called it, lifts the self in the direction of "the One," while outside the self and now clearly distinguishable from it are the swarming impulses, the chaotic sensations on the periphery of consciousness, and the crowding confusion of the surrounding world—"the Many."[6]

The duality which More found in himself he found also in the universe. In the commingled flux and order of nature he saw the same two principles struggling with each other for mastery: the superior centripetal power, holding both the stars and the atoms in their orbits, and by its regularity bearing witness to an overarching design in its activity; and the inferior centrifugal power, always pulling away from control toward the abyss—the force of negation, dark, formless, resistant to design, indefinable, "the disorder underlying all order."[7] In its largest sense, "the One" More associated with the Divine Being.

To that sludge which blocks or resists the will in the personal life More gave the Greek name, *rhathymia*—slackness, inattention, and the willingness to drift aimlessly.

. . . The last discoverable source of evil in the soul [is] . . . that slackness which succumbs to the fatigue of holding fast to higher things and turns to the ease and comfort of change, the vanity that flatters us into believing we have no other end than to be ourselves and to follow our inclinations. Slackness and vanity, these together are the dark remote origin of our guilt; they are the cause of our fall, and then of the misbehavior of the soul amid the trials which it has brought upon itself, whereby it is plunged ever deeper into the abyss of evil.[8]

Human history was just this agony to surmount the residual chaos of nature and bring the ideal down to earth and into life. The various codes of law, the sacred myths and customs, the universal longing for a golden age now passed away,[9] all bore testimony to the existence of an Upper World, a realm of transcendent ideals, as Plato expressed it, which holds us in its charge and after which we fashion our own imperfect models of personal and social order.[10] What is the theme of Sophocles's *Oedipus* but the stark moral responsibility of man and his inability to understand why he has it?

More summed up human experience in the sorrowful words he used repeatedly: "We are intellectually incompetent and morally responsible; that would appear to be the last lesson of life."[11]

I

For More, history's Himalayan peaks were in the far past, the lofty central range of events occurring between 400 B.C. and A.D. 400. The revolution of thought that came with Socrates, always taken together with the towering expositions of that thought in Plato; the incarnation of the Word for those few years in Palestine; and the formulation of a creed expressive of the wisdom of the early Church fathers at Chalcedon: these were the Everests of history's great divide. Summits of magnificent height glow lower on the distant horizon—the ages of Homer, of Moses, and of Buddha—but they only lead to the higher moments, they are not the consummative moments themselves.

Below these pinnacles of history More saw crowded foothills, sudden chasms, wandering valleys, and misty swamps. The upper light was clear enough in the landscape, but darkness obscured the better part of it, like a Doré landscape of the inferno. The undulating shadows had an explanation. Man, never content with the truths of his duality, always had to be thrashing out some "new" explanation for his suffering—for God, evil, accident, and the indifference of nature—another "final" answer which would put the cursed contradictions into a flawless, logical unity. In order to fashion this monism he had to omit or compromise one or the other of the two factors in the duality of existence; he would find, for example, by suppressing the reality of the empirical world, that the cosmos was a kind of glorified mathematics extrapolated out of an irresistible Absolute; or he would find by looking past the permanent attributes of the spiritual world that the universe was an improbable accident drifting aimlessly into a pointless future.

Looking back over history More saw several periods when man's rage either to over-rationalize on the one hand or to surrender to impulse on the other had formed spiritual swamps, from whence poisonous intellectual rivulets flowed to the perpetual pollution of the human spirit and civilization. One of these dank tarns was the ancient Alexandrian era (A.D. 50–400).

After Plato, Greek philosophy slipped back with astonishing speed into one or another kind of rationalistic monism. Explanations which profess to unify the material and the spiritual into one grand system of thought have always appealed to human beings. Spice such metaphysics with mystery and superstition, and one has a formula for instant and widespread popular acceptance. Such was the appeal of Neoplatonism and Gnosticism.[12] With Plotinus the First Cause ceased to be the Father of creation, as had been true with Plato, and became "a naked nucleus of mechanical necessity" without heart, will, or sight, and out of which the cosmos drops down, sphere by sphere, into the bosom of Vacuity.[13] Here in Plotinian absolutism, asserts More, is the seedbed of every variety of Western mysticism, from Augustine to J. A. Symonds.[14] Classical civilization was crumbling, and Plotinus offered a way of escape for the troubled minds of his time.[15] He promised that through an intellectual ascent the soul could pass from this world of disordered passions up through the planes of discursive (and dismaying) reasoning and out of its own activity into the Final Vision of the Absolute, where all was peace.[16] Philo Judaeus was equally implicated in the transformation of Platonism into mysticism, and most of the philosophical Fathers of the Church were influenced by him, especially Origen and Clement of Alexandria.[17] The sink of ancient spirituality was Gnosticism, that deathbed whereon all the myths of Oriental and Occidental antiquity crowded together for a last convulsion.[18] Portentous for modern history, however, and the worst of the persisting delusions to emerge from this era, was romanticism, that thing wrought of Greek egoism and the Oriental idea of infinity as an "escape" from dependence upon the finite. Here was the origin of the "insatiable personality" with its extravagant passions, its craving for whatever is unlimited, its self-torment and "confusion of the sensuous and the spiritual," illustrated in the heresy of Valentinus, the tales of idealized love, and the romantic epic going back as far as Apollonius of Rhodes, one of the masters of the library at Alexandria.[19] Entering into the bloodstream of Christianity, the romantic malady came to the surface first in the medieval idea of the infinite, especially in the monkish mysticism of Pseudo-Dionysius and St. John of the Cross; from thence the infection broke out in the rationalizations of the Scholastics, especially those of Duns Scotus and Occam.[20] Kept in check by orthodoxy and the occasional revivals of classical standards, romanticism was at times almost lost from view; only with the triumph of naturalism in the late seventeenth and the eighteenth centuries did it reassert its ancient hold over the imagination of man.

In the seventeenth century, especially in England, the imagination and the practical sense were divided into hostile camps.[21] Rationalistic science, begun by Bacon and Descartes and perfected by Aldravandus of Padua, Newton, and Locke, broke the hold of the supernatural, preparing the way for Hume in the eighteenth century to find morality entirely within nature.[22] The Puritans, surrendering imagination in religion for a hard, rationalistic piety, broke the hold of Christian sacramentalism and so paved the way for deism, atheism, and the watertight materialistic determinism which later arose in the nineteenth century.[23] Reason, no longer associable with any supernatural realm, began to be viewed only as another aspect of nature.[24] It was only to be expected that, in the eighteenth century, nature should become an intricately balanced machine, set in motion by a benevolent Deity, and left in its perfection to run by rational principles immanent in its structure. Whatever was left of the religious enthusiasm of the seventeenth century soon evaporated into the dry rationalism and pseudoclassicism of the age of Anne.[25]

There were two brave spirits of the seventeenth century who held a special place in More's affection because of their resistance to the science and naturalism of that age. The lesser of the two was Sir Thomas Browne, who wanted above all to reconcile the new science with the old religion and whose writings were for More an enchanting illustration of the triumph of the religious imagination over the tyranny of the senses and reason;[26] the greater of the two was Blaise Pascal, whose *Pensées* were in More's thought the purest expression of reasoned faith from that day to this.[27] Pascal had the power to make ideas living things, especially the idea of eternity, which, once man has caught a glimpse of it, he is "no longer content in the diversions of this life" and spends the remainder of his days yearning for the sight of God and immortality.[28] In a day of rampaging rationalism, Pascal and Browne secured the *heart*, meaning not the emotions alone, but the combination of reason and feeling in "the spirit of intention which is faith."[29]

Unfortunately for most men of the time, reason and feeling did not combine into an "*O Altitudo*" of religious certainty. The imagination, severed from tradition by science and sectarianism, was left the prey of that side of human nature neglected by both Puritan and Deist: the emotions. The human sense of the deep cleft within had been denied; now it was to be sublimated and falsified as a conflict between reason and the emotions and eventually externalized as a conflict between the individual and society. The romantic spirit, so long suppressed, now asserted itself again with a vengeance. The all-sufficient human ego, set free from the restraints of religion and encouraged in a militant expansiveness by the proud conquest of nature, soon saw itself as wholly a part of nature, unfolding with the growing universe into ever newer assertions of its unlimited powers. Once again the insatiable yearnings of ancient Alexandria were loosed upon the world, but now they were combined with a devotion to nature which could only end in abasement before the instincts. Philo and Plotinus had lost themselves in the One; the men of modern times were losing themselves in the Many.[30]

The steps downward should be taken in order. First came the liberation of the "feelings." The rationalistic revolution of the seventeenth and eighteenth centuries had equalized the positions of reason and emotion in man by making them both "natural." Superficially, reason appeared to be supreme; in fact, it was held to be a totally "natural" faculty, a product of nature and wholly within nature. Therefore, by an unexpected transposition, the "natural" feelings and instincts were put on an equal footing with the rational faculty and had only to assert their right to be attended to if they wanted to be heard, with the result that the door was left open for poets like Blake and rebels like Rousseau to raise the insubordination of impulse and unrestrained private feeling.[31] Blake lifted the revolt against the pseudoclassicism of the day in the name of a new spirituality, which was mistaken by many for a return to spiritual insight but in fact was only a capitulation to subrational impulses and wandering visions. The liberty of the Enlightenment passed quickly into the libertinism of the Romantic Movement, properly so called, which regarded human life as primarily an opportunity for the limitless expansion of the emotions.[32]

It was Rousseau, however, summing up in himself all of the elements opposing what was classical and humanistic and submitting them to the world as if entirely new, who sealed the fate of succeeding centuries. In *Émile*, Rousseau makes the aim of education the freeing of a child's instincts from the perverting control of schoolmaster and society and allowing them to develop "naturally." Starting with the assumption of the innate goodness of the natural man, Rousseau was forced to find man's corruption outside of himself; banishing the true dualism of the human spirit, he had to erect a false dualism between nature and civilization, between man and the state. Evil with Rousseau became a social phenomenon, a conspiracy of property and law against the freedom of the individual. In this view anyone who would escape the corruptions of the world would have to return to nature; only there could he find the sympathy denied him in society; there alone could he recover the peace and innocence missing among men and commune with the benign voices of field and brook. Reason had no share in this religion, except that of certifying the conviction that God was somehow in nature, united with her by a sympathy corresponding to that which human beings felt in her presence.

Hume transformed the world into a flux;[33] Berkeley identified world and idea, thus preparing the way for the romantic notion of the unlimited, fluctuating ego;[34] Adam Smith located the origin of virtue in sympathy;[35] and Rousseau said that the force of sympathy innate in mankind had to be called into action as the *volonté générale*, the embracing of the "desires of individuals into one harmonious purpose."[36]

The Romantic liberation of the feelings becomes for Rousseau the basis of a new social purpose, the feelings being harnessed to the *general will* for the good of all. The religion of nature, based on the subjective, by being changed into something "objective," becomes the religion of the state.[37] After Rousseau, when Romanticism passes from France into Germany, the doctrine of social sympathy becomes a chief doctrine of Romantic sentimentality and the basis of our modern ethics of humanitarianism.[38]

The arrival of humanitarianism, the doctrinaire organization of eighteenth-century sentimentalism, More saw as the second fateful step taken in the West toward our own times. Rousseau's double ethic of self-love and sympathy was eventually to culminate in the various forms of individualism and socialism of the nineteenth and twentieth centuries, both tendencies strangely cooperative despite their mutual repugnance. The extreme individualism practiced by the post-Romantics of Edwardian England, the French decadents, and the American realists combined easily with the socialism of the Marxists, the Fabians, and the Progressives on a platform of rebellion, which would result in our time as personal disorder, *ennui*, surrender to instinct, then to impulse, and finally to tyranny.

The rebels justified their principles on humanitarian grounds, and it is still humanitarianism which holds these disciples of egotism and brotherhood together.

Humanitarianism might not have been enough to keep the egotistical and collectivist tendencies from flying apart had not science come to her assistance. Essentially, humanitarianism was romantic self-pity translated into pity for all mankind, indeed for the whole of suffering nature. No longer directed from above by supernatural laws, men were to join each other in a spirit of fraternal love for bringing justice, peace, and plenty to the earth. Dominated by humanitarianism, men now looked to their feelings and impulses when they wished to make judgments, write poetry, or plan cities.[39] The result was moral and esthetic impressionism, surrender on a grand scale to the flux.[40] Rationalistic science, however it had appeared since Bacon's day to be preoccupied with empirical fact, and so excluding sentiment from the serious business of life, was nevertheless as much subservient to the law of change as were art and public sentiment. Forever experimenting, the scientist was always discovering new facts or new methods of organizing the facts; his "openness" to phenomenal change was a part of his approach to life. It was to be expected, therefore, when he turned to the humanities, that he would be the impressionist *par excellence*: "he simply carries into art the law of change with which he has dealt in his proper sphere, and acknowledges no principle of taste superior to the shifting pleasure of the individual."[41] Practical philosophy, which is in part the effort of reason to come to grips with the dominating spirit of an age in terms that the age can understand, followed science in finding only "an indefinite congeries of changes" (Dewey, Bergson, Whitehead) at the heart of the universe.[42] Personal whim and fellow-feeling now were sanctified by scientific "law" and the philosophical jargon of Pragmatism. Change was lord; the self was all-sufficient in things spiritual; sympathy and social experiment were the goals of society. The dogma of evolution had shown that the world had by its own innate powers developed man from a germ; why could it not be expected that man and his society would not also "progress" by unlimited experiment to an immeasurably beautiful future? And so humanitarianism, buttressed by science, was linked to a new doctrine of progress and sanctified by grandiose hopes. This was the third step leading to the immediate present.

We are commonly told, said More, that the distractions from which the men of the modern world suffer are the result of conflicting philosophies of life; but the case is otherwise. What we really see are the self-contradictions within a single philosophy which as certainly dominates the thought of men today as the Church did in the thirteenth century. Our innumerable isms all go back to the ism of Change because we have turned our minds to *things* and insisted "upon mastering nature by regarding ourselves as a part of nature." The result is that modern man has become a slave of the Absolute once again, this time absolute naturalism. Two philosophical currents flow from this overriding naturalism, seemingly contradictory, yet equally logical from the premises. The one stresses that the universe runs by an intricate system of self-perpetuating laws, all causally related and ostensibly decipherable were it not for man's limitations of life and energy. Contemporary sociopolitical philosophers call this view behaviorism, so far as it concerns man.[43] The other current of thought stresses the infinite accidentalness of nature and says that the universe is an incalculable flux of contingencies without plan or meaning. In this view man is merely a "passive channel for an ever-flowing stream of sensations."[44] In literature the first current gives us sentimental realism and the view of man as a helpless victim of overpowering hostile circumstances; it spawns social and political programs aimed at transforming man's environment instead of man himself; it nourishes hatred of the past and an unlimited number of adjustments to the present on the basis of what is momentarily most pleasant (or least painful); and it encourages an escape into the future as a relief from its own snares. The second current abandons man almost completely in order to focus attention on the units of impulse, instinct, and emotion which go to make up the man; man under this second view is not so much a victim as nothing at all; socially and esthetically, the viewpoint encourages abandonment to every passing impulse, escape from standards, expressionism, eccentricity for its own sake, Dadaism, the glorification of drift—the hippie movement.[45] The first

current tends to be epicurean and pessimistic; the second, hedonistic and nihilistic.[46] Both spring from monistic naturalism.

Of one thing More was sure: modern civilization would not survive an unbridled lust for change. At the present rate of their surrender to impulse, literature and art would simply cease to be. Thereafter social and economic order would disappear. Humanitarian socialism, far from being a bulwark against the war of all against all, would at least turn inward upon itself:

> In a world made up of passions and desires alone, the attempt to enter into the personal emotions of others will react in an intensifying of our own emotions, and the effort to lose one's self in mankind will be balanced by a morbid craving for the absorption of mankind in one's self. . . .[47]

Having tracked Western thought from Bacon through Rousseau and Darwin up to Dewey and Whitehead, More concludes:

> I should assert that our vacillating halfheartedness is the inevitable outcome of the endeavour, persistent since the naturalistic invasion of the Renaissance, to flee from the paradox of life to some philosophy of life which will merge, no matter how, the mechanical and the human together.[48]

II

For More, the chief failing of human thought throughout history was its habitual tendency to find "perfect" explanations for all of man's persistent problems. Using reason as an all-sufficient guide, men would construct first one philosophical system and then another in terms of either one or the other of the two modes of being, the One or the Many, in order to explain reality. Some systems based everything on motion, others were all for seeing reality as matter, still others held out for spirit, or energy, or Mind, and what not. The evil was not in using reason to make investigations; rather, it was the tendency to absolutize or even divinize the explanation of reason. It was one of the weaknesses of reason, said More, that it could not be content with approximate explanations of reality. In this respect the self-assertion of reason was only another aspect of man's self-destructive pride. What was needed was the leavening influence at all times of humility and commonsense, or "the Humility of Commonsense," as he titled one of his essays.[49]

> The rationalism I denounce has no affinity to the reasonableness of commonsense; it is rather just that defalcation of the reason to its own unreal abstractions which, obscuring the true function of the master faculty of our composite being, reduces the soul of man to a nonentity controlled by fatalistic law or to a puppet tossed in the winds of irresponsibility.[50]

"The Demon of the Absolute," More called this disturber of man's spirit: "reason run amok."[51] So long as it accepted the actual data of experience, reason was a guide and friend; but when it acted in disregard of factual matter and set up its own absolutes as truth it became delusory. The usurpations of reason constituted in More's mind the better part of the story of philosophy since the days of Heraclitus and Parmenides, who had set the wrangle going over whether ultimate reality were all unity and rest or all flux and multiplicity; it had been also the story in political history, he said, whenever men had attempted to set up the unchecked authority of the State, whether it be the tyrant or the people; it had been the case in religion when men were asked to choose between an Absolute Being who was causally connected to everything that had happened, good or evil, and no God at all; or when they were forced to choose between an infallible Church and un-

checked religious individualism.[52] In the days of Valentinus and Philo, religion was dressed in the mystical robes of idealized intellectual abstractions, and God was simply the highest, most unlimited abstraction of all; in the thirteenth century, the Church usurped infallible Papal authority to itself; in the seventeenth century, the fallacy transformed itself into an infallible Bible; in the eighteenth came infallible reason; in the nineteenth, infallible feeling, infallible nature, infallible science, infallible progress; and in the twentieth, infallible democracy and infallible change. There was always some system of rationalistic abstractions to seduce the pride of man and fix him in a new monism.

The paradox of the twentieth century was that the monism dominating the age was based on pluralism and relativism. The existentialism, pragmatism, and process philosophy of the age were only manifestations of the same old naturalism which had dominated men's minds since the seventeenth century. The spate of "liberated" moralists, "frank" fictionalists, "process" theologians, "progressive" educationalists, and ordinary people "doing what comes naturally"—what were they but instruments of the philosophy of change? And it was this divinization of change, this apotheosis of "the newest," this glorification of the flux, this deification of the teachers of relative values which constituted the new absolutism.[53]

This was dangerous enough, but added to the new absolutism was a phenomenon unique in human culture, making the modern situation perilous almost beyond remedy—the *enfeeblement of the imagination*.[54] Other cultures had been dominated by one absolute or another, but always there had been a respect for the past, some carry-over of wisdom from previous ages which had eventually helped to correct the life and thought of the time. For what was imagination in the high historical sense but "the indwelling of the past in the present?"[55] But the twentieth century seemed committed to the abandonment of its cultural heritage and the repudiation of everything but what concerned the immediate present or future.

More's doctrine of imagination is one of the most important categories of his thought and deserves brief attention in passing, particularly as it relates to his assessment of the twentieth century. He held that the American domination of modern culture was portentous, since as early as Franklin (who, he said, was the real father of the country), it was apparent that the American genius would be supereminently "practical," absorbed in problems of the present and the immediate future, and driven by a kind of unresting energy to tinker with the mechanico-empirical environment.[56] Morse, Edison, Ford, and Firestone were as much representative of the American imagination at one level as Dewey, Woodrow Wilson, and James Branch Cabell were at another. None of them had an ear for those remote voices murmuring the symbolic meaning of the puppet-actions of this world; none had any feeling for that obscuring shadow which hovers over the present out of the past and smiles ironically at the repetitious "originality" of men who have simply forgotten the lessons of history; not one had the power of visualizing the incorporeal and the eternal.[57]

The saddest feature of the American consciousness of the twentieth century was the absence of the religious side of this historical imagination: the power of seeing the dispersed fragments of reality under a unifying symbol of Divine guidance. Men, more than ever before, seemed incapable of recognizing that the solid-seeming phenomena of nature and empirical science "are but the shadow, too often distorted and misleading, of the

greater reality which resides within the observer himself." In their haste they had lost the power of subjecting the lesser to the greater and "of finding through the many that return to the one, which was the *esemplastic* function of the imagination."[58] Men must have that "sense of something other and different lurking beneath natural law" if their rationality is not to lead them into the quicksand. It was this inability, in Sir Thomas Browne's words, to teach "haggard and unreclaimed reason to stoop unto the lure of faith" which was dooming the modern world.[59]

World War I had been made possible, More argued, by liberals like Lord Morley, who had sanctioned the very forces which were destroying the traditions and values they claimed to be defending.[60] There was a new enslavement to the subhuman, all too evident in both the mechanized butchery of the war and the cynical emancipation of limitless animality in the years following it.[61] "The strange, unwilling brotherhood" of anarchic individualism and humanitarian collectivism, gotten up by Protestant socialists and Europe's proletarian intellectuals,[62] had been formed on the two principles most at work in society since the time of Rousseau, the *lust for power* and the *lust of irresponsibility*.[63] Even the modern university had sold out to the doctrines of power and human service.[64] The fear of God was now replaced with a debased fear, the fear of emptiness, of purposelessness, illustrated so vividly in the art of Proust,[65] Baudelaire,[66] and Joyce.[67] Modern men were educated in no exercise save that of thinking about themselves, "and in *le néant* beyond the phantasmagoria of unsatisfied and forever insatiable desires the only reality for them [was] the grinning figure of Fear."[68] Existentialism, as a popular term, had not come on the scene in More's day, but when More spoke of "the void, the nothingness" as being the prime immediate of contemporary metaphysics he had his finger on what was already there and soon to sprout a name.[69] In contemporary philosophy and art, More wrote in a moment of passionate visualization, "we appear to be adrift on a waste expanse of racing shadows" and the events through which we pass rise out of the storm "like isolated rocks" only to "melt into fluctuant forms like the waves that toss about them."[70]

Was there hope? If there was, it was only in the restoration of the religious imagination. While More at times permitted himself to dream about possible programs of action, he knew that civilization could not be saved or renewed without the restoration of a fundamental religiousness. God could not be driven from His universe, but men seemed bent on trying to forget Him. Never had pride exalted itself so stridently against the holy; never had the permanent things been so blasphemed. The collectivist principle, whose power lay in the universal sentimentality of the populace, was now dominant on so vast a scale, because of technical skills, as to constitute an entirely new kind of satanism on earth.

III

In his earlier years More had been content to propound a return to dualism as the answer to modern degeneracy;[71] ultimately he came to identify the "something permanent" with the Logos of the New Testament:

> To believe seriously in the otherworld of God and ideas, to lift the mind habitually to the contemplation of supernatural realities until it learns of a certainty that its home is there, to live in that realm wholeheartedly, yet without shrinking or denying the claims of nature, to centre the distracted will upon God as the King of righteousness, to see in this maze of gliding phenomena, or to know without seeing, the obscured presence of

veritable justice and beauty, to retain faith in a divine purpose at work within the world despite all the persuasions of infinite illusion, to take one's part valiantly in the eternal conflict of truth—that is not a light choice or a feeble task.[72]

More refused baptism and never took the communion in spite of his heavy emphasis on the Eucharist. He was content to rest, he said, in its potency over his imagination.[73]

> For if creation is a slow and painful redemption of the world of matter for spiritual ends, and if the Incarnation may be regarded as a summary act condensing in one tense moment the will and benevolence of the Creator, with all they cost, and by its appealing force bringing man back to a consciousness of his share in the glorious task; then the Eucharist may be taken as man's response to the appeal and as an enactment in human hands complementary to the divine drama that had its close on Calvary. We are here, already incarnate, soul and body, Word and flesh; it is for us, imitating our great exemplar, so to live in purity and holiness, in faith and charity, that the full man shall be made ready for enjoyment of the Ideal world. And in the invocation of the Holy Ghost upon the elements I see, as it were, an epitome of the religious life, a presentation in foreshortened form of the slow spiritualization of the flesh.[74]

"The slow spiritualization of the flesh." This is More's best summary of his own view of history. The Word had become flesh so that flesh could become Word. That "one intense moment" at the summit of human experience, when the will of the Creator was concentrated in the death and resurrection of the Nazarene, was the pledge of God's continued interaction with the upward longings of men and a promise of their own eventual redemption. Men are called to share in the glorious task of ransoming nature for spiritual ends.[75] This is their true purpose. Civilization is nothing, if it is not proof of this; culture

in the true sense has no meaning if it does not mean this; art, literature, and philosophy express this, or they express nothing to the point; and history is a nightmare, hope a bubble, if men are not gods in the making and if it is not their duty here below to trace the operations of the *Logos* in all of their duties and joys and to hold such truth "in fee for the generations to come."[76]

NOTES

[1] The latest and best is Francis X. Duggan's *Paul Elmer More*, in *Twayne's United States Authors Series*, #106 (New York: Twayne Publishers, Inc., 1966).

[2] T. S. Eliot, "Paul Elmer More," *Princeton Alumni Weekly*, February 5, 1937.

[3] There are eleven volumes in the first series of *The Shelburne Essays* (1905-1921); three in the second series, called *New Shelburne Essays* (1928-1936); four volumes in *The Greek Tradition: The Religion of Plato* (1921), *Hellenistic Philosophies* (1923), *The Christ of the New Testament* (1924), and *Christ the Word* (1927). *Platonism* (1917; rev. 1926) and *The Catholic Faith* (1931) are complementary works to *The Greek Tradition*. More was first literary editor and then editor of *The Nation* from 1906 to 1914 and wrote a critical column for the *Independent*, the New York *Evening Post*, and a score of periodicals. His many other writings include two volumes of poetry, an epistolary novel, an edition of Byron's works, a biography of Franklin, and the beautiful *Pages from an Oxford Diary*, published after his death in 1937.

[4] Paul Elmer More, *The Sceptical Approach to Religion. New Shelburne Essays*, Volume II (Princeton: Princeton University Press, 1934), 2. Hereafter *SAR*.

[5] Knowledge is limited to what we have, not by inference from something else, but directly and without the intervention of inferential reason." *Ibid.*, p. 1.

[6] For a full discussion of More's dualism, see "Definitions of Dualism," in his *The Drift of Romanticism. Shelburne Essays: Eighth Series* (New York: Phaeton Press, 1967), p. 245ff. The volumes in the *Shelburne Essays* will be referred to hereafter as *SE*, I, *SE*, II, etc.

[7] Paul Elmer More, *The Religion of Plato. The Greek Tradition*, Volume I (Princeton: Princeton University Press, 1921), p. 215. See also p. 205. Hereafter *RP*.

[8] Paul Elmer More, *Hellenistic Philosophies. The Greek Tradition*, Volume II (Princeton: Princeton University Press, 1923), p. 201. Hereafter *HP*.

[9] See More's "The Theme of 'Paradise Lost'," *SE*, IV, pp. 239-53. Also More's *The Christ of the New Testament. The Greek Tradition*, Volume III (Princeton University Press, 1924), p. 78.

[10] *RP*, p. 309ff.

[11] *Ibid.*, p. 78; *SAR*, p. 191.

[12] *SAR*, p. 57.

[13] *Ibid.*, pp. 92-8.

[14] Paul Elmer More, *The Catholic Faith* (Princeton: Princeton University Press, 1931), pp. 306-12. Hereafter *CF*. More traces Plotinus's Absolute to Aristotle (*RP*, pp. 313-18).

[15] *HP*, p. 194 and rest of chapter, "Plotinus."

[16] *Ibid.*, pp. 189-92.

[17] *RP*, pp. 315-17.

[18] Paul Elmer More, *Christ the Word. The Greek Tradition*, Volume IV (Princeton: The Princeton University Press, 1927), p. 70. See also pp. 30-52. Hereafter *CW*.

[19] Valentinus (d. 160); Apollonius of Rhodes (B.C. 3rd cent.).

[20] *CF*, p. 260ff.; *CW*, pp. 268-9; also p. vi.

[21] *SE*, X, pp. 134-5.

[22] *SE*, VI, p. 160; *SE*, VIII, pp. 158-9.

[23] *SE*, VI, pp. 189-93; *SE*, VIII, p. 217.

[24] *SE*, VIII, p. 229.

[25] *SE*, VII, pp. 11-13; *SE*, X, pp. 106-7; *SE*, III, pp. 46-48.

[26] *SE*, VI, pp. 154-86.

[27] *Ibid.*, p. 153.

[28] *Ibid.*, pp. 101-2, 146, 152.

[29] *Ibid.*, p. 149.

[30] *SE*, III, p. 256ff.

[31] *SE*, VIII, p. 230.

[32] *Ibid.*, p. 234.

[33] *Ibid.*, p. 161.

[34] *SE*, X, pp. 221-2.

[35] *SE*, VIII, p. 164.

[36] *Ibid.*, p. 168.

[37] *SE*, VI, p. 234.

[38] *SE*, VIII, p. 169.

[39] Paul Elmer More, *The Demon of the Absolute. New Shelburne Essays*, Volume I (Princeton: Princeton University Press, 1928), p. 32ff. Hereafter *DA*.

[40] *SE*, VIII, pp. 161-9.

[41] *SE*, VII, p. 251.

[42] *Ibid.*, pp. 252-3.

[43] *DA*, pp. ix–x.

[44] *Ibid.*, p. xi, 49.

[45] *Ibid.*, pp. 39-41; *SE*, VII, pp. 259-60.

[46] *SE*, VIII, p. 186ff.

[47] *Ibid.*, p. 186.

[48] *DA*, p. 51.

[49] See Norman Foerster, ed., *Humanism and America. Essays on the Outlook of Modern Civilization* (New York: Farrar and Rinehart, Inc., 1930), pp. 52-74.

The essay in this work was taken from sections IV and V of the title essay in *DA*.

⁵⁰ *DA*, p. xii.

⁵¹ *Ibid*., p. 1.

⁵² *Ibid*., p. 2.

⁵³ Paul Elmer More, *On Being Human. New Shelburne Essays*, Volume III (Princeton: Princeton University Press, 1936), pp. 137-43. Hereafter *OB*. See also *SE*, VIII, pp. 208-10; *DA*, pp. 6-7; 39ff.

⁵⁴ *SE*, II, p. 189.

⁵⁵ *SE*, IV, p. 154.

⁵⁶ *Ibid*., pp. 129-30, 152-3.

⁵⁷ *Ibid*., p. 130, 152, 154. For another definition of the religious imagination see *HP*, p. 239.

⁵⁸ *SE*, VI, pp. 167-8. More borrows "esemplastic" from Coleridge, whom he refers to in passing.

⁵⁹ *Ibid*., p. 169.

⁶⁰ *SE*, XI, pp. 212-22.

⁶¹ *SE*, VIII, p. 238; *DA*, p. 39ff, 69ff, 98, 118.

⁶² *SE*, X, 297ff.

⁶³ *OB*, pp. 109-16.

⁶⁴ *SE*, XI, p. 244.

⁶⁵ *OB*, pp. 48-9.

⁶⁶ *Ibid*., pp. 106-9, 113.

⁶⁷ *Ibid*., pp. 79-89, 91-6.

⁶⁸ *Ibid*., p. 56.

⁶⁹ *Ibid*., p. 57.

⁷⁰ *Ibid*., pp. 48-9.

⁷¹ ". . . The only salvation is in the recognition of some superior guiding and dividing law of just rule and right subordination, in the perception, that is, of something permanent within the flux." *SE*, VII, p. 267.

⁷² *CF*, p. 312.

⁷³ Paul Elmer More, *Pages from an Oxford Diary* (Princeton: Princeton University Press, 1937), p. 74.

⁷⁴ *Ibid*., p. 73.

⁷⁵ *CW*, p. 328.

⁷⁶ *Ibid*., p. 301.

[XIII, Summer 1969, 277–288]

[20]

T.S. Eliot and the Critique of Liberalism

GEORGE A. PANICHAS

George A(ndrew) Panichas (1930–), since 1962 professor of English at the University of Maryland, is the fourth editor of Modern Age: A Quarterly Review. *His teaching and writing have centered on the period between the two world wars and also on the interdisciplinary relations between literature and politics, education, history, philosophy, and religion. His major critical books include* The Reverent Discipline: Essays in Literary Criticism and Culture *(1974),* The Burden of Vision: Dostoevsky's Spiritual Art *(1977), and* The Courage of Judgment: Essays in Criticism, Culture, and Society *(1982). He is also the editor of* Promise of Greatness: The War of 1914–1918 *(1968),* The Simone Weil Reader *(1977), and* Irving Babbitt: Representative Writings *(1981).*

Are you aware that the more serious thinkers among us are used . . . to regard the spirit of Liberalism as the characteristic of the destined Antichrist?
—JOHN HENRY NEWMAN (1841)

EXCEPT FOR FRAGMENTS, the critique of modern liberalism has not been written. It cannot be otherwise. Our experience of liberalism, whether at this point of cruel history it is that of a moribund liberalism or of a *meta*-liberalism, remains dynamic. We can record the cumulative effects of the process, its inclusive progressions, but we can hardly determine its complete and final ending. We shall have to be content with the fragments that contain the substance of the critique of modern liberalism. Julien Benda, José Ortega y Gasset, and Nicolas Berdyaev on the Continent, T. E. Hulme and Christopher Dawson in England, Irving Babbitt and Paul Elmer More in the United States— it is to writers like these that we need to turn in order to compile such a critique. Unquestionably, the name of Thomas Stearns Eliot figures prominently in this hierarchic list, despite the fact that his social writings now seem to be read only by literary scholars. They are largely dismissed, except to be ridiculed or damned, by most critics and cultural historians. Yet Eliot's contribution to the critique of modern liberalism is considerable. That his contribution has been misunderstood and misrepresented as an example of "right-wing millennialism," reflects not upon the quality of Eliot's thought but rather upon twentieth-century intellectuals who, as Benda once pointed out, do not have enough moral stamina to carry the weight of their culture.

Modern man has still to acquire those

high items of civilization that Eliot admired in Virgil's world, a "more civilized world of dignity, reason and order." Eliot was thoroughly aware of the dominance of those forces leading to the decline of Western culture. "The forces of deterioration are a large crawling mass," he said, "and the forces of development half a dozen men." From the beginning he knew on which side of the cultural argument he belonged. That is, he refused to accept indiscriminatingly the view that cultural change is the law of life—a view that liberal ideologues have stoutly defended. This view epitomized for Eliot precisely the heresy that leads to cultural breakdown. "The heretic," he insisted, "whether he call himself fascist, or communist, or democrat or rationalist always has low ideals and great expectations." Eliot chose to resist the liberal doctrine no less than the liberal trend that he saw ascendant in the world. He made his choice knowing its alienating consequences. "What Machiavelli did not see about human nature is the myth of human goodness which for liberal thought replaces the belief in Divine Grace," Eliot wrote in those tough and unflinching terms that liberals have neither forgotten nor forgiven.

In essence, liberalism was for Eliot a temper and an attitude and a habit of mind culminating in a particular ethos of response to the human condition. He did not approach liberalism as a specifying ideology or dialectic in the way that, say, an aristocratic liberal like Bertrand Russell or a reform liberal like John Dewey did. Instead, he saw the crisis of liberalism largely from a religious and poetic sensibility, not from a scientific and statistical perspective. His assessment of liberalism, though "disinterested" in delineating defined valuations—the disinterestedness of a "steady impersonal passionless observation of human nature"—was moral and not programmatic or administrative. Not

the principles of liberalism so much as the pattern—the shaping forms, curves, and colors—that liberalism took in civilization were what concerned Eliot. "For the question of questions," he says in "The Literature of Politics" (1955), "which no political philosophy can escape, and by the right answer to which all political thinking must in the end be judged, is simply this: What is Man? what are his limitations? what is his misery and what his greatness? and what, finally, his destiny?"

Eliot's response to liberalism must be seen not in the special and limiting framework of the unity or the continuity of his thought *per se*, its development to be plotted, indexed, and aggregated, but in its totality, in what Eliot himself spoke of as "one's total harvest of thinking, feeling, living and observing human beings." What Eliot thought and said and wrote emerged from a profoundly reflective process: determining, contemplating, discerning, judging. In his critique of liberalism he employed no Alexandrian theological design: He did not set out to write a *contra Haereticōs*. As a poet-critic, not a man of action, Eliot in his cultural opinions was not concerned with the political attainment of influence or with the goal of effecting an immediate change in human affairs. When Eliot said that he belonged to "the *pre-political* area" rather than to the political, he particularized further "the stratum down to which any sound political thinking must push its roots, and from which it must derive its nourishment." Such an area encompasses ethics and, in the end, theology.

Eternal rather than pragmatic principles inform Eliot's assessment of liberalism. To say that Eliot's writings on liberalism bear the imprint of a religious philosophy is to say that in these he discloses an apocalyptic bent, for he sees that modern man lives in an apocalyptic time in which an internal judgment of history reveals itself. Within the strict, measured Bradleyan economy and scrupulosity of his pronouncements, there is ever present a vatic energy that makes one aware of Eliot's judgmental view of man's destiny in the historical process. Against what he sees as liberalism's relativism he posits the absolute; against its meliorism he asserts the tragic element; against its naturalism he upholds the supernatural; against its secularism he places the Incarnation. For Eliot, then, liberalism is a creed equatable with the collapse not only of "ancient edifices" but also of spiritual values and certitudes. Such a creed, with its methodological proclivity and its scientific image of man, leads to the kind of devaluation, or desacralization, that, Eliot felt, negates order and confounds moral law and spiritual authority. As such, liberalism "is a movement not so much defined by its end as by its starting point; away from, rather than towards, something."

What some of Eliot's critics mistake for lifelessness and escapism—a "liberal conservative" like Peter Viereck spoke of Eliot's advocacy of "an artificial clerical unity" as being a symptom of the Waste Land in "its self-hate"—is actually a diagnostic exploration of the most serious problems confronting Western culture. It is the writer's task, Eliot declares in his essay "The Man of Letters and the Future of Europe" (1945), to speak out on issues affecting the fate of one's country, particularly its "cultural map," and "to take a longer view than either the politician or the local patriot." And what "the man of letters" should guard against, according to Eliot, is what he associated with the technologico-Benthamite liberal view and what he saw crystallizing even more explosively at the end of World War II: ". . . the idea of peace is more likely to be associated with the idea of *efficiency*— that is, with whatever can be *planned*."

For Eliot the crisis of liberalism was tied inseparably to the greater crisis of culture. The methodology of liberalism had become the ontological substance, as discriminating standards of inclusion and exclusion were neglected or dissolved in the name of social-political expediency. Nor did he fail to see that in its acceptance of instrumentalism the liberal mind in time surrendered to the technic spirit and ultimately, too, to the principle of an organized social order: "Not the least of the effects of industrialism is that we become mechanized in mind, and consequently attempt to provide solutions in terms of *engineering*, for problems which are essentially problems of *life*." Political and economic thinkers who embrace the idea of social engineering disregard cultural consequences; only "the man of letters is better qualified to foresee them, and to perceive their seriousness." The qualitative aspects of cultural life had to be upheld against a state of mind that measures all things by number and linear extension and that expects human and social perfection to emerge from the historical process. Eighteenth-century rationalism, nineteenth-century utilitarianism, and twentieth-century collectivism embodied for Eliot an evolving historic, secular process contributing to overcentralization and uprootedness, the two most rife conditions of this century's cultural malady. Eliot's rejection of liberalism as "the wave of the future" was total and incontrovertible.

From the standpoint of clarity and rhetorical economy, John Dewey's *Liberalism and Social Action* has classical standing for its espousal of liberalism in its history, its theory and doctrine, its problems and its promise. From the standpoint of connection with Eliot's indictment of liberalism, it also has the remarkable coincidence of advantage of containing Dewey's Page-Barbour Foundation lectures, given at the University of Virginia and published in

1935. The publication of these lectures came a year after Eliot's own Page-Barbour lectures appeared under the title *After Strange Gods*, in which Eliot bluntly stated his position: "In a society like ours, worm-eaten with Liberalism, the only thing possible for a person with convictions is to state a point of view and leave it at that." No indication is found anywhere in *Liberalism and Social Action* that Dewey was attempting to answer any of Eliot's charges, though the first two sentences of Dewey's book must inevitably place Eliot in the hostile camp: "Liberalism has long been accustomed to onslaughts proceeding from those who oppose social change. It has long been treated as an enemy by those who wish to maintain the *status quo*." In any event these two books present the two sides of a great debate. There could have been no more appropriate or intellectually respectable spokesmen for their opposing judgments about value in Western civilization.

Now, nearly forty years later, Dewey's arguments have a timely ring, nowhere better heard than in his declaration that "If radicalism be defined as perception of need for radical change, then today any liberalism which is not also radicalism is irrelevant and doomed." Much of the New Left ideology of the contemporary period is both a continuation and a variation of Dewey's theme, but it often lacks either his devotion to liberty or his courage of honesty. The difference between Dewey and his successors is the difference between true and false liberals, between, in Irving Babbitt's apt expression, a "spiritual athlete" and "cosmic loafers."

"Organized social planning," Dewey repeatedly emphasizes, "is now the sole method of social action by which liberalism can realize its professed aims." A gradualistic, nonviolent combination of "organized intelligence," of "scientific method," and of "technological application," we are told, will topple the old

morality and bring about a social order that frees man from the coercion and oppression of a dead past and prepares him for a place in the "great society." Conquer material wants and deprivations, runs the all too familiar argument, and spiritual rehabilitation of man is inevitable. Dewey's portrayal of liberalism speaks volumes about the historical promise of a "new deal" to be reached in the twentieth century:

> Flux does not have to be created. But it does have to be directed. It has to be so controlled that it will move to some end in accordance with the principles of life, since life itself is development. Liberalism is committed to an end that is at once enduring and flexible: the liberation of individuals so that realization of their capacities may be the law of life. It is committed to the use of freed intelligence as the method of direct change. In any case, civilization is faced with the problem of uniting the changes that are going on into a coherent pattern of social organization. The liberal spirit is marked by its own picture of the pattern that is required: a social organization that will make possible effective liberty and opportunity for personal growth in mind and spirit in all individuals. Its present need is recognition that established material security is prerequisite of the ends which it cherished, so that, the basis of life being secure, individuals may actively share in the wealth of cultural resources that now exist and may contribute, each in his own way, to their further enrichment.

If these are the words of a philosopher of a continent, of the New World, and if, incidentally, they underline the perennial but parochial dream of an "American Eden" (for "We are," Dewey said, "a new body and a new spirit in the world"), they also have the implicit, the reminding and representative, power of summarizing so much that missionary technic liberalism, regardless of time and place, prescribes. And it is this prescriptiveness of liberalism that Dewey, no less than earlier political moderns as, say, John Locke, Jean-Jacques Rousseau, or Jeremy Bentham, enshrined in his writings. Apostles of the liberal spirit all, they refused to be intimidated by the more strenuous concept of human limitation and fallibility. Dewey accepted what is modern in human civilization: the belief in change, in social organization, in the "law" of progress, in the planned human will. "The task is to go on," he proclaims, "and not backward, until the method of intelligence and experimental control is the rule in social relations and social directions." Regardless of the insight and wisdom of its lessons, the historical past, Dewey maintained, was nothing as compared with the new scientific method that merely needed cooperative, experimental application. *That history in being a process of change generates change not only in details but also in the method of directing social change*": this was something that could not be overlooked, he insisted. Indeed, this was the revealed fact of the modern world and of which he became one of its prophets of acceptance, leading him to posit a recurring question that in recent years has been the subject of acerbic debate between Dr. F. R. Leavis and Lord Snow: "And what is scientific technology save a large-scale demonstration of organized intelligence in action?"

Eliot's vision of the historical process was the vision of a *Weltdichter* unafraid to see the world as it exists both in and between illusion and disillusion. In this vision Eliot possessed the poetic insight that Dewey and his liberal precursors and successors have lacked and that makes the difference between the creative and the technic minds so startling. "But the essential advantage of a poet," we hear Eliot saying, "is not to have a beautiful world with which to deal; it is to be able to see beneath both beauty and ugliness; to see the boredom, and the horror and the glory." Combining what he calls "a Cath-

olic heritage, and a Puritanical temperament" and affirming the requirements of "prayer, observance, discipline, thought and action," Eliot may have given a picture of the death-motive in life, the loathing and horror of life. And yet, as Eliot stresses, "the hatred of life is an important phase—even, if you like, a mystical experience—in life itself." His diagnostic truths resulted precisely from his possessing a *préoccupation morale*; his poetic vision of life could hardly sanction the blank kind of empiricism found in the legacy of Charles Sanders Peirce, that "truth is that concordance of an abstract statement with the ideal limit toward which endless investigation would tend to bring scientific belief."

Reverence for what Eliot called "permanent truths about man and God and life and death,"—the "permanent things" that Bentham derided as "nonsense on stilts,"—is at the center of *After Strange Gods*. Seen together, Eliot's book and Dewey's *Liberalism and Social Action* present the quarrel between the pronouncement of tradition and the proclamation of revolt. *After Strange Gods* can be interpreted as a condemnation of the intellectual revolution that Dewey's thought crystallized. (In *After Strange Gods* Eliot points to China as "a country of tradition"—"until the missionaries initiated her into Western thought, and so blazed a path for John Dewey.") What Eliot condemns is the spirit of indulgence that pervades liberalism. The results of such a softness bring decay of cultural standards. Assuming "the role of moralist," Eliot stresses that what he has to say is not undertaken as "exercises in literary criticism." Rather, he is concerned with developing "certain ideas in illustration of which I have drawn upon the work of some of the few modern writers whose work I know." In delineating these ideas Eliot employs moral criteria, for he believes that "the struggle of our time [is] to concentrate, not to dissipate; to renew our association with traditional wisdom; to re-establish a vital connexion between the individual and the race; the struggle, in a word, against Liberalism."

After Strange Gods has been attacked as the most offensive of Eliot's social-religious writings. Typically critics charge that the book is "full of inverted psychology and perverted sociology," a "defeatist" example of "neo-scholastic" reversion to "dogmatic theology" and "ecclesiastical orthodoxy." Eliot was aware of this reaction to his book, which, after two printings, he did not permit to be reissued. "I regarded the tone of much of its contents as much too violent and sweeping; some of my assertions I should qualify and some I should withdraw," he declared in 1960. Yet, although he may no longer have agreed with certain of his opinions in *After Strange Gods*, he did not repudiate their essence. In the development of a writer's thought later qualifications must not be equated with outright rejection of earlier views. In this connection, it is interesting to note that John Hayward edited, "with the author's approval," a selection of Eliot's critical writings under the title *Points of View*, published in 1941 by Eliot's own firm of Faber and Faber. "Designed as an introduction to the author's work in prose," the book contains representative passages, from a single paragraph to a complete essay, from Eliot's writings published between 1917 and 1939. Two passages from *After Strange Gods* are included: the first under the caption " 'Romantic' and 'Classic,' " the second under the caption "Thomas Hardy."

With all its problematic history *After Strange Gods* remains a valuable clue to Eliot's critique of liberalism. His misgivings about the book, curiously blending humility and irony, resulted from literary considerations, not from basic theses. In applying "the standard of orthodoxy to contemporary literature," Eliot focused on some of the writings of Ezra Pound, William Butler Yeats, Thomas Hardy, and D. H. Lawrence. In these he detected "deviations from the inherited wisdom of the race," that is, a denial or neglect of "a living and central tradition"; an extreme individualism in views; an absence of moral principles stemming from growing disenchantment with the validity of religious tradition as maintained and refined by the supervision of orthodoxy. Poets and novelists have become "promoters of personality" who claim that for a man to achieve his "sincerity" he should " 'be himself.' " Such a view of personality is, for Eliot, an example of "heresy," which he coupled, as a consequence and concomitant, with the glorification of personality: " . . . the *unregenerate* personality, partly self-deceived and partly irresponsible, and because of its freedom, terribly *limited* by prejudice and self-conceit, capable of much good or great mischief according to the natural goodness or impurity of man: and we are all, naturally, impure." What Eliot was attacking was the "organizing" ethos of liberalism, as proclaimed by Dewey, and its optimist ideal of personality, as defined by another liberal oracle, L. T. Hobhouse, who wrote in 1911: "Liberalism is the belief that society can safely be founded on this self-directing power of personality, that it is only on this formulation that a true community can be built. . . ."

From his condemnation of the liberal view of personality Eliot never deviated. Whatever regrets he later expressed came not from the substance of his traditionalist convictions but rather from the form in which he presented them. Thus Eliot acknowledged "errors of judgment" and "errors of tone: the occasional note of arrogance, of vehemence, of cocksureness or rudeness." No doubt Eliot remembered his infamous statement in *After Strange Gods* that "reasons of race and religion combine to make any large number of free-thinking Jews undesirable." Whatever the insinuations, usually from critics who fail to distinguish between dogma and prejudice, Eliot's anti-Judaism was not anti-Semitism. For a Christian to be racist and to hate Jews, he later said, is forbidden—"is a sin"; and no other modern poet has been more aware of sin. It is enough to assert in Eliot's defense that his was a kind of Christian anti-Judaism that is opposed not to the Old Testament but to Talmudic-rabbinic Judaism, which developed after the Jews' refusal to accept Christ.

Eliot no doubt also remembered the travesty of his attack on D. H. Lawrence in *After Strange Gods*:

> The man's vision is spiritual, but spiritually sick.... I fear that Lawrence's work may appeal, not to those who are well and able to discriminate, but to the sick and debile and confused; and will appeal not to what remains of health in them, but to their sickness.

Above all Eliot had towards the end of his life reappraised some of his hard-line Bloomsbury valuations of Lawrence. Lawrence and Eliot were, at least in their critical overview of the dialectic of liberalism, of the same party without, it seems, knowing it, though as Eliot does say, "it matters a good deal in what name we condemn it." Lawrence's critique of liberalism nevertheless has its echoes in Eliot:

> ... they want an outward system of nullity, which they call peace and goodwill, so that in their own souls they can be independent little gods, referred nowhere and to nothing, little mortal Absolutes, secure from question. That is at the back of all Liberalism, Fabianism and democracy. It stinks. It is the will of the louse.

"When morals cease to be a matter of tradition and orthodoxy—that is, of the

habits of the community formulated, corrected, and elevated by the continuous thought and direction of the Church—and when each man is to elaborate his own, then *personality* becomes a thing of alarming importance": to this thesis Eliot was to return again and again. If his use of Lawrence was a tactical error in the struggle against liberalism, there were other writers who could better illustrate the pitfalls of liberalism. Could Eliot have had this in mind in permitting the long paragraph on Thomas Hardy, from *After Strange Gods,* to reappear in *Points of View?* Hardy, he charges, is an example of a writer living "in an age of unsettled beliefs and enfeebled tradition" with no loyalty to any metaphysics or tradition; a writer extremely self-absorbed in his novels, in which most of his characters come alive only "in their emotional paroxysms": "This extreme emotionalism seems to me a symptom of decadence; it is a cardinal point of faith in a romantic age, to believe that there is something admirable in violent emotion for its own sake, whatever the emotion or whatever its object." Hardy exemplifies a form of what Eliot found to be the same indiscipline that his Harvard mentor Irving Babbitt and the other New Humanists equated with the absence of the "inner check upon the expansion of natural impulse." In circumscribing Hardy from this angle of criticism Eliot surely had in mind the limitations of the liberal doctrine; the ultimate as opposed to the scientific fact that, as Eliot wrote of Hardy's rendered *"personal view of life"* (which, he said, referring at the same time to liberalism, "is merely part of the whole movement of several centuries towards the aggrandisement and exploitation of personality"), "unless there is moral resistance and conflict there is no meaning."

That man should be free to regulate his own moral progress: such constituted the climate of relativism that was at the core of Eliot's critique of a flourishing liberalism. The liberal view that morals are a kind of humanistic science and that, in consequence, as the liberal ideologue would have it, "for the rational man, the world begins anew each moment," led to "a spirit of excessive tolerance" that, Eliot believed, "is to be depreciated." Whatever reservations Eliot was to have about the tone of *After Strange Gods* or about the harshness of its opinions as he came to see them, he was never to repudiate the social and religious perspectives he delineated in his "primer of modern heresy." His preoccupation with "orthodoxy of sensibility and with the sense of tradition" was to remain pivotal. Without this sense of tradition—"all those habitual actions, habits and customs, from the most significant religious rite to our conventional way of greeting a stranger, which represent the blood kinship of 'the same people living in the same place' "—instability and moral debilitation are inevitable. Eliot stamped his moral perspectives with "a definite and theological standpoint," that is, with a clear-cut and present Christian metaphysics insofar as he said in his essay "Francis Herbert Bradley" (1927), "Morality and religion are not the same thing, but they cannot beyond a certain point be treated separately." Eliot's critique of liberalism could hardly be more explicit in all of its developing and informing referents in *After Strange Gods* than in these words:

> If you do away with this [moral] struggle, and maintain that by tolerance, benevolence, inoffensiveness and a re-distribution or increase of purchasing power . . . the world will be as good as anyone could require, then you must expect human beings to become more and more vaporous.

In liberalism Eliot discerned the quintessence of another form of secularism, another of the seductive "philosophies without revelation," springing from "titanism, or the attempt to build a purely human world without reliance upon grace." Liberalism was to underline a contemporary example "of the permanent force of the world against which the spirit must always struggle," as Eliot expressed it in an acute but neglected essay which he contributed in 1937 to a symposium entitled *Revelation*, edited by John Baillie and Hugh Martin. As always in his probing of secular philosophies, he returned to the moral element, or, better, to the absence of "the possibility of that frightful discovery of morality." In facing the *données* of liberalism, for example, those of Bertrand Russell's "enervate gospel of happiness," he unfailingly castigated the liberals' contention that only in the adventure of unrestrained experience will truth ever emerge. Such a conviction he associated with what he believed to be the constitutives of modernism, "newness and crudeness, impatience, inflexibility in one respect and fluidity in another, and irresponsibility and lack of wisdom." Ultimately he saw that the promise of liberalism was mechanistic, part of the great, secular experiment conspiring "to form a civilized but non-Christian mentality." In his major prose writings appearing after 1934, Eliot continued to answer the "liberal-minded," who, as he put it in his essay "Religion and Literature" (1935), "are convinced that if everybody says what he thinks, and does what he likes, things will somehow, by some automatic compensation and adjustment, come right in the end."

That this conviction is untenable is a subject of Eliot's *The Idea of a Christian Society* (1939). *After Strange Gods* offended readers because of its demarcation, from an overtly Christian position, of "the organisation of values, and a direction of religious thought which must proceed to a criticism of political and economic systems." The judgmental tone of this book is no less severe than that of *After Strange Gods*. So relentless and uncompromising is it, that the book infuriated liberal critics, especially, and predictably, one of Dewey's disciples, who denounced its tractarian stance as "a vulturous idea decked out in doves's words." But there could be no relenting tone, no easy choice of tactics or of tact. In *The Idea of a Christian Society,* consisting of lectures delivered at Corpus Christi College, Cambridge, in March 1939, Eliot said exactly what he thought about the nature, end, and function of social order at almost exactly the time when Winston Churchill was warning the House of Commons, "The danger is now very near . . . dark, bitter waters . . . are rising fast on every side." It was a time of history, even of a judgment upon history, that, as Eliot said in his conclusion, provoked "a doubt of the validity of a civilisation," made already more anguishing for "many persons who, like myself, were deeply shaken by the events of September 1938, in a way from which one does not recover; persons to whom that month brought a profounder realisation of a general plight." And in an appended note dated September 6, 1939, Eliot wrote that the whole of *The Idea of a Christian Society* "was completed before it was known we should be at war." He emphasized, however, that since the possibility of war was always present in his mind, he has only two additional observations to make: "first, that the alignment of forces which has now revealed itself should bring more clearly to our consciousness the alternative of Christianity or paganism; and, second, that we cannot afford to defer our constructive thinking to the conclusion of hostilities—a moment when . . . good counsel is liable to be obscured."

Here, too, Eliot continued his examination of the environment of modern society that, as he had written in *After Strange Gods,* was hostile to faith and produced few individuals "capable of being injured by blasphemy." A modern society without the "assurance of first principles" becomes either like the United States religiously "neutral" or like Soviet Russia "pagan." Eliot was unbending in his distrust of "secular reformers," whose reforms merely generalize man and impose a mechanistic psychology over moral philosophy. His quarrel with an emergent modernism therefore was a quarrel precisely with the liberal concept of the evolution of morals in direct relation to the concrete results of social action. This legislative view, as it might be called, signified for Eliot moral flabbiness. "But because Christian morals are based on fixed beliefs which cannot change," he wrote, "they also are essentially unchanging: while the beliefs and in consequence the morality of the secular world can change from individual to individual, or from generation to generation, or from nation to nation." The image of Eliot as an "anxious pilgrim" rather than an intrepid explorer is no doubt understandable in any appraisal of *The Idea of a Christian Society.* But for Eliot the impelling idea of human exploration always had its limits; indeed, the whole of Eliot's poetic and critical achievement, in principle and in intent, ultimately affirms sacral limits, that is, knowing when to stop in reverence before the "burning bush," or as Eliot phrased it: "For only in humility, charity and purity—and most of all perhaps humility—can we be prepared to receive the grace of God without which human operations are vain."

Eliot's remarks on liberalism in *The Idea of a Christian Society* were made in the course of his envisaging the end to which "the community of Christians" must be directed, "a society in which the natural end of man—virtue and well-being in community—is acknowledged for all, and the supernatural end—beatitude—for those who have eyes to see it." Indubitably the religious attitude that he affirmed was set against the secular attitude and, more specifically, against the liberalism that he saw permeating men's minds and affecting their attitudes towards life. His treatment here of liberalism is brief but devastating. There is no doubt that he had given long and careful thought to the subject, that he knew its magnitude, that he had to speak his mind on the subject clearly and categorically, for the record, for history. Eliot also knew full well the intricate power of the enemy and the evil of which it is capable: "It [liberalism] is a necessary negative element; when I have said the worst of it, that worst comes only to this, that a negative element made to serve the purpose of a positive is objectionable." The historical role of liberalism in the neutralization and paganization of modern society cannot go unchallenged or unpunished, Eliot seemed to be saying. Consequently, the section that he devoted to liberalism has such a concentrated power of thought, of controlled scorn, such care of expression and confidence of view, that it sounds like the bursting of a rocket in a war of faiths. No better example of Eliot's pronouncements against liberalism can be found than in this passage:

> By destroying traditional social habits of the people, by dissolving their natural collective consciousness into individual constituents, by licensing the opinions of the most foolish, by substituting instruction for education, by encouraging cleverness rather than wisdom, the upstart rather than the qualified, by fostering a notion of *getting on* to which the alternative is a hopeless apathy, Liberalism can prepare the way for that which is its own negation: the artificial, mechanised or brutalised which is a desperate remedy for its chaos.

At the same time Eliot prophetically pointed out that liberal attitudes were disappearing, inasmuch as the sphere of private life which liberalism traditionally defends was being steadily diminished. For out of liberalism, he noted, come philosophies that deny it, as we move "from Liberalism to its apparent end of authoritarian democracy." Liberalism signified for Eliot the legacy of disorder, "and not the permanent value of the negative element," which he saw as essential to cultural growth and maturity, an integral aspect of what he later labeled "internal cultural bickering." With critical liberalism, as it might be termed, Eliot disagreed, but for him this disagreement was a dimension vitally important to an emerging "definition of culture." He was too much the creative genius to discredit dialectical tension. Still, Eliot was to take a long view of things, to make his judgments and choices according to his concept of "last things," according to what he regarded as the needful return to an assurance of "first principles." Only these could overcome and transcend that "liberalised or negative condition of society [which] must either proceed into a gradual decline of which we can see no end, or . . . reform itself into a positive shape which is likely to be effectively secular." For Eliot there was a third possibility, "that of a positive Christian society." For him the dogma of "the primacy of the supernatural over the natural life" was irrevocable. Christian theology provided Eliot with precisely the answers to why things are wrong in the world: "What is right enters the realm of the *expedient* and is contingent upon place and time, the degree of culture, the temperament of a people. But the Church can say what is always and everywhere *wrong*." He refused to accept what the secular mind speaks of as the urgent need for "greater plasticity and bolder exploration of human possibilities." Eliot sought for permanent answers to ultimate questions.

Man's possibility for evil, as Eliot underlined in *The Idea of a Christian Society*, was unlimited; hence, the problem of man was the problem of motives and of law. Eliot could not accept the secularist's view that politics, being, to use a phrase, "the art of the possible," especially when embodied in the highest forms of intellect and governance, was superior to the prior creation of a temper of mind in people equipping them to see and know "what is wrong—*morally* wrong—and why it is wrong." Eliot affirmed the teleological priority of Christian doctrine. Hence, the year 1939, which for W. H. Auden brought to an end "a low dishonest decade," for Eliot marked the epochal crisis of modernism in all of its ramifications. The war embodied for Eliot the most brutalizing consequences of the liberal spirit, in short, the modern offshoots of secularism either as the neutralization or the paganization of civilization, or as both. In holding to such a view he resolutely opposed what John Dewey espoused as modern man's need "to translate the word 'natural' into 'moral.'" *The Idea of a Christian Society* was to contain Eliot's answer to the liberal concept of human nature; in it he included his world-view. This view was hardly optimistic, but historical developments since 1939 (let alone since 1914, that penultimate year of crisis) validate what liberal critics denigrate as Eliot's "peculiar gloom." Dewey's belief that "the future of democracy is allied with the spread of the scientific attitude" cannot but be tinged today with a more deepening irony, as Eliot had foreseen.

Dewey's *Freedom and Culture* appeared in the same year as did Eliot's *The Idea of a Christian Society*. The earlier debate now continued as the crisis of 1939 emerged. No other two books could more sharply focus on increasingly opposing viewpoints. The positions stated and defended, in terms of each writer's special sense of historical crisis, are irreconcilable. For Eliot the crisis of history and the problem of man conjoined in the need of

"the perpetual message of the Church: to affirm, to teach and to apply, true theology." For Dewey the crisis instanced the basic failures of modern society to subscribe more fully and boldly to the "scientific attitude" and to the belief in the infinite adaptability of human nature. Neither man's corruptiveness nor man's avarice, which Eliot called "the dominant vice of our time," contained explanations for Dewey. It was not a matter of the tragic outlook but rather of man not plumbing his capacity and exploring his possibilities, to use the liberal's terminology. Employing the logic of argumentation that makes Eliot's critique of liberalism all the more understandable in its antithesis, Dewey surveyed the crisis of his time in terms of the surviving relics of coercion instead of cohesion. The threat to the cause of democratic freedom, Dewey observed, lay not in the existence of totalitarian states but in man's own attitudes and within man's institutions: "A culture which permits science to destroy traditional values but which distrusts its power to create new ones is a culture which is destroying itself." Invoking the liberal's faith, Dewey was to stress in *Freedom and Culture* that no problem was too big nor crisis too overpowering if only man confronted it "with all the resources provided by collective intelligence operating in cooperative action."

Eliot's concept of the modern cultural situation is closely tied to his indictment of the liberal ethos, particularly its pragmatism, with its pluralistic, indeterministic, and melioristic habits of thought. Democratic liberalism presented Eliot with no theory or standards for the growth and survival of culture. "A democracy in which everybody had an equal opportunity in everything would be oppressive for the conscientious and licentious for the rest," he observes coldly in *Notes Towards the Definition of Culture* (1948), his sequel to *The Idea of a Christian Society*. He is still assaying, though on a broader level, the consequences of the liberal outlook. Here, too, his pronouncements remain consistently critical. Secularism is the enemy. "Culture . . . is of divine origin and must perish among people who lose belief in a supernatural world," he warns. Eliot marks his cultural views in irrevocably religious contexts insofar as, he claims, one cannot escape the religious point of view, "because in the end one either believes or disbelieves." For him culture is "the incarnation . . . of the religion of a people"; "what is part of our culture is also part of our *lived* religion"; "the formation of a religion is also the formation of a culture." The informing religious tone in *Notes Towards the Definition of Culture* is one of reverence: the reverence that Richard M. Weaver epitomized in his *Visions of Order* (1964) when he wrote: "While culture is not a worship and should not be made a worship, it is a kind of orienting of the mind toward a mood, a reverence for the spirit on secular occasions."

Although Eliot retains an inherent concern with the process of de-Christianization, his chief concern in this book is with religious values in their cultural meaning. (There is some truth to Father Walter J. Ong's observation that "Eliot's writings are often concerned with 'religion' but seldom explicitly with Christ.") Eliot no doubt recognizes in *Notes Towards the Definition of Culture* the expansion of the irreligious and anti-religious tempers in the modern world. World War II, "a period of unparalleled destructiveness," must be seen as the background against which he defends his religious concept of culture. If this book discloses a certain and pronounced hesitancy, even an impreciseness of definition and of critical application, and if it lacks that force of assurance found in *The Idea of a Christian Society*, these weaknesses must be viewed against the backdrop of the war. The question that now plagued Eliot more than ever was: Had not the world since 1939 moved beyond chaos, into the zero-zone in which, as Samuel Beckett has said, there is an absolute absence of the absolute? If Eliot had had, through Prufrock and Sweeney, his vision of horror, he now understood it in its most radical implications. A tormented note of defensiveness was the communicated consequence of such an experience, and its scars were visible. Fear, too, was a feeling that Eliot revealed here, leading to almost agonized supplication:

> If Christianity goes, the whole of our culture goes. Then you must start painfully again, and you cannot put on a new culture ready made. You must wait for the grass to grow to feed the sheep to give the wool out of which your new coat will be made. You must pass through many centuries of barbarism. . . . But we can at least try to save something of those goods of which we are the common trustees: the legacy of Greece, Rome and Israel, and the legacy of Europe throughout the last 2,000 years. In a world which has seen such material devastation as ours, these spiritual possessions are also in imminent peril.

The problem of culture and religion, of "the whole way of life," has grown immensely difficult, as Eliot showed. The conflict between social tradition, as the maintenance and transmission of standards of culture, and the common standards enforced by the decrees of social planners and of politicians was moving towards a secular victory. In the aftermath, Eliot also saw the religious decline against which he was fighting. Again, the seductiveness of liberal theory was all too evident. Common standards result in "common faith," to use the title of John Dewey's credo published in 1934. "A body of beliefs and practices," Dewey says, "that are apart from the common and natural relations of mankind must . . . weaken and sap the force of the possibilities inherent in such relations. Here lies one aspect of the emancipation of the religious from religion." The allurements of such a liberal dictum were (and are) no doubt mighty for the masses that naturally dislike "historic encumbrances" and succumb to the miracle of technics. Eliot's recognition of the cultural power of these "new methods of inquiry and reflection," as "the final arbiter of all questions of fact, existence, and intellectual assent," to use Dewey's own words, is inherent in *Notes Towards the Definition of Culture*. The metaphysical essences of a transcendent "otherness" and otherworldliness, Eliot could hardly escape noticing, were jeopardized by a world in which a religious concept of culture would increasingly fall victim to the radical metaphysics of liberal doctrine, the metaphysical pluralism that one authority describes as follows: "There can be no ultimate system, for each new system must like all others be limited by its categories and hence must take its place in an infinite series" (Henry Alonzo Myers, *Systematic Pluralism*, 1961).

The purpose and function of education also figure prominently in Eliot's critique of liberalism. Liberalism, he stresses in his essay "Modern Education and the Classics" (1932), along with exciting a "superficial curiosity," has fallaciously tried to equalize subjects of study. Radicalism, the offspring of liberalism, has proceeded "to organize the 'vital issues,' and reject what is not vital." As a result, liberal concepts of education, as of politics, have led to the steady decline of standards. "In a negative liberal society," Eliot observes in *The Idea of a Christian Society*, "you have no agreement as to there being any body of knowledge which any educated person should have acquired at any particular stage: the idea of wisdom disappears, and you get sporadic and unrelated experi-

mentation." The question of education is tied to the principles of order. To think of education in terms merely of adapting it to a changed and changing world is to ignore what must remain the inviolable "permanent principles of education." Education is not to be measured pragmatically or scientifically, "dominated by the idea of getting on" as "many ardent reforming spirits" believe. "A high average of general education is perhaps less necessary for a civil society than is a respect for learning," Eliot writes in *Notes Towards the Definition of Culture*. His view of the close relationship between education and culture is evident: If "culture can never be wholly conscious . . . it cannot be planned because it is also the unconscious background to our planning." Such a truth for Eliot more specifically accentuates "the delusion that the maladies of the modern world can be put right by a system of education." It underlines also the commensurate truth that in education, as in culture, "one thing to avoid is a universalised planning; one thing to ascertain is the limits of the plannable."

No less than other aspects of modern life, education, Eliot believed, was stamped by a secularist liberalism. In his essay in *Revelation* he writes:

The whole tendency of education (in the widest sense—the influence playing on the common mind in the forms of "enlightenment") has been for a very long time to form minds more and more adapted to secularism. . . .

Such a liberalism can appeal to only the "experiential test," and not to the permanencies of order, of unity, and of wisdom. "What happens in our thinking about education is, of course, only a special instance of what happens to human consciousness," Eliot told his audience in his lectures on "The Aims of Education" at the University of Chicago in November 1950. At the heart of his criticism here, as elsewhere, was Eliot's distrust of changes that have external, material ends. Educational reforms, albeit humane, lack centrality of the kind that can neither "change the will of those who worship false gods" nor "sustain an entire society." Such reforms, as the products of liberal theory, remain unfinished, for their success is socially oriented and derivative, fostering surrogates that also create new perils:

> The restoration of a kind of order in people's private lives . . . when it is made in the name of a social purpose only, furthers the reduction of men to machines, and is the opposite from the development of their humanity.

Eliot never wavered in his belief that liberalism contains the kind of secular faith that conceives of the evils of the world as external to man. He rejected the liberal view of the human condition. He refused, in short, to subscribe to the scientific concepts of the future of man, precisely that "new age" which John Dewey saw as inseparable from scientific knowledge as the paradigm of all reliable knowledge. Eliot readily admitted that his approach to education was "orthodox." It was, in other words, metaphysical and theological. "There are two and only two finally tenable hypotheses about life: the Catholic and the materialistic," he writes in "Modern Education and the Classics." There were, then, limitations and retributions that no scientific liberalism could ever overcome. These limits were, whatever the temptations of liberal doctrine, implicit in the very fabric of life. No liberal educational theorist, he maintained, could afford to ignore the insoluble contradictions that Simone Weil, whom Eliot admired, saw "afflicting" the human condition. Eliot saw fit to quote from Simone Weil's *Gravity and Grace* in "The Aims of Education":

> Our life is impossibility, absurdity. Everything that we will is contradicted by the conditions or by the consequences attached to it. That is because we are ourselves contradiction, being merely creatures. . . .

The key word to much of Eliot's critique of liberalism is found in these words.

Eliot considered education a cultural rather than a social phenomenon. His concern was always with cultural health achieved through standards, a concern informed by this statement in *Notes Towards the Definition of Culture*: "For it is an essential condition of the preservation of the quality of culture of the minority, that it should continue to be a minority culture." In holding such a view, and especially in the attendant indictment of modern collectivist social theory, of "mass-culture," Eliot continued his conflict with liberalism and specifically with the liberal educational views propounded by John Dewey, who once more helps provide a positive frame of reference in historical antithesis. "One needs the enemy," Eliot writes in *Notes Towards the Definition of Culture*. "So, within limits, the friction, not only between individuals but between groups, seems quite necessary for civilisation. The universality of irritation is the best assurance of peace." It is Dewey, of course, who in the twentieth century has presented the liberal philosophy of education at its best. But it was not just a philosophy of education but a philosophy of ideals, the major ideal being Dewey's conception of education as an agency of social adjustment, one in which the individual's "privacy of reflective self-consciousness," as it has been put, is notoriously expendable. As a liberal ideologue of education, Dewey resisted any "externally imposed ends." All values, he argued in his influential *Democracy and Education* (1916), a work that Walter Lippmann hailed as expressing "the best hope of liberal men," come from experience and not from contemplation. All distinctions, moreover, are social. All matters of moral significance and discrimination are derived solely from the relations between man and man and not from what lies within man. To the question What is education?, Dewey therefore replied: "It is the reconstruction or reorganization of experience which adds to the meaning of experience, and which increases ability to direct the course of subsequent experience."

Such a reply obviously was a liberal fallacy that Eliot connected with the spread of the materialistic view and ends. The Deweyan view sought for "the wrong things." Inherent in his rejection of such a view was Eliot's belief that it was not only "wrong" but also abstract. He wrote in *Notes Towards the Definition of Culture*:

> Education in the modern sense implies a disintegrated society, in which it has come to be assumed that there must be one measure of education according to which everyone is educated simply more or less. Hence *Education* has become an abstraction.

Eliot thought that a proper system of education should "unify the active and the contemplative, action and speculation, politics and the arts." For Dewey—for the liberal—this approach signified the kind of philosophical dualism that was unprogressive. Education, Dewey stipulates in "My Pedagogic Creed" (1897), which he was to refine and enlarge upon in his later educational works, "is a process of living and not a preparation for future living"; "is the fundamental method of social progress and reform"; is "the art of thus giving shape to human powers and adapting them to social service . . . the supreme art." Such testaments incorporate the liberal creed. They also signalize the unfortunate fact that "we have always new problems, and the old ones in new forms," as Eliot observed in "The Aims of Education." He could hardly have been more right or the Deweyan liberals more wrong in their dismissal of Eliot's thinking on

education (his reflections—for he distrusted conclusions) as having only "an antiquarian interest." Eliot's picture of higher education in America in the early thirties, as he painted it in "Modern Education and the Classics," could not be more prophetic of the contemporary plight:

> And when you have sunk so much money in plant and equipment, when you have a very large (though not always well-paid) staff of men who are mostly married and have a few children, when you are turning out from your graduate schools more and more men who have been trained to become teachers in other universities, and who will probably want to marry and have children too; when your whole national system of higher education is designed for an age of expansion, for a country which is going indefinitely to increase its population, grow rich, and build more universities—then you will find it very difficult to retract.

That there were forces in the late 1920's fighting the manifold consequences of the liberal doctrine of endless experiment and expansion Eliot was fully aware. He particularly applauded the new Humanism of Irving Babbitt and his disciples for its diagnosis of the ills of the modern world, arising, at least in one major respect, from what Babbitt termed the liberal theory of "free temperamental expansion." Eliot shared with Babbitt a distrust of the liberal pragmatists and other philosophers. No less than the humanists was he critical of monistic postulates, and no less did he seek for what a humanist like Norman Foerster called the "principles of order and construction" to help contain "the tumult of the times disconsolate." But no less than they did Eliot insist on what Babbitt himself termed "a careful determination of boundaries." If, therefore, Eliot joined the humanists in opposing what the latter spoke of as the gospel of Occidental "naturism," he could not overlook their lack of a Christian standard or their voluntary alienation from a central spiritual tradition. For the humanists the struggle against liberalism had to rely on the staying power and persuasiveness of "ethical will." Humanism was essentially a nonreligious philosophy, though nobler in its aspirations as it stood against the materialism and the "naturism" of a profane age. This humanism, Foerster writes in "Humanism and Religion" (in *The Forum*, September 1929), "attracts persons who are content to be human, but not worldlings." It provided, as both mediator and reconciler, an alternative to "the ideal of the religious man" by offering "the ideal of the civilized man." Its roots, Foerster stressed, were Hellenic, pre-Christian:

. . . the choice of the humanist is that vision of a proportioned totality, that selective comprehensiveness, that just relation of the planes of life which was more nearly attained in the Greece of Pericles than any subsequent time or place.

Despite his support of humanism, Eliot found its forms, ancient and modern, inadequate, just another "attempt to devise a philosophy of life without a metaphysic." In his essay "The Humanism of Irving Babbitt" (1927) Eliot centers on the "obscurities" of humanism, resulting from its primary failure to accept any dogma except that of human reason. The humanist, by suppressing the divine element as the revelation of the supernatural, was left with the ever-corruptible human element. Humanism was "sporadic" and "impure"—"merely the state of mind of a few persons in a few places at a few times"—rather than, in irreversible historical contexts, "continuous" and "constructive" like Christianity. To be sure, humanism was, Eliot confessed in "Second Thoughts About Humanism" (1928), "necessary for the criticism of social life and social theories, political life and polit-

ical theories." But the battle against liberalism, against the chaos of the modern world, needed, Eliot believed, more than the positive and exclusive things that humanism offered, *i.e.*, "breadth, tolerance, equilibrium and sanity." Here Eliot was as critical of Babbitt's humanism as he was of Matthew Arnold's philosophy of culture (he, in fact, believed Arnold to be a forerunner of humanism). In both positions he condemned the great *élan* towards usurping the place of revealed religion. By no means did Eliot reject either the virtues or the values of humanism, but these, too, he was careful to define in the priority of their appropriateness. He wrote in "Religion Without Humanism," an essay he contributed to Norman Foerster's *Humanism and America* (1930):

Without humanism both religion and science tend to become other than themselves, and without religion and science—without emotional and intellectual discipline—humanism tends to shrink into an atrophied caricature of itself.

Only what Jacques Maritain called "*humanisme intégral*," humanism with a "metaphysics of transcendence," was to embody for Eliot a genuine spiritual ally in the war against liberalism. Singleness of vision and not a choice of vision was what mattered in the end. Certainly, the humanists did proffer wisdom against the liberals' "gospel of mediocrity," words Eliot used in writing about Bertrand Russell's *The Conquest of Happiness* (1930). "But wisdom is one thing without Christian wisdom, and another thing with it," Eliot writes in his essay "The Christian Conception of Education" (1941); "and there is a sense in which wisdom that is not Christian turns to folly." To repeat, Eliot insisted always on defining and ordering priorities. Humanism, under the circumstances, was a positive but secondary view of life. It was as admirable as it was effectual in combatting liberal fallacies, particularly in education. In this same essay Eliot singled out for praise Dr. Leavis's statement that "the problem of producing the 'educated man'—the man of humane culture who is equipped to be intelligent and responsible about the problems of contemporary civilization—becomes that of realizing the Idea of a University in practical dispositions appropriate to the modern world." But Eliot was careful to pose questions about the thinking behind such a humane culture. That is to say, humane culture by itself is not enough; it becomes an anthropocentric *cul-de-sac*. The ideas of humanism can never be consummate insofar as humanist "alternatives" and "auxiliaries" to religion fail in the long run. As G. K. Chesterton was to observe: "Humanism may try to pick up the pieces; but can it stick them together? Where is the *cement* which made religion corporate and popular, which can prevent it falling to pieces in a débris of individualistic tastes and degrees?" To such questions Eliot gave unequivocal answer:

> It [humanism] can only appeal to a small number of superior individuals; it can help them to recognize what is wrong, but it cannot provide them with the power to influence the mass of mankind and to bring about what is right. It can appeal to those people who have already the humanists' feelings and desires: but it cannot change the will of those who worship false gods. It is powerless against the drifting desires or torrential passions which turn by turn provide the motive force for the mass of natural men.

Liberal critics will continue to dismiss Eliot's contribution to the critique of modern liberalism. The charge that Eliot's sociocultural views are "irrelevant" will continue to be broadcast. Nor does there seem to be any letup in the derision of Eliot's "elitist politics." (Nor at the same time is there any real attempt to grapple with the substance of Eliot's belief that

"The pursuit of politics is incompatible with a strict attention to exact meanings on all occasions.") For the most part critics will continue to be curiously one-sided in their evaluation of Eliot's quarrel with liberalism, though such evaluation accords fully with the long-standing refusal of liberalism to see that man belongs to two planes of being and that man's rights cannot be separated from his responsibilities. Philip Rahv, the founding co-editor of *Partisan Review*, reflected this one-sided critical reaction (that too often sets a party-line judgment) when he wrote of Eliot: "His commitment to orthodox beliefs must have answered an irresistible inner demand of his nature for a discipline to shore him up against chaos. . . . In this sense it was no more than an anodyne." There is nothing wrong with society, we are told by such pundits, that the "organizational impulse" will not solve. John Dewey, in his ninetieth year, uttered a common liberal sentiment when he declared that "the one thing of prime importance today is development of methods of scientific inquiry to supply us with the humane or moral knowledge now conspicuously lacking." Yet, Dewey's valedictory, no less than Rahv's clinical judgment, is as one-sided as the Benthamism that, as John Stuart Mill writes, "can teach the means of organizing and regulating the merely *business* part of the social arrangements."

The events of time must render the final verdict. But it is clear by now that in his social criticism Eliot has become one of the great modern prophets. He saw not only into but beyond liberalism. Eliot, it has been said, "has the 'uncynical disillusion' of a tempered religious sensibility." This constitutes no shortcoming in his vision. What makes Eliot's thought so forceful is his ability to size up the human situation with a prophetic sensibility that is missing in the liberal mentality. "If liberalism," Lionel Trilling reminds us, "has a single desperate weakness, it is an inadequacy of imagination: liberalism is always being surprised." Eliot's was a vision of unromanticized compassion, and in this compassion lay that endurance and serenity of ordered thought leading to the kind of thinking that informs the following observation in "The Aims of Education":

> And so long as we are capable of resenting control, and of being shocked by other people's private lives, we are still human. We are, at least, recognizing that man is something more than merely a social animal: that there should be limitations to social control. And by being shocked (when it is something more than a prejudice that is shocked) we are recognizing, however dimly, that there is some law of behaviour which is something more than a duty to the State.

Toughness of thought is a characteristic of Eliot's social criticism. This toughness was a quintessential principle of order needed to resist some of the consequences of liberalism that Eliot detected especially in the nineteenth century and about some of which he wrote in his essay "Arnold and Pater" (1930): "The dissolution of thought in that age, the isolation of art, philosophy, religion, ethics and literature, is interrupted by various chimerical attempts to effect imperfect syntheses." This "dissolution," Eliot saw, remained unchecked, the enemy as combative as ever. Sir Arthur Quiller-Couch, lecturing at Cambridge University in 1934, exhibited the kind of scorn that has greeted Eliot's views. Eliot's concept of liberalism, he said, "is anything which questions dogma: which dogma, to be right dogma, is the priestly utterance of a particular offset of a particular branch of a historically fissiparous Church." Sir Arthur went on to give his own estimate of liberalism which, he claimed, "reveals itself rather as Tradition itself, throughout Literature (which is Thought worth setting down and re-cording) the organic spirit persisting, aër-ating, preserving, the liberties our ancestors won and we inherit." But surely the voice of liberalism heard here is the sentimental voice of the world. And the world, Eliot stated, "The world insists upon being right. It insists upon being virtuous. It is right, it is virtuous, it is damned."

"It seems to me," Eliot wrote to Herbert Read in 1924, "that at the present time we need more dogma, and that one ought to have as precise and clear a creed as possible, when one thinks at all. . . ." If, in time, Eliot did change his mind about some of his literary valuations, he did not alter his social views. To the end he remained critical of the process of de-Christianization, as well as of dehumanization, that he connected with liberalism. And to the end he believed that history, despite the deep contradictions and mysteries of human existence, has spiritual meaning. His social criticism marks him essentially as a man of wisdom, not, like John Dewey, a man of influence. "To be understood by a few intelligent people," Eliot said, "is all the influence a man requires." His quarrel with liberalism was moral; it must be seen as a creative quarrel that raised disturbing conceptual questions. Only a few liberals have been willing to read Eliot and to answer his questions with the sense of responsibility demanded of any scrutiny of ultimate issues that affect not only the structure of life but, more important, man's inner life. Certainly it is true that Eliot spoke as a conservative in his social criticism; yet he endowed his conservatism with a creativeness exceptional in its discriminations. Even if this conservatism, to use here John Stuart Mill's words regarding Samuel Taylor Coleridge, "were an absurdity, it is well calculated to drive out a hundred absurdities worse than itself."

[XVIII, Spring 1974, 145–162]

[21]

Willmoore Kendall: Conservative Iconoclast

GEORGE H. NASH

George H. Nash *(1945–   ) was educated at Amherst (B.A., 1967) and Harvard (M.A., 1968; Ph.D., 1973). The author of articles on Josiah Quincy, Jr., and Charles Stelzle, he has also published articles in* National Review, The Alternative, Labor History, *and other periodicals. His comprehensive multivolume biography of Herbert Hoover was commissioned by the Hoover Presidential Library Association; the first volume has already been published:* The Life of Herbert Hoover: The Engineer, 1874–1914 *(1983), and he is currently completing the second volume. His extended study of American conservatism—* The Conservative Intellectual Movement in America Since 1945 *(1976)—has commanded wide and serious attention, for, as he noted: "In 1945 'conservatism' was not a popular word in America, and its spokesmen were without much influence in their native land. A generation later these once isolated voices had become a chorus, a significant intellectual and political movement which had an opportunity to shape the nation's destiny."*

I

Few who met Willmoore Kendall ever forgot him. He was born in Konawa, Oklahoma, in 1909, the son of a blind Southern Methodist minister. Kendall's early years were spent in little prairie towns where his father preached—towns like Konawa, Idabel, Mangum. He was a child prodigy who learned to read at the age of two by playing with a typewriter. He graduated from high school at thirteen, entered Northwestern University the same year, and graduated from the University of Oklahoma at eighteen. By the time he was twenty he had published a book on baseball and was teaching in a

"prep" school. He was, in the words of a friend, "the boy wonder of Oklahoma."[1]

After completing all non-thesis graduate work in Romance Languages at the University of Illinois, Kendall became a Rhodes Scholar in 1932; his next four years abroad in many respects changed his entire life. It was at Oxford that he enrolled in the philosophy, politics, and economics (P.P.E.) program and discovered his future intellectual passion: political philosophy. One of his tutors was the distinguished philosopher R. G. Collingwood, who, Kendall later remarked, was a major influence. The years in England were ones of excitement, challenge, and intellectual exploration, and in this at-

234

mosphere Kendall thrived. He was argumentative, even quarrelsome, and soon earned a reputation as a brilliant, eccentric, and sometimes impossible fellow. He loved to shock people into debate, taking on all comers in disputation far into the night. Kendall's sister provides a glimpse of his arguments with his father—which suggest the pattern at Oxford and wherever he went:

> . . . it was not unusual for him and Dad to engage in heated debate of a political issue, ending with one or the other storming out of the room in anger—and then hear them, a few hours later, pick up the same subject, each taking the opposite side of the question under discussion. . . . It was for them, I think, a very stimulating kind of mental gymnastics—and it made artists of argumentative technique out of both of them.[2]

While Kendall's pugnacious probing at Oxford was generally good-humored, his temperament helps to explain the later troubled personal and academic life of this strangely driven man.

While abroad in the 1930's, Kendall became known as a man of the Left—even (some believed) the Trotskyist Left. While the precise evolution of his beliefs in this period is in some dispute,[3] the testimony of those who knew him at Oxford is solid on one point: he was an enthusiastic admirer of the Spanish Republic. In 1935 he left Oxford for a sojourn as a United Press correspondent in Madrid. There is little doubt that this experience, which ended shortly before the civil war broke out on July 18, 1936, was in political terms one of the decisive moments of his career. Passionately in favor of the leftist Spanish Republic, Kendall became associated with a number of prominent Spanish Trotskyists in Madrid.[4] According to Kendall's first wife, whom he married in 1935, Kendall's affinity for the Trotskyists was in large part a reaction against Stalinism. In the turbulent cockpit of Spanish political warfare, Kendall's detestation of Stalin and the Moscow-oriented Communists grew.[5] The dictatorial, totalitarian, anti-democratic aspects of Communism appalled him. He later told a friend that as Spain slid toward civil war he could tolerate the Communists' blowing up the plants of opposition newspapers. But when they deliberately killed opposition *newsboys*—this was too much.[6] Exposure to the Spanish Republic "really shook Willmoore up," one friend recalled, and within a few months "his thought crystallized into fervent anti-Communism."[7] This theme—militant, uncompromising hostility to Communism—became one of the dominant features of his thought. The disintegration of Spain, the awful specter of civil war, started a disillusioned man on the road to the Right. Like so many other postwar conservatives (Whittaker Chambers, Frank Meyer, and more), in Kendall's past was a god—or, more likely in his case, only a demigod—that failed.[8]

But if Kendall's anti-Stalinism was the genesis of a later, broader anti-Communism, it did not make an instant conservative out of him. Returning to the University of Illinois in the fall of 1936, Kendall continued to be a man of the Left. He supported the cause of Republican Spain and was even accused of recruiting students for the Abraham Lincoln Brigade. His first scholarly articles in the late 1930's were of a decidedly left-wing cast—articles in which he advocated, for example, government ownership of the press[9] and contended that an "economic oligarchy" had always held political power in America.[10] Ever distrustful of elites, Kendall enunciated a radical democratic viewpoint—a position somewhat in vogue in the late 1930's during the debate over majority rule versus the "nine old men" on the Supreme Court. In 1938 he advocated the Ludlow Amendment, under which the United States could not officially go to war (except in case of invasion) until a national referendum was held. "There are those of us," he declared, "who believe that the best judges of a nation's welfare are the people who live in it; and once that belief has been set aside, the door is thrown wide open to the most violent excesses of minority rule."[11]

Meanwhile Kendall continued his study of political philosophy. Changing his field from Romance Languages, he obtained his Ph.D. from the University of Illinois in Political Science in 1940. His dissertation adviser was Francis Wilson, one of the pioneers of the postwar conservative renascence. Kendall's dissertation, published a year later, was true to his temperament: daring, relentlessly argued, and unorthodox.[12] Challenging the conventional notion that John Locke was the champion of inalienable natural rights, Kendall meticulously contended that Locke was actually a "majority rule" democrat. To be sure, Locke talked of natural rights, but in the last analysis he "would entrust to the majority the power of defining individual rights."[13] ". . . Locke's natural rights are merely the natural rights vouchsafed by a legislature responsible to the majority. . . ."[14] The society is sovereign, not the individual, whose rights are "a function of, not a limitation on" the society.[15] How could Locke have both "rights" and majority dominance? Because, said Kendall, of his "latent premise" that his kind of majority "would never withdraw a right which the individual ought to have."[16]

Kendall's work, which was recognized as a major piece of scholarship on the Locke "problem," inaugurated one of the most unusual academic careers of his time. After government service during and after World War II (including a high position at the Central Intelligence Agency),[17] Kendall joined the Yale University faculty

in 1947 and stayed for fourteen tumultuous and bitter years. His letters from this period are full of stories of departmental warfare; never, although he had tenure, did Yale grant him a promotion from associate professor. Finally, in 1961, when Kendall believed it clear that he would never go higher at Yale, he offered to leave—if Yale "bought up" his tenure rights. Yale agreed and paid him a sum in the tens of thousands of dollars. Kendall told a friend that he was "the only man that Yale ever paid to resign from its faculty."[18]

In his early years at Yale,[19] Kendall's principal scholarly enthusiasms were "majority-rule democracy" and the related critique of the "open society." He called himself "an old-fashioned majority-rule democrat," by which he meant that the people in a democracy had "not only the right but the *duty* . . . to use public policy as an instrument for creating the kind of society their values call for. . . ." He was therefore flatly against attempts to limit majorities by bills of rights;[20] such attempts were, ipso facto, undemocratic. Why was he so unremittingly hostile to the natural rights philosophy? A passage from a critique of one of his favorite targets—John Stuart Mill—provides a clue:

> Start out with Mill's principles, and you end, as Mill himself did, with the anarchistic view that there are no limits whatever upon the degree of "diversity" a society can stomach and still survive (wherefore we must today tolerate, for instance, anti-semitic utterance by our neighbors, because prohibiting it would infringe their "rights" to freedom of speech).[21]

Again and again, in articles and on debate platforms, Kendall denounced the "heresy" that all-questions-are-open-questions. He insisted that all societies (including democracies) do have, ought to have, and must have an orthodoxy, a consensus, a will-to-survive that they may rightfully defend against those who fundamentally challenge the very core of what they hold dear.[22]

To Kendall these considerations were no airy theoretical fancies. They were truths applicable to the greatest domestic debate of the late 1940's and early 1950's: the status and influence of Communism in American life. Into this fray he moved with characteristic vigor and flamboyance, soon emerging as one of the most capable of the academic defenders of Senator Joseph McCarthy, whom he knew personally. Tirelessly he defended McCarthy's crusade, Whittaker Chambers, and the determination of many Americans to declare Communists beyond the bounds of public protection. He criticized Alger Hiss and J. Robert Oppenheimer[23]—activities not likely to smooth the ruffled feathers of some of his enemies on the Left. Discussing the Nixon-Mundt bill to control Communism in 1950, Kendall even suggested deportation as a possible sanction against Communists (and, back in the 1930's, Nazis, too). Kendall acknowledged that "liquidation of a minority" must be a very careful undertaking. But he insisted on two principles:

> . . . (a) that a democratic society that has a meaning to preserve, as I think ours still does, must stand prepared to make such decisions, and (b) that the surest way for it to lose its meaning is for it to tell itself, and its potential dissidents, that where dissidence is concerned, the sky's the limit.[24]

In another letter several years later Kendall amplified his point. *His* campaign against Communists did not depend on proving that domestic Communists were a clear and present danger. Indeed, at the moment they were not a *clear* and *present* danger at all. His argument was different: "we do not make sense as a community so long as we tolerate Communists and pro-Communists in our midst."[25] Or as he put it on another occasion: "The reason for striking at [domestic] Communists is not so much that they are dangerous as that they are incapable of participating in democratic government."[26]

A few years after the McCarthy episode faded into history, Kendall applied his perceptions to an attempt to explain the true meaning of McCarthyism. The basic issue had not been McCarthy himself; after all, people were "mad" at one another in the Hiss case, long before McCarthy was heard of. Nor had the issue simply been one of different opinions about the seriousness of the Communist threat; this answer could not explain the intensity of the dispute—indeed, its "civil war dimension." The issue had not been one of the executive versus the legislative branch, either; people do not become *that* angry over abstract "separation of powers." The clue to the proper explanation, rather, lay in the fact that each side was really accusing the other of "heresy." The battle was a debate—"with genuine civil war potential"—over the fundamental nature of American society. Were we, or were we not, an "open society"? Could the United States proscribe and "persecute" an "undesirable" movement like the Communists *even if* there were no immediate peril? Did the United States have a consensus—an orthodoxy—which could be defended by legal and other sanctions? Were all questions "open" questions, or did we hold certain truths? In all the confusion and maneuvering of the dispute, said Kendall, "McCarthyites" (that is, broadly speaking, the Right) answered these questions one way, and "anti-McCarthyites" (the Left) another. The McCarthy episode was thus an intellectual and spiritual crisis of the gravest dimensions.[27]

Long after the McCarthy controversy subsided, Kendall labored on—almost

quixotically, it seems—in defense of
America's deepest meaning as he saw it.[28]
There was irony and perhaps pathos in
his odyssey: a dissenter pleading the cause
of orthodoxy, an individualist who detested notions of absolute rights, a rebel
who suffered the displeasure of the local
orthodoxy of liberal Yale. Kendall knew,
too, the price he was paying for his relentless, irrepressible iconoclasm: hostility
at Yale, the obstacles to professional advancement, the charges that he was a
fascist, an authoritarian, a warmonger.
Why, one wonders, was he such a persistent, perhaps compulsive, "aginner"?
Without attempting to probe Kendall's
extraordinary personality (someone has
aptly said he was too complicated a man
to psychoanalyze), and without wishing
in the least to "explain away" his philosophy, we draw attention to two profound
and probably formative experiences in his
life. First, he said that he learned his
deepest lessons about democracy from the
closed little towns of his Oklahoma boyhood.[29] Second, the shattering nightmare
of Spain, one strongly suspects, first taught
him the horror of a society without a
consensus, a society at war with itself, a
society where everybody was free to talk—
and talked themselves into war. These
truths were too dear to him to surrender
for the sake of tranquillity in academe.

There was more to his anti-Communism than that. Kendall genuinely believed that Communism was a danger to
America and that it simply had to be
exposed. Francis Wilson, his dissertation
adviser, explained Kendall's convictions:

> Apparently, liberal and kind-hearted Amer-
> icans believe all men are good and that all
> issues can be resolved by a little amiable
> conversation; hence, the communists could
> hardly be in any case a menace to the security
> of the United States. But Kendall (and all
> conservative critics of communism) have

> held that this is not so: communists are just
> not like this. They are engaged in a world-
> wide conspiracy to bring about the com-
> munist revolution everywhere, and the
> greatest enemy of communistic progress
> after World War II has been and is the
> United States.[30]

This unrelenting anti-Communism was
undoubtedly a key to his transition from
Left to Right. In the 1930's, of course,
(and later, too), one could be both a man
of the Left *and* an anti-Stalinist—a fact
which, James Burnham believed, motivated Kendall's "Trotskyism."[31] But to
someone like Kendall, the Left in the late
1940's and early 1950's was no longer a
likely haven. Certainly not Henry Wallace's Progressivism, which he denounced
fiercely. Nor "containment" liberalism,
which, to its critics, did not contain.[32] To
Kendall, who advocated a "liberation"
strategy,[33] the Truman-Acheson foreign
policy was hopelessly inadequate.[34]

Kendall's fervent anti-Communism was
only one of a number of factors pushing
him toward conservatism in the 1940's.
As the decade wore on, signs of his estrangement from liberalism multiplied.
One early wedge was the great foreign
policy debate of 1939–1941. Staunchly
anti-interventionist (although still at that
time a leftist in domestic affairs), Kendall
grew increasingly saddened as many of
his friends and heroes on the Left began
to support war with Germany. Writing to
a friend early in 1942, Kendall revealed
his disenchantment with the nation's political Establishment:

> It is not, in short, my faith in the majority
> which I've lost. The majority has, in sober
> truth, arrived at no conclusions in the last
> couple of years that, on the evidence offered
> to it, I could fairly have expected it to reject.
> My concern, and disillusionment, is with the
> people who could have given them evidence
> of another kind—with, if you like, the most

gigantic and unpardonable *trahison des clercs* of which History offers any record. To think of it makes me sick at heart.[35]

Vehemently anti-Roosevelt, Kendall voted for Willkie in 1940 and hoped for a Republican victory in 1944. He was pleased by the Republicans' gains in the 1946 elections; perhaps, he explained to a friend, he would finally see what he had so long yearned for: "a Congress really asserting its prerogatives vis-à-vis the Executive."[36] None of these positions made Kendall an orthodox "conservative"; indeed, his correspondence indicates that he was in many respects a man of the Left at least until 1946.[37] But his was a left-wing stance of a decidedly idiosyncratic kind. It is not so surprising, then, that when the great "civil war" over loyalty and Communism erupted in the late 1940's, Kendall moved with apparent ease from Left to Right. So many of his enemies were *already* on the Left.

And one enemy above all: the liberal philosophy of natural rights and civil liberties. In a sense one can say that Kendall in the late 1940's did *not* change fundamentally at all; the Left did. For in the era of Joseph McCarthy, many Americans on the Left asserted with new fervor the value of civil liberties, individual rights, due process of law, checks and balances, and "pluralism." Back in the 1930's, it had been easy to applaud popular sovereignty and sweeping majority rule when the enemy was the Supreme Court, "economic royalists," and Spencerian natural "rights." With the advent of McCarthy and other zealously anti-Communist legislators, however, pure majoritarianism lost much of its appeal. Perhaps the people could be misled, by a *demagogue*; perhaps we needed *institutions* and *elites* to limit the untamed general will. To this reorientation in liberal thought, Willmoore Kendall—student of Rousseau,[38] foe of elitism, enemy of John Stuart Mill—

was impervious. Others might abandon their undiluted majoritarianism; not Willmoore. Well into the 1950's, he strenuously maintained his old position.[39] This unyielding theoretical consistency was one more ingredient in Kendall's deepening antagonism toward liberalism.

So Kendall ended on the Right. At first a supporter of Senator Taft in 1952, he voted for Eisenhower over "Addlepai" Stevenson, "the Ivy League Will Rogers." He even planned at one point (he had so many plans) to write a *Confession of an American Imperialist Reactionary*, which would be "a declaration of war on the intellectuals."[40] Many of his closest student friends at Yale went on to become conservative spokesmen—William F. Buckley, Jr., L. Brent Bozell, Stanley Parry. In 1955 Kendall became a senior editor of *National Review*.

And always he played the role of iconoclast, the man who loved to defend the seemingly impossible cause. In a stunning analysis of Plato's *Apology* and *Crito* in the late 1950's, for example, Kendall attacked head-on the view that Socrates was a faultless hero unjustly persecuted by an ignorant mob. If Athens were so utterly without reason, why did Socrates deliberately elect to stay there and die? If the laws had no legitimate claim over him, why did he not escape? The true point of Plato's drama was the "sheer inevitability of the failure" of Socrates, the tragedy of a conflict of truths. On one side was a man inspired by God, a man with a "divine mission," a "revolutionary agitator" (in the eyes of the Assembly) who candidly and radically questioned the way of life of the *polis*. On the other was Athens, which did *not* savagely persecute him but first gave him a full hearing *and was not convinced*. How could it have been otherwise? Socrates made it plain that he would not, could not, cease to preach (in effect) the overthrow of the city. He was not harmless; already he had many devoted youthful followers. Therefore, Plato was saying, punishment of Socrates was unavoidable. Athens had offered him all that it possibly could—the laws, freedom to speak in his own defense, even a chance to flee—and still survive. And Socrates understood this fact. He *refused* to become a modern liberal asserting his absolute "right" to speak regardless of other considerations. He spoke instead in the name of a shattering Truth, of God, *not* in the name of relativistic, "open-minded," free discussion in search of truths-that-don't-exist. *We* may prefer Socrates, Kendall concluded, but we must "forgive" Athens for its "second-best" choice which was actually more "realistic" than that of the man who forced it to condemn him.[41]

Meanwhile another fundamental reorientation of Kendall's life began to occur in the 1950's—a transformation as important as his earlier shift from Left to Right. Writing in 1954 to Henry Regnery, William F. Buckley noted a "metamorphosis" in his mentor:

> In 1949, he was rather cynical about the great truths that you had dedicated your life to pressing upon our society. Slowly, but inexorably, he has lost the cynicism he acquired as a precocious scholar at Oxford and as a young and gifted teacher in the turbulent '30's, to the point where he has become, in my experience, one of the few fine and intensely moral figures of our time.[42]

In 1956 Kendall, long a religious skeptic, joined the Roman Catholic Church—impelled in part, he said, by the Church's centuries and centuries of tradition.[43] It is possible that the Church's anti-Communism also had something to do with his conversion.[44]

What were these "great truths" which Kendall increasingly expounded? During the 1950's he became profoundly influenced by two men whose thought, he believed, inaugurated a "revolution in political theory scholarship": Eric Voegelin and Leo Strauss.[45] These two men, he acknowledged freely, dramatically changed his scholarly career. Kendall called Strauss "*the* great teacher of political philosophy, not of our time alone, but of any time since Machiavelli."[46] Under Strauss's influence Kendall modified his view of John Locke[47] and in fact became so affected by the "revolution" that his scholarly standards "changed drastically" and the pace of his own scholarship slowed down. He felt the duty to combat what Strauss called the "illegitimate" (that is, behaviorist, relativist, "value-free") branches of political science.[48] Above all, Kendall absorbed the great Straussian distinction between the Great Tradition and the rebellion against it inaugurated by Machiavelli, Hobbes, and Locke.[49]

In numerous ways, Kendall held, the "moderns" deviated from the older and better conception of political man. The Great Tradition believed that man and society were "coeval"; the "contractarians" saw society as an "artifact" to be altered at will. The Great Tradition emphasized that man is social by nature; the contractarians emphasized instead the self-contained individual, isolated and fearful in a state of nature, who merely made a "contract" or compact to which he gave "consent." The Great Tradition emphasized man's "perfection" or "end"; the contractarians, merely man as he (supposedly) was. The Great Tradition especially emphasized natural law and the duties of men; the "modern" rebellion spoke only of natural "rights" which were not bound by duties or by any moral obligation at all. The only ultimate right, really (said the moderns), was mere self-preservation or self-interest. Indeed, the contract philosophers denied that a higher law existed. That was the question for

Kendall: "whether there is or is not a higher law, independent of agreements and contracts, among men."[50]

This new direction in Kendall's thought may seem puzzling on the surface. Natural law, truth, justice, the denigration of "consent"—how was this emphasis compatible with his former "absolute majoritarianism"? Was not the thrust of his "Straussian" views at least in spirit antidemocratic? Perhaps. But Kendall was a complicated thinker, and one should note the deep continuities between his earlier (Leftist) and later (Rightist) phases. In *both* periods, for example, he detested "individual rights" philosophies. In the earlier years he did so in the name of a majority (unhindered by formal bills of rights) eager to create and sustain an orthodoxy. Under Strauss's influence he called forth the natural law and duties. Perhaps there is an affinity between "absolute" majoritarianism and the "absolute" priority of justice and virtue over freedom and self-interest. At any rate, although he abandoned his absolute majoritarianism in the late 1950's, he did not surrender his belief that the majority should rule. Instead, he now began to speak of *kinds* of majorities, some good, some evil— a transition reflected in his "Two Majorities" article in 1960.[51] What happened, perhaps, was only this: the upholder of the propriety of public orthodoxies had found *the* Orthodoxy to defend.

II

In the final decade or so of his life, Willmoore Kendall became increasingly absorbed by a new task: the application of his political philosophy to the American tradition. Well before *National Review* was founded, Kendall was, of course, interested in American political institutions[52] and their rescue from both Communists and liberals. But the demonstration that our heritage was reconcilable with the Great Tradition became a dominant theme only in his last years.[53] Animating his writing was the conviction that traditional America was fighting off a "war of aggression," a "liberal revolution" which sought to set up, "in Machiavelli's phrase, *new modes and orders*." Conservatism could be empirically defined as the resistance to this revolution.[54] Of what did the liberal threat consist? First, the effort to create a totally "open society"; second, the ceaseless attempt to change the Constitution into a merely "plebiscitary" system; and third, the attempt to institutionalize a coarse egalitarianism.[55] Kendall contrasted true, conservative criteria for evaluating regimes (justice, the common good) with false, liberal criteria (individual rights, equality).[56] Indeed, there lay the "ultimate issue": natural law versus relativism and self-interest, the Great Tradition versus liberalism. Since liberalism was Lockeanism, conservatism must oppose both.[57]

And so an issue that frequently troubled the postwar conservative movement burst out once more. The "official literature" (to borrow a phrase of Kendall) taught that the American tradition was inherently liberal. The "official literature" said that Locke decisively influenced the Founding Fathers, that America was (or ought to be) "open," equal, and solicitous of natural rights. Kendall disagreed.

Consider, for example, Kendall's interpretation of the Declaration of Independence. If, as liberals often said, the "all-men-are-created-equal" clause was our preeminent national commitment in 1776, why was equality not even mentioned in the Preamble to the Constitution only eleven years later? Surely the Fathers did not simply forget to include among the supreme defining purposes of the Constitution the one which everybody supposedly knew underlay all the rest. And why did the *Federalist Papers* also neglect equality? And the Bill of Rights? And what did the word connote, anyway? To Kendall it meant a universal right to justice, to government under law, to treatment as a human being. Equality did not mean liberal egalitarianism—the notion that men should be made equal in a material way. That notion emerged only much later, with Abraham Lincoln, whom Kendall found guilty of a tragic "derailment" of our tradition because of his claim that the Declaration of Independence had "constitutional status." Why, it had not even set up a nation—only "a baker's dozen of new sovereignties." The signers actually refused to condemn slavery in the Declaration and gave other indications that the document's phrases had no binding or compelling meaning. Kendall argued that to make the Declaration's equality clause a paradigmatic slogan was to distort grotesquely its limited intent.[58]

Nor did the Constitution or Bill of Rights embody the absolute natural rights theory. Again, the Preamble spoke of insuring justice, tranquility, and other goals, not absolute individual "rights." Moreover, and astoundingly, the Philadelphia Convention of 1787 had unanimously (and properly) rejected George Mason's proposal to include a bill of rights! How, if the Founders had been such thoroughgoing Lockeans, could they ever have done that? Moreover, there was no "mandate" or genuine popular demand for a bill of rights, and the one which was adopted was conspicuously not the sort of document Justice Hugo Black later thought it was. It did not proclaim the United States an "open society"; that question was not even "up" in 1790. The First Amendment did not proclaim a right to free speech. It merely constrained Congress and gave a monopoly of "suppression" to the states! The First Amendment was simply a states' rights amendment.[59]

Moreover, relying on the scholarship of Leonard Levy,[60] Kendall claimed with delight that history vindicated his analysis. Levy showed that the sainted Founding Fathers did not intend (and did not act as if they had intended) to set up a wide-open, do-your-own-thing society. The First Amendment was not believed at the time to abolish the common law of seditious libel. Indeed, said Kendall,

> "the people," whose representatives wrote and who themselves ratified the first amendment, with its apparent guarantees of freedom of expression, had no tradition of free speech or a free press, no statesmen who were urging the need for these guarantees, and no political philosophers who had made out a case for them.[61]

Even Jefferson himself had what Levy (but not Kendall) called his "darker side": this verbal libertarian "*did*, while in office, appear to act on the principle that no government should permit qualms about individual rights to get in the way of its policies."[62] Now a critic might berate Jefferson and the Founders for failure to be twentieth-century libertarians. Or he could reprove Jefferson for "ill-considered" grandiloquent pronouncements out of office that could not possibly meet the test of "prudential considerations" in office. Kendall took the latter course.[63]

In fact, he wondered, just where *did* this notion of free-speech-open-society come from? Clearly ordinary Americans had no such understanding. In 1955, for instance, two-thirds of them would not even permit Communists and atheists to speak in their town or high school.[64] Now whether this be a sign of intolerance or higher wisdom, it did, Kendall argued, make one wonder whether Americans had ever meaningfully adopted John Stuart Mill's ideas on free speech. It seemed to Kendall—in an extreme, if humorous, statement—that the true American tradition was not "preferred freedoms" but "riding somebody out of town on a rail."[65]

And that was the point. America was *not* in theory *or* in practice an open society. The liberals were *wrong*—wrong on the Founding Fathers, wrong on the Bill of Rights, wrong on our day-to-day functioning tradition. Whatever the merits of their philosophy, they could not claim the American tradition as a support. That tradition was *ours*—the conservatives'— and liberalism was at best a recent accretion, a "foreign" body, not organic and not viable.

How could the Left say otherwise? The very fact that American politics is a constant battle about *liberal* proposals demonstrated, said Kendall, that the tradition itself was conservative.[66] The liberals had not made our country "open" or "equal." From J. Allen Smith to James MacGregor Burns, they had not succeeded in converting our Constitution into an instant-majority-rule document. The French Revolution had not yet occurred in the United States.[67] The liberal rebellion had not captured the barricades.

What barricades? It was not enough for Kendall to deny that the American tradition was exclusively or predominantly liberal. He had to show wherein our tradition was conservative. How did we know that what happened out there in America away from enclaves of liberals was not mulishness or ignorance but wisdom?

That something was indeed happening which conventional theory could not explain was the thesis of Kendall's path-breaking article, "The Two Majorities." Noting the familiar fact of conflict between a "liberal" President and a "conservative" Congress in recent decades, Kendall sought to understand "an unexplained mystery": the fact that "*one and the same electorate maintains in Washington, year after year, a President devoted to high principle and enlightenment, and a Congress that gives short shrift to both.*"[68] The liberals, of course, had an easy explanation for

this behavior: the Congress was undemocratic. First, they said, the Constitution itself—by such means as bicameralism, staggered elections, and rural overrepresentation—obstructed the translation of popular sentiment into decisive action. Second, the internal procedures of Congress—like the filibuster and seniority system—further thwarted majority rule. To Kendall this analysis was superficial and greatly misleading. How could one accuse the Founding Fathers of erecting barriers to a plebiscitary system when such a system was still unheard of? Moreover, the presidential system as we know it was only later "engrafted" onto our system. Citing numerous passages from the *Federalist*, Kendall contended that the Fathers were majoritarians—but of a special sort.

For what the Fathers wished to achieve *was* majority rule, but a majority decision articulated after "a process of deliberation among virtuous men representing potentially conflicting and in any case different 'values' and interests." This process of deliberation did *not* occur during the ritual of elections, as modern liberals would like. It did not involve deciding at elections between airy principles and visionary programs. It did not involve creation of a binding "mandate" at the polls. Ours was not the British system of government as that is usually perceived. Instead, the central process was that of deliberation by the Congress itself—a Congress of good men elected by structured local constituencies and *uninstructed* by them, yet always and inevitably aware of them. It was the task of Congress not to "carry out" packaged campaign promises but to weigh and consider, to obtain "feedback" from the local communities—in short, to deliberate. For what purpose? To achieve a "deliberate sense of the community," a *consensus*—not a bare, ragged majority produced after a shrill clash of grandiose principles. It was this undramatic congressional majority that expressed the way the system was originally intended to operate. And rightly so:

> ... insofar as the presidential election encourages the electorate to overestimate its dedication to moral principle, the congressional election encourages them, nay obliges them, to take a more realistic view of themselves, and to send forth a candidate who will represent, and act in terms of, that more realistic view. By remaining pretty much what the Framers intended them to be, in other words, the congressional elections in the context of the engrafted presidential election, provide a highly necessary corrective against the bias toward quixotism inherent in our presidential elections.... And it is well they do; the alternative would be national policies based upon a wholly false picture of the sacrifices the electorate are prepared to make for the lofty objectives held up to them by presidential aspirants. And executive-legislative tension is the means by which the corrective works itself out.[69]

Long before it had become fashionable, Kendall was a critic of the "imperial Presidency."

In siding with Congress and the local constituencies against the President and the centralizing liberals, Kendall, of course, ended in the same camp as most other conservatives. But—and this point is crucial—he came to that position in an "old-fashioned" majoritarian way. Here were no stirring appeals to natural rights, no Goldwaterish blasts at "big government,"[70] no exaltation of abstract individual freedom, no denunciations of universal suffrage or "the tyranny of the majority." Instead, Kendall denied J. Allen Smith's contention (tacitly accepted by many conservatives) that the Constitution was essentially undemocratic.[71] It was not, he insisted, hostile to majority rule *per se*. Even the Bill of Rights was not really a check on popular sovereignty.

> ... Madison's Bill of Rights, correctly read, ... leaves the natural rights, in the areas Justice Black correctly regards as crucial, subject to the general Federalist principles that the deliberate sense of the American community is to be trusted, and that any attempt to put parchment barriers in its way will as a matter of course be ineffective.... If the people wills to do itself hurt—or, we may safely add, good either—who is to say it nay? And the answer, for the American system, would appear to be: in the crucial area, nobody.[72]

But what *kind* of majorities should prevail? Not the plebiscitary ones, which, he stated in one article, "are not good instrumentalities for making public policy" and furthermore tend "to divide us, to make us bad friends with one another."[73]

> We must learn, we conservatives, that the issue is *not* whether the American system is or is not "democratic," but which of two competing definitions of "democracy"—that which equates it with government by the "deliberate sense" of the people, acting through their elected representatives, and that which equates it with direct majority rule and equality—should prevail, and in doing so, learn to expose the falseness of the Liberal's claim that the reforms he proposes can properly be defended in the name of democracy.[74]

In a rousing debate with James MacGregor Burns in 1964, Kendall cheerfully admitted that the American political system as he understood it was not an effective instrument for "translating popular will into action" or "getting government to do things for the people." But that was precisely its design and its virtue:

> Our system was devised by men who feared and disliked *above all things* the operation in politics of sheer naked will.... It was devised for purposes that had nothing to do with simplistic formulae like "the will of the people." ... It was devised to effectuate not the will of the people, but rather, as *The*

Federalist puts it, the deliberate sense of the community, the *whole* community, as to what ought to be done, what policies ought to be adopted.[75]

From the majoritarianism of his radical days Kendall had moved to a subtle, "Madisonian," majority-rule posture.

Kendall freely conceded that nothing explicitly written in the Constitution required "deliberate sense" or "consensus" majorities. Indeed, the document itself had—on paper—extraordinary "plebiscitary potential."[76] Consider afresh its words alone. It did not explicitly incorporate any notions of "separation of powers"; in fact, it was virtually a "congressional supremacy" document. An aroused, sustained majority in Congress could, if it wished, run roughshod over the other two supposedly equal branches. By impeachment and the power of the purse it could control the President. By such tactics as "court-packing" or regulation of appellate jurisdiction it could, if it wished, subdue the Supreme Court. Nothing forbade the emergence of a "mandate" system; Article V, in fact, even allowed the most drastic alterations of the Constitution to be adopted by the country. Clearly Kendall was no ordinary "strict constructionist."

And yet this most unconservative constitutional potential had never been actualized. Congress had refrained from using all its powers to dominate the government or to become the vehicle of every passing majority. Our system, said Kendall, has accepted the rise of judicial review, although, as L. Brent Bozell had now "conclusively demonstrated," the Constitution did not, in the eyes of those who wrote it, empower the Court to declare legislative acts unconstitutional. But Kendall held that We the People had, in our wisdom, adopted various political "habits" such as the filibuster, the seniority system, the avoidance of polarized, ideological parties, and the resistance to being "mobilized" for such ends as drastically amending the Constitution. We had absorbed, in short, a particular "constitutional morality."[77] Its purpose—the purpose of these "habits"—was not to thwart majority rule but to create a certain *kind* of majority rule.

And whence had this morality come? Above all, it was articulated in a book which Kendall tirelessly extolled as a "sacred" text: the *Federalist Papers*. It was "Publius" who persuaded Americans to accept a certain interpretation of the Constitution and a certain process by which the country was to be governed. In a luminous passage in an essay on the civil rights movement, Kendall summarized his distinctive teaching:

> ... what I do take sides on is the thesis of the *Federalist Papers*, namely: That America's mission in the world is to prove to the world that self-government—that is, government by the people through a representative assembly which, by definition, calls the plays—is possible. What I do take sides on is our solemn obligation, as Americans, to value the good health of the American political system—the system we have devised in order to prove to the world that self-government is possible—above the immediate demands, however right and just, of any minority. What I do take sides on is government by consensus, which, I repeat, requires of minorities demanding drastic change that they bide their time until they have pleaded their case successfully before the bar of public—not merely majority—opinion. What I do take sides on is the Preamble of the Constitution which gives equal status to justice and domestic tranquility, and so pledges us to pursue them simultaneously and not even in the "case" that seems "dearest" to a protesting minority, subordinate domestic tranquility to justice.[78]

To Kendall, one of the great strengths of the American system was its ability to prevent the rise of "pockets of irredentism that produce crises."[79] Perhaps in the back of his mind he was thinking of Spain.

Kendall was shrewd enough to realize that he could not base his defense of a tradition on a single book that might be dismissed as propaganda.[80] In a posthumously published book he attempted to uncover the "basic symbols" of America's heritage.[81] Employing the methodology of Eric Voegelin, Kendall argued that any society's self-understanding could be explored by scrutiny of its myths and symbols—in America's case, her formative public documents from the Mayflower Compact to the Bill of Rights. According to Kendall, the true tradition—of which even the Declaration of Independence, properly interpreted,[82] was a part—was:

> the representative assembly *deliberating* under God; the virtuous people, virtuous because deeply religious and thus committed to the *process* of searching for the transcendent Truth.[83]

And, argued Kendall, this commitment had never been abandoned. In blunt contrast to nearly every other conservative of his time, many of whom were deeply skeptical of the masses, Kendall stated, time and time again, that We the People had not ceased to be "virtuous," to keep the faith of the Fathers. Oh, the people were inarticulate—he knew that. Yet they had succeeded in carrying the tradition (the Great Tradition) "in their hips"—a favorite phrase he attributed to Lincoln Steffens. Kendall called himself an "Appalachians-to-the-Rockies patriot." Even in the dark days of 1964 he maintained that "the overwhelming majority of the American people" were conservative.[84] A frequent undercurrent of his writings, in fact, was the conviction that in the local communities political wisdom could still be found. He had faith in "neighborliness," which "knocks the edges off the

tendency to be doctrinaire."[85] The Liberal Revolution—construed especially as an assault on the structure, not the substance, of our politics—had not been consummated. The American people were still bound by a consensus. They had not converted our system to "reliance on the sheer, naked will of the majority."[86] In their hips they knew they were right.

Even the civil rights movement, Kendall said in one of his last essays, had been obliged to conform to the still vital American system. In 1964, a few years before he died, Kendall had predicted that this allegedly revolutionary force would precipitate a "constitutional crisis comparable to and graver than that which precipitated the Civil War. . . ."[87] The American political system, based on government by "consensus" or "the deliberate sense of the community," and biased against "governmentally-induced drastic change,"[88] would clash with a group that demanded such change and that would not take "no" for an answer. Three years later, even as American cities were wracked by riots, Kendall announced that the civil rights movement had been "killed." His earlier prediction of a constitutional crisis had not come true. Why this unexpected development? First, the movement had lost "steam" because it had been "deserted" by many white liberals. Second, its greatest victories—the congressional legislation of 1964 and 1965—had been won at the price of increasing opposition and of moving the scene of battle from the South to the "more difficult terrain" of the North. Third, by altering its objectives from legal equality to "substantial" equality for blacks, it had increased the obstacles to further success. In other words, the more radical it became, the lesser the likelihood of victory. Finally—and this was Kendall's "favorite" explanation—the crisis had been averted because the civil rights forces had been made "a prisoner of the traditional

American political system and thus of consensus politics." The movement had been "softened in order to restore equilibrium in the American political system. . . ." How? Precisely by the legislation of 1964 and 1965, which Kendall, virtually alone among conservatives, hailed as "great Conservative victories." Congress had skillfully given the civil rights advocates the appearance of triumph, had domesticated the movement, without giving it in practice what it had conceded in principle.[89] The system still stood.

Still, there was no denying that America faced a massive rebellion. It had been initiated, Kendall said on one occasion, by Abraham Lincoln, whose "legitimate offspring" were today's liberals, "dedicated like Lincoln to egalitarian reforms sanctioned by mandates emanating from national majorities. . . ."[90] Kendall, like many other postwar conservatives, was uneasy about Lincoln, whom he perceived as a prototype of the modern, liberal, "strong" President. He said he found "hair-raising" the idea of

a political future made up of an endless series of Abraham Lincolns, each persuaded that he is superior in wisdom and virtue to the Fathers, each prepared to insist that those who oppose this or that new application of the equality standard are denying the possibility of self-government, each ultimately willing to plunge America into Civil War rather than concede his point—and off at the end, of course, the cooperative commonwealth of men who will be so equal that no one will be able to tell them apart.[91]

The rebellion was fanned, said Kendall, by a Liberal Propaganda Machine[92] and advanced by the Warren Court. The "cancer" that threatened "the very survival of the American political system" was not, however, judicial review as such (which had the sanction of tradition) but the "due process" and "equal protection" clauses of the Fourteenth Amendment, without

which the desegregation and school prayer decisions, for instance, would never have been made.[93] On one occasion he even called for the repeal of the Amendment— or at least a "clarification" of it or perhaps a congressional removal of the offending clauses from the Court's jurisdiction.[94] On a later occasion he pointed to an ambiguity in one of these clauses:

Does the Fourteenth Amendment call for the equal protection of existing laws? Or does it call for revising existing laws until they confer equal protection?[95]

To Kendall the former meaning was correct—and it had been accepted by the Supreme Court for decades.[96]

Kendall was less interested, however, in determining the original intention of the Amendment than he was in the meaning of the Court's new interpretation of our entire system. The original Constitution, he noted, had clearly given the monopoly of power in the fields of suffrage, education, religion, and legislative apportionment to the states. The original government, which included the Court, "was to keep its hands off. . . ." This was, as he put it in his distinctive idiom, the "original deal," which the Tenth Amendment "merely hammers down." There was "nothing . . . sacred" about the ideal that "couldn't be revised as time went on." If, he went on, the equal protection clause of the Fourteenth Amendment merely meant "that all are entitled to the impartial application of existing laws," then the "original deal . . . is still on." But if the other meaning was in force, then the Fourteenth in effect repealed the Tenth! The Supreme Court, by opting for this other meaning, had grossly changed the "deal." It had done so by ignoring the proper process of alteration: constitutional amendment.[97] But, he warned conservatives, do not waste time arguing about the legality of judicial review. Instead, challenge the wisdom of Court decisions. And "get busy and amend the Fourteenth Amendment."[98]

Yet if the menace from the Left was so profound, how could Kendall be sure that We the People would remain "virtuous"? In an essay on Richard Weaver, he gave his answer: a "select minority" (Ortega's phrase) must serve as guardians and teachers of the truths of their culture. To Kendall, Weaver was such an exemplar, and Weaver's *Visions of Order* (1964) was actually the "missing section" of *The Federalist*, the section which would tell us how the virtue requisite to republican self-government would be maintained.[99] Kendall ranked Weaver among the greatest contemporary conservative intellectuals.[100] It was evident from Kendall's writings that Leo Strauss was another such teacher. And it was evident that still another would have to be Kendall himself.

For Kendall was thoroughly dismayed as he surveyed the ranks of those who should serve as the teachers of the virtuous people: the contemporary conservative intellectual movement. Time and again Kendall revealed his exasperation with his fellow intellectuals of the Right. They were, he believed, generally a "poor lot,"[101] full of "false teachers."[102] The movement was disturbingly "rent" by divergent opinions about the very nature of the system it was supposed to be defending. Indeed, it even seemed at times "to be in the *business* of being unprepared intellectually for the next thrust of the Liberal Revolution."[103] There was, for instance, Frank Meyer, "the false sage of Woodstock" (New York),[104] John Chamberlain, and all the other libertarians who perpetuated the "Liberal lie" that our tradition was one of "individual rights."[105] There were those—he mentioned Frank Chodorov and Meyer, but nearly all were guilty—who railed against "big government," *per se*, as inherently evil. *The Fed-*

eralist should have taught them otherwise.[106] There were those who ceaselessly lamented that the Right was losing to the Left. The truth was that the Right had not been routed at all.[107] He found Meyer's influential *In Defense of Freedom* (1962) "rather frightening."[108] He was "horrified" at the rejoinders of Meyer, Russell Kirk, and M. Stanton Evans to M. Morton Auerbach in the *National Review* in 1962 on the nature of contemporary conservatism.[109] He thought that his revisionist article on the Bill of Rights would "end up getting me expelled from intellectual conservative circles." He noted that *National Review* had once refused to publish an article he wrote on the Declaration of Independence.[110]

Moreover, Kendall was relatively indifferent to laissez-faire economics—perhaps because he had immersed himself in John Maynard Keynes's thought at Oxford in the 1930's.[111] His conservatism, he proclaimed, had "sworn no vow of absolute fidelity . . . to free enterprise à la [Ludwig] von Mises. . . ."[112] Indeed, he even attacked the widespread conservative belief that political freedom and free enterprise were inseparable: "Given an appropriate public opinion, I see no reason why a free political system and a socialized economic system couldn't co-exist on one and the same piece of real estate."[113] Kendall, like other conservatives, definitely did believe in "private initiative" and economic freedom; he was no egalitarian socialist. But unlike many other conservatives, he did not believe that the primary threat to "private initiative" came from government at all:

. . . if the future of individual initiative depends on . . . containing the advance of levelling for the sake of levelling, of principled egalitarianism, then . . . we can safely say that private initiative is safe for the foreseeable future because, as far as this threat is concerned, there exists in America a healthy public opinion which, when the chips are down, is against levelling.[114]

In fact, some of the most serious dangers came from the private sector: "the bureaucratization of business enterprise" and "the rise of the meritocracy."[115] Once again we observe his lifelong distrust of elites—wherever they existed.

It was not surprising that this self-styled "Appalachians-to-the-Rockies" conservative was often incensed at the man he labeled "the benevolent sage of Mecosta": Russell Kirk.[116] Privately he called his own *The Conservative Affirmation* a "declaration of war" against Kirk, who must be shunted aside as an influence on the conservative movement.[117] For one thing Kendall disliked Kirk's recurrent appeals to Edmund Burke. While Kendall found Burke a useful guide on some matters,[118] he repeatedly emphasized that American conservatism must be grounded in *American* experience, expressed in American terms; he repudiated the "Burke 'cultists.' "[119] Burke's thought, for example, too often stressed "the tried and true" as the "essence" of conservatism. But "principled, general opposition to change . . . was not characteristic of our Founding Fathers, was never in American conditions, and is not today, a possible political posture. . . ."[120] In many other ways also, Burkean thought was irrelevant to America's heritage.[121] Moreover, Kirk was inculcating an " 'antipower' mystique" that was liberal, not conservative:

The essence of the American political tradition . . . lies in the exclusion of political power itself from certain *spheres* of human activity, thus *not* in the "separation" or "division" of powers—in *limited government* . . . not, I repeat, in any mystique about power in the spheres assigned, rightfully, *to government*. . . . [The] contemporary conservative movement . . . must learn to regard power as *morally neutral*. . . .[122]

Privately Kendall claimed on one occasion that Kirk was really a liberal.[123] On another, he contrasted Kirk's "literary" conservatism with his own "marketplace conservatism, not very elegant."[124]

Kendall's conservatism, in short, was unique. His was a political conservatism, concerned not so much with particular programs as with a process of making decisions. He was quite willing, he said, to let issues be settled "on their merits" in the political arena.[125] And let those decisions be made, he insisted time after time. He explicitly dissociated himself from the "Tenth Amendmentite anxieties" that James J. Kilpatrick and Russell Kirk expressed in *A Nation of States*.[126] As far as he was concerned, it was part of "the proper business of the American constitutional system to decide when powers reserved to the states and the people shall be moved 'across the line' " to the federal government. Indeed, "the sky's the limit . . . *provided* . . . we do not stumble into a constitutional crisis. . . ."[127] Perhaps there was a deeper reason for his divergence from so much conservative thought and his startling unconcern about so many right-wing apprehensions. From the 1930's to the late 1960's, the American Right was often haunted by a fear: what if the majority of the people irrevocably abandons the truths that we hold dear? Deep down inside, Willmoore Kendall, the Middle American boy from Oklahoma, seems never to have felt that fear. Konawa, Idabel, Mangum: the virtuous people, Yes.

And it was to the heartland that he returned toward the end of his life. In 1963 he accepted a position at the University of Dallas, a conservative, Roman Catholic institution. There he seemed at last to be happy. He was idolized: Saint Willmoore, they called him. "Kendall for King," proclaimed some student sweat shirts. After two unsuccessful marriages he was happily married at last.[128] Kendall knew, too, that he had come home. In the spring of 1963, just after visiting Dallas and confirming the job offer, he wrote with pride and relief:

> At Dallas, I can be Moses back from the 40 years of his preparation, among *his* people— I found myself sinking into the local accent, which was mine forty years ago, as a weary man sinks into a warm bath.[129]

"[J]'ai survéçu," he told Francis Wilson, "and without . . . any compromise on *any* point."[130] He had escaped the "World of the Buckleys" and felt "surrounded with the warmth and affection of *home*."[131]

Willmoore Kendall died in 1967. Several years earlier, Leo Strauss had told him that he was the best American political theorist of his generation.[132] Nearly everybody—friend and foe alike—agreed that he was one of the most brilliant and remarkable men they had ever met. He was universally regarded as a matchless teacher. His was a life of restless eccentricity. William F. Buckley, Jr., later called him "the most difficult human being I have ever known. . . ."[133] It was said at *National Review* that he was never on speaking terms with more than one associate at once—and never the same one.[134] Even his closest friends regarded him as "perverse."[135] One referred to Kendall's "raging compulsion to expose error and force recognition of sound principles here and now."[136] In part because of his combativeness, in part because of his marred academic career, Kendall's influence on his profession and the conservative movement was limited in 1967. For these reasons, plus his ardent "egghead McCarthyism,"[137] he never gained while he was alive the full, careful attention of his profession which he deserved. Yet the time would soon come when some conservatives and political scientists would begin to feel that he had been ahead of his time.[138]

Some conservatives had their doubts about him. Frank Meyer believed that his effort to reconcile his early left-wing absolute majoritarianism with his later right-wing "Madisonian" majoritarianism was a "mistake."[139] Russell Kirk stressed that Kendall was a "natural aginner" who was too majoritarian, too much influenced by Rousseau's concept of the "general will"— a position "disastrous" to conservatism.[140] Writing to Peter Viereck in 1954, Kirk noted that Kendall was a "devotee" of both Rousseau and Senator McCarthy, and then added: "significantly enough."[141] Similarly, the sociologist Robert Nisbet, who regarded Rousseau as "the real demon of the modern mind,"[142] was cool toward many of Kendall's positions.[143]

These comments by fellow conservatives highlighted one of the distinctive characteristics of Kendall's conservatism: its "populist" overtones. This word, to be sure, is a tricky one, with all sorts of connotations, and Kendall himself eventually repudiated "populist" (that is, pure, untrammeled, plebiscitary, undeliberative) democracy.[144] His was a special blend of "majoritarian" and "anti-majoritarian" perspectives. Nevertheless, in the thought of this native son of rural, Democratic Oklahoma, certain themes commonly called "populist" emerge. The Westerner's distrust of the East and what he once called the "world of the Buckleys." Faith in the inarticulate common man and distrust of "undemocratic" elites—a feature of his thought throughout his life.[145] Belief in the virtue still residing out there in the heartland of America. Kendall was in these respects a "populist" and a conservative.[146] The contrast with much aristocratic, even explicitly anti-populist, conservatism in the postwar period was striking.[147]

What had he offered? The most comprehensive and daring reinterpretation of America's political heritage developed by anyone on the Right since World War II.

Some have gone further. Professor Jeffrey Hart of Dartmouth College, for instance, has written:

> Willmoore Kendall remains, beyond any possibility of challenge, the most important political theorist to have emerged in the twenty-odd years since the end of World War II.[148]

He offered a plausible,[149] "non-Lockean" rejoinder to the "rebels" against the Great Tradition in the United States. An undeniably American conservatism—an important legacy to a movement that had often, since 1945, turned to European models in its search for an identity. He once indicated to a friend that he wanted to be, for the contemporary era, an American equivalent of Edmund Burke.[150] At least as much as any other conservative of his time, Willmoore Kendall had a right to make this claim.

NOTES

[1] This biographical portrait is based on a large variety of published and unpublished sources. Rather than burden the text with a citation for every single biographical datum, I shall list here the material used. For published information on Kendall's life, see George W. Carey, "Willmoore Kendall, 1909–1967," *Western Political Quarterly*, 20 (September, 1967), 799; Neal B. Freeman, "Recollections of an Impossible Man," *Rally*, 2 (September, 1967), 22, 28; Jeffrey Hart, "Willmoore Kendall: American," in Nellie D. Kendall, ed., *Willmoore Kendall Contra Mundum* (New Rochelle, 1971), pp. 9–26; Charles S. Hyneman, "In Memoriam," *P.S.: Newsletter of the American Political Science Association*, 1 (Winter, 1968), 55–56; and "Kendall, Willmoore," *Encyclopedia of Biography* (n.d.; copy supplied by Mrs. Nellie D. Kendall). I have been permitted to read "Willmoore Kendall: American Conservative," an unpublished tribute by Professor Leo Paul S. de Alvarez, a former colleague at the University of Dallas. In addition, more than thirty-five individuals have supplied (by correspondence and, in many cases, interviews as well) information about Kendall. They include some of his relatives, his first and third wives, three of his tutors at Oxford, and friends and professional colleagues from every phase of his career. I am very grateful for their interest and cooperation. Large numbers of Kendall's letters are in the Francis Wilson Papers, University of Illinois, and in the William F. Buckley, Jr., Papers, Yale University Library. Furthermore, four old friends and associates of Kendall—Professors Alfred Balitzer, Charles Hyneman, Austin Ranney, and Henry Wells—have very kindly allowed me to examine their letters from him. The responsibility for fact and interpretation, of course, is mine alone. The remark about Kendall as "the boy wonder of Oklahoma" was made in a letter from Prof. Arthur Larson to the author, December 29, 1971.

[2] Letter from Yvona K. Mason (Kendall's sister) to the author, April 20, 1972.

[3] Kendall's sister and Lyle H. Boren (an old friend) have stated their belief (in letters to the author) that Kendall was never a full-fledged "Trotskyite." (Mrs. Mason did say, however, that after returning from Spain he did for a time "argue in favor of certain aspects of that philosophy.") On the other hand, several who knew him at Oxford have recalled that he was left-wing, and even (more or less) a "Trotskyite." Kendall himself, in a letter to Henry Wells on April 20, 1942, referred to his "notorious Trotskyite sympathies from 1935 down to 1938." Copy in possession of the author. In a letter to the author on January 7, 1973, James Burnham recalled that although Kendall was never a Trotskyist member in the late 1930's, he was "on the fringe" of a loose group of "fellow travelers of the Trotskyite faction." This "satellite group," said Burnham, included Sidney Hook, Suzanne LaFollette, Mary McCarthy, and Dwight MacDonald. "Most of these intellectuals swerved toward Trotsky primarily because of Trotskyism's anti-Stalinism (which for many of them, as for me, was in reality potential anti-Communism) and, related to this, the issue of the Moscow Trials. Most of them, including Kendall, supported the committee that arranged the countertrial in Mexico." Probably Prof. Mulford Sibley—another old friend of Kendall—has most accurately summed up the matter: "If he was not actually a Trotskyite, he was at times close to their position." Letter to the author, January 6, 1972.

[4] One of his closest friends was Juan Andrade, a leader of the semi-Trotskyist Partido Obrero de Unificación Marxista (P.O.U.M.).

[5] Interview (by telephone) with Mrs. Katherine Kendall (Kendall's first wife), October 21, 1973.

[6] Interview with Prof. Charles Hyneman, Washington, D. C., March 8, 1974.

[7] Letter from Lyle H. Boren to the author, May 17, 1972.

[8] Prof. Austin Ranney of the University of Wisconsin recalls that Kendall told him that his experience in Spain was a great formative influence on

him: it made an anti-Communist out of him. Interview (by telephone) with Prof. Austin Ranney, December 30, 1971.

[9] See Kendall, "Should the Government Control the Press?" *The Quill*, 27 (May, 1939), 10–12.

[10] See Kendall, "On the Preservation of Democracy in America," *Southern Review*, 5 (Summer, 1939), 53–68.

[11] Kendall, "A Letter to a Congressman," *The American Oxonian*, 25 (April, 1938), 93. Full article: 91–94.

[12] Kendall, *John Locke and the Doctrine of Majority Rule* (Urbana, Ill., 1941; reprinted, 1965).

[13] *Ibid.*, p. 54.

[14] *Ibid.*, p. 58.

[15] *Ibid.*, p. 101.

[16] *Ibid.*, p. 135.

[17] He was Chief of the Latin American division of the C.I.A.'s Office of Reports and Estimates. The author is grateful to Mrs. Nellie D. Kendall for supplying a *curriculum vitae* of Kendall.

[18] Letter from John Fischer (a friend of Kendall from Oxford days on) to the author, January 20, 1972. Kendall appears to have been paid $42,500— the equivalent of five years of his salary.

The merits of Kendall's controversy with Yale are impossible to weigh here and are, at any rate, largely irrelevant to the issues at hand. The "case" did attract considerable comment within the profession. At one point late in the 1950's Kendall, in desperation, had a substantial number of academic friends write to Yale attesting to his scholarly reputation. Apparently Yale contended that his record of publications was inadequate. In addition, there was probably some animus against his immersion in "non-professional" work as a senior editor of *National Review*. Personal factors were also undoubtedly important.

[19] Actually he was on leave much of the time. From 1950 to 1954, for example, he was a major in the Air Force in the area of psychological warfare. His work (which included analysis of the effectiveness of propaganda and preparation of manuals) took him frequently to the Far East.

[20] Kendall, letter to the editor, *Yale Daily News*, April 28, 1950.

[21] Kendall, book review in *Journal of Politics*, 8 (August, 1946), 427. For Kendall's most extended critique of Mill, see his *The Conservative Affirmation* (Chicago, 1963), Chapter 6.

[22] This was a persistent theme in his writings, early and late. See, for example, *The Conservative Affirmation*, especially Chapters 3, 4, and 6.

[23] See William F. Buckley, Jr., ed., *Odyssey of a Friend: Whittaker Chambers' Letters to William F. Buckley, Jr., 1954–1961* (New York, 1970), pp. 53–54;

William F. Buckley, Jr., "The Ivory Tower: Professor Kendall Speaks at Harvard on Oppenheimer," *National Review*, 3 (May 4, 1957), 430.

[24] Kendall, letter to the editor, *Yale Daily News*, April 28, 1950.

[25] Letter from Kendall to Austin Ranney, April 13, 1954. Copy in possession of the author.

[26] Quoted in *Yale Daily News*, April 18, 1950.

[27] See Kendall, *Conservative Affirmation*, Chapter 3: "McCarthyism: The Pons Asinorum of Contemporary Conservatism."

[28] In a letter to the author on November 25, 1972, Kendall's sister pointed out that he persisted in defending what people called "McCarthyism" after others had stopped. Francis Wilson said: ". . . it is probable that toward the end of his life he may have been among the very few who were willing to stand before a university audience and affirm the danger of communism and the necessity of exposing communists." Francis G. Wilson, "The Political Science of Willmoore Kendall," *Modern Age*, 16 (Winter, 1972), 45.

[29] Kendall's colleague Leo Paul S. de Alvarez has remarked that Kendall often said this. See de Alvarez, "Difficult, Singular, and Legendary," *National Review*, 23 (August 24, 1971), 935–936.

[30] Wilson, "Political Science of Willmoore Kendall," 44.

[31] Interview with James Burnham, Kent, Conn., February 4, 1972. Burnham also believed that Kendall's political shift paralleled Burnham's own from anti-Stalinist Left to anti-Communist Right.

[32] In a noted speech before the European Center for Documentation and Information in 1957, Kendall asserted: "American Europe can become free, can resume the living of the good life as Europe has always conceived it, only by liberating itself and the rest of Europe from every form of subjection to Communism. And this it can do only by destroying the military power of the Soviet Union." Quoted in Rafael Calvo-Serer, "They Spoke for Christian Europe," *National Review*, 4 (July 27, 1957), 109.

[33] Charles Hyneman recalls that he advocated preventive war during the early Cold War years. Interview with Hyneman, March 8, 1974.

[34] For an important example of Kendall's critique of liberal foreign policies and assumptions about Communism in this period, see his "Introduction" to A. Rossi, *A Communist Party in Action* (New Haven, 1949), pp. v-xxiv.

[35] Kendall, letter to Henry Wells, April 20, 1942. Copy in possession of the author.

[36] Kendall, letter to Henry Wells, November 6, 1946. Copy in possession of the author.

[37] Quite in contrast to many conservatives in the mid-1940's, for example, Kendall disliked Friedrich

Hayek's influential critique of socialism, *The Road to Serfdom*. Instead, he praised Herman Finer's rebuttal, *The Road to Reaction*.

[38] After Kendall completed his dissertation on John Locke, he planned to write an equally revisionist study of Rousseau. But although he studied the French philosopher intensively throughout his life, and although he translated two of Rousseau's books, Kendall never completed his projected work.

[39] See, for example, his "Prolegomena to any Future Work on Majority Rule," *Journal of Politics*, 12 (November, 1950), 694–713.

[40] Kendall, letter to Henry Wells, Oct. 24, 1952. Copy in possession of the author.

[41] Kendall, "The People Versus Socrates Revisited," *Modern Age*, 3 (Winter, 1958–1959), 98–111.

[42] Letter from William F. Buckley, Jr., to Henry Regnery, September 25, 1954, Buckley Papers.

[43] The author is indebted here to Professor de Alvarez's unpublished memorial essay, listed above. One of Kendall's students, Father Stanley Parry, appears to have been a significant influence on his religious conversion.

[44] Lyle Boren suspects that this was the case. Letter to the author, May 17, 1972.

[45] Kendall, review of David Spitz, *The Liberal Idea of Freedom*, in *American Political Science Review*, 59 (June, 1965), 473.

[46] Kendall, "Who Killed Political Philosophy?" *National Review*, 8 (March 12, 1960), 175. Kendall also called the Straussian interpretation of modern political philosophy "the decisive development in modern political philosophy since Machiavelli himself." Kendall, review of Strauss's *Thoughts on Machiavelli*, in *Philosophical Review*, 75 (April, 1966), 251–252. Full article: 247–254.

[47] See his "John Locke Revisited," *Intercollegiate Review*, 2 (January–February, 1966), 217–234.

[48] Letter from Kendall to Francis Wilson (received by Wilson, March 4, 1960), Wilson Papers. Kendall attributed his low productivity at this point to the fact that Strauss and Voegelin had "changed drastically" Kendall's "standards." In this letter Kendall described Strauss's *Thoughts on Machiavelli* (1958) as very unsettling—"the most upsetting work of our time."

[49] See especially Kendall, *Conservative Affirmation*, pp. 83–99.

[50] *Ibid.*, p. 99. This paragraph is also based on Kendall, "Social Contract," *International Encyclopedia of the Social Sciences* (1968), XIV, 376–381.

[51] Kendall, "The Two Majorities," *Midwest Journal of Political Science*, 4 (November, 1960), 317–345.

[52] See Austin Ranney and Willmoore Kendall, *Democracy and the American Party System* (New York,

1956), a combination explanation/defense of the system, using "absolute" majority rule criteria. This book was begun several years before Kendall joined *National Review*.

[53] This new orientation meant, of course, that Kendall had to change his mind on many things. For example, in his radical days he had highly regarded J. Allen Smith's *The Spirit of American Government*. By the late 1950's and 1960's Kendall perceived Smith's book as the origin of the twentieth-century " 'Liberal attack' on the inherited political system of the United States." See Willmoore Kendall and George Carey, eds., *Liberalism Versus Conservatism: The Continuing Debate in American Government* (Princeton, 1966), p. xvi. See also Kendall, *Contra Mundum*, pp. 285–286. Kendall's correspondence indicates that he occasionally dreamed in his later years of writing a full-scale rejoinder to Smith's book.

[54] See Kendall, *Conservative Affirmation*, pp. 8, 10. See in general pp. 1–20.

[55] Kendall, "Three on the Line," *National Review*, 4 (August 31, 1957), 179–181, 191.

[56] *Kendall*, "The Cure That Kills," *National Review*, 11 (November 18, 1961), 346.

[57] *Kendall, Conservative Affirmation*, p. 99.

[58] Kendall talked about these matters often. See especially Kendall, *Conservative Affirmation*, pp. 17–18, 249–252; Kendall and George Carey, *The Basic Symbols of the American Political Tradition* (Baton Rouge, 1970), Chapters 5 and 6; Kendall, *Contra Mundum*, pp. 350–352.

[59] See Kendall, "The Bill of Rights and American Freedom," in Frank S. Meyer, ed., *What Is Conservatism?* (New York, 1964), pp. 41–64.

[60] Leonard Levy, *Legacy of Suppression* (Cambridge, Mass., 1960) and *Jefferson and Civil Liberties: The Darker Side* (Cambridge, Mass., 1963).

[61] Kendall, review of Levy, *Jefferson and Civil Liberties: The Darker Side*, in *Stanford Law Review*, 16 (May, 1964), 759. Full article: 755–767.

[62] *Ibid.*, 764.

[63] *Ibid.*, 765.

[64] See Samuel Stouffer, *Civil Liberties, Communism, and Conformity* (Garden City, N.Y., 1955). Kendall called this "a very favorite book of mine." Kendall, *Conservative Affirmation*, p. 81.

[65] *Ibid.*, p. 82. Kendall was not "opposed" to "free speech." In fact, he said (*Conservative Affirmation*, p. 77) that he sided "temperamentally" with the "let-em-speak" people rather than the "shut-em-up" people. But he refused to make a universally true, always applicable, absolute doctrine out of his preference.

[66] Kendall, "Three on the Line," 180.

[67] This was a major point of Willmoore Kendall

and George Carey, "Towards a Definition of 'Conservatism,' " *Journal of Politics,* 26 (May, 1964), 406–422.

[68] Kendall, "The Two Majorities," 328.

[69] *Ibid.,* 344.

[70] In a debate with James MacGregor Burns in 1964, Kendall explicitly denied that he was the kind of conservative who believed "The more government, the less freedom." *Dialogues in Americanism* (Chicago, 1964), p. 112.

[71] This was a change from the late 1930's when Kendall—still on the Left—believed that an "economic oligarchy" had always controlled political power in America and that the Constitution, "as it now operates, is as little congenial to majority-rule as it could possibly have become without abandoning the make-believe of democratic leanings." Kendall, "On the Preservation of Democracy for America," *Southern Review,* 5 (Summer, 1939), 54, 58.

[72] Kendall, "The Bill of Rights and American Freedom," pp. 63–64.

[73] Kendall, "Three on the Line," 181.

[74] Kendall, *Contra Mundum,* p. 417.

[75] Kendall in *Dialogues in Americanism,* p. 136.

[76] Kendall, "Three on the Line," 181.

[77] This paragraph is based primarily on Kendall, "Three on the Line," and Kendall's essay, "How to Read 'The Federalist,' " reprinted in *Contra Mundum,* pp. 403–417. Kendall's conception of a "constitutional morality" is similar to Bozell's idea of the "unwritten Constitution." Kendall's reference to Bozell's "conclusive" research is in *Contra Mundum,* p. 413.

[78] Kendall, "What Killed the Civil Rights Movement?" *Phalanx,* 1 (Summer, 1967), 43.

[79] Willmoore Kendall and George Carey, "The 'Intensity' Problem and Democratic Theory," *American Political Science Review,* 62 (March, 1968), 22. One outstanding element in the American political system was the political parties, which Kendall vigorously endorsed. See Kendall and Ranney, *Democracy and the American Party System.* For example: "Fostering consensus, then, is the phase of popular consultation on which our parties make their best showing . . ." (p. 517). Kendall was a great believer in government by consensus. He was very impressed by the "civil-war potential" in American society (*ibid.,* pp. 464–467). Political parties helped to counteract this danger.

[80] Charges that he attempted to refute in his essay on *The Federalist.* See Kendall, *Contra Mundum,* pp. 403–417.

[81] Kendall and George Carey, *The Basic Symbols of the American Political Tradition,* cited above.

[82] While Kendall often appeared to attack the Declaration of Independence, his targets were slightly different: the liberal (he thought Lincolnian, too) *interpretation* of the document, and the effort to make the document (or one clause of it) the single absolute American principle before which all else was to be sacrificed. He could on occasion acclaim the Declaration on conservative grounds. Following John Courtney Murray, whom he called "the true sage of Woodstock" (Maryland), he appeared, in an unfinished essay, to approve the Declaration's emphasis on absolute truths ("we hold these truths") in opposition to the relativism of the liberals. See Kendall, *Contra Mundum,* pp. 74–89, especially pp. 88–89.

[83] Kendall and Carey, *Basic Symbols,* p. 154.

[84] Kendall, *Contra Mundum,* p. 360. The author has been told that Kendall voted for Lyndon Johnson in 1964. It is clear that he was not enthusiastic about Senator Goldwater.

[85] Kendall, "American Conservatism and the 'Prayer' Decisions," *Modern Age,* 8 (Summer, 1964), 258.

[86] Kendall in *Dialogues in Americanism,* p. 141.

[87] Kendall, "The Civil Rights Movement and the Coming Constitutional Crisis," *Intercollegiate Review,* 1 (February–March, 1965), 54.

[88] *Ibid.,* 60, 57, 61.

[89] Kendall, "What Killed the Civil Rights Movement?" 37–43.

[90] Kendall, "Source of American Conservatism," *National Review,* 7 (November 7, 1959), 462.

[91] *Ibid.*

[92] A phrase he used frequently in his column for *National Review.* Kendall did not use this phrase in any literal, conspiratorial sense. Rather, he meant to convey by it what later conservatives meant by the "Liberal Establishment."

[93] Kendall, "American Conservatism and the 'Prayer' Decisions," 254.

[94] *Ibid.*

[95] Kendall, *Contra Mundum,* p. 354.

[96] *Ibid.,* pp. 354–355.

[97] *Ibid.,* pp. 354–357.

[98] Kendall, "American Conservatism and the 'Prayer' Decisions," 255, 259.

[99] See Kendall, "How to Read Richard Weaver: Philosopher of 'We the (Virtuous) People,' " *Intercollegiate Review,* 2 (September, 1965), 77–86.

[100] *Ibid.,* 83. Kendall had enthusiastically approved Weaver's *Ideas Have Consequences* when it appeared in 1948. In a review of this book Kendall unabashedly nominated Weaver for "the captaincy of the anti-Liberal team." Kendall, review in *Journal of Politics,* 11 (February, 1949), 259–261.

[101] Kendall, book review in *American Political Science Review,* 57 (June, 1965), 473.

[102] Kendall, "How to Read Richard Weaver," 81.

[103] Kendall, "American Conservatism and the 'Prayer' Decisions," 250.

[104] This was Kendall's epithet for Meyer and the projected title of a chapter on Meyer in Kendall's never-finished *Sages of Conservatism*. Interview (by telephone) with Frank Meyer, September 4, 1971.

[105] Kendall, "How to Read Richard Weaver," 81.

[106] *Ibid.*, and Kendall, *Conservative Affirmation*, p. xi.

[107] Kendall, "How to Read Richard Weaver," 81–82.

[108] Letter from Willmoore Kendall to Francis Wilson (received by Wilson, August 17, 1962), Wilson Papers.

[109] Letter from Willmoore Kendall to Francis Wilson, February 3, 1962, Wilson Papers. Auerbach's critique of conservatism, and various rebuttals, appeared in *National Review*, 12 (January 30, 1962), 57–59, 74.

[110] Letter from Willmoore Kendall to Francis Wilson (received by Wilson, December 4, 1962), Wilson Papers.

[111] The author learned this fact in correspondence with two of Kendall's surviving tutors.

[112] Kendall, *Conservative Affirmation*, p. xi.

[113] Kendall, *Contra Mundum*, p. 601.

[114] *Ibid.*, p. 600.

[115] *Ibid.*, p. 605. See in general, pp. 594–608 (a speech Kendall delivered in 1966).

[116] See *ibid.*, pp. 29–57 for an analysis of Kirk's conservatism.

[117] Letter from Willmoore Kendall to Francis Wilson (received by Wilson, April 11, 1963), Wilson Papers.

[118] See Kendall and George Carey, "Towards a Definition of 'Conservatism,' " cited above.

[119] Kendall, "How to Read Richard Weaver," 83. See also the introduction to Kendall, *Conservative Affirmation*.

[120] Kendall, *Contra Mundum*, p. 37. See in general pp. 29–57.

[121] *Ibid.*, pp. 46–47.

[122] *Ibid.*, pp. 53–54.

[123] Letter from Willmoore Kendall to Francis Wilson (received by Wilson, March 7, 1963), Wilson Papers.

[124] Letter from Willmoore Kendall to Francis Wilson (n.d.; probably March, 1963), Wilson Papers.

[125] Kendall in *Dialogues in Americanism*, p. 112.

[126] Robert A. Goldwin, ed., *A Nation of States* (Chicago, 1963).

[127] Kendall, "The Civil Rights Movement and the Coming Constitutional Crisis," 53–54. It should be noted that Kendall was discussing what *could* be done under our political system, not what *ought* to be done. On many, probably most, policy issues of the day, Kendall agreed with his fellow conservatives.

[128] Even in private life Kendall was unusual. Thrice married, he may have been the only person in the history of the Roman Catholic Church to have two marriages annulled simultaneously.

[129] Letter from Willmoore Kendall to Francis Wilson (n.d., but spring, 1963), Wilson Papers.

[130] Letter from Willmoore Kendall to Francis Wilson, May, 1963, Wilson Papers.

[131] Letter from Willmoore Kendall to Francis Wilson (received by Wilson, January 13, 1964), Wilson Papers.

[132] Letter from Leo Strauss to Willmoore Kendall, May 14, 1961, Wilson Papers.

[133] William F. Buckley, Jr., *Cruising Speed—A Documentary* (New York, 1971), p. 73.

[134] In 1963 Kendall resigned as senior editor of *National Review*. Letter from Kendall to William F. Buckley, Jr., September 22, 1963, Buckley Papers.

[135] Both Frank Meyer and George Carey used this word to describe (but certainly not dismiss) Kendall. Interview with Meyer, September 4, 1971; George Carey, "How to Read Willmoore Kendall," *Intercollegiate Review*, 8 (Winter-Spring, 1972), 63.

[136] Charles S. Hyneman, "In Memoriam," *P.S.: Newsletter of the American Political Science Association*, 1 (Winter, 1968), 56.

[137] Kendall used the term "unabashedly egghead McCarthyism" to describe his article on "The Open Society and its Enemies." Letter from Kendall to Francis Wilson, August 4, 1960, Wilson Papers.

[138] In his memorial essay on Kendall, Charles Hyneman stated that "few of his generation in American political science can match his claim for attention over the decades immediately ahead." Hyneman, "In Memoriam," 56.

[139] Interview with Meyer, September 4, 1971.

[140] Interview with Russell Kirk, Cambridge, Mass., April 21, 1971.

[141] Letter from Russell Kirk to Peter Viereck, August 5, 1954. Copy in possession of the author.

[142] Letter from Robert Nisbet to Russell Kirk, September 10, 1953, Russell Kirk Papers, Clarke Historical Library at Central Michigan University.

[143] Letter from Robert Nisbet to Russell Kirk, January 3, 1963, Kirk Papers. On the other hand, Nisbet did acknowledge that Kendall was a "formidable" and "towering" figure for those who knew his work. Interview with Robert Nisbet, Northampton, Mass., November 29, 1971.

[144] See his late essay with George Carey, "The 'Intensity' Problem and Democratic Theory," *Amer-*

ican Political Science Review, 62 (March, 1968), 5–26, especially Part IV.

[145] See his early essay "The Majority Principle and the Scientific Elite," *Southern Review,* 4 (Winter, 1939), 463–473.

[146] These remarks are not, of course, meant to imply that Kendall was in any way an unsophisticated individual.

[147] Compare, for example, "new conservative" Peter Viereck's attacks on "populist" McCarthyism in *The Unadjusted Man* (Boston, 1956).

[148] Jeffrey Hart, "Willmoore Kendall: American," in Kendall, *Contra Mundum,* p. 9. John P. East, a political scientist at East Carolina University, has recently concurred with Hart's appraisal. East declares that Kendall must be placed on any "list of the most important political scientists of the post-World War II era. Moreover, as regards the American political tradition, it is easily argued that Kendall is the most original, innovative, and challenging interpreter of any period." John P. East, "The Political Thought of Willmoore Kendall," *Political Science Reviewer,* 3 (1973), 201.

[149] An analysis of the merits of Kendall's thought would require a separate and different study. As Garry Wills has said, "One has to answer Kendall in books—the mark of an important thinker." Garry Wills, review of Kendall and Carey, *Basic Symbols,* in *Commonweal,* 93 (December 18, 1970), 306. Our own concern here, of course, is not the validity but the history of Kendall's thought.

[150] Thus one should not conclude that Kendall "disliked" Burke. He sought rather to "translate" him—where applicable—into American vocabulary. Nor should one conclude that because Kendall was such a fervent American he was any less at home in Europe; he spent many years abroad. He was, for example, very interested in Spain. Frederick Wilhelmsen (a close friend) stated that Kendall once said to him upon seeing Spain's Escorial, "This is my favorite church in all Christendom." Wilhelmsen, letter to the editor, *National Review,* 24 (June 23, 1972), 672–673. On the other hand, Kendall was not any less an American because of his "Europeanness," either. He was indeed a complex man.

[Part I: XIX, Spring 1975, 127–135. Part II: XIX, Summer 1975, 236–248]

[22]

Leo Strauss and American Conservatism

JOHN P. EAST

John P(orter) East (1931–1986), a professor of political science at East Carolina University (1964–1980), served as a United States senator from North Carolina (1980–1986). He was a member of the editorial advisory boards of Modern Age *and* The Political Science Reviewer. *Just prior to his death he completed* The American Conservative Movement: The Philosophical Founders, *in which he examines the writings and thought of seven scholars who laid the modern philosophical foundations of the American Right: Russell Kirk, Richard M. Weaver, Frank S. Meyer, Willmoore Kendall, Leo Strauss, Eric Voegelin, and Ludwig von Mises.*

I

Leo Strauss (1899–1973) was a native of Germany. "I was," he reported near the end of his life, "brought up in a conservative, even orthodox Jewish home somewhere in a rural district of Germany."[1] Strauss received his doctorate from Hamburg University in 1921. To escape the Nazi holocaust, in 1938 he emigrated to the United States and commenced teaching political science and philosophy at the New School for Social Research. Joining the faculty of the University of Chicago in 1949 as a professor of political philosophy, Strauss subsequently was named Robert Maynard Hutchins Distinguished Service Professor at that institution. After his retirement in 1968 from the University of Chicago, Strauss held teaching positions at Claremont Men's College in California and at St. John's College in Maryland. At the latter institution he was named Scott Buchanan Distinguished Scholar-in-Residence, and he held that position at the time of his death.

A prolific scholar, Strauss authored over a dozen books and in excess of eighty articles. Moreover, he spawned a generation of admiring students who have attained the highest ranks in the academic profession. One admirer eulogized, "At the University of Chicago his lectures at the Hillel Foundation were events. In a university that prided itself on intellectual distinction, he was widely regarded as most distinguished."[2] Another admirer offered, "He surely was the most learned man of our time in the great writings . . . worth being learned in. . . ."[3] In particular, conservative intellectuals were enamored with Strauss's work. For example,

257

Walter Berns succinctly explained, "He was the greatest of teachers."[4] In his assessment, Dante Germino concluded, "Strauss' impact on American philosophy and political science has been one of almost astonishing proportions."[5] With unreserved praise, Harry V. Jaffa wrote, "For us who have had the privilege of knowing him as a teacher and as a friend, we can only say that of the men we have known, he was the best, and the wisest and most just."[6] William F. Buckley, Jr., observed that Strauss "is unquestionably one of the most influential teachers of his age," while the always exacting Willmoore Kendall referred to Strauss as "*the* great teacher of political philosophy, not of our time alone, but of any time since Machiavelli."[7] Among Strauss's books, those having the greatest impact upon American conservative thought would include *The Political Philosophy of Hobbes* (1936), *Natural Right and History* (1953), *Thoughts on Machiavelli* (1958), and *What Is Political Philosophy?* (1959). Concerning the latter two works, Kendall exclaimed, "Both of these should be not required reading but scripture for everyone who likes to think of himself as a conservative."[8]

What was the essence of this powerful spell that Leo Strauss cast over his students—nay, his disciples? His message was disarmingly simple. He commenced with this admonition:

> However much the power of the West may have declined, however great the dangers of the West may be, that decline, that danger, nay, the defeat, even the destruction of the West would not necessarily prove that the West is in a crisis: the West could go down in honor, certain of its purpose. The crisis of the West consists in the West's having become uncertain of its purpose.[9]

The key to the resolution of the crisis lay in a restoration of the vital ideas and faith that in the past had sustained the moral purpose of the West. It was necessary to go back to the origins and to explore deeply the fundamental problems. Specifically, it was imperative to study the great thinkers of the past, be they teachers of good or evil, and to pore over their enduring works; it was essential to understand these thinkers as they understood themselves, and from that base the task of revitalization could commence. Who are the teachers of Good? They will be found, Strauss responded, in the Classical Greek and biblical heritages; inescapably, the soul of the historical West is rooted in these intellectual traditions, and here are found the metaphysical foundations of what Strauss called "The Great Tradition" of Western politics.

II

Strauss's affection for classical Greek political philosophy is a pervasive characteristic of all his work. Strauss cautioned that when a person "engages in the study of classical philosophy he must know that he embarks on a journey whose end is completely hidden from him. He is not likely to return to the shores of our time as exactly the same man who departed from them."[10] Why study the classics? Strauss instructed, "It is not . . . antiquarianism nor . . . romanticism which induces us to turn . . . toward the political thought of classical antiquity. We are impelled to do so by the crisis of our time, the crisis of the West."[11] The fact that classical political philosophy had been replaced by modern utopian ideologies was, according to Strauss, "the core of the contemporary crisis of the West"; consequently, "the indispensable starting point" for rekindling the idea of "the very possibility of high culture" lay with a return to the classics.[12] Indeed, Strauss concluded, "After the experience of our generation, the burden of proof would seem to rest on those who assert rather than on those who deny that we have progressed beyond the classics."[13]

A subtle yet key point in Strauss's affinity for the classical heritage is his preference for the Platonic emphasis over that of the Aristotelian. Although generally laudatory of Aristotle, it is in Plato that Strauss finds the *summum bonum* of classical political thought. Strauss elaborated:

> Plato never discusses any subject . . . without keeping in view the elementary Socratic question, "What is the right way of life?" . . . Aristotle, on the other hand, treats each of the various levels of beings, and hence especially every level of human life, on its own terms.[14]

Or as Strauss wrote on another occasion, "Aristotle's cosmology, as distinguished from Plato's, is unqualifiedly separable from the quest for the best political order. Aristotelian philosophizing has no longer to the same degree and in the same way as Socratic philosophizing *the character of ascent*."[15]

"The character of ascent," Strauss contended, leads to the Great Tradition of political philosophy:

> The Great Tradition of political philosophy was originated by Socrates. Socrates is said to have disregarded the whole of nature altogether in order to devote himself entirely to the study of ethical things. His reason seems to have been that while man is not necessarily in need of knowledge of the nature of all things, he must of necessity be concerned with how he should live individually and collectively.[16]

The ascent commences with acknowledgment that the highest calling of man is in the role of philosopher, for he alone relentlessly pursues "knowledge of the whole"—and it is essential to underscore that the quest is for knowledge (*episteme*), not opinion (*doxa*). The philosopher perceives a "nature of things" which is "intelligible" and "knowable," and to a comprehension of the Truth of this whole he bends his will and talents. In keeping with the Socratic heritage, to Strauss the first step in seeking comprehension is *piety*: "The beginning of understanding is wonder or surprise, a sense of the bewildering or strange character of the subject matter."[17] More simply, "[P]iety . . . emerges out of the contemplation of nature," and in so doing man learns "to see the lowliness of his estate."[18] In perceiving his lowliness, man is acknowledging a hierarchy of being. At the pinnacle of this hierarchy is transcendent Truth or the Good. To know the Truth, to go out of the Platonic cave and to know fully the essence of the sun, would be inexpressibly exhilarating and would be the ultimate in attainment and satisfaction for the philosopher. Needless to say, total comprehension of the whole, including the Truth at the pinnacle, eludes the full grasp of mortal man; yet, it is from knowing in the marrow of his intellectual being that the hierarchy of the whole exists that the philosopher is driven unrelentingly in pursuit of knowledge of the whole. To the philosopher the logic of the matter is inexorable: man is not self-produced; he is a part of a larger scheme of things; and no greater challenge lies before man than to attempt to discern, however dimly, the essence of that whole.

As imperfect as our knowledge is, from the Platonic-Strauss perspective we have learned some truth; that is, there is such a thing as human knowledge, and, in fact, knowledge about important matters. For example, we know in our understanding of the whole that things have unalterable essences; more particularly, we know "that there is an unchangeable human nature."[19] Similarly, individual men have fixed natures that are not amenable to fundamental alteration or change. The initial task is to know ourselves, to perceive our fixed natures, and to attune ourselves accordingly. To the extent that we know our inner beings and accept our fixed essences as integral parts of the hierarchy of the whole, we have glimpsed the essence of classical Justice: "We shall then define justice as the habit of giving to everyone what is due to him according to nature."[20] Conversely, "Justice means attending to one's own business, bringing oneself into the right disposition with regard to the transcendent unchanging norm."[21]

The political implications of classical Platonic thinking are profound. As a consequence of the general concern for ascent, piety, knowledge, truth, justice, and kindred concepts, the Platonic tradition stresses the quest for "the best political order"—the summit of the political hierarchy. As Strauss explained, the best political order entails government by "good men":

> The claim to rule which is based on merit, on human excellence, on "virtue," appeared to be least controversial [in classical Platonic thought.] . . . Good men are those who are willing, and able, to prefer the common interest to their private interest and to the objects of their passions, or those who, being able to discern in each situation what is the noble or right thing to do, do it because it is noble and right and for no ulterior reason.[22]

Thus virtue emerges as the controlling ingredient in establishing the best political order: "[T]he chief purpose of the city is the noble life and therefore the chief concern of the city must be the virtue of its members. . . ."[23] And what is the hallmark of virture?: "Pseudo-virtue seeks what is imposing and great, true virtue what is fitting and right."[24] Moreover, "Virtue is impossible without toil, effort, or repression of the evil in oneself."[25] Strauss summarized:

> The classics had conceived of regimes (*politeiai*) not so much in terms of institutions as in terms of the aims actually pursued by the community or its authoritative part. Accordingly, they regarded the best regime as that regime whose aim is virtue. . . .[26]

It was then "the character, or tone, of a society" which was the key datum to the classical thinkers in the quest for the best regime. The cornerstone in building the best political order was the character of the individual. As the society was only the individual writ large, it was "the formation of character" in the individual that preoccupied the classical thinkers. Neither institutions, environmental changes, nor science, according to classical thought, were capable of redeeming man and ushering him into the political promised land. Indeed, it was beyond the potential of mortal man to redeem himself; however, he could seek the best attainable by aspiring to ascend, and this required developing the intellectual and moral character of the individual.

There is the element of universalism in classical political thought: "By the best political order the classical philosopher understood that political order which is best always and everywhere. . . . 'The best political order' is, then, not intrinsically Greek: it is no more intrinsically Greek than health."[27] This quest for the finest universally is not to be confused with egalitarianism; in fact, it is the antithesis of egalitarianism: "But just as it may happen that the members of one nation are more likely to be healthy and strong than those of others, it may also happen that one nation has a greater natural fitness for political excellence than others."[28] The concept of the hierarchy of things, that moving from lower to higher was an immutable component of classical thinking, and it indelibly etched an anti-egalitarianism into classical political thought. Strauss observed, "The basic premise of classical political philosophy may be said to be the view that natural inequality of the intellectual powers is, or ought to be, of decisive political importance."[29] Similarly, he wrote, "The founding of the good city started from the fact that men are by nature different and this proved to mean that they are by nature of unequal rank."[30]

Although classical political thought sought an understanding of the ideal or best political order in order that man might aspire to ascend, it was categorically anti-utopian. Strauss explained, "The classics thought that, owing to the weakness or dependence of human nature, universal happiness is impossible, and therefore they did not dream of fulfillment of History. . . . [T]hey saw how limited man's power is. . . ."[31] In contrast to the utopian, Strauss noted,

> [T]he philosopher . . . is free from the delusions bred by collective egoisms. . . . [H]e fully realizes the limits set to all human action and all human planning . . . , he does not expect salvation or satisfaction from the establishment of the simply best social order.[32]

Concisely stated, "The best regime and happiness, as classical philosophy understood them, are impossible."[33]

"Perhaps Socrates," Strauss speculated, "does not primarily intend to teach a doctrine but rather to educate human beings—to make them better, more just or gentle, more aware of their limitations."[34] In sum, classical political philosophy "is free from all fanaticism because it knows that evil cannot be eradicated and therefore that one's expectations from politics must be moderate. The spirit which animates it may be described as serenity or sublime sobriety."[35] We return to that originating principle of piety, or as Strauss explained, "Classical political philosophy was liberal in the original sense."[36] Conversely, Strauss concluded, "The classics were for almost all practical purposes what now are called conservatives."[37]

III

In Strauss's thinking the Judeo-Christian heritage is the second pillar of the Great Tradition of political philosophy. Unequivocally, he found the religious tradition of the West as vital to the Great Tradition as he did the classical heritage. Revealing of Strauss's affinity for the religious basis of Western thought is his intense admiration of Moses Maimonides, described by Strauss as "the greatest Jewish thinker of the Middle Ages."[38] Maimonides' major work was *The Guide for the Perplexed*, which is directed, Strauss explained, "[T]o those believing Jews who have, by reason of their training in philosophy, fallen into doubt and perplexity. . . ."[39] Or as Maimonides himself wrote:

> I address those who have studied philosophy and have acquired some knowledge, and who while firm in religious matters are perplexed and bewildered on account of the ambiguous and figurative expressions employed in the holy writings.[40]

Did Strauss feel that Maimonides had been successful in resolving this perplexity? Strauss answered, "*The Guide* as a whole is not merely a key to a forest but is itself a forest, an enchanted forest, and hence also an enchanting forest: it is a delight to the eyes. For the tree of life is a delight to the eyes."[41]

Maimonides "is the Jewish counterpart" of St. Thomas Aquinas: "Maimonides reconciles reason and revelation by identifying the distinctive aim of . . . divine law, with the aim of philosophy."[42] Regarding their respective emphases upon the classical heritage, Strauss noted a basic difference between Aquinas and Maimonides:

> For Thomas Aquinas, Aristotle is the highest authority . . . in political philosophy. Maimonides, on the other hand, could not use Aristotle's *Politics*, since it had not been translated into Arabic or Hebrew; but he could start, and he did start, from Plato's political philosophy.[43]

Thus Maimonides did out of necessity what Strauss had done by choice: both drew more heavily from Platonic than Aristotelian thought. Maimonides was able to harmonize the Platonic and Judaic traditions, Strauss related, for both heritages sought the Ideal; specifically, Judaism became the "perfect law in the Platonic sense" of the Ideal.[44]

Strauss's admiration for Maimonides takes on a particularly important dimension in view of the deep religious orthodoxy of Maimonides. In Strauss's words: "The remedy for this perplexity [the perplexity the philosopher has about religion] is the . . . explanation . . . that restores the faith in the truth of the Bible, that is, precisely what Maimonides is doing in *The Guide*."[45] The basic tenet of Maimonides' thinking is rooted in Platonic-Biblical piety: "Maimonides finds . . . that given man's insignificance compared with the universe man's claim to be the end for which the world exists is untenable."[46] According to Maimonides "human reason is inadequate for solving the central problem"; consequently, he affirms the indispensability of revealed religion.[47] As Strauss concisely stated the matter: "Maimonides defines his position by two frontiers. In the face of orthodoxy he defends the right of reason, in the face of philosophy he directs attention to the bounds of reason."[48]

Profoundly significant in terms of impact upon Strauss's professional career was the approach in studying scripture recommended by Maimonides. Maimonides offered these maxims: "The *deeper sense* of the words of the holy Law are pearls, and the literal acceptation of a figure is of no value in itself"; "Their *hidden meaning*, however, is profound wisdom, conducive to the recognition of real truth"; and "Your object should be to discover . . . the general idea which the author wishes to express."[49] As to reading *The Guide*, Maimonides requested, "*Do not read superficially*, lest you do me an injury,

and derive no benefit for yourself. You must study thoroughly and read continually; for you will then find the solution to those important problems of religion, which are a source of anxiety to all intelligent men."[50] Maimonides then concluded with an observation which Strauss could only relish:

> Lastly, when I have a difficult subject before me—when I find the road narrow, and can see no other way of teaching a well established truth except by pleasing one intelligent man and displeasing ten thousand fools—I prefer to address myself to the one man, and to take no notice whatever of the condemnation of the multitude; I prefer to extricate that intelligent man from his embarrassment and show him the cause of his perplexity, so that he may attain perfection and be at peace.[51]

The technique of study advocated by Strauss in his professional career is unmistakenly vintage Maimonides. There is that emphasis upon careful textual analysis in which one eschews literalism and looks for the "deeper sense" and "the hidden meaning." In addition, as noted, there is that strong Platonic-biblical willingness, if necessary, to ignore "the multitude" and "to address" oneself to "one intelligent man." Indeed, the point is compelling: Strauss not only drank deeply of the substance of Maimonides' thought, he not only attempted to reconcile the classical and biblical views, but in addition he borrowed extravagantly from Maimonides' method of study, and it is not too much to say that he cast himself in the role of a modern Maimonides.

Further underscoring Strauss's commitment to the biblical heritage is his disdain for Spinoza. Maimonides and Spinoza were both of Jewish heritage. The former was devoted to preserving the biblical roots, while the latter through his major work, *Theologico-political Treatise*, sought to free himself and his readers from biblical guidance. Strauss was lavish in his praise of Maimonides, and unsparingly critical in his analysis of Spinoza. Strauss wrote, "Spinoza rejects both Greek idealism and Christian spiritualism. . . . Spinoza's God is simply beyond good and evil. . . . Good and evil differ only from a merely human point of view; theologically the distinction is meaningless."[52] Spinoza's initial error is to reject the classical-biblical concept of piety: "To humility Spinoza opposes composure of mind as the joy that springs when man contemplates himself and his power of action."[53] Having rejected piety, Spinoza, according to Strauss, called for "an open attack on all forms of orthodox biblical theology." Spinoza "denies . . . revealed religion"[54] and rejects outright the biblical conception of sin:

> Does there exist [in Spinoza's thinking], apart from all humanly constituted law, a law plainly imposed on all men, and of which transgression is sin? Is there human action which contravenes the will of God? For Spinoza, *this* is the question regarding the *lex divina*, and to the question understood in this sense his answer is No.[55]

As Strauss explained even more succinctly, "Spinoza's real view [is that] . . . every man and every being has a natural right to everything: the state of nature knows no law and knows no sin."[56]

Strauss continued, "Spinoza . . . charges full tilt . . . with the whole-hearted scorn of the realist free of illusions who knows the world."[57] According to Spinoza, Strauss noted, the error of religion is that it causes man to place "his trust in others rather than in himself, rather than in his own powers of rational reflection. . . ."[58] Thus, unlike Maimonides, Spinoza was "convinced . . . of the adequacy of human capacities for the guidance of life," and he demanded of "Judaism that it should justify itself before the tribunal of reason, of humanity."[59] In sum, Spinoza, "taking

his stand on the unambiguous evidence of experience and of reason," points directly to the mind and spirit of the Enlightenment:

> Interest in security and in alleviation of the ills of life may be called the interest characteristic of the Enlightenment in general. This movement sought in every way open to it to assure greater security and amelioration of life. . . . Nothing could be more odious to the Enlightenment than the conception of God as a terrible God, in which the severity of mind and heart, and the spirit of the Book of Deuteronomy, finds its ultimate justification.[60]

What is the end result of Spinoza's view?: "[T]he humanitarian end seems to justify every means; he plays a most dangerous game; his procedure is as much beyond good and evil as his God."[61] More specifically, Strauss wrote, "The explicit thesis of the *Theologico-political Treatise* may be said to express an extreme version of the 'liberal' view," and thus Spinoza ultimately "found his home in the liberal secular state."[62]

Not only in his differing reactions to Maimonides and Spinoza does one see the religious facet of Strauss's thinking. In stating directly his personal views, Strauss reveals a deeply religious dimension. Note this somewhat cryptic remark: "It is true that the successful quest for wisdom [that is, philosophy] might lead to the result that wisdom is not the one thing needful."[63] Extensively throughout his work Strauss employs this biblical phrase, "the one thing needful." And is there any doubt as to the religious implications of this statement by Strauss?: "The insecurity of man and everything human is not an absolutely terrifying abyss if the highest of which a man knows is absolutely secure."[64] Strauss contended that reason is inadequate for a comprehensive explanation, for it "knows only of subjects and objects."[65] Similarly, naturalism is inadequate, for it "is completely blind to the riddles inherent in the 'givenness' of nature," and finally "humanism is not enough. . . . Either man is an accidental product of a blind evolution or else the process leading to man, culminating in man, is directed toward man. Mere humanism avoids this ultimate issue."[66]

The answer lay, Strauss reasoned, "only by surrendering to God's experienced call which calls for one's loving Him with all one's heart, with all one's soul and with all one's might can one come to see the other human being as one's brother and love him as oneself."[67] In addition, Strauss cautioned, "The absolute experience will not lead back to Judaism . . . if it does not recognize itself in the Bible and clarify itself through the Bible. . . ."[68] Concerning the Bible, Strauss wrote, "[I]t is true . . . I believe . . . that the Bible sets forth the demands of morality and religion in their purest and most intransigent form . . . ," and he further reflected, "[T]he orthodox answer rests upon the belief in the superhuman origin of the Bible."[69] Strauss charged that without "biblical faith" it was not possible to see "human beings . . . with humility and charity. . . ."[70] Moreover, men of "unbelief" are "haunted men. Deferring to nothing higher than their selves, they lack guidance. They lack thought and discipline. Instead they have what they call sincerity."[71] Strauss continued with this profoundly religious observation: "One can create obstinacy by virtue of some great villainy, but one needs religion for creating hope."[72] Compelling is this final observation, "The genuine refutation of orthodoxy would require the proof that the world and human life are perfectly intelligible without the assumption of a mysterious God."[73] There is no question that Strauss looked upon biblical knowledge of this "mysterious God" as an in-

dispensable step toward "knowledge of the whole."

Although his personal heritage was Jewish, there is not a trace of antagonism in Strauss's writings toward Christianity; indeed, probably the most moving dimension of Strauss's thinking was his effort to afford "recognition of that common ground" between Judaism and Christianity:

> What can such recognition mean? This much: that Church and Synagogue recognize in each the noble features of its antagonist. Such recognition was possible even during the Christian Middle Ages: while the Synagogue was presented as lowering its head in shame, its features were presented as noble. . . . Even the pagan philosophers Plato and Aristotle remained friends . . . because each held the truth to be his greatest friend. The Jew may recognize that the Christian error is a blessing, a divine blessing, and the Christian may recognize that the Jewish error is a blessing, a divine blessing. Beyond this they cannot go without ceasing to be Jew or Christian.[74]

In pursuing his "common-ground" theme, Strauss argued:

> The common ground on which Jews and Christians can make a friendly *collatio* to the secular state cannot be the belief in the God of the philosophers, but only the belief in the God of Abraham, Isaac, and Jacob—the God who revealed the Ten Commandments or at any rate such commandments as are valid under all circumstances regardless of the circumstances.[75]

As Strauss viewed it, "The agony of the Jew and the agony of the Cross belong together; 'they are aspects of the same agony.' Judaism and Christianity need each other."[76] Thus to Strauss it was essential to understand that "over against scientism and humanism Judaism and Christianity are at one."[77]

Beyond "the common-ground" argument, Strauss wrote with affection for the specifically Christian contributions to Western thought. For example, regarding Catholicism he observed:

> Anyone who wishes to judge impartially of the legitimacy or the prospects of the great design of modern man to erect the City of Man on what appears to him to be ruins of the City of God must familiarize himself with the teachings, and especially the political teachings, of the Catholic church, which is certainly the most powerful antagonist of that modern design.[78]

Be it in their "common ground" or in their separate contributions, he spoke then approvingly of the Jewish and Christian heritages. It is to be cautioned that Strauss was not advocating a maudlin ecumenical synthesis of Judaism and Christianity. Strauss insisted, as noted, that beyond "the common ground" neither faith could go "without ceasing to be Jew or Christian." Strauss did not conceive it as the task of mortals to dilute the essence of either faith; to attempt to do so would reflect impiety in its rankest form.

IV

To Strauss the issue was clear: "Western man became what he is and is what he is through the coming together of biblical faith and Greek thought. In order to understand ourselves and to illuminate our trackless way into the future, we must understand Jerusalem and Athens."[79] As had Maimonides and Aquinas, Strauss saw, in spite of certain irreconcilable antagonisms, a mutuality of interest between "Plato and the prophets." To commence with, both the classical and biblical heritages renounced human pride or *hubris* and commended piety as the key virtue: "According to the Bible, the beginning of wisdom is fear of the Lord; according to the Greek philosophers, the beginning of

wisdom is wonder."[80] Moreover, as a corollary premise, Strauss noted both traditions "made very strict demands on self-restraint. Neither biblical nor classical morality encourages us to try, solely for the sake of our preferment or our glory, to oust from their positions men who do the required work as well as we could."[81] Similarly, "Neither biblical nor classical morality encourages all statesmen to try to extend their authority over all men in order to achieve universal recognition."[82]

In addition to instructing on the virtues of piety and self-restraint, "Plato teaches, just as the Bible, that heaven and earth were created or made by an invisible God whom he calls the Father, who is always, who is good and hence whose creation is good."[83] Furthermore, in biblical and classical thought "justice is compliance with the natural order" of creation.[84] The wisdom of Jerusalem and Athens requires discernment of the natural order of things and man's attuning himself to that order. That is, man is not the Creator, he is the creature; he is not the potter, he is the clay. It is then man who adapts to creation, not creation to man—to propose the latter is to propose perverting the natural order of things. On these essentials, on the essence of God, creation, and Justice, Plato and the prophets were as one.

In his analysis of the "coming together" of the wisdom of Jerusalem and Athens, Strauss cautioned, "Yet the differences between the Platonic and the biblical teaching are no less striking than the agreements."[85] First, there is the inescapable problem of "the opposition of Reason and Revelation." By its essence Reason accepts as true only that which has withstood the probing power of human logic and scientific understanding. In contrast, by its nature Revelation assumes there are truths beyond the intelligence of man to grasp. Man is finite and limited in his understanding; therefore, those ineffable truths beyond the ken of human reason are knowable only through Revelation. Thus the clear thinker yields: from the human vantage point, because of their respective essences, Reason and Revelation are not fully reconcilable.

Likewise, Jerusalem and Athens take opposing positions on the fundamental question of whether we are pursuing truth or whether we already possess truth. Strauss explained:

> The philosopher is the man who dedicates his life to the quest for knowledge of the good, of the idea of the good. . . . According to the prophets, however, there is no need for the quest for knowledge of the good: God "has shewed thee, O man, what is good; and what doth the Lord require of thee, but to do justly, and to love mercy, and to walk humbly with thy God."[86]

Plato and prophets are agreed that truth is the goal, but by the very nature of their differing perspectives, the clear thinker again concedes that from the standpoint of human understanding complete reconcilability is not possible; differing essences cannot be forced into a common mold; to attempt to do so does violence and irreparable harm to the vital nature of each.

As he had done in his efforts to find "the common ground" between Judaism and Christianity, so Strauss had done in his analysis of the classical and biblical views. He looked for the mutual foundations and artfully defined and boldly asserted them; however, he resolutely refused to force either component into an unnatural synthesis of human design. The essence of things had to be respected. The philosopher-theologian could carry the matter of synthesis to the highest level possible consistent with his understanding of the nature of things; yet, it was gross error—perversion—to force the unnatural union of differing essences. We would

have to learn to reconcile ourselves to the irreconcilable. This was acceptable to learned men, for classical and biblical piety had instructed it was not in the nature of things that mortal man should have total knowledge of the whole.

V

The cardinal error of modern ideologies was to war against the nature of things, and to attempt to superimpose a strictly new design solely human in origin. With the thinking of the Renaissance, Strauss wrote, commenced the heresies of modernity: "[W]ithin the Renaissance an entirely new spirit emerged, the modern secular spirit. The greatest representative of this radical change was Machiavelli. . . ."[87] In Machiavelli, Strauss contended, lay the theoretical foundations of the modern age:

> The founder of modern political philosophy is Machiavelli. He tried to effect, and he did effect, a break with the whole tradition of political philosophy. He compared his achievement to that of men like Columbus. He claimed to have discovered a new moral continent. His claim is well founded; his political teaching is "wholly new." The only question is whether the new continent is fit for human habitation.[88]

Machiavelli launched the "first wave of modernity" as he broke sharply with the classical and biblical heritages, as he broke with the Great Tradition of Western political thought. Regarding Machiavelli's break with the classical tradition, Strauss observed, "Machiavelli refers so rarely to philosophy and philosophers: in *The Prince* and *The Discourses* taken together there occurs only one reference to Aristotle and one reference to Plato."[89] Concerning the key concept of piety in classical thinking, Strauss noted, "[O]ne does not find a trace of pagan piety in Machiavelli's work."[90] Similarly, "Wisdom is not a great theme for Machiavelli because justice is not a great theme for him"; consequently, there is "a movement from excellence to vileness" as Machiavelli, in departing from the classical view, "denies that there is an order of the soul, and therefore a hierarchy of ways of life or of goods."[91] In repudiating the classical view, Machiavelli denied "the possibility of a *summum bonum*," and thereby "Machiavelli abandoned the original meaning of the good society or of the good life."[92] The "character of ascent," characteristic of classical thought, is destroyed by Machiavelli.

Nor, Strauss continued, is Machiavelli any less devastating in his attack upon the biblical tradition. In his clever and subtle attack upon the biblical legacy, Machiavelli employs a conspiracy of silence: "He silently makes superficial readers oblivious of the biblical teaching."[93] "As one would expect," Strauss explained, "Machiavelli is silent about God's witnessing or the relation between the conscience and God."[94] Moreover, in neither *The Prince* or *The Discourses* does Machiavelli make a "distinction between this world and the next, or between this life and the next; nor does he mention in either work the devil or hell; above all, he never mentions in either work the soul."[95] On this latter point, Strauss concluded, "[H]is silence about the soul is a perfect expression of the soulless character of his teaching: he is silent about the soul because he has forgotten the soul, just as he has forgotten tragedy and Socrates."[96] Thus "Machiavelli unambiguously reveals his complete break with the biblical tradition, and . . . he ascribes to all religions a human, not a heavenly, origin."[97] Briefly, Machiavelli "is certain that the Christian religion will not last forever. It is [merely] 'the present religion'."[98]

The cleavage between Machiavelli and Christianity is sharply reflected in fundamentally differing attitudes on the meaning of "virtue." To Machiavelli virtue (*virtù*), properly understood, meant the pursuit of worldly power and honor. As Strauss elaborated, "Not trust in God and self-denial but self-reliance and self-love is the root of human strength and greatness."[99] Succinctly, "God is with the strongest battalions."[100] In contrast, to Machiavelli Christian virtue had "led the world into weakness . . . by lowering the esteem for worldly glory [and by] regarding humility, abjectness and contempt for things human as the highest good."[101] In summing up Machiavelli's position, Strauss wrote, "The sins which ruin states are military rather than moral sins. On the other hand, faith, goodness, humility, and patience may be the road to ruin, as everyone understanding anything of the things of the world will admit."[102] Machiavelli was indifferent to the truth of the biblical view; he proceeded to substitute politics for religion; and in his "spiritual warfare" on the historical faiths of the West he raised a banner which proclaimed "there is no sin but ignorance."[103] Had Machiavelli's assault upon the established faiths succeeded? Strauss retorted, "The problem posed by biblical antiquity remains behind him like an unconquered fortress."[104]

Yet in spite of his failure to convince Strauss, the latter acknowledged the powerful impact Machiavelli has had upon the modern mind. Machiavelli was a bold "innovator" who sought to discover "new modes and orders" in the moral realm. He was "a rebel against everything that is respected," and he "liberated himself completely from belief in any authority."[105] Indeed, he attempted to establish a new authority spun from wholly new cloth. This new authority was rooted in Machiavelli's well-known proclamation "that all armed prophets have conquered and unarmed ones failed." This meant, Strauss explained, that the primacy of Love must be replaced by the primacy of Terror. . . . Therefore the perfection envisaged by both the Bible and classical philosophy is impossible. . . . Man cannot rise above earthly and earthy humanity and therefore he ought not even to aspire beyond humanity.[106]

In Machiavelli is found then an "attempt to replace humility by humanity," and the practical result is "to lower man's goal."[107] The purpose in lowering the goal is "to increase the probability of its attainment."[108] The new standard is "low but solid" and "its symbol is the Beast Man as opposed to the God Man: it understands man in the light of the sub-human rather than of the super-human."[109] Machiavelli's conception of the Beast Man leads to the threshold of modern tyranny which "has its roots in Machiavelli's thought."[110] Ironically, Strauss observed, "A stupendous contraction of the horizon appears to Machiavelli and his successors as a wondrous enlargement of the horizon."[111]

In reference to *The Prince*, Strauss wrote, "The characteristic feature of the work is precisely that it makes no distinction between prince and tyrant; it uses the term 'prince' to designate princes and tyrants alike."[112] In Machiavelli's own words:

> [F]or how we live is so far removed from how we ought to live, that he who abandons what is done for what ought to be done, will rather learn to bring about his own ruin than his preservation. . . . Therefore it is necessary for a prince, who wishes to maintain himself, to learn how not to be good. . . .[113]

In pursuing worldly honor and the praise of men, Machiavelli further instructed that the prince "must imitate the fox and the lion," must, that is, alternate between cunning and violence, and "in the actions of princes, from which there is no appeal, the end justifies the means. Let a prince therefore aim at conquering and maintaining the state. . . ."[114] Strauss summed

up Machiavelli's instructions to the fledgling prince-tyrant: "He must pursue a policy of iron and poison, of murder and treachery. . . . [T]he patriotic end hallows every means however much condemned by the most exalted traditions both philosophic and religious."[115] "There can be no doubt regarding the answer," Strauss concluded, "the immoral policies recommended throughout the *Prince* are not justified on grounds of the common good, but exclusively on grounds of the self-interest of the prince, of his selfish concern with his own well-being, security and glory."[116]

An additional result in Machiavelli's "lowering the goal" is that he "replaces God . . . by Fortuna."[117] "Fortuna is malevolent," Strauss explained, and she "mysteriously elects some men or nations for glory and others for ruin or infamy."[118] Furthermore, "[T]he end which Fortuna pursues is unknown, and so are her ways toward that end."[119] In brief, Fortuna is what is conventionally called chance, and she is the essence of human existence. Unlike the classical and biblical views, Machiavelli sees no hierarchy of order, nor does he perceive that things have essences and substances, that there is a "nature of things" independent of man's will. From the classical-biblical perspective man is a vital component of the whole, but he is not creator of the whole, nor does he have full dominion over it. The matter is otherwise with Machiavelli Strauss noted, for "Fortuna is like a woman who can be vanquished by the right kind of man." Thus "if Fortuna can be vanquished, man would seem to be able to become the master of the universe. Certainly Machiavelli does not recommend that Fortuna be worshipped: she ought to be beaten and pounded."[120] As Machiavelli himself explained, in the case of "great men . . . fortune holds no sway over them."[121]

If fortune holds no sway over man as Machiavelli proclaimed, and "if there is no natural end of man" in the Machiavellian view, then, Strauss maintained, "[M]an can set for himself almost any end he desires: man is almost infinitely malleable. The power of man is much greater, and the power of nature and chance is correspondingly much smaller, than the ancients thought."[122] And what are the practical implications of the notion that man is "infinitely malleable"? Strauss elaborated:

> Machiavelli takes issue with those who explain the bad conduct of men by their bad nature: men are by nature malleable rather than either bad or good; goodness and badness are not natural qualities but the outcome of habituation.
>
> [Thus] what you need is not so much formation of character and moral appeal, as the right kind of institutions, institutions with teeth in them. The shift from formation of character to the trust in institutions is the characteristic corollary of the belief in the almost infinite malleability of man.[123]

It was to "the young" that Machiavelli took his call to join with him, as with a bold Columbus, in establishing "new modes and orders" and in settling a new "moral continent." Machiavelli stated, "I certainly think that it is better to be impetuous than cautious, for fortune is a woman. . . . And therefore like a woman, she is always a friend to the young, because they are less cautious, fiercer, and master her with greater audacity."[124] "Machiavelli tries," Strauss continued, "to divert the adherence of the young from the old to the new teaching by appealing to the taste of the young," and thereby "he displays a bias in favor of the impetuous, the quick, the partisan, the spectacular, and the bloody over and against the deliberate, the slow, the neutral, the silent, and the gentle."[125] In Machiavelli's thought, Strauss reasoned, "Reason and youth and mod-

ernity rise up against authority, old age, and antiquity." The result is "the birth of that greatest of all youth movements: modern philosophy. . . ."[126]

In *The Prince* Machiavelli instructed youth with this superficial and callow doctrine: "Only those defences are good, certain and durable, which depend on yourself alone and your own ability."[127] "Machiavelli thus establishes," Strauss wrote, "a kind of intimacy with his readers par excellence, whom he calls 'the young,' by inducing them to think forbidden or criminal thoughts."[128] Strauss asked, "How can we respect someone who remains undecided between good and evil or who, while benefiting us, benefits at the same time and by the same action our worst enemies?"[129] "If it is true," Strauss maintained, "that only an evil man will stoop to teach maxims of public and private gangsterism, we are forced to say that Machiavelli was an evil man."[130] After all, Machiavelli himself had proclaimed in *The Discourses* that "evil deeds have a certain grandeur."[131] In sum, the Florentine is "a teacher of evil," and it is only "the incredibility of his enterprise which secures him against detection, *i.e.*, against the detection of the intransigence and awakeness with which he conducts his exploration of hitherto unknown territory and thus prepares the conquest of that territory by his brothers."[132]

VI

Although Machiavelli had laid the primary theoretical foundations, Strauss considered Thomas Hobbes as one of those "brothers" assisting in launching the "first wave of modernity." In fact, earlier in his writing career Strauss had viewed Hobbes as the key figure in introducing modern Western thought; however, subsequently, he wrote, "Hobbes appeared to me [earlier] as the originator of modern political philosophy. This was an error: not Hobbes, but Machiavelli, deserves this honor."[133] "It was Machiavelli, that greater Columbus," Strauss decided, "who had discovered the continent on which Hobbes could erect his structure."[134] To understand this "structure" erected by Hobbes, it was imperative, Strauss instructed, that "the fundamental difference" between Hobbes's thinking "and the classical as well as the Christian attitude should be grasped."[135] Succinctly stated, it was essential to understand that "the shifting of interest from the eternal order to man . . . carried to its logical conclusion . . . leads to Hobbes's political philosophy."[136] As had Machiavelli, Hobbes broke completely with the Great Tradition of Western thought.

Under the tutelage of Plato, the classical perspective yearned for "the truth hidden in the natural valuations and therefore [sought] to teach nothing new and unheard-of "; rather, it sought to discover and articulate the "old and eternal." In contrast, Hobbes lusted after the "future and freely projected"; he searched for the "surprising, new, unheard-of-venture."[137] Hobbes then, at war with the classical legacy, unleashed a violent outpouring of the modern spirit. He denied the notion of the soul, and he rejected the idea that there was a supreme good. Moreover, he denied the concept of the natural law; he repudiated the notion that there was an order of being and that there was a hierarchy of value and gradation in the nature of things. Likewise, Hobbes renounced any ideal of an objective moral order, that justice could be perceived, and that there was a natural end of man. As Strauss reported it, Hobbes was "elated by a sense of the complete failure of traditional philosophy."[138]

Hobbes turned with comparable vehemence on the biblical heritage, and, Strauss maintained, he preached a doctrine of "political atheism." As to the Christian

tradition, Hobbes differed with it "by his denial of the possibility that just and unjust actions may be distinguished independently of human legislation."[139] To Hobbes man "has no reason to be grateful to the 'First Cause' of [the] universe," and "there is then no reason for believing in the authority of the Bible."[140] Thus "unbelief is the necessary premise of his teaching about the state of nature."[141] Shockingly, in Hobbes's hands impiety is converted into a virtue.

According to Strauss, Hobbes taught a corollary doctrine of "political hedonism." In the Hobbesian scheme of things, death is "the primary and greatest and supreme evil, the only and absolute standard of human life, the beginning of all knowledge of the real world."[142] As fear of death is the primary evil, it follows that "self-preservation" is the most basic of all rights, particularly self-preservation against violent death. In effect Hobbes upended the classical and biblical heritages and made self-preservation the *summum bonum* of the human experience; thus the ultimate sacrifices of self by Socrates and Christ in the pursuit of truth become odious perversions—evil—in the Hobbesian view. Self-preservation is the supreme Right; it is the foundation of political morality, and it is antecedent to all things political. Classical and biblical notions of duty, service, and sacrifice to higher transcendent callings are summarily rejected. The Hobbesian goddess is sovereign power, for she alone can offer security against violent death, the supreme evil. Strauss wrote, "[O]ne may call Hobbes' whole philosophy the first philosophy of power."[143] He did find a nuance of difference between Hobbes and Machiavelli: "[W]hereas the pivot of Machiavelli's political teaching was glory, the pivot of Hobbes' political teaching is power."[144] Power and glory emerge then as key pillars of modern thought; they stand in stark contrast to the classical-biblical notions of piety and service.

After Machiavelli and Hobbes, Strauss maintained, "The second wave of modernity begins with Rousseau. He changed the moral climate of the west as profoundly as Machiavelli."[145] Rousseau unleashed the romantic radical spirit of modern Jacobinism. Whereas Machiavelli and Hobbes had subtly (and even on occasion gracefully) undermined the Great Tradition, Rousseau with glee and bravado wielded the ideological sword against the classical-biblical heritage. He was obscenely impious: he repudiated God and reason and declared human passion as the center and measure of all things. Through Rousseau's concept of the General Will, which is no more than collectivized human passion, we see erected the modern idol of collective man. The wreckage lies all around and the end of the destruction is not yet in sight. Strauss concluded, "[T]he restitution of a sound approach is bound up with the elimination of Rousseau's influence."[146]

Upon the heels of Rousseau, Strauss asserted, Nietzsche ushered in "the third wave of modernity." At least in Rousseau there had been the potentially redeeming virtue of the "noble savage" exuding compassion in his tranquil and blissful state of nature. However, Nietzsche offered no redeeming virtue; rather, he raised the preaching of evil to the *n*th power. He struck savagely at the twin pillars of the Great Tradition; with barbaric frenzy and sadistic pleasure he openly and explicitly condemned Jerusalem and Athens. The heritage of Plato was rejected out-of-hand because of its emphasis upon reason in the pursuit of the Good. As had Rousseau, Nietzsche turned from reason to sentiment and passion, and he repudiated categorically any notion of an existing transcendent Good. Rather than the "character of ascent" of the classical view,

Nietzsche led to descent into the world of the animal—the beast. In speaking of man, Nietzsche had written, "[The] hidden core needs to erupt from time to time, the animal has to get out again and go back to the wilderness."[147] In the same breath, Nietzsche renounced the biblical view by declaring "God is dead." In addition, he uttered the heretofore unthinkable blasphemy that "man is god in the making," and dismissed Christianity as no more than a "slave morality."

In place of the classical Good and Christian love, Nietzsche offered the "will to power." He wrote, "A living thing seeks above all to discharge its strength—life itself is will to power; self-preservation is only one of the indirect and most frequent results."[148] In the Nietzschean view, Strauss observed, "Man derives enjoyment from overpowering others as well as himself. Whereas Rousseau's natural man is compassionate, Nietzsche's natural man is cruel," and the result is that the "harmony and peace" of the classical biblical view are replaced by "terror and anguish."[149] Nietzsche prefers Dionysus to Apollo; that is, he prefers the egotistic and orgiastic to the humble and contemplative. In converting man, the creature, into God, the creator, Nietzsche commits the ultimate blasphemy. The result is, Strauss wrote, "Man is conquering nature and there are no assignable limits to the conquest."[150] As God, Nietzschean man knows no authority higher than himself. He repudiates all authority and guidance provided by traditional theology, philosophy, and history. Released from the restraining forces of classical reason and biblical love, with a frenzied craze Nietzschean man grasps for the levers of power and deliberately directs that power to the destruction of man—to the obliteration of self. Strauss concluded, Nietzsche "thus has grasped a more world-denying way of thinking than that of any previous pessimist," and the result is the "adoration of the Nothing."[151]

VII

In breaking with the Great Tradition of the classical and biblical legacies, Machiavelli, Hobbes, Rousseau, Nietzsche, and kindred spirits spawned the modern "isms." Foremost among these are positivism and historicism. "These are the two most powerful schools in the West today," Strauss observed.[152] Strauss underscored the positivist dimension in Machiavelli's thinking: "He may be said to exclude dogmatically all evidence which is not ultimately derived from phenomena that are at all times open to everyone's inspection in broad daylight."[153] Precisely stated, "Positivism is the view according to which only scientific knowledge, as defined by modern natural science, is genuine knowledge."[154] Positivism looked only to the factual and the material; it refused to think in terms of the transcendent and the spiritual—in sum, the essences of the Great Tradition were beyond its comprehension.

"Positivism," Strauss explained, "necessarily transforms itself into historicism."[155] From the viewpoint of the historicist, "History . . . became the highest authority. . . . [N]o objective norms remained."[156] Strauss elaborated, "The typical historicism of the twentieth century demands that each generation reinterpret the past on the basis of its own experience and with a view to its own future. It is no longer contemplative, but activistic. . . ."[157] To the historicist, values "change from epoch to epoch; hence it is impossible to answer the question of right and wrong or of the best social order in a universally valid manner."[158] Historicism led its followers to the pursuit of temporal honor and glory as successful "sons-of-the-times." In substance, the modern historicists were ancient sophists in new garb. Machiavelli was a historicist in his pursuit of "Power," "realism," and "new modes and orders"; similarly, Hobbes and Rousseau in their respective pursuits of "sovereign power" and the "General Will" were historicist in orientation; and Nietzsche's individual "will to power" was, Strauss maintained, no more than an extreme form of "radical historicism." Although varying in technique, in all cases these thinkers had repudiated notions of the transcendent and enduring; they sought solace and understanding in the mortal clay of specific times and places; and in so doing they broke with the Great Tradition and laid the foundations of modern historicism.

Historicism fragmented into corollary isms. The "radical historicism" of Nietzsche led to existentialism. Strauss asserted, "[I]t became clear that the root of existentialism must be sought in Nietzsche. . . ."[159] Existentialism rejected "the assumption that being is as such intelligible," and it pitted the "will to power" of each individual against an indifferent, sometimes hostile, and always meaningless universe. It was a pathetic mismatching of power; the individual invariably lost, for in searching solely within himself for the resources to prevail, man found his stock of private resources woefully inadequate, and he inevitably succumbed to his infinitely more formidable opponent, blind fate. Under these despairing circumstances, the ineluctable end was nihilism. "Let us popularly define nihilism," Strauss wrote, "as the inability to take a stand for civilization against cannibalism."[160] Indeed, to those caught up in the depressing web of existentialism and nihilism, cannibalism was an acceptable alternative, for it offered escape even though through self-destruction.

Finally, the "three waves of modernity" led to the great heresy of utopianism. The classical and biblical traditions were rooted in piety, and thus though they strove powerfully to perceive the transcendent Ideal, there were no illusions that the human condition was perfectible; it was not inherent in the nature of things; from the classical perspective mortal man could never expect to completely escape the limitations of the Platonic cave, and in the biblical view only God's grace, not human effort, could fully redeem. The philosophical founders of the modern age contended otherwise; they did promise an earthly utopia. Machiavelli had proclaimed that Fortuna or chance could be conquered, and that man could be "master of the universe"; Hobbes assured his listeners that "not divine grace, but the right kind of human government" would allow man to escape the limits of nature; Rousseau likewise maintained that man was "infinitely perfectible" and that there were "no natural obstacles" to human progress; and Nietzsche brazenly asserted, in Strauss's words, "that man is conquering nature and there are no assignable limits to that conquest."[161] As Strauss assessed the impulse of modern utopianism, it was predicated on the notion of "man's conquest of nature for the sake of the relief of man's estate."[162] Hence "[t]he modern project . . . demands that man should become the master and owner of nature," and it holds out the promise not only of "emancipation" but of "secular redemption."[163] This was a powerful ideology which had come to grip the modern imagination, and it moved with confidence and relentlessness.

To Strauss, modern utopianism was little more than ancient tyranny. Its essentials were well known to classical and biblical thinkers (after all, "there is nothing new under the sun"), and it was antithetical to the Great Tradition of Western political thought. While the latter tradition stressed piety, the order of things,

truth, justice, love, service, hope, and the attunement of man to the ordained nature of things, the legacy of tyranny was founded upon pride, egalitarianism, relativism, perversion, terror, power, despair, and the rebuilding of the human condition from new foundations of strictly human design. Strauss summarized, "In limitless self-love, in frenzied arrogance, the tyrant seeks to rule not merely over men but even over gods."[164] Tyranny was a massive heresy; its roots were Machiavellian; and it found its fullest expression in modern totalitarianism, in National Socialism and Communism.

The armed ideology of National Socialism had been halted by World War II, and in that Strauss rejoiced. It was the relatively unchecked growth of contemporary Communism, the ultimate in tyranny, that deeply troubled him. "The victory of Communism would mean," Strauss wrote, "the victory of the most extreme form of Eastern despotism."[165] What of those "new" political scientists who expected Communist regimes "to transform themselves gradually into good neighbors?"[166] They were "criminally foolish," retorted Strauss; they knew nothing of the immutable ideological character of the Marxist-Leninist mind; and because these thinkers had ceased to draw intellectual and spiritual nourishment from the Great Tradition, as "old fashioned political scientists" had done, they appeared incapable of discerning tyranny, let alone condemning it. In probably his most famous statement, Strauss lamented:

> Only a great fool would call the new political science diabolic: it has no attributes peculiar to fallen angels. It is not even Machiavellian, for Machiavelli's teaching was graceful, subtle, and colorful. Nor is it Neronian. Nevertheless one may say of it that it fiddles while Rome burns. It is excused by two facts: it does not know that it fiddles, and it does not know that Rome burns.[167]

In Conclusion

Although Strauss saw contemporary Western society gravely threatened by the modern isms, he was not a teacher of despair. "Not anguish but awe is 'the fundamental mood,'" Strauss advised, and he added it is false to assume "that a prophet is true only if he is a prophet of doom; the true prophets are also prophets of ultimate salvation."[168] Even when confronted with the monstrous evils of contemporary totalitarianism, Strauss counseled, "There will always be men who will revolt against a state which is destructive of humanity or in which there is no longer a possibility of noble action and of great deeds."[169] This rich prophecy, perhaps symbolized in the figure of a Solzhenitsyn, gives assurance that out of the very crucible of degradation springs hope and thereby power; thus out of evil itself emerges good. If this was the case, and Strauss contended it was, hope inhered in the nature of things. There is cause then for joy, not despair. The bottom metaphysical line in Strauss's thinking is one of affirmation, not negation.

Building successfully on the foundations of hope is not likely to be accomplished through merely offering alternative isms of a more alluring and comforting nature. John Locke, whom conventional wisdom considers the theoretical patron saint of American democracy, does not point to the needed solution, for "Locke is closer to Machiavelli than he is generally said or thought to be": "Locke enlarged self-preservation to comfortable self-preservation and thus laid the theoretical foundation for the acquisitive society."[170] The Lockean tradition negated notions of duty and service, of excellence and virtue, and offered instead tantalizing visions of ever-expanding rights which fostered egoism—Locke was a "political hedonist." Nor, continued Strauss, did libertarianism in general possess the theo-

retical strength and depth to withstand the evils of the modern isms. Rooted also in hedonism and egoism, libertarianism soon produced cloying and aimlessness, and life degenerated into "the joyless quest for joy."[171] Libertarianism left the "ultimate sanctity of the individual as individual unredeemed and unjustified."[172] Similarly, there was no redemptive power in modern statist liberalism. Its ethical foundations were appallingly thin: it challenged no one to virtue and service; rather, it openly, unrelentingly, and arrogantly pandered to hedonism by promising material surfeit through governmental planning and edict. Knowledge no longer had "the character of ascent" toward the transcendent and enduring; it existed exclusively to serve the ever escalating material demands of the unrestrained human ego. Strauss concluded, "There is undoubtedly some kinship between the modern liberal and the ancient sophist."[173]

Moreover, it was unlikely that some form of traditionalism alone could restore the needed metaphysical foundations. Strauss was not hostile to traditionalism if it were properly understood as a corollary to a deeper metaphysic. As a corollary theorem, it had the value of restraining men from engaging in mindless and reckless innovation; it served as a preventive to impiety, the rankest and most ancient of heresies. However, the potential error of unassisted traditionalism was its equating "the good with the ancestral."[174] Strauss warned, "But not everything old everywhere is right."[175] "Prudence," Strauss cautioned, "cannot be seen properly without some knowledge of 'the higher world'—without genuine *theoria*."[176] In sum, the ultimate goal is ascent to the Truth, and unexamined traditionalism frequently serves as a deterrent to that upward thrust.

The only course open to a restoration of the essential theoretical foundations seemed clear. Contemporary man had succumbed to the petty dogmas and harsh ideologies of the modern thinkers. To restore the intellectual vitality of the Western tradition, to alleviate the crisis of modernity and to avert disaster, it was imperative to reject the modern isms and to repair to the restorative powers of the classical and biblical heritages—to the Great Tradition of Western politics. Strauss never defined his intellectual position as "conservative"; perhaps there was the risk that any newly spawned ism, no matter how nobly conceived, would degenerate into another fleeting variant of historicism. Yet American conservatives happily accepted Strauss on his terms; they drew incalculable sustenance from him; many shared his belief in the restorative powers of the Great Tradition; and finally, conservatives instinctively knew that Strauss, the teacher, was correct: to endure and to prevail it was imperative to escape the stifling clutches of historicism.

NOTES

[1] *The College* (April, 1970), 2.
[2] *Commentary* (August, 1974), 64.
[3] *The Academic Reviewer* (Fall-Winter, 1974), 5.
[4] *National Review* (December 7, 1973), 1347.
[5] *Beyond Ideology* (1967), 149.
[6] *National Review* (December 7, 1973), 1355.
[7] *American Conservative Thought in the Twentieth Century* (1970), 398; *National Review* (March 12, 1960), 175.
[8] *National Review* (March 12, 1960), 175.
[9] *The City and Man* (1964), 3 (hereafter cited *CM*).
[10] *Social Research* (September, 1946), 331.
[11] *CM*, 1.
[12] *Ibid.*, 2, 11.
[13] *What Is Political Philosophy?* (1959), 101 (hereafter cited *WPP*).
[14] *Natural Right and History* (1953), 156 (hereafter cited *NR*).
[15] *CM*, 21 (italics added).
[16] *Xenophon's Socratic Discourse* (1970), 83.
[17] *Social Research* (March, 1947), 129.
[18] *On Tyranny* (1963), 108; *History of Political Philosophy* (1972), 45 (hereafter cited *HPP*).
[19] *Jerusalem and Athens* (1967), 22 (hereafter cited *JA*).
[20] *NR*, 146–7.
[21] *The Political Philosophy of Hobbes* (1952), 161 (hereafter cited *PPH*).
[22] *WPP*, 85–6.
[23] *CM*, 31.
[24] *PPH*, 146.
[25] *HPP*, 17.
[26] *NR*, 193.
[27] *WPP*, 87.
[28] *Ibid.*
[29] *Social Research* (December, 1947), 485.
[30] *CM*, 113.
[31] *WPP*, 131–2.
[32] *Ibid.*, 120.
[33] *Thoughts on Machiavelli* (1958), 243 (hereafter cited *TM*).
[34] *CM*, 59.
[35] *WPP*, 28.
[36] *Liberalism Ancient and Modern* (1968), 29 (hereafter cited *LAM*).
[37] *TM*, 298.
[38] *Persecution and the Art of Writing* (1952), 9.
[39] *Spinoza's Critique of Religion* (1965), 163 (hereafter cited *SCR*).
[40] *The Guide for the Perplexed* (Dover Press, 1956), 5.
[41] *LAM*, 142.
[42] *SCR*, 165.
[43] *Isaac Abravanel* (1937), 96.
[44] *Ibid.*, 99, 104.
[45] *LAM*, 170.
[46] *SCR*, 190.
[47] *Ibid.*, 158.
[48] *Ibid.*, 148.
[49] *The Guide*, 6, 8 (italics added).
[50] *Ibid.*, 8 (italics added).
[51] *Ibid.*, 9.
[52] *SCR*, 18.
[53] *Ibid.*, 201.
[54] *Ibid.*, 200.
[55] *Ibid.*, 171–2.
[56] *Ibid.*, 203.
[57] *Ibid.*, 225.
[58] *Ibid.*, 222.
[59] *Ibid.*, 164, 160.
[60] *Ibid.*, 172, 209.
[61] *Ibid.*, 21.
[62] *WPP*, 226; *SCR*, 170.
[63] *NR*, 36.
[64] *SCR*, 11.
[65] *Ibid.*, 9.
[66] *Interpretation* (Summer, 1971), 7; *The State of the Social Sciences* (1956), 420 (hereafter cited *SSS*).
[67] *SCR*, 8–9.
[68] *Ibid.*, 9.

276

JOHN P. EAST

69 *TM*, 133, 32.
70 *LAM*, 261.
71 *Ibid.*, 261.
72 *TM*, 150.
73 *SCR*, 29.
74 *LAM*, 266.
75 *Ibid.*, 265–6.
76 *Ibid.*, 267.
77 *Ibid.*, 270.
78 *WPP*, 281.
79 *JA*, 3.
80 *Ibid.*, 5.
81 *WPP*, 111.
82 *Ibid.*
83 *JA*, 20.
84 *Political Philosophy: Six Essays by Leo Strauss* (1975), 86 (hereafter cited *PP*).
85 *JA*, 21.
86 *Ibid.*, 27.
87 *Church History* (March, 1961), 101.
88 *WPP*, 40.
89 *TM*, 224.
90 *Ibid.*, 175.
91 *Ibid.*, 295.
92 *WPP*, 180; *NR*, 178.
93 *TM*, 176.
94 *Ibid.*, 194.
95 *HPP*, 278.
96 *TM*, 294.
97 *Ibid.*, 142.
98 *Ibid.*, 170.
99 *Ibid.*, 190.
100 *Ibid.*, 199.
101 *Ibid.*, 178–9.
102 *Ibid.*, 191.
103 *Ibid.*, 13.
104 *Ibid.*, 94.
105 *Ibid.*, 132, 136.
106 *Ibid.*, 167.
107 *Ibid.*, 207–8.
108 *NR*, 178.
109 *TM*, 296–7.
110 *Ibid.*, 13–14.
111 *Ibid.*, 295.
112 *WPP*, 289.
113 *The Prince*, ch. 15.
114 *Ibid.*, ch. 18.
115 *TM*, 67–8.
116 *Ibid.*, 80.
117 *Ibid.*, 209.
118 *Ibid.*, 214–15.
119 *Ibid.*, 215.
120 *Ibid.*, 221.
121 *The Discourses*. Book Three, discourse 31.
122 *WPP*, 42.
123 *TM*, 279; *WPP*, 43.
124 *The Prince*, ch. 25.

125 *TM*, 82.
126 *Ibid.*, 127.
127 *The Prince*, ch. 24.
128 *HPP*, 287.
129 *TM*, 282.
130 *Ibid.*, 9.
131 *The Discourses*, Book One, discourse 27.
132 *TM*, 9, 107.
133 *PPH*, xv.
134 *NR*, 177.
135 *PPH*, 5.
136 *Ibid.*, 100.
137 *Ibid.*, 163–4.
138 *NR*, 170.
139 *PPH*, 23.
140 *WPP*, 185.
141 *Ibid.*, 189–90.
142 *PPH*, 23.
143 *NR*, 194.
144 *WPP*, 48–9
145 *PP*, 89.
146 *Social Research* (November, 1939), 539.
147 *Genealogy of Morals*, 476–7
148 *Beyond Good and Evil*, in *Basic Writings*, 211.
149 *PP*, 97–8, 94.
150 *Interpretation* (Winter, 1973), 112.
151 *Ibid.*
152 *The Predicament of Modern Politics* (1964), 91 (hereafter cited *PMP*).
153 *TM*, 203.
154 *PMP*, 91.
155 *WPP*, 25.
156 *NR*, 17.
157 *Ibid.*, 59.
158 *PP*, 82.
159 *Relativism and the Study of Man* (1961), 151.
160 *SSS*, 422.
161 *NR*, 292, 221, 184, 271; *Interpretation* (Winter, 1973), 112.
162 *SCR*, 2.
163 *Ibid.*, 15, 17.
164 *PPH*, 147.
165 *CM*, 3.
166 *Essays on the Scientific Study of Politics* (1962), 317.
167 *Ibid.*, 327.
168 *WPP*, 260; *JA*, 25.
169 *WPP*, 130.
170 *WPP*, 218; *HPP*, 273.
171 *NR*, 251.
172 *Ibid.*, 294.
173 *LAM*, 56.
174 *NR*, 319.
175 *Ibid.*, 83.
176 *Ibid.*, 321.

[XXI, Winter 1977, 2–19]

[23]

Voegelin Read Anew: Political Philosophy in the Age of Ideology

ELLIS SANDOZ

(George) Ellis Sandoz, Jr. (1931–   ), a member of the editorial advisory board of Modern Age, *is professor of political science at Louisiana State University. A native of New Orleans, he studied at Louisiana State University, at the University of Heidelberg, and under Eric Voegelin at the University of Munich. Sandoz's* The Voegelinian Revolution: A Biographical Introduction *(1982), the first comprehensive exegesis of the entire Voegelin canon, interweaves the events of this great thinker's life with the philosophical inquiry to which that life was devoted. Similarly, Sandoz's earlier work,* Political Apocalypse: A Study of Dostoevsky's Grand Inquisitor *(1971), is a perceptive exploration of major philosophical questions and existential issues: life and death, good and evil, man and God, order and disorder, history and eternity.*

ANY OSTENSIBLE discussion of Eric Voegelin's critique of behavioralism in political science labors under a peculiar disability: he never has had much to do with behavioralists or behavioralism and has nowhere conducted a discursive critique of this approach to political study. There is, to be sure, the passage in the "Introduction" to *The New Science of Politics* in which the positivist doctrines are examined briefly and shown to be a contradictory and defective basis for a comprehensive science of man; and what is said there no doubt has pertinence. There also are scattered comments here and there in "What Is Political Reality?" in the *Anamnesis* (1966) volume, in more recent essays such as "Immortality: Experience and Symbol,"[1] where he mentions "behaviorism," and in the paper entitled "On Classical Studies,"[2] where he alludes to "theoretical illiteracy" and notes the frequent equation of "critical theory" with "irrational, nihilistic opining." Then there was the fabled verbal exchange with Harold Lasswell on a panel at the annual meeting of the Southern Political Science Association in Gainesville, Florida, in 1953 about which I have heard rumors and recollections. But Voegelin never has engaged in a considered critique of the work of Truman or Easton or Lasswell or Eulau or Dahl, political scientists all, or any other eminence of the behavioralist movement

277

and I very much doubt that he ever shall; he long ago left that wearisome controversy aside and busied himself otherwise.

Still the topic is not entirely inopportune. For it is true that Voegelin's "new science" comprises a major alternative for political scientists to the now faded orthodoxy of the past two decades, and it certainly implies a rejection of the heady pretences of the more sanguine exponents of behavioralism. Moreover, insofar as behavioralism rests at all upon any definable theoretical foundation, that foundation lies in positivism; and the deft critique of the principal tenets of that doctrine as it has application in political science conducted in 1951 is fatal to it, so that no more need be said.

"But why not?" one may perhaps be forgiven for obtusely asking: "What about dialogue and all that? Would not patient explanations be of value in leading the confused out of the *Sheol* of the mind and spirit?" Bluntly stated, Voegelin's evident refusal to engage in "dialogue" with the proponents of behavioralism (or of any of the other "isms") rests on the perception, as I remember his once phrasing it, that "against the vulgarity of the ideologue one can do nothing. The less one says the better." He is inclined neither to shouting matches nor to fatuous verbal exchanges with dogmatists of this or that "persuasion"—to use the word in Eulau's sense. I do not think this is snobbery. Rather it is a reflection of the sober conviction, resting on good empirical evidence, that the doctrinaire exponent of this or that creed is incapable of scientific debate, so why waste effort of anguish and words?

Voegelin's work is remarkably free of polemics, a fact that the partisan zealots on all sides seem incapable of recognizing. The attitude of the man to the work of behavioral political scientists, it must be stressed, is far from being contemptuous.

He values this dimension of the discipline for what it contributes to the pragmatic understanding of politics. But he finds the approach is hopelessly inadequate for a comprehensive science of politics just because it reduces politics and science to a single strand of reality when the whole must be explored. Hence, it is only this reductionist feature that Voegelin flatly rejects, this untenable, methodologically dictated narrowing of the horizon of political science and of rational endeavor itself. He does not in the least doubt that political behavior must thoroughly be studied. Unfortunately many arrogantly have insisted that behavioral science is the only *scientific* approach to politics, and Voegelin's work is, in a sense, partly a critique of that ill-founded dogma.

As to "dialogue" his attitude is as old as Hesiod who, you will remember, was approvingly cited by Aristotle at the beginning of the first treatise on political science:

> Far best is he who knows all things himself;
> Good, he that hearkens when men counsel right;
> But he who neither knows, nor lays to heart Another's wisdom, is a useless wight.[3]

Rational discussion is only possible with fellow *spoudaioi* and with those who are sufficiently attuned to the pulls of the Golden Cord as to be attentive to wisdom when it is spoken. The utterly useless types of Hesiod-Aristotle (the "fools" of Isaiah [32:6]) include the dogmatists of all stripes, and with these one simply cannot discuss theoretical matters. These considerations bring to focus the particular questions which I want briefly to address here: What are the conditions essential to rational debate? How can Voegelin's work over the past quarter century be related to such demanding conditions? The person possessed of dogmatic certitude is incapable of persuasion (this time and hereafter, the word is used in Plato's sense [*peitho*]) by rational means (Hesiod's third type).

THE TWENTY-TWO year period which has elapsed since Voegelin's Walgreen Lectures were delivered at the University of Chicago[4] is characterized by attributes which militate against rational debate, and, more generally, the Life of Reason (Aristotle's *bios theoretikos*) even among the few men intrinsically capable of it. This current "climate of opinion," in Joseph Glanville's seventeenth-century phrase, composes the "given" circumstances in which life has been lived for the past two decades; and, of course, this period is only the most recent phase of a historical configuration going back to the time of Glanville.

The "climate" of the contemporary period prominently displays certain features inhibiting the successful prosecution of philosophical science. By way of a general characterization one may say that it is intellectually dominated by the conflict among ideological deformities of a variety of types which (whatever the dissimilarities) are alike in being dogmatically held and urged as exclusive Truth. This enforces a closure of the soul against rational persuasion and against the asking of questions of a fundamental kind. Ideological constructs compose Second Realities superimposed upon the one true First Reality systematically to obscure it. The range of "isms" and jargon of newspeak are here denoted: positivism (behavioralism), Marxism, fascism, communism, national socialism, nihilism, Freudianism, scientism, liberalism, conservatism, neo-Thomism, relativism, and so on. The life of the mind, then, tends to be perverted by a polemical *dogmatomachie* which renders reality impenetrably opaque and substitutes dreamworlds of this or that tincture for the world of experience illuminated by science and philosophy. And this perversity is institutionalized especially in the "seats of learning"—the universities and the intellectual community at large—thereby massively screening existence and ruthlessly enforcing irrationality, false consciousness, and bad faith.

Social dominance through institutionalization of deformation is attained not only through the universities, but through educational systems at all levels; through political activism resulting in defective policy and legislative decisions; through ubiquitous communication of the mass media. And the result is a psychic destruction and pneumatopathology that desperately elevates Pascalian *divertissement* into a way of life. The phenomenon is sufficiently evident that a Howard Cosell can, in disgust, diagnose a society to be sick which relies upon televised football as a national cult.

The syndrome also includes the collapse and dispersal of the key sources of social cohesiveness and order through fragmentation of the historical consciousness and destruction of the stabilizing traditions of society. The churches no longer serve as mediators of revelation. The universities rarely perceive themselves primarily to be mediators of science and rational knowledge—a complaint voiced by Mario Savio while a student at Berkeley in 1964. The family, which is the focus of habitual tender personal relationships indispensable to private and public virtue, rootedness in existence, and the commonsense rationality requisite for political order in a free society under free government, suffers profound crisis and poor prospects as a viable social institution.

The picture is a bleak one, for climates of opinion are not easily dispelled, and social pathologies of the depth of the contemporary ones—with their roots in more than three centuries of development—cannot as such be countered by private initiatives. As Whitehead observed in 1925, "modern philosophy has been ruined." And so also has been the Life of Reason as a conventional endeavor. Yet dismal as is the setting, the past quarter century has rightly been proclaimed one of the great ages of humane science. And if this is so, it is because climates of opinion and, more generally, the hold that social environment has on a man—pernicious and oppressive of the spirit as they may be—cannot *obliterate* the nature of man itself. In every society there always will be the few gods and beasts among men whose actions are done despite the politics of the times. There is inevitable laceration of the consciousness in the solitary life, for man is truly a political being; but this saving contradiction—the mysterious and exceptional capacity to be freed from the Cave—provides the perennial alternative to psychic mutilation at the hands of maniacal social forces.

"Work in silence is a free enterprise," Voegelin once remarked; and it has been through retreat into the privacy of his existence that achievement as a thinker has come. Whether hounded from a university chair by Nazis in Vienna or exiled to the hinterlands of American academia in Louisiana, Voegelin has pursued his remarkable work in the silence of the study. Such a life in freedom, it needs be said, is also one of very great courage. Nor is it without political impact. For even though society be ponderously unresponsive to the philosophers in its midst in the short run—preferring to poison and stone them rather than give praise—the impact over the long haul is more assuring. Despite the Athenians, Socrates is the progenitor of us all. Even in the immediate present, the work of a single man becomes more than merely a life of solitude. For a man of courage and insight creates around himself an enclave of order in the midst of existential disorder from which radiates a more than negligible influence even into those societies in which the authority of the spirit is most perfectly divorced from political power. Something of the kind has occurred in the present instance, for Voegelin's books are published and read; he has won prominence in Europe, and, belatedly, in America as well.

CERTAIN OF THE questions he has addressed arose directly out of the hostile milieu of his life and work. These are of particular interest on this occasion, for it is important to discern the strategy underlying noble work in silence. If the proposition be accepted that the philosopher's life is, first of all, an effort at salvation for himself and, then, for his fellowmen, it follows that such a philosopher as Eric Voegelin teaches and writes both in enactment of the process of meditative inquiry and in persuasiveness toward fellowmen. How can the latter dimension of the theoretical activity be done amidst the ruins of the Life of Reason just sketched?

The head-on approach at the level of ideas already has been precluded: "dialogue" with ideologists is fruitless because existential persuasion (the aim of rational discussion) is an impossibility known at the outset. Persistence on this track leaves the critical questions untouched, since the decisive errors lie in the premises. These are placed beyond debate by the prohibition against the asking of fundamental questions—Marx's *denke nicht, frage mich nicht.* . . . But, if discussion is persisted in anyway, then it inevitably derails into trivia and the polemics of dogmatic assertiveness indistinguishable from ideological diatribe.

The problem becomes clearer if one ascertains the minimal conditions under which rational debate is possible. Voegelin has written especially of this question in two places: "On Readiness to Rational Discussion" (1959) and "On Debate and Existence" (1961).[5] The first presupposition of rational debate is common agreement, as the starting point, on the terms of reality and on the place of man as a reflective participant in this reality of which he is not himself the creator, *i.e.*, agreement in the rootedness of the existent *man* and, hence, of rational inquiry in the *condicio humana*, a condition structured by the ontological tensions represented by the terms *God, man, world*, and *society* as symbolisms of the sectors by which being is articulated. From this initial agreement, secondly, there also follows agreement upon the *topoi* or the topics, questions, and issues for debate which are of interest to everybody: "the why and how of existence, the questions of the nature of man, of divine nature, of the orientation of man towards his end, of just order in the actions of man and society, *etc.*"

If these two conditions cannot be met (as they seldom can be today), then debate at the level of reason and intellect must inevitably fail. The current situation may be contrasted, in this respect, with that of Thomas Aquinas, for example. St. Thomas could debate with the Jews on the basis of the mutually accepted authority of the Old Testament; with the heretics on the basis of the authority of the New Testament; and with the Moslems on the basis of natural reason, because they were the transmitters of Aristotle to the West and shared a common noetic order. But the modern debate can find no such common ground. There is no common reality, set of *topoi*, scriptural authority, or (so thoroughgoing has been the destruction of noetic rationality since Locke) common reason.

The alternatives remaining are two. One can engage in a hidden debate exclusively with the few (one thinks of Spinoza) with whom the stipulated conditions can be met and ignore or deceive the many. But this is a highly volatile even if acceptable and widely practiced solution which is related to the question, When should one return to the Cave? Not only are companions scarce, but intellectual and even physical attrition diminishes their number and reliability by reason of the inroads upon the few achieved by the many who monopolize power, institutional controls, communications, and the means of reward and penalty in society at large. Existential disorder presses in not only upon the many (who cannot bear it), but also upon the few who may with difficulty be capable of sustaining life in truth; for the disease of the soul is a political contagion of which all men *qua* men are more or less susceptible. Empirically grounded clinical studies of the limits in these matters might be undertaken in such settings as the *samizdat* activities of the Medvedevs, Amalriks, Marchenkos, Gorbanevskayas, and Solzhenitsyns, if an updating of Plato's analysis in the *Republic* is desired—and if only the KGB would open its files.

Perhaps a sounder alternative is the one indicated by Plato in the *Gorgias*: without hoping for too much, to return to the Cave of pre-philosophical discourse and seek to communicate in existentially meaningful ways at the level of the *pathos* shared by all men by virtue of their common humanity. Only in this way can persuasion of truth rationally be attempted under conditions of intellectual collapse in society. And one must be reminded that the task is today not merely the old one of existential communication with *hoi polloi* through popularization of insights, or merely with the few in the face of ruthless and powerful adversaries who may control public means of retribution; but it is the task of communicating with and persuading the potential *spoudaioi* engulfed by the pervasive deculturation that has inundated the entire intellectual world in the ideological age in which we live. This far more formidable task of alleviating the "eclipse of reality" in an era of ruined minds receives its distinctive mark from the fact that, not only can one not know with any certainty which among his students, auditors, and readers is potentially a philosophical man or woman, but also that the best among them are those likely to be most perfectly deformed by a milieu differentiated by psychic deformity as its norm and standard. In short, the most and best educated and educable persons in our midst are likely also to be the most perfectly corrupted; but *only* these have the capacities requisite for grasping highest truth. Here lies the pragmatic dilemma Voegelin attempts to resolve as a teacher.

The foregoing inventory of the preconditions and possibilities provides a clue for partly understanding the directions taken by Voegelin in his work over the past two decades. The abandonment in about 1945 of his project for a *History of Ideas,* triggered by the reading of Schelling's philosophy of myth and revelation, was at least partly dictated by these considerations. There is no history of ideas but a history of experiences of order and their symbolization. When the intellectual culture has desiccated and crumbled away because no longer supported by the ground of common experience, then a break occurs such as the one reflected on in the works of Plato and Aristotle; or that seen in the period of late Scholasticism and reacted against by Francis Bacon, Descartes, Hobbes, and Locke; or even that continued into the contemporary period as reflected in such startling and disparate manifestations as D. H. Lawrence on sex (Mellors hated words) and Jesus Freaks on Christianity. The denominator here is the attempt to escape from logorrhea and recapture the savor and content of fun-

damental experiences which, at once, compose the *pathos* of existence for all men and supply the foundations of ordered existence.

Every man loves *something,* and these loves structure existence—even when ideational communication and traditional symbols cease to evoke that order and deteriorate into curious artifacts and deadening abstractions at odds with experienced reality and isolated from it. Callicles and Socrates claimed two loves apiece, one immanent and one transcendent of purely personal existence: a human favorite each, and the *demos* by the one, divine *Sophia* by the other. Just here one can always lay the finger on what *is.* The symbolism of Plato's *Gorgias* implies the composite and essential nature of man as well as the hierarchical structure of being itself. These are correlated and linked through erotic participation at various levels arising out of the depths of existential *pathos* immediately present in the concrete consciousness of Everyman. This common ground remains accessible to all men by virtue of their humanity; and it forms the substance of autobiography (for example, as Bergson's *durée réelle*) no less than the stuff of meaning in history. To speak with Emerson:

> We are always coming up with the emphatic facts of history in our private experience and verifying them here. All history becomes subjective; in other words there is properly no history, only biography.

THE DRIFT of Voegelin's major work as it continues into the present may then be interpreted as the attempt philosophically to recover the truth of existence for himself and to propagate it as a teacher and writer through procreative persuasion in the souls of the youth and other of his fellowmen. Three facets of the endeavor can be distinguished.

Central is the penetration through symbolisms and ideas evidenced in historiographic documents into the underlying experiential sources of existence whence these symbolisms arose; then the interpretation of these engendering experiences with full attention to existential content—*i.e.,* to the infusing substance or feeling which prompts orientation toward known truth and thereby makes meaningful the life of men and the history of nations. Out of this endeavor issued concretely the multifold classification of types of controlling experience as cosmic-divine, noetic, and pneumatic and the classification of forms of symbolization as myth, philosophy, and revelation set forth in *Order and History.*

These meditative and scholarly activities are seen to be in essential conformity with the theoretical activity of the Hellenic philosophers of antiquity. Hence, meticulous analysis of the process of human consciousness and of the noetic structure of being emerged as cardinal tasks; philosophical inquiry seeks both to explore, and to represent imaginatively and ideationally, the form and content of the controlling modes of experience of the salient dimensions of reality. These experiences provide the sovereign means of understanding and communicating those fragments of the truth of reality grasped by human cognition thus far in history. Indeed, the centrality of experience to philosophy and all science is such as to require the supplementation of the earlier discussion in this paper. It is only partly, as was said, as a strategy of persuasion that common experience of a pathetic kind was appealed to by Socrates in the *Gorgias* and by Voegelin in the wake of his reading of Schelling. No less damning than Whitehead's assessment of modern philosophy is Voegelin's blunt statement that "the history of philosophy is in the largest part the history of its derailment."[6] The explanation of this perversion (*pa-*

rekbasis) is the divorcement of philosophy from the experiences out of which it initially arose, and the simultaneous transformation of the symbols developed for articulating these experiences into topics of immanentist speculation. Hence, the appeal to the pathetic experience common to all men, the ground of existential communication (and its only possibility under unfavorable intellectual circumstances) is the starting point, but not the end of reliance upon experience. It may be said that the *pathos* of existence in Everyman stands to the differentiated experience of a Plato or Aristotle as does common sense to noetic rationality. The experience of divine Being of the mystic philosopher outstrips the pathetic experience of Everyman; and philosophy as a mode of scientific cognition remains bound to experience. Indeed, philosophy is identical to the noetic experience of the divine Reality; it is its symbolic articulation through consciousness and very essence, in the Life of Reason first named by Aristotle. This work is best seen in *Anamnesis* and in subsequently published essays.

Finally, the uncovering and declaring of truth implies the reflexive discernment of falsehood; and in the contemporary plight of men, this especially entailed some attention to the Second Realities which massively hinder the former effort and provide its immediate backdrop. These then are explored with regard both to their delineation as constructs but more especially to their motivating experiential basis as deformed "structure[s] of existence in untruth." The concrete result is the analysis and compilation of the pathologies of politics and existence exemplified by the second half of *The New Science of Politics* and the Inaugural Lecture at Munich, *Science, Politics, and Gnosticism.*[7]

On this reading, then, Voegelin's work is one of the philosophical science of politics. It seeks redemption from exis-

tence in untruth for the philosopher himself as well as for those around him.
Integral to this life's effort is a diagnosis
of the disorders of existence and of the
age which prescribes their therapies
through Reason in an act of ministering
love.

NOTES

[1] *Harvard Theological Review,* 60 (1967), 254ff.

[2] *Modern Age,* vol. 17, no. 1 (Winter 1973), pp. 2–8.

[3] Cited from *Nicomachean Ethics,* 1095b10: Hesiod, *Works and Days,* lines 293ff. W. D. Ross's translation.

[4] Entitled "Truth and Representation," and published in 1952 as *The New Science of Politics.*

[5] The dates given are of initial publication. The essays can be found in the following places: the first in Albert Hunold, ed., *Freedom and Serfdom: An Anthology of Western Thought,* trans. R. H. Stevens (Dordrecht, Holland: D. Reidel, 1961), pp. 269–84: the second in *The Intercollegiate Review,* 3 (1967), 143–52. See also "The Eclipse of Reality," in Maurice Natanson, ed., *Phenomenology and Social Reality: Essays in Memory of Alfred Schutz* (The Hague: Martinus Nijhoff, 1970), pp. 185–94.

[6] *Order and History,* III, p. 277.

[7] Published by Henry Regnery Co. (Chicago); for a fuller discussion of Voegelin's work see further my "Voegelin's Idea of Historical Form," *Cross Currents,* 12 (1962), 41–63; "The Science and Demonology of Politics," *Intercollegiate Review,* 5 (1968–69), 117–23; "The Foundations of Voegelin's Political Theory," *Political Science Reviewer,* 1 (1971), 30–73; and "The Philosophical Science of Politics Beyond Behavioralism," in George J. Graham, Jr., and George W. Carey, eds., *The Post-Behavioral Era: Perspectives on Political Science* (New York: David McKay Co., 1972), pp. 285–305.

[XVII, Summer 1973, 257–263]

[III]

Roots of American Order

[24]

The Heresy of Equality:
Bradford Replies to Jaffa

M. E. BRADFORD

M. E. Bradford (1934–   ) first appeared in Modern Age *in 1966 and has been an associate editor since 1979. Currently he is chairman of the English department of the University of Dallas. The author of numerous essays on rhetoric, literature, and American politics, he has frequently focused on the Southern Agrarians in such books as* Rumors of Mortality: An Introduction to Allen Tate *(1969) and* The Form Discovered: Essays on the Achievement of Andrew Lytle *(1973), as well as on earlier periods of American history and literature in such works as* A Better Guide Than Reason: Studies in the American Revolution *(1979). His most recent book is* Remembering Who We Are: Observations of a Southern Conservative *(1985).*

I

Let us have no foolishness, indeed.* Equality as a moral or political imperative, pursued as an end in itself—Equality, with the capital "E"—is the antonym of every legitimate conservative principle. Contrary to most Liberals, new and old, it is nothing less than sophistry to distinguish between equality of opportunity (equal starts in the "race of life") and equality of condition (equal results). For only those who *are* equal can take equal advantage of a given circumstance. And there is no man equal to any other, except perhaps in the special, and politically untranslatable, understanding of the Diety. *Not intellectually or physically or economically or even morally. Not equal!* Such is, of course, the genuinely self-evident proposition.[1] Its truth finds a verification in our bones and is demonstrated in the unself-conscious acts of our everyday lives: vital proof, regardless of our private political persuasion. Incidental equality, engendered by the pursuit of other objectives, is, to be sure, another matter. Inside of the general history of the West (and especially within the American experience) it can be credited with a number of healthy consequences: strength in the bonds of

---

* This essay is a direct response to Harry Jaffa's "Equality as a Conservative Principle," *Loyola of Los Angeles Law Review,* VIII (June 1975), pp. 471–505, which is itself a critique of *The Basic Symbols of the American Political Tradition* by Willmoore Kendall and George W. Carey. Lincoln's reading of the Declaration of Independence is the central subject of this entire exchange. Jaffa's piece invites direct comparison with mine.

community, assent to the authority of honorable regimes, faith in the justice of the gods.

But the equality of Professor Jaffa's essay, even in the ordinary sense of "equal rights," can be expected to work the other way around. For this equality belongs to the post-Renaissance world of ideology—of political magic and the alchemical "science" of politics. Envy is the basis of its broad appeal. And rampant envy, the besetting virus of modern society, is the most predictable result of insistence upon its realization.[2] Furthermore, hue and cry over equality of opportunity and equal rights leads, *a fortiori*, to a final demand for equality of condition. Under its pressure self-respect gives way in the large majority of men who have not reached the level of their expectation, who have no support from an inclusive identity, and who hunger for "revenge" on those who occupy a higher station and will (they expect) continue to enjoy that advantage. The end result is visible in the spiritual proletarians of the "lonely crowd." Bertrand de Jouvenel has described the process which produces such non-persons in his memorable study, *On Power*.[3] They are the natural pawns of an impersonal and omnicompetent Leviathan. And to insure their docility such a state is certain to recruit a large "new class" of men, persons superior in "ability" and authority, both to their ostensible "masters" among the people and to such anachronisms as stand in their progressive way.

Such is the evidence of the recent past—and particularly of American history. Arrant individualism, fracturing and then destroying the hope of amity and confederation, the communal bond and the ancient vision of the good society as an extrapolation from family, is one villain in this tale. Another is rationalized cowardice, shame, and ingratitude hidden behind the disguise of self-sufficiency or

the mask of injured merit. Interdependence, which secures dignity and makes of equality a mere irrelevance, is the principal victim. Where fraternity exists to support the official structure of a government, it can command assent with no fear of being called despotic or prejudiced in behalf of one component of the society it represents. But behind the cult of equality (the chief if not only tenet in Professor Jaffa's theology, and his link to the pseudo-religious politics of ideology) is an even more sinister power, the uniformitarian hatred of providential distinctions which will stop at nothing less than what Eric Voegelin calls "a reconstitution of being": a nihilistic impulse which is at bottom both frightened and vain in its rejection of a given contingency and in its arrogation of a godlike authority to annul that dependency.[4] As Robert Penn Warren has recently reminded us, distinctions drawn from an encounter with an external reality have been the basis for the intellectual life as we have known it: prudent and tentative distinctions, but seriously intended.[5] With the reign of equality all of that achievement is set at peril.

II

So much in prologue. Concerning equality Professor Jaffa and I disagree profoundly; disagree even though we both denominate ourselves conservative. Yet this distinction does not finally exhaust or explain our differences. For Jaffa's opening remarks indicate that his conservatism is of a relatively recent variety and is, in substance, the Old Liberalism hidden under a Union battle flag. To the contrary I maintain that if conservatism has any identity whatsoever beyond mere recalcitrance and rationalized self-interest, that identity must incorporate the "funded wisdom of the ages" as that deposition comes down through a particular national experience. Despite modifications within the prescription of a continuum of political life, only a relativist or historicist could argue that American conservatism should be an utterly unique phenomenon, without antecedents which predate 1776 and unconnected with the mainstream of English and European thought and practice known to our forefathers in colonial times. Jaffa of course nods toward one face of Locke and, by implication, the chiliastic politics of Cromwell's New England heirs.[6] And I have no doubt that he can add to his hagiography a selective (and generally misleading) list of earlier patrons of his view. I cannot in this space encounter the full spectrum of Straussian rationalism. To specify what I believe to be lacking in Jaffa's conservative model (and wrong with the intellectual history he uses in its validation), it will serve better for me to concentrate first on how I read the Declaration of Independence and then append, in abbreviated form, my estimation of Lincoln's lasting and terrible impact on the nation's destiny through his distortions upon that text. This of course involves me incidentally in Jaffa's quarrel with Kendall/Carey and *The Basic Symbols of the American Political Tradition*. But it must be understood that my object is not to defend these worthy gentlemen. To the contrary, my primary interest is in a more largely conservative view of the questions over which they and Professor Jaffa disagree. And, therefore, incidentally with the operation and quality of my adversary's mind which lead him to conclusions so very different from mine. With those concerns I propose to organize and conclude my remarks.

III

Professor Jaffa begs a great many questions in his comments on the Declaration. But his greatest mistake is an open error, and supported by considerable precedent in both academic and political circles. In truth, his approach is an orthodox one, at least in our radical times. I refer to his treatment of the second sentence of that document in abstraction from its whole: indeed, of the first part of that sentence in abstraction from its remainder, to say nothing of the larger text. Jaffa filters the rest of the Declaration (and later expressions of the American political faith) back and forth through the measure of that sentence until it has (or so he imagines) achieved its baptism in the pure waters of the higher law. He quotes Lincoln approvingly that "the doctrine of human equality was 'the father of all moral principle [amongst us].' "[7] Jaffa sets up a false dilemma: we must be, as a people, "committed" to Equality or we are "open to the relativism and historicism that is the theoretical ground of modern totalitarian regimes." The Declaration is, of course, the origin of that commitment to "permanent standards." And particularly the second sentence. The trouble here comes from an imperfect grasp of the Burkean calculus. And from the habit of reading legal, poetic, and rhetorical documents as if they were bits of revealed truth or statements of systematic thought. My objections derive primarily from those antirationalist realms of discourse. For I assume, with Swift, that man is a creature capable of reason, *capax rationis*, but not a rational animal. Therefore the head and heart must be engaged together where instruction is attempted. The burden of poetry and rhetoric is inherent in the form through which that idea is embodied: its meaning *is* its way of meaning, not a discursive paraphrase. And it achieves that meaning as it unfolds. According to this procedure we are taught from of old that the soul may be composed, the sensibility reordered. Reason enters into this process with modesty and draws its sanction for whatever new truth it may advance from cooperation with sources and authorities that need produce no credentials nor prove up any title with the audience assumed. For in poetry as in law and rhetoric all matters are not in question. There is a prescription, or something equivalent to what Burke calls by that name. And usually a theology to channel and gloss the prescript. Tropes and figures, terms weighted more or less by usage, norms of value configured and dramatic sequences of associated actions discovered through an unbroken stream of place and blood and history operate in this mode of communication as something logically prior to the matter under examination. And likewise the law, especially where the rule is *stare decisis*. Where myth or precedent or some other part of the "wide prejudice" of a people is presupposed and identity therefore converted into a facet of ontology, a providential thing ("inalienable" in that word's oldest sense, not to be voted, given, or reasoned away), there is nothing for mere philosophy to say. And that *philosophe* abstraction, political Man, who once theoretically existed outside a social bond, is nowhere to be seen. As a wise man wrote, "Where the great interests of mankind are concerned through a long succession of generations, that succession ought to be admitted into some share in the councils which are so deeply to affect them."[8] For the "moral essences" that shape a commonwealth are "not often constructed after any theory: theories are rather drawn from them"—the natural law, made partially visible only in the prescription, but made visible nonetheless.[9]

IV

To anyone familiar with English letters and the English mind in the seventeenth and eighteenth centuries, the Declaration of Independence is clearly a document produced out of the *mores majorum*—legal, rhetorical, poetic—and not a piece of reasoning or systematic truth. No sentence of its whole means anything out of context. It unfolds *seriatim* and makes sense only when read through. Furthermore, what it does mean is intelligible only in a matrix of circumstances—political, literary, linguistic, and mundane. Nevertheless, no one trained to move in the rhetorical world of Augustan humanism would take it for a relativistic statement any more than they would describe Dryden's *Religio Laici*, Addison's *Cato*, Johnson's *Rasselas*, or Burke's *Reflections on the Revolution in France* in that fashion.[10] Jaffa revives the error of his master, Leo Strauss, in speaking of the bugbear historicism and of "mere prescriptive rights."[11] For it is in our day the alternatives which carry with them a serious danger of the high-sounding despot. Radicals (to use his term, meaning the Liberals who see in politics a new "Queen of the Sciences" and employ a sequence of private revelations to exalt her condition) believe in a "higher law"—have done so at least since the politics of secularized Puritanism first appeared in European society.[12] Even Marxists finally worship the demiurge of history—and rest the remainder of their argument upon that authority. And the goddess Reason is still with us, available to sanction whatever her hand finds to do in erasing all that survives from what Peter Gay rightly labels the mythopoeic vision.[13] I agree with Professor Jaffa concerning the danger of relativism. A Christian must. And also about behavioristic political science. Such study is description only, or else mere manipulation. But, hunger for the normative aside, we must resist the tendency to thrust familiar contemporary pseudo-religious notions back into texts where they are unlikely to appear. Any Englishman of 1776 (colonial or not) should not be expected to construe natural rights so rigorously as Justice Black—except perhaps for hyperbole and in argument. In between our day and that first July 4 stand a number of revolutions, especially the French. And also two hundred years of liberal and radical thought. We are bemused by the spectre of Locke (an authority to some of the revolutionary generation, but read loosely and in the light of Sir Edward Coke and William Petyt, and the 1628 Petition of Right, and the 1689 Declaration of Rights).[14] The legacy of English common law is lost upon us. And in the process we have forgotten, among other things, that Edmund Burke is our best guide to the main line of Whig thought: *not Locke or Paine, or even Harrington, but Burke*. It is, of course, a truism that all colonial Americans did their political thinking inside the post-1688 Whig legal tradition.[15] Some years ago Professor Jaffa attempted to counter this line of objection to this Lincolnian construction of the Declaration by setting Paine and Locke (plus an irrelevant bit of Blackstone) upon Daniel J. Boorstin's excellent *The Americans: The Colonial Experience*. But in so doing he only evaded his antagonist and obfuscated the question of what is typically Whig and behind our "revolution."[16] For Locke is not so consistent a source of equal rights as Jaffa would lead us to believe. Indeed, that worthy theorist of liberty was an eager part to the creation of a slaveocracy in South Carolina.[17] And on occasion he justified the peculiar institution with nothing more sophisticated than an appeal to race or right of conquest.[18] Blackstone, for his part, was a high Tory and a poor sponsor for equality of any sort. And Paine relates to very little that became American in our Constitution of 1787. Recent scholarship on early American history has, by and large, exhibited an anachronistic tendency to ignore all patriotic utterances that do not

sound like Locke in his highest flights of freedom or Paine before the Mountain: like the Whig "Left," in other words.[19] They have ignored the problems in logic set up by "all men are created equal" when understood as one of Lincoln's beloved Euclidian propositions and the larger problems for libertarians determined not to call for equality of condition when they start from such a postulate.[20] Along with the political philosophers they have approached the task of explication as if the Declaration existed *sui generis*, in a Platonic empyrean.[21] A gloss upon what transpired in a real (*i.e.*, intellectually "messy") convention in a real Philadelphia seems not to interest these sages: what with reason could be expected to occur?[22] With a non-Lockean Whig machinery (and as a practicing rhetorician) I will attempt to draw the inquiry down toward such probabilities.

V

Contrary to Professor Jaffa, it is my view that the Declaration of Independence is not very revolutionary at all. Nor the Revolution itself. Nor the Constitution. Only Mr. Lincoln and those who gave him support, both in his day and in the following century. And the moralistic, verbally disguised instrument which Lincoln invented may indeed be the most revolutionary force in the modern world: a pure gnostic force.[23] The Declaration confirms an existing state of affairs, even in its announcement of a break with George III. For the colonies existed as distinctive commonwealths with (and out of) English law. Yet they were English with a difference. It required only a fracturing of spiritual bonds that it be made official. In the spring and summer of 1776 things came to a head. As Jefferson wrote, a British army was descending upon Long Island: an army bent on putting an end to petitions, inquiries, declarations, and all such irritants. The King had declared the members of the Continental Congress rebels, without the law. And likewise those who thought themselves represented by that body. No security from deportation for trial, summary execution and confiscation were the alternatives to unconditional submission and allegiance outside the law.

Rhetorical criticism begins with a careful description of circumstances antedating composition.[24] For without that information well established, the meaning of language is uncertain; and a piece of literature may be treated as if it had been prepared only for the gods. Connection of a document with a set of writings made and/or exchanged before or after its appearance is certainly such necessary information. There is no Declaration apart from it. Effacing himself, Thomas Jefferson wrote what completed a conversation concerning the law which had gone back and forth across the Atlantic for many years before exhausting its purpose. Everything in this sequence appeals to the *consensus gentium* of sensible men (common reasonableness, but not philosophy) and to English law. James II had set himself outside that rule, using the dispensary powers to invent a new equality of rights. This usurpation resulted in a royal "abdication" and a new king who promised to uphold the charters and ancient laws and thus to preserve to Englishmen and their posterity the rights they had inherited through a providentially blessed history. This was the common understanding of that period. It is implicit in the dialogue between Philadelphia and Whitehall and in the antecedent quarrel between the Crown and various colonial assemblies after the Stamp and Declaratory Acts and the Albany Congress. The American "parliament" first convened in September of 1774 and soon issued its "Declaration and Resolves of the First Continental Congress, October 14, 1774." Even there it is unmistakably clear that a composite identity is addressing a related composite identity, that the mode of address is forensic (determining praise or blame between respective parties in dispute over the meaning of a "given" phenomenon), and that the point of reference is not divine revelation or a body of doctrine maintained according to the precepts of philosophy, but rather a wisdom inherited as prescription, to be applied reasonably, but not in *Reason's* name. This particular declaration makes it plain that Englishmen are in dispute with Englishmen, groups with groups, and on English grounds. The colonial charters set up this situation. At law they connect the colonies to a paternal source, even while they set them apart. They create an ambiguity in relations with the English parliament and the independent reality of other governments. And they leave law and king and common enemies to hold the mix together.[25]

In their first declaration we learn that the remonstrants are entitled to "life, liberty and property"; that these basic rights come from their ancestors (God perhaps acting through them); that removal over the sea can involve no alienation of such inherited rights; that such alienation is now proposed by way of taxation *and by the machinery for enforcing that tax*; and, finally, that kindred offences against "immunities and privileges granted and confirmed" by royal charters and "secured by their several codes of provincial law" are in prospect. Here and in the later (and similarly argued) "Declaration of the Causes and Necessities of Taking up Arms, July 6, 1775," we can recognize the lineaments of a position finally developed in July of 1776. And also a line of thought coming down directly from the Great Charter of 1689—or even more remotely from Bracton and Fortescue.

The king is the king, the subject the subject, only within the law. The American colonies are by blood and law part of the English *res publica*, set apart from the old Island Kingdom by England's destruction of that organic relationship. To repeat, it is well to remember that the king declared them "rebels" (Prohibitory Acts, August 1775) well before they accepted that title for themselves. As they insist, it is for no "light or transient causes" that they make his appellation official. Their charters have become mere paper. By virtue of relocation across the seas they have been defined as alienated Englishmen, without security even in such fundamental matters as life, liberty, and the fruits of their labors. And all men recognize these rights as being the precondition of submission to any government. Their fathers had, of course, grown violent over much smaller affronts. But the "authors" of the Declaration are determined to keep within the law and to appear as unusually conservative men. Only when the king denies them all representation, asserts his right to bind them *collectively,* to seize their goods *collectively,* to quarter an angry army upon them, and to punish their entreaties that he restrain his servants to observe the Bill of Rights—only then will they close with a last "appeal from reason to arms."

VI

We are now prepared to ask what Mr. Jefferson and his sensible friends meant by "all men" and "created equal." Meant together—*as a group.* In rhetoric, it is a rule to ask how the beginning leads through the middle to the end. If end and beginning consort well with one another, if they point in one direction, that agreement defines what may be discovered in between.[26] The last three-fourths of the Declaration (minus the conclusion, its

original draft) is a bill of particulars.[27] The king (their only acknowledged link with England) has decapitated the body politic and hence is no longer king on these shores. The law/prescription cannot otherwise be preserved. And these men intend such a preservation. Something in existence declares itself in possession of "honor" and "sensible of the regard of decent men," prepared to draw a new charter out of those it possesses, to act as an entity in forming a confederal government. But first these commonwealths must file an official bill of divorcement, designed to the pattern of a countersuit in an action already initiated on the other side. The generation of a new head for this body is not yet, but will, we can assume, present no problem when a necessity for its creation is made explicit.[28]

The *exordium* of the Declaration begins this appeal with an argument from history and with a definition of the voice addressing the "powers of the earth!" It is a "people," a "we" that are estranged from another "we." The peroration reads the same: "we," the "free and independent states," are united in our will to separation—and prepared to answer to high and low for that temerity. They act in the name (and with the sanction) of the good people whose several assemblies had authorized their congregation. This much formally. No contemporary liberal, new or old, can make use of that framework or take the customary liberties with what is contained by the construction. Nor coming to it by the path I have marked, may they, in honesty, see in "created equal" what they devoutly wish to find. "We," in that second sentence, signifies the colonials as the citizenry of the distinct colonies, not as individuals, but rather in their corporate capacity. Therefore, the following "all men"—created equal in their right to expect from any government to which they might submit freedom from corporate bondage, genocide, and massive confiscation—are persons prudent together, respectful of the law which makes them one, even though forced to stand henceforth apart: equal as one free state is as free as another.

Nothing is maintained concerning the abilities or situations of individual persons living within the abandoned context of the British Empire or the societies to be formed by its disruption. No new contract is drawn. Rather, one that exists is *preserved by amputation*. All that is said is that no component of a society can be expected to agree, even though it is part of that society by inheritance, that it is to be bereft of those securities that make life tolerable simply by geographical remoteness. And, if even the Turk and infidel would not as a people submit to a government such as George III proposes to impose through Lord Howe's army, how can Englishmen be expected to agree to that arrangement? So much is "obvious" to everyone, in other words, "self-evident." Thus even if the law of nature and of nations is drawn into our construction of "endowed by their Creator," what is left to be called "inalienable" with respect to American colonials and demonstrative of a certain minimal equality of rights in their collectivities is not so much. What happens in the remainder of the Declaration, following sentence two, is even more depressing to the contemporary Jacobin who would see in the new beginning a departure from the previous political history of Western man. Note particularly the remarks concerning the part played by the king's servants in encouraging a "servile insurrection," the xenophobic objections to the use of foreign mercenaries, and the allusion of the employment of savages as instruments of royal policy. Note also Jefferson's ironic reference to "Christian Kings" and anger at offences to the "common blood." These passages

draw upon a received identity and are not "reasonable" in character. Certainly they do not suggest the equality of individual men. But (and I am sure Professor Jaffa will agree with me on this), even though racist, xenophobic, and religious assumptions have no place in the expression of philosophic truth, they can readily operate in an appeal to prescriptive law. And therefore, I say, in our Declaration of Independence.

VII

Though I agree with Kendall/Carey that there is a distance between the Declaration and the Constitution of 1787, and that silence on equality in the latter reflects a conscious choice, I agree also with Professor Jaffa that the two are not in conflict. The Constitution, like the Articles of Confederation before it, built a structure of common government (to handle all difficulties made by being one and thirteen) upon a common legal inheritance, common origins, and an established unity of purpose. It *is* a limited contract, resting on an external and prior bond of free and independent states, perfecting or improving their union.[29] It *does not* abrogate what it rests upon. The Declaration was a necessary prologue to its adoption. But, in logic, the Declaration is not implicit in the Constitution except as it made possible free ratification by the independent states. In truth, many rights are secured under the Constitution that are not present in the Declaration, however it be construed. Yet not equal voting rights in state or federal elections. Or economic rights in taxation. Or rights for women. Or even equal footing for various religions—or species of irreligion. To say nothing of slaves. All of this is well known. But, if we reasoned as do some gifted scholars, it might be maintained that the Constitution takes us even further away from equality for slaves than does the Declaration.[30] For in Article I, Section 9, provision is made that no law shall be passed by Congress to restrict the slave trade prior to 1808. Slavery exists by acknowledgment of the same document. Yet it encourages that there be more slaves in the Republic than are present in 1787. More in a proportion that twenty-one years can be expected to provide. Hence this provision can be described in logic as presenting Negro slavery as a positive good. For reasons of history I do not insist upon this commentary. The evidence of what lies behind the text suggests another view.[31] And for the same reasons I cannot follow the practical advice of the late Everett McKinley Dirksen and "get right with Lincoln."[32]

VIII

It would be unreasonable for me to attempt to develop in this essay all that I wish to say in objection to the politics of Abraham Lincoln. For it is a great deal and will perhaps involve some years. Therefore I must, in returning the courtesy of this review, raise only my primary objections, most of them proceeding from Lincoln's misunderstanding of the Declaration as a "deferred promise" of equality. I am of course close to the late Professor Kendall in these matters and have learned much from him and from Professor Carey.[33] For one thing, I agree with those gentlemen that Lincoln's "second founding" is fraught with peril and carries with it the prospect of an endless series of turmoils and revolutions, all dedicated to freshly discovered meanings of equality as a "proposition." I do not, however, look so much as they do to New England. It is not my preference for a colonial precedent to the national identity.[34] The millenarian infection spread and almost institutionalized by Lincoln (and by the

manner of his death) has its impetus from that "other Israel" surrounding Boston.[35] And its full potential for mischief is yet to be determined. What Alexander Stephens called Lincoln's "religious mysticism" of Union, when combined in "cold, calculating reason" to the goal of "equal rights" and an authoritarian (that is, irrational) biblical rhetoric, constitutes a juggernaut powerful enough to arm and enthrone any self-made Caesar we might imagine: even an unprepossessing country lawyer from Illinois. For by means of that mixture and solution a transfer of authority and energy is effected, from the Puritan dream of a New Jerusalem governed by an elect to the manifest destiny of American democracy led by keepers of the popular faith. Both are authorized from on High to reform the world into an imitation of themselves—and to lecture and dragoon all who might object. Both receive regular intimations of the Divine Will through prophets who arise from time to time to recall them to their holy mission. And both operate from that base to paint all prospective opposition in the darkest of colors, the rhetoric of polarity being a fundamental correlative of all genuinely Puritan activity, with no room for shadings in between and no mercy for the wicked.

This is, of course, not to minimize the role played in Lincoln's rise to power by the tireless "engine" of his ambition. Nor his political gifts—for which I have an ever-growing admiration. As is announced obliquely in the "Address Before the Springfield Young Men's Lyceum, 1838," Lincoln was, very early, touched by a Bonapartist sense of destiny. His papers (all ten volumes, plus a recent supplement) reflect a steady purpose, an inexorable will to rise, to put his stamp upon the world.[36] Yet there was always another side to his nature—glum, ironic, pessimistic, self-deprecatory: in a word, inscrutable. It has deceived and puzzled many. Yet, as is ordinary in a Puritan, this meandering reflected private doubt of the wisdom behind personal choices and (perhaps) the status of motives which directed him toward their enactment: self-doubt, but not doubt of ideals. And he knew how to cure the ailment—by "striving to finish the work." He had his ends in mind, his religion of Union *in* Equality, but he left it to the "providential" flow of history to carry them to realization. However, after 1854 he condescended to give that flow a little help. The Kansas-Nebraska Act *made* the political career of Abraham Lincoln, opened the door for the "Reign of Reason," made it possible to put behind the "living history" of the revolutionary generation ("oaks," an organic image), and provided for an opportunity to roll out the big guns of priestly language to give what he meant by "freedom" that "new birth" he came to speak of at Gettysburg. He played with consummate skill the circumstances of free-soil reaction in '54 and then the tumult surrounding the campaigns of '58 and '60. Nor are there many scholars who do not find some mystery or subtle craft in his first months as President, to say nothing of his subsequent conduct. But that story, as I read it, is a large book—larger than Professor Jaffa's. Suffice it to say that Lincoln was indeed a man whose "policy was to have no policy."[37] He loved to quote from *Hamlet* that "there's a divinity that shapes our ends, / Rough-hew them how we will."[38] And from the total pattern of his conduct we can extract the following formula: Wait, set up or encourage pressure, then jump, and call it God. The original behind this procedure could be any one of a dozen historic tyrants, all of whom announced a noble purpose for their acts. But when the pattern is encapsulated by the high idiom of Holy Scripture (the authority of which no man can examine),

the Anglo-Saxon prototype emerges as Oliver Cromwell, the Lord Protector. And in searching for what is significant in that analogy, the logical point of departure is the House-Divided speech to the Illinois Republican convention of June 1858.

IX

Lincoln's political gnosticism does not come to a head in the House-Divided speech, and does not begin there. For even in the Springfield Lyceum address (made when he was twenty-nine), he concludes on a Puritan note: Let us refound the Union, and "the gates of hell shall not prevail against it." The new founder, having propped up the temple of Liberty/Equality on the solid pillars of "calculating reason," will therefore be, in relation to the powers of evil (*i.e.*, those who do not care for the arrangement) as was the faith of Peter to the Christian church after its foundation. And God is thus, by implication, the security for the quasi-religion of Equality. In a similar fashion Lincoln finds God as a verification for his rectitude as President in his address to Northern moderates, men who loved the old "divided" house, which we find in his Second Inaugural. Here is the heresy of a "political religion" at the beginning of Lincoln's political career, and also at its end. But one prudent shift is observable. Except for an occasional mention of "propositions" or their equivalent, the debt to European rationalism (the source of Lincoln's puzzling theological heterodoxy), fades into the background once Honest Abe appears on the center of the national stage in Peoria, Illinois (October 1854). And in the opposite direction the biblical element grows to be more and more dominant after 1858. But we should not infer from this that Lincoln's design changed after he got the Republican nomination against Douglas. Only his perception (drawing from the abolitionists) of the proper instrument for its execution.

The House-Divided speech was, beyond any question, a Puritan declaration of war. And therefore also Lincoln's election on the basis of its contents as transcribed in the Republican platform of 1860. A Lincoln admirer, Don E. Fehrenbacher, in his *Prelude to Greatness: Lincoln in the 1850's*, calls it "Garrisonian."[39] The South saw it that way, as did much of the North. And neither forgot those words:

> A House Divided against itself cannot stand. I believe this government cannot endure, perpetually half *slave* and half *free*. I do not expect the Union to be *dissolved*—I do not expect the house to *fall*—but I *do* expect it will cease to be divided. It will become *all* one thing, or *all* another.

Yet we should not abstract the speech from the intellectual milieu to which it belongs. By means of his political manipulation, Lincoln, in the words of his one-time friend, Alexander Stephens, "put the institution of nearly one-half the states under the ban of public opinion and national condemnation." And, continued Stephens, "this, upon general principle, is quite enough of itself to arouse a spirit not only of general indignation, but of revolt on the part of the proscribed."[40] Other people in those days made noises like Lincoln. After 1854 they got a good hearing. One of them, old John Brown, received beatification from the Northern newspapers which supported Mr. Lincoln in 1860. What this juxtaposition signified, despite certain cluckings of disapproval among Republican stalwarts, no one could mistake.

Of course the central motif of the House-Divided speech, as quoted above, echoes the Bible (Mark 3:25): Christ speaking of the undivided hosts of Satan.[41] Lincoln's authority is thus, by association, elevated to the level of the hieratic. But he adds

something to the mixture. The myth that slavery will be either set on its way to extinction by an official gesture on the part of the federal government or else all states will eventually become slave-states establishes a false dilemma, describes a set of conditions which, once fixed in the minds of his free-soil audience, was certain to create in them a sense of alarm. Thus he participates in what Richard Hofstadter calls the "paranoid style" in politics.[42] Fear of the slave power (Southern political and economic domination) and racist hostility to the idea of massive Negro influx, free *or* slave, into the North made predictable that one of these alternatives would be perceived as intolerable—and we can guess which one. Thus the size of the Republican Party might be augmented from the ranks of persons who despised Abolition and all its works.

For Lincoln to say after 1858 that the Constitution and the laws were sacred to him, that he would "preserve" the "old Union of the Fathers," is mere window dressing. For to argue that your enemy is evil incarnate (the burden of his rhetoric), in league with Satan, and then add that you respect him and his legal rights, is to indulge in pietistic arrogance—as Alexander Stephens specified in the passage I quoted just above. Jaffa confuses matters no end in maintaining that Lincoln addressed a real danger in his imaginary "division." As the South perceived the question, the real issue in Kansas and Nebraska was whether or not there could be a federal policy on the "morality" of its conduct in any connection not covered by the original federal covenant: whether they could stay under the gun.

For houses are always divided, in some fashion or another. And, no doubt, should slavery be gone, some new infamy was bound to be discovered by the stern examiners whose power depends upon a regularity in such "crusades." A law prohibiting slavery in the territories, in that it affected the ability of a new state to grow to maturity as a child of the total Union, would define the South as outside of that communion. Furthermore, it would set in motion a chain of circumstances that could be used against the region in any connection where antinomian morality could be read into law—could touch slavery or any other "peculiarity," unless a Constitutional amendment (requiring a three-fourths vote of the states) existed to protect it. A Union of this sort was not the old Union. Nor was its issue, a Union by force—in 1865 or *now*. Whatever the intent of armies in blue, it could not be the same—not the contract ratified by all the states who were party to it. Rather, it involved Lincoln's worship of the law as the Constitution *with the Declaration drafted into (and over) it*—Lincoln's Declaration: and therefore (*vide supra*), no worship of the law whatsoever, but instead devotion to perpetually exciting goals, always just beyond our reach. Thus, under the aegis of a plurality president, the principle of assent is put aside for the sake of an idea (read ideology) which only a small minority of Americans could be expected to approve, either in 1860 or today. And the entire project accomplished by rhetoric—Kendall's "magic." On the record of American history since 1858, Lincoln stands convicted as an enemy of the "founding."[43] Which is to say, as our new Father—even though many of us still refuse to live in the cold uniformitarian temple he designed.

Of course, military resistance to radical Union (*i.e.*, statism covered by a patina of law) ended in 1865. Lincoln saluted these developments at the beginning of his second term. And I must conclude my remarks on Lincoln's politics with some observations on that address. His conduct in using the presidential powers has been treated to my satisfaction by Gottfried

Dietze.[44] What that conduct amounts to is the creation of an Eastern priest/king—an epideictic personage such as we hear in the voice at Gettysburg. Speech and deeds together did change the country—and in respects more important than the abolition of Negro slavery: together opened the door to portentous changes that finally touch even liberty.[45] The argument of this essay is, in sum, that what Lincoln did to preserve the Union by expanding and enshrining equality left the prescription of the revolution of law in our national beginning and the "unwritten constitution" of our positive pluralism very much in doubt. Such was his purpose. But (and I again repeat) this plan is something which he concealed until he prepared the Second Inaugural—where in victory he became a scripture in himself.

X

There is of course a clear conflict between the Cooper Union speech, the First Inaugural, Lincoln's letters of the time, and the posture Lincoln assumed a few weeks before Lee's surrender. If we would discover in father Abraham the "crafty Machievel," the conflict between his assent to a constitutional amendment making slavery "perpetual" where established and the House-Divided speech is our point of departure. But the Lincoln who kept Kentucky and Missouri from secession is hard to penetrate. It is wise to assume that he followed the times. For it cannot be demonstrated that he never really attempted to pacify Southern anxieties without reconstituting the Republic. Certainly he wanted no peace on any grounds but unconditional surrender. And in 1865, he looked back on his five years as national leader, "scanned the providences," and "found himself approved."

When seen in the context of his career after 1858 and within the pattern of a lifetime of deliberate utterances, Lincoln's Second Inaugural turns out to be something very different from what most Americans have believed it to be: a completion of a pattern announced in the House-Divided speech, unfolded in its fullness at Gettysburg, and glossed in a letter to Thurlow Weed written just before his death. Historically, the misconception of this performance may be attributed to a disproportionate emphasis upon the final paragraph of the Second Inaugural treated (once again) as if it had an independent existence outside the total document. Furthermore, what Lincoln means by "malice toward none" and "bind up the nation's wounds" is, even within this single paragraph, modified beyond recognition by "as God gives us to see the right." For he means here revelation, not conscience. Americans are so accustomed, since Lincoln's time, to a quasi-religious rhetoric in their public men that the combination has passed without notice for a century and more. But to discover its full meaning we must look up into the body of the speech. There it becomes clear what Lincoln is about behind his mild forensic tone.

Said another way, what I here contend is that the attribution of his own opinions to an antinomian revelation of divine will as regards America's political destiny is more completely and intensively visible in this particular Lincoln document than in any other. For what he does in the Second Inaugural is to expand the outreach of his rhetorical manicheanism beyond the limits made familiar to us in a thousand expressions of piety toward the Union (and most particularly at Gettysburg) to include not only his obviously beaten enemies in the South but also all those who accepted the Union as it had existed from the Founding until 1860. Indeed, the targets of his rhetoric on this occasion are all moderate Unionists who did not afore-times recognize, as did their prophet for the day, the necessity for a greater perfection in their bonds. The war was long, says Father Abraham, not simply because the rebels were wicked but furthermore because many of their adversaries were reluctant. In the letter to Weed (March 15, 1865) Lincoln observes, in speaking of the unpopularity he expects to be the fate of the remarks in question, that "men are not flattered by being shown that there has been a difference of purpose between the Almighty and them. To deny it, however, in this case, is to deny that there is a God governing the world."[46] Since no Southerners were present to be offended by the Second Inaugural, and since Lincoln's teaching in that address refers chiefly to those who had been patient with the divided house, it is evident that his targets in interpreting long war and heavy judgment are those who did not see *before secession* the necessity of conflict. How this reading of the American teleology could be expected to bind up wounds in any conventional sense is difficult to determine. But the end result is to give Lincoln a rhetorical upper hand he had not sought at any point in his presidency and to prepare him to do whatever he means by "finish the work." It is to leave him, finally, alone as the agent of his master, beyond the most ultraRepublicans as an instrument of providence and with an authority few mortal men have ever aspired to hold in their hands. Death confirmed him (or rather, his design) in that condition. Consider for an illustration Edward M. Stanton's words after reading the Gettysburg Address to an 1868 political audience in Pennsylvania: "That is the voice of God speaking through the lips of Abraham Lincoln. . . . You hear the voice of Father Abraham here tonight. Did he die in vain?"[47] Such politics are beyond reason, beyond law, though they may embody a rationalist objective. They are also Jaffa's model—from authority and passion. And with consequences I shall now consider.

XI

"Style," Alfred North Whitehead once observed, "is the ultimate morality of mind." By style I would understand him to mean all the elements that go into the composition of a piece of rhetoric, its structural elements as well as its textural; and, in examining the "style" of this particular essay, I find an extraordinary laxity—which suggests that Professor Jaffa is not at his best. Indeed, I can hardly recognize here the consummate and ethical rhetorician of *Crisis of the House Divided,* a work which I obviously admire—though from a certain distance. The argument of this later essay is loose and meandering, like some ancient river that is constantly winding back on itself. Lincoln as a young legislative candidate once advocated (like a good, money-minded Whig) the straightening of such rivers by cutting off the neck of the loops. In closing, I shall attempt to do the same for Mr. Jaffa's argument, if only to indicate the tortuous nature of the "moral" impulse which lay behind its composition.

In the first place, as my metaphor suggests, this is an old river, an ancient argument which need not be developed again in detail since everyone is familiar enough with its tenets (*i.e.,* the equation of the social-contract theory with some theory of equality). What is new in this lengthy diatribe is no more than the ostensible targets of Professor Jaffa's attack, Kendall and Carey. And indeed they could be a valid point of departure for an egalitarian like Professor Jaffa, since Kendall and Carey do define the true American political tradition as both conservative *and* hostile to Equality.

But unfortunately Kendall and Carey do not raise their standard on that spot

of polemical ground where Professor Jaffa would like to do battle. They do not become overly preoccupied with slavery; and for obvious reasons Professor Jaffa would rather talk about slavery than the political documents which are the announced topic of *Basic Symbols.* And so he does, curving around obstacles to reach the sacred subject, turning his argument in that direction by charging that Kendall and Carey never mention the word in their study and that such an omission avoids the essential question of the American political experience. He repeats this charge several times during the windings of his thesis, despite the fact that it is unfounded (pp. 479, 486 and 491). For instance, he ignores the following comment on page 92 of *Basic Symbols,* a passage that raises perhaps a most difficult question for him to consider:

> However, the assembly that approved the Declaration would not subscribe to the denunciation of slavery that Jefferson sought to include, so that we might be led to believe that the signers were talking of equality of men in a sense far short of that which modern egalitarians hold.

Small wonder that Professor Jaffa's rhetorical river veers sharply away from this high ground. Was it forgotten or ignored in order to avoid the issue it raises? Whatever the reasons, it flows off in that direction, attacking Kendall's review of *Crisis of the House Divided,* a Kendall essay in which the issues are relevant to slavery and furthermore a matter of historical interpretation. Soon we are curling and gliding through familiar territory, much of it mythic in nature and therefore simpler and purer than life. In Jaffa's imaginary history of the United States, Jefferson is the drafter of the Declaration, but *not* the slaveholder who wrote in *Notes on the State of Virginia* of his suspicion that blacks "are inferior to the whites in the endowments both of body and mind" and that this "unfortunate difference of colour, and perhaps of faculty, is a powerful obstacle to the emancipation of these people"; and *certainly not* the Virginian who called "Equality" a "mere abstraction" and its devotees a "Holy Alliance." There, Locke is the philosopher of *The Second Treatise*, but *not* the man responsible for *Fundamental Constitutions for Carolina.* Antebellum slavery is a kind of Buchenwald;[48] and the United States Constitution is drafted with a tacit understanding that "all men are [really] created equal," that this is a proposition with "constitutional status," *in spite of the fact* that the Constitution itself recognized the established legal institution of slavery and discouraged interpolation into its provisions of what is not clearly there. All of these oversimplifications ignore one overriding question, the question that Kendall and Carey raise and which Professor Jaffa is careful not to consider. Some "truths" are more important than the Truth. Even the Truth that we have a political tradition that is conservative and contrary to Lincoln. Thus, though the river of Professor Jaffa's argument seems erratic, its wanderings (like the wanderings of a real river) have a predictable pattern; they follow the course of least resistance. And it is in the pattern—tortuous and circuitous—that one can see the relationship between his "style" and his "ultimate morality of mind."

Yet we cannot entirely blame Professor Jaffa for these aberrations, this great falling away from scholarly rectitude and right reason. His errors are endemic among his kind—such Old Liberals as identify their politics with the Lincolnian precedent. As I have tried to indicate, such errors constitute what amounts to a "genetic flaw" within that intellectual tradition, a fracture impossible to heal. Trying to preserve property, secure tranquillity,

and promote equal rights, all at the same time, insures that none of these purposes will be accomplished. And insures also a terrible, unremitting tension, both among those in power and among those whose hopes are falsely raised. Especially with persistence in thinking of men outside of all history that is not Lincoln, and apart from the durable communions of craft and friendship, faith and blood. It has been, however, a distinctive trait of American political thought to do its worst as it touches upon the Negro: to break down when unable to make it through the aforementioned impasse of objectives. Class struggle has been the result, to say nothing of race conflict. And that failing attaches by definition to the Republican identity, flawing it perhaps forever as a viable conservative instrument. Said another way, the more a people derive their political identity from Lincoln's version of Equality, the more they are going to push against the given and providential frame of things to prove up the magic phrase. And, therefore, the more they will (to repeat one of my favorite images) kick the "tar baby."[49] And we all know how that story ends.

NOTES

[1] When pressed in debate by the righteous minions of Equality, an antebellum Northern congressman once called sentence two of the Declaration a "self-evident lie." Consider also *The Federalist,* No. 10.

[2] See Helmut Schoeck, *Envy: A Theory of Social Behavior* (New York: Harcourt Brace Jovanovich, 1970).

[3] *On Power: Its Nature and the History of Its Growth* (Boston: Beacon Press, 1962).

[4] See Eric Voegelin, *Science, Politics and Gnosticism* (Chicago: Henry Regnery Co., 1968), pp. 99–100.

[5] Robert Penn Warren, "Democracy and Poetry," *Southern Review,* XI (January 1975), p. 28.

[6] See my "A Writ of Fire and Sword: The Politics of Oliver Cromwell," in No. 3 of *The Occasional Review* (Summer 1975), pp. 61–80.

[7] Doctrine is a loaded word. It is here suggestive

of theology, revealed truth, though Lincoln means by it the kind of demonstrable "abstract truth" of the sort Jefferson "embalmed" into a "merely revolutionary document." See Lincoln's letter to Messrs. Henry L. Pierce & Others, April 6, 1859, on pp. 374–376 of Vol. III of *The Collected Works of Abraham Lincoln* (New Brunswick, N.J.: Rutgers University Press, 1953). The usage is thus a device for "having it both ways," as does Jaffa when claiming that the commandments of Sinai are knowable by unassisted human reason. For the commandments are explained only in Christ—a scandal to the Greeks.

[8] Edmund Burke, *Reflections on the Revolution in France* (Chicago: Henry Regnery Co., 1955), p. 240.

[9] Ibid., p. 244. See also on this manner of thinking Louis I. Bredvold's *The Intellectual Milieu of John Dryden* (Ann Arbor: University of Michigan Press, 1934) and also *The Brave New World of the Enlightenment* (Ann Arbor: University of Michigan Press, 1961) by the same author. Swift is a major illustration of this intellectual *habitus*. I identify with it.

[10] I borrow from the title of Paul Fussell's *The Rhetorical World of Augustan Humanism* (Oxford: The Clarendon Press, 1965). In the same connection see J. T. Bolton's *The Language of Politics in the Age of Wilkes and Burke* (Toronto: University of Toronto Press, 1963).

[11] See Jaffa's *Equality & Liberty: Theory and Practice in American Politics* (New York: Oxford University Press, 1965), p. 122; and Leo Strauss' *Natural Right and History* (Chicago: University of Chicago Press, 1953), pp. 1–9.

[12] Jaffa accepts the Puritan typology for the American venture. There are, we should remember, alternative formulations (*Equality & Liberty*, pp. 116–117)—formulations less infected with secularized eschatology. And if Jaffa pursues his analogue, he should remember that there was slavery in Israel and among the ancient Jews a racism so virulent that they considered some neighboring peoples too lowly even for enslavement and fit only for slaughter. Or too wicked (Indians, the Irish at Drogheda, etc.).

[13] Peter Gay, *The Enlightenment: An Interpretation* (New York: Alfred A. Knopf, 1966), pp. ix–xiv.

[14] See Maurice Ashley, *The Glorious Revolution of 1688* (New York: Scribner's, 1966), pp. 97–106.

[15] And this of course includes certain established rights, plus a balance between the values of liberty and community. I do not mean to minimize the value of these achievements. Clearly I identify with them.

[16] *Equality & Liberty*, pp. 114–139. For correction (in some respects), see Leonard Woods Labaree's *Conservatism in Early America* (Ithaca: Cornell University Press, 1959), pp. 119–122; and Clinton Ros-

siter's *The Seedtime of the Republic* (New York: Harcourt, Brace & World, 1953), especially p. 345; also Ashley, op. cit., pp. 193–198.

[17] David Duncan Wallace, *South Carolina: A Short History, 1520–1948* (Columbia: University of South Carolina Press, 1966), p. 25.

[18] Peter Laslett, *John Locke, Two Treatises of Government: A Critical Edition with Introduction and Apparatus Criticus* (Cambridge, England, 1960), p. 159.

[19] For examples consider Bernard Bailyn's *The Ideological Origins of the American Revolution* (Cambridge, Mass.: Harvard University Press, 1967); and Gordon S. Wood's *The Creation of the American Republic, 1776–1787* (Chapel Hill: University of North Carolina Press, 1964). Somewhat better are H. Trevor Colbourn's *The Lamp of Experience: Whig History and the Intellectual Origins of the American Revolution* (Chapel Hill: University of North Carolina Press, 1965); and Merrill Jensen's *The Founding of a Nation: A History of the American Revolution, 1763–1776* (New York: Oxford University Press, 1968). These last two books are especially good on the "reluctant rebels," who were Burkean, not Lockean Whigs, postulating law, not a state of nature (*i.e.*, where a full-scale, new contract can be drawn). See also Wallace (*op. cit.*, p. 273) for an account of a prescriptive South Carolina patriot—William Henry Drayton.

[20] In strict logic there is a problem with quantification if the proposition is supposed to be universal: a universal proposition would read "every man is created equal to every other man." Jefferson's phrase is merely a loose generalization, when seen in this light. For the libertarian the trouble goes the other way around: if all men are by nature equal (morally, in will, intellect, etc.), then only circumstances can explain the inequalities which develop. And these circumstances are thus offences against nature and the Divine Will—offences demanding correction. What some libertarians try to get out of "created equal" is "created unequal, but given an equal start." Jefferson's phrase will not submit to this.

[21] An exception is Russell Kirk's *The Roots of American Order* (La Salle, Ill.: Open Court, 1974).

[22] One has the temptation to say, as Socrates did of the rhapsode in Plato's *Ion*, that they understand the subject not by art or knowledge but by "inspiration."

[23] I began to develop this view in "Lincoln's New Frontier: A Rhetoric for Continuing Revolution," *Triumph*, VI, No. 5 (May 1971), pp. 11–13 and 21; VI, No. 6 (June 1971), pp. 15–17. I use the term from Eric Voegelin's *New Science of Politics* (Chicago: University of Chicago Press, 1952).

[24] For a chronicle of these events see Jensen (*op. cit.*) and Lawrence H. Gipson's *The Coming of the*

Revolution, 1763–1775 (New York: Harper & Brothers, 1954).

[25] *Charter* and *compact* are usually synonyms in the language of the Whigs, and usually imply a relation of unequals.

[26] There is no room for "secret writing" in public declarations.

[27] I cite Volume I of Julian P. Boyd's edition of *The Papers of Thomas Jefferson* (Princeton: Princeton University Press, 1950), pp. 315–319 and 414–433. Carl Becker, in his valuable *The Declaration of Independence: A Study in the History of Politics and Ideas* (New York: Vintage Press, 1958), argues unreasonably that this bill of particulars is not really important to the meaning of the Declaration. He was, however, as we should remember, an admirer of the *philosophes*—and no rhetorician.

[28] The image here is drawn from one of the Fathers of English law, from chapter 13 of the *De Laudibus Legum Angliae* (1471) of Sir John Fortescue (Cambridge, England: Cambridge University Press, 1949), the edition and translation by S. B. Chrimes.

[29] Jaffa's argument that one national Union was decided upon in 1774–1776 or before is easily refuted by John R. Alden's *The First South* (Baton Rouge: Louisiana State University Press, 1961); in Alden's *The South in the Revolution, 1763–1789* (Baton Rouge: Louisiana State University Press, 1957); and in Donald L. Robinson's *Slavery in the Structure of American Politics, 1765–1820* (New York: Harcourt Brace Jovanovich, 1971), p. 146 *et passim*. More than one Union has always been a possibility to be entertained by deliberate men. See Staughton Lynd's "The Abolitionist Critique of the United States Constitution," in *The Antislavery Vanguard: New Essays on the Abolitionists,* ed. Martin Duberman (Princeton: Princeton University Press, 1965), pp. 210–239.

[30] For instance, Professor Jaffa in forcing the notion of a Union before the Constitution into the "We the People" of the Preamble. Few scholars deny that the people acted through the states to ratify—as they had to form a Constitutional Convention. To this day they act through the states to amend. They existed at law through the maintenance of their several freedoms in battle. They formed the Confederation. The Declaration was only a negative precondition to a Union and to the firmer connection that followed. Underneath all of this may stand an unwritten Constitution, joining the partners of the Declaration in more ways than are specified in 1787. And perhaps also committing them to other ends: ends which Professor Jaffa would not care to consider. That compact was the prescription which sanctioned the Continental Congress—a creature of the chartered colonies. If the Declaration commits to anything, it is to that prescription—a compact of

"the living, dead, and yet unborn." The continued operation of a society united in such a compact constitutes assent, regardless of official legal relations. New members are the only ones who are "sworn in."

[31] For instance, the 32 acts passed by Virginia's colonial House of Burgesses which called for a restriction of the trade, all of them negated by the Crown at the behest of Northern traders. Reports of the Constitutional Convention of 1787 indicate the same sort of pressures, resolved there by reasonable men determined to close out a divisive subject.

[32] See "Getting Right with Lincoln," pp. 3–18 of David Donald's *Lincoln Reconsidered* (New York: Vintage Press, 1961).

[33] And especially from Kendall's "Equality: Commitment or Ideal?" *Phalanx,* I (Fall 1967), pp. 95–103, which answers some of Jaffa's complaints about Kendall's silences. I find it curious that Jaffa does not mention this piece.

[34] Except for reasons of strategy (guilt by association), I cannot see why Jaffa identifies *Basic Symbols of the American Political Tradition* with the South. For Kendall and Carey begin with Massachusetts and Connecticut.

[35] See p. 226 of Jaffa's own *Crisis of the House Divided.*

[36] See Edmund Wilson's magisterial *Patriotic Gore: Studies in the Literature of the American Civil War* (New York: Oxford University Press, 1962), pp. 99–130. Surely Wilson cannot be mistaken in arguing that Lincoln saw himself in his portrait of the "new founder." For Lincoln clearly knows the animal he describes on a more intimate basis than mere speculation or observation could provide. Wilson compares Lincoln (pp. xvi–xx) to Bismarck and Lenin—the other great founders of our age. Another useful analogue (a firm higher-law man, and no legalist or historicist) is Adolf Hitler. For he writes in *Mein Kampf* that "human rights break state rights," calls for illegal as well as legal instruments in "wars of rebellion against enslavement from within and without," observes that all governments by oppression plead the law, and concludes, "I believe today that I am acting in the sense of the Almighty Creator . . . fighting for the Lord's work." (I cite the edition of 1938, published in New York by Reynal and Hitchcock, pp. 122–123 and 84).

[37] Donald, *op. cit.,* p. 131.

[38] Roy P. Basler, *The Touchstone for Greatness: Essays, Addresses and Occasional Pieces about Abraham Lincoln* (Westport, Conn.: Greenwood Press, 1973), pp. 206–227.

[39] Jaffa praises Fehrenbacher's work.

[40] *A Constitutional View of the Late War Between the*

States (Philadelphia: National Publishing Co.,1868), Volume II, 266.

[41] Lincoln's use of this passage is curious. For, as the context makes clear, Christ's point in setting up the dichotomy is that the Devil would not help his servants to ruin his own plans.

[42] See David Brion Davis's *The Slave Power and the Paranoid Style* (Baton Rouge: Louisiana State University Press, 1969), especially pp. 10–11.

[43] I use quotation marks because I deny that they were ever founded, in that term's strict sense.

[44] *America's Political Dilemma: From Limited to Unlimited Democracy* (Baltimore: Johns Hopkins Press, 1968), pp. 17–62. He is supported by papers published in *National Review* by the late Frank Meyer (Aug. 24, 1965; Jan. 25, 1966).

[45] Liberty is clearly the American value of greatest traditional authority—meaning "liberty to be ourselves," a nation which assumes an established, inherited identity. On the part played by the Get-tysburg Address in this process, see my *Triumph* essay cited above.

[46] Lincoln, *Collected Works*, Volume VIII, p. 356.

[47] Donald, *op. cit.,* p. 8.

[48] This analogy smacks of Stanley Elkin's now discredited theory in *Slavery: A Problem in American Institutional Life* (Chicago: University of Chicago Press, 1959). For correction see Eugene D. Genovese's *Roll, Jordan, Roll: The World the Slaves Made* (New York: Pantheon Books, 1974). Also consider the fact that Jews were proscribed under Hitler—all Jews, in the same way—while antebellum Southern blacks could be slaves or freemen or even slaveholders.

[49] "A Fire Bell in the Night: The Southern Conservative View," *Modern Age*, XVII (Winter, 1973), pp. 9–15. In these pages I maintain that an expansive view of "natural rights" with respect to Negroes has undermined our inherited constitutional system.

[XX, Winter 1976, 62–77]

Equality, Justice, and the American Revolution: In Reply to Bradford's "The Heresy of Equality"

HARRY V. JAFFA

Harry V(ictor) Jaffa (1918–   ) received a B.A. from Yale in 1939 and a Ph.D. in political science from the New School of Social Research in 1951. He is Henry Salvatori Research Professor of Political Philosophy at Claremont McKenna College and president of the Winston S. Churchill Association. A follower of Professor Leo Strauss, his strong admiration for Abraham Lincoln caused him to clash with other conservatives such as Frank S. Meyer, Willmoore Kendall, and Francis G. Wilson. He is the author of numerous books, among which are The Crisis of a House Divided *(1959),* Equality and Liberty *(1965), and* How To Think About the American Revolution *(1978).*

"LET US HAVE no foolishness indeed," writes Professor Bradford, in his reply to "Equality as a Conservative Principle," echoing my echo of Willmoore Kendall:*

Equality as a moral or political imperative, pursued as an end in itself—Equality, with the capital "E"—is the antonym of every legitimate conservative principle.[1]

In *The Federalist*, No. 51, Madison writes that "Justice is the end of government. It is the end of civil society. It ever has been and ever will be pursued until it be obtained, or until liberty be lost in the pursuit."[2] But what is justice? Let me

---

* "The Heresy of Equality: Bradford Replies to Jaffa," *Modern Age*, Vol. 20, No. 1, Winter, 1976, pp. 62–77. The original title of Professor Bradford's essay, which he was kind enough to send me in typescript, was "Black Republicanism Redivivus: A Reply to Harry Jaffa." I greatly regret the change in title. Professor Bradford and I are carrying on a debate which reached a climax in the 1850's. His original title accurately indicates the political character of our differences. In applying to me the appellation that belonged above all to Abraham Lincoln, he has paid me a compliment that, however undeserved, I cannot forgo. As Prof. Bradford explains in a note in his *Modern Age* essay, he is replying to my "Equality as a Conservative Principle," Loyola of *Los Angeles Law Review*, VIII (June

1975), pp. 471–505, which is a critique of *The Basic Symbols of the American Political Tradition*, by Willmoore Kendall and George W. Carey. As Professor Bradford correctly notes, "Lincoln's reading of the Declaration of Independence is the central subject of this entire exchange." But see also "Time on the Cross: Debate," in *National Review*, March 28, 1975, pp. 340–342, and 359. Here Bradford and I crossed swords for the first time.

enter into the record of our differences a passage from the *Nicomachean Ethics* which I would hope Professor Bradford might accept as canonical. In Book V, Chapter 3,[3] both the unjust man and the unjust action are said to be unequal. Every action admitting more or less, says Aristotle, admits also of a mean, which is the equal. "If then," he continues, "the unjust is the unequal, the just is the equal."

Aristotle divides justice into two kinds. The one, the justice that is in exchanges. The other, the justice that is in distributions either of honors or profits. As an example of the first kind, consider an exchange of shoes for grain. Somehow the quantity of shoes exchanged for a quantity of grain must be made equal. A common measure is needed, such as money. The shoes and the grain should then both be valued by the same amount of money. If they are so valued—things equal to the same thing being equal to each other—then the transaction may be said to be just. As an example of the second kind of justice, consider the honors or prizes awarded at the end of a race. The first-place prize should go to the first-place finisher, and the second-place prize to the second-place finisher. Or, 1/1 equals 2/2. The first kind of justice—in exchanges—is an equality of number: ten dollars worth of shoes equals ten dollars worth of grain. The second kind of justice—in distributions—is an equality of proportions. In both cases, however, the justice is a species of the equal.

Equality is a conservative principle because justice is conservative, and equality is the principle of justice. Where exchanges are just—that is, where one party does not overreach the other—and where distributions are just—that is, where rewards are proportioned to merit—men tend to become friends. Where the opposite is the case, they tend to become enemies. In Book V of the *Politics*[4] Aristotle declares that the most general or universal cause of *stasis* (faction or sedition) is inequality. Inequality—whether numerical or proportional—tends to disrupt and destroy political communities, and equality tends towards their harmony and their preservation. Equality as the ground of justice is then both good in itself and good for its consequences.

In the course of my praise of equality I had referred to a New Conservatism, properly so-called, as being identical with the Old Liberalism, which was in my view the Liberalism of the Founding Fathers of the American regime. For the Liberalism of the Founders, in my understanding, was not merely that of locally disaffected British Whigs. Once the separation from the British crown was decided upon, they set out to build a new and more radically just political order than had existed in practice in any antecedent model. It was indeed intended to be the *novus ordo seclorum*, the new order of the ages, announced on the great seal of the United States. It was to decide, as Hamilton announced in the first *Federalist*, whether "societies of men [might be] capable of establishing good government [by] reflection and choice," or whether mankind was forever destined "to depend for their political constitutions on accident and force." From the perspective of the American founding, all previous governments, including that of Great Britain, however excellent some of their features, did not embody that reasonableness implied in the human capacity for "reflection and choice."[5] But the American founding was intended to do just that. The rule of priests and kings, and of priestly kings, and the legal privileges of hereditary orders generally, were regarded by our Founders as elements of unjust inequality in all European constitutions, including the British. The forbidding of the issuance of patents of nobility, either by the States or by the United States, the prohibition of any religious test for office, the absence of any property qualification for office, in the Constitution of 1787, all attest to the revolutionary thrust against inequality. So does the prohibition of slavery in the great Northwest Ordinance, which was adopted by the old Congress, even as the Constitution was being drafted. Professor Bradford plays upon our present familiarity with many of these things to inform us that "the Declaration of Independence is not very revolutionary at all. Nor the Revolution itself. Nor the Constitution." But this is to read history backwards, to pretend that the man was never a child, or that something was never new because it is no longer so!

I have observed many times that the independence of the United States was accomplished by a Declaration that constituted a political act without parallel in the history of the world. Professor Bradford opposes this thesis in writing that

> only a relativist or historicist could argue that American conservatism should be an utterly unique phenomenon, without antecedents which predate 1776, and unconnected with the mainstream of English and European thought and practice known to our forefathers in colonial times.[6]

But I never said or implied that the principles of the American Revolution were "without antecedents." No one would insist more than I that the colonies had enjoyed a learning process, of nearly two centuries, in constitutionalism and the rule of law. Some of the ideas incorporated into the Declaration—including the connection between equality and justice—had a history of more than two thousand years. But the rooting of constitutionalism, and the rule of law in a doctrine of universal human rights, in the political act of a people declaring independence, *is* unique and unprecedented.[7] Professor Bradford denies that the Declaration is revolutionary—or that it is unique—because he denies that it contains a decla-

ration of universal human rights. And, I admit, if there were no such declaration, then the Declaration would cease to be everything I have claimed for it. Our debate turns upon what it is we find in the famous second paragraph. Professor Bradford, like Willmoore Kendall—and indeed like Chief Justice Taney in the case of Dred Scott—expends a great deal of ingenuity in pretending that the words do not mean what they plainly do mean.

> We hold these truths to be self-evident, that all men are created equal, that they are endowed by their Creator with certain unalienable rights, that among these are life, liberty, and the pursuit of happiness.

Because of the rights here affirmed—but only because of them—the American people are said to have a right to resist any attempt "to reduce them under absolute despotism." Professor Bradford thinks that white Americans had the right to resist despotism, because somehow such a right had become prescriptive under British tradition. Leaving aside the question of how such a tradition could have originated, we merely insist that that is not what the Declaration says. It says that *all* men have a right to resist despotism, and because all Americans are men, all Americans have this right. The right to resist despotism, that is, the right *not* to be slaves, is possessed equally by every human being on the face of the earth. That some might not have the capacity to make good this right, lacking either the power or the inclination, is nothing to the purpose. The form of the proposition contained in the second paragraph implies, by unbreakable necessity, that unless the rights mentioned are possessed by everyone, they are possessed by no one. That is what the Signers said, and that, I am convinced, is what they meant.

The proposition that all men are created equal is, on the most elementary level, a principle of political obligation. It occurs in a context in which men are withdrawing their allegiance from an authority that has lost its legitimacy, and are transferring that allegiance to a new repository of legitimate authority. It is a principle for distinguishing when it is that men are, and when they are not, under a duty to obey. For anyone to argue, as does Professor Bradford, that the Signers of the Declaration did not understand their principles to apply to all men—in particular that they did not apply to Negro slaves—it would be necessary for him to find evidence that they (or anyone of the Revolutionary generation who had deliberately subscribed to the principles of the Declaration) considered that slaves had a *duty* to obey. That slaves may have been under a *necessity* to obey—or that the Signers or anyone else considered it expedient to place them under such a necessity—is nothing to the purpose. Abraham Lincoln, and many others, argued that in some sense American slavery was a necessity, imposed by circumstances, on both masters and slaves. Whether or not such an argument was disingenuous we need not enter into here. What is relevant is that such an argument in no way contradicts the opinion that the rights set forth in the second paragraph of the Declaration are universal rights. To say that white men have such rights, but that black men did not, would indeed have been inconsistent with the language of the Declaration. Professor Bradford is on common ground with the Marxist and Black Power historians of recent years, who have all along maintained that the Declaration was a bourgeois or racist document, never intended to be understood in the universalistic sense in which it is expressed. None of them has produced any such evidence of inconsistency as I have demanded, nor have they tried to show why any other evidence ought to be acceptable. I shall look forward to seeing

whether Professor Bradford can supply this defect in his brief.

Professor Bradford's polemic against what he is pleased to call "the heresy of equality" occurs on at least two levels. On the one hand, he denies that there is any politically relevant sense in which it can be said with any truth that all men are created equal. On the other hand, he denies that the Signers of the Declaration meant it in any of the politically relevant senses attributed to it by Jefferson or the arch-heretic, Abraham Lincoln. Professor Bradford launches his attack by denying that there is any difference between what I had called the Old Liberalism—which demands equality of opportunity (which Professor Bradford correctly identifies with equality of rights)—and the New Liberalism, which demands equality of results. "Contrary to most Liberals, new and old," he writes,

> it is nothing less than sophistry to distinguish between equality of opportunity (equal starts in the "race of life") and equality of condition (equal results). For only those who *are* equal can take equal advantage of a given circumstance. And there is no man equal to any other, except perhaps in the special, and politically untranslatable, understanding of the Deity. *Not intellectually or physically or economically or even morally. Not equal!* Such is, of course, the genuinely self-evident proposition. [Emphasis by Bradford.][8]

We have already seen that Professor Bradford maintains that neither the Declaration, the Revolution itself, or the Constitution are ("contrary to Professor Jaffa") very revolutionary. They became revolutionary, he says, "Only [because of] Mr. Lincoln and those who gave him support, both in his day and in the following century."[9] This is Bradford's expression of Kendall's thesis, that Abraham Lincoln had somehow "derailed" an American political tradition that had not heretofore worshipped the golden calf of equality.

Yet Bradford, like Kendall, is doing little more than paraphrase Senator John C. Calhoun, in his great speech on the Oregon Bill, in the Senate, June 27, 1848. All the essentials are there, only with this difference: the arch-heretic is Jefferson instead of Lincoln!

In his speech, Calhoun calls "the most false and dangerous of all political errors" a proposition which, he said, "had become an axiom in the minds of a vast many on both sides of the Atlantic," a proposition which is "repeated daily from tongue to tongue, as an established and incontrovertible truth." [10] This is the proposition that "all men are born free and equal," a proposition which occurs in this precise form, not in the Declaration of Independence, but in the Massachusetts Bill of Rights (1780). But the doctrine it embodies was endemic to political public opinion in the revolutionary generation, as I have demonstrated by citing its variant expressions in seven of the original state constitutions, in "Equality as a Conservative Principle."

Calhoun refutes this dangerous falsehood by declaring that men are not born, that on the contrary only infants are born! And infants are so far from being either free or equal, that they are in a condition of perfectly unfree dependence.[11] He then takes up the proposition in the Declaration of Independence, that "all men are created equal." This form of expression, he says, "though less dangerous, is not less erroneous." Calhoun does not explain why it is less dangerous, but we may suppose that to call all men by nature free, is more directly subversive of slavery than to call them equal. Calhoun then continues as follows:

> All men are not created. According to the Bible, only two—a man and a woman—ever were—and of these one was pronounced subordinate to the other. All others have come into the world by being born, and in no sense, as I have shown, either free or equal.[12]

Now Calhoun knew that he was here merely taking words in their wrong sense. He knew that when Jefferson had penned his immortal lines—for the universal approval of his patriot fellow-citizens—he was making assertions, not about particular individuals in any particular state of individual or social development, but about the entire human race, seen in the light of the Creation. He was distinguishing man, as man had been distinguished in philosophic discourse even before Socrates, from the beast on the one hand, and from God or the gods on the other. Indeed, he was distinguishing man, as man had been distinguished in the first chapter of *Genesis*, when God gave him dominion over all the brute creation, while subject to Himself. Jefferson was laying down a premise by which despotic rule might in certain cases be regarded as natural and legitimate: the case of man ruling beast, or God ruling man. But by this same premise it was seen that man does not differ from man, as man differs from beast, or as man differs from God. As Jefferson rephrased the same thought fifty years later, shortly before his death, some men are not born with saddles on their backs, and others, booted and spurred, to ride them! Legitimate government does not then arise directly from nature; and therefore it does arise from consent. As the citizens of Malden, Massachusetts, declared, in their instructions to their representatives in the Continental Congress, May 27, 1776, "we can never be willingly subject to any other King than he who, being possessed of infinite wisdom, goodness, and rectitude, is alone fit to possess unlimited power."[13] It is in this eminently reasonable sense that the proposition that all men are created equal is to be understood. And so it was understood, until the serpent of slavery tempted some Americans to understand it differently.

Professor Bradford has declared with strident emphasis, that no man is equal to any other, intellectually, physically, or morally. In his speech on the Dred Scott decision,[14] Abraham Lincoln also asserted that the Signers of the Declaration did not intend to say that men were equal in color, size, intellect, moral development, or social capacity. And where Professor Bradford agrees with Abraham Lincoln we have, I suspect, a good practical definition of self-evident truth. But why cannot Professor Bradford understand that equality of *rights* is perfectly consistent with inequality of ability? Indeed, why cannot he understand that equality of rights is the *only* ground upon which inequality of ability can properly manifest itself?

Let us consider again the case of an exchange of shoes for grain. Should such an exchange be governed by the relative I.Q.'s, or moral reputation, or color, or the physical strength, of the buyer and the seller? Or should it be governed by the equal money value of the shoes and the grain? At bottom, an exchange of shoes for grain is an exchange between a shoemaker and a grain-grower. But what qualities of the shoemaker and the grain-grower are relevant to a just exchange, except those manifest in the shoes and the grain? Now good shoes should bring more money—and hence more grain—than poorly made shoes. But the good shoemaker can be known only by his shoes. To return less to the shoemaker for his labor, not because of the quality of the shoes, but because he is black (or, for that matter, because she is female), is manifestly unequal and hence unjust.

Professor Bradford has made the extraordinary assertion that it is sophistry to distinguish equality of opportunity from equality of results. He observes that "only those who *are* equal can take equal advantage of a given circumstance." I confess myself unable to assign any intelligible meaning to this assertion. Does he mean that a fair start in a race is advantageous only to someone who is fast enough to win it? But this is nonsense. The purpose of the race is to find out who *is* the fastest, and this can be done only if the start of the race is fair. I think it useful here to distinguish an open race from a handicap race. Only an open race is a true race—that is, only a race in which every runner has a chance to compete, can reveal who it is who can run the fastest. And a true race is one in which everyone starts from the same line at the same time, and runs the same distance. Moreover, it is one in which none of the runners are hobbled, and none are given packs to carry. Or, alternatively, if hobbles or packs are part of the race, then everyone must be hobbled or burdened in exactly the same way. But it is precisely when everyone starts together in a fair race, that they do *not* end together. According to Professor Bradford, the "hue and cry over equality of opportunity and equal rights leads, *a fortiori,* to a final demand for equality of condition." But is it not evident; indeed, is it not *self-evident,* that the truth is the exact opposite? In a fair race, the natural inequalities of the runners emerge in the results, and these inequalities are expressed in the order of the finish. The only equality which we see—or wish to see—in the result, is the proportional equality of unequal prizes for unequal finishers.

Now what is a handicap race? A handicap race is one designed to overcome the natural inequality of the runners. It is one designed to give the slower runner an *equal* chance with the fastest runner. The handicapper does this by assigning a longer distance (or a later start) to the fast runner, and a shorter distance (or an earlier start) to the slow runner, and in theory, a perfectly handicapped race would be one in which everyone finished together. In practice, a perfectly handicapped race introduces the greatest amount of uncertainty into the outcome. Both theoretically and practically, handicapping overcomes natural ability in favor of equality of results. But Professor Bradford's prescriptive rights, in particular the prescriptive right of a master to own slaves, as against the equal natural rights he opposes, bring about a handicapped society. That they do produce a spurious "equality of results," is the testimony of the supreme spokesman for the old South.

In Calhoun's Oregon speech, speaking in defense of that social order which, Professor Bradford would have us believe, was a partnership in every virtue and all perfection, the Senator declared that

> With us [of the South] the two great divisions of society are not the rich and poor, but white and black; and all the former, the poor as well as the rich, belong to the upper class, and are respected and treated as equals, if honest and industrious; and hence have a position and pride of character of which neither poverty nor misfortune can deprive them.[15]

What a confession of moral blindness is this! All whites are assigned upper-class status (if honest and industrious!), with pride of position and character assigned to them, without regard to their inequality of achievement or excellence. And all blacks are assigned lower-class status (however honest or industrious) simply because they are black (free blacks not being distinguished from slaves). All distinctions of virtue or intelligence are, in the decisive respect, assimilated to the single distinction of color. All intrinsically important human qualities are debased and degraded from the honors due to them, by the distinction of color alone.

And except for the *inequality* resulting from color, the antebellum South, according to its most distinguished spokesman, produced the most perfect *equality of results*, in the race of life, that the world has ever seen!

Professor Bradford's case against the "heresy of equality" rests upon both logical and historical grounds. That is, he regards it both as false in itself, and false as a doctrine ascribed to the Founding Fathers. He denies that the doctrine of equal human rights can properly be found in the Declaration of Independence. To find it there is, he maintains, to misread the Declaration. Professor Bradford's argument is a theme with many variations, and it is sometimes difficult to detect the theme within the variation. But his case as a historical scholar—as distinct from a political philosopher—comes down to this. When the Declaration reads "all men are created equal," we are not to understand "men" to refer to *individual* human beings, but only to human beings in their *collective* capacity, acting politically within civil society as members of a "people."

> We are now prepared to ask [writes Professor Bradford] what Mr. Jefferson and his sensible friends meant by "all men" and "created equal." Meant together—*as a group.* . . . [16]

Professor Bradford, be it noted, thought Jefferson's *friends* were sensible. What they meant *as a group* (the emphasis is Bradford's) must be sensible, because of the friends. Jefferson's well-known strictures against slavery make it impossible for Professor Bradford ever to regard him as a sensible *individual*. However, one can only wonder why those sensible friends were so agreeable to having the nonsensible Jefferson draft the Declaration in the first place.

> The *exordium* of the Declaration begins . . . with an argument from history and with a definition of the voice addressing "the pow-

ers of the earth!" It is a "people," a "we" that are estranged from another "we." The peroration reads the same: "we," the "free and independent states," are united in our will to separation. . . . No contemporary liberal, new or old, can make use of that framework or take the customary liberties with what is contained by the construction. Nor coming to it by the path I have marked, may they, in honesty, see in "created equal" what they devoutly wish to find. "We," in that second sentence, signifies the colonials as the citizenry of the distinct colonies, not as individuals, but rather in their corporate capacity. Therefore, the following "all men"—created equal in their right to expect from any government to which they might submit freedom from corporate bondage . . . [hence] equal as one free state is as free as another. Nothing is maintained concerning the abilities or situations of individual persons. . . .[17]

We have quoted at length here, because we wished there to be no doubt that any assertions we make concerning Professor Bradford's text, are solidly grounded in that text. We observe, first of all, that Professor Bradford and I do not differ at all concerning the proposition that when the Signers of the Declaration speak of "one people" or "we" or "these united colonies," they were referring to themselves, and those whom they represented, in a corporate or collective, or political capacity. Indeed, I suspect that I go further than Professor Bradford, since I am convinced that "one people" meant just that, and that the several "peoples" of the several colonies or states were already formed into one single people. And I hold—with Presidents Jackson and Lincoln—that the several states also were formed into one indissoluble union. But how in the world can the expression "men" be synonymous with "people"? Consider the text: "We hold these truths to be self-evident, that all men are created equal, that they are endowed by their Creator with certain unalienable rights. . . ." The

first "We" is indeed the colonials, or the former colonials, citizens of the formerly distinct (but now united) colonies. But why are "we" endowed with "certain unalienable rights"? According to Professor Bradford, it is because they possessed those rights as colonials. But why should they possess those rights when they are no longer colonials? Rights granted by civil society are rights which can be taken away by civil society. But the Declaration here is most explicit. The rights of which it speaks are not civil or political rights, rights resulting from human or positive law. They are rights with which they had been "endowed by their Creator." Unless therefore Professor Bradford believes that the Creator endowed colonial Americans with rights with which he had not endowed other human beings, then the "men" in the phrase "all men are created equal" *must* be a more comprehensive category than the men in the "we" who hold these truths.

It is also a rule of interpretation for archaic documents that the meaning of words and phrases is to be sought in the light of contemporary usage. In Calhoun's Oregon speech, he assumed as a matter of course that "all men are born free and equal," and "all men are created equal" were mere variations of expression for the same fundamental idea. The former was, as we have noted, taken from the Massachusetts Bill of Rights. Article I of that document reads in full as follows:

> All men are born free and equal, and have certain natural, essential, and inalienable rights; among which may be reckoned the right of enjoying and defending their lives and liberties; that of acquiring, possessing, and protecting property; in fine, that of seeking and obtaining their safety and happiness.[18]

Can anyone doubt that the "men" referred to here are *individuals,* not societies of men in any collective sense? Instead of being "endowed by their Creator" with certain rights, they are born with them. And the rights with which they are born, are said to be "natural, essential, and inalienable," the three terms clearly being synonymous. But Professor Bradford's reading, as we have seen, regards the rights which the collective "we" declares to be rights held only "in their corporate capacity." Such rights are ineluctably civil or political, they could not possibly be called "natural" or "essential," any more than they could be called "inalienable."

But we may, I think, settle the matter beyond cavil. In the very Preamble of the Massachusetts Bill of Rights, we find the following:

> The body politic is formed by a voluntary association of individuals; it is a social compact by which the whole people covenants with each citizen and each citizen with the whole people that all shall be governed by certain laws for the common good.[19]

Since the Massachusetts Bill of Rights was adopted in 1780, I submit further these lines from the Virginia Bill of Rights, adopted less than a month before the Declaration of Independence.

> That all men are by nature equally free and independent, and have certain inherent rights [inherent being synonymous with natural, essential, and inalienable], of which when they enter into a state of society, they cannot by any compact deprive or divest their posterity. . . .[20]

Can there then be any reasonable doubt, can there indeed be any possible doubt, that, for the revolutionary generation, human beings, as human beings, as men, had rights antecedent to, and independent of, civil society? Or that civil society, properly so-called (that is, legitimate civil society), resulted from an agreement among men possessed of such rights? Can there then be any doubt that when the Declaration speaks of "all men" being

created equal, it does indeed then refer to individuals?

This record is not, contrary to Professor Bradford, an invention of liberals, new or old. Had John C. Calhoun, when he delivered his Oregon speech in 1848, had the slightest suspicion that this interpretation of the Declaration was a perversity of abolitionist propaganda, he would certainly have been as forward as Professor Bradford in pointing it out. Yet in the peroration of that speech he declared that

> We now begin to experience the danger of admitting so great an error to have a place in the declaration of our independence. . . . It had strong hold on the mind of Mr. Jefferson, the author of that document [Calhoun did not see the difference between Jefferson and his sensible friends], which caused him to take an utterly false view of the subordinate relation of the black to the white race in the South; and to hold in consequence, that the latter, though utterly unqualified to possess liberty, were as fully entitled to both liberty and equality as the former; and that to deprive them of it was unjust and immoral.[21]

Clearly, it never occurred for a moment to Calhoun that the "men" in "all men are created equal" did not refer to Negroes, however erroneous he may have believed the proposition to have been. We see then that the American Civil War resulted from a new revolution, a revolution in opinion in the South. That revolution denied the axiomatic premise of the older, better Revolution, which had declared—and meant—that all men are created equal.

Professor Bradford has a great many things to say about Abraham Lincoln, none of them complimentary. His remarks cover a spectrum that ranges all the way from the nonsensical to the absurd. As a specimen, we cite one which even he felt constrained to put into the small print of the endnotes. After observing a comparison of Lincoln to Bismarck and Lenin by Edmund Wilson, he adds:

> Another useful analogue (a firm higher-law man, and no legalist or historicist) is Adolf Hitler. For he writes in *Mein Kampf* that "human rights break state rights," calls for illegal as well as legal instruments in "wars of rebellion against enslavement from within and without," observes that all governments by oppression plead the law, and concludes, "I believe today that I am acting in the sense of the Almighty Creator . . . fighting for the Lord's work."[22]

I think that if Professor Bradford had searched long enough he might have found a documented quotation from Hitler, in which he had said that some of his best friends were Jews. Such a quotation would have had exactly the same significance as the one presented above.

Professor Bradford does not like Lincoln's attachment to higher-law doctrine. In particular, he does not like the fusion, in Lincoln's rhetoric, of higher law drawn from both the natural law, as expressed in the Declaration of Independence, and from the divine law, as found in the Bible. Let us concede that Lincoln was the greatest master of this rhetorical fusion. But it is utterly misleading to suppose that it was his invention, or that it was more characteristic of him than of any one of a large number of his contemporaries, North or South.

According to Professor Bradford, the House-Divided speech—with which Lincoln opened the campaign for Douglas' Senate seat in 1858—"was, beyond any question, a Puritan declaration of war." It was so, says Bradford, because, quoting the words of Lincoln's "one-time friend, Alexander Stephens," it " 'put the institution of nearly one-half the states under the ban of public opinion and national condemnation.' " Bradford continues:

> Of course the central motif of the House-Divided speech . . . echoes the Bible (Mark 3:25): Christ speaking of the undivided hosts of Satan. Lincoln's authority is thus, by association, elevated to the level of the hieratic. But he added something to that mixture. The myth that slavery will either be set on its way to extinction . . . or else all states will eventually become slave states establishes a false dilemma. . . . Thus he participates in what Richard Hofstadter calls the "paranoid style" in politics.[23]

Later on, Bradford adds, in words which he italicized for emphasis:

> *For houses are always divided, in some fashion or another.*[24]

Thus Lincoln, invoking the higher law, natural and divine, against slavery, demanding that the house be undivided, was introducing a revolutionary, gnostic, antinomian morality, as the ground of politics. He was thus assuring that politics would forever after be a crusade against sin, the sin to be defined, not by priests, but by egalitarian, ideological politicians.

Since Bradford has introduced Alexander Stephens as a witness against Lincoln, it would be particularly instructive to see how Stephens' views of the crisis of the divided house compared with Lincoln's. In December 1860, shortly after South Carolina had adopted its Ordinance of Secession, Lincoln wrote to Stephens, saying that

> you think slavery is *right,* and should be extended, and we think it is *wrong,* and should be restricted. That, I suppose, is the rub. It certainly is the only substantial difference between us."[25]

Stephens, it should be remarked, was a Southern moderate. As an old Whig, he was a strong Unionist, and fought against secession in his state of Georgia as long as he could. But he went with his state when it left the Union, and became Vice President of the Confederate States of America. After the adoption of the Confederate Constitution, he propounded a defense of the new regime, which has come down in history as the "Corner-Stone" speech. It has its name from precisely the same source as Lincoln's House-Divided speech. Both are built around biblical texts. Stephens certainly elevates his doctrine to the level of the hieratic, as Bradford puts it, every bit as much as Lincoln. But Stephens' speech is more than a defense of the new regime. It is the most comprehensive Southern reply to *all* of Lincoln's speeches, from 1854 to 1860, of any that the record of the times shows. What the speech proves, beyond doubt, is that Lincoln was perfectly accurate when he said that Stephens' thinking slavery right, and Lincoln's thinking it wrong, was the *only* substantial difference between them. In every other respect, as we shall see, Stephens was in *agreement* with Lincoln, and in *disagreement* with Professor Bradford.

Lincoln held, in virtually all his speeches between 1854 and 1860—notably in the debates with Douglas, and in the Cooper Union speech—that the Founding Fathers had all regarded slavery as a great moral wrong. They had inherited slavery as part of their colonial legacy, and its presence among them imposed certain "necessities" which they were powerless to change. But they supposed that slavery was nonetheless on a "course of ultimate extinction," and although they gave guarantees to slavery while it should last, they did not expect it to last. Its presence was tolerable because, but only because, they expected it gradually to die out. The House was not a Divided House, in Lincoln's sense, if the moral wrong of slavery were acknowledged, and public policy based upon that acknowledgement as a premise. What does Alexander Stephens say about this?

> The prevailing ideas entertained by [Jefferson] and most of the leading statesmen at the time of the formation of the old Constitution, were that the enslavement of the African was in violation of the laws of nature: that it was wrong in principle, socially, morally, and politically. It was an evil they knew not well how to deal with, but the general opinion of the men of that day was, that somehow or other, in the order of Providence, the institution would be evanescent and pass away.[26]

We see now that Jefferson's sensible friends were no more sensible than he! It is axiomatic for Stephens that "most of the leading statesmen" of the time, were antislavery. All of them understood "all men are created equal" to include *all* men, and therefore to include Negroes. It was the "general opinion of the men of that day" that slavery was a transient phenomenon. Hence general opinion agreed with Lincoln that at the Founding slavery was on a course of ultimate extinction, and that the House of the Founders was not a Divided House.

Stephens does not disagree by one iota with Lincoln's interpretation of the Founding. *But he disagrees with the Founding.* "Those ideas," he writes, viz., of the Founding Fathers,

> were fundamentally wrong. They rested upon the assumption of the equality of the races. This was an error. It was a sandy foundation, and the idea of a government built upon it; when the "storm came and the wind blew, it fell."[27]

The quotation by Stephens is taken from Mark, 7:26, 27. Jesus is speaking, and says, "And every one who hears these words of mine and does not do them will be like a foolish man who built his house upon sand: and the rain fell, and the floods came, and the winds blew and beat against the house, and it fell; and great was the fall of it." What was the sandy foundation? It was the doctrine that the races were equal. And what is the rock which, asserts Stephens, is the truth upon which a government can stand? What is it for which he claims, by analogy, the hieratic authority of Jesus himself?

> Our new government [declared Stephens] is founded upon exactly the opposite idea; its foundations are laid, its corner stone rests upon the great truth that the negro is not the equal to the white man. That slavery—the subordination to the superior race, is his natural and normal condition.
>
> This our new Government [the Confederate States of America] is the first in the history of the world, based upon this great physical and moral truth. This truth has been slow in the process of its development, like all other truths in the various departments of science. . . .[28]

We have seen Professor Bradford's distaste for political novelty. Time and again, he has defended the cause of the Confederacy as the cause of traditional society attempting to preserve tradition against a radical break with the past, a break enforced by Lincoln's militant, uniformitarian Unionism. But here we find a most eminent apologist for the Confederacy, its supremely articulate Vice President, in March 1861, declaring the cause of the Confederacy to be the *exact opposite* of what Professor Bradford has declared it to be.

Not only does Stephens say that the Confederacy is the first government of its kind in the history of the world, but he says that it is based upon a truth that has emerged from the progress of science. Although he says that such truths are slow in their process of development, it is also the case that they cause profound upheavals where they make their appearance. The examples which Stephens himself gives span less than two centuries. The fault of the Founding Fathers was not that they were perverse, but that the progress of science had not enlightened them. Stephens' doctrine is then not merely a commitment to novelty, but a commitment to a perpetual revolution of morals

and politics, whenever the progress of science shall reveal new truths. It is the most radical denial possible of that "funded wisdom of the ages" in which Professor Bradford would have us place our faith. It is a denial of such permanent standards as are incorporated in the natural-law teaching of the Declaration of Independence.

Stephens compares the new truth about the races to the discoveries of Galileo, Adam Smith, and Harvey. Harvey's theory of the circulation of the blood, he says, was not admitted by "a single one of the medical profession living at the time," yet now it is "universally acknowledged." "May we not," asks Stephens,

> therefore look forward with confidence to the ultimate universal acknowledgement of the truths upon which our system rests? It is the first government ever instituted upon principles of strict conformity to nature, and the ordination of Providence, in furnishing the materials of human society. Many governments have been founded upon the principle of certain classes; but the classes thus enslaved, were of the same race, and in violation of the laws of nature. Our system commits no such violation of nature's laws. The negro, by nature, or by the curse of Canaan, is fitted for that condition which he occupies in our system.[29]

Surely, Abraham Lincoln never set forth the case for an undivided house with greater assurance or conviction! Nor did Lincoln appeal to greater authority, either natural or divine, in support of his version of what the undivided house should be. Yet there is something self-contradictory in Stephens' appeal, as there is not in Lincoln's. Why should it have come to be known only so recently that the Negro is fitted by nature only for slavery? Especially if the "cause" of that nature is the curse of Canaan? Whence could it have arisen, that so enlightened a generation as that of the Founding Fathers should have been so completely wrong about so fundamental a reality? For it is clear that Stephens *does* regard them as enlightened, in all respects except one. The many governments which, he says, were founded upon "the principles of certain classes," is certainly meant to encompass all the unequal regimens of the old world. The founding that began on July 4, 1776, is certainly, albeit indirectly, endorsed by Stephens, in precisely the sense in which we have endorsed it. It too must have been the "first in the history of the world," in just the way in which we have described it above. Stephens has no quarrel—any more than did Calhoun—with a system which is radically egalitarian as far as white men are concerned. But, like Calhoun, he thinks that this egalitarianism can only be properly realized upon the foundation of Negro slavery. From Stephens' perspective the Revolution accomplished by the Declaration and the Constitution was perfect in its kind. There is no question but that that Revolution represented a break with everything that went before it. But it needed one further step forward in enlightenment—the step represented by the discovery of the inferiority of the Negro race. (Never mind if this opinion is inconsistent with the idea of unknowable future scientific progress.)

The architect, in the construction of buildings, lays the foundation with proper materials. . . . The substratum of our society is made of the material fitted by nature for it, and by experience we know that it is best, not only for the superior, but for the inferior race that it should be so. It is indeed in conformity with the ordinance of the Creator. . . . The great objects of humanity are best attained when conformed to His laws and decrees, in the formation of government, as well as in all things else. Our Confederacy is founded upon principles in strict conformity with these laws. This stone which was first rejected by the first builders "is become the chief stone of the corner" in our new edifice.[30]

Thus ends the first and greatest apology for the Confederacy, made in the flush of its confidence in long life and prosperity. Stephens' apology *after* the Civil War, contained in his *Constitutional View of the War Between the States*, is very different. The "corner stone" sinks from sight, and States' rights, as the ground of constitutionalism, replaces it. But I think the Corner-Stone speech is the more authentic, as revealing the character of the Confederacy when it felt full confidence in its principles. The "corner stone" quotation comes from Psalms, 118:22. "The stone which the builders refused is become the head stone of the corner." It appears however in both Matthew and Mark, where Jesus quotes it, and quotes it in such a way as to indicate that he, or his teaching, is the stone in question. Certainly Stephens yielded nothing to Lincoln, in his assumption of what Bradford calls "hieratic" authority.

We began this part of our essay by giving Professor Bradford's quotation from Adolf Hitler, in which he shows that Hitler, like Lincoln, was a "firm higher-law man." Hitler, we saw, like Lincoln, believed that "human rights" take precedence of "state rights"; and that Hitler, like Lincoln, believed he was "fighting for the Lord's work." But we see now that Union and Confederate causes did not differ, with respect to being higher-law causes. Had Hitler looked back for precedent, it is not likely that he would have looked to Abraham Lincoln. All the precedent he would have needed in the higher-law sense was certainly present in Stephens' Corner-Stone speech. And in the decisive sense, that speech, like the cause it represented, would have been entirely congenial. Certainly Hitler's doctrines of racial inequality went much beyond that of Stephens. Yet when Hitler spoke of "human rights," he certainly did not do so in the sense of Lincoln or Jefferson. "Human rights" were for him primarily and essentially the rights of the master race. And the Confederate States of America represented the first time in human history that a doctrine of a master race was fully and systematically set forth as the ground of a regime. More precisely, it was the first time that such a doctrine was set forth *on the authority of modern science*. It was this authority that made it so persuasive, and so pernicious.

National Socialism and Marxist Communism are, as I have argued elsewhere,[31] alternative versions of the social Darwinism that was so rife in nineteenth-century thought. They are alternative foundations of the totalitarian tyrannies that have so blotted and befouled the life of man in our time. That at least one of them never took root in the United States we owe, more than to any other man, to Abraham Lincoln. Let us carry on his work, building upon that rock upon which he built his undivided house, the teaching that, with respect to the rights to life, liberty, and the pursuit of happiness, *"all* men are created equal."

NOTES

[1] "The Heresy of Equality," *loc. cit.*, p. 62.

[2] Modern Library Edition, p. 340.

[3] 1131 a 10 to 1131 b 24.

[4] 1301 b 27.

[5] Modern Library Edition, p. 3.

[6] "The Heresy of Equality," *op. cit.*, p. 63.

[7] "It was not because it was proposed to establish a new nation, but because it was proposed to establish a nation on new principles, that July 4, 1776, has come to be regarded as one of the greatest days in history." And again: "But we should search these charters [of the Dutch and of the British] in vain for an assertion of the doctrine of equality. This principle had not before appeared as an official political declaration of any nation. It was profoundly revolutionary. It is one of the corner stones of American institutions." President Calvin Coolidge, speaking on the one hundred and fiftieth anniversary of the Declaration of Independence, in *Foundations of the Republic: Speeches and Addresses* by Calvin Coolidge (New York and London: Scribner's, 1926), pp. 445, 447.

[8] "The Heresy of Equality," *op. cit.*, p. 62.

[9] *Ibid.*, p. 66.

[10] *The Works of John C. Calhoun*, Richard K. Cralle, ed. (New York: Appleton, 1854), Vol. 4, p. 507.

[11] *Ibid.*

[12] *Ibid.*, p. 508.

[13] *Documents of American History*, Henry Steele Commager, ed. (New York: Appleton-Century-Crofts, Seventh Edition, 1963), pp. 97, 98.

[14] *The Collected Works of Abraham Lincoln*, Roy P. Basler, ed. (New Brunswick, New Jersey: Rutgers University Press, 1953), Vol. 2, pp. 398–410.

[15] Calhoun, *op. cit.*, pp. 505, 506.

[16] "The Heresy of Equality," *op. cit.*, p. 67.

[17] *Ibid.*, pp. 67, 68.

[18] Commager, *op. cit.*, p. 107.

[19] *Ibid.*

[20] *Ibid.*, p. 103.

[21] Calhoun, *op. cit.*, p. 512.

[22] Bradford, "The Heresy of Equality," p. 77 (note 36).

[23] *Ibid.*, pp. 70, 71.

[24] *Ibid.*, p. 71.

[25] *Collected Works*, Vol. 4, p. 160.

[26] *The Political History of the Great Rebellion*, Edward McPherson, ed. (Washington, D.C., 1865), p. 103.

[27] *Ibid.*

[28] *Ibid.*

[29] *Ibid.*, p. 104.

[30] *Ibid.*

[31] E.g. in "On the Nature of Civil and Religious Liberty," *Equality and Liberty* (Oxford, 1965), pp. 169–189.   [XXI, Spring 1977, 114–126]

[26]

The Rhetoric of Alexander Hamilton

FORREST McDONALD

Forrest McDonald (1927–   ) is a professor of history at the University of Alabama, where he specializes in United States history before 1800, cultural pluralism, and economic and business history from 1890 to the present. A Guggenheim fellow from 1962 to 1963, he has been the recipient of a number of honors and awards, including the Fraunces Tavern Book Award in 1980. He is the author of widely acclaimed works, including We The People: The Economic Origins of the Constitution *(1958),* E Pluribus Unum: The Formation of the American Republic *(1965),* Novus Ordo Seclorum: The Intellectual Origins of the Constitution *(1985), and works on the presidencies of George Washington and Thomas Jefferson.*

THE POLITICAL RHETORIC of the Founders of the American Republic has received scant attention from scholars. The relative neglect is understandable. On the one hand, the very concept of rhetoric has, in modern times, all but lost its classical signification, and has come to mean empty verbosity or ornament. On the other, the political achievements of the Founders—the winning of independence, the establishment of a durable federal Union on republican principles, the creation of a system of government which is itself bound by law—were of such monumental proportions as to make their methods of persuasion seem of pedantic and picayune consequence. And thus, though every student of the epoch is at least vaguely aware that the general level of public discourse in late eighteenth-century America was extraordinarily high, perhaps unprecedentedly so, we tend to regard the way the Founders spoke and wrote as only incidental to what they did. I would contend, on the contrary, that it was their commitment to and practice of open, dispassionate, informed, and reasoned discussion of public questions which made their achievements possible. Their rhetoric, in other words, was not a mere by-product of their accomplishments: rather, their accomplishments were the product of their rhetorical interchange.

I

In the most general proper sense of the term, rhetoric is the art of persuasion through written or spoken language. In the classical and eighteenth-century usage, however, it meant persuasion according to certain formal rules. The Founding Fathers studied and practiced the art in accordance with the Aristotelian model, and at the risk of boring those of you who know far more about the subject than I

319

do, I shall begin by pointing out a couple of the implications inherent in that model.[1]

First, Aristotle ruled out the relationship of rhetoric to pure knowledge, insisting instead that, since it was founded upon opinion rather than upon absolute truth, it was concerned only with matters of probability. I shall clarify that point later. For now, what is important is that consciousness of that limitation of the art was of immense value in the building of American republican institutions, for it meant that public discourse could not be conducted in terms of ideological certainties of the sort that perverted the French Revolution and, indeed, most other revolutions. Instead, discussion of public questions was at its best a trial-and-error process of moving toward ever-greater probabilities of truth without succumbing to the fatal sin of gnosticism, the belief that one has arrived at absolute Truth.

Second, though the rules required that persuasion be based on reasoned argument, they permitted two additional forms of "proof" besides logical proof. These were ethical proof, which was designed to win from the audience a favorable attitude toward the author or speaker, and emotional proof, which was aimed at putting the audience in a receptive frame of mind. Given the Founding Fathers' understanding that men are governed by their passions—that is, drives for self-gratification—and by habits and sentiments, and that reason is normally the servant rather than the master of the passions, this meant that their rhetoric and their view of the nature of man could complement and reinforce one another. It also meant that they were enabled to (as they were obliged to) work toward raising the level of public sentiments as well as the level of public understanding. This was put simply and clearly by the celebrated author of the 1767 *Letters from a Farmer in Pennsylvania,* John Dickinson. In his seventh letter Dickinson quotes at length from speeches that Lord Camden and William Pitt had given in Parliament, praises the "generous zeal for the rights of mankind that glows in every sentence," and analyzes what it was that made their rhetoric so powerful: "Their reasoning is not only just—it is, as Mr. *Hume* says of the eloquence of Demosthenes, 'vehement.' It is disdain, anger, boldness, freedom, involved in a continual stream of argument."[2]

Historians, in dealing with the Founding Fathers, have paid too much attention to the "justice of their reasoning" and not enough to their "vehemence." If a proper balance were brought to a study of the writings of the Founders, I believe, the result would be an enormous contribution to our understanding of them. If I were outlining such a study, I would suggest a rhetorical analysis of a half-dozen patriotic tracts written between the 1760's and 1776: Dickinson's *Letters,* John Adams's *Novanglus Letters,* James Wilson's *Considerations on the . . . Authority of the British Parliament,* Thomas Jefferson's *Summary View of the Rights of British America,* Thomas Paine's *Common Sense,* and the Declaration of Independence.

I would also suggest that the student be sensitive to certain nuances of eighteenth-century political writing which have eluded most investigators. One concerns the meaning of words. The meaning of many crucial words has changed so radically that, without an *Oxford English Dictionary* at one's side, one is likely to commit grave errors of interpretation. In a moment I shall offer some fairly dramatic examples of the ways that meanings have changed; meanwhile, a related subtlety is that there were then, as there are now, a variety of code words in common currency. For instance, there was the phrase "Great Man." In one of my early books I missed entirely the connotations of the phrase: having noticed that it was frequently used to describe the financier of the Revolution, Robert Morris, I misread it to mean that even Morris's enemies viewed him with a touch of awe. Much later I learned that it had been used by English Oppositionists as a contemptuous description of Sir Robert Walpole, then applied to the corrupt and wealthy aristocrats who dominated English politics in mid-century. It was the Oppositionists' ideological heirs in America, anti-Federalists and Jeffersonian Republicans, who applied the term to Morris—as they did also to Hamilton and Washington—and they were using it as a form of condemnation.[3] Finally, there are literary conventions which can sometimes be revealing. For example, pre-Revolutionary political tracts abounded in typographical variations—the use of italics, all capital letters, and extravagant punctuation—designed to achieve emphasis, indicating that the authors were thinking in terms of speeches to small, tangible audiences. Upon the emergence of a truly national politics and the large, impersonal audience that that implied, typographical variations were abandoned, indicating that the writers now intended their words to be read rather than heard.[4]

II

Enough of preaching: it is time to start practicing. I have been speaking of a study that someone should make; let us turn to one that I have made, of the rhetoric of Alexander Hamilton. As we do so, we immediately face three formidable obstacles, all of which arise from Hamilton's historical reputation. It is commonly alleged that Hamilton was contemptuous of public opinion; that he created a system based upon greed, in disdain of public spiritedness; and that he was hypocritical, saying one thing in private and another in public. These allegations, if true, would

make analysis of his rhetoric pointless, save perhaps as an exercise in the study of duplicity. Each must therefore be considered before we proceed.

The first allegation rests mainly on a misreading of Hamilton's language. After the Whiskey Rebellion in 1794, Hamilton said in a letter to Washington that he had "long since . . . learnt to hold popular opinion of no value." If those words are read in their twentieth-century sense, they are pretty damning, and they seem conclusive; and that is the sense in which historians have read them. Richard H. Kohn, for instance, though usually a careful scholar, quotes Hamilton's remark, adds that President Washington "knew he could not govern on such principles," and cites with approval Secretary of State Edmund Randolph as saying that "Hamilton's ideas 'would heap curses upon the government. The strength of a government is the affectation of the people.' "[5]

But let us consider Hamilton's language more carefully. The operative words are "popular" and "opinion." I do not have space here (even if I knew enough) to do full justice to the etymology of the word "popular" or to the historical distinction between it and the word "public," but I can summarize briefly. In its ancient forms and in its seventeenth- and eighteenth-century usage, "popular" comprehended everybody; in meaning, though not in its roots, it was akin to "common" or "vulgar." It also had a specific political connotation, namely left-wing (significantly, Hamilton's remark was apropos of political attacks in Philip Freneau's left-wing newspaper, *The National Gazette*). "Public," by contrast, was derived from the same root as the word "pubic," meaning manhood; it referred individually to those who had attained the full status and responsibilities of manhood and referred collectively to the political society or body politic itself. Interestingly, "virtue"—which Montesquieu and others regarded as the actuating principle of a *re*public—was also derived from a root word meaning manhood. Thus the phrases "public virtue" and "republican virtue," which had considerable currency in eighteenth-century America, were somewhat tautological, whereas "popular virtue" would have been a contradiction in terms, the component words being mutually exclusive. As for the word "opinion," it was used in at least three distinct ways in the eighteenth century. One was the Aristotelian usage, as a technical term associated with probability, with the assembly and the courts, and thus with rhetoric. More frequently, it was used in the present sense, meaning belief or prejudice. Still a third usage signified confidence, esteem, high regard. Following an essay of David Hume's, Hamilton had indicated in the Constitutional Convention that he used the term in the third sense. In other words, he was saying in 1794 that he held it of no value to be well-regarded by the rabble and by rabble-rousers—or, to phrase it differently, that statesmanship is not a popularity contest.[6]

That is a far cry from expressing contempt for what the public thinks and believes. Hamilton made his meaning clearer in the rest of his letter to Washington: after saying that he had learned to hold popularity of no value, he added that his reward for service to the public would be in "the esteem of the discerning and in internal consciousness of zealous endeavours for the public good." Historians have somehow managed to omit that part of his letter, just as they have managed to ignore the fact that Hamilton probably expended more energy, thought, and words trying to create and guide an informed public opinion than did any of his contemporaries.

The second allegation, that Hamilton's policies represented an effort to build a political system on greed rather than on civic virtue, stemmed from more complex roots. It originated in the charges of his political enemies. Some (William Maclay, for example) were economically interested in discrediting Hamilton; others (Jefferson and Madison, for example) were politically interested in doing so; still others (John Taylor of Caroline, for example) were ideologically interested in doing so. But that view of Hamilton has also been expounded by an impressive array of modern scholars, including E. James Ferguson, Gerald Stourzh, J. G. A. Pocock, and, most recently, Drew R. McCoy. The eighteenth century, as these historians have pointed out, witnessed the development of a school of political theory that espoused what Pocock calls "the movement from virtue to interest" as the activating principle of government: it began with Bernard de Mandeville's *Fable of the Bees* (1714), holding that private vice was the wellspring of public virtue, and ran through Adam Smith and his often-quoted passage which begins, "It is not from the benevolence of the butcher, the brewer or the baker that we expect our dinner, but from their regard of their own interest." According to McCoy, the "powerful, economically advanced modern state" which Hamilton envisaged "would stand squarely on the worldly foundations of 'corruption' that Bernard Mandeville had spoken of."[7]

The case is persuasive. Though Hamilton never read Mandeville, as far as I am aware, he did read and on several occasions quote from David Hume's essays in a similar vein, and he read and was influenced by Adam Smith. Moreover, in 1783 he clearly advocated the consolidation of national authority through appeals to the interests of public creditors and financial and commercial groups, and in 1784 he said flatly that "the safest reliance of every government is on men's interest." I myself have been guilty of writing that Hamilton's program as Secretary of the Treasury depended upon tying the interests of public creditors to the fate of his measures.[8]

But I was wrong, and so are the others. Two things happened to Hamilton between 1783 and 1789 which radically altered his thinking on this subject: he learned from observing and participating in state politics that state governments could be more effective in employing avarice to win political support than could a national government, and he learned from study of the principles of natural law that morality, in the long run, was a more stable foundation for government than was economic self-interest. Despite the abundance of charges, there is no evidence whatsoever that Hamilton used the lure of personal gain in seeking congressional support for his measures. Moreover, he expressed himself clearly on the subject in a remarkable private document he wrote in 1795. In drafting his plan for assuming the state debts, he admitted, he had taken into account the tendency of assumption "to strengthen our infant Government by increasing the number of ligaments between the Government and the interests of Individuals. . . . Yet upon the whole it was the consideration upon which I relied least of all." Even on purely practical grounds, had this been "the weightiest motive to the measure, it would never have received my patronage." And, he added in a marginal note to himself, "such means are not to be resorted to but the good sense & virtue of the people." [9]

The third common allegation against Hamilton, that he was hypocritical in his public utterances—and, most particularly, that he spoke contemptuously of "the people" in private and sang a different tune for public consumption—is likewise without foundation. It is true that, in his youthful disillusionment with the way the Revolutionary War was going, he expressed his disgust with the people. In 1779 he wrote his intimate friend John Laurens that "the birth and education of these states has fitted their inhabitants for the chain, and . . . the only condition they sincerely desire is that it may be a golden one." The next year he wrote Laurens that "Our countrymen have all the folly of the ass and the passiveness of the sheep in their composition. . . . The whole is a mass of fools and knaves." In maturity, however, he arrived at a different and more balanced view and expressed it in public and private alike. I shall return to that later. Meanwhile, the measure of his duplicity, or lack of it, is to be found in comparing his public writings, from *The Federalist Papers* through the 1790's, with his private correspondence. Such comparison reveals a record of virtually perfect consistency. The truth is that Hamilton was, as Fisher Ames said of him, "the most frank of men"; and, as he said of himself in a letter to an intimate friend, "what I would not promulgate I would avoid. . . . pride makes it part of my plan to *appear truly what I am*." Indeed, his passion for candor more than once led him to transcend the boundaries of prudence—as he did, for instance, in publishing the details of his sexual affair with Maria Reynolds so as to protect the integrity of the office he had filled.[10]

III

Hamilton's rhetoric may be fruitfully examined by considering separately his employment of each of the Aristotelian forms of proof. Thorough analyses of two of his performances have been made along those lines: Bower Aly's study of Hamilton's speeches in the New York ratifying convention, published in 1941, and Larry Arnhart's study of the rhetoric of *The Federalist*, delivered before the Midwest

Political Science Association in 1979. Some of what I have to say in the following pages draws on these two studies.

Logical proof, as opposed to ethical and emotional proof, carries the greatest portion of the burden in Hamilton's rhetoric. In the Aristotelian system, logical reasoning is of two broad kinds: deductive, which means reasoning from general propositions to arrive at particular conclusions, and inductive, which means reasoning from a number of particular observations to arrive at general propositions. The principal device of deductive reasoning is called a syllogism, and it is something we all employ even if we have never heard the word. A syllogism consists, in order, of 1) a major premise, 2) a minor premise, and 3) a conclusion, as in this example: 1) no man is immortal, 2) John Smith is a man, and 3) therefore John Smith is not immortal.

But deductive reasoning in rhetoric, though having the same structure as that in other forms of logic, is not quite the same in substance. In rhetorical reasoning, one uses a special kind of syllogism called an enthymeme. The main difference between a pure syllogism and an enthymeme is in the nature of the major premise. In a pure syllogism the major premise is absolutely true, as in "the square of the hypotenuse of a right triangle equals the sum of the squares of the other two sides." In an enthymeme, the major premise is based instead upon the reputable beliefs of the audience, which are only probably and relatively true, as in the statements "people are creatures of habit," or "honesty is the best policy."

Hamilton described the two kinds of premises, as well as deductive reasoning as he practiced it, in Federalist 31. "In disputations of every kind," he said at the beginning of that essay, "there are certain primary truths or first principles upon which all subsequent reasonings must de-

pend. These contain an internal evidence, which antecedent to all reflection or combination commands the assent of the mind. . . . Of this nature are the maxims in geometry, that 'the whole is greater than its parts;' " and so on. "Of the same nature are those other maxims in ethics and politics, that there cannot be an effect without a cause; that the means ought to be proportioned to the end; that every power ought to be commensurate with its object; that there ought to be no limitation of a power destined to effect a purpose, which is itself incapable of limitation."[11]

A couple of aspects of this description want special notice. One is that Hamilton tends, in the passage quoted, to treat the two kinds of premises as equally valid. Doing so was an effective rhetorical device as well as a reflection of his personality—he was nothing if not positive and forceful—but he knew the difference. The first kind was what, elsewhere, he called "geometrically true," the other what he called "morally certain." The second subtle aspect of the passage quoted is that there is a progression in his examples of "maxims in ethics and politics," from one which nobody would question to one that many members of his audience might challenge. The listing itself is almost a process of deduction. That, too, was both an effective rhetorical device and a reflection of his personality.

As for Hamilton's inductive reasoning—that is, reasoning from experience, observation, or example—he always employed it, his mixture of inductive and deductive varying with the audience. Temperamentally, he distrusted the deductive and preferred the inductive. "A great source of error," he wrote early in his career, "is the judging of events by abstract calculations, which though geometrically true are false as they relate to the concerns of beings governed more by passion and prejudice than by an enlightened sense of their interests." In Federalist 20, echoing a sentiment shared by most of the Founding Fathers, he and Madison said that "Experience is the oracle of truth; and where its responses are unequivocal, they ought to be conclusive and sacred." In any event, as Arnhart has pointed out, he made clear to his audience whether he was using one or the other or both by introducing his arguments with such phrases as "theory and practice conspire to prove."[12]

I shall not go into a detailed analysis of all the rhetorical techniques Hamilton employed in his logical proof. Aly has done so at great length: in regard to speech after speech, Aly points out where Hamilton has employed dilemma, antecedent probability, analogy, exposure of inconsistency, reduction to absurdity, causal relation, turning the tables, and other devices. For those who are interested in pursuing the matter further, I recommend Aly's work.

But there are three additional aspects of Hamilton's method of using rhetorical logic which, while compatible with the Aristotelian model, were unique to him. One was that his approach was always positive, never negative. As the editors of his law papers put it, "His habit of thought even when acting for the defense was affirmative; in other words, he was always carrying the war to the enemy." That habit reflected his personality, but it was also a deliberate choice of rhetorical strategy and tactics. In this regard, it is instructive to observe the brief notes Hamilton recorded from Demosthenes' Orations (which he studied while in the army). " 'Where attack him, it will be said? Ah Athenians war, war itself will discover to you his weak sides, if you will seek them.' Sublimely simple." And again, "As a general marches at the head of his troops, so ought wise politicians, if I dare to use the expression, to march at the head of affairs;

insomuch that they ought not to await the *event*, to know what measures to take; but the measures which they have taken, ought to produce the *event*." In addition to being effective, this positive style had a special advantage that is related to the inner logic of rhetorical reasoning. The speaker or writer is limited, in attempting to persuade his audience, by the fact that the premises from which he can argue are restricted to what the audience already accepts as an established truth. Hamilton's practice of seeking the enemy's weak sides and seizing the initiative "to produce the event" enabled him to broaden the range of acceptable premises, and thus to educate as well as to persuade his audiences.[13]

The second of Hamilton's special qualities was an intuitive sense of the heart of a subject combined with an awesome capacity for mastering its details. As William Pierce wrote of him in the Constitutional Convention, "he enquires into every part of his subject with the searchings of phylosophy . . . there is no skimming over the surface of a subject with him, he must sink to the bottom to see what foundation it rests on . . . and when he comes forward he comes highly charged with interesting matter." His speeches and writings were characteristically long, for he was rarely content to rely upon only one approach to an argument, even when he was confident of winning in a single stroke. His celebrated opinion on the constitutionality of the bank affords an excellent example. He disposes of Randolph's and Jefferson's arguments in six brief but devastating paragraphs—piercing immediately to the heart of their position, showing the false premise on which it rests, indicating the appropriate premise, and drawing from it the only reasonable conclusion. But then he goes on for another 15,000 words, ringing every imaginable change on the argument. The beauty of this technique is again its educational value: it goes beyond successful persuasion in the particular instance and establishes new foundations for further persuasion on the morrow.[14]

Hamilton's third special quality is more difficult to describe. He was sensitive to the difference between the two nontechnical connotations of the word "opinion": belief, judgment, prejudice on the one hand, approval, esteem, regard on the other. In conventional rhetorical theory, it was opinion in the first sense, belief, that supplied the premises for deductive logical proof; opinion in the second sense, approval, would fall under ethical proof, having to do with the audience's favorable view of the author or speaker. Hamilton perceived that in the circumstances in which he labored—the attempt to establish a durable republican system of government—the two were so interrelated as to be inseparable. Each supported the other: the tasks of winning belief and approval went hand in hand. As a statesman he was seeking to establish public "credit" in the broad sense of credibility or confidence as well as in the narrow financial sense; indeed, in some respects he viewed the latter as only a means of attaining the former. Moreover—and this is crucial—he understood that opinions derive as much from perceptions as they do from facts. "A degree of illusion mixes itself in all the affairs of society," he wrote; "The opinion of objects has more influence than their real nature." Or, as he said in his First Report on the Public Credit, "In nothing are appearances of greater moment, than in whatever regards credit. Opinion is the soul of it, and this is affected by appearances, as well as realities." There is an extremely subtle point here: one central aim of Hamilton's public life was to replace the prevailing law of contract, based upon the medieval concepts of just price and fair value, with a modern theory of contract based upon

consent in a free market. Thus Hamilton's attention to the effect of appearances on opinion, like his other two special qualities, was an extension of the dimensions of logical proof, for it broadened the possible range of premises available within the rules of reasoning with enthymemes.[15]

Most of the techniques I have been describing can be illustrated by a brief analysis of one of Hamilton's greatest performances, the Report on Manufactures presented to Congress in December, 1791. The rhetorical situation was different from what it had been when Hamilton had given his reports on the public credit and the bank. On the earlier occasions the audience agreed with the first premise, that it was imperative to establish a system of public credit; Hamilton's task of persuasion was to convince Congress that it was desirable to do so in a particular way. In regard to the Report on Manufactures, the body of beliefs shared by most members of the audience, which we may describe in shorthand as the agrarian ideal, was hostile to Hamilton's objective, the promotion of industry. His task of persuasion was to convince Congress that it was desirable to encourage manufacturing, whatever the means.

He began by isolating and attacking the enemy's weakest side. The agrarian ideal itself was an impregnable bastion of prejudice, but the economic theory used to justify it—the physiocrat's rather silly notion that land is the source of all wealth and that the labor of craftsmen adds nothing to the value of things—was highly vulnerable. Hamilton demolished the physiocratic theory by quoting and paraphrasing at length from Adam Smith's *The Wealth of Nations*, a work whose free-trade doctrines the audience regarded with great respect. He was careful, however, not to draw any conclusions beyond what his argument demonstrated: all he claimed at that stage was that manufacturing could produce wealth, probably about equally with farming.

Hamilton's rhetorical strategy so far, that of using one body of acceptable premises to displace another, was effective, but it created a new rhetorical problem. The use of Smith's work had the advantage of establishing, as a premise for further argument, that the wealth of a nation could be increased. On the other hand, it also had a disadvantage, for Hamilton was advocating active governmental promotion of manufactures, and Smith had championed the doctrine of noninterference—the idea that human industry, "if left to itself, will naturally find its way to the most useful and profitable employment." To overcome that difficulty, Hamilton again sought the weakest sides of the argument. Smith, as Hamilton paraphrased him, had laid down seven new premises to prove that manufacturing could increase the wealth of a nation—the principle of the division of labor, the advantages of the use of machinery, the possibility of enlarging the labor pool by pulling normally idle people into it, and so on. As Hamilton developed each point, he corrected Smith by using inductive rather than deductive reasoning, which is to say by employing the awesome array of factual data which Hamilton had laboriously gathered for the purpose. By that means he transformed Smith's premises into his own. To put it another way, he had taken premises acceptable to the audience, from which it was not logically possible to conclude that governmental activism was desirable, and altered them in such a way that it could logically be shown that such activism was not only desirable but in fact necessary.

Now Hamilton brought the cumulative effects of previous argumentation into play. Given the proposition that manufacturing should be encouraged, the fact remained that the United States, as an undeveloped country, was woefully short of the necessary capital. That obstacle was readily overcome, Hamilton said, and he showed how by reviewing his reports on public credit, where he had demonstrated that the public debt could be institutionally manipulated in such a way that, with the support of public opinion, it would be turned into a great pool of liquid wealth or capital. From there to the end of the report, Hamilton had smooth sailing: all he had to do was propose a series of practical steps to be taken to bring about the desired ends.

I described the Report on Manufactures as one of Hamilton's greatest performances. Historians, however, will recall that Congress did not act on the report; and rhetoricians, armed with that datum, will conclude that the performance was not a great one at all. Let me construct the enthymeme: excellent rhetoric persuades the audience, Hamilton's report failed to persuade the audience, and therefore the report was not excellent rhetoric. But Hamilton's audience did not consist exclusively of the members of the Second Congress. In his rhetoric as in his statesmanship, Hamilton was addressing posterity and building cumulatively toward the future. In the course of time, the nation would begin the active promotion of manufactures, and for more than a century Hamilton's report would provide the rhetorical foundation for such a policy. Indeed, the report itself became a first premise.

IV

There remains the task of reviewing briefly Hamilton's use of ethical and emotional proof and, finally, his style. In regard to the first two I shall depend, for my theoretical underpinnings, largely on Arnhart, for he has put the matter extremely well. For the last I shall return exclusively to my own analysis, for there is an important dimension to Hamilton's style which he and others have overlooked.

Since the time of John Locke, logicians and rhetoricians have tended to share Plato's suspicion of traditional rhetoric because of its admission of irrational appeals to the audience. If ethical and emotional proofs are made in adherence to Aristotle's standards, however, they can in fact contribute to rational discourse. As for ethical proof, Aristotle says that a speaker will be most persuasive if he shows himself to be possessed of prudence, virtue, and good will. The persuasiveness of a speaker's character, based upon those criteria, can scarcely be dismissed as irrational: it is obviously quite reasonable to judge the reliability of a writer or speaker as being proportionate to his prudence, his virtue, and his good will. Besides, the more an author or speaker establishes his own credentials on those foundations, the more he conditions the audience to expect and demand them of other authors and speakers—and thus contributes to raising the general level of the rationality of the audience, which in turn elevates the rational possibilities available to the author or speaker.[16]

Hamilton's use of ethical proof was calculated to obtain just that end. His techniques varied with his audience, of course, as they necessarily must. In dealing with Washington, for instance, the appropriate tone was one of deference—not of flattery, which the president would instantly have regarded as showing an absence of character, but of respect for the presidential office and for the president's own character. In other words, one gained Washington's respect by showing respect in a proper manner. Washington was a special case, but in a sense that was the way Hamilton employed ethical proofs in more conventional rhetorical situations. That is to say, Hamilton normally

sought to establish his good character among the members of his audience not by reciting his own virtues but by appealing to theirs. He appealed to his audiences to judge his arguments dispassionately, openly, and in a spirit of moderation tempered by zealous concern for the happiness of their country. By urging them to be prudent, virtuous, and possessed of good will, he avoided the necessity of claiming to have those qualities himself; and, to the extent that he succeeded, he actually instilled them in his audiences.[17]

As for emotional proofs, they are legitimate in Aristotle's scheme of things only insofar as the passions with which they deal are rational ones. Now, passions are passions and reason is reason, to be sure; but passions can be shortsighted or prudent, biased or open, hastily formed or carefully considered. After all, there is such a thing as reasonable fear, and in some circumstances to be unafraid is to be unreasonable. Hamilton sometimes appealed to the fears of his audience, as when, in numerous of the Federalist essays, he declared that failure to adopt the Constitution would result in anarchy, tyranny, and war—and when, in essays on the French Revolution, he warned of the perils of emotional or ideological attachment to foreign powers. There are those of us who believe those fears were entirely reasonable. More characteristically, however, Hamilton's appeals were to noble and positive passions: pride, honor, love of liberty, love of country. There are those of us who believe that stimulation of those passions is likewise reasonable.[18]

Lastly, there is the matter of Hamilton's literary style. His style changed and improved over the years, as one might expect (though few scholars seem to have noticed); but what is more significant is that it evolved in a direction. Whatever one thinks of the intellectual merits of his earliest political writings, the 1774–1775 polemics entitled *A Full Vindication of the Measures of Congress* and *The Farmer Refuted*—unlike most other Hamilton scholars, I regard them as extremely muddleheaded—one is struck by their sophomoric literary quality. *The Farmer Refuted*, especially, is studded with strained metaphors, pretentious words, Latinisms, citations of authorities (many of whom young Hamilton had obviously not read), and other displays of affected erudition. By 1781–1782, when he wrote *The Continentalist* essays, and 1784, when he wrote the *Letters from Phocion*, he had discarded most of that excess baggage, but there was still more than was necessary. By 1788, when he co-authored *The Federalist*, he had almost reached his mature form, but not quite: though he made far fewer classical allusions than Madison did, he was still making unnecessary ones, and though he rarely attempted a consciously ornate metaphor, his unconscious metaphors were sometimes mixed or strained. Thereafter, he had arrived: from 1790 until the end of his life his prose style was straightforward, clear, lean, hard, and energetic.[19]

That course of evolution paralleled the growth of Hamilton's commitment to making a success of the American experiment in constitutional government. More than most of his countrymen, he doubted that the experiment could succeed; more than any of them, he was dedicated to making the effort. He perceived clearly that political rhetoric of the highest order was necessary to the attempt, for such is essential to statecraft in a republic. Now, we hear a great deal these days about the public's "right to know." That is a perversion of the truth, even as modern public relations, propaganda, and political blather are perversions of classical rhetoric. If the republic is to survive, the emphasis must be shifted from rights back to obligations. It is the obligation, not the right, of the citizen of a republic to be informed; it is the obligation of the public servant to inform him and simultaneously to raise his standards of judgment. In adapting his style to his audience, Hamilton was fulfilling his part of the obligation.

V

I would close with a postscript.[20] Despite Hamilton's efforts, and despite the efforts of other patriotic souls, the level of public discourse degenerated rapidly in the late 1790's. A plague of unscrupulous scribblers infested the nation, spewing venom, scurrility, deception, and hysteria throughout the land. Hamilton himself was subjected to as much abuse as any man, and possibly more. But he remained true to his principles until the very end.

One of his last and most celebrated cases as a lawyer arose from the frenzied partisan propaganda warfare that had developed. Harry Croswell, editor of a small-town newspaper, published a report that Jefferson had paid the notorious pamphleteer J. T. Callender to slander Washington, Adams, and other public men. The charge against Jefferson was true; but the Jeffersonians, who had stoutly defended freedom of the press when in the opposition, thought a "few wholesome prosecutions" were in order once they came to power. The Jeffersonian attorney general of New York, Ambrose Spencer, brought proceedings against Croswell for libel. On conviction, he appealed, and Hamilton became his counsel in the arguments before the state supreme court.

The key point at issue was that the judge in the trial court had refused to admit testimony regarding the truth of the statement as defense. English common-law doctrine, to which Republicans adhered, held that truth was not a defense. Hamilton scored effectively with a bit of emotional proof, showing that the doctrine itself was questionable since it had originated not in common-law courts but in the odious Star Chamber, as a departure from older law. But he was particularly concerned with the suitability of the doctrine in a republic. Libel, he said, was "a slanderous or ridiculous writing, picture or sign, with a malicious or mischievous design or intent, towards government, magistrates, or individuals." Intent was crucial, and truth was relevant to determining intent. Truth was therefore a defense, though not an absolute one. If it were used "wantonly; if for the purpose of disturbing the peace of families; if for relating that which does not appertain to official conduct," it was not acceptable. "But that the truth cannot be material in any respect, is contrary to the nature of things. No tribunal, no codes, no systems can repeal or impair this law of God, for by his eternal laws it is inherent in the nature of things. . . . It is evident that if you cannot apply this mitigated doctrine for which I speak, to the cases of libels here, you must for ever remain ignorant of what your rulers do. I never can think this ought to be; I never did think that the truth was a crime; I am glad the day is come in which it is to be decided; for my soul has ever abhorred the thought, that a free man dared not speak the truth."

NOTES

[1] In my comments on Aristotelian rhetoric, I have been guided by Larry Arnhart, "The Federalist as Aristotelian Rhetoric," paper presented at the Annual Meeting of the Midwest Political Science Association, Chicago, April, 1979. Professor Arnhart kindly supplied me with a copy. I find his argument that the Founding Fathers followed the Aristotelian model entirely convincing. His forthcoming "Aristotle on Political Reasoning: A Commentary on the *Rhetoric*," is scheduled for publication by Northern Illinois University Press in 1981. See also Bower

Aly, *The Rhetoric of Alexander Hamilton* (New York, 1941).

[2] Forrest McDonald, ed., *Empire and Nation: Letters from a Farmer in Pennsylvania, John Dickinson, Letters from the Federal Farmer, Richard Henry Lee* (Englewood Cliffs, N.J., 1962), 45n.

[3] Forrest McDonald, *We the People: The Economic Origins of the Constitution* (Chicago, 1958), 54; Rodger D. Parker, "The Gospel of Opposition: A Study in Eighteenth Century Anglo-American Ideology" (Ph.D. dissertation, Wayne State University, 1975); Harvey Mansfield, Jr., *Statesmanship and Party Government: A Study of Burke and Bolingbroke* (Chicago, 1965); Philadelphia *Freeman's Journal*, October 10, 1783; George Clinton to John Lamb, June 28, 1788, quoted in Aly, *Rhetoric of Hamilton*, 164n; Edgar S. Maclay, ed., *Journal of William Maclay, United States Senator from Pennsylvania, 1789–1791* (New York, 1890).

[4] The change is readily observed by comparing Dickinson's essays with Lee's in McDonald, ed., *Empire and Nation.*

[5] Hamilton to Washington, November 11, 1794, in Harold C. Syrett, ed., *The Papers of Alexander Hamilton* (26 vols., New York, 1961–1979), 17:366; Richard H. Kohn, *Eagle and Sword: The Federalists and the Creation of the Military Establishment in America, 1783–1802* (New York, 1975), 172.

[6] This analysis is based upon *The Oxford English Dictionary*, supplemented by many years of study of usages in eighteenth-century political writings. I have been given informative suggestions on earlier usages by my colleague, Professor Michael Mendle.

[7] E. James Ferguson, "The Nationalists of 1781–1783 and the Economic Interpretation of the Constitution," in *Journal of American History*, 60:241–261 (1969–1970); Gerald Stourzh, *Alexander Hamilton and the Idea of Republican Government* (Stanford, 1970); J. G. A. Pocock, *The Machiavellian Moment* (Princeton, N.J., 1975), 531; Drew R. McCoy, *The Elusive Republic: Political Economy in Jeffersonian America* (Chapel Hill, 1980), 13–47, 133. The Smith quotation is in the condensed version of *The Wealth of Nations* edited by Bruce Mazlish (Indianapolis, 1961), 15; it is found in Book 1, Chapter 2.

[8] First Letter from Phocion, January 1784, in Syrett, ed., *Papers of Hamilton*, 3:494; Forrest McDonald, *The Presidency of George Washington* (Lawrence, Kansas, 1974), 67.

[9] The Defence of the Funding System, July, 1795, in Syrett, ed., *Papers of Hamilton*, 19:40–41. Regarding Hamilton's growth and maturity in the 1780's, see Forrest McDonald, *Alexander Hamilton: A Biography* (New York, 1979), 49–94.

[10] Hamilton to Laurens, September 11, 1779,

June 30, September 12, 1780, to Robert Troup, April 13, 1795, in Syrett, ed., *Papers of Hamilton*, 2:167, 347, 428, 18:329; Ames to Rufus King, July 15, 1800, in Charles R. King, ed., *The Life and Correspondence of Rufus King*, 3:275–276 (New York, 1894); McDonald, *Hamilton*, 227–230, 237, 243–244, 259, 334–336.

[11] Federalist Number 31, in Syrett, ed., *Papers of Hamilton*, 4:456. Arnhart analyzes this argument in "The Federalist as Aristotelian Rhetoric," 15–16.

[12] *Ibid.*, 17–18; Hamilton to ——— ("Generations of H scholars have not been able to . . . determine its addressee with any certainty." Syrett, ed., *Papers of Hamilton*, 2:234), December 1779, and Federalist 20, in Syrett, ed., *Papers of Hamilton*, 2:242, 4:395. Arnhart (p. 19) points out that Publius uses two kinds of experience, that derived from the study of history and that derived from observation of ongoing affairs. He does not point out—what close analysis of *The Federalist* reveals—that Madison was much more given to citing historical examples, Hamilton to citing current and recent experience.

[13] Julius Goebel, Jr., and others, eds., *The Law Practice of Alexander Hamilton: Documents and Commentary*, 1:3 (New York, 1964); Hamilton's Pay Book notes, 1777, in Syrett, ed., *Papers of Hamilton*, 1:390.

[14] Max Farrand, ed., *Records of the Federal Convention of 1787* (4 vols., New Haven, 1937), 3:89; Opinion on the Constitutionality of an Act to Establish a Bank, February 23, 1791, in Syrett, ed., *Papers of Hamilton*, 8:97–134. Aly comments on Hamilton's practice of ringing the changes on the arguments in his speeches in the New York ratifying convention; *Rhetoric of Hamilton*, 171 and elsewhere.

[15] The quotations in this paragraph are from Hamilton to ——— (see footnote 12 above), December, 1779, and "Report Relative to a Provision for the Support of Public Credit," January 9, 1790, in Syrett, ed., *Papers of Hamilton*, 2:242, 6:97. The generalizations are my own, derived from long study of Hamilton.

[16] Arnhart, "The Federalist as Aristotelian Rhetoric," 22–24.

[17] Hamilton's approach to Washington varied, of course, with the situation, the circumstances, and the vicissitudes of the relationship between the two men. For examples, see McDonald, *Hamilton*, 24, 124, 204, 289–296, and the documents cited therein. Both Aly and Arnhart point out that Hamilton's use of ethical proof was essentially as I have described it.

[18] Arnhart, "The Federalist as Aristotelian Rhetoric," 25–29; Aly, *Rhetoric of Hamilton*, 142–145, 157–158; Federalist numbers 1, 9, 15, 30 and others. For one of Hamilton's many warnings against emotional or ideological attachments to France, see Pacificus No. IV, July 10, 1793, in Syrett, ed., *Papers of Hamilton*, 15:82–86.

[19] The writings referred to may be found *ibid.*, vols. 1, 4, and 5.

[20] Documentation of what follows is to be found in Goebel, ed., *Law Practice of Hamilton*, 1:775–848; the quoted passages are at pages 813, 820–821, and 822.   [XXV, Spring 1981, 114–124]

[27]

Orestes Brownson and the Political Culture of American Democracy

ROBERT EMMET MOFFIT

Robert Emmet Moffit (1946–   ) received a B.S. in political science from La Salle College in Philadelphia, as well as a Richard Weaver fellowship, in 1969; he acquired his M.S. (1971) and Ph.D. (1975) in political science and theory from the University of Arizona. Currently the deputy assistant secretary for legislation in the United States Department of Health and Human Services in Washington, D.C., Moffit has contributed to such journals as The Political Science Reviewer, The Catholic Historical Review, *and* Vital Speeches.

I

The electioneering campaign of 1840, carried on by doggerels, log cabin, and hard cider, by means utterly corrupt and corrupting, disgusted me with democracy as distinguished from constitutional republicanism, destroyed what little confidence I had in popular elections, and made me distrust both the intelligence and the instincts of the masses.[1]

So wrote Orestes Augustus Brownson in his autobiography, *The Convert*, seventeen years after Van Buren's defeat. A once powerful enemy of orthodoxy in politics and religion, Brownson's desertion of the "radical" democratic camp marked a turning point in his fascinating public career. A writer among the first rank of American men of letters, he enjoyed a colorful, though checkered, career

as a controversialist and a journalist. Editor of the famed *Boston Quarterly Review*, he was the most radical of the transcendentalists, a scourge of New England conservatives, and a harbinger of social and economic criticism notoriously similar to that of Karl Marx. No greater loss was to be endured by the proponents of radical democracy in America than the loss of Brownson's brilliant pen.

Brownson's disillusionment with the methods and results of the 1840 election occasioned a reconsideration of the premises of his political thought. Plunging into a study of the classical works of political science and the history and constitutions of ancient and modern states, he forged a comprehensive political theory, featuring continuity and balance, an elaboration of fundamental themes seemingly immune from his notorious changes of political and theological opinion.[2] His theoretical investigations culminated in what is perhaps the most systematic elaboration of political theory by a nineteenth-century American, *The American Republic*, published in 1865.[3]

In *The American Republic*, Brownson sets forth an analysis of the origin and ground of government, a profound discussion of the roots of authority and political obligation, and a meticulous examination of the structure of the American constitutional order. He praises the unique contributions of American Federalism, and suggests means to resolve problems created by the Civil War and Reconstruction compatible with the preservation of the nation's constitutional integrity. But the great question that sustains Brownson's attention, a major theme of much of his writing since the 1840's, was the advance of democracy in America.

The forces of democracy were gathering strength in every quarter of the nation, he observed, like a "silent revolution," perceptibly transforming the character of American political institutions. How was democracy to be understood? Was it simply a means or process of rule whereby the sovereign people of civil society express their will in and through specific constitutional or federal legal forms? Or was it an investiture of absolute power in an amorphous mass outside of the peculiar historical, legal, and political patrimony, a patrimony institutionalized by the Philadelphia Convention of 1787? Did the commitment to the exercise of popular will transcend one's commitment to republican order, leaving the people boundless, free of restraints of any kind?

These and similar questions preoccupied him. But the basic question was not the *form* of rule, the rule of the many as opposed to the rule of the few; and Brownson never, in his long public career, even after the cruel shattering of his lofty

optimism in popular wisdom in 1840, argued for any form of political elitism.[4] Rather, it was the philosophical explanation used in the promotion or defense of democratic processes, and the long-term impact of that exegesis on the political culture, the values and beliefs of the society, that preoccupied him with the democratic tendencies in America. Political history was determined by ideas, and not simply by institutional arrangements.

Brownson composed his *American Republic* during the Civil War. He viewed it as a personal contribution to the Union cause and a guideline for statesmen intent upon preserving the special genius of the American constitutional order amidst the pressures and passions of war. One of the remarkable features of the treatise was his interpretation of the great struggle as the culmination of a deep cultural conflict between opposite tendencies in the North and the South, a theme later developed by such writers as W. J. Cash and Richard Weaver.

He saw the South as the land of hearty yeoman individualists. Blessed with a natural leadership in peace and war, they were sons of the soil; their gentry resembled that of the old European feudal order. The culture of the antebellum South was unfriendly to innovations that might disturb the long-established prejudices and customs of the region. Values were generally nonmaterialistic, basically religious, and unapologetically hierarchical. Southern leadership was prone to put much stock in personal relations, surely far more than in legal or commercial relations. Personal honor ranked high among the manly virtues. There did exist a distinct complex of common understandings, a Southern "way of life." In defense of this, the white South waged war.

The North, on the other hand, was a land of great contrasts, a center of bustling industrial enterprise. The social and eco-nomic structure was equally hierarchical, but the relationship among men was not that of either personal service or the recognition of social or cultural superi-ority, but that of the cold and impersonal "cash nexus." Financial and commercial "aristocracies" entrenched themselves largely through securing legislation pro-tective of their special interests. Northern class conflict was real, and social divisions could be healed only through legislation that would break the power of special interests. Brownson's constant champi-onship of free trade was motivated by his desire to assure the poorer classes greater access to goods and services at market prices.[5] Always sympathetic with the in-terests of "the poorer and more numer-ous" classes, he nevertheless came to de-spise the socialists and the communists even more than the business interests favorable to protectionism or inflationary economic expansion. Want, misery, and barbarism were the ends of the communist experiment. "Communism, if it could be carried out, would not, then, as the com-munists dream, secure to all the advan-tages of wealth, but would result in the reduction of all to the most abject pov-erty—the very thing which they are ready to commit any crime or sacrilege in order to escape."[6]

Even more important than the social and political divisions within Northern industrial society was the prevalent cul-tural orientation. Values reflected the dy-namism of that society, which was a source of both its strength and its weakness. In contrast to the South, there reigned an unquenchable thirst for change and in-novation, a materialistic world view largely generated by the insecurity that accom-panies a rapidly industrializing economy, and an almost instinctive inclination to egalitarianism in theory if not in practice. Religion was quite elastic, easily trans-formed into a secularized philanthropy, and often accompanied by a lachrymose sentimentality.

The cultural and the intellectual lead-ership of Northern industrial society was to be found in New England. The children of the Puritan fathers exhibited the very best and the very worst traits of Yankee civilization: "The New Englander has ex-cellent points, but is restless in body and mind, always scheming, always in motion, never satisfied with what he has, and always seeking to make the world like himself, or as uneasy as himself. He is smart, seldom great; educated, but seldom learned; active in mind, but rarely a pro-found thinker; religious, but thoroughly materialistic: his worship is rendered in a temple founded on Mammon, and he expects to be carried to heaven in a softly cushioned railway car, with his sins care-fully checked and deposited in the bag-gage crate with his other luggage, to be duly delivered when he has reached his destination. He is philanthropic, but makes his philanthropy his excuse for meddling with everybody's business as if it were his own, and under pretence of promoting religion and morality, he wars against every generous and natural instinct, and aggravates the very evils he seeks to cure. He has his use in the community; but a whole nation of such as he would be short-lived, and resemble the community of the lost rather than that of the blest. The Puritan is a reformer by nature, but he never understands the true law of prog-ress, and never has the patience to wait till the reform he wishes for can be prac-tically effected. He is too impatient for the end ever to wait the slow operations of the means, and defeats his own purpose by his inconsiderate haste. He needs the slower, the more deliberate, and the more patient and enduring man of the South to serve as his counterpoise."[7]

These two competing cultural patterns

gave rise to two different conceptions of democracy in America. The democracy of the South Brownson labeled "personal democracy." It was essentially the democracy of American individualism, tracing its heritage in political theory back to the sophisticated rationalism of Thomas Jefferson, and yet further, to Master John Locke. Within this famous tradition, the primary value in social and political life was individual freedom. Government was understood to be a product of convention; and its purposes were necessarily limited to the stipulations set forth by free and equal individuals in the original compact. Political order was thus an artificial legal structure within which the individualist could pursue his rational self-interest, developing his personality according to his own lights. Society was to be liberated from artificial encumbrances. Social relationships were naturally superior to political relationships; for the political existed for the social, and not the social for the political, as among the ancient Greeks. Men were to be protected from pesty political incursions into their personal affairs, for such interventions did little more than retard the multidimensional progress of social and personal life.

The state in "personal democracy" was a voluntary association in which each of its constituent parts remained free and equal. Founded either actually or hypothetically in compact, government had no authority but that originally ceded to it, or otherwise derived from the "consent of the governed."

Brownson keenly observed the paradoxical fact that the high political leadership of the South, the representatives of an essentially illiberal social and political order, adroitly employed the tenets of eighteenth-century liberal compact theory in defense of "States' Rights." The American mind had been long since liberated from the bondage of classical thought, especially in reference to the nature and origin of the state. Neither the metaphysics of Greece nor the historical nationalism of men such as Burke accounted for much in the high counsels of the Republic. Chief theoretician of the Southern cause, John C. Calhoun, a gentleman for whom Brownson retained the highest admiration, knew that the logic of the Southern position, grounded in the premises of the vast majority of his countrymen, was impregnable. Liberal political theory made eminent good sense; men compact to form the state; men of the various states compact to form the Union. The Union was thus genetically dependent upon the agreement of the *sovereign* states, states united to protect their territorial integrity, welfare and prosperity. At the point at which their welfare was either injured or threatened by continued participation in membership, the states—as sovereign or supreme unto themselves—could simply withdraw. Liberal political theory, thought Brownson, naturally broke the bonds of the Union. Secession was logical, theoretically coherent, and perfectly legitimate on the premises of conventionalism and state sovereignty.

The sociological foundation of "personal democracy," the democracy of the South, was the slave-holding aristocracy. The social structure of the South fostered a sense of personal power among the ruling class, the landed aristocracy, unmatched anywhere else in the nation, except perhaps among "border ruffians" or "wild frontiersmen." Every lord of the plantation, every landed master, had ample reason to believe he was a power unto himself, and carried about a fierce sense of independence "in his breast."[8]

The Southerner was right, Brownson agreed, in affirming the inescapable truth of human personality, but his fierce individualism blinded him to the equally inescapable truth of the "solidarity of the race."[9] His observations on the real character of Southern political thought, not mere theorizing, brought him to this conclusion. Had not Calhoun, in his famous *Disquisition*, declared forthrightly that few people were entitled to liberty? Not the ignorant, the degraded, those incapable of either understanding or appreciating liberty, but only the intelligent, the patriotic, the virtuous, and the deserving had just claims to the blessings of liberty. Such rationalizations found wide appeal. For the Southerner rights and duties were preeminently personal. He understood not the abstract rights of man, but only the concrete "rights of men." Political authority itself was too often perceived as the right of those who could assert and maintain it; liberty was all too often reduced to a Hobbesian exercise of raw, personal power. The particular was everything; the abstract nothing. Black slavery in the South was predicated on the theoretical and the practical exclusion of the Negro people from the human race.

No doctrine, no matter how erroneous, was without an admixture of truth. Southern "personal democracy" was no exception. In spite of its minimization or denial of the "solidarity of the race," the "personal democracy" of the South was a positive force for strengthening individual freedom, local independence, and diversity within the constitutional order of the United States.

Southern "personal democracy," once such a powerful ideological force in the august councils of the Republic, so eloquently expounded by luminaries such as Jefferson, Taylor of Caroline, Randolph of Roanoke, and John C. Calhoun of South Carolina, suffered decisive defeat in American political culture with the fall of the Confederacy. Surviving among small groups of disaffected individualists, it was never more to recover its former strength

and dignity in American political life. The age of hearty, yeoman individualism and state sovereignty was gone forever. It had died with the collapse of the valiant armies of the Confederacy.

II

Brownson wrote to Senator Charles Sumner in February, 1863: "We are now in the crisis of our future, and are more in need of statesmanship than generalship, though much we need of both."[10] The centralizing pressures of war rose like extraordinary tides, and threatened to engulf and wash away the American constitutional order. Southern "personal democracy" had aggressive champions, bent upon extending the evil institution of slavery into the territories. The political theory of "personalist democracy," as interpreted in the South, had threatened the Union. Now, with the recession of the Southern threat, as he remarked to Horace Greeley, there arose another danger to the American constitutional order: an enthusiasm for moral and political regeneration in the form of "humanitarian democracy."

"Humanitarian democracy" was the democracy of the North. Anti-individualistic, with a decided tendency to exaggerate the social element at the expense of individual rights and prerogatives, the "humanitarian democrat" was prone to overlook traditional distinctions and political forms. Longing for a return to affective community, motivated by a sentimental idealism peculiar to rapidly changing industrial civilization, the "humanitarian democrat" fixes his attention almost exclusively on the "solidarity of the race," thus rushing in the direction opposite that of the Southern "personalist democrat." The humanitarian imagines the birth of a new community, practically realized through socialistic reform measures; he envisions a new brotherhood of men based upon the "solidarity" or the unity of the human race. Where the "personalist democracy" of the South was individualistic, empirically oriented, and supportive of variety in social, cultural, and political life, the "humanitarian democracy" of the North was suffused with a vague, alluring ideal of a future egalitarian community. Victims of an enthralling vision, particularity, individuality, geographical or territorial divisions or cultural distinctions are to be sacrificed directly to the higher ideal of egalitarian community. For the humanitarian of the North these elements of concrete social and political reality constitute at least an annoyance, at worst a mortally sinful obstruction of high-minded Yankee idealism.

The new Northern democrats tended towards radicalism, and found an outlet for their moral crusades in the radical wing of the Republican Party. Their politics was of the "rationalist" or "metaphysical" sort. Brownson knew this exaggerated "metaphysicalism" was not so much the product of rigorous, disciplined philosophical cogitation, as of a sentimental preoccupation with pleasant abstractions. So long enamored of elaborate systems of thought, especially those transported from Europe, Brownson himself was supremely conscious of the pervasive disinterest in higher philosophy among his fellow American intellectuals, noting well their earthy pragmatism and sublimation of "common sense."[11] But this characteristic practicality of American thought in no way dampened the adolescent enthusiasm among Northern intellectuals for novel social and political schemes.

Unity was an *idée fixe* among "humanitarian democrats." They were obsessed with the ideal of humanity united by the principle of equality in a new fraternal community. Though a vague notion, it invariably generated a gushing sentimentality, elevating the most dedicated visionaries to new heights of moral and emotional intensity. "The humanitarian is carried away by a vague generality, and loses men in humanity, sacrifices the rights of men in a vain endeavor to secure the rights of man, as your Calvinist or his brother Jansenist sacrifices the rights of nature in order to secure the freedom of grace."[12] The egalitarian vision, then, was the source of rapture, the origin and end, the motivating force of the humanitarian enterprise. But vision alone has an ontological status akin to products of the imagination. In the attempt to realize the vision, the humanitarian must negate reality itself, sacrificing as Brownson remarks, the concrete rights of men to the abstract Rights of Man. He sacrifices the empirical for the ideal, the particular for the general, the person for the race, the present for an imaginary future. Feverish and evangelical, his political crusades constitute a war on the order of being, a metaphysical assault on reality itself:

> Individuals are, and as long as there are individuals will be, unequal: some are handsomer and some are uglier, some wiser or sillier, more or less gifted, stronger or weaker, taller or shorter, stouter or thinner than others, and therefore some have natural advantages which others have not. There is inequality, therefore injustice, which can be remedied only by the abolition of all individualities, and the reduction of all individuals to the race, or humanity, man in general. He can find no limit to his agitation this side of vague generality, which is no reality, but a pure nullity, for he respects no territorial or individual circumscriptions, and must regard creation itself as a blunder. This is not fancy, for he has gone very nearly as far as it is here shown, if logical, he must go.[13]

The frenetic reformist politics of the humanitarian is grounded in a distorted psychology and a false ontology. Neither idealism nor metaphysics is itself at fault. The politics of Orestes Brownson, though similar in emphasizing the historical evolution of the state, is not the politics of a Burkean, one pained by the very sound of metaphysical abstractions. Political reformers are not wrong in asserting metaphysics as the basis of a sound politics, but only in asserting the wrong metaphysics. Platonism, Manicheanism, and Calvinism asserted radical separation between matter and spirit, the realm of the real and the realm of the ideal, the reality of nature and the reality of grace. And the humanitarian follows suit. It is on this crucial point that he is wrong. Reality is not radically disjoined; it is synthetic and dialectic; a harmonious balance subsists among distinct, though inseparable, elements.[14] One could not have, or even know for that matter, the ideal without the empirical, nor the general without the particular. One could not assert the race without individuals, nor individuals without the race. Individuality and sociability are two real, vital, and ineluctable elements of the human condition. It is simply bad political theory to sacrifice one to the other. A distorted ontology gives rise to a grotesque politics.

This negation of the individual, the particular, the concrete, borne of a theoretical denial of the duality of human nature, rendered the "humanitarian democracy" so pernicious. Personality was bound to be sacrificed to Moloch-like generalities. Humanitarian political action continuously exalted the social whole at the expense of the individual parts, the collective society over and above the particular persons who necessarily comprise it. The person was subordinate to the mass; his relationship to the society as a whole was that of an inferior to a superior.

It was this principle of subordination that was the defining element of "socialism" for Orestes Brownson. The "human-

itarian democracy" was the American version of "socialist democracy," and, if triumphant, would usher in an era of "social despotism." Socialists wrongly held for the primacy of economics over politics. To the contrary, Brownson affirmed that politics, and beyond that, philosophy and religion, determined economic organization and structure. Socialism was not simply social or political control of the means of production and distribution for the alleged benefit of the commonwealth—though collectivist economic organization logically and naturally follows, but rather, the fundamental assertion of the "rights of society" over and above individual rights and distinctions as a matter of principle.[15]

III

Writing of Brownson's prescient insights into the character of radical, humanitarian or socialist democracy, Russell Kirk observes, "He seems to have been the first writer to describe Marxism as a Christian heresy, a concept since adopted by Christopher Dawson, Arnold Toynbee, and other leaders of Twentieth Century opinion."[16]

Brownson knew that modern, Northern "humanitarian democracy" was ideologically rooted in "liberal" Christian movements and sects, the various reformist elements with which he was intimately familiar as a leader and active participant in the 1830's and 1840's.[17] In particular, he viewed the rise of "humanitarian democracy" towards the middle of the nineteenth century as the logical progression of a secularized New England Calvinism. Northern Protestant Christianity, in New England especially, had weakened its sacral character in excessive concern with the things of the world. Worldliness was replacing the old Puritan Godliness, and social rejuvenation was replacing personal salvation. The root assumption of this embryonic American democratic socialism, as with socialism elsewhere, was that man's good lies in the natural or the temporal, as opposed to the supernatural or the spiritual order, and that this good was unattainable by personal effort.[18]

The New England culture had generated the philanthropic socialism in the process of the evisceration of the Protestant Calvinist religion:

> Veiling itself under Christian forms, attempting to distinguish between Christianity and the church, claiming for itself the authority and immense popularity of the Gospel, denouncing Christianity in the name of Christianity, discarding the Bible in the name of the Bible, and defying God in the name of God, socialism conceals from the undiscriminating multitude its true character, and, appealing to the dominant sentiment of the age and to some of our strongest natural inclinations and passions, it asserts itself with terrific power, and rolls on its career of devastation and death with a force that human beings, in themselves, are impotent to resist. Men are assimilated to it by all the power of their own nature, and by all their reverence for religion. Their very faith and charity are perverted, and their sublimest hopes are made subservient to their basest passions and their most grovelling propensities. Here is the secret of the strength of socialism, and here is the principal source of its danger.[19]

The inefficacy of individual effort to achieve temporal good logically entailed collective or social action, which naturally translated into political action. It was henceforth the duty of the state, or the communion of true believers through the state, to rectify structural evils and secure human goodness. The state was to become the moral enforcer, the agency of a sort of humanitarian inquisition. If the natural inequalities of the extant human condition were the source of intolerable social dislocations, obstructing the realization of the egalitarian community, the future good life, the course of action was eminently clear. The state was charged with abolishing such particularities until the envisioned fraternal unity was achieved.

Where the sociological foundation of "personal democracy" had been the landed aristocracy of the antebellum South, the popular base of the "humanitarian democracy" was New England, among the burgeoning philanthropic and reform movements, zealous to combat real or imagined evils. Private morality was a matter of public concern, and temperance leagues and feminist organizations found little difficulty in recruiting among New Englanders. But the primary engine of "humanitarian democracy" was the Abolitionist movement; for the Abolitionists enlisted the highest humanitarian sentiments in warring against Negro bondage as a crime against humanity itself. Preservation of the constitutional system was subordinate to the goal of ridding the nation of so vile an institution as slavery.

Largely Protestant in composition and spirit, such philanthropic and reform movements naturally gained few adherents among the largely immigrant Catholic populations of the urban industrial North, themselves periodically victims of social ostracism and bigotry. Repelled by the puritanical tone, especially in its secular manifestations, Brownson shrewdly predicted that the urban, immigrant Catholic North would join with the South in opposing such movements. These two diverse elements would provide the sociological, the cultural, and eventually, the political basis of resistance against future humanitarian encroachments upon traditional order. The political culture of the Southern people, rooted in their "habits," "sentiments," and "convictions" was hostile to humanitarian enthusiasms: "They are and always will be an agricultural people, and an agricultural people are and always will be opposed to socialistic dreams, unless unwittingly led for a moment to favor it in pursuit of some special object in which they take a passionate interest."[20] Roman Catholics would oppose the socialistic democracy because ". . . their church everywhere opposes the socialistic movements of the age, all movements in behalf of barbarism, and they may always be counted on to resist the advance of the socialistic democracy."[21]

The nature and scope of "humanitarian democracy" was not simply defined by domestic philanthropic and reform movements. From the ideological wellsprings of the old world came new dissidents, in the aftermath of the 1848 upheavals, chiefly distinguished by a near hysterical hatred of Roman Catholicism and the conservative political establishments of Europe. Jacobinical democrats, "red republicans," and militant secular liberals formed a new, and highly politicized, émigré community.[22] The new Europeans found allies among the domestic philanthropists, and American humanitarians likewise applauded the revolutionary undertakings of European liberals and "red republicans." The influx of the radical émigrés provided a cosmopolitan leaven to domestic humanitarian idealism.

A religious fervor captivated the humanitarians. The social order, like a fallen woman, had to be purified and set aright. The overriding passion for egalitarian social and political unity, manifest in concrete measures to further centralize the American Republic during the Reconstruction era, was reflective of a deep longing for a pious simplicity, a liberation from gaudy rituals or ornamental distinctions, standards, and conventions. Hearkening to pleadings for the integrity of the constitutional powers of the several states was akin to abiding temptation. The Radical Republicans best exemplified the political style of "humanitarian democracy."

To Brownson's mind, the moral fervor underpinning this drive for social salvation was, as previously noted, a secular variant of the stern religious tradition of the New England Calvinists.[23] The imperious Puritan ardor was not lost, only adapted to worldly causes. Prophets of the new secular social order were still called upon to curb lax conduct and fight moral depravity, especially among the unreconstructed remnants of the bad, old, sinful social order. New rules and regulations, no matter how minuscule or pestiferous, were not beyond the pretensions of the custodians of social goodness.

A triumphant "humanitarian democracy," fueled by a puritanical fervor, would end in repression, Brownson believed. Society itself would be reduced to an aesthetic disaster, an ugly, dull, drab, mass conformity. Searching always for a common denominator in human affairs, desperate to realize that tantalizing social unity, the agents of "humanitarian democracy" would smother the richness and the variety of life, the beauties of particularity and diversity, robbing the American Republic of its pleasing and distinctive heterogeneity. That which did not, or could not, conform to the preordained socialistic ideal was doomed to labor under suspicion or the threat of ultimate extinction. While Brownson sharply took issue with the Classical Liberals on the origin and nature of the state, opting instead for the natural law tradition of Aristotle and Aquinas, he nonetheless shared their dread of the Leviathan state. He conceded to no man a greater disdain for agents of mindless conformity and political centralization.

IV

The Northern victory in the Civil War strengthened "humanitarian democracy." Its chief effect on the constitutional system was an unprecedented centralization of the American Republic. Under the pretext of the "war powers," the Lincoln administration expanded the executive prerogatives out of all proportion to the original grant of constitutional authority. Brownson feared that the constitutional system, especially the authority of the several states, would be rapaciously violated by this new growth of untrammeled federal power. Lincoln's seeming ignorance or disregard of constitutional limitations appalled him. "The President is no statesman, is no constitutional scholar, and has no conception of our unique system of government," Brownson hotly warned Senator Charles Sumner.[24] But Sumner's close collaboration during the course of the war was to end with Reconstruction. He came to lead the very political faction which best represented the interests of the "humanitarian democracy," the Radical Republicans. Brownson himself sided with these Republicans in their efforts to assure vigorous prosecution of the war; he broke with them in their efforts to impose a draconian peace.[25]

Black liberation from slavery and the removal of the civil encumbrances of former servitude were to be assured, but not at the price of the peerless American constitutional order, the unique federal system, itself the major bulwark of American liberty.[26] Brownson's commentaries on the constitutional questions surrounding the Civil War and Reconstruction rank him among the most original of American political theorists. But his most penetrating insight into the transitional phase of nineteenth-century intellectual life was his perception of the totalitarian character of political order cut off from a transcendent ground of moral truth. He viewed the Jacobin democracy, socialism, or the triumphant Northern "Humanitarian Democracy" as the germinal carrier of the new absolutist disease.

For the humanitarian radical, man, not God, was the object of religion; the social rather than the supernatural order was the object of missionary zeal. Brownson saw the triumph of this secularism in humanitarian guise as the victory of the Angel of Darkness in the dazzling finery of an Angel of Light. In denying or ignoring the supernatural order, the humanitarian rendered the natural order henceforth supreme; and political man was himself supreme over the natural order. With nothing above himself, man has only himself to whom he can be called accountable. It makes only a procedural difference whether he appeals to majority or minority rule, and nothing more. He can do with himself what he will, setting himself up as the final arbiter of good and evil, life and death. He has absolute freedom; he is his own God.

The problem, of course, is that this imperfect god has pretensions to perfection. Imperfect man strives to act as Perfect God, and, in the process, reduces himself to an agent of misery, oppression, and murder, a being too hideous to behold. For good and evil are abolished, or—what amounts to the same thing— reduced to matters of mere personal opinion. Brownson pondered well Dostoevsky's dictum: if God is not in his Heaven, then all is permitted.

Above all else, Brownson loathed political absolutism. He recognized that "political atheism," the separation of the political life of man from the laws of God, was the necessary precondition of political absolutism. Thus, religion was the very antithesis of political absolutism. Man's relationship to a transcendent God was sacred, not secular; the effect of religion was thus to insulate an activity of the mind and spirit, the inner life of man, his most important life, from the intervention of the state. In that vital respect, the very existence or profession of religion undermines totalitarian claims. The totalitarian claim is rendered impotent against the transcendental ground of conscience. But to deny the transcendental ground of conscience is to leave men at the mercy of history, convention, or whatever else the political chieftains wish to absolutize.

Brownson's startling conversion to Roman Catholicism in 1844, his acceptance of its authoritarian structure, spiritual austerity, discipline, and claim to infallibility in matters of faith and morals, was nothing less than a counterrevolutionary affirmation. He defied all the secularizing tendencies of his age. The Church unapologetically held for the superiority of the supernatural order and the supernatural destiny of man, against which all human actions would be judged. The Church claimed to stand as the divinely authorized, transhistorical bulwark of truth, amidst the fleeting confusions of the world. The Church claimed magisterial authority in the moral life, an authority for prince and pauper alike. This appeal to religious authority and the emphasis on man's transcendental destiny, this defiance of boundless secular authority, was not unlike that of Aleksandr Solzhenitsyn in our own day. For Brownson and Solzhenitsyn, despite radically different personal experiences, both pose the same question for modern men: Is it possible, in the face of the massive power of the modern state, to assert personal liberty without being anti-secularist, or putting the question in institutional terms, to be anti-totalitarian without being pro-clerical?

It must be understood that Brownson's strictures on "humanitarian democracy" did not constitute a condemnation of popular rule. Popular sovereignty, political equality, and majority rule are the three constituent principles of a democratic politics.[27] Brownson was a steadfast proponent of the doctrine of popular sovereignty, but in a distinctly republican sense. He viewed the people of the state, as vested by God through the Natural Law, as the repository of political authority, as opposed to any particular caste or class. Political inequalities he held incompatible

with the special genius of the American people; and for all of his legalistic qualifications, recognized the full enfranchisement of the newly liberated blacks as a natural development of the American idea. He likewise accepted majority rule as the conventional right of the people of the Republic to effect such changes as they deemed necessary or convenient, but only in and through the rule of law and the constitutional order.

It was his great hope that the American Republic could achieve a balance between the native spirit of individuality, so powerful to the South, and human sociability, so exaggerated to the North:

> Its idea is liberty, indeed, but liberty with law, and law with liberty. Yet its mission is not so much the realization of liberty as the realization of the true idea of the state, which secures at once the authority of the public and the freedom of the individual— the sovereignty of the people without social despotism, and individual freedom without anarchy. In other words, its mission is to bring out in its life the dialectic union of authority and liberty, of the natural rights of man and those of society. The Greek and Roman republics asserted the state to the detriment of individual freedom; modern republics either do the same, or assert individual freedom to the detriment of the state. The American Republic has been instituted by Providence to realize the freedom of each with advantage to the other.[28]*

NOTES

[1] Henry F. Brownson (ed.), "The Convert," *Brownson's Works* (New York: AMS Press, 1966), V, p. 120; hereafter cited as *Works*. See also: Brownson, "Democracy and Liberty," *Works*, XV, pp. 258–259.

---

* I should like to acknowledge the kind and generous assistance of Father Thomas Blantz and his staff at the Archives of the University of Notre Dame. Their aid in helping me locate various letters among the *Brownson Papers* greatly facilitated my research into Brownson's political theory.

2 Much has been written on Brownson's notorious ideological instability, his propensity for change and shifting allegiances. Recent scholarship, happily, has more closely scrutinized the conventional "instability thesis," emphasizing the continuity and the developmental character of Brownson's thought. See, in particular, Per Sveino, *Orestes Brownson's Road to Catholicism* (New York: The Humanities Press, 1970); Hugh Marshall, *Orestes Brownson and the American Republic* (Washington: Catholic University Press, 1971); Leonard Gilhooley, *Contradiction and Dilemma: Orestes Brownson and the American Idea* (New York: Fordham University Press, 1972); and Thomas R. Ryan, *Orestes Brownson* (Huntington, Indiana: Our Sunday Visitor Press, 1976). Perhaps no better insight into the course of Brownson's thought has been made than that of William Ellery Channing, Brownson's contemporary and the esteemed Unitarian minister of Boston. In commenting upon a recent publication, Channing wrote: ". . . I am disposed to look upon your changes not as fluctuating, but as steps of rational progress, and I wish you joy in your consummation." Channing to Brownson, June 10, 1842. *Orestes Augustus Brownson Papers*, University of Notre Dame Archives, Notre Dame, Indiana, Folder I-3.f., Correspondence 1841–42; hereafted cited as *Brownson Papers*.

3 The classic work has recently been republished. Americo Lapati has brought out an annotated edition for the College and University Press of New Haven in 1972. Augustus Kelley Company has reprinted the work in a facsimile edition. High praise for the treatise has been expressed by a great number of outstanding scholars in the field of American political thought including Woodrow Wilson, Arthur M. Schlesinger, Jr., Edward R. Lewis, Charles Merriam, Ralph Gabriel, Francis Graham Wilson, and Russell Kirk.

4 Brownson strongly believed in the social value and utility of a class of "first families," an established leadership of virtue, talent, and manners, to set the right tone for the social order. But neither social value nor utility logically entitled any elite to exercise political authority, or the ethical right to rule. His mature thought was decidedly anti-elitist. As he observed in the *American Republic*, aristocracies tend to their own interest before that of the commonwealth: "I have ranked feudalism under the head of barbarism, rejected every species of political aristocracy, and represented the English Constitution as essentially antagonistic to the American, not as its type." *American Republic* (New York: P. O'Shea, 1865), p. xi.

5 The use of government by financial, banking, or corporate interests to better their position at the expense of consumers, especially the poorer classes, was a practice that continuously agitated him as a radical, a democrat, a constitutionalist, and a conservative. He was unsparing in his attacks. Early in his career, Horace Greeley was moved to complain: "We of the Protective School contend that we are not understood, at any rate not fairly presented by your side of the house. You invariably present us as advocative of local against universal interests, which we deny." Greeley to Brownson, June 16, 1843. *Brownson Papers*, Folder I-3.g., Correspondence 1843–1844.

6 Brownson, "The Democratic Principles," *Works*, XVIII, p. 237.

7 Brownson, "Liberalism and Progress," *Works*, XX, p. 346.

8 Brownson, *American Republic*, p. 351.

9 *Ibid.*, p. 353.

10 Brownson to Sumner, February 1863. *Brownson Papers*, Folder I-4.b., Correspondence 1863.

11 The similarity between his views and those of Alexis de Tocqueville on the style of American thinking are striking. In correspondence with the great French metaphysician Victor Cousin, he remarked: "We have but few scholars, and these are rarely lovers of philosophy. We have been in the habit of sneering at metaphysics and praising common sense." Brownson to Cousin, September 6, 1839. *Brownson Papers*, Folder I-3.e., Correspondence 1823–1840. He expressed impatience with the American neglect of "first principles," especially in political theory, throughout his public career.

12 Brownson, *American Republic*, p. 363.

13 *Ibid.*, pp. 364–65.

14 This so-called "synthetic philosophy," largely developed through the influence of French philosophy, especially that of Cousin and Pierre Leroux, remained the cornerstone of Brownson's thought from 1842 until his death in 1876. His metaphysics was the key to a correct understanding of his political theory. This fact he acknowledged in an essay on the American constitutional system: "It will be seen from what we have said that the Constitution of the United States, or, as we prefer to say, the American State, is profoundly philosophical, and accords perfectly with that synthetic philosophy which we have for years defended. We even doubt, if we had not found in that philosophy a key to it, we should ever have been able to fully understand it." Brownson, "The Federal Constitution," *Works*, XVII, p. 499.

15 Brownson, *American Republic*, p. 355.

16 Russell Kirk (ed.), *Orestes Brownson: Selected Essays* (Chicago: Gateway Editions, 1955), p. 9.

17 "Affecting to be Christian, these advocates invoke the name of Jesus and appeal to Holy Scripture, the text to which, with a perverse ingenuity, they accommodate to their socialistic purpose. May Al-

mighty God forgive us the share we had in propagating what we called the *Democracy of Christianity!* We have nothing to palliate our offence or to hide our shame; for if we knew no better at the time, we might have known better, and our ignorance was culpable. All we can say is, we followed the dominant sentiment of the age, which is a poor excuse for one who professed to be a preacher of the Gospel." Brownson, "Socialism and the Church," *Works*, X, pp. 91–92.

[18] *Ibid.*, p. 95.

[19] *Ibid.*, p. 92.

[20] Brownson, *American Republic*, p. 376.

[21] *Ibid.*, p. 379.

[22] Brownson, "The Native Americans," *Works*, XVIII, p. 292; see also, "What the Rebellion Teaches," *Works*, XVII, pp. 282–283.

[23] Jacobinism is Calvinism, without its long face, pious garb, and guttural tone. . . ," Brownson told his son Henry, in a letter dated November 12, 1870. Henry F. Brownson, *Latter Life* (Detroit: Henry F. Brownson Publisher, 1900), pp. 493–494.

[24] Brownson to Sumner, February 1863. *Brownson Papers*, I-4.f., Correspondence 1863.

[25] "The government is strong enough to afford to be generous and severity would now be only a proof of weakness or cowardice. The honor of our country is at stake." Brownson to Horace Greeley, June 4, 1865. *Brownson Papers*, I-4.c., Correspondence 1864–66.

[26] It was a view from which he never deviated, a continuous theme on the issues of slavery and race from the 1840's through the Reconstruction era. "With me, I own, the Negro holds only a subordinate position, and I am more interested in maintaining our marvelous political system than I am in securing the Negro equality." Brownson to an unidentified Member of Congress, 1865. *Brownson Papers*, I-4.c., Correspondence 1864–66.

[27] *Cf.* Currin V. Shields, *Democracy and Catholicism in America* (New York: McGraw-Hill Company, 1958).

[28] Brownson, *American Republic,* p. 5.

[XXII, Summer 1978, 265–276]

[28]

They Took Their Stand:
The Agrarian View After Fifty Years

ANDREW LYTLE

Andrew (Nelson) Lytle *(1902–   ), longtime distinguished editor of* The Sewanee Review *and professor of English at the University of the South and at Vanderbilt, has been prominent in American letters for some fifty years. Born in Murfreesboro, Tennessee, he had a varied education: the Sewanee Military Academy, Vanderbilt University, a year of study in France, and two years of graduate work at the Yale School of Drama. He even briefly considered making the theater his career, writing several plays and acting professionally in New York. Farmer, novelist, poet, and stylist, he is one of the last of the Southern Agrarian movement. He now resides in retirement in Monteagle, Tennessee. His article is based on "The South and American Conservatism," presented to the Philadelphia Society meeting held in New Orleans in October 1979.*

THIS TITLE IS for me ambiguous. Of the twelve agrarians who wrote the symposium *I'll Take My Stand*, only three are alive: Robert Penn Warren, the poet and novelist; Lyle Lanier, a psychologist and former executive vice-president of the University of Illinois; and myself, a writer and reader of fiction. I don't presume to speak for either Warren or Lanier, and I don't know how to address myself to myself in the past tense. Perhaps I am not here at all. Secretly I've had the feeling I was killed at the Battle of Brice's Cross-Roads, taking the bullet meant for General Forrest. You understand it was Forrest who, if he'd been let, could have been decisive in winning the war of the Northern Rebellion. Too often Confederate forces won the field only to retreat later on. Brice's Cross-Roads, fought in Mississippi, was a perfect battle. It should be an example of such in the textbooks of war colleges. Forrest combined his forces at the right time, defeated an enemy with odds of two to one against him, and then pursued the enemy and drove him out of the state—not to speak of the seizure of supplies, which was large. So perhaps it will be all right to speak of myself in the third person, along with my companions in arms who must of necessity be so addressed, if what you see here is not me but my ghostly presence. But if I am a ghost, what are you?

And what then are all those good men and true who find their beliefs disembodied? For as there is God, no idea, principle or belief is ever defeated. Men are. Except

345

those men who continue to believe and take the proper risks. I cite you Thermopylae. As military science and tactics are never either defensive or offensive but both, so no surrender need be final, not even unconditional surrender. There was a moment when the agrarians thought this, a particular moment when the country suffered the 1929 stock-market crash. The book coming out after that made us seem prophets. We did not so see ourselves in the writing of it. None of us was a politician or intended, I think, any pragmatic action. We were protesting an unhappy condition of Southern affairs and a continuing conquest. Today it is clear to me, at least, that we were better prophets than we knew. I don't feel that any of us at the time could have imagined that the conditions we protested could become so rapidly worsened.

So, after the crash, for a while at least, we had hopes of making the word flesh. It was a lot of fun. We addressed one another as generals, I hope you understand facetiously but not entirely. The depression was upon us, and it was heavy. People were stealing corn in broad-open daylight, and my father turned his head. I know of a fireman in Trenton, New Jersey, who rode his bicycle into the country and stole apples to keep his family from starving. William Dodd, historian and ambassador to Germany, tried to persuade Roosevelt that he might do well to listen to what the agrarians had to say. He got the dollar-a-year men. I spoke to Senator Bankhead. All he could come up with was forty acres and a mule. (There were mules then. They are curiosities now.)

Before I go on, I must remind myself how pervasive was a growing acceptance of the new materialism we attacked as industrialism. The South had prospered during the First World War. In the euphoria of victory there was a general

feeling that we were back in the Union. The New South propaganda of progress everywhere said as much, and most of the media of news and public information took it for granted. Farming was looked down upon. Tired of poverty and honest work, the young began to desert the land and go to town, and in town the ambitious youth took the train to New York City, as did many young men from the West. The educational world began to change its curricula. The Chancellor of Vanderbilt University announced at a crucial moment of an agrarian fight that he wanted to graduate bankers, not writers or farmers. Rumor had it that the English building, ordered by him, was to be as much like a factory as possible, and the architect obliged. It was not the Church's Thanksgiving that we chanted. A New England holiday was universally celebrated as the national Thanksgiving. This salvation of the Puritan fathers after their hard winter was instilled into the minds of Southern children as the salvation of their founding fathers. One of my projects in kindergarten was cutting out and painting turkeys and tall-hatted men with bibs to paste in front of a log cabin made out of twigs. At home *Uncle Remus* was read to me, but in public it was John Alden, why don't you speak for yourself, John? that we were read. We were not told that Captain John Smith, sailing the Atlantic coast, brought smallpox to the Indians at Plymouth and so let the Puritans land in safety. Always it was the New England story which concerned the genesis of the nation. Not the other John, John Rolfe, who courted the Indian maiden, Pocahontas. Their subsequent marriage made an elevating and romantic story of amity between races. No teacher knew enough to reveal the historic meaning of this incident. It was the first instance recorded in English of the Indian woman's preference for the European. The betrayal of her tribe for the white man's favors was a constant element in the pattern of Indian defeat. Nancy Ward, a beloved woman of the Cherokees, saw nothing wrong in sitting in council while living with one of the enemy. Her betrayal indicates the complexity of the Indian mind, for she never left the council and remained beloved and respected.

Whoever wins an internecine war writes the history of that war. And the textbooks as well. Lost in diaries and obscure histories, there yet survived many stories about the settlements in Middle Tennessee, both of Indians and of Americans, which would have told our young of stamina and courage. The attack on the stations around Nashville, the skillet and the kettle at a bend in the Tennessee River, or an account of that one man Spencer who lived in the arm of a hollow sycamore, alone during the hardest winter that country had known, with only half a skinning knife for protection and food. It must have been some tree, for he was so big a man that a French trader, seeing his footprints, jumped into the Cumberland River and swam away. He thought he was fleeing a monstrous bear. Later at a militia muster Spencer intervened between two young men who were fighting. One tried to get rough with him, whereupon he picked him up and threw him over the nine-foot fence surrounding the stockade. The man called back, "If you will just throw my horse over, Mister Spencer, I'll be getting on my way." There are a number of these tales which, along with more formal documents, carry the truth about a history, the quality of a tradition.

It was not long before some of us, at least, suffered a disillusionment: it was not clear that we were back in the Union. There were two incidents which had a good deal to do with this; at least they gave some propulsion to reforming our opinions and informing our judgments. One was the Dayton or Monkey trial in Tennessee. The trial concerned a law forbidding the teaching of evolution in the schools of the state. This law was loudly proclaimed as an attack on academic freedom. Almost alone at Vanderbilt, our philosophy professor, Dr. Herbert Sanborn, a New Englander, exposed the fallacies in scientism's argument. I first met Allen Tate in New York City. We at once began discussing the trial as a liberal attack on our traditional inheritance. Now I see it as an advanced phase of Reconstruction. Maybe they are one and the same thing. After the economic exploitation of the South, this religious attack on the Southern spirit seemed to have a double purpose: to denigrate us before the country and the world and to make us laughable as backward and ignorant. But the real aim was more insidious, a forced acceptance of belief in a secular instead of a divine order of the universe. Practically this would have meant a total, instead of an economic, dominance by the Northeast. But the soul is not so easily traduced, especially of a people who live by or close to the land. These people are religious by nature because they enjoy and suffer nature, or they starve. Of course the defense at Dayton was inadequate, depending as it did upon a strict construction of the Bible with its literal fallacy. But the Liberal attack was equally fallacious, that scientism (there is not science, only sciences) was the only truth about man and nature. Along with the Monkey trial came H. L. Mencken's journalistic description of the South as "the Sahara of the Bozarts." This is like the thief who robs a house the second time and complains that the owners do not eat with silver.

How far such calumnies influenced the twelve I won't try to say, except for myself. One of the dangers of this kind of a discussion is inflicting your own responses upon your fellows, who certainly spoke for themselves. It set me to studying American and Southern history, about which I knew little to nothing. I kept at it for seven years, with Frank Owsley to guide me. One of our professional historians, Owsley's life work was to replace biased or inaccurate accounts with the truth. Soon Tate was writing the biographies of Stonewall Jackson and Jefferson Davis, and Warren a biography of John Brown. I was at work on Forrest. At any rate all the writers were Southern and most of them, by accident, were associated with Vanderbilt University. These men were already known or were to become distinguished in their proper occupations, whether it was history or psychology or literature. Their agrarian writings merely displayed their common cultural inheritance, which was Christian and European. Let me quote a paragraph from the statement of principles in the Introduction to *I'll Take My Stand:*

> Opposed to the industrial society is the agrarian, which does not stand in particular need of definition. An agrarian society is hardly one that has no use at all for industries, for professional vocations, for scholars and artists, and for the life of cities. Technically, perhaps, an agrarian society is one in which agriculture is the leading vocation, whether for wealth, for pleasure, or for prestige—a form of labor that is pursued with intelligence and leisure, and that becomes the model to which the other forms approach as well as they may.

Surely, then, it must be taken that a poet, a farmer, a banker, a historian, a schoolteacher, must live in a certain place and time and so exhibit the kind of belief and behavior defined by the manners and mores of that time and place. It was not necessary to be a farmer to be agrarian. It was merely the basic occupation of a commodity-producing society. The Lib-

eral cartoons attacking us showed us with our heads under a mule's tail, or a lone privy, or Necessary as George Washington called it, with a half moon cut over the door and the door closed. It left to the imagination what was behind the door. Allen Tate remarked that he preferred an indoor commode so long as he didn't have to kneel down and worship it before using it.

Only the Liberal mind could confuse equipment with the thing itself, but then the Liberal is always promising to relieve us of our common ills at somebody else's expense. He is the propagandist of the power we opposed. It is an old fight and the agrarians were not the first to enter it. This is no time to reargue the case. The books are there to be read, and read in light of our present circumstances. I do want to emphasize that agrarianism was not an effort to reconstitute an ideal state, a utopia, unless, in the sense of Sir Thomas More's utopia, an allegory criticizing his king's English and European policies. An outright statement would have lost him his head much earlier. The agrarian effort was towards the preservation of an inherited way of life, a way which was threatened but still in existence. I said it was an old fight. Napoleon tried to restore the legitimacy of kingship, but London, the center of international banking, defeated him. At St. Helena, he told Las Cases, "Agriculture is the soul, the foundation of the Kingdom; industry ministers to the comfort and happiness of the population. Foreign trade is the superabundance; it allows of the due exchange of the surplus of agriculture and home industry; these last ought never to be subordinate to foreign trade." This country's policy has reversed the order: foreign trade first, industry, agriculture a poor third. Each day news reports witness to the folly of this order.

Shortly after the American Revolution

the cogent opponent to what he called the paper and patronage aristocracy was John Taylor of Caroline County, Virginia. His question was: Why set up in this country the same power we fought a war to be free of? He was speaking against banking and central government. He was a Jeffersonian but more agrarian and more lucid than Jefferson. He refused to put any hope in men themselves, but always in principles. In 1813 he published *Arator*, a collection of essays on farming and politics. The thesis was this: agriculture and politics are the sources of wealth and power. Both contain good internal principles, but both are subject to practical deterioration. If agriculture is good and the government bad, we may have wealth and slavery. If the government is good and agriculture bad, liberty and poverty. We must remember that at this date nearly ninety percent of the American population made its living by or on the land. From 1940 to 1974, the number of farms in the U.S. declined from approximately six million to a little over two million, 62 percent of our family units. Since the Second World War, thirty-million people have left the country for the city. You don't need more than one wrong idea to destroy a state.

I am not talking from statistics, but this great acceleration of such widespread loss of farms and families sustains my argument, which is this: at the time we wrote there were enough families living on the land and enough privately owned businesses in small towns and cities to counterbalance the great industrial might, which was a fact and had to be reckoned with. If our proposal had been listened to, this necessary industry might have been contained, might not have grown into the only idea of the kind of life everybody must be forced to accept. A family, and I mean its kin and connections, too, thrives best on some fixed location which holds the memories of past generations by the ownership of farms or even family businesses. Not only sentimental memories but skills passed down and a knowledge of the earth tended. And a knowledge particularly of the bloodstreams, so as to be warned and prepared for what to expect in behavior. Industry today uproots. It's like the army without having the army's raison d'être. Promotion, except among the basic workers, means pulling up roots and being sent elsewhere, with the promise of a better car and another room to the house. The children, just as they are making friends and getting used to school, must begin all over again. This is a modification of the Spartan state, which reduced the family to a minimal role.

The most irresponsible of our critics accused us of the self-indulgence of nostalgia, of foisting on our readers a myth, and by myth was meant something that never existed. All societies are sustained by a myth. Such a myth is of necessity metaphysical, but it was not this kind of myth the critic had in mind. He had mischosen his word. He meant fantasy, something that had no grounding in fact. It was unfortunate for this kind of argument that many of us were historians, and in Frank Owsley we had the best of professional historians. I speak of Owsley rather than Nixon because it was he and his wife, Harriet, who exposed the alien "myths" about the South—that it was composed of large plantations with Old Marster sipping juleps while the slaves sang; and on the fringe were the one-bale (if that) cotton farmers called "poor whites." He simply went to the census records where the facts were. Also to diaries and county records, but the federal census carried particular authority. One instance of this: Presumably the black-belt counties would be the area of the large plantations. Now the census taker went down the road, stopping in order at this farm and that, as he went along. The Owsleys discovered the greatest diversity in ownership, large plantations by moderate-size farms, small farms, a plantation of two-thousand acres with no slaves, a man owning slaves and no land. I won't go on, as the authority is here to correct or amplify me, if she so wills. You see the South was never solid until after the war. Defeat made it solid.

The misunderstanding, even among the most sympathetic critics, like Louis Rubin, have assumed that a commodity-producing society, such as the South and West, had not a chance of sustaining itself before the successive triumphs of the financial corporate role of money. And this kind of money is always international. They were vague about this corporate rule, but they accepted as absolute the *ex post facto* assumption of the relative poverty of the Southern farm and its ultimate doom. The confusion lies just here. The communities composed of families with real property and private businesses still existed. The fight was on, but the outcome was uncertain. The depression was a heavy blow. Cotton cost seven cents a pound to grow and it brought, on what is essentially the world market, five cents. The only answer Roosevelt's government could give was plow under a fourth of your labor, cotton, corn, hogs, and cattle. This is the most immoral fiat ever handed down from afar: destroy your handicrafts and life for an abstract stock-market purpose. Where was the Joseph to talk of lean and fat years, store away instead of destroy.

The communities were the shape of society, even after the First World War. I was there. I lived in them. Most of the towns in the South, and cities, too, lived by the country. My argument in two essays was this: the small farm upholds the state. I didn't give any number of acres. What I meant was a family-owned and operated place. If the place has no mortgage, you

live in a dwelling-house without paying money for rent. If you plow with a team, you grow your own fuel. You grow most of your food. You do grow crops for money, but you are not completely in the money economy. You live at home with security. And you are part of a living community, with other families in your situation, some better-to-do than others, as will always be the case.

Now witness the county seat. I'm speaking from experience again. All the roads radiating from the seat were privately owned. They had tollgates every five miles, and to pass through cost so much, a buggy, twenty-five cents, so much a head for sheep. I used to go with my father to collect toll, and the money, all coin, would be stacked in order, silver dollars, halves, quarters, on down to dimes and nickels, and they all smelled of snuff. There were very few paper bills. This meant that you didn't leave home idly. You lived in a community with a radius of, say, five miles. This lasted almost until I went to college. The automobile was in its infancy. It was a toy for those who could buy. The ladies wore veils and everybody wore dust-coats when "the machine," as it was called, took you out for a short spin. People would call and ask if you were going to bring it out. It scared their mettlesome carriage horses. And rightly so. It was the horses' doom. But it took some years before it broke up the community. Thirty miles an hour was fast. The roads were not fit for speed. It took the greater part of the day to go from Huntsville, Alabama, to Guntersville, forty miles away. Punctures were frequent, or a mud-hole with brush in it would delay you for maybe an hour, until you could find somebody to hitch up his team and pull you out. Of course unless the team was obviously nearby and the hand out. My father had a Ford tractor. It could break four acres a day, but so could a good team. He used it for disking, as broken ground is hard on animals. This was for Cornsilk, a twelve-hundred-acre place, which the T.V.A. stole and covered up with water.

This family farm I talked about earlier (here I am not referring to Cornsilk) was dismissed as a "subsistence farm." In the first place, there is no such thing as a subsistence farm. That is an adjective used by a voice who thinks milk comes out of bottles, or a term that applies possibly to land so poor that no insurance company would give it a mortgage. But even land such as this is no subsistence farm. Even this has its place in society. If it has little money and no credit to buy advertised products, it still has a life of its own. When the T.V.A. began to build all those dams, making of the best land a permanent flood to control floods, it had to buy a little place near Muscle Shoals. This place was so poor it had no mortgage against it, but the shack did have a chimney whose fire had not gone out in a hundred years. "Eminent domain" or not, the T.V.A. had to move that chimney, the coals covered and hot, to its new location. The point is not that the move cost more than the price of the farm. The point is that from the mirage of history, fire on the hearth has been the symbol of the home. Neolithic man "identified the column of smoke that rose from his hearth to disappear from view through a hole in the roof with the Axis of the Universe, saw in this luffer [*i.e.,* louver] an image of the Heavenly door, and in his hearth the Navel of the Earth." The man who cherished that chimney and forced a sovereign power to preserve it was not a man who thought much of comfort, that euphemism which disguises the perfidious intention of turning man into an appetite, to be perpetually bloated by some new appeal of an expanding economy, expanding until the resources on the earth and beneath it are exhausted.

In 1928, Allen Tate, his wife, and child, and I travelled in a secondhand Ford from New York to Alabama, going over the battlefields. There were no Interstates (maybe the Pennsylvania Turnpike), but many narrow paved roads and roads with gravel, all rough in places. The outskirts of Philadelphia ended easily in the country, with its farms—and not just Amish either. (Today, from Trenton to Philadelphia there is a flow of houses which obliterates the state lines, and at night becomes one long blur of light.) Through Maryland into Virginia we camped by the side of the road or in a farmer's lot and picked his turnip greens and cooked them in a pot with sowbelly. I knew how to make a hoecake. The water and greens were free, as was the campground. If we felt we could afford it, we would stop in a village or at some courthouse with buildings about it and eat a lunch for thirty-five cents. If it was forty-five, we might drive on.

There was only one tourist camp the entire way, no buildings but a common washroom and commodes. This was outside Richmond. We pitched our pup tents here. Sometimes we washed and dressed and went into town on invitation, which was always welcome as a change of diet. The night-watchman was the great-nephew of General John Bankhead Magruder, late of the Confederacy. The superintendent was the great-nephew of General A. P. Hill of the Army of Northern Virginia, whose name was called by both Lee and Jackson in their dying speech. This was the familiar world all of us were born in, and I hope I am making it clear that now I am not speaking only of the Southern terrain.

Later, I went on alone to Mississippi, where Forrest often rode. I can't believe it had changed much from war days. Going through the backcountry to Tupelo, I stopped to inquire the way. Teams were hitched about the courthouse fence; a political meeting was afoot. The patriarchs, in black hats and with white beards, sat on the platform with their hands on hickory sticks. It was obvious that little of folly would take place in their presence. I was asked to "take-out" and join the crowd. I was not asked to park my Ford. I thanked the man but told him I was running late. Could he direct me to Tupelo. I was told to go down the road, and he pointed which way, until I came to a widow-woman's house, where I was to turn left. I thanked him and went on. I had no trouble finding the widow-woman's house. It had no stovewood stacked in the yard.

I've often asked myself: Why was it that so few people listened to us, although most were sympathetic. The kind of life they knew was at stake. I think the reason of their seeming indifference is this: Nobody could imagine the world they were born in, had lived in, and were still living in could disappear. Well, it has.

As my final word, I think we should have found a larger word than agrarian, for it was this whole country's Christian inheritance that was threatened, and still is. But let there be no misunderstanding. We still are subjects of Christendom. Only we have reached its Satanic phase. I can't believe that any society is strong which holds physical comfort as its quest. There is only one comfort, and it is the only thing that has been promised: the gates of Hell will not finally prevail.

[XXIV, Spring 1980, 114–120]

[29]

World War II and the War Guilt Question

KURT GLASER

Kurt Glaser (1914–   ), professor of political science in the Department of Government at Southern Illinois University in Edwardsville, has been an associate editor of Modern Age *since 1972. Coeditor with David S. Collier of a number of books in the* Foundation for Foreign Affairs *series, he has also been associated with the educational activities of the Freedoms Foundation of Valley Forge. He is the author of* Czecho-Slovakia: A Critical History *(1961) and coeditor of* Accelerated Development in Southern Africa *(1974) with John Barratt, Simon Brand, and Collier, as well as of several volumes of essays on Eastern Europe and numerous articles and reviews.*

As is doubtless the case in most other countries, historiography in the United States is dominated by a historical orthodoxy, the tendency if not the function of which is to defend the foreign policy of the past and to support that of the present. It is important for political science to understand the historical orthodoxy of a nation, since history provides the conceptual framework in which current foreign policy is shaped.

Historical orthodoxy in America is both the expression and the supporting ideology of a political attitude characterized as "legalism-moralism" by the perspicacious analyst George F. Kennan. This attitude was most clearly manifested in the political ethics of Woodrow Wilson and Franklin D. Roosevelt, as well as in the "non-recognition doctrine" of Secretary of State Stimson. The essence of legalism-moral-ism lies in the attempt to apply to the international politics of sovereign states the same principles of law and morality that individual members of civilized communities observe in their interpersonal relations.

The classical orthodox account of the outbreak of World War I is Professor Bernadotte Schmitt's *The Coming of the War, 1914.*[1] Since the Allies understood better than the Central Powers how to camouflage their goals of power politics behind a democratic ideology, Schmitt—who accepted Allied "idealism" at face value—confirmed for the most part the verdict of the Versailles Treaty. This orthodox perspective is shared by America's best known diplomatic historians, Samuel F. Bemis, Thomas A. Bailey, and Dexter Perkins.

Confronting the orthodox school, the

353

intellectual lights of which are too numerous to mention here, are the so-called revisionists, among whom Charles A. Beard enjoyed the greatest prominence. Beard's successor as elder statesman of this group was the late Harry Elmer Barnes, who led the way for Charles Callan Tansill and Sidney B. Fay. Revisionists prominent since World War II have included William Henry Chamberlin, George Morgenstern, Freda Utley, and, in a more popular vein, John T. Flynn, Austin J. App, and Edward L. Delaney.

The ideological roots of legalism-moralism reach back into the first half of the nineteenth century. The American people were at that time preoccupied with the expansion of commerce and industry and with the realization of "Manifest Destiny"—that is, with the conquest and exploitation of a continental *Lebensraum.* Alongside these practical concerns, however, there arose a utopian idealism, the alienated character of which was noticed by the French observer de Tocqueville, and which culminated in the messianic conviction that the American Union was the model for the future federation of mankind. Ignorant of the problems of other regions but deeply impressed by the flamboyant exploits of democratic heroes such as Bolívar, Mazzini, Kossuth, and Garibaldi, American idealists assumed uncritically the identity of national liberation struggles with their own revolutionary tradition. No consideration was given the certainty that the uninhibited quest for national statehood by minor, minuscule, interlocking and overlapping European nations would lead to a series of bitter wars and to majority tyranny between these wars.

With the Monroe Doctrine, the United States assumed an anti-imperialist position. As the historian Hans Kohn has observed, however, American politicians defined imperialism as *overseas* expansion—a category that specifically excluded the continental expansion of their own "Manifest Destiny."[2] When the United States pushed beyond its own maritime boundaries by annexing Samoa, Hawaii, and the former Spanish possessions, a vehement quarrel arose between opponents of expansion, among whom the Democratic leader William Jennings Bryan and Professor W. G. Sumner of Yale were to be found, and the "imperialist" faction led by Senator Albert J. Beveridge. The disagreement was resolved by a compromise that reconciled idealist conceptions with practical interests: the United States retained its new possessions and secured the Panama Canal Zone in the bargain, but embraced the principle of systematic disapproval of the imperialist adventures of *other* powers. This principle was applied to the encroachments of other powers against Chinese sovereignty in the "Open Door" policy introduced by Secretary of State John Hay. As Kennan observes, this policy, which was never backed with enough military force to make it effective, stemmed from an incorrect evaluation of the situation in China and contributed greatly to arousing the Japanese to eventual war against the United States.[3]

Legalism-moralism assumed concrete form as a principle of foreign policy after the outbreak of World War I. American history books show little agreement as to why the United States entered the war. Some authors claim that the German resumption of unrestricted submarine warfare in February 1917 was the deciding factor; others agree with Walter Lippmann that the U-Boats merely provided a convenient pretext, and that the real reason lay in the fear (which Lippmann and most academic historians find justified) that the power constellation after a victory of the Central Powers might be dangerous for the United States.

The historiography of the 1920's and

1930's was dominated by revisionism, which annihilated whatever factual basis the war-guilt clause in the Versailles Treaty had seemed to possess. The most important American revisionist studies of European diplomacy were Harry Elmer Barnes's pioneer book, *Genesis of the World War* (1926) and the more exhaustive two-volume study by Sidney Fay, *The Origins of the World War* (1928). Barnes considers the Russian diplomats Izvolski and Sazonov and the French politicians Poincaré, Viviani, and the Cambons the principal perpetrators of the war, and assigns a somewhat lesser responsibility to Grey and Berchtold. Fay, on the other hand, distributes the burden of war guilt more equally between the two sides, but with emphasis on Allied responsibility. Fay was the first to document the complicity of the Belgrade government in the murder of Archduke Franz Ferdinand. Space does not permit a more detailed survey of revisionist writings between the wars.

At this point, however, an important fact must be registered. The opponents and the supporters of American entry into World War I proceeded for the most part from the same legalist-moralist premises that had become traditional in our foreign-policy thinking. The ethical considerations that led William Jennings Bryan to resign as Secretary of State rather than sign the second *Lusitania* note, which he judged a step toward war, were the same that motivated President Wilson to insist that the note be dispatched. *This common legalism-moralism was inherited by both orthodox and revisionist historians.* Since under legalist-moralist rules the aggressor in war is automatically wrong (the sinking of the *Maine* having served as "aggression" in the war with Spain), American revisionists simply reversed the sign on an existing equation to the extent that they shifted the "guilt" for World War I to the Allies or distributed it symmetrically. By establishing that Germany and Austria were not solely or not even primarily responsible for starting the war, they proved to their own satisfaction that the United States should have stayed out of the war, even at the cost of victory by the Central Powers. The sensational findings of the Nye munitions investigation compounded the impression spread by books such as Walter Millis's *Road to War* (1935) that America had been maneuvered into war by selfish Europeans. Public clamor arose for a law that would banish forever the danger of involvement in foreign wars.

The specific result of American revisionism was thus the neutrality legislation of the late 1930's—legislation which temporarily paralyzed American foreign policy, particularly with regard to the Spanish Civil War. Neither the orthodox nor the revisionist historians had really faced, let alone analyzed, the basic question of national interests. The American people therefore remained incapable of producing a workable foreign policy for their encounter with the rival totalitarian systems of National Socialism and Communism.

Whatever judgment is passed on the causes of American entry into the First World War, the sources now available make one thing manifestly clear: that a majority of the American people found itself in war without at first knowing why, and in any case without awareness of a clearly defined national interest. Two weeks after the declaration of war, the British propaganda headquarters at Wellington House reported a disappointing lack of enthusiasm on the part of the American press and public.[4] The way into the war had to be justified *ex post facto,* a task to which President Wilson and his energetic propaganda director George Creel addressed themselves.

As a reformer in the Puritan tradition, Wilson rejected any justification of belligerency on the basis of national interest as "Machiavellian" and therefore incompatible with the American conscience. The justification thus had to be drawn from the war itself, a psychological process that Kennan describes as follows:

A democracy is peace-loving. It does not like to go to war. It is slow to rise to provocation. When it has once been provoked to the point where it must grasp the sword, it does not easily forgive its adversary for having produced this situation. The fact of the provocation then becomes itself the issue. Democracy fights in anger—it fights for the very reason that it was forced to go to war. It fights to punish the power that was rash enough and hostile enough to provoke it— to teach that power a lesson it will not forget, to prevent the thing from happening again. Such a war must be carried to the bitter end.

... a line of thought grew up, under Wilson's leadership, which provided both rationale and objective for our part in fighting the war to the bitter end. Germany was militaristic and antidemocratic. The Allies were fighting to make the world safe for democracy. Prussian militarism had to be destroyed to make way for the sort of peace we wanted. This peace would not be based on the old balance of power. Who, as Wilson said, could guarantee equilibrium under such a system? It would be based this time on a "community of power," on "an organized common peace," on a League of Nations which would mobilize the conscience and power of mankind against aggression. Autocratic government would be done away with. Peoples would themselves choose the sovereignty under which they wished to reside. Poland would achieve her independence, as would likewise the restless peoples of the Austro-Hungarian Empire. There would be open diplomacy this time; peoples, not governments, would run things. Armaments would be reduced by mutual agreement. The peace would be just and secure.[5]

Wilson's idealistic war ideology proved very convenient for the Allied statesmen. Their use—and in the opinion of many misuse—of it has been documented in detail by the late Wenzel Jaksch, a Social Democratic leader in the Czechoslovak and later in the West German parliament. As Jaksch points out in his study of wartime politics, the Allies in World War I suffered an embarrassing lack of plausible war aims.[6] Masaryk, for instance, summarized a conversation with Briand in February 1916 as follows:

It is no exaggeration to say that our policy of resolving Austria into her constituent parts gave the Allies a positive aim. They began to understand that it would not be enough to overthrow the Central Powers and to penalize them financially and otherwise, but that Eastern Europe and Europe as a whole must be reorganized.[7]

The following winter Wilson's peace offensive, aborted by the President's own lack of persistence, caused Doctor Beneš to fear a "premature end of the war"— which in his opinion would have frustrated Czech national aims. "Morally," he admitted, "this was a painful situation." Democratic war ideology, which took off from legalist-moralist premises to transform a power struggle between fundamentally similar states of the same cultural community into a crusade against supposed international criminals, provided a "moral justification" for goals of power politics which never could have been justified on their own merits. That only those peoples with the acumen to shift to the victorious side at the proper moment would enjoy the self-determination so glorified by Wilson was an inevitable result to the crusade psychology of the war.

In Article 231 of the Treaty of Versailles Germany was forced to accept "the responsibility of Germany and her allies for causing all the loss and damage to which the Allied and Associated Governments and their nationals have been subjected as a consequence of the war imposed upon them by the aggression of Germany and her allies." A few years after the war, Lord Grey admitted to the historian G. P. Gooch, "It was a very bad mistake to attribute the whole responsibility for the war to the Central Powers in the Treaty of Versailles. . . ."[8] The opinion that finally prevailed was that the notorious war-guilt clause constituted a superfluous and annoying appendage to the treaty, and that the Allies in their own interest would have done better to dispense with it. In reality, however, article 231 was the ideological core of the Peace of Paris.

Had the standards of international morality under which World War I was fought still prevailed during the 1930's, a second war launched by Germany—let us say by a nontotalitarian Germany in order to set aside the special problem of National Socialism—for the purpose of treaty revision would have been considered a just war or at least a tolerable war, inasmuch as the Versailles Treaty, resting squarely on the war-guilt clause, was by then generally recognized as a falsified verdict. In the meantime, however, American legalism-moralism, reinforced by a new international legalism-moralism with its seat in the League of Nations, had staked itself a higher goal: to change the rules of international politics through a categorical prohibition of war, which was proclaimed to the world in the Kellogg-Briand Pact of August 27, 1928. This pact is of historical importance, not because it ever prevented a war, but because it provided the juridical basis for convicting the so-called war criminals—in reality for convicting Germany—in the Allied trials at Nuremberg at the close of World War II.

Article I of the Kellogg-Briand Pact reads:

The High Contracting Parties solemnly declare in the names of their respective peoples that they condemn recourse to war for the solution of international controversies and renounce it as an instrument of national policy in their relations with one another.

Almost all states in the world, including the German Reich and the Soviet Union, adhered to the pact, which the public greeted with groundless optimism, especially in the United States, but which diplomats tended to regard as a pious wish rather than a valid legal norm. The principle of the Kellogg-Briand Pact also forms the basis of Article II, paragraph 4, of the Charter of the United Nations, which reads:

All members shall refrain in their international relations from the threat or use of force against the territorial integrity or political independence of any state, or in any other manner inconsistent with the Purposes of the United Nations.

The prohibition of war contained in the Kellogg-Briand Pact and repeated in Article II, paragraph 4 of the United Nations Charter constituted the legal basis for the Nuremberg trial. The organizers of the International Military Tribunal were fully aware that the practical application of this legal thesis was an innovation. In a commentary to the charter of the court, the American chief prosecutor, Justice Jackson, explained that the "crime against peace" consisted in *starting* a war, not in *causing* it. "We must make clear to the Germans," he said, "that the wrong for which their fallen leaders are on trial is not that they lost the war, but *that they started it*. And we must not allow ourselves to be drawn into a trial of the causes of war, for our position is that *no grievances or policies will justify resort to aggressive war*."[9]

The proposition, however, that aggressive war is forbidden by a truly valid principle of international public or criminal law—in the form of the League of Nations Covenant, the Kellogg-Briand Pact, or the Charter of the United Nations—such as would find application in trials lacking the political motivation of Nuremberg, is open to the greatest doubt. The Kellogg-Briand Pact was ratified by most of its signatories with reservations going far beyond the right of self-defense specified in the letter circulating the treaty. In addition to wars of national defense and in execution of sanctions imposed by the League of Nations, major powers exempted wars for the defense of specific regions and vital national interests as well as those in fulfillment of treaty obligations from the scope of the pact. As Professor Edwin M. Borchard, who held the chair of international law at Yale, declared in a lecture at the time of ratification, the reservations expressly stated were so numerous and comprehensive as *to sanction almost every conceivable war in advance.* France, in particular, reserved the right to take military action against Germany should the latter concentrate troops in the Rhineland in violation of the Locarno Pact.

In contrast to the Locarno treaties, the specific provisions of which represented a true extension of international law, the Kellogg-Briand Pact was, in the words of the diplomatic correspondent Sisley Huddleston, who witnessed its signature, "not worth the paper on which it was written." Anticipating the possibility that aggressive war might be justified against a concentration-camp regime, Professor Wesley L. Gould of Purdue University observes that:

Definition of the term "aggression" becomes a problem of placing the law in support of justice before placing force in support of law. If this is not done, then international law, at least in its treatment of war, would be of as much value as municipal law that gave a cornered criminal a license to kill with impunity if a policeman fired the first shot.[10]

The most interesting point of view is that of the former Vienna Professor Hans Kelsen (most recently at the University of California in Berkeley), who regards the war-guilt clause of the Versailles Treaty as a specific application of the doctrine of *bellum justum,* which permits war as a reaction against a violation of international law. Kelsen describes the legal effect of the Kellogg Pact as follows:

The Kellogg Pact forbids war, but only as an instrument of national policy. This is a very important qualification of the prohibition. A reasonable interpretation of the Kellogg Pact, one not attempting to make of it a useless and futile instrument, is that war is not forbidden as a means of international policy, especially not as a reaction against a violation of international law, is an instrument for the maintenance and realization of international law. This is exactly the idea of the *bellum justum* theory.[11]

Kelsen's reasoning that the *bellum justum* theory forms the basis of the Treaty of Versailles, especially of Article 231 which provides the rationale for its various punitive provisions, opens the way to the following conclusions: the legal validity of a unilaterally imposed punitive treaty, such as that of Versailles, depends upon the qualification of the war that has been fought as a *bellum justum* and of the treaty as punishment of an offense against international law. If, however, this condition is removed through the process of historical revision, as happened in the case of World War I, the war then turns out to be a *bellum injustum* insofar as it went beyond restoring the situation that had existed before the war. The punishment imposed by the victors is then likewise revealed as a violation of international law, the correction of which is an *inter-*

national concern dictated by justice and not mere national interest. Once efforts to secure peaceful revision have definitely failed, a war to change a treaty violative of international law may be considered a *bellum justum,* according to Kelsen's construction of the Kellogg-Briand Pact.

Since the presidency of Woodrow Wilson, but more particularly since the outbreak of World War I, American foreign policy has moved within the framework of a doctrine of *bellum justum,* which is explained lucidly by Professor Robert W. Tucker in a short book entitled *The Just War* (1960).[12] According to this American doctrine, the moral character of belligerency as good or evil is determined, not by the deeper causes of the war and even less by the issues in dispute, but solely by the circumstances under which hostilities are opened. Whichever state first invokes military force in pursuit of its national interests becomes *ipso facto* the aggressor, whom "international justice" demands to be *not only defeated* but also *punished.*

This form of the "just war" doctrine is, however, political rather than legal in nature. It is only employed when it happens to coincide with the political policy of the time. (Its nonapplication to Vietnam is notorious: if punishment were a necessary instrument of international politics, then the Hanoi government and the Russians and Chinese who incite its aggressions would certainly be targets.) When the doctrine is invoked, the language is always that of unsullied rectitude, as in the opening speech of chief prosecutor Jackson at Nuremberg:

> Our position is that whatever grievances a nation may have, however objectionable it finds the *status quo,* aggressive warfare is an illegal means for settling those grievances or for altering those conditions.[13]

A defensive war in the strict sense must be limited to those measures needed to repel the attack and to restore the *status quo ante bellum.* Since, however, the American doctrine of "just war" demands punishment of the aggressor, it sanctions total warfare aiming for unconditional surrender and not shrinking from the use of mass-destruction weapons. It furthermore permits the victor who has defeated aggression to exploit the fortunes of war in order to obtain political and territorial gains that would otherwise be forbidden objects of military campaigns. After both world wars, American administrations were not opposed to territorial changes at Germany's expense; the question was only "how large?"

Our present context does not include analysis of the reasons that moved President Roosevelt to lead, or if one prefers, maneuver the United States into World War II. Suffice it to say that the fashionable "legalism-moralism," of which Roosevelt himself was a prominent representative, forbade the justification of war policies with arguments of supposed national interest. To move from the "semi-war" of Lend-Lease to a full state of war, it was necessary that the United States be attacked. "The question was," Secretary of War Stimson wrote in his diary after a cabinet meeting on November 25, 1941, "how we could maneuver them [the Japanese] into firing the first shot without too much danger to ourselves."[14] Since the Japanese fulfilled Stimson's (and evidently Roosevelt's) wish on December 7, 1941, the Administration was able to lead the nation into war without qualms of conscience and with the full support of a united though badly deceived American people.

American World War II revisionism has dealt mainly with the chain of events that led to Pearl Harbor and only incidentally with the outbreak of the European war. In Europe, serious revisionism has been limited to the Munich crisis and certain aspects of Allied strategy during the war; the politics and diplomacy of the German-Polish dispute of 1939 have been left largely untouched. The court historians of America, who are inclined to hold Poland and Britain blameless in the affair, are supported by a West German school of historical orthodoxy, the philosophy of which can be summed up in a sentence widely quoted in popular books and newspapers: "Whoever casts doubt upon the exclusive guilt of Germany for World War II thereby destroys the foundation of postwar politics."[15] Few academicians on either side of the Atlantic have been disposed to question what the orthodox Professor Walther Hofer calls "Nuremberg historiography" (*das Geschichtsbild von Nürnberg*)—the axiom that the "catastrophic personality" of Adolf Hitler, his totalitarian rule, and his territorial expansionism constituted the single decisive cause of World War II.[16]

The possibility that respectable historians might challenge the Nuremberg thesis was indicated when the British historian A. J. P. Taylor produced a slim volume entitled *Origins of the Second World War* (1961), the main contention of which was that neither Hitler nor the British cabinet really wanted war, which nevertheless broke out as the result of inept diplomacy. Yet no German historian of repute has come forth with a revisionist book about 1939, despite the fact that such a book would have an instant market since it would fulfill two wishes: that of Germans generally for an acquittal of their country, and that of former National Socialist functionaries for an exoneration of Adolf Hitler and thus of their own past.

An extensive study of the published diplomatic documents (and some unpublished documents) and considerable secondary literature having to do with the 1939 crisis—the details of which are too voluminous to report here—has convinced this writer of the correctness of a number of theses that can be classified as revisionist, since they conflict with "Nuremberg historiography." These theses, which are in each case supported by the pertinent documentation, may be summarized as follows:

1. Hitler and Ribbentrop complained repeatedly to the Polish foreign minister, Colonel Beck, and his Berlin ambassador Lipski indicating that Germany regarded the situation in Danzig and that of the Germans in Poland as intolerable. They proposed various compromises for the settlement of German-Polish differences. The acceptability of these proposals is of course a matter of opinion.

2. Against the advice of his colleagues, Colonel Beck rejected every opportunity to reach solutions re. the Danzig Corridor, and minority questions acceptable to Germany, although he must have known that renitent insistence on the *status quo* of Versailles would inevitably provoke the Hitler regime to violence. During the fall and winter of 1938–39 he followed a policy of dragging things out; after the British guarantee of March 31, 1939, Beck refused any serious negotiation on these controversial questions and indulged in an openly anti-German policy.

3. Hitler made serious efforts to achieve a settlement of German-Polish differences as the basis for a rapprochement of the two governments. In so doing, he insisted on the return of Danzig to the Reich and on extraterritorial transit rights through the Corridor as the essential minimum for Germany. Only after the British guarantee, when Polish obduracy seemed to prove the impossibility of reaching an agreement, did Hitler decide to destroy Poland militarily. The documentation so far available does *not*, however, prove that Hitler was still willing to negotiate in late August 1939. It must also be observed that Beck, particularly after March 1939, had every reason to fear that fulfillment

of Hitler's initial demands would lead to further demands and perhaps to the total dependency or destruction of the Polish state.

4. After September 1938, the British foreign minister, Lord Halifax, succeeded in recapturing control of British foreign policy from Prime Minister Chamberlain, who had managed the British end of Munich singlehandedly and without keeping the cabinet fully informed. By 1938 at the latest, Halifax reached the conviction that Hitler's power system represented a direct danger for England. His post-Munich policy was directed at achieving a decisive defeat of the Third Reich—through diplomatic means if possible, otherwise with armed force.

5. To make the war morally and politically acceptable to the British people (and, what is more important, to the American people), Germany had to be induced to commit aggression. For this purpose, Halifax needed a trip-wire—a role that Poland was admirably suited to play. His diplomacy was therefore calculated to stiffen Polish resistance against German demands, but with a surface tone of moderation so that London could claim credit for appeasement to the bitter end. Cleverly backing his minister's policy, the British ambassador in Warsaw, Sir Howard W. Kennard, undermined any tendency toward Polish accommodation with Germany. Although the British public would not have supported a war on account of Danzig, the unconditional guarantee against German attack worked as a pledge against German reannexation of the so-called "Free State."

6. That England was interested in Poland mainly as a trip-wire is obvious, since geography rules out England as a base for the effective defense of the Polish western border. When Poland asked in June 1939 for sixty million pounds sterling to purchase war materials, Halifax responded with a credit of only eight million pounds restricted to purchases in England, under which no deliveries actually took place. The British government did *not* guarantee the Polish eastern border against Soviet annexations. Churchill's negotiations with the Polish exile government in 1944 were mainly devoted to persuading the Poles to accept Stalin's territorial demands.

Once we can make up our minds to depart from the legalist-moralist standpoint, we will judge the war not according to who fired the first shot, but on the basis of the larger issues at stake. In this case, the proof that Halifax deliberately permitted a German-Polish war to take place with the purpose of Franco-British intervention does not lead automatically to the conclusion that he thereby committed an international crime.

Two important observations must be made at this point:

1. The question as to the specific chain of events that let to the outbreak of World War II and the roles of the various actors in these events is a very different question from that concerning the nature and long-range goals of National Socialism. Each question must be answered separately.

2. The National Socialist program of expansion must be rigorously distinguished from genuine German national interests, including that of treaty revision.

Since the facts of prewar diplomacy disprove the thesis of *unprovoked* German aggression in World War II, Allied warfare against Germany to the point of unconditional surrender cannot be justified as a war of retribution—even on legalist-moralist premises. The question remains whether a war to overthrow the Hitler regime was justified. Since two totalitarian systems were fighting each other after June 1941, the question necessarily arises as to the extent to which warfare *by the Germans* was justified.

The moral question of World War II—

a question we must answer again in our confrontation with Communism—is whether and under what circumstances war for the elimination of a totalitarian regime is justified, as a war of aggression if need be. The traditional doctrine of sovereignty would suggest a negative answer, since each state is considered entitled to manage or mismanage its internal affairs. The advent of modern totalitarianism has, however, broken down the barrier between domestic and foreign policy, for the following reasons:

1. The doctrine of internal sovereignty within the Western cultural community is based on the assumption that governments will adhere to the rules of civilized statesmanship, which is not the case with totalitarian regimes.

2. Human responsibility does not stop at political boundaries. Since the contemporary technology of weapons, propaganda, and political control favors inordinately those who exercise state power, totalitarian dictators in particular, the overthrow of a totalitarian regime without outside help has become almost unthinkable. Because human rights are universal, mankind is under a universal obligation: the fight for freedom is the cause of all men of good will.

3. The dynamics of totalitarian systems, which prevent the achievement of internal political balance, propel these systems automatically into expansionist adventures. Communism, exactly like National Socialism, requires conflict with an external or at least externalized enemy as an element of internal stability.

It is obvious from these reasons that the question of free systems versus totalitarian systems must be included in every realistic evaluation of contemporary history and politics. The German annexation of Austria in March 1938 presents values quite different from those involved in the proposed *Anschluss* of German Austria

with the then constitutional Weimar Republic, which the Allies prevented in 1919 and again in 1931.

Long before Hitler rose to power, the Versailles peace was recognized in America as the main cause of the expected Second European War. Most Americans were firmly determined to remain neutral in this war. The slogan in the early 1930's was: "We'll sit this one out."

The factor that moved America to give Great Britain its unconditional support and finally to take part in World War II was *not* the German aggression against Poland, but the brutality of the Hitler regime and particularly its persecution of the Jews. If a *nontotalitarian German government* had invoked military force to secure the return of Danzig and extraterritorial transit rights through the Corridor after the failure of diplomatic efforts, Warsaw would have fought alone. None of the West European powers, and much less the United States, would have seen its national interest served by a second world war to prevent the overthrow of a territorial settlement already recognized as fragile and dangerous. In this case the German war against Poland, while it might not have qualified as a "just war" under pseudojuristic American doctrine, would in any case have been a tolerated war in political practice. While there may remain room for dispute as to how responsibility for the German-English and German-French war of 1939 is to be distributed, there is no doubt whatever that the totalitarian nature of National Socialism and not German aggression provoked the Western declarations of war.

As soon as the reality-alienated "Nuremberg historiography" is dispensed with, World War II is seen, not as a fight between aggressors and victims of attack, but as the struggle of free men against the unfreedom of totalitarian dictatorship. Only the maintenance of human freedom and the restoration of the threatened values of Western culture can justify the sacrifice of millions of human lives and the destruction that was militarily unavoidable. (The latter category does not include the bombing of Rotterdam, Dresden, or Hiroshima.)

Once the ideological nature of World War II is recognized, the front lines necessarily appear both complex and contradictory. The conflict of constitutional and totalitarian systems was interlocked with a series of simultaneous and only loosely related national wars in such a fashion that the armed forces of *both sides* were fighting *both for and against freedom* at various times and places.

Large-scale war might perhaps have been avoided by granting the German claim to treaty revision in the East—a claim that the constitutional government of the Weimar Republic had also asserted in refusing to sign an eastern Locarno. The Reich had a justified *and limited* claim against Poland. Experience with Hitler and with Communist dictatorships raises the question, however, whether a totalitarian system is capable of waging a national war. Insofar as national interest, conceived in organic, geopolitical terms, is overshadowed by the messianic pretensions of a totalitarian ideology, the question seems to demand a negative answer.

The specific justification of the ideological war against Hitler's totalitarian Reich had the effect of determining and limiting its morally admissible war aims. The ideological goal was the removal of Hitler and the restoration of a stable rule of law in continental Europe. This goal was not fulfilled but frustrated by the total liquidation of German political and military power.

Whether the ideological struggle against Hitler's Germany justified an American war against Japan is another question altogether. A national interest in such a

war did not exist; the total value of American investments in the Far East was only a few billion dollars, and the projected Japanese "Greater East Asia Co-Prosperity Sphere" did not at any point overlap the area of predominant American power. Inasmuch as the Hitler regime avoided carefully any collision with the United States, however, President Roosevelt chose the "back door": the provocation of Japan. The tactics through which he incited Japan to its foolhardy attack on Pearl Harbor have been described in detail by Tansill, Beard, Morgenstern, and W. H. Chamberlin, whose historical thesis—that the Roosevelt Administration deliberately sought war—has found general if grudging acceptance. Four days after Pearl Harbor, the Hitler regime fulfilled Roosevelt's wish with a declaration of war against the United States.

In Chapter III of his *American Diplomacy, 1900–1950*, George F. Kennan shows that the American conflict with Japan represented no true national interest, but only the expression of a rigid legalism-moralism with little relation to political reality. Whether the ideological interest in the defeat of Hitler, had that aim been pursued without presenting half of Europe to Soviet Russia, was worth the price of an unnecessary war with Japan, with its consequences of the bolshevization of China and a series of limited wars that pin down American troops in Asia to this very day, is a question that need not be answered here. Insofar as Western strategy merely replaced one dictatorship with another, equally vicious, the American sacrifice was not worthwhile.

In the European theater of war, the ideological goal of overthrowing Hitler dictated unqualified Western support of the German resistance. This would have included the offering of acceptable peace conditions to a non-National Socialist German government willing to vacate the

occupied territories in western and northern Europe and to make restitution for
damages caused by the war and the occupation. The politics of unconditional
surrender frustrated this ideological goal,
undermined the anti-Hitler underground, and transformed the Second
World War into a senseless national war.
It may well be contended that the last
nine months of the war—from July 20,
1944 to May 8, 1945—and the deaths and
destruction that took place during this
interval, are a direct result of this perverse
policy, chargeable to Washington and
London, not to Hitler and even less to
the German *Wehrmacht*.

Through the involvement of Soviet
Russia, the European war assumed an
ambivalent aspect. Stalin and his henchmen had always been enemies of freedom
and of European culture, the material
output of which they hoped to confiscate.
The German-Soviet Pact of August 23,
1939 fulfilled the Communist aim of provoking war among the capitalist powers,
so that, when both sides were in a state
of exhaustion, the "second wave of world
revolution" could roll unhampered.

Under these conditions, the politics of
freedom indicated sufficient help to the
Soviet Union so that the German armies
would bog down there, but in no case
enough to permit a Communist conquest
of Europe. Few Western statesmen understood the fact that Stalin remained their
enemy through all phases of the war and,
with revolutionary weapons, *waged uninterrupted war against the West*.[17] Stalingrad
was the great turning point of the war.
After the encirclement of General Paulus
and his army and the destruction of German offensive force, the most urgent
danger for Europe was no longer that of
a continuation of National Socialist rule,
the days of which were numbered, but
that of a continental Communist dictatorship. *After Stalingrad, the German army was*
fighting for Europe. Had the Western powers appreciated this and planned their
strategy accordingly, so as to end the war
with the eastern front as far removed as
possible, the history of the last two decades
would have been very different. In fact,
however, Allied, principally American,
deliveries of trucks, tires, weapons, airplanes, and other war materials to the
Soviet Union were stepped up enormously in 1943 and 1944, while the German forces were already in continuous
retreat. The continuation of "Lend
Lease" to the U.S.S.R. to the end of the
war and to a total figure of eleven billion
dollars—although the Russians had major
reserves of men and materials—gave the
Red Army the mobility it needed to advance to the center of Europe.

The saving of East-Central Europe was
totally incompatible with the policy of
"unconditional surrender." A continuity
of the German state and the German
military command was urgently necessary
in the interest of the West. The security of
Europe required that the Balkans, Poland,
and as much of the Baltic lands as possible
be held by German troops, while the Allies
assumed the functions of military government until national governments could
be restored. The only way to avoid the
Soviet filling of power vacuums was not
to create such vacuums.

The events at the end of the war,
including the sovietization of East-Central
Europe and the expulsion of national and
ethnic Germans from the eastern *Reich*
and *Volksdeutsche* settlements into what
was left of Germany, were a consequence,
not only of World War II as such, but
also to a very large degree of Allied war
policy, which guaranteed war "to the bitter
end." For the fact that things did not turn
out even worse we can thank those elements of the *Wehrmacht* who took care
that the Russians were not the first to
cross the Rhine.

Seen in this perspective, World War II does not present a black-and-white picture, but a mosaic in diverse shades of gray. Whatever the importance of National Socialism as one of the decisive causes of war, it must be kept in mind that totalitarianism is an endemic disease of modern society, the germs of which are present in every country and which becomes virulent in times of national crisis. The nation that has fallen victim to totalitarianism should be liberated and healed, not punished. Even the most uncompromising opponent of Communism would never think of demanding that the Russian people "expiate the sin of Bolshevism."

Once the concept of "war guilt" is given a concrete and realistic meaning—responsibility for political or military measures that did not serve freedom or were actually injurious to freedom—then it is obvious that the answer to the "war guilt question" must be complex. Both sides offended against freedom and the dignity of man; both sides forgot the strategy of prudence and let themselves be swept to disaster by the passions of war. The common people of both the former Allies and the former Axis Powers are with indistinguishable differences guilty or innocent: World War II brought them a common destiny that must now be mastered. Individual crimes should be impartially punished by due process of whatever law existed at the time of their commission. The German people as a whole, however, has no reason for particular guilt feelings; it was the first victim of National Socialism and today occupies the front line against totalitarian Communism. It is absurd to maintain that Germany has a particular obligation, not shared by the other nations of Europe, to make special sacrifices in the liquidation of World War II. That war was a common catastrophe with multiple causes. If it is essential to have a villain,

that role can only be filled by the exaggerated nationalism of the late nineteenth and early twentieth centuries, which shattered the concert of Europe and brought forth a half century of conflict, but is now yielding to a restored sense of European unity.

NOTES

[1] Bernadotte E. Schmitt, *The Coming of the War, 1914* (New York: H. Fertig, 1958).

[2] Hans Kohn, *Reflections on Colonialism*, Memorandum Number Two, Foreign Policy Research Institute, University of Pennsylvania (Philadelphia, 1956).

[3] George F. Kennan, *American Diplomacy, 1900–1950* (Chicago: University of Chicago Press, 1951), pp. 44–48.

[4] Harold Lavine and James Wechsler, *War Propaganda and the United States* (New Haven: Yale University Press, 1940), pp. 31–32.

[5] Kennan, *op. cit.*, pp. 67.

[6] Wenzel Jaksch, *Europe's Road to Potsdam*, translated and edited by Kurt Glaser (New York: Praeger, 1963), pp. 118–22 and 142–47.

[7] Thomas G. Masaryk, *The Making of a State* (London: G. Allen & Unwin, 1927), p. 103.

[8] Verbatim quote from G. P. Gooch, *Studies in Diplomacy and Statecraft* (London: Longmans Green, 1947), p. 107.

[9] *Department of State Bulletin*, 1945, XII, p. 228.

[10] Wesley L. Gould, *An Introduction to International Law* (New York: Harper, 1957), p. 607.

[11] Hans Kelsen, *General Theory of Law and State* (New York: Russell and Russell, 1961), p. 334.

[12] Robert W. Tucker, *The Just War* (Baltimore: Johns Hopkins Press, 1960).

[13] Quoted, *ibid.*, p. 12.

[14] Quoted in U.S. Congress, *Pearl Harbor Attack* hearings of the joint committee (Washington, 1946), Volume XI, p. 5433. Richard N. Current has undertaken to explain this entry in his article "How Stimson Meant to 'Maneuver' the Japanese," *Mississippi Valley Historical Review*, XL, No. 1 (June, 1953), pp. 67–74. Current contends that Stimson anticipated a Japanese attack on British or Dutch, rather than United States possessions. But he also points out that Stimson told FDR of his preference that U.S. bombers from the Philippines attack the Japanese naval force that had been observed moving southward, without a declaration of war.

[15] This is an incorrect but widely repeated version of a statement by Professor Theodor Eschenburg, in a newspaper article reprinted in *Institutionelle Sorgen in der Bundesrepublik* (Stuttgart: Schwab, 1961),

p. 164, that recognition of the unquestioned and exclusive guilt of Hitler was "a foundation of the politics of the Federal Republic."

[16] Walther Hofer, "Entfesselung oder 'Ausbruch' des Zweiten Weltkrieges?, eine grundsätzliche Auseinandersetzung mit dem Buch von A. J. P. Taylor über die Ursprünge des Zweiten Weltkrieges," re-printed in: *Die Vorgeschichte des Zweiten Weltkrieges—Legende und Wirklichkeit* (Zürich: Buchverlag Neue Zürcher Zeitung, 1963), p. 23.

[17] See George B. deHuszar, "The Success of Kremlin Policy," in George B. deHuszar, ed., *Soviet Power and Policy* (New York: Crowell, 1955), pp. 8–14.

[XV, Winter 1971, 57–69]

[30]

The End of the Old America

HARRY ELMER BARNES

Harry Elmer Barnes (1889–1968), one of the best-known American historians, devoted much of his life to studies of the causes and course of World War II; an isolationist, he was up to the time of his death still reflecting on Pearl Harbor after a quarter of a century. Considered the dean of American "revisionist" historians, he was the author of textbooks and studies that ranged from A History of Historical Writing *(1938) to* Social Institutions in an Era of World Upheaval *(1942) to* Perpetual War for Perpetual Peace *(1953), a significant post-World War II volume that he edited and that influenced a generation of scholars.*

A NEW BOOK, true to its title, describes the most momentous and ominous transition in American history. The racial and segregation issue, which is so warmly debated at present, is surely an important item charged with political and social dynamite. But it is a relatively trivial matter when compared to the abandonment by the United States of the benign neutrality, international modesty, and pacific inclinations that generally guided our relations with other countries for nearly a century; and the wholehearted, even passionate, espousal of globaloney, world-meddling, and perpetual war for perpetual peace. Indeed, it is no exaggeration to state that even the Civil War was of less importance than the revolution in American policies on world affairs since 1917. However deplorable a permanent disruption of the Union might have been, its results probably would not have been as momentous to American life and values

as the loss of our neutrality and its aftermath since 1917. As the late Garet Garrett pointed out, this change has made our country, as it existed before 1941, and especially before 1917, veritably "Ex-America."

This transition has been one from the tradition of Monroe to the Orwellian system which now dominates the majority of the civilized world—all of it except the "neutrals." In regard to the United States, it may also be the harbinger of another menacing development, namely, that our country will become the new Byzantine Empire, devoted chiefly to bolstering up what remains of the British Empire, in the same way that the Byzantine Empire acted as the receiver and protector of the decaying Western Roman Empire. This was pointed up by the crisis in Cyprus, the "Eisenhower doctrine" on the Middle East and the Syrian crisis, the disputes growing out of the seizure of the Suez

Canal, and the almost frantic Anglo-American collaboration after the release of the "sputniks." It is a rather striking coincidence that the most specific date and action connected with our entry into the Orwellian era came in March 1947, when President Truman took over the international burdens and responsibilities which Britain could no longer shoulder in the very center of ancient Byzantine glory and later distress, Greece and Turkey. The temporary clash with Britain over the latter's attack on Egypt in November 1956 was quickly smoothed out, and American power was pledged to maintain the *status quo* in the Middle East, so vital to what remained of the British Empire.

Opponents of state enterprise can get little comfort out of either Orwellianism or the new Byzantine trends. The enormous increase of statism, military state capitalism, inflation, debt, and the like, has been inseparably connected with the Orwellian pattern of basing economic "prosperity" and political tenure upon cold and phony war, a gigantic armament industry, and a vast "giveaway" program. The lessons of history drawn from the experience of the Byzantine Empire indicate that any neo-Byzantinism would be equally fraught with danger to economic liberty. The eminent medievalist, the late Professor James Westfall Thompson, thus characterized the economic results of the Byzantine efforts to bolster and protect a disintegrating empire:

> The industrial structure of the Eastern Empire at the beginning of the sixth century was a mass of exclusive trade and industrial corporations under governmental regulation. . . . The economics of the Byzantine Empire was one supreme socialistic organization; but a selfish one, for its regulation was governed in the interests of the ruler and his government and not primarily in the interest of society. Industry was a state affair.

In what was probably the most timely and vitally important article in an American periodical in a decade, Felix Morley set forth the evidence that the United States may be on its way to Empire and decadence, in the first issue of *Modern Age* (Summer 1957).

Essential Nature of Professor Drummond's Apology for Roosevelt

As I implied earlier, Professor Drummond's book bears out its title in describing "the passing of American neutrality." It shows very adequately how our neutrality was lost. It does not deal with the subject in its broad theoretical principles and institutional developments, but is limited to the diplomatic maneuvers and intrigues whereby this momentous change was accomplished. It is unquestionably the best one-volume book on our entry into the Second World War that is also devoted to vindicating the alleged wisdom and integrity of the Roosevelt-Hull foreign policy from 1937 to 1941, which, in reality, means the Roosevelt foreign policy. It is not as lengthy and comprehensive as the gigantic and erudite apology for Churchill and Roosevelt in the two-volume Langer and Gleason treatise. But it is far superior to Walter Millis's fantastic defense of Roosevelt and his entourage in *This Is Pearl!*, and the effort of Basil Rauch to portray Roosevelt as a pacific benefactor of all mankind. The bibliography is fairly full, but is carefully selected to serve the author's purposes. Such basic and fundamental revisionist volumes on the background of the Second World War as W. H. Chamberlin's *America's Second Crusade*; F. R. Sanborn's *Design for War*; George Morgenstern's *Pearl Harbor*; the symposium *Perpetual War for Perpetual Peace*, edited by the reviewer; and Admiral Theobald's *The Final Secret of Pearl Harbor*, are not listed, nor is there any evidence that the author has used them.

Despite this, the book resembles the *magnum opus* of Langer and Gleason in making available to those scholars in actual search of the truth a large amount of material very directly useful to the revisionist interpretation of events between 1937 and 1941, when presented or interpreted in a forthright and logical manner. It is also true, however, that many events and acts of the greatest significance for the record and a full understanding of the international situation between 1937 and 1941 have been omitted because they would so obviously support the revisionist interpretation, and undermine the approach and conclusions of Professor Drummond and his fellow-apologists for intervention. This is especially apparent in the author's treatment of the immediate background of Pearl Harbor.

As a sample of these omissions, and surely one of the more crucial, we may cite the attempt to obscure the real purpose of the Roosevelt-Churchill meeting off the coast of Newfoundland in August 1941. By this date, it had become evident to these two collaborators in the effort to get the United States actively into the war that there was little hope of inciting Hitler and Mussolini to execute acts of war that would enable the United States to enter the war by the front door of Europe. Hence, as Professor Charles C. Tansill, Dr. Charles A. Beard, and others, have shown, they arranged this meeting at sea to explore the possibility of finding a back door to war by inciting Japan to attack in the Far East. The possibility of a naval war with Japan had also been in Roosevelt's mind since his first cabinet meetings in March 1933, a fact revealed by James A. Farley in his memoirs. Professor Drummond omits the overwhelming evidence relative to the "back door" program and

portrays the meeting as primarily concerned with the idealistic effort of Roosevelt to circumvent any attempt of the British to involve him in a repetition of the secret treaties of the First World War. This effort, acccording to Professor Drummond, resulted in the Atlantic Charter, the supreme achievement of the meeting.

An "assistant president," Forrest Davis, and a specially favored political writer, Ernest K. Lindley, prepared a quasi-official book on this subject in 1942, *How War Came*. Here, on pages 9 to 15, they blurted out the truth about the "back door" plan, and showed that the only difference between Roosevelt and Churchill relative to the scheme was in the matter of timing. Churchill wished to kick the back door open at once, but Roosevelt demanded that he be allowed to "baby the Japanese along" for three months in order to gain time for further American preparations for war. This vital confession is omitted entirely. Indeed, there is no mention of the Davis and Lindley account. When he was later cornered by newspapermen in Washington, Roosevelt admitted that the charter was essentially a hoax and a protective propaganda stunt. The fraud was nailed down by John T. Flynn in his *The Roosevelt Myth* (pp. 385–386).

Import of the Missing "Kent Documents"

Friends of Roosevelt, Churchill, and the interventionist version complain that the revisionists like Beard, Tansill, Sanborn, Chamberlin, Morgenstern, et al., are extreme to the extent of unfairness or malice in their criticisms of the Roosevelt-Churchill actions and policies from 1939 to 1942. Yet these books are more moderate and generous than the ultimate verdict may be, if and when all the evidence is in and is available to scholars.

While there are other reasons for this statement, a main basis lies in the fact that far and away the most damaging evidence against Roosevelt and Churchill has never been opened for use even to the apologists for these men. On the contrary, there have been almost frantic efforts to prevent its use, and it is not impossible that the alarm over any future use of this material will lead, or has already led, to the destruction of the dangerous documents. We have reference here to the so-called Kent Documents, namely, the nearly two-thousand secret messages illegally exchanged between Roosevelt and Churchill in the American code beginning in September 1939. Roosevelt used the code name of POTUS (President of the United States) and Churchill the title of "Former Naval Person." Churchill himself has told us that these documents contain most of the really vital facts about the collaboration of himself and Roosevelt in their joint effort to bring the United States into the war, contrary to Roosevelt's public assurances and the obvious and repeatedly expressed wishes of the American people. As Churchill expressed it in *Their Finest Hour*: "The chief business between our two countries was virtually conducted by these personal exchanges between him and me."

That these Kent Documents contain diplomatic and historical dynamite of the first order is very apparent from the concern, if not alarm, expressed by Churchill lest they be used, even by historians notoriously favorable to the Roosevelt-Churchill policies and intrigues. Professors Langer and Gleason were subsidized to the amount of some $150,000 to produce the semi-official "court history" of the origins of the Second World War and American entry therein. It was well known to the historical profession and Washington officials that these able scholars intended to go to any reasonable length to defend Roosevelt and Churchill, and the latter was fully acquainted with all this. Yet he felt it necessary to forewarn Langer and to threaten him with a court suit if he made any use of the Kent Documents.

If and when the latter are made accessible to scholars intent upon the truth, we may rest assured that the indictment already presented in the books by Beard, Tansill, Sanborn, Chamberlin, and Morgenstern will seem almost like apologies for the Roosevelt-Churchill epic. No one can well doubt that if this material would refute, or even moderate, the revisionist indictment of Roosevelt and Churchill there would be no such alarm over its use; instead, it would have been brought forth already in their defense. I conclude that the Kent Documents would make the case against them much stronger than the revisionist verdict as it stands in 1958. These documents—supposing they still exist—are, along with Roosevelt's commitments to Eden in December 1938, and to George VI in June 1939, perhaps the most closely-guarded top-secret material in our national archives and the Roosevelt Library.

It may be argued that because the present writer has not read the Kent Documents, he has no right to comment on them. But one does not have to read them to grasp the fact that if these documents would clear Roosevelt and Churchill, they would have been made available long since to scholars. And probably this writer knows as much about the Kent Documents as anyone can who has not read them. I had a day-long conference with Tyler Kent within forty-eight hours after he arrived in this country, following his illegal imprisonment in England, and have talked with him about them several times since. Both Mr. Kent and this writer are prevented by Federal law from divulging the contents of the documents.

Omissions and Admissions

Professor Drummond presents a picture of Roosevelt in prewar diplomacy as a pacifically-inclined statesman who hated war, sought to prevent any European conflict, tried to end the war after it broke out, and resisted pressure to get the United States involved. As he summarizes the first two items on page 375: "Roosevelt brought his counsels of restraint to bear in all major European crises from 1938 to the outbreak of the war." There is no mention of Ambassador Kennedy's confession to James Forrestal that Roosevelt was urging Kennedy to "put iron up Chamberlin's backsides," so he would make no more conciliatory gestures after Munich, or of the evidence in the authentic captured Polish documents that Roosevelt both directly, and through his Ambassador in Paris, William C. Bullitt, pressed Poland to resist the reasonable German demands in 1938–39, and urged the British and French to back up the Poles in the policy and actions that led straight to war at the beginning of September 1939. It is not revealed that Roosevelt's support of the Munich appeasement was not due to his love of peace but to his feeling that, if war broke out in 1938, the odds against Hitler would be so great that the war would be over before Roosevelt could lead the United States into it. In conjunction with Churchill, Roosevelt resisted all the efforts of Mussolini and Hitler to end the war both after the Polish defeat and after Dunkirk.

In regard to Roosevelt and the entry of the United States into the war, Professor Drummond agrees with Dexter Perkins that the President was cautious, loath to become involved, and rather reluctantly pushed along by events and American public opinion. He does not agree with the frank admission of another eminent fellow-interventionist, Professor Thomas A. Bailey, that Roosevelt deliberately snared this country into war because he thought that the great majority of American citizens were too dumb in 1939–1941 to know what was good for them and their country.

In treating the outbreak of the war in 1939, the Polish-German dispute is passed over hurriedly, and the completely misleading impression is given that the Germans were wholly in the wrong. No mention is made of the admitted evils of the Corridor arrangement, the Polish persecution of the German minority, the reasonableness of the German demands on Poland in 1938–1939 and the unreasonable Polish responses, or of the fact that Hitler decided to call off military action on August 25, only to be met by Polish resistance and mobilization. This the British approved but requested that it be kept as secret as possible, much like the French reaction to Russian mobilization in 1914. It has also been shown that Lord Halifax, the British Foreign Minister, and Mr. Kennard, the British Ambassador in Poland, did everything possible to discourage the Poles from taking any diplomatic action which would remove the war threat in late August and the beginning of September 1939.

The German invasion of Norway in early April 1940, is interpreted as unique, unilateral aggression. There is no mention of the fact that Britain had laid plans for the invasion of Norway even before Hitler did. The old myth of a direct Nazi threat to the United States is repeated and emphasized (p. 370), although even Langer and Gleason admit that Hitler did not have the most remote intention of striking at the United States. Indeed, there is plenty of evidence in Professor Drummond's book to refute this thesis.

The treatment of Japanese activities and interests is equally partisan. If we were to credit Professor Drummond's story, our cracking of the Japanese code ("Magic") in August 1940, only enabled us to learn of *aggressive* Japanese policies, rarely or never of their sincere efforts to preserve peace with the United States. Conciliatory and pacific Japanese efforts are either omitted altogether, glossed over, or minimized, from the several Japanese efforts to obtain a pacific arrangement with the United States, rather than enter the Axis, right down to the attack on Pearl Harbor. Even the strenuous and repeated efforts of the Japanese Premier, Prince Konoye, to meet with Roosevelt in the late summer and early autumn of 1941 and work out some reasonable means of preserving peace are passed over as of no real importance, although Konoye subscribed in advance to terms that Hull admitted would have fully protected American interests in the Far East.

While omitting, dismissing or depreciating the sincere Japanese peace efforts from the amazing offer of January 1941, to the final efforts of November, Professor Drummond several times stresses with apparent seriousness the transparent hoax of Roosevelt's message to the Japanese Emperor, which was sent on the night of December 6 and did not reach the Emperor until a few minutes before the Japanese attack. Even Hull admits that it was concocted and sent only for the diplomatic "record."

The evasions and omissions in treating the immediate background of Pearl Harbor would require more than the space of this review for a mere listing. It is either directly implied or specifically stated that the Washington authorities had little reason to expect any attack at Pearl Harbor, even on December 7, 1941, that the reception of the Japanese reply to Hull on December 6–7 did not make Roosevelt feel certain about anything beyond the probability of war, that General Marshall was fully on the alert in first taking a leisurely horseback ride and then getting

to his office at nearly 11:30 on the morning of December 7, and that he then did his best immediately to warn General Short by the most rapid available means of communication. Admiral Theobald's refutation of all this is not mentioned, nor is his book listed in the bibliography.

Some vital items are omitted from the Pearl Harbor account: the fact that, of all the American outposts that the Japanese might have attacked, they made inquiry only through their espionage agents about the situation at Pearl Harbor, and that this careful checking and reporting by Japanese spies went on for months in full knowledge of the Washington military and political leaders; that Pearl Harbor had been denied a decoding ("Purple") machine as early as April 1941, although one was even sent to Panama; the total omission of the "East Wind, Rain" message, picked up on December 4 and making it clear that war was imminent and that it would be against the United States and Great Britain; the fact that by around 8:30 A.M. on the morning of the 7th, Admiral Stark was in his office and realized that war would break out at any moment, surely by 1:00 P.M., but refused to warn Kimmel; that Marshall sent his already absurdly delayed warning to General Short about noon on December 7 by ordinary commercial radio, not even marked "urgent" (Professor Drummond incorrectly implies that the message reached Short far too late—long after the Japanese planes had returned to their carriers—only because its transmission was delayed by operational difficulties on a rapid means of transmission); that the commander of the Japanese task force moving to attack Peart Harbor had been ordered to turn back if any diplomatic settlement had been reached, and that Nomura and Kurusu were unaware of the impending Pearl Harbor attack when they delivered the Japanese reply to Hull on the afternoon of the 7th.

Nevertheless, Professor Drummond's treatment of the background of Pearl Harbor is preferable to that of Herbert Feis, who avoids dealing with the damaging evidence against Roosevelt by virtually ignoring the events of December 3 to 7, or that of Langer and Gleason, who go to the utterly preposterous extreme of stating that: "Of Hawaii there was apparently no thought" on the part of Roosevelt and his circle on December 6 and 7.

Just where General Marshall was on the night of December 6, 1941, perhaps the most dramatic night of his life, remains one of the major unsolved mysteries of the Pearl Harbor fiasco. Prior to the Congressional investigation of Pearl Harbor, Marshall had been frequently pictured as having a simply prodigious memory akin to that of Lord Macaulay, but when questioned by the Congressional Committee early in December 1945, he maintained that he could not recall where he spent this momentous night. If Senator Homer Ferguson had revived the Pearl Harbor investigation in 1947, when the Republicans controlled Congress, instead of making his disastrous foray into the doings of Howard Hughes and his "cuties," this mystery could have been solved by subpoenaing the orderlies assigned to accompany Marshall on the night of December 6.

Only a complete simpleton could imagine that Marshall did not *actually* recall where he was on the night of December 6. Hence, it is evident that his denial must have been motivated by a desire to cover up an embarrassing reality. Since Marshall was a good family man of exemplary personal habits, there is little likelihood that he needed to conceal any morally shady behavior on that crucial night. He certainly did not spend the night in a brothel, a gambling den, or the apartment of a mistress. Confession of where he was on the night of the 6th must have involved something *politically* rather than morally

embarrassing to Marshall and his administrative superiors. If this be true, then it follows rather directly that he must have been in conference with Roosevelt. There would have been no reason for his hiding the fact that he visited Stimson or any other member of the Cabinet or the military forces. But the revelation that he had visited Roosevelt would have opened Marshall to sharp questioning by Senator Ferguson as to what went on at such a meeting, a matter which would have been delicate, to say the least, in the light of Marshall's strange behavior on the following day (December 7).

The Washington newspaperman who is best informed on this particular item, has informed me personally that he has evidence which leads him to feel certain that Marshall was summoned to the White House on the night of the 6th, after Lieutenant Schulz had delivered the first thirteen portions of the Japanese reply to Hull, to Roosevelt and Hopkins in the White House. It may well be that Marshall then and there received his orders from Roosevelt to stay away from his office as long as possible the next morning and not send Short any warning before noon, which would be far too late for Short to take any defensive action that might scare off the Japanese from an attack on Pearl Harbor. Since we know that Roosevelt talked to Admiral Stark on the phone after the latter left the theater on the night of the 6th, he may well have then given Stark his orders not to warn Admiral Kimmel at Pearl Harbor. As Stark knew by about 8:30 on the morning of the 7th that the Japanese were in all probability going to make an immediate attack on Pearl Harbor, presumably at 1:00 P.M. Washington time, and yet *never* warned Kimmel, such action on the part of an intelligent and patriotic officer can only be explained on the basis of his having been ordered by Roosevelt not to send any warning.

When, between 8:30 and 9:00 A.M. on the morning of December 7, Stark received the Japanese message indicating the attack at 1:00 P.M., he "cried out in great alarm" and exclaimed: "My God, this means war! I must get word to Kimmel at once!" He did nothing of the kind and his astounding failure to do so has never been explained. It may be that his exclamation was the automatic response of a trained naval officer, and that his later lapse was the result of recalling his phone conversation with Roosevelt the previous night. Anyone with a better explanation is welcome to produce it.

If Stark had been free to act in an independent and unhampered manner, there is no doubt that he would have remained awake and alert all night on December 6, seeking all possible information as to the time of the Japanese attack. At least, he would have demanded that all information of this sort be brought to him immediately. The Japanese message which indicated that the attack on Pearl Harbor would come at 1:00 P.M. Washington time was available at the Navy Department at 5:00 A.M. Had Stark been ready to receive this information, some seven hours before the attack, and immediately transmitted it to Admiral Kimmel, there would have been plenty of time to have moved the fleet out of the harbor and dispersed it in battle formation. General Short could have put his planes in the air and gotten the antiaircraft guns in readiness. There was still time for an effective warning at 9:00 A.M. We now know that had all this taken place the Japanese task force would have turned tail and started back home without even trying to drop one bomb. Professor Drummond calls Kimmel's failure to go on the alert without any warning, "unaccountable."

Apologists for Roosevelt grow indignant when such cogent and highly plausible circumstantial evidence is brought forth without absolute documentary proof. But it fits in with the logic of the circumstances and developments very perfectly and explains otherwise completely mysterious actions of the utmost importance. Such protests from the Roosevelt partisans come with poor logic when they, themselves, support such statements as those of Langer and Gleason, Feis, Millis, and Jonathan Daniels, who contend that Roosevelt and his group had no idea or evidence whatever that Pearl Harbor would be attacked, and were completely surprised by the assault.

This contention is disproved by a mountain of evidence. No evidence has been produced to prove that Roosevelt did not order Marshall and Stark to refrain from warning Short and Kimmel in time to avert the Japanese attack. In the light of the fact that both Marshall and Stark knew by the night of the 6th that there was every probability that the Japanese might strike at Pearl Harbor the next day, there seem to be only three possible explanations of why they did not warn Short and Kimmel: that they were idiots, that they were traitors, or that they had orders from Roosevelt not to do so. The last explanation appears the most plausible.

The present writer has been criticized by partisans of Roosevelt for listing these three possibilities. I have repeatedly challenged these critics to list other possibilities. They have not taken up the challenge. They cling still to the thesis that Roosevelt was completely surprised by the Pearl Harbor attack—that he had no idea it was in the making. Professor W. L. Langer puts this concisely: "Of Hawaii there apparently was no thought." Readers of the material in this present review-article may form their own opinion of the plausibility of this alternative.

It would appear that Roosevelt partisans will never concede his responsibility for the failure to warn the Pearl Harbor commanders unless revisionist historians produce a full confession in his own handwriting, signed by a notary public, with the notary's commission attested by a county clerk. Such a document is not likely to be produced.

Roosevelt and his circle had been alarmed on December 5 and 6 lest the Japanese might move deep into the South Pacific and compel Roosevelt to make war, even though the Japanese did not attack American territory or vessels. Roosevelt had approved a secret promise made to the British and Dutch at Singapore, late in April 1941, to do just this, a violation of his 1940 campaign pledge. But when Schultz brought to Roosevelt the Japanese reply on the night of December 6, all such worries vanished. On the 7th, Roosevelt was fully relaxed over his stamp collection, while Harry Hopkins fondled Fala, the President's Scotty terrier.

I offer here only a few samples of Professor Drummond's statements which support the revisionist position. The unneutral attitude of the Roosevelt administration is conceded by the statement on page 376: "Although neutrality remained its official text, every major aspect of United States policy was thus (by early 1940) oriented toward Great Britain and France." Again, it is remarked that the United States was virtually at war by the middle of March 1941: "By the middle of March 1941, therefore, the United States had assumed almost its full place in the world crisis. Nothing short of an immediate declaration of war could have rendered its alignments more clear."

One of the most important admissions is the explicit and repeated statement that from June 22, 1941, onward, Stalin seemed far more concerned about what he could grab *after* the war was over than in sound military strategy and the best means of winning the war. Nothing could make

clearer the mistake of Churchill and Roosevelt in expecting Stalin to be interested in a war for idealism, democracy, peace, or justice. He showed his hand from the start. His policies and demands flew in the face of the quasi-bogus Atlantic Charter.

Stalin's attitudes and policies were well known to Churchill and Roosevelt many weeks before Pearl Harbor. They attested to the wisdom of the pleas made after Hitler's invasion of Russia in June 1941, by former-President Hoover and Senators Taft and Truman, that the United States remain aloof from the conflict and permit the two dictators to battle themselves to a stalemate which would leave them both in too weak a condition to offer any threat to democratic countries.

Again, it is acknowledged that Japan was really forced into war by the economic acts and diplomatic aggression of the United States in July and August 1941, and that no Japanese diplomatic actions, however conciliatory, could well have averted war: "The freezing order, taken in conjunction with the warning of August 17, reduced the Japanese government, for all practical purposes, to a choice between surrender and war." In discussing the efforts of Prince Konoye to meet Roosevelt in August and September 1941, and preserve peace, Professor Drummond details fully (p. 306) the fact that Konoye was willing to agree in advance to "the four principles laid down by Hull in April as a basis for a Japanese-American settlement."

Summary of the Facts about Pearl Harbor

In the light of the effort of Professor Drummond and other anti-revisionist historians to demonstrate that Roosevelt and his circle had no reason to believe that there was any basis for fearing a Japanese attack on Pearl Harbor in early December 1941, it may be useful here to summarize briefly the more important, but by no means all of the evidence that refutes any such contention. First, as to the reasons for expecting that the attack would be made at Pearl Harbor.

For years before the Pearl Harbor attack, practice maneuvers of the American Navy in the Pacific had envisaged a surprise Japanese attack on Pearl Harbor, and in 1938 the aircraft carrier *Saratoga* had launched a successful surprise attack on Pearl Harbor from a point only a hundred miles distant. It was well recognized by the American Navy that Japan could not rationally risk a war with the United States unless it could deal an initial smashing blow against our Pacific fleet. Leading naval officers, including Admirals Stark and Richardson, had opposed bottling up the main Pacific fleet at Pearl Harbor, where the ships would be exposed like "sitting ducks" to a surprise Japanese attack. Roosevelt was so annoyed by the opposition of Admiral Richardson, commander-in-chief of the Pacific fleet, that he removed Richardson from his post.

Ambassador Grew had sent a warning from Tokyo that he had received an authentic "leak" to the effect that, in the event of a war between the United States and Japan, the latter would launch its part of the hostilities by a surprise attack on Pearl Harbor. The leading Washington authorities then admitted the probable validity of this warning.

Most important of all was the fact that, of all possible points of attack on American outposts, the Japanese demanded reports on American military and naval details only at Pearl Harbor from their espionage agents, but they did lay great emphasis on the Pearl Harbor reports and, after November 15, 1941, required that they be turned in at least twice a week. All this was well known to Washington authorities for months as a result of our breaking the Japanese code in August 1940.

The fact that, very early, the Administration apparently decided to make it impossible for the Pearl Harbor authorities to obtain their own warnings of a possible Japanese attack is underlined by the Washington decision to deny Pearl Harbor a decoding ("Purple") machine to intercept Japanese messages, although a machine was sent to the Philippines and Panama, and even to London. This decision came in April 1941, at the very time when American Army and Navy representatives were making the secret agreement with the British and Dutch to go to war, even if the Japanese did not attack American territory or ships. This agreement made it all the more desirable to promote a Japanese attack on Pearl Harbor, so as to assure American popular support for the war. Hence, whatever orders Roosevelt may have given Marshall and Stark on or before the night of December 6 to refrain from warning Short and Kimmel, the idea of leaving the latter two in the dark as to the facts about Japanese war plans long antedated December. It would appear that, even as early as April, it had been decided not to permit Short and Kimmel to know or do anything that might possibly avert a Japanese surprise attack at Pearl Harbor. In the light of all this evidence, no serious and informed person can well doubt that Roosevelt and his circle knew well enough by December 1, 1941, *where* the Japanese would, in all probability, launch their surprise attack.

How thoroughly Short and Kimmel would have been prepared for the Japanese attack if they had possessed a decoding ("Purple") machine to use on the spot at Pearl Harbor can be discerned from the fact that Panama, with such a machine, went on an all-out alert on November 29, days before the far more alarming intercepts were picked up by our Intelligence force on December 3 and 4. Indeed, Short and Kimmel would certainly have taken steps which would have led to the abandonment of the attack. This we now know from the Japanese documents about their task force which we have obtained since the war.

The answer to the question of *when* the surprise attack would be made was just as slowly but surely built up by December 6 and 7. The "Magic" intercepts, which had been going on ever since August 1940, had repeatedly revealed not only the basic Japanese desire for peace with the United States but also the clear determination of the Japanese, after the embargo and freezing actions of the United States in July 1941, to go to war if no diplomatic settlement was reached. It was rather generally agreed among both the political and military authorities in Washington that these economic, financial, and political actions of July and August 1941 meant war with Japan unless they were rescinded, and there was no intention on the part of Roosevelt and Hull even to modify them. It was fully recognized by Roosevelt, Hull, Stimson, Knox, and others in Washington that Hull's ultimatum to Japan on November 26, 1941, ended diplomatic relations with Japan and meant certain war with Japan. Hull himself frankly admitted this at the time. Hence, the Washington authorities knew that the Japanese reply to the ultimatum would be the signal for war on the part of Japan.

Remembering the proclivity of the Japanese to begin a war by a surprise attack and to make such an attack on a weekend, the more alert Washington authorities expected that the attack might even come on November 30. A Japanese message had been intercepted on the 28th which stated that diplomatic negotiations were to be broken off in "two or three days." When the attack did not come on the 30th, there was far greater expectation that it would fall on December 7. Hence, after November 30, more careful attention was given by the Intelligence officers picking up the intercepts of the Japanese messages to discover any information that would throw some possible light on the probability of war coming on December 7. They found plenty of evidence of this.

On December 3, a crucial Japanese message ordering the destruction of code machines and documents in all the main Japanese embassies was intercepted. This was recognized as proof of war at any moment. The next question was whether the war would be against Russia or against the United States and Britain. This was settled when the "East Wind, Rain" message was picked up on the 4th. Through previous intercepts, our Intelligence staff knew that this meant that the war would be against the United States and Britain, not against Russia. By the late afternoon of the 6th, the Japanese reply to Hull's ultimatum began to come in, and it was immediately apparent that this rejected the ultimatum and would break off diplomatic relations. From this time onward, it was evident that war would break out at any moment through a Japanese attack on Pearl Harbor. By 8:00 on the morning of December 7, the decoded final point in the Japanese reply to Hull, and an accompanying message to the Japanese envoys in Washington, revealed the fact that the Japanese would, in all probability, strike at Pearl Harbor at 1:00 P.M. Sunday afternoon, Washington time. When the Intelligence officers brought in the decoded final point to Stark, they told him just this. Therefore, by morning on December 7, both the time and place of the Japanese attack were known to the top political and military authorities in Washington.

The exact time when Roosevelt ordered Marshall and Stark not to warn Short and Kimmel is not known. It has been suggested that it might have been when Roosevelt phoned Stark late on the night of the 6th and during his likely conference with Marshall in the White House that same night. Others think it must have been as early as the alarming intercepts of November 28, and December 3 and 4. Admiral Robert A. Theobald, who has made the most careful study of the subject, logically concludes that it must have been *before* the afternoon of the 6th. By mid-afternoon of that day the Army Intelligence had decoded the so-called Japanese Pilot Message which announced that the ominous reply to Hull's ultimatum was about to be delivered. As Theobald concludes:

> The Washington silence which followed the receipt of the Pilot Message was the most vital key to the Pearl Harbor story. War, within 24 hours, initiated by a surprise attack which, according to all evidence, would be delivered on the U.S. Fleet in Hawaii, stared General Marshall and Admiral Stark in the face from that moment onward, and they made no move during 21 of the 22 hours which intervened before the attack to inform Admiral Kimmel and General Short. Nothing but a positive Presidential order could have so muzzled them after the receipt of the Pilot Message.

Some of this evidence is admitted, even if reluctantly, by Roosevelt apologists, unless they prefer to dodge the issue by ignoring most of the events after November 26. But they try to go on defending the "surprise" doctrine and the "Day of Infamy" myth by contending that, just before the attack, Roosevelt and his associates had forgotten all about Pearl Harbor in their momentary panic of December 5 and 6—mainly on the 6th—lest the mounting Japanese naval movements into the south Pacific would compel Roosevelt

to make good on the secret agreement of April 1941 with the British and Dutch to go to war even though the Japanese did not attack American territory or ships. This would, indeed, have been most embarrassing to Roosevelt. It would not only have been contrary to the Democratic campaign pledge of 1940, but would have deprived Roosevelt of the indispensable popular support which he could count on in the event of a prior Japanese attack, especially a surprise attack. Therefore, there is no doubt that he and the war group in Washington were actually in a panic on the 6th when they received the news of the advancing Japanese ship movements in the South Pacific.

But this temporary excitement and distraction ended on the evening of December 6, when Lieutenant Schulz brought to the President the Japanese reply to Hull. Roosevelt could then breathe a sigh of relief, return to the Pearl Harbor situation, and see to it that Short and Kimmel had no warning which would incite them to take any steps that might scare off the Japanese task force from executing its mission at Pearl Harbor. Indeed, it is evident that the panic on the 6th was based more on political fears than strategic realism. There was little probability that the Japanese would launch a war against the United States in the South Pacific without first attempting to destroy the American fleet, and this was anchored helplessly at Pearl Harbor.

It is also obvious that any Washington panic as late as the 5th or 6th day of December provides no excuse whatever for the failure of Roosevelt, Marshall, and Stark to warn Short and Kimmel in ample time. The sending of the Hull ultimatum on November 26, the intercept of the 28th revealing the imminent breaking off of diplomatic relations, the intercept of December 3 concerning the destruction of Japanese code machines, and the intercept of the 4th making it certain that the imminent attack would be against the United States and Britain all came before the 5th.

The revisionist historian who has made the most exhaustive study of the nature and amount of antiwar sentiment in the United States on the eve of Pearl Harbor has come to the conclusion that the only real panic on the part of Roosevelt and the war party in the White House was one based on the fear that the Japanese might *not* attack Pearl Harbor. Antiwar sentiment was so strong and widespread throughout the nation, even as late as December 6, 1941, that Roosevelt realized that he simply *had* to have a Japanese attack on American territory and forces to lead the United States into war with any success and popular enthusiasm.

Striking confirmation of the previous assertion that the intercepts of Japanese messages provided ample prior knowledge of the impending attack on Pearl Harbor has recently come to us from British sources. London had a "Purple" machine which had been denied to Short and Kimmel. General John N. Kennedy, Director of Military Operations in World War II, has recently published his memoirs, *The Business of War*. In these memoirs he reveals the fact that the British had picked up the information on December 3 that the Japanese were about to attack. This accords definitely with what we know about the Japanese messages, for it was on the 3rd that they ordered the destruction of the coding machines and diplomatic documents in their embassies, an act that was universally recognized as indicating the immediate onset of war. There is little doubt that the British believed that this attack would take place at Pearl Harbor. It is highly likely that the able and alert British Intelligence Service would have picked up the Japanese messages directing their espionage agents to report on American military and naval activities at Pearl Harbor, and not elsewhere. Hence, there is every probability that Churchill was as fully aware of the coming attack as was Roosevelt.

One may rest assured that neither Churchill nor Kennedy made any effort to warn Roosevelt and urge him to alert the commanders at Pearl Harbor. They were far too eager for American entry to do that. Earlier, Kennedy had noted that: "I am sure that we can make a plan for losing the war, but the only way to end it quickly is to get America in. We must concentrate on that." And, on the 3rd, he observed: "Japan looks like it is coming into the war at once. If we can get America in we shall gain on balance in the long run." Churchill heartily agreed. Whether Churchill and Roosevelt were in close secret communication between the 3rd and the 7th, while holding their breath in expectation of the Pearl Harbor attack, is not known at present, but it is highly likely that they were.[1]

Official Historians Now More Willing To Present the Truth than the Academic Fraternity

That there is a real danger in the work of court and official historians cannot well be doubted. But, in all fairness, it must be said that, thus far, the official historians have shown a greater inclination to face the facts about the coming of World War II than have the academic historians, fairly represented by Professor Drummond. As far back as the meeting of the American Historical Association in December 1954, two official historians, Dr. Stetson Conn and Dr. Louis Morton, reviewed the background of the Second World War and American participation in more realistic fashion than Professor Drummond or any other academic historian has done, outside the handful of revisionist professors. And in an article on the literature of the American entry: "Pearl Harbor in Perspective," in the *U.S. Naval Institute Proceedings,* April 1955, Dr. Morton dealt with the books on this hotly debated topic in a far more competent fashion than does Professor Drummond or any of his academic associates. This may be explained by the fact that, whatever the reluctance of academic historians to admit the factual justification for such a policy, the United States has gradually adopted a "revisionist" political and military attitude toward Western Germany and Japan since 1945 which can be defended logically only on the basis of revisionist historical evidence. Official historians are more likely to assimilate and reflect such official changes in policy than are their academic brethren.

NOTE

[1] Lest any reader get the false impression that I have clutched at every possible straw to indict Roosevelt, it may be pointed out that there is considerable new and important material on Pearl Harbor which I have not cited because of limitations of space, although I have examined it. It confirms or amplifies the interpretation given in the above article, but affords no grounds for altering any statement. Such material is Walter Lord's *The Day of Infamy,* which especially emphasizes how jittery the commander of the Japanese task force really was and how certainly he would have turned back if there had been any evidence that the Pearl Harbor commanders had any inkling of a prospective Japanese attack; *Admiral Kimmel's Story,* which reveals how thoroughly he and General Short were prevented from having available any of the vital "Magic" intercepts between November 26 and December 7, and how easy it would have been to prevent or intercept the Japanese attack if this material had been sent to them; Don Whitehead's *The F.B.I. Story,* which shows how the F.B.I. agents in Hawaii were prevented from cooperating with Short and Kimmel in putting before them discoveries which would have enabled them to anticipate the Japanese attack; the book by the Japanese Foreign Minister at the time of Pearl Harbor, Shigenroi Togo's *The Cause of Japan,* that stresses the Japanese efforts for peace in November 1941, and shows how Japan was forced into war for self-preservation; and the admirable series of articles by George Morgenstern in the Chicago *Tribune* bringing together the latest information on the Pearl Harbor attack. A Japanese spy was detected signalling the task force from Hawaii. Another vitally important document was left on a desk on December 6th (Saturday) ostensibly for editing on the following Monday, although its crucial content was readily apparent. None of this information reached Short or Kimmel.

[II, Spring 1958, 139–151]. Review of *The Passing of American Neutrality, 1937–1941,* by Donald F. Drummond, Ann Arbor: University of Michigan Press.

[31]

The United States as a "Revolutionary Society"

STEPHEN J. TONSOR

Stephen J. Tonsor (1923–   ) is professor of history at the University of Michigan and an associate editor of **Modern Age**. He lectures on European intellectual history and historiography and is the author of important studies on education, conservatism, neo-conservatism, national socialism, and the idea of equality, as well as of numerous articles and reviews in both popular and scholarly journals. He was educated at Blackburn College in Carlinville, Illinois, the University of Zurich, and the University of Illinois. He has received numerous prizes and awards, including an honorary D.Litt. from Blackburn College in 1972.

THE ASSERTION THAT two hundred years after a revolution reluctantly made and a Constitution which strengthened rather than weakened the conservative character of American political institutions and arrangements, American society and politics are still revolutionary is, I suggest, a rather daring thesis. Other revolutions have run their courses from high hopes to Thermidorian reaction in the passage of a few brief years and while the Russians and the Chinese have talked of "permanent revolution" they have exhibited only too clearly the ways in which revolutionary elites, while proclaiming themselves the handmaidens of popular revolution have become in fact new privileged and exploiting classes. It is odd and very nearly contradictory that a conservative revolution now two centuries old should be the only "permanent revolution" history has

known, a revolution which has perennially transformed the structure and the nature of life in the United States.

It is not obvious to everyone at the present time, however, that the United States is still a revolutionary society. There have been a good many recent assertions that American society has hardened into a totalitarian mold, that repression is the chief characteristic of American political life and that there is both less liberty and less social justice in America than in many contemporary Marxist states. Perhaps, then, I would not be ill advised were I to first present my reasons for believing America to be still and increasingly revolutionary before I go on to explore the reasons why I believe America has been able to maintain and to broaden its revolutionary base.

It is important that we demonstrate

381

clearly the truly revolutionary character of the events of 1776 and their continuing impact upon American society. It has become fashionable on the left to assert that there was no genuine revolution or that if a revolution took place it was strangled by the ensuing conservative reaction. The study of American history has produced many stern judges and doubting Thomases. None was tempted to take a more critical attitude than were Charles and Mary Beard. When, however, they came to make an assessment of the American revolution in their *Rise of American Civilization* (p. 296) they pointed unhesitatingly to the truly revolutionary character of the events they described:

> If a balance sheet is struck and the rhetoric of the Fourth of July celebrations is disconnected, if the externals of the conflict are given proper perspective and background, then it is seen that the American Revolution was more than a war on England. It was in truth an economic, social, and intellectual transformation of prime significance—the first of those modern world-shaking reconstructions in which mankind has sought to cut and fashion the tough and stubborn web of fact to fit the pattern of its dreams.

But even without the Beards's respected view we know that there was a genuine revolution because we live out its enduring consequences and its continuing ramifications. Indeed, one of our least admirable contemporary attitudes is our retreat from the novelty and the implications of our revolutionary heritage and our search (a vain one to be sure) into what we think to be the quiet reaches of the past for a golden age of tranquillity. Surfeited on change we imagine that at some golden moment in some magical American Camelot men were free of the necessity to choose and to change; the necessity that the initial revolutionary transformation of our society has imposed on all of us. While the Left sees insufficient change of a particular socioeconomic and political type,

the Right rejects those changes which necessarily follow from the principles of the revolution.

That the American revolution was indeed a "world-shaking reconstruction" as the Beards insisted it was is borne out by the testimony of diverse observers of American society. Several years ago, for example, John W. Holmes, director general of the Canadian Institute of International Affairs, was interviewed by John Chancellor of NBC News. In that interview Holmes made the following important point:

> The United States is a pioneer society even in its adversities. In spite of what many young Americans say, it is not counter-revolutionary—it is still a revolutionary society. It seems to me that you are going through a further and very turbulent extension of democracy. All sorts of people are participating in the policy-making process who never did before, and this is a trial other countries have yet to cope with.

Mr. Holmes's observations concerning the revolutionary character of contemporary American society are not entirely original. Much the same observations were made by a Frenchman, a man of the political Left, Jean-François Revel, in his book *Without Marx or Jesus*, published in 1970 at the very peak of our recent "time of troubles" and self-doubt:

> . . . To my mind, present day America is a laboratory of revolution—in the sense that eighteenth century England was to Voltaire . . . (p. 266). The stuff of revolution, and its first success, must be the ability to innovate. It must be mobility with respect to the past, and speed with respect to creation. In that sense, there is more revolutionary spirit in the United States today, even on the Right, than there is on the Left anywhere else. (p. 123)

One might enlarge both the number of quotations and the number of authors. The fact is that America is a revolutionary society, has been such from the outset, and derives a great deal of its revolutionary *élan* from the events and ideas of its initial revolutionary movement.

But even if we admit that the United States is a revolutionary society in which the processes of political, economic and social transformation are constantly at work we must, in search both of historical and self understanding, ask the question "why?" There have been other revolutions in other places and other times and the consequences have been far more ambiguous; far less clear, far less progressive and optimistic. If one studies the history of France in the nineteenth and twentieth centuries it becomes clear that a well-intentioned and successful revolution is not enough to energize permanently the forces of progressive change in a society. For the past two centuries France has vacillated between the poles of anarchy and authoritarian Caesarism. There have been brief and extended periods of liberal and even democratic government but these have not been characterized by any high degree of certainty and self-assurance. England alone has shown throughout this whole period of the past two centuries the continuity of development in the direction of liberal and democratic institutions comparable to the American experience, but that development has at best been tardy, grudging and complicated by ancient social and cultural encrustations and deep-seated class divisions and antagonisms. One is tempted to argue that innovative and democratic societies do not often arise from liberating revolutions.

And so we must return to the question of why the revolutionary tradition has maintained its vitality in the American setting, why America in this respect has been so much more fortunate, so much more creative, and so much more dynamic than other societies which have passed through a revolutionary experience.

And no doubt good fortune, pure luck played a role. "*Amerika, du hast es besser,*" the German poet Goethe wrote in 1823. Freely translated he said "America, you're lucky," though he hastened to add as his reasons, "the lack of inner confusion, a useless fixation on the past and vain conflict." Others have adduced different reasons for considering America a fortunate, a lucky land. There were the nearly empty continent, the favorable geographic and climatic factors, the untapped and abundant natural resources, the immense land area, the promise and the actuality of Eldorado even though the fountain of youth and the earthly paradise remained a dream. And yet it could not have been luck alone, or even chiefly, which accounted for the peculiarly American progressive dynamism. The Great Russian peoples entered the underpopulated and resource-rich vastness of Central Asia and Siberia and their authoritarian institutions were not transformed. Latin America was not so different geographically from North America and yet its political and cultural experience was wholly different. They too had liberal revolutions, often modeled on the revolution which had taken place in the Thirteen Colonies and yet they relapsed very shortly into political patterns of authority and tyranny. Even Australia and New Zealand seem stodgy and conservative in comparison with the cultural, social and political experimentation which has characterized the United States. The existence then of a great, empty, unexploited land is not the answer to our question of why the United States has been characterized by a revolutionary dynamism.

Long ago men identified a "restless temper" with the private enterprise of democratic societies; societies in which men gloried in being thrown upon their own resources and encouraged to make their own decisions. On the eve of the outbreak of the Peloponnesian War Thucydides, in Book I, Chapter 6, puts into the mouths of the Corinthian ambassadors to Sparta a speech concerning the Athenians which must remind us at nearly every point of peculiarly American characteristics.

> Then also we think we have as much right as anyone else to point out faults in our neighbors, especially when we consider the enormous difference between you and the Athenians. To our minds, you are quite unaware of this difference; you have never yet tried to imagine what sort of people these Athenians are against whom you will have to fight—how much, indeed how completely different from you. An Athenian is always an innovator, quick to form a resolution and quick at carrying it out. You, on the other hand, are good at keeping things as they are; you never originate an idea; and your action tends to stop short of its aim. Then again, Athenian daring will outrun its own resources; they will take risks against their better judgment, and still, in the midst of danger, remain confident. But your nature is always to do less well than you could have done, to mistrust your own judgment, however sound it may be, and to assume that dangers will last for ever. Think of this, too: while you are hanging back, they never hesitate; while you stay at home, they are always abroad; for they think that the farther they go the more they will get, while you think that any movement may endanger what you have already. If they win a victory they follow it up at once, and if they suffer a defeat, they scarcely fall back at all. As for their bodies, they regard them as expendable for their city's sake, as though they were not their own; but each man cultivates his own intelligence, again with a view of doing something noble for his city. If they aim at something and do not get it, they think they have been deprived of what belonged to them already; whereas, if their enterprise is successful, they regard that success as nothing compared to what they will do next. Suppose they fail in some undertaking; they make good the loss immediately by setting their hopes in some other direction. Of them alone it may be said that they possess a thing almost as soon

as they have begun to desire it, so quickly with them does action follow upon decision. And so they go on working away in hardship and danger all the days of their lives, seldom enjoying their possessions because they are always adding to them. Their view of a holiday is to do what needs doing; they prefer hardship and activity to peace and quiet. In a word, they are by nature incapable of either living a quiet life themselves or of allowing anyone else to do so.

Thucydides, as Herodotus before him, had no doubt that this "restless temper" which characterized Athens was a consequence of her democratic institutions. Of course democracy did play a major role both in Athens and in America in energizing the forces of innovation. But democracy alone was not the explanation, for Sparta too was, in its strange way, democratic, and there are contemporary democratic societies which one could hardly describe as dynamic. The explanation for our peculiar dynamism is not democracy alone but democracy coupled to the spirit of enterprise. That "restless temper" was most manifest when it was coupled to the desire for unique individual expression and the compelling drive to self-advantage. Self-fulfillment and free choice have been in America extended into every aspect of life. From the abandonment of primogeniture, titles and hereditary status to the right of every man to build the biggest, costliest, and ugliest house in the neighborhood or to live in the meanest, shabbiest shack in town, the motive has been the same. Americans have believed that every man should be free to seek his bliss and his advantage on his own terms. The basic liberal assumption that private advantage redounds to public benefit has been the essential and fundamental assumption. From the outset democratic politics was related directly in fact and in theory to freedom of enterprise in economics. John Stuart Mill after reading

Tocqueville on *Democracy in America* quoted with approval the lines in which Tocqueville expressed his belief that the links between capitalism and democracy were fundamental:

> As soon as land was held on any other than feudal tenure, and personal property began in its turn to confer influence and power, every improvement which was introduced in commerce or manufactures was a fresh element of the equality of conditions. Henceforward every new discovery, every new want which it engendered, and every new desire which craved satisfaction, was a step toward the universal level. The taste for luxury, the love of war, the sway of fashion, the most superficial as well as the deepest passions of the human heart, co-operated to enrich the poor and to impoverish the rich. From the time when the exercise of the intellect became a source of strength and wealth, it is impossible not to consider every addition to science, every fresh truth, every new idea, as a germ of power placed within the reach of the people. Poetry, eloquence, and memory, the grace of wit, the glow of imagination, the depth of thought, and all the gifts of providence which are bestowed by providence without respect of persons, turned to the advantage of democracy; and even when they were in the possession of its adversaries, they still served its cause by throwing into relief the natural greatness of man; its conquests spread, therefore, with those of civilization and knowledge; and literature became an arsenal, where the poorest and the weakest could always find weapons to their hand.

Tocqueville saw in this movement such evidence of inevitability that he assumed it to be the work of providence. Today we are less certain of the inevitable march of equality however basic the drive for equality may be as an element in human behavior. It is clear, however, that the energies released through the free exercise, not only of the franchise, but of every human gift and talent unencumbered by tradition and unimpeded by society or the state, has transformed and continues to transform the very conditions of human existence. No doubt there are many Americans who would be delighted were that "restless temper" to be quieted, were the revolutionary energies of our society to be stilled or stopped. Sometimes as I walk across the campus I yearn to see the year when the approach of spring does not mean that the grounds will be dug up, that old buildings will come down and new buildings rise, that old ideas will be in the discard and that a band of young turks will be pressing for change and innovation—and the campus is our society in microcosm; change is the overriding aspect of our existence. It is the most characteristic feature of our society. My purpose is not to praise or to laud change or even to assert my admiration for a society which is constantly in flux. Indeed, my own conservative sympathies lead me to mistrust change and to feel uneasy when I am caught up in some rapid transition. My personal feelings, however, are of little importance; what is important is that we recognize what the full consequences of freedom have been in our society. No doubt some of the consequences have been unacceptable to many men but we cannot doubt that there has been revolutionary change. Those who have lived through a revolution know it well enough. Things are simply different than they were before. The color, the texture and the mode of life have changed and these changes have drawn us all into their circle.

We all know, moreover, that freedom has been either the remote or the immediate cause for these changes. Revolutions have a way of petering out; their mighty currents sinking into the sand in the course of a few decades or even less. That this has not happened in the United States has been due to that "restless temper" and that in turn has been in sub-

stantial measure the reflection of a peculiarly American economic and intellectual
pattern. In each generation the drive to
innovation and the retesting of our institutions has been due, above all, to the
institutions of a market economy and the
spirit of enterprise. In the intellectual
sphere it has been a reflection of our
dedication to freedom of the press and
general access to education. We have continued to be a revolutionary people then
because we have maintained a free market
in goods and a free market in ideas.

Many of the complaints which thoughtful men have lodged against private enterprise are the same arguments, or arguments parallel to those, which they have
lodged against a free press. They have
said that it is wasteful, that it produces a
society that is materialistic, vulgar, corrupt
in taste, and indifferent in morals; that it
produces a world in which the mediocre
rather than the best prevails, that it rewards indifference to the truth and the
fast-buck artist, the con-man and the literary hack. And no doubt all these charges
are true. The competition of goods and
the competition of ideas are no doubt in
the short run wasteful, and their effects
lead some men to mediocrity and vulgarity. But this system which rewards innovation and guarantees it through free and
open competition is the only method any
society has of arriving in the long run at
both the truth and abundance, at not only
those things which are good but those
things which are the best available. The
central dictum of the philosophy of Charles
Sanders Peirce, the key to his philosophy
of science was, "Do not block the way of
inquiry." As theorists of market economics
have demonstrated over and over again
the market is not simply an economic
device but a discovery mechanism as crucial in its way for knowing as the work of
scientific laboratories. We have remained
politically resilient because we have re-

warded innovation and difference, because we have encouraged men to do
their own things and because we have
asserted always that the long-range welfare of the individual is more important
than the short-range welfare of the group.
In short, the founding fathers gambled
on the desirability and the permanency
of change.

Although the frontier alone neither
produced liberty nor insured its survival,
it did provide the habitat in which freedom flourished. One need not subscribe
completely to the Turner thesis in one of
its variations in order to accept the evidence of the impact of the American
landscape and American conditions upon
the political and social institutions of the
United States. It was precisely in this
environment where geographic mobility
paralleled and fostered social mobility that
our "restless temper" found its expression
eased and strengthened. There was, in
the very facts of geography, an invitation
to expansiveness and the abundance and
bounty of the land encouraged men to
what must at times have seemed a wasteful
experimentation. Men were induced by
nature to try their luck, and life-styles
which were both innovative and imper-
manent appeared and disappeared with
bewildering rapidity. Of course experimentation was not always rewarded, there
have been tragedies enough in the American past to remind us of that, but there
have always been the bonanzas, too, the
big but seemingly foolish idea that paid
off handsomely. Ours is a landscape which
has encouraged the far-out, the grandiose, the individual, the deviant, the violent
and the unusual. It has been a landscape
which has seemed in natural league with
the other forces of liberty to assure the
continued existence of freedom on this
continent; a landscape rich enough to
encourage the wildest hope, and the most
magnificent of ambitions, yet challenging

enough to ensure that the dictum of Darius which we find in Herodotus that "soft lands make soft men," would never be applied to the American scene.

Perhaps the most important characteristic of that landscape in its impact on politics and society has been its diversity. By diversity I do not mean the "regionalism" which has played such a large role in the explanations of American politics and history, particularly in the form given those explanations by Frederick Jackson Turner and his followers. Regionalism has been based on dividing and defining differences and I am concerned with those smaller gradations and shades which make the garden I grow in my backyard different from that of my friend who lives only two-hundred miles away. In Europe we take the impact of those differences for granted, for there variety has been entrenched in history. In our new land with its endless variations and differences we often fail to see our daily encounter with a complex and variegated environment as a source of the most profound differences in character and mood in American political life. In periods characterized by the rapid shift of population such as has taken place during the past three decades, we fail to note the influence of those differences inherent in the landscape. It is likely those great movements of population are now drawing to a close and we shall once more discover how widely we differ from one another rather than how like one another we are.

Diversity, even the subtle diversity of the landscape, is an important source of liberty and an important fount of change. One of the most important theoretical questions debated by Americans in the years of the Republic's foundation was the question of whether or not republican institutions could survive in an extended and sizeable state or, to put the question in the words of Alexander Hamilton in

The Federalist No. 9, "the necessity of a contracted territory for a republican government." Ancient precedent and modern opinion seemed to agree that republican institutions could survive and prosper only in the narrow territories of the small state. The Federalist papers turn to this question again and again and Jay, Hamilton, and Madison each in turn deny the validity of that assertion. Their reasons for denying it are all interesting and correct, but one in particular commands our attention at the present time. The chief threat to liberty in the view of the writers of the Federalist papers was the concentration of power especially as it is reflected in an unchecked and tyrannical majority. In *The Federalist* No. 51, either Hamilton or Madison argues that the chief way of preventing such a concentration of power is through diversification of interest. The argument runs as follows:

It is of great importance in a republic not only to guard the society against the oppression of its rulers, but to guard one part of the society against the injustice of the other part. Different interests necessarily exist in different classes of citizens. If a majority be united by a common interest, the rights of the minority will be insecure. There are but two methods of providing against this evil: the one by creating a will in the community independent of the majority—that is, of society itself; the other, by comprehending in society so many separate descriptions of citizens as will render an unjust combination of a majority of the whole improbable, if not impracticable. The first method prevails in all governments possessing an hereditary or self-appointed authority. This, at best, is a precarious security. . . . The second method will be exemplified in the federal republic of the United States. Whilst all authority in it will be derived from and dependent on the society, the society itself will be broken into so many parts, interests and classes of citizens, that the rights of individuals, or of the minority, will be in little danger from interested combinations of the majority. In a free government the security for civil rights must be the same as that for religious rights. It consists in the one case in the multiplicity of interests, in the other in the multiplicity of sects. The degree of security in both cases will depend on the number of interests and sects; and this may be presumed to depend on the extent of country and the number of people comprehended under the same government. . . .

Consequently the greatest and most telling defense of size in the republic is the fact that size itself will help to guarantee diversity and multiplicity. It is diversity alone which in the long run will prevent the tyranny of the majority in any society and guarantee that freedom which has always been the great boast of our American polity. The drive to diversity in the actuality of American life was even greater than its theoretical formulation in the Federalist papers. It has been a drive, moreover, which has not slackened with time but which in our own days has taken on a sharp and powerful new meaning. The racial and ethnic claims to full and distinctive participation, not as individuals but as members of an identifiable minority group, participation in both the culture and the polity has created a wholesome check on what threatened to become an unexamined consensus. Submerged minorities, cultural, political, sexual, and social, have emerged within the last few decades to challenge an older complacency and to demand the right to participate fully after their own unique fashion in the shaping of American life. They represent a vast potential for the renewal of the American system and they provide, as the founding fathers anticipated, a dynamic to drive on the engine of liberty.

It is apparent, even from what I have so far said, that a powerful tension exists in the American polity and American society between the ideals of complete liberty and full equality. I am highly unoriginal in pointing this out. We have chosen to absolutize neither the ideal of liberty nor the ideal of equality, sacrificing the one to the other as has happened in the French, Russian, and other revolutions. Rather we have tried to have it both ways; demanding achievement and status and yet insisting, perversely perhaps, upon equality; boasting of our liberty yet willing from time to time to see that liberty attenuated and diluted in order that we may all enjoy a bit more equality of condition. So much I think has often been observed and remarked on. It has not been so often pointed out, however, that this relationship of tension and reciprocity in the American system is one of the major sources of its ability to transform and to change the conditions of American life. We have remained in a state of flux because we have refused to become totalists with respect to our ideals. We have refused to succumb to the beguiling power of a single good idea and have alternated in an unseemly but very practical fashion between liberty and equality. In questions of class conflict, race, education, and minority rights in recent times we have sacrificed a measure of liberty in order to secure a greater degree of equality but there are limits, as evidenced by the busing controversy and the question of open admissions to colleges, to cite only two examples, chosen at random; limits beyond which the American people will not go in sacrificing liberty to equality. A shifting adjustment between liberty and equality is always in process in American life and we have managed because of it to become both more free and more equal. Whether or not in the years ahead we shall be able to maintain this feat of social prestidigitation remains to be seen. Should we lose it I believe the system itself will falter and slow and we will find ourselves like so many other political systems and sects ruined by one good idea taken to its extreme.

We now stand at the end of a decade in which anti-institutionalism has been a major force. Political, cultural, social, and religious institutions during the past ten years have not only had a bad press, they have been vigorously attacked and denounced by the trendy intellectual elites of the Western world. That has happened before and is not necessarily a sign of danger. More important, however, is the fact that ordinary men and women have lost faith and confidence, in those institutions and often not without reason. The courts have not functioned well. The holder of the highest office in the land has laid himself open to charges which, if true, exhibit a contempt for the values of our system almost unprecedented in our history. To argue that these developments came at the end of a period during which federal powers have been surrendered by the states and concentrated in Washington; that in this period the office of the presidency moved from republican simplicity of manner to imperial grandeur and in this period of time more and more of the everyday decisions of our public lives were made at a great remove from the people whom those decisions affect— to say this and to add that other recent presidents appear to have acted no better, simply compounds the problem and deepens public pessimism. Nor do Congress, state legislatures, and state administrative officers fare better in the public estimate.

It may seem presumptuous then to argue that the basic structure of our institutions as set forth in the Constitution is sound and functioning and that the self-correcting powers of the system have asserted themselves and are, in fact, even now producing the necessary changes.

For the Constitution, conservative in temper, liberal in principle, has been, it seems to me, one of the chief reasons for ordered change in our society. That conservative temper of the Constitution is reflected in its evaluation of men and their motives and its ability to employ even self-interest in the pursuit of the common good. Federalist paper No. 51 (which surely is one of the most remarkable documents in all of the American state papers) puts the case in the following words:

> . . . Ambition must be made to counteract ambition. The interest of the man must be connected with the constitutional rights of the place. It may be a reflection on human nature, that such devices should be necessary to control the abuses of government. But what is government itself, but the greatest of all reflections on human nature? If men were angels no government would be necessary. If angels were to govern man, neither external nor internal controls on government would be necessary. In framing a government which is to be administered by men over men, the great difficulty lies in this: you must first enable the government to control the governed; and in the next place oblige it to control itself. A dependence on the people is, no doubt, the primary control on the government; but experience has taught mankind the necessity of auxiliary precautions.

Those "auxiliary precautions" have been written into the fabric of the Constitution. They lie at the heart of our self-correcting system. It is they which, even and particularly, at the moments of greatest crisis have enabled us to proceed in our public and private lives with a measure of assurance making those changes, in the sum revolutionary, which have enabled us to live in ordered freedom. How sad, then, "the fact," as Irving Kristol recently pointed out, that, "at our major universities it is almost impossible to find a course, graduate or undergraduate, devoted to *The Federalist*." (How important those papers are may be determined by anyone who cares to read No. 65 written by Alexander

Hamilton on the subject of impeachment.) And so, in the final analysis, it is our basic institutions and the founding instruments of the Declaration of Independence and the Constitution which have perpetuated our values and given our system its elasticity and its dynamism.

The men who made the American Revolution were reluctant rebels. They did not deliberately set out to create an ideal society and forge the fabric of a new nation in the fires of war. They were surprised at their own audacity and fearful of its consequences. And when they sought to justify their actions to themselves and to the world at large they rested their arguments on an appeal to the British Constitution and a demand that their traditional rights as Englishmen be recognized. Few, if any, revolutions have been so conservative in their inspiration.

Yet once those liberties and historical rights were taken seriously, once they had become the central principle of a new polity, they changed and transformed the whole texture of American political and social life. It was, indeed, as though the American Revolution had salvaged the great vital principle that stood at the heart of the English historical experience and had given it new life and meaning. Far from being a break with the past and its institutions, the new American nation sheltered, preserved and quickened political ideas, constitutional forms and political institutions that were temporarily in eclipse in Europe.

Sometimes an act of conservation is a truly revolutionary action. The concrete realization of specific liberties, no matter how partial or incomplete, was in the instance of the American revolution the great device by which liberty permeated the totality of American life in the years that were to come. That process has not ended and I would like to remind you that success as well as failure exacts a price.   [XIX, Spring 1975, 136–145]

[IV]

Law, Legislation, and Liberty

[32]

Criminal Character and Mercy

RUSSELL KIRK

Russell Kirk (1918–   ), the founding editor of Modern Age, *1957–1960, is a leading exponent of philosophical conservatism in America. For his achievement of four decades as a man of letters—during the course of which he wrote the celebrated* The Conservative Mind *(1953),* Enemies of the Permanent Things *(1969),* Eliot and His Age *(1972),* The Roots of American Order *(1974), etc.—he received the Weaver Award of the Ingersoll Prizes in 1985. Kirk has been professor or visiting distinguished professor at several universities and colleges. The only American to earn a Doctor of Letters degree from St. Andrews University in Scotland, where in idyllic surroundings he saw "the metaphysical principle of continuity given visible reality," he has also been awarded many honorary degrees.*

TO PERCEIVE TRUTH, we require images. As G. K. Chesterton put it, all life is an allegory, and we can understand it only in parable. I am about to offer some observations concerning mercy: that is, mercy toward deadly criminals. I believe that the capital penalty has a compassionate function. I propose to make my point through presenting a series of images— some of them drawn from perceptive works of fiction, others taken from my own experience and acquaintance in the course of a wandering life.

My introductory image is extracted from a memorable short story by the German writer Stefan Andres, "We Are God's Utopia." This is a realistic episode from the Spanish Civil War, and it takes place in a desolated convent in a deserted walled town. One faction—the Reds, apparently—have confined two hundred prisoners of the opposing faction in the cells of a convent. These prisoners will be executed if the battle goes against the faction to which the jailers belong.

The captors are commanded by a lieutenant, Don Pedro, who already has committed indescribable atrocities. The memory of the worst of these acts will not permit the lieutenant to sleep—not in this very convent where he tortured the nuns to death.

Among the prisoners here is a former priest, Paco, taken in arms. Don Pedro implores Paco to hear his confession, so that he may sleep again. Although no enthusiast himself for the rite of confession, Paco consents to receive this dreadful penitent. In the course of the lieutenant's confession, Paco learns that Pedro, when a boy, had tortured cats hideously; that he had beheaded the puppets in his own puppet-theater; that he had flung to his death the kindest man Paco had ever

393

known; that he had kept the nuns screaming in agony all night long. Yet Teniente
Pedro has taken no real pleasure in these
acts; they have made him sad, at the time
of their commission and thereafter. He
says to Paco, "I dwell in myself as though
in a grave!"

The sometime priest absolves Pedro,
for at the moment of absolution he is
contrite. (Half an hour later, nevertheless,
he will direct the massacre of the prisoners.) But before granting absolution,
the confessor instructs his penitent, who
kneels before him:

> "I tell you, it would be good for you if you
> were to die in the war." The voice was silent;
> after a pause it went on. "Yes, pray to God
> for death. According to the laws of man—
> but no, you know that!—no sin can separate
> you from God if you want to come back to
> Him, but it can separate you from life. For
> this reason, the death penalty for certain
> crimes has a decidedly compassionate char-
> acter. You are a criminal of this sort. Pray
> to God for death!"

To Don Pedro, death would bring relief
from his ghastly sadness and the moral
solitude in which he had suffered since
childhood; relief from the tormenting
memory of his atrocious crimes; relief
from the depravity of his own nature.
Like most murderers, Pedro is not totally
corrupt: he is capable of some kindly acts
and of gratitude. But there is no way in
which he can be redeemed or relieved of
the torment of being what he is, in the
flesh—except through death. To such a
one, capital punishment would be an order of release. Sin already has separated
the atrocious homicide from true life; yet,
through grace in death, even the slayer's
soul may be redeemed. Death is not the
greatest of evils. In the language of orthodoxy, indeed, death is no evil at all.

At this point, it may be objected that I
have offered merely a fictitious instance.
But great works of fiction are more true

than particular incidents of the actual:
that is why they are recognized as great.
Andres gives us in this story a kind of
distillation from mankind's experience of
spirit. Those of us who have knocked
about the world have encountered our
real Teniente Pedros. It is not pleasant to
meet them in confined quarters. A friend
of mine spent much of his life in the
company of conspicuous specimens of
such unregenerate humanity. Permit me
to offer you, then, a different sort of
image: that of my friend the late Clinton
Wallace, very much flesh and blood.

Clinton was the most heartfelt advocate
of capital punishment that ever I have
met. At the age of fourteen, Clinton had
run away from a brutal father. Thereafter,
until he came to live in my house, Clinton
spent his life either on the roads or in
prisons. His convictions were for petty
offenses against property—usually the pil-
fering of church poor-boxes—or for endeavoring to escape from prisons. He was
a giant in size and strength, and an innocent.

I do not mean that Clinton was a fool:
the prison psychiatrists wrote him down
as "dull normal," but Clinton was neither
dull nor normal. He did not drink, except
for one glass of beer on especially conviv-
ial occasions; did not smoke; did not curse;
did not offend against women or children.
His only vice, aside from petty larceny in
time of necessity, was indolence. (Like
Don Pedro, though, Clinton dwelt in himself, as in a grave.)

Clinton could recite a vast deal of good
poetry, could make himself amusing, loved
children, and prided himself upon being
non-violent. The worst aspect of life in
prison, Clinton told me once, was not the
boredom, or even the loss of liberty, but
the foul language of the convicts—their
every other word an obscenity. In recent
years, Clinton added, prison conversation
had grown monotonous—everybody dis-

cussing interminably the pleas of Miranda and Escobedo.

My wife once asked Clinton—who lived with us for six years near the end of his tether—how many of the men in prison are innocent.

"They're all innocent, Annette," Clinton replied. "You only have to ask them." He chuckled briefly. "They're all guilty, really, guilty as sin. Many of them are animals, brutes that ought to be put out of their misery."

From the worst forms of degradation at the hands of fellow prisoners, Clinton had been saved by his size, strength, and stentorian power of lung. But he had not been spared the company of the depraved. For some months, in one prison, Clinton's cellmate had been a man who had taken off his wife's head. That missing head had never been discovered. Clinton (who, like Don Pedro, had trouble getting to sleep) used to lie awake in his bunk at night, watching his cell-mate in the opposite bunk and stroking his own throat to reassure himself.

Clinton went on, in his kitchen-table conversations with us, to talk of the horror and the danger of existence in company with such men. Any tolerably decent person who had been sentenced to confinement might find himself at their mercy. "They're lower than beasts." Out of compassion for the other prisoners and for the guards, Clinton argued, the death penalty ought to be imposed upon men who had committed deliberately those crimes once called capital.

"Nobody can reform you," Clinton would continue. "There's no such thing as a 'reformatory' or a 'correctional facility.' The only person who can reform you is yourself. You have to begin by admitting to yourself that you did wrong. Then you may begin to improve a little."

Clinton Wallace had concluded from much observation and painful experience that very few deadly criminals possess either the ability or the intention to reform themselves. It is their nature, outside of prison, to prey beast-like upon whomever they may devour; and if confined within prison, these human predators are impelled by their very nature to ruin the other inmates. From the time he first was imprisoned—for truancy, at the age of fourteen—Clinton had been flung behind bars with such men. To make a swift lawful end of them, he declared, would be a work of mercy for all concerned.

My acquaintance with convicts is not confined to Clinton Wallace. For armed robbery, my friend Eddie was sentenced to three to thirty years imprisonment. (It was his first offense, committed under the influence of a kinsman and perhaps of drugs.) Within the walls, Eddie's religious yearnings of earlier years returned to him, and he grew almost saintly amidst the general corruption. As a reward for his good conduct, the warden was ready to assign him to an open-air work detail in the Upper Peninsula of Michigan. "For God's sake," Eddie cried, "don't do that to me! Put me in solitary if you have to, but keep me behind these walls! In a camp like that, I wouldn't have a chance against the gangs."

Eddie was a rough-and-ready young man, a seaman by trade, courageous to the point of recklessness. He did not labor under any illusions concerning the character of the dominant spirits within prison walls. He knew that no adequate punishment could be imposed upon any "lifer" who might take it into his head to do Eddie a mischief—including as "mischief" a knife between Eddie's ribs. So Eddie was no advocate of gentleness with the brutally violent.

Both Clinton and Eddie, flesh and blood though they were, have appeared as characters in short stories of mine—Clinton in my best-known tale, "There's a Long,

Long Trail a-Winding"; Eddie in my more recent story "Lex Talionis." I drew them with affection from the life. The final penalty called capital punishment does something to protect those men behind bars, like Clinton and Eddie, who may yet redeem themselves.

I have been suggesting through these incidents and images that capital punishment possesses certain merciful aspects. It may be merciful, first, in that it may relieve a depraved criminal of the horror of being what he is. It may be merciful, second, in that it can help to protect the less guilty from the more guilty. And in a third way, which I am about to touch upon, capital punishment may mercifully protect the guiltless from the more extreme forms of violence.

Here the arguments concerning "deterrence," already widely discussed, may emerge afresh. But let me assure you that I have no intention of returning to the theoretical and statistical considerations advanced so often. Instead I offer you now another image which strongly impressed itself upon my consciousness, early. It is an image formed out of a real happening—the kidnapping of my grandfather.

Although that abduction occurred when I was a small boy, I recollect all the details clearly. Frank Pierce, my grandfather, was a bank manager, a well-read man, kindly and charitable, the leading spirit of our Lower Town by the great railway yards outside Detroit. During the 1920's he repelled several attempts at robbery of his bank. (He carried a tear-gas fountain pen and kept a pistol handy in a drawer, but always had succeeded in baffling the robbers without using either instrument.) On one occasion, for all that, my grandfather lost the contest.

As he walked from his house toward his bank, very early in the summer morning, an automobile drew up alongside him, a submachine gun was pointed at him, and he was persuaded to enter the car. His captors were two: a vigorous voluble man and an armed thug who, muffled in women's clothes, never spoke—possibly a disguised man.

They took my grandfather to his bank, long before any customers would appear, and ordered him at gunpoint to open the safe. He would not do so. The two robbers sat down to converse with Mr. Pierce; there was plenty of time yet. The voluble robber, in rather friendly fashion, recounted the story of his own life. He had been a victim of circumstances, he said; but he had transcended them by taking up the robbing of banks. He held a theory of law and society rather like that of Thrasymachus, it seemed to my historically-minded grandfather: that is, the robber maintained that might is right, and that he was by nature one of the strong, which truth he was presently demonstrating. He then requested Mr. Pierce, once more, to open the safe. My grandfather still refused.

"Then, Mr. Pierce, though I've come to like you, I'm going to have to kill you." The voluble robber explained that, for the sake of his very reputation and livelihood, it was regrettably necessary for him to shoot bankers who set him at defiance. How otherwise could he subsist at his trade? So, if you really won't . . .

Convinced of his companion's sincerity, my grandfather opened the safe. The robbers took the money and drove away with my grandfather to an isolated barn. They left him inside, very loosely tied about his wrists, with the admonition that, if he should come out within ten minutes, he would be shot. But my grandfather emerged as soon as he heard the robbers' car roar away. It had been his one defeat.

Years later, in an Illinois prison, a police officer who had known my grandfather happened to talk with Machinegun Kelly, generally believed to have been the author of the St. Valentine's Day Massacre in Chicago. According to my grandfather's acquaintance, Kelly told him that the Plymouth bank-robbery had been one of his jobs, and that he had taken a liking to Mr. Pierce, the banker. Whether or not there was truth in this confession, certainly the man who kidnapped my grandfather was an accomplished professional criminal without scruples. Against him my grandfather could have been a convincing and convicting witness. Then why did he let my grandfather live? Perhaps because this robber was a highly rational criminal who calculated chances and weighed penalties. Pursuit for a murder is more intense than for a mere robbery, and penalties are heavier.

As others have suggested, the degree of deterrence provided by any severe penalty depends in part upon the calculating intelligence of the criminal—or the lack of reckonings and calculations on his part. From what I have observed, systematic bank robbers and safecrackers commonly are cold, egoistic, calculating persons who rank Number One very high indeed, look out carefully for Number One, and therefore weigh disadvantages and penalties. Fairly often they, like my grandfather's kidnapper, develop ideological apologies for their actions. Upon such mentalities, the final penalty of death may exercise a prudent restraint.

I have digressed at this length to suggest that the death penalty may be merciful toward the victims of certain types of crimes, committed by certain types of persons. In such cases, heavy penalties—and capital punishment especially—tend to deter a rational offender from covering up one crime by committing a worse. The instance of my grandfather's misadventure early fixed in my mind, at least, a certain healthy prejudice in favor of stern deterrents.

Doubtless many people could tell us of more dreadful cases of criminality, within their personal experience, than these three vignettes drawn from my own past which I have just presented. The breakers of violence sweep ever higher up the beaches of our civilization. We have supped long on horrors. About four years ago, my wife was kidnapped—though she escaped, chiefly through her gift of persuasive talk. (That episode also has gone into a short story of mine, "The Princess of All Lands.") Everyone knows how the previous exemptions from criminal depredations have been cancelled. That, I suppose, is why we are discussing the possible restoration of capital punishment.

The meliorists of the nineteenth century took it for granted that by a century after their time—by the year 1980, say—violent criminality would be virtually extinguished through universal schooling, better housing, better diet, general prosperity, improved measures for public health, and the like. They assumed that capital punishment was a relic of a barbarous and superstitious age: Capital punishment, they thought, was merciless; and they were themselves evangels of mercy. Their intellectual descendents did succeed, by the 1950's, in abolishing the death penalty throughout most of the civilized world.

But they did not succeed in abolishing hideous crimes of the sort formerly labelled "capital." In the most affluent of great countries, the United States, the rate of serious crimes rose most steadily and rapidly. At a time when the need for restraints upon criminality appeared to be greater than before, penalties were diminished. All this was done in the name of mercy.

Yet to whom was this mercy extended? Was it mercy toward the criminals? The recent insistence of two murderers in this country upon being executed according to sentence is no peculiar phenomenon. Doubtless many of the unfortunates being worked slowly to death in the prison-camps of the Soviet Arctic would find a firing-squad far more merciful than the pretended mercy of a thirty-year sentence. But we need not turn to totalist lands.

Is it not refined cruelty to keep alive, in self-loathing, a man who is a grave danger to the innocent and a grisly horror to himself? And to do such a thing in countries long admired for the justice of their laws? Once, walking Dartmoor, I came within sight of Dartmoor Prison, celebrated in so many English detective yarns, but abandoned since my stroll nearby. At that time there was immured in Dartmoor Prison a little man with a talent for escaping. Although serving a life term there, he had managed to get out four or five times. And every time he contrived to elude his pursuers long enough to find, ravish, and kill a small girl. That done, he would submit in apathy to arrest and return to Dartmoor Prison.

This pitiable, loathsome being, after recapture, would be overwhelmed by remorse and would beg for death—which would be denied him, although yet another sentence of imprisonment for life would be imposed. For what purpose was his life so carefully preserved? His continued existence here below was of benefit only to the gutter press of London, which regaled the public with details of his atrocities. To whom was this policy merciful? To the twisted creature himself? To the other inmates of Dartmoor, compelled to associate with this creature? To the rural population of Devonshire, among whom the creature repeatedly committed his depredations? What sort of human dignity was this abstinence from capital punishment upholding?

Georgia's most talented writer of this century, the late Flannery O'Connor, once read aloud to me the most famous of her short stories, "A Good Man Is Hard to Find." Flannery was no sentimentalist and no meliorist; blameless herself, she nevertheless perceived the whole depravity of our fallen nature. In her art, she agreed with T. S. Eliot (who never read her stories) that the essential advantage for a poet "is to be able to see beneath both beauty and ugliness; to see the boredom, and the horror, and the glory."

In "A Good Man Is Hard to Find," Miss O'Connor describes the roadside murder of a whole family by an escaped convict, called The Misfit, and his chums. (Flannery told me that she had got The Misfit's sobriquet from Georgia newspapers—their appellation for a real-life fugitive from justice quite as alarming as Flannery's character.) The Misfit, like Teniente Pedro in "We Are God's Utopia," is not without his amiable qualities: he apologizes to the grandmother (whom he kills a few minutes later) for not having a shirt on his back. He is a psychopath who had been "buried alive" in the penitentiary. Like many others of his dreadful nature, he has drifted through existence:

> "I was a gospel singer for a while," The Misfit said. "I been most everything. Been in the arm service, both land and sea, at home and abroad, been twict married, been an undertaker, been with the railroads, plowed Mother Earth, been in a tornado, seen a man burnt alive oncet," and he looked up at the children's mother and the little girl who were sitting close together, their faces white and their eyes glassy; "I even seen a woman flogged," he said.

After a nightmare conversation about how "Jesus thown everything off balance," the grandmother impulsively touches The Misfit; and he shoots her three times. His helpers return from disposing of the other members of the helpless family.

> "She would of been a good woman," The Misfit said, "if it had been somebody there to shoot her every minute of her life."

"Some fun!" Bobby Lee said.

"Shut up, Bobby Lee," The Misfit said.

"It's no real pleasure in life."

Aye, a good man is hard to find; in Adam's fall we sinned all; yet the depth and extent of our depravity varies from one person to another; and for the safety—perhaps the survival—of our species, it was found necessary in all previous ages to put out of their misery such criminals as The Misfit. Their physical presence among us cannot well be tolerated; the ultimate mysterious judgment upon their souls—so Flannery O'Connor implies—we leave to God.

To the Dartmoor child-ravager or the Jesus-accusing Misfit, what sort of mercy was burial alive in a penitentiary? Why, such preservation at public expense is merciful only if the mere prolongation of life here on earth is viewed as the chief purpose of existence; it is merciful only if one assumes that death brings annihilation—in Eliot's lines,

> *whirled*
> *Beyond the circuit of the shuddering Bear*
> *In fractured atoms.*

The abolition of capital punishment, I mean, is one of the products of humanitarianism—that is, of the belief that man's cleverness will suffice for all purposes, without need for knowledge of the transcendent and the divine.

Yet humanitarianism is now a decayed creed, worthless as a defense against the ideologues and the terrorists of our age, insufficient even to induce men and women to perform the ordinary duties which are supposed to bring the rewards of ordinary integrity. In a world that has denied God the Father, God the Son, and God the Holy Ghost—why, today the Savage God lays down his new commandments. The gods of the copybook headings with fire and slaughter return. The humanitarian who finds nothing sacred except (mysteriously) human life (so long as it is a criminal's life, not the life of an unborn infant) soon goes to the wall, throughout most of the world, in our time.

Flannery O'Connor, a woman of humane letters, was no humanitarian. She was aware that this brief existence of ours—in her case, a brief life of physical suffering—is not the be-all and end-all. She did not mistake physical death for spiritual destruction.

One of the many consequences of the widespread decay of belief in the resurrection of the flesh and the life everlasting has been the revulsion against capital punishment. But our understanding of the human soul begins to revive—encouraged, strange though it may seem to some people, by the speculations of physicists. No longer does it seem absurd to deny the suppositions of materialists and mechanists; no longer is it a mark of ignorance to declare that man is made for eternity. For a popular treatment of this renewed awareness of the realm of spirit, I refer those interested to Morton T. Kelsey's recent book *Afterlife: the Other Side of Dying*; I might cite also a score of other serious books, among them certain studies of what time is and of what energy is.

The rejection of capital punishment in any circumstances thus is becoming an attitude which belongs to the intellectual and moral era that is passing. If the deprivation of life by human agency amounts only to opening the gate of another realm of existence—why, Death has lost its sting.

Why do some people retain so extreme an aversion to capital punishment that they would deny the death penalty even to condemned murderers who desire to be executed? Because of the fear of death—the dread of the void, of annihilation. Their dread of extinction—even if repressed in their conversation—for themselves is so powerful that they cannot abide the terminating of others' lives, not even the lives of Don Pedros and Misfits.

It is an illogical dread, this terror of the inevitable: for we all die, just the same. John Strachey, as the Labour party was about to push the Churchill government out of power, promised the electorate that, under socialism, the ministry of health would work such wonders that human life itself would be prolonged indefinitely. That did not come to pass. No statutes can assure immortality, except perhaps for corporations.

Yet why is death so dreadful? On my recommendation, the American Book Awards people have chosen as one of the five best religious books of 1979 Peter J. Kreeft's *Love Is Stronger Than Death*; "Death makes the question of God an empirically testable question," Kreeft writes. "Death makes the abstract God-question concrete. Instead of 'Is there a God?' the question becomes 'Will I see God?' It is a dramatic thought, the thought of meeting God at death. Death gives life to the God-question. Perhaps we shall find death giving life to many other things too."

We have lost all our absolutes today except one. Once, we had God, truth, morality, family, fidelity, work, country, common sense, and many others—perhaps too many others. Now in the age of absolute relativism, one absolute is left: death. Death is the one pathway through which all people at all times raise the question of the absolute, the question of God. The last excuse for not raising the God-question is Thoreau's "one world at a time." Death removes this last excuse.

The zealots against capital punishment fear to raise the God-question. Yet death, as Peter Kreeft tells us, can be a friend, a mother, a lover. Those who do not fear to clasp darkness as a bride die well, and are not extinguished. For all of us, in the end, death is the ultimate mercy. I do not understand why we should deny that mercy to slayers whose earthly existence is a grave; nor why we should deny a merciful protection to the guiltless whose purpose in this world may be undone by those guilty slayers.   [XXIV, Fall 1980, 338–344]

[33]

How Much Justice?

ERNEST VAN DEN HAAG

Ernest van den Haag (1914–   ) has been contributing to Modern Age *since the Winter 1958–1959 issue, when he wrote a proposal for making "tax honesty" rewarding. A man of intellectual accomplishment and varied interests, he is a psychoanalyst in private practice as well as a Distinguished Scholar at the Heritage Foundation, John M. Olin Professor of Jurisprudence at Fordham University, a contributing editor at* National Review, *a fellow of the American Sociological Association, a Guggenheim fellow, and a senior fellow of the National Endowment for the Humanities. Books he has written include* The Death Penalty: A Debate *(with John P. Conrad; 1983),* Passion and Social Constraint *(1963), and* Punishing Criminals: Concerning a Very Old and Painful Question *(1975). He is also the editor of* Capitalism: Sources of Hostility *(1979).*

SOCIAL CHANGES in America so far have tended toward equality in three major respects. The distance between those who have more and those who have less income has decreased. Between 1936 and 1950, the income of the top five percent of all recipients rose by fourteen percent, and the income of the highest quintile of all income recipients rose by thirty-two percent. The income of the lowest quintile rose by 125 percent—four times as much. The trend toward equalization has pervaded the income structure as a whole, although its steepness varied in different periods and in different segments of the structure. To illustrate further: from 1956 to 1967, median white income rose 46.6 percent while median black income rose 76.2 percent; by 1970 there remained no difference between the incomes of young (under 35) husband-and-wife families, white or black. The rate of change has slowed down lately, but the trend toward more equality is continuous with the past, and promises to continue in the future.

Distribution has become more equal also with respect to the relative size of income groups. The size of the groups at the lowest end of the distribution has decreased, while the size of the groups in the middle and upper ranks has increased: in 1920, fifty percent of all families were poor (*i.e.,* below the present government poverty standard adjusted for changes in purchasing power); in 1962, only twenty percent; and in 1967, less than eleven percent were poor—an amazing decrease in so short a period. The proportion of the poor in the total population continues to decrease, though at a much slower rate; by now a plateau has been reached.

The political effects of these changes help explain why poverty was "discovered," to become an exciting social problem, just when it had been reduced so precipitously. Contrary to naive expectation shared by revolutionaries (who fear contentment) and by reformers (who hope for it), the shortening of the distance between them and others increased the resentment of the poor. When rich and poor were as "two nations," the resentment of the poor was vague and unfocused; they experienced and envied each other more than the remote rich. No longer isolated by vast and apparently insurmountable distances in education and living conditions, the poor now share much of the common outlook. They share, in particular, the consuming ambitions of the non-poor, brought home to them by TV. But they still lack the means to fulfill them and resent more than ever what they now feel is "deprivation." Further, while the habitual is regarded as inevitable and the inevitable is tolerated, the inadequate is resented. Improvement as a process is always felt to be inadequate— it can never keep pace with the rise in expectations it generates; at least temporarily, it often increases dissatisfaction.

In the past, finally, the proportion of the poor in society was so great they saw their condition as natural. So did everybody else. But nobody any longer can. The poor are comparatively few now. Rather than separate and different, they feel isolated and passed by, while the rich, in turn, feel guilty for having left them behind.

The social perception of poverty has altogether changed. No one—rich or poor—any longer believes that poverty can be an individual responsibility or fault of the poor, let alone part of a divinely sanctioned, just, or even tolerable social order. Poverty is now seen as an injustice committed by the rich, guilty of depriving the poor. ("*Cui bono?*" is proof of their guilt.) No longer accepted as part of the *physiology* of the body social, poverty has come to be regarded as social *pathology*.

Since poverty has been revealed as a disease of the body social, the government must try to cure it. However, progress is hindered by the very reduction of poverty which has confronted the government with the task of eliminating what remains of it: those who were poor solely because of external conditions probably no longer are. Those who stayed poor often did because of endogenous (or internalized) disability, or psychopathology, which hindered utilization of available job opportunities. It cannot be overcome by creating jobs—or by anything tried so far. Nonetheless, it has become the objective of the government to banish poverty altogether. Meanwhile, it is to be made materially less depriving and punishing than it was. Welfare agencies are to help the employable poor to earn decent incomes; and to grant unemployables an equivalent income; or to make available to them goods and services essential to satisfy human needs without the economic *quid pro quo* which they cannot afford.

If to be poor meant only to have less than a biologically defined minimum needed to survive, poverty would affect only a few among those called poor in the U.S. But "poverty" is defined by history and society, and refers not to incomes, high or low, but to the social judgment passed on income differences. In the U.S., people whose living scale is less than half of the (median) average are judged to be poor, regardless of the absolute size of their incomes. Because roughly only 10–12 percent of all families remain poor even by this social definition, the temptation to regard poverty as curable pathology and to "wage war" against it is hard to resist. Yet, though many battles have been won, and more can be, the war cannot be won since anything other than a totally equal distribution of income puts some people at the top and others at the bottom. The top group will be called rich, the bottom group poor.

The size of the bottom group and its distance from others can be changed. Not enough, however, to make us perceive the remaining distance as insignificant: those at the bottom continue to be regarded as poor by themselves and others, just as those at the top will be perceived as rich.

Even if the "needs" of the poor were met by making "essentials" available to all, regardless of ability or effort, poverty could only be alleviated but not banished, for, unlike survival minima, needs are not biologically given. They are socially generated desires. Biologically dispensable things become "essentials" when they are perceived as essential—whether they be kinds of food, housing, TV sets, cigarettes, legal and medical services, education, recreation or plumbing. As Shakespeare realized (*King Lear*):

> . . . Our basest beggars
> Are in the poorest things superfluous. . .

As more things become available to most of society through higher incomes, more things are felt to be essential to meet needs created by these things. The poor feel no fewer needs now than people who earn average incomes. Hence these needs cannot be met while they are poor, *i.e.*, as long as they have much less than the average.

Yet, however chimerical the hope of banishing poverty, we must continue to help those made miserable by nature, misfortune, society, or themselves. Charity, as preached by all our religions, demands as much; moreover a community indifferent to the fate of its poor would cease to be. Whatever its merits, after "the revolution" an immense amount of misery must still be dealt with, just as before. The question thus is not whether, but how, the poor, not should, but can be helped.

Attempts to help them meet a dilemma which has not been faced fully. As we make poverty less depriving and punishing, some otherwise employable poor people become unable or unwilling to accept employment at market rates. Thus, either welfare grants must be kept within very narrow limits, or reduced employability must be accepted.

It had been thought that the poor will work for the sake of additional income, even when needs are satisfied by welfare grants. Generous grants might actually increase employability by making available essentials such as training. As it became obvious that public agencies have been unsuccessful in training potentially employable adults, and seem unlikely to succeed at a justifiable cost, expectations were reduced. But many studies still profess to show that people on welfare are as interested in working as others. Typically, Leonard Goodwin[1] finds that "[the poor] express as much willingness [to work]" as others. He concludes they are as willing—as though such expressions were evidence for future behavior, and not merely for ideas about it. But labor market and welfare statistics prove that the willingness of the poor to take available jobs at available wages clearly is weakened by welfare grants. (By the reasoning which led to Mr. Goodwin's conclusions, we also would have to conclude that, when convicts express willingness to be law-abiding, they will be. Though touching, such faith is unlikely to reduce the crime rate.)[2]

To be sure, the employable poor would accept employment if the difference between the standard of living available through employment and that available without were large enough. If "large enough" is defined as the difference which leads anyone to seek employment, the problem is solved—by definition. The frivolous nature of this "solution" is barely disguised by code words such as "dignified jobs" or "living wages" which stand for jobs and wages which would be acceptable—but are not available. The problem is: will the poor take the actually available jobs at market rates? not: would they take available jobs for higher-than-market pay? If essentials are granted free, the difference between the standard of living provided by grants, and that yielded by available jobs at market rates, is not sufficient to induce all of the employable poor to seek employment. The problem would disappear if "essentials" were not provided by grants if poverty remained depriving. That "solution" is not acceptable. What then?

The nineteenth-century half-truth was that the poor are a shiftless lot, never willing to work. Unless we want simply to replace it with an opposite half-truth—that the poor are always willing to work, however high the welfare grant—we must distinguish three groups of employable poor. If granted essentials without working, members of the first group prefer not to work, whatever they would earn. They do not share the "Protestant ethic." They enjoy life more with fewer conveniences and no work. Unless shorn of "essentials," they will not be motivated to work by any rewards. Even among middle-class youngsters raised in the "work ethic," some now shun work as long as they are not painfully deprived. This marginal group has always existed, including "hobos," or "bums," as well as some "rentiers." One can only speculate upon the present size of the group. Members of a second group would only take jobs for which their actual skills do not qualify them; or if the gap between income from work and income from not working is much larger than the available wages and benefits make it. Members of a third group will work for the rewards available on the market, even though not working would not deprive them of essentials.

We do not know how many of the current poor are in the last group. But statistics unmistakably suggest that when the difference between income from grants and income available through employment at market rates is reduced, so is this group. From 1960 to 1969 the number of persons on welfare in New York City tripled while the rate of unemployment was halved and poverty decreased. In the same period there was a notorious shortage of unskilled labor in New York (including office boys, cleaning personnel, stock boys, file clerks, elevator operators, janitors). Obviously when the welfare standard approaches that of the lowest segment of the gainfully employed, low-paying jobs will be unfilled, and the number of welfare clients will rise, even as poverty diminishes.[3] The price of reducing the poverty of non-workers is an increase in their number. How then can we subsidize the poor so that poverty, the disease to be cured, does not increase and spread because of the subsidy?

We might reduce the welfare problem to manageable size by applying an economic theorem hitherto ignored by the social workers who have formulated welfare policies. The supply of anything subject to human control—anything producible or marketable, anything for which money is paid—responds to many factors, including the price offered. Other things being equal, supply depends on the price offered and on price-elasticity—the change of the supply in response to each price offered. Supply of some things is inelastic because production is: the supply of aged persons is inelastic as is that of paintings by Rembrandt (although the portion marketed is not). But the supply of poverty is elastic and rises when the price offered for it (the welfare grant) does. The supply of marketed poverty, of applicants for relief, has risen accordingly, and production, *via* unemployability, probably has risen almost as steeply.

Elasticity varies with the control of the

causes of poverty by those who are, or become poor. The least elastic supply of poverty rises least when the price rises; wherefore poverty produced by age rises least. The most elastic supply of poverty rises most; wherefore poverty produced by dependent children or drug addiction rises most. Once the price offered exceeds the income available through low-paid jobs, the supply rises very steeply. However, poverty produced by drug addiction or motherhood is upward more than downward elastic: increases in the price offered increase production, but price reductions, while reducing the rate of production, do not greatly decrease the supply already on the market. The supply of poverty from other sources (*e.g.*, the employable but unemployed poor) may be more downward than upward elastic.

Because eligibility was narrow in the past, and welfare grants were small, what disincentive effect they had was symbolic, and quantitatively not significant enough to worry about. Grants, therefore, were scaled according to need. Since their needs were supposed to be met by the subsidies granted, the income some recipients managed to earn on their own was subtracted so as not to give them an unfair advantage over other recipients, or even non-recipients. The practice was equitable (if not charitable) but left no economic incentive to earn money. Wherefore we can no longer afford it.

Welfare policies usually have been designed to deal with a fixed supply of poverty or, at least, with a supply independent of the price paid for it. Yet any price increases the supply over no price.

And a price which substantially subsidizes current poverty must encourage the production of significant increments, for which it secures a satisfactory market. Therefore, welfare policies should consider not only the need of recipients, but also the effect of grants on the supply of poverty. This has not been done. The situation is analogous to that of the penal system which must consider not only the effect of punishment (or non-punishment) on the convict, but also on the supply of criminals. Unfortunately many policy makers seem unable to envisage social effects and focus exclusively on individual suffering. This has contributed both to high welfare and high crime rates. It is this that must be changed.

NOTES

[1] *Do the Poor Want to Work?* (Brookings Institution, Washington, D.C., 1972). I am aware of Mr. Goodwin's attempts to test the meaning of the responses obtained, but not convinced that they support his conclusions.

[2] Such reasoning also implies that convicts have no distinctive psychological characteristics whatever—which would make rehabilitation efforts more quixotic than they are. With respect to the characteristics of the poor, Edward Banfield, *The Unheavenly City* (Little, Brown, Boston, 1970), is more realistic.

[3] In 1968 a family of four in New York received $333 per month in welfare grants (the allowance is tax exempt; various services may be added) whereas the potential breadwinner would have earned $277 if he received the minimum wage. If he abandoned it, the family would receive a slightly reduced allowance while he could keep the $277. Hence the rate of abandonment was high.

[XIX, Winter 1975, 71–75]

Law, Legislation, and Liberty:
Hayek's Completed Trilogy

ARTHUR SHENFIELD

Arthur Shenfield (1909–   ) is a British economist, writer, and barrister-at-law who has frequently taught at various universities in America. In 1977 he was regents' professor of economics at the University of California; in 1978 he was visiting professor of law and economics at the University of San Diego Law School; he has also been a visiting professor at such institutions as the University of Dallas and Temple University. A past president of the Mont Pelerin Society, he resides in Old Windsor, Berkshire, England, at the Dower House.

IN 1973 Professor Hayek published the first volume, under the heading *Rules and Order*, of a trilogy entitled *Law, Legislation, and Liberty*.[1] Its place in the long development of his thought in the field of legal and political theory was examined in "The New Thought of F. A. Hayek" (*Modern Age*, Winter 1976), which offered the observation: "If we may judge from the standard established by the first volume, the scholarly world can await a feast of analysis and argument of masterly vigor and profundity. The whole three-part work will surely be a landmark in the development of fundamental political and legal philosophy."

The trilogy has now been completed. The second volume, *The Mirage of Social Justice*, was published not long after the first, but the world had to wait until May 1979 for the appearance of the third, *The Political Order of a Free People*. It is now possible to see whether the high expectations aroused by the first volume have been fulfilled.

The Mirage of Social Justice opens with an examination of the rules governing the spontaneous order or cosmos, which was presented as the order of the free society in the first volume of the trilogy. The rules, we are told, are a device for coping with our inevitable ignorance of more than a small part of our relationships with other persons in the Great Society. If we were omniscient, there would be little need for general rules, for we could then deal with each other in the *ad hoc* way which we normally apply within our small families. Here Hayek rests his analysis on what has been for many years the rock bottom of his most profound work, namely the role of knowledge, or more importantly the absence thereof, in human relationships. It is because freedom's famous but too often misunderstood "invisible hand" enables us to produce a system, despite the narrow limits of our knowledge, that the free society is so superior to all unfree societies, which need a degree of knowledge beyond the capacity of man to encompass. This is not a matter only of economic relationships. It extends to all the relationships which make up the spontaneous order of the Great Society.

The rules of a spontaneous order are abstract, normally negative in character, and long-term in application. Thus the commandment "thou shalt not steal" names no specific article or person of which or from whom there is to be no theft, lays down only a negative, not a positive, duty in relation to other people's property, and has a timeless horizon. By contrast the rules of a made order are concrete, positive, and subject to frequent change. Hence there arises the fundamental difference between the functions of a judge or lawgiver and those of an administrator.

What is the relation between the rules of a spontaneous order and justice? In the first volume of his trilogy Hayek lingered for a considerable time on the nature of law, but here he takes it further in an onslaught on the doctrines of legal positivism, namely that all law is the expression of the will of a legislator, and that justice has no meaning other than the prescription of such law. From Hobbes, Bentham, and Austin to Kelsen these doctrines have had a powerful influence, all the more because they have been expounded by scholars of very high eminence.

Hayek is not the first to criticize these doctrines, but his insight into the difference between a spontaneous and a made order gives his criticism a thrust which is especially his own. Thus he says (page 46): "It is evident that so far as legal rules of just conduct, and particularly the private law, are concerned, the assertion of legal positivism that their content is always an expression of the will of the legislator is simply false. This has been shown again and again by the historians of private law and especially of the common law. It is necessarily true only of those rules of organization which constitute the public law; and it is significant that nearly all the leading modern legal positivists have been public lawyers and in addition usually socialists—organization men, that is, who can think of order only as organization, and on whom the whole demonstration of the eighteenth-century thinkers that rules of just conduct can lead to the formation of a spontaneous order seems to have been lost."

And (page 53): "Legal positivism is in this respect simply the ideology of socialism and of the omnipotence of the legislative power"; and further (page 55): "It was the prevalence of positivism which made the guardians of the law defenseless against the new advance of arbitrary government."

Hayek's lengthy and painstaking analysis of legal positivism ranks with the most profound work which he has ever produced, and by itself would make this volume of his trilogy an outstanding achievement. But it is only an introduction to the volume's central argument.

Who can be just or unjust? asks Hayek. Only human beings acting purposively. Hence individuals can be just, groups acting as groups can be just, governments can be just. But society cannot. For society is an abstract or spontaneous order, not a purposive group. Social or distributive justice is meaningless in a spontaneous order (a cosmos); it can have meaning only in an organization (a taxis). Hence the idea of social justice is a mirage. It is well known that in practice it turns out to be institutionalized envy and hatred. But it is worse than that, for it is built on ideological sand. As between men justice and injustice have meaning only when it is men who do right or wrong. We all understand that it makes no sense to talk of human injustice if a volcano or lightning kills one man and not another, if it rains gently on one farmer but destructively or not at all on another, or if some are born clever and others stupid, for no man was responsible for fortune or misfortune in these cases. We also understand that if a virtuous woman whose price is beyond rubies chooses to marry one man and not another, the latter cannot claim to be the victim of injustice, even though here purposive human action is the cause of his discomfiture; for no man has a right to command the affections of any woman, and the woman in this case has done no injustice in exercising her choice. We may even understand that it is not injustice if some are born with the cultural heritage of an Eskimo and others with that of a European, though here again chains of human action are behind the difference. But when we see one man to be richer than another, with no discernible moral superiority or perhaps with a clear moral inferiority, many of us easily succumb to the seductive notion that injustice must be at work. Hence those who talk of social justice can persuasively declare in such a case that success (except their own) is due to injustice, and that therefore they must take by force from the more successful to give to the less successful (as long as the latter are their clients). In practice, as we shall see below, they only promise to give to the less successful. Once they have the power so to do, what they do turns out to be somewhat different.

In the spontaneous order of freedom, the best society known to us, income or wealth arises from payment freely agreed and given by those whose wants are satisfied to those who satisfy them. Hence differences in income or wealth have no relation to merit unconnected with the satisfaction of human wants. Saints and sinners may reap their just rewards in a future life, and they may perhaps get some spiritual rewards in this life, but their material rewards can only be determined by the value which others, free from compulsion, put upon their services. In some fields this is or used to be well understood. By all accounts the late Babe Ruth was a man of odious personal character, but the fans made him rich because they prized not his personal merits but his ability with a baseball bat. Henry Ford was a pitiable ignoramus outside engineering and industrial management, and not very pleasant a man; but the people, acting without compulsion, made him a multimillionaire not for his moral or intellectual qualities but for his ability to put them on wheels at an unprecedentedly low cost. Nowadays the Babe Ruth case continues to be understood: thus rich sportsmen and entertainers are generally exempt from assault by champions of social justice. But the Henry Ford case has changed. Now his wealth would be assailed as unjust even if he were a saint or an intellectual titan as well as a marvellous producer of wealth.

We still understand that surgeons must pass examinations before they can be certified competent to operate upon us, and that it is just to pay surgeons for their competence in surgery, not for any other merit or any need which they may have. A surgeon of mediocre skill who is known to be a saint or to have numerous children to support would not receive payment from us on the scale of one of high skill, and in this we do not think that we act unjustly. But too few of us understand that where men are free, they conduct similarly just examinations every moment of the day as they decide whom to reward for the service of their wants, and whom not to reward.

This principle is sometimes misunderstood even by supporters of free enterprise. In the Samuel Smiles and Horatio Alger type of exposition, there is a tendency to stress the moral qualities of materially successful men, giving the impression that it is these qualities which we reward. Of course the man who makes two blades of grass grow where there was formerly one, or the man who makes a better mousetrap, may be led to do so by his high moral qualities, but he receives his just payment for the abundance of the grass or the quality of the mousetrap and for nothing else. Sometimes his achievement is justified on the ground that it has social value or a value to society. However there is no such thing as a value to society, except the value of its rules. Goods and services can have value only to persons, or to groups of persons acting as a group. Society does not so act.

It is common at this point to argue that wealth differences may be justified by personal success in the satisfaction of wants, but that the inheritance of wealth cannot be justified since the legatee satisfies no wants. Many supporters of the rights of private property have needlessly agonized about this. In a free society the state has no part in the transactions which put the property in the hands of the testator except that of guardian of the rules, and the state has no more *locus standi* to take it out of the hands of the legatee (except for its taxing power, which has a quite different basis) than any other bystander. That it may tax the legatee does not mean that his inheritance belongs to it, any more than its power to tax incomes means that it owns the incomes. When the state claims the right to deprive the legatee of his inheritance, apart from the taxing power exercised for other purposes, it does so on the false pretense that it is itself the society or is in some manner clothed with the rights of

society, which is the essential claim of the totalitarian state.

The mirage of social justice beckons men to the unattainable goal of substantive equality. Though the goal is unattainable, the pursuit of it is one of the most corrosive of all human influences. It not only produces envy and hatred. It also drives men into submission to tyranny, for only tyranny can plausibly offer to reach the unattainable goal; and with tyranny there also comes poverty. Thus are lost the blessings which men came upon when almost inadvertently they constructed the Great Society.

Hayek expounds the nature and consequences of the pursuit of substantive equality with his customary insight, thoroughness, and felicity. For many it will be almost equally important that he also explodes the concept of the alternative which is commonly called equality of opportunity. If by this is meant *la carrière ouverte aux talents*, it is unexceptionable, but that is not equality of opportunity. If equality of opportunity is truly meant, it is as unattainable as substantive equality and its pursuit is almost as destructive as that of the latter.[2] The only form of equality consistent with the rules of the free society is equality before the law.

A most important aspect of the pursuit of substantive equality is that, since genuine equality of condition is highly repugnant to almost everyone and extremely difficult to define or even conceive, right from the beginning the self-styled champions of substantive equality pursue something else. In its more obviously odious form it is the desire to pull down certain selected groups who are declared to be immorally rich but who often are neither rich nor immoral. In its less obviously odious form, which is indeed widely approved by men of goodwill, it is the protection of accustomed or established positions. This is so obviously different from equality that it is only the remarkable perversity which is so often found among ideologues and their political pupils that enables the one to be sought under the banner of the other. Few persons command so ready a sympathy as those who, without apparent fault, lose their jobs because those who have bought their produce now decide to buy from some cheaper source, especially if that source is foreign. Since Hume, Smith, and Ricardo, economists have always understood the folly of allowing this sympathy to propel us into protectionism, and of course Hayek knows all about this. Here however he goes deeper than the exposition of mere economic folly. He demonstrates with a full and acute analysis that the protection of established positions strikes at the heart of the spontaneous order, and all the more once that order has expanded into the Great Society.

Thus we come to Hayek's conclusion on social justice. It is a *cri de coeur* from a scholar who has spent a lifetime watching the corrosive effect of this slogan upon many minds which might have been expected to perceive its true character (page 97): "What I hope to have made clear is that the phrase 'social justice' is not . . . an innocent expression of goodwill towards the less fortunate, but has become a dishonest insinuation that one ought to agree to a demand of some special interest which can give no real reason for it. If political discussion is to become honest it is necessary that people should recognize that the term is intellectually disreputable, the mark of demagogy or cheap journalism which responsible thinkers ought to be ashamed to use because, once its vacuity is recognized, its use is dishonest. I may, as a result of long endeavors to trace the destructive effect which the invocation of 'social justice' has had on our moral sensitivity, and of again and again finding even eminent thinkers thoughtlessly using

the phrase, have become unduly allergic to it, but I have come to feel strongly that the greatest service I can still render to my fellow men would be that I could make the speakers and writers among them thoroughly ashamed ever again to employ the term 'social justice.' "

If the cry of "social justice" does cease to be heard in the land, no man in all the history of political and legal philosophy will have done more to produce that devoutly desirable consummation than Hayek.

Let us now pass to the third volume of the trilogy, *The Political Order of a Free People*. In the first two volumes Hayek laid a foundation for a program for the renovation of the once-liberal, once-successful, but now sadly crumbling, Western political order. In the third volume the program is set out in much detail and with a full envelope of argument.

However, though this program is in an important sense the culmination of Hayek's thought on the problems of society, it did not arise in his mind as a late flowering of his analysis of law, order, and justice in society. There is no surprise in finding that all Hayek's ideas are the product of a long, slow development in his mind, so that they display the rich maturity to be expected from years of thought and experience, of examination and re-examination, of testing and re-testing. Thus those who have followed the development of Hayek's work will already be familiar with the essentials of his proposals for a new political order. He first presented them in a brief discourse to the Mont Pelerin Society at Vichy in 1967. He offered them in more developed form in 1973 in his "Economic Freedom and Representative Government."[3] In this volume he presents them in what is perhaps their finished form, though it will not be open to us to think of any of Hayek's ideas as having reached their ultimate form until he lays down his pen once and for all.

Why is the Western political order crumbling about our ears? And why do we need to devise fundamentally new political machinery to preserve such freedom as we have, restore the freedom we have lost, and give all our freedoms that protection of a stable order? Because, Hayek argues, we have failed to distinguish between nomos and thesis, between the rules of just conduct and the orders required for the tasks of government, between legislation in the true sense and administration.[4] We entrust the same body, Parliament, Congress, National Assembly, etc., with the task of deliberating upon and determining both nomos and thesis. From this, in Hayek's view, the degeneration of modern democracy has developed.

The degeneration of democracy into plebiscitary dictatorship and perhaps ultimately into totalitarian tyranny proceeds visibly before our eyes, but we are powerless to arrest it, Hayek tells us, as long as, while still prizing the principle of democracy, we think that existing democratic forms are the only forms. For it is by these very forms that we are betrayed.

We are surely right to prize the principle of democracy. A system in which government is responsible and accountable to the governed offers the best chance for liberty under law, for peaceful political change and peaceful rivalry for office or power that mankind has known. Yet if it be the case that existing democratic forms are a mechanism for the decay of democracy, the time will come, and perhaps soon even in the apparent citadels of democracy of the North Atlantic, when the people will abjure democracy. For as it decays, mounting disorder will arise in which even democrats will come to believe that only the agonizing choice between authoritarian and totalitarian government

remains open to them. Fortunate will be those who then get an authoritarian Franco, Salazar or Pinochet rather than their alternatives. Yet the authoritarian dictator fails to produce a durable system. His system tends to last no longer than he himself. Where has there been a better dictatorship in modern times, if dictatorship people must have, than the "*ditadura sem ditador*" (dictatorship without a dictator) of Salazar? How many rulers have given the Spanish people as long a period of peace and prosperity as did Franco? Yet Salazar and Franco were not long in their graves before their peoples dismantled the systems which they had so laboriously constructed. The lesson is clear. If democracy can be saved, there can be no higher political duty than to save it.[5]

The process of democratic degeneration displays itself as the general interest becomes subordinated to various sectional group interests, so that the legislature ceases to be a forum for the determination of the general interest (for which the rules of just conduct are the basis), but becomes an arena in which special interests jostle and bargain with each other for the favors of the state. The democratic process thus comes to betray not only the general interest but majority rule itself. It is not the wishes, still less the interests, of the majority which prevail, but the desires of fluctuating coalitions of minorities. Each group in the coalition bargains with other groups so that each may feed at the public trough, and the rapacity of each is thus constrained not by any attention to, or concept of, the commonweal but by the need to accommodate itself to the rapacity of the others. However, such a system is unstable. It is not merely that its true nature cannot be concealed from the people, however adept at camouflage by way of democratic slogans and mob flattery the coalition leaders may be. What must bring it down and in due course end even the pretense of majority rule is the fact that it must produce mounting discontent, which by the irony of the gods turns out to be even more destructive among the coalition in-groups than among the outer groups which are the victims of their plunder. For in the first place the betrayal of the general interest itself undermines economic stability and produces general unease as well as reducing the scope for plunder; and in the second place the appetite for plunder grows with eating. Hence the coalitions must constantly regroup themselves, enmity among them growing apace, until the strongest among them, probably with a charismatic leader at their head, assume full power. When this happens the majority of the people sigh with relief as chaos yields to apparent order, and the forms of democracy follow the long-evaporated principles of democracy into oblivion.

We may readily accept this account of degeneration and yet ask why the failure to distinguish between nomos and thesis, and to separate their determination, is the spring and origin of this process. Because, Hayek argues, the powers of government offer seductive gains to those who can capture them. Hence if the same persons determine both the deployment of governmental powers and the rules of just conduct, the seductions of the former will in time submerge the constraints of the latter. The most striking example of this process is shown by the very country, Britain, which first in modern times established responsible government and was long its great exemplar. The Parliament which once forced the Crown to submit to the rule of law, has itself become an engine for lawless government, having assumed the uncontrolled sovereignty which it denied to the Crown, and having abandoned the self-imposed conventional restraints which made it conform to the rule of law for some two centuries after the defeat of the Crown in 1688. The irony for parliamentary democracy is that the sovereignty of Parliament is now only formal, the power to use it having reverted to the Crown's successor, the Cabinet and its party machine, which, behaving like a true plebiscitary dictator, is restrained only by the need to manipulate success in the next plebiscite, which in turn depends mainly on skill in manipulating the competition between various pressure groups.

The analysis indicates the remedy. The determination of nomos and thesis must be separated and entrusted to two different bodies, both of which must be democratically elected, so that neither can claim to be invested with greater democratic sanctity than the other (thus avoiding the process which enabled the British House of Commons to emasculate the House of Lords and effectively destroy its revising powers). However, though the two bodies will have equal democratic authority, their constituencies, modes and periods of election, and qualifications for election, should be different.[6]

Hayek examines the possible modes, periods, and especially qualifications, for election to the true law-making body (*i.e.,* that dealing with nomos, which we may call the legislative assembly) in penetrating and illuminating detail. Its members (whom Hayek with his alert eye for classical Athenian parallels, calls the *nomothetae*) would lay down the general rules of just conduct which would govern the deliberations of the thesis-making body (which we may call the governmental assembly) and the exercise of the powers of government. In such a constitution there would be a need for a supreme court not merely for the conventional task of construing the decisions of the two assemblies, but also for adjudication in case of disputes between them.

It is impossible within the short compass of this article to do justice to the depth and amplitude of Hayek's analysis. For example his exposition of the proper functions of government, and in particular of the correct approach of authority to problems of competition and monopoly, is a marvel of surefootedness as he picks his way to a sound conclusion with immense skill through a minefield thickly strewn with lethal errors. The above statement of his argument is therefore a barely adequate attempt at a very compressed account of its most essential elements.

His diagnosis of the process of democratic degeneration surely merits ready acceptance, but with this qualification which has a bearing upon the effectiveness of his remedy. The entrustment of nomos and thesis to the same deliberative body would not have the baleful effect which he rightly describes without the grip on the minds of citizens and legislators of the intellectual errors which he exposes in the first two volumes of his trilogy. Hence his remedy is unlikely to be successful unless at the same time the influence of these errors is removed. But if this influence disappears, it is arguable that his remedy becomes unnecessary.

Consider the case of the United States. The same process of democratic degeneration is visible there as elsewhere, though it may not have gone so far as in some other countries. Yet, though it does not appear to be the case at first sight, it is arguable that the United States already has Hayek's system in its essentials, and has had ever since the Supreme Court invested itself with the power of judicial review.

The essence of Hayek's system is twofold. First, a body concerned with the rules of just conduct which is separate from a second body which deliberates upon the administration of government, and which sets the framework of law for the decision of that second body. Secondly, at least equal popular legitimacy for the first body as for the second, so that when the former's rules restrain the latter's itch for action, the people will accept them and approve the restraint.

The two bodies in the American system are the Supreme Court and Congress, which look different from Hayek's system but, it may be argued, are not. In theory the function of the Supreme Court is to apply the provisions of the Constitution. In practice it has tended to apply its concept of what is right and just (*i.e.*, has sought to distil out of the Constitution Hayek's rules of just conduct), especially during the past forty years or thereabouts. The shift from theory to practice presents little difficulty if one proceeds from the assumption that the Constitution is itself essentially a comprehensive statement of what is right and just. It then calls for no great effort from the judges to find that the Constitution really means whatever they currently believe to be right and just. If they are good lawyers, accustomed to intricate argument, their skill in construction enables them to reach this conclusion. If they are not, they ride off on the principle that the Constitution is a flexible document which is intended to breathe the spirit of the age, and so they reach the same conclusion as their more competent brethren. It is true that there have been and are judges described as strict constructionists, but a scrutiny of their judgments will show that they too follow what they believe to be just, though their concept of justice is of an older lineage than that of their less traditionalist brethren.

This process was especially obvious in the decisions of the Warren Court. It is well known that Chief Justice Warren, knowing little law himself and having little skill in legal analysis, would react irritably to counsel who submitted a web of legal argument, saying "Never mind these legal points. The question is, is it right, is it just?" Of course a judge of such a caliber is contemptible, and it is true that when a competent judge deduces what he considers to be right and just from the Constitution, he does it in such a manner that the thread of legal construction handed on by his predecessors is as far as possible unbroken. Nevertheless Warren differed from his predecessors, colleagues and successors only in his naiveté and ignorance. They too have generally sought to find and apply what they have believed to be the rules of just conduct, free from the trammels which bind the lower courts. In countries where there is no power of judicial review (*e.g.,* the United Kingdom), it is common for the highest court in the land to say "We find that the law in the case before us is unjust, but we are bound to apply the law as we find it. It is for the legislature to rectify the injustice by amending the law." In the United States the parallel would be "We find that the provisions of the Constitution in the case before us are unjust, but we are bound to apply them as we find them. It is for Congress and three-quarters of the States to rectify the injustice by amending the Constitution." How often has the Supreme Court said this?

It follows that the Supreme Court at least in some measure attempts to perform the function of Hayek's legislative assembly; and that the fact that Congress attempts to deal with both *nomos* and *thesis* is not a fatal impediment since its acts are subject to judicial review. As for popular respect and allegiance, it is stronger for the Supreme Court than for Congress even though it is not founded on democratic election. Thus when Franklin Roosevelt was at the height of his democratic popularity, having carried 46 out of 48 states in the 1936 election, he was unable to carry the people with him in his assault on the Supreme Court.

The matter can be tested further. Suppose that Hayek's system had existed in the United States in the 1930's. Would the Legislative Assembly have resisted the popular clamor for the acts and policies of the President and Congress which have done so much damage to the American economy and polity? It is hardly likely. After all, from 1937 the Supreme Court itself succumbed to the fashionable myths and errors, although it had a greater power to stand aloof from popular emotion than a Legislative Assembly would have had. Indeed those myths and errors have become so ingrained in the thinking of most judges, that the Supreme Court has now become in some ways an even more powerful engine for the degeneration of liberal democracy than the Congress. Could a Legislative Assembly have resisted the *Zeitgeist* better?

Hence I suggest that Hayek's remedy will not work unless his assault on the intellectual errors of our time first succeeds. But is it true that if he wins the intellectual battle, his remedy becomes unnecessary? The answer, I believe, is No. First, there are important countries (*e.g.,* notably Britain and those which have inherited her system) which will save their liberties only by fundamentally new constitutional arrangements; and Hayek's remedy is at least as good as the only other probable workable alternative, the original prescription of the American Republic (but including judicial review). Secondly, his remedy would consolidate the intellectual victory. Indeed, as intellectual battles are never complete and tend to stretch out over long periods, his new constitutional arrangements would be needed to forestall the effects of the local and occasional reverses which even victorious armies suffer.

NOTES

[1] F. A. Hayek, *Law, Legislation, and Liberty*, three volumes (Chicago: University of Chicago Press, 1973–1979) and (London: Routledge and Kegan Paul); Vol. I: *Rules and Order* (1973), xi + 184 pp.; Vol. II: *The Mirage of Social Justice* (1976), xiv + 195 pp.; Vol. III: *The Political Order of a Free People* (1979), xv + 244 pp.

[2] See my article, "The Wiles of Satan," *Modern Age,* Spring 1978, p. 168.

[3] The Wincott Lecture, 1973, published by the Institute of Economic Affairs, London. 2nd impression, 1976.

[4] In the interest of brevity I am doing some slight violence to Hayek's distinction between nomos and thesis. The underlying distinction is between found law and made law. Hence some element of thesis enters into the determination of rules of just conduct. But for the purpose of this article's discussion the distinction stated here will serve.

[5] As the degeneration of democracy may lead to disgust with its very name, Hayek suggests that we might have recourse to the other Greek word for rule and call his regenerated system "demarchy."

[6] Of course this should not be confused with the case of the American Senate and House of Representatives because, though they do indeed differ in their constituencies, periods and qualifications for election, and to some degree in their powers, they both deal with nomos *and* thesis.

[XXIV, Spring 1980, 142–149]

[35]

Government by Judiciary

PHILIP B. KURLAND

Philip B. Kurland (1921–   ) is the William R. Kenan, Jr., Distinguished Service Professor in the College, and professor of constitutional law in the Law School, of the University of Chicago. In the 1950s he was twice a Guggenheim fellow and, since 1960, he has been the editor of the annual Supreme Court Review. *Since 1972 he has also been connected with the law firm of Rothschild, Barry and Myers in Chicago. The author or editor of a number of distinguished works, he has written at least three books on Supreme Court Justice Felix Frankfurter and even more on the Constitution, as well as* Religion and the Law *(1962) and* The Great Charter *(1965).*

Judges ought to remember that their office is *jus dicere*, and not *jus dare*—to interpret law, and not to make, or give law.
    FRANCIS BACON, *Essays* LVI (1625).

ON THE THIRD of January in this bicentennial year, the Chief Justice of the United States delivered his annual report on the state of the judiciary.* To some of us that report seemed both oversanguine and underinclusive. An unwarranted optimism filled the opening and closing paragraphs, while the middle was devoted to some unedifying statistics suggesting that "case flow" is to judicial business what "cash flow" is to economic enterprises. The opening words were:

At our 200th anniversary of nationhood we find, in common with most other countries, that confidence in our institutions, public and private, seems to be eroded. The judicial system by and large, however, is working well, and this is reflected in the relatively high popular esteem of the courts. The faults and frailties of our judicial branch are, for the most part, recognized and correctable—and there is much activity toward improvement.[1]

The Chief Justice then reported, in what is the current vogue among academics of almost all disciplines, statistical data. This time the numbers told about how many cases the federal courts were handling, how many cases the federal courts were not handling, and the need for more workers on the production line to make the outflow of judgments equal to the input of cases filed. His optimistic conclusion was put in these words:

As we try to look forward into what another century will bring, we can be optimistic about the prospects of justice in this country, provided we relate the burdens placed on

---

* The title of this article is borrowed from two volumes under that name, written by Louis Boudin and published in 1932. While the point of view here expressed is rather different from that of Mr. Boudin, the complaint is the same.

416

the courts to their capacity to perform and provide the necessary tools and personnel.[2]

A chief justice of the United States may be forgiven for speaking like an econometrician, for he is forbidden by the unwritten code to speak publicly about those issues that have come before the Supreme Court, are presently before that tribunal, or could be there for judgment in the near future. Since today's judicial system is likely to be called on to decide any social, political, or economic question, his range of subject matter was necessarily limited.

The implicit assumption of the Chief Justice's report is that the difficulties with the federal judicial system are quantitative and that, to the degree there are qualitative problems, they are due to these quantitative deficiencies. My opinion is that the Chief Justice has the cart and the horse misplaced. It is the judicial system's qualitative deficiencies that have given rise to whatever quantitative problems that it may have.

I am suggesting that, were Congress tomorrow to give the Chief Justice all the additional judges he has asked for—and more—the primary problems raised by contemporary judicial behavior would be exacerbated rather than resolved. In part this is true because courts are like modern superhighways: additional courts, like additional roads, are likely only to increase the traffic rather than to diminish the congestion. But that is the smallest of the difficulties.

Essentially the problem is that we have become a society overburdened by laws, whether they be statutes, or executive orders, or regulations, or guidelines, or judicial decrees. And contrary to the tenets of the American Revolution, an "imperial judiciary"—the phrase belongs to Professor Nathan Glazer[3]—provides legislation without representation.

I obviously have reached my conclusion too quickly, so let me turn back to the beginning.

The Beginning

When Alexander Hamilton was engaged in selling the proposed Constitution to the citizens of New York, he wrote in the 78th *Federalist* to quiet fears about a federal judiciary. The fears were not imaginary, they were grounded in the abuses before the Revolution of the prerogative courts and the courts of vice-admiralty. Hamilton there said:

> Whoever attentively considers the different departments of power must perceive that, in a government in which they are separated from each other, the judiciary, from the nature of its functions, will always be the least dangerous to the political rights of the Constitution; because it will be least in a capacity to annoy or injure them. The executive not only dispenses the honors but holds the sword of the community. The legislature not only commands the purse but prescribes the rules by which the duties and rights of every citizen are to be regulated. The judiciary, on the contrary, has no influence over either the sword or the purse; no direction either of the strength or of the wealth of the society, and can take no active resolution whatsoever. It may truly be said to have neither *force* nor *will*, but merely judgment; and must ultimately depend upon the aid of the executive arm even for the efficacy of its judgments.

Obviously, Hamilton was better at argument than at prognosis. From the beginning, Marshall and his colleagues on the federal courts repeatedly caused the transfer of power from the states to the national government, whether by interpretation of the Commerce Clause,[4] the Necessary and Proper Clause,[5] the Contract Clause,[6] or what have you. And, necessarily, in the course of these adjudications, they enhanced and enlarged the power of the judiciary.[7]

Thus, almost from the outset, and indeed as a result of his own arguments,[8] Hamilton was proved wrong with regard to the suggestion that the judiciary had no *will*. For some time, however, it could be said that Hamilton was right in stating that the courts could "take no active resolution whatsoever." In short, with some egregious exceptions, deriving from the combination of the injunctive power and the contempt power,[9] the judicial branch of the national government, while continually authorizing expanded national legislative and executive power, served primarily as a limiting force on governmental authority generally.

Until recent times, therefore, the judiciary of the national government was essentially a brake on the other branches of government, state and national. It did not purport to tell them what to do, but it did tell them what not to do, especially in the realm of economic and social affairs. And so it was that the judicial branch enjoyed particularly warm support from the conservative and business elements in the community.

The following language may sound familiar to you, but you must concede that you wouldn't associate these words with the 1924 Calvin Coolidge campaign, from which they are indeed taken:

> It is frequently charged that this tribunal is tyrannical. If the Constitution of the United States be tyrannical; if the rule that no one shall be convicted of crime save by a jury of his peers; that no orders of nobility shall be granted; that slavery shall not be permitted to exist in any state or territory; that no one shall be deprived of life, liberty or property without due process of law; if these and many other provisions made by the people be tyranny, then the Supreme Court when it makes decisions in accordance with these principles of our fundamental law is tyran-

nical. Otherwise it is exercising the power of government for the preservation of liberty. The fact is that the Constitution is the source of our freedom. Maintaining it, interpreting it and declaring it are the only methods by which the Constitution can be preserved and our liberties guaranteed. . . .

> Some people do not seem to understand fully the purpose of our constitutional restraints. They are not protecting the majority, either in or out of the Congress. They can protect themselves with their votes. We have adopted a written Constitution in order that the minority, even down to the most insignificant individual, might have their rights protected.[10]

In the 1924 campaign, therefore, both Calvin Coolidge and his opponent, John W. Davis, spoke the same language in opposition to what was labelled "The Red Terror of Judicial Reform," sponsored by the Progressives of the period, who were advocating recall by referendum of judicial opinions and even of judges.

It was during the New Deal that the issue last came to a head, with Franklin D. Roosevelt almost succeeding in his famous—or infamous—Court Packing plan.[11] And so it was that Robert Jackson, the devil himself to much of the business community during his service as a lawyer for the New Deal, just before he ascended the high bench, wrote a book in which he condemned the concept of "Government by Lawsuit."[12] In the chapter with that heading he pointed out:

> Judicial justice is well adapted to ensure that established legislative rules are fairly and equitably applied to individual cases. But it is inherently ill suited, and never can be suited, to devising or enacting rules of general social policy. Litigation procedures are clumsy and narrow, at best; technical and tricky, at their worst.[13]

Among the reasons for this adverse conclusion about the desirability of government by lawsuit is that its control falls entirely to lawyers who are not suited to the task. Jackson thus wrote:

> Custom decrees that the Supreme Court shall be composed only of lawyers, though the Constitution does not say so. Those lawyers on the bench will hear only from lawyers at the bar. If the views of the scientist, the laborer, the businessman, the social worker, the economist, the legislator, or the government executive reach the Court, it is only through the lawyer, in spite of the fact that the effect of the decision may be far greater in other fields than in jurisprudence. Thus government by lawsuit leads to a final decision guided by learning and limited by the understanding of a single profession—the law.
>
> It is no condemnation of that profession to doubt its capacity to furnish single-handed the rounded and comprehensive wisdom to govern all society. No more, indeed not nearly so much, would I entrust only doctors, or economists, or engineers, or educators, or theologians, to make a final review of our democratically adopted legislation. But we must not blink the fact that legal philosophy is but one branch of learning with peculiarities of its own and that judicial review of the reasonableness of legislation means the testing of the whole social process by the single standard—of men of the law.[14]

Thus the argument went—and had gone almost from the beginning—between those who decried the inhibitions on government imposed by the federal courts, usually the proponents of social legislation, and those who saw the courts as the guardians of constitutional principles, especially as seen through the wisdom of Herbert Spencer. When Coolidge was talking about the protection of minorities, he was apparently not speaking about minorities described by race, sex, ethnic background, religion, or whatever the current meanings of the much-abused word may be. The wealthy were and continue to be among the smaller minorities. His clientele was the minority of one

or the few, and not least the conglomerates of capital which had, by grant of the Supreme Court, become persons for the purposes of the Fourteenth Amendment.[15]

Obviously the rewriting of the Fourteenth Amendment to conform with the *will* of the justices of the Court is not a contemporary device. And thus, to some, the controversy over the behavior of the federal courts depends on whose oxen are gored. For many, the courts are just one more political instrument which deserve approbation when the judges' predilections conform with their own and damnation when they do not. Neither attackers nor defenders of this kind can honestly resort to the condemnation that the Court is not an instrument of popular will. It was not intended to be such.

If we were to be concerned only with the question of when a court may impose a veto on the actions of the branches of the government directly responsible to the people, we could come no further than the wisdom of Mr. Justice Holmes as predicated by Judge Learned Hand, perhaps the greatest of American judges in our history. Speaking of Holmes, Hand wrote:

> Men ask more than scholarship, however, of a judge, and in this they are right, for while scholarship may clear the thickets it can build little. In the end, and quite fairly, a judge will be estimated in terms of his outlook and his nature. He cannot evade responsibility for his beliefs, because these are at bottom the creatures of his choice. The temperament of detachment and scrutiny is not beguiling; men find it more often a cool jet than a stimulus, and it is a little curious that they ever can be brought to rate it highly. Yet, in the end, it has so obvious a place in any rational world that its value is forced upon their notice and they look behind to the disposition which produces it. If they do, they find it anything but cold or neutral, for the last acquisition

of civilized man is forbearance in judgment and to it is necessary one of the highest efforts of will.

It is in his position on constitutional questions that this has been most apparent in Justice Holmes. However we may view it, these are nearly related to policy and preference. There are two schools, rather two tendencies; one is to impose upon the Constitution the fundamental political assumptions which for the time being are dominant; it views the general clauses of the amendments as protecting the individual from the vagaries and extravagances of faction. The other does not depart from the first in theory but in application is more cautious. That caution in the end must rest upon a counsel of scepticism or at least upon a recognition that there is but one test for divergent popular convictions, experiment, and that almost any experiment is in the end less dangerous than its suppression. Of the second school, Justice Holmes was one of the earliest and has been one of the foremost members. His decisions are not to be read as indicating his own views on public matters, but they do indicate his settled belief that in such matters the judges cannot safely intervene, that the Constitution did not create a tri-cameral system, that a law which can get itself enacted is almost sure to have behind it a support which is not wholly unreasonable. . . .

Forty years ago, when Justice Holmes went upon the Supreme Court of Massachusetts, this doctrine was getting its foothold, that the court should be the bulwark against improvident, selfish, and uninformed legislation. That doctrine he did not assent to then and he has not since. Whatever it was, the capaciousness of his learning, the acumen of his mind or his freedom from convention, forbade him to interject the judge into heated controversies best settled by political impacts. . . .[16]

In popular terms, in the contest between judicial restraint and judicial activism, we know only that "the accomplished judge," a judge of "sagacity, insight, and acuteness; courtesy, dignity and humor; wisdom, learning and uprightness" has come down on the side of restraint. To this, the judicial careers of Holmes and Brandeis, of Stone and Hughes, of Frankfurter and Black, of Jackson and the second Harlan give witness. But it must be seen that these judges were of a different era, working under a different constitution, directing themselves to a different kind of question. The issue no longer is whether the Court should undertake a veto of legislative or executive action. And there is little point in speaking of today's problems in terms of yesterday's conflicts.

A New Nation

There emerged from the New Deal and the Second World War a different nation. The words of the Constitution have remained the same, but their meaning has totally changed. The service state has arrived, with the result that the classic description of American freedom has been destroyed. It was once said of the English system and, *a fortiori,* of the American, that it allowed its citizens freedom to do anything that was not specifically forbidden, while the European systems allowed freedom to do only that which the government authorized. Since the Great Depression, we have been moving from the first toward the second, or, at least more laws inhibit individual freedom more and more.

A nation that brought a unique concept of federalism and divided sovereignty between nation and states has changed into one in which all governmental authority has been concentrated in a central sovereignty. And a nation that was founded on the concept of division of authority among three branches, with checks and balances of each upon the other, has been drastically changed if not destroyed. The popular will that purports to be expressed by the legislative branch has become a diminished, all but obliterated, element in government. It doesn't make any difference whether the power was voluntarily surrendered by the Congress or usurped by the executive and judicial divisions. The fact remains that Congress is today all but impotent.

Some will argue that Congress is impotent because the multitude of areas in which government has taken control from the individual are too complex for legislative competence. Others, that Congress lacks the expertise and information to perform its function. And so authority has developed, not upon the President himself, but on the vast bureaucracy that is the national government, including what is known as the Office of the White House. It is not only the Congress but the President who has lost capacity to perform the duties assigned by the Constitution.

The Constitution says in Article I that Congress shall "make all laws which shall be necessary and proper for carrying into Execution the foregoing Powers, and all other Powers vested by this Constitution in the Government of the United States, or in any Department or Officer thereof." The Constitution says in Article II that the President "shall take Care that the Laws be faithfully executed." The fact is that Congress does not any longer make the laws nor does the President execute them. The laws are now largely made by the bureaucracies who also execute them. But they are also now made and executed by the judicial branch, which was created to have neither *will* nor *force* but only judgment.

It is of the latter situation that I am here to make complaint. And of course, in the confines of a single short essay I will speak of the judicial problem only in terms of examples. While I may deplore them, I do not despair of them. For with Learned Hand: "I answer, like Carlyle: The Present is our Indubitable Own; we can shape it, for we can shape ourselves; we can shape them as near to the Heart's Desire as we have constancy and courage."[17] But first to see the problem.

The Judge as Legislator

In 1967, Adolph A. Berle delivered the Carpentier Lectures at Columbia University. His opening words were intended to shock his audience, but they were received as commonplace. He started by saying: "The thesis can be briefly stated. Ultimate legislative power in the United States has come to rest in the Supreme Court of the United States."[18] His position was that this was not only a necessary but a good thing. And his plea was for providing assistance in terms of expertise and data so that the Court could better perform its legislative duties. The preface to the printed lectures explicates his position:

> This is a report on a revolution. The unique fact is that the revolutionary committee is the Supreme Court of the United States.
>
> The first of the three essays relates to the acquisition and exercise by the Supreme Court of senior legislative power in the United States, particularly in the field of education and local government. . . .
>
> Use of the word "revolution" implies no criticism of the Court. I think it could not have acted otherwise than as it did. Far from arrogating to itself power it did not have, the Court's latent constitutional powers granted it by the Fourteenth Amendment were activated by the pace of technical and social change. When this history is written, it will probably be found that the Supreme Court's action saved the country from a far more dangerous and disorderly change.
>
> [This language is somewhat reminiscent

of the arguments of military juntas who impose dictatorships to prevent "far more dangerous and disorderly" takeovers, *i.e.,* by someone else.]

Yet this situation does impose on the federal government problems of power which must be solved if the Supreme Court is not to endanger or lose its mandate through tides of political action. Revolutionary progress does fuse judicial and legislative power, and possibly a degree of executive power as well. A common sequel is liquidation of that power as increasing sectors of opposition or fear become active.[19]

Let me underline Berle's proposition that "revolutionary progress [fuses] judicial and legislative power, and possibly a degree of executive power as well." I would suggest that the revolutionary aspect is the rejection of the concept of separation of powers and checks and balances. In short, the proposal is that Articles I, II, and III of the Constitution be merged. But, it should be readily seen that the notion of merger does not necessarily imply exclusive or monopoly power over all legislation or execution of the laws in the judicial branch or any other. And so the question remains, even after the basic conceptions of the Constitution are rejected, who is to do what with regard to the creation and execution of the laws?

Of course, one need not be a revolutionary, even in A. A. Berle's use of the term, to accept the proposition that the law courts are makers of the law. Historically, this is the very essence of the common law, from which many of our constitutions derive. And, although Mr. Justice Brandeis, speaking for the Court in 1938, proclaimed that there is no such thing as a general federal common law, because the Constitution prohibits it,[20] federal common law continues to be made openly by Brandeis's successors.[21] The constitutional ban on a federal common law of

crimes[22] purports to remain in existence but is easily bypassed.

Since lawmaking is not a novel aspect of the judicial function in common-law countries, it can hardly be considered a "revolutionary" conception. So, too, courts have long engaged in their fundamental function of executing the laws. In sum, both courts and legislatures in common-law countries engage in lawmaking. How then to distinguish between them or to confine each to its rightful place? The distinction is, perhaps, so subtle as to elude my capacity to put it in adequate language. The problem of definition here is much like the problem of defining hard-core pornography for purposes of the First Amendment, because, like Mr. Justice Stewart in that area, I cannot tell what judicial legislation is. "[B]ut I know it when I see it."[23]

For Mr. Justice Holmes, for example, it was a question of more or less. In 1917, in a dissenting opinion, he wrote:

> I recognize without hesitation that judges do and must legislate, but they can do so only interstitially; they are confined from molar to molecular motions. A common-law judge could not say I think the doctrine of consideration a bit of historical nonsense and shall not enforce it in my court.[24]

And, while he was accurate in his prediction that no court would jettison the concept of consideration, many courts have modified it almost beyond recognition.[25]

What Holmes was saying was that the limited scope of judicial discretion was so well bred into lawyers and judges that it was not likely to be exceeded, particularly where needed reforms could be effectuated by legislative action. The answer, therefore, was not quite so easy with reference to public law as with regard to private law. And this is particularly true with regard to constitutional law which is not subject to legislative control. And whenever an attack is made on the Supreme Court for going beyond its proper realm, the answer comes back in terms of the opinions of Chief Justice Marshall in such cases as *McCulloch* v. *Maryland*,[26] *Gibbons* v. *Ogden*,[27] or *Marbury* v. *Madison*.[28] And, of course, this argument from precedent is sound. For, if any opinions have constituted judicial legislation, these fundamental decisions have. The opinions can only be justified retrospectively by history and not by earlier precedents or contemporary reason. Constitutional adjudication is more than an essay in the adjudicative process, it is also an essay in statesmanship, and the appeal is basically to the future not to the past.

Yet, there is the solidly held belief that even in the constitutional area there must be limits to judicial legislation. Thus, Professor Felix Frankfurter, immediately before his elevation to the Court, could say what he was wont to say even after he became a Justice:

> "Judicial power," however large, has an orbit more or less strictly defined by well-recognized presuppositions regarding the kind of business that properly belongs to the courts. Their business is adjudication, not speculation. They are concerned with actual, living controversies, and not abstract disputation. While adjudication has phases of lawmaking, legislatures not courts are policy-makers in the larger meaning of the term. Courts, therefore, act within relatively narrow bounds of discretion. Their jurisdiction is contingent upon the means of illumination and the resources for judgment to which the technique of an Anglo-American litigation limits them. To be sure, these are the historic deposits of the operations of courts in the English-speaking world for centuries. That is precisely the strength of the doctrine of self-limitation. But these considerations, rooted as they are in the profound empiricism of the common law, had special signif-

icance when applied to the Supreme Court in our federal scheme.[29]

These amorphous concepts of judicial restraint are adumbrated by the language of the Constitution itself. Article I, speaking to the legislative power, is a mighty catalogue of subjects which the Congress is authorized to address. And, except for impeachments, that same document prohibits the Congress to undertake adjudicative functions. Article III, on the other hand, confines the judicial power to resolution of "cases and controversies" and "under such Regulations as the Congress shall make." The two Articles emphasize the distinction between a legislative process meant to establish rules of general applicability and the judicial process, the essence of which is the resolution of disputes between identified and affected parties.

When, then, does a judicial body overstep its role and encroach upon the legislative function? It is not merely when it announces new rules, especially if the new rules are revisions of those that it has previously made. What we must keep in mind is that the prime function of a court is not to promulgate rules, it is to resolve disputes. In the course of such resolutions, it will establish the reasons for its decisions, those reasons will be utilized in the future to resolve later disputes that come before it, disputes which come within the rationalization of the first decision.

1. Rhyme without Reason

I would say, then, that a court oversteps its bounds when it reaches a decision without adequate reasoning to support it, especially reasoning establishing the need for change. Judges are not expected to decide cases in terms of their personal predilections. While one cannot exclude the personality of the judge from the conclusions he may reach, he is required to decide the case in terms of the law. To use Felix Frankfurter's words: "We do not sit like a kadi under a tree dispensing justice according to considerations of individual expediency."[30] That of course was a normative statement and not a descriptive one. Today, the kadi and the federal judge look like twins.

Erwin Griswold, former dean of the Harvard Law School, former member of the Civil Rights Commission, former solicitor general of the United States, recently commented: "Some Supreme Court Justices employ the ruse of saying, 'What we are doing is interpreting the Constitution' when what the Court is doing is deciding what is good for the country."[31] What is good for the country is a question for the representatives of the people to decide, not an unelected, politically selected, group of lawyers.

Professor Paul Freund has pointed out that one of the prime difficulties with the assumption of power by the judiciary is the absence of reasons for its decisions, as well as false reasons. The Supreme Court "should not play a shell game in making such decisions—it should tell us what it is doing."[32] And, of course, the same admonition is valid with regard to courts other than the Supreme Court.

I expect that the most important recent decision that is without rational justification in constitutional terms is the abortion case.[33] I have no quarrel with the result; I like it. Were I a legislator, I would vote for it. But the question whether abortion may be banned by the state in the first, second, or third trimesters of pregnancy is not a question that can be answered by the history or language of the Constitution and certainly does not fall within the expertise of the nine robed men in the

marble palace. There would appear to be reasons why the result was not justified by the opinion.

2. Lord High Executioner

I think, too, that the courts enter the legislative area when, in the absence of legislative mandate, they take the huge step from forbidding action that is prohibited by the negative provisions of the Bill of Rights and the Fourteenth Amendment to commanding the effectuation of programs of their own creation. My example, here, would be the reapportionment cases, where the federal judicial system has undertaken to replace what might well have been an invalid allocation of legislative offices with a system described by a slogan—"one man–one vote." It is a standard that never existed in the past; it is a standard that was clearly rejected by the framers of the national constitution for the national government, and it remains a standard unjustified by the Court itself.[34] It is one thing to say that specific malapportionment cannot be tolerated under the loose limits of the Constitution. It is quite another to prescribe how a state must apportion its legislative districts, state and federal—and even local. A similar situation occurred when the courts shifted from a ban on racial segregation to a command for "racial balance."

The courts also seem to me to go beyond their province when the judgment is not directed to remedying the wrongs done to a particular litigant or litigants, but when they use the judgment in a particular case to assert administrative authority over a large number of people and activities that were not the subject of the case or controversy before them. This is the fact with some school desegregation remedy cases, of which Boston is the most egregious recent example. The Boston school system is now in "receivership," which means that the federal district judge determines where repairs are to be made and how much is to be spent for them; whether students are to receive instruction in laboratories and shops or classrooms; which school should get a new piano. In short, the judge has replaced the school board and, whatever expertise he may have as a jurist, I don't believe that he qualifies in any manner, shape, or form as an educational expert.

There is some reason to doubt judicial expertise as to most desegregation plans. Judge Skelly Wright ordered the desegregation of the schools of Washington, D.C., which are now ninety-seven percent black as a result. Certainly this makes it difficult to integrate the student body. Similar instances of rigidity resulting in catastrophe are to be found in Atlanta and other cities.

I do not mean, by rejecting the validity of judicial action, to condone the use of force to oppose judicial orders that are plainly grounded in constitutional bans on invalid state actions.

> Compliance with decisions of this Court, as the constitutional organ of the supreme Law of the Land, has often, throughout our history, depended on active support by state and local authorities. It presupposes such support. To withhold it, and indeed to use political power to try to paralyze the supreme Law, precludes the maintenance of our federal system as we have known and cherished it for one hundred and seventy years.[35]

Thus spoke Felix Frankfurter in the *Little Rock* case. And the proposition is no less relevant to Northern and Western communities than to those of the South and Border states. But that kind of opposition is not likely to decrease when a court

decides that it will not only execute its own functions but those of the school board as well. Or, for another example, when it assumes the authority for administering a prison system, rather than simply forbidding the violations of prisoners' rights, which may be occurring.

3. Legislation Pure and Simple

When it comes to promulgating rules that are meant to control the behavior of others than those who are litigants before the courts, there can be little doubt that the judiciary is engaged in the legislative role. This is frequently done through the fiction of class actions, which assume that the relevant universe is divided into two groups, those like the plaintiff and those like the defendant, and any decision of such a case is therefore binding on everyone. But there are even more specious approaches to the legislative realm by the judiciary. I will mention just two. The first, by which decisions are intended to govern the behavior of those who were not parties, *i.e.,* those clearly outside the case or controversy before the court for adjudication. The second, where the courts simply rewrite the words of the legislative authority in order to effectuate its own will rather than that of the representatives of the people.

The first of these may be seen in a longstanding rule of the federal courts that excludes evidence of guilt because of the misbehavior of the police.

Evidence is sometimes secured by means that cast dubiety on its veracity. Of course, such evidence of doubtful probity should be excluded from consideration because of its implicit weakness. Other evidence is often excluded, but not because of its intrinsic infirmity. And, as Mr. Justice Jackson once wrote:

That the rule of exclusion and reversal results in the escape of guilty persons is more capable of demonstration than that it deters invasions of right by the police.... Rejection of the evidence does nothing to punish the wrong-doing official, while it may, and likely will, release the wrong-doing defendant.... The disciplinary or educational effect of the court's releasing the defendant for police misbehavior is so indirect as to be no more than a mild deterrent at best.[36]

Again, I do not mean to condone police misbehavior. It is one of the banes of our system of criminal justice. But there is more than abundant evidence that such misbehavior is not inhibited by the exclusionary rule. If it is to be controlled it must be made the basis for direct punishment of the wrong-doers. To argue, as do the supporters of the ever-broadening exclusionary rule, that while that rule really does not do any good in correcting official misbehavior, they know of no more efficient rule, is, I submit, a legislative judgment and not properly a judicial one; it has nothing to do with the proper resolution of the case or controversy before the court.

It is equally true that the legislative province is invaded by the judiciary when it moves in the opposite direction of making crimes of actions that the legislature has not defined as criminal. An example here is to be found in the judicial administration of the so-called "mail-fraud" statute which, as a result of judicial action, requires only a gossamer connection with the use of the mails and no fraud at all. As I have noted, the federal courts are not constitutionally competent to create common-law crimes. But in this instance, they have made bricks without straw, by allowing trial courts and juries almost absolute discretion to decide whether a person accused of "mail fraud" should be subjected to punishment, although the acts charged clearly do not fall within the ban of the statutory language. An exacerbation of the problem has resulted because federal prosecutors—especially those with political ambitions—have utilized this power to political ends.

If the utilization of laws beyond their language, purpose, and intent is judicial legislation, as I contend it is, the administration of laws in the direct face of legislative language to the contrary is even more offensive. This form of judicial legislation, the transmuting of congressional language into its opposite in order to meet the personal judgments of the courts rather than the expressed judgments of Congress, is endemic in the American judicial system. Let me spell out one example that I have chosen because the Attorney General has recently spoken publicly if erroneously on the subject. The issue is whether Congress has, by Title VII of the 1964 Civil Rights Act, commanded racial balance in employment. Like the Attorney General, I have a personal interest, because both of us are counsel—on opposite sides—in cases involving the question of the proper construction of the law.

The news story of the Attorney General's remarks appeared in the Chicago *Sun Times* of March 18, 1976. The headline was: "Levi hits Congress on job-bias laws." The lead paragraphs are as follows:

> Anyone trying to understand the judicial and administrative law on discrimination in employment is confronted with the "view of a madhouse," Atty. Gen. Edward H. Levi said Wednesday.
>
> In the field of equal opportunity, Levi said, the federal courts have been given the "tremendous burden" of doing "what Congress does not care to state plainly."

With all respect, Congress has stated its intention plainly in the language of the statute and in the congressional history of the statute. It forbids, in so many words, racial or ethnic or sex quotas in employment. It bans "racial balance" as a legislative standard.

> Nothing contained in this title shall be interpreted to require any employer, employment agency, labor organization, or joint labor-management committee subject to this title to grant preferential treatment to any individual or to any group because of race, color, religion, sex, or national origin of such individual or group on account of an imbalance which may exist with respect to the total number or percentage of persons of any race, color, religion, sex, or national origin employed by any employer, referred or classified for employment by any employment agency or labor organization, admitted to membership or classified by any labor organization, or admitted to, or employed in, any apprenticeship or other training program, in comparison with the total number or percentage of persons of such race, color, religion, sex, or national origin in any community, state, section, or other area, or in the available work force in any community, state, section, or other area.

Like the language of the statute, its legislative origins make clear the ban on "racial balance." Thus, the floor managers of the Civil Rights Act of 1964, Senators Joseph Clark and Clifford Case, submitted a memorandum explaining this part of the proposed law to their colleagues. It read in part:

> There is no requirement in Title VII that an employer maintain a racial balance in his work force. On the contrary, any deliberate attempt to maintain a racial balance, whatever such balance may be, would involve a violation of Title VII because maintaining such a balance would require an employer to hire or refuse to hire on the basis of race. It must be emphasized that discrimination is prohibited as to any individual. While the presence or absence of other members of the same minority group in the work force may be a relevant factor in determining whether in a given case a decision to hire

or to refuse to hire was based on race, color, etc., it is only one factor, and the question in each case would be whether that individual was discriminated against.[37]

In 1964 the Department of Justice prepared a memorandum in support of the bill at the behest of the bill's sponsors. It said:

> Finally, it has been asserted that Title VII would impose a requirement for "racial balance." This is incorrect. There is no provision, either in Title VII or in any other part of this bill, that requires or authorizes any Federal agency or Federal court to require preferential treatment for any individual or group for the purpose of achieving racial balance.
>
> No employer is required to hire an individual because that individual is a Negro. No employer is required to maintain any ratio of Negroes to whites, Jews to gentiles, Italians to English, or women to men. The same is true of labor organizations. On the contrary, any deliberate attempt to maintain a given balance would almost certainly run afoul of Title VII because it would involve a failure or refusal to hire some individual because of his race, color, religion, sex, or national origin. What Title VII seeks to accomplish, what the civil rights bill seeks to accomplish is equal treatment for all.[38]

Far from being what Mr. Levi calls a failure of Congress to state its rule plainly, we have a series of decisions by the courts, made at the insistence of the Department of Justice, that fly in the face of the legislative command. The judicial rulings are that a want of racial balance in an employment force is a violation of Title VII and that the remedy for that violation is a decree imposing racial balance on that work force. If the Attorney General sees the judicial and administrative law as "a madhouse," it is the Department of Justice and the courts that are both the inmates and the operators of the "Cuckoo's Nest." But, as usual, someone else, the persons deprived of jobs because of their race, color, religion, sex, or national origin, must pay the costs of maintaining the inmates.

Maybe the 1964 Civil Rights Act should have been written as the executive and judicial branches of the federal government desire. It is clear, however, that such a declaration of social policy belongs to the Congress and it has not been delegated, although it may have been usurped by the bureaucrats and the judiciary.

Again, I would reject the notion that judicial interpretation of legislative language is not a judicial task, and a difficult task. It is only when the judges, as so many of them now do, rewrite the statute to their own preference, that they violate their judicial oaths. Judge Learned Hand's words are more revealing than any I could adduce:

> There are indeed political philosophers who insist that a judge must inevitably choose between the dictionary and tabula rasa; but there is a plain distinction in theory between "interpretation" and "legislation," as well as a clear boundary in practice. Let the judge go as far afield as he will, in seeking the meaning of an "enactment"; if he is honest, he will never substitute his personal appraisal of the interests at stake, or his personal preference between them. It is true that he is not engaged in historical reconstruction, as he is when determining an issue of fact; his task is more difficult, so difficult that it is impossible ever to know how far he has been successful. For it is no less than to decide how those who have passed the "enactment" would have dealt with the "particulars" before him, about which they have said nothing whatever. Impalpable and even insoluble as that inquiry may be, the method which he must pursue is toto coelo different from that open to him, were he free to enforce his own choices.[39]

Where a legislative act gives no clear direction as to its application to the facts before the court, a judge requires extraordinary talent to divine the legislative will. And, we cannot expect all our judges to have the talents of a Learned Hand or a Thomas Swan, much as we should like that. One should not chastise them, therefore, when, in an ambiguous situation, their personal values are necessarily involved in their judgments. But the same cannot be said where, as in the Title VII cases, the legislative will is clear if unpalatable to both the administrators of the law and the courts. When, in conjunction, the bureaucracy and the judiciary supplant the legislature, they are acting unconstitutionally.

Conclusion

I have spoken of judicial invasion of legislative function as the primary deficiency of current judicial behavior. Except in terms of partisan interest in the outcome of particular cases, I am not among those able to see the desirable results of such judicial hegemony. Again, I would take my stand with Judge Learned Hand:

> Another supposed advantage of the wider power of review seems to be that by the "moral radiation of its decision" a court may point the way to a resolution of the social conflicts involved better than any likely to emerge from a legislature. In other words, courts may light the way to a saner world and ought to be encouraged to do so. I should indeed be glad to believe it, and it may be that my failure hitherto to observe it is owing to some personal defect of vision; but at any rate judges have large areas left unoccupied by legislation within which to exercise this benign function. Besides, for a judge to serve as communal mentor appears to me a very dubious addition to his duties and one apt to interfere with their proper discharge.[40]

Dean Griswold was, perhaps, more pragmatic in his objections to judicial activism: "Judges may be doing good things in the name of activism today, but activism can also be used to order bad things if the principle of intervention is accepted."[41]

One word of—shall I call it—"hope." When we talk about the federal judiciary we tend to think in terms of the Supreme Court. There are signs, however, that there is a movement away from judicial activism by the Supreme Court. The recent decision that rejected the lower federal court's desire to take over the management of the Philadelphia police department is an example.[42] What we may have begun to witness is that an inherited judicial activism continues to grow in the lower federal courts. At the same time, there seems to be a reticence on the part of the Supreme Court to rein in that activism. The immediate future may see a Supreme Court that will try to turn the federal judiciary from its constant overreaching.

If the Supreme Court does not impose judicial restraint on its lower court brethren, the Chief Justice will continue to report each year—regardless of new appointments—that the federal courts cannot meet the burdens that they impose on themselves. All law will turn into federal law, especially if the lower courts have their way with the post-Civil War Reconstruction Civil Rights acts. All laws will be judge-made, except for that which is made by the bureaucracy. All institutions will be the subject and object of judicial management. Perhaps it is not insignificant that federal trial judges, like American presidents, now speak of themselves in the first person plural: the royal "we."

This will certainly bring no improvement on present government incompetence. No more than other governmental agencies is the federal bench burdened by brilliance. Indeed, as Horace Binney wrote in 1835 in his biography of John Marshall, patron saint of judicial activism:

"The world has produced fewer instances of truly great judges than it has of great men in almost every other department of civilized life."[43] Government by judiciary is neither democratic nor efficient. Its only justification is that Congress and the President prefer politics to government, and opinion polls show that while the people do not think highly of the judiciary, they credit it more than they credit either the executive or legislative branches.

NOTES

[1] "Chief Justice Burger Issues Yearend Report," 62 *A.B.A.J.* 189 (1976).

[2] *Ibid.* at 190.

[3] Glazer, "Towards an Imperial Judiciary?" *The Public Interest*, #41, p. 104 (1975).

[4] *E.g., Gibbons* v. *Ogden*, 9 Wheat. 1 (1824).

[5] *E.g., McCulloch* v. *Maryland*, 4 Wheat. 316 (1819).

[6] *E.g., Dartmouth College* v. *Woodward*, 4 Wheat. 518 (1819).

[7] See Powell, *Vagaries and Varieties in Constitutional Interpretation* (1956).

[8] See Konefsky, *John Marshall and Alexander Hamilton* (1964).

[9] See *In re* Debs, 158 U.S. 564 (1895); *Truax* v. *Corrigan*, 257 U.S. 312 (1921).

[10] Speech at Baltimore, Md., September 6, 1924, quoted in Kurland, ed., *Felix Frankfurter on the Supreme Court* 158–159 (1970).

[11] See Leuchtenburg, "The Origins of Franklin D. Roosevelt's 'Court-Packing' Plan" 1966 *Supreme Court Review* 347.

[12] Jackson, *The Struggle for Judicial Supremacy* c. IX (1941).

[13] *Ibid.* at 288.

[14] *Ibid.* at 291–92.

[15] *Santa Clara County* v. *Southern Pacific R.R. Co.*, 118 U.S. 394 (1886).

[16] "Mr. Justice Holmes at Eighty-Five," in Hand, *The Spirit of Liberty*, 27–28 (Dillard, ed., 1952).

[17] "At Fourscore," Hand, *Supra* note 16 at 262.

[18] Berle, *The Three Faces of Power*, 3 (1967).

[19] *Ibid.* at vii–viii.

[20] *Erie R.R. Co.* v. *Tompkins*, 304 U.S. 64 (1938).

[21] See Friendly, "In Praise of Erie—and of the New Federal Common Law," in *Benchmarks* 155 (1967); cf. Kurland, "The Romero Case and Some Problems of Federal Jurisdiction," 73 *Harvard Law Review* 817 (1960).

[22] *United States* v. *Hudson*, 7 Cranch 32 (1812).

[23] *Jacobellis* v. *Ohio*, 378 U.S. 184, 197 (1964).

[24] *Southern Pacific Co.* v. *Jensen*, 244 U.S. 205, 221 (1917).

[25] See Gilmore, *The Death of Contract* (1974).

[26] 4 Wheat. 316 (1819).

[27] 9 Wheat. 1 (1824).

[28] 1 Cranch 137 (1803).

[29] Kurland, *supra* note 10, at 339–40.

[30] *Terminiello* v. *Chicago*, 337 U.S. 1, 11 (1949).

[31] *U.S. News & World Report*, 19 Jan. 1976, p. 29.

[32] *Ibid.*

[33] See Epstein, "Substantive Due Process by Any Other Name: The Abortion Cases," 1973 *Supreme Court Review* 159.

[34] See Casper, "Apportionment and the Right to Vote: Standards of Judicial Scrutiny," 1973 *Supreme Court Review* 1; Neal, *"Baker* v. *Carr*: Politics in Search of Law," 1962 *Supreme Court Review* 252.

[35] *Cooper* v. *Aaron*, 358 U.S. 1, 26 (1958).

[36] *Irvine* v. *California*, 347 U.S. 128, 136–37 (1954).

[37] 110 *Congressional Record* 7213 (8 April 1964).

[38] *Ibid.* at 7207.

[39] "Thomas Walter Swan," in Hand, *supra* note 16, at 164.

[40] Hand, *The Bill of Rights* 70–71 (1958).

[41] Note 31 *supra*.

[42] *Rizzo* v. *Goode*, 96 S. Ct. 598 (1976).

[43] Binney, *The Life and Character of Chief Justice Marshall* xx (1835).

[XX, Fall 1976, 358–371]

[36]

The Well-Intending Judges

C. P. IVES

C(harles) P(omeroy) Ives *(1903–1982) started his career at* The New Haven Journal-Courier *as a reporter in 1928 and went on to become editor of that newspaper in 1932. He joined* The Baltimore Sun *as an editorial writer in 1939, and for twenty years wrote a weekly column on public affairs. He retired in 1973. Particularly interested in twentieth-century jurisprudence, he contributed numerous articles on that subject to* Modern Age *and other scholarly publications.*

IN JUNE 1968 the Chief Justice of the United States announced his intention to retire; in the same month the Pentagon issued Defense Department Directive No. 3025.12: "Subject: Employment of Military Resources in the Event of Civil Disturbances." Few noticed the Pentagon directive, but the Court announcement was widely published. Neither could have been foreseen a short three years earlier, much less any relationship between the two. But on January 19, 1965, a dissenting opinion in the Supreme Court enables us, by hindsight, to understand how directive and announcement interact to signal the formal ending of the Roosevelt-Warren era, the middle third of the American twentieth century.

The case decided by the Supreme Court on January 19, 1965, was Cox v. Louisiana, a plea for reversal of convictions under a Louisiana statute prohibiting picket lines intended to "impede" or "influence" courts in the performance of their duties. The appellant Cox had been a leader of some 2,000 college students who had picketed a jail and court house in Baton Rouge to protest the arrest of 23 of their number in demonstrations at segregated lunchrooms. The Supreme Court majority ruled for the appellants, on the ground that the police officer in charge at the scene had authorized the picketing. But four dissenters, speaking through Justice Hugo L. Black ". . . fail to understand how the Court can justify the reversal . . . because of a permission which testimony in the record denies was given, which could not have been authoritatively given anyway, and which, even if given, was soon afterward revoked. . . ." And then, moving to something like prescience:

. . . the streets are not now and never have been the proper place to administer justice . . . and minority groups . . . are the ones who always have suffered and always will suffer most when street multitudes are allowed to substitute their pressures for the less glamorous but more dependable and temperate processes of the law. Experience demonstrates that it is not a far step from what to many seems the earnest, honest, patriotic, kind-hearted multitude of today to the fanatical, threatening, lawless mob of tomorrow.... *Those who encourage minority groups to believe that the United States Constitution and Federal laws give them a right to patrol and picket in the streets whenever they choose, in order to advance what they think to be a just and noble end, do no service to those minority groups, their cause, or their country....* (Italics supplied.)

Just five months later in the Watts section of Los Angeles a routine arrest for speeding and drunkenness touched off a rage of civil disturbance in a hundred American cities over the next four years and moved the Pentagon at length to Directive No. 3025.12—"in order to preserve domestic tranquillity."

I

Why should the majority justices in Cox v. Louisiana have rejected an argument which, as stated by Black, would surely have persuaded most thoughtful Americans attuned to the classical American constitutionalism? Because by the time Black spoke, a court majority, shifting from time to time in pace and personnel, but implacable over a period of three decades, had transcended not merely the older juridical exegesis but the original norms of the judicial process itself. One strategically positioned herald of this great change was the late Jerome N. Frank in an address to the Association of American Law Schools on December 30, 1933. Frank was then one of the rising young lawyers in the new administration, general counsel of the Agricultural Adjustment Administration, later chairman of the Securities and Exchange Commission (SEC), and finally a United States circuit judge for the Second Circuit. A prolific legal writer, Frank had led in a new philosophical jurisprudence variously labelled "re-

alistic," "pragmatic," "factualist," "experimental," "scientific," "positivist," then well in command of many of the brightest young teachers in such elite law schools as Columbia and Yale.

Frank entitled the law school association address, "Experimental Jurisprudence and the New Deal." He began by dividing the government lawyers then in Washington into two groups, the Mr. Try-Its and the Mr. Absolutes. The Mr. Absolutes had great difficulty in adjusting to many of the new administration's proposals, but the Mr. Try-Its enjoyed drastically updated resiliences:

Especially do they repudiate fixed beliefs as to the eternal validity of any particular means for the accomplishment of desired ends.... Most of these experimentalists, too, are characterized in these troubled days, by their primary regard for the immediate. ... For the new deal as I see it, means that we have taken to the open road. We are moving in a new direction. We are to be primarily interested in seeking the welfare of the great majority of our people and not in merely preserving, unmodified, certain traditions and folkways, regardless of their effect on human beings. That important shift in emphasis is the vital difference between the new-deal and the old-deal philosophy. It is the leaders of this new movement whom the experimentalist lawyers in government find it delightful to serve. ...

Writing about the same time another of the new philosophers put it more briefly—and bluntly: "... Rules and principles are empty symbols.... Legal science is slowly being washed with 'cynical acid.' ... The ideal of a government of laws and not of men is a dream. ..."

But of course the idealization of a government of laws animates the whole older Anglo-American jurisprudence. The institutionalization of political tradition and folkways—"the law of the land"—is explicitly what a constitution *is*—written or unwritten. The short formula is consensus to constitution to consent. The United States Constitution as originally conceived was nothing if not a fixed, that is, a reified, belief, out of recent tyrannies experienced and remoter tyrannies vigilantly studied, in the eternal validity of narrowly particularized means for the accomplishment of desired ends. Its whole rationale and intent were to temper the impact on human beings of political authority by slicing sovereignty horizontally into two layers, subdividing the lower layer vertically into an indefinite number of regional segments, and partitioning all the segments in both layers into separate executive, legislature, and judiciary. The bearing on these older concepts—intricate, awkward, designed as much to impede as to ease political action—of Frank's address was not immediately understood by the public, perhaps not even in its full scope and import by all those who heard it—perhaps not even by Frank himself!

But its implications began to clarify almost at once and came into dazzling relief three years later, on February 5, 1937. That was the day the experimentalist President sent to Congress a proposal to reorganize the Supreme Court more closely to his own views. Frank had explained in the law school address that just as there were Mr. Try-It and Mr. Absolute lawyers, so there were Try-It judges and Judge Absolutes. Glossing Frank, as it were, some 14 years later, Professor Max Rheinstein told how

> ... despairing of the possibility of moving legislatures, these scholars set their hopes in the judges, especially the future judges who would arise from the ranks of their own pupils. Let the judges be aware of their powers, and let them be well-trained and well-intentioned and they will be the initiators of the good society. . . .

The President's purpose, never seriously denied, in the court-reorganization message, was to add enough result-oriented Try-It judges to out-vote the Judge Absolutes who still relied more on principle as a guide to decision. The Congress responded, as would have been expected of legislators under oath to support a constitution of folkways and traditions embodying consensual beliefs in the eternal validity of fixed procedures for conducting the public business. By overwhelming vote, after a Judiciary committee report of almost unprecedented severity, the Senate rejected the court reorganization plan.

But the victory of constitutionalism was merely formal, and for reasons suggested early in the debate by a court reorganization proponent in testimony knitting the Court plan into the full assumption and perspective of the Try-It jurisprudence. The witness, dean of a famous "experimental" law school, talked less of constitutional principle than of immediate results: given the obduracy of the Justice Absolutes on the Court, the plan would short-cut the otherwise necessary amendment process and so expedite validation of reform measures whose instant need was indicated by the confrontation at that very moment of armed troops and striking workingmen in automobile plants in Michigan.

And indeed, the President had launched his proposal in a time of nation-wide industrial turbulence climaxing in Michigan with the political campaign of November 1936, in which his friend and protégé, the late Frank Murphy, was elected Governor. The President had assigned Murphy as High Commissioner to the Philippines in 1935 with clear suggestions that he would be brought home in time to run in the next year's campaign. Simultaneously, the newly organized Congress of Industrial Organizations had launched its drive to unionize the motor industry. John L. Lewis, CIO chief, spoke publicly of heavy campaign contributions by his United Mine Workers and expected "... the administration to ... help the workers. . . ." Soon after Murphy's election, automobile employees occupied several General Motors plants by way of the sit-down strike device, borrowed from left extremist trade unions in France. The corporation secured court orders clearing the plants by February 5, but Murphy, pleading the risk of bloodshed, declined to enforce them. That was the February 5 on which the President sent the court message to Congress.

When Murphy ran for re-election in 1938, the sit-down strike crisis of the previous year was a major issue. The Communist party, some of whose members had been involved, announced formal support for Murphy, but he was defeated. That was on November 8. Two months later, January 1, 1939, the President named Murphy Attorney-General of the United States, chief law enforcement officer of the federal government. Within a few months Jerome Frank, by then chairman of the Securities and Exchange Commission, was assuring Murphy that "I know of nothing that has occurred in the history of the New Deal which has been as stimulating as the manner in which you have been administering the Department of Justice. . . ." One of Murphy's early acts as Attorney-General had been to recommend William O. Douglas, then chairman of the Securities and Exchange Commission, and a leader of the new experimentalist jurisprudence in his years as a law teacher at Yale, for nomination to the Supreme Court. The President complied, Douglas took the oath in April 1939, and was succeeded by Frank at the SEC.

But Murphy's career was still short of its climax. On January 4, 1940, the experimentalist President named him to an unexpected vacancy on the Supreme Court. There he became the fifth Roosevelt nominee, taking his seat on February 5, 1940. That was three years to the day from the court-reorganization message and Murphy's simultaneous refusal to enforce the Michigan court order for clearing the seized automobile plants.

Murphy's brief term as Justice—he died in 1949—was marked by two extraordinary opinions in which he spoke for the court. In Thornhill v. Alabama he ruled that a labor picket line in an industrial dispute was really a form of publication, a means of communication, like a newspaper or a book, and like a newspaper or book, enjoyed the protection of the First Amendment. Three years later, in Schneiderman v. U.S., Murphy announced for a passionately divided court that an official of the Communist Party-USA could not, on that ground alone, be judged to lack that faithful attachment to the United States constitution which was required by law of naturalized citizens. In a note to Murphy, Justice Felix Frankfurter had proposed the following gloss on his Schneiderman opinion: "The American constitution ain't got no principles. The Communist party don't stand for nuthin'. The Supreme Court don't mean nuthin'. Nuthin' means nuthin', and ter Hell with the USA so long as a guy is attached to the principles of the USSR." Murphy's latest biographer, J. Woodford Howard, Jr., who supplies the Frankfurter comment, labels a key chapter "Tempering Justice with Murphy."

In fairness to Murphy, it should nevertheless be said that he seems to have been reluctant to quit the Philippines and to join the Court. A modest and introspective man, he took each step out of humble loyalty to the President's judgment on strategical necessities along the "open road."

Four years later, however, and in a labor crisis even graver than that of 1937, the President had readier collaboration from his friends. In September 1941, under threat of a nation-wide strike on the railways, he set up a five-man emergency board to survey the union and management positions and make quasi-judicial recommendations for a settlement. The Board was named under the National Railway Labor Act, then 15 years old, and widely labelled as the "model labor act," because rail strikes had practically disappeared under it. It represented very much a "particular means for the accomplishment of desired ends." But when the emergency board (headed by Wayne L. Morse, not yet a Senator of any party) reported, the unions took the all but unprecedented step of rejecting the recommendations. Five operating unions fixed the date for a nation-wide railway strike—December 7, 1941.

In the meantime, as we now know, official Washington was aware of the threat of hostilities from Japan in the Pacific. The President reconvened the railway emergency board and pressed it for immediate settlement of the dispute. Board members protested that their report, being quasi-judicial, could not be altered, so the President turned them into a mediatory body with instructions to work out arrangements acceptable to the unions. And how had this enterprise been managed? A union spokesman supplied the answer in formal testimony before the second Morse board:

> Immediately following the filing of the [original] report by this board . . . the report was released by the President as public information without comment. I don't know whether that has any significance to you: it has a lot to me. . . . You were asked by [the President] to help him find an answer. . . . You advised him; he said, "That is not enough. I want some more." Do you know the President has never asked us [the unions] to accept this [first] report?

In other words, by the union spokesman's uncontradicted testimony the President did not once call on his union friends to accept the quasi-judicial recommendations on the merits of his own hand-picked board, though a nation-wide strike threatened on the date that proved to be that of Pearl Harbor. "At four separate times he tried to settle the dispute after a decision on the merits had been handed down," Morse testified in Senate debate five years later. ". . . Strikes have occurred in the past, and they will occur in the future whenever the [unions] believe they have sufficient power in connection with specific disputes to obtain a modification of a decision through mediation or intervention by the Chief Executive." Almost continuous failure since 1941 of the Railway Labor Act and the Taft-Hartley emergency strike provisions modelled thereon, support Morse's expert testimony. This was "experimentalism."

II

By the early 1940s even non-scholarly observers were beginning to examine not merely the forward implications but the roots and philosophical relationships of political strategies and matching jurisprudential departures quite new to American practice. The Absolutes, after all, on the bench, at the bar, and in public service generally partook of insights and outlooks broader than the United States and older than the present. What about the new men and the innovating ideas that Frank was describing in 1933?

A clue was already available to careful newspaper readers in a 1937 dispatch from Germany quoting *Hamburger Fremdenblatt* on the President's defeat in the court-reorganization controversy:

> [The conflict] revealed that the oldest real democracy is also the most reactionary and that its various divided portions will unite in opposition whenever something new is proposed. President Roosevelt has been de-

feated through the trickiness of a constitution. . . .

This comment, so close to what the discomfited court reorganizers were saying that summer in the United States, was instantly recognized by scholars as a journalistic echo of the jurisprudential philosophy then dominant in Germany. In 1940, Professor Lon L. Fuller of the Harvard Law School had commented on a legal essay of some 14 years earlier by a leading German law writer. It discussed

> . . . the extent to which in Germany public law and political science have become passively positivistic. [The German author] remarks that the foreign writings most esteemed abroad were unacceptable in Germany, because, being tainted by ethics and natural law, they were not deemed sufficiently "scientific." . . . One cannot read [this article] today without some sense of the doom which [then] hung over the German social structure. . . .

Thirteen years after Fuller wrote, Professor Leo Strauss, born in Germany and arriving in the United States in 1938, discussed the post-World War I emergence of "scientific" positivism in American social science. "It would not be the first time," said Strauss, "that a nation defeated on the battlefield, and, as it were, annihilated as a political being, has deprived its conquerors of the most sublime fruit of victory by imposing on them the yoke of its own thought. . . ."

More explicit was Professor Arthur Nussbaum—then on the Columbia law faculty though Berlin born, who reached the United States in 1934:

> During the last few decades legal thinking in a number of countries has been pervaded by a reform movement which has become variously known as "realistic," "sociological," or "functional." . . . Germany and the United States have been the main scenes of that novel jurisprudential evolution. The German movement began earlier than the

American. . . . The new realistic movement did not move forward in Germany until the decade preceding the [first] World War. . . . [Eugen] Ehrlich [who lectured in the United States] constitutes a distinct link between the two movements. . . .

But what really arrested American observers of the new American "experimentalism" was the address delivered by the Governor-General of Poland, Hans Frank, to a meeting of National Socialist jurists at Berlin on December 4, 1939:

> Pale phantoms of objective justice do not exist for us any more. Today our law of war is the reality of war itself. The Leader now has placed us in a world of reality filled with values that are independent of formal rules. The decisive principle is, who is stronger, who is more determined, who has better nerves? Whoever does not admit this is a pale theorist and is no good for politics, or, in the deepest sense, for creative law-giving. . . .

As Professor Nussbaum wrote the next year, "The National Socialist government, it seems, favors the realistic approach."

It remained for an American judge to put statements like these into full context and perspective for Americans. Twelve years after Jerome Frank addressed the American Law School Association, six years after Hans Frank spoke to the National Socialist jurists, Justice Robert H. Jackson of the Supreme Court was named chief prosecutor for the United States in the Nuremberg trials of war criminals. In his preparatory readings, perhaps in the German jurisprudence, Jackson (a court reorganizer in 1937) seems to have suffered a sudden pang of recognition. Two weeks before his departure for Nuremberg, he spoke in a public address of

> a school of cynics in the [American] law schools, at the bar and on the bench . . . [who teach] that law is anything that can muster the votes to be put in legislation, or directive, or decision, and backed with a

policeman's club. . . . Law to those of this school has no foundation in nature, no necessary harmony with higher principles of right and wrong. . . . It is charitable to assume that such advocates of power as the sole source of law do not recognize the identity of their incipient authoritarianism with that which has reached its awful climax in Europe. . . .

III

Yet Justice Jackson may have been uncharitable in imputing to the American experimentalists a total failure to sense their own true direction. "We have built up new instruments of public power," Mr. Roosevelt conceded in 1936. But "in the hands of a people's government this power is wholesome and proper. . . ." In the court reorganization of 1937, he seemed to be differentiating between American and foreign programs to convert courts into instruments of policy: "You who know me will accept my solemn assurance that in a world in which democracy is under attack . . . I seek to make American democracy succeed. . . ."

The quick of the matter was that the new judges would use realism, experimentalism, the positivism which measurably emancipated them from precedent and principle, for good ends. Rheinstein thought such ideas were "to a large extent held unconsciously," and would be applied "in conformity with the value judgments of that society of which [the judge] is a functionary"—their premise being, of course, that judges would know better than legislators what the value judgments of society really were. It was as though consciously or otherwise they were caught red-handed in the German and related doctrines which had shaped Hans Frank; but was not the very essence of the scientism they had espoused that the law as such was neutral, washed with cynical acid, a mere instrument, a means to an

end? If German positivism had been put to the uses of the totalitarian state, then the American positivists would hasten the evolution of the good society. Hans Frank rejected the pale phantoms of objective justice because they cramped tyranny. For Jerome Frank's Judge Try-It, fixed belief in eternal verities obstructed welfare and reform.

But if "despairing of legislatures," judges themselves are to "initiate the good society," how can they bend judicial techniques to what is clearly a legislative task? A fateful logic led them again and again to the Fourteenth amendment. By new applications of, by invisible radiations from, by projections of anterior curbs on the central government through this great ordinance to curb the states, much of the juro-legislation of experiment and innovation has been accomplished. Yet the turbulent history of the Civil War amendments might have warned prudent jurists against employing the Fourteenth too generally beyond "the absolute compulsion of its words." The exceptional manner of its ratification has been much rationalized, even euphemized, but Bernard Schwartz in his history of the Supreme Court was candor itself. The Fourteenth

was imposed upon the South as part of the price of defeat on the battlefield. Without a doubt, the post-Civil War amendments were intended to work hardships on the South and to do so without regard to southern inclinations and desires; that is the normal purpose of terms imposed upon a defeated power and particularly after a civil war.

The operative word is "imposed": from the first it has taught the attentive how much the Civil War amendments were *sui generis*, of a different quality, sounding in assumptions distinct from all the rest of the constitution. To repeat commonplaces repeated earlier, the constitution, like legislation itself, is consensual. The Constitutional Convention was, qualitatively, like a special one-act parliament. The charter drafted at Philadelphia announced consent, as did the several ratifications in consenting states. The Civil War amendments are coercive, ratified in the South under duress; they are an exercise of will, the will of a conqueror whose army remained in occupation for twelve agonizing years to see that the will was done (as in the end it was not, and is not yet).

It is true that some critics of our parliamentary arrangements say unlimited debate in the United States Senate converts that body intermittently from consensus to coercion. One scholar justifies judicial intervention in the school segregation controversy "because of the stranglehold which one section of the country had upon the Congressional windpipe. . . ." A minority filibuster, this well-worn argument runs, can parry the majority will. But a two-thirds vote in the Senate can always close debate, and has. And knowledgeable parliamentarians know that a majority may tacitly acquiesce in minority intransigence because the majority members know their constituents tacitly acquiesce. The ultimate reason that legislation fails in Congress is the lack of consensus.

None of this suggests for a minute, obviously, that the Fourteenth amendment, however distinct in tone and texture, is not truly a part of the Constitution of the United States. Nor is there the slightest doubt that its stated purpose was to apply nation-wide—the abomination of human slavery and all its enumerated incidents were to be extirpated wherever they existed, in Maine and Oregon as in Mississippi. The propriety of court intervention aside, Brown v. Board of Education was well within the exact and literal subject matter announced in the plain words put before the states and sufficiently ratified.

But experimental jurists have magni-

fied that narrow and explicit purpose into a crypto-legislative remaking at large of state criminal laws, state legislative apportionment, state laws defending property and against pornography. Even in Brown v. Board, Chief Justice Warren conceded that the history of the Fourteenth amendment was "at best . . . inconclusive" in its bearing on school desegregation. There was very much less support for generalized applications of a reach and severity hardly contemplated by the bitterest of the Republican Radicals. The victorious states meant to impose their will in one carefully defined particular not to surrender at large to the central government.

There was, of course, Radical disapproval when the Supreme Court made its first interpretation of the Fourteenth amendment, but prudent opinion undoubtedly concurred. "We doubt very much," said Justice Miller in the Slaughterhouse cases, "whether any action of a state not directed by way of discrimination against the Negroes as a class, or on account of their race, will ever be held to come within the purview" of the enforcement provisions. But that was in 1873, and it must at once be added that of the several testimonies of fallibility in the *United States Reports,* this is still among the most spectacular. Within five years Justice Miller was protesting that "the docket of this court is crowded with cases in which we are asked to hold that State courts and state legislatures [some outside the South] have deprived their own [white] citizens of life, liberty and property without due process of law."

But the new "experimentalists" are at least in logic estopped from using this Fourteenth amendment expansionism to support their own. What Justice Miller complained of was the early symptoms of one of the great and famous "scandals" of our jurisprudence, as seen by progressives of all schools. In a one-two exercise in expansionism, the court majority first held that a business corporation was a "person" within the meaning of that term in the Fourteenth amendment; then that such "persons" could not be deprived of property without Fourteenth amendment due process of law. Fourteenth amendment due process, in turn, came to mean that state legislation aimed at regulating or controlling the raucous capitalism of the time would have to pass the scrutiny of federal judges. And Oliver Wendell Holmes was merely the most eloquent of several dissenting Justices who insisted that Supreme Court majorities were writing their pro-property predilections into constitutional law against the sovereignty of the states. Holmes said:

> There is nothing I more deprecate than the use of the Fourteenth amendment beyond the absolute compulsion of its words. . . . I cannot believe that the amendment was intended to give us carte blanche to embody our economic or moral beliefs in its prohibitions.

This Holmesian theme, sharpened and even envenomed in the bitter Depression days, largely animated the 1937 attack on the Supreme Court in the first demonstrable surge of the new "experimentalism" in our judicial history: unconstitutional, and indeed, unconscionable pro-property bias was the central allegation against the Nine Old Men. But when with Justice Murphy an "experimentalist" majority emerged on the court itself, the earlier arguments for an aseptic literalism were abruptly jettisoned in an altogether characteristic "primary regard" for a new "immediate": "it began to seem as though, when 'personal' rights were in issue," wrote Learned Hand, that "something strangely akin to the discredited attitude . . . of the old apostles of the institution of property was regaining recogni-

tion. . . ." The strict constructionists of very recent years were translated in a wink to Fourteenth amendment expansionism of quite unexampled hardihood and scope.

IV

Now it is surely not unfair to put experimentalists to the test of results and pragmatists to that of workability. If philosophies used for evil in other places are to be redeemed by good deeds, the deeds are to be examined. Jurists who repair the lack of consensual legislation out of the old warrant for coercion must still depend on consensus in the end. So a surge of federal juro-legislation abridging state police powers counters the German criminal jurisprudence of gun and gallows—but at length the President in the capital city itself must propose detention before trial to reduce crime in the streets. The Germans burned books and wrecked printing presses, and the Americans debilitated state censorship laws—but pornography flaunts on every screen and drugstore bookstand.

The German positivists fought communism and fawned on the propertied classes which controlled the steel mills and munitions plants. The American Judge Try-Its stretch the First and Fourteenth amendments in a dozen ways useful to communism, the anti-property archetypes; and withdraw progressively from property the protections guaranteed to it equally with liberty and life itself—"whether this court likes it or not," cries Justice Black in a recent dissent, "the Constitution recognizes and supports the concept of private ownership of property."

The German positivism of bad intent generated street fighting and *Kristallnachts*, as has the well-intentioned positivism of the Americans. When student militants draw on the factory seizures of the thirties to seize universities in the sixties, they rely, as well, on systematic suspension, over 35 years, of peace and property laws in behalf of earlier and no less reckless minorities.

In an ultimate horror, the Germans proscribe the Jews: and the Americans break out of a century of neglect to accord to American Negroes everything promised in the Civil War amendments and much that goes beyond anything contemplated in the 1860s or even in the 1950s. At the same time, Justice Try-It pronounces prayer decisions dimming in the public schools the Judaeo-Christian doctrines of brotherhood which alone make the new school integration policies comprehensible.

But by 1968, Robert L. Carter, former general counsel for the NAACP, reports that Brown v. Board's ". . . indirect consequences have been awesome. . . . [It] has promised more than it could give, and therefore has contributed to black alienation and bitterness, to a loss of confidence in white institutions and to the growing racial polarization of our society." Polarization by residence leaves too few white children "to go around" in school desegregation programs. It translates one-man, one-vote apportionment (the good positivists' retort to the bad positivists' dictatorship) into still more rigid concentrations of the political power represented by 80 percent of the population. The National Advisory Commission on Civil Disorders has just found "white racism" pandemic not merely in the South but through the nation as a whole. (Was this the true explanation of the Senate filibusters which the court moved to supervene by its own diametrically opposite reckoning of public sentiment?)

When race militants employ the time-hallowed abuses and immunities of trade unions against trade unionist teachers, macabre and ultimate Nemesis revives Nazoid anti-semitism in the streets of New York. And across a century of truly drop-sical distention of the Fourteenth amendment, the force and will of Reconstruction echo in Defense Department Directive No. 3025.12.

V

The intimations seem to be that those who reject pale phantoms of objective justice come to common grief, no matter how their motives differ. "We know that in practice," says A. H. C. Chroust, "there is hardly a more eloquent claimant of [human] rights than the legal positivist or realist who spends most of his time disproving 'scientifically' the very existence of or truth of those rights." To intend good ends does not decontaminate septic means. Means are, in our constitutional assumptions, among the ends: maintenance of constitutional due process, of separate powers and consensual legislation was the end which would legitimate and fortify all the other ends. What are the chances of converting means into ends again, and ends into means? If the Roosevelt-Warren third of the century is ending, what happens next?

The first thing is obvious: getting controversy off the streets and college lawns and back into the "less glamorous but more dependable and temperate processes of the law." In early 1969 optimists might find prospects for this at least fair, with resumption in race matters of the quiet progress before 1954 and continuing in some vital areas since. A graver index to the larger future is available in recent government trends now very strong, probably irreversible, possibly able to be slowed down, and quite aside from jurisprudence. In 35 years we have clearly regressed in political conceptualism and institutional articulation—check and balance wobble, separation of powers fuzzes. As early as 1930, Dean Pound of the Harvard Law School was proclaiming "The New Feudalism": in "the original fundamental idea [of the old feudalism] . . . the single individual . . . was not thought of as self-sufficient. . . . He commended himself to some lord. . . ."

We do not generally concede how broadly we commend ourselves to a state which nurses, houses, feeds, educates, pensions, and buries always increasing numbers of us. Not inappropriately does the Secretary of Health, Education and Welfare describe a new welfare reform plan under study at the White House as "the most sweeping since the Elizabethan poor laws." Those who defend the trends as inevitable can cite overwhelming evidence much beyond medieval Europe that pyramidal and patriarchic government is the norm for mankind, and our own brief two centuries of self-help and constitutional limit an exception and, perhaps, an eccentricity. They are equally persuasive when they argue that a government of plenary commitments must have plenary power to discharge them. Here, too, they can cite history, particularly the late English feudalism romanticized by Lord Bolingbroke from whose Patriot King the Americans broke so sharply in the eighteenth century.

We know that in medieval theory the king and his council nurtured and ruled all, with the council including relatively undifferentiated judges and legislators. "The chief justices," says William Holdsworth, "have as members of the king's council, a real voice in the making of laws. . . . In fact, the legislative, executive and judicial authorities have not as yet become so completely separated that they cannot occasionally work together." Holdsworth was speaking of the reign of Edward II (1307–1327), but the discussion will not seem wholly foreign to contemporary Americans. As we have seen, the warmest friends of the Warren Court do not deny—they proclaim—that it has already recaptured much of the legislative function in a widely accepted authority to make new law when national or state

legislators fail for reasons which the one judge who completes a quorum considers insufficient.

A working intimacy of American executives and judges is quite in the medieval pattern. Lincoln had his Davis and Harding his Taft (or vice versa), but Johnson moved forward. Considering at least two Justices for Chief Justice, he named one. The Justice he named (because he "was a pragmatist") assisted at closed executive meetings and remonstrated with citizens who spoke unkindly of executive policy. The Justice (by now ex-Justice) he did not nominate served at least once while on the Court to "pick the administration's chestnuts out of the fire in a secret meeting" with a Cabinet official and a great labor magnate on a troubled question of wages (Associated Press, January 1, 1965); and later embarked on executive business as an ambassador to a foreign court, having resigned as a judge.

Holdsworth recalls that in 1312 "Bereford, C. J., directed the parties to an action in which circumstances were unusual to 'sue a bill to parliament'; and after debate in parliament judgment was given for the plaintiff." Our separation of powers has hardly decomposed that far—though surely it is maintained only in form when the Court does the legislating itself! Of one thing we may be quite sure: a constitution designed for limit and oriented toward *laissez-faire* will prove increasingly inappropriate to an organic, nurturing, and patriarchal state. And to political exigencies that cannot wait on legislative consensus, a juro-legislation insulated against electoral rebuke may increasingly respond.

To say all of which does not rule out as at least conceivable a "great and stately" jurisprudence in which human rights—including security of person and property—would still have recognition. The earliest judges in the Anglo-American tradition believed, after all, in a natural law transcending human affairs, but mindful of humanity made on a very high model. In subjection to this "brooding omnipresence" and its impress on conscience, the old judges began long before Edward II to shape the concepts which grew into petitions, remonstrances, and bills merely elaborated and consolidated in our Philadelphia charter. The "experimentalists" teach that this natural law is mere "mythmaking and fatherly lies," impossible of belief because "to us who have eaten from the tree of knowledge, that happy state of innocence is no longer possible," as Professor Rheinstein puts it.

Yet it may depend on whether those who ate from the tree really ate or merely nibbled. The American positivists who read Defense Directive No. 3025.12 and the Walpurgis nightscape which it reflects have now more than nibbled and are less than refreshed. One who fed to the teeth was the late Gustav Radbruch, author of a German textbook in legal positivism. Emerging physically intact from what he called the "twelve-year dictatorship" (1933–1945), Radbruch prepared another edition of the original work—but announced a new point of view:

> The legal positivism that ruled unchallenged among German scholars . . . this view was helpless when confronted with [National Socialist] lawlessness. . . . Legal philosophy must restore to consciousness a wisdom that is centuries old and that was common to antiquity, the Christian Middle Ages and the Enlightenment. During these periods men believed that there was a law higher than mere enactment, which they called the law of nature, the law of God or the law of Reason.

Americans know about it, as Professor Filmer S. C. Northrop says:

> New England was founded in major part by nonconformist Protestants who came to the western hemisphere to escape from the rule of the religious majority. Like Jefferson [they] were heavily under the influence of the philosophy of natural rights and natural law of Locke. With the opening of the frontier this living law spread to the middle west and the far west. . . . It is exceedingly unlikely that legal positivism has seeped down . . . to the masses to a sufficient extent to alter this original and basic philosophy of American culture. The coming of Roman Catholics in large numbers brought in a natural law philosophy also. These two positions of the living law of the United States constitute a statistical majority of the people.

Northrup was writing in 1957, but nothing that happened November 5, 1968, is inconsistent with his analysis.

To be sure, the older transcendentalism may be past revival, and it can encourage rather than restrain judicial law-making when the judge equates his own predilections with the divine will. But humility, always the major yield of a true sense of transcendence, is perfectly possible among judges who reject natural-law doctrines. This Felix Frankfurter and Learned Hand, positivists both, indicated in their steadfast practice of the "passive virtues" described by Alexander Bickel, one of their ablest disciples. The difference is between judges who use their release from higher sanctions to indulge their own ideas of public desire and judges who see in their lack of divine guidance all the weightier curb on any temptation to substitute the private will of unelected and lifetime jurists for the consensus of the people's frequently elected legislature.

VI

In sum, if there is a rise in judicial self-aggrandizement, there may be a decline. Jurists dizzied by early success can learn humility from ultimate failure. A national majority with at least lingering commitment to transcending law and limit on judges will still have judicial notice in the least representative of American political institutions. Already the constitutional legislature has denied the chief justiceship to a positivist jurist who left the Yale law faculty for Frank's Agricultural Adjustment Administration in the year of Frank's "Experimentalist" address to the law school association; and a generation later struck even colleagues on the Supreme Court as over-prone to juro-legislation. Now the chief justice for the next stage has been named by President Nixon, learned in the law and acutely observant of affairs over the three decades of legal positivism. There is another vacancy and others may follow. The people's elected legislators still command the confirming power, and may temper, if not abate, "experimentalism."

On the court even under Warren, time has not always favored Rheinstein's law professors who despaired of legislators and hoped to train up future judges from among their own pupils to juro-legislate the good society. The Yale positivists, Douglas and Fortas (resigned) were joined on the bench by Justices Stewart and White, of a younger Yale law generation. Stewart dissented from a one-man, one-vote decision grounded in an uttermost Fourteenth amendment stretch because "I could not join in the fabrication of a constitutional mandate . . . uncritical, simplistic and [a] heavy-handed application of sixth-grade arithmetic."

In a Fourteenth amendment rewrite of state criminal law by the majority, White dissented because ". . . law enforcement . . . will be crippled and its task made a great deal more difficult, all in my opinion, for unsound, unstated reasons, which can find no home in any of the provisions of the Constitution. . . ." Nicholas deB. Katzenbach, one of the younger Yale law alumni, warned, as Attorney-General of the United States, that in recent decisions enlarging the defense in criminal procedure, "I believe the judges have left the public behind, and even among judges, the margins of the consensus have been passed. . . ."

VII

To criticize the Supreme Court of the United States is a grave undertaking. The critic sometimes finds himself in unappetizing company. Moreover, the juro-legislation of the Roosevelt-Warren court is a very small part of its total performance—the tip that shows above the surface of the waters, as it were. Below it has gone about its elevated version of the appellate judge's normal work, mindful of principle, respectful of precedent, aware that "continuity with the past is not a duty, it is only a necessity." Criticism there is there, too, again quite normal—from disappointed suitors, from academic commentators, for results reached, or for lack of art in reaching them.

But it is the political decisions, the juro-legislation, which will make the new Court look most carefully to its "moral sanction," without which it cannot prosper. We have seen how Robert Carter believes that, promising too much (more accurately, perhaps, by not stressing enough the limits on its promise), the Brown decision ". . . contributed to a loss of confidence in white institutions. . . ." The Court is a white institution as Carter uses the term. "Since the Nuremberg post-mortem on the Hitler régime," said Justice Jackson, "few will believe that these positivist doctrines are weapons in the struggle to preserve liberty." If it is supposed permissible for the judge "covertly to smuggle into his decisions his personal notions," warned Learned Hand, "compliance will much more depend upon a resort to force, not a desirable expedient when it can be avoided. . . ."

It can be avoided if non-positivist judges continue what they are; and if positivist judges will reread Jackson on the ideological affinities of American legal positivism; Black on earnest multitudes and feral mobs; Hand on humility—and then embrace one least canon of judicial self-restraint: so to judge as to minimize the use, even atrophy the need, of Defense Department Directive No. 3025.12, the unloveliest monument to the Roosevelt-Warren jurisprudence.

This article was completed some months before the recent extraordinary events in the history of the Supreme Court. These I do not propose to discuss, though I think none incompatible with the discussion as it stands. One more recent episode is to me so striking, as rounding out a symmetry of thirty years, that some account may be of interest.

When President Roosevelt sent the court-reorganization message of February 5, 1937, to the Congress, I was a special student in the Yale Law School, finishing the second year of graduate study required at Yale for the M.A. degree. The proposal by the executive branch to enlarge the court with judges compliant to the presidential will seemed to me shocking. I looked at once to the law school faculty for protest and resistance, but many of the professors, led by the Dean himself, announced instant and zealous support. This dismayed me even more, and when it came time to choose a subject for the essay required of M.A. candidates, I decided to examine the new jurisprudential philosophy then blooming at Yale, Columbia, and other leading law schools, which seemed to me to have motivated the court plan, or at least the law professors who spoke for it.

The more I read into the background of this "legal realism," and checked its contemporary affinities, the more my concern grew. In my final chapter I suggested that it might well corrode the old symbolism of consensual law and order by which we had lived, even usher in what I called a "rule of iron." To sharpen my point I quoted a contemporary description by Professor Hans Kohn (delivered at Harvard in its tercentenary year, 1936) of the political and social climate then prevailing in the Third Reich.

> Might creates right. The objectivity of law is declared a liberal prejudice. Right is what helps in the struggle for power. In a world like that all security has disappeared. The abstract majesty of law is gone. The concrete situation alone and its supposed needs decide.... Fear grows everywhere and fear only begets more fear....

My theme was not universally applauded in the Yale ambiance of 1938, but the essay was read by a committee of three professors who certified my eligibility for the M.A. degree awarded in due course shortly thereafter.

Almost exactly 31 years later, on April 30, 1969, three Columbia University professors stood in the entrance to Fayerweather Hall on the Columbia campus. They were among several faculty members who had volunteered to "interpose ourselves" against new seizures of university buildings by student militants. Several students charged them, and, said one of the three, "One [student] held my arm behind my back and another hit me across the face with a stick. I was shoved to the floor. One student took the brass nozzle of a fire hose and was about to hit me with it when I scrambled away...." (As quoted in the *New York Times*.)

When the students grabbed this man, his two colleagues were shoved roughly aside. One of them had been a member of the committee of three at Yale which had read my M.A. essay in 1938. At Fayerweather Hall in 1969 a student bystander was heard by a *New York Times* reporter to say: "What a terrible business! This is straight out of Germany in the nineteen thirties...."

[XIII, Summer 1969, 233–247]

The Supreme Court's Civil Theology

FRANCIS WILSON

Francis (Graham) Wilson *(1901–1976) received his Ph.D. from Stanford in 1928 and taught at the University of Washington, in Seattle, from 1928 to 1939. As a professor of political science at the University of Illinois from 1939 to 1967, he directed the doctoral dissertation of Willmoore Kendall (Ph.D., 1940), published as* John Locke and the Doctrine of Majority-Rule *(1941). One of the pioneers of the post-World War II conservative renascence, Wilson has been analyzing the nature of conservatism in America for many years in articles like "The Ethics of Political Conservatism" and "A Theory of Conservatism" and books such as* The American Political Mind *(1949) and* The Case for Conservatism *(1951).*

WE HAVE PLAINLY reached the nit-picking stage in the discussion of religious liberty in the United States. The Justices of the Supreme Court, dominated as they are by the secular-liberal ideology (as L. Brent Bozell has named it), have reached for power against history and tradition, against the historical allocation of powers provided in the Constitution, and against the religious feelings of perhaps a majority of the nation. The ultimate in non-judicial absurdity was probably reached in the DeKalb, Illinois, prayer decision early in 1968, in which a verse recited by kindergarten children was declared unconstitutional and contrary to the First Amendment. The lines recited by the children said, *inter alia:* "We thank you for the flowers so sweet, etc." One might add that this decision was accepted by a docile people, just as the same docile people seem unwilling to organize a political drive for the so-called Prayer Amendment sponsored by Senator Dirksen of Illinois.

No doubt there are numerous reasons for the failure of busy people to organize against the Supreme Court's suspension of the decision of public questions by majorities. The issue extends from local government, the local school board, and state governments to the freedom of Congress to deal by internal (and popular) majority with issues under the First and Fourteenth Amendments. The decisions of the Supreme Court have removed important religious freedom issues from a customary and long-established tradition of majority control in the different levels of American government.

Aside from other reasons, we have been taught from our childhood that we have the most wonderful system of government in the world and that under it we have more freedom and more democracy than any other people on the face of the earth. We shudder at the rampaging barbarians in our streets, but we do nothing. We wait patiently for stuffy party pronouncements, verbose political speeches, and the relatively meaningless elections (in terms of the course of events) which every biennium and every quadrennium bring forth.

Our belief in the greatness of our system is, no doubt, the most persuasive of reasons for inaction. But there are others. We seem to be persuaded that all men are good (like Rousseau's teaching of the Vicar of Savoy) and that education merely gives skills that are added to their innate virtues. The people who burn, kill, and camp in our cities in our summertimes are not evil; they are misguided and they need more kindness by the police, more federal money, and no harshness in the courts in the punishment of criminals. In a little while, some say, there will be a restoration of national consensus. Yet are there not darker reasons? Have we not really lost our religious faith, and do Christians really believe in the articles of their faith? We cannot organize and act publicly because we have little belief in anything. Toleration has become so latitudinarian that we may at times believe more in the doctrines of the other fellow than in the platform which we publicly profess. By the same token we have ceased to teach the Constitutional tradition; instead we accept the proposition that the Constitution is just what the judges say it is at the moment.

And what great doctrines of the American constitutional past do we affirm today? Surely not federalism, but there does seem to be some revival of "locality" government sentiment by the minorities who are seeking to control their local schools. The spokesmen of the traditional and formerly dominant middle class hardly say a word in defense of local government as a foundation of democracy—or of religious liberty! The "angry conservative" has come to believe that our heritage is being frittered away in policies generated by liberal ideology. But it is an ideology

that our founding thinkers, like John Adams, would faintly recognize in the mind of some of the French philosophers of the eighteenth century.

I

The liberal ideology has in recent years taken its stand on the theory of the "open society." Liberals have often defined themselves simply as the defenders of liberty which in turn has been identified with the open society. The open society doctrine seems to say that all questions must be considered open questions. But it does not do so in fact, for at least the denial of the open society is not an open question. Not only is the use of history in the open society theory confused (was there ever an open society? or, did it end with Plato?), but the interpretation of the "classics of the open society" leaves much to be desired. The theorists or advocates seldom discuss the exceptions to the open society in the literature, and even so there are suspiciously few documents on which these ideas can rely. List the "Trial and Death of Socrates," Spinoza's Chapter XX in the *Tractatus Theologico-Politicus*, Locke's late *Letters on Toleration*, Milton's *Areopagitica*, some sentences from Jefferson and Tacitus, and J. S. Mill's *Essay on Liberty*, and you have just about covered the historical material. If you start with what the authors of each will not tolerate, one comes to the conclusion that even the so-called advocates of the open society operate with many closed issues. Like Locke and Rousseau, they seem to say: "We will tolerate those who are committed to toleration, but this is something we must judge. If we say that someone is not to be tolerated because he will not tolerate, we will not admit by that judgment that we ourselves become intolerant, however logical it may seem to the authoritarian-minded critics of liberty."

Whenever the state starts out to give liberty a paradox is involved. For the liberty that is given to some is denied to others. Liberty is, thus, transitive; "to give liberty" is not an intransitive expression. The public liberty given to some implies the duty of others to recognize and to sustain it. The burden of respect for the enjoyment of others involves very often the threatened imposition of civil and criminal responsibility. The anarchist may say that a removal of legal duty and enforcement will give liberty to all, except that the record of the anarchist is a cruel madness, as in Spain under the Second Republic or in the anarchist murders of the nineteenth century. Prince Kropotkin retired to his English flower garden during his last years and all who talked with him loved him. But this was not so with the American anarchists in the Chicago Haymarket in 1886, or in the violence of the Sacco-Vanzetti brotherhood just after World War I. Have we forgotten that an anarchist was blown to pieces by his own bomb in front of Attorney-General Palmer's house in Washington, just about the time of the anarchist crimes in Massachusetts?

Liberty at best is a dark paradox. It is nowhere more contradictory than in dealing with religion, that is, in the modern efforts to expand and contract religious liberty. A world that is governed by our Supreme Court is governed by bitterly aggressive liberals like Earl Warren and the left-wing lawyers who have come from the left-wing law schools of the Ivy League. These legal minds have matured in posts of power in the bureaucracy, in the foundations, and in the higher learning institutions in America.

Anyman's and Everyman's doctrines and practices of liberty should logically begin with the liberties that would be denied. Let us ask of any theory of liberty, or any conception of the so-called open society, who are the people or advocates who would be condemned first intellectually; and second, who are the people on whom the power of government would be used to deny the liberty they seek?

My proposition is that we are, under the current sovereignty of the courts, giving more liberty to secular rebels, including Communists, than to Christians. The liberty of Christians to get together to build their communities, either under the pennants of majority rule or under their utopian withdrawal from activity in the community has been restricted. The politics of liberty centers greatly on the politics of the child and the family. Because of our emphasis on public education, the contradictions keep coming angrily forward. For example, there seems to be no reconciliation in the New York City schools between the professional educators on school boards, nor in Washington, D.C., including the teachers' union, which struggles to control the public schools, and the rising demand of Negro parents to determine what their children shall be taught and who shall teach them. Legislatures seem to struggle in vain toward the resolution of such issues. At the same time the professor of education may point to the private school and say: "There is the really divisive force in our society." Their manifesto has long declared: "There shall be only one public system of education in America." But this single educational system shall be controlled by the epigoni of John Dewey and by those who profess a secular philosophy of education. (It would appear that the next stage in the resolution of this problem is to appropriate public money for the support of non-religious private education. It might be possible to spend tax money as a subsidy for families to spend on education for their children as they may decide. But direct support of religious private education seems a long way in the future. In the fifty states of the American Union there is notable variation in the relation of the government to private education, religious and otherwise.)

II

The proper way to begin the consideration of any theory of liberty or toleration, therefore, is to find out who will not be tolerated. There is apparently no theory of human order which allows complete liberty in the choice of expression and behavior. Not even the philosophical anarchists have such a theory. Under these circumstances every theory of religious liberty is a theory of the denial of liberty in some of its details. But a distinction must be noted. In modern speculation the *libertas philosophandi* has been defended more vigorously than the rights of religious bodies. For Immanuel Kant, the one secret article in the treaty for lasting peace was that the philosophers should be allowed to speak their piece. Otherwise, the transcendental principle of freedom was that all governmental actions and public documents must be compatible with publicity. The philosophers, with a customary modesty, put their own liberty above that of any others, just as today the academic community places its assertion of "academic freedom" above the freedom of others who are not orthodox, secular liberals. Theories of religious toleration, of the open society, and of intellectual freedom generally, seem always to have some limitations. These limitations are, in the eyes of proponents, compatible with the proper extent of liberty. In these cases at least the statement of freedom is also the statement of the limitation or the denial of freedom, and the support of liberty is also the defense of the non-liberty of those who may be restricted. In the totalitarian regimes we expect the expansion and

contraction of liberty in both expression and behavior. We note with scholarly appreciation the thaw in Communist regimes, and recently we have begun to speak of the maturity of anti-democratic systems, as well as the development of consensus within them.[1] While in democracies there are specific restrictions, for example, the advocacy of racism, there is a voluntary, though implicit and unexpressed, censorship of the means of public communication.

The liberal practice of our times is to turn primarily to seventeenth-century writers, such as Hobbes, Spinoza, and Locke. But perhaps the most widely assigned documents in university classes in this area are J. S. Mill's *On Liberty* and some of the "Trial and Death of Socrates" literature. But that liberal practice seldom notes the limitations on freedom that crop forth in the "freedom literature." J. S. Mill, for example, said his theory was unsuited to barbarians who should be governed despotically. Nor was it suitable for those under the age of full legal capacity.

Just why Hobbes should be a favorite of the secular-minded, I am not sure, except that religion is made a function of the state under both a positive and a negative civil theology, and liberty is defined under positive law primarily as the silence of the law or pretermitted action. The non-religious and pro-political personality can live pleasantly under a state according to Hobbes; for him, obedience to the sovereign is not repugnant to the laws of God.

We have here one version of the "natural theology" argument, for the theology allowed to exist outside the power of the state is limited indeed. As Rousseau said, let us have a few simple doctrines, and before him Hugo Grotius tried to limit the state to a few understandable and acceptable doctrines. But in Hobbes we also have a version of "deism," which was the name the atheists and libertines of an earlier time took in order to protect themselves against the thrust of official religion. To anticipate our argument, we may say that today we have much in common with Hobbes, for a Christian in America should believe in a Christianity that is being defined negatively by the First Amendment decisions of the Supreme Court. When we obey the Supreme Court are we not obeying aright the word of God? Our deistic, natural theology grows faster by judicial enactment than by the discourses of theologians, or by the decrees of church councils.

The peculiar form of intolerance that is being propagated by the Supreme Court has, as I have suggested, historical roots. It has been said that we took the Whig tradition from the English and made it the foundation of our constitutional liberty. Few Americans have ever questioned the assassination of character perpetrated on James II and the Stuart kings by Thomas Babington Macaulay. We still repeat the "slings and arrows of outrageous" Whig propaganda as historical truth. In this sense, James II and Senator Joseph R. McCarthy have much in common. One thing must be noted: However valuable the Whig tradition has been to us constitutionally, there was little religious liberty in it in the seventeenth century when it was being formulated. On June 8, 1789, when James Madison was discussing his proposals for a bill of rights, he observed: "In the declaration of rights which that country [Great Britain] has established, the truth is, they have gone no farther than to raise a barrier against the power of the Crown; the power of the legislature is still left altogether indefinite. . . . Their Magna Charta does not contain any one provision for the security of those rights, respecting which the people of America are most alarmed.

The freedom of the press, the rights of conscience, those choicest privileges of the people, are unguarded in the British constitution."

The Whigs made no effort to modify the long and inglorious series of penal statutes against the Irish and their Catholicism, nor were the laws against Catholics in England taken from the books, though they were enforced irregularly in the eighteenth century. Toleration by the non-enforcement of penal stipulations is an old practice, as many a Latin liberal can testify. Whiggery served well in the American Revolution, and even the opponents of Andrew Jackson sought to restore the force of the name of Whig, as in the political activity of David Crockett, or among those who established the Whig Party in the United States. But whatever the practice of Whiggery in practical politics and in constitutional history, it served little purpose in the development of modern views on religious pluralism. One may say that the continent was generally ahead of the British in the establishment of religious liberty in principle in public policy. Religious liberty came in America perhaps primarily as a matter of nonenforcement of law, or as a recognition of social necessity. It is really only since 1925 when the First Amendment freedoms began to be incorporated in the Fourteenth Amendment that the Supreme Court has added its version of religious liberty to what we call the Whig tradition.

In Hobbes's *Leviathan* there are many passages which affirm the right of the sovereign to judge what doctrines are fit for the public peace, and there is hardly a distinction between doctrine and the public practice of religion. Spinoza took much the same view in Chapter XIX of his *Tractatus Theologico-Politicus*. "God has no special kingdom among men except in so far as he reigns through temporal rulers," he said. All outward observances must be in accordance with the public peace, "if we would obey God aright." The Kingdom of God exists among men through the means of sovereign power; however, we must keep our religious dogmas sharply separated from philosophy, for the philosophers, according to Chapter XX, have their special freedom of the mind.

John Locke's various *Letters on Toleration* are commonly cited as the beginning of the modern Anglo-American doctrine of religious liberty and the separation of church and state. The recent publication of Locke's early tracts shows that in 1660 at least he was not interested in religious toleration,[2] though by the time of the publication of the *Epistolae* he had modified his earlier Whig intolerance. In the *First Letter*, which is today cited virtually to the exclusion of the other three, there is clearly a doctrinal and practical toleration to a much greater extent than before. Catholic doctrine is regarded as speculative, but Catholic practice, he thinks, is very probably seditious. Thus, Catholics who break oaths and atheists who do not know the meaning of an oath are not to be tolerated. He stated in his *Letter* the formula later used by Rousseau that only those who tolerate are to be tolerated. One should observe, of course, that Locke did not give a religious conscience the right publicly and legally to declare that it is right.

Locke's views must be regarded as a significant advance over Milton's *Areopagitica*, for it seems clear than Milton would tolerate only English Protestants who did not break "the unity of Spirit." Toward the end of the *Areopagitica*, Milton says:

> Yet if all cannot be of one mind, . . . this doubtless is more wholesome, more prudent, and more Christian: that many be tolerated, rather than all compelled. I mean not tolerated Popery, and open superstition, which as it extirpates all religions and civil supremacies, so itself should be extirpated, provided first that all charitable and compassionate means be used to win and regain the weak and the misled: that also which is impious or evil absolutely either against faith or manners no law can possibly permit, that intends not to unlaw itself; but those neighboring differences, or rather indifferences, are what I speak of, . . . which though they may be many, yet need not interrupt *the unity of spirit,* if we could but find among us *the bond of peace.*

While Milton favored suppressing speculative theology, Locke was trying to reach the conclusion that only seditious action should be suppressed. Whether he reached such a point may well be debated, but it is surely one of the ground-rules of contemporary argument for suppression: We have no obligation to tolerate those who are seditious or who are actively trying to overthrow the political system. The Supreme Court agreed in 1968 that those occupying public posts may be asked properly to take a positive oath to support the Constitution of the United States.[3] In general, the critics of Communists argue that they are inherently engaged in a conspiracy against public order and the constitutional system. Membership in the Communist Party in and of itself commits the Communist to revolutionary action designed to overthrow the American system of government. It would seem obvious that the effort to say that only those who tolerate may be tolerated will not stand the test of application, for those who judge others to be intolerant become themselves intolerant and subject to self-condemnation. Obviously, Rousseau's phrase that we will not tolerate those who do not preach tolerance "in mere matters of religion" is remote from any empirical or legal application, unless, of course, the determinations of the doctrines of a negative civil theology, such as Supreme Court rulings, are accepted as four square with true Christianity, or perhaps with nonsectarian Christianity. Such a degeneration of "natural theology" and deism into a negative civil theology, not unlike that of Hobbes, Spinoza, Locke, and Rousseau, is for us a kind of twentieth-century final stage of deism.

III

No doubt, many of our "natural theology" ideas of today fit into Jacques Maritain's notion of contemporary atheism: It is a practical atheism which is lived or practiced without the bother to affirm or deny any doctrine. From doctrine in the past we have moved to moral theory and to ethical doctrines, and today we have passed from an ordinary Christian morality to a morality that tastes of socialism. We have become silent on traditional sex standards and hostile toward the religious family. But if we are silent on sex, we have become noisy on racial equality, and equality in housing and property. Such a shift among non-religious speakers and writers has long been underway, but today religious radicals have turned from the historical foundations of the Creed to economic reform.

Who defends today the historic Constitution, now an archaic document, which in its historical form is dead, according to L. Brent Bozell? Deists do not believe in prayer, and of course they would be hostile to the proposed Prayer Amendment, but do the masses of presumptively religious people believe in prayer today? We seem no longer to support a firm theological position, while we are taught in mass communication to feel guilty about the inequalities we may enjoy. We certainly no longer enjoy watching the privileged enjoy their privileges. The death of God theology carries with it the death of property. We could not even settle today for Bertrand Russell's proposal in

1918 that anyone might be entitled to a vagabond wage. And the crisis for the ordinary man is repeated in the crises of the clergy, where some of them even became involved in Guatemala with Communist revolutionaries in 1967. In curious contrast, for some rebellious students an anti-theological position has gone with an anti-political theory of the social revolution; but the anarchism of students will end as for other rebels against government in becoming totalitarian in fact.[4]

The sources of modern heresy and social revolt seem clear enough. It is both the best and the worst of the thought of the eighteenth century. It has been given expression in hundreds of forms, and its opposition has been stated in like volume. The criticism of the Enlightenment is found in the arid Toryism and traditionalism of David Hume, and in the warm love of the past and of national tradition to be found in Edmund Burke. But the secular-liberal intellectuals have not gone to Hume or Burke for inspiration. As much as any, Rousseau has symbolized the liberalism and optimism of the eighteenth century, which is a source of much of the present-day antagonism toward religious liberty, that is, the liberty of the churches to carry on their preaching, the administration of the sacraments, and education, especially in the whole vast Communist empires.

The warmest, most eloquent document of the modern attack on tradition is Rousseau's piece on the ideas of the Vicar of Savoy. Few defenders of natural theology, deism, the goodness of human nature, and the inevitability of progress have risen to the height reached by Rousseau in his *Emile*. In the profession of faith of the "Vicaire Savoyard" we have a priest who continues to administer the sacraments, but who surely believes not a word of it in the sense at least in which the Catholic Church has taught its doctrines. The Savoy Vicar, no doubt, has his counterpart in the modern deviationism of Teilhard de Chardin, who was once in recent years condemned by the Pope but who is now explicated in some Catholic seminaries. The Vicar of Savoy contemplated the order and sublimity of the universe, and he saw goodness and intelligence in man as he stands upon the earth as part of the earth. One needs no Bible, which is written in languages the ordinary man does not understand, but one does need to contemplate the beauty and order that is all about him. Both the Vicar and Teilhard de Chardin see beauty and purpose in the world, and both apparently believe that progress is inevitable.[5] It has been said that Rousseau did not believe it was necessary to educate man in the virtues of reason and morality. Perhaps Teilhard de Chardin is not far from such a position. At any rate they both make a mighty appeal to the secular and non-religious intellectual. Rousseau argued in the *Contrat Social* that the government should establish a few simple dogmas as the civil religion, with the death penalty for those who dared to resist. The decisions of the Supreme Court on what the Justices believe is religious liberty come close to being this kind of civil religion, without, however, the death penalty for those who disagree. If all this is true, Rousseau and his eighteenth century were never closer to corrupting us than today. As with Rousseau, the function of the American schools is to teach the simple and noble doctrines of a civil order which has departed from any acknowledged and historical form of theology.

IV

What are the doctrines of our negative civil theology? The affirmations of religious liberty in America, or in the traditional forms of Latin anti-clericalism, have a peculiarly negative aspect. It is affirmed that the members of a community may not do certain things as an expression of their religious consensus. Thus, there is affirmed as well a conflict between the decrees of the sovereign and the "members of consensus," a conflict in which the only reconciliation of the religious with the sovereign is submission to the statements of the law. The irreconcilable element has sometimes produced disobedience to the decisions of the Court. This has often been the case with the decisions of the Court against religious instruction in public school buildings. Of course, the decision was strictly observed in Champaign County, Illinois, where the issue first arose. The later approval of released-time religious teaching away from the school premises gave rise to the possibility of confusion between the two situations.

What we have first of all is the doctrine that the teaching of Western religions, including all forms of Christianity, is compatible with the Court's interpretation of the First and Fourteenth Amendments. Thus, like Hobbes and Spinoza, we can say that if we would obey God we must obey the sovereign. Though this became the authoritarian doctrine of the seventeenth century, it has always been a Christian doctrine in the sense that when there is no conflict between the Emperor and the Church, it is the will of God that we should obey the government. However, there is an important distinction between Gelasian dualism and the Hobbesian doctrine of civil theology, for in Gelasian dualism it was the Church which determined if there were a conflict between the word of God and the command of the Emperor. If we consider Justice Douglas's statement that our institutions presuppose the existence of a Supreme Being, we must also be willing to accept the worthy Justice's definition of God. I would hazard the guess that what he had in mind was some form of deism, some idea of God as the benevolent architect of the universe, or God as the great watchmaker who started the universe and then went off about His business. Might we not ask if the ambiguity of the dictum of the Court has any the less failed to imply that a radical deism has become a kind of state religion for America? Of course, one might say that these negative determinations of religious freedom are, on their positive side, a kind of affirmation that an ecumenical view of religion is the truth of Christianity, as well as of Judaism, and Mediterranean remnants of Classical religion. But it would be a truth that logically all of the sects and divisions of Christianity must accept as the truth of our time. And logically it might be said that any sectarian Christian denial of these principles would be a heresy from religious truth as formulated in the Constitution.

Furthermore, the decisions of the Court have stated in effect that the separation of church and state as defined by the Court is the true religious liberty of the Christian. An idea of the distinctness of religion and government is ancient indeed, and it is found in the Classical religious tradition, as well as in the Judean and Christian versions of the religious life. There are two orders of life, two ways of life, and two final authorities who state the principles that govern us. But if we take the seventeenth-century Puritan view, the Church defines morality, and sin that may have a criminal flavor, while the magistrates undertake to enforce these standards under the formulation of the positive law, such as the Common Law and the liberties and statutes enacted by the legislative body. For example, the Church has defined the moral code under which we should live, and it has been the duty of the government to enforce this code, as far as possible, in the education and behavior of the young. Let us be

clear: The historic separation of church and state was something very different from the separation as it has been defined by the Supreme Court. Our Supreme Court speaks more like a Roman Emperor before the rise of Christianity than like an Emperor in the days of Ambrose or of Augustine.

Thus, the separation of church and state has become to us, in its judicial definition, a common doctrine of the sovereign and the church. It has meant that religious belief has become almost wholly a private or family matter without public implications. As with Locke, Hobbes, or Spinoza, one may not affirm the rightness of his conscience in a public capacity, that is, in the law as it is enforced by the sheriff and the police. It is said that the state should not offer support to churches, though the Education Act of 1965 provided support for children who may incidentally be associated with parochial schools. But what about chaplains in the armed forces, or in Congress, or religious words on the coins of the realm? Should not one say that chaplains are ecumenical chaplains, and that in so far as they have public money in their salaries for public functions under the law they are not acting in any orthodox or doctrinal capacity? In our public ceremonies, pluralistic religious views are supposed to be recognized, with the understanding that those who pray at commencement and other ceremonies will appeal only to God and not to Christ, as a Christian might. It is understood that the state shall not support churches, but what about the building of chapels on military posts or on the grounds of military and naval hospitals? The interfaith chapel has become compatible, it might seem, with the deistic ecumenism of the Justices of the Supreme Court. Catholic, Protestant, and Jew will worship in the same building.

In 1925, the Supreme Court declared

the right of private schools to exist, provided adequate standards of secular education were observed in conformity with compulsory school laws. The child is the greatest of all political issues, and the battles over education through the centuries are evidence of it. Many of our current definitions of religious liberty involve the school, and they involve, generally, prohibitions or restrictions on what may be done in a school in a religious sense. These prohibitions are, in effect, restrictions of the citizens of a community who in accordance with their tradition may want to include some observance of religion in the content of their publicly supported educational program. The proposition of ecumenical deism is that religion must be separated from public education, and if private education should receive public funds it must observe many of the same restrictions.

The secularists state that religion must be separated from education, though presumably some elements of civil and Biblical virtue may be taught along with reading, writing, and ciphering (as it was said in the eighteenth century). The believer in religious education may want money to support his school, but he surely wants religious freedom to teach his faith more than he wants affluence at the expense of the taxpayer.

The Supreme Court has been willing to admit that Sacred Writings may be used in education for literary and historical purposes, but the Bible is not to be taught as the word of God. The believer in religious education must demand that the Bible and church doctrine be taught as the truth, and not mere myth, fiction, symbol, or literature. If we may not pray in school, there is hardly any use in teaching the Bible as a book of history or

poetry. But the logic of the Supreme Court would suggest that we obey God aright when we take the Bible in education as literature and not as the word of God. What saves us from bitter religious controversy in American education is that the family is generally free in religion.

We do, indeed, have enough religious freedom to enable us to accept the theology of the judicial stretching and pulling of the Constitution. Should we come to an acute constitutional crisis, we might have a wide-ranging development of private education. Such a development could restore religion to the schools and it could avoid the more rasping aspects of the race conflict. If there is energy enough in localities and communities, public support for religious schools ought in the end to be a relatively inconsequential matter.

NOTES

[1] Carl J. Friedrich, "Totalitarianism: Recent Trends," *Problems of Communism*, XVII (May–June 1968), pp. 32–43.
[2] John Locke, *Two Tracts on Government*, edited with an introduction by P. Abrams, 1967.
[3] There is an extensive and notably controversial literature on the issues discussed here. My point is that the exceptions to liberty or toleration are properly and necessarily a part of the teaching of these writers. Among the distinguished studies of toleration are some of the writings of the late Willmoore Kendall. See "How To Read Milton's *Areopagitica*," *The Journal of Politics*, 22 (1960), pp. 439–473; "The Open Society and Its Fallacies," *The American Political Science Review*, LIV (1960), pp. 972–979, which is largely a critical study of J. S. Mill.
[4] See Donald A. Zoll, *The Twentieth-Century Mind*, 1967, for an important philosophical and political statement of our times.
[5] One should include in this comparison George Santayana's *The Idea of Christ in the Gospels or God in Man* (1946). Santayana in his interpretation of the New Testament is, obviously, closer to Teilhard de Chardin than to Jean Jacques Rousseau.

[XIII, Summer 1969, 248–257]

[38]

Judicial Verbicide:
An Affront to the Constitution

SAM J. ERVIN, JR.

Sam(uel) J(ames) Ervin, Jr. (1896–1985), a United States senator from North Carolina, was well-known for his role in the Watergate hearings but undeservedly less well-known for his work as chairman of the Senate subcommittees on the Separation of Powers and on Constitutional Rights, concerned with the rights of individual privacy and with judicial usurpation of the legislative authority and functions. His eventful and very interesting life— including service in World War I, in which he was twice wounded and twice cited for gallantry in action and for which he was awarded a Purple Heart with oak leaf cluster and the Silver Star—is summed up in his autobiography, Preserving the Constitution *(1985).*

Judicial Verbicide

Jim's administrator was suing the railroad for his wrongful death. The first witness he called to the stand testified as follows: "I saw Jim walking up the track. A fast train passed, going up the track. After it passed, I didn't see Jim. I walked up the track a little way and discovered Jim's severed head lying on one side of the track, and the rest of his body on the other." The witness was asked how he reacted to his gruesome discovery. He responded: "I said to myself something serious must have happened to Jim."

Something serious has been happening to constitutional government in America, and I want to write about it. My motive for doing so is as lofty as that which caused Job Hicks to be indicted and convicted of disturbing religious worship in the Superior Court of Burke County,

North Carolina, my home county, 75 years ago. Job revered the word of the Lord. An acquaintance of his, John Watts, took a notion he had been called to preach the Gospel, and adopted the practice of doing so in any little country church which would allow him to occupy its pulpit. While he was well versed in his profession as a brick mason, John Watts was woefully ignorant in matters of theology. One Sunday, Job Hicks imbibed a little too much Burke County corn liquor, a rather potent beverage. After so doing, he walked by a little country church, saw John Watts in the pulpit, and heard him expounding to the congregation his peculiar version of a biblical text. Job Hicks entered the church, staggered to the pulpit, grabbed John Watts' coat collar, dragged him to the door, and threw him out of the church.

When the time came for the pronouncement of the sentence upon the

455

jury's verdict of guilty, Judge Robinson, the presiding judge, observed: "Mr. Hicks, when you were guilty of such unseemly conduct on the Sabbath Day, you must have been too drunk to realize what you were doing." Job Hicks responded: "It is true, Your Honor, that I had had several drinks, but I wouldn't want Your Honor to think I was so drunk that I could stand by and hear the Word of the Lord being *mummicked up* like that without doing something about it."

Although I am completely sober, I am constrained to confess I am like Job Hicks in one respect. I cannot remain silent while the words of the Constitution are being *mummicked up* by Supreme Court Justices. This is so because I entertain the abiding conviction that the Constitution is our most precious heritage as Americans. When it is interpreted and applied aright, the Constitution protects all human beings within our borders from tyranny on the one hand and anarchy on the other. William Ewart Gladstone, the wise English statesman, correctly described it as the most wonderful work ever struck off at a given time by the brain and purpose of man.[1]

I entitle this essay "Judicial Verbicide: An Affront to the Constitution." I am prompted to do so by this trenchant truth which was told by Dr. Oliver Wendell Holmes in his *Autocrat of the Breakfast Table*:

> Life and language are alike sacred. Homicide and verbicide—that is—violent treatment of a word with fatal results to its legitimate meaning, which is its life—are alike forbidden.[2]

Why the Constitution Was Framed and Ratified

The term "Founding Fathers" is well designed to describe those who framed and ratified the Constitution and its first ten amendments. For ease of expression, I also apply it to those who framed and ratified subsequent amendments. The Founding Fathers knew the history of the struggle of the people against arbitrary governmental power during countless ages for the right to self-rule and freedom from tyranny, and understood the lessons taught by that history.

As a consequence they knew these eternal truths: First, that "whatever government is not a government of laws is a despotism, let it be called what it may;"[3] second, that occupants of public offices love power and are prone to abuse it;[4] and, third, that what autocratic rulers of the people had done in the past might be attempted by their new rulers in the future unless they were restrained by laws which they alone could neither alter nor nullify.[5]

The Founding Fathers desired above all things to secure to the people in a written Constitution every right which they had wrested from autocratic rulers while they were struggling for the right to self-rule and freedom from tyranny. Their knowledge of history gave them the wisdom to know that this objective could be accomplished only in a government of laws, *i.e.,* a government which rules by certain, constant, and uniform laws rather than by the arbitrary, uncertain, and inconstant wills of impatient men who happen to occupy for a fleeting moment of time legislative, executive, or judicial offices.

What the Constitution Was Designed To Accomplish

For these reasons, the Founding Fathers framed and ratified the Constitution, which they intended to last for the ages, to constitute a law for both rulers and people in war and in peace, and to cover with the shield of its protection all classes of men with impartiality at all times and under all circumstances.[6] While they intended it to endure for the ages as the nation's basic instrument of government, the Founding Fathers realized that useful alterations of some of its provisions would be suggested by experience.[7]

Consequently, they made provision for its amendment in one way and one way only, *i.e.,* by combined action of Congress and the States as set forth in Article V. By so doing, they ordained that "nothing new can be put into the Constitution except through the amendatory process" and "nothing old can be taken out without the same process;"[8] and thereby forbade Supreme Court Justices to attempt to revise the Constitution while professing to interpret it.[9]

In framing and ratifying the Constitution, the Founding Fathers recognized and applied an everlasting truth embodied by the British philosopher, Thomas Watts, in this phrase: "Freedom is political power divided into small fragments." They divided all governmental powers between the Federal Government and the States by delegating to the former the powers essential to enable it to operate as a national government for all the states, and by reserving to the states all other powers. They divided among the Congress, the President, and the federal judiciary the powers delegated to the federal government by giving Congress the power to make federal laws, imposing on the President the duty to enforce federal laws, and assigning to the federal judiciary the power to interpret federal laws for all purposes and state laws for the limited purpose of determining their constitutional validity.

In making this division of powers, the Founding Fathers vested in the Supreme Court as the head of the federal judiciary the awesome authority to determine with

finality whether governmental action, federal or state, harmonizes with the Constitution as the supreme law of the land, and mandated that all federal and state officers, including Supreme Court Justices, should be bound by oath or affirmation to support the Constitution.[10]

The Founding Fathers undertook to immunize Supreme Court Justices against temptation to violate their oaths or affirmations to support the Constitution by making them independent of everything except the Constitution itself. To this end, they stipulated in Article III that Supreme Court Justices "shall hold their offices during good behaviour . . . and receive for their services a compensation, which shall not be diminished during their continuance in office."

In commenting upon the obligation of Supreme Court Justices to check unconstitutional action in his dissenting opinion in *United States v. Butler,* Justice (afterwards Chief Justice) Stone made this cogent comment: "While unconstitutional exercise of power by the executive and legislative branches of government is subject to judicial restraint, the only check upon our own exercise of power is our own sense of self-restraint."[11]

Wise Americans Condemn Judicial Activism and Verbicide

Some exceedingly wise Americans, who understood and revered the Constitution, have expressed opinions concerning Justices who do not exercise the self-restraint which their oaths or affirmations to support the Constitution impose upon them, and the impact of their derelictions upon constitutional government. George Washington, who served as President of the convention that framed the Constitution before becoming our first President under it, gave America this solemn warning in his *Farewell Address*:

> If in the opinion of the people, the distribution or modification of the constitutional powers be in any particular wrong, let it be corrected by an amendment in the way which the constitution designates. But let there be no change by usurpation; for though this, in one instance, may be the instrument of good, it is the customary weapon by which free governments are destroyed. The precedent must always overbalance in permanent evil any partial or transient benefit which the use can at any time yield.

Chief Justice Marshall emphasized the supreme importance of a Supreme Court Justice accepting the Constitution as the absolute rule for the government of his official conduct by declaring that if he does not discharge his duties agreeably to the Constitution his oath or affirmation to support that instrument "is worse than solemn mockery."[12] Another great constitutional scholar, Judge Thomas M. Cooley, asserted that such a Justice is "justly chargeable with reckless disregard of official oath and public duty."[13]

Benjamin N. Cardozo, Chief Judge of the New York Court of Appeals and Justice of the United States Supreme Court, stated in *The Nature of the Judicial Process* that "judges are not commissioned to make and unmake rules at pleasure in accordance with changing views of expediency or wisdom" and that "it would put an end to the reign of law" if judges adopted the practice of substituting their personal notions of justice for rules established by a government of laws.[14]

Constitutional Obligations of Supreme Court Justices

No question is more crucial to America than this: What obligation does the Constitution impose upon Supreme Court Justices? America's greatest jurist of all time, Chief Justice John Marshall, answered this question with candor and clarity in his opinions in *Marbury v. Madison* and *Gibbons v. Ogden*.[15] In these indisputably sound opinions, Chief Justice Marshall declared:

1. That the principles of the Constitution are designed to be permanent.
2. That the words of the Constitution must be understood to mean what they say.
3. That the Constitution constitutes an absolute rule for the government of Supreme Court Justices in their official action.

In elaborating the second declaration, Marshall said:

> As men whose intentions require no concealment generally employ the words which most directly and aptly express the ideas they intend to convey, the enlightened patriots who framed our Constitution, and the people who adopted it, must be understood to have employed words in their natural sense, and to have intended what they have said.[16]

Judicial Activism and Verbicide

Judges who perpetrate *verbicide* on the Constitution are judicial activists. A judicial activist is a judge who interprets the Constitution to mean what it would have said if he instead of the Founding Fathers had written it. Contrary to popular opinion, all judicial activists are not liberals. Some of them are conservatives. A liberal judicial activist is a judge who expands the scope of the Constitution by stretching its words beyond their true meaning, and a conservative judicial activist is one who narrows the scope of the Constitution by restricting their true meaning. Judicial activism of the right or the left substitutes the personal will of the judge for the impersonal will of the law. The majority opinion in *Miranda v. Arizona* is the product of liberal judicial activism, and the majority opinion in *Laird v. Tatum* is the product of conservative judicial activism.[17]

Judges are fallible human beings. The temptation to substitute one's personal notions of justice for law lies in wait for all occupants of judicial offices, and sometimes ordinarily self-restrained judges succumb to it. Nobody doubts the good intentions of the judicial activists. They undoubtedly lay the flattering unction to their souls that their judicial activism is better than the handiwork of the Founding Fathers, and that America will be highly blessed by an exchange of the constitutional government ordained by the Constitution for a government embodying their personal notions.

Before accepting these assurances as verity Americans would do well to ponder what Daniel Webster said about public officials who undertake to substitute their good intentions for rules of law. Webster said:

> Good intentions will always be pleaded for every assumption of authority. It is hardly too strong to say that the Constitution was made to guard the people against the dangers of good intentions. There are men in all ages who mean to govern well, but they mean to govern. They promise to be good masters, but they mean to be masters.

Alexander Hamilton's Assurance Concerning Judicial Activism and Verbicide

When the Constitutional Convention of 1787 submitted the Constitution to the states, Elbridge Gerry, who had been a delegate from Massachusetts, and George Mason, who had been a delegate from Virginia, opposed its ratification because it contained no provision sufficient to compel Supreme Court Justices to obey their oaths or affirmations to support it.

Gerry complained that, "There are not well defined limits to the judiciary powers" and that "it would be a herculean labour to attempt to describe the dangers with which they are replete." George Mason said that "the power of construing the laws would enable the Supreme Court of the United States to substitute its own pleasure for the law of the land and that the errors and usurpations of the Supreme Court would be uncontrollable and remediless."

Alexander Hamilton, a delegate from New York, rejected these arguments with the emphatic assertion that "the supposed danger of judiciary encroachments . . . is, in reality, a phantom." To support his assertion, Hamilton maintained in much detail that men selected to sit on the Supreme Court would be chosen with a view to those qualifications which fit men for the stations of judges, and that they would give that inflexible and uniform adherence to legal rules and precedents which is indispensable in courts of justice.[18]

By his remarks, Hamilton assured the several states that men selected to sit upon the Supreme Court would be able and willing to subject themselves to the restraint inherent in the judicial process. Experience makes this proposition indisputable: Although one may possess a brilliant intellect and be actuated by lofty motives, he is not qualified for the station of judge in a government of laws unless he is able and willing to subject himself to the restraint inherent in the judicial process.

Fruits of Judicial Activism and Verbicide

Hamilton's prediction about the qualifications of the men to be selected to serve as Supreme Court Justices proved valid for generations. Unfortunately, however, for constitutional government in America, Hamilton's phantom has now become an exceedingly live ghost. While they have acted with reasonable judicial decorum in ordinary cases, the tragic truth is that during recent years some Supreme Court Justices have adopted and exercised the role of judicial activists with more or less abandon in cases involving the place of the states in the federal system, cases involving prosecution for crimes in federal and state courts, and cases having emotional, political, and racial overtones.

A high proportion of these cases have been decided by a sharply divided Court. Limitations of language and space compel me to confine my remarks in respect to them to the handiwork of the Supreme Court Justices who have enacted the role of judicial activists and to omit reference to that of their brethren whose vigorous dissents have protested such actions.

By committing verbicide on the Constitution, the judicial activists concentrate in the federal government powers the Constitution reserves to the states; diminish the capacity of federal executive officers and the states to bring criminals to justice; rob individuals of personal and property rights; and expand their own powers and those of Congress far beyond their constitutional limits.

In Milton's poetic phrase, the cases in which the Supreme Court has committed *verbicide* upon the Constitution have become as "thick as autumnal leaves that strow the brooks / In Vallombrosa."[19] The number and variety of these cases make it impossible to detail them within appropriate limits. If anyone should detail them in their entirety, he would be justly chargeable with forsaking time and encroaching upon eternity. Merely to indicate how judicial verbicide performs its wonders, I cite a few of the innovative decisions an activist Supreme Court has handed down since 1968. They are *Jones*

v. Alfred H. Mayer Co., 392 U.S. 409; *Sullivan v. Little Hunting Park,* 396 U.S. 229; *Tillman v. Wheaton-Haven Recreation Association,* 410 U.S. 431; *Johnson v. Railway Express Agency,* 421 U.S. 454; *Runyon v. McCrary,* 427 U.S. 160; and *McDonald v. Santa Fe Trail Transportation Company,* 427 U.S. 273.

By committing colossal verbicide on the plain words of the Thirteenth Amendment and the Civil Rights Act of 1866, Supreme Court Justices have assigned to themselves and Congress powers to dominate and punish the private thoughts, the private prejudices, and the private business and social activities of Americans which are repugnant to the powers given them by the Constitution.

A Chorus of Protest Against Judicial Activism and Verbicide

In charging, in Chief Justice John Marshall's unhappy phrase, that some Supreme Court Justices are making a solemn mockery of their oaths to support the Constitution, I am not a lone voice crying in a constitutional wilderness. I am, in truth, simply one member of a constantly expanding chorus.

Judge Learned Hand, Alexander Bickel, Philip B. Kurland, and other profoundly enlightened constitutional scholars have made similar accusations. These charges are corroborated in detail by these recent books: *Government by Judiciary,* by Raoul Berger; *The Price of Perfect Justice,* by Macklin Fleming; and *Disaster by Decree,* by Lino A. Graglia. Besides, the apostacy of the activist Justices to the Constitution is highlighted in numerous vigorous dissents by their brethren on the Supreme Court bench.

One of the most lucid comments on the judicial verbicide of activist Supreme Court Justices is that of Justice Jackson in his concurring opinion in *Brown v. Allen*, 344 U.S. 443, 542–550. In deploring the perverted use of the great writ of habeas corpus to rob the verdicts and judgments of state courts in criminal trials of any finality, Justice Jackson said:

> Rightly or wrongly, the belief is widely held by the practicing profession that this Court no longer respects impersonal rules of law but is guided in these matters by personal impressions which from time to time may be shared by a majority of the Justices. Whatever has been intended, this Court also has generated an impression in much of the judiciary that regard for precedents and authorities is obsolete, that words no longer mean what they have always meant to the profession, that the law knows no fixed principles.

Justice Jackson closed his observations on judicial verbicide with this sage comment:

> I know of no way we can have equal justice under law except we have some law.

Excuses for Judicial Activism and Verbicide

Candor compels the confession that many Americans commend the usurpations of the activist Justices, especially when they harmonize with their wishes. These erring ones seek to coerce critics of judicial activism into silence. To this end, they assert that all Supreme Court decisions are entitled to respect, and that those who criticize any of them are unpatriotic. This assertion is contemptuous of the wisdom of the Founding Fathers in incorporating in the First Amendment for the benefit of all Americans guarantees of freedom of speech and the press. Besides, it is downright silly.

Like other official action, judicial decisions merit respect only when they are respectable, and no decision of the Supreme Court is respectable if it flouts the Constitution its makers have obligated themselves by oath or affirmation to support. As Justice Felix Frankfurter so rightly declared: "Judges as persons, or courts as institutions, are entitled to no greater immunity from criticism than other persons or institutions. . . . Judges must be kept mindful of their limitations and their ultimate public responsibility by a vigorous stream of criticism expressed with candor however blunt."[20]

Chief Justice Stone concurred with Justice Frankfurter's view by stating that "where the courts deal, as ours do, with great public questions, the only protection against unwise decisions, and even judicial usurpation, is careful scrutiny of their action, and fearless comment upon it."[21] Apologists for the *verbicidal* attacks of Supreme Court Justices upon the Constitution attempt to justify them by these arguments:

1. They are necessary to keep government abreast of the time because the amendatory process established by Article V is too cumbersome and dilatory.
2. They are desirable because they make pleasing amendments to the nation's supreme law which Congress and the states are unwilling to make.
3. They prove that the Constitution is a living instrument of government.

The Invalidity of the Excuses

There are two incontestable answers to these arguments in their entirety. They are, first, that tyranny on the bench is as reprehensible as tyranny on the throne; and, second, that the ultimate result of judicial activism on the part of the Supreme Court Justices is the destruction of the government of laws the Constitution was ordained by the people to create and preserve.

There are also separate irrefutable an-

SAM J. ERVIN, JR.

swers to each of the arguments. As James Madison, the Father of the Constitution, stated, the Founding Fathers created the amendatory process of which the apologists complain to ensure that Congress and the states will act with deliberation when they consider proposed changes in the Constitution and will refrain from acting unwisely in making them.

The Founding Fathers knew that a Constitution is destitute of value if its provisions are as mutable as simple legislative enactments,[22] and they certainly did not intend that decisions of constitutional questions by the Supreme Court should ever be rightly compared as they were by Justice Roberts in a colorful phrase with restricted railroad tickets, good for this day and train only.[23]

The second argument of the apologists is the stuff of which tyranny is made. Its underlying premise is their apprehension that Congress and the states acting in combination may have too much wisdom to amend the Constitution in ways pleasing to them. Hence, they maintain that for their pleasure Supreme Court Justices ought to usurp and exercise the power the Constitution vests exclusively in the people to have the Constitution amended only by the representatives they choose to act for them at congressional and state levels.

The usurpation of this power by Supreme Court Justices does not prove that the Constitution is a living instrument of government. On the contrary, it proves that the Constitution is dead, and that the people of our land are being ruled by the transitory personal notions of Justices who occupy for a fleeting moment of history seats on the Supreme Court bench rather than by the enduring precepts of the Constitution.

Despite *Miranda's* disapproval of confessions, I am going to make an honest one. Those who abhor tyranny on the

bench as much as tyranny on the throne are unable to devise any pragmatic procedure to compel activist Judges to observe their oaths or affirmations to support the Constitution.

Judicial aberrations are not impeachable offenses under Article II, Section 4. No earthly power can compel activist Justices to exercise self-restraint if they are unable or unwilling to do so, and the soundest criticism is not likely to deter activist Justices from their activism and verbicide when they honestly believe their handiwork is better than that of the Founding Fathers. It is obvious, moreover, that Congress and the states cannot protect constitutional governments adequately by adding new amendments to the Constitution. This is true for these reasons: First, it is folly to expect activist Justices to obey new constitutional provisions when they spurn the old; and, second, it would complicate simplicity and convert the Constitution into a confusing document as long as the *Encyclopaedia Britannica* to rid us of all the judicial usurpations of recent years.

In Conclusion

All history proclaims this everlasting truth: No nation can enjoy the right to self-rule and the right to freedom from tyranny under a government of men. The Founding Fathers framed and ratified the Constitution to secure these precious rights to Americans for all time. Judicial verbicide substitutes the personal notions of judges for the precepts of the Constitution. Hence, judicial verbicide is calculated to convert the Constitution into a worthless scrap of paper and to replace our government of laws with a judicial oligarchy.

A great Senator, Daniel Webster, warned America in eloquent words what the destruction of our Constitution would entail. He said:

> Other misfortunes may be borne, or their effects overcome. If disastrous wars should sweep our commerce from the ocean, another generation may renew it; if it exhaust our treasury, future industry may replenish it; if it desolate and lay waste our fields, still under a new cultivation, they will grow green again, and ripen to future harvests.

> It were but a trifle even if the walls of yonder Capitol were to crumble, if its lofty pillars should fall, and its gorgeous decorations be all covered by the dust of the valley. All of these may be rebuilt.

> But who shall reconstruct the fabric of demolished government?

> Who shall read again the well-proportioned columns of constitutional liberty?

> Who shall frame together the skillful architecture which unites national sovereignty with States Rights, individual security, and public prosperity?

> No, if these columns fall, they will be raised not again. Like the Colosseum and the Parthenon, they will be destined to a mournful and melancholy immortality. Bitterer tears, however, will flow over them than ever were shed over the monuments of Roman or Grecian art; for they will be the monuments of a more glorious edifice than Greece or Rome ever saw—the edifice of constitutional American Liberty.

Finally, I reiterate some inescapable conclusions: The distinction between the power to amend the Constitution and the power to interpret it is as wide as the gulf which yawns between Lazarus in Abraham's bosom and Dives in hell. The power to amend is the power to change the meaning of the Constitution, and the power to interpret is the power to determine the meaning of the Constitution as established by the Founding Fathers.

The Founding Fathers did not contemplate that any Supreme Court Justice would convert his oath or affirmation to support the Constitution into something worse than solemn mockery. On the contrary, they contemplated that his oath or affirmation to support that supreme instrument of government would implant indelibly in his mind, heart, and conscience a solemn obligation to be faithful to the Constitution.

A Justice who twists the words of the Constitution awry under the guise of interpreting it to substitute his personal notion for a constitutional precept is contemptuous of intellectual integrity. His act in so doing is as inexcusable as that of the witness who commits perjury after taking an oath or making an affirmation to testify truthfully.

We must not despair because there is no way by which law can compel activist Supreme Court Justices to subject their personal wills to the precepts of the Constitution. This is true because it is not yet unconstitutional for Americans to invoke divine aid when they are at their wits' end.

Hence, we can pray—hopefully not in vain—that the activist Justices will heed the tragic truth spoken by Webster and their own oaths or affirmations to support the Constitution, and become born-again supporters of the most precious instrument of government the world has ever known.

NOTES

[1] William Ewart Gladstone: *Kin Beyond the Sea*, North American Review, September–October, 1878.

[2] Oliver Wendell Holmes: *Autocrat of the Breakfast Table.* (The Limited Editions Club, 1955), Chapter I, p. 9.

[3] *The Writings and Speeches of Daniel Webster*. National Edition, Vol. 2, p. 165.

[1] George Washington: *Farewell Address*.

[5] *Ex Parte Milligan*, 4 Wall. (U.S.) 2, 120–121.

[6] *Ibid*.

[7] James Madison: *The Federalist* No. 43.

[8] Frankfurter, J.: *Ullman v. United States*, 350 U.S. 422, 428.

[9] Cardozo, C.J.: *Sun Printing and Publishing Association v. Remington Paper and Power Company*, 235 N.Y. 338, 139 N.E. 470. See, also, *West Coast Hotel Co. v. Parrish*, 300 U.S. 379, when Justice Sutherland stated in a dissent: "The judicial function is that of interpretation; it does not include the power of amendment under the guise of interpretation. To miss the point of difference between the two is to miss all that the phrase 'Supreme law of the land' stands for and to convert what was intended as inescapable and enduring mandates into mere moral reflections. If the Constitution, intelligently and reasonably construed in the light of these principles, stands in the way of desirable legislation, the blame must rest upon that instrument, and not upon the court for enforcing it according to its terms. The remedy in that situation—and the only true remedy—is to amend the Constitution."

[10] *The United States Constitution*.

[11] *United States v. Butler*, 297 U.S. 1, 78.

[12] *Marbury v. Madison*, 1 Cranch (U.S.) 137, 180.

[13] Thomas M. Cooley: *Constitutional Limitations*, pp. 88–89. See Volume 1, p. 153, of the 8th Edition of this treatise where Judge Cooley makes this statement: "Whoever derives power from the Constitution to perform any public function is disloyal to that instrument, and grossly derelict in duty, if he does that which he is not reasonably satisfied the Constitution permits. Whether the power be legislative, executive, or judicial, there is a manifest disregard of the constitutional and moral obligation by one, who having taken on oath to observe that instrument, takes part in any action which he cannot say he believes to be no violation of its provisions."

[14] Benjamin N. Cardozo: *The Nature of the Judicial Process*, pp. 68, 136.

[15] *Marbury v. Madison*, 1 Cranch (U.S.) 137, 175, 180; *Gibbons v. Ogden*, 9 Wheat. (U.S.) 1, 188.

[16] *Gibbons v. Ogden*, 9 Wheat. (U.S.) 188.

[17] *Miranda v. Arizona*, 384 U.S. 486; *Laird v. Tatum*, 408 U.S. 1.

[18] Alexander Hamilton: *The Federalist* Nos. 78, 81.

[19] John Milton: *Paradise Lost*, Book I, line 292.

[20] Frankfurter, J., in *Bridges v. California*, 314 U.S. 252, 289–290.

[21] Alpheus Thomas Mason: *Harlan Fiske Stone, Pillar of the Law*, (1968 edition) p. 398.

[22] James Madison: *The Federalist* No. 43.

[23] Roberts, J. in *Smith v. Allwright*, 321 U.S. 649, 669.   [XXV, Summer 1981, 234–242]

[39]

American Conservatism and the "Prayer" Decisions

WILLMOORE KENDALL

Willmoore Kendall (1909–1967), the son of a Southern Methodist minister, was born in Konawa, Oklahoma, and spent his early years in the Midwestern prairie towns where his father preached. A child prodigy who learned to read by the age of two, his genius flowered at Oxford University, where he arrived, as a Rhodes scholar, in 1932. His transition from a near-Trotskyite leftist in the Red Decade to a fervent anti-Communist who had, by 1955, become a senior editor of National Review, *is described in vivid detail by George H. Nash in his essay on Kendall in this volume. Kendall was the author of* The Conservative Affirmation *(1963).*

"CHILDREN STILL PRAY IN SCHOOL." "Massachusetts town defies the Supreme Court." So the title and sub-title of a spread in a recent issue of *Life* magazine;[1] and the accompanying text and photographs amply justify both headings: The school board of North Brookfield, Mass., the text relates, finds itself confronted with (1) a 137-year-old state law that requires prayers in the public schools, (2) three widely-publicized Supreme Court decisions that seem to imply that that statute is unconstitutional, and (3) a State Attorney General's ruling to the effect that the 137-year-old statute is indeed null and void in consequence of the Supreme Court decisions.[2] The school board has deliberated and voted no less than four times on the question "Whom—what law—shall we obey?"; and on each of these occasions it has decided to obey the state

legislature, and so disobey—defy, if you like—the Supreme Court and the Attorney General. North Brookfield's 3,616 residents, the text continues, mostly agree with the school board: among 418 students at North Brookfield's high school, only 17 (reflecting, perhaps, the views of their parents) have been willing to sign a petition demanding reversal of the school board's decision. ("You're against *God*," the more vocal of the non-signers tell the lad circulating the petition.) Classes in North Brookfield's schools "still" begin—not "keep right on" beginning but "*still*" begin (by analogy, one supposes, with "the flag was still there")—with *viva voce* reading of a verse from the Bible and recitation of the Lord's Prayer. And there are some fascinating quotes which are not the less revealing, I think, because they clearly come from the "extremists" in the controversy: "We," says Board Member William Boyd, "will challenge and defy the world movement toward atheism." "This is Massachusetts, the cradle of liberty," says Board Member Lawrence Delude, ". . . here is where the first shots are going to be fired"—shots, one gathers, that are intended to be "heard 'round the world," *inter alia* in Moscow, Peking, and Washington; Boyd and Delude are conscious not merely of making history, but of making it on a stage that is neither merely local nor merely national. Against them they have William Smith and Joseph Durkin: "It's futile," says Smith, "to continue challenging the Supreme Court decision." "They"—Durkin observes of the Board's victorious majority—"are for God, for prayer, and they're *simple.* . . . The whole thing should never involve your feeling about prayer. That's not an issue. The law is the issue." North Brookfield's stand, Smith and Durkin ominously insist, "makes us look like Governor Wallace." We look further and find, presiding over the whole spread (as we should expect?), a photograph of 10-year-old Ellen Waydaka, head bowed, hands clasped reverently on her desk, hair and eyes whose brunette quality may or may not have ultramontane associations for most of *Life*'s readers, and the chilling pronouncement by the editors of *Life*: "Around the country *thousands* of school children"—I'd guess millions, but never mind—"[are] starting their day the same way. . . . Several states are openly disobeying the ruling and, even in states that officially comply, some schools still continue prayer."

Life, to be sure, chose to subordinate its spread on North Brookfield to a grand exposé of "The Bobby Baker Bombshell." But I confidently predict that history will longer remember, symbolically at least, the events in North Brookfield than those in Baker's motel. I propose, therefore, to take the crisis in North Brookfield (for surely it is a crisis) as my point of departure for this article. The events there hold in deposit, force upon our attention even in *Life*'s account, the crucial aspects of the problem I want to explore. And these events seem to me to warrant at least the following preliminary comments:

1. North Brookfield is divided—angrily divided—on the issue of religious observances in its public schools—which, day before yesterday, the people of North Brookfield had never thought of as conceivably becoming an issue. For, day before yesterday, an objector to North Brookfield's long-established custom of beginning the schoolday with a verse from the Bible and the Lord's Prayer would have been told in effect: "Look, your youngsters aren't required to participate; they are not even required to be present; the rest of us, which is to say pretty nearly all of us, deem it a religious duty to see to it that our youngsters begin their day in school as we began our day in school— that is, with a reminder that God exists, that we are His creatures, rightfully subject to His will. Moreover, North Brookfield is not peculiar about this: the same thing happens all over Massachusetts, and what's more always did; besides which, state law—the same state law that requires us to maintain public schools and authorizes us to collect taxes for their support— *requires* it to happen. Do you expect us to change our way of doing things just because you and a few other people don't happen to like it?" And if the objector had answered: "It isn't a matter of what I happen to like; I take my stand on the Constitution, which prohibits the 'establishment of religion' in the United States," he would have been told: "Your understanding of the establishment clause is not ours; it certainly does not prohibit religious observances in the public schools." The objector, in short, would have been

told that he did not have a leg to stand on, and that would have ended the discussion. Day before yesterday, I repeat, no issue could have arisen in North Brookfield over the topic. If the town is in crisis, it is in crisis because of a disturbance that has come from *outside*. From, concretely, three unprecedented and wholly unexpected decisions by the United States Supreme Court.

2. North Brookfield's crisis is indeed a crisis, a crisis moreover of the worst kind that can possibly overtake a political community. Its citizens face a problem from which, in Lenin's wonderful phrase, "there is no way out." Why? Already divided against itself, North Brookfield faces a future in which the wedge that has been driven between its majority and its minority must as time passes be driven deeper and deeper, forcing majority and minority ever further—ever more angrily—apart. That fact cries up at us even out of *Life's* meager data, which oblige us to say: Blessed no doubt are the peace-makers, but in North Brookfield, alas, they have no role to play. The issue that has arisen there cannot be side-stepped, cannot even be postponed; either the schoolday does begin with Bible-reading and prayer, or it doesn't; either the watchword is to be, "Out, out brief prayer," as the minority demands, or established custom will prevail, as the majority is clearly determined it shall. There is no middle course between Yes, having prayers in school, and No, not having prayers in school, no chance of what Mary Follett used to call the "integrated solution" (which so disposes matters that everybody gets his way and ends up happy). Middle courses have been excluded by the manner in which the issue has been drawn—first by the Supreme Court, later, now, by the spokesmen for the two "parties" in North Brookfield. "You are against God," cries one party, "And what's more, freedom is at

stake!"—from which, in America, it is always a brief step to "Give us liberty or give us death!" "We are a government of laws not of men," cries the other party, "and the law says there shall be no religious observances in the public schools; you, sirs, are against the law, and the law, cost what it may, must be enforced." Each position, be it noted, is essentially *theological*—I shall substitute another word for "theological" later, but for the moment let it stand—basing itself ultimately upon high principle of the kind that *eo ipso* places itself beyond discussion and beyond compromise. Ineluctably, therefore, the anger generated by the dispute must take on increasingly the mood and quality of *odium theologicum*. ("I've got my P.T.A. members," says Mrs. Richard Walther, a substitute teacher at North Brookfield high school. "We call them minutemen. . . This is like the Revolution all over again.") In brief: North Brookfield cannot, even if *per impossibile* it brings to bear upon the controversy all the resources of imagination and good will that it has at its disposal, *cannot* resolve its crisis—any more than a man can chew a morsel of beef-steak by describing an arc with his upper teeth. Nobody from now on, nobody in sight anyhow, can restore peace except the United States Supreme Court itself. And it can do so only by restoring the *status quo ante*—which, I suppose, nobody thinks it is going to do.

3. We, say in effect the two dissident school board members, are going to "look like Governor Wallace." Indeed they are going to look like Governor Wallace, to begin with for the same reason that Governor Wallace looks like Governor Wallace: certain strategically-situated persons—among them, off at the end, no doubt, the President himself—are going to see to it that they do. Nay, more. The suggested analogy with Governor Wallace will stand on more legs than the Board

dissidents may have had in mind: some North Brookfield, somewhere (which, in what state, of course doesn't matter), is indeed slated to play, in the working out of the prayer decisions, the role of Little Rock in the working out of the school desegregation decision. One day some district court will—will, because under the Supreme Court ruling in the "prayer" cases, it must—*order* the school board in some North Brookfield to abolish religious observances in the schools for which it is legally responsible. At that point, to be sure, the story may take any of several turnings—of which none, however, is going to improve matters in North Brookfield: The school board, its members, like Governor Barnett, not wishing to go to jail and pay an out-size fine for contempt of court, will surely order its teachers to discontinue the Bible-reading and the recitation of the Lord's Prayer, may even put teeth in the order by promising to fire any teacher who refuses to go along. That will keep the school board members out of jail, but (a) the teachers must now choose between "defying" the school board and "defying" the State legislature, besides which (b) unless North Brookfield is a mighty peculiar American town, which up to now it gives no evidence of being, the school board's reversal of its earlier stand is *just* what it will take to harden the majority's *odium theologicum* into sullen, we-won't-take-No-for-an-answer determination—to have religious observances in the schools or bust. The teachers obey the school board? The youngsters, with a little coaching at home, can recite the 23rd Psalm and lead themselves in prayer; and, to quote Harry Truman, The Buck Stops Here. We are still a government of laws not of men? Then the parents stand in contempt of court—and must not the law, with them as with Governor Barnett, have its pound of flesh? And the question forthwith becomes, How

many parents can the federal marshals of the district accommodate in their jails, especially as the pray-in-school-or-bust movement has by now snowballed—who can doubt that it will have?—into neighboring towns? Legally, remember, it is no longer merely a question just of praying or not praying in school, but of obedience or non-obedience to a command from a federal court, of the sanctity of the law and of legal process, of order against anarchy no less. Yet the prayers in school do remain the crucial dimension, and I defy any reader of this article to come up with the dodge by which the White House that sent troops to Little Rock and Oxford can now—without looking so foolish that it must go back and undo Little Rock and Oxford, which would not be easy—refuse to send troops to North Brookfield. And *then*—the imagination balks, but we must proceed—the question becomes, What can a soldier with a fixed bayonet do to Ellen Waydaka? Force her hands apart? Hold her head erect by main force? Seal her lips with adhesive tape? Very well; but once the federal troops are withdrawn, the prayers—for the movement will by now have become a crusade—will start all over again. A caricature, you say? I answer: Little Rock was a caricature, and the White House, nowadays, is normally occupied by a specialist in caricature. (To be sure, we have it on the high authority of Walter Berns that "There is reason to believe that federal marshals will not be ordered to swoop down upon the nation's schoolrooms and arrest teachers leading their children in daily prayer."[3] But Professor Berns is silent as to his reasons for this judgment; and who would have guessed in, say, 1950 that federal authorities would one day escort Negro students into Central High School, or serve as bodyguards for a Senior at Ole Miss?) I repeat: the dissident school board members are on solid ground when they point up the analogy between the controversy over desegregation of the public schools and that over—if I may coin a phrase—their *deorisonation*.

4. The issue that has been drawn in North Brookfield is one on which no Liberal—unless an occasional odd-ball like Bishop Pike—will have any difficulty "taking sides," or any difficulty saying why he takes the side he takes. What is in question, for him, is what I have called in a recent book the Liberal Revolution,[4] which is to say the wave of the future. The majority in North Brookfield, as the Liberal sees it, is impudently resisting the Liberal Revolution, just as the White Southerners are impudently resisting it. Both must, quite simply, be prevailed upon to abandon the positions they have adopted—preferably of course by persuasion (that is, by instruction in the principles of democracy); if not by persuasion then by legal fiat, at the margin and if necessary, by coercion. The North Brookfield majority, as the Liberal sees it further, just isn't with it: the First Amendment prohibits any and every Congressional enactment "respecting an establishment of religion"; the Fourteenth Amendment "extends" that prohibition to the state legislatures, and to state agencies like the school board of North Brookfield; the Supreme Court has now spelled the prohibition out in, so to speak, words of one syllable, which it becomes the business of the citizens of North Brookfield to cognize, to take to heart, and to obey. For them to refuse to obey is tantamount to their declaring war on American democracy, which for present purposes at least we may take as the Highest Good, and having declared war they may fairly expect to be treated like enemies. Send troops to North Brookfield to enforce a court order implementing the Supreme Court ruling? If we must, we will. Freedom of conscience is just as necessary to democracy as freedom from

racial discrimination, and both just as necessary as freedom of speech and press, freedom of assembly, and freedom to petition. I repeat: North Brookfield's crisis poses no problems for which the Liberals are less than fully prepared, both as regards where, politically, they are going, and why, doctrinally, that is where they ought to go. Nor could the North Brookfield crisis take any turn for which the Liberals would not have a ready strategy and a carefully worked out doctrinal justification.

Not so, however, with the Liberals' putative opponents, the Conservatives. Many of them could not say for sure whose side they are on in North Brookfield; some, I venture, would side, however reluctantly, with the dissidents on the school board (some because they too believe in the absolute "wall of separation" between Church and State, some because they too are not about to encourage disobedience to orders emanating from federal courts, some because they think, here as with "Civil Rights," that any battle that might once have been worth fighting against this aspect of the Liberal Revolution is already lost, so that there's nothing for it now but an orderly retreat from yesterday's Conservative positions). If, moreover, as I do suppose to be true, most would side with the North Brookfield majority, the reasons they would give for doing so would vary greatly from individual to individual. And if, as I suppose also to be true, many would say "Look, the problem can't be decided in North Brookfield," and "The question is what we are going to do *nationally*," these again would disagree as to what ought to be done nationally. To put it otherwise: the prayer decision has caught the Conservatives intellectually unprepared—just as, in 1954, the school desegregation decision caught them unprepared intellectually; and just as, hard after the turn of the century, the Liberal attack on the American Political System—beginning as it did with the publication of J. Allen Smith's *Spirit of American Government*—caught them unprepared intellectually.[5] American Conservatism, one is tempted to say, seems to be in the *business* of being unprepared intellectually for the next thrust of the Liberal Revolution; the Conservatives never do their homework until after they have flunked the exam. If the resistance to the Liberal Revolution had been left up to them, the Revolution would be over and the American Red Widow (a Red Grass-Widow, no doubt, automated on top of that) would have settled matters for the Conservative intellectuals, once and for all. Certainly most of the effective resistance to the Revolution, up to now, has come precisely at the intellectual level of the majority in North Brookfield—at, if you please, the level appropriate to the North Brookfield slogan: "You're against *God*," to planting your feet in the mud and saying to the enemy, "You shall advance no further," but *not* appropriate to the elaboration and implementation of Conservative solutions. Such solutions and the necessary prior penetration of problems, as they arise, through skillful and realistic analysis, only the Conservative intellectuals can provide—they, moreover, only if they are good at their job. And that they will never be until, like the Liberal intellectuals, they have developed a theoretical base from which, carrying their rank and file with them, they can strike right to the heart of each issue as it presents itself, and promptly identify the Conservative strategy called for. We have Brent Bozell's word for it that fifty—yes, fifty—proposals for constitutional amendments, all inspired by the prayer decision, now lie before Congress (none of them, I might add, with a Chinaman's chance of reaching the floor of either House). Moreover—handily enough for purposes of my pres-

ent point—the thesis of the Bozell article to which I refer is that *no* constitutional amendment is needed at all![6] We are a movement—assuming that is that we are a movement—rent not merely by divided counsels, but also by sharply conflicting views of political reality and, above all, of the American political system itself, and the proper role of Conservatives with respect to its proper functioning, its good health, and its preservation. The condition of our learned literature, moreover, offers little hope of our ceasing, any time soon, to be that kind of movement.

Now: We shall not move, in this article, from intellectual unpreparedness to intellectual preparedness. But we might, just might, take a step or two in the right direction; and I have, to that end, the following theses to propose:

A) We Conservatives must stop frittering away our energies in *argument* with the Supreme Court—whether about the intention of the Framers of the Constitution and the First Amendment[7] (and we may now add the Fourteenth Amendment) or about the "clear meaning" of the words "Congress shall make no law respecting an establishment of religion, or prohibiting the free exercise thereof," and "equal protection of the laws," and "due process of law." Concretely, we must withdraw from the great current debate on the so-called "broad" interpretation versus the so-called "narrow" interpretation of the "establishment" clause I have just quoted, which debate let me explain briefly as follows: According to the "narrow" interpretation, we are committed under the First Amendment merely to a policy of governmental neutrality over against the numerous religious groups into which we are divided: government action must not tend to strengthen the hand of the Baptists against the Methodists, or that of the Protestants against the Catholics, or that of the Christians against the Jews, or that of the "Judeo-Christians" against Mohammedanism or Bahai. According to the broad interpretation, by contrast, our commitment goes much further: government must be neutral over against all possible states of conscience or belief (including, one supposes, cannibalism provided you don't actually eat anybody, and certainly including the Black Mass, provided it be celebrated behind closed doors and so without offense to public standards of decency); governmental action must be of such character as not even to strengthen the hand of religion against irreligion. I am not saying, of course, that it is a matter of indifference which of these two views prevails (assuming for the moment that one of them is to prevail), or that the Conservatives who are doing battle on behalf of the "narrow" interpretation are incorrect in preferring it to the broad interpretation: Let the broad interpretation prevail and, as Leonard Levy puts it in a brilliant statement of the Liberal position,[8] "even government aid that is impartially and equitably administered to all religious groups is barred by the First Amendment." Let the broad interpretation prevail, and not merely Bible-reading and prayers in the public schools have to go: released-time programs must go, too, along with Christmas plays and public *crèches* and even religious songs; so must invocations and benedictions at school graduation exercises; so—to bump the problem up to another level—must chaplains in the Armed Forces and, one supposes, in Congress; so must the words "In God We Trust" from the nation's coinage; so must—above all perhaps—the exemption of the property and income of religious groups from taxation (which certainly does have the effect of forcing the irreligious to help propagate the superstitions of the religious). Somewhere along that line, I suppose, any American Con-

servative except perhaps R. P. Oliver[9] is going to begin to feel misgivings about our famous "wall of separation," and come out against the First Amendment so construed; and, as I have already said, in my opinion rightly, as far as he goes. On the narrow interpretation, by contrast, all the goods I have named, if goods they be, would be safe, which I am prepared to assume they ought to be. My quarrel, then, is not with the *animus* of the Conservative defenders of the narrow interpretation; I merely call upon them, in the first instance, to stop "argue-barguing" with the Supreme Court about which of the two interpretations the First Congress intended and, short of that, which of the two interpretations the actual language of the First Amendment adds up to. This for a number of reasons that, in so brief an article, I can hardly do more than adumbrate in the following summary manner: (a) There is no reason to suppose that the Supreme Court is ever affected by such arguing, or even listens to it; the inertia of the Supreme Court is a forward inertia, and always in the direction of the Liberal Revolution. (b) If the purpose of the arguing be to appeal over the heads of the Supreme Court justices to public opinion, the advocates of the narrow interpretation are indeed frittering away their energies: Mr. Dooley to the contrary notwithstanding, the Supreme Court precisely does *not* follow the election returns; besides which—look again at North Brookfield—there is *no* reason to suppose, up to now anyhow, that public opinion is other than basically sound on the First Amendment issue. (c) The argument, insofar as it turns on the intention of the Framers of the First Amendment and the clear meaning of the establishment clause is—how curious that no Conservative publicist has ever stepped forward to say so!—in its present phase a silly argument, and silly on the very face of it. For in its

present phase *all* that is in question is
what our 50 *states* (and their subordinate
agencies) can or cannot do under the First
Amendment, which is a matter about
which the Framers of the First Amendment, directed as it is exclusively at Congress ("Congress," it reads, "shall make
no law," etc.), certainly had no discoverable intent; about which, therefore, the
language of the First Amendment certainly has no meaning *sensu stricto* except
this meaning: the States are free, under
the Constitution of the United States, to
do exactly what they please "respecting
an establishment of religion" and about
"prohibiting the free exercise thereof."
The question of possible limitations upon
the power of the states in this area was,
quite simply, not "up." (Except, we may
pause to notice, in the mind of Madison,
who indeed included in the original draft
of the Bill of Rights a provision that would
have extended the "Bill of Rights" limitations upon the power of the Federal
government to the states; but the First
Congress made short shrift of that.) (d)
The energies that Conservative publicists
fritter away on the current argument
ought to be channeled into another kind
of argument altogether, namely: What
policy *should* we adopt—we the people of
the United States, that is to say—with
respect to the problems that have arisen
amongst us under the general heading:
"church and state, government and religion"? For as Conservatives, that is, as
disciples of Publius, what we should want
above all is that the relevant questions
shall be decided by the "deliberate sense
of the community"—and the deliberate
sense of the community *not* about the
intent of the Founders (it was, above all,
that we should govern ourselves, and so
prove to mankind that self-government is
possible); and not, Talmudically, about the
meaning of verbal formulae penned by
the dead hand of the past, but about the

merits of the competing policy alternatives
amongst which we, as a self-governing
people, are obliged to choose. Which is
to say: about the *appropriateness* of competing policies to our conception of ourselves as a people, to our historic destiny
as *we* understand it, to our settled views
as to the nature of the good society. That
is the argument into which we ought, I
say, to be channeling our energies—that
and the further argument: What is it we
are going to have to do to the American
political system in order that (look again
at North Brookfield) the deliberate sense
of the community *shall* prevail, as, generally, we believe it to have prevailed
always in the not-too-remote past. Those,
I say, are the kinds of questions into which
Conservative publicists should be pouring
their energies. Yet—so it seems to me, as
a student of the relevant literature—it is
an argument that nobody amongst us
seems to be conducting except John
Courtney Murray. (His *We Hold These
Truths* should, in my opinion, be the take-
off point for all future Conservative discussion of the establishment problem.)

So much for my first thesis—we must
stop arguing with the Supreme Court—
and the reasons I offer in its support.

B) My second thesis, which I believe
reaches to the remote source of Conservative helplessness and indecision in these
matters, is this:

*We must seek a way out of the apparently
exhaustive dilemma: Either give the Supreme
Court its head* (even if giving it its head
leads to North Brookfield—and Birmingham), *or strike at the whole business of judicial
review.* I assume here, correctly I think,
that what keeps Conservatives from taking
sides (and all of us the same side) in North
Brookfield is—I have intimated as much
above—that we see no way to take the
side to which we are instinctively drawn
without ourselves defying the Supreme
Court and, off at the end, not merely

questioning its power under the Constitution to set itself up as a legislature but also deciding to try to eliminate that power from the American political system. I assume also that the reasons for which we hesitate to strike at the Supreme Court, hesitate even to think of striking at the Supreme Court, are sound. For one thing, they have behind them a tradition that reaches as far back as *Marbury v. Madison* and *The Federalist*. For another, the explicit case for judicial review, as urged by Marshall and Publius, is a case well nigh impossible to answer in the Conservative idiom. We judge, and with good reason, that judicial review is the chief institutional barrier that ultimately protects us against (as I like to call it) the *plebiscitary potential* in our Constitution, that is, its potential for transforming itself into something very like the British Constitution. Nor is that all. The Conservative intellectuals must never forget that those good folk of North Brookfield, who are today defying the Supreme Court, are *their* constituents, and only too likely to turn against them the day they set out to "do something" about judicial review (it was, remember, they, precisely they, who rose in their fury against FDR's Court-packing plan). And, all that apart, it is by no means certain that the American political system, insofar as it is *federal*, would be workable without judicial review at least of the acts of the states and of state agencies (which, not judicial review of acts of Congress, is the kind of judicial review that has precipitated the "Civil Rights" crisis and the "prayer"-decision crisis). At the present moment, to be sure, the temptation to strike at judicial review is indeed very great. The Court hardly keeps up even the pretense, these days, that it is not legislating. Instead of merely postponing governmental action until there exists a deliberate sense of the community, which was its traditional practice, it today

situates itself far out ahead of that deliberate sense. Very far from moving to blur divisions amongst us that might undermine civil peace, it has taken to creating divisions where yesterday there were none, and then, as it seems, does what it can to aggravate them. Its decision in the *Nelson* case (though that, of course, involves the other, the Congressional aspect of judicial review) involved a kind of judicial aggression of which, so far as I know, it had never before been guilty.[10] Smaller wonder, then, that we shall soon hold in our hands an important Conservative book—the first, I think—that will summon us, in the name of the good health of the American political system, to take any steps that may be required now in order to *curb* the Court.[11] Our dilemma, in consequence, is a painful one. That indeed is *why* we argue-bargue with the Court: the alternatives to argue-barguing—giving the Court its head, curbing the Court—we find too horrible to contemplate. Now: we must, I say, stop the argue-barguing, because it is the political equivalent of the sin of Onan. But we must also, I am saying, hit upon a means of escaping between the horns of our Supreme Court dilemma, and confer upon the making good of the escape the very highest priority in the American Conservative movement. Nor, once you put it that way, can there, I think, be any doubt where we have to go: We must recognize that the cancer that threatens not merely the good health but the very survival of the American political system is not judicial review (which unlike a cancer confers great goods upon the body politic); it is those clauses of the Fourteenth Amendment—*equal protection of the laws* and *due process*—that, as we see now, make of it an invitation to the Supreme Court to tamper, in the teeth of the Tenth Amendment, with our traditional division of powers between the federal and state governments. But for those clauses (they were of course never intended for the purpose for which they are being used, but let us not insist on that; to do so belongs under our general heading of arguing with the Supreme Court), the Court could not have catapulted itself into either the school-desegregation decision or the deorisonation decision. Those clauses, I repeat, are the cancer, and so the point at which we must apply the knife, which we can do in any one of several ways: Repeal the Fourteenth Amendment as a whole, telling ourselves—as with good conscience we can—that the purposes for which it was enacted were long since accomplished (it lay dormant through the decades that divided the Reconstruction crisis from the Gitlow case, which was the case in which the Supreme Court first took it into its head to extend the so-called Bill of Rights limitations on the federal government to the states). Or, short of repealing the Amendment as a whole, amend it so as to get rid of the offending clauses. Neither of these things, I think, need be particularly difficult to do if we set out to mobilize, behind repeal or amendment, the resentments engendered by the desegregation, deorisonation, and apportionment decisions (making the most we can, of course, of the procedural irregularities that were involved in the adoption of the Fourteenth Amendment to begin with). Or, if repeal or amendment seems too big a job, let us then call upon Congress (where, unlike the Supreme Court, we *are* listened to) to clarify the Fourteenth Amendment (as the Supreme Court has itself, on occasion, invited it do to)—clarify it, of course, in the direction to which I have just been pointing. Or, finally, let us call upon Congress to remove the offending clauses from the appellate jurisdiction of the Supreme Court—over which, so far as we know to date, it has complete control.

It does not much matter, I think, which of these alternative means we adopt for achieving the desired proximate end, which is to leave judicial review untouched while exercising *our* rightful control over the Constitution of which the Supreme Court is the guardian—which means we use, I repeat, does not matter, *provided* we get it through our heads that the present situation, alike in North Brookfield and in Birmingham and in Austin, is intolerable; that *no* less drastic remedy can meet the test of Conservative principle; and that we, as Conservatives, have *no* reason to suppose our political resources inadequate for bringing it off (whether by legislative enactment or by amending the Constitution). To which let me add: a campaign to draw the teeth of the Fourteenth Amendment would give us something to do in life, which apart from our pipedream of a committed Conservative in the White House is exactly what we have never had. I reiterate: *We must escape between the horns of the dilemma:* suffer the Supreme Court, curb the Supreme Court; and soon, for in these matters time presses and, as Cabell's Jurgen remarks, in pressing sets us an admirable example.

C) We must learn—and having learned make the most of it—to distinguish between the *legality* of a decision handed down by the Supreme Court and the *prudence* of such a decision. Then, if argue with the Supreme Court we must, we must learn to confine our part in the debate to the *prudential* area. And no, I by no means agree, from the point of view of Conservative doctrine and strategy, that this distinction is "jesuitical," or a distinction without a difference. Challenge the *legality* of a Supreme Court ruling based upon its interpretation of the language of the Constitution, and you get yourself into an argument that is (a) endless, and (b) impossible to win. Challenge the *prudence* of such a Supreme

Court ruling, or at least of its enforcement within the foreseeable future, and you situate yourself upon different and altogether more promising ground. This for a number of reasons: The claim of the Supreme Court to the last say as to the *meaning* of a constitutional provision, as I have already noticed, is pretty well unanswerable in terms of our traditional constitutional theory—and legally unanswerable altogether. Attack it, and you attack an aspect of our political system that, to go no further, now has behind it nigh onto two centuries of prescription. Attack it, and you must not only meet the case for judicial review as worked out by Hamilton and Marshall, but meet it to the satisfaction of your neighbors (who, as one of the dissenters on the North Brookfield school board reminds us, are pretty sure to be "simple"). The case for the Supreme Court's last say on the meaning of the Constitution is on the same footing, like it or not, as the case for papal infallibility within the Roman Catholic Church. And from all this it follows that one enters an argument with the Supreme Court about legality before, so to speak, a packed jury. On the other hand, no one, so far as I know, has ever worked out a case for deeming the Supreme Court infallible in the realm of prudence, or for supposing the American political system unworkable unless the Supreme Court have the last word on whether, given the current lay of sentiment and opinion in the American community, immediate enforcement of this or that inspired ruling by the Court would be so destructive of civil peace, so certain to produce those divisions among the people that threaten the whole process of government by the deliberate sense of the community, so likely to eventuate in bloodshed, or, as in North Brookfield, in impossible situations, as to be (I deliberately use Dwight Eisenhower's magic phrase) "unthinkable." The Supreme Court

has a right, nay a duty, to say what, in a given case, the Constitution *means*, and thus to the inside track in an argument about its meaning. It does not have the right and duty to add to its rulings, as further constitutional doctrine, *ruat coelum*—which as matters stand, with the President apparently having accepted a general cost-what-it-may obligation to enforce all federal court orders in any conditions anywhere, and Congress a similar obligation to keep hands off, is *just* what it does in effect add to its rulings. "Let the Heavens fall!" But this, I contend, is under the Preamble to the Constitution ("in order to form a more perfect Union," it says) impossible constitutional doctrine in America, once it is brought skillfully out into the open where you can get at it. But back to my distinction: I hazard the guess that the reluctance of the Congress to resort to its control over the appellate jurisdiction of the Court as a means of sidestepping an unacceptable Court ruling—it has, I think, resorted to it only twice—may be a matter of Congress' seeing no way to resort to it, on a given ruling, without seeming to question the Supreme Court's last say on the *law*. Let Congress, I say, taught by Conservative publicists, learn to assert its own last say about what will go down in the American community, along with its own final responsibility, together with the President but *not* the Supreme Court, for the maintenance of civil peace. The Supreme Court, remote as it is from the brute facts of American life, is not in a strong position for talking back in an argument about what is prudent (in strict theory, indeed, it is not even supposed to take prudential consideration into account in handing down its decisions). And it would be terrible to think that the responsibility for confining governmental action within the bounds of prudence lies nowhere in the American political system.

D) One thesis more, and I shall have done. I have spoken above of restoring the *status quo ante* in North Brookfield, that is, the *status quo* that obtained before the New York Regents' case, and with the apparent implication that everybody is clear what that *status quo ante* is. I have also spoken above of a choice between the so-called "narrow" interpretation of the establishment clause and the new "broad" interpretation, with the apparent implication that the choice between them is an exhaustive choice. In both instances, let me say now, I was merely postponing problems; and I owe it to my readers, in conclusion now, to meet those problems head on. As regards the *status quo ante*—the relation between church and state, religion and government, before the Engel case—I must make the two-fold point: First, there *was*, generally speaking, no particular *status quo ante;* and second, insofar as there was a particular *status quo ante* it was *not* what we commonly pretend it to have been. As regards the choice between narrow interpretation and broad interpretation, that choice is not exhaustive at all—and is not likely to be in our time. Here, let me emphasize, is one of those matters in America that one can see clearly only with a carefully-cultivated *innocent* eye, an eye whose owner has *deliberately* removed from it the blinders of constitutional myth and often-repeated, never-challenged verbal formulae, so that it actually sees that which is actually "given" to it by reality—a rare gift, I happen to think, among students of politics. Now: The First Amendment, we are in the habit of telling ourselves, establishes a "wall of separation" between church and state, between religion and government, that it is the agreed business alike of Congress, the States, and at the margin the Supreme Court to maintain. To which I answer: that is an Old Wives' Tale, from which, if we are to make sense of our affairs, we

must speedily emancipate ourselves. In point of fact, the wall of separation in America has always been as full of holes as a kitchen sieve. This is not, moreover, wonderful; the religion clauses of the First Amendment (which are the only verbal formulation we have of our wall of separation) went into our constitutional law, and similar clauses have gone into our state constitutions, not as a matter of high principle, not as a sacred presupposition of freedom, but (as Father Murray has shown, though I deliberately use unpriestly language)[12] as a *deal*—a *deal* rendered necessarily by the fact that we are a people divided not only pluralistically (Father Murray's point) but *spottily* (my point over and beyond his) amongst a wide variety of religious persuasions. We the people have always known that the absence of any wall of separation at all must lead to the undermining of civil peace; but we have always known also that a complete wall of separation is out of the question. The deal—my understanding of it differs from Father Murray's—was a deal, so to speak, for having it both ways about civil peace on the one hand and a little-not-too-much penetration of the governmental sphere by religion—both ways, if you like, about on the one hand the wall of separation (in the absence of such a wall, civil peace will be broken because some religious people will seek too great a penetration of the civil order, and other people will resent it) and on the other hand that minimum of religious penetration of the civil order that you cannot, in America, begrudge religious people without, as at North Brookfield, breaking civil peace. The American answer to the problem of having it both ways here, the *traditional* American answer, which to our misfortune we have all too rarely tried to put into words, has been this: Maintain a wall; celebrate it in myth and song even as the Great Wall of

China was celebrated in myth and song; celebrate it, indeed, as a wall that cannot and must not be breached. But let the wall be *porous*; and if now and then here or there, some moisture seeps through from one side of the wall to the other, that is, from religion to government (though not the other way 'round), use some common sense, of which we expect you to have some, in deciding how excited to get about it. Americans carry that answer, I like to think, not so much in their minds as (in Lincoln Steffens' phrase about T. R.) in their hips; they apply it to their affairs, if I may put it so, instinctively, and without need of assistance from their intellectual betters. Thus the chapels, maintained at public expense, in our service academies; thus cadets required by law to turn up in them on Saturday or Sunday, or explain why not; thus church organizations testifying before Congressional committees (which, as Peter Drucker has pointed out, would not be tolerated for a moment in any country deadly serious about the "wall of separation"); thus a score of yet other Congressional acts of defiance against the "clear" language of the First Amendment, and thus the systematic tacit acquiescences of the Supreme Court in all these acts of defiance; thus, *most* especially, the continuing phenomenon of religious observances in the public schools throughout our history and pretty much all over the land. (I give it as my educated guess that the biggest surprise of the Engel decision, for most Americans, must have been the discovery that the public schools *are* "state" or "government" at all; *who,* they might well ask, were they, like their intellectual betters, a little more articulate, who ever *heard* of such a thing?) The public schools of America, as we all know off at the back of our minds, were originally established in America with a legal mandate to foil the Old Deceiver Satan by providing religious

and moral instruction for the young; nor, except spottily (in the big cities especially, of course) has the average American ever ceased for one moment to expect them to perform that function; nor, over most of the country, have the public schools ever stopped performing it in some fashion or other—often, to be sure, half-heartedly, often formalistically only, often with the religion so purged of doctrinal or sectarian content as to be hardly recognizable as religion, but still in a manner oceans apart from the genuine neutrality toward religion, or even enmity towards religion, that is characteristic of, say, our great secular universities. There are exceptions? No doubt; indeed the point I am leading up to could hardly stand if there were not some exceptions. For my point is going to be: Insofar as there has been a general rule, it has been: go ahead with your religious observances in the public schools, *provided* you keep the peace. But that is only another way of saying there has been *no* general rule except, surprising as it may be to see it down in black and white, this rule: let the local community decide: in favor of virtual exclusion of religious observances if you like (as in California), in favor of a wee little bit of religious observances (that, one gathers, was the decision in New York, with the well-nigh meaningless Regents' prayer), in favor of quite a bit of religious observances (as in, say, Massachusetts or Connecticut). Let the local community decide, but on the tacit condition that it recognize and live up to its local responsibility for keeping the peace, for not having people at each others' throats. Our history in this matter, moreover, as I proudly believe, has been an impressive one.

The real significance and danger of the "prayer" decisions lies, then, precisely in the attempt to lay down a general rule on religious observances in the schools where formerly there was none—and to accomplish this by setting aside a universally understood (if never articulated) general rule on another matter, namely: Let the people of the local community work the matter out, as part of their general problems of living together on their little portion of American real estate.

That way of slicing it, so familiar to us that it is difficult to put into words, had certain very great advantages as compared with any alternative way of slicing it—advantages, we must now notice, tied up with the relevant rules, commandments even, that have, I believe, been generally observed in our local communities. These are:

I. Thou shalt not be *doctrinaire* about religious observances in the public schools (that is, thou shalt assert no high principles, allegedly governing this matter, that thou placest beyond discussion or negotiation). (Doctrinaire, of course, is the word I promised to substitute for "theological"; and now I have kept my promise.)

II. Thou shalt keep thy sense of humor (on pain of being laughed at and, ultimately, laughed out of town).

III. Thou shalt bear in mind, in the course of thy face-to-face negotiations with thy neighbors on this matter, that tomorrow thou must live neighbors with them.

These three commandments, like the Ten, are parts of one and the same *ethos*, and are for that reason members one of another. Not being doctrinaire makes for greater neighborliness, as neighborliness knocks the edges off the tendency to be doctrinaire. Both neighborliness and the avoidance of doctrinairism increase the chances of people keeping their sense of humor, as sense of humor cements neighborliness and wears down, still a little further, the tendency to be doctrinaire. The fact that the relevant negotiations

are and must be conducted face-to-face, and are presided over by the necessity of living together tomorrow, sets a stage on which alike neighborliness, sense of humor, and the avoidance of doctrinairism can thrive like the green bay tree. Are we going to permit the Supreme Court to uproot them, in the name of spurious and novel doctrine?[13] If not, then let us get busy and amend the Fourteenth Amendment.

NOTES

[1] *Life,* November 8, 1963.
[2] *School District of Abingdon Township v. Schempp, Murray v. Curlett* (83 Supreme Court 1560, 10 Lawyer's Ed. 2nd. 844, 1963). *Engel v. Vitale* (370 U.S. 421, 82 Supreme Court 1261, 8 Lawyer's Ed. 2nd. 601, 1962).
[3] Walter Berns, "School Prayers and 'Religious Warfare,'" *National Review,* April 23, 1963, pp. 315–318.
[4] Willmoore Kendall, *The Conservative Affirmation.* (Chicago: Henry Regnery Co., 1963), Chapter I, *passim.*
[5] J. Allen Smith, *The Spirit of American Government* (New York: The Macmillan Co., 1912).
[6] L. Brent Bozell, "Saving Our Children From God," *National Review,* July 16, 1963, pp. 19–22.
[7] For a skillful though in my opinion wrongheaded explication of this issue, see Leonard W. Levy, "School Prayers and the Founding Fathers," *Commentary* 34, 225–230.
[8] *Ibid.*
[9] R. P. Oliver, "Conservatism and Reality," *Modern Age,* Fall 1961, pp. 397–406.
[10] *Pennsylvania v. Nelson* (350 U.S. 497, 1956).
[11] This book, by L. Brent Bozell, will be published in 1965 by Henry Regnery Co.
[12] John Courtney Murray, *We Hold These Truths* (New York: Sheed and Ward, 1960), Chapter II.
[13] How far people quickly go—in the direction of doctrinairism and loss of sense of humor—emerges clearly in the following Letter to the Editor from the complainant in the Maryland "prayer" case: "I am the Maryland Atheist, Sirs: I am a principal in one of the cases now pending before the Supreme Court concerning the reading of the Bible and prayer recitation in the public schools.
"The Atheist's position (I am that Maryland Atheist you mentioned) is one arrived at after considerable study, cogitation and inner search. It is a position which is founded in science, in reason and

in a love for fellow man, rather than in a love for God.

"We find the Bible to be nauseating, historically inaccurate, replete with the ravings of madmen. We find God to be sadistic, brutal, and a representation of hatred, vengeance. We find the Lord's Prayer to be that muttered by worms, groveling for meager existence in a traumatic, paranoid world.

"This is not appropriate untouchable dicta to be forced on adult or child. The business of the public schools, where attendance is compulsory, is to pre-pare children to face the problems on earth, not to prepare for heaven—which is a delusional dream of the unsophisticated minds of the ill-educated clergy.

"Fortunately, we atheists can seek legal remedy through our Constitution, which was written by deists (not Christians) who had *enough* of religion and wanted to grow toward freedom from it, not enslavement in it.

"Signed, Madalyn Murray, Baltimore, Maryland."

[VIII, Summer 1964, 245-259]

[V]

The Place of Christianity

[40]

The Freedom of Man in the Freedom of the Church

JOHN COURTNEY MURRAY, S. J.

John Courtney Murray, S.J. *(1904–1967), "one of the most creative Christian intellectuals of our time," was the son of an attorney. Born in New York City, he planned to be a lawyer. In 1920, however, he became a Jesuit. In the midst of a distinguished theological and academic career, he found himself, in the 1950s, a center of controversy when he proposed that the Vatican bless the relationship between church and state in America. By 1954 his Jesuit superiors had demanded that he stop writing and lecturing. But during Vatican Council II, when Cardinal Francis Spellman invited him to Rome, Murray became the most widely admired peritus at the Council. He was instrumental in framing the* Declaration of Religious Freedom *(1965). Most of his theses were presented in essays in* Theological Studies, *of which he became an editor in 1941, and in his books, among them* We Hold These Truths *(1960),* The Problem of God *(1963), and* Problems of Religious Freedom *(1965).*

AS THE STANDPOINT for my remarks I shall assume that we now stand at the "end of modern times." The phrase, in one or other variant, has come into common use. Whether "modern times" began with the fall of Constantinople in the fifteenth century, or with the rise of Gnosticism in the second century, is a matter of dispute. But there is some scholarly agreement today that the spiritual era known as "modern" is running to a close. A new era is beginning. Almost everything about it is unpredictable, save that it will be an era of unprecedented dangers. The danger of violent destruction threatens the physical fabric of civilization. And the spiritual nature of man himself is men-aced by more insidious corruptions. I have no wish to be a prophet of *Untergang*; I do not believe that downfall is our inevitable civilizational fate. But I do think that confusion is the present civilizational fact. . . .

Is the Problem today rightly identified, in one word, as "freedom"? The point might be argued. In any case, the Problem is not "freedom" in the sense in which modernity has understood the term. So rapidly have the generations slipped beneath our feet that the prophets of modernity and of its "freedom"—the Miltons and the Mills, the Madisons and the Jeffersons—have already begun to seem slightly neolithic figures to our backward glance. Certain of their insights retain validity. But the adequacy of their systems can no longer be upheld. The broad question has arisen, whether the problem of freedom in the post-modern era can be satisfactorily dealt with in terms of philosophies (and theologies) which bear too heavily the stamp of modernity.

The problem does not center on some minor malfunctions of the mechanisms of freedom. Our "free institutions," in their procedural aspects, are working today as well as they ever have worked or ever will work. Some tinkering with them may be needed. But tinkering is not our full task. It is characteristic of the present moment that all the serious talk is about Basic Issues.

The initial difficulty is that these Basic Issues are not easily located and defined. Perhaps rather abruptly, I shall venture a twofold formulation.

First, the Basic Issues of our time concern the spiritual substance of a free society, as it has historically derived from the central Christian concept, *res sacra homo*, "Man is a sacredness" (only the abstract noun can render the Latin rightly). Second, the Basic Issues concern the fundamental structure of a free society. I do not mean its legal structure, as constitutionally established; few of the real problems today are susceptible of solution, or even of statement, in legal language. I mean rather the ontological structure of society, of which the constitutional order should be only the reflection. This underlying social structure is a matter of theory; that is, it is to be conceived in terms of a theorem with regard to the relation between the sacrednesses inherent in man and the manifold secularities amid which human life is lived.

This twofold formulation is very general. I set it down thus to make clear my conviction that the Basic Issues today can only be conceived in metaphysical and theological terms. They are issues of truth. They concern the nature and structure of reality itself—meaning by reality the order of nature as accessible to human reason, and the economy of salvation as disclosed by the Christian revelation.

But these general formulas may not be useful for purposes of argument. And argument, I take it, is our purpose. Therefore a more pragmatic approach to our problem is indicated. No philosopher today will uphold the crude tenet of an older outworn pragmatism, that whatever works is true. But any philosopher must acknowledge the more subtle truth, that whatever is not true will somehow fail to work. Prof. Hocking has stated the case in his book, *The Coming World Civilization*: "For whatever is real in the universe is no idle object of speculation; it is a working factor in experience or it is nothing. Consciously or subconsciously we are always dealing with it; to entertain false notions about it, or simply to neglect it, will bring about maladjustments which thrust this neglect forward into consciousness. A false metaphysic, engendering empirical malaise, calls for a new work of thought, begetting an altered premise."

The statement suggests a method of inquiry. What are our malaises today? That is, what are the discomforts and uneasinesses that trouble, not the surface of mind and soul, but their very depths? Are these distresses somehow traceable to falsities in the philosophy that has inspired the political experiment of modernity? If so, what new work of thought is needed? And what alterations in the premises of the modern experiment are called for?

A process of questioning, more or less inspired by this method, has been going on of late; and in the course of it many ideas dear to a later modernity have found their way into Trotsky's famous "dustbin of history."

For instance, we no longer cherish the bright and brittle eighteenth-century concept of "reason"; we do not believe in the principle of automatic harmony nor in the inevitability of progress. We have rejected that principle of modernity which asserted that government is the only enemy of freedom. We see that the modern concept of freedom itself was dangerously inadequate because it neglected the corporate dimension of freedom. We see too that modernity was wrong in isolating the problem of freedom from its polar terms—responsibility, justice, order, law. We have realized that the modern experiment, originally conceived only as an experiment in Freedom, had to become also an experiment in Justice. We know that the myopic individualism of modernity led it into other errors, even into a false conception of the problem of the state in terms of the unreal dichotomy, individualism vs. collectivism. We have come to disbelieve the cardinal tenet of modernity which regarded every advance in man's domination over nature—that is, every new accumulation of power—as necessarily liberating. We have begun to understand the polyvalence of power. In fact, we know that we are post-modern men, living in a new age, chiefly because we have begun to see what modernity never saw—that the central problem is not the realization of the Cartesian dream. This dream today is largely reality; man is the master of nature. Our problem now is the dissolution of a nightmare that never visited Descartes—the horrid vision of man, master of nature, but not master of himself.

It may be useful here to carry this process of questioning further, and to an altogether basic level. This can best be done, I think, by viewing the modern political experiment in its continuity with the longer liberal tradition of the West. My generalization will be that the political experiment of modernity has essentially consisted in an effort to find and install in the world a secular substitute for all that the Christian tradition has meant by the pregnant phrase, the "freedom of the Church." This freedom, though not a freedom of the political order, was Christianity's basic contribution to freedom in the political order. Some brief articulation of the concept will initially be necessary. Modernity dropped the phrase out of its political vocabulary, and eliminated the thing from its political edifice, and installed in its place a secular surrogate—this will be my second assertion. Thirdly, I shall attempt to identify some of the more acute stresses and distresses currently being experienced at our present stage in the modern experiment. Finally, I shall attempt to state some of the spiritual issues which lie, I think, at the origin of our empirical malaises. It will be sufficient for my purpose simply to present these issues for argument.

I

In his book, *Libertas: Kirche and Weltordnung im Zeitalter des Investiturstreites* (a broad study of the basic issues involved in that great medieval struggle between opposed conceptions of the nature and order of Christian society which centered around Gregory VII), Gerd Tellenbach writes: "In moments of considered solemnity, when their tone was passionate and their religious feeling at its deepest, Gregory VII and his contemporaries called the object towards which they were striving the 'freedom' of the Church." More than six centuries earlier the same idea had inspired Ambrose in his conflicts with Gratian and Theodosius. And eight centuries later, Leo XIII used the same phrase to define the goal of his striving in a more radical conflict between the Church and modernity, now fully developed not only as a spirit but also as a polity. In more than sixty Leonine documents the phrase, the "freedom of the Church" appears some eighty-one times.

On any showing, even merely historical, we are here in the presence of a Great Idea, whose entrance into history marked the beginning of a new civilizational era.

It is an historical commonplace to say that the essential political effect of Christianity was to destroy the classical view of society as a single homogeneous structure, within which the political power stood forth as the representative of society both in its religious and in its political aspects. Augustus was both *Summus Imperator* and *Pontifex Maximus*; the *ius divinum* was simply part of the *ius civile*; and outside the empire there was no other society, but only barbarism. The new Christian view was based on a radical distinction between order of the sacred and the order of the secular: "Two there are, august Emperor, by which this world is ruled on title of original and sovereign right—the consecrated authority of the priesthood and the royal power." In this celebrated sentence of Gelasius I, written to the Byzantine Emperor Anastasius I in 494 A.D., the emphasis laid on the word "two" bespoke the revolutionary character of the Christian dispensation.

In his book, *Sacrum Imperium*, Alois Dempf called this Gelasian text the "Magna Charta of the whole 'freedom of the Church' in medieval times." It was the charter of a new freedom, such as the world had never known. Moreover, it was a freedom with which man could not enfranchise himself, since it was the effect of God's own "magnificent dispensation," in Gelasius' phrase. The whole patristic and medieval tradition, which Leo XIII reiterated to the modern world, asserts the freedom of the Church to be a participation in the freedom of the Incarnate Son of God, the God-Man, Christ Jesus.

For our purposes here we can consider this new freedom to be twofold. First, there is the freedom of the Church as a spiritual authority. To the Church is entrusted the *cura animarum*; and this divine commission endows her with the freedom to teach, to rule, and to sanctify, with all that these empowerments imply as necessary for their free exercise. This positive freedom has a negative aspect—the immunity of the Church, as the suprapolitical sacredness (*res sacra*), from all manner of politicization, through subordination to the state, or enclosure within the state as *instrumentum regni*. Second, there is the freedom of the Church as the Christian people—their freedom to have access to the teaching of the Church, to obey her laws, to receive at her hands the sacramental ministry of grace, and to live within her fold an integral supernatural life. In turn, the inherent suprapolitical dignity of this life itself claims "for the faithful the enjoyment of the right to live in civil society according to the precepts of reason and conscience" (Pius XI). And this comprehensive right, asserted within the political community, requires as its complement that all the intrapolitical sacredness (*res sacra in temporalibus*) be assured of their proper immunity from politicization.

This concept, the *res sacra in temporalibus*, had all the newness of Christianity itself. It embraces all those things which are part of the temporal life of man, at the same time that, by reason of their Christian mode of existence, or by reason of their finality, they transcend the limited purposes of the political order and are thus invested with a certain sacredness. The chief example is the institution of the family—the marriage contract itself, and the relationships of husband and wife, parent and child. Included also are other human relationships in so far as they involve a moral element and require regulation in the interests of the personal dignity of man. Such, for instance, are the employer-employee relationship and the reciprocal relationships established by the political obligation. Sacred too is the intellectual patrimony of the human race, the heritage of basic truths about the nature of man, amassed by secular experience and reflection, that form the essential content of the social consensus and furnish the basic guarantee that within society conditions of freedom and justice, prosperity and order will prevail, at least to some essential human degree.

Instinctively and by natural inclination the common man knows that he cannot be free if his basic human things are not sacredly immune from profanation by the power of the state and by other secular powers. The question has always been that of identifying the limiting norm that will check the encroachments of secular power and preserve these sacred immunities. Western civilization first found this norm in the pregnant principle, the freedom of the Church.

I should perhaps emphasize that the phrase must be given its full meaning. As a matter of history, the liberal tradition of Western politics did not begin its lengthy, slow, and halting evolution because something like Harnack's wraith-like *Wesen des Christentums* began to pervade the dominions of imperial Rome. This pale phantom would have been altogether unequal to the task of inaugurating a new political history. What appeared within history was not an "idea" or an "essence" but an existence, a Thing, a visible institution that occupied ground in this world at the same time that it asserted an astounding new freedom on a title not of this world. Through the centuries a new tradition of politics was wrought out very largely in the course of the wrestlings between the new freedom of the Church and the pretensions of an older power which kept discovering, to its frequent chagrin, that it was not the one unchallengeable ruler of the world and that its rule was not unlimitedly free.

In regard of the temporal order and its powers and processes this complex Existent Thing, the "freedom of the Church," performed a twofold function. First, the freedom of the Church as the spiritual authority served as the limiting principle of the power of government. It furnished, as it were, a corporate or social armature to the sacred order, within which *res sacra homo* would be secure in all the freedoms that his sacredness demands. Men found their freedom where they found their faith—within the Church. As it was her corporate faith that they professed, so it was her corporate freedom that they claimed, in the face of the public power and of all private powers. Within the armature of her immunities they and their human things were immune from profanation. Second, the freedom of the Church as the "people of God" furnished the ultimate directive principle of government. To put it briefly, the Church stood, as it were, between the body politic and the public power, not only limiting the reach of the power over the people, but also mobilizing the moral consensus of the people and bringing it to bear upon the power, thus to insure that the king, in the fine phrase of John of Salisbury, would "fight for justice and for the freedom of the people."

This was the new Christian theorem. I leave aside the historical question, whether and to what extent the theorem was successfully institutionalized. What matters is the theorem itself: the freedom of the Church, in its pregnant meaning, was conceived to be the key to the Christian order of society. What further matters is the historical fact that the whole equilibrium of social forces which under the guidance of this theory made (however imperfectly) for freedom and justice within society was destroyed by the rise of the national monarchies and by the course of their political evolution in the era of royal absolutism.

II

The basic effort of modern politics, as I have suggested, looked to a re-establishment of the equilibrium. In a much too rapid description of it, the process was simple. The early Christian dualism of Church and state (or better, the dyarchy of Gelasius' "Two there are") was in a sense retained—that is, it endured in a secular political form, namely, in the distinction between state and society which had been the secular political outgrowth of the Christian distinction between Church and state. However, the freedom of the Church, again in its pregnant sense, was discarded as the mediating principle between society and state, between the people and the public power. Instead, a secular substitute was adopted in the form of free political institutions. Through these secular institutions the people would limit the power of government; they would also direct the power of government to its proper ends, which are perennially those of John of Salisbury—the fight for justice and for the freedom of the people.

The key to the whole new political edifice was the freedom of the individual conscience. Here precisely lies the newness of the modern experiment. A great act of trust was made. The trust was that the free individual conscience would effectively mediate the moral imperatives of the transcendental order of justice (whose existence was not doubted in the earlier phases of the modern experiment). Then, through the workings of free political institutions these imperatives would be transmitted to the public power as binding norms upon its action. The only

sovereign spiritual authority would be the conscience of the free man. The freedom of the individual conscience, constitutionally guaranteed, would supply the armature of immunity to the sacred order, which now became, by modern definition, precisely the order of the private conscience. And through free political institutions, again constitutionally guaranteed, the moral consensus of the community would be mobilized in favor of justice and freedom in the secular order. This, I take it, has been in essence the political experiment of modernity. It has been an attempt to carry on the liberal tradition of Western politics, whose roots were in the Christian revolution, but now on a new revolutionary basis—a rejection of the Gelasian thesis, "Two there are," which had been the dynamic of the Christian revolution.

I take it, without fear of contradiction, that the rejection of the Gelasian thesis has been common to all the prophets of modernity, from Marsilius of Padua onwards. All of them have been united in viewing the freedom of the Church, in the sense explained, as a trespass upon, and a danger to, their one supreme value—the "integrity of the political order," as the phrase goes. Two citations may be given as illustrative. Rousseau complains: "Jesus came to establish on earth a spiritual kingdom. By separating the theological system from the political system he brought it about that the State ceased to be one, and caused internal divisions which have never ceased to agitate Christian peoples. From this twofold power there has resulted a perpetual conflict of jurisdiction which has rendered all good politics impossible in Christian states. No one has ever been able to know which one to obey, priest or political ruler." Thomas Hobbes put the same issue with characteristic bluntness and clarity: "Temporal and spiritual government are but words brought into the world to make men see double and mistake their lawful sovereign," which is Leviathan, the Mortal God.

In this indictment of Christianity for having made the state "cease to be one," and in this protest against men who "see double," one hears the authentic voice of the secular power as modern history has known it.

It would not be difficult to demonstrate that this monistic tendency is somehow inherent in the state, in two of its aspects— both as an expression of reason and also as a vehicle of power. Nor would it be difficult to show how this monistic tendency has been visible in practically all the states that have paraded across the stage of history, even in states that bore the name of Christian. In any case, the tendency has achieved its most striking success in the modern era. It is the most salient aspect of political modernity. Over the whole of modern politics there has hung the monist concept of the indivisibility of sovereignty: "One there is." This has been true even in those states in which the sovereignty, remaining indivisible, has been institutionalized according to the principle of the separation of powers.

The dynamism behind the assertion, "One there is," has, of course varied. In the seventeenth and eighteenth centuries it was royal absolutism, whose theorists— Widdrington, Barclay, James I—proclaimed a social and juridical monism in the name of the divine right of kings. In the nineteenth century the dynamism was the Revolution, that whole complex of forces which created Jacobin democracy and proclaimed the *république indivisible* in the name of the sovereignty of the people understood as the social projection of the absolutely autonomous sovereignty of individual reason. In the twentieth century the most successful dynamism has been Soviet Communism, which makes the assertion, "One there is," in the name of the unitary class which is destined for world sovereignty, and in the name of its organ, the Party, whose function is to be the servant and ally of the materialist forces of history.

In the twentieth century too, as the modern era runs out, the ancient monistic drive to a oneness of society, law, and authority has also appeared in the totalitarianizing tendency inherent in the contemporary idolatry of the democratic process. This democratic monism is urged in the name of something less clear than the *république indivisible*. What is urged is a monism, not so much of the political order itself, as of a political technique. The proposition is that all the issues of human life—intellectual, religious, and moral issues as well as formally political issues—are to be regarded as, or resolved into, political issues and are to be settled by the single omnicompetent political technique of majority vote. On the surface the monism is one of process; Madison's "republican principle" affords the Final Grounds for the Last Say on All Human Questions. But the underlying idea is a monism of power: "One there is whereby this world is ruled—the power in the people, expressing itself in the preference of a majority; and beyond or beside or above this power there is no other."

The inspiration of democratic monism is partly a sentimentalist mystique—the belief that the power in the people, in distinction from all other powers, is somehow ultimately and inevitably beneficent in its exercise. But the more radical inspiration is the new idea, unknown to medieval times, which modern rationalism thrust into political history. Christianity has always regarded the state as a limited order of action for limited purposes, to be chosen and pursued under the direction and correction of the organized moral conscience of society, whose judgments are formed and mobilized by the Church, an independent and autonomous community, qualified to be the interpreter of man's nature and destiny. It has been specific of modernity to regard the state as a moral end in itself, a self-justifying entity with its own self-determined spiritual substance. It is within the secular state, and by appeal to secular sources, that man is to find the interpretation of his own nature and the means to his own destiny. The state itself creates the ethos of society, embodies it, imparts it to its citizens, and sanctions its observance with rewards and punishments. Outside the tradition of Jacobin or Communist dogmatism, the modern democratic secular state does not indeed pretend to be the Universe or to speak infallibly. But it does assert itself to be the embodiment of whatever fallible human wisdom may be available to man, because it is the highest school of human experience, beyond which man can find no other School and no other Teacher.

Professor Hocking has put the matter thus: "Outside the Marxist orbit the prevalent disposition of the secular state in recent years has been less to combat the church than to carry on a slow empirical demonstration of the state's full equivalence in picturing the attainable good life, and its superior pertinence to actual issues. As this demonstration gains force the expectation grows that it will be the church, not the state, that will wither away. Where the fields of church and state impinge on each other, as in education and correction, the church will in time appear superfluous. Where they are different, the church will be quietly ignored and dropped as irrelevant." This, says Hocking, is the "secular hypothesis." It is, he adds, the premise of the "experiment we call 'modernity'." In the language I have been using, the hypothesis asserts: "One there is by which the world is ruled."

The "one" here (sc., outside the Marxist orbit) is the self-conscious free individual, armed with his subjective rights, whose ultimate origins he may have forgotten but whose status as legal certitudes he cherishes. This individual, the product of modernity, has been taught by modernity to stand against any external and corporate authority, except it be mediated to him by democratic processes; to stand against any law in whose making he had no voice; to stand finally against any society which asserts itself to be an independent community of thought, superior to the concensus created by the common mind of secular democratic society, and empowered to pass judgment, in the name of higher criteria, on this common mind and on the consensus it assembles.

Outside the Jacobin and Communist traditions this "one ruler," the modern man, does not object to religion, provided that religion be regarded as a private matter which concerns only the conscience and feelings of the individual. In his more expansive moments he will not object even to organized religion—the "churches"—provided they accept the status of voluntary associations for limited purposes which do not impinge upon the public order. But he will not tolerate any marring of his image of the world as modernity conceives it—the image of democratic society as the universal community whose ends are coextensive with the ends of man himself. It is the One Society, with One Law, and with One Sovereign, the politically equal people. Modernity has declared the Gelasian doctrine to be heretical and has outlawed it, in the name of modern orthodoxy, which is a naturalist rationalism.

This dominant image of democratic society as ultimately monist in its structure (whatever may be its constituent and subordinate pluralisms), and as ultimately secular in its substance (whatever historical tribute it may have levied on religious spiritualities), represents the refined essence of political modernity. Its significance lies in the fact that it confronts us with an experiment in human freedom which has consciously or unconsciously been based on a denial or a disregard of the essential Christian contribution to human freedom, which is the theorem of the freedom of the Church.

III

We come now to the uneasiness stirring in the world of post-modern man, and in his soul too. The first may be quickly run over, although it is most profoundly serious. I mean all the uneasiness aroused by our confrontation with international Communism. Communism is, of course, political modernity carried to its logical conclusion. All that is implicit and unintentional in modernity as a phenomenon in what is called the West has become explicit and deliberate in the Communist system. The "secular hypothesis," in Hocking's phrase, has been lifted to the status of a dogma. And Hobbes' prohibition has seen most vicious enforcement; man is not allowed to "see double and mistake his lawful sovereign." The operations of the Communist system would seem to offer an empirical demonstration of the fact that there can be no freedom or justice where God is denied and where everything meant by the freedom of the Church is deliberately excised from the theorem on which the life of the community is based.

The measure of human malaise within the Communist orbit cannot be estimated accurately. In any case, the malaise cannot be geographically contained. Stress and distress are the condition of the whole world. And we ourselves feel them, or at least should feel them, most sharply in the form of the question, whether we are spiritually and intellectually equipped to meet the communist threat at its deepest level.

Communism in theory and in practice has reversed the revolution which Christianity initiated by the Gelasian doctrine: "Two there are by which this world is ruled." This new system has proposed with all logic an alternative to the basic structure of society, and a surrogate of society's spiritual substance, as these are defined in the Christian theorem. And the question is, whether there are in the spirit of modernity as such the resources whereby the Christian revolution, with all its hopes of freedom and justice, can be reinstated in its course, and the reactionary counterrevolution halted. The issue is clear enough; two contrary views of the structure of reality are in conflict. And the issue is certainly basic—too basic to be solved either by military measures or by political techniques. Free elections, for instance, have their value. But of themselves they leave untouched the basic issue, which is joined between the clashing assertions: "Two there are," and "One there is."

The second post-modern uneasiness derives from the current experience of the "impotence of the state." Here I adopt Hocking's phrase and the thesis it states, as developed in the first part of his book, already cited. (With certain of his subsequent analyses and theses, and with their Gnostic overtones, I have serious difficulties.) The net of it is that the modern state has, as a matter of empirical fact, proved impotent to do all the things it has undertaken to do. Crime and civic virtue, education, the stimulus and control of economic processes, public morality, justice in the order and processes of law—over all these things the modern state assumed an unshared competence. But it has proved itself incompetent in a fundamental sense. The reason is that "the state depends for its vitality upon a motivation which it cannot by itself command." As long as this motivation can be assumed to be existent in the body politic, the order of politics (in the broadest sense) moves with some security to its proper ends. But if the motivation fails, there is no power in the state itself to evoke it.

We confront again the dilemma which modernity resolved in its own sense. Is the life of man to be organized in one society, or in two? Modernity chose the unitary hypothesis, that the state itself is the highest form of human association, self-ruled, and self-contained, and self-motivating. But the unitary hypothesis has not been able to sustain itself under the test of experience. Post-modern man has become most uneasily aware of the limitations of the state even in the discharge of its own functions.

The challenge here is to the validity of the suprapolitical tenet upon which modernity staked the whole success of its political experiment. This tenet, I said, was that the individual conscience is the sole ultimate interpreter of the moral order (and of the religious order, too), and therefore the sole authentic mediator of moral imperatives to the political order. But the truth of this tenet, confidently assumed by modernity, is now under challenge from a battery of questions.

Is the failure of motivation within the state somehow due to the falsity of this tenet? Is the pragmatic law in operation—that whatever is not true will somewhere fail to work? Or again, is the individual conscience, in modernity's conception of it, equal to the burden that has been thrust upon it—the burden of being the keystone of the modern experiment in freedom? Is it disintegrating under the burden? If so, what of the free society which it undertook to sustain? Will it perhaps disintegrate in one or other of the two ways in which a political structure can disintegrate—into a formless chaos or

into a false order? Will the modern experiment then prove to be simply an interlude between despotisms—between the known and limited despotisms of the past, and the unknown depotisms of the future, which may well be illimitable? In a word, in consequence of having been enthroned as the One Ruler of this world, has the *conscientia exlex* of modernity succumbed to *hubris*, and is it therefore headed for downfall—its own downfall, the downfall of the concept of the moral order amid the bits and pieces of a purely "situational" ethics, and the downfall of the political order projected by the spirit of modernity?

From another point of view the same questions return. It was an essential part of modernity's hope that the moral consensus upon which every society depends for its stability and progress could be sustained and mobilized simply in terms of a fortunate coincidence of individual private judgments, apart from all reference to a visibly constituted spiritual and moral authority. Has this hope proved valid? Is it perhaps possible that the profound intellectual confusions in the mind of post-modern man, which make necessary today a conference on the essentials of freedom, are somehow witness to the fact that modernity's hope has proved to be hollow? If there be no consensus with regard to what freedom is, and whence it comes, and what it means within the very soul of man, how shall freedom hope to live within society and in its institutions?

There is a final malaise upon which I should touch. It is, I think, related to the fundamental ambiguity of modern times. Modernity, I said, rejected the freedom of the Church, in the twofold sense explained, as the armature of man's spiritual freedom and as a structural principle, of a free society. Initially the rejection was addressed only to a truth of divine revelation. The whole system of moral values, both individual and social, which had been elaborated under the influence of the Christian revelation was not rejected. I mean here all the values which form a constellation about the central concept, *res sacra homo*. As a matter of fact, these values are adopted as the very basis for the modern political experiment. Modernity, however, has maintained that these values are now known to be simply immanent in man; that man has become conscious of them in the course of their emergence in historical experience; and that, whatever may have been the influence of the Christian revelation on the earlier phases of this experience, these values are now simply a human possession, a conquest and an achievement of humanity by man himself. Now that I have arrived, said modernity, Christianity may disappear. Whatever aesthetic appeal it may still retain as a myth, it is not needed as a dynamic of freedom and justice in this world. *Res sacra homo* is now under a new patronage—singly his own.

This is what Romano Guardini has expressively called the "interior disloyalty of modern times." He means, I think, that there has occurred not only a falsification of history but a basic betrayal of the existential structure of reality itself. If this be true, we are confronted by the gravest issue presented by the whole experiment of modernity. The issue again is one of truth. Upon this issue hangs the whole fate of freedom and justice, if only for the pragmatic reason already advanced, that the structure of reality cannot with impunity be disregarded, even less by society than by the individual.

It will perhaps be sufficient if I simply present the issue as I see it, without undertaking to argue it. Here are its terms. On the one hand, modernity has denied (or ignored, or forgotten, or neglected) the Christian revelation that man is a sacredness, and that his primatial *res sacra*, his freedom, is sought and found ultimately within the freedom of the Church. On the other hand, modernity has pretended to lay claim to the effects of this doctrine on the order of human culture—the essential effect, for our purposes here, being the imperative laid on John of Salisbury's "king" (say, if you will, the state in all its range of action) to fight for justice and for the freedom of the people. In terms of this denial (or ignorance) and of this pretension (or hypothesis) modernity has conceived its image of political man. Justice is his due, and his function, too; but not on the title of his sacredness as revealed by Christ. Freedom is his endowment, and likewise his duty; but not on the title of the freedom of the Church. A fully human life is his destiny; but its fulfillment lies within the horizons of time and space.

The question is, whether this modern image of political man be a reflection of reality (historical, philosophical, theological), or a mirage projected by prideful human reason into the *terra aliena* of a greatly ignorant illusion. Undoubtedly, this question will be answered by history, in which the pragmatic law operates. But it would be well, if possible, to anticipate the operation of this law by embarking upon a "new work of thought, begetting an altered premise."

In any case, the sheerly historical alternatives are clear enough. I shall state them in their extremity, using the method of assertion, not of interrogation.

On the one hand, post-modern man can continue to pursue the mirage which bemused modern man. As he does so, a spiritual vacuum will increasingly be created at the heart of human existence. But this vacuity cannot remain uninhabited. It will be like the house in the Gospel, swept and garnished, its vacancy an invitation to what the Gospel expressively calls the "worthless spirit" (*spiritus ne-*

quam). He then will enter in with seven spirits more worthless than himself, and there set about the work that befits his character. He is the Son of Chaos and Old Night; his work is to turn vacuity into chaos.

Less figuratively, if post-modern man, like modern man, rejects the Christian mode of existence, the result will be that an explicitly non-Christian mode of existence will progressively come into being at the heart of human life. It will have its own structure and its own substance. And since it exists, it must manifest its existence and its dynamism. And it will do so—in violence, in all the violence of the chaotic. Violence is the mark of the Architect of Chaos, the Evil One, whose presence in the world is part of the structure of the world. It is not by chance that the mark of violence should have been impressed so deeply on these closing decades of the modern era, and that the threat of violence should hang so heavily over post-modern man as he takes his first uncertain steps into the new era. It was Nietzsche, I think, who said that the non-Christian man of modern times had not yet fully realized what it means to be non-Christian. But in these last decades the realization has been dawning, as we have watched the frightening emergence and multiplication of that "senseless, faithless, heartless, ruthless" man whom Paul met on the streets of non-Christian Corinth and described in his Letter to the Romans.

This development, into a dreadful chaos of violence in which justice and freedom alike would vanish, is not inevitable. An alternative is possible. The way to it lies through a renunciation by post-modern man of the "interior disloyalty of modern times." Thus the new era would have a new promise on which to pursue the experiment in freedom and justice which political society perennially is. However, I must quickly add that this renunciation is not a political act. If one accepts the doctrine of the Second Council of Orange (A.D. 529) it is the work of the Holy Spirit, who "corrects the will of man from the infidelity unto faith."

Nevertheless, the "new work of thought" to which post-modern man is impelled as he reflects on the increasing fragility of the "secular hypothesis" will not be irrelevant to the fortunes of the future. If only we do not deny our malaises or seek to drown them, the experience of them can be turned to rational account. It is, after all, not beyond the power of reason to recognize illusion when the results of illusion are encountered in experience. Hence reason itself, and its high exercise in argument, could lead us to the recognition of a law, even more basic than the pragmatic law, which our forebears of the modern era most seriously failed to reckon with. It is the law of reality itself: "Only that ought not to be which cannot be." This perhaps would be the altered premise—a rational premise—that a new work of thought might beget.

[I, Fall 1957, 134–145]

[41]

Political Theory:
The Place of Christianity

JAMES V. SCHALL, S.J.

James V. Schall, S.J. (1928–   ) has been contributing to Modern Age *since the Spring 1960 issue, when he was a Jesuit scholastic completing his doctoral dissertation on "Immortality and the Foundations of Political Theory" at Georgetown University. A member of the California Province of the Society of Jesus, he also teaches political theory at Georgetown. Among his recent books are* Liberation Theology *(1982),* The Distinctiveness of Christianity *(1983), and* The Politics of Heaven and Hell *(1984).*

IN AN ESSAY on "Teaching History to the Rising Generation," Russell Kirk told of the textbook his daughter was assigned in the sixth grade of a Roman Catholic grammar school. "In the whole of the textbook there is no mention of Christianity or Christ, no mention of Catholicism or of any other Christian or Jewish persuasion . . . . One is left to conclude that none of (the) large (historical) themes has been influenced by religion in any way."[1] The question can also be asked quite naturally at a higher educational level and not only in a parochial environment: Is the treatment of Christianity much better at the university level, and this not merely in history? In particular, is the academic discipline of political theory, with its various conferences, journals, departments, and curricula so designed in practice that it can be presented as if Christianity did not and does not exist? Anyone familiar with the field, no doubt, will suspect that

the latter is largely the case. Christianity is not in practice seen to be connected with the core integrity of the discipline itself. At most, it is a marginal theoretic issue, of some importance in certain past eras, quite often with harmful results. There is, it would seem, some need to state the opposite position, at least for the sake of argument, namely, that political philosophy cannot be fully itself without understanding the relationship of Christianity to its premises and contents. The relative neglect of Christianity must, then, itself be accounted for.

"Too much politics, like too much education, is a sign of social decline," V. A. Demant wrote in his essay "The Theology of Politics." "The temptation of the natural man is to seek one unifying principle short of God. This is sought in some immanent fact of the natural and historic process."[2] Politics remains the most natural and human substitute for God, since

495

politics is, in its own right, a "unifying principle." This is why, intrinsic to itself, political theory requires a reason to be limited and *self*-limiting. The essential contribution of theology to political theory is, on this basis, philosophical. That is, by locating ultimate being outside of the legitimate tasks open to mankind to accomplish by its own efforts, theology at its best prevents political theory from becoming its own metaphysics, prevents it from being, again in Demant's words, "some immanent fact of the natural and historical process." For metaphysics, however it be called, is a discipline that presumes, on its own grounds, to account for all being—all natural and historical being, itself implicitly identified with *that which is*.[3] When this latter effort appears under the guise of political theory, it limits total reality to that which appears under the methodological processes available to the study of politics.

Without the transcendent, however, politics has no intrinsic limits, since in itself, it is, properly, the highest of the practical sciences, as both Aristotle and Aquinas held. Without a theoretic limit, politics naturally tends to become absolute, a discipline designed to place everything under its scope. On the other hand, an authentic political theory will be, even in its sense of its own reality, essentially "self"-limiting, to the extent it realizes that the whole of being and reality is *not* to be identified with that aspect of reality which is human, which deals with man as precisely "the mortal," as Hannah Arendt used to say.[4] In this connection, then, we are able to suggest that to explore political theory is first to examine its natural and also extrinsic limits. The import of this position can clearly be sensed if we recall the traditional idea that theology was the "queen of the sciences." We should not, then, easily pass over what Professor Leo Strauss wrote at the beginning of his *The City and Man*:

It is not sufficient for everyone to obey and to listen to the Divine Message of the City of Righteousness, the Faithful City. In order to propagate that message among the heathen, nay, in order to understand it as clearly and as fully as is humanly possible, one must consider to what extent man could discover the outlines of that city if left to himself, to the proper exercise of his own powers. But in our age it is much less urgent to show that political philosophy is the indispensable handmaiden of theology than to show that political philosophy is the rightful queen of the social sciences, the sciences of man and of his affairs.[5]

Whether, some twenty years later, the urgency is still in the direction Professor Strauss suggested, can be questioned. But anyone familiar with the central line of Western tradition will immediately recognize in his reflections themes from Aristotle and Augustine, Plato and Aquinas.

Yet, it is safe to say that few Christian thinkers have recognized the enormous implications to theology contained in Leo Strauss' monumental works.[6] For his subtle argument was to ask about the limits of the "queen of the social sciences," political philosophy itself, in order to allow a space for revelation or at least its possibility. He understood, in other words, that even on its own grounds, political theory could not account for everything that guided and influenced nature and man. Hence, in urging political philosophers to "discover the outlines of that City if left" to themselves, Strauss recognized that self-limitation was the natural consequence in a discipline that was not itself a true metaphysics. This both legitimated the enterprise of political theory itself, with its own relative autonomy, what the Christians called, "rendering to Caesar," while not requiring political philosophy to explain precisely everything, *all that is*, a task proper to man, even though not a political task. This is why Aristotle said that even the little we could know of the divine things was worth all our efforts, even though politics was "proper" only to man.[7] In de-emphasizing the "handmaiden" relationship, Strauss evidently made a place for the same function within the discipline of political philosophy itself, or at least tried to.

Political theory, for its part, has also something very basic to say to contemporary theology and religion. From the ordinary viewpoint of the political theorist, theology seems presently to state its case before the world precisely in political terms and guises, yet with few of the limits to which political reflection, at its best, is subjected. This makes theology seem more and more unreal, even naive. It often advocates lethal policies in the name of "justice" without ever even suspecting where political things actually go, without ever having heard of the chapters in Plato and Aristotle on the decline of states. Today, it is not the theologian who complains about the encroachment of politics, but rather, the political theorist, surveying what is purported to be theological reflection, who wonders if theology has anything at all to say other than the political, a political that seems but a determined image of contemporary ideology. The curricula of theology or religion departments and seminaries often vaguely parallel those of government departments, with little clear notion of any differences in content or procedure. From the viewpoint of academic political theory, then, the major encroachment today is not from the political to the theological, but, particularly in the area of economics and development and "rights," in the founding and rule of the new and poorer nations, from the theological to the political. Theology almost seems to have admitted that politics is indeed an autonomous metaphysics, contrary to the tradition of Aristotle and Aquinas.[8] Today, there are priests who want to become politicians (even after the papal decree to the contrary).[9] In the Christian tradition, however, as in the case of Ambrose of Milan, it was the politicians who became bishops and priests. The hierarchy of value was reversed.

What political philosophy has to tell religion, then, is the grounded estimate, based on judgment, experience, and law, of what can be expected in terms of virtue and practice from the generality of mankind as each person exists in a given culture. Ironically, this is what religion used to tell politics, before religion began to claim for itself the advocacy of the ideal human good, as it has tended to do more and more in conformity with modern revolutionary utopias, especially Marxism.[10] To deny that men can always be "better" is, therefore, as "un-Christian" as to expect them actually to produce the Kingdom of God on earth.[11] "We can hardly measure what the modern doctrine of individualism must owe to the Christian belief that men are spiritual beings, born for eternity, and having a value incommensurate with anything else in the created universe," the great Protestant historian, Professor Herbert Butterfield, wrote in his essay on "Christianity and Politics."[12] But, as he went on to suggest, the doctrine of universal sin, with particular attention to one's own sinfulness, was designed precisely "to be a serious check on the many evils and mistakes in politics." Likewise, G. K. Chesterton, in his still even more formidable *Orthodoxy*, found the political connected with this doctrine: "Christianity is the only thing left that has any real right to question the power of the well-nurtured or the well-bred. . . . If we wish to pull down the prosperous oppressor we cannot do it with the new doctrine of human perfectibility; we can only do it with the old doctrine of Original Sin."[13] Only if *all* men and women are sinners can we realize that our governments, composed as they likewise are of these same men and women, must be designed to prevent these same people who actually rule us, even with our own advice and consent, from also abusing us.

Thus, by itself, politics could not know how valuable each person really was. All it could do is to project, with a Professor Rawls, that we all must be important because we all would, with various veils of ignorance, project the same fate for ourselves. Yet, not by itself could politics know and account for the depths of evil and disorder that are operative and to be somehow expected among men. The holocausts we describe and acknowledge do not prevent their repetition among us. They only guarantee that the destiny of the sufferers cannot be finally accounted for by politics alone. The saint, Aquinas remarked, is above the law, because he observes the law, knows it, whereas the politician must account for the majority of us who are not saints.[14] The politician who does not understand how men can abuse one another, who does not believe that holocaust is *possible*, is simultaneously a bad politician *and* a bad theologian. He does not know how to rule because he does not know what to expect.[15] Thus, when once the truth of the value of each person *and* his concrete sinfulness is comprehended, it becomes the legitimate task of politics to account for their realities within the political realm, to account for the absolute dignity and for the possibility of mass political destruction and the more frequent lesser evils.[16] This is why, then, that politics ultimately does have something to teach theology even about itself. For it is the politician who must confront men also in their sinfulness, however it be called, while leaving a real space for their virtue, a space that does not "coerce" a particular definition of goodness on men. The politician must seek a "common good" even among the less than perfect, the kind of people Aquinas held to be the primary objects of civil law.[17] The task of political theory, as Plato had already in-

timated in *The Republic*, the first book of the discipline, is to find a place for the Good that transcends the ordinary political experience of the normalcy of men. Specifically Christian political theory begins with the Incarnation, with Augustine's realization that the Good, happiness, was indeed a necessary aspect of human reflection and endeavor, but that its fullness was not proper to this world, not achievable by human, particularly political, means.

In his still perceptive essay, "St. Augustine and His Age," the Catholic historian, Christopher Dawson, pointed out why the reality of transcendence, the dignity of the person, and the persistence of evil and sin—each a foundation of politics and of what is *beyond* politics—can become the basis of a new kind of social order that results from the effect of the Christian stimulus in the world. "In the West, however," Dawson wrote, "St. Augustine broke decisively with this tradition by depriving the state of its aura of divinity and seeking the principle of social order in the human will. In this way, the Augustinian theory, for all its otherworldliness, first made possible the ideal of a social order resting upon the free personality and a common effort towards moral ends."[18] This idea that the social order was to be based upon the dignity of individual persons, who had the capacity to "will"—the philosophical discovery the late Professor Hannah Arendt in her *The Life of the Mind* attributed directly to Christianity—this capacity to direct human actions to moral or immoral ends even within the political order, seemed to make political theory free from any scientific determinism, even from sociology or psychology.[19] The "causes" of social disorder or progress, therefore, had to be located in the vices or virtues, in the various definitions men gave to the actual existential happiness which they individually sought, choices eventually reflected, as Aristotle knew in the First Book of his *Ethics*, in the forms of government described in *The Politics*.[20]

"Value-free" political theory, consequently, as Professor Strauss and Professor Voegelin were quick to note in famous studies, explained everything but politics and that which transcended it.[21] The late E. F. Schumacher, in his remarkable *A Guide for the Perplexed*, was thus mostly correct in his observation that "The modern experiment to live without religion has failed, and once we have understood this, we know what our 'post-modern' tasks really are."[22] The post-modern endeavor for political theory is, consequently, precisely the rediscovery of specifically Christian political theory, a theory which does not, when it is itself, allow politics to become effectively a secular religion or substitute metaphysics, as it has, in effect, tended to become in the recent past, particularly in academic political theory. This would, likewise, be a theory that does not allow theology to destroy the things of Caesar.

There is, then, rather much truth in the ironical remark of Father Robert Sokolowski, Professor of Philosophy at Catholic University, when he remarked: "Perhaps we can say Christians forget that justice is a reflection of the image of the good and not the good itself. It is curious that Christians look for the divine in social order at a time when the social order itself has so much of the inhuman in it."[23] The rapid legalization of what were called in classical natural law theory properly "vices" has made it more and more imperative that political theory retain its principled foothold in theology and metaphysics, in a source that would prevent it from completing Machiavelli's modern project of identifying absolutely what men do with what they ought to do. The public order is more than ever being arranged so that we be not allowed to state the "untruth" of the laws and practices we have enacted against the classical norms.

"To speak knowingly the truth, among prudent and dear men, about what is greatest and dear, is a thing that is safe and encouraging." (#450) Such penetrating words of Socrates in the Fifth Book of *The Republic*, of course, are very circumspect. For the number of "prudent and dear men," among whom Socrates felt himself to be discussing where political thought ultimately led, is indeed too few. When, however, this same truth is spoken among the multitudes, it can be quite dangerous, as Socrates himself soon was to find out. Realization of this very danger was the background of Professor Strauss' emphasis on "secret writing," about what he called "persecution and the art of writing."[24] The social sciences had to search their own limits because, if men suspected such limits led to or arose from revelation, they would, perhaps stubbornly, refuse the search for the truth. This is why it is no accident that both Paul VI in his Vatican II Document on Religious Liberty (1965) and John Paul II, in his address to the United Nations (October 2, 1979), took special and careful pains, from the side of religion, to insist precisely upon the obligation of each person in himself not merely to pursue but to accept the truth on its own grounds, even the truth of revelation if it persuades. Truth may indeed make us free, but, as Solzhenitsyn and Strauss knew, it may also lead to persecution and tyranny by its rejection. The truth of political theory, from the viewpoint of the truth of original sin, may indeed lead to what does happen in actual political experience, to persecution of the just and the honest *because* they are just and honest. Man, in other words, always retains will as well as intellect.

The suspicion that the truth of political theory was bound up with the truth of metaphysics and revelation, then, has been

500 JAMES V. SCHALL, S.J.

the guiding principle of Western political theory—Christian, Jewish, and Muslim—until the modern era, until what the textbooks call, from Machiavelli, "modern" political theory.[25] The modern theoretical project, however, the one that now normally dominates the discipline, is based upon the intellectual "autonomy" of political theory. This means that the discipline contains within itself not only an historical *canon*, as Professor Pocock called it, a baker's dozen of basic authors from Plato to Augustine to Hobbes, Locke, Rousseau, and Mill, through which political theory is understood, but also a methodology and independent ground which is self-explanatory and self-justifying.[26] The extreme position was meant to be something quite different from Aristotle's notion of a "practical science," as he developed it in the Sixth Book of *The Ethics*. It is different because, for Aristotle, the ends of the practical sciences were found in the metaphysical order.[27] Man did not "make" himself to be man, as Aristotle said, so that politics presupposed what made man to be man. Man's relation to himself, in other words, was not primarily one of self-making, but of self-discovery. And we can, properly, only "discover" what we ourselves do not make. Political theory appears in most academic and scholarly programs as the "history" of political theory, even though Professor Strauss warned that political philosophy ought not to be confused with the *history* of political thought.[28] Usually, political theory will be divided into the following categories: classical Greek and Roman; Jewish–early Christian–Roman Empire; Feudal and Christian Medieval; Modern, and 20th Century. However, the same enterprise can be divided in another fashion, according to the themes of "The Great Political Thinkers." The narrative histories of Professor Sabine or the more recent work of Professor Sibley would fill

in the gaps of practice and theory for the less than "great."[29]

A third approach not infrequently used would be the "isms" analysis, as, for example, that used by the late Professor Ebenstein.[30] Here, attention would be paid rather to a single doctrine or ideology with its contents and problems. We would find in such an approach treatments of capitalism, democracy, communism, nazism, fascism, socialism, nationalism, behaviorism, corporatism, authoritarianism, anarchism, internationalism, and, perhaps, "developmentism," in the various offshoots of Professor Rostow's now famous pioneer thesis about the "five states" of economic growth.[31] Finally, not a few endeavors would like to exorcise altogether the "history" of political theory to replace it with some procedure subject to "verifiable," scientific tools. In this way, political theory would, presumably, declare its independence from the tyranny of the past, of revelation, of metaphysics, even of history.[32]

In recent years, in most academic programs and official political science journals and associations, even in professedly "Christian" universities, a distinct intellectual "silence" has existed about the content and philosophical import of Christianity in political thought and affairs. One need only to inquire of even good undergraduate classes—it is little better in graduate classes—about the identity of the Good Samaritan or the precise meaning of the Incarnation, Original Sin or the "City of God," all the common fare of the West for centuries and centuries, to realize that the terms of shared discourse are no longer readily available in the general academic community.[33] Official political science journals will too often—there are exceptions—return essays on formal Christian political theory and its implications in the discipline with the polite suggestion that they would be more "fitting" for perhaps theological journals. (And, alas, the quality of political discourse in the theological journals is often appalling.) We no longer suspect that William of Occam, for example, in his analysis of the divine freedom, might have had something to do with the absoluteness of later, more modern political theory.[34] We do not see why the denial of the divinity of Christ is related to salvific ethos in much modern ideology.[35]

This severing of much connection of political theory from religion and theology, this studied "reductionism," however, has unfortunately served to separate them precisely at a moment when religion, under the curious aegis of "liberation theology," is gaining an unprecedented political influence.[36] One has only to glance at the average weekly religious magazine, Protestant or Catholic, or diocesan newspaper, to realize that the major drift is political.[37] Political theorists, for their part, find themselves ill-equipped to handle the political overtones of the murder in a Central American Cathedral of an archbishop or the elevation of a revolutionary priest to the Office of Foreign Affairs, or why it is not "illiberal" for the Roman Pope in Brazil to exclude the clergy from politics. Moreover, this self-isolation of political theory, the result of its own modernist methodology, is itself in part responsible for the radicalization of theology because this latter discipline almost never receives the sobering wind of analysis that ought to come from political theory at its best about what we might expect of men in the world.[38] Thus, contemporary theologians, when it comes to politics, too often are the successors of the Dr. Price who so incensed Edmund Burke in his *Reflections on the Revolution in France*: "It is somewhat remarkable that this Reverend Divine should be so earnest for setting up new churches, and so perfectly indifferent concerning the doctrine

which may be taught in them." [39] Today's divines are equally earnest, though not equally unconcerned about the direction of the doctrines they espouse. Only today, they are concerned not with setting up new churches, but new governments and nations. Rendering to Caesar has become, paradoxically, a clerical occupation, or at least a clerical ambition, as the cynics have always suspected it would.

Ironically, then, the classical roles are almost reversed, so that religion lacks the "realism" once expected of it, that source of sensibility Reinhold Niebuhr once found in Augustine.[40] The doctrine of the Fall did have political consequences in the very areas of property, coercive government, and labor, areas so related to modern theory and ideology.[41] Political theory, on the other hand, appears unable to articulate a coherent version of man or common good that would permit "the political" to be less than a substitute metaphysics, as it has become implicitly in so much contemporary theory. This would seem to suggest that, even for its own health, political theory must have addressed to it certain basic ideas and religious affirmations that force and convince politics to limit itself to its own proper sphere.[42] Likewise, religion will not long remain balanced if the experience of politics is not included as a basic element in the analysis of how religion impacts on the world, how human dignity is to be defended. The very nature of man's intellect does, in classical reflection, give him a real source for political knowledge.[43] "It may be accepting a miracle to believe in free will," G. K. Chesterton wrote in *The Well and the Shallows*,

but it is accepting madness, sooner or later, to disbelieve it. It may be a wild risk to take a vow, but it is quiet, crawling and inevitable ruin to refuse to make a vow. It may be incredible that one creed is the truth and others are relatively false; but it is not only incredible, but also intolerable, that there is no truth either in or out of creeds, and, all are equally false.[44]

The "miracles," "the wild risks," and the "incredibilities," which arise from a Western tradition that includes, to be itself, both faith and reason, seem precisely those innovations that allow us to keep our politics sane and sensible.[45]

This, ultimately, is why Christianity cannot be avoided, along with the Old Testament, in the study of political theory, why religion needs to acknowledge that Caesar is to be rendered unto, within limits, to be sure.[46] This is why, too, the most remarkable part of Christ's famous distinction was not that God was before Caesar, but that Caesar did have a place by right. In limiting politics, Christianity limited religion.[47] Christian political theory is the intellectual limitation of the political precisely by removing from Caesar what is not his. In Aristotelian terms, this leaves the "highest of the practical sciences," the "queen of the social sciences," to be what it is. The "Divine Message of the City of Righteousness, the Faithful City," then, ought to be sought, even listened to by political theory, for that is part of its discovery of itself. This is the place of Christianity in political theory, and the place of political theory in Christianity.

NOTES

[1] Kirk, *Educational Update*, Winter, 1980.

[2] V. A. Demant, *Theology of Society*, London, 1947, p. 218.

[3] J. M. Bochenski, *Philosophy—an Introduction*, New York, 1972.

[4] Hannah Arendt, *The Human Condition*, 1959, p. 19.

[5] Leo Strauss, *The City and Man*, 1964, p. 1.

[6] Cf. J. Steintrager, "Political Philosophy, Political Theology, and Morality," *The Thomist*, July, 1968; Charles N. R. McCoy, *The Structure of Political Thought*,

New York, 1963; D. Lowenthal, "The Case for Teleology," *The Independent Journal of Philosophy*, 1978.

[7] Aristotle, 981b25-983b29; 11412a31.

[8] J. Schall, "The Recovery of Metaphysics," *Divinitas*, #2, 1979.

[9] Address of January 28, 1979.

[10] Cf. R. Heckel, *The Theme of Liberation*, Rome, Pontifical Commission on Justice and Peace, 1980.

[11] Cf. J. Schall, "From 'Catholic Social Doctrine' to the 'Kingdom of God' on Earth," *Communio*, Winter, 1976.

[12] *Herbert Butterfield: Writings on Christianity and History*, 1979, p. 44.

[13] G. K. Chesterton, *Orthodoxy*, 1908, pp. 116, 141.

[14] Aquinas, I-II, 96, 2; 96, 5.

[15] Cf. J. Kirkpatrick, "Dictatorships and Double Standards," *Commentary*, November, 1979.

[16] Cf. J. Schall, "Displacing Damnation: On the Neglect of Hell in Political Theory," *The Thomist*, January, 1980.

[17] Aquinas, I-II, 96, 2.

[18] C. Dawson, in *St. Augustine*, New York, 1957, p. 77; cf. also J. East, "The Political Relevance of St. Augustine," *Modern Age*, Spring, 1972; H. Deane, *The Political and Social Ideas of St. Augustine*, New York, 1963.

[19] H. Arendt, *The Life of the Mind*, New York, 1978, Vol. II, *Willing*; V. Bourke, *Will in Western Thought*, Chicago, 1955.

[20] Cf. J. Schall, "The Best Form of Government," *The Review of Politics*, January, 1978.

[21] Cf. L. Strauss, *Natural Right and History*, Chicago, 1950; E. Voegelin, *The New Science of Politics*, Chicago, 1952.

[22] E. F. Schumacher, *A Guide for the Perplexed*, New York, 1977, p. 139.

[23] R. Sokolowski, Letter to the Author, 1979.

[24] L. Strauss, *Persecution and the Art of Writing*, Glencoe, 1952.

[25] Lerner and Mahdi, *Medieval Political Philosophy*, Ithaca, 1972; L. Strauss, *Thoughts on Machiavelli*, Chicago, 1958; McCoy, *ibid.*

[26] J. Pocock, *Politics, Language, and Time*, New York, 1973, pp. 5–15.

[27] McCoy, *ibid.*, pp. 29–60; E. Midgley, "Concerning the Modernist Subversion of Political Philosophy," *The New Scholasticism*, Spring, 1979.

[28] Strauss, *City, ibid.*, p. 8; Pocock, *ibid.*, R. Dahl, *Modern Political Analysis*, Englewood Cliffs, 1976.

[29] Cf. G. Sabine, *A History of Political Theory*, New York, 1963; M. Sibley, *Political Ideas and Ideologies*, New York, 1970; Foster and Jones, *Masters of Political Thought*, Boston, 1957; Elliot and McDonald, *Western Political Heritage*, Englewood Cliffs, 1957; L. McDonald, *Western Political Theory*, New York, 1968.

[30] W. Ebenstein, *Today's Isms*, Englewood Cliffs, 1973.

[31] W. Rostow, *The Stages of Economic Growth*, London, 1960.

[32] Cf. H. Eulau, *The Behavioral Persuasion in Politics*, New York, 1963.

[33] Cf. J. Schall, "On the Teaching of Ancient and Medieval Political Theory," *Modern Age,* Spring, 1975.

[34] Cf. J. Pieper, *Scholasticism*, New York, 1964.

[35] Cf. "Neomarxistisches Jesusbild," *Stimmen der Zeit*, März, 1980.

[36] Cf. M. Dodson, "Prophetic Politics & Political Theory in Latin America," *Polity,* Spring, 1980; Cf. also M. Novak, *The Theology of Democratic Capitalism*, forthcoming.

[37] Cf. E. Norman, *Christianity and the World Order*, New York, 1979; J. Ellul, *The Betrayal of the West*, New York, 1978; E. Lefever, *Amsterdam to Nairobi: The World Council of Churches and the Third World*, Washington, 1978; J. Hitchcock, *Catholicism and Modernity*, New York, 1979.

[38] Cf. M. Novak, "The Politics of John Paul II," *Commentary*, December, 1979; Graham and Carey, *The Post-Behavioral Era*, New York, 1972; Gould and Thursby, *Contemporary Political Thought*, New York, 1969.

[39] E. Burke, *Reflections on the Revolution in France*, Chicago, 1955, p. 24.

[40] R. Niebuhr, in *Perspectives on Political Philosophy*, New York, 1971, (1953), V. I, pp. 243–57.

[11] Cf. J. Schall, "Political Theory and Political Theology," *Laval Théologique et Philosophique*, Février, 1975.

[12] Cf. F. Wilhelmsen, *Christianity and Political Philosophy*, Athens, GA., 1978; H. Jaffa, *Thomism and Aristotelianism*, Westport, CT., 1952 (1979).

[13] Cf. J. Maritain, *The Social and Political Philosophy of Jacques Maritain*, South Bend, IN., 1955 (1973); J. Pieper, *The Silence of St. Thomas*, Chicago, 1957; E. Schumacher, *ibid.*

[14] G. K. Chesterton, *The Well and the Shallows*, New York, 1937, p. 82.

[15] Cf. E. Gilson, *Reason and Revelation in the Middle Ages*, New York, 1938 (1966); Pieper, *Scholasticism, ibid.*, and *Silence, ibid.*; M. de Wulf, *Philosophy and Civilization in the Middle Ages*, New York, 1922 (1953); C. Cochrane, *Christianity and Classical Culture*, New York, 1940 (1977); C. Dawson, *Religion and the Rise of Western Culture*, Garden City, 1958; G. Meilaender, *The Taste for the Other: The Social and Ethical Ideas of C. S. Lewis*, Grand Rapids, MI., 1978; McCoy, *ibid.*; J. Senior, *The Death of Christian Culture*, New Rochelle, NY, 1978; J. Schall, "The Recovery of Metaphysics," *ibid.*

[16] Cf. J. Schall, "The Old Testament and Political Theory," *The Homiletic and Pastoral Review*, November, 1979.

[17] Cf. J. Schall, "The Death of Christ and Political Theory," *Worldview*, March, 1978.

[XXV, Winter 1981, 26–33]

[42]

Faith and Reason

FREDERICK D. WILHELMSEN

Frederick D. Wilhelmsen (1923–　　) has contributed to Modern Age *since its first issue. Professor and chairman of the Department of Philosophy and Politics at the University of Dallas, he has taught in Iraq, Spain, and Central and South America and is the author of over ten books, including* The Metaphysics of Love *(1962) and* The War in Man: Media and Machines *(1970). A convert to Roman Catholicism and a biographer of Hilaire Belloc, Wilhelmsen, like T. S. Eliot and Richard M. Weaver, cherishes the idea of a Christian society. He looks back to medieval Christianity to see what is missing in the modern age, lamenting that "We conservatives have lost our kings and our chivalry; our craftsmen are gone, and our peasantry is fast disappearing." In short, he concludes, "We have nothing to offer the world but our vision."*

FAITH DIVORCED FROM REASON is piety crowned and reason divorced from faith is pedantry enthroned. Both proclaim a universal sovereignty and these illegitimate lords challenge one another to a duel to the death—their battleground is the geography of the human spirit. This war has erupted periodically in Western history: Tertullian preached an arrogant faith that reduced reason to sin, and centuries later the same disease broke out as would the pox in the Rhine valley where the "brotherhoods" reproved men who sought wisdom from the schoolmen; the Latin Averroists in the High Middle Ages insinuated into the universities a paganism that flagrantly insulted the conscience of the Latin West and the Averroists countered by insisting that philosophy had nothing to do with religion. Believe with your right hand, my boy! think with your left! be certain that your right knows not what your left is doing!

Some have argued that this split between what we believe and what we think goes back to the Fall of Man. Be that as it may, there is undoubtedly an itch in the human thing to shatter the unity of his own existence and to scatter the fragments of his being to the scavengers of history. The supposed opposition between faith and reason is an instance of this suicidal imitation of Humpty Dumpty. And this supposed opposition has returned to the American academy where it occupies the very highest posts of power in the most prestigious as well as in more modest institutions of higher learning in the nation. Theology is becoming mindless and philosophy is becoming incorporeal. The vacant-mindedness of the former and the insubstantiality of the latter are breeding theological idiocy and philosophical irrelevance. The study of theology has been radically divorced from the great tradition of scholastic philoso-

504

phy and the reading of much scripture substitutes for the recognition of the middle term in a simple piece of reasoning. Much Greek and no logic mark the vast majority of our seminaries today. In the very moment in which theology departments divide the time of their students into pondering biblical texts and espousing the social gospel, philosophy departments increasingly teach their discipline as though Christianity had never happened, as though philosophical discourse grows up in a hothouse university building having little or no intercourse with the world without and practically none with the Western tradition. An alienation from the Christian tradition is a *condition sine qua non* for a doctor's degree in philosophy in most of the universities in this nation supported by the tax money of believing Christians.

But the Thomist ought to be peculiarly wedded to the conviction that faith must not be separated from reason and that reason, at its best, was married to faith. The reflections molding this essay and the reasoning which is its excuse for being are the work of a Thomist who is disturbed to note that faith seems to have abandoned philosophical reasoning and that philosophy seems to have abandoned faith. Being a philosopher, my observations will fall largely upon this latter issue. Some definitions are in order and some reasoning therefrom is imperative. Disorder always involves a scattering of what ought to be knit together in the catalyst of existence. The divorce between faith and reason is disorder: scattering, shattering, smashing. And the office of the philosopher—does not Aristotle teach me this and did not St. Thomas reiterate it in the first sentence of the *Summa Contra Gentiles?*—is to establish order. And there is an order in the lively business constituting the interplay between faith and reason. To that order I now turn, addressing myself initially to the structure of faith

with the hope of elucidating experiencially some verifiable relations between faith and reason.

First, we must ask believers what it means to believe, not only—let us say—in a church but in the word of my neighbor or in the truth of my own civilization. To believe is to assent to the truth of a proposition which is communicated to the believer through its being heard, not seen. Assenting to the being true of some predicate in a subject, the mind assents because moved by the will. Such propositions, primed by the immediacy of experience, are not reducible thereto. I cannot, for example, believe that I face a typewriter as I write these words because that truth is simply evident to me. Were I to doubt the evidence of my senses—in this instance, principally the senses of sight and touch and secondarily the sense of hearing—I would be a candidate for a rest home.

Nor can I believe—if I am a mathematician—that "the angles of a triangle are equal to two right angles": as a mathematician I would know that this conclusion is engendered by synthesizing two previously understood propositions bearing on the definition of triangle and the concept of a parallel line drawn through the apex. I know the truth in question thanks to having produced that conclusion by reasoning.

Belief is neither a judgment of direct experience (nor a judgment reducible to it), nor is belief a conclusion which is the product of reasoning. Assume further, however, that I am a mathematical idiot but otherwise a fairly bright fellow: I am told by a mathematician that "the angles of a triangle are equal to two right angles." I understand the meaning of the proposition but I assent to its being true only because some authority in matters geometrical has communicated that truth to me. I hear the man tell me these things: a fact of experience; I have cogent evidence leading me to conclude that this man is not a fraud but a competent expert in his field: a reasoned fact; I assent, altogether without any doubt, to the truth of what he says about triangles: a matter of belief, a reasonable as opposed to unreasonable belief, but belief nonetheless. In placing my trust in the word of the mathematician, my will has responded to his authority. Belief always involves at least three aspects: (1) an intellectual grasp of the meaning of the terms of a proposition; (2) an assent to the truth of the proposition which is: (3) prompted by a free act. If there be no understanding of the meaning proposed for belief, there is no belief: totally blind belief is a contradiction. If there is evidence of the truth of the proposition presented directly or indirectly in experience; or if there be a movement of the mind concluding to the truth from at least remotely evident premises, there is no belief but rather either experience or reason.

The weight of two thousand years of Christian teaching insists that belief in Jesus Christ as expressed in the historic Creeds is precisely that: belief; faith: hence the symbol of *The* faith and the admonition to "keep the faith." Could I demonstrate the truth of Christianity, as claimed by one enthusiastic Cartesian in the eighteenth century, I would have knowledge, *epistēmē, scientia*. This knowledge would be pleasant to have but I am afraid that it is reserved for another order of things. If I had a direct experience, let us say a mystical rapture, of the risen and glorified Lord, I would not have belief—in any event not at the moment of the experience. In a word: you cannot both simultaneously know or conclude to and believe in the same truth. The word "belief" has been so debased in our time that people can tell us that they "believe" or "do not believe in capital punishment": civilized usage demands that we respond by asking them if they mean that they believe that capital punishment exists or does not exist. "Belief" is not approval: belief is an assent to existence on the testimony of a witness.

Catholic Christianity of the Latin West, after centuries of hesitation and debate, came to conclude that not only is there no contradiction between faith and reason but that both buttress one another. That theology in our time has progressively shaken off reason in the name of a fideistic return to scriptural tradition is a sign of a malaise disturbing the well-being of theology itself. As a philosopher I shall leave that problem to the theologians. I am more interested in the topics clustering around the role of both experience and faith in the exercise of philosophical reasoning. If I have a target towards which I shall be bending and winging arrows from my quiver, that target is the contention that philosophy is a work of rationality foreign to faith. Presuppositionless philosophy is no saint of my devotion and I would be less than candid were I to dissemble my conviction that such an understanding of philosophy not only divorces philosophy from its sources in history but shrivels it into an enterprise utterly boring to men of flesh and blood, as Unamuno might have put it.

Neither faith nor reason can be divorced from experience. My thesis, therefore, stands or falls with my demonstrating the truth that experience is a kind of "middle term" mediating the synthesis of faith and reason in the actual exercise of philosophical thinking.

But what is experience? The Latin "*experior*"—"to try" or "to put to the test," thus Cicero's customary use of the verb; "to measure one's strength with another," "to try in a hostile manner," thus Caesar's more military employment of the verb; "to experience," "to find," thus Livy's understanding of the word, a sense very close to contemporary English usage—comes from "*ex*" and the root "*per*": *exper*, "to come out of" (*ex*) by "going through" (*per*). Hence "*experientia*" in Ciceronian prose means both "trial" and "experiment"; finally, by extension, "knowledge gained by experiment or experience": "*multarum rerum experientia cognitus*"—the line is from Tacitus, but the usage was already Cicero's. In turn, the "*experimentum*" of "experience" indicates the results of the "*experientia*." In the medieval Latin of St. Thomas Aquinas—his usage here seems typical of his time and certainly is typical of the meaning given the term in scholastic Latin throughout the past seven centuries—"*experientia*," while remaining a trial undergone such as a "trial by arms," is more usually understood to be "a trial of learning—through experience"; thus the man of experience is contrasted to the man without experience: "*inexperientia*." When associated with Aristotle's teaching on "the searching intelligence," the "*experimentum*" was understood to be the fruit of repeated experiences which finally yielded intelligibility or meaning. Through trial and error the chef mixes his condiments and relishes, spices, and the rest. Finally, the soup savors for the palate and from that *experimentum* the active intelligence, other conditions being equal, can illuminate the causal structure at work and the chef thus comes up with a recipe. The recipe is *epistēmē* or *scientia* if it includes the "why" of the successful soup. The cause of knowing the cause is the *experimentum*: "*Causa causae est causa causati*." "Trial," originally "trial by arms" or at a court of law in the Latin of Caesar and Cicero, now means "trial and error" in the searching for meaning until the sensibility produces a unified perceptual whole within which the intellect grasps the working of form in matter or, possibly, entelechy or finality in this moving and changing world.

Experience, involving—as it does—man's sensorial marriage with a world whose being is saturated in time and the restlessness of matter, is a "going through" a kaleidoscope of what originally are isolated impressions for the sake of "coming out" with a patterned whole whose symbolic structure can be penetrated intelligently. All men do this in order that they might survive; subsequently, some men do this in order that they might contemplate. So highly did Aristotle value experience that he tells us that he prefers the man of experience who knows no theory to the man of theory who has no experience. Not all the theory in the world about how to swim will substitute for one brief splashing about in a pool. Nonetheless, only the most primitive romanticism would despise theory in favor of experience. Romantic mystification of experience violates experience. Experience is not merely a "going through" (*per*); experience is also a "coming out" (*ex*). I come out of the experienced, the passion underwent or suffered or gloried in, not in the sense of abandoning it, but in the sense of understanding what has happened to me. Experience exists for the sake of cognition: even more, there is no human cognition without experience. Because of these considerations, both Aristotle and Thomas Aquinas insisted that sensation is the first principle of human knowing. But sensation does not know being. Brute animals do not affirm or deny and therefore they are singularly inept at producing civilizations. Human sensation is saturated by mind.

Although our concept of experience could exclude cognition and could be restricted to the immediacy of sensorial life, *à la* Bergson, I think that such a narrowing of the meaning of experience does violence to the subject. In the normal course of a man's life, he is conscious of nothing that precedes cognition or some intellectual penetration of the perceived: were he so conscious, consciousness would precede itself and men would understand before they understood. This Alice in Wonderland Fun House composed of charming "unbirthday birthday parties" belongs to controlled fantasy but not to experience prior to any conscious attempt to control it. Controlled experience objectifies an activity, better yet, a synthesis of activities both sensorial and intellectual, bodily and spiritual. Man quite literally is—as Karl Rahner insists—"Spirit in the World," *Geist in Welt*. If God is pure spirit creating *a* world; if the angels are spirits sent as messengers *to* a world, then man's spirit is constituted *in* a world: man becomes what he is by acting in and through his body. Man's soul is not a motor which pushes a body as though it were a go-cart. The soul is itself an act in and through the body. Again, the doctrine advanced is both Aristotle's and Aquinas', although understood by these two geniuses in their own distinctive ways.

Consciously we are already in a world before we commence to think deep thoughts about this odd situation; indeed, the situation itself does not even begin to seem odd at all until we back away from it and thus separate ourselves from the way in which we exist prior to signing up for Philosophy 101. Signing up for Philosophy 101 is often today signing away our humanity. The trick of the Cartesian and rationalist *cogito* consists in inviting us, often with the threat of an "F" grade, to separate our knowing of X from the X without which our knowing would not be a knowing at all because the knowing is *of* X. Secondly, the rationalist and Cartesian (possibly positivist or phenomenologist) schoolmaster will ask us to separate our knowing (already now separated from the known-X) from ourselves who are doing the knowing. Once this double sleight of hand has been accomplished,

this lonely knowing which is not a knowing of anything or a knowing by anybody converts itself into idealism or criticism or phenomenology or whatever and commences to confer doctoral degrees on I know not whom.

For the overarching purposes of this essay, I offer the following observation: experience escapes both faith and reason in the sense of being prior to both, prior because—although faith and reason can be brought to bear upon experience in an effort at evaluating it—the judgment of experience, itself principiated by sensation and perception, is an ultimate. With ultimates in life we quarrel at the peril of our sanity. Sensation—the pun seems to be worked into the fabric of the language—is the *touch*stone of existence. According to Hilaire Belloc anyone questioning this proposition ought to be baptized with a pint of beer in the name of the five senses.

We reason for the purpose of concluding but we conclude only thanks to something previously understood. There is an exceedingly curious factor about reason which makes it—as an act—as ultimately unjustifiable by anything prior to itself as is experience. I do nothing at all curious or untoward if I ask the reason why the angles of a triangle are equal to two right angles. But I do something very curious and untoward indeed if I ask for a reason for reasoning. Such a presumptive reason would be concluded to by reasoning and we would be presuming to already know what we set out to prove. This cart before the horse situation points to the somewhat alarming truth that there is no reason for reasoning. We reason because we want to and because we must, because of volitional and emotional needs: if I am locked in a room, I think about ways to free myself; if I philosophize to dispel ignorance, I do so because I fear ignorance. An overarching skepticism about the capacity of reason to achieve truth cannot be dispelled rationally. Such skepticism can only be overcome existentially: possibly all absolute skeptics ought to be locked in rooms and told to find the only clue that will free them: this could shake their doubts about reason's capacity to do what reasoning does: conclude. Given in its own way as is experience in its way, reason is an absolute. This is the way we are: reasoning animals.

Experience and reasoning as delineated follow the pattern that Aristotle sketched in describing these ontological structures in the *Posterior Analytics*. But the concept of experience can be broadened to include the whole spatial-temporal world in which man exists. Experience need not be limited to evident judgments made about the here-and-now or reducible to the here-and-now. The continuum of life is woven out of a pattern of immediate judgments, mediated judgments, evident judgments, self-evident judgments, and judgments made in faith or belief. All of this accumulated knowledge constitutes a history, a culture. Understood broadly, this corporate experience is traditional wisdom, the inheritance of a *populus*. Every people has its presuppositions: let us think only about the Western technical presuppositions that permit us all to move about in an ordinary day's work; they may have been demonstrated rationally by learned gnomes lurking in distant laboratories, but they are given credence by men at large because society imposes its own authority and validates that authority, so to speak, sensibly. The man buying a new car ought to read carefully the manual instructions the manufacturer gives him with his purchase. Prudent faith in the authority might avoid breakdowns and subsequent drain upon the wallet. Hume can teach us something here.

Reason, all reason, operates within the prescriptions and suppositions of some social order because reasoning cannot take its point of departure from itself: the act of a man, reasoning is lodged in him; and—very profoundly—is *his* product: we produce our own conclusions; we do not capture them on the wing as though they were Platonic ideas floating in a void. In life, reason is always operating on faith and faith is always operating on reason, and both of them are stirred out of the broth of experience.

The man who would drive a wedge between Reason and Faith—capitalized—does so on the grounds that the one is not the other. This reasoning is not very good reasoning: man is not woman but this argues to no necessary divorce. Reason is not faith but both have a common source permitting them to nourish one another: experience. The posture which stakes out an opposition between faith and reason and which does so in the name of philosophical reason is no sacred cow: the advocates of the position advance it as philosophically sound, and hence open to rational questioning. Therefore they can have no objection to their position being evaluated by another philosopher who adheres to a different order of things.

The reason-faith divorce court posture advances itself under the rubric, as suggested earlier, of a "presuppositionless philosophy," a rational body of teaching which depends on nothing prior to itself and which is therefore hermetically sealed from the influence of faith, especially religious and most especially Christian faith. The mind can, of course, entertain the proposition according to which philosophy ought to have no presuppositions. The mind can equally well entertain its contrary. *A priori*, before taking a look at the actual practice of philosophy, there is no inbuilt self-evident structure insisting that philosophy have or not have any presuppositions. That reason operates in total isolation from faith is, on logical grounds, not a first principle. There is nothing particularly unintelligible about the "presuppositionless" position—except that such a philosophy in fact has one: namely, that philosophy should have none! And this altogether without a shred of proof! The business cannot be settled in advance of some act of philosophizing and the conditions for that act can only be disengaged once the act is performed. The business must be resolved experientially and historically: what happens when men think philosophically? In truth, no philosophy ever mushroomed into being like Topsy without anterior causes rooted in experience. We all know about the unsuspecting freshman who signs up for Philosophy 101 and who hears instructor X tell the class never to accept any authority in philosophy and we all know that the poor devil writes down in his notebook: "Teacher says never to accept any authority in philosophy." Being a good little student, he swallows this nonsense, thus entering his putatively short-lived career in philosophical studies marked with the sign of contradiction.

Anyone with a modicum of realism and what Kierkegaard called a sense of the comic knows that this is not what happens. Philosophy departments and individual professors have their preferences, some may even have made their commitments. Students who stray into their classes or who are told by others, hence, take it on faith that this man or the other university teaches sound philosophy, and commence their study already specified by faith in some authority. In differing cultures and at different moments of time this or that philosophy is the rage of the hour or the public orthodoxy of the academy. Faith in the orthodoxy or in the fashion are the motor powers which get the wheels of philosophical thinking spinning. Be it the French rationalism of the seventeenth century; the German idealism of the eigh-

teenth and nineteenth; the phenomenology or existentialism of the twentieth; the enduring positivism of the Anglo-American tradition; or any other philosophical tradition—each and all of them fashion young minds who tend to accept the authority of their cultures or tend to become the apes of contradiction and are thus defined by what they reject.

Very few human beings have the capacity or the time to master thoroughly one great philosopher and it is my guess that the most that could be mastered by anybody in a lifetime is two. Philosophy is as much a risk as is the life of which philosophy is a part. I might be duped in giving ten or twenty years to studying this or that system but I will be able to evaluate rationally what I have studied only *after* I have studied it, after I have gambled time and money and—possibly—a life. When I commence, I go where I go because of some authority: I take a culture or a person or a school and I make of it my authority. My decision, possibly but usually not free, may be motivated by sound reasons; more often, it is the product of sheer luck, good or bad. Nobody ever entered into a philosophical life because of a philosophical decision: there are no philosophical decisions: there are only philosophical conclusions. If philosophy caused a man to study philosophy, he would be a philosopher before he became one. The so-called "life of reason" begins with an act of faith. I am not proving anything here: I am simply pointing to the way things are.

If I may be permitted a personal observation by way of illustration, I am a Thomist. Today I am a Thomist by conviction, philosophical and rational conviction. But I commenced my studies in the thought of St. Thomas Aquinas because he was recommended to my consideration by the *Magisterium* of the Church which centuries earlier had declared him The

Common Doctor. I began my career with an act of faith—but then again so does everybody else. What is at stake on this level is which authority are you going to choose and whose word are you going to believe, instructor X in Philosophy 101, the *Zeitgeist*, or the authority of Christ's Church?

So much for the facts: nobody ever philosophized in an hermetically sealed box. If philosophy be understood to be a body of reasoned conclusions achieved by a man moved to wonder about the world of being and who wills to dispel ignorance with knowledge; if all reason, including—of course—philosophical reason, takes its point of departure from experience; if, again, experience is not solipsistically sealed in some suitcase; if, in a word, the aspirant to philosophical truth is a man who lives in a world; if these conclusions be sound—and this essay has so argued—then it follows that the questions men formulate when they commence to philosophize will be structured or specified by their experience, by life, by history; and, finally, because these questions include a tissue of propositions previously entertained on faith although not coextensive therewith, no philosophy could possibly get off the ground unless carried by the wings of experience.

Philosophical speculation poses questions and then tries to answer them. A questioning stance is consubstantial with the wonder from whence philosophy begins. Most questions admit of affirmation or negation. Both look to the actual existence of the content mounted in the subject-predicate structure of the question. I use the word "content" to mean intelligibility, thinkability—meaning. (Meaning is not being: by "being" I mean "existing." Were meaning being, erroneous judgments would be unthinkable. The judgment declaring that "Great Britain is a peninsula" is false but the terms of the proposition are easily intelligible to anyone who has heard about or lived in Great Britain and who understands what the geographical term "peninsula" means.) Now the terms of all propositions are derived, ultimately, from experience. It follows that I cannot reason about, hence affirm or deny, positions unknown to me. Aristotle never denied that the world was created *ex nihilo*, "out of nothing," because Aristotle never heard of the Jewish and Christian doctrine insisting that it is. Even philosophies which negate the presuppositions of a going order—the public orthodoxy, a term I coined a number of years ago—are defined and specified by what they deny. It follows that an impoverished historical order asks impoverished questions, just as a household, impoverished imaginatively and intellectually, busies itself with trivialities. Because experience is accumulative and hence traditional, a betting man would be wise to put the odds on a superior philosophy emerging out of a superior culture.

I take it that I need not argue the proposition that nobody gets answers to questions that he does not ask. Further, I take it that questions run ahead of answers in the sense of specifying them. Philosophies can be evaluated in two ways:

1. Do the conclusions follow logically from their first principles? Making a man take his own point of departure seriously can often result in hoisting him on his own petard: *e.g.*, Descartes' use of the principle of causality to prove the existence of an external world when he had previously told us that he was suspending doubt about everything hitherto held by him to be true and at a moment in which he knew only two truths, his existence as a thinking principle and the existence of God; Kant's postulation of *das Ding an sich* after he had located all judgment in experience and had excluded the "Thing-

In-Itself" from experience. (Fichte caught him on *that* one.)

2. From what questions do these particular conclusions follow? Further, for whom are the questions worth asking? Possibly, these questions do not interest me because in no sense do they enter into my experience of the real. Ortega y Gasset was a brilliant philosopher who probed splendidly the subtleties of the *dolce vita*. Ortega was a philosopher for a duchess with a dog in his explorations of the intricacies of charm and flirtation. His world tempts me from time to time but it is not really my own. In a lengthy bookshelf of writings, the *obras* of Don José contain only about six pages concerning God and the destiny of the soul. A philosopher of this world, Ortega was not concerned about matters that have absorbed the lives of other philosophers. Philosophical speculation always exists in an existential context which has already annealed the questioner in the catalyst of his own corporate response to the real. In this sense, if only in this, heart dictates to head.

Christian philosophy is marked by conclusions whose springboard has been Christian convictions: The Faith. There is nothing in pagan antiquity that is remotely comparable to the sophisticated body of philosophical doctrine that grew up around the Christian belief in the intrinsic dignity of the person; the providence of God over each man; creation out of nothing by a God whose name is "I Am"; the basic dignity of the family; the distinction between nature and person; natural and international law. In-

stances could be multiplied but all add up to one conclusion. Christians have asked superior questions in philosophy because those questions have been quickened by faith in the word of God.

Questions, from which philosophical reasoning grows, are themselves not ultimate intelligibilities because every question is an at least implicit judgment about the status of the question, the terms at play. Asking any question at all, most especially a sophisticated question, involves a world in which somebody halts the projector of time and freezes a slice of reality into a problem weighed. The probing mind must have experienced, gone through—*per*, a history. That history, in turn, will have been congealed into a symbolic structure from which the light of intelligence illuminates meaning. That meaning is first conceptualized and questioned, pondered over, scaled by evidence and eventually affirmed to have existence effectively in the real in this or that way, or even absolutely. The truth known in an ultimate judgment will be truth about being; illuminated in the stream of history.

Reason can never escape experience and therefore reason can never escape its twin, faith. Both are born of the same mother. There are those who have known as their mother the experience of Faith and the history it created. Their reasoning about the ultimate things issues therefrom. Then again there are those who have not known the history of salvation and their reason issues from their experience. Every man is free to look at the fruits because by their fruits ye shall know them.   [XXIII, Winter 1979, 25–32]

[43]

Liberalism and Christianity

WILHELM RÖPKE

Translated by Patrick M. Boarman

Wilhelm Röpke (1900–1966), one of the leading free-market economists of the world, was the author of numerous and important works focusing on International Order and Economic Integration *(1959) and* A Humane Economy *(1960). Professor of economics at the University of Geneva's Graduate School of International Studies, he spoke his mind before an audience in Frankfurt on the barbarism of Nazism one week after Hitler took power. As a result, he was dismissed from his professorship and exiled to Turkey and Switzerland. But he lived to see his economic and political philosophy adopted by the post-Hitler* Bundesrepublik *in the restoration of a free economy in Germany. Of him Chancellor Ludwig Erhardt said: "My own services toward the attainment of a free society are scarcely enough to express my gratitude to him who, to such a high degree, influenced my position and conduct."*

TEN YEARS AGO, a group of eminent men from the United States and several European countries met at Mont Pélérin, in Switzerland, to discuss the conditions under which a society of free men can exist today.[1] They had in common a social philosophy which might be called "liberal," if this word had not become the source of many misunderstandings.

None of us there believed that a socialist economy could result in anything but misery and serfdom, and we all were convinced that collectivism in all its forms is the real danger threatening our civilization. We discussed the necessity for reestablishing a regime of active competition; and in the course of our meetings we touched upon technical questions in the spheres of economics and jurisprudence. Most of us, indeed, were economists, familiar with the theories of supply and demand, of the prices of the factors of production, and of money. There was no one among us who was an active representative of the Catholic faith.

Then there happened something which shows strikingly the almost funereal gravity of our present hour. In this circle of technicians, the discussion turned upon the increasing conviction that if we intend to win the battle for freedom, we must pay attention not primarily to supply and demand, but to quite different things; and once the ice was broken, we "hardened liberals" spoke of what Christianity means for freedom—and, inversely, of what freedom means for Christianity. We were conscious that in speaking in the first place as Christians *or* liberals concerned for freedom and human dignity,

513

we were on common ground: ground we did not share with the enemy.

One of us, Professor Eucken—who, since then, has died before his time—spoke of the experiences of the Third Reich, where men finally were driven to ask themselves if a man might be a Christian under a totalitarian regime, since such a domination deprives him of the freedom of moral decision essential to Christianity. He added that common suffering had overthrown the old confessional barriers, and that both Protestants and Catholics worked in the same direction, or even together, to attain a common goal: the development of a political and economic order which would be the opposite of a totalist society and economy, and which would express both Christian and liberal ideals. Since then, this collaboration has culminated in Germany in the foundation of the Christian Democratic party, led by Dr. Adenauer.

In the course of our discussions at Mont Pélérin, we entered fully into the question of the relationship between liberalism and Christianity. I believe that this question can no longer be neglected. It merits a fresh examination. In this undertaking, it is desirable to speak of liberalism in a double sense: first, in the general sense of an idea which expresses the essence of our civilization; and, on the other hand, in the narrower and more specific sense of an intellectual, economic, and political ideology, born in the nineteenth century under the influence of certain factors proper to that period. In the first sense we are, indeed, all liberals so soon as we are anti-totalitarians. But if the word is taken in its second meaning, it is doubtful if any one of us can still call himself a liberal. Liberalism in the first sense is, as I have written elsewhere,[2] a giant tree which blossomed in a respectable age: under its ample foliage we are at this moment assembled with the feeling in our hearts that we have something in common

to defend, whether we be conservatives or democrats, liberals or socialists, Protestants or Catholics. In its second meaning, on the contrary, liberalism is only the newest offshoot of this tree, and more than one person is wondering if it is not a savage growth. It would be criminal to wish to cut down the tree because the newest branch does not suit us; nevertheless, a thousand hatchets are already at work to commit this crime.

He who counts as precious the essential values and ideals of our Western civilization, so precious that he would be willing to defend them to his last breath—such a man knows what we mean when we speak of this tree, that is to say, of liberalism in its large and loftier meaning. For in the shape of this tree he honors the valuable work of centuries, yes, even of millenniums, a heritage which goes back to the origins of our civilization, to the Ionian Greeks, to the men of the Stoa, to Aristotle and Cicero. He reflects on all those thinkers of antiquity who were among the first to speak of human dignity and of the absolute nature of the individual soul in terms that could be understood by all rational men—who discovered the kingdom of ideas, who opposed human caprice, who proclaimed the inviolability of an order beyond the State—ideals which became the guiding stars of Western thought. What the *animae naturaliter Christianae* launched was completed in a grand way by Christianity and transmitted to us as Christian natural law. Christianity was necessary to wrest man, as a child of God, from the grasp of the State and to undertake (in the words of Guglielmo Ferrero) the destruction of the "Pharaonic spirit" of the State of antiquity.

Most of us are still moved to wonder how it was possible for the Ancients to have had a concept of freedom so different from our own.[3] In effect, their notion of the collective freedom of the "sovereign people" did not exclude the total subjection of the individual; we find the idea of freedom in this form in the ancient *polis*, and it occurs again in Rousseau; it is at the base of the doctrinaire ideology of modern democracy. Our idea of freedom, on the other hand—the Western idea—is of a freedom which guarantees the rights of the person, limits the action of the State, and comprehends the rights of the individual, of the family, of the minority, of the opposition, of religious groups. Western man has been at pains to point out that the wall which at this point separates him from the Ancients is Christianity, that Christianity to which we owe the phrase: *Render unto Caesar the things which are Caesar's, but to God the things which are God's.* If we reflect upon the whole meaning of this phrase, we recognize that it expresses, after all, what is in our minds when we speak of liberalism in its widest sense.

It is, therefore, our common inheritance from antiquity and Christianity with which we are concerned here. Both are the true ancestors of a philosophy which defines the always tenuous relationships between the individual and the State in accordance with the postulates of universal reason and of human dignity—a philosophy which conforms to the nature of man, and thus opposes personal freedom to the power of the State. A précis of liberalism could be written using only the orations of Cicero, the *Corpus Juris,* and the *Summa* of Aquinas; it would be vividly contemporary. In all of these works, we discover the venerable patrimony of the personalist philosophy, but perhaps nowhere do we find it more distinctly than in the political philosophy of the Catholic Church through all of its changes and vicissitudes.

WITHOUT BIAS, and excluding resolutely any ideas merely negative, we ought to examine Catholic social philosophy in all its sources, works, and documents, and in all its aspects, to find out if it is akin to our idea of universal liberalism. This is a tempting task. To those of us who are concerned with the philosophical bases of liberalism and who seek to free liberalism of the fatal errors of the nineteenth century, such a study may reveal the extent of the debt we owe to Catholic thought. It may also show that a goodly number of liberal thinkers—among whom are Tocqueville and Acton—were good Catholics, and that even a man like G. K. Chesterton did not hesitate to call himself a liberal. Perhaps in this way we may overcome the hesitancy of more than one Catholic to make an unbiased re-examination of the case for liberalism.

For the grave problems of the modern age oblige us, regardless of our position, to examine afresh our social philosophy, that we may realize exactly where the common front lies, and thus avoid useless controversy. I may illustrate what I mean here by referring the reader to that solemn document of the Catholic Church, the Encyclical *Quadragesimo Anno,* which appeared on the 15th day of May 1931. While I have space only for a brief investigation of this document, I should like to suppose that the serious reader is interested in learning of the attraction it has for a Christian and a liberal who is not a member of the Catholic Church—although one who pretends to no skill in exegesis. But such a man—and this is the essential point—who in the higher and more general sense can call himself a liberal, will not hesitate to declare that this Encyclical is one of the most impressive, profound, and noble of manifestoes, in which many things close to the hearts of all of us are expressed with a dignity, with a vigor of conviction, and with a comprehensiveness of view which are rare. Indeed, the "liberal" quintessence of this document cannot be denied, so long as we take this word in its large and eternal sense of a civilization based on man and upon a healthy balance between the individual and community; so long, in short, as we accept liberalism as the antipodes of collectivism.

I know that in making this brief observation I shall encounter the objections of those who are accustomed to see in the Encyclical an anti-liberal program of the "Corporate State," and who hold it in good or bad memory depending on their political opinion. It seems to me that this is the result of an erroneous interpretation which today might well repel the favorable opinion the Encyclical merits. He who takes the trouble of reading it with care and without bias (and, in case of doubt, refers to the Latin original) will have difficulty in seeing how the Encyclical could have been interpreted as a program of Corporatism were this interpretation not based upon a confusion of ideas to which the term "Corporatism" can certainly lead, but a confusion which cannot be excused today.[4] Let us not forget that the corporate state and the corporate economy are expressions which have meaning only if the "corporation"[5] (*ordo* in the original) becomes the structural principle of the State or of the economy. If it is made the basis of the State, it will replace the principle of existing democracy (representative, parliamentary, or direct), and will make of the corporations, organs which express the general will. Likewise, if the corporation becomes the structural principle of the economy, it will replace the existing principle, notably the market, by the concord or discord of the corporations (skeptics would say by vested interests). In the first case (the case of the corporate state), corporatism is opposed to all democracy; in the second case (that of the corporate economy), it destroys the *economy of the market*.

Even with the best will, I have been unable to find any trace of such a corporatism in the Encyclical, not to speak of the disapproving way in which the Encyclical treats the corporatism of Fascist Italy of the period. In each place where the "ordines" are mentioned and where their establishment is recommended, it is done simply with the social purpose of obtaining an improvement of the relations between employers and employees, that is to say, with the aim of dissipating the class struggle, and not of killing competition in the market. Even in this restricted meaning of corporation (*professional community* as we would translate the word *ordo* in our day), as an instrument of social reform (and not of economic reform), the Encyclical stresses free will before all else. One is continually under the impression that the author of the Encyclical had before his eyes the dangers arising from an imprudent recommendation of corporations, and that to avoid an anarchy of "group interests," he endeavored to restrict this organization to the sphere of social reform.

This impression is, moreover, confirmed when, in answering the question whether the structural principle ought to be collectivist or non-collectivist, the Encyclical decides in favor of the market economy (*haec oeconomiae ratio*) and against a controlled economy. Such a position, obviously, does not exclude rejection of the aberrations of the market economy. I have been unable to find in the Encyclical any passage sanctioning the belief that an order based on the market economy should be replaced by another which can only be a collectivist order, exception being made for the sector in which an autonomous peasant economy prevails. The latter is given its due estimation. (III.1).

In my opinion, one of the very great merits of the Encyclical is that it makes a clear distinction between the principle of the market economy as such and its numerous deviations. It does this precisely in order to attack the latter and save the principle of the market, and thus rescue our economic system from an omnivorous collectivism. This is exactly what the representatives of neo-liberalism hold, though they formulate it in a different way. This is more clearly realized when we note that the Encyclical sees the degradation of the market economy not only in the excesses of an outdated policy of laissez-faire, but also in the progressive disfiguration of the competitive order by monopoly. Doubtless, I would here emphasize certain things which the Encyclical does not, and occasionally, perhaps, I would express myself in different language to obviate misunderstanding. Thus, I hesitate to accept the Encyclical's point of view on monopolies, which it imagines to be the creations of free competition; in my opinion, they are rather the result of insufficiencies in the legal framework and of a certain brand of state interventionism. But I can only acquiesce with joy when the Encyclical goes to war against monopoly (*oeconomicus potentatus*) and its disastrous economic and political consequences (in particular III.1).

When it stigmatizes the "debasement of the dignity of the State which should place itself above the quarrels of special interests," it directs itself against a monopoly sclerosis of the market economy and against group anarchy—diseases which, on the one hand, paralyze the market by making impossible any just balance between what is given and what is taken in return and, on the other hand, dissolve the State by their "pluralism." We cannot at the same time fight the "special interests" and recommend economic policy which would sanction and even aid their fatal growth. That, however, is what corporatism would do; only the reestablishment of real competition can provide a remedy at this point. It would impugn the perspicacity of the author of the Encyclical to understand him as meaning anything else.

If the concentration of power in the hands of private persons is a great evil, it becomes a still greater evil in the hands of an all-powerful State armored with political sanctions. This truth does not escape the Encyclical despite its emphasis on rendering to the State the things which are the State's. Thus it is led, as are all of us, to a war on two fronts: against the individualism and economic policy of laissez-faire, and against collectivism. The fact that the Encyclical should reject collectivism and individualism with equal intransigence is all the more significant in view of the omnipresent danger to see in socialism (collectivism), in its theory at least, a genuine Christian doctrine, or at least an emphasis on moral values and sentiments which are specifically Christian. The very fact that it has clearly taken a position is the great merit of the Encyclical; now that we are again hearing vague talk about a "Christian Socialism" we would do well to recall these clear and authoritative words: " . . . whether Socialism be considered as a doctrine or as an historical fact, or as a movement, if it really remains Socialism, it cannot be brought into harmony with the dogmas of the Catholic Church, even after it has yielded to truth and justice in the points we have mentioned; the reason being that it conceives human society in a way utterly alien to Christian truth." (III.1). Even the "moderate socialists" receive a severe warning (Communism being considered as beyond discussion). If their moderation resides in the fact that they confine their activity to certain reforms which can just as well be supported by a non-socialist ideology (e.g., the struggle against monopoly concentration), "then," says the Encyclical, "they abuse the term Socialism."

The Encyclical has taken up its position between two extremes so that it may seek a "third road" to avoid the "dangers both of individualism and collectivism." In what direction does this third road lead us? On this point the Encyclical furnishes some remarkable details. I shall speak first of its exposition of the problem of Property. In our industrial age of huge corporate holdings, the concept of property needs redefining, if it is to withstand criticism. The Encyclical speaks of the double nature of property, of its individual and social functions; and it proves that exaggeration of the latter leads to collectivism. Though it underlines the responsibility which attaches to the possession of the means of production, a responsibility which arises out of the social function of property, the Encyclical is no less emphatic in affirming the inviolability of property. In view of the recurring temptation to make of property a relative thing by appeal to the Gospels, the Encyclical takes a further stand: "Man's natural right of possessing and transmitting property by inheritance must be kept intact and cannot be taken away from man by the State. Hence, the domestic household is antecedent, as well in idea as in fact, to the gathering of men into a community." The final remarks of the Encyclical may be added here: "Those who are engaged in production are not forbidden to increase their fortunes in a lawful and just manner: indeed, it is just that he who renders service to society and develops its wealth should himself have his proportionate share of the increased public riches." (III.3b).

It is upon this eminent social philosophy which respects a rational natural order that the third part of the Encyclical is based (II.1). This is the part which treats of social questions and in my opinion it surpasses all the others. The high point of its argument occurs when the Encyclical, without undervaluing traditional social policy, rightly situates the real problem in a process of decomposition, a decomposition which is not essentially material but spiritual and anthropological; a process which may be summed up in the word: *proletarianization*. The solution of the social problem and the solution to the problem of de-proletarianization (*redemptio proletariorum*) are inseparable; and the Encyclical further declares, with justice, that our civilization hangs upon the solution of these problems. It is impossible here for me to give an adequate summary of the many other considerations which ought to be taken into account. I confine myself to the observation that the world would long since have done well to impregnate itself with the social doctrine and the spiritual tradition of this Christian philosophy.[6]

It would be superfluous to dilate further on the fact that such a program of de-proletarianization is at the same time a program of economic, social, and political decentralization, or better, a program of the "aerated society" (Gustave Thibon); that it is in every respect the opposite of economic collectivism and of political totalitarianism—a program, too, which has nothing in it of the romantic but is rather built on realism since it considers man in his milieu and as subject to his natural necessities, and since, finally, it puts reason above the unreal or the anti-natural of the actual world.

Behind this Encyclical we sense the able economist who does not lose himself in vague postulates, but, like the "liberal" economist, remains aware of the interdependent relationships of economics. Because he has carefully avoided viewing the social problem merely as a question of wages, the author of the Encyclical makes the legitimate observation that it will not suffice to raise wages without considering these interdependent economic relationships. He makes it plain that an arbitrary raise in wages, indeed, is closely linked to unemployment. (III.3c).

The informed economist is once more revealed when the reform of industrial corporations is seen as an important condition for the improvement of economic life (III.3).

Only now and then does the Encyclical mention the problems of the international economy. Considering the importance of this domain, this omission is regrettable. If I am not mistaken, the position of Catholic social philosophy is least definite with respect to these problems. But it seems that recently an increasing number of voices have declared that on the international level, the sociological and economic principles of the Encyclical lead to adherence to the principles of a free, "multi-lateral" world economy. That is precisely the kind of international economic order desired by truly liberal thinkers.[7]

Perhaps the average Catholic may balk at speaking in terms of a "liberal" world economy. It is not easy to abstract what is essential from the association of nineteenth-century ideas implied by the word "liberal"; there is an understandable hesitation to employ this word in its general meaning—that meaning which, nevertheless, expresses so well a social philosophy specifically Catholic.

In the last analysis, it may be answered that words count for little. What matters is that we recognize our entry into the decisive phase of the battle for freedom and the dignity of man; and, or in this battle, the patrimony of Christian social philosophy which, increasingly, merges with all that is essential and enduring in liberalism.

NOTES

[1] The group included Wilhelm Roëpke, William Rappard, and Hans Barth from Switzerland; Jacques Rueff and Bertrand de Jouvenel from France; Luigi Einaudi and Carlo Antoni from Italy; Walter Eucken from Germany; Friedrich Hayek, Lionel Robbins, John Jewkes, E. Eyck, Michael Polanyi, and S. R. Dennison from England; Karl Brandt, Henry Hazlitt, Ludwig von Mises, and George Stigler from the United States.

[2] In my book *Mass und Mitte* (Zurich, 1950).

[3] Perhaps the most noteworthy treatment of this question is the essay by Benjamin Constant: "De la liberté des anciens comparée à celle des modernes." (*Oeuvres Politiques*, Editions Louandre, 1874).

[4] Here I refer the reader to my own books, in particular, *The Crisis of Our Time* (University of Chicago Press), and *Civitas Humana* (W. Hodge, London, 1948).

[5] "Corporation" as used in this context is a general term meaning a group of persons organized on professional lines. It must not be confounded, therefore, with the business corporation of American law.

[6] In addition to the writings of G. K. Chesterton (especially *Outline of Sanity*) and of H. Belloc, Goetz Briefs' *The Proletariat* must be mentioned. Also, the wholesome and refreshing works of the French Catholic peasant philosopher Gustave Thibon (*Diagnostics, Essai de Physiologic sociale, Retour au Réel*). Of Belloc, see especially: *An Essay on the Restoration of Property*.

[7] See the interesting book by the former editor-in-chief of *L'Osservatore Romano*, Guido Gonella, *Presupposti di un ordine internazionale* (Vatican City, 1942). For my own ideas, see my book *Ordnungbeube* (Zurich, 1954), and my English lecture delivered at the Academy of Internatial Law, "Economic Order and International Law" (Leyden, 1955).

[I, Fall 1957, 128–134]

[44]

The Western Dilemma:
Calvin or Rousseau?

ERIK VON KUEHNELT-LEDDIHN

Erik von Kuehnelt-Leddihn (1909–   ), a Roman Catholic from the Austrian Tyrol, received his doctorate in political science from the University of Budapest in 1929. A gifted linguist who has mastered all the principal languages of the world, he taught in the 1930s in England, crossing the Atlantic to lecture at such Roman Catholic American colleges as Georgetown, Fordham, Chestnut Hill, and St. Peter's College in Jersey City, where he later chaired the Department of History and Sociology. In the early 1940s, under the pseudonym Francis Stuart Campbell, he wrote The Menace of the Herd *(1943). Following World War II, he resettled in Austria. In his* Liberty or Equality *(1952) and as an Austrian columnist for* National Review, *he has kept in close touch with the United States, where he returns each year on a lecture tour. He is also the author of the novel* Black Banners *(1954) and a study in the history of political theory,* Leftism *(1974).*

I

Nearly everyone who saw the film called *The Third Man* remembers a sardonic gibe by one of the leading characters: "And what has Switzerland given to the world? The cuckoo clock!" Many, even among those who like and respect the Swiss, believe this to be the lamentable truth. Switzerland, they tell themselves, may have excellent trains, clean well-managed hotels, an efficient postal system, and fine chocolate; but as for great ideas and higher intellectual and cultural contributions, it is too small and too materialistic to have achieved them. Such a view reflects the monumental ignorance that characterizes so many of our contemporaries. As a matter of fact, Switzerland, situated at the crossroads of Europe, has always been an intellectual and spiritual powerhouse—not so much perhaps in the fine arts but certainly in the domains of philosophy, technology, the natural sciences, medicine, psychology, and above all, theology.

At the middle of this century the three most influential theologians of the Reformed Church were Swiss: Karl Barth, Emil Brunner and Oscar Cullmann.[1] In the age of the Reformation itself two of the three leading Reformers worked and preached in Switzerland. Indeed, were it possible to excise from the map and from history just a single Swiss city, our Western

520

civilization would not be what it is, for by eliminating Geneva we should eliminate two of the most powerful influences on the modern Western mind: Jean Calvin, French-born though he was, and Jean Jacques Rousseau. Without the one the puritan capitalist "work ethics"—Max Weber's *Protestantische Wirtschaftsethik*—would probably never have taken root, and without the other the course taken by the French Revolution would have been unthinkable.

To understand the Western world's dilemma, its vacillations between the Calvinist and the Roussellian way, one needs above all a thorough understanding of the true significance of the Protestant Reformation. It is too frequently regarded—as for example in de Rochemont's film about Luther[2]—as the beginning of liberalism and democracy with their various sequels, such as the United Nations and medicare; yet it was, to the contrary, a *conservative* revolution. The birth of the Reformation was not in 1517, the date on which Luther nailed up his ninety-five theses, but a half dozen years earlier in the winter of 1510–1511 which Luther spent in Rome. It was there in the Eternal City that the German Augustinian friar made his first contact with modernity. Before then he had encountered Humanism only in its literary form; in Rome he found himself face-to-face with the synthesis of Christianity and Antiquity, whereby the mediaeval concept of the world as a circle with God as its center had been replaced by the concept of an ellipse with two focal points—God *and* man. Luther had no patience with what Karl Barth has called *das katholische Und*, "the Catholic And." Neither could he accept the Catholic-Humanist doctrine that everything true, everything beautiful, whatever its origin, had to be embraced and integrated into the treasurehouse of Christianity. To Luther the spirit and climate of the Renaissance were a treason to Christ. The new age, visibly perfected in Italy, was the revival of paganism; it represented a triumph of rationalism, estheticism, and secularism, all of which he detested and rejected.

Thus it is a mistake to think of Luther as "the first modern man"—a designation more appropriately applied to Nicholas of Cusa—or as "modern" in any sense; rather he was a Gothic man who came from a very new German university in a truly "colonial" area, for from the wall of Wittenberg one could then look over the thatched roofs of the cottages of the indigenous Slavic inhabitants. When Luther learned to his horror that Ulrich Zwingli, one of the few Humanists among the Reformers, believed in the possible salvation of pagans and was looking forward to conversations with Plato, Aristotle, and other Greek sages in Heaven, he furiously denied Zwingli's right to call himself a Christian. The other leading Humanists of the epoch—Reuchlin, Erasmus, Adelsmann, Pirckheimer—all originally favorable to reformation, became fiercely anti-Lutheran as soon as they recognized the friar's real position. Thus it is clear that the Reformation began as a reaction *against* Humanism and the spirit of the Renaissance.[3] In Germany the movement was distinctly illiberal and anti-intellectual.[4] It supported royal absolutisms as against the later mediaeval conception of the monarch restrained by law, the principle of *rex sub lege*; but at the same time Lutheranism was an organic outgrowth of the mediaeval spirit.[5] While Catholicism moved on from the Renaissance to the Baroque, and from the Baroque to the Rococo,[6] the world of the Reformation continued to adhere to the Gothic style, to the old order and the common law. For a long time the Reformed Church remained the most conservative force in Europe.

II

It is impossible, of course, to think of Calvin without Luther, yet the two are in many ways different, though the differences have sometimes been wrongly evaluated. The patently fallacious notion of Luther as the inaugurator of a liberal-democratic outlook has been transferred to Calvin. He has been represented as the father of political liberties and of the right of resistance to tyrannical rule. In reality, Calvin's political attitudes were aristocratic or oligarchical. He considered arbitrary government to be a chastisement divinely ordained, *un ire de Dieu*,[7] to be endured with humility and patience. In this he agreed entirely with Luther. It was not until more than a century after his death, that is until after Louis XIV's revocation of the Edict of Nantes in 1685, that a Calvinist theory of the right to resistance, largely inspired by earlier Jesuit teachers, was developed by Pierre Jurieu. As for predestination, we should remember that Luther, too, was a predestinarian, as is shown in his essay *De servo arbitrio*, although Melanchthon, another Humanist and an early ecumenist, made sure that Luther's position in this matter was not incorporated into the Augsburg Confession. Calvin's view of predestination did not wholly erase the older Christian tradition of free will, and though it was a strong factor in the shaping of the "Protestant" mind,[8] it never became the same fatalistic force as Kismet in Islamic religion. Western man may accept the idea of belonging to an elect few, but his dynamic nature does not allow him to think of himself as a mere puppet manipulated by God. It is significant that Karl Barth, founder of a neo-Calvinist orthodoxy, has rejected Calvin's theory of predestination.[9]

Both Luther and Calvin were true wrestlers with Christ. The doctrines of both were strictly theocentric—more so, in a sense, than those of the Catholic Church. The outlook of both was essentially monastic[10] and, in Calvin's case at least, decidedly ascetic.[11] Both were severe types, convinced that without strict discipline man is destined to founder because he is by nature a sinful wretch bent on mischief. They condemned those elements in the Catholic tradition and temperament which were anthropomorphic, sensual, artistic, personalistic, intellectual and rational. The Catholic Counter-Reformation for its part was frequently inclined to take positions directly opposite to those held by the Reformers.

III

In the eighteenth century we encounter in the Western world the twin phenomena of Rationalism and the Enlightenment, both derived from Catholic culture and civilization. Rationalism, as J. Bochenski has pointed out, is the grandchild of Scholasticism,[12] and the Enlightenment is a late product of the Renaissance spirit. Both emphasize the power and the glory of man. Both—to borrow the phrase of Romano Guardini—are expressions of *menschliche Selbstbehauptung*, human self-assertiveness. The catastrophic consequence of these two currents was the French Revolution. The genius of that revolution, as Hegel wisely observed,[13] finally triumphed in the Reformed rather than the Catholic orbit. The reason for this paradox was that, thanks to the character it had acquired in the Renaissance,[14] the Catholic world had been "vaccinated," so to speak, against the new ideological infection. The influence exerted by Rationalism and the Enlightenment had little or no permanent effect on the Catholic world, but with the churches of the Reformation it was another story.[15] There the influence was profound and divisive; thereafter these churches developed in one or the other of two distinct directions—either along a line determined by the deposit of faith established by their founders, or taking a radical turn away from that line, following the road of secular liberalism on to relativism. Since then almost every "Protestant" church has had two branches: an orthodox Christian—though not necessarily fundamentalist—branch and a secularized and relativist one.[16]

Thanks to this intrusion of the secular—and to a degree the Renaissance-Catholic—spirit into the post-Reformation world, we find in the nineteenth century, though not until then, a growing belief that "Protestant" nations are somehow enlightened, progressive, advanced, intellectual and individualistic, whereas Catholic nations are ignorant, backward, uninventive, sterile, mediaeval, and so forth. Such views are due to a profound confusion of facts in the semantic order. The notion that Catholics live under an ecclesiastical autocracy which denies them the pleasures of life is held only by those "Protestants" who no longer share the spiritual and cultural values of the Reformers but live instead in the shadow of liberal relativism. In the eyes of a true Reformation-Christian the Catholic ethos is one of "Rum, Romanism, and Rebellion," or, to put it in somewhat kindlier terms, one of pagan *joie de vivre*, the Renaissance spirit, and anarchical inclinations. If you doubt this, just compare the views expressed about the Catholic faith by a dominie of the *Nederlandse Gereformeerde Kerk* in Groningen and those expressed by a minister of the Marble Collegiate Church on Fifth Avenue, New York. You will find them diametrically opposed.

The person chiefly responsible for the change of outlook was that other Jean of Geneva, Jean Jacques Rousseau, who for a brief period of his youth had accepted the Catholic religion. His view of human nature was exactly opposite to Calvin's. Whereas Calvin, the adopted son of Geneva,[17] had held that man is a creature so vile that his sins can be washed away only by the Blood of the Lamb, Rousseau, the native Genevois who lived most of his life abroad, believed that man is by nature wholly good. If man shows signs of wickedness, external circumstances alone are to blame: "Man is born free, but he is everywhere in chains." Everything, therefore, depends upon a right order. Rousseau is the philosophical coordinator of a not-very-rational rationalism and of an Enlightenment which, as we can now perceive, heralded the coming of an age of darkness. His contradictory message consists of an appeal to man's innate goodness, especially in his natural state as the noble savage, to a concept of liberty which has a purely collective character, and to a most unclearly defined political order which is entirely restrictive. No wonder that his books were burned at Geneva or that during the French Revolution his remains were transferred to the Pantheon. Rousseau is the one who anticipated the Grand Inquisitor's message to Christ in *The Brothers Karamazov*:

> The time will come when mankind, through the mouth of its philosophers and scientists, will proclaim that there is no such thing as crime, perhaps not even sin, but only hungry people. On the banner they will carry against You will be written: "Feed them first and then you can ask virtue from them!" and with this they will destroy Your cathedral.

The numberless contradictions in Rousseau's thought merely reflect the contradictions in his personality[18] and in the ideas he spawned and which are still effective today. Vague notions of freedom and of collective slavery, inherent in his concept of the *volonté général*, alternate with exaggerated notions of the efficacy of "education." We must not forget that, with all his totalitarian ideas, Rousseau is perhaps not so much a child of the Enlightenment as the central figure in the Romantic movement with its ambivalent veneration for sophistication and simplicity, its adulation of *philosophes,* shepherdesses and peasants, its craving for absolutes combined with a latent anarchism, its sentimentality coupled with a trend toward the utmost brutality.[19] In fact, if we consider the antagonism between Classicism and Romanticism, as brilliantly formulated by Irving Babbitt,[20] we can say that if Calvin was a classicist—which, unlike Luther, he certainly was—then Rousseau represents Romanticism *par excellence.*

IV

The dilemma of Western Man, torn between Calvin and Rousseau, is less perceptible in Europe than in the United States. In the Old World so many other painful alternatives offer themselves—Adam Smith *versus* Karl Marx, Burke and de Maistre *versus* Sade and Robespierre, the First Rome *versus* the Second and Third—that the only real choice at issue, the occupied tomb of Lenin *versus* the empty tomb of Christ, is obscured. In the New World, however, where the tables of history are not rewritten over and over until they become almost illegible, the transition from Calvin to Rousseau stands out in stark relief. If we call the American statesmen of the late eighteenth century the Founding Fathers of the United States, then the Pilgrims and Puritans were the grandfathers and Calvin the great-grandfather. In saying this, one need not exclude the Virginians because Anglicanism has essentially Calvinistic foundations still recognizable in the Thirty-nine Articles, and the Pilgrim Fathers, like the Puritans generally, represented a kind of re-reformed Anglicanism. Though the fash-

ionable eighteenth century Deism may have pervaded some intellectual circles, the prevailing spirit of Americans before and after the War of Independence was essentially Calvinistic in both its brighter and uglier aspects. They were a hardworking, frugal, plain-spoken, intensely nationalistic people,[21] aware and proud of their moral standards which included the "Protestant work ethics."[22] As a nation of such virtues they aroused the admiration of the world[23] and in their own self-esteem they were convinced that their nation had a messianic mission to save the world through a *novus ordo seclorum.*

At the end of the eighteenth and the beginning of the nineteenth century religion played a much larger role in America than in Europe, not so much perhaps among the intellectual and social leaders,[24] as among the people generally. "Pluralism" was not then the cant word it has become today, but it was much more the fact, and the sectarian divisions served to strengthen rather than to weaken religious zeal. It is worth remembering that the Colonial wars against the French had something of the character of crusades against Popish idolatry and popular enthusiasm for the War of Independence was helped along by a belief—absurd as it was—that George III had secretly become a Catholic and by the Quebec Act of 1774, granting religious toleration to French Canadians, which the Colonists considered a direct threat to their liberties.[25]

American Catholics were for a long time, as was shown in their puritanical ways, a tiny minority much influenced by the Protestant culture that surrounded them, their religious sobriety, their clericalism[26] and legalism and total acceptance of Thomistic theology.[27] They were at the same time culturally Calvinistic and intellectually mediaeval[28] and this was the occasion of many misunderstandings between them and their Continental European coreligionists. To many American and Irish-American Catholics the Italian immigrants seemed more pagan than Christian. Indeed, as Everett Dean Martin has pointed out, the American spirit was— and to a small extent still is—more mediaeval than modern. D. H. Lawrence came to much the same conclusion.[29] Martin thought the American was not a modern man because he had missed the liberalizing influences of the Renaissance; Lawrence maintained that the Renaissance influence was precisely what the Pilgrim Fathers had fled from. Before the First World War most colleges and universities, some banks and a good many millionaires' palaces were built in the Gothic style and some skyscrapers had Gothic pinnacles. Even the so-called Gothic letters were deemed to have a sacred character and were favored for religious inscriptions and the advertising of liturgical objects. But perhaps the contrast between the Gothic American and the Renaissance European may be best understood by comparing the faces and figures in Grant Wood's famous work of portraiture with the "baptized goddess" in Botticelli's *Birth of Venus*.

While European peoples within the Catholic orbit generally pursued the sweetness of life, the United States, thanks to its Calvinist psychology and virtues, became a world power. The Spanish-American War and its aftermath marked the radical turning point. Under the banner of John Calvin the American saga began to unfold. Forgotten were the days when the aid of two Catholic monarchs, Louis XVI of France and Charles III of Spain, had been eagerly welcomed by the nascent Republic. When in 1917 the United States came to the rescue of the Anglo-French Allies against the Catholic-Lutheran Central Powers, French Calvinist writers expressed their satisfaction and

delight.[30] George D. Herron, Woodrow Wilson's left hand in foreign policy and perhaps his chief ideologist, persuaded him to propose Geneva as the seat of the League of Nations because it was the source and origin of both puritan theology and the French Revolutionary dynamism.[31] It was a symbolic indication that the United States, although still Calvinist in spirit, was already on the steep and slippery road laid out by Rousseau in the *Discourses* and *The Social Contract*. The descent to a moral and political Avernus had begun.

V

Of course the American propensity to withdraw from Calvin toward Rousseau did not begin just yesterday. Some aspects of Jefferson's thought are distinctly Roussellian and we find still stronger evidences in Thomas Paine, a champion of the French Revolution. The cult of deism is violently opposed to the Calvinist ideas of God. Freemasonry, a considerable factor in the American Revolution, is decidedly deistic in temper, and its conception of human nature is much more "Catholic" than "Protestant," that is to say much closer to the Renaissance than to the mediaeval notion of the condition of man. Yet the American retreat from Calvin was never a complete one, nor is it so even today. His influence continues to run like a dark, subterranean stream through the American subconsciousness. The presence of *Maistre Jehan* of the Genevan theocracy can be felt throughout all great American literature and to a lesser degree through all other forms of American artistic expression. For all their superficial optimism, Americans cannot wholly rid themselves of the notion that man is a wretched creature totally crippled by Original Sin and that God's grace alone can save him. Beneath all the frenetic activity, the restless pursuit of pleasure, a certain somberness pervades American life and finds expression in a folk music which is profoundly Calvinistic, expressing in its own way what Jacques Chardonne, a Catholic, has called *les terribles vérités chrétiennes*.[32] No doubt Calvinism gives an enormous impetus to those who believe themselves to be saved, to be among the predestined elect—a belief held collectively by the American people. But the Calvinist doctrine of election and reprobation can also crush the lesser souls, those troubled by an inferiority complex; hence the bitter and biting nature of poverty in all countries where the Reformed Faith and its ethics prevail, and where the pauper and the beggar are outcasts.

A delayed historical reaction, however, caused a large sector of American thought to be deflected in a direction opposite to Calvinism. The prevailing temper became one of buoyant optimism which made itself felt even in the national folklore. This was in harmony with the new political trend toward egalitarian democracy which the Founding Fathers in 1787 had sensed and rejected, a fact that is too often willfully ignored. The popular distinctions drawn between Jeffersonian and Jacksonian democracy[33] ought not to obscure the fact that Washington, Hamilton, Adams, Gouverneur Morris, and Fisher Ames were as hostile in their way to democracy—and to the French Revolution—as were later the diehards of the Holy Alliance, though for somewhat different reasons. But throughout most of the nineteenth and all of the twentieth century we can observe the gradual democratization of the American Constitution concurrent with the psychological democratization of American society in which birth,[34] wealth and learning had once[35] played an important part. The Rousellian notion that man by nature is intelligent and good, that he is politically

knowledgeable and responsible, began step by step, to permeate the American outlook. Americans began to consider themselves masters of an Island of the Blessed where these "self-evident truths" were recognized and understood. The picture of Europe as a continent whose shores were teeming with "wretched refuse" enslaved and oppressed by kings, aristocrats and priests became an addition to American folklore, though it was never accepted by such hardy spirits as Herman Melville, Irving Babbitt, and H. L. Mencken.[36]

By the middle of the twentieth century the deification of the Common Man, heralded by his prophet Henry Wallace, was complete. The ancient moral disciplines were replaced by a new gospel of permissiveness. For Calvin's *Soli Dei Gloria* was substituted the worship of human agglomerates, entire races, entire nations, entire classes—or, by contrast, the worship of the alienated individual, the non-hero. If there is anything wrong with any of these, whether collectively or individually, the fault is not in themselves but in external circumstances—in economic oppression, faulty education, traumata due to minority status, exclusion from clubs, fraternities and sororities, inadequate sexual "outlets," socially imposed *tabus*, authoritarian fathers, run-down neighborhoods, unsuitable toilet facilities, lack of recreational opportunities, ethnic discriminations, and so on *ad infinitum*.

For all its predestinarianism, Calvinism had fostered an ascetic manner of life. Though God may have decided from the beginning of time just who was to be saved and who was not, mankind was never absolved from the duty of at least striving for eternal happiness through prayer, hard labor, and the chastening of appetites, by severity to oneself and charity to others, by obedience, discipline and the reading and following of the Holy Scripture, by reception of the two sacraments and by general personal saintliness. In Calvin's eyes man, though inescapably born into sin, was nevertheless a responsible creature. In Rousseau's eyes, man is at once good and irresponsible—a creature of circumstance. Though nature may permit physical and intellectual inequalities, one man is essentially as good as another, a notion now deeply imbedded in American folklore. A wayward Christian theology has indorsed the notion by asserting that "we are all equal in the sight of God." But the Scriptures speak nowhere of equality; we are given varying amounts of Grace. Christ did not love all his disciples equally, and if Judas had been admitted to be the equal of St. John, Christianity would have had to close shop. There is no equality in Heaven, nor for that matter in Purgatory, but there may very well be equality in Hell, where it belongs.[37]

It is sad to reflect that the gradual transfer of the Christian imagination from the Calvinistic to the Roussellian concept of human nature has been fostered by various denominations, especially in their liberal branches, and that it has been accompanied by a smuggling of secularism into their theologies. Instead of *leading* their flocks, the clergy began to *follow* the secular trends, heedless of Chesterton's warning that the Church is the only thing that saves us from the degrading slavery of becoming children of our times. In this respect the Catholic Church, too, in America and elsewhere has failed her followers. In her counter-reformatory zeal, she ran full speed away from Calvinism, only to have her apologists end too often in the arms of Jean Jacques.

The constant, lachrymose chatter about "the dignity of man" is depressing. Of course it exists, but it can easily be forfeited. Dignity is something that must be regained every day; it is not to be taken for granted,[38] nor is it to be automatically conceded to every little windbag or to every scoundrel great and small.

In some Catholic theological quarters of late there has been a respectful revaluation of the personality and teachings of Martin Luther. A similar reassessment of John Calvin would be a more difficult matter both doctrinally and psychologically, for where Luther was choleric but warmhearted, Calvin was hard, cold and balanced. Still, it has been Calvin rather than Luther who has had enduring significance and has changed the world; and as between Calvin—after all a Christian theologian of genius—and Rousseau the pagan *philosophe*, there should be no doubt about which merits the appreciation of Catholics.

VI

It is in the social and political spheres that the shift of loyalties from the religious reformer to the philosophic romanticist has wrought the greatest mischief. In the conduct of both domestic and foreign affairs the actual or potential wickedness of human nature is willfully overlooked. Since nobody anywhere is deemed really guilty of anything, social conditions must be constantly criticized and corrected; thus one noble experiment follows upon the failure of another, a good example being the socialist experiments in Soviet Russia. That human beings can be lazy, deceitful, avaricious, envious, spiteful, and just plain stupid is apparently never allowed to enter the neo-Roussellian mind. Original Sin and its manifestations are, of course, at the core of the Calvinist theology. The dominant Catholic doctrine on the subject is less severe: "Man is deprived of his extraordinary gifts and wounded in his nature." We are left with an enfeebled will, a darkened understanding, and a strong inclination to evil. With the aid of grace sought and obtained, however, the inclination may be resisted, thus allowing the possibility of salvation by free choice as well as by divine election. But the contemporary tendency is toward a total rejection of the doctrine. In place of a mankind corrupt by nature we are given an image of man as naturally good, sometimes weak perhaps, but aspiring always to goodness, truth and beauty. Since the evident facts so often contradicted this pleasant theory, it was necessary to democratize it. Majorities are always good, always right, were it not for the existence of inimical minorities—aristocrats, capitalists, Jews, priests, generals, bankers, manufacturers, certain politicians or certain intellectuals, as occasion may require. The majority, representing the average, consists, as the popular idiom would have it, of the good guys, the minority, representing the exceptional few, of the bad ones.[39] The doctrine of the *volonté générale* allows no room for minorities and all the ideological movements stemming out of the French Revolution—Jacobin democracy, socialism, communism, fascism, national socialism—are theoretically intolerant of them. The notion of an infallible majority ruling by a kind of divine right has become part of the American political and social folklore; hence the suspicion of conspiracies by the few. The Nuremberg trials, for example, were based on the charge of a conspiracy by the Nazis, though everyone knows, or should know, that the Nazis were the largest party in Germany, voted for by the good people in free elections, and so came to power by the democratic process. Similarly, the Italian Communists today are hoping to gain power by the democratic process, without a conspiracy, without a revolution.

The attitude of most Americans and many Europeans toward conditions in Latin America affords another example of distorted political perspectives. To the liberal mind it seems obvious that the social structure in Latin America must be all wrong since the virtuous masses there are frustrated in their effort to find work that will earn them better living standards, and are therefore turning to communism, just as the exploited Italian masses have done. The truth is that virtually all the leaders of the radical leftist movements in Latin America are the children of oligarchs or of the bourgeoisie; the masses so far have remained unmoved by them. Nor have the masses shown much enthusiasm for the bourgeois way of life or the bourgeois virtues of hard work and thrift. Our contemporaries tend to cling to the unhistoric notion that history is strictly rational, that action and reaction follow in a logical and mathematical fashion.[40] The superstition underlying this belief is again Roussellian, though it also derives in part from a certain Catholic naïveté which has placed too much emphasis on the Aristotelian and Scholastic concept of man as a rational animal. The notion of a "communism of the stomach" fits easily into the concept. So does the interpretation of the Bolshevik revolution as a reaction to Czarist oppression, as a rebellion of landless peasants against feudal landlords. Yet except for Kalinin and Dybenko, none of the Bolshevik leaders of 1917–20 was a proletarian. The leaders were nobles like Lenin and his wife, like Chicherin, Dzerzhinski, Lunacharski and Alexandra Kollontay, or Jewish bourgeois like Trotsky, or ex-seminarians like Stalin and Mikoyan. Besides it was not the Bolsheviks that overthrew the Russian monarchy; that was largely the work of other liberal-democratic elements. In 1917, moreover, only 23 percent of the arable land in Russia—as compared to 55 percent in Great Britain—belonged to large landowners.

VII

The belief that man is good and becomes bad only in desperation is utter nonsense. The Portuguese proverb, *Castigo o bom, melhorará, castigo mao, peorará*—"Punish a good man and he becomes better, punish a bad man and he becomes worse"—is far more realistic; suffering separates the wheat from the chaff. One must face the fact that man is a sinner, that he is weak and inclined to be wicked. No scientific or philosophical preparation is needed to recognize this sad truth: all we need do is look into our own lives and into our own souls to realize that we have at least the potentiality for great evil. This is something that the neo-Roussellian, whether a democrat, a socialist, a communist or an anarchist, wishes to ignore. He prefers to believe in the inexhaustible capacity of man for good. The *liberal* Roussellian expects him to achieve it through a boundless permissiveness, the *illiberal* Roussellian would have him find it in "systems" and utopias. But total dissolution and total regulation both mean death.

Political, social, and economic history, even the history of religions, shows us clearly that though saintliness and altruism do exist in the world, the prevalence of envy, malice, hatred, cruelty and avarice can never be safely ignored.[41] Nor does history give any assurance that the good will eventually triumph. Good governments as well as bad have been destroyed in revolutions, good rulers and statesmen have been murdered, scoundrels and monsters have succeeded, evil causes have prevailed. By comparing Luther's concept of this world as *des Teufels Wirtshaus*, the Devil's Inn, and Rousseau's concept of the limitless perfectibility of man on earth, it becomes evident where both the lesser error and the greater arrogance lie.

We are living today in an age of Roussellian triumphalism. Bolshevism is only one evidence of its victory; another is the hippie movement of the intellectual *Lumpenproletariat*. Rousseau is the grandfather of the concentration camps and also of those armed brothels that we continue to call universities. We have with us on one hand the Old Left, a finished product of *l'éducation sentimentale*, with its bent for social engineering and its tendency to identify its own plans and policies with the *volonté génerale*; on the other the New Left which has taken up the slogan *Retournons à la nature!* exemplified in the rabble of unwashed, unkempt, debauched, unbridled ignoble savages who look to the Third World of the underdeveloped for inspiration. Its heroes are Chairman Mao with his Little Red Book, Ché Guevara, Ho Chi Minh, Holden Roberto, the Harlem criminals and the pistol-packing priests. The New Left will continue its game until its time is up, and that will be either when the Roussellian dissolution engulfs us all or—as we should rather hope—when out of the deeper recesses of the American subconscious memories of the other Genevois rises to a new life. That will be a new day for Maistre Jehan, a great day and a bitter one for the rest of us.

NOTES

[1] The three most outstanding living *Catholic* Swiss theologians of world fame are Hans Urs von Balthasar, Otto Karrer, and the controversial Hans Küng.

[2] The *Frankfurter Allgemeine Zeitung* remarking on the complete lack of modern scholarship which characterized this film, called it *Der amerikanische Luther*, the very caricature of the Reformer.

[3] On the profoundly Christian character of the Renaissance and Luther's reactions cf. H. W. Rüssel, *Gestalt eines christlichen Humanismus* (Amsterdam: Pantheon, 1940), esp. pp. 142—147; G. Toffanin, *Storia del umanesimo* (Rome: Perella, 1940); Fred Bérence, *La Renaissance Italienne* (Paris: La Colombe, 1954), p. 16.

[4] The resistance of the German universities (and university cities) to Lutheranism is well described by Herbert Schöffler, *Die Reformation* (Frankfurt: V. Klostermann, n.d.), pp. 20, 42, 50.

[5] In Catholic American colleges the character of the Reformation was always taught "the other way round." All this went with an excessive and naïve

praise of the Middle Ages (versus the wicked Renaissance). James J. Walsh's *The Thirteenth, Greatest of Centuries* was then the most popular book. (Heaven knows what it is today!)

⁶ The greatest praise for the Renaissance and the strongest criticism of the Middle Ages written by a Catholic are perhaps contained in Giovanni Papini's *L'imitazione del padre. Saggi sul Rinascimento* (Florence: Le Monnier, 1942), pp. 4–5, 8–9, 18–19, 27.

⁷ Cf. Calvin, *Institutions*, IV, xx, 25.

⁸ We put this term in brackets as it is a term of opprobrium invented in the sixteenth century by the Counter-Reformers who began to use it more generally a hundred years later. It has no *official* standing on the European continent. The explanation that "Protestant" comes from *pro-testare*, i.e. to stand witness, is a nineteenth century legerdemain.

⁹ Cf. H. U. v. Balthasar, *Karl Barth. Darstellung und Deutung seiner Theologie* (Cologne: Jakob Hegner, 1951), p. 186.

¹⁰ Sebastian Franck (1499–1543) exclaimed that one merely thought to have escaped the monastery but now everybody had to be a monk. Cf. A. Rüstow, *Ortsbestimmung der Gegenwart* (Erlenbach: Rentsch, 1952), Vol. 2, p. 291. It is, however, significant that the revival of monasticism among the Reformation faiths came primarily from Calvinists—vide Taizé.

¹¹ On Geneva under Calvin and his successors cf. F. W. Kampschulte, *Johann Calvin. Seine Kirche und sein Staat in Genf* (Leipzig: Duncker und Humblot, 1869 and 1899), 2 vols. esp. Vol. 1, p. 444 sq.

¹² Cf. I. M. Bochenski, *Der sowjetrussische dialektische Materialismus* (Bern: Francke, 1956), p. 14.

¹³ Cf. F. W. Hegel. "Philosophie der Geschichte" in *Werke* (Berlin: Duncker und Humblot, 1948), Vol. 9, pp. 541–542.

¹⁴ We should say that without a real grasp of the Renaissance and the Baroque spirit an understanding of the Catholic world is well-nigh impossible. The only Catholic country which has escaped these influences, significantly enough, is Ireland.

¹⁵ In German Lutheranism auricular confession (which Luther himself practiced to his dying day) fell victim to Enlightenment. It was revived and reinstated only in 1956.

¹⁶ It is one of the common errors of the American Catholic who ignores the very healthy survival of the former (though in a certain isolation from the big world), to see in the latter the real representative of "Protestantism." No wonder, because he still believes that Luther stood for "private interpretation." Luther did nothing of the sort. Woe to the man who disagreed with him!

¹⁷ On Calvin and Rousseau cf. also A. M. Cornelissen, *Calvin en Rousseau* (Nijmegen-Utrecht: Dek-

ker, 1931) and Corrado Eggers-Lecour, "Calvino y Rousseau o la ambivalencia ginebrina" in *Razón y Fé*, Vol. 165 (May 1962), pp. 481–494.

¹⁸ Rousseau who had written so beautifully on education put all his children into an orphanage. He could not be bothered with them.

¹⁹ On Marx as an organic product of German Romanticism cf. Ernst Kux, *Karl Marx, Die revolutionäre Konfession* (Erlenbach: Rentsch, 1967).

²⁰ Cf. Irving Babbitt, *Rousseau and Romanticism* (Boston: Houghton Mifflin, 1919).

²¹ Is there a connection between the theatrical figure of Chauvin (Chauvinism) and Calvin? The meaning of the Latin-French word is originally the same.

²² The attitudes of Jefferson and Franklin towards money were similar—counting, calculating, cautious.

²³ Jefferson, too, was convinced that the United States (due to its agrarian character but also for other reasons) was more virtuous than Europe where nascent republicanism identified virtue as the essence of the republic while the monarchic system was "depraved." Honesty, fortitude, chastity, veracity became *vertus républicaines*.

²⁴ Alexander Hamilton, however, seems to have been a truly religious man. This is evident from his farewell letter to his wife before his duel with Aaron Burr. Cf. *The Basic Ideas of A. Hamilton* edited by R. B. Morris (New York: Pocket Library, 1957) p. 451.

²⁵ Cf. Ray Allen Billington, *The Protestant Crusade 1800–1860* (New York: Macmillan, 1938), p. 17 and John C. Miller, *Origins of the American Revolution* (Boston: Little, Brown, 1943), pp. 190–191, 373–374.

²⁶ Genuine clericalism exists only in "decapitated" societies where the priests can assume the function of the First and Second Estate. For this reason clericalism existed or exists in Ireland, Holland, French Canada, Slovenia, Slovakia, but never in Spain, Bavaria, etc.

²⁷ It is significant that there were in the United States during the nineteen-forties and nineteen-fifties three Catholic theological reviews called *Modern Schoolman, New Scholasticism* and *The Thomist*. To uphold a non-Thomist view in Catholic circles was considered extremely "rash" if not down-right heretical. Today the fashion aims at the other extreme.

²⁸ There were several Catholic clubs in the United States calling themselves *The Medievalists*.

²⁹ Cf. Everett Dean Martin, *Liberty* (New York: W. W. Norton, 1930), pp. 79 and 81; D. H. Lawrence, *Studies in Classic American Literature* (New York: Doubleday, 1953), p. 15.

³⁰ Cf. Emile Doumergue, "Calvin et l'Entente de

Wilson à Calvin" in *Revue de Métaphysique et de Morale*, Vol. 25 (Sept.–Dec. 1918).

[31] Cf. Herron's Letter to the President, dated March 20, 1919. In the *Herron Papers*, Box of Docum. VII a. (Hoover Institute, Stanford) He wrote: "We are in the bounds of historic truth when we say that the Puritan Revolution, the French Revolution, the American Revolution, all had their springs in Geneva." Indeed, they had, but Calvin and Rousseau were two different men and Cotton Mather no more than George Washington would have accepted Danton as brother under the skin.

[32] There is a tombstone at the *Stadtpfarrkirche* in Klagenfurt which carries the inscription *NASCI, PATI, MORI*. To see the switch from Calvinist seriousness (and Christian devotion) to modern hedonism (and illusionism) one must compare ancient New England graveyards with modern "Memorial Parks."

[33] Jackson was undoubtedly a democrat, but the position of Jefferson is by no means clear. In all his collected works (Washington edition) he only *once* spoke out (indirectly) in favor of democracy when in a letter to Dupont de Nemours he called the "temper" of the American people democratic. Yet in a letter to Mann Page (Aug. 30, 1795) he spoke about the "swinish multitudes." Cf. *The Writings of Thomas Jefferson*, ed. P. L. Ford (New York: Putnam, 1896), Vol. 7, p. 24. His outlook was essentially elitarian and he proposed the establishment of harems so that superior men (like himself), could have a large progeny. Cf. L. J. Cappon, *The Adams-Jefferson Letters* (Chapel Hill: U. of N. Carolina Press, 1959), Vol. 2, p. 387.

[34] On America in the early nineteenth century cf. Francis J. Grund, *Aristocracy in America* (New York: Harper Torchbook, 1959), *passim*.

[35] Richard Hofstadter, *Anti-Intellectualism in American Life* (London: Jonathan Cape, 1964), *passim*.

[36] Today it ought to be evident to all and sundry that suppression by such enlightened and uncrowned "leaders" as the late Adolf Hitler or Joseph Stalin, Fidel Castro or Mao Tse-tung, Ernest Gerö or Antonín Novotny was worse than that of kings in times bygone.

[37] Equality invoked by our theologians is usually *adverbial* equality. We have equally souls (but, of course, not equal souls), we are equally children of God (but not equal children of God), etc. If we have equally banking accounts, it does not mean by any means that we have equal bank accounts.

[38] It could, however, be argued that in no political system is the dignity of man so challenged than precisely in those stemming from the French Revolution, i.e. those inspired by Rousseau. "Democracy" belongs to the same group. Here man is a mere cypher, an arithmetical, not an algebraic unit. Long ago Aristotle remarked that men in democracies are counted by numbers and not according to worth.

[39] Locke was convinced that "right is what the majority wills—what the majority wills is right." Cf. Willmoore Kendall, "John Locke and the Doctrine of Majority Rule," in *Illinois Studies in the Social Sciences*, Vol. 26, No. 2 (1941), p 132. This notion is very Roussellian. It would certainly not have been shared by Voltaire who belonged to the Enlightenment, but not to Romanticism. His contempt for Rousseau was impressive. Cf. his exchange of letters with d'Alembert in *Oeuvres complètes de Voltaire* (Paris: Société Littéraire; 1785), Vol. 68.

[40] The worst upheavals in Latin America are taking place in that former Model-State, the Latin American Switzerland—Uruguay. This is a strictly dereligionized welfare state with a very balanced social structure. There are neither grave social nor racial problems. The leaders of the terroristic *Tupamaros*, however, are sons (and daughters) of well-to-do or even rich families. The *Tupamaros* are called after Tupac Amaru, an Indian-Peruvian eighteenth century rebel . . . . but there are *no* Indians in Uruguay.

[41] Envy according to the late Earl Bertrand Russell is the driving motor of democracy. Cf. his *The Conquest of Happiness* (New York: Horace Liveright, 1930), pp. 83–84. [XV, Winter 1971, 45–56]

[45]

The Institutional Church and Political Activity

RENE DE VISME WILLIAMSON

René de Visme Williamson (1908–   ) blends two important disciplines in his expertise as a political scientist and a committed Presbyterian churchman. A graduate of Rutgers University (B.A., 1931), he earned both the M.A. (1932) and Ph.D. (1935) degrees at Harvard University. A retired chairman of the Department of Political Science at Louisiana State University with a specialization in political theory, comparative government, and international law, Williamson held professorships at Princeton University, Davidson College, Beloit College, and the University of Tennessee, as well as visiting professorships at numerous American colleges and universities and at the University of Napal in Durban, South Africa. From 1949 to 1953 he was editor of the Journal of Politics *and from 1959 to 1960 he was president of the Southern Political Science Association. He is the author of five books, including* Politics and Protestant Theology *(1976) and* Independence and Involvement *(1964), and many articles.*

THE IDEA THAT there exists a necessary relationship between the Christian faith and politics is, of course, not new. The subject is an exceedingly difficult and controversial one. It is something which sharply divides all the mainline Protestant denominations. We have had, for instance, the so-called Social Gospel in the nineteen twenties. The Social Gospel demanded that ministers devote their sermons to political issues and that church bodies make pronouncements on these issues to guide the conscience of members and influence public policy.

The Nature and Rise of Social Activism

Now, however, the involvement of the church in political activity is being advocated and pushed much further. The demand is that the church move from words to deeds. Sermons and pronouncements are not enough. There must be active lobbying for decisions by legislative, executive, and judicial bodies. There must be direct personal participation by church members, ministers, and denominational officials in mass demonstrations, some violent and some nonviolent. Following

532

the current slogan that we must put our money where our mouth is, church bodies are withdrawing denominational funds from enterprises they disapprove of and investing them in enterprises that meet with their approval. Individual church members are urged to follow the denominational party line in their own private investments. This political use of denomination and private funds is urged upon us as an imperative of the Christian faith and described as corporate responsibility.

This push for what has become known as Social Activism is not limited to domestic affairs such as when we are urged to withdraw funds from businesses that have defense contracts or to invest funds in high risk black-controlled enterprises. It spills over into foreign affairs. It demands church use of a financial club in the domestic affairs of South Africa, Rhodesia, and Portugal—but not, curiously enough, in the domestic affairs of Communist countries. It demands the support of so-called liberation movements in Africa and revolution in Brazil. It has caused a group of high officials of the Presbyterian Church in the United States to go to Paris and consult with the North Vietnamese and Viet Cong delegations in the very midst of governmental negotiations—in violation of the Logan Act, I might add. It has caused the United Presbyterian Church to send money to a Protestant group in Colombia in spite of the vehement protests of the Colombian Presbyterian Church. These interventions in foreign affairs are to some extent funnelled and directed by the World Council of Churches.

Social Activism is finding its place in ecclesiastical structures. In my own denomination, the Presbyterian Church in the United States, which is going through a thoroughgoing restructuring, Social Activism is recognized in a new division in

the general executive board designated as corporate responsibility. A new office has also been created, that of Washington communicator, with a salary of $20,000 a year. He is in fact a lobbyist, and it remains to be seen whether he is required by law to register as such. Most mainline denominations have some structural recognition of Social Activism called by various names such as Council on Church and Society.

The movement from the Social Gospel to Social Activism is not very old. It probably owes its impetus, if not its birth, to the civil rights movement and was further strengthened by the controversies over the Vietnam War. Its latest reinforcement has come from the Women's Liberation Movement and is taking the form of a demand for quotas (the word is usually avoided) for women as well as ethnic groups in denominational structures. As we observe the impact of anti-war groups, civil rights groups, and Women's Lib on the life of the church and we remember the Great Commission, one wonders who is converting whom and to what.

A Personal Frame of Reference

Anyone who tries to answer this question and appraise Social Activism cannot do so in an ideological or theological vacuum. He must do it on the basis of his own convictions, and fairness demands that he make clear from what standpoint he makes his judgments. In response to this demand, let me say that I am a member of the Presbyterian Church in the United States, subscribe to the Standards of my church (*i.e.* the Confession of Faith, the Larger and Shorter Catechisms, and the Book of Church Order), adhere to the Calvinist Reformed theology, and believe that a Christian's position in all things should be Bible-based and Christ-centered. In other words, I am a conservative in religion.

In politics I am and have been a lifelong Democrat. For much of my life I have supported liberal candidates and policies. I do not regret this insofar as those earlier years are concerned, but in later years I have become a conservative. I do not mean that I have become a prisoner of the status quo or lost the compassion for the underprivileged and the dedication to political and social ideals which once caused me to be a liberal. But I do mean that, in my firm opinion, times have changed so much that the issues of earlier years are no longer the same and different approaches and remedies are called for. By way of example, I have come to the belief that crucial social problems like poverty and racial tensions are too complex to be solved by the mere expenditure of federal funds and the extension of governmental power.

*The Conceptual Approach
to Religion and Politics*

Turning to the relation of religion and political science, I have no difficulty in affirming the relevance of the Christian faith to my chosen professional field. For most of my life, I have tried to rethink the basic concepts of political science in the light of the Christian faith and written a book in which I reviewed such concepts as state, law, constitution, civil rights, citizenship, and representation in that light. I believe this kind of rethinking is a very fruitful endeavor because it yields a truer and deeper understanding of these concepts and delivers the political scientist from being the victim of gadgetry and all that which is merely technical. Political institutions and processes are illuminated

and brought into perspective as they are linked with the purposes which have or should have brought them into existence. Moreover, the confrontation of Christian theology and political science exposes false values, many of which lie hidden under various labels like behaviorism. I would like to see the kind of intellectual reconstruction required by this enterprise extended to all other fields, particularly those of philosophy, psychology, history, economics, and sociology because they deal directly with human life. Obviously, the vastness of human knowledge puts this task beyond any would-be twentieth-century Thomas Aquinas. Furthermore, this necessarily collective task can only be undertaken by scholars who are as well versed in theology as they are in their professional fields, and that is something which is rare indeed. We should observe, too, that this is a task primarily for laymen and not ministers. Ministers may well be useful as resource persons, but they are not equipped to do the job themselves.

Rethinking the concepts of one's professional field in the light of the Christian faith, valuable and illuminating as it is, cannot solve the problem of Social Activism. It touches it, to be sure, but it does not solve it. A concept is one thing, and a public policy is quite another. The first refers to thought, while the second refers to action. The most that I can say for the conceptual approach in relation to Social Activism is that it may produce enough insight into the issues to be faced and the context in which they arise to enable public officials to make the right decision as Christians. It may supply resources for an answer, but not the answer itself. This is commendable and desirable, but it is not enough. At this point, I know of no way to proceed except by grappling with specifics and seeing whether doing so can lead to guiding principles.

The Issue of Civil Disobedience

The first issue I shall discuss is that of civil disobedience. Perhaps it would be well to begin by reminding ourselves of the difference between civil and criminal disobedience. Civil disobedience can be identified by three criteria: (1) high-minded motives arising out of religious convictions, (2) the unavailability of legal means to obtain redress of legitimate grievances or to promote a righteous cause, (3) the willingness to accept the consequences of disobedience. Criminal disobedience fails to meet the first and third criteria: the motives are reprehensible like greed and revenge, and there is a total unwillingness to accept the consequences. The second criterion is obviously inapplicable. Civil disobedience was resorted to rather extensively by people in the civil rights movement. Some of these people met the first and third criteria. Whether or not they met the second criterion has been much debated. The issue depends on a judgment of fact, *i.e.* whether the alternative legal means of peaceful persuasion, voting, and access to the courts were sufficiently effective and prompt to achieve the legitimate demands of the blacks. There is considerable disagreement on this point and probably always will be.

The General Assembly of the Presbyterian Church in the United States has endorsed the principle of civil disobedience, much to the dismay of large numbers of Presbyterians. It seems to me, however, that a Christian must conclude that the General Assembly was right insofar as the principle itself is concerned. If the early Christians had not disobeyed the commands of the constituted authorities of their day by following the admonition of the apostle Peter that we must obey God rather than man, Christianity would have died with the first generation. Nor would Protestantism exist, including its Presbyterian form, if the early Reformers had not followed the example of Martin Luther when he uttered the famous words, "Here I stand, I can do no other, so help me God."

It should be observed, however, that endorsing the principle of civil disobedience—even if all three criteria are scrupulously met—should not be regarded as an automatic invitation to apply it. Every human being, and especially a Christian and the church to which he belongs, must carefully consider all the consequences of his acts to the best of his ability. Church bodies must realize that their pronouncements easily and often do lead to misunderstandings with the result that civil disobedience degenerates into criminal disobedience, and lawlessness, in turn, is apt to bring brutal repression. Young men who publicly burned their draft cards—a clearly illegal act—are a borderline case. Even if we grant them the benefit of the doubt as to motives and recognize their willingness to accept the consequences, they fail to meet the second criterion for civil disobedience because they had the option to get classified as conscientious objectors. But even here, some people might stretch a point by arguing that these young men had no real legal alternative because it took a dramatic gesture like card-burning to press their cause upon the public. Conceding this point merely for the sake of argument, the fact still remains that such a gesture can have serious consequences. It may result in military defeat induced by low domestic morale in a war which, in fact, is necessary for national survival and the safeguarding of the Christian values of Western civilization.

It will do no good to invoke Christ's admonition to turn the other cheek. Jesus did not instruct his disciples to turn other people's cheeks, and governments are responsible for the welfare of peoples and not just themselves. A church body or a high church official who condones or encourages young men to burn their draft cards may become morally responsible for national disaster. It is this matter of political responsibility which may prevent the granting of amnesty to draft dodgers and deserters of the Vietnam War. Of course draft dodgers and deserters are guilty of criminal disobedience because they do not fit any of the criteria for civil disobedience. The point is that these people have no moral right to amnesty and the government has no moral duty to grant it. Whether amnesty is granted or not is a matter of public policy based on a judgment as to what is most conducive to the national interest. To act on principle alone without regard to consequences can lead to the most atrocious sacrifice of human life, welfare, and happiness, whether performed by individuals, churches, or governments. It might be noted, in passing, that our Social Activists are not always consistent, for they insist on the moral right to disobey the draft law and, with equal fervor, insist on the most uncompromising obedience as a moral duty to busing pupils from one end of the city to the other so that racial balance may be achieved.

The Issue of Corporate Responsibility

The second issue I shall discuss is that of corporate responsibility. This issue, as we have already observed, deals with money and, more especially, with investment. It arises from the fact that religious denominations have very large sums of money at their disposal running into many millions. Not all of that money is spent on denominational programs. Much of it is invested in stocks, bonds, land, and buildings. Large amounts are also deposited in banks. Some of the money, of course, is spent for the salaries of ministers and denominational board executives, for operating expenses, and for benevolences. It is noteworthy that benevolences is an elastic term which can include many causes. In the Presbyterian Church in the United States, for example, the Birthday Offering of the Women of the Church for 1973 amounted to more than $400,000, and half of this sum was assigned to the relief of world hunger—an imperceptible drop in one enormous bucket.

The Social Activists contend that the possession of those vast sums creates a moral responsibility for churches (and individual church members as well) which no Christian can rightly ignore. As the slogan goes, churches and church members should put their money where their mouth is. Let us note, in passing, that this slogan is not consistently adhered to, for the Social Activists raise a loud outcry when conservative church members diminish or withhold their contributions to denominational causes and support because they do not approve the uses which the denomination makes of them. In this case, the slogan is quite forgotten. In general, one can say that the concept of corporate responsibility discards the usual economic criterion of investing money where the highest returns are after due consideration to the element of risk. Considering the size of denominational funds, it is easy to see that if the demands of the Social Activists were met, the impact on eonomic life would be great, especially if large numbers of individual church members took parallel action.

The suggestion that the investment and spending of money should be governed by moral rather than economic criteria would appear to be an economic rather than a political matter since we are dealing with money. In a way, of course, it does. At bottom, however, it is a political matter because the causes for which it is proposed that money be invested, spent, or withheld are usually clearly political and always have strong political implications. The concept of corporate responsibility, therefore, necessarily means a profound involvement of the institutional church in political activity, political activity not being understood in the modern sense of a mere struggle for power (though such a struggle is always involved) but in the old Greek sense of a collective pursuit of the good life.

Let us admit that there is validity to the principle that moral considerations are relevant to the investment and spending of money. These considerations may be decisive in some cases. For instance, I believe every Christian would agree that churches and churchmen should not invest their money in houses of prostitution, no matter how high the rate of return might be.

Nevertheless, admitting the principle requires that moral considerations be carefully identified in concrete situations, that the proper occasion for acting upon them be dependably determined, and that the probable consequences of political action be thoroughly ascertained and evaluated beforehand. Such an analysis always depends upon a judgment of facts, facts which are not theological or moral but political, social, and economic. And respect for facts, whether palatable or unpalatable, is essential in applying Christian principles. There is no place in the Christian life for untruth, distortion, wishful thinking, or prejudice. This aspect of the application of moral principles calls for a professional knowledge and expertise which ministers and church bodies seldom possess. It is something which falls in the domain of laymen, *i.e.* businessmen, educators, lawyers, government officials, military officers, political scientists, economists, sociologists, and (in the case of ecology) of natural scientists. Any political involvement of the institutional church which neglects or disregards professional knowledge and expertise is irresponsible and must be condemned on Christian grounds.

Unfortunately, most of the involvement of the institutional church in political activity with which I am acquainted belongs to the category of irresponsible activity because the judgments of facts on which they are based are faulty and the moral motivation which prompts it is marred by prejudice. Space does not permit me to go into all the cases I have in mind, so I shall illustrate what I mean by pointing to only one example, namely Social Activist attitudes and actions dealing with South Africa.

Many of the mainline Protestant denominations, among which are the United Church of Christ, the United Methodist Church, and the United Presbyterian Church have condemned South Africa in the harshest terms and sought to apply their concept of corporate responsibility to that country. The World Council of Churches has done the same. All these bodies defend their position in the name of the Christian faith. What is wrong with that?

In the first place, this position fails to take into account the magnitude of the problems which South Africa is facing. Some legitimate questions should be asked of our churches. What right have they to expect the white people of South Africa to bring millions of blacks from the most primitive tribalism into the twentieth century in one generation when it took the white peoples of Europe over two thousand years to reach it? How great a financial burden can four million whites carry to raise the standard of living of sixteen million blacks without killing the goose that lays the golden eggs? How do you govern and promote peace and harmony in a country that is multi-national, multi-racial, multi-lingual, religiously and culturally diverse? To ask such questions is to answer them or, rather, to confess one's inability to answer them. Certainly our Social Activists have never replied to the late Prime Minister Verwoerd's challenge to the Commonwealth Conference in London some years ago: what else would you do?

In the second place, this position is faulty because it judges South Africa in terms of black and white when what you have got is various shades of grey—or brown. There is no doubt whatever that there are South African policies which are morally indefensible, *e.g.* some measures which are characteristic of police states, some features of petty *apartheid* which affront human dignity, the breakup of families in labor compounds. But no account is taken of the fact that townships have replaced ghettos and more money is spent on the housing, education, and health of the blacks than in any of the black republics to the north, an amount vastly larger in proportion to what is spent on the blacks in our own country. No account is taken of the policy of creating Bantustans whereby blacks are being trained for self-government with independence as the ultimate goal. One trouble is, of course, that many of our critics have no conception of what a Bantustan is. A recent report of an official body to the 1973 General Assembly of the United Presbyterian Church obviously confused it with townships. No account is taken of the fact that the most informed and severest attack on what is wrong with South African policies are to be found publicly expressed in South African newspapers and universities. No account is taken of the fact that large numbers of blacks from the republics to the north are migrating

to that House of Horrors, as the title of a recent book calls South Africa. These migrants apparently know better!

In the third place, the above described one-sidedness is based on more than ignorance. It reeks of virulent prejudice. How else can one explain that our Social Activists shed crocodile tears over poverty and disease in the Transkei but are dry-eyed over worse conditions in Lesotho and Botswana—not to mention the black republics to the north? How else can you explain the condemnation of townships like Soweto while not one word is said about the ghettos of Rio de Janeiro and Lima which I have seen with my own eyes and which are among the worst in the world? Where is the condemnation of the Brazilian and Peruvian governments for adopting a policy of letting them rot? Why is it that the police state measures of South Africa are denounced while the much more severe ones of the Communist states are given the silent treatment?

In the fourth place, racial segregation in South Africa is judged by reference to American, not South African, conditions. Segregation by law in the United States was indeed an evil which we have abandoned *de jure* and are trying to abandon *de facto*. But in South Africa, segregation is made necessary by the vast cultural, economic, social, and health conditions of the peoples who live there. To integrate in that country would cause an explosion—a repetition of the famous Durban riots when the Zulus tried to exterminate the Indians, violent expulsions of peoples like that of the Asians in Kenya and Uganda, bloodshed as in the massacre of Arabs by blacks in Zanzibar. Those who cannot get along must be separated, and people of like origins, language, and culture naturally gravitate toward each other. Curiously enough, the one case in which South African segregation policies are indefensible is the very one never mentioned by our Social Activists, namely the application of *apartheid* to the two million Coloureds who live in the Cape Province and whose position with respect to the South African whites is almost identical with that of our American blacks.

In the fifth place, our Social Activists do not think through the consequences of withdrawing American business investments in South Africa. It would seem elementary to see that the first victims of such a withdrawal would be the blacks—the very ones which our Social Activists claim to be most concerned with. Many blacks would lose their jobs as well as the beneficial effect of the higher wages paid by American business on the policies of South African business. Also lost would be the broadening effect of the American presence on the tendency of South Africans to a parochialism born of geographic isolation.

This necessarily brief survey of the application of the concept of corporate responsibility to South Africa illustrates the terrible vulnerability of that concept to error in judgment of fact, to prejudice in the moral realm, and to political irresponsibility.

The Issue of Compensatory Action

What has become known as compensatory action is a response to the plight and pressure resulting therefrom of groups which are and have been the victims of unfair discrimination. It springs mainly from ethnic groups and women who have received unequal treatment. These groups demand equal pay for equal work. They protest against discrimination in employment on the basis of race, national origin, or sex. They point to the fact that their members are the last to be hired and the first to be fired. Almost everyone concedes that their cause is a just one. Their legit-

imate demands resulted in legislation designed to assure equal rights for everyone in fact as well as in law, by private employers and groups as well as public bodies. In the case of women, an amendment to the Constitution has been endorsed by Congress and is now pending before the state legislatures for ratification—a veritable Pandora's box.

The movement for equal rights and nondiscrimination has gone beyond the achievement of equality in the hitherto recognized sense. The call now is for what is labelled compensatory action. What this call means was most dramatically propounded by the Negro James Forman who appeared before top denominational bodies and demanded that they hand over many millions of dollars to black organizations to compensate for the years of slavery and the discriminations which followed emancipation and for which he held the white churches responsible. He described his demand as a call for reparation, which is another word for compensatory action.

The movement for compensatory action was taken up by the federal government through the Department of Health, Education, and Welfare and the Office of Equal Opportunity. This has meant the application of federal pressure on the federal bureaucracy, private employers, and universities to force them to hire more blacks and women to the point where a "balance" has been achieved, and to rectify salary scales and status in rank for these groups at an accelerated rate to bring them up to the level of those already on the payroll. Public school children are to be bused regardless of time, expense, and distance to the extent of achieving a "racial balance" and public school teachers are to be reassigned with the same end in view. In all this the term "quota" is not officially recognized because so much opposition to it has developed, but its substance is disguised and retained under such terms as "proportionate" and "plans for affirmative action." Needless to say, the Social Activists are strongly in favor of compensatory action and they strain every effort to support it.

Compensatory action is having a great impact on ecclesiastical structures. As is the case in so many other instances, the impetus for compensatory action came from the government rather than the churches, and the churches are merely responding to a secular movement outside. The Social Activists are pushing for structural changes which would give a representation to ethnic minorities and women that would correspond to the relative number of these groups in the church membership. In addition, Social Activists are pushing for special recognition for youth, usually defined as people under thirty. These changes are applied to denominational courts and assemblies, boards and agencies, and church colleges and seminaries. The effect on local congregations is less marked and will probably be slower to appear, but I have heard of a sixteen year old boy being elected to the status of Ruling Elder in a Presbyterian church, and the number of women ministers and church officers is increasing.

We have now reached a point where we must appraise the concept of compensatory action. Is it a Christian concept which the institutional church is bound in conscience to approve and apply? Before I try to answer this question, let me first dispose of the James Forman argument that reparation is due to those who have been victimized. That argument is clearly bad theology. There is no way to pay for two centuries of slavery, discrimination, and exploitation. There is no amount of money that can cure broken hearts, deep-seated feelings of inferiority, and the agony of personal insecurity. Similarly, where blessings, privileges, and opportunities have been conferred on someone, there is no way by which the recipient can begin to pay for what he has received and enjoyed. Grace is free. All he can do is to pass on the blessings he has not earned to others who do not deserve them either.

The real and authentically Christian basis for a government's social policy is response to human need. What is done is done and cannot be undone. What counts are the present and the future, because these are things we can do something about. The question, therefore, must be reformulated in the following way: is compensatory action a proper response to human need?

The argument which is made for compensatory action is that when things are out of balance they are one-sided, and to get them into balance, more weight must be placed on the other side. If women are to occupy that position in political, economic, and social life to which their abilities entitle them, special extra efforts must be made to achieve that end. The men do not need such efforts because they occupy that position already. If the potentialities of the black people are to be actualized, special extra efforts must be made, efforts which need not be made for the dominant white people. It must be conceded that there is a good deal of validity to this argument. Thus, parents who have two children, one who needs a great deal of medical attention and one who does not: more money will have to be spent on the first than on the second, and neither the parents nor anyone else will think that there is anything unfair about it. Parents try to meet the needs of their children and recognize that those needs are not the same in either character or extent. On the family level, therefore, any Christian should endorse the concept of compensatory action.

But endorsing this concept as a basis

for action by governments and churches raises serious problems which Social Activists generally ignore. One of these is the logical inconsistency inherent in affirming compensatory action on the one hand and the principle of equality without regard to race, national origins, or sex on the other. You simply cannot have it both ways. Compensatory action only transfers discrimination from one group to another. To grant favored treatment to blacks in employment means to discriminate against the whites. Individual job seekers no longer stand on their own merits but as members of a particular race, and that is precisely what is normally meant by racism. This is especially true when it is argued, and it is by some of the more extreme Social Activists, that a less qualified applicant should get a position because he is black. It is generally admitted that such employment policies are illegal and immoral when the less qualified applicant happens to be white. Why is it not equally illegal and immoral when this applicant happens to be black? What all this amounts to is that it takes two wrongs to make a right and that injustice must be perpetrated that justice may be achieved.

There are people who, recognizing the logical inconsistency of affirming both compensatory action and nondiscrimination, frankly choose the former. They do so in order to achieve ultimate equality. Ultimate equality is taken for granted, accepted as an axiom. But is it really such? Any survey of society, past and present, shows that inequality is an inseparable and inescapable part of life. Christians will agree that God loves all human beings equally right down to the individual person, but no one can contend that God has endowed them all equally. To argue that ultimate equality is a Christian objective cannot be sustained. God singled out the Jews as His chosen people, not the Egyptians, the Assyrians, and the Babylonians.

Jesus chose twelve disciples, not one hundred or one thousand. Equality in the Christian religion is absolute in the sense that we are not called to do and to be more than God enables us to do and to be. That is all we have a right to expect.

As is true with all principles, compensatory action should not be applied without the most careful and conscientious consideration of probable consequences. Assistance to one group should not inflict injury on other groups. In the case of busing, churches should adopt a flexible attitude and not consider it as a dogma to be universally applied without regard to time and place. In some places, busing results in interracial friendships among black and white children, thus paving the way for adult harmony in the future. In other places, busing results in physical injury and disorder to the point where no education is possible for either blacks or whites because all school time must be devoted to discipline. Furthermore, no busing or other form of compensatory action should operate to the detriment of excellence and merit. It can also happen that the money used for busing might be better spent for other purposes advantageous to both races, such as raising teacher salaries and improving school equipment. The Christian view of busing, therefore, must be flexible enough and open-minded enough to take circumstances into account and see to it that Christian principles have Christian consequences.

Criteria for Involvement of the Institutional Church in Political Activity

One of the most obvious observations concerning Social Activism is that Jesus was not a Social Activist. He sympathized with the poor and fed the five thousand who came to hear him, but he did not feed all the people in Palestine nor suggest an anti-poverty program. He said not one word about the institution of slavery so prevalent in his day. He did not join the zealots or denounce Roman policies. He approved the payment of taxes to Rome and urged the Jews to render unto Caesar (who was a pagan) what is Caesar's. He attended the synagogue regularly. He honored the Temple, so much so that he was indignant at its profanation by money changers. In short, Jesus was not a revolutionist or a Social Activist in any sense that we would recognize. Jesus was concerned with the transformation of the mind and heart of men. He looked upon social and political evils as symptoms and dealt with the source. Why prescribe palliatives when you have the cure?

Neither can our Social Activists find much comfort in the epistles. Instead of preaching the abolition of slavery, the apostle Paul urged slaves to obey their masters not only as a matter of prudence but of conscience. He told wives to obey their husbands and children to obey their parents. He said that magistrates should be honored and not resisted. When the apostle Peter converted the centurion Cornelius, he did not tell him to quit the Roman army. It is true that the apostle James loved the poor and said some harsh things about the rich, but even he did not come up with an anti-poverty program, and he ascribed the existence of war not to social or political causes but to the human heart.

The New Testament position being what it is, the Social Activists fall back on the Old Testament, particularly the prophets. They are fond of saying that the church should speak with "a prophetic voice," by which they mean a fervent and ceaseless denunciation of current political, social, and economic evils. This reliance on the Old Testament makes it necessary for us to determine just what the role of a prophet in ancient Israel was and to deduce from

this what are the criteria which should govern the involvement of the institutional church in political activity.

In the first place, it should be noted that the prophets were speaking for God, not for themselves. Time and time again, they would say: Thus saith the Lord. They were not voicing personal opinions, sociological conclusions, or debatable propositions. God spoke to them and gave them a message. They were utterly convinced of this fact and needed no sociological surveys and computerized data to give them the certainty and authority with which they spoke. It would appear, therefore, that churchmen and church bodies should be similarly convinced to the depth of their being that they are speaking for God at God's specific and unquestionable direction, or else they should keep silent. Few church pronouncements indeed show signs in the language and the context in which they are made that they originate in that kind of certainty and authority.

In the second place, the ancient prophets spoke unwillingly and did so only under divine duress. They did not enjoy their message at all. Moses did his best to argue himself out of his commission to deliver the people of Israel from Egyptian slavery. Jonah tried to escape his commission by fleeing to Spain which, in his day, was thought to be the end of the earth. Jeremiah pled with God that he not take up his role as a prophet and lamented over the events he was obliged to prophesy. And Jesus himself, let us not forget, wept over the fate of Jerusalem which he foresaw. Yes, the role of a prophet is a heavy and painful one which nobody in his senses would seek and relish. In contrast, most of our modern would-be prophets seem to enjoy their message and luxuriate in denunciation.

In the third place, the ancient prophets ran enormous personal risks, unpopularity being the least of these. Jeremiah was thrown into prison, a dungeon where he sank in the mire. Daniel was thrown into a fiery furnace. Elijah fled for his life into the desert from the wrath of Jezebel and Ahab. John the Baptist was beheaded. In contrast, our modern would-be prophets speak their uncostly message from comfortable, air-conditioned, and well equipped offices and enjoy the protection of constitutional guarantees of freedom of speech. Among them, I can think of only three who ran great personal risks and paid a high price for it, namely Martin Niemoeller, Dietrich Bonhoeffer, and Martin Luther King. Niemoeller was sent to a Nazi concentration camp. Bonhoeffer was executed by the Nazis after a term in prison. King was in prison several times and was the victim of an assassin's bullet. But these martyrs are few indeed and not at all typical of our modern would-be prophets.

In the fourth place, the ancient prophets never limited themselves to denunciation and purely negative messages. They were like Isaiah who held up visions of peace, of a new heaven and a new earth, of forgiveness whereby blood-stained souls would be white as snow. They offered the people something to live for and to live by. In contrast, our modern would-be prophets are mostly negative, and when they venture to say something positive, it has none of the power, precision, and color which characterized the message of the ancient prophets. Martin Luther King was an exception, and people still remember with nostalgia his famous sermon, "I have a Dream." In that sermon, he stood in the tradition of the ancient prophets.

In the fifth place, when the ancient prophets spoke, they did so with foreknowledge. Under divine inspiration, they saw the future in all its infamy and all its glory. They knew that when you prophesy, you had better be right! And they

were. Nor was this a matter of giving forth ambiguous Delphic utterances. Thus, when king Zedekiah inquired of Jeremiah if there was a word from the Lord, Jeremiah replied: "There is: For thou shalt be delivered into the hand of the king of Babylon." This is exactly what happened. Again: in the fifty third chapter of Isaiah we find a description of Christ so detailed, so specific, and so accurate that it is startling. Let the scholars argue whether these words were written seven hundred or three hundred years before the birth of Christ. It does not matter. We have here a clear case of foreknowledge either way. Let the Jews argue that Isaiah was describing not Jesus but Israel. It does not matter either, for Jesus was the incarnation of everything Israel was supposed to be, with the result that both the Christian and the Jewish interpretations are right. In contrast, it is evident that our modern would-be prophets do not have foreknowledge. They do not even claim it. And yet, if they are true prophets, they should have it, whether it come to them from predictions based on the most thorough research and understanding of the facts or by direct perception of the future as was the case with the ancient prophets.

If the would-be prophets, past and present, in the World Council of Churches like Eugene Carson Blake and Philip Potter are to be real prophets, if those who so loudly demand that the churches speak with a prophetic voice are to be believed, they ought to meet the five criteria we have just described. If these criteria are not met, it becomes impossible to distinguish preaching from propaganda. The worst aspect of Social Activism is that it plunges the churches so deep in politics that the necessary theological foundation is ignored and the Gospel is lost.

No Christian should lack a social conscience and ignore political issues, but he should approach them with an intellectual humility that knows the limitations of finite minds, the complexity of social and political issues, and the distorting effect of human sin on human judgment. He should approach them with a compassionate heart that embraces all political contestants in its love. He should cultivate his personal moral and spiritual life, and sensitize his conscience so that he can rely on the invisible resources which God grants to those who love Him and believe in Him. Finally, in the midst of much that is evil, he should remember the sovereignty of God and not act and speak as though any man or group of men can claim omniscience and omnipotence.

If it be said that my analysis of the involvement of the institutional church in political activity results in a serious curtailment of that activity and puts a powerful brake on Social Activism, the answer is that it does and that I intend that it should. Church involvement in political activity should be reserved for cases where the principle and its consequences are indisputably clear, as was true in the condemnation of the Nazi regime abroad and compulsory racial segregation at home.

[XVIII, Spring 1974, 163–174]

[46]

Christian Faith and Totalitarian Rule

WILL HERBERG

Will Herberg (1909–1977), who received his Ph.D. from Columbia in 1932, was Andrew V. Stout graduate professor of philosophy and culture at Drew University. Well known for his work in social philosophy and biblical theology, he was a native of New York City and was an active Communist in the late 1920s and early 1930s. Expelled from the party for ideological reasons, he worked for the International Ladies Garment Workers Union from 1935–1948, lectured and taught for several years at various institutions, and then joined the faculty of Drew University in 1955. He wrote widely on social, cultural, and religious questions and was the author of Judaism and Modern Man: An Interpretation of Jewish Religion *(1951),* The Writings of Martin Buber *(1956), and* Faith Enacted as History: Essays in Biblical Theology *(1976). He was a member of the Medieval Academy of America, the American Theological Society, and the American Judicature Society.*

THE TWENTIETH CENTURY is the age of totalitarianism. Not only does a great portion of the human race live under pervasive totalitarian rule, but totalitarianism emerges as a crucial problem at every level of twentieth-century life, and is largely at the source of the great conflicts, economic, political, and spiritual, that are tearing apart the contemporary world.

What has Christianity to say about this massive historical reality that gives our century its characteristic aspect? The utterances and interventions of influential Christian spokesmen in recent decades can hardly be regarded, most of them, as contributing to the clarity and responsibility so desperately needed in this time of crisis. The confusion in the churches is itself a major factor exacerbating the crisis and facilitating the advance of totalitarianism on many fronts. The effort to achieve a Christian understanding of totalitarianism, therefore, involves a drastic criticism of many things that have been said and done by the churches, and in the name of the churches, in their fateful confrontation with totalitarianism.

I

Our Western political institutions, especially our Western political conceptions, derive, in large part, from the experience of the ancient Greek city-state, and from the political philosophy developed around

545

it. For Aristotle, it will be remembered, the *polis*, the State, was "by nature." Man, according to Aristotle, was "by nature a political animal," that is, a being with a nature that demanded organized community for its proper life, and was always straining to establish it. Indeed, for Aristotle, as for Plato before him, and for the intelligent, educated Athenian of their time, the *polis* was, in fact, the *human-making* institution, in which man's human potentialities could be actualized and perfected. The full perfection of humanness could be achieved only within and through the *polis*. When the Greek city-states began to lose their autonomy and vitality, political philosophers began to talk of a "universal *polis*," a *polis* of the cosmos, a cosmopolis—sometimes identified with the Roman Empire, sometimes conceived as a "heavenly city" of the wise and the virtuous. But Greek political philosophy still remained essentially *polis*-thinking.

Greek experience, and Greek philosophy founded on this experience, did not, and apparently could not, distinguish between society and State. Man's sociality, which makes society "natural" to him, was made to cover the coercive organization of society as well. In Greek political thought, therefore, there was a strong totalistic element: the pervasiveness of society in bringing forth, educating, and molding the individual into a civilized human being was easily understood as the total jurisdiction of the State as a mind- and character-forming power. Even Aristotle, a careful, moderate, and realistic thinker, complained that

> in most states, these matters [education, occupations, domestic affairs, etc.] have been neglected [by the authorities]; each man lives as he likes, ruling over wife and children in the fashion of the Cyclops. The conclusion to which we come is that the best course is to have a system of public and proper provision for these matters (*Nic. Eth.*, 14; 1180a14).

In any well-conceived community, in other words, such matters as marriage, vocation, and domestic life, would properly fall under the jurisdiction and control of the State. The fact is that, *in principle*, though fortunately not always in practice, Greek political rationalism, as Hajo Holborn points out,

> has no organ for the free individual. The idea of the right of the individual to possess a sphere of his own [Holborn goes on] was alien to the Greeks. The government was in total control of the community, and whatever freedom the individual might acquire, he could gain only through participation in government. The Greek soul [apparently] did not demand a field all to itself beyond the social order (Hajo Holborn, "Greek and Modern Concepts of History," *Journal of the History of Ideas*, Vol. X, No. 1, Jan. 1940).

The distinction between society and the State was well understood by the Jews of the time as a result of their own experience and the traditions about the kingship coming from the Old Testament; the early church fully shared their way of thinking. Community, conceived in terms of ever-widening circles of covenant, was part of God's creation, and therefore (using the Greek vocabulary) "natural" to man. But the State, as the *coercive* organization of society, most emphatically was *not*! The State, with its vast, complex machinery, was the outcome not of human nature, but of human *sin*. And yet, it was ordained of God, indirectly but no less truly. Here is how Paul, in that celebrated thirteenth chapter of Romans conceives it:

> Let everyone be subject to the governing authorities [Paul admonishes], for there is no authority but from God, and the powers that be are ordained of God. Therefore he who resists the authorities resists what God had ordained, and those who resist will incur judgment. For rulers are not a terror to good-doing, but to evil-doing. Would you have no fear of the magistrate who is in authority? Then do what is good, and you

will have his approval, for he is God's minister for your good. But if you do evil, be afraid, for he does not bear the sword in vain; he is the minister of God to execute his wrath on the evil-doer. Therefore, one must be subject [to the authorities] not only to avoid God's wrath, but also for the sake of conscience. For the same reason you also pay taxes, for the authorities are the ministers of God. . . . (Romans 13:1-6)

What one may call the theopolitical logic here is clear enough. Were it not for man's sinfulness, were it not for man's propensity to do evil, there would be no necessity for the coercive State, for the magistrate with his sword. But since man is sinful and prone to evil-doing, God, in his infinite mercy, has instituted the political order as an *order of preservation*, to save mankind from itself, to save it from destroying itself through its sinful self-aggrandizement. Hence, the State authority, from the Emperor down to the local magistrate, is carrying out a divine vocation: the ruler is, in Paul's forceful language, a "minister of God," though he may not himself know or acknowledge it—remember that the "public authorities" Paul is talking about are the pagan Emperor Nero and his pagan officials throughout the Empire! The magistrate with the sword is necessary, and must be obeyed by the Christian out of his Christian conscience; but he is made necessary by the dreadful consequences of human sinfulness, and he is to be obeyed not on his own claim, but out of obedience to God.

Paul's sweeping injunction, "Obey the governing authorities!" finds its own limitations elsewhere in the New Testament. There is, first, Peter's declaration, "We must obey God rather than man" (Acts 5:29); this, however, was strictly limited in scope, meaning that a Christian could not obey the magistrate when the magistrate called to idolatry, or forbade the proclamation of the Gospel. Much more

fundamental was the teaching that emerges out of Revelation 13. Romans 13 defines the *legitimate* government, ordained by God as a divine order of preservation. Here, in Revelation 13, we have the definition of the *illegitimate* government, which is an agency, not of God, but of the Devil. Here is the operative section of Revelation 13:

> Then, out of the sea, I saw a Beast rising. . . . The Dragon conferred upon it its power and rule. . . . The whole world went after the Beast in wondering admiration. Men worshiped the Dragon who had conferred his authority upon the Beast; they worshiped the Beast also, and chanted: "Who is like unto the Beast? Who can stand against him?" (Rev. 13:1-5)

This powerful passage has a reference that is directly political. The Dragon, of course, is Satan. The Beast is the Roman Empire, or the Emperor. Here, the "public authority," which Paul had seen as the minister of God, is denounced as a servant of the Devil. And how is its diabolical character discerned? By its self-exaltation against God! Instead of confining itself to its God-ordained function of preserving society against sinful evil-doing, it now claims to be worshiped and exalted. (The chant, "Who is like unto the Beast? Who can stand against him?" is, of course, a devilish parody of the Song of Moses, Ex. 15:1-18: "Who is like unto Thee, O Lord. . . ?") Because it claims for itself what is owing only to God, the State is no longer to be obeyed as an order of preservation, but it is to be opposed as an agency of Satan, in rebellion against God. This is the *illegitimate* State, in fact, the anti-State.

The Pauline conception of the State as an institution not of the created, or "natural" order, but of the sinful world, to protect mankind against itself, came to govern the thinking of the Western Fathers, most thoroughly the thinking of the great Augustine. For Augustine, the political order, embodied in the coercive

State, is emphatically not "by nature," as an order of creation. On the contrary, it is *"propter peccatum,"* because of sin. In the order of creation, there is no rule of man over man; that emerges, as Paul had shown, out of the necessity for curbing man's evil-doing, his sinful self-aggrandizement, which, uncurbed, would destroy the entire human race. The State is, therefore, not only *propter peccatum*; it is also *remedia peccati*, a remedy for, a protection against, sin. One must, therefore, obey the public authorities, except when they order something *contra legem Dei*, which, to Augustine as to the other Fathers, meant, as in the New Testament, a call to idolatry, a prohibition to preach the Gospel, or both. Under such circumstances, the Christian would have to obey God rather than man; but his disobedience to earthly authorities would always remain passive, leading to martyrdom. Of the distinction between the legitimate and the illegitimate State, there is only the most shadowy suggestion; it seemed so little relevant to the new age of the Christian emperors.

We cannot sufficiently admire the profundity and realism of this biblical-patristic view of the State. To the Christian, it should be self-evident that political power, to be in any sense legitimate, must ultimately come from God, the true Sovereign Lord. Where else is the legitimacy of an arrangement that gives some men power over others to come from? From the mere will and power of the ruler—whether monarch or people? That would be the sheerest idolatry. If I am to recognize the legitimate authority of the rulers, be they kings or parliaments, I must see these rulers, whether they themselves acknowledge it or not, as ministers of God, and their authority as authority coming from God, conferred upon them for preservative purposes. This view carries with it, let us never forget, implicit limitations on the scope of this authority

of the State: those limits passed or violated, the State loses its legitimacy, and becomes a diabolical agency for the oppression and subversion of mankind.

But our admiration of the profundity and truth embodied in the Pauline-Augustinian doctrine cannot blind us to one glaring defect. For, if the State is justified by the necessity of curbing the evil-doing that comes out of the sinful self-aggrandizement of men, how is it that the ruler—whether prince or parliament—is overlooked? Is not a ruler a man, a sinful man, driven on, as are other men, by sinful self-aggrandizement, by the *libido dominandi*, the "lust for dominating," which Augustine sees as the paramount "law" of the Earthly City? Does not the ruler, therefore, need curbing on his part as well? This germinal idea of a constitutional order setting restraints on the power of rulers, however legitimate, seems to have been completely overlooked until the Middle Ages—or, perhaps, not entirely overlooked since there was some notion of the Church acting as a check on the inordinances of the State. In any case, the groundwork of the Christian understanding of the State, its nature and its limits, was firmly laid.

II

This conception, however, did not fully satisfy Thomas Aquinas in the thirteenth century. He was engaged in a massive enterprise of reconciling, by proper distinction and redefinition, the philosophical and the Christian traditions, Aristotle with Augustine, Augustine with Aristotle. And so he revived the Greek doctrine of the State "by nature," while retaining the Pauline-patristic teaching of the State as an order of preservation made necessary by sin. Thomas effected this reconciliation by an acute distinction. There are two kinds of subjection of man to man, he said. The first is *subjectio civilis*, civil subjection, the kind made necessary by the very nature of civil society, in which the various positions and tasks would require some sort of public authority for their allocation, even if every citizen were a saint: this kind of subjection is "by nature," and is presumably the kind Aristotle had in mind in his book on politics. On the other side, though, men are obviously and emphatically not all saints; they are sinners, and act out of sinful self-aggrandizement, and have to be curbed in their evil-doing. Here the subjection is *subjectio servilis*, servile subjection, the kind Augustine had in mind. Hence, therefore, the State is both by nature and by sin.

The tenability of this appealing synthesis has been much argued. For our purposes, however, no conclusion on this question is necessary. What is necessary, most emphatically necessary, is to note that, for all his desire for reconciliation, Thomas brought out even more clearly the fundamental points of difference between the Greek and the biblical views. Although Aristotle did not, and could not, distinguish between society and State, Thomas could and did: He translated Aristotle's characterization of man as *"zoon phusei politikon"* ("by nature a political animal") with *"animal naturaliter sociale et politicum"* ("by nature an animal social and political"), thus making the vital and far-reaching distinction between society and State. But even more important, of really fundamental importance, as Jacques Maritain has pointed out, is Thomas' emphasis on the transcendence of the human person beyond all social collectivities and institutions, beyond society itself. Consider these two texts from St. Thomas:

> Every individual person is related to the entire community as part to whole (*S. Th.* II-II, qu. 64., art. 2).

> Man is not ordained to the body politic according to all that he is and has (*S. Th.* I-II, qu. 21, art. 4, ad. 3).

Here we have the first clear and explicit challenge to totalitarianism. Although by nature part of civil society, the individual person is not to be swallowed up whole in society or State. On the contrary, by virtue of certain aspects of his being—what Kierkegaard was later to call his "God-relationship"—man as such is elevated above political society and the social order. It is man's ordination to the divine that thus raises him above everything social and political that would totally engulf him. Who denies this, denies both God and man.

Not only does St. Thomas make explicit the Christian rejection of totalitarianism, which is radical and uncompromising; he also makes quite plain the meaning of legitimate and illegitimate government. Government is instituted by God, but the divine ordination may operate through a variety of ways and institutions, all the way from dynastic succession to popular election. The ruler must remember that he is there to keep order, dispense justice, and maintain the law, which it is his to make only to a very limited degree. The ruler must be careful that, on the one side, he does not go *contra legem Dei*, against the law of God; and, on the other, he does not drive *ultra vires*, beyond his proper powers, as these are defined by natural and public law, by custom, tradition, charter, coronation oath, and the like. If he avoids violating the divine law, and if he keeps within what may now be properly called the constitutional limits of his power, as publically defined, he is a legitimate ruler, and is entitled to honor and obedience, without qualification. But, if he deliberately, systematically, and incorrigibly insists on violating the divine law and running beyond his constitutional powers, he becomes an illegitimate ruler, a tyrant. And, against tyrants, as is well known, St. Thomas, in the last resort, allows rebellion (on the part of the magnates of the community) and even tyr-

annicide. With St. Thomas, the Christian
doctrine of legitimate government against
tyranny is well established. The Reformers did not go beyond. Both Luther and
Calvin called for unqualified obedience to
constituted authority, so long as it remained legitimate in the biblical-Augus-
tinian sense; both permitted resistance
when the ruler went *contra legem Dei*; both
required that this resistance be passive,
leading to martyrdom, though both allowed a loophole, subsequently enlarged
(by the Calvinists), to permit armed rebellion and tyrannicide, along Thomist
lines. One more point, though: Calvin's
keen sense of the involutions of sin as
libido dominandi led him to make an explicit
argument in favor of republicanism as
government by committee against government by the will of a single ruler.

> The vice or imperfection of man [Calvin
> argued], therefore renders it safer and more
> tolerable for the government to be in the
> hands of many, that they may afford each
> other mutual assistance and admonition,
> and that, if anyone arrogate to himself more
> than is right, the others may act as censors
> and masters to restrain his ambition. (*Insti-
> tutes*, IV, 20: *viii*.)

III

Direct and conscious confrontation with
totalitarianism did not arise for the mass
of Christians in Western Europe and
America, and for the Church as such,
until the appearance of Nazism as a massive power on the continent of Europe.
Both in Soviet Russia and in Fascist Italy,
totalitarianism had emerged earlier, but
it had emerged slowly, and concern over
it was pushed to the background by excitement over other aspects of the new
regimes (the atheism of Soviet communism, e.g., or the imperialist adventures
in Africa on the part of the Mussolini
regime). Indeed, in Germany itself, it was

not until 1935 that even Karl Barth came
to realize that the Nazi State was not an
ordinary State in the sense of Romans 13,
legitimate, to be prayed for, though unfortunately harassing the Church, and
acting with painful injustice in many ways.
In fairness, however, it must be noted
that it was largely the writings of Karl
Barth in the years that followed that
revealed the inner nature of totalitarianism and its demonic character from the
Christian standpoint—though Barth's
strange reversal at the end of the war,
when it became a matter of communism
rather than Nazism, has no doubt been a
major factor making for confusion and
demoralization in Christian ranks
throughout the world.

What is it that characterizes totalitarianism as a special kind of a State, a State
radically different from the kind of State
designated as legitimate in the tradition
of Paul, Augustine, and Thomas?

1. The totalitarian State of its very nature recognizes no majesty beyond itself;
it exalts itself as its own highest majesty,
its own god, and demands to be "worshiped" as such. In short, it demands for
itself what is owing only to God: worship
and absolute submission.

2. The totalitarian State, in line with
its own self-absolutization, claims jurisdiction over all of life, public and private,
and over every aspect of life. "Everything
in the State, and through the State; nothing outside the State." In principle, the
State swallows up society, State and society
swallow up the individual person; and, in
practice, every device of modern mass
control is employed to implement the
totalitarian claim. Nothing outside the
State, nothing truly voluntary or private,
can be tolerated.

3. The totalitarian State refuses to recognize in man any dimension of his being
or doing that carries him beyond the

totalitarianized social order. For man to claim such a dimension of being is regarded, and quite logically in its own terms, as the most radical challenge not merely to the regime, but to the totalitarian idea and system as such.

Such is totalitarianism in its essence. It is not merely an oppressive regime; indeed, in principle, it does not have to be particularly oppressive at all, at least not to large sections of the population. What is involved is something much more fundamental. The old-fashioned despot demanded obedience, taxes, and manpower for his armies. The totalitarian regime wants much more: "It's your souls they want," as someone once put it, referring to the Nazis. It's total possession of the whole man they want; and they will brook no rivals in engaging man's loyalties, hopes, and affections. The totalitarian rulers will sometimes tolerate less than they, in principle, demand; but this "moderation" is only temporary, pending more favorable conditions. A real abatement of their total claims is not to be expected.

It needs no extended argument to show that the totalitarian State, thus described in its essence, is the contemporary embodiment of the *illegitimate* State pictured in Revelation 13, and further defined by Augustine and Thomas. It deifies and exalts itself; it demands a quasi-religious commitment on the part of its subjects; it runs constantly *contra legem Dei*, and it operates systematically *ultra vires*, beyond the inherent constitutional limits of States. And, finally, it refuses to recognize, and strives incessantly to destroy, man's personal being and his God-relationship.

But we cannot leave it at that. Every established order, every society, and every political system, has its inner totalistic strivings. Sören Kierkegaard, himself a thoroughgoing political conservative, was among the first to see this. Over a century and a quarter ago, he pronounced these impassioned words:

> The deification of the established order is the secularization of everything. . . In the end, one secularizes also the God-relationship . . . [This God-relationship] must be, for individual man, the absolute; and it is precisely this God-relationship of the individual that puts every established order into question. The established order refuses to entertain the notion that it might consist of . . . so loose an aggregation of individuals, each of whom severally has his own God-relationship. The established order desires to be totalitarian, recognizing nothing above it, but having every individual under it, and judging every individual who is integrated in it. . . . (*Training in Christianity*, Princeton, 1951, p. 92.)

"Every established order desires to be totalitarian," exalting itself, and demanding everything. But there is a difference: the legitimate state, especially the modern constitutional state, possesses built-in institutions and traditions of resistance to these totalitarian "desires" and strivings, while the totalitarian State is the very political embodiment of these totalistic potentials, and lives only to promote and implement them.

IV

On the basis of this analysis, what is indicated as the Christian attitude to totalitarianism, the totalitarian State, and the actual totalitarian regimes in operation today? Certain points, I think, deserve emphasis.

1. Since the totalitarian State is so obviously the diabolical State of Revelation 13, the illegitimate State of Christian tradition, the Christian as Christian owes it no allegiance, no support or obedience whatever; on the contrary, the Christian as Christian stands in radical opposition to the totalitarian State and all its works,

for the totalitarian State is, in fact, an instrument of the Devil against mankind. It is war without possibility of compromise.

Many Christians find it hard to understand or go along with this notion. Some Christian leaders have even allowed themselves to become so bemused with the idea of "socialism" as a kind of wave of the future, and with the "liberal" delusion that the "enemy is always at the Right," that they cannot see the flagrantly totalitarian character of the Soviet, East German, Chinese, and other Communist regimes, because these regimes are allegedly of the Left, and tend to adopt attitudes running from friendly "neutralism" and "critical cooperation" to outright support. I will not elaborate further, but I venture to say that this betrayal of the Church will not, in the end, pass off entirely unrequited.

But for large numbers of Christians, these are not the considerations that make them so embarrassed at the intransigent opposition to totalitarianism that I have suggested as the truly Christian attitude. The fact is that many Christians, especially on the Continent, have been so habituated to the Pauline doctrine of Romans 13 that opposition to government, let alone such intransigent opposition, is entirely out of their field of vision; they cannot conceive that something like it might become their Christian duty. They cannot see that the totalitarian State is a very different kind of thing, a diabolical thing, a device of the Devil. We are now paying for the superficial, unreal, even plainly misleading political education of the Church in recent decades and centuries.

2. This radical opposition to totalitarianism as the work of the Devil does not itself entail public disobedience or outright rebellion at every point. It does entail a total inner withdrawal of allegiance and obedience. But, let us not forget, that along with this inner posture of radical opposition, there are considerations of prudence and worldly responsibility that cannot be ignored. Revolution against the totalitarian State is, in principle, always justified in the Christian conscience; but the actual translation from principle to action must depend on a careful and realistic assessment of the situation. I do not want to lay down rules: sometimes a demonstrative action without much hope of success may be in place; but sometimes, too, prudence may have to be carried to a far point indeed. All this must necessarily be left to the conscience and good sense of those who live and suffer under totalitarianism.

3. There is still another consideration of far-ranging importance. The primary function of the State, it will be recalled, is to curb evil-doers, and to assure the community its security and justice. The totalitarian State is prone to pervert even this elementary function, politicalizing its justice, and converting the security it affords into a weapon of State control. But in totalitarian countries, as in all others, the elementary preservative services must be carried out or else the society itself would go under. Fires must be put out, traffic must be regulated, theft and burglary and non-political crimes of violence must be suppressed, and so on. Now it seems obvious to me that responsible inhabitants of a totalitarian country, no matter how uncompromising their opposition to the State, would have to give some support to the activities of the State in these elementary preservative areas. Augustine somewhere speaks of a man held captive for ransom by a robber band, and therefore obliged to live in the robber community for months, perhaps even for years. Obviously, he will feel it necessary and proper to support the efforts of the bandit leaders to maintain order in the bandit community, preventing violence, fighting fires, dispensing its very limited and partial kind of justice ("Even a robber

band has its justice," as Plato pointed out). The captive will do this without in the least recognizing the legitimacy of the bandit government, or abdicating his right to escape if possible, or helping destroy the entire bandit enterprise, if circumstances prove favorable. This kind of "co-operation," if "cooperation" it can be called, is very different from the cooperation offered by many radical Christians to the totalitarian regime. The cooperation they offer in East Germany, e.g., is to help build "socialism," the name given to the State-controlled economies of such countries. In the one case, the totalitarian program is being supported and promoted; in the other case, it is only those activities of the State without which it would be impossible to live that come into consideration.

These conclusions are not, I admit, particularly sensational; and I do not want them to be. They are simply some of the more obvious conclusions one may draw from the fundamental Christian understanding of the State, the legitimate State of Romans 13, and the illegitimate, self-deifying State of Revelation 13. We might put it this way:

The legitimate State of Romans 13 (whether democratic or not) the Christian acknowledges as a divine order, and is bound in conscience to obey, unless it commands what is *contra legem Dei*, against the law of God. On the other hand, the illegitimate State depicted in Revelation 13—in our time, the totalitarian State—must be denied the allegiance and support of the Christian, and there is no obligation in conscience to obey it, though where it serves an elementary preservative function, the Christian can support these activities without commitment. This, I think, is basic.

I am sure it has been obvious from my discussion that we must not fall into the egregious error of identifying the legitimate State with the democratic State. The legitimate State is not identifiable with any particular system, and can find expression in any one of a variety of regimes, provided it meets the requirements I have described. The absolute monarchy of the eighteenth century was certainly not democratic; but it was quite legitimate in the proper sense: (1) it recognized a higher majesty beyond itself; (2) it did not claim total jurisdiction over all of life, many areas being left, in theory and practice, to institutions and agencies outside the State, or to the individual himself; (3) it never questioned the reality of the God-relationship that raised the individual human being at some point beyond every social order, including the absolute monarch's own political order; and (4) it acknowledged the preservative function of the State, and fulfilled it with not inconsiderable success. There are self-styled democracies that have not met, and do not meet, these requirements as well. So let us keep clearly in mind what we really mean when we speak of legitimate and illegitimate States.

In the last analysis, the struggle against totalitarianism and the totalitarian State is, for the Christian, a religious struggle, a struggle for men's souls. For the totalitarian State is not simply a political institution; it is, as Karl Barth saw so clearly when it was a matter of Nazism, an "anti-Christian counter-church," making an "inward claim," and "demanding the adoption of a particular philosophy of life," utterly opposed to Christianity. With this kind of State no Christian who is serious about his Christian faith can make his peace. [XI, Winter 1966–67, 63–71]

[47]

Dawson on Education in Christian Culture

LEO R. WARD

Leo R(ichard) Ward (1893–1984), a leading American disciple of Cardinal Newman's educational principles, was an editorial adviser of Modern Age *since the journal's inception in 1957. A Roman Catholic priest and professor of philosophy at the University of Notre Dame, his eighteen books on ethics and education as well as on social philosophy and regional literature have had a friendly reception by both Catholics and Protestants. Although he received his education under a faculty largely trained in Europe (he submitted his doctoral dissertation, "St. Thomas' Theory of Moral Values," to the faculty of philosophy at the Catholic University of America in 1929), he was always an American philosopher and humanist who addressed the domestic issues of the day, such as living wages, farming cooperatives, oil profits, mining conditions, the Grangers, and ward politics.*

ABOVE ALL OTHER twentieth-century men, the late Christopher Dawson took seriously the two theses developed by Newman over a century ago. Newman's theses were that only the liberally educated is really educated and that a person without an introduction to theological lore lacks an ingredient necessary for liberal education. Dawson wanted to know what, given our situation, could be done about a liberal education and about an effective acquaintance with transcendent purpose in and through education. Is either a liberal education or an education in divine transcendent things now possible? Could we have both and combine and integrate the two? Could it be undertaken at all in American universities, in France or Italy or East or West Germany or in South American countries?

Aware of the difficulties, Dawson said it could be done through "education in Christian culture." Education need not be shut once for all into an enclave marked "Secular and illiberal," and Dawson outlined a course of studies in Christian culture covering two to four years; in this attempt he was more radical and thorough than any secular, Catholic or Protestant college or university in America. He claimed that some such studies are needed if youth is to receive a liberal education relevant to today's world. To grasp what he meant we must first see how he understood the relation of religion to culture and to society in general.

Dawson's central thesis, repeated for forty years, was the relation, as he conceived it, between religion—any religion, primitive, Christian, Buddhist—and a living and healthy culture. This is an anthropological, historical and sociological question, and his treatment of it in his Gifford Lectures[1] and elsewhere showed that it is also a philosophical question. What have religion and culture—occasionally called civilization or society—to do with each other? And what has education in religion to do with a liberal education? But the other part of the question—what has religion to do with culture?—is more inclusive and it comes first in time and in his opinion first in significance. Dawson's reply was that a strong living culture has to have a strong living religion; if religion is on the downgrade, culture is on the downgrade. There is a correlation between the two, so that, as religion lapses, culture lapses, even though outwardly the society or culture may be prosperous. Dawson claimed that a people cannot have a great and lasting culture unless the worship of the gods is basic to it and co-creative with it. He held that it is a mistake to think that the great cultures are the creators of religions, it is truer to say that religions are creators of cultures.

Dawson knew that his assertion would have shocked nineteenth century liberalism, which assumed that it is all the same to society and culture whether people ever bother their heads about religion, and the routine liberal view that society is as well off without religion: the secular city is self-sufficient. Religion is a matter of social and cultural indifference; the arena of political, economic and military involvement is too rough for religion to count. That is what the liberal-secular man has concluded, partly because religion has long been regarded by both liberals and conservatives and by believers and unbelievers as a private matter between a man and his God, with no social function; religion is seen as faith and a matter of private interpretation. Irreligion is nonfaith. One man believes, another does

not; one society is religious, another is not. That is all there is to it. Whether people are of the faith kind or of the nonfaith kind is a matter of individual taste and preference and of no concern to society and culture. As Dawson read history, this opinion is an error with serious social consequences.

Culture is an organized way of life based on a common tradition and adapted to a particular environment. It requires some specialization of tasks and channeling of social energies, as is clear among the Eskimos or Bushmen. It is the life style worked out under particular circumstances, and its formation involves a community of work and a community of thought as well as of place and of blood. Any people with any considerable "community" and adaptation to its environment automatically has a culture. The culture, said Dawson, is a living whole from roots in the soil and peasants' and fishermen's instinctive lives up to achievements in artists' and philosophers'. We may think the Bushman culture retrograde, but it is the result of a free and intelligent activity, and expresses itself in an art and folklore richer and more original than that of many civilized peoples.[2] A people's culture may be high or low, healthy or decadent, but is sure to be existent.

Dawson's hope for the West was that at least some youths would concentrate on the study of Christian culture in an objective way, since, in addition to the fact that this culture could be the content of a liberal education, he held that it would be extraordinarily important to have Christian culture diffused and recreated. This is because Christian culture has been central to whatever we have been for centuries. But what precisely is it? Christian culture is the Christian people's way of life: "Christian culture is simply the Christian way of life in its historical development."[3] When we study this or any culture, we are studying man, and, said Dawson in 1942, "Primitive man is just as much dependent on cultural traditions as civilized man." We speak of and for Christian culture, but mindful that we may justly speak of Pueblo or Grecian or Chinese culture. Seen in this way, culture is a remarkably democratic concept, and Christian culture is one among many cultures.

Dawson was temperamentally an aristocrat and conservative, yet here again he was liberal and democratic. Man, he said, is religious, and secularized modern man, refusing the overall religious way of mankind, is an illiberal maverick with a penchant for aristocracy, uppish and as if too good for the human race. Religion is the bond between man and God, between human society and the spiritual world.

> What we are concerned with here is not literary culture but spiritual culture—the training of the mind in the way of the divine law. Some such process is implicit in the conception of human relations with superhuman reality which is the very essence of religion according to our definition. . . . [Involved in religion is an inner discipline which renders the soul capable] of transcending the ordinary level of humanity.[4]

Man reaches above and beyond himself and enjoys a vision of the divine. His thus linking himself to God is the religious phenomenon and datum. The strange occurrence, said Dawson, is our modern widespread secularism. If it is true that man is the worshipping animal and incurably religious and if he can turn a man or a nation into his god, it is still not strange that some man should think himself not religious or a worshipper; after all, a man here or there has thought himself the man in the moon. The strange thing, Dawson proceeded, is that an age at least in some leading lights should in effect declare itself secularist, not bound to God. He described the irreligious man

as the man who lives on the surface of existence and recognizes no ultimate spiritual allegiance.

Losing the religious and theological dimension in Western society has been a long and complex story. Although from Plato's time, Hellenic "paideia" was a humanism in search of a theology, the religious traditions of Greek culture were not deep enough to furnish one. Somewhat similar is the modern situation. Progressively controlling education, the state is nevertheless religiously badly off; it needs a spiritual bond other than law and the power of the sword. But how are we to achieve such a bond which we have needed ever since society lost contact with the faith of Christendom? Modern society has sought this bond in each of three ways; in the democratic ideal of a natural society and its general will, the common American method; secondly in the nationalist cult of a racial community, the Fascist-Nazi model, and in the Communist faith. In each instance we see a substitute religion or counterreligion with a quasi creed, a cult and priesthood, transcending the political community and creating a kind of secular church.[5]

A major event secularizing Western man is the split in Christianity; this has made education in Christian culture difficult. The break meant a break in Christian culture, a culture which, as Dawson's *The Making of Europe* shows, had been a thousand years in process of formation. This culture had struggled trying to discover itself, making its way past a sort of presumed commitment solely to the supernatural until it encountered an extremely natural and naturalistic world. Tension was inevitable and remained for centuries: a dualism between the natural barbarian warrior and the supernatural man with his faith in a transcendent being and transcendent society. Eventually, it became the custom to accept, at least as

provisional and transitory, any good political rule and any good temporal conditions and institutions. This attitude held
when the ruler was, from Charlemagne's
time on, anointed and regarded as in
some way sacred, and it still holds in the
coronation of British rulers. Tension and
dualism between temporal and spiritual
must always remain in a Christian society.[6]
The Church-State social body was quasi
theocratic, and yet the guilds turned society in effect into a community of communities. The guilds combined secular
and religious activities, and medieval society was much like one organism, "an
ordered spiritual structure that reaches
from earth to heaven."[7]

The organic structure was broken by
the dividing of Christendom in the sixteenth century. In a volume on this subject, Dawson summarized thus:

> For when the age of religious war was over,
> Europe was still divided (and America also)
> by a difference of moral values and psycho-
> logical antipathies. And these differences
> are harder to surmount than the theological
> ones, because they go so deep into the un-
> conscious mind and have become a part of
> the personality and the national character.[8]

Much common belief and common tradition has remained, but for a long time
the gap in ways of life has been so wide
that we cannot speak of modern Western
culture as a common Christian culture,
and the fissure is so deep that we cannot
see a solution in the present period and
under existing historical circumstances.

In education, common ground long
remained because the Renaissance afforded higher education a common classical background and it furnished common norms for value judgments
transcending national and political frontiers and forming the European republic
of letters of which every scholar was a
citizen. This intellectual community was
presupposed in primary and secondary

education, the primary school taught children their letters, grammar school taught
them Latin and Greek, so that educated
men everywhere possessed a common
language and the knowledge of a common
literature or two common literatures.
Classical education could perform this
unifying task, said Dawson, because it was
built on a common spiritual tradition; by
itself, it was less than half the European
system of education: below it was the
religious education common to all, and
above was the theological education special to the clergy. Whatever its merits and
former success, Dawson had not the slightest illusion about its present feasibility;
after so long a run in Great Britain and
on the Continent, classical education is
completely antiquated as a common denominator in education. Dawson was convinced that we must nevertheless seek a
unifying factor. But this cannot be found
in prevailing specialisms and much less in
technology. We suffer for a unifying element, given the centrifugal forces of spe-
cialism and vocationalism and the disori-
entating forces of Communism and
nonrevolutionary secularism.

That is one side of the picture—education has lost common and unifying factors. At the same time, modern Western
society has made education universal; the
effect on the whole is good, but has been
bought at a high price. It has meant the
substitution of quantitative for qualitative
standards and inevitably changed the relations of education to the state:

> . . . there is no power left outside politics to
> guide modern civilization, when politicians
> go astray. For in proportion as education
> becomes controlled by the state, it becomes
> nationalized, and in extreme cases the serv-
> ant of a political party. This last alternative
> still strikes us here in England as outrageous,
> but it is not only essential to the totalitarian
> state; it existed before the rise of totalitari-
> anism and to a great extent created it, and

it is present as a tendency in all modern societies, however opposed they are to totalitarianism in its overt form.[9]

To be brief, education is state education, the state tending to control the mind of man. These ideas were stated by Dawson in *Lumen Vitae* in 1949 as part of his earliest and (he said in a letter to the author) his most important article on educational philosophy. As Dawson saw the situation, our culture lacks a common understanding of nature or of man and any transcendent aim for person or society, each of the deficiencies a serious matter. Three mighty contemporary faiths, democratic, fascist and communist, successfully transcend the individual, but none of them succeeds in transcending either the secular or temporal. In America, continued Dawson,[10] faith in science tends to supplant theological orthodoxy and this faith merges unconsciously with faith in democracy. A cultural uniformization is more and more demanded; in educational theory men of distinction have said that to be democratic and American all must attend public schools; and to be up-to-date, all must applaud the same television shows and Hollywood stars. Dawson regarded those who have their own schools as in some measure saving educational and cultural freedom.

The individual person transcends the political arena, since he is not totally subject to it, and for Dawson the cultural body should also transcend that arena. In totalitarian nations, both culture and the person are at the mercy of the state. The effect is the invasion of the human soul by the hand of power, the original sin of every totalitarian system. Common understanding and transcendent purpose—does anything now promise these values in education? Must we give up hope that a culture with common understanding and transcendent purpose can be created and perpetually recreated? Dawson's re-

ply was that those values are available, but not on a secularist basis. We need a new ground for educational process, and the time when secularism could conceivably provide an acceptable philosophy of education and culture is past.

Dawson's reply to the cited deficiencies and threats was always the same—it was "education in Christian culture." We must face the problem as a whole and remember the common spiritual foundations of the learning for centuries available to Western man. But while we use Christian culture as content, we must hold this culture off from ourselves and study it as we would any given object. Dawson was not appealing for indoctrination nor speaking primarily of cult and commitment, but of Christian culture as a basic area of study.

This content could be studied with appreciation and respect as the old classical matters were studied, and like these with dispassion and freedom, and could serve as what Dawson called the "means" of liberal education. Moreover, the study of Christian culture in its formation, its peak and its periods of decline could be useful. Spending so many years in school, we certainly want to discover how we ourselves came to be. To do this we must study, not vocational specialisms and not primarily modern civilization, important as this is, but the older order of Christian culture which is the historic basis of our civilization. Our coming to be modern was through a struggle of centuries and even a series of prolonged struggles. Let at least some Western youths have the chance to become liberally educated by a straightforward study of how we and our culture came to be. Such a study could be useful in face of domestic and world problems, it could be both liberal and utilitarian.

To carry this study through, teachers would have to acquire much knowledge now passed over. Also a devotion akin to that once felt for the classics and now for scientific studies would have to be experienced by teachers and students. We would need a new renaissance. Another handicap is the fact that in most universities it has become nobody's business to consider Christian culture. But Dawson claimed that the reasons making its study difficult are reasons in its favor as educational matter; difficult, but integrative:

> it is an integrative subject involving the cooperation of a number of different specialized studies, in the same way as the study of *litterae humaniores* in the Greats School at Oxford involves the cooperation of philosophers and historians as well as philologists and literary critics.

In every culture, education teaches children some know-how, how to hunt and fish and cook, to read and write, and its massive overall work is to initiate youth into the social and spiritual inheritance of the community. It always does this whether or not the community has formal schools. Today we would need to understand our particular culture, English, Mexican or Dutch, as

> the first step to understanding the culture of the past. From this point of view I have much sympathy with Dewey's theory of education—that it should be a means of participating in the total experience of life in a community. But whereas his community is contemporary secular society, our community is a universal one in the fullest sense of the word: it is the community of the *civitatis Dei*. The whole purpose of Catholic higher education should be to actualize or realize this citizenship which we all accept as a truth of faith, but which we should realize as the membership of a true community more real than that of the state or nation and more universal than modern civilization because past and present coexist in it.[11]

Taken in its widest sense education is simply the process by which the new members of a community are initiated into its way of life and thought from the simplest elements of behavior up to the highest tradition of spiritual wisdom. Christian education is therefore an initiation into the Christian way of life and thought, and for one thousand two hundred years, more or less, the peoples of Europe have been submitted to this influence. The process has been intensive at some points, superficial at others, but taking it as a whole it may be said that nowhere else in the history of mankind can we see such a mighty stream of intellectual and moral effort directed through so many channels to a single end. However incomplete its success may have been, there is no doubt that it changed the world, and no one has any right to talk of the history of Western civilization unless he has done his best to understand its aims and its methods.[12]

Through homes and churches and private schools we now receive some of this initiation, but actual curricula in Europe and America generally avoid Christian culture content.

The education for which Dawson spoke would be national, but also transnational and transpolitical. All of us say with Aquinas that it is against nature for man to be "subordinated in all that he is to any political community;"[13] man is of the political community and naturally transcends it. People want their children to learn with and for the political community, but through their learning and culture to transcend that community. That was Dawson's position. Citizens should know and love the national community and know and love beyond it—a view, he remarked, unacceptable to revolutionary or other secularists. Dawson thus parted company with secularists of whatever brand. Writing in *Studies*, he remarked that even in Western democratic society which in intention consciously rejects totalitarian solutions, state control and political direction of schooling inevitably tend to increase—a control due to the fact that the state has taken the place of homes and independent organs of culture as the paymaster and controller, first of universal public education, and eventually of higher education and scientific research.

> Hence it is not surprising that some leading representatives of democratic educational theory, like the late Professor Dewey, go as far as the Communists in their subordination of education to the needs of the political community. In Professor Dewey's view the function of education is not to communicate knowledge or to train scholars in the liberal arts: it is to serve democracy by making every individual participate in the formation of social values and contribute to what he calls "the final pooled intelligence" which is the democratic mind.
>
> No doubt Dewey's democratic community is not so crudely political as that of the totalitarian ideologists. What he has in mind is not the political organization of the state but the community of popular culture. But it is no less fatal to the traditional concept of culture since it reverses the natural relation between the teacher and the taught and subordinates the higher intellectual and moral values to the mind of the masses. It is indeed difficult to see on these principles how any of the higher forms of culture could ever have arisen. For even the most primitive and barbarous peoples known to us achieve Dewey's ideals of social participation and communal experience no less completely by their initiation ceremonies and tribal dances than does the modern educationalist with his elaborate programmes for the integration of the school with life.[14]

Dewey's final word was initiation into the ways of the democratic community, a *ne plus ultra*. But it was not Dawson's final word, since he held that the person transcends the best sociotemporal community; and not only the person, but the culture also transcends it. Education should serve the good society and help to initiate men into it, but also serve other important ends—to liberate the person's judgment,

and teach all, as Dewey insisted, to respect the socially liberated state of man. Along with these values, it should help to initiate men and culture into the transnational, transpolitical and transtemporal world. This higher objective, necessary at any time, just now is especially needed to counter the totalitarian mind, and it seems to us that Dewey remained unaware of such a demanding goal of education. The secular city is always unaware of it.

It is difficult to separate education as initiation into the particular culture from a people's religious life, since this is part of the culture. As the people believe and worship, so we may expect their theory and practice of education to be. Almost always the tradition of a learned priesthood lies at the heart of the great civilizations, and even when a culture has been secularized, the tradition of a priesthood is not wholly lost, as was clear (said Dawson) in Matthew Arnold and Emerson who saw themselves as priests of culture; a culture always has its high priests. The sacred order exists in any society, serves as a law and norm, being not merely social or political, since, seen in anthropological and historical light, law requires divine origin and sanction. Such a view is stock in trade in Judaism and is found in one form or another in the world religions and the ancient civilizations; in the Pueblo culture where a remarkably durable society is based on sacred ritual; and in China:

> [with] all the characteristic features of the religion of the archaic culture preserved at least formally intact in one of the most highly developed and refined forms of civilization the world has known. Down to 1912 the Emperor still offered the great sacrifice of the winter solstice at the Altar of Heaven with all the ritual of a remote, almost prehistorical past, and every spring he performed the ceremony of the sacred ploughing which opened the agricultural year. For

the ancient Chinese religion like that of the other archaic societies was based on the principle of a perfect coordination of the heavenly and the earthly orders by a cycle of ritual actions.[15]

Granting so much, what have such anthropological and historical facts to do with a modern philosophy of education? Dawson's answer was that to jettison the coordination between sacred and earthly and of a priestly group guarding a sacred tradition of culture could not be done without disorienting and impoverishing the culture in question. Yet this has occurred in the secularization of modern Western culture, where, as in any culture, some social embodiment of the higher spiritual principle remains a fundamental condition of an enduring social order. If religion is vital to culture, then religion is not a matter of indifference to education, and neither is it a matter of sentiment or private interpretation; on the contrary, religion is integral to social realities and is the root of every living culture.

In the tendency toward secularization, and in the case of Communist nations, in the violent secularistic imposition, education has a dual task. First, it has to help us desecularize our minds—and in a society bursting with affluence and freedom, this may be difficult—and help us to understand our present condition, and this also will demand much. Dawson spoke strongly on this point:

> It is only by the rediscovery of the spiritual world and the restoration of man's spiritual capacities that it is possible to save humanity from self-destruction. This is the immense task which Christian education has to undertake. It involves a good deal more than any Christian or any educationist has yet realized.

We cannot tear the two apart—a Christian learning and a Christian culture or society. However, the chance for education in Christian culture suffers attacks arising from two unlikely sources: a religious source, and an academic source. In the latter, the tendency is to sacrifice everything to science and technology and these themselves to political power. In the religious field, theological study is shut into an airtight cell and thereby in effect, so far as education is concerned, social realities are secularized. Education also suffers disabilities of its own. For two centuries, it has faced an insistent vocational and industrial demand, resulting in a sort of subculture. The dualism of religious and secular and the utilitarian tendency are further complicated by a massive social fact which Dawson called an "extroverted hedonistic mass culture."

> The recovery of a Christian culture is therefore the essential educational and religious task, and it is inseparable from the social ideal of Christendom—of the Christian people—*plebs Christiana*—*populus Dei*. This ideal . . . lies at the very heart of Christianity.[16]

Christian culture is a natural and inescapable subject of study for anyone wishing to understand the Western world. What, then, would it be like? How would it be broken into areas or fields? On Dawson's plan, it would be a study in history, philosophy, theology, in art and literature and social institutions, and be a study for anyone, Jew, Moslem or agnostic, who wished to understand that world, since without Christian culture the Western world does not exist and cannot be studied. Dawson claimed that such a study would be of greater educational importance than most matters studied now in school and university, and because of its immersion in historical data, it would be more relevant, especially in theology and philosophy, than the courses now given in many Catholic or other Christian schools. Within this manifold called "Christian culture," we would have fields and objects of study—Greek and Latin civilization, the Near East, many sciences and Oriental cultures along with Christian culture. Dawson felt that we must bypass both textbook courses and nationalist separatism in the study of Western society. We need to "study the old spiritual community of Western Christendom as an objective historical reality," since there is a living tradition "reaching back through Petrarch and John of Salisbury to Alcuin and Bede and Boethius, and it was this that built the spiritual bridge across the ages" bringing us classical humanism.

> The existence of this spiritual community or psychological continuum is the ultimate basic reality which underlies all the separate activities of modern Western societies and which alone makes Western education possible.[17]

The educational and cultural task would mean a conversion and spiritual transformation, even to begin to think of the task would take effort. The alternative, in Dawson's view, is a robot utopia combined with a bankrupt secular humanism; we have samples of this combination and can see that it is "inhuman in the absolute sense—hostile to human life and irreconcilable with human nature itself." Science without wisdom will not answer, nor science in the hands of power. But a thorough social science, of anthropology, history and sociology, teaches that man is the worshipping animal, that religion is essential to a living culture and that education is an initiation into the social and spiritual inheritance of the community. We want facts brought forward integrally

with an understanding of whole ways of life. We want to know man, and Dawson held that we have the opportunity and the need to know and to assimilate Christian culture.

NOTES

[1] Christopher Dawson, *Religion and Culture* (New York: Sheed and Ward, 1948); *Religion and the Rise of Western Culture* (New York: Sheed and Ward, 1950).

[2] For Dawson's concept of culture, see his *Age of the Gods* (London: J. Murray, 1924); *Progress and Religion* (New York and London: Longmans, 1928); *Religion and Culture*, and *Religion and the Rise of Western Culture*.

[3] Dawson, *The Commonweal*, 61 (April 1, 1955), p. 678.

[4] *Religion and Culture*, p. 176.

[5] Christopher Dawson, *The Crisis of Western Education* (New York: Sheed and Ward, 1961), pp. 102–111.

[6] *Religion and the Rise of Western Culture*, pp. 75–76, 170, 180–181.

[7] *Ibid.*, pp. 91, 205–212.

[8] Christopher Dawson, *The Dividing of Christendom* (New York: Sheed and Ward, 1965), p. 16. Parenthesis in the original.

[9] Christopher Dawson, *Understanding Europe* (New York: Sheed and Ward, 1952), pp. 4–7; also Dawson, "Education and the State," *The Commonweal*, 65 (January 25, 1957), pp. 423–427.

[10] *The Crisis of Western Education*, Chapters 6 and 8.

[11] Dawson, "Dealing With the Enlightenment and the Liberal Ideology," *The Commonweal*, 60 (May 14, 1954), p. 139.

[12] *Understanding Europe*, p. 242.

[13] Saint Thomas Aquinas, *Sum. Th.*, I–II, q. 21, a. 4, ad 3.

[14] Dawson, *Studies*, 42 (Autumn, 1953), p. 298.

[15] *Religion and Culture*, Chapter 8.

[16] *Understanding Europe*, p. 254.

[17] *Ibid.*, Chapters 1 and 13.

[XVII, Fall 1973, 399–407]

[VI]

Not for Marx

[48]

Not for Marx

DAVID LEVY

David Levy (1947–   ) received a degree in history from Oxford University and then for a time began studying law until, still influenced by Robert Nisbet's The Sociological Tradition *(1966), which he had been reading at Oxford, he registered for a master's degree in sociology at the London School of Economics. During his year of study there, he considerably broadened the view of Marxism reflected in his essay found in this selection. Now living in South London, Levy has been a lecturer in sociology at Middlesex Polytechnic, Enfield, England, and literary editor of* Monday World. *The author of* Realism: An Essay in Interpretation and Sociology *(1981) and a philosophical treatise on thought and order, he has contributed articles and reviews to journals in England, France, Germany, and the United States.*

OVER THE LAST FEW YEARS much of my intellectual development has been motivated by the desire to combat the influence of Marxism. Marxism is a pervasive influence in the intellectual world today and nowhere more so than in the social sciences where my teaching responsibilities lie. As a philosophy it has the peculiar character of enabling its adherents to dismiss in advance any objections that may be brought against it by ignoring the content of the objections and concentrating their counterattack on the motives of the detractors and the political results of their work. Since the political results, if any, of the writings of such critics of Marxist theory as Karl Popper will be to discourage people from accepting the Marxist analysis and adhering to Marxist movements, the faithful can be spared the trouble of refuting Popper's criticism with the assurance that his opposition to Marxism (and psychoanalysis) "was determined in the last instance by the bourgeoisie's political need to deny these sciences any objective validity, since they presented a massive threat to bourgeois ideology."[1]

No one, in Marxist eyes, ever rejects Marxism because by a process of independent intellectual inquiry he discovers the falsity of its basic assumptions and a critic is always "in the last instance" (a favorite Marxist phrase) determined in his rejection by external economic or ideological forces of which he may be completely unaware. True to Althusser's view that "Philosophy is, in the last instance, the class struggle in theory," and to the belief that it is the class struggle and the eventual victory of the proletariat which will establish the only "truth" that man will ever know, the social system of communism, the closed world of Marxism defines out of existence the man or woman

565

who could show its illusory character. In other words there is no way out of the Marxist web unless one breaks with basic assumptions of the theory of which many of its adherents may be less than half aware.

Though no convinced Marxist will believe me, my opposition to Marxist politics and my support for anti-Marxist individuals, groups and interests is determined by my intellectual rejection of Marxist philosophy and not vice-versa. Marxists believe that political action will establish the truth of the human condition sometime in the future, while I believe that that truth is always present to be discovered by the intellect. If their politics determines their philosophy, then I claim that my philosophy influences my politics, for the truth about man and his social existence is there to be discovered and not created by a more or less bloody process of revolution. Thus while accepting the close connection between philosophy and politics, which Marxists so often employ as a stick with which to beat the backs of their opponents, I reverse its significance. For Marxism is not only a creed of lecturers and professors, and there are worse dangers in its advance than the rather grey aura that it tends to spread over any department or faculty where it becomes the orthodoxy. Marxism provides the intellectual armory for internal revolutionary organizations and external aggressive powers who differ among themselves but who all threaten the future of our society; and, while Western society is not and never can be the imagined paradise of life without external constraint, it can be and is a great deal more free than anything the Marxists have been able to construct after their revolutions and misnamed "wars of liberation." My opposition to Marxist philosophy is based on the view that it gives a largely false picture of the human condition it pretends to explain. My rejection of Marxist politics is founded in a conviction that the essence of Marx's political message is a utopian belief in the possibility of a total transformation of the nature of man and the character of human existence for which neither history, philosophy nor the social sciences give us any warrant.

Utopian hope and impatience before the complexities and limitations of man's real situation in the world, and not scientific demonstration and rational argument, explain the widespread appeal of Marxism, and the undoubted sophistication of many Marxist arguments often disguises unfounded premises whose true nature is seldom made clear but which alone give any credibility to the reasoning built upon them. These considerations have led me to the view that, in parody of Marx's own view of religion, the criticism of Marxism is today the beginning of all criticism.

Of course such a criticism would have to be developed at greater length than is possible in an essay. It would have to investigate fully the formative influences on Marx's mind, to picture what I like to think of as Marx's metaphysical cradle, set in the shadow of Hegel and rocked by the left Hegelians who developed the revolutionary and atheist possibilities hidden in the master's system. For I am convinced that it is the Hegelian idealist inheritance which is at the root of the illusory conception of the nature of politics and history which flowered in Marxism. The criticism of Marxism would also take account of the diverse branches which sprang from this common root, including the positivistic Marxism of Kautsky and the Second International, the recently fashionable, more openly Hegelian Marxism associated with the names of Lucacs, Korsch, and the Frankfurt school, and the new wave of structuralist Marxism represented by Althusser and his school.

The treatment of each of these would overflow the space I can allow myself here. Nor could a full critique of Marxism be limited to a refutation of the common philosophical premises that these apparently differing factions share; it would also have to contain a sociological element based on the impossibility of reconciling the utopian aspirations of Marxist post-revolutionary society with the necessary social conditions of human existence.

Robert Tucker quotes an amusing example of what happens when this incompatibility is uncovered by Marxists themselves. In a famous passage in his early writings Marx says:

> in communist society, where nobody has one exclusive sphere of activity but each can become accomplished in any branch he wishes, society regulates the general production and thus makes it possible for me to do one thing today and another tomorrow, to hunt in the morning, fish in the afternoon, rear cattle in the evening, criticize after dinner, just as I have a mind, without ever becoming hunter, fisherman, shepherd or critic.

Faced with the reality of organizing an industrial system the Soviet economist V. M. Kriukov remarks that

> An unintelligent person and philistine might form his own picture of communism approximately as follows: you rise in the morning and ask yourself, where shall I go to work today—shall I be chief engineer at the factory or go and head the fishing brigade? Or shall I run down to Moscow and hold an urgent meeting of the presidium of the Academy of Science?

As Tucker points out, the view of the "unintelligent person and philistine" is precisely that of Marx himself as expressed in the quoted passage. While no one would claim that Kriukov and the Soviet theoretical journal *Kommunist* that printed his text have any special claims on the one "true" Marxist message, it is likely that the governors and apologists of the Soviet system have rather more idea of the imperatives of running a social system than the myriad generous hearted idealists who really believe that the more extravagant positions of Karl Marx, which are those which usually attract the converts, represent a realistic social or political option.[2]

Beyond the sociological elements of the critique there would also have to be sections on the psychological and economic illusions tied up in the Marxist package and, naturally, a specifically political side to the argument. For I do not suppose that I should ever have become committed to the struggle against Marxism if I had not come to think that totalitarian dictatorship was the necessary consequence of the active pursuit of the Marxist utopia. I have often been struck by the fact that the only non-Marxist regime in a developed country that has matched the brutality of Marxist revolutionaries in this century has been the only other regime that has envisaged its mission in terms of an all inclusive transformation of reality. Nazis share at least this with Marxists, that both seek to force the reality of the human world into a mould it was never meant to fit. I can quite see that the classless kingdom of freedom promised by Marxism is in a different and abstractly superior ethical class to the racially pure empire of the Aryan race pursued by the Nazis, but in these matters an ounce of realism about what is and what is not appropriate on the human scale is worth a ton of superior intentions and pious hopes. However highly one estimates the ethical value of the goal of Marxist politics in comparison with that of the Nazis it remains true that much of the brutality and most of the totalitarian dynamic of both systems in action is bound up with the nightmarish pursuit in reality of an impossible dream.

The development of the above points would alone require treatment at book length and this is not the moment to attempt it. Instead I shall adopt a different approach and use elements of my intellectual autobiography to show the way my anti-Marxism has been built up over the years through the synthesis of influences from many different sources. When I came down from Oxford I was the possessor of a mediocre degree in history and the flimsiest possible understanding of Marxism. Most of my friends at Oxford, insofar as they were politically minded at all, were Tories. Like them my attitude to Marxism was one of political hostility unenlightened by much real intellectual understanding. In the course of the Spring and Summer terms of 1968 Oxford had its own pale reflection of the student riots of Paris and the continental universities. The Oxford leftists were organized as the "Oxford Revolutionary Socialist Students" and the parades, chanting, and banner waving of that particular long defunct coalition of malcontents and visionaries (among whom there were few who knew much more about Marxism than I did) offended and amused us in about equal proportions. In retrospect I think that I probably took the Oxford disorders much more seriously than they deserved but, at the same time, my disquiet, expressed in the founding of a blue-bannered group which I called the Social Defense Union, had a small but solid basis in my limited knowledge of the ideas of Marx himself.

Marx was one of the main figures studied in the political philosophy course which formed a small part of the history degree: but my first serious consideration of his theory arose not from the formal teaching but out of long conversations which lasted far into the night with a friend of mine in Trinity College who was at that time a member of the Communist Party. To those conversations, as much as anything, I owe the fact that the political animal I had always been became a philosophical one as well. I can never adequately express my gratitude.

At that stage I knew that Marx had explained the course of human history in terms of the growth and organization of human productive power and that he saw the changing forms of political and social institutions as corresponding to the stage of development reached by the forces of economic production. History proceeded in stages and each social/political system, which embodied in its institutions the social relationships required by the pattern of economic ownership, was in time shattered by the revolution of the class whose rise had been favored by previous economic trends but whose ambitions were limited by the old social and political system. Feudalism had given way to capitalism and capitalism would give way to socialism. The dictatorship of the proletariat would overthrow the rule of the bourgeoisie, private ownership would be abolished, the forces of production would be socialized and the kingdom of freedom ushered in.

I took it for granted that Marx was a determinist and was very impressed by the fact that many of his prophecies had not been fulfilled. But I was also puzzled by his apparent assumption that the abolition of private ownership would lead to a drastic qualitative change in the nature of social life and that a freer egalitarian society would be the result. Even then I saw more conflict than natural harmony between freedom and equality but, more important, I now realize that my puzzlement was only the surface manifestation of a basic difference between the Marxist conception of the relationship of human nature and social organization and my own.

I had always assumed that there was a

relatively stable human nature which combined aggressive and cooperative elements and that social orders, in all their variety, reflected the character of the human animal that made them up. I alternated between an Aristotelian view of man as a naturally political animal and a more Hobbesian conception of society as a collective defense against the anti-social murderous side of human nature. I did not then see, and cannot accept now, Marx's assumption that what we call human nature is only a reflection of the social arrangements made by men themselves and that the reason why men will achieve a near utopian existence under communism is that the socio/economic arrangements will be such as to prevent the rise of new patterns of dominance. Marx expresses this principle in the 6th of his *Theses on Feuerbach*, which states that "Human nature is no abstraction inherent in each separate individual. In its reality it is the ensemble of social arrangements," and it is noteworthy that it is precisely this point that Althusser regards as the locus of the "epistemological break" between Marxian science and the merely ideological theories of Marx's predecessors. Althusser has a case here though I see its significance in an altogether different light. The principle of the 6th *Theses on Feuerbach*, the principle that makes of human nature a product of more or less manipulated social arrangements and rejects explicitly any prior inherent limiting human nature actualized in man's social existence, is alone what makes it possible for the utopian speculation on the communist future of man to mask itself as science. While I do not deny that different social arrangements can encourage the manifestation of different human characteristics, those characteristics are precisely elements of man himself, none of which is ever exhausted and all of which are coeternal with human existence. All the evidence we have confirms the view that human nature is fundamentally unchanging and that in consequence social and political systems will always be more or less satisfactory variations on themes as old as man himself.

It was my interest in pursuing the theme of the unchanging character of human nature and society through the apparent chaos of historical events that led me into the study of sociology. A year or so after coming down from Oxford I read Robert Nisbet's *The Sociological Tradition* and was extremely impressed by the way in which such nineteenth century social thinkers as Le Play, Comte, Durkheim, Toennies and Weber had pointed out the negative characteristics of the breakup of the old regime in Europe. Some of these men, Comte for instance, thought of the problems of modernity as essentially problems of a more or less brief transitional "critical" period between the stability of the old and the coming stability of the new regime, but others, like Weber, rejected any such a historicist way out of the dilemma. "Not a summer's bloom lies ahead of us, but rather a polar night of icy darkness and hardness, no matter which group may externally triumph now," Weber told his Munich listeners shortly after the German revolution of 1918, and while I have never been able to accept a pessimistic historical determinism any more than its optimistic other face I was open to the evidence of overwhelmingly likely trends in areas of reality where no hard and fast historical "laws" are to be found.[3]

The difference between historical trends and so-called natural laws of history is that the first are open to diversion and even reversal when they have been understood while the latter can only be borne with the patience of resignation. It was adherence to the first rather than the second conception of historical movement that made me receptive to the conception of politics found in the work of Charles Maurras. Maurras figures in most English and American books, if at all, as a proto-fascist, a writer of considerable talents who diverted his undoubted skills into the murky waters of reactionary and anti-semitic journalism. But while Maurras undoubtedly said many unjust things and fell into considerable political errors there is at the center of his work an insistence on the value of human intelligence in politics and an understanding of man's need to measure himself and his projects against a preexisting reality which reveal a perceptive realist of the first order. By his verbal excesses and the sheer quantity of his journalistic output Maurras makes it difficult for the newcomer to penetrate to the heart of his thinking. I was naturally curious about a man now so vilified but who had exercised such an enormous influence in his country and abroad and what I read in consequence certainly sharpened my understanding of the issues at stake in seemingly abstract political discussions. If my conversations in Trinity made me intellectually curious, then it was my readings of Charles Maurras that gave me my central belief, which I have carried through a positivist phase to my present philosophical position, in the objectivity of reality and its openness to intellectual penetration.[4]

Obviously it was the anti-utopian character of much nineteenth century social theory, in contrast to the boundless hopes of the ideologues of the French Revolution, that struck me. My attitude to social change was not wholly negative but I did realize that a gain in one area will have to be paid for in another. I was convinced by Comte's arguments for the inevitability of hierarchy in society even though I found his excited anticipation of a dictatorship of social scientists macabre and absurd. Total solutions, in political and social matters, are always wrong.

I suppose it was at this time that I also read for the first time Jacob Talmon's *Origins of Totalitarian Democracy* which argues that there was a necessary connection between the regime of the Terror in revolutionary France and the utopian ambitions and ideologies of the men who made the revolution. The parallel between France and Russia, Jacobin and Bolshevik dictatorship, still seems very revealing. The abolition of marks of rank, so apparently harmless in itself, is a case in point. Beneath the ubiquitous terms "Citizen" or "Comrade" is created, in subterfuge, a web of power relationships in which one individual has life and death power over his formal equal to an extent scarcely imaginable in a system where distinctions of rank are openly recognized. Citizen Robespierre and Comrade Lenin held, and employed, a power of which Louis XIV might have dreamed, and what is true at the top of the power ladder is true all the way down the rungs to the last little agent of revolutionary dictatorship checking his neighbors for insufficient enthusiasm.[5]

I was sufficiently interested in the sociology and political philosophy I was now reading to give up reading for the Bar and register to do a master's degree in sociology at the London School of Economics. The L.S.E. had a reputation for radicalism in the country as a whole. That reputation was based on the disorders of the two previous years which had been more serious there than in most other English colleges but still was nothing compared with the activities of our continental neighbors. In fact I knew from friends of mine studying there that the L.S.E.'s reputation as a hotbed of Marxist activity was grossly overblown; I must admit, though, that in comparison with what I had known before the Marxist flavor of the place was strong. A small minority of Marxist staff and a larger minority of students combined with the place occupied by Marx's writings in the social science courses to bring me face to face with the need to work out my own position more fully.

During my year of study there I learned a great deal more about Marxism. I was impressed by the coherence of what I heard but in no way convinced. I attended Ralph Miliband's lectures on Marx and remember him announcing in his splendid but oddly hesitating tones that, "The Marxist project is only comprehensible in terms of the aim of the transcendence of domination." I also participated in Dr. Miliband's political sociology seminar. Many of my fellow students there were American new Leftists, self-styled Marxists with an insatiable capacity to absorb the unsuspectedly rich theoretical fare they complained of missing in their first degree courses. In most cases their previous acquaintance with the master was confined to a reading of *The Communist Manifesto*. Miliband patiently unravelled their confusions, and mine as well, leaving each of us to reformulate our views in the light of his astute criticism. They became, I suppose, better Marxists, while I became more certain than before that in Marxism I was facing less a school of social science than a messianic hope dressed up in the language of academic discourse. For even while I was listening to Dr. Miliband's patient attempts to sophisticate his new Leftist admirers I was learning, from my readings of Mosca, Pareto and Durkheim, how little sense there was in thinking in terms of "the transcendence of domination." At the time Durkheim and Pareto were my masters in sociology. I described myself as a positivist and opposed the authority of "social facts" to what I saw as the wildly speculative arguments of the Marxists.

Durkheim gave me a conception of society as a unity of interdependent groups. Of course there is such a thing as class conflict and, under certain conditions, it may lead to such extreme hostility within a society that the political institutions may be shattered but the roots of such revolutions are seldom to be found, as Marxists claim, in patterns of ownership. They are much more likely to derive from the failure of particular classes to carry out their specific functions in the general business of society. As for the prospect of a classless society, it all depends on how you choose to define class. If you decide that a society without private ownership is *ipso facto* a classless society then it is quite possible to achieve it, though at considerable cost. But nothing in what you have created will prevent the reestablishment of chains of command and authority structures, and these of themselves are likely to give rise to most of the phenomena that Marxists associate with class society. It is entirely unrealistic to expect a group occupying a privileged position in the power structure of a society not to derive a certain material or cultural advantage from it. And, as Max Weber argues, there are organizational imperatives that assert themselves in any complex society. Industry has its own imperatives and whether it is privately owned or managed by a state appointed, or approved, board of directors, which is the social reality behind the concept of "socialization," will not make much difference to those employed within it: though like Weber I have a strong suspicion that private ownership is more efficient and more responsible than state control in industry and nothing in the sorry history of socialized industry has dispelled that suspicion.[6]

At this time I also read Robert Michels' *Political Parties* which combined with the influence of Mosca and Pareto to convince me that the so-called "iron law of oligarchy" was one of the few sociological "laws" that positivist social science has been able to formulate. "He who says organization says oligarchy" is, I think, a proposition that has yet to be refuted and if, since Karl Popper, no one feels secure enough to claim that any such proposition can be verified, it is no less irresponsible to base one's social and political action on the rejection of an unrefuted hypothesis that happens to have the whole weight of historical evidence on its side. Marxist talk of the dictatorship of the proletariat, or Maoist theories of the action of revolutionary masses, disguises the fact that someone or group acts in the name of the proletariat (as with the Bolshevik party) or stirs up the movement of more or less discontented masses (as with revolutionary agitators). Some societies are more vulnerable than others, and at one time rather than another, to such revolutionary outbreaks, and sociology can tell us a great deal about the conditions that make it so, but there never was, and never can be, a society without discontented elements on whose discontent the revolutionary can play. Social life is inseparable from the tensions arising in the fact that it is built on the compromise between our common and often long term good and the more immediate satisfaction of partial individual or group ends. These goods are irreducible to each other and neither ought ever to be wholly sacrificed to the other, for while the continued existence of the wider society alone gives security and the conditions of fulfillment to individuals and groups, security and fulfillment themselves presuppose the acceptance by society of the private, and sometimes inconvenient, aspirations of its component parts. The limits of social tolerance cannot be laid down once and for all but must depend on a common sense calculation of reciprocal advantage and disadvantage between the component parts of society and mutual interest in the survival and prosperity of the whole. History, espe-cially the mythical path of Marxist history, cannot deliver us from this condition though it can provide us with the political solution of totalitarianism, whose most powerful ideological support is the myth of existence without tension and whose political survival is assured by the suppression of the men and ideas who provide evidence to the contrary, the reign of the lie and the labor camp.

I had already seen the inadequacy of Marx's view of human nature but as I continued my sociological studies I came to supplement my original explanations of social structure in terms of the demands of human nature with the further notion of the human condition or situation. Existentialist philosophers have used the concept of "the human condition" as a substitute for that of human nature, arguing that man has no determinate nature as such but merely finds himself in a certain situation in a more or less inexplicable universe. In contrast my view has always been that the understanding of the human condition or situation is a supplement to rather than a substitute for the understanding of man's nature. The human condition is the result of the interaction of a particular sort of being, man, with the other animate and inanimate beings found in the universe, each of which also has an inherent character determining the parameters of its possibilities of transformation. I have never thought that this amounted to saying anything more than that men are men and mountains are mountains and that in dealing with either we must take account of the sort of beings they are. This trail led me, in philosophy, beyond David Hume and positivism toward Aristotle and St. Thomas Aquinas. In the development of my relationship to Marxism it led to a new interest in the philosophical background to Marxist theory. It seemed clear that Marxists paid, at least in the order of ends, no respect to the notion of inherent limitations in either human nature or the human condition and that they habitually attributed all deficiencies and disappointments to defective but eminently changeable social arrangements. This was particularly obvious in the more open utopians among them, such as Ernst Bloch, but it is also, I think, the underlying assumption in the rest.

The book which most influenced me at this stage of my Marxist studies was Robert C. Tucker's *Philosophy and Myth in Karl Marx*. Tucker firmly places Marx against the background of the development of German idealism from Kant to Hegel and Feuerbach. He shows that the idealist theory of knowledge, according to which the human mind orders or even creates reality, is the starting point for the development of Marx's own theory of social transformation. From his earliest writings Marx believed that the world could be brought into line with what he thought desirable. This is the great importance of his original atheism as expressed, for instance, in the preface to his doctoral dissertation,[7] for in order that the world may be totally malleable it must be theoretically emptied of any determinate structures. We have already seen how this is done with human nature, and to accomplish the same trick with the rest of surrounding reality it is necessary to deny, explicitly or not, the existence of any fixed character to its defining elements. In other words we must substitute man for God as creator of the nature of things. Tucker quotes a passage from the young Engels which puts the matter clearly: "Hitherto the question has always stood: What is God? and German philosophy has resolved it as follows: God is man." It is precisely the God-like properties attributed to Marxian man that allows the assumption that the world can be recreated in his image.[8]

In *The Rebel* Albert Camus provides a vivid picture of what happens when the human impulse to rebel against a situation perceived as unjust becomes bound up with the myth of the total transformation of the universe. Metaphysical rebellion, which Camus argues is the hard center of the cult of revolution, involves the blurring and eventual dissolution of the distinction between what is man-made and can be changed and what is not. Camus' atheism, which is better understood as a Mediterranean paganism of place and fate, is altogether different from that of Marx. It leads to the realistic conclusion that man's life is unavoidably bound to be played out against the background of a preexisting reality which defines the limits of achievement. At worst men must try to make the best of a bad job and at best the achievements of the human spirit are there for all to see. A nonreligious humanism like that of Camus can, ironically, be suffused by the religious sense of absolute dependence on transcendent reality, a sense which permits pride as well as shame before the various works of man's history. But where this sense is lost, as in the substitute creation envisaged by Marx, there is no independent measure for man and no way of distinguishing the objectively real from the subjectively desired. I have always thought that Camus' testament is particularly important, coming as it does from an atheist and man of the Left, for Camus was a natural rebel who detested even those minor injustices inseparable from social life but who understood the terrifying climax of totalitarianism inherent in the Marxist rejection of the limits of human reality.

Camus should be required reading for students of Marxist ideas because it is to the sense of social injustice that Marxism makes its first appeal. At the moment the appeal is made we must be clear about the point from which it is sounding. Is the call to revolutionary commitment aimed at the achievement of a goal of whose possibility we have some reasonable evidence or is it a cry from the imagined peaks of utopia? For the solution to real problems can only be found in reality itself and the real problem the utopian ultimately faces is the need to hide from himself and others the impossible character of his goal. Thus what purports to be a road to freedom turns out to be a path to deception and deprivation. The utopian may blind you with false science until you fall in with his plans and he may destroy the social and political conditions which he imagines to stand in his way but his problem remains. His hopes are always betrayed, his promises ever broken. At that stage his program must turn from the destruction of particular institutions, social groups, and individuals to the suppression of reality itself. Of course reality cannot be suppressed on the level of existence, things still remain what they are, but it can be suppressed on the level of consciousness through the propagation of a total ideology that systematically distorts and falsifies the evidence of reality. Alongside this, as its only guarantee, must come the elimination of anyone who sees through the veil. This is the worm of totalitarianism which lurks in the bud of every utopia.

Marx began as a rebel. Against the established political reality he set up his own imagined paradise of freedom. His later turn to political economy, culminating in *Das Kapital,* was never designed to do anything more than to show why the subjectively desirable was historically necessary. The utopianism of this enterprise was probably unconscious: (a background in German idealism is enough to confuse anyone interested in distinguishing the possible from the impossible) but the fact remains that Marx, beginning his years of labor on detested economic statistics in the British Museum, already knew the answers he would find to the problems he brought with him from philosophy. In the case he made against the established political and economic system he was like a corrupt detective framing a suspect by the selective accumulation of evidence. The suspect was capitalism and class society in general and, as with most real individuals under investigation, there was plenty of dirt to uncover. But to the evils really resulting from the system Marx added every other charge he could find. The trick at the heart of his science of revolution was to attribute all evil to the object of his investigation leaving socialist "man," freed of the incubus of private ownership, to develop toward his fulfillment in a Communist utopia.

The procedure was illegitimate from the start: some of the "evils" analyzed were unreal, and most could by no stretch of the imagination be laid at the door of any particular system of economic arrangements. Nevertheless the theory that emerged was compelling for several reasons. It was simple in that it found a single culprit for a mass of social, psychological and philosophical evils. It was satisfying because it assuaged man's sense of his own limitations with the promise of a perfect world to come, not after death and in a scarcely imaginable disembodied state but in the world of sensible experience itself. And it was timely, being phrased in just the sort of apparently scientific terms that could command respect in a world seeking certainty in the absence of any universally accepted religious truth. But Marxism was, and is, profoundly wrong in its failure to take account of those circumstances that permanently preclude the achievement of its goal. It was an imagined and imaginary future, itself a variation of the old theme of heaven on earth, that set the intellectual adventure of Marxism in motion as it was later to justify the crimes of Stalin and his henchmen. Whatever the differences between the various critics of Marxism, they share the recognition that there is nothing accidental in this historical association between the Marxist rhetoric of total liberation and the Marxist practice of total coercion. That has also been my own conclusion and it goes far toward explaining why I am and ever will be against Marx.

NOTES

[1] Alex Callinicos, *Althusser's Marxism*, 1976, p. 81.

[2] Robert C. Tucker, *Philosophy and Myth in Karl Marx*, 1969, p. 199.

[3] Weber's two magnificent postwar lectures "Politics as a Vocation" and "Science as a Vocation" have been translated by H. H. Gerth and C. Wright Mills in *From Max Weber: Essays in Sociology*, 1970.

[4] A good one volume selection of Maurras' writings is provided in *De la Politique Naturelle au Nationalisme Integral*, Paris, 1972.

[5] The messianic character of modern revolutionary creeds including Marxism is a theme common to many critics of Marxism. To Professor Talmon's name one should add those of Eric Voegelin, Thomas Molnar and Christopher Dawson.

[6] In other words it is because of its superior performance in assuring prosperity that I prefer private to public ownership. I have no dogmatic preference one way or the other, it is by its good works rather than on faith that free enterprise takes its place in a conservative program and there are cases where I can well see that a measure of socialization is necessary.

[7] A detailed discussion of the important part played by atheism in the development of the Marxist system is provided by George Cottier in *L'Atheisme du Jeune Marx: ses Origines Hégéliennes*, Paris, 1969.

[8] Much of Tucker's analysis is based on psychological interpretation of the development of German philosophy after Kant. Perhaps under the influence of Santayana's *Egotism in German Philosophy* the play of philosophical ideas traced by Tucker struck me as more significant than the psychological tensions on which he lays so much emphasis.

[XXI, Winter 1977, 20–29]

[49]

Fifty Years of Communist Power

WILLIAM HENRY CHAMBERLIN

William Henry Chamberlin (1897–1969), a revisionist historian whose America's Second Crusade *(1950) was a major post-World War II text, was a Moscow correspondent early in his career. Initially enthusiastic about the Russian "experiment," he reacted against such horrors as the artificial famines of the 1930s with a disillusioned isolationism, seen in such works as* Collectivism: A False Utopia *(1937) and* The Confessions of an Individualist *(1940). One of the original creators of the conservative intellectual movement in America, Chamberlin was probably closest to being a classical liberal in his rejection of state interference with the political, social, and economic freedom of the individual. In his* The Evolution of a Conservative *(1959), Chamberlin saw conservatism as a defense against "the revolt of the masses, when the equality of man threatens the quality of man." Perhaps his best-known work was* The Russian Revolution, 1919–21 *(1935).*

ONE TEST OF THE significance of a revolution is the stability of the institutions which it has created, and the well-being of the people who live under those institutions. By this standard the American Revolution is easily the most successful in history, not least because its founding fathers abjured utopian goals and unfulfillable promises.

Another test is the spread and sweep of the upheaval, the scope of the innovations, the effect on the life and thought of hundreds of millions of people outside the country where it occurred. By this test the Russian Communist revolution that took place fifty years ago, on November 7, 1917, whether its legacy may be considered good or evil, on general balance, is unmistakably one of the great events of the twentieth century.

Lenin's seizure of power transformed communism from the speculative faith of a few small and isolated groups into the operative doctrine of a mighty Eurasian empire. Its totalitarian politics and collectivist economics opened up new methods of harnessing individual citizens to the service of an all-powerful state and were curiously reflected in the practice of the rival system, fascism, which arose in struggle against communism and also repudiated guarantees of human liberty and limitations on the power of the government.

Although it was quarantined in Russia after the First World War, communism, by a mixture of force, propaganda, and quick exploitation of power vacuums created by World War II, became the ruling creed over a vast area of eastern and central Europe and also in the historic empire of China. Communist power displayed considerable capacity for national adaptation and acclimatization. Outside the Soviet Union communism assumed a protean variety of forms, from the fanatical egalitarianism and organized mob rule of Red China to the reluctant conformism of the Soviet satellite states, the reformist trends in Yugoslavia, and the respectable image of left-wing socialism in the Communist parties of France and Italy. In some cases there has been skill in exploiting and utilizing nationalist and anti-imperialist movements, although here the record has been somewhat mixed. In many African and Asian lands communism has experienced sharp rebuffs, with Indonesia perhaps the most vivid example.

What happened in 1917 to make Russia, long regarded as the bulwark of reaction, the policeman of Europe, the fountainhead of international subversion? It should first be noted that the repressive authoritarianism of Tsarism carried with it the probability that, should revolution ever come, it would take extreme, not moderate forms. A surprising number of predictions to this effect can be found, not only in the writings of revolutionists, but in the reflections of Russians of quite conservative views.

So the Minister of the Interior in the sternly reactionary reign of Alexander III voiced the opinion, in a letter to Prince Bülow in 1884, that the fall of the monarchy would lead to "communism pure and simple, the communism of Mr. Karl Marx of London, who has just died and whose theories I have studied with interest and attention." A police state that interfered in every department of life, that looked suspiciously on the mildest educational experiments, gave no opportunity for moderate liberals to acquire experience in practical problems of self-government, and drove many students and intellectuals to espouse extreme schemes of social reconstruction.

There was also the immense potential for upheaval, once the strong hand of government was withdrawn, of a vast mass of landless and land-poor peasants, who looked hungrily and greedily at the fine estates of the nobility and the gentry. And successive generations of young revolutionaries, although imprisoned and exiled to Siberia in thousands, and often spurned with suspicion by the very masses whom they wished to organize, had sown seeds of discontent throughout the empire.

Yet it is conceivable that Russia might have avoided revolution of the violent and sweeping type had it not been for one factor, the First World War. Between the abortive 1905 Revolution, which Lenin called a dress rehearsal for 1917, and 1914 there was a considerable economic upswing, accompanied by an improvement in living conditions. A statesman of foresight and intelligence, Count Sergius Witte, with the help of an inflow of foreign capital, had achieved substantial results in the development of industry and transportation. A Prime Minister of force and insight, Peter Stolypin, besides stamping out the embers of the 1905 upheaval by a liberal use of death sentences imposed by court-martial, had tried to strike at the heart of the peasant problem by legislation designed to facilitate the break-up of the traditional village system of partially communal farming and to build up a class of well-to-do peasant proprietors.

After the explosive outbursts of 1904–1906, the workers' strikes, the peasant land seizures and burning of manor-houses, the mutinies in the armed forces, the old regime seemed to be again firmly in the saddle. Less than two months before Tsarism collapsed Lenin was sadly telling an audience of young socialists in Zurich, where he lived in exile, that "we of the older generation may not live to see the decisive battles of the coming revolution."

But when Nicholas II signed the order for Russian mobilization in 1914 he was unconsciously signing his own death warrant. The unsuccessful war with Japan had helped to touch off the abortive revolt of 1905. The equally unsuccessful and far more costly war with Germany was the obvious primary cause of the collapse of the imperial regime, which, in turn, led to the Bolshevik coup eight months later.

Although in the beginning the war with Germany was fairly popular (some old revolutionaries favored Russian involvement, on the ground that France and Great Britain were more liberal than Germany and Austria-Hungary), defeats and heavy casualty lists depressed morale. The war created problems of supply, for the troops and for the civilian population, with which the old-fashioned administration could not cope. It took a heavy toll of experienced officers, commissioned and noncommissioned, and the replacements were sometimes of much more dubious loyalty to the monarchy. Disaffection grew, even in normally monarchist circles, excited by the hypnotic influence which a disreputable monk, Rasputin, had acquired over the nervously susceptible Empress. There were rumors, apparently unfounded, of treason, of German influence at court.

In these circumstances it took only a small number of comparatively trivial incidents, a lockout at the big Putilov metal works, demonstrations in honor of International Working Women's Day, a temporary interruption of the bread supply in some districts of Petrograd, to bring the imposing structure of the Romanov autocracy crashing to its fall. Several days of demonstrations and clashes with the police led up to an unforeseen and unexpected climax on March 12, 1917, when the soldiers of the Petrograd garrison refused orders to fire on the demonstrators and joined them in wild celebration of the downfall of the old regime.

Never was a big revolution so spontaneous, so leaderless, so completely unplanned. If vigilant police work could have saved the monarchy it would have been saved. No prominent revolutionary was in Petrograd; all were in exile abroad or in remote parts of Russia. The scope of the upheaval took everyone by surprise, the weak, rather passive Tsar and his entourage, the opposition in the Duma (the parliament of limited powers, elected on a rigged franchise, which existed at the time), the leaders of the more radical parties.

Out of what might have been sheer chaos two centers of authority emerged, a Provisional Government and the Petrograd Soviet, an organization of elected representatives of workers and soldiers, with representatives of left-wing political parties. These Soviets (the word in Russian means council) were set up in provincial towns and in military units at the front, more slowly among the peasants. Improvised and tumultuous organizations though they were, the Soviets soon became the most effective authority in what was practically a power vacuum.

Because it represented mainly the privileged and propertied minority of the population, the Duma could assert no effective claim to leadership. And the obliteration of Tsarism was complete. Not only in the capital, but throughout the country, not a hand was lifted for its defense or restoration. Even when there was very considerable discontent with the Communist regime and the country was racked from end to end with civil war there was no movement to restore the Tsarist rule. The dynasty of the Romanovs, in the Chinese phrase, had exhausted the mandate of heaven.

News of the downfall of the Tsar and the formation of a liberal Provisional Government was greeted at first with enthusiasm in the United States. The image of the old Russian autocracy was a negative one and the revolution was hailed on the double ground that it meant the emergence of a new democratic Russia and an assurance of Russian determination to prosecute the war more vigorously. Woodrow Wilson referred to the new Russia as "a fit partner in a league of honor" in his war message to Congress. But these hopes faded as it became increasingly evident that Russia was in the throes of a violent social revolution and that the Russian army had virtually disintegrated as a fighting force.

The Provisional Government, first composed mainly of liberals, later with a predominance of moderate socialists, found it easy enough to proclaim and put into effect a program of full political and civil liberties. It foundered and was eventually wrecked because of four elemental movements that gained increasing momentum throughout the summer and autumn.

These were growing refusal of the soldiers to fight, the demand of the peasants for the land of the big estates, the revolt of the industrial workers against the rights of private ownership of factories, and the impulse of the non-Russian nationalities to seek separation from Russia in separate states. All these movements had roots in Russian social history; no one of them could have achieved such large dimensions had it not been for the popular feeling that the iron hand of state authority had disappeared with the Tsar.

It became increasingly clear that the soldier would not be punished if he failed to salute an officer or refused to carry out an order, that no police action would follow if peasants encroached on the neighboring big estate, that the workers could defy the manager or foreman with impunity, that there were no military forces that could be sent to suppress secession. Bit by bit Russia lapsed into virtual anarchy, presenting a master of revolutionary strategy with an unrivalled opportunity to plan and execute a strike for power.

This master was Vladimir Ilyitch Ulyanov, better known under his revolutionary pseudonym of Lenin, leader of the Bolshevik, or left-wing faction of the Russian Social Democratic Party. Lenin was a dogmatic disciple of Karl Marx, but with a considerable streak of sympathy with some of the nineteenth-century revolutionaries who cherished the belief that a revolutionary elite must direct, guide, even coerce the masses for their own good.

Lenin's goal was not a parliamentary regime, with freedom to vote for several parties. It was what he called the dictatorship of the proletariat, or industrial working class. And in Russia, as in other lands where communism has come into power, this has meant the rule of the Communist Party, which is conceived as a ruling elite. Although Lenin made use of the slogan, "All Power to the Soviets" in 1917, he had no more use for freely elected Soviets than for a freely elected legislature. The Constituent Assembly, the convoking of which had been a professed aim of Bolshevik party propaganda, was allowed to meet in January, 1918, but was promptly dissolved when it appeared that the Bolsheviks (or Communists, as they later called themselves) held only about 25 per cent of the seats. And other socialist parties were systematically expelled from the Soviets, which soon became mere rubber stamps for registering and administering the decisions of the Communist party.

Lenin skillfully associated his party with the demands of large masses of the people for land and peace. All the efforts of Alexander Kerensky, moderate socialist who headed the Provisional Government in the later phases of its existence, to rally support for continuation of the war and for patience in waiting for the Constituent Assembly before adopting decisions on the land question were in vain. By October Lenin, who had been urging the necessity of an armed uprising to overthrow the weakening Provisional Government, won the acceptance of a revolution in favor of such an uprising from the majority of the Party Central Committee.

The uprising took place on November 6–7 and succeeded in the capital, Petrograd, with little bloodshed. Leon Trotsky, principal organizer of the revolt in Petrograd, had contrived to win over the soldiers of the garrison, who very much feared being sent to the front, to an attitude of friendly neutrality, while the more active operations, such as the seizure of government buildings and the storming of the Winter Palace, headquarters of the Government, were entrusted to such Bolshevik sympathizers as armed workers, so-called Red Guards, and the sailors in the nearby base, Kronstadt.

The coup was also coordinated with the meeting of the second Congress of Soviets, which, in contrast to the first, where the majority consisted of members of the moderate socialists, possessed a Bolshevik majority. Russia was proclaimed a Republic of Soviets and decrees were rushed through for immediate opening of peace negotiations and for abolishing private property in land, which was to be distributed among the users on an egalitarian formula, each peasant family receiving shares in proportion to the number of its members. This was not the solution of the land problem of which the Bolsheviks approved in theory, because it looked to the establishment of widespread peasant proprietorship. But Lenin recognized the necessity of this step as a means of winning the support of the poor and "middle" peasants. The radical character of the new regime was further emphasized later by decrees confiscating foreign enterprises and repudiating Russia's state debts, owed to foreign creditors. Still later there was wholesale nationalization of all industrial plants and other undertakings employing hired labor.

One other point should be emphasized in connection with the Bolshevik Revolution. All its leaders, notably Lenin and Trotsky, regarded it as the first step toward an international revolution that would embrace, if not the whole world, at least the leading European industrial countries. As Marxists they did not believe that an isolated socialist revolution could hold out indefinitely in Russia, where the industrial working class was small and the majority of the population consisted of property-minded peasants. A world, or European revolution was, to them, the remedy for the failures and deficiencies of their attempt to build up a socialist, or communist (Marx used the terms interchangeably) order in Russia.

With a view to promoting this end a Third, or Communist International was formed in Moscow in 1919, designed to draw off the more revolutionary elements who had belonged to the pre-war Second International. This organization was referred to rather grandiloquently as the general staff of the world revolution and drew up many schemes, published and private, for the subversion of what were called capitalism and imperialism, both in the economically more developed countries of the West and in the Colonial and semi-colonial lands of Asia.

But, despite this ambitious attempt at organizing revolutions on the Russian model, communism between the two wars, while it won several temporary victories, was never able to take over and hold a country. Contrary to many explicit predictions of Lenin himself, the Russian Revolution stopped at Russia's frontiers. After the respite of the new economic policy (1921–1929) the problem of the independent peasant proprietor was solved with Asiatic brutality by abolishing, or "liquidating" him. The "kulaks," or more prosperous peasants, were deported with their families to forced labor; the remainder of the peasants were dragooned into membership in so-called collective farms, where they were completely under the authority of the all-powerful state as to what they should plant and how much they should receive for their labor.

World War II brought a further expansion of the frontiers of communism. This occurred in Europe, with the possible and partial exception of Yugoslavia, not by spontaneous national revolutions, but by the occupation of a large part of eastern and southeastern Europe by the Red Army. This made it possible to impose Communist patterns of government, regardless of the wishes of the people, on Poland, Hungary, Bulgaria, Rumania, Czechoslovakia and East Germany, as also on the little Baltic states, Latvia, Lithuania and Estonia, which gained their independence after World War I, only to lose it after World War II.

Somewhat different was the case of mainland China, where the Soviet contribution to the success of Mao Tse-tung was peripheral, not decisive. As General Albert Wedemeyer has plausibly suggested, World War II had much the same effect on China as World War I on Russia. Eight years of unsuccessful war and Japanese occupation of the largest Chinese cities ruined the currency, upset the administration and social order and in various ways prepared the way for the Communist sweep in 1949.

The long and fierce polemics between the Soviet and Chinese Communist leaders, together with Yugoslavia's successful assertion of independence from Moscow and the smaller gains in the direction of enlarged autonomy in the Soviet satellite states, go far to disprove the possibility of a Communist world state, ruled from Moscow. At the root of the Soviet-Chinese feud is the fact that Russia is a more economically advanced, psychologically more satisfied power, while China, especially under Mao's recent paranoid prodding, is more inclined to stress the early

Leninist doctrine of support for universal proletarian revolution in all its rigor. Moreover, China, especially in regard to Formosa, considers itself a have-not power.

Half a century is a long enough span to make possible some conclusions about the system that, in one form or another, now dominates the lives of about one-third of the population of the world. Communism may be appraised in two ways, in terms of its original ideals and in terms of comparative performance with developments in non-Communist countries.

One of the obvious casualties of experience has been the ideal of material equality, which figured in Lenin's early thinking and has been a powerful factor in attracting the poor and discontented to the Communist cause. Wages and salaries are as sharply differentiated in the Soviet Union as anywhere else in the world; the difference is sharper than in Western countries because the standard of living is much lower.

There have been other substantial changes in Communist policies and attitudes since the early period of the Soviet Republic. At that time education was highly permissive; experimental art, literary and theater forms were encouraged; national patriotism was disparaged. Now education is sternly disciplined, even to the point of restoring the uniforms which school children wore before the Revolution. Soviet writers, artists, and musicians are required to shun "formalism," the use of abstract forms of expression. The outstanding figures of the Russian past again are given full appreciation. Military rank and hierarchy, reduced to a minimum in the first years of the Red Army, have been fully restored. Contrary to a general impression abroad, the Soviet Union today is socially and culturally a rather conservative, even puritanical country. Marriage, virtually abolished by early Soviet legislation permitting divorce at the desire of either partner, is now surrounded with stabilizing safeguards. Undue emphasis on sex in magazines, pictures, and on the stage is forbidden.

Two characteristics of Soviet communism have remained constant through all these changes and have made for a prodigious concentration of political and economic power in the hands of the Soviet state and the ruling Communist Party. These are the system of government by a single party and the operation by the state, in one public form or another, of all branches of the economy: factories, transportation, stores, mines, even down to small stores and handicraft enterprises.

The Soviet Communist Party has worked out a formula for staying in power which is extremely effective. This is a combination of government by terror and government by propaganda. Political and civil liberties are non-existent. Anyone who speaks out against the existing regime may be arrested, sent to a concentration camp, in extreme cases executed. The intensity of the terror has varied; it was most intense during the quarter of a century of Stalin's absolute rule, from 1928 until 1953, when millions of people were uprooted from their homes and deported, millions more were sent to slave-labor concentration camps and executions took a very heavy toll, not least among Communist Party members who fell victim to Stalin's paranoid fantasies. Conditions became much milder under Khrushchev and under Khrushchev's successors, Brezhnev and Kosygin. But the threat of police repression is always in the background.

Side by side with this repression there is a nonstop campaign of organized propaganda of almost unimaginable intensity. Suppose that in the United States the government controlled every newspaper and magazine, that no book could be published without state censorship approval, that schools and youth organizations, theaters and broadcasting stations were all pressed into service for the purpose of making the people believe what the government wishes them to believe. Given this situation for half a century, besides the severe penalties for activity that could be called counter-revolutionary, and the natural result would be a pretty conformist population, with the sceptics and dissenters keeping their opinions to themselves.

At its best communism is a system of intellectual dullness, of far-flung abortion of creative thought and achievement, of amazing blank spots, even in the minds of educated Soviet citizens, about the world outside Soviet frontiers. At its worst it is the sheer horror of Stalinism. There is a Russian saying that victors are not judged. Stalin could never be brought before an international tribunal on charges of waging aggressive war and of a long list of crimes against humanity. If one could imagine such a trial here are a few of the items in the prosecuting attorney's bill of indictment:

That you killed, by various means, all the six fellow-members of the Politbureau (highest steering committee) of the Communist Party at the time of Lenin's death;

That you caused the arrest and shooting of 98 of the 139 members of the Central Committee of the Soviet Communist Party, chosen at its Seventeenth Congress in 1934.

That you created something unknown in Russian history, with its long record of political persecution and repression, the show trial in which the defendants eagerly incriminated themselves in monstrous crimes, of which not a shred of material evidence existed. That you achieved this sinister result by wholesale use of torture, ranging from brutal physical violence to threats against the members of the defendants' families.

That, without any semblance of legal procedure, you uprooted about a million peasant families, the so-called kulaks, from their homes, confiscated all their property, and shipped them in freightcars to remote places of forced labor.

That, by heavy grain requisitions in a year of poor harvest, 1932, you deliberately caused the death of some 5 million Russian and Ukrainian peasants, refusing to import foreign grain or to permit foreign relief activity. This for the purpose of finally breaking the resistance of the peasants to your policy of taking away almost all their privately owned land and regimenting them in collective farms.

That, on August 23, 1939, you concluded with Adolf Hitler a mutual aggression pact, taking as your part of the spoil the Baltic Republics of Latvia, Lithuania, and Estonia, the eastern part of Poland, and the Rumanian territories of Bessarabia and Northern Bukovina. This procedure, involving the subjugation of 25 million people, was carried out in violation both of elementary principles of international law and of specific non-aggression treaties in force between the Soviet Union and the countries concerned.

That, on November 30, 1939, again in violation of a non-aggression treaty, you launched a military invasion of the republic of Finland and annexed the town of Viipuri and other ethnically Finnish territory.

That, following the military occupation of Eastern Poland and the Baltic states, you carried out mass deportations of about 1,200,000 people from Eastern Poland and of several hundred thousand from the Baltic states under circumstances of such brutality that about one-quarter of the victims perished.

That, early in April, 1940, you murdered some 14,000 Polish officer war prisoners, over 4,000 in the Katyn Forest, near Smolensk, the remainder in some place or places unknown. The attempt to attribute responsibility for this crime to the Germans was so devoid of supporting evidence that, after being advanced at the Nuremberg war crimes trial, it was quietly dropped.

That the regime of utter lawlessness and contempt for human rights which characterized your rule in the Soviet Union was extended to all areas of eastern and central Europe which fell under the permanent or temporary occupation of your troops. And that you made no effort to prevent your troops from committing in Berlin, Vienna, Budapest and other occupied cities and towns enormous and systematic excesses of murder, rape, and looting without precedent in the previous behavior of Russian troops in Europe or in the practice of war among civilized nations.

The verdict of an informed impartial tribunal on every count of this indictment could only have been: Guilty, as Charged.

The system that could produce the monstrous record of Stalinism, still unpunished, still unatoned for, stands self-condemned on moral, cultural, and humanitarian grounds.

The Soviet Union has made impressive material progress during the half century of its existence. New cities, built around huge modern factories, stand where formerly herdsmen grazed their flocks. The celebrations that will center in Moscow's Red Square this November will put forward many comparisons of pre-revolutionary and present-day Russia, and these comparisons will by no means be mere propaganda. New natural resources have been discovered; there have been daring ventures in polar exploration; education has been made available to far more people. Soviet achievements in nuclear arms development and space exploration have attracted world acclaim.

Without in the least detracting from

WILLIAM HENRY CHAMBERLIN

these genuine achievements, two qualifications must be borne in mind. First, Russia under any political and economic system would have gone ahead rapidly over a span of five decades. The pre-revolutionary Russian growth rate was higher than that of Western Europe. Russia in the twentieth century is somewhat similar to the United States in the nineteenth, with vast new territories east of the Urals to explore, develop and exploit. The chances are that Russia under a system of private enterprise would have achieved substantial progress, less spectacular, perhaps, in some fields, but more even and without the frightful toll of human suffering involved in Stalin's Genghis Khan methods of pushing industrial development and collective farming.

The second qualification is the extreme disparity of Soviet economic development. If Russia ranks with the United States in space exploration and nuclear weapons development, it is more comparable with Bulgaria and Romania in terms of standard of living for the average citizen. Its record in agriculture has been a productive disgrace. While the United States, with 6 per cent of its population engaged in farming, gives its own people an ample varied diet and produces large surpluses for less fortunate lands, the Soviet Union, with almost half its people still in state and collective farms, has never resumed its pre-revolutionary status as a large exporter of grain and as late as 1963 depended on grain purchased from the United States, Canada, and Australia, with their individualist farm systems, to prevent serious shortage, if not downright starvation. This same phenomenon may also be observed in Communist China.

The absence of the element of individual ownership and initiative is also keenly reflected in the chronic shortage and poor quality of what is produced by handicraft

industries and of goods offered in the state stores. It is abundantly clear from the Soviet experience that the elimination of the economic incentive of private ownership and operation is equivalent to removing a dynamo from a machine.

Neither morally nor materially is Soviet communism, on its fiftieth anniversary, a serious challenge to the economically developed countries of North America and Western Europe. In the poorer lands of the southern hemisphere the propaganda appeal of communism, of the Russian or Chinese model, is higher, although even there the lasting Communist successes have been fewer than might have been exacted.

The military, political, and diplomatic weight of the Soviet Union is considerable. But the launching deliberately of an aggressive war by Moscow, in this age of nuclear destructive power, seems improbable.

The confrontation of the two systems that now divide the world will presumably go on indefinitely, although both systems are subject to internal pressures for change and neither is altogether static. The individualist system is now less vulnerable to Communist propaganda than it was when there were periodic severe depressions, with mass unemployment and paralysis of existing industrial equipment.

Those old enough in Russia to remember the grey days in November, 1917 when the Soviet regime was born may well reflect that the revolution achieved more in some ways, less in others, than it had promised. It achieved more in building up, in a country close to disintegration in 1917, an impressive modern industry, a powerful army, a leading place in the European balance of power. It realized vastly less in realizing such goals as material equality, kindlier and more humane relations among its citizens, security for the individual against a police state more ruthless and more efficient than that of the Tsars.

Among the unsolved problems of Soviet communism two are outstanding. These are the failure to create a peaceful legal machinery for the transfer of power at the top and the unmistakable contradic- tion between the desire of the more broadly educated youth for more freedom to travel abroad, to speak and write, and the old and often obsolete Marxist dogmas to which conformity is required.

[XI, Fall 1967, 364–373]

[50]

Two Socialisms

GERHART NIEMEYER

Gerhart Niemeyer (1907–   ) was born in Essen, Germany, and studied at Munich and Cambridge universities; he was awarded the J.U.D. degree (Doctor of both Civil and Canon Law) from Kiel University in 1932. Now professor emeritus of government at the University of Notre Dame, his academic career also included teaching at Princeton, Madrid, and Oglethorpe universities, and in 1981 he was ordained as an Episcopalian priest. He is the author of many distinguished works, among which are Law Without Force *(1941),* Between Nothingness and Paradise *(1971), and* Deceitful Peace *(1971). His* An Inquiry into Soviet Mentality *(1956) revealed Niemeyer to be one of the most important conservative political thinkers of our time, capable of understanding the irrationality of the Soviet mind.*

"THE ISSUE TODAY is between socialism and freedom." Those who state their conviction in this way fear that the gradual expansion of government here at home will ultimately turn out to have been the road to communism. Is their fear well-founded? What precisely is socialism? Strictly speaking, the term connotes public ownership of the means of production. Today in the United States, socialism is a derisive name for any tendency of Washington to plan what must not be planned, to organize what should regulate itself, to regiment what ought to move in freedom. The fear of government invasion in certain areas of life bespeaks the premise that government has proper limits, that wide areas of human life should remain beyond its reach. We speak of a public and a private sphere. "Private" is not only the life of each individual person, and his relations with family and friends, but

"private" designates also an entire system of social order in which not the government but the decisions of numberless individuals and their action upon each other keep house. The fear of "socialism" implies that this pattern of individual decisions constitutes a genuine order, an order that is valuable not only because it has intrinsic merit but also because its unhampered functioning guarantees the freedom of personal autonomy to all competent individuals who can exercise responsible self-control.

Public discussion of these problems is emotional and somewhat fuzzy. Clarity can be achieved only when one penetrates beyond the slogans to the underlying problems. The problems are institutional, but the institutional concepts are formed by theoretical premises. Thus when we speak of the limited state, which has been one of the perennial political problems of

586

Western civilization, we must go further and examine the assumptions on which the notion of the limited state is founded. This takes us to the basic ideas about man, his ultimate destiny and his aspirations in life. The concept of man, in turn, inspires that of an order of life that lies beyond government action. In modern times, this idea has taken the form of a "natural order." No more can be done here than roughly to indicate the direction of this kind of inquiry. Thus we shall explore the connection between the modern notion of the limited state and socialism, the difference between the welfare socialism of the Western variety and Marxist socialism, and the role which both socialisms play in the crisis of Western civilization. I shall try to show that socialism in the West, being a variety of liberalism, differs both in fundamental philosophies and policies from communism, but that both socialisms constitute relations between rulers and ruled that are alien to the spirit of freedom and friendship.

I

Aristotle said that the political community is the highest and most comprehensive of all communities. He argued that every community among men exists for a particular good, but the political community aims at the good of the whole life. Hence government, the art of politics, is the master art of them all, for it determines the respective importance and scope of all the other arts. There is nothing limited about this concept of the state. The limited state is a creation of Christian thinking, particularly of Augustine. It arose from the fundamental experience of the Incarnation, the appearance of God in human form at a definite place and time of human history. Christian thinking about politics was based on a new discovery about the destiny of man: man lived in order to attain fellowship with God. Augustine distinguished in this world two great communities among men: those who were drawn to each other by the common love of God, and those who understood each other in the similarity of the love for themselves. The first he called the City of God. In its orientation toward eternal life, this community ranks highest among all human associations. Augustine, in other words, could not share Aristotle's idea that the purely temporal institution of government represents the royal order, the master order. The City of God ranks higher. The state cannot be its master and director. Thus Augustine, for the first time in human history, assigned to the state a merely practical task of procuring a rudimentary sort of peace and a modicum of justice.

As a result, an entire sphere of human life, the spiritual sphere, was not only distinguished from the temporal order but deliberately put beyond the reach of the government. The spiritual and moral life of man, with its purpose of salvation, was left to the autonomous authority of the Church. The significant feature of this arrangement was that the center of gravity shifted from the state to the nonpolitical aspects of life. Man's chief purpose in life was pursued in an order which the government had not created and did not direct. The government, in turn, provided what amounted to a mere auxiliary framework of temporal peace and justice. Its function was limited not only in scope but also in dignity. The state's proper activity is legislation, and legislation cannot save men's souls. In the autonomy of the spiritual sphere from government Western man achieved both the social order characteristic of our civilization and the Western form of freedom. For the limitation of government to peace, public order, and justice also permitted and facilitated the freedom of human reason, represented by the Western institution of the university.

A decisive change in this pattern occurred when the rationale of the limited state was secularized by John Locke. Locke taught that "the great and chief end of men uniting into commonwealths" is property, the acquisition of wealth. This teaching, which was almost universally accepted in the West, shifted the center of gravity of human life from man's relation with God to man's relation with nature, from the concern for his soul to the concern for his estate. Man's economic activity was seen as that for the sake of which governments performed their auxiliary functions. Thus Locke continued to think of the state as an order limited in scope and in dignity. Instead of being limited in favor of the autonomous order of salvation, however, he conceived it to be oriented to the service of men's economic purposes which antedated the state. The state was seen as an order of peace, public safety, and judicial certainty, which enabled men to acquire wealth more effectively than would have been possible otherwise. Beyond the state lies the great private sphere of economics, a sphere which the state with its laws has not created and cannot create because the state has been created by it. This secular sphere of men's chief end differed from the spiritual order in more than one respect. Above all, unlike the spiritual order, it could not be conceived or experienced as a community beside the state. Rather, it was a sphere of self-seeking activities of a multitude of men, each pursuing his own advantage, an aggregate of private personal interests. The relation of the social order to these interests was one of means to end, so that the purpose of society would be attained as the private interests of multitudes of individuals were more or less satisfied, according to each person's abilities. The contribution of the state to this end was the procurement of suitable conditions that would facilitate each individual's success as much as is possible.

To this new version of the limited state Adam Smith contributed the idea that the total aggregate of self-centered individual economic activities constitutes a natural pattern of order. Smith's symbol was the "Invisible Hand," the force that in the circulation of goods produces a general harmony. As each individual "intends only his own gain," he is "led by an invisible hand to promote an end which was no part of his intention," and "by pursuing his own interest he frequently promotes that of the society more effectually than when he really intends to promote it." Individual self-interest thus was seen as a social function, the motor which propels not merely individual wealth but the wealth of nations. As self-seeking individual activities produced an ordered pattern for the whole, unhindered economic initiative must eventually result in the widest possible individual satisfaction. This is the concept of a natural economic order, an order on which the intentional pursuit of society's interest by the government could not possibly improve. Locke had said that man's economic purposes constitute the *raison d'être* of the state. Smith added that these purposes were unconscious parts of a self-executing harmony which could function perfectly only when left autonomous, and which would procure the end of society, namely the best possible satisfaction of individual material welfare. Thus the economic natural order and its laws now turned into the ultimate cause for the sake of which the state should be limited to minimal activity.

The Locke-Smithean limitation of the state involves also a concept of man that differs radically from that of the Christian tradition. Augustine's limitation of the state had derived from a psychology that sees men's loves as the decisive factor in any community, and the love of God as the most significant fact of human life. The community formed by the love of God is then recognized as that which embodies man's highest destiny. By contrast, Locke's psychology sees man as significantly self-centered and self-seeking. This follows from the assumption that man's essential relationship is not that with God but rather that with nature. Foreshadowing Marx, Locke centers man's social interests in property, and derives property from human labor creating value out of nature's matter. We have here the difference between what Mircea Eliade has called "religious man," the man who conceives his entire existence in the light of the Creation and his relation to the Creator, and modern man, who vaunts his mastery over material nature. To these two concepts of man correspond two concepts of the limited state. For Augustine, the community of men in the love of God is a fact of life. As the highest conceivable community, its order lies untouchable beyond the reach of merely temporal authority. For the modern *homo oeconomicus,* the natural order of the Invisible Hand is his proper realm, an order of intrinsic value which involves the actuality of human freedom as well as the promise of human welfare. One cannot possibly overemphasize the importance of this change from the traditional to the modern notion of the limited state. The state is limited now for the sake of unhindered economic production rather than for the sake of the love of God; the autonomous realm limiting it is no longer the spiritual order of salvation but the natural order of economic harmony.

The difference is not merely philosophical. Unlike the order of salvation, the Invisible Hand implies a pragmatic postulate. It is supposed to function here and now, and there are tangible criteria

of its functioning. What is more, the idea that the economic system's harmonious functioning entails benefits for all arouses certain definite expectations. These soon begin to take the form of demands which people make on their society. We have noted that the task assigned to government was to procure the conditions under which individual interests could attain maximum fulfillment. Society thus became an arrangement for the ultimate purpose of a well-functioning economic order. A corresponding change occurred in the concept of the common good. Traditionally identified with justice, it now takes the form of a macro-economic perspective of society, in which individual material welfare is a function of the overall balance of productive forces. The new orientation, however, has taken a most ironic turn. For the same concepts which first instructed government to stay within limits drawn more narrowly than ever before in history later prompted an ever expanding role of government in the management of the economic system. It is the concern with the health of the economic system as a whole, for the sake of its expected benefits for the individual members of society, that has brought about the gradual incursion of the government into the economic realm and created Western welfare socialism.

II

The limitation of the state, as postulated by Locke's concept of man and Smith's concept of the natural order of society, has a tendency to give way to ever expanding government interference in the economic system. This is the thesis I am here submitting, a thesis that can of course not be adequately substantiated in so brief a space. Only the main arguments can be briefly sketched.

The role of government is to ban from

human existence certain evils. When the limits of government are circumscribed by man's ultimate spiritual destiny and the autonomous life of moral and spiritual order, the business of government will be seen in the "punishment of wickedness and vice, the maintenance of true religion, and virtue." When man's purpose, however, is seen as the acquisition of wealth, and the aggregate of individual pursuits of wealth postulated as an order of natural harmony, the evil on which government should concentrate must be found wholly in external conditions which somehow are disturbing the natural harmony of things. Government thus becomes increasingly a device to procure favorable circumstances. The concept of evil is externalized, the source of evil no longer sought in the human heart but in certain undesired conditions that can be removed in order to achieve a more perfect functioning of the social order. Once this is the accepted notion of government's role, there is room for widely divergent opinions on what precisely are the disturbing circumstances, and what should be done to eliminate them. The limitation of government will be prescribed by these opinions. Locke, for instance, felt that the only thing man lacked for his existence was the assurance of a smooth-functioning judicial system. It was not so much justice that he demanded but rather the predictability in human relations that comes from publicly promulgated laws, impartial judges, and assured enforcement. In other words, men could live well, if only government would see to it that society observed certain "rules of the game." Now this is one idea of the conditions which man needs in order to live the good life, but not the only one. Other conditions can be postulated, particularly when attention has been drawn to the macro-economic context of the good life. When one begins to wonder under what conditions the economic system as a whole would probably operate as postulated, one may hit upon all kinds of things. The government may be called upon to provide tariffs or other means of protection, to regulate credit, even to lend a supporting hand to the pricing system,—all in the name of macro-economic health. Such measures will of course be disputed by those who say that here the government is no longer engaged in the business of securing favorable basic conditions but is rather trying to run the economy, thereby disturbing the laws of the natural order. The point, however, is not whether such government interferences are or are not well conceived and compatible with premises of the Invisible Hand. Once the entire problem of order and disorder has been shifted from the human heart to external conditions, and men begin to blame circumstances rather than themselves for the evils of their social existence, and expect their government to change these circumstances, there is really no cogent reason why any external condition should be kept from government's correcting hand. Thus the dispute between classical liberals and modern liberal socialists is one conducted on common premises. The premises are that the overall economic order of society is the basis of the good life, that it has inherent value, and that its functioning depends on certain basic conditions to be secured by the government. Given this assumption, the decision of what conditions are an impediment to the system's smooth operation and what means are required to remove them is one on which opinions may vary widely.

A tendency toward socialist policies thus is built into the assumptions underlying our modern world, since with Locke we see man as the *homo oeconomicus* whose habitat is the acquisitive society. A socialist government is one that concerns itself authoritatively with the functioning of the economic system. The economic order of which Adam Smith spoke is supposed to engender its own equilibrium, but it is also, on the Lockean premise, supposed to provide individual welfare. The concept of welfare in terms of material well-being is a thoroughly modern one, differing from Aristotle's happiness as identical with virtue, and Augustine's goal of fellowship with God. Welfare is what modern man expects of society. The promise of welfare as the result of a well-functioning economic order can almost be called the charter of modern society. Once this promise was grasped by the masses in an age of universal suffrage, the voters would build up enormous pressures on the government to make up for any failures of the Invisible Hand to fulfill it. The welfare state is thus the psychologically and politically unavoidable consequence of the welfare concept of society that stems from John Locke.

One should distinguish between the problem of human welfare and welfare as the utilitarian rationale and purpose of the political order. The latter results from the turn which political philosophy took in the seventeenth and eighteenth centuries. The modern welfare problem, by contrast, is a product of the industrialized and urbanized society as it emerged in the nineteenth century. Masses of individuals found, and are still finding, themselves exposed to indigence of health and estate which they are unable to handle with the resources of rented apartment dwellings and wage income. Facilities larger than those at the command of the urban family are required to cope with many personal emergencies that typically arise in modern existence. We are still groping for the most humane forms of organization capable of dealing with these problems. There is, then, a modern welfare problem. One must, however, resist the temptation of jumping from the awareness of a welfare problem to the conclusion of the welfare state. The welfare state is more than an answer to an urgent need: it embodies a concept of man's purpose in life and the function of political association that far antedates as well as transcends the welfare task in an industrial society. Western welfare socialism has arisen from the relatively recent merger of urban welfare problems and utilitarian political philosophy, compounding the fallacies of the latter with a fallacious intellectual shortcut that makes government instrumental to the solution of almost any human task.

Socialism in the West thus is merely one of the possible variants of Western liberalism, the concept of society centered in the individual and his material aspirations. It is an ultimate concern for private utility and individual welfare that converts itself here into an expanding public management of economic processes and resources. To be sure, the "Individual" is not the concrete living person, whom nobody really consults, but rather a type that is authoritatively defined, together with his presumed needs and aspirations, by the political thinker or government planner. Still, the motivation of Western welfare socialism stems from the same sources as that of Western classical liberalism. It is an individualist rather than a collectivist approach to man and society. It conceives of government as the servant of the ultimate value, acquisitive individual self-interest, and merely occupies one of the extremes of a wide range of conditions that can be conceived as meeting the postulate of welfare.

III

The socialism of Marx and Lenin has roots in entirely different ideas. To begin with, its underlying concept of human nature is collectivist rather than individualist. Marx saw man as being wholly defined by the process of labor. To Aristotle's formulation "More than anything else, reason is man" Marx might have retorted: "More than anything else, labor is man." Man is a being whose distinctive feature is that he creates his own life through the objects that he makes out of nature, and who becomes himself in the relations with the objects of his creation. Any kind of separation between him and the fruit of his labor, or between him and his labor process, deprives him of his humanity. This view of man leads Marx into the concept of a collectivist order of labor as man's proper way of life. For in any other economic system, man would be alienated from his fellow beings and himself, by being alienated from his labor and its products. Private property of the means of production, for instance, enables one man to make another work for him. It also entails a division of labor by which a person is constrained to do the same kind of work all his life, so that he becomes functionally dependent on others. Only if labor were organized under the management of the entire community, and the means of production became the property of all could man become the master of his own labor process as well as of nature and nature's laws. It is clear that the Marxist view of man differs as much from that of Locke as from that of Augustine or of Aristotle. The individual as a separate entity is rejected. Freedom and a human life is seen as possible only in a collective arrangement of the labor process. All individualism, above all however acquisitive individualism, is condemned as injustice, oppression, and dehumanization. Marx, together with Locke, looks for man's "chief end" in his relation with nature, but unlike Smith does not assume that there is a humane self-executing order of economic production, as long as private property and individual self-interest is the basis of the economic system.

Marxist socialism, however, is more than the postulate of a collectivist order of labor. More than anything else, it centers in a view of history that asserts a necessary movement of history from one type of society to another by means of revolution. Marxism-Leninism assumes that the conceivable types of society are limited, in fact that there are only five such types, and that the last of these, which is still to come, is the collectivist society in which human nature finally comes into its own. This last society of history will grow out of the revolution of the proletariat, the class of propertyless workers that arises in the last but one society in the series, the capitalist society. The struggle of the proletariat against the class of the bourgeoisie, i.e. the owners of the capitalist means of production, is thus the decisive struggle of history. Through it, the proletariat will overthrow its masters and then use political power dictatorially to "expropriate the expropriators." The proletariat is described as the only "really revolutionary class" because it fights not for the establishment of any interests of its own but for the radical destruction of the bourgeois society and all its vestiges. Thus Marxist socialism is more than merely a vision of collectivist production. It is also a doctrine of protracted and irreconcilable struggle, a declaration of total war against every now existing social order. It proclaims the action of revolutionary forces, of revolutionaries who pride themselves in having nothing in common with all other fellow-beings and are committed to a radical attitude of hostility until every trace of the now existing society has been eliminated.

For the same reason, Marxist socialism is not a doctrine of state supremacy, particularly not of state management of the economic system. Marx, Engels, and Lenin agree in characterizing the state as merely an instrument of class rule which will disappear when class society gives way to classless socialism. The ultimate vision of these communists includes a society with no political order, a society held together only by the discipline of collective labor. This is not the place to pass judgment on that vision. The point is to note that Marxist socialism, unlike Western welfare socialism, sees no role for the state in the ultimate order of economic harmony which it expects. The state is, however, extremely important in the period of transition from capitalism to communism. This is the period in which the Communist Party is still relatively weak, the forces hostile to it still powerful, the dangers of a relapse into the past lurking everywhere, and the new socialist society still in gestation. Man is still beset by the habits acquired under capitalism, and therefore he is still selfish, individualistic, acquisitive, obstreperous. In this period the state must be powerful to hold down the enemies of the Revolution, to enforce labor discipline, to destroy what Lenin called the "terrible force of habit," and to press men into a new mold. Thus in Marxist communism the state is above all an instrument of combative power, the major weapon in that protracted struggle that is to fill the entire period of transition from capitalism to communism. It must be totalitarian because the Communist Party is engaged in a total struggle against everything that has existed, because its power is supposed to be adequate to the task of re-making human beings into something they never have been, and, as far as we know, do not want to be. The communist state is totalitarian because the Communists want to play God. They intend to master the human soul, to converge all its powers of loyalty on the Party, to create the world according to their idea of what it should have been. In this enterprise,

the state's monopolistic management of the economy plays an important role, but it is the role of engendering more and more power for the Party. In the period of transition, unlimited and unlimitable power is the Party's main concern. State management of labor and production represents not yet the way of life, the social order for which communism ultimately hopes. Rather, it is another manipulative operation designed above all to suppress and eradicate everything in the hearts and minds of men that is not wholly amenable to the Party's leadership.

IV

There is, then, a Western socialism distinct from the Marxist variety. Between the two there are fundamental differences in assumptions and motivations. The socialism that is a noticeable tendency in this country stems from the liberal tradition of Locke-Adam Smith-John Stuart Mill. Its basis is the concept of the acquisitive individual who expects from society the satisfaction of his material interests. Its orientation is toward a nebulous value called welfare. Marxist communism comes from the tradition of speculations about history that runs from Fourier and Saint-Simon to Hegel and Comte. Its basis is the expectation of a wholly new and transfigured world that is to emerge from the revolution of the proletariat. Its orientation is toward the requirements of the struggle that precedes the coming of that world. The difference of assumptions and motivations results in different policies and legal forms. Western socialism emphasizes the supremacy of government in the economic process, but one may say that with all that it is not wholly committed to the abolition of private property or the free labor contract, so that it is likely to retain these institutions while putting an ever heavier hand of government regulation on the freedom of their use. Marxist communism can never reconcile itself with any part of the existing order, but it will readily make use of existing institutions to further its power strategy. One could trace these differences in many details, and one is likely to come out with the clear-cut result that, no matter how objectionable Western socialism may be, it is in no way a road to the regime of Communists. That is an enterprise of quite a different nature.

The differences, however, should not induce us to overlook the similarities among all kinds of socialisms. After all, one could possibly discover still more varieties of socialism around, for instance, the unity-oriented socialism of the Fascists, and the modernity-oriented socialism of Nehru and Nasser. What characterizes all socialism in an institutional respect is the combination of political power with the power of controlling the means of material existence. Political power, we all would agree, consists in the authority to make laws that bind people's wills in conscience and obligation. Thus, the individual citizen can properly be said to be *subject* to political authorities. Now if the same set of people or the same agency that makes laws also holds the key to every person's livelihood and material betterment, the individual is not merely subject to, but *dependent* on, the government. There is quite a difference between subjection to authority and dependence on controlling power. Not only does a government combining both political and economic power become impossible to control, but it also acquires the means of manipulating people into unresisting subservience. It does not even require the open and harsh methods of compulsion, such as penalties, jails, police force. It needs only to withhold employment, deny advancement, raise the bread basket or lower it, as its interests may require. Instead of addressing the citizens,

through the command of laws, as moral beings capable of rational obedience, it controls them as natural creatures who cannot escape their animal needs for food, shelter, cover. In a socialist system, the entire relation between rulers and ruled is changed. A normal political relationship is cast in terms of rational moral assumptions and persuasion within that framework. Under the socialist type of authority, the relation between ruler and ruled is based on the people's dire necessity, a necessity to which the government alone holds the key. Even should a socialistic government conceive of itself as the servant of people's needs rather than the exploiter of people's dependence, it would still be that government which determines which needs should be recognized, and in what way people should be served. The entire public order is distorted when it centers in the material aspects of life where men are by necessity unfree, rather than in the rational-moral order where man, by virtue of the spirit, is free.

In conclusion, we may ask the question why socialism, seeing that it perverts the public order, attracts so much support. The answer can be submitted only in the form of an hypothesis which cannot be proven. It has nothing but plausibility to recommend it. It claims that socialism is a reaction meant to counteract the void left by a state limited on a purely secular basis, a void that left Western man without any order or guidance for his soul and his spirit.

The limited state has been created by Christian political thought. In the Christian order of things, it was man's community in God that imposed limits on government. Because God himself had created this community, the government was reduced to the practical function of procuring peace, public order, and a modicum of justice. But throughout the Christian era, the government discharged this function side by side with the Church. Thus the realm beyond the temporal order was also a kind of public order, one concerning the spiritual and moral aspects of human life. The temporal and the spiritual order together covered the fullness of human life. The two realms were separate but co-ordinate, and this arrangement allowed for greater human freedom than had ever been achieved before. The limited state could operate within its bounds because beyond its limits the Church provided guidance and community.

The modern era began when the Church first was split, and then rejected by the European intelligentsia. A number of perceptive thinkers then noticed that, with the dropping out of the Church from the public order, a dangerous gap had opened. There was now no publicly recognized spiritual and moral community. Hobbes and Rousseau, among others, attempted to fill that gap by the creation of a "civil theology," a minimal public philosophy that would be substituted for the spiritual community of the Church. These attempts, as we know, came to nothing. Instead, the place of the former autonomous order of the Church was taken by the autonomous economy. It is for the sake of the system of production that limits were now imposed on government action. This provided for a rationale of the limited state, but not for community. For in his economic activities, man is centered on himself, competing rather than communing with others. And the economic system as a whole is a pattern of regularities rather than one of common values. The new limitation thus placed the state side by side with a realm of public order that spiritually is a void. Man, in so far as he was left to himself by the state, found himself individually alone, or at most embedded in a business company. Society outside of the state became a statistical universe rather than an experienced community. The modern world presents itself to individuals as a medium through which one must claw one's way to individual goals. As the last remnants of the former community fell victim to the freedom of modern *homo oeconomicus,* complaints about the emptiness of human existence began to multiply. Man's loneliness, that is, his lack of community with others, has become the dominant theme of our time, from Riesman's sociological analysis to the elevation of loneliness to a philosophical axiom by the Existentialists and its endlessly varied representation in modern art.

In this situation, socialism has offered itself as a kind of patent medicine to cure man's illness. It postulates an extension of the state's order to embrace the whole man, through the medium of the care for individual material welfare. There is a feeling that somehow, if only the economic system can be managed by the government as the common authority, the economy can become the vehicle of true community. Needless to say, this hope is illusory. Under socialism, man's loneliness has not decreased. Rather, it has been compounded by boredom resulting from the absence of risk, adventure, and personal achievement which are characteristic of an individualistic economy. We are gradually beginning again to recognize that community among men is a matter of the spirit. It resides only in the acknowledgment of common truths, common meaning, common values, which in turn are rooted in a publicly shared theology or philosophy, a recognized view of what is man, society, nature, and the meaning of life.

The characteristic feature of Western political order is the "civil government," that is a government barred from publicly entertaining theological or philosophical orthodoxies. The state that is thus limited can administer a true social order only in combination with an antonomous unity representing spiritual truth, be it spontaneous or directed. Our limited state in itself is unable to provide a full social order, and it cannot represent a communal order if supplemented by nothing but the economic system. People can be united only by a shared view of the meaning of life. In other words, the limited state makes sense only in combination with religious community. This does not mean a community of abstract contemplation or mere cult: in the West, spiritual community must always entail active brotherhood and mutual help. The sharing of transcendent truth creates common responsibilities of practical love. It is in the framework of a spiritual community that the task of providing for the welfare of the needy must be solved if that task is not to degenerate into an occasion for the soulless bureaucratic power of an apparatus over dependent beings.

This view could be criticized as a mere personal preference if it were not for the massive evidence of the totalitarian movements that have threatened us in our time. In both cases, we have a kind of substitute church, the totalitarian party, designed to take its place beside the state to provide meaning and coherence to the whole. Needless to say these parties are profound perversions of what a church is and should be. The question is not how we should judge them. The question is why so many millions have acclaimed these perverted churches as filling a deeply sensed need. We cannot have any doubt as to the answer, for the evidence is overwhelming: the people recoiled from the social structure of the West in which they failed to find satisfaction for their spirit's hunger. We have traditionally kept the authority of faith and that of reason apart from political authority. This order, the glory of the West, worked as long as "separate" meant also "coordinate" and "together." The crisis of the West cannot be solved merely by falling back from totalitarianism to the system of free enterprise. There must be a re-creation of an order of the spirit, in conjunction with which limited government alone is capable of ordering human life.

[VI, Fall 1962, 367–377]

[51]

Marxism, Anarchism, and the New Left

KARL A. WITTFOGEL

Karl A(ugust) Wittfogel (1896–1988) was born in Woltersdorf, Germany, and received his Ph.D. from the University of Frankfurt in 1928. A research associate at the Institute für Sozialforschung in Frankfurt, 1926–1933, and social researcher at Columbia University, 1934–1939, he became in 1939 the director of the Chinese History Project (sponsored by the University of Washington) at Columbia's Low Memorial Library. After 1947 he was professor of Chinese history at the University of Washington, Seattle. The author of articles on the economics, ecology, and institutional development of conquest societies in Asia and Russia, he wrote a number of books on such topics as The Natural Foundations of Economic History *(1932),* Oriental Despotism *(1957), and* Russia and the East *(1936). Wittfogel's important contribution to American academic conservatism is delineated by G. L. Ulmen in his* The Science of Society: Toward an Understanding of the Life and Work of Karl August Wittfogel *(1978).*

1. The New Left: "The Anarchist Element" plus . . .

The New Left considers itself a revolutionary force. Taking this designation without making a value judgment, we can agree that this is so. The new activists want radical social and political change—and they want it now. Some profess an affinity to older civil disobedience movements; but those who do are increasingly stressing their conditioned allegiance to the principle of nonviolence. And most of the New Leftists frankly advocate the use of violence, either with a qualification (against institutions and things) or without this qualification, recognizing that struggle against institutions and things usually involves struggle against humans or subhumans ("pigs").

The members of the New Left are revolutionaries. For the most part they raise red flags, but some raise black flags. The anarchists have used the black flag since 1883.[1] But they have not used it everywhere. The Chinese anarchists preferred the red flag when the young Mao Tse-tung was under their spell. They did not then dissociate themselves sharply from the Marxist-Communists. And during the Spanish Civil War the anarchists displayed red and black flags, thus underlining their wish to maintain an uneasy alliance with the Marxist-Communists.

Those who consider the New Left a camouflaged Communist movement may find it difficult to understand that the red flag is raised conspicuously. Others who recognize that there really is something new in this movement may be surprised that the number of black flags is relatively small, although quite a few prominent activists and ideologists are taking an "antiauthoritarian" position (e.g., Dutschke), or are identifying themselves with such revolutionary anarchists as Makhno (e.g., Cohn-Bendit), or, as Marcuse does, are stressing the great significance of "the anarchist element" for the new radicalism.

Marcuse asserts that he is not a spokesman for "the movement of 'angry students,'" and that others are much more daring in the revolutionary fight: "Ché Guevara, Debray, Rudi Dutschke, etc. . . . have truly risked and are still risking their lives in the battle for a more human society." But with apparent modesty, he does state his role: "I participate in this battle only through my words and my ideas." He gives very practical reasons to explain why he does not join the anarchists: "I am not an anarchist because I can not imagine how one can combat a society which is mobilized and organized in its totality against any revolutionary movement, against any effective opposition; I do not see how one can combat such a society, such a concentrated force—military force, police force, etc.—without any organization." But he feels that the New Left definitely needs "the anarchist element": "I do believe that the anarchist element is very powerful and very progressive, and that it is necessary to preserve this element as one of the factors in a larger and more structured process."[2] Marcuse fails to explain what, in his opinion, the "anarchist element" is like and what its function is. He is somewhat more explicit with regard to the other forces that give the revolutionary process a larger

dimension and more structure. In his *Liberation* pamphlet he praises the French rebellion of the spring of 1968 for having briefly recaptured "the libertarian power of the red and black flags." Among those who march under the red flag, the Communists are, of course, the outstanding force. And in the French unrest of 1968, the Communists, who briefly joined ranks with the anarchist-led students were not only followers of Mao, Ché, and Ho, but of the large and organized masses of Moscow-attached Communists.

2. A New Political Syncretism

Obviously then, what is new in the New Left movement is primarily the appearance of an anarchist element. But although avowedly this element is very powerful, its character is not clearly defined even by those who identify or associate with it.

Highly instructive in this respect is the attitude of the brothers Daniel and Gabriel Cohn-Bendit. In their book about the French uprising of 1968, *Leftism: Remedy Against the Senile Disease of Communism*, they sharply attack what they consider the degeneration of Soviet Communism. But they do not discuss the Marxist tradition in Leninist Communism or the hostility of the original Marxists against anarchism. They cannot be bothered with the history of "the contradiction between anarchism and Marxism"; in fact they find this contradiction "false and uninteresting."

The classical revolutionary anarchists responded quite differently. Although they were greatly impressed by Marx' critique of capitalism, they rejected his political doctrine and strategy. Not so the new anarchists and pro-anarchists. Dutschke embraces the "true" Communists of China, Cuba, and Vietnam who, I need hardly add, consider themselves Marxist-Leninist

Communists; and he condemns all types of anti-Communism. What he wants is a scientific socialism without "isms."

The brothers Cohn-Bendit prefaced the German edition of their *Leftism* book with a programmatic statement. In it they hail the New Left movement as a revival of a revolutionary "tradition" that has found expression in the persons of three anarchists—Bakunin, Makhno, and Durutti (Durutti was a particularly ruthless anarchist terrorist prior to and during the early days of the Spanish Civil War[3])—and two Marxists: Marx and Rosa Luxemburg. The attempt to be the inheritors of this tradition without facing up to the deep contradictions within it amounts to a syncretism that is as problematic intellectually as it is significant politically.

What are the elements in this tradition that today need clarification? In the confines of the present analysis I can answer this question only by identifying certain key tenets of revolutionary anarchism that overlap, or contradict, Communist Marxism and that affect the ideas and actions of the New Left.

3. A Side-Issue: Nihilism

There is not one major revolutionary socialist movement, but there are two: Marxist Communism and anarchism. And there is also not one major type of anarchism, but there are two: reformist anarchism and revolutionary anarchism. Nihilism connotes the total rejection of existing ideas and institutions, and as such it has a place in the literature of modern radicalism. The anarchists themselves have applied it to members of their group.[4] But nihilism never became a political movement. And the knowledge that the word nihilism occurs in the literature is no substitute for the serious study of anarchism.

4. Types of Anarchism and Civil Disobedience

The term "anarchism" is, of course, old. During the French Revolution certain types of violence and tumult were considered "anarchist." And during this same time, William Godwin pleaded in his *Enquiry into Political Justice* for a society that would be just and free, and therefore not in need of a state and laws. Godwin believed that only reason, education, and gradually achieved improvements could bring such a society into being.

Proudhon, who in 1840 referred to himself as a (positive) "anarchist," expected that only through radical economic reform could his "participatory" stateless society become a reality. Bakunin and his followers insisted that a just and free society could replace the old evil, private-property-based society only through an anarchist revolution that would totally destroy all major existing institutions: "ramparts." In the English translation that is now circulating in the U.S.A., this term occurs in a passage that mentions six "ramparts," four political (the state, the courts, the army, and the police), one educational (the university), and one religious (the church).[5]

Bakunin was thinking primarily of direct revolutionary action when he requested the total destruction of these targets. But he also suggested indirect methods of attack. One way to destroy "the university" (almost everywhere in continental Europe controlled by the state) was to hand it over to the community. The church could be weakened by taking away the bulk of its property. Through Bakunin, anarchism became a doctrine of, and strategy for, total destruction. Kropotkin modified this doctrine; and he suggested tactics that were—in some respects—more specific and more formidable.

Since Bakunin's time the two major, and some in-between, currents of anarchism are clearly discernible. Reformist anarchism which owes much to Godwin cannot be discussed in any detail here. The various civil disobedience movements of the nineteenth and twentieth centuries cannot be discussed in any detail here either. But as types of resistance that fall between nonviolent and violent anarchism they certainly deserve analysis, classification, and political attention.

Thoreau suggested civil disobedience, and he dreamed of a resistance movement. But he made no effort to initiate one. He wanted a stateless society, and he was not averse to a revolution that involved bloodshed. But the violence he envisaged followed the early American tradition. There is no evidence to indicate that he was attracted by the "anarchist" patterns of total violence and tumult that emerged during the French Revolution.

Benjamin Tucker wanted a stateless society; and to attain it, he proposed a flexible policy of "passive resistance." But although he accepted certain types of violence, including outright terror, he concluded that in general and under western conditions, a nonviolent approach was most "expedient."

Tolstoy recommended a policy of "nonresistance," which was to be completely nonviolent. Although he too wanted a stateless society, he separated himself sharply from all revolutionary anarchists—and socialists and communists as well.

Gandhi's civil disobedience movement was directed toward national liberation, not toward social revolution or the establishment of a stateless society. And, like Tolstoy's, it was to be completely nonviolent. Some of Gandhi's friends, among them Romain Roland, who recognized his integrity, feared that the mass character of his movement might at times override

the Mahatma's peaceful intent,[6] which indeed it did.

Godwin discussed at considerable length the problem of resistance against established authority. Quite possibly he gave the term "resistance" its present meaning. But he definitely rejected the policy which was involved because, in his opinion, it would lead to violent revolution, perhaps even to the "universal violence and tumult" of "anarchy." Violent revolution could hamper the cause of freedom; anarchy could damage it irreparably. In view of Godwin's rational approach to the stateless society, his objections have greatly embarrassed the revolutionary anarchists. Kropotkin, who praised Godwin as a trailblazer of the philosophy of anarchism, criticized him for his withdrawal from some of the political views he had supported in the first edition of his *Enquiry*. But Kropotkin did not squarely face the core of Godwin's final arguments which were as timely and hard to answer in his day as they are timely and hard to answer today.

5. Revolutionary Anarchism—The Ideology and Practice of Revolutionary Russian Peasants?

The Marxist Leninists claim that Bakunin's revolutionary anarchism was a "petty-bourgeois" peasant movement. This interpretation is crudely simplistic. The peasants cannot be equated with the petty bourgeoisie despite important similarities in their proprietary positions. Furthermore, Bakunin's ideas certainly did not mirror the condition of the Russian peasantry. After Bakunin left Russia in 1840, he adopted a number of significant western attitudes and he included, for the West, the workers into his strategy.

But while the Leninist correlation is faulty, it is important to recognize that

Bakunin was indeed deeply affected by a type of mentality in traditional Russia that found expression in the ways in which the Russian peasant revolutions had been fought—and crushed. Pushkin pointed to this mentality when he exclaimed: "Save us, oh Lord, from the Russian insurrection, which is without sense and mercy." Bakunin believed that, with certain modifications, the Russian peasant uprisings could still serve as a model for the uprisings he envisaged for Russia; and the workers whom he expected to launch the anarchist revolution were supposed to be close to the peasants in their beggarliness and illiteracy.

Kropotkin developed more ties to the West than Bakunin. But he too remained strongly attached to Russia, the Russian countryside, and the Russian peasantry. This is eminently clear in his autobiography; and it is confirmed in his revolutionary pamphlets that were published in Europe and largely directed at European readers. Roger Baldwin, who in 1927 edited a collection of these pamphlets in New York, was convinced that when Kropotkin thought of the masses, "he unconsciously pictured to himself peasants oppressed by landlords and Czars, quite capable of handling themselves or handling their own affairs when a revolutionary upheaval once gave them freedom." [7]

To repeat: It is not enough to consider Bakunin's and Kropotkin's attitude as reflecting conditions of the traditional Russian peasantry, just as it is not enough to consider Marx' and Engels' attitude as reflecting the conditions of the industrial workers of nineteenth century Europe. It is necessary to place Bakunin's and Kropotkin's development within the framework of a conflict-ridden Russian society in which conflict-sensitive young men could easily envisage an increasingly dissatisfied peasantry as the potential storm-center in a growing societal crisis. And it is equally necessary to place Marx' and Engels' development within the framework of a conflict-ridden Europe in which conflict-sensitive young men could easily envisage a growing proletariat as the potential storm-center in a growing industrial society.

These views do not explain why Bakunin and Kropotkin on the one hand and Marx and Engels on the other responded to their respective settings and potential storm-centers as they did. Singular features interlock with general historical trends.[8] But in all the above cases the result has been a definable social orientation for Bakunin and Kropotkin toward peasants of the Russian type, for Marx and Engels toward western industrial workers.

The spokesmen of the New Left are certainly aware of all manner of conflicts. They certainly try to utilize them. And they strive to associate themselves with major social forces in their homeland and abroad. But these efforts have remained strikingly ineffectual. Why is this so? Could there be something in the political attitude of the New Left that impedes such associations?

6. Instinct versus Science

Bakunin was perfectly willing to call the peasants "ignorant." But he asserted at the same time that they had "profound common sense" and, most importantly, a sound political instinct. Their instinct for justice qualified them for their revolutionary mission. And the workers? Eager to place them and the peasants on the same level, Bakunin declared that the revolutionary "greatness" of the workers was based, "not on their education, which was little, but on their instinct for justice, which incontestably was great."[9] In a pamphlet written in 1869, whose authorship has been debated but whose ideas are certainly Bakunin's, the young Russian revolutionaries were asked rhetorically: "Should we instruct the people?" The answer was: "That would be stupid. The people know better than we what they need. . . . Our task is not to instruct the people, but to arouse them." [10]

Bakunin was convinced that the success of the anarchist revolution did not depend on scientific knowledge. In other contexts he explained why he thought so. Science was "immobile, impersonal, general, abstract, insensible." It was "bookish" and unable to cope with the richness, creativity, and spontaneity of life. Moreover, whatever value as a clarifying agent science might potentially have was being thwarted by the interests of the ruling classes, who dominated the officially recognized sciences.

Bakunin's class argument explains his negative attitude toward the universities. His "bookish" argument explains his negative attitude toward "scientific socialism," especially Marxism: being doctrinaire, the Marxists were harming rather than helping the social revolution.

Marx and Engels, when in 1873 they wrote their anti-Bakunin pamphlet, did not know all facets of Bakunin's arguments against science. But the information they possessed enabled them to refer to "Bakunin's hatred against science." In their opinion, his *Appeal to the Young Brothers in Russia* (1896) glorified the "cult of ignorance." [11]

Bakunin's critique of scientism was not adequate; and Marx' and Engels' treatment of Bakunin's antiscientism was not adequate either. But despite these deficiencies (which do credit to neither side) and despite Bakunin's tendency to confuse the issue (which is part and parcel of his way of arguing) the controversy over science reflects basic differences in the doctrines and practical policies of the two camps.

The difference is not a matter of moral or social values; it is a difference in instrumentalities. Other circumstances being equal, the more rational ("scientific") approach, which systematically uses past experiences to foresee future developments, is potentially more realistic, even if some of the "scientifically" obtained data are problematic. Two forces trying to find their way through a poorly known territory may be equally equipped technically, and equally imbued with the will to reach their destination. But they may be unequally prepared in terms of information and analysis. The members of one force will be eager to use an available map, which, though crude, presents what has been learned through earlier explorations; and they will carefully analyze and use this information in their decisions. The members of the second force may despise this map as "bookish" (which in a way it is) and depend instead on impressionistic appraisals and improvised action.

The intellectual difference between the two approaches is evident. Equally evident is the operational superiority it gives to the Marxist Communist map-users as compared with the anarchist improvisers—and the New Left radicals who distrust all ideology, including the fact-oriented and macroanalytic "ideology" ("theory") of the Marxist Communists.

The New Left movement came into being at the end of the fifties. The *New Left Review* first appeared in January 1960; and in the fall of that year, it published Wright Mills' article, "The New Left." Mills' thinking did not noticeably induce his admirers to read books or study theory. In 1965 in an article in the magazine *Liberator*, David McReynolds asserted that the New Left was hostile, not only to adults, but also to "ideology." In an article written in 1967/68, Marcuse expressed his hope that the New Left would turn toward theory. But he confirmed it harbored "a deep distrust of all ideology, also of the socialist ideology."[12]

The brothers Cohn-Bendit know, of course, that in the tradition they are hailing, theory is important for understanding the conditions and possibilities of the revolution. But while they acknowledge this, they are not at all disturbed by the present a-theoretical mood of their movement.[13]

7. The Voluntaristic Trend

If science cannot explain life except in "general" and "abstract" terms, then there is not much use in scientifically examining the preconditions for the revolution. Not much use, but some. Bakunin's acknowledgement that science has a "clarifying" function leaves the door open for a rational (scientific) analysis of the economic, political, national, and international factors that affect a given situation. And from time to time, and perhaps in anticipation of Marxist criticism, he acknowledged the importance of external conditions for the chances of a successful revolution; and he avoided referring to himself as a voluntarist. However, in general he paid little attention to these conditions.

One important exception was Bakunin's response to the German invasion in France in 1870. For a while he believed that this situation might be propitious for a revolutionary French "war of liberation." But even at this time he did not seriously study the military, economic, and political factors affecting the national and international scene as did the Marxists. And once the French crisis receded, he reverted to the doctrinal position he

had taken prior to it. Thus for all practical purposes Bakunin's attitude was that of a voluntarist. And this attitude has prevailed in the revolutionary anarchist movement ever since.

We cannot trace here the anarchist influences on the pre-Communist and Communist Mao Tse-tung. These influences—which are well documented—explain certain features of his policy. And they go far to explain the voluntaristic trend in his thinking. His Communist opponents have criticized this trend as "subjectivistic," "petty bourgeois," and "adventurist." Today many members of the New Left find it eminently appealing.

8. Marxist and Anarchist Programs— Differently Structured and Argued

Bakunin's revolutionary programs reveal crucial differences between his voluntaristic position and the "scientific" position of the Marxists. The Marxist programs— from *The Communist Manifesto* to the Gotha and Erfurt programs of the German socialists and the programs of the Russian Marxists—all begin with a lengthy "theoretical" section that sets forth the socio-historical background of their respective movements and the conditions that favor or discourage the advance of the revolutionary forces at various "stages" of their struggle. In later sections, all these programs outline the policies that the revolutionary Marxists should pursue in these various stages—short-range policies aimed at immediate tasks, and long-range policies aimed at overthrow of the capitalist order and the establishment of a socialist society.

Bakunin's programs—some of which were quite long—were differently structured and differently argued. Instead of explaining the socio-historical background of the revolution and the conditions for its advance, they stressed the "principles" of the existing order (its class character, inequalities, injustices, and oppressiveness) and the revolutionary "principles" of equality and justice that induce the people to attack and ultimately destroy this order.

Bakunin's indictment of the old society was as total as the social revolution that was to overthrow it. There could be no in-between solution, and there must be no compromise. In the secret program of the International Alliance, Bakunin declared that the international Brothers "reject any policy of transition and compromise, and they consider any movement reactionary which does not have as its immediate and direct aim the triumph of its principles." Indeed, "the revolution, as we understand it, must from the first day radically and totally destroy the state and all state institutions."[14] Around this statement of "principles," Bakunin built elaborate directives concerning the psychological, social, and personal preconditions for revolutionary action and the forms this action should take.

9. "Evil Passion" and Direct Action

The psychological precondition for revolutionary action was not just instinct, although instinct was basic to it. The instinct of justice gives the people the correct orientation; but passion gives them the proper drive. From 1842, when Bakunin termed "the lust for destruction . . . a creative lust," he never tired of hailing the "evil" and "diabolical" revolutionary passions, the urge for destruction, total destruction. Kropotkin later envisaged this urge as a positive force; but on the basis of a newly found philosophy of life, he too considered it the psychological

mainspring of the revolutionary anarchists.

It was under such an irresistible inner urge that trail-blazing revolutionary deeds were accomplished. And it was these trail-blazing deeds that broke the spell of legality, that destroyed respect for existing laws and institutions. Bakunin called revolutionary action "the most potent deed, the most irresistible form of propaganda." Kropotkin asserted that the transformation from revolutionary thought to revolutionary will was attained thus, and only thus: "Action, the continuous action, ceaselessly renewed, of minorities, brings about this transformation." The concepts of the "propaganda of deed" and of "direct" action are rooted in this principle.

Particular passions spark the revolution. Particular social groups give it a grassroots basis. And particular methods of operation provide the members of the movement with the means by which to attain the revolutionary goal: the disintegration of the existing order and its total destruction.

10. Leadership Qualifications, Old and New

The leaders must have sufficient education to serve the revolutionary needs of the culturally backward masses. But in order to do so they must dissociate themselves from the upper-class setting in which they were bred. They must be *declassed*.

Most of the revolutionary leaders should be *young*. To be sure, Bakunin found a place for some older revolutionary leaders (e.g., "*citoyen* B."). But his major hope was centered on the young since it was easier for them than for older persons to break "heroically" with their social and cultural origins. Statistical evidence shows that among the revolutionary Russian terrorists of the nineteenth and twentieth centuries many were between twenty-one and twenty-five years of age, and not a few between fifteen and twenty.

Bakunin's young declassed leaders were expected to be *unwashed* and *half-educated*. Those who neglected their appearance were, of course, symbolically rejecting their earlier ways of life. But this also fulfilled a practical purpose. The young Russian revolutionaries who dressed as poorly as the peasants would be less easily recognized by the police, since in appearance they merged with the mass of the toilers whose fate they were trying to share.

The young Russian revolutionaries who remained half-educated also fulfilled two purposes. They dissociated themselves from upper-class culture; and they came closer to the working classes who distrusted this culture, which they considered unattainable and potentially hostile.

Not a few young declassed revolutionaries smoked; but among the extremists this was considered a weakness. Chernichevsky's hero, Bakhmetov, who inspired generations of Russian rebels, spoke of his cigar-smoking as a minor "vice." He despised the conventional matrimonial tie, but he was equally critical of sexual indulgence and, of course, of intoxication. For the young revolutionaries drug addiction was virtually unthinkable.

The New Left activists approach Bakunin's revolutionary qualifications for leadership in several respects. But in some instances, superficial similarities hide deep differences. The rebels, who to Marcuse are today the main revolutionary hope, are "the nonconformist youth," "the militant intelligentsia" that has "cut itself loose from the middle classes" (cf. Bakunin's "young" and "declassed"). These new rebels express their protests by "the sensuousness of long hair," by a "body unsoiled by plastic cleanliness" (cf. Bakunin's "unwashed"). They assume a seemingly surrealist cultural tradition (they reject classical music, "Beethoven, Schu-

bert") and a distrust of integrative thought: theory (cf. Bakunin's "half-educated"). Their new attitudes are manifested by the advocacy of an extreme sexual "liberation" that rejects the very sublimation[15] which, according to Freud, is the foundation of civilization.

And then there are the drugs. Marcuse is not entirely uncritical of their use. The narcotic "trip" he sees as "artificial" and "private." But the claims of the users have a "kernel of truth": "The artificial and 'private' liberation anticipates, in a distorted manner, an exigency of the social liberation."[16]

11. The New Working Classes Reject the New Left

The new radicals are certainly no Bakhmetovs. And certainly the politically alert members of the working classes are not awed by them. As Marcuse notes, even in France and Italy the student rebels in 1968 received only "precarious" and "passing" aid from leftist labor organizations, and in West Germany and the U.S.A. "they met with vociferous and often violent hostility of the people and of organized labor." In a summarizing statement he declares that "the student opposition meets with all but pathological hatred on the part of the so-called 'community,' including large sections of organized labor."[17]

For reasons that defy simple "Marxist" explanations, the new working classes find the New Left repulsive. They are not at all impressed with the new rebels' rejection of standards of cleanliness that in most industrial countries are now generally accessible and relished. And they resent the new rebels' hostility to educational and cultural assets that are now widely attainable and that the mass of the toilers are working hard to acquire for themselves and their children.

Recent developments have resulted in the emergence of several new, or newly shaped, classes with new forms of class consciousness. What has happened in this respect behind the Iron Curtain is often studied without recourse to the experiences that have been gained in the long history of total power. What is happening in this respect in the non-Communist world is often being studied with equally inadequate means. In the industrial core areas of the non-Communist world there originated a new type of working class composed of blue and white collar employees, which is definitely not bourgeois (occupying the large center of the new society it may be called a new middle class). This class is developing a new self-confidence. It lacks the guilt feelings that today paralyze not a few members of the bourgeoisie and bourgeois intelligentsia; and it is more liberty-conscious. Hence it is less patient with the New Left attacks on our basic freedoms than are many members of the new bourgeoisie.

12. The Issue of the Negro Minority

In the U.S.A. the racial issue has been creating very serious social, psychological, and political problems. This has lead the New Left ideologists to believe that "the ghetto population" has been cut loose from "the organized working class."[18] But those who cherish this view have a static and obsolete concept of capitalism. Industrial capitalism, which was indeed ruthless at the time of the Industrial Revolution, was already in Marx's days beginning to assume a new "social" quality.[19] It was already then suggesting the possibility of something like a "partnership capitalism." (John Stuart Mill, *Marx*).[20]

Marx recognized this possibility in his later writings, which, like his earlier ones, reflect his urge for truth as well as his urge for power. While he continued to look for a proletarian revolution in the West, he increasingly recognized the ameliorative capacity of capitalism[21] which manifested itself in "the physical and moral rebirth" of industrial labor.[22] In the U.S.A. this development has raised the majority of the workers to the new level of well-being and self-confidence indicated above. And today this development is also beginning to affect the black minority. The radical Negro ideologist, Harold Cruse, grimly and without making his peace with the Establishment, acknowledges the strength of this trend. "American capitalism's dynamic, plus the federal and state power," he writes in criticizing Robert Williams, "can take every one of what he calls the essential demands of 'our people' and use them to buy off and absorb every militant wave of the entire Negro movement, as fast as they emerge."[23]

Thus the New Left activists cannot count on revolutionary mass support in industrially advanced countries, as did Marx and Bakunin—each in his own way. Nor can they, in the colonial and quasicolonial countries of the Third World, count on the mass support of the peasants. The prominent Third World ideologist, Frantz Fanon, warns against this expectation. According to his experiences, the "native peasant" is basically conservative: he "defends his traditions stubbornly."[24]

13. The Issue of the Lumpenproletariat

In consequence and much more than the old revolutionary anarchists, the new anarchists and their friends are compelled to seek alliances with the "scum" of society, with the "lumpenproletariat." (According to Marx' and Engels' definition, the lumpenproletariat did not engage in work, as did the proletarians; in *Das Kapital*, Vol. I, Marx saw this group composed of "vagabonds, criminals, and prostitutes".) Bakunin placed his main hope for the revolution in what he called the "beggarly" proletariat; and by equating this group with Marx' and Engels' lumpenproletariat, he implied a willingness to work with elements that Marx and Engels completely rejected. But although Bakunin and his followers propounded a pan-environmentalist interpretation of crime, and although they kept the door open for revolutionary cooperation with criminals, they did *not* openly associate themselves with the lumpenproletariat (as Marx and Engels accused them of doing).[25]

Lacking the mass support which the Old Left took for granted, the New Left (insofar as it is a "new" political force and not under the sway of the Communists) is impelled to associate itself more closely with lumpenproletarian methods and elements. In the U.S.A. this linkage has so far been mainly factual.[26] In France it has been defiantly sloganized. In the spring of 1968, the French authorities claimed that the real force behind the student uprising was the underworld, *la pégre* (the fraternity of thieves). In contrast to the French workers of 1830 and 1848, who sharply rejected "the thieves" and occasionally shot them, the new radicals have solidarized themselves with these elements: "We are all thieves (*nous sommes tous la pégre*)."[27]

14. The Third World Version of the Issue

With regard to the Third World, Fanon has been very outspoken in his insistence that revolutionary peasant support being unavailable, it is the lumpenproletariat that in these areas is the spearhead and hope of the revolution.[28] Fanon's glorification of the lumpenproletariat is worth studying because of the methods of revolutionary guerrilla warfare that he demands to be used in countries of the Third World, and even more so because of the admiration with which many New Left radicals in Europe and America study his strategy as a guide to action within their own countries. Sartre, who, of course, is aware that Fanon is speaking primarily to his fellow natives in the Third World, feels that "we" in the West also need the "decolonization" that Fanon is promoting there. Out of Fanon's book, Sartre fashioned "a remedy for Europe." Since Engels no one has succeeded like Fanon in "bringing the processes of history into the clear light of day."[29]

Sartre's appeal did not go unheeded. According to Seale and McConville, in the spring of 1968 many young French rebels were "acting out the colonial revolution in the heart of a Western capital"; and they did so, while searching for "the heroic revolution" among whose patrons Fanon ranked first.[30] In the same spirit, leading West German New Left radicals, such as Dutschke, have been promoting "the radical reception of the theories of the Third World," usually with emphasis on Ché Guevara and especially on the author of *The Wretched of the Earth*, which continues to discuss the North African experiences within the wider framework of decolonization.[31] The "black-colony" thesis, which the Black Panthers proclaim in paragraph 10 of their program, is being interpreted as reflecting the lessons of the battle of Algiers, which the Panthers "seem to have over-learned."[32]

What is Fanon's version of this lesson? In his decolonization theory Fanon, envisaging the towns as the core area of the revolutionary struggle, is convinced that the rebellion will find its urban spearhead "at the core of the lumpenproletariat." Coming from the countryside and the forests and unable to find work in the towns, declassed rural elements "took to stealing, debauchery, and alcoholism." The authorities declared them a mass of " 'young hooligans' who were disturbing the social order." Fanon considers the destructive potential of these elements enormous: "The lumpenproletariat is like a horde of rats; you may kick them and throw stones at them, but despite your efforts they'll go on gnawing at the roots of the tree." Once constituted, the lumpenproletariat "brings all its forces to endanger the 'security' of the town. . . . So the pimps, the hooligans, the unemployed, and the petty criminals, urged on from behind, throw themselves into the struggle for liberation like stout working men. These classless idlers will be militant and decisive action will discover the path that leads to nationhood. They won't become reformed characters to please colonial society, fitting in with the morality of its rulers; quite on the contrary, they take for granted the impossibility of their entering the city save by hand grenades and revolvers. These workless less-than-men are rehabilitated in their own eyes and in the eyes of history. The prostitutes too, and the maids who are paid two pounds a month, all the hopeless dregs of humanity, all who turn in circles between suicide and madness, will recover their balance, once more go forward, and march proudly in the great procession of the awakened nation."[33]

The New Left radicals' attempt to apply Fanon's strategy of decolonization to France, Germany, and the U.S.A. is bound to fail, if the modern industrial society, properly alerted, asserts its "dynamics" constructively and protectively. But even such writers as Ronald Steel, who sympathizes with the American decolonizers, does not hide his apprehension: "The United States today is not Algeria of 1954, nor Cuba of 1958, nor even France of 1968. It is a deeply troubled, but none-theless largely stable society."[34] But the process of getting alerted involves the realization of the new national and international (institutional and ideological) crisis and of the new policies of disintegration that are being formulated and tested today. Among these policies Fanon's lumpenproletarian strategy of decolonization is a reality that must be carefully examined.

15. The New Left: The New Trends Summarized

These are some features of the new development. What do they mean in terms of our comparative analysis of the old and new radicalism? They mean that the identification of the New Left must proceed not only on one level of differentiation, but on two. The New Left radicals are not Marxist Communists. Despite certain syncretistic trends, which facilitate an uneasy alliance with the Communists, the New Left radicals consider themselves essentially revolutionary anarchists, not Marxist Communists (Level One). And while they share important features with the classical revolutionary anarchists, they exhibit several social and ideological peculiarities that give their movement a specifically neo-anarchist quality (Level Two).

To begin with the first difference: The drive of the New Left for direct revolutionary action has little appeal for the mass of the white and blue collar workers. But its manipulators use all sorts of educational, political, and racial discontents (some of which have a genuine basis in fact) and an unprepared public (that often neither understands its own condition or that of the nation), to instigate such actions in vulnerable zones of our multicentered and open society. There are, first of all, the radical students (including not a few high school students) and their academic and nonacademic allies. The old revolutionary anarchist movement valued radical students essentially when they left the campus in order to lead nonacademic rebels in off-campus uprisings. In the present sociohistorical setting, our liberalized campuses provide extremist students with legal, communicational, and psychological opportunities for starting rebellions that may have national and even international repercussions, but that, first of all, are campus rebellions.

Extremist elements within the racial minorities are trying to develop these minorities into a grass-roots base for revolutionary assaults on the existing order. As stated above, in the long run these efforts are bound to fail in countries with a "dynamic" capitalism. But temporarily they may be strongly divisive. This is the second differentiating feature in the New Left movement.

A third differentiating feature has to do with the lumpenproletarian elements. Take the Russian Revolution of 1917. Under the shadow of the black flag many criminal acts were committed; but the revolutionary anarchists became so influential in the factory committees that for a time they challenged the Bolsheviks within the proletarian core area of the revolution. And take the Spanish Civil War. Again many criminal acts were committed; but in certain territories, particularly in Catalonia, the revolutionary anarchists were more deeply rooted in the working classes than the Communists.

The New Left activists have scored no similar successes, not because they do not want working-class support (many of them do), but because the new working classes dislike their extremist policy. This fact probably explains, at least in part, the increased significance of lumpenproletarian methods and elements in the New Left movement.

16. The New Ideological Trends Summarized

Hand-in-hand with a different social orientation goes a different intellectual attitude. Bakunin distrusted science; but he made allowance for the clarifying function of scientific procedure, and he did not reject integrative ideas ("principles"). He was in fact deeply interested in them. The New Left activists do not elaborate on their rejection of science, especially social science; and they profoundly distrust all integrative thought, "ideology." Their totally negative attitude in this respect does not mean the elimination of all ideology (or ideologists) from the movement. But it does favor a particularly shoddy type of ideology and a particularly shoddy type of ideologist.

To be sure, the fact that an ideology is shoddy does not mean that it is ineffective. The ideas with which Mussolini and Hitler imbued their followers—the most irrational strata of the populations—were shoddy indeed. But it can hardly be said that for this reason they were ineffective.

17. Functional Ignorance

From the standpoint of what the New Left radicals are trying to accomplish, their extreme aversion to intellectual clarity is eminently understandable. A movement that fiercely attacks academic institutions as oppressive, the industrial-military "establishment" as all-powerful, and non-Communist agrarian conditions as unjust, and at the same time invokes Communist China, North Vietnam, and Cuba as models, or at the least as acceptable allies, has to keep the intellectual level of its followers extremely low.

How much academic freedom is there in Communist China, North Vietnam, and Cuba? None. The New Left agitators do not even attempt to prove that such freedom exists under Mao, Ho, and Castro (who developed his system of total intolerance with the help of Ché Guevara). In these and other Communist regimes, whatever industry there is is interlinked through an all-powerful managerial bureaucracy with the military complex—"establishment," if you will. And in Mao's China, the central position of the military complex was openly proclaimed at the very time when New Left spokesmen were denouncing with increasing fury the American "industrial-military establishment" (which happens to be controlled by many countervailing forces)—and this in the name of Mao (whose industrial-military establishment lacks any such controls).

And as to the agrarian issue. In almost all Communist countries an initial "land reform" that gave a part of the land to a part of the peasants, was followed by a collectivization that took away all of the land from all of the peasants. This being the case, it is certainly misleading to appeal to the peasants of the non-Communist world in the name of Mao, Ho, and Ché—and in some instances also in the name of the alleged welfare state of post-Stalin Russia.

It is equally misleading to justify an uneasy alliance with Moscow-attached Communists by presenting the USSR as a "senile" form of Communism (cf. the title of the Cohn-Bendit book). Moscow's recent activities in Cuba, North Vietnam, and the Near East are anything but senile. And Moscow's policy in East Germany (in 1953), in Hungary (in 1956), and in Czechoslovakia (in 1968) certainly gives little evidence of decrepitude.

The Soviet Union was not senile after it came of age. And it was not proto-socialist when it came into being. According to core ideas of Marx and Lenin (which include the classical concept of a special

"Asiatic" society dominated by an "Oriental" despotism), the nascent Soviet regime was no incipient socialist society, but an incipient *Oriental despotism*—that is, the very antithesis of the socialist order, whose principles Marx outlined in 1871 (in *Civil War in France*) and Lenin adopted in 1917 (in *State and Revolution*). Anyone who presents this Orientally despotic regime as "socialist" runs into serious trouble if those he wants to follow him know the crucial facts concerning Russian society and revolution and the "Asiatic" interpretation of these phenomena given by Marx, Engels, Plekhanov, and Lenin.[35]

I do not say that a Dutschke and a Cohn-Bendit are intentionally trying to mislead when they disregard the pertinent ideas of Marx and Lenin. I prefer to think that they have never taken the trouble to study the classical elements in Marxism and that instead they are content to swallow a distorted version of orthodox Marxism which, at best, can be looked upon as vulgar Marxism, and when dealing with such a vital issue as this one, can only be considered *lumpen* Marxism.[36]

This is not exactly a noble ideology. But can the New Left radicals afford anything more rational? Evidently not. Being hemmed in by their sectarian drive for total destruction, ignorance in these matters is virtually a necessity if they want to maintain an anti-anti-Communist alliance with the Marxist Communists.

18. Cui Bono?

The communist regimes of all varieties are closely watching the New Left. And the strong antiauthoritarian criticism that many New Left spokesmen have been leveling at some of these regimes has resulted in considerable annoyance and strong counter-attacks. But whatever Communist critics may say about the "petty-bourgeois" and "subjectivist" character of the New Left movement, all shades of the Marxist Communist world profit "objectively" from the extremists' efforts to discredit, demoralize, and disintegrate the democratic institutions of the non-Communist world.

And what will the Communist beneficiaries do when the revolutionary anarchists have served their purpose? The Spanish example, although instructive, is not conclusive, since the Spanish Civil War did not culminate in the victory of the Communist forces. The Russian example is both instructive and conclusive, since Lenin's Communist forces did prevail in the October revolution.

What happened in 1918 was foreshadowed in a remark made by one of the "Jacobin" leaders of the French February Revolution of 1848, Caussidière, who observed the behavior of the budding revolutionary anarchist, Bakunin, on the barricades of Paris. Said Caussidière: "On the first day of the revolution, he is a perfect treasure, on the second day one ought to shoot him."

The Cohn-Bendits are aware that the Russian Marxist Communists followed this pattern in 1917 and 1918 respectively.[37] From the standpoint of their own movement it would therefore be better if they were less bored with the contradictions between anarchism and Marxism. For it is within the framework of these contradictions that the Marxist Communists temporarily cooperate with the revolutionary anarchists. Being much stronger and much more purposeful than were Caussidière and his friends, the Marxist Communists can fully utilize the wrecking activities of their uneasy allies "on the first day of the revolution," because they are confident that, when, "on the second day," the revolutionary anarchists oppose the centralist Marxist policy with their "commune" program, they will not only

have the wish, but also the power to shoot them.

NOTES

[1] Specific evidence for this and subsequent statements will be given in my forthcoming book *Revolutionary Anarchism*. Only when an issue suggests the desirability of immediate documentation will the exact reference be given in this account.

[2] *The New York Times* Magazine, October 27, 1968, p. 29.

[3] See Gerald Brenan, *The Spanish Labyrinth*. Cambridge 1967, pp. 250 f.

[4] See Michael Bakunin's *Sozial-politischer Briefwechsel*, ed. by Michael Dragomanow. Stuttgart 1895, pp. 132, 161. Hereafter cited as Bakunin 1895. Cf. also Kropotkin's *Revolutionary Pamphlets*, ed. by Roger N. Baldwin, New York 1927, pp. 83, 86. Hereafter cited as Kropotkin 1927.

[5] See *The Political Philosophy of Bakunin*, ed. by G. P. Maximoff. Glencoe 1953, p. 374. Hereafter cited as Bakunin 1953.

[6] Romain Rolland, *Mahatma Gandhi*. New York, London p. 145.

[7] Kropotkin 1927, p. 3.

[8] See Karl A. Wittfogel, "Ideas and the Power Structure," in *Approaches to Asian Civilizations*, ed. by Wm. Theodore de Bary and Ainslie T. Embree. New York 1964, pp. 94 f.

[9] See Michael Bakunin, *Oeuvres* (6 volumes, Paris 1907–1913), Vol. II, p. 94. Hereafter cited as Bakunin O.

[10] Bakunin 1895, p. 357.

[11] *Karl Marx, Friedrich Engels Werke.* (Berlin 1957 ff), Vol. XVIII, pp. 400 and 443. Hereafter cited as MEW.

[12] Herbert Marcuse, *Psychoanalyse und Politik.* Frankfurt, Wien 1968, pp. 55, 65.

[13] Gabriel and Daniel Cohn-Bendit, *Linksradikalismus—Gewaltkur gegen die Alterskrankheit des Kommunismus.* Hamburg 1968, p. 12. Hereafter cited as Cohn-Bendit 1968.

[14] Bakunin 1895, pp. 324, 335.

[15] Herbert Marcuse, *An Essay on Liberation.* Boston 1969, pp. 35 ff. and 51 f. Hereafter cited as Marcuse 1969.

[16] Ibid. p. 37.

[17] Ibid. p. 60 f.

[18] Ibid. p. 52.

[19] MEW 16, p. 11.

[20] See John Stuart Mill, *Principles of Political Economy.* London 1909, p. 764; MEW 23, p. 320. Mill foresaw the possibility that, in a reformed capitalism, labor might enter into a partnership relation with owners of individual factories. Marx suggested that

the restrictions imposed on the capitalists and workers by the advancing factory legislation might lead to something like a "modest *Magna Carta*" situation. The *Magna Carta* was the result of an agreement between four forces: the crown, the Church, the nobles, and the towns. At the time of its creation, these forces were of very different strengths, but nevertheless all were considered "partners." Since the thirteenth century the power of the English middle classes has grown enormously and the power of the Crown has shrunk conspicuously. Since 1867 the power of labor in legal, economic, social, and political affairs has also grown enormously, and the power of certain other groups has been greatly restricted.

[21] The term is mine. The present national and international crisis makes it imperative to reevaluate recent socioeconomic developments in the light of Marx's *Magna Carta* concept, which is bolder and less "orthodox" Marxist than is generally assumed.

[22] MEW 23, p. 312.

[23] Harold Cruse, *The Crisis of the Negro Intellectual*. New York 1967, p. 383.

[24] Frantz Fanon, *The Wretched of the Earth*. New York 1968, pp. 111 f. Hereafter cited as Fanon 1968.

[25] MEW 18, p. 440.

[26] Marcuse has shied away from a clear and consistent identification of the lumpenproletariat as a revolutionary force. In a statement he made in 1964 he suggests that it was such a force; but in another made in 1969, he denies that he intended any such identification. (Marcuse 1964, p. 256; *idem,* 1969, pp. 51 ff.) Did Marcuse in 1969 no longer believe in the revolutionary importance of the "outcasts" and "unemployables"? He does not say. Nor does he explain his attitude to the arguments of Marx, Engels, and Bakunin regarding the lumpenproletariat which are crucial for a clarification of the underlying issue.

[27] Patrick Seale and Maureen McConville, *Red Flag/Black Flag*. New York 1968, p. 14. Hereafter cited as Seale and McConville 1968.

[28] Fanon 1968, p. 129. Fanon starts out in the conventional Leninist Communist (and Bakuninist) manner by declaring that in the colonial countries "the peasants alone are revolutionary." But he at once qualifies this statement by referring to "the starving peasants outside of the class system"; and he ends up by contrasting the peasants proper who, in his opinion, are conservative, with the "fraction of the peasant population" that has left the countryside and become the core of the urban lumpenproletariat. (Ibid. 61 and 129 f.)

[29] Ibid. p. 14 (Sartre's Preface to Fanon's book).

[30] Seale and McConville 1968, pp. 88, 89.

[31] Rudi Dutschke, "The Contradictions of Late Capitalism, the Anti-Authoritarian Students and their Relation to the Third World," in *Rebellion of the Students or The New Opposition*. An Analysis by Uwe Bergmann, Rudi Dutschke, Wolfgang Lefevre, Bern Rebehl, Hamburg 1968, pp. 62, 71, 80, 91, 92.

[32] "Ronald Steel, Letter from Oakland: The Panthers," *The New York Review,* September 11, 1969, p. 22. Hereafter cited as Steel 1969.

[33] Fanon 1968, pp. 129–130.

[34] Steel 1969, p. 22.

[35] See Wittfogel, *Oriental Despotism*. New Haven 1957, pp. 375 passim; *idem.* "The Marxist View of Russian Society and Revolution," in *World Politics,* Vol. XII, July 1960, pp. 487 passim.

[36] This statement implies that at least four major aspects of Marxism can be distinguished: "classical" Marxism (the classical elements in Marx's thought and their development by him), "orthodox" Marxism (the adjustment of Marx's truth-oriented views to a power-oriented programmatic Marxism), "vulgar" Marxism (a crude version of Marx's orthodox and classical ideas), and *"lumpen"* Marxism (the deliberate perversion of Marx's thoughts especially in the ruling ideology of the various Communist regimes).

[37] See Cohn-Bendit 1968, pp. 238 and 241 ff.

[XIV, Spring 1970, 114–128]

[52]

Marxist Revisionism: A Commentary

THOMAS MOLNAR

Thomas Molnar (1921–   ) was born in Budapest, Hungary. A student at the University of Brussels early in World War II, he was arrested by the Nazis for his activities in a Catholic resistance group, imprisoned at Buchenwald and Dachau, and liberated by American troops on the day on which his execution was scheduled. Now professor of French literature at the City University of New York and professor of European literature at C. W. Post College, he is a member of the editorial advisory board of Modern Age *and contributes to many of the serious journals in America and France. His numerous publications include* The Counter-Revolution *(1969),* God and the Knowledge of Reality *(1973), and* Le Socialisme sans visage *(1976).*

THIS COMMENTARY does not intend to exhaust the whole subject of revisionism of Marxist doctrine, and its sole purpose is to indicate the general—and perhaps necessary—direction of revisionist thought. It is enough to mention one reason why a complete study could not even be undertaken. Jean-Paul Sartre has written that we in this century live in an intellectual (he said "philosophical") universe created by Marx's genius, and that we cannot, even if we tried, withdraw ourselves from this pervasive influence. In other words, we cannot philosophize outside the circumference of Marxism.

From this statement it would follow that the number of Marxist writers is so vast (each bringing some minor modification to the *corpus*) that one may attempt to list, but not to discuss them, in a short space. I do not think, however, that one cannot philosophize outside the magic circle drawn by Marx; in fact, I believe one can easily philosophize in such a way as to create an even larger "circle" so as to include— and critically analyze—Marx's teaching. This may be achieved, as I have tried to do elsewhere, by showing that Marxism itself is a particularly successful species of the utopian genus; if we examine the latter's assumptions and structure, as well as the terminological parallelisms, we indeed reveal a schema in which Marxism conveniently finds its natural place as a subclass.

Most "revisionists," since the 1920's, have tried to do, in a sense, just that: noting the successive failures of practiced Marxism to live up to the utopian ideal, they strove, wittingly or unwittingly, to relink it to its more starkly utopian roots. If the specific difference, Marxism, displays some flaws, they seemed to say, then let us return to the *genus proximum* and begin anew our investigation along the same lines but more carefully. In the

613

process the revisionists remained, of course, Marxists since they claimed to use Marx's dialectical method, made their own his analysis of history, and assigned to mankind generally Marxian objectives. Yet, at the same time they were also "revisionists" because they wanted to save the utopian core from the infection of reality—an effort which has created the oft-chronicled clashes between the communist parties and the revisionists in their ranks and outside their ranks.

In the present confusion of Marx's followers and camp-followers (a confusion due to the phenomenon suggested by Sartre's statement: the saturation of the intellectual world by Marxism), it is important to distinguish between "revisionists" and "critics." Here we shall consider only the former, that is, those who move inside the utopian universe of discourse. One may say that their principal intention is the rehabilitation of the "young Marx" who, of course, is not only the Marx of 1844 and the early manuscripts, but is present in all major works of maturity and old age. The revisionists argue that this Marxism, the true content of the doctrine, has been hidden by both capitalist bourgeoisie and the Soviet state: the first, through its variations, never ceased fragmenting and falsifying our consciousness, the worker's consciousness, to be sure, but in proportion as the industrial state absorbed all citizens in its operations, also the consciousness of all men. This happens, let us remember our Marx, because consciousness is a reflection of the material conditions and interpersonal relationships, which are thoroughly vitiated by capitalistic production methods and by the bourgeois superstructure they determine.

"True Marxism" is also hidden by the Soviet state, the revisionists charge, insofar as Moscow has, at best, slowed down if not outright distorted the Marxian ev-olution towards a classless society. Communist leadership and cadre have turned themselves into a "new class." Thus the capitalist and the (official) Marxist state work along the same line, they both *alienate* man.

Let us take now a passage from the work of 1844 which fairly summarizes Marx's thesis at the time, and consequently the revisionist thesis too: since man is part of nature, and his natural condition is harmony with nature in all his activities, this primordial relationship is broken when man-as-a-worker finds in work the source of his misery instead of a joyous reunion with the source of his being. Misery then necessarily spreads to all man's other activities conditioned by the central activity, work. He is alienated from himself as well as from his fellows. The source of this chain of evils is private property because both the propertied and the propertyless live in an anti-natural milieu. In contrast, writes the young Marx, "the suppression of private property suppresses all alienation; man will return from religion, state, family, law, morals, science and art to his true human, that is social existence."

This, I think, has remained the core-ideal of all revisionists. Their activities may be described as efforts to persuade the official exponents of Marxism to return to this objective. What they do not seem to tolerate is that although private property had officially been suppressed half a century ago in Soviet Russia, the rest of the process of liberation did not follow: first, there is still a state which, in Marxist language, means that the class-character of society is still intact, although there has been a radical change of the ruling class. In the second place, not only is the state evident in its presence and its power, it now reinvents new forms of religion, morals, politics and law, that is, new forms of alienation. As the Polish

Adam Schaff charged some time ago, communist society too knows the phenomenon of man's alienation: of the intellectuals from the Party and from the mass-culture (sic!) it promotes; of the Jew who meets the walls of discrimination; and so on. True, Marxism, like other utopian systems, is able to justify these delays of paradise and reversals of hope by insisting that a certain time is bound to elapse between the death of capitalist society and the emergence of the communist one, a time supposedly filled with "revolutionary transformations" which may stretch over, as Bukharin insisted, a very long period. But the revisionists assume that the promises of Marx, founded on science, may be realized without the time-gap of the proletarian state and are, consequently, unwilling to put up with what they consider the hardly-disguised bourgeois-type abuses of which the communist state is now guilty.

The strange thing is that non-Marxists of a conservative persuasion must oppose both the "orthodox" and the "revisionist" Marxists. The first, because of their extreme cult of the state embodied in a totalitarian party, the second because revisionism too is completely opposed to human nature in its wild utopian expectations. In fact, it is easier to understand the reasons why the state and its institutions do not "wither away" even though now the "proletariat" is supposed to have taken power in it, than to imagine as many revisionists do a structureless community of perfect cooperators existing without conflict and friction and pursuing mutually ennobling tasks.

Fact is, from the early revisionist critics to the most recent ones, the central thesis contradicted the Marxian premises. The latter were based on Marx's materialistic ontology which assumed that man is part of nature, that his consciousness is determined by what goes on "outside," and

that therefore radical changes in the economic infrastructure would result in a similarly transformed intellectual-cultural superstructure. The revisionists never directly challenged this dogma, certainly not while Stalin ruled. But it was always evident that it went against their own philosophical inclinations to assume that the intellect is a mere copying machine of material circumstances. They wanted to assert, and to make Marx say, as the essence of his so-called "humanism," that intellectual ideas may also decisively influence economic modifications in a kind of interaction. This would be fine and acceptable, but it is no longer Marxism. Indeed, the latter stands or falls depending on whether it maintains a consistently materialistic position; if it does not, it must be demoted from its scientific pedestal and ranged among the many nineteenth-century socialist reform movements which can no longer validly analyse conditions in the twentieth.

THE FIRST NOTABLE revisionist was the Hungarian George Lukacs, who died earlier this year at the age of 86. He displays the impatience with the period of "revolutionary transformations" mentioned earlier as characteristic of revisionists. For Lukacs maintained that economics was a bourgeois invention by which this class was hiding from its victims' eyes the totality of social processes. Man and his activities cannot be naturally fragmented, and, for example, one is not justified in elevating to the rank of a separate science (economics) that part of his activities which deals with *work*. The communist objective is, therefore, to abolish the world in which work as such dominates human relationships, and to bring about another kind of world in which all human actions may flourish in harmony.

This would be the world of *culture*, putting an end to the "scandalous degeneration produced by capitalism." (For Marcuse, the "scandalous degeneration" produces the "one-dimensional man.") Culture, communist culture, is the content of the revolution, so that in the truly Marxist world, Lukacs taught, historical materialism will no longer be the correct doctrine, the correct law of the historical process.

Now this view does not substantially contradict Marx who also said that history would lift mankind from the realm of necessity (economics) to the realm of freedom (social harmony, collective culture). Yet, revisionist impatience is there as a corrosive element, and it is there in the name of the Hegelian contradiction to Marx, the importance of the (mental) superstructure which is able to accelerate even the laws of economic transformations.

Lukacs himself was first among leading Marxists to call attention to Marx's Hegelian roots, and we must understand now how this embarrassed the Soviet leadership in the 1930's. Stalin, like all communist leaders after him in Russia and elsewhere had every interest to *prolong* the period of "revolutionary transformations." This was his interest as the head of the new class, and this was also sheer necessity. Yet Lukacs and others proposed a quicker solution as if history did not have, for the Marxian orthodox, its own rhythm which one may study but not modify. The conflict was bound to appear each time that the "revisionists" came to power, but it was also bound to be short-lived since the revisionists were unable to resist the Party's immediate and forceful counterattacks (Budapest, Prague, etc.). When, for example, workers' councils were set up in Warsaw or Budapest (in the latter case at Lukacs' personal initiative in 1956), the Party intervened at once and liquidated these "counterrevolutionary" groups as *not yet* corresponding to the

economic realities. This *not yet* signals the clash between the Party and those impatient men who want to contemplate "socialism with a humane face."

Ernst Bloch, another grand old man of revisionism, goes beyond Lukacs in a more overt critique of Marx whom he accuses of depriving communism of its genuine millenaristic aspects. This statement thus places the entire Marxist thesis in question, and one may wonder if Bloch does not merely utilize Marxism for his own purposes. What is interesting for our study is, however, the fact that Bloch too criticizes Marx for his insistence on political economy and for seeing in the various millenaristic and utopian movements mere "stimulations" for the communist grand design. For Bloch himself, on the contrary, a revolutionary figure like Thomas Münzer in the early part of the sixteenth century is central to history's highway to utopia. Münzer did not wish merely to secure for his followers a more just distribution of goods, but to found a Mystical Republic where creatureliness would be abolished and all men would be divine.

Thus parallel to the supposedly inexorable laws of economic evolution, Bloch, who does not pay much attention to these laws anyway, suggests another, more important line of development, one which goes from "not-yet-being" to utopia. He misuses the whole theory of dialectics by expanding it to truly unverifiable dimensions; he maintains that the present world of facts, the world as it is and as it has been from the beginning is only *thetic,* that is, it forms the thesis of history with an immense future unfolding ahead about which nothing can as yet be said. Fine, but then how do we know that we live in the *thesis* period, how do we know that, as Bloch states, "world history is an experience aimed at a just and proper world"? The history of philosophy itself, he adds (in *A Philosophy of the Future*), is an anticipation of an "omega instant" in which appearance and essence will merge in full identity, to be reached in utopia. At the entrance of this socialist utopia Bloch sees the following inscription: "The end of the object with the liberated subject; the end of the subject with the unalienated object."

Until this final point is reached, world history remains "an imperilled *fieri*," an always fragile *becoming*. A clear contradiction to Marx who pretended to possess the science telling him at what point of history society was standing at a particular moment, and to judge that the advanced stage of capitalist decay must, by historical necessity, usher in a socialist form of production. No room for the "fragility" of history was left in the Marxian system, no room either for a Mystical Republic. On the other hand, Bloch leaves no room for Marx's thorough-going materialism and scientific calculations of the phases of history. History, for Bloch, is simply not yet, and the only ontology he recognizes is that of the "not-yet-being."

Utopianism is also the central preoccupation of Leszek Kolakowski.

> The Left gives forth utopias as the pancreas discharges insulin . . . . The Left is a quest for change . . . a movement of negation toward the existent world . . . . It [the Left] is defined by the nature of its Utopia.

It follows from these revealing statements that the Marxian Left is also only a phase in the interminable sequence of leftist "discharges," and that history is not bound by the laws of dialectics to reach an end. That utopias are endlessly superseded by other utopias is demonstrated by Kolakowski in his voluminous book, *Christians without a Church*, in which he studies the sixteenth- and seventeenth-century Dutch and German Lutheran, Calvinist, etc., sects. Their history shows a regular alternation of attempts to break up established churches and to establish new churches by those who had been anti-establishmentarians and nonconformists. "Church" may also be called "Party" (to work out this analogy may be Kolakowski's real intention) so that the Polish revisionist philosopher chronicles in reality the history, past and present, of "utopians without a party."

He does not seem to be aware that by doing so he has hit upon a new law of history, other than Marx's, namely the law one might call of "recurrent alienation." This "law" seems to have only a tenuous relationship with political economy, and its processes take place in the mind rather than in the clash of owners and victims of the means of production. Nor does this "law" seem to lead to the solution of history's enigma—which Marx claimed to have solved. True, Kolakowski admits with Marx that "the basic Marxist rule is to analyse social life by seeking the basic divisions separating societies into antagonistic groups." But Marx claimed he had found the way to heal for ever all antagonisms and thereby transform society into a harmoniously cooperating one. Nothing of the sort can be detected on Kolakowski's horizon: he simply puts his hopes in a "Marxist humanism" which, at closer inspection, reveals itself as a general receptacle for discarded dreams.

The case of Milovan Djilas is a *sui generis* one because he seems to have travelled farthest from orthodox Marxism, and according to my earlier distinction he appears today perhaps more as a critic than as a revisionist. In *The New Class*, which fell like a bomb on placid and conformist Marxists about a dozen years ago, in *Conversations with Stalin*, and recently in *The Un-perfect Society*, Djilas can be said to have undermined, from inside, the communist society no matter under what new label it may parade in the foreseeable future. What is more interesting, however, is his increasingly clear insight in the philosophical foundations of Marxism itself, something which shows a greater intellectual courage than the denunciation of factual abuses. In the winter 1971 issue of *Survey* he writes: "The mere fact that Marxism believes in its own scientific nature prevents changing Marxism into any kind of communism which would not be Stalinist." At the same time he criticizes Lukacs, Marcuse, Garaudy, and others as non-creative and utopian, as men unable to think "outside the Marxist canons of thought."

Djilas seems to base his attack on Marxism's pretensions to be a "science" on the realization (expressed, I think, for the first time in *The Un-perfect Society*) that the laws of dialectics—if indeed they are laws—are those of the domain of thought, but not of the domain of nature. Thus he effects a salutary dissociation between the world of concepts and the world of external reality, a major heresy in the Marxist universe of dogmas where concepts are supposed to translate, indeed to copy, external reality without a margin of error.

This is of course an important step in the direction of the de-Marxization of Marxist philosophy of which Djilas remarks in the *Survey* article that it "has not yet passed through the fire of creative criticism." Of what such a criticism will consist, is hard to tell since in the quoted text at least Djilas suggests that Kolakowski may be able to perform it. Most unlikely, as we have seen. But it may be that Djilas merely paid a gratuitous compliment to his Polish colleague. He begins to see quite clearly that after failing as a social system and as a regime, Marxism must also fail as a philosophy. In a recent issue of *Encounter* (May 1971) Djilas concluded that "alienated man is one of the aspects of mankind" and that without being "alienated" man could not be creative, could not be a man. "Even if he came to know what his Being and his Essence were, man could not return to them, for he has never departed from them. He is what he is." ("On Alienation.")

This shows that Djilas understands now, after an interesting and to all appearances honest evolution, that the horrible temptation of Marxism is to divinize man. He writes now that "man is not, and cannot be, a God," he does not create "out of his head alone." In sum, Djilas denies that Marxism is either science or religion. What remains is a "ceaseless movement into new circumstances and new possibilities." I think Djilas would grant that Marxism was such a movement, as we said at the beginning of this essay, a social reform movement of the nineteenth-century type, although particularly violent.

NATURALLY, DJILAS' conclusion does not settle the issue of revisionism we are discussing, it merely sheds more light on its interminable attempts to "save" a doctrine which cannot be saved unless we place it *inside* the much larger circle of utopianism. That is, of course, where the revisionists can be located.

It would be tedious to review here a more complete list of revisionists, perhaps from Trotsky himself to Marcuse, Sartre, Roger Garaudy and Jürgen Habermas—without even mentioning the political offshoots like Guevara or Mao Tse-tung. I think the substance of revisionism is now fairly clearly before us, so that we may understand that by its very nature, plus certain external circumstances, revisionism will continue its course.

A recent open letter (published in the *New York Times* of February 4, 1971, and elsewhere) by Vladimir Dedijer and addressed to J.-P. Sartre, is almost a classical illustration of a degenerate Marxism such as revisionists of the third or fourth vintage are able to present. In the name of the past generation that failed to bring forth a better world, Dedijer calls upon

Marxist Revisionism: A Commentary

Sartre, another member of that generation, to put his hope in the American
New Left. The short text abounds in
revisionist rhetoric that Marx himself would
hardly recognize as being in his own
lineage because in it revisionism seems to
have returned to the formulas of utopian
impatience, more naive than even what
Engels once denounced in his *Socialism,
Utopian and Scientific*.

The United States today, writes Dedijer
exultingly, is a real "Noah's Ark with all
kinds of rebels whose effort is to liberate
man in all his repressive relationships:
social, ethical, esthetical." If this sentence
echoes the already quoted one from the
Marxist texts of 1844, the next sounds
like Kolakowski: the American radicals,
writes Dedijer, are determined *not* to create a new Establishment that can become
the master rather than the servant of the
revolution—and this they hope to achieve
by "hard thinking to formulate a new
ideology."

The writer then administers the proof
as he sees it: the efficiency with which the
American New Left, in its fight against
the Vietnam War, has succeeded to "smoke
out a President from the White House"
is greater, according to Dedijer, than that
of the French Communists who had opposed in vain the Indochina and Algerian
wars! In conclusion:

> The future of the world depends so much
> on the American New Left. Nowhere are
> the social contradictions deeper, and no-
> where does a rebel have a greater oppor-
> tunity to demonstrate the firmness of his
> convictions than here. Therefore it is the
> greatest country in the world.

If the present article dealt with a critical
analysis of revisionism, it would be easy
to point out the *non sequiturs* in Dedijer's
panegyrics of the American New Left: to
cite only one, the assumption that a single
event (the pressure of radicals on Washington) prefigures a universal mutation of
the human condition. This is a clear symptom of "enthusiastic" or emotional thinking for which *passionate will* is equivalent
with the modification of the structure of
reality. For much less than that Marx and
Engels used to pour their scorn on Proudhon, Weitling, Godwin and others.

Yet, we are not analyzing now Dedijer's
thought processes, but continue to examine if this thought is still Marxian.
Marx's great, although false, assumption
was that history follows an iron law whose
processes bring about by necessity the
new society. His epigoni, like all epigoni,
are struck by the nondelivery of the child
with which history is allegedly pregnant,
and they invent all sorts of explanations
and excuses for the delay. Meanwhile,
again like typical epigoni, they realize that
the constantly postponed birth means not
only a deficiency in the timetable of revolutionary achievements, but also an ever-
new rearrangement of facts and data in
contradiction to Marx's "iron law." Thus
nationalism, religion, the state, the structures of capitalism, the breakthroughs in
technology, all of them phenomena interpreted by Marx in a certain way, do
not develop or degenerate according to
the expected pattern.

But Marx at least elaborated a theory
of economic development which provided
the "iron law" with substance, and served
as a system of verification at every phase
of the historical process. Needless to say,
the theory has proved to a large extent
irrelevant, it was one of the huge nineteenth century constructs which in Marx's
mind no longer proposed a philosophy
but a blueprint for action. Nevertheless,
it *was* a philosophical construct, with its
theory of knowledge, anthropology, and
cultural vistas. Yet, no matter how defective it proved to be, the epigoni are unable
to formulate a genuinely novel one, although they find themselves compelled

to abandon that of their master. Let us summarize it by saying that they still are committed to the "iron law," but no longer know how to substantiate it.

The inevitable occurs: the epigoni, involved in situations very different from those which surrounded Marx, and philosophically also less prepared, choose the road of eclecticism and syncretism, formulate strange and short-lived ideologies, launch new excommunications and initiate new dialogues. Thus Marcuse adopts Freud and abandons the proletariat in favor of youth; Garaudy is fascinated by a Christianity which refuses to die and speaks of man as a "budding divinity"; Dedijer sees a new red dawn in America; etc., etc. Such restless inventions are habitual phenomena during the eclipse of an orthodoxy and the rise of a pale syncretism in the minds of less original thinkers. In some respects one is reminded of early Islamic history when fanatic orthodox preachers turned into vulgar activists, although no less fanatic.

Indeed, we are far from the Marxist generation which produced biased but more serious scholars, such as Kautsky, Plekhanov, the Adlers, Lukacs himself. So that if we need proof that Marxism is unable to change the world as Marx had triumphantly announced, all we have to ponder is that Marxists are unable even to break the rules of ideological behavior, that is, to conduct themselves differently from the adherents of other historical movements of the past. Marxism simply follows the destiny and developmental rhythm of these movements: after the initial iron legion of thinkers and men of action, it has produced two or three waves of increasingly banal revisionists whose subjective and superficial eclecticism fragments the whole, creates clashes among sects, and reduces the great ambition of changing the world to mere noises and their echoes.

[XVI, Summer 1972, 301–308]

[53]

The Cold War of the Mind: Regimentation in East Germany

GRACE RICHARDS CONANT

Grace Richards Conant (1898–1985) had an excellent opportunity to study the situation in East Germany that she writes about in this essay. She lived for some years in Germany with her husband, James Bryant Conant, United States ambassador to the Federal Republic of Germany and the president of Harvard from 1933 to 1953. The daughter of one of her husband's most famous professors, Theodore William Richards, she was also the granddaughter of William T. Richards, a talented artist. Before marrying Conant in April 1921, she studied to be a painter at the Boston Museum of Fine Arts; she spent much of her honeymoon in the art galleries of Europe. An accomplished linguist, she mastered German more quickly than even her husband, who said her facility with the language and her social grace considerably ameliorated his duties as ambassador.

The state of education and culture in the "Democratic Peoples' Republic."

IT IS DIFFICULT for Americans to realize the scope and impact of thought control in a modern police-state. We need not fear that the police will be informed if we pick up a newspaper in the subway or listen to a forbidden radio program. We read what we choose. It is not dangerous for us to applaud in the theatre a striking line about liberty. No one indoctrinates our little children with fear and loathing of "the enemy." We do not need to watch, day in, day out, for ideological spies, both young and old, in our schools and universities. We find it almost impossible to comprehend that academic and cultural institutions, which we cherish as sources of enlightenment, can be degraded into training-squads and rallying-points in the cold war of the mind.

Yet this is what happened in Hitler's Germany. And today from West Berlin one can look across to the so-called "German Democratic Republic," the puppet-state set up by the Soviets in their zone of occupation, and see from year to year the frightening process of systematic intimidation and control of all free minds. The directives of the Communist functionaries, fanatics, and opportunists in the seats of power are implemented under the prying eyes of an elaborate spy-system and supported by the ever-present threat of force. Nearly 40,000 teachers, scholars, and students have escaped from this tyranny. The refugees who still come over to West Berlin in thousands every week tell poignant stories of intrigue, blackmail, and persecution.

The ruthless application of Communist techniques embraces all manifestations of cultural life and all phases of education. Children must pass a course that indoctrinates them to hate the capitalistic enemy before they can be promoted to the next grade. In 1958 the practice of training children to stand watch at vacation camps was defended because the enemy would not hesitate to attack them on holiday. Political significance—a "provocative" allegiance to the West—is read even into the personal attire of the young (blue jeans!) and their choice of dance-music is considered a "class issue." School textbooks are permeated by propaganda. School-teachers must write out their own treatment of a subject before presenting it in class, and hand it in to the responsible authority, so that there is little chance to evade the party line. Any deviation is regarded as suspicious and may be denounced as "sabotage of the Socialist state."

The pressure in many ways is grimmer, the spy-system more ramified, than in Nazi days. Under Hitler, the fervent and prolonged applause of Berlin audiences for a line in one of Schiller's plays—"Give us freedom of thought, sire!"—amounted, as the *New York Times* correspondent reported at the time, to a political demonstration against the Nazi régime. Such a demonstration is unlikely today in East Germany. After 15 years of Communist rule the people have learnt to preserve their masks; the "deutscher Blick" (a glance over each shoulder before committing one's self to anything) has become a habit. The people have been trained to watch for ideological traps that may lead to police interrogation and perhaps jail. They know that a scene in an opera, a line of poetry, even an article on art must be interpreted in terms of political loyalties and the power conflict between Communism and the West.

To us it may seem absurd that the history of art, for instance, must be taught from the Marxist point of view, and that philosophy is considered primarily a weapon against the "capitalist bandits." History is deliberately twisted to add to its lethal power. For "the criterion of scholarliness of our political and legal studies is their usefulness for the practical purposes of socialism," as Ulbricht, the Communist boss of East Germany, recently declared. All intellectual attitudes and cultural undertakings in the "German Democratic Republic" have political implications. Religion is no longer a private spiritual aspiration, but an enemy of the Communist state. The famous theological faculty in Leipzig is now a center for the teaching of materialism.

The Communist leaders have often declared that the highest duty of a teacher is to mold his pupils into convinced Marxists. They insist that the upbringing of children cannot be regarded by the state as a private affair. From the "socialist christening," which in East Germany has now almost replaced religious christenings, to the atheistic "youth consecration" designed to replace confirmation, the child is to be dominated by "socialist principles." The new school law explicitly states that home influences must follow these lines. For, as Grotewohl, Ulbricht's second in the Communist hierarchy, declared at a meeting called in 1959 to discuss the planning of *Kulturpolitik*, "morality is what serves the cause of Socialism" (read "Communism"). Religious parents in East Germany once again suffer from the painful conflict of conscience which they endured in Nazi times. Shall they speak honestly to their children and take the risk that a child may quote them to some teacher eager for advancement? Or should they rather relinquish the attempt to inculcate their own beliefs in their children and leave them to party indoctrination?

There has been no "thaw" worthy of the name in East Germany. Stalin's statue still stands in East Berlin in the place of honor on the spacious avenue that bears his name. His disciple, Walter Ulbricht, long chief of the S.E.D., the Communist party in the "German Democratic Republic" and now officially the head of the state, continues to enforce a repressive policy which rankles all the more bitterly because it must be endured by a people already once "liberated" from dictatorship. There is a grotesque similarity between the methods of the German Communist functionaries and those of the Nazis. It all seems like a bad film beginning again—the exploitation of culture in the service of a totalitarian régime striving to dominate Germany.

Hitler believed that "power comes from culture." By a thorough-going purge of those who stood for creative freedom in art, science, and scholarship, the Nazis strove to exclude all but Nazi ideas, "Aryan" science, art, and literature. The official Nazi praise of "Nordic culture" sounds like raving to our ears. But a similar chorus is to be heard daily in East Germany with a new refrain—praise of the "Soviet man" and his achievements, coupled with denunciation of Western imperialists and their corrupt culture. All are warned that what the West regards as culture is but a trap to beguile the innocent into the greedy jaws of "monopoly-capitalism."

The East German functionaries strive to exploit the great figures of German history for the purposes of the Communist cause. They struggle to show the continuity of German culture leading, as they put it, to the "socialist triumphs" of their puppet state. Sometimes their propaganda efforts miscarry. During the Schiller

anniversary year (1955) they endeavored to enlist Schiller as a fellow-traveler, and benefit from the veneration in which he is held all over Germany. Perhaps they should have been warned by the memory that the Nazis had found this passionate crusader a prickly bedfellow. Eventually Goebbels was forced to banish "Wilhelm Tell" even from the school-room because of its ringing appeals for liberty.

The verse of Schiller selected in the anniversary year for propaganda use by the East German régime seemed nicely in line with official policy. It read "We want to be a people of united brothers." This reinforced the constant appeals of the Soviets for negotiations between the "two Germanies"—"all Germans at one table," as the gaudy streamers plastered on public buildings in East Berlin put it. But when these few words from Schiller appeared prominently displayed on a large red and white sign near an East zone railway station, an experienced American observer immediately prophesied that "this will not work" as propaganda—it could not be allowed to remain!—because of the disastrous echoes it would awaken in every German mind. The German people know their Schiller well, and the line which seemed to support the political policy of their oppressors would serve to remind them of the verses which immediately follow it in the poet's text: *We want to be free as our fathers were. Rather death than slavery!*" Three weeks later the sign had disappeared, as prophesied.

The official Communist exploitation of drama and music for political purposes reached a high point when the Soviet zone government could announce the re-opening of the East Berlin opera-house. In free West Berlin, essential rebuilding of housing and industry and care for the thousands of refugees who since 1952 have come over every week from the East were given first priority by the city authorities. Even now the West Berlin opera is still performing in makeshift quarters, although the completion of a new house is hoped for late in 1961. But a totalitarian régime can overlook humanitarian scruples and arbitrarily channel great sums into a favored official project. By 1955, the East Berlin opera-house had been splendidly rebuilt and decorated, and a gala première was planned to add luster to the capital of the "German Democratic Republic." This great occasion should have been a glorious victory, but instead, at the eleventh hour, it turned into a dramatic reversal. Shortly before he was to preside at the première, Erich Kleiber, the famous conductor who had recently been appointed Musical Director of the East Berlin opera, escaped to the West. In his farewell letter, the conductor complained that the promises of the management had not been kept; he had come to feel that "politics and propaganda will not come to a halt outside the door of this temple." The Director of the opera immediately published an angry open letter in rejoinder, implying that the West had conspired to subvert the great musician. This remarkable document underlines the political implications of all culture in a totalitarian state. "The Dulles and Adenauer intriguers realize the worth of such a man to opera in the East," he wrote. "If only Kleiber's ear for politics were as good as his ear for music!"

One footnote may be of interest as exemplifying the intense emotional significance that a work of art can carry in the war for men's minds. Here Beethoven emerges—like Schiller a torchbearer for liberty, and deeply revered by all Germans. For the gala opening night of the restored opera-house in East Berlin the production of Beethoven's *Fidelio* was originally announced. But at the last moment the Executive Committee of the S.E.D. substituted *Die Meistersinger*—"a national folk opera standing for the unity of the Fatherland," to quote from the official statement. Such a decision would hardly be made on the basis of musical values alone. To understand the factors involved, one must realize that *Fidelio* has a special message to those who have suffered under tyranny. This opera has become a deeply loved symbol of liberation. Many Berliners will testify that, at the first performance after the Nazi defeat, the entire Berlin audience broke down and wept. The scene where gaunt political prisoners come up out of their dungeon to the light of day was to the Berliners a picture of their own life. The Communist officials in East Berlin had good reason for their second thoughts about scheduling *Fidelio*. The sight of released political prisoners, even on the stage, so soon after the revolt of 1953 and the many following arrests, would have cast a dark cloud over the occasion. In this connection a *New York Times* dispatch from Budapest in the summer of 1957 is significant. It reported that in Szeged, a city in southern Hungary, the manager of the opera had announced that in future some of the scenes in *Fidelio* would be altered, to avoid the demonstrations that had been taking place at every performance.

The effort to impress the great figures in the German past into the Communist army and to prove that only since the triumph of Communism has it been possible to understand their contribution to the German cultural heritage leads to surprising re-evaluations. For instance, to quote from a statement of the Executive Committee of the S.E.D. inaugurating the celebration of the Bach anniversary year: "a truly objective evaluation and appreciation of Bach has only been possible since the destruction of German fascism by the defeat of the German imperialists at the hands of the armies of the Socialist Soviet Union." Reading further, we find that the significance of Bach in musical history is that he burst the "ecclesiastical fetters" of music. He represents the bourgeois opposition to a decaying feudal society, and by introducing folk songs and dances into his music, he "secularized" church music! A specimen of the results of the process of secularization, a sample of the proletarian and materialistic music of the Soviet zone, was performed by an East German choir at an all-German music festival in Coburg. The "White Bread Cantata" by Hans Eisler shocked and angered those attending the festival from West Germany by its deliberately blasphemous propaganda line: "For a man who has no white bread .... Jesus was never born."

It is a curious fact that an article exists written in 1937 by Ulbricht, the very man responsible for Stalinist repression in East Germany, in which he echoes Schiller's line "Give us freedom of thought." There has been no freedom of thought in East Germany since 1945, except for dialectical materialism. Ulbricht now echoes the view of his Moscow patron, Khrushchev, who in a famous speech in 1957 declared: "In the world of today a bitter struggle is going on between two ideologies and in this struggle no one can be neutral." Earlier in the same speech Khrushchev said: "For an artist who truly serves his people, there is no question about whether he is free or not." A German translation of this speech was prominently on display in the East Berlin bookshop where I bought my copy a year ago.

In the face of vilification, threats, and reprisals, the writer and the artist in East Germany have been forced to take sides and become cultural hacks and government mercenaries in the cold war of the mind. On the surface they must conform. Their private opinions and creative efforts must be hidden away, as in the Nazi time, in the "literature of the desk drawer." The

writing demanded by the Communist régime is a militant literature, "a literature of rolled-up shirt-sleeves."

The most brilliant star in the East German literary galaxy was the late Bertolt Brecht, the revolutionary playwright. A few poems recently published in the West seem to testify to his secret disillusionment and sense of guilt. But whatever his inner conflicts may have been, during his lifetime he accepted the privileged position accorded him by the Communist police-state without any public indication that he repudiated its sickening excesses. Another member of the literary "avant-garde," Johannes R. Becher, became a government functionary. Until his recent death he occupied the impressive post of Minister of Culture in the "German Democratic Republic." His career as a bureaucrat had a pronounced effect on his literary style. I quote the last lines of one of his "activist" poems:

> The mining collective calls thee.
> The tractor challenges thee.
> Be thou also a power-plant!

Ulbricht has often declared that the highest task of the writer—as of the teacher—is to build up socialism. At a conference in East Berlin in April, 1960, he called on the workers to "storm the heights of culture." The importance of art and literature in his program is emphasized by the fact that, according to an official journal, the party-controlled trade unions in East Germany now have almost a quarter of a million "culture functionaries" attached to them. The workers themselves are now being urged to "seize the pen" and compose "progressive literature." For, to quote a line by Heinrich Mann which was featured at one East German culture conference, "the books of today are the deeds of tomorrow."

Ulbricht has often repeated with approval Stalin's dictum that "artists have the task of being engineers of the human soul." In East Germany, art and literature are skills to be harnessed for the indoctrination of the masses and for the prestige and greater glory of the state. As one shrewd Swiss observer put it, "art is nothing but the continuation of politics by other means."

It is not surprising that some of the painters who in Nazi times were "well-tried soldiers of the cultural war" and did their best to exalt "the prototype of Nordic man" are now busy under other colors. Their task in East Germany is to express the "heroic" optimism of "socialist realism." They paint in a naturalistic-sentimental style reminiscent of their Nazi days such subjects as girls driving tractors, Red soldiers being kind to children, "worker and soldier clasping hands," and "peasant delegation meets with brigade of socialist artists." Modern art is taboo as it was under Hitler's rule. The few modern pictures that were left after the confiscations and bonfires of the Nazis have been returned to the museum cellars. Many artists, unable to exhibit, have fled to the West. Functional modern architecture, so brilliantly developed elsewhere by the architects Hitler banished, is condemned in East Germany with Marxian smear-words ("cosmopolitan," "eclectic," "formalist"). Its steel construction has been alleged to reveal "imperialist preparations for war." The pretentious new buildings on Stalinallee in East Berlin are patterned after the Moscow confectioners' pseudo-classic style. The directive laid down in 1951 by Otto Grotewohl, then Prime Minister of the "German Democratic Republic," is still being followed in East Germany. "Literature and the arts," he said, "are subordinate to politics. The idea of art must follow the line of march of the political struggle."

But in spite of sixteen years of systematic repression and indoctrination, the "German Democratic Republic" is not yet completely sovietized. Compulsory inoculation with Marxist-Leninist philosophy has not worked well. Fifty per cent of the refugees escaping to West Berlin are under 25 years old. These young people have been conditioned for years by a socialist education. They represent a large government investment, and their loss is a bad blow to the future of the economy. The intellectuals who have escaped to the West report much spiritual misery among those skilled professional groups most needed in a modern industrialized society. The leakage of technical personnel has resulted in serious gaps in the staffing of many institutions. Some hospitals are served only by Russian or Bulgarian doctors. Massive "crash" programs have been announced to train teachers and technicians to overcome the shortages. But the flight to the West continues, month after month. It seems at the least doubtful whether any crash program can compensate for the repudiation of the communist state by so many of its unhappy, enslaved inhabitants.

Communizing East Germany is a more difficult task than the clamping of ideological fetters on a primitive or backward country. In this highly industrialized and literate society the attempt to eliminate "bourgeois ideals" has created bitter resistance. The East Germans are proud of their academic tradition and consider their level of civilization far above that of the "Soviet man." Furthermore, protestant Christianity is strongly rooted in East Germany. Professors in the universities whose posts depend on their support of the régime find it difficult to subscribe to the dogma that "there is no co-existence possible between science and religion." Is a man who has church affiliations fit to teach physics? The Communists say no. They urge that anyone who sees a teacher at church or at a religious christening must report the fact. Students are questioned by the secret police about the religious discussions of their fellows. In East Germany conflicts of conscience long stilled in Russia are still acute.

The aim of Ulbricht and his colleagues is to convert the schools and universities into instruments of the state—"smithies to forge the cadres of the workers' and peasants' power." This aim has been largely achieved. The new school law of December, 1959, anchors "socialist principles" in every stage of the schools. Higher education is more and more the privilege only of those students who "unreservedly support the cause of socialism." All students entering a university must now take an oath of loyalty to the Communist régime and pledge themselves to its defense. Ninety per cent of them are supported by government stipends and therefore subject to official intimidation.

The recent "socialist reforms" of university organization and control were first announced in 1958 at the time of the 400th anniversary celebration of the famous University of Jena. The Rector of the university was to be the star witness at an official press conference set up to give publicity to the government program. But a few days before the press conference he and his family escaped to West Berlin. His defection at that moment drew the attention of the German academic world—as Kleiber's had that of the musical world—and amounted to a serious Communist defeat in the cold war of the mind.

The massive flight of intellectuals from East Germany in the last two years has been called a "bleeding of the intelligentsia." But the Communist officials continue to exert an inexorable ideological pressure. Professors are now on contracts which must be renewed every six months; loyalty to the régime is implicit in the renewal of the contract. University senates

are packed with representatives of Communist organizations who control all decisions, and government secretariats have the last word on academic affairs. Censorship, party control of publishing permits and limitation of paper quotas, party discipline and party reprisals (including jail sentences) have combined to stifle all independent voices. As the Minister for Security put it in 1956, "It goes without saying that in the German Democratic Republic no so-called free discussion can or should be tolerated which leads to the smuggling in of foreign anti-democratic and anti-socialist ideologies."

To give an impression of the climate of opinion among intellectuals, I quote from an article in "Einheit," the official scholarly journal of the East German Communist party (S.E.D.). The author, Jurgen Kuczynski, is defending himself against a criticism by Walter Ulbricht: "Of course I have no thought of denying the leading role of the party," he cries, "because as a comrade and especially as a scientist I do not wish to ruin myself ideologically. I have no intention of throwing away the compass of my political and scientific life or committing social suicide." Nothing could be much more abject, and this is only a sample.

I recommend a systematic reading of "Einheit." Any one who believes that Communism in East Germany can be reconciled with integrity of mind and conscience, or that the creative spirit of man can transcend party lines, should study this journal. To struggle with its double talk is a dizzying and almost nauseating experience. I quote two statements on the role of art: "When the artist renders the reality of life in the form of high art, he will arrive unconditionally at Marxism.". . . "The decadent art of American monopoly-capitalism has the very real task of infecting the German people with cosmopolitanism, robbing them of all true national pride, all will to struggle for unity and sovereignty, and making them ripe for a life of slavery under American rule."

There is no doubt that the rulers of a totalitarian state are right in their stern measures against the intelligentsia,—right from their own perspective. There is no danger to a dictatorship so great as free-thinking minds. Hitler's purges of the intellectuals were based on a sure instinct. The serious disturbances in Poland and the uprising in Hungary in 1956 were both preceded by unrest and agitation in literary and academic circles. Adam Wazyk's terrible "Poem for Adults" * was published in Poland in 1955, and the next year at a gathering of writers in Warsaw

---

* Wazyk, a leading Communist poet, describes in harrowing terms the squalor, vice and tragedy of the great industrial center, Nowa Huta, near Cracow. He flays the betrayal of the "great aims of education":

when students are imprisoned in textbooks without windows,
when language is reduced to thirty slogans,
when the lamp of imagination is extinguished.
He continues:
There are boys forced to lie,
there are girls forced to lie. . . .
there are the weary, dying of tired hearts,
there are people slandered, spat upon,
there are people stripped in the streets by common bandits. . . .
there are people who wait for a slip of paper,
there are some who wait for justice. . . .
And he concludes:
We make demands on this earth. . . .
for a clear truth,
for the bread of freedom,
for flaming wisdom.
We demand these every day,
we demand through the Party.

"socialist realism" was bitterly attacked as "political-literary blackmail." The courageous leadership of Hungarian intellectuals in the struggle for freedom has been amply documented. Their example aroused echoes in East Germany. The young university teacher, Dr. Wolfgang Harich, who was sentenced in 1957 in East Berlin to ten years' imprisonment, was charged with planning an uprising after the Hungarian model. He advocated a "humanized socialism." As Khrushchev said in the speech already quoted, we must not forget "the lessons of events in Hungary where the counter-revolution exploited various writers for its dirty purposes."

The East German government officials are endeavoring to maintain and extend their control by more of the same brutality from which so many have fled. Their thesis is: "The right is what is right for the party, and what is not right for the party is wrong." Johannes R. Becher, the late Minister of Culture, in one of his speeches added a Communist definition of freedom. He said: "Our kind of freedom is the endless freedom of humanity *which exists only on the basis of party membership.*" (Italics mine.) These statements together define accurately the harsh ideological strait-jacket in which 17,000,000 Germans have to live. The Communist police-state in East Germany shows clearly both in its theory and its practice the issues that are at stake for all of us in the cold war of the mind.

[V, Spring 1961, 117–124]

[VII]

The Anatomy of Terror

[54]

The Anatomy of Perdition

J. M. LALLEY

J(oseph) M(ichael) Lalley (1896–1980), who has been called "the best book-reviewer in America," was a reporter for The Baltimore Sun *from 1923 to 1925, when he left to work in advertising in Baltimore and New York. In 1937 he became an editorial writer for* The Washington Post. *He contributed book reviews to* New Yorker *magazine in 1947 and 1948 and was book review editor from 1947 to 1950 for* Human Events Newsletter. *Following his retirement from the* Post *in 1961, he served as an associate editor of* Modern Age *from 1963 until his death. His essays, short stories, and articles appeared in many publications, including* Smart Set, H. L. Mencken's *magazine of the 1920s.*

I

The authors of these two books * about life, terror, and death in the Soviet slave camps were for several years prison companions and firm friends. They met for the first time in the *sharashka*, or privileged prison for scientists and technologists useful to the régime, afterwards made famous as the setting for Solzhenitsyn's novel, *The First Circle*. Nearly all the characters in that novel were drawn from the life and many of them reappear in this powerful memoir by Sologdin-Panin, who it seems is now living in Paris, a devout convert to the Roman Catholic Church. In the darkest hour of his captivity in the camp

hospital at Vyatlag, wasted almost to a skeleton by weeks of pellagrous dysentery, he turned to religious meditation and was rescued from death by what he firmly believes to have been a miraculous intervention of Providence.

As for Solzhenitsyn, despite his protestation that to convey all the "savage meaning" of the Stalinist terror "is beyond the capabilities of one lonely pen," he has with his rare literary genius and fierce fervor for truth and justice put before the world in *The Gulag Archipelago* a great and terrifying epic, a panorama of horrors and heroisms without counterpart in history. It is impossible to read him without shudders or without fears that what has happened to the Russian and the German societies may be but the prelude to what will happen in our own. Solzhenitsyn is one of those who see in the apocalyptic terrors of our time the culminative effects of the philosophic forces and social ten-

* Review of *The Notebooks of Sologdin*, by Dimitri Panin, translated by Thomas Moore, New York: Harcourt Brace Jovanovich, 1976, and of *The Gulag Archipelago*: *An Experiment in Literary Investigation*, Volume 2 (Parts III & IV) by Alexandr Solzhenitsyn, translated by Thomas P. Whitney, New York: Harper & Row, 1975.

dencies set loose by the Enlightenment. Both Solzhenitsyn and Panin make much of the reversal of moral and legal values involved in the transition from nineteenth century humanitarian liberalism to twentieth century totalitarian dogmatism, and both ascribe it to the declining influences of religion. We need not look very far from home to find incipient analogies to the inverted notions of guilt and innocence reflected in the transfer of judicial solicitude from the victims of violent crime to the perpetrators of it. Solzhenitsyn cites the severe restrictions placed on the traditional right of self-defense in the Soviet Criminal Code of 1926. Under one of its articles a citizen who may be attacked on the street by a mugger is forbidden to unsheath his knife until after the criminal has unsheathed his own: "you could stab him only after he had stabbed you." Solzhenitsyn mentions the case of one Aleksandr Zakharov,[1] a Red Army man, who was attacked by a thug, for apparently no particular reason, and badly beaten. Zakharov managed to extract a small folding penknife from his pocket and to open a blade, and with this killed his assailant. He was found guilty of willful murder and sentenced to ten years imprisonment.

"Why, what was I supposed to do?" the astonished Zakharov asked the court.
"You should have fled," snapped the prosecutor.

The twenties, the thirties, the fifties! Who does not remember that eternal threat hovering over the citizen: Don't go where it's dark! Don't come home late! Don't wear your watch! Don't carry money with you! Don't leave the apartment empty! Locks! Shutters! Dogs! . . .

In the file of the *Literaturnaya Gazeta* for September, 1955, Solzhenitsyn found an account of a man who was beaten to death in a Moscow street alongside a house occupied by two families who watched the performance from their windows but made no effort to interrupt it. Another witness, however, this one a retired officer and an Old Bolshevik, became indignant and demanded that the two families be charged with abetting a murder. The editor of the *Gazeta*, to whom the complaint seems to have been brought, agreed that the incident was indeed deplorable but unhappily not illegal. Some who read this may recall the case, a decade ago or thereabouts, of a Miss Kitty Genovese whose screams drew no response when she was similarly attacked and murdered in full view of dozens, perhaps hundreds, of freeborn, freedom-loving American apartment-house dwellers, not one of whom bothered even to inform the police.

II

In the Marxist scheme of things, as Solzhenitsyn explains, common criminals—such as thieves, muggers, murderers, rapists and so on—are deemed authentic members of the *Lumpenproletariat* with a wholly commendable disdain for the institution of private property. Thus in the eyes of the Party ideologues they constitute a "friendly element" and are seen as potential allies or auxiliaries in the class war, and are accordingly treated with special consideration. In the prison camps to which it is occasionally necessary to consign them—as when for example they fail to remember the important distinction between *state* and *private* property—they constitute a privileged caste—something close to an élite. It is an axiom sanctified by the Marxist revelation that criminals are what they are, not because of Original Sin or any other form of innate wickedness, but solely because of an unfavorable environment created by capitalist greed and oppression. So it was that the Bolsheviks after their triumph in 1917 recognized the Russian criminals as a revolutionary force that had to be guided into the mainstream of the proletariat . . . and this would constitute no difficulty. An unprecedented multitude of newcomers grew up to join them, consisting of orphans of the civil war and famine—homeless waifs, or *besprizorniki*, and hoodlums. They warmed themselves at asphalt cauldrons during the New Economic Policy, and for their first lessons they learned to cut ladies' purses off their arms and to lift suitcases through train windows. . . .

Observing this, the Party theoreticians began to say to themselves and to one another:

> . . . Let us reeducate these healthy lumpen-proletarians and introduce them into the system of conscious life! And the first communes came into existence for this purpose, and the first children's colonies, and the motion picture, *The Road to Life*. . . .
>
> Now, when more than forty years have gone by, one can look around and have doubts. Who educated whom? Did the Chekists reeducate the thieves or the thieves the Chekists? The *urka*—the habitual thief—who adopted the Chekist faith became a *bitch*, and his fellow-thieves would cut his throat. The Chekist who acquired the psychology of the thief became the energetic interrogator . . . or else a resolute camp chief—such men were appreciated. They got the promotions. . . .

A *bitch* in the Gulag jargon meant a criminal who collaborated with the camp authorities and became a spy and informer. Such persons—for they included both men and women—acquired powers of life and death over other inmates and were greatly feared and bitterly hated, not only by the political prisoners but even more so by the other criminals who held to a curious code of honor, which though it might sanction the stealing of food rations and clothing from the helpless and starving, drew a line at the betrayal of one's own kind. They would kill the *bitches* without compunction whenever opportunity offered, as frequently it did.

Solzhenitsyn is as scornful of the criminals who held fast to their code as of those who turned informer against their own comrades in crime. "No matter how much I saw of one and the other, I never could see that one rabble was nobler than the other." Those were presumably "honorable thieves" who knocked out the gold teeth of Estonian prisoners and drowned Lithuanian prisoners in the toilets at Kraslag for refusing to turn over a food parcel; who would plunder prisoners condemned to death; who would murder a cellmate for the sake of getting a new interrogation and trial and so of spending the winter in a warmer place.

The one effect of Marxist education on the lumpenproletarians seems to have been to strengthen their hostility to private property, and in this respect, says Solzhenitsyn, their hatred of the bourgeoisie was real enough, but it extended equally to Communist bureaucrats who owned dachas and motor cars. All the rest of Marxism-Leninism-Stalinism they dismiss as twaddle. Their attitude to life is summed up thus:

> Everything they come across on life's path they take as their own (if it is not too dangerous). Even when they have a surfeit of everything, they reach out to grab what belongs to others because any unstolen article makes a thief sick at heart. They wear the clothes they have stolen while they have novelty, until they tire of them, and soon afterward lose them at cards. Card games that last several nights on end give them their most powerful sensations, and in this respect they have far outdone the Russian nobility of past eras. They can even gamble *an eye* for stakes (and tear out the loser's eye on the spot). They can also play for . . . the right to use the loser for perverted [sexual] enjoyment. . . .

And Panin, it seems, knows of incidents where the loser at cards was obliged to carry out a murder prescribed by the winner.

III

Unlike Solzhenitsyn, however, Panin has some sympathy for the criminals, at least for those who obeyed their "code of honor." He agrees that in some historical situations criminality may be the effect of a hostile environment and that this was true for many of the first post-revolutionary generation whose only choice, especially after the great state-provoked famines, was between thievery and starvation. Besides the new government in both pattern and conduct was criminal, for Panin has pointed out how Lenin had recruited his Bolshevik Party on the very principles employed by a bandit chieftain in selecting and disciplining the members of his band; *viz*:

1. blind submission to the will and orders of the boss;
2. periodic "purges" to eliminate possible violators of underworld law, "trials for offenders and vindictive sentences, antihuman ethics";
3. excommunication and destruction of renegades (*"bitches"*);
4. a sharp distinction between members of the gang bound together by the code and the common herd of non-criminals.

Panin had not been long in the camps before deciding that each of them is a microscopic mirror of Soviet life in general.

> The camp's criminal element corresponds to the ruling Communist Party element, just as the Communist Party had modeled itself after an underworld gang. The most vicious segment among the criminals performs duties comparable to those of the Chekists, while the rest of them act as spies and informers. Their chiefs fulfill the functions of the judges. The *frayers*, the *muzhiks*, and the *Sidor Polikarpoviches* correspond to the

ordinary masses outside the party. These people, like their kind outside, are isolated, timorous, cowardly, mean, easily swayed by rumors, without confidence in their own powers. . . .

Panin, though a Christian who believes the whole message of Christianity to be contained in the Lord's Prayer, nevertheless insists that the killing of informers is a justified measure of defense against the evil power of the political police. "All my life," he writes,

> I had been opposed to terrorism in any form and had always supported the struggle against it. But in conditions of unabated Chekist terrorism against prisoners in the camps, informers became instruments of terror, and were, in effect, terrorists themselves. Under those circumstances the elimination of a notorious informant who had caused the death of several prisoners and undermined the health of many others was an act of self-defense and self-preservation. . . . One had to cut off the tentacles of an octopus. . . .

In the "hard labor" camp at Ekibastuz where Panin and Solzhenitsyn spent some of the latter months of their captivity informers were being done away with by the other prisoners at the rate of something like five or six a month, and without them the Chekists became virtually impotent. It was at Ekibastuz that a big riot and strike occurred in which Panin was a leader.

IV

Solzhenitsyn's research has demolished a myth still fondly cherished by some Western liberals, and after the Twentieth Party Congress promoted by some Soviet historians:[2] that Stalin alone was responsible for the creation of the slave camps and that they represented a complete departure by the tyrant from the humanitarian concepts of Marxism and Leninism. They were, on the contrary, an inescapable corollary of the class war, which Lenin from the first was prepared to wage with all rigor and ruthlessness. Marxist and Leninist, too, was the principle of forced labor; prisoners of the workers' regime were not to waste time reading books or writing poems or arguing with one another about abstruse points of political theory, as the revolutionary forefathers had often been allowed to do in the latter days of the tsarist dispensation. Class enemies under Communism would atone for their sins against the dialectic of history by wholesome and productive labor. Or if any should prove so unregenerate as to refuse to labor at building Communism, his proletarian jailers were simply to forget to feed him. *Si quis non vult operari, nec manducet:*[3] it is perhaps the one point at which the Marxian and the Pauline scriptures accord.

If there was a slight delay about getting this salutary program into practice, it was because of the Left Socialist Revolutionaries. Having helped the Bolsheviks in October 1917 they were allowed for a brief time afterward to share the power with them to control among other things the ministry of justice. These Left Essars, as the sarcastic Solzhenitsyn puts it, were tainted by "rotten petty-bourgeois concepts of freedom" and showed no disposition to adopt and enforce "the progressive principle of forced labor." But in July, 1918, the Left Essars were purged from the government, suppressed elsewhere, and haughtily relegated by Comrade Trotsky to the "dustbin of history." The prisons which had been pretty well emptied under the provisional government began to fill up rapidly with various sorts of class enemies and new prisons were created by seizing monasteries and convents and evicting the monks and other religious. The first of the great arctic prison camps was created in the Solovetsky Islands of the White Sea where a

famous monastery had existed since mediaeval times, to which a cathedral and a score of other churches had subsequently been added, and where a kremlin, or fortress, had been built by the tsars to discourage invasions from Scandinavia.

At Solovetsky there seem to have been at first few criminal prisoners and only a handful of Chekists. The administration seems to have been mostly in the hands of the prisoners themselves and discipline, often cruel and erratic, left oddly enough to former White officers from the armies of Kolchak, Denikin, and Wrangel. There were acute shortages of everything, but particularly of clothing, and in the arctic winter many prisoners had nothing to wear but burlap sacks into which apertures had been cut for the head, arms and legs. Prisoners condemned to be shot were required to strip themselves naked before being taken to the place of execution. Solzhenitsyn tells of a debonair aristocrat named Georgi Mikhailovich Osorgin, who was sentenced to die on the very day he was expecting a visit from his beautiful young wife.

> Osorgin begged his jailors not to spoil his wife's visit for her. He promised that he would not let her stay more than three days and that they could shoot him as soon as she left. And here is the kind of self-control this meant, the sort of thing we have forgotten because of the anathema we have heaped upon the aristocracy, we who whine at every petty misfortune and every petty pain. For three days he never left his wife's side, and he had to keep her from guessing the situation! He must not hint at it even in one single phrase! He must not allow his spirits to quaver. He must not allow his eyes to darken. Just once (his wife is alive and she remembers it now) when they were walking along the Holy Lake, she turned and saw that her husband had clutched his head in torment. "What's wrong?" "Nothing," he answered instantly. She could have stayed still longer, but he begged her to

leave. As the steamer pulled away from the wharf, he was already undressing to be shot.

V

Among the many other visitors to Solovetsky was the great proletarian literary light, Maxim Gorky. He seemed especially impressed by his inspection of the children's colony, where a bit of Potemkin magic, similar to that performed for Mrs. Roosevelt's benefit at Butyrik Prison,[4] had been hurriedly attempted. Gorky observed with pleasure the neatness and comfort of the appointments and the happy faces of the children who gathered round him and his entourage of G.P.U. officers.

> All of a sudden a fourteen-year-old boy said: "Listen, Gorky! Everything you see here is false. Do you want to know the truth? Shall I tell you?" Yes, nodded the writer. Yes, he wanted to know the truth. . . . And so everyone was ordered to leave, including the children and the accompanying *gaypayoosh-niki*—and the boy spent an hour and a half telling the whole story to the lanky old man. Gorky left the barracks, streaming tears. He was given a carriage to go to dinner at the villa of the camp chief. And the boys rushed back to the barracks. "Did you tell him about the *mosquito treatment*?" "Yes." "Did you tell him about the *pole torture*?" "Yes." "Did you tell him about the prisoners hitched up instead of horses?" "Yes." "And how they roll them down the stairs? And about being made to spend the night in the snow?" And it turned out that the truth-loving boy had told all. . . . But we don't even know his name. . . .
>
> On June 23 [1929] Gorky left Solovetski. Hardly had his steamer pulled away from the pier than they shot the boy. . . . And that was how faith in justice was instilled in the new generation.

VI

At about this point in Solzhenitsyn's narrative a strange and sinister genius named Naftaly Aronovich Frenkel makes his entrance. There is a persistent legend that it was Frenkel who conceived the whole scheme of the "corrective labor camps," as they are still called, but Solzhenitsyn, as we have seen, has traced them to Lenin and to the very first year of the Bolshevik dispensation, and the germinal idea of them back a century to Marx and Engels in their *Critique of the Gotha Program*. What Frenkel actually did, however, was to draw up and put into effect a reorganization of forced labor out of which arose the vast Gulag empire and enabled Stalin in a few short decades to transform Russia from a backward feudal and agricultural society into a powerful modern industrial state. Frenkel, observes Solzhenitsyn,

> was one of those successful men of action whom History awaits and summons to itself. . . . Every genuine prophet arrives when he is most acutely needed. Frenkel arrived at the Archipelago just at the beginning of the metastases.

He was not a Russian and perhaps never at any time a Marxist at heart. He was a Jew born in Constantinople and became at an early age a big-sale entrepreneur and a millionaire. He owned steamships and a newspaper and in late tsarist times controlled a great lumbering industry in the Black Sea region with headquarters at Mariupol in the southeastern Ukraine. In the First World War he is said to have trafficked for a time in arms, but in 1916, sensing the approach of revolution, he returned to Turkey, but was afterward lured back to Russia by the opportunities opened to his special talents by Lenin's New Economic Policy. Solzhenitsyn says that it was at the instigation of the G.P.U. that Frenkel opened a black market operation for the buying of gold and other valuables with paper rubles; the gold went into the Chekist treasury, but when the NEP came to an end Frenkel's ungrateful partners threw him into their Lubyanka. Whether it was there or at Solovetsky—

to which he was presently transferred—that Frenkel drew up his master plan of reorganization is uncertain. What is certain is that:

> One day in 1929 an airplane flew from Moscow to get Frenkel and brought him to an appointment with Stalin. The Best Friend of the Prisoners (and the Best Friend of the Chekists) talked interestedly with Frenkel for three hours. . . . It was Frenkel in person, apparently on that precise occasion, who proposed the all-embracing system of prisoners . . . which left no leeway to the camp chiefs and even less to the prisoner: everyone not engaged in providing essential services for the camp, not verified as being ill, and not undergoing correction in a punishment cell must drag his workload every day of his sentence. The world history of hard labor has never known such universality! It was Frenkel who outlined a unified system of redistribution of the meagre food supplies for the whole Archipelago—a scale for bread rations and a scale for hot-food rations which was adapted by him from the Eskimos: a fish on a pole held out in front of the running dog team. . . .

This was the Frenkel who told the Party bosses that, "We have to squeeze everything out of a prisoner in the first three months," meaning no doubt that this was about as long as the prisoner under camp conditions could be expected to carry his full work load and to draw his ration.

After the interview with Stalin Frenkel was of course set free and as a beginning placed in charge of the fearful White Sea-Baltic canal project to which so many tens of thousands of lives were to be sacrificed. Because of the absence of machinery and of such vital requirements as steel and concrete it was an almost impossible assignment, but by sheer will and ruthless expenditure of flesh and blood he managed somehow to push it through to completion. For this he received the Order of Lenin, though it was only the first of his many grandiose exploits of construction. The wastage of lives and manpower was the least of his problems, for there was an exhaustless reservoir of replacements which included virtually the whole population. Under one or another article of the Criminal Code almost anyone could be sent to the camps for anything, including Chekists whose leaders had fallen into disgrace. Solzhenitsyn offers some bizarre examples: a former diplomat sentenced for saying that Gorky was not a good writer; a certain Skvortsov given fifteen years for comparing the proletarian Gorky unfavorably with the bourgeois Pushkin; a tailor putting aside his needle by sticking it into a newspaper and inadvertently piercing the eye of a photograph of Kaganovich and thereby getting himself ten years for terrorism; a saleswoman who got the same sentence for the same offense because she allowed one of several pieces of soap she was holding to fall on a newspaper portrait of Stalin; a shepherd, enraged by a cow that refused to obey him, called her a "collective farm whore," and so became another terrorist; a young woman arrested after leaving a church and accused of having prayed—silently of course—for the death of Stalin. The list of such juridical lunacies could no doubt be extended indefinitely, and Solzhenitsyn in fact extends it over several pages.

Ten years ago, as he was working on the final phases of this book, Solzhenitsyn decided on a brief and surreptitious visit to the first great monument to Stalin's economic transformation of Russia on which the party propagandists had expended so much exultation—where Naftaly Frenkel won the first of his accolades and where such a multitude of famished and exhausted prisoners found their graves. Solzhenitsyn was astonished to discover that the world-famous White Sea-Baltic Canal was virtually devoid of traffic and presently learned the reason. It is only sixteen feet deep and hence unnavigable by vessels of any considerable draft.

It is also, he was told, frozen solid for about half of every year.

VII

These books, and especially Solzhenitsyn's, are much more than extended and important addenda to the long catalogue of titanic cruelties, maniacal stupidities, and ideologic bigotries compiled from the revelations of other survivors of the Gulag empire, beginning more than a generation ago with Professor Tchernavin's *I Speak for the Silent*. Of even greater and ominous import is their testimony to the almost universal corruption of a society in which treachery and slander are accounted the highest civic virtues, where out of fear, envy, secret malice, or mere ambition men, women, and even children are led to deliver neighbors, colleagues, bosom friends and even close kindred to the merciless political police and to the horror of the slave camps. Wives renounced their husbands, and *vice versa*, children renounced their parents. "And thus," says Solzhenitsyn, "they save their lives." Sometimes, too, their careers. One thinks for example of Sergei Vavilov who retained his job as head of the Soviet Academy of Sciences and the ostensible favor of Stalin, while his brother Nikolai Vavilov, the world-famous geneticist, after enduring four hundred ordeals by interrogation and refusing at any to confess his crimes against Darwin, Marx, and Trofim Lysenko, died of starvation in an arctic camp.

NOTES

[1] Not of course to be confused with Andrei Sakharov, the Nobel Prize-winner who is proving himself as much a headache to the Soviet Establishment as Solzhenitsyn had been.

[2] *Cf. Let History Judge: Origins and Consequences of Stalinism* (New York: Alfred A. Knopf, 1972).

[3] "If any should not work, neither should he eat." *II Thessalonians*, 3:10.

[4] See *The First Circle*, Chapter 54 (London: Collins & Harvill Press, 1968).

[XX, Summer 1976, 327–333]

[55]

The Kravchenko Case

DAVID J. DALLIN

David J(ulievich) Dallin (1889–1962) was a student at the University of St. Petersburg from 1907 to 1909. Arrested in 1909, he spent the years 1910–1917 in exile. Returning to Russia after the Revolution, he was an opposition deputy at the Moscow Soviet until 1921. Again forced to leave Russia, he lived in Germany, Poland, and France while writing for magazines and newspapers on political and economic questions from 1921 to 1940. Arriving in the United States in 1940, he went on to author eleven books on Soviet Russia, three of them written during World War II. He was one of the few historians to unravel the mysteries of Russian domestic and foreign policies during the critical years when they were proving so puzzling to many leaders in England and the United States. Dallin wrote this account of an escape to freedom shortly before his death on February 21.

WHEN VICTOR KRAVCHENKO, an official of the Soviet Purchasing Commission, arrived in Washington, D.C. from Russia in July 1943, his intention to quit the Soviet service was firm. It had ripened in the six long years that had passed since his arrest and maltreatment by the NKVD. Just as clear to him, however, were the hardships and difficulties attending such a step. He had no friends, and his only acquaintances were the few men and women working in his office and the members of his Communist cell in Washington, career Communists, always afraid and therefore loyal.

In his division in the Purchasing Commission, however, there were a few non-Communists who obviously belonged to another world: translators, technicians, and accountants employed to perform their specialized tasks and considered more or less as outsiders by the other officials.

Kravchenko often listened to their conversation and watched their behavior. Slowly it became clear to him that here he might find a channel to the non-Soviet world. With great care, he devised a plan for approaching the interpreter in his division, Mrs. Rita Holiday, an immigrant, and Kravchenko knew from his party cell that Communists were to use caution in dealing with Rita Holiday.

On Sundays Kravchenko occasionally went to the Library of Congress to look through Russian émigré writings. He discovered a number of publications—books and magazines—in which his own ideas and his own criticism of the Stalinist system found clear and adequate expression.

One Monday Mrs. Holiday chanced to ask him how he had spent his Sunday. Kravchenko decided to risk telling her about his visit to the Library, about the books he had seen, and the sentiments they had expressed. He wanted to see if she would denounce him, as every Soviet employee is expected to do. Days passed and nothing happened. Kravchenko's confidence in Mrs. Holiday grew as his contacts with her increased. Finally Kravchenko asked her to help him contact politically independent, non-Communist people, speaking Russian. Thus it was that Rita put Kravchenko in touch with me.

One evening in late January 1944, a tall, dark-haired gentlemen of about thirty-five or forty came to my home and introduced himself as Vladimir Sergeevich Gromov, the name by which we were to know Kravchenko until he chose to reveal his real name. I had anticipated Gromov's visit with mixed feelings. By that time my reputation as an anti-Communist writer was established. It seemed more than strange that a Soviet official would dare visit me at home if he was not himself a secret Soviet agent. And if he was, what was his real motive? This question was to worry me for a long time.

During his first visit Kravchenko asked no questions. Most of the time he did the talking—about his life in Russia, the Communist party, collective farms, the industrial plant where he had served as manager before the war, and about his experience with the NKVD in 1937. He told me that his job with the Purchasing Commission required him to travel frequently to New York where he supervised the loading of cargo ships for the Soviet Union. Only at the very end of his visit did he reveal his intention to defect and to remain in this country: "For years," he said, "I have been preparing myself for this moment; I have long wanted to go abroad so I might tell the truth about the real state of affairs in Russia."

The next evening he came again, and again stayed late into the night. The more he told about himself, the more interest-

ing he became. Still my suspicions were not dissipated. He told us that his wife, against her will, was connected with the NKVD. He wanted her to join him abroad so that they could defect together. He mentioned further that his superiors in Washington had offered him a better job which would entitle him to have his wife brought to this country. But it was also possible that he would be ordered back to Russia during the coming summer.

Slowly his background was becoming clearer to me. The son of a railway worker, he had not enjoyed a good education. At the time when he studied engineering, the Technical Institute was still the scene of chaotic Soviet educational experiments. Therefore, Kravchenko did not acquire the knowledge, experience, and broad outlook characteristic of the young Russian intellectuals before the revolution. By his own confession he had been a staunch and devoted member of the Communist party. When he talked to me, it was apparent that much of what he had embraced as a younger man, what had given sense to his earlier life was still very much alive. Despite a bitter personal disappointment, despite his hatred for Stalin, the NKVD, the kolkhoz system, he could not conceive the future of Russia in terms of a private economy. Nor did he admit the possibility of a restoration of the old political system, least of all the Russian monarchy.

Personal comfort and the amenities of life meant very much to "Gromov." Not without pride he told us that his salary in Moscow had reached 3,000 rubles a month. At the same time he had great sympathy for the social underdog in Russia as well as in America, and the conviction that social changes would one day abolish poverty and oppression was still alive in his heart. He was interesting to me because I was sure that thousands of the new Soviet intellectuals combine this urge for freedom and comfort with great ideals which—right or wrong—will guide them even after all traces of Stalinism disappear.

A week or two later Gromov came back to New York and again spent a few evenings at my home. He was preoccupied now with his plans for defection, and hundreds of details had to be considered. One major question tortured him. Since he entered this country as a Soviet official, would he not be deported home if he quit the Soviet service? I had no doubt that he would be permitted to stay here as a political refugee, but he could not rely on my conviction. I, therefore, had to help get an authoritative answer to this question.

Yet even as I committed myself to help him, I was very much aware that the man remained an enigma. Here is a Soviet official—I said to myself—who has lived in Russia all his life, who has been a party member for fifteen years, who is perhaps even now being shadowed by the Washington NKVD, and he regularly visits a "reactionary" to discuss with him the techniques of desertion. Is he not an *agent-provocateur* planted by the secret service of the Soviet Embassy and intending to "expose" me and any others who help him?

Toward the end of February, Gromov told me that he would have no assignments in New York for some time and therefore no opportunity to see me. In order to continue our planning, he asked me to meet him in a small Pennsylvania town which he would have to visit for two days. He would call me from Washington and give me the details. His call came, and on the appointed day I boarded the train for Lancaster, Pennsylvania. On my way to his hotel, I decided to discuss matters with him in the lobby instead of going to his room, just in case this was a final move in a well-laid trap. But the lobby was full of smoking, drinking, and shouting people, and there was no place where our delicate problems could be discussed. With considerable misgivings, I agreed to go to his room on the fourth floor. As it turned out, my fears were groundless; his only intent was to continue our planning.

For a few hours we discussed various matters. Gromov elaborated on his concern about his legal status and his financial situation. I asked, in turn, when approximately he intended to make his break. He replied within a month or so; a longer delay was risky because of his possible recall to Russia.

After we parted, I decided on my own course of action to help "Gromov." The man to see was William Bullitt, our first Ambassador to the USSR and one of the few prominent Americans I knew. Bullitt was reliable; the war climate had not turned his head, and I was sure he would not betray us to our "great ally." But after I had told him my story, he appeared reluctant to offer an opinion. He disappeared long enough to telephone someone, and when he returned he asked only where I could be reached the next morning. "There are agencies," he said enigmatically, "which will have to deal with the Gromov affair." That was all.

Next morning I was interviewed by a man of about thirty-five, dark-haired and rather bold. He gave his name as Watson and told me he was there at Mr. Bullitt's request; he mentioned J. Edgar Hoover as his chief. I repeated the questions Gromov wanted answered. After listening for a period, Watson suddenly, and curtly, informed me that there was no Vladimir Gromov in the Purchasing Commission or in any other Soviet agency in this country. Like Bullitt, Watson was reluctant to comment on the case, and I interpreted his hesitation as a suspicion that "Gromov" was in reality an NKVD agent.

Watson intimated that someone would probably contact me soon—and this was the meager result of my trip to Washington.

About mid-March "Gromov" again appeared in New York. He was not happy about the report of my dealings with the FBI and asked me for the name and address of Mr. Watson. He now revealed his true name as Victor Kravchenko.

A new question was bothering Victor: should he herald his desertion with a comprehensive political statement to the press and thus arouse the energies of the secret service and jeopardize his life? Or should he quit in silence and simply mail his documents to the Soviet authorities and disappear so that the NKVD would get no clue in their search and no reason to become very much interested? He still feared that no real protection would be given him by the U.S. government, and this made him afraid of the first alternative. And the second plan—to disappear unnoticed—was unrealistic. The Soviet Embassy would certainly seek to persuade the American authorities that the defector was guilty of such crimes as the embezzlement of money or the acceptance of bribes from American clients of the Purchasing Commission. Then Kravchenko would be obliged to make refutations which might not seem entirely convincing. Even if then permitted to stay in this country, his name would become associated with obscure rumors. The NKVD is a great expert in such things, and the only way to disarm it in this case was to seize the initiative. "You must put yourself," I therefore told him, "under the protection of American public opinion."

Not entirely convinced and still undecided, Kravchenko returned to Washington.

THE REASON THE FBI was hesitant is obvious: if Kravchenko had been a stooge sent by the NKVD, he could then have reported to the Soviet agency on the "techniques" used by the FBI to lure Soviet officials into the American net. But Kravchenko interpreted their reluctance as a refusal and decided on a dangerous step—to go himself to FBI headquarters— and this in a city where several hundred Soviet officials were stationed.

Without telling me his plans, he one day telephoned Mr. Watson of the FBI, gave his name, and asked for an interview in the evening hours. Assuming the great risk of being observed, he walked into FBI headquarters on Pennsylvania Avenue and stayed from seven until eleven P.M. (this must have been between the fifteenth and twentieth of March, 1944). The discussion was friendly, but Kravchenko failed to get a clear commitment from the FBI. Nevertheless, he now decided that on the first of April he would quit his job. This date was convenient because it was a Saturday, and it gave him a weekend to make good his escape.

My next job was to find a channel to the press. I got in touch with Joseph Shaplen of *The New York Times* and, without mentioning names or dates, told him of the imminent defection. I inquired whether, despite the wartime atmosphere of friendliness, the *Times* would publish the anti-Communist statement of this Soviet official. Shaplen was sure the *Times* would run it, particularly if it were an "exclusive" story.

The next days were uneventful. On Saturday, April 1, Kravchenko went to the accountant of the Purchasing Commission (the office was open half a day on Saturdays), got his pay, and accounted for every penny so that no embezzlement charges could be made against him. Kravchenko complained to his colleagues of a headache and fever. They advised him (much as he had hoped they would) to stay in bed for a few days. He assented, adding that this indisposition might cause him to be absent on Monday. In the afternoon Kravchenko packed his two suitcases, waited until dark, and then went to the railroad station. At the entrance to the station he saw a Soviet colonel walking up and down. For a moment he was petrified. Quickly he slipped by, entered a coach car for New York, and sat immobile for the four-hour trip which carried him from Soviet servitude to freedom.

I met Kravchenko at Penn Station, and together we went by taxi to a hotel where I had reserved a small room for him. When we entered the room and switched on the little lamp, Kravchenko exclaimed: "But this is a coffin . . . a room for committing suicide!" I tried to remind him that economy was imperative and that it was only a temporary arrangement, but he kept repeating, "So this is how my new life starts. . . ."

The following day Kravchenko and Shaplen met at my home to prepare Kravchenko's political statement. Victor did the writing and Shaplen the translation, a process which involved much give-and-take. During these discussions Kravchenko frequently got angry, nervous, and aggressive. In turn, Shaplen, who was used to quick newspaper work, also got irritated. As they clashed, I grew increasingly worried.

At this time I knew Kravchenko mainly from his absorbing personal stories. I did not realize that his experience at home had made him bitter and hot-tempered. Now as I saw him disputing words, rejecting suggestions, insisting on trifles, I asked myself how this extremely nervous man with no knowledge of English, no money, and virtually no friends could manage to live. I felt an enormous responsibility not only for his security but for his very life.

That evening as Kravchenko and Shaplen continued their discussions, I telephoned Eugene Lyons and insisted on seeing him immediately. After hearing my whole story, Lyons observed that the climate of wartime pro-Sovietism would result in little support for Victor, and he would advise him to return to the Soviet fold if that was still possible.

With a heavy heart I returned home. This was precisely what I myself thought; now it was confirmed by a man in whom I had considerable confidence. I decided to tell Kravchenko frankly our opinion; in the bottom of my heart I hoped, however, that he would reject our advice. By the time I returned, Shaplen had left, carrying with him Kravchenko's political statement. I began to talk; I explained all the hardships that lay ahead, his precarious position, and the great risks. I offered to take him to the station and get him back before anyone could notice the "escapade." His reply: "No. Definitely, no."

There was a finality in this no. No arguments, no discussion. He rejected our advice emphatically. I was greatly relieved, almost happy for him and for myself. That same night, on his insistence, I took him to my apartment, where he stayed until we could arrange other more comfortable and relatively secure quarters.

The following day passed uneventfully. It was the Monday Kravchenko was supposed to be ill, and his superiors were thus unaware of his defection. His statement had not yet appeared in the press. After dark we went for a walk, not realizing in the comparative calm of those hours that this was the last night Kravchenko was an unknown person, a "man in the street," and also, at least for a number of years, it was his last night of relative security. It was late when we stopped for a copy of *The New York Times*. On the front page, dated Tuesday, April 4, 1944, was Kravchenko's statement. It read in part:

> For many years I have worked loyally for the people of my country in the service of

the Soviet Government and have followed closely the development of Soviet policy in its various stages. For the sake of the Soviet Union's interests and her people I tried hard to overlook many aspects of the situation which were repugnant and alarming. But I cannot keep silent any longer. The interests of the war effort and of my suffering, tortured people compel me to keep silent on many things, but they demand that I speak out on fundamentals of the policy pursued today by the Soviet Government and its leaders affecting the war and the hopes of all peoples for a new international order of peace and reconstruction.

I can no longer support the double-faced political maneuvers directed at one and the same time toward collaboration with the United States and Britain while pursuing aims incompatible with such collaboration.

The real plans and aims of the Soviet Government as distinct from its public professions, are in contradiction with the interests and the needs of the Russian people and of the cause for which the peoples of the United Nations are fighting. While professing to seek the establishment of democracy in countries liberated from fascism, the Soviet Government at home has failed to take a single serious step toward granting elementary liberties to the Russian people.

The Russian people are subjected, as before, to unspeakable oppression and cruelties, while the NKVD (Soviet secret police), acting through thousands of spies, continues to wield its unbridled domination over the peoples of Russia. In the territories cleared of the Nazi invaders, the Soviet Government is re-establishing its political regime of lawlessness and violence, while prisons and concentration camps continue to function, as before. The hopes of political and social reforms cherished by the Russian people at the beginning of the war have proved to be empty illusions.

I maintain that more than any other people the Russian people require that they be granted elementary political liberties—genuine freedom of press and speech, freedom from want and freedom from fear. What the Russian people have had from their Government has been only lip service to these freedoms. For years they have lived in constant dread and want. The Russian people have earned a new deal by their immeasurable sacrifices, which have saved the country as well as the existing regime itself, and through which they have dealt such decisive blows to fascism and determined the course of war.

Being aware of the methods of struggle employed by the Soviet rulers against political opponents, I fully expect that they will now be used against me—the methods of slander, provocation and possibly worse. I declare that I have never committed any acts detrimental to my people, the ruling party and the Soviet Government, and have always tried to perform my duties to my country, my party and my people honestly and conscientiously.

I hope to have the opportunity of continuing to devote my experience and energy to the war effort in this country. I, therefore, place myself under the protection of American public opinion.

Kravchenko had added in an interview:

I can no more imagine Churchill as a member of the Communist party than I can conceive of Stalin without the Comintern or its substance. The Comintern continues to function but by different methods and in other forms.

The story was a sensation! It produced its greatest shock in Soviet circles in Washington. We soon learned that in Kravchenko's division of the Purchasing Commission, all work ceased on that Tuesday: people raced in and out; small conferences were held; telephone calls about the "traitor" went on incessantly; everyone was excited and presumably indignant. Not a few of his colleagues and superiors had reason to fear for their own fate since, in Soviet tradition, someone had to be made responsible. The precise punishment meted out to the scapegoats has remained a secret. It is known that a few of Kravchenko's superiors and party supervisors were ordered back to Moscow and they have never returned.

As SOON AS Kravchenko's statement appeared in the *Times,* Mr. Watson of the FBI called me in order to locate Kravchenko immediately. A group of men from the New York FBI office wanted to visit him. I was amazed at the changed attitude of the "Bureau"; formerly so cool and reluctant, they now were insistent and vigorous. It seemed unlikely that Kravchenko's public statement alone had convinced J. Edgar Hoover that he was sincere.

Conversations between the FBI and Kravchenko grew frequent, even though the latter was not in a mood to reveal everything he knew. "I could tell you a lot of things about the NKVD," he said frankly, "but I do not intend to reveal any military secrets, even if I knew them." He still considered himself a Russian anti-Stalinist, not an American patriot. What he wanted from the FBI was protection; the recent tragic fate of other Communist defectors was well known to him. The FBI pressed him to work for the agency in return for an apartment, car, revolver, and one or two guards. But Kravchenko refused; he had not broken with the Soviets to become a servant of the police, even in a democratic country.

Without letting him know, the FBI watched him from time to time, shadowing him on the street, in elevators, in trains. Its intent may have been both to find out whether he still had any contacts with Soviet agencies, and to discover if he was being shadowed by the NKVD. The FBI tapped his telephone—and mine. As a matter of fact, Soviet agencies in this country were shadowing Kravchenko and gathering information about him. In addition, there was frantic press and diplomatic activity to have him surrendered to the Soviet authorities. As for Victor himself, he knew he was being followed; beyond that, he frequently could not distinguish NKVD from FBI men, nor could he know their motives or plans.

Shortly thereafter, Kravchenko started publishing a series of articles in *The Cosmopolitan* magazine. It was then that he received a letter in Russian from a Mrs. Steiner in Detroit, who expressed great sympathy for Kravchenko and his courageous act. Victor answered, and a correspondence developed, in the course of which Mrs. Steiner and her husband, both German refugees, invited him to their home in Detroit. I tried to dissuade Kravchenko from the folly of going to visit people he did not know; but he was intent on living quietly for a few weeks and wanted to meet these devoted friends. What he did not know was that the Steiners had already determined that there were no legal objections to former German citizens' harboring a refugee from Soviet service during the war with Germany.

Kravchenko left by the night train. Early next morning he called from Detroit to tell me a strange story. At the Detroit station he had been met by the Steiners—but also by three men obviously waiting for him. When Victor drove away with the Steiners, they were followed by the three men. Unwilling to reveal his address to the strangers, Steiner drove aimlessly through the city, but he failed to lose the shadowing group. Finally he stopped at a police station to ask for help, and only then did the other car disappear.

Obviously the NKVD had learned of Victor's trip to Detroit and had assigned its agents to find out his whereabouts, and possibly to act. As long as he stayed in Detroit, the NKVD continued to shadow him. It all was very disturbing and certainly did not provide conditions for the "quiet" rest which Victor had longed for.

Meantime I committed an error of the

first magnitude, an error which I did not recognize as such and for which I was not really responsible. In an effort to find friends for Kravchenko I got in touch with a number of Russian-speaking people, interested in Russia—among them Russian émigrés. I tried to be very cautious in this choice, of course. I could not have suspected, however, that one of the "anti-Stalinists" whom I put in touch with Kravchenko was Mark Zborowsky, a secret agent of the NKVD. (It was not until 1955 that the truth about his activities was revealed.) Zborowsky, whom I had met in France in the late 'thirties, posed as a Trotskyite and Stalin-hater. He came to the United States in 1941, and it was precisely this agent whom I presented to Kravchenko as his "protection" against the NKVD. That nothing happened to Victor is certainly due to the reluctance of the Soviet police to commit crimes on American soil at a time when United States aid was still needed in the war.

THE SOVIET GOVERNMENT made several attempts to have Kravchenko extradited by the U.S. authorities. At times Moscow apparently entertained real hopes that the "deserter" would be turned over for investigation and punishment. It took the Soviets exactly a fortnight to decide how to open conversations with the State Department in the issue. Referring to Kravchenko as an official on "temporary" duty in the United States, the Soviet Embassy informed the State Department in its note of April 18, 1944, that Kravchenko was no longer connected with the Purchasing Commission, and that, since he had been serving in the Soviet armed forces during his stay in Washington, he was guilty of "deserting" his post. The short note contained no request for extradition nor any other demands; no answer was expected or given to this communication.

It was only on May 6, 1944 that the Embassy presented an *Aide-mémoire* to the State Department. Victor Kravchenko, the document stated, inspector of the Purchasing Commission of the USSR, being on active military service and temporarily on duty in the United States, had violated the military code of the USSR and his own personal military duty. "Deserter" Kravchenko, the note went on, had covered up his crime by a slanderous statement trying to give it political coloration, hoping thereby to avoid extradition. The note concluded with a direct request that the United States return Kravchenko to the Soviet government "for prosecution for desertion."

The State Department never seriously intended to comply with the Soviet demand; as a matter of fact, its attitude was negative from the beginning. Only Harry Hopkins, then in regular contact with the Soviet Embassy on lend-lease matters, once asked Charles Bohlen why "we keep a Soviet deserter here." Bohlen explained, and Hopkins dropped the matter.

This was wartime, however, and the Soviet Union was an ally; furthermore the second front was finally scheduled to be opened in a matter of weeks. At such a moment the State Department preferred to stall and maneuver rather than to give a blunt refusal. No written reply was given to the Soviet note despite repeated prodding from Ambassador Andrei Gromyko. Half a year passed, and there was still no answer. On November 24, the Embassy submitted a new *Aide-mémoire*. Referring to the note of May 6, it stated that the Soviet government was sure it would meet with full understanding on the part of the U. S. government, since desertion in wartime was particularly "unsupportable." The document reaffirmed the request of May 6 and stressed its hope to receive a prompt and favorable reply.

Secretary of State Edward Stettinius

obviously felt that some kind of answer was called for. In a friendly letter to the Soviet ambassador (dated December 18), he offered assurance that he personally, along with the Department of Justice, was working on the Kravchenko matter. A preliminary investigation by the Justice Department, Stettinius wrote, revealed that, in the absence of any extradition treaty or any other Soviet-American agreement covering cases of this nature, the issue of deportation fell within the purview of the domestic laws of the United States. The Executive Branch of the Government, Stettinius wrote, could act only with and under the authority of the pertinent law of the United States. Delaying a definitive answer, Stettinius once again assured the embassy that he was making every effort to have the Department of Justice expedite its consideration of the case and that he hoped to be able to give further information in the near future.

Not satisfied with this delay, Gromyko went to see Stettinius on December 26. Gromyko referred to the fact that he had raised the Kravchenko issue several times before and that his government was "very anxious" to receive an answer. Stettinius, in turn, referred to his note of the previous week, but Gromyko retorted that the note "did not say a thing." Once again the Secretary of State assured Gromyko that he was giving the matter his personal attention and that the moment he could make a statement, he would communicate promptly with the Soviet Embassy.

On January 5, 1945, the State Department requested the Soviet Embassy to supply proof that Kravchenko belonged to the Red Army at the time he defected. On January 13, 1945, the Soviet Embassy replied with a new note. It summed up all information on Kravchenko which the Embassy had given previously; apparently the Soviets were aware that their argument concerning Kravchenko's status as a member of the Soviet military force was not foolproof. When Kravchenko's visa to enter the United States had been requested in Moscow in 1943, he had been referred to simply as an engineer of the People's Commissariat of Local Industry. Therefore in its new note the Embassy gave a detailed record of Kravchenko's service with governmental agencies and the Red Army. It added that when he left for the United States, Kravchenko, like a number of other military persons, remained in the Soviet armed forces.

Soon after this Soviet note the Yalta conference took place. Among other things, the repatriation of Soviet citizens, chiefly from German-occupied Europe, was discussed; Soviet military personnel in the West were to be turned over to the Soviet authorities. This agreement could have had significant repercussions on the Kravchenko case. Chances were that, in the climate of strengthened American-Soviet friendship, the U. S. government would accede to Soviet demands.

One day in the early spring of 1945, at his regular meeting with his FBI contacts, Kravchenko heard with some trepidation a frank statement by one of the FBI officers: "We cannot foresee how the President will act if Moscow continues to insist on your extradition. Don't blame us if one day we have to take you to Ellis Island until your fate is decided. Our advice to you is to go underground so we can't find you or arrest you. If you should be arrested, you must fight the extradition order. In this country no agency has the right, without due process of law, to extradite you to Russia and thus condemn you to death. You must find a lawyer; your friends must alert the press; and you yourself must protest, fight, and resist."

This friendly, but disheartening, advice proved superfluous, however, because things shortly took a turn for the better.

On April 12, 1945, the day President

Roosevelt died, and over a year after Kravchenko's defection, the State Department finally delivered a definite answer to the Soviet Embassy. The U. S. government had explored every avenue, the note said, to find a solution satisfactory to the Soviet government and at the same time consistent with the laws of this country. The Department of Justice had reached the conclusion that although Soviet domestic law may have viewed Kravchenko's status as a military one, he had been granted a U. S. visa as an engineer and not as a member of the Red Army; therefore he must be dealt with under U. S. law as a civilian. As a civilian he could be deported only as the result of a regular statutory deportation proceeding in which he would be entitled to obtain permission to depart from this country voluntarily to any country of his choice. The note concluded that there appeared to be no legal basis upon which Kravchenko could be turned over to the Soviet authorities for prosecution.

This was the end of the extended diplomatic correspondence on the Kravchenko case. The Soviet engineer had gained the right of asylum in this country and from then on his personal security was guaranteed. One mystery remained, however. For years the FBI tried to identify and locate the Soviet spy who had informed the NKVD of Kravchenko's plans and activities. The agency had obvious and unquestionable indications that the NKVD in the United States was in possession of this information. It wasn't until 1955 that Alexander Orlov, formerly a high ranking NKVD official, who had been living in this country for over a decade, pointed to a certain "Etienne," as the carrier of this information. Closer investigation proved that "Etienne" was none other than the Soviet spy whose real name was Mark Zborowsky, the man in whose "protection" I had placed Kravchenko against NKVD actions. In 1944 Zborowsky had been assigned by the NKVD to observe and report fully on Kravchenko's activities.

As time passed, everything was quieted down for Victor Kravchenko. Extradition was ruled out and kidnapping by the Soviet police was made rather difficult by precautionary measures and the great caution which was observed by him. A few articles in *The Cosmopolitan* magazine provided the means for existence, and then, in 1947, when his best-seller *I Chose Freedom* appeared in the United States and was translated into all languages of the world, Kravchenko's star rose high. Even today, despite everything, Kravchenko prefers obscurity to publicity successes. Because, as the Russians say, habit is the man's second nature. . . .

[VI, Summer 1962, 267–276]

[56]

The Last of the Anarchists

FRANCIS RUSSELL

Francis Russell (1910–   ) has been called "one of the liveliest and most versatile essayists in the United States," as seen in his contributions to American Heritage, Antioch Review, Harvard Magazine, Horizon, Modern Age, National Review, The New England Quarterly, The New York Review of Books, *and* The Observer. *Among his many books are* The World of Dürer, 1471–1528 (1967), A City in Terror: The 1919 Boston Police Strike (1975), *and* Sacco & Vanzetti: The Case Resolved (1986). *Now living in Cape Cod, he has been studying and writing on Sacco and Vanzetti for over twenty-five years, retelling their story convincingly and with great narrative force, as well as describing the equally fascinating "keepers of the flame": the scholars, politicians, teachers, and writers who have kept the case of Sacco and Vanzetti alive in the years since they died.*

ON THE EVENING of January 11, 1943, a tall middle-aged man in a wide-brimmed hat locked the door of his small third-floor office in the building at the corner of New York's 15th Street and Fifth Avenue. He then walked down the narrow darkened stairs—a little stiffly because of his bulk. A great scar running down his left cheek showed up even in the shadows, in spite of the pointed gray beard grown to conceal it. He looked watchfully aggressive, but this air of subdued pugnacity was belied by the mildness of his eyes behind his pince-nez. From his appearance he might have been Scandinavian. He was accompanied by a smaller, darker man, who was obviously Italian.

The building had two entrances, one on 15th Street and one on Fifth Avenue. The men walked out of the 15th Street entrance into the dank, dim street and headed eastward for Fifth Avenue. The

time was 9:30 P.M. After they had covered the seventy-five feet to the corner, they crossed over. They had intended to stop at a tavern on the other side of Fifth Avenue, but momentarily the traffic signal was against them. As they stood waiting under the dimmed street light, a man stepped up behind them, snatched a pistol from his pocket and fired four shots. The bearded man dropped to the pavement, one bullet in his back, a second imbedded in his brain. The other two shots went wild. Before the smaller man could grasp what had happened, the gunman sprang into a dark sedan that disappeared down 15th Street. The bearded man died almost instantly. He was Carlo Tresca, the last leader of the American anarchists.

From his haberdashery shop at 100 Fifth Avenue, Samuel Sherman heard the shots, saw the car disappear, and called the police. When they arrived and searched

649

the vicinity, they found a loaded .38 calibre revolver in an ashcan at the Fifth Avenue entrance to the building. Since the bullets found in Tresca's body were from a .32 calibre automatic, they reasoned that there must have been a gunman waiting at each entrance. After the first gunman had fired, the second had evidently thrown away his pistol and slipped off.

Two passers-by had a fleeting glimpse of the murderer. He seemed to them a man of between thirty-five and forty, about five feet five inches tall. Several hours later the police found a Ford sedan abandoned beside the 18th Street subway entrance near Seventh Avenue, five blocks northwest of the site of the murder. All four doors of the sedan were open, and a group of keys hung from the ignition lock. Tresca's friend, Tony Ribavich, recognized the car from its unusual side mirror. A driver of a similar car with the same sort of mirror had tried to run Tresca down two days before as he and Ribavich were walking past the New School for Social Research on West 12th Street.

The abandoned car had been licensed in the name of Pappas, a non-existent man with a non-existent Queen's County address. The Con-Field Automobile Company at 1902 Broadway had sold it to "Charles Pappas" on December 22. Two days after the killing the police arrested a thirty-two-year old paroled convict, Carmine Galante, who had been seen entering the car only an hour and a half before Tresca was shot.

On that evening Galante had made his routine weekly report to the Parole Office at 80 Centre Street. He left the building at 8:10. Because the supervisor of parole inspectors had learned that Galante was again associating with criminals, he assigned two parole officers to follow him. During this period of gasoline rationing the officers did not have the use of a car,

so they followed Galante on foot, expecting him to take the subway. Instead, about a block away, he stepped into a Ford sedan that had apparently been waiting for him. The officers could not follow him further but they managed to get the number on the car's license: 1C-9272. It was the same number as the one on the plates of the abandoned Ford.

On his arrest Galante denied that he had been in any car that night. He said that he had gone uptown by subway with a girl to the Hollywood Theatre, and had seen Casablanca. Under questioning he contradicted himself, stating he had met the girl after the show. He was vague about the details of the film. His story was that after the show he had gone to his home in an outlying section of Brooklyn where he arrived at half-past ten—in spite of the fact that the length of Casablanca (102 minutes) would have made this impossible.

Galante had already served two terms in prison. In 1926 he had been sentenced to two-and-a-half to five years for attempted armed robbery. Then, in 1930, he was apprehended with two other petty gangsters holding up a collector for a Brooklyn brewery. Before being taken into custody he fired four shots at the police. For this holdup he was sentenced to fifteen years in Sing Sing penitentiary. To avoid a longer sentence as a second offender, he pleaded guilty to "attempted robbery in the first degree, unarmed." The judge and the district attorney accepted this plea, and Galante's lawyer thanked them for their "wonderful co-operation."

When Galante was arrested in 1943, he told the police he was employed by the Knickerbocker Trucking Company. This turned out to be a shadowy concern with desk room at 520 Broadway and only one truck. For three months a trucking company had been paying Galante twenty-five dollars a week—for doing nothing.

After his arrest he was held in the Tombs for eight months. Although the police were convinced that he had killed Tresca, they could obtain no confession from him. "Prison-wise and a tough witness to crack," the district attorney described him. Galante had never known Tresca or anything about him, and he would have had no motive for killing him—so the police reasoned—unless he was hired for the job. In some shadowy way Galante seemed to be associated with the gangster chief Vito Genovese, and through him with the Brooklyn racketeer group known as Murder, Incorporated.

From the Tombs Galante was returned to Sing Sing for violation of his parole, and on completion of his term he was released in December, 1944.

In September, 1943, a second murder suspect was arrested. He was Frank Nuccio, a small-time racketeer who lived less than a block from where the police had picked up Galante. Nuccio ran an eight-car garage; it was here that the escape car had been kept until the night of the killing. The police had traced the garage through the keys found in the ignition lock of the Ford. A locksmith who had made one of the keys said that he had changed the lock on Nuccio's garage a few hours before Tresca had been shot—presumably to prevent the sedan from being returned there afterwards. Nuccio—as uninformative as Galante—was held for two months; then his bail was reduced and he was released.

There the investigation came to an end. On various unrevealed grounds neither the district attorney's office nor the mayor nor the United States Attorney General seemed to have much interest in solving the mystery of Tresca's death. "Is there some political reason?" Tresca's old Boston friend Aldino Felicani asked in an open letter to Mayor LaGuardia, published in his miniscule anarchist monthly,

Countercurrent. "Would it complicate our international relations . . . if the forces which inspired that murder were revealed at this time?" Those questions remained unanswered, as well as the major question: Why was Carlo Tresca killed? The answer was there, but Tresca's whole life lay behind it.

In his earlier years Tresca had been a doctrinaire anarchist, a believer in—if not a practitioner of—the propaganda of the deed. But as he grew older—in spite of his broad-brimmed anarchist hat and black butterfly tie—he became less involved in anarchist theory and more and more concerned with the rights and freedom of individuals. Fascists and communists—those who talked of breaking eggs to make omelets and who would suppress the individual for the sake of the cause—came to hate him. Others, whatever their politics or religion, could not resist his abounding personality. Even the police who arrested him became his friends—and he was arrested some thirty-six times, on charges ranging from blasphemy, libel, disorderly conduct, incitement to riot and criminal obscenity to conspiracy, sedition and murder. Even the district attorney, who denounced him as an enemy of society, would eat and drink at his table. He relished the mere fact of being alive, and he loved to the full the personal things life had to offer him—women and wine, talk, food and song. "Big, bearded, boastful, life-loving," his friend Eugene Lyons saw him as, "and as unlike the embittered anarchist of popular tradition as possible. Priest-baiting and spaghetti were among his chief passions, and his hairbreadth escapes from enemy bullets everywhere, from Abruzzi to the copper empire of Montana, were ample proof of his charmed life." Suzanne La Follette remembered him as "tall, very heavy, with gray hair and beard and the kindest blue eyes twinkling through glasses. (If my memory is correct he wore a pince-nez with a black cord.) He always wore a black hat with a rather low crown and wide brim. Altogether a most impressive looking man; warmly affectionate toward his friends, wise and humorous, without a touch of the fanatic about him."

Tresca's funeral was held in the old Manhattan Opera House on 34th Street; even that building was too small.

> It was packed [Suzanne La Follette wrote] and as one looked and listened one knew that these people were no mere sensation-seekers; they were mourners—mourners of all sorts and conditions, sharing a common grief and a common awareness that with Carlo a vital warmth had gone out of their lives that could never be rekindled.

Carlo Tresca was born in 1879 in Sulmonia, ancient hill town in the Abruzzi set in a high valley of the Apennines. Like Galleani, Malatesta and many of the anarchist leaders, he came from an upper-class family, his father having been the wealthiest landowner in the vicinity. He became a socialist before he left school, and at the age of twenty he organized a local branch of the Socialist party and mustered and marched his father's peasants behind the red flag. He also founded a little revolutionary paper called *Il Germe* (The Seed). Oddly enough, his radical views caused no family conflict. Eventually he was even able to convert his father to a socialist point of view. At twenty-two the buoyant and irrepressible Carlo had become secretary of the Italian Railroad Workers' Union and had distinguished himself as one of the most popular of the undesirable citizens in southern Italy. The tone of *Il Germe* was hardly scholastic. Tresca took politicians and landlords as his natural target, and his aim was exuberantly accurate. Soon he was indicted for libelling the political boss of Sulmonia, his father's friend. To defend their bright young man the socialists sent two celebrated lawyers, one of them the world-famous criminologist Enrico Ferri. Tresca was so certain that Ferri had won his case that while the jury was debating on a verdict he went across the square to a café to celebrate with his friends. While they were drinking a toast to Garibaldi and the new war for freedom, the bailiff appeared on the courthouse steps shouting "Carlo! Carlo!" Tresca dashed over to the courthouse with a bottle of wine in one hand and a piece of cheese in the other to hear himself pronounced guilty and sentenced to a year-and-a-half imprisonment. His lawyers entered an appeal, he was released—and then he *forgot* to file his appeal!

With incarceration near, Tresca fled to Switzerland and an exile that would endure a lifetime. For a while he associated with a group of Italian radicals in Geneva. Among those noisy café exiles, one of the noisiest was a comrade by the name of Benito Mussolini. He and Tresca did not take to each other. Mussolini thought that Tresca was not enough of a radical. Tresca thought that Mussolini talked too much.

In 1904 Tresca sailed for the United States. He still considered himself a socialist, although in those days the boundaries between socialists, communists, and anarchists were much less rigid than they were later to be. For several years in the coal mining district near Pittsburgh he edited *La Plebe*, the paper of the Italian Socialist Federation. Whatever remaining energy he had—and it was much—he spent organizing and leading his Italian compatriates, the workers who had now replaced the Irish at the base of the American economic pyramid as a source of exploitable labor. The America that he knew in those years was scarcely more than an extension of Italy. He learned only a few words of English; he would never really master the language. After a few months editing *La Plebe* he found himself in jail for libelling the local priest. On his release he was warned by the more militantly pious to leave town. Shortly afterwards, as he was leaving his office, someone seized him from behind and slashed his face with a razor from the left nostril down to his collar. Instinctively he raised his shoulder and managed to protect his jugular vein. Spurting blood, he staggered into a drugstore and sat down, certain that he was dying. A policeman— one of those who had seen the attack— followed him in to arrest him. Tresca was still able to muster enough strength to shout: "Why don't you take a dead body to the morgue?" Instead they took him to the station and, after he fainted there, to the hospital. It required twenty-six stitches to bring his face together. The man who slashed him was caught and tried, but even though the three policemen testified that they had seen him lunge at Tresca and flash the razor, he was acquitted.

In June, 1905, the one-eyed giant Big Bill Haywood, Daniel DeLeon, "Mother" Jones and other militant varieties of socialists founded the Industrial Workers of the World, soon to be known as the Wobblies. In the decade of their strength the Wobblies organized the masses of unskilled and transitory workers and led strikes in New England textile mills, Minnesota iron mines and Pennsylvania steel works, that were as much social rebellions as economic conflicts. The Wobblies were syndicalists whose goal was not to have the state own all the means of production but to have the mines owned and run by the miners' union, the land by a union of agricultural workers, the factories by textile workers, all in a vast non-capitalistic, non-nationalist co-operative society. Tresca was attracted to the I.W.W. at once, although the anarchist element was initially small. Later the anarchist influence expanded as the Wobblies put the theories of direct action into violent practice. Tresca

at this period considered himself an anarcho-syndicalist.

It was the strike in the textile mills of Lawrence, Massachusetts, beginning on January 12, 1912, that stamped the letters I.W.W. in burning red on the American imagination. The year before, the Massachusetts legislature—with the best of liberal intentions—had passed a law reducing the working hours of women and of children under eighteen from fifty-six to fifty-four hours. When the law went into effect, the mill owners countered by reducing wages correspondingly. Since many of the juvenile mill workers received $5 a week or less, the reduction amounted to only about twenty-five cents, but its calculated meanness so infuriated the workers that they surged out of the factories, smashing the looms as they left. Twenty-three thousand workers struck in aimless anger. They were a polyglot mixture of Italians, Germans, French-Canadians, Poles, Lithuanians, Belgians and Syrians with a scattering of Russians, Jews, and Greeks. After a number of riots between strikers and police, the governor called out the militia.

It was then that Joe Ettor of the I.W.W. executive board came in from New York with the radical poet Arturo Giovannitti to give the strike force and direction. The winter was unusually bitter and the workers suffered greatly from cold and hunger. Sympathy for them grew as the wretchedness of their condition became known. "Their demands were justified," William Allen White wrote in distant Kansas, "and there was no excuse for the violence by police and military." Contributions came from labor organizations all over the country, and eleven soup kitchens were set up. However, the attempt of a committee, headed by Margaret Sanger, to send the needy Lawrence children to other cities was halted by the police.

With the passing of weeks, clashes between the I.W.W.-led strikers and the militia became more and more frequent, the Wobblies flaunting red banners reading "No God! No Master!" the soldiers replying with bayonets. Finally, one afternoon as police and militia charged a picket line, shots rang out and a girl striker, Annie Lopizza, fell dead. No one ever determined who shot her, but the police welcomed the chance to arrest the "troublemakers," Ettor and Giovannitti, as accessories to the murder.

With the strike leaders in jail, the Wobbly hero, Big Bill Haywood, came in from the West to take charge. He himself had been on trial for murder five years before in Boise, Idaho, in connection with the dynamiting of ex-Governor Steunenberg, and by now he was the most noted and notorious radical leader in the United States. He arrived in Lawrence at about the same time as the slim, dark-haired, blue-eyed "East Side Joan of Arc," Elizabeth Gurley Flynn. Decades later, in an antithesis unanticipated by Marx, her almost spherical figure was to be seen waddling in militant complacency across the platform of all Communist conventions until her apotheosis as General Secretary of the Communist party of the United States. But at Lawrence she appeared in the slender fire-breathing charm of her indignant youth.

By March the textile owners capitulated, granting the strikers pay increases of from 5 to 20 per cent. Ettor and Giovannitti still remained in jail, however, awaiting trial. Tresca had long been a friend of Giovannitti's, but at this time he was again serving time in Pennsylvania on another libel conviction for an article in another newspaper. As soon as he was released Tresca hurried to Lawrence to help in the organizing of mass agitation for Ettor's and Giovannitti's release. On the day that the Italians' trial began, he arranged for a twenty-four-hour protest

strike, and every mill in Lawrence shut down. Everything that Tresca did had a way of turning into an adventure, and on his arrival in Lawrence he was a marked man. Early one morning a militia squad came to arrest him at the tenement in which he was staying, and he escaped out a rear window, dashing stark naked through a network of alleys. At another time, when he was leading a memorial parade to lay wreaths on Annie Lopizza's grave, the police did corner him, but a group of workers formed a flying wedge to snatch him away. Two policemen were injured, and after that the police preferred to look the other way when they saw Tresca coming.

Lawrence made the I.W.W. famous, and for a while it seemed to the Wobblies and their sympathizers a harbinger of social revolution in the United States. Vincent St. John, who would succeed Haywood as general secretary of the I.W.W., wrote him: "A win in the Lawrence mills means the start that will only end with the downfall of the wage system." As if to underline this, Ettor and Giovannitti were acquitted. Soon, however, the flame of indignation fanned so assiduously by the I.W.W. died down, the workers shed their militancy, and Lawrence relapsed into its grubby obscurity.

Lawrence had a more lasting effect on Tresca, for in a May Day parade he met Elizabeth Gurley Flynn. Her combination of beauty and radicalism he found irresistible. He had married, in Italy, a shadowy figure of a wife, with a shadowy infant, who had followed him to America only to separate from him shortly afterwards. "I no like married life," he once explained to Max Eastman in his not quite basic English. "I like one woman an' then time pass an' I like another. I make many good friendship with women because I always say ver' frank: 'Don' trus' me. My character ver' emotional. I have gran' an' real passion now, but when dat gone, I gone too!' " His grand passion for Gurley—as she was called—outlasted all his others. They lived together until 1923. She too had been married and separated, but all that remained of her marriage was a two-year-old son.

After Lawrence, Tresca moved to New York and began to publish and edit another anarchist paper, *L'Avvenire* (The Future). He and Gurley were soon up to their necks in the strike of the Hotel and Restaurant Workers, most of them foreigners, whose degrading working conditions had turned them from the gradualism of the American Federation of Labor to the militancy of the I.W.W. A meeting of the strikers in Bryant Hall on Sixth Avenue, with a squad of hostile police standing by, transformed itself into a riot. Tresca, as the most conspicuous person present, was at once arrested. When a group of strikers tried to rescue him, a policeman pointed his revolver at Tresca's head and stopped the rescuers in their tracks by threatening to shoot him. Gurley had a finger broken by a police night stick in the scuffle. Somewhere between the hall and the patrol wagon to which they were hurrying him Tresca lost a pocket edition of Elizabeth Barrett Browning's *Sonnets from the Portuguese* that Gurley had given him with an affectionate inscription and with many of the tender passages underlined—to the embarrassment of both of them when photographs and accounts of the "hidden I.W.W. romance" appeared in the next day's newspapers.

The hotel strike was merely a prelude to the prolonged silk strike in Paterson, New Jersey. Paterson was known both as the silk-weaving center of the United States and as the Red City. Most of the workers were Italians, and the Red City had a long and turbulent anarchist tradition. Luigi Galleani had thundered revolution there weekly in his *Cronaca Sovversiva*. The in-ternational anarchist leader, Errico Malatesta, had been shot at while on a visit. Gaetano Bresci, the editor of an earlier anarchist paper, had left Paterson in 1900 and had sailed for Italy to assassinate King Humbert. The city was a dreary, smoke-encrusted industrial hinterland with interlaced streets of minute ramshackle workers' houses, seared by poverty and at the same time belligerently class-conscious.

The strike broke out in February when the mill owners introduced a system increasing the number of looms each weaver had to tend. Twenty-five thousand workers walked off their jobs, and violence broke out at once. Before the strike ended, all the leaders and a thousand strikers had been arrested. Two workers were shot dead in clashes with the police. Tresca and Gurley arrived within days of the walkout to help organize a general strike committee. They were arrested by the police at their first platform appearance and were charged with conspiring to cause an unlawful assemblage as well as to "routously and riotously and tumultuously disturb the peace of New Jersey." Big Bill Haywood hurried to Paterson, as did the fledgling revolutionary John Reed, lately hatched from Harvard. Haywood and Reed were of course arrested, Reed spending a dynamic interlude teaching the imprisoned strikers songs of the French Revolution and writing such realistic accounts of imaginary filth and vermin in the jail that the furious sheriff finally had "that writing son of a bitch" ejected to freedom.

In and out of jail, Reed, Tresca, Gurley and Big Bill kept right on speaking, but it was Reed who, with the help of his friends in the New York theatrical world, organized the Silk-Strike Pageant that was presented in the old Madison Square Garden. New York had never seen anything like this cast of 1,200 strikers. Skillfully staged, a massive and moving spectacle that was both a pageant and an industrial morality play, it thrilled its non-proletarian audiences with the feeling that a new proletarian art form had been born. There were five scenes. The first showed the strikers streaming out of the mills. In the next scene pickets and police clashed, and a striker was killed. Scene three showed the funeral; the coffin of the dead worker was carried down the aisle followed by the massed strikers singing the *Funeral March of the Workers* which Reed had taught them. Tresca, Gurley and Big Bill then stood before the coffin heaped with red carnations and repeated the same speeches that they had made before an actual striker's grave in Paterson. In scene four the strikers' children left their families to go to friends in other cities. The Pageant ended with a strike meeting, the actor-strikers facing the platform with their backs to the audience so that the audience itself became an extension of the strikers. Haywood on the platform sonorously told the workers what they were fighting for; then everyone stood and sang the *Internationale*. On the night of June seventh, the letters I.W.W. shone out from the top of the Garden's tower under Diana's statue. To middle-class Manhattanites those glaring red letters seemed to be the modern abbreviation for Mene, Tekel, Upharsin.

Unfortunately for Reed the Garden expenses were heavy, and when after a single performance the Pageant closed it had added much more to the notoriety of the strike than it had to the funds of the strikers. Some of the disgruntled Paterson workers accused the New York committee of profiting at their expense. Ironically, the closing of the Pageant was followed shortly afterwards by the collapse of the strike.

To enthusiasts like Haywood, Tresca, Gurley and Reed, each new strike in its moment of incandescence seemed a dynamic thrust forward towards a new dawn. The pattern, however, became static—an initial spontaneous walk-out; agitation and organization; violence, in which more often than not a striker or policeman was killed. Sometimes, as in Lawrence, the strikers won, sometimes, as in Paterson, they lost. In any case, the life of the gray industrial communities soon moved much as before, a little better or a little worse, but with no beguiling prospect of revolution just around the corner.

In 1916, when Tresca was on a speaking tour in California, Haywood asked him to help organize a strike of iron miners in the Mesaba Range of Minnesota. Haywood's Western Federation of Miners— the genesis of the I.W.W.—had long conducted what was almost a civil war with the feudalistic mine owners of the great western ranges. The miners at the Mesaba Range struck for an eight-hour day. The companies responded by importing strike-breakers and gunmen. In that bleak countryside of scarred red earth, where even the landscape seemed violent, the law was an irrelevant abstraction. Both sides were willing to fight. When Tresca arrived with a group of speakers and organizers, he was at once hustled off to the Duluth County jail.

While he was locked up, four Mesaba deputies forced their way into a Montenegrin worker's house and when the man's wife objected they beat her up. Three boarders jumped to the woman's defense, there was a scuffle, shots were fired, and an instant later a deputy lay dead on the floor. The boarders and the woman were held for murder. Tresca and three organizers were charged with being accessories.

In spite of Tresca's predicament, Haywood did not come to the Mesaba Range. At this point he was preoccupied with setting up central offices for the I.W.W. in Chicago. With this developing centralism, the old direct-action agitator began to show signs of turning into a bureaucrat. Even the various I.W.W. foreign-language papers, he decided, were now to be moved to Chicago. To Gurley and the others in Minnesota, his interest in the strike appeared unhappily remote. They, on the spot, made what they considered the best deal they could with the state's attorney. Since the latter wanted to avoid a long, spectacular and expensive murder trial, he was willing to allow the three boarders to plead guilty to manslaughter. After serving one year of a three-year sentence, he informally agreed, they could be released. The Montenegrin wife, Tresca, and the organizers would be freed. When the boarders appeared before the judge on the next day they—to the shock of Gurley and Tresca—received sentences of five-to-twenty years. From Chicago, with no knowledge of the details, Haywood furiously denounced the outcome. Actually the prisoners were released after three years, but Haywood's arbitrary long-distance reaction to the episode was enough for Tresca. He scornfully severed all connections with the I.W.W.

He returned to the Little Italy of New York and to editing *L'Avvenire*. His interest in unions was now limited to those of predominantly Italian membership, such as the Amalgamated Textile Workers and certain insurgent movements within the United Mine Workers. From this time on, according to Elizabeth Gurley Flynn, "he wrote and spoke only in Italian and made little or no effort to learn English or to participate in American affairs. His preoccupation was with Italian affairs, his friends were predominantly Italian anarchists."

Like all anarchists he opposed the First World War and America's entry into it. When he wrote flaming editorials in *L'Avvenire* denouncing conscription he found his paper banned from the mails. After President Wilson's declaration of war the United States Government moved against the I.W.W.; Tresca, Gurley, Ettor, Gio-

vannitti, Big Bill Haywood, and 164 others were indicted in Chicago under the new espionage and sedition laws; ninety-three of them were sentenced by Judge K. M. Landis to prison terms. Tresca and Gurley were released, since they were fortunate enough to have broken with the I.W.W. before April, 1917. Others were not so lucky. America's first Socialist congressman, Victor Berger, was deprived of his seat in the House of Representatives. Tresca's friend Eugene Debs received a ten-year sentence under the Espionage Act. The anarchists Emma Goldman and Alexander Berkman, who had organized the No-Conscription League, were sentenced to two years and then deported.

Undaunted by his narrow escape and by further possibilities of jail, Tresca travelled through the Italian enclaves of the East, denouncing Wilson's imperialist war and proclaiming that the real war for freedom was being fought by Lenin and Trotsky in Russia. Because he proclaimed in Italian to Italians he managed to escape the more assiduous attentions of the monolingual police, although at one such enclave—in Canton, Ohio—he came as close as he ever had to dying. When he arrived in Canton the police were waiting for him at the station platform but he, wise in their ways, managed to leap off the train just outside the station. He made a detour through back alleys to the hall where he had been billed to speak, only to discover that it too had been taken over by police. An anarchist comrade spotted him on the street and took him home. There, among his Italian friends, he was relaxing over a meal in the kitchen when the police burst in, led by the chief with a drawn revolver who hysterically asked where the books were, and then fired almost point-blank at Tresca. The men shouted, a woman screamed, but Tresca seemed bullet-proof.

"Arrest me," he told the chief, "but stop shooting at my friends!" He did not notice at first that an old friend sitting beside him had slumped forward mortally wounded. Years ago he and that friend had marched behind the red flag in Sulmano, but the young radical had crossed the ocean to become, in middle-age, a conservative businessman. He had merely dropped in with a bottle of wine to chat reminiscently with the friend of his youth.

Such wild happenings were the very substance of Tresca's life. When Mussolini, after his march on Rome, began to organize the overseas Italians, Tresca organized his own direct-action groups to drive the New York *fascisti* from the streets of Little Italy. It was his boast that from 1925 on he had made it impossible for the fascists to hold meetings in New York. Stung by such obduracy the Duce arranged to have a New York gunman eliminate his former comrade. But Tresca's apparently bullet-proof figure was so formidable and his popularity in Little Italy so strong that the gunman hesitated. His hesitation became panic when the Mafia for inscrutable reasons of its own "suggested" that Tresca was not to be harmed. Finally the would-be assassin came to Tresca, confessed his intentions and begged forgiveness.

Unlike many of his comrades Tresca never felt the protective need of carrying a weapon. But during his struggle with the New York *fascisti,* when for the first time he found himself compelled to use a bodyguard, he decided to buy himself a revolver. Then, on the very day he bought it, he accidentally pulled the trigger while he was trying to fit it into his trousers pocket and shot himself in the foot, an accident that he considered even more comic than did his friends.

President Wilson's crusade "to keep the world safe for democracy" stopped short of anarchists and other radical dissenters. Ever since the Haymarket Massacre of 1886, when six policemen had been killed by a bomb thrown at a Chicago anarchist

meeting, the name "anarchist" in America conjured up the cartoonists' image of the bearded foreigner with a bomb in his hand. Anarchism's own vision was of a golden age when all governments would be done away with and each individual would accept his innate responsibilities in a world of voluntary cooperation; the means to this goal—in Malatesta's portentous words—would be revolutionary destruction; the immediate instrument, terrorism, the politics of the deed. By spectacular acts of political assassination, anarchists would stamp their image on the world. One bomb, the anarchist high priest Kropotkin insisted, made more propaganda than a thousand pamphlets, and to demonstrate this the direct-action anarchists had emerged from their obscurity to strike down presidents, emperors and kings. Denjiro Kotoku tried to kill the mikado, Mateo Morral made an attempt on the King of Spain, Luigi Luccheni assassinated the Empress of Austria, Santa Ceserio killed the French President, Carnot. President McKinley had been shot by the half-mad half-anarchist Leo Czolgosz, and his death resulted in the first restrictive immigration act, through which aliens who advocated the overthrow of the government by violence could be deported. Although after the First World War the anarchists lost much of their mass support to the Communists, their individual acts of violence continued. At the Peace Conference in 1919 the anarchist Emile Cottin shot and wounded Clemenceau. Most anarchists—like Emma Goldman in her later days—rejected the politics of the deed, but they were not prepared to reject their comrades who did not. Nor did modern Americans, who generally attributed spectacular disasters like the 1920 Wall Street explosion to anarchists, make any distinction between theorists and bombers.

The year following the war seemed to

bring more problems to the United States, or at least more disillusioning problems, than the war itself—nation-wide strikes, the High Cost of Living (as inflation was then euphemistically known), a crime wave, jobless ex-servicemen. And in their wake came distrust of foreigners and the search for a scapegoat. The scapegoat itself accommodatingly turned belligerent. Radicals, anarchists, socialists and the two nascent Communist parties saw a great light in the East, and hailed the Bolshevik Revolution as the harbinger of the second American Revolution. John Reed expected such an overturn almost momentarily. Even the mild Eugene Debs announced that he was a Bolshevik "from the crown of my head to the tips of my toes."

The flamboyant Attorney General of the United States, A. Mitchell Palmer, had little in common with John Reed but his belief in the imminence of revolution, which he predicted for the following May Day. Under Palmer's direction the Department of Justice's "Red raids" were organized. Large numbers of foreign-born individuals, whether naturalized or not, were suddenly, illegally and often brutally rounded up and herded into detention centers. Those aliens among them who could be identified as Communists and anarchists were deported.

To this blunt harassment the direct-action anarchists replied even more bluntly with dynamite. Bombs were found in the mail addressed to the Attorney General, the Postmaster General, the Secretary of Labor, the Commissioner of Immigration, Judge Landis, J. P. Morgan, John D. Rockefeller, and others. In May the leader of the American anarchists, the leonine Luigi Galleani, editor of *Cronaca Sovversiva,* was deported under the 1903 law. His deportation was followed by reprisal bombings in eight cities. The chief target was Attorney General Palmer in Wash-

ington. Just as he was going to bed a bomb exploded on his doorstep, destroying the whole front of his house. Apparently the bomb had gone off prematurely and killed its carrier, for fragments of a body were found up and down the street.

The disintegrated man was Carlo Valdinoce, a former associate of Galleani on *Cronaca Sovversiva.* In time Department of Justice officials would come to suspect that he was the dead bomber, but they would never be wholly certain. One of the few who knew with certainty was Tresca, who now replaced Galleani as informal leader of the anarchists in the United States. Without any intention, merely by the force of his own personality, the now gray and bearded leader assumed the role of father figure for comrades and associates who in theory at least did not believe in father figures and leaders. He initiated a new anarchist paper, *Il Martello* (The Hammer), that he was to publish and edit for the rest of his life. In the sea of troubles in which the anarchists found themselves, theorists and direct-actionists turned to him almost automatically. He knew their thoughts and their deeds, he shared their innermost secrets. He gave them his skilled and unstinted help. They in turn gave him their admiring trust.

Flyers calling for the proletariat to smash the tyranny of capitalism, signed by "The Anarchist Fighters," had been found scattered in the neighborhood of Attorney General Palmer's shattered house. Government agents finally managed to trace them to two anarchist printers in Brooklyn, Roberto Elia and Andrea Salsedo, who had once worked for Galleani. Elia and Salsedo were taken to the Manhattan offices of the Department of Justice, where they were detained for some weeks. Tresca and a committee he had formed to aid the Palmer raid victims tried without success to help the two men. Elia was eventually deported, Salsedo—who gave evidence and then regretted it—committed suicide by jumping out of the fourteenth-floor window. While the printers were still confined by the Department of Justice, an obscure anarchist, Bartolomeo Vanzetti, arrived at Tresca's office from Boston on April 26, 1920. He had been sent by his comrades to inquire about the two prisoners. Nine days before there had been a hold-up murder in South Braintree, Massachusetts. Eight days later Vanzetti, along with Nicola Sacco, would—by sheerest chance—be plucked off a Brockton streetcar a dozen miles from South Braintree and held on suspicion of this murder.

When Sacco and Vanzetti were arrested, the Boston anarchists hired local lawyers for their defense. Vanzetti was identified by several witnesses as having participated in an earlier robbery attempt at Bridgewater, Massachusetts, where although there was much shooting no one was killed. Vanzetti was tried first on this lesser charge. He was found guilty of attempted armed robbery and sentenced to twelve to fifteen years in State Prison.

Tresca was furious at what he considered the bungling of the Boston anarchists and their local lawyers. He now engaged the bohemian radical lawyer, Fred Moore, a former general counsel to the I.W.W., to assume the defense. Moore had worked with Tresca in the Lawrence strike and had known him in many a struggle afterwards. He had just returned from Oklahoma, where he had successfully defended an I.W.W. organizer, "Big Boy" Krieger, on a framed-up charge of dynamiting the house of a Standard Oil official. Tresca met him in New York and persuaded him to go to Boston. Moore drove up in his own car, somewhat annoyed, for all his radicalism, at two anarchist gunmen on the run whom Tresca had tucked in with him.

If Massachusetts lawyers had been left

to defend Sacco and Vanzetti, the obscure Italians, whether convicted or acquitted, would never have shed their obscurity. It was Moore, with his flair for propaganda and his contacts with many radical labor groups all over the country and abroad, who made the fate of the two immigrants into an international issue that blazed round the world. Tresca, by sending Moore to Boston, originated the Sacco-Vanzetti case. But for Moore, their linked names would today mean nothing, even though as an ironic aftermath he came to the conclusion that they were probably guilty.

Tresca's attacks on the Duce and the Italian monarchy were duly noted by the Italian Embassy in Washington. When in 1923 he printed a small advertisement in *Il Martello* for a book on birth control, the Embassy complained to the postal authorities and Tresca was prosecuted for sending "obscene matter" through the mails. He was convicted and sentenced to a year and a day in the Federal Penitentiary in Atlanta. H. L. Mencken in protest reprinted the advertisement in the *American Mercury* and vainly challenged the government to prosecute him.

Congressman Fiorella La Guardia managed to persuade Coolidge to pardon Tresca after the latter had spent three months in Atlanta. Tresca passed the time in the manner of a star boarder as soon as it was learned that he was a friend of Eugene Debs. Debs had served his time in Atlanta earlier, and his genial nature and simple goodness had made an unforgettable impression on both guards and prisoners.

On the way back from Atlanta Tresca stopped off at Washington like any tourist to look at the public buildings. A group of children happened to be standing before the main gate of the White House and Tresca, as he passed, stopped to talk to them. He was fond of children and, like a benign uncle, soon found himself in the middle of a chattering circle. Suddenly a White House attendant appeared and beckoned to them to come inside. The children insisted on taking Tresca along, and they all ended a tour of the White House by shaking hands with President Coolidge. It must have been an incongruous sight when the ebullient anarchist grasped the hand of the taciturn Yankee. Reporters thought so when they spotted Tresca on the way out. Next day the headlines announced: TRESCA AT WHITE HOUSE, CRIMINAL ANARCHIST RELEASED FROM ATLANTA MAKES PEACE WITH PRESIDENT. Tresca's embarrassment was voluble. Coolidge's was not, but the attendant who brought in the anarchist with the children lost his job.

Anarchism as a world movement reached its peak before the First World War. In the twenties it was an obviously dwindling cause, its more violent adherents absorbed by the Communist wave, the others turning to socialism. Only in Spain did it retain any mass support. In America the emerging second-generation Italians for the most part forsook the radical politics of their fathers to become Democrats and Republicans. Tresca changed too, in emphasis if not in theory. In his middle years, he turned more and more from the heady dream of an international working class to the defense of the individual against oppression. "Carlo fought injustice from one end of the country to the other," Benjamin Gitlow wrote of him. "He defied authority and went to jail. . . . Essentially a man of action, he did whatever he did because he thought it was right. He was a sworn enemy of the state, holding that no institution is superior to the individual. He worked on behalf of common causes with every group in the radical movement from Communists to socialists to Trotskyites, though he viewed with contempt the theories of the political Marxists."

Just as in the circle of political thought the discipline of fascism and the compulsion of communism come to coincide, so anarchism and conservatism, with their emphasis on the responsibility of the individual, come to approach one another. Tresca, the last great anarchist leader, ended in the conservative belief that the ultimate discipline is self-discipline and that the just society must be built on loving kindness.

In 1919, as Emma Goldman with 248 other anarchists and Communists was deported on the *Buford,* "the Soviet Ark," to the Soviet Union, she thumbed her nose at receding America. To her, Russia was a northern Promised Land. The promise, however, lasted only the few months it took her to learn that the Russian anarchists were being liquidated by the secret police in the cellars of the Lubianka. In 1921, after Trotsky's merciless suppression of the anarchist revolt of the Kronstadt sailors, she managed to escape to Latvia just a step ahead of the Soviet liquidators. For the rest of her life she remained a bitter enemy of the Soviet Union, convinced then that its brutalities far exceeded anything known in the capitalist world.

Tresca, immersed in his American activities and chiefly concerned with fighting the imported *fascisti,* did not react as did Emma Goldman. He continued to cooperate with the Communists even when the Boston Sacco Defense Committee in the later stages of the case was bitterly and publicly denouncing them. In 1925, when James P. Cannon on orders from Moscow organized the International Labor Defense as a subsidiary of the Communist International Class War Prisoners Society, Tresca allowed his name to be included among the non-Communist decoy minority on the executive committee. Not until 1934, when the Communists maneuvered to disrupt the big New York hotel strike, did he break with them, and two years later he was still willing to co-operate with the Popular Front to support the Spanish Republic in the civil war. But word soon came to him of the ruthless Communist control of the international brigade volunteers and of the Communist liquidation of the anarchist militia. His old friend Professor Camillo Berneri, an Italian anarchist intellectual, was assassinated by OGPU agents in the streets of Barcelona. Communists seized and executed another acquaintance of his, the Trotskyite Andrés Nin, who had been for a time Minister of Justice in the Catalan Government.

Whatever the vagaries of politics and policy, Tresca never let them interfere with his emotions. The end of his relationship with Gurley came when a man presented her with a package of love letters that Tresca had written to the man's wife. After Tresca had left Gurley he developed an affair with a well-known Communist sculptress, and lived for a while in a *ménage à trois* under her roof, with the roof expenses provided by the sculptress' husband. OGPU agents often dropped in at the studio, and Tresca remained on friendly terms with many of them until the Spanish Civil War. Subsequently he had a much more serious and lasting affair with another Communist, Juliet Stuart Poyntz. Juliet Poyntz—with a hard veneer of physical attraction, a Daughter of the American Revolution, aristocratic in appearance and revolutionary in ambition—was until 1934 a member of the Communist District Executive Committee. Then she officially dropped out of the party to become a spy for the OGPU. Following the Kirov assassination she was called to Moscow and took part in some of the OGPU interrogations there. The horror of what she saw was too much for her. When she returned to New York, broken in nerve and belief, she refused

to accept new OGPU assignments but remained in isolation writing her memoirs. Orders to eliminate her came from the OGPU chief, Yagoda, in Moscow. It was her murder by the OGPU, as a culmination of similar murders in the Spanish Civil War, that set Tresca irrevocably against the Communists. From that time on he fought them with the same enthusiastic single-mindedness with which he had combatted the *fascisti* in the twenties.

Juliet Poyntz disappeared in the autumn of 1937, the same year that the Communists drove the anarchists to the wall in Barcelona. She left her room in the American Women's Hotel, an unfinished letter on her desk and none of her clothes missing, and was never seen again. Tresca would not let her disappearance rest. He was certain that she was dead, although it took him several years to piece together enough bits and pieces of the elusive facts to discover what had happened.

She had apparently been enticed from the hotel by a telephone call from one of her lovers, Shachno Epstein, an associate editor of the New York *Freiheit*. He, fearful to the point of collapse, had been forced by the OGPU to act as a decoy. The two met at Central Park Circle, and then walked through Central Park. Epstein led her along an isolated walk and close to a large parked car. Then he stopped. Two OGPU agents sprang out of the car, seized her, forced her inside and drove away, leaving Epstein shaking and alone. With the woman muffled in back, they drove through Westchester and into Dutchess County. Not far from the Roosevelt estate, in a remote wooded area, they garroted her and buried her body.

Tresca, when he felt he had gathered enough clues about her disappearance, went to the district attorney's office and demanded an investigation. Communist publications at once began to refer to him as a police spy, and party members hinted that he would be next on the OGPU list. Tresca, through his Italian followers, let it be known if anything happened to him, the Communist Party Secretary, Earl Browder, would be killed in retaliation.

For the Communists, Tresca committed the unpardonable sin when he agreed to serve on John Dewey's commission to sift the treason charges made against Trotsky in the Moscow Trials. After sittings held in New York, Washington and Mexico City, the commission found Trotsky innocent. Afterwards Tresca was singled out for attack by the *Daily Worker,* and the Italian Communist leader, Pietro Allegra, published a pamphlet calling attention to Tresca's "moral suicide" and demanding the "elimination from society of beings who are hateful to themselves and to society."

It was of singular and long-standing annoyance to the Communists that Tresca was able to keep them out of the Garibaldi Society, the leading organization of Italian anti-fascists. Even in the hothouse period of Russian-American friendship during World War II, he continued to bar the way to their infiltration. In 1942 the Office of War Information organized the Italian-American Victory Council to arrange overseas broadcasts and prepare for political changes in Italy after the war. So great was Tresca's influence that in spite of OWI objections he was still able to exclude the Communists as well as the ex-fascists from the new organization. For the fellow travelers of the Italian section of the OWI Tresca was as formidable an obstacle as he was to the Communists.

When the awkward obstacle was eliminated, it seemed both simple and convenient to let the blame fall on elusive ex-fascists. Washington was willing to let it go at that. So was New York's Mayor La

Guardia, tipped off by his friend, Congressman Vito Marcantonio. So was the district attorney. Investigation might embarrass Soviet-American relations. Galante, the killer suspect, was turned loose. The man who directed Tresca's murder remained officially unknown.

He had not been unknown to Tresca, however. His name was Vittorio Vidali, alias Carlos Contreras, alias Enea Sormenti, a Communist agent who had come from Mexico on a special mission to eliminate Tresca. "Where he is, I smell death," Tresca told a friend a few days before he was shot down, when he learned that Vidali had been seen in the city.

"A human deadend, squat as a toad, his face wart-like, cruel and liking cruelty." So Ralph de Toledano described Vidali. Tresca had known him in New York without hostility in the twenties. In 1928 Vidali had been deported to Mexico. There he developed his talent for political assassination by arranging the murder of Antonio Mella, a Cuban ex-Communist who turned against the party and was living in exile.

With the outbreak of the Spanish Civil War, Vidali went to Spain and under the *nom de guerre* of Colonel Carlos Contreros became the implacable political commissar of the Fifth Brigade, which conducted the bloodiest of the Communist-organized purges. It was by his arrangement, and in spite of the protests of the Spanish Republican Prime Minister Juan Négrin, that Andrés Nin was executed. At the war's end Vidali escaped to Mexico where he directed the first attempt on the exiled Trotsky's life.* In May 1942 Tresca denounced him on the front page of *Il Martello* as a "commandant of spies, thieves and assassins" who had committed hor-

---

* Vidali is at present the leader of the Communists in Trieste.

rible crimes in Spain. Within months Vidali took his revenge. Possibly he was the gunman near the Fifth Avenue entrance to Tresca's office building; almost certainly he was in the getaway car.

Carlo Tresca's death marked the end of the great anarchist leaders. Kropotkin, Merlino, Malatesta, Galleani, were all gone. Three years before Tresca was killed, Emma Goldman died. "A mountain of integrity," Rebecca West called her. The same was true of all the anarchist leaders. They were what they said they were, they believed what they said they believed, and no cause or end was for them worthy of a lie.

When Tresca sent Moore on to Boston on that August morning in 1920 as counsel in an obscure murder trial, he created the Sacco-Vanzetti case. It developed into one of those world-encompassing issues that occur once in a generation and that polarize a society. Conservative New Englanders defiantly insisted that the two men were guilty. But in the liberal intellectual world that prevailed outside New England it became a dogmatic conviction that Sacco and Vanzetti were two innocent radicals wilfully done to death for their political beliefs by a reactionary and corrupt social order. According to this dogma their innocence was self-evident, the trial a frame-up, the jury twelve Yankee bigots, the district attorney a corrupt scoundrel and the judge a senile and profanely biased old man. Massachusetts itself became the arch-criminal when the governor and a special committee appointed by him refused to revoke the death sentences.

The dogma of the innocence of Sacco and Vanzetti was embraced with such passionate tenacity by liberal opinion that it was as if the dogma itself filled some vital inner need. Men and women identified themselves so intimately with the fate of Sacco and Vanzetti that their deaths came to seem an irreparable personal loss.

James T. Farrell remembered how he walked the streets of New York sobbing the morning after the execution. Eugene Lyons, when he saw the news flash over the wire, felt the constricting grief that he was later to feel when he watched at his father's coffin. A few minutes before the electrocution, Ferris Greenslet, the biographer of the Lowells, stood with a crowd in front of the Massachusetts State House staring up at the oval lighted windows of the governor's office, "hoping, doubting, despairing."

The dozens of books, the hundreds of pamphlets and plays and poems and articles that have appeared for over a generation of the Sacco-Vanzetti case have all taken the dogma of the men's martyrdom for granted. To do otherwise would have seemed intellectually contemptible and politically perverse. Outside the backwater of Massachusetts, the dogma became fixed and unchallenged, closed to debate, a liberal canon. Yet, the man who shaped the canon was the man who shattered it.

If there was one man who held the ultimate inner knowledge of the Sacco-Vanzetti case, that man was Carlo Tresca. From their leader the anarchists had no secrets. Just as Tresca had known that it was Valdinoce who had blown himself up on the steps of Attorney General Palmer's town house, so he knew the whole hierarchy of direct-actionists. A few weeks before he died he was talking with Max Eastman who, whatever his own shifts in politics, had remained his close friend over the years. Some time before, Eastman had written a Tresca "Profile" that appeared in *The New Yorker*. Eastman was perplexed by recent rumors he had heard about Moore's doubts. "Carlo," he asked his friend suddenly, "would you feel free to tell me the truth about Sacco and Vanzetti?" Tresca could have said many things. He could have said No. He could have said that he did not know the truth. He could have said that the men were innocent. Instead, and without hesitation, he told Eastman: "Sacco was guilty, but Vanzetti was not."

And with the unqualified honesty of his reply, in those seven bare words, he rent the most cherished liberal myth of the century.   [VIII, Winter 1963–64, 61–76]

The Purloined-Letter Syndrome

JOHN RUSSELL

John Russell *(1928–)* *is professor of English at the University of Maryland, where he teaches modern literature and particularly British fiction. His publications include works on* Anthony Powell: A Quintet, Sextet, and War *(1970),* Henry Green: Nine Novels and an Unpacked Bag *(1960), and* Style in Modern British Fiction *(1978). He has been a longtime contributor of essays and reviews to* Modern Age *and has also contributed to* Kenyon Review *and* Modern Fiction Studies, *among other journals.*

CALLED *The Climate of Treason* when it came out last year in England, Andrew Boyle's *The Fourth Man* owes its changed title to the recent notoriety it has effected. Really about the trio of spies from the British Establishment who fled to Russia— Philby, Maclean, and Burgess—it made enough stir about the "fourth man" who abetted these traitors to cause his identity to be revealed via parliamentary enquiry. Now stripped of his title, this turns out to have been Sir Anthony Blunt, adviser on art these many years to the Queen.

The Fourth Man stands as a good title anyhow, if taken allegorically (even though Blunt has but a small role in the text)— for it can represent the whole governing class of England, almost incarnated as one composite person, who stood aside and allowed brazen catch-me-if-you-dare antics to go on for years in front of its imperturbable face. The figures of Burgess and Maclean and Philby cried out for detection and the detectors simply would not oblige—becoming themselves the "fourth man" writ large, who took

every trouble to endorse the traitors' "safe conduct" and speed them on their way.

Of course the Foreign Office and the Secret Intelligence Service did not *want* the men they harbored to betray them, so that early on one is apt to feel "this can't be true." In other words, one may be led to suspect Mr. Boyle's objectivity: he sounds so caustic. When Guy Burgess was recruited by the Communists in 1932 (right out of Cambridge, just like the others), Boyle reports that "the conversion of Burgess unleashed a willful and sometimes malignant demon on the University." Even a hundred pages in, the demonic note keeps seeming to produce overstatements about Burgess and Maclean: "For Burgess had already introduced Maclean, the emancipated Calvinist-turned-Communist, to the sad pleasures of sodomy, the irrepressible Guy wryly boasting about it as if he had thereby earned the Victoria Cross for valour beyond the call of duty." Why all these tags, it might be asked. Why the sneer-words "emancipated" and "irrepressible"; why the editorial "sad pleasures" (plain "sodomy" would have done); why the egregious reference to the Victoria Cross?

Yet in the last analysis, this language is accurate. Boyle has only barely begun to document his principals' doings, and they will indeed attain heights of repulsiveness that warrant hyperboles like "beyond the call of duty." Not by design, the extravagant *social* behavior of the three men turned out to be their "cover." It was the classic case of Poe's "purloined letter"— hide the evidence by displaying it flagrantly under the investigator's nose. For instance, one of Burgess' desks at the Foreign Office literally stank; he kept there "a half-gnawed clove of garlic" and he himself reeked along with the detritus on his desk. If he happened to have a tapeworm—and he did—he would let everyone know how he intended to blackmail an innocent restaurant on account of it. So the refrain develops, and what applies to Burgess comes to apply to all three: "The likelihood that any self-respecting foreign intelligence service would ever have stooped to recruit [them] was utterly preposterous."

For this extraordinary reason the three spies remained unsuspected—it was inconceivable that anyone would have tapped them for work requiring, above all, continued discretion. Yet the collective "fourth man," respectable Great Britain, in both public and private guises, *did* employ them and condoned their wallowing in positions of trust. This amazing fact supplies a full excuse for Boyle's legitimately caustic tone. If no self-respecting spy network could have risked them, how could any self-respecting and above-board agency have countenanced such employees? The attack in this book, in the end, is not on a nation's leadership that has let itself be duped, but on one that has—in its permissiveness—lost all connection with self-respect.

Before the war, as the most reluctant Communist agent of the three (but still a Communist agent), Maclean had begun his career in the Foreign Office. He would ultimately reveal the most important secrets, connected with atomic experimentation and stockpiling, because he'd risen to First Secretary rank in the American Embassy (1944–1948). Burgess and Philby, also agents since 1932, were originally freelancers, but their "cover" was just as impeccable, Burgess working for the BBC and Philby as a *Times* correspondent. Both were taken into the secret service in the war, and while from then on Burgess oscillated among mainly propagandistic jobs, Philby was elevated to the two most ironical SIS posts imaginable for a Communist spy: he was first in charge of anti-Soviet counter-espionage, and during the cold war was sent to America as chief liaison man with our CIA and FBI. It was these agencies who had begun to smoke out the treachery of Maclean (by now transferred to Cairo), and so Philby was in a position to warn him and to depute Burgess to effect Maclean's escape in 1951—Burgess accompanying the latter to Moscow. Twelve years later Philby would make the same bolt, when evidence had finally been garnered—as though by smoke signals taking twelve years to reach Whitehall—that would condemn him.

But to return to dissoluteness: the first half of the book tends to dwell on the excesses of Burgess, a violent homosexual, and Philby, just as arrant a womanizer. (He efficiently put his first two wives aside, the second drugging herself to death after being abandoned.) Maclean, who married but a single wife and sported the remnant of a conscience, is by contrast kept under wraps. But two hundred pages in we learn of a "stage managed orgy" of Burgess which enabled him to get blackmail photographs of Maclean and other males participating in erotic acts. And it eventuates that Maclean thenceforward went on periodic homosexual drinking binges ("bouts of almost uncontrollable schizophrenia"), providing Burgess with leverage for later bullying whenever Maclean wavered as a Communist. "Maclean, the waverer," we are told, "had to be driven into line under the lashing tongue of Burgess. The treatment worked."

The most miserable of the three—and it could be the most despicable—was this half-conscienced man Maclean. Anthony Powell, in his own recent memoir *Messengers of Day,* describes meeting him, and his underlying theme is no different from Andrew Boyle's. Powell was disturbed by "an emanation of shiftiness positively creepy" on their first meeting, which was borne out after the war. By then Maclean

> had become quite a talked-of personality. His drunkenness and violence were referred to with awe as an example of what you could not only get away with, as a member of the country's diplomatic corps, but actually turn to good account in augmenting your reputation as a rising man. I can vouch for the fact that Maclean broke a colleague's leg . . . [so does Boyle vouch for it, giving chapter and verse on this ugly matter from which Maclean escaped unscathed on his last mission to Egypt].

Powell also met the young Burgess, "well known in London as a notorious scally-wag, to whom no wholly baked person, among those set in authority, would ever have dreamt of entrusting the smallest responsibility. . . ."

Does there seem to have been a death-wish among constituted English authorities, when to these men's proclivities there had to be added their undisguised Communist sympathies that accompanied them throughout their careers? Men sick of their country and demonstrably sick as well? Of their ends there is little to say. Burgess dying, supposedly nostalgic for England, evokes about as much sympathy as Kim Philby abandoned by his third wife, who fled back to the free world after she discovered that Kim was cuckolding his comrade David Maclean in Moscow. That cuckolding presumably still goes on. Burgess might have found a way to take pictures of it had he not died. Meanwhile, one of the extra signs of intelligence in *The Fourth Man,* congruent with its acerbic tone, is the fact that it is not illustrated. One can't conceive of a reader wishing to know what at any point in their careers these chameleons would have photographed up as. Presumably an editorial decision was made not to illustrate Boyle's text, and if so it was right. Graphic erasure suits them.

[XXV, Winter 1981, 76–78]. Review of *The Fourth Man,* by Andrew Boyle, New York: Dial Press, 1979.

[58]

Europe on the Eve

FELIX MORLEY

Felix (Muskett) Morley (1894–1982) was editor of The Washington Post *and later president of Haverford College. He won the Pulitzer Prize for editorial writing in 1936, three years after he was named editorial page editor of the* Post. *An antimilitarist and anti-imperialist political philosopher, he was a contributor to* Modern Age *beginning with its first issue. He was the author of* The Power in the People *(1949) and wrote several books on American foreign policy as well. His study* Freedom and Federalism *(1959) was described by Roscoe Pound as "a notable contribution to political science and indeed to jurisprudence."*

ON MAY 5, 1937, I was told by Eugene Meyer, then publisher of *The Washington Post,* that he would like me, as editor of the paper, to make a trip of observation and reporting in Europe with him. He had reservations on the *Normandie* in two weeks' time, accompanied by Mrs. Meyer, their daughter Florence and a maid, these to be established in Paris for six weeks while he and I would travel around together. He would not go to Germany, because of the Nazi persecution of the Jews, but would be glad if I could make investigations there. All my expenses would be covered by the paper and my salary, while I was absent, paid directly to my wife.

It was, of course, a command performance, but not less attractive for that reason. Events in Europe were obviously coming to a crisis. Hitler was moving towards *Anschluss,* or union, with Austria, and was threatening to annex the German-speaking part of Czechoslovakia. In Britain, France and Russia there was grave ap-

prehension, but no coordinated policy of resistance to these or further Nazi demands. I had lived a total of nearly six years in Europe, spoke French and German adequately and was familiar with the history and politics of the entire area. To "write up" the tense situation in an objective manner would be not merely a journalistic service but a pleasure. So I accepted immediately.

Nevertheless I knew in advance that there would be some travail in this travel. The plan was for the two of us to interview celebrities together, with the editor writing a series of informative articles on our findings for front-page display in *The Post.* The publisher had numerous European connections and rightly thought that his international financial know-how would serve to broaden my outlook. On the other hand, Mr. Meyer had little interest in average opinion and by refusing to visit Germany would miss the key to the entire situation. Moreover, he was unfamiliar with the techniques of newspaper correspondence, in which I had years of experience.

A good reporter does not argue with the person from whom he seeks information. He must, of course, question in a manner showing that he is both well-informed and alert to propaganda. But his basic function is to present a *tabula rasa* on which the selected interviewee is invited to express opinions, whether wise or otherwise. When the questioner considers these deficient he does not directly contradict but seeks another source to present opposing viewpoints and thus obtain a balanced picture. Editorial opinion should be most sparingly used in writing a news story and never if the report is set forth as strictly factual.

This procedure was not Mr. Meyer's habit. In the triangular interviews throughout the trip he was not hesitant in expressing his own, well-informed ideas. To these the statesmen interviewed would always listen courteously, which did not justify the assumption of agreement. When the publisher heard a viewpoint in accord with his own he seldom thought it necessary to look further. In writing my articles, therefore, I was under intangible pressures never before experienced. Nor was it easy to grind out the correspondence at the end of exhausting days, while my colleague was socializing.

The social relationship was also somewhat anomalous. In some respects I served as a courier, making many of the appointments as well as travel and hotel arrangements. This was important, since my publisher was not accustomed to handling details for himself. Taking a taxi to the station, after an overnight visit to Brussels, I noticed that my chief was leaving without his suitcase and inquired. "I guess I thought the valet would pack it for me!" said Mr. Meyer ruefully. The editor could not refrain from observing that few newspapermen could depend on such auxiliary service.

I also functioned as a traveling companion. Mr. Meyer liked to talk and his wealth of experience, depth of knowledge and wide-ranging interests made him a fascinating conversationalist. But it was clear that the subordinate's role was to listen rather than to dilate himself and as time went on the unilateral pattern became a little tiresome. Such annoyance, however, was offset by the publisher's unfailing generosity. He paid for almost everything, including tips. Federal Reserve notes fairly showered the decks of the *Normandie* as we disembarked. "It should not be a difficult trip," I confided to my journal, "as long as Meyer's bottomless purse stands back of me."

The Meyer ladies left the ship at Cherbourg, to establish a Paris base. Eugene and I, headed for London, went on to Southampton, passing through a big flotilla of the British fleet still assembled in the Solent following the Coronation Review for George VI. That night in London my brother Frank had us both to dinner at the Oxford and Cambridge Club, along with several mutual journalistic friends including Jim Bone of the *Guardian* and my old friend Hamish Miles, now a member of *The Times'* editorial staff. The blowout must have been a strain on the fraternal pocketbook, immediately following a vacation trip to Salzburg, but Frank stood to it as the perfect host. It was the last time I would see Hamish, a cherished comrade from World War I days. In a few months the still youthful Scot would be stricken by an inoperable brain tumor. It seemed improbable that this delicate aesthete would get on well with so forceful a character as the aggressive Jewish publisher. But with individuals Eugene Meyer had an almost chameleon power of adaptation and the pair were simpatico.

The Imperial Conference was sitting in London, considering bonds soon to be tested in the furnace of war, and I spent the next morning with contacts made for me by old friends on the League of Nations' Secretariat—Raymond Kershaw for Australia and Craig McGeachie, a clever and attractive woman, for Canada. I lunched alone with my brother at Simpson's, afterwards meeting Meyer at the U.S. Embassy for a quiet conference with Ray Atherton, now much more favorable to coordinated Anglo-American policies than had been the case when I had talked with this career diplomat in London a year earlier. Then publisher and editor caught a late afternoon train to Oxford where they were royally entertained overnight at Rhodes House, completed since my last presence at this Alma Mater, fifteen years earlier. Little else, however, was changed in Oxford and I had pleasure in acting as cicerone to my appreciative boss. By invitation we dined in Hall at New College (founded in 1386) where several old Dons of my time as a Rhodes Scholar received us cordially. Then there was port, in the Senior Common Room, and a moonlight stroll through well-remembered quadrangles and streets. "What a glorious old place it is," I wrote in my diary, "how unrivaled, how redolent of the finest human aspirations!" Next morning there was even time for a visit to Blackwell's famous bookshop before returning to London and lunch with Goeffrey Dawson, editor of *The Times*, who had in, among others, Lord Lothian (the former Phillip Kerr), newly appointed Ambassador to Washington. Dawson was moderately pro-German, to the extent of regarding that country's overthrow of the Treaty of Versailles as justified. But more outspoken in this regard was elderly James L. Garvin, famous editor of *The Observer*, who argued strongly against any British—or American—policy that could lead towards an alliance with Soviet Russia. Communism, for Garvin, was much more of a threat than Hitler to Western civilization.

There were many more talks, with Labor Party leaders, economists, financiers and businessmen, during the crowded nine days in England. I found it exhausting, having had to produce articles, generally late at night, on the often conflicting impressions with which the daytime hours were crowded. This writing, featured in *The Post* as my copy streamed in, had to be objective, clear and convincing, also much more "in depth" than ordinary cable correspondence. I had the necessary background and Meyer's comment, as we reviewed what we had heard, was often luminous and always helpful. But the publisher, for all his keen thinking, was congenitally unable to write a single paragraph of comprehensible newspaper English, so that I had to compose to satisfy both. This was wearisome and when the weekend came I struck for time off, to leave London and visit quietly with my parents who had come over to make a visit to rural Woodbridge, the ancestral Morley home.

I was always grateful for this overnight stop in the placid, almost unchanging, East Anglian town. My father, now nearly 77, chatted happily of his boyhood days there, as we strolled along the river and through the familiar winding streets. We visited the abandoned Quaker Meeting House, then up for sale, and Professor Morley identified the simple family headstones in its little yard. The feverish panorama of this world's politics seemed far away. The old mathematician, back in his mid-Victorian childhood and never much concerned with current events, gave little thought to the developing madness. In time, but not yet, I would assume the same protective armor. That night I was in London again, picking up threads with Eugene Meyer. More interviews had been scheduled before leaving, 24 hours later, by the comfortable train ferry to Dunkirk and Paris. The small French port with a Scottish name—the kirk on the dunes—was familiar to me from the 1914 war. In the one impending it would become very widely known.

For the day of arrival in Paris an older sister of Mr. Meyer, wife of the Brazilian Ambassador there, had arranged a cozy lunch with the then Premier of France, Leon Blum, as honor guest. Afterwards I talked at length with this leader of the uneasy Popular Front government, finding him surprisingly temperate towards Germany. "Blum," I wrote in my journal that night, "finds Czechoslovakia in the position of Poland at the end of the Eighteenth Century, which would seem to carry a certain implication of an eventual partition." But this pacific and gentle Socialist, who would oppose the Munich settlement, be interned by the Germans and surface briefly after World War II, was at the moment on the eve of overthrow by the Chamber of Deputies. Another Premier, Camille Chautemps, was in office a few days later. With him, as well as with former Premier Herriot, Georges Bonnet, René de Chambrun, Pierre Comert, Bertrand de Jouvenel, André Philip and other influential French friends, I conferred at length. It was cumulatively evident that France, far more than Britain, was both physically unprepared and psychologically unwilling to stand up to German demands, a fact of which the *Führer* was certainly well aware.

The stay in Paris was broken by an overnight trip to Brussels, for a talk arranged with Prime Minister Paul Van Zeeland. The Belgian leader was about to visit Washington and welcomed the backstage advice which Mr. Meyer was both competent and glad to give him. Van Zeeland, a forceful and able conservative, was more anxious to ask than to answer questions but asserted that Belgium could successfully maintain its newly-announced neutrality in the event of another war. He made plain his concern about French political weakness, with all

the implications for a small adjacent country unable to resist alone. It made me the more anxious to get a slant on the Nazi attitude, when I took the sleeper from Paris to Berlin the night of June 9. I would have a scant four days in the German capital, before rejoining Mr. Meyer in Prague.

Though necessarily brief, the editor looked forward to this dip into the Third Reich with keen anticipation. It was his first visit to Germany since 1931 and Berlin he had not seen for sixteen years. Thus he was in an excellent position to observe the changes brought by the Nazis, the more so because of familiarity with the language. In casual conversation it was easy for him to pose as a curious German-American, on a first visit to the *Vaterland* since childhood. The approach always brought an interested and seemingly frank response. Also he was fortunate in having good friends at the U.S. Embassy: Jimmy Riddleberger, well up the diplomatic ladder since their Geneva acquaintance; Lloyd Steere, the agricultural attaché, whom he had known in Washington, and Douglas Miller, a Rhodes Scholar of his vintage, then serving as commercial attaché.[1] Foremost among German friends was former Judge Karl von Lewinski who described his country as a *"sehr orderliches Gefängnis"* (very orderly prison). Another old friend, Paul Leverkuehn, a reserve officer, was at the time away on maneuvers.

In Berlin, however, there was little evidence of armed force, some said because military preparedness was so unpopular. Persecution of Jews and Communists was still relatively restrained and I was disposed to think the police-state stories somewhat exaggerated. I had been told that my baggage would certainly be secretly examined and therefore, on reaching the Adlon Hotel, arranged papers in my unlocked suitcase so that it would be obvious immediately if they were at all disturbed. Somewhat to my disappointment there was no evidence of this. On the other hand, von Lewinski told me of the police agents employed as doormen for every apartment house and anticipated questioning about my visit.

Germany seemed in a more pacific mood than expected. Certainly the "man in the street"—taxi drivers, waiters, shopkeepers—deplored the possibility of another war. Uninvited but welcomed I joined a random student group for a *Bierabend* in a popular restaurant. The songs were all sentimental—nothing patriotic—and the boys and girls alike were unanimously critical of Hitler's saber-rattling. I went with von Lewinski to watch the Davis Cup tennis match with Belgium and noted how punctiliously the audience applauded points scored by the outplayed foreigners. Nor did the atmosphere seem exceptionally repressive. That evening the judge took his daughter and son-in-law, an Austrian architect named Wiedemann, along with their visitor to dinner at the big outdoor restaurant in the Zoologischer Garten. Towards the end of a merry meal the young Austrian pulled a lock of his black hair down his forehead, held a small pocket comb so that it looked like a trim moustache, and began a high-pitched gabble obviously imitative of the *Führer*. I was appalled, expecting immediate arrest by the Gestapo. But people at nearby tables only smiled. "For the moment one Austrian can make fun of another," said von Lewinski. Nevertheless Wiedemann, like everyone else, rose to his feet for mass singing of the Horst Wessel Lied and followed it with the Nazi salute from which I alone refrained. The architect was no Nazi but he viewed the German-Austrian *Anschluss* as inevitable. "There was no work for me in Vienna," he said. "I had to come to Germany for employment. Either Germany takes over Austria or half

my countrymen will migrate here, where jobs are plentiful."

It was extremely hot in Berlin—37° centigrade *im Schatten,* people complained—and the renowned energy of the inhabitants was somewhat subdued thereby. Having made no advance arrangements I could not get to talk with either Hitler or Goering, which was regrettable. However, with the help of the Embassy, I made appointments with several lesser Nazi functionaries. Notable among these was Dr. Walther Darré, Minister of Agriculture and Nutrition, a big man who received the visitor in a baggy and unseasonable suit which he proudly explained had just been made from beechwood fibre. "The process will save us imports of wool," said the Minister. "And it is developing so well that we plan to plant thousands of beech trees in this area"—pointing to a big wall map—"where the beech flourishes." A few hours later, at the Air Ministry, the editor was told of plans for a new commercial airport north of Berlin, located for him on an identical map in the same area that Dr. Darré had designated for forestation. I asked whether this would eliminate previous farmland. "Practically none," replied the official. "It's very poor soil, growing nothing but beech trees useful only for firewood." Like big bureaucracies everywhere the National Socialist planners were often working at cross-purposes. But this particular contretemps was doubtless straightened out by Goering, who was at the time director of both aviation and forestry.

Dr. Darré convinced me that "in case of need" Germany would prove more self-sufficient than had been the case in the first war. That this "need" was not imaginary I was forced to conclude from my most significant interview, with Dr. Karl Haushofer, the geopolitician said to have been largely responsible for guiding Hitler's foreign policy. Though gracious, this scholarly old man would talk about his "Heartland" theory only under a pledge of no quotation or attribution "since Americans are so prone to misunderstand." With this reservation, Haushofer spoke eloquently. The "Heartland" of Europe, he explained, is the great prairie which extends without significant natural interruption from the Elbe River to the Ural Mountains. It is for the most part invulnerable to sea power and too huge for successful air attack. "Whoever dominates that plain will control the destiny of the Continent." Currently, he said, using a map and pointer in professional manner, Prussia and Poland control the western part of this vital area, the bulk of which is in Russian hands. Should Russia take over Poland and Eastern Germany, then Communism would be the master of all Europe and, working with a Red China, would control the Eurasian land mass and, in effect, the world. It was therefore in the interest of the West that Germany work out an arrangement with Poland, keeping a large part of the "Heartland" from Russian domination. This meant modification of the Polish Corridor, by which the Treaty of Versailles had inexcusably split East Prussia from the rest of Germany. To that end Nazi diplomacy was dedicated and he hoped his visitor would recognize that such a settlement was in the interest of all. There was no question of Haushofer's sincerity. His presentation was thoughtful and I felt able to present its essence, without mentioning the source, in one of my articles.

On the last morning of his stay the editor went for a drive on the much advertised, and beautifully engineered, *Autobahn*, then visiting the *Vier Jahre Zeit* exposition with Douglas Miller. The name expressed the four more years of power which Hitler asked in order to complete his program of German regeneration.

Actually four years from that date would see the German armies plunging deep into their eventual disaster in Russia. But the exposition, focussing on industrial accomplishment, was impressive. At the entrance was a big painting with the title from the Gospel of St. John: *Am Anfang war das Wort*—"In the Beginning was the Word." This somewhat sacrilegious representation showed Hitler talking to a group in a cellar, during the proscribed period of the Nazi movement. His small audience was evidently intended to depict his appeal to all elements of German society. There was a one-legged war veteran, a college student, an old Hausfrau knitting as she listened, a peasant, a beautiful blonde maiden, a businessman in stiff collar with briefcase under his arm and other symbolic figures. I have often wondered about the fate of that starkly propagandist painting.

That afternoon the correspondent was formally invited to the U.S. Embassy, where he had tea *à deux* with William E. Dodd, the much-tried Ambassador who was soon to give up his not too successful tenure of office there. In reply to questioning as to my findings I emphasized the contrast between the despairing German mood of 1921 and the completely self-confident, not to say arrogant, Nazi attitude in 1937. The Ambassador, a student of history, nodded his head sadly. "The wheel has turned too quickly," he said, confirming von Lewinski's gloomy prediction that Hitler henceforth would show little restraint. That night, after mailing a couple of articles to catch a German express steamer, I took the train for Prague. There was a brief stopover in lovely Dresden; then across the contested frontier and through the seething Sudetenland to meet Mr. Meyer for breakfast at his hotel in the capital of Czechoslovakia.

Prague was no longer quite as picturesque a city as I remembered from a visit in 1921. During the intervening years Czech passion for modernization had swept away much of the medieval huddle around the Karluvmost, oldest and most decorative of the dozen bridges across the Vltava river. It had been called *Karlsbrücke* and the correspondent found the rigidly enforced change from German to Czech nomenclature confusing. He could not accustom himself to speaking of the beautiful old *Theinkirche* as *Tynskykostel*. The Christmas Carol helped with the one named after St. Wenceslaus. But local pronunciation of the great Gothic Cathedral of St. Vitus was never absorbed. That seemed a particularly appropriate patron for a people as nervously energetic as the Czechs.

But there was little time for sightseeing. Mr. Meyer had secured an appointment with President Edward Benes and by mid-morning we were at his office, in the great hilltop castle of Hradcany. It is said to contain 868 separate rooms and certainly many stately halls were traversed before the visitors were ushered into the huge audience chamber where the President, a small and sharp-looking man, seemed both physically and metaphorically lost. He sat at a royal desk with a magnificent view over the far-flung city with the winding river cutting through its middle. Through the tall windows of this room, onto the rocks far below, several unpopular governors of Bohemia had been unceremoniously ejected some centuries ago. This crude form of justice was euphemized in the official guidebook as "defenestration." I had no premonition that Jan Masaryk, foreign minister of the Republic and son of its first President, would be similarly "defenestrated" when the Communists took control of Prague, early in 1948.

The interview was conducted in English, which Benes spoke with extraordinary lucidity. It soon demonstrated that a prevalent English criticism of his policy—its extreme Czech nationalism—was fully justified. Czechoslovakia, a hybrid creation of the Paris Peace Conference, bore little resemblance to the ancient kingdom of Bohemia which was supposed to give it historical justification. The artificial boundaries included big blocs of discontented Germans, Magyars, Moravians, Poles and Ruthenians to whom the governing Czechs and Slovaks allowed little autonomy. Since there was also bad feeling between its two dominant elements Czechoslovakia reproduced, on a less stable basis, all the political weakness of the Austro-Hungarian dual monarchy from which it had been arbitrarily carved by the Paris peace-makers. And no minority president could hope to inspire the solidifying loyalty with which the Hapsburgs had cemented the old regime.

According to Dr. Benes his country had no problems that could not be solved with a little more time and a little less Hitler. Unquestionably the latter was working zealously to stir discontent in the heavily Germanic part of Czechoslovakia. But this only made the Czech leaders more adamant in refusing to Sudeten Germans the same right of self-determination with which the former had so eloquently clouded Woodrow Wilson's vision. Even in 1937, I believe, a really federalized republic, emphasizing home rule, might have solved the problem. Dr. Benes could not see it that way so it was ironic that a decade later he would have to accept the Kremlin's solution, annexing the tail of Czechoslovakia and making the remainder a vassal "people's democratic republic." Yet, as a predominantly Slavic country, it was a not unnatural fate for an area doomed by geography alone to a precarious independence. There was little apprehension among the merry group of Czech officials who took the editor to dinner that evening at a beautiful river-side restaurant. Since the United States had pre-sided over Czechoslovakia's rise, they told him, Americans would surely prevent its fall. It was the same unhappy assumption that would later involve us in Korea, Vietnam and Israel. I wondered about this assumed "commitment" as I took the sleeper for Vienna, where Mr. Meyer had preceded me by plane. But I was certain, from what I had learned in Germany, that the Nazi hammer would fall first on Austria.

Though no plebiscite on the issue was ever held it is probable that, in 1937, a large majority of Austrians looked favor-ably on union with Germany. The larger country was much more prosperous than the truncated remnant of Hapsburg gran-deur and the Nazi movement had not by then wholly disgraced itself, except in Jewish eyes. The faded magnificence of Vienna only emphasized the poverty of the mountainous sliver to which the old dual monarchy had been reduced and in the disproportionately huge capital one worker in every three was unemployed. Scars from recent street fighting were apparent and the government of mod-erate Chancellor Schuschnigg wavered helplessly between the Nazi and Com-munist factions. Hope of stability had vanished with the assassination of Chan-cellor Dollfuss, three years earlier, and everyone seemed to agree that a German takeover, though feared by many, was inevitable. Again the sorry consequences of the Versailles "peace" were all too apparent.

The principal Vienna informant of *The Post* correspondent was the U.S. Minister, George S. Messersmith, a career diplomat who had previously been Consul General in Berlin and was familiar with the eco-nomic as well as political aspects of the situation. He confirmed the report, heard by me in Berlin, that Mussolini had with-drawn his earlier objections to *Anschluss*,

thus making the Austro-German union virtually certain. The question was no longer *whether* but only *when* and *how* it would take place, a subject much debated at the Café Louvre where the foreign correspondents gathered to exchange re-ports and rumors. I felt so sure of the ground on *Anschluss* that I predicted it in one of my articles, following an interview with timid Foreign Minister Schmidt. This was at the famous Ballhausplatz where the Congress of Vienna, by refusing to humiliate and crush Napoleonic France, had worked out a contrastingly durable peace. Meyer got virtual confirmation of the Hitler-Mussolini accord when he called upon Chancellor Schuschnigg the eve-ning that I left for Munich, "*Hauptstadt der Bewegung*" (Chief City of the Move-ment), where I felt it important to look into the mechanics of Nazi operation.

Not the least illuminating meeting of the Vienna stay was one with Helena Kollmann, the Austrian girl who had cared for our small daughters in Baltimore and then accompanied the family to Geneva in 1928. Helena had risen to the position of inspector in a textile factory and was engaged to an expert woodworker, Hans Mareda, who came with her to the dinner I arranged in a modest restaurant. Hans was unable to find work, even as a plain carpenter, because of the cessation of almost all construction in Vienna. Con-sequently Helena could not marry, her own small wage being scarcely sufficient to support her widowed mother. Nobody could have been less of a Nazi than Helena but her comment on *Anschluss* was: "Most of my friends think that is our only hope." It would be nearly nine months before Hitler would actually incorporate Austria in the Third Reich. But certainly nobody should have been surprised when he fi-nally moved to do so.

At the British Embassy, in Berlin, I had been advised to make contact with His

Majesty's Consul General in Munich. This Mr. Gainor was said to be unusually well-informed on details of National Socialist organization. By prearrangement, therefore, the correspondent went direct from the railroad station to the British Consulate where this high-type civil servant described the "apparatus" built up by Hitler and his associates to control and direct the German people. It was a terrifying analysis of the manner in which principles of business management can be applied to keep an entire population in efficient subjection. Then I reported to the *Presse Abteilung* and was sent on with an escort to the famous "Braunhaus," national headquarters of the Nazi Party. Here, as everywhere, I was well received and shown in operation the complex organization which Gainor had already described. Great batteries of filing cabinets contained individual cards for every party member, cross-indexed both for localities and skills. When a job of any magnitude was to be filled, either in industry or the professions, particulars had to be sent to the Braunhaus. If a registered Nazi met the requirements he or she would be "recommended" to the employer, whether that was a school board in Silesia or an insurance office in the Rhineland. In reply to a question the reporter was assured that there was no "legal" obligation to employ the referred *Partei Mitglieder* in preference to another applicant. "But we haven't set up this system just for the fun of it," the official added with a smile.

This careful melding of Nazi members and directive positions was curiously distorted in the highest echelons of government. There executive appointments were often given to obviously unqualified persons, merely because they had been associated with Hitler in the early days of the movement. Ribbentrop, soon to become Foreign Minister, was one illustration of this bad staff work and a number of incompetent generals were equally disastrous. Goering was everywhere regarded as an able man, and also Dr. Goebbels in his twisted way. But when war came most of those in the Fuehrer's intimate circle could not be called competent, still less distinguished. This was a point much emphasized by my Russian Embassy friend, Nehmann, whenever I argued with him in Washington that the Communist and Nazi dictatorships were essentially similar. "To be a Nazi," said Nehmann, "you need only goosestep and shout 'Heil Hitler.' To be a Communist you must first and foremost be well trained. Stumblebums do not last long in the Communist hierarchy."

A pleasant young official from the Press Bureau—Eric Gassner—was assigned as escort and on request took me to the "Temple of Honor" where Hitler's comrades killed in the premature Putsch of 1923 were buried. I had heard that this illustrated German sentimentality at its most maudlin. In a deeply excavated shrine, reached by a ring of marble steps, a dozen great granite sarcophagi were aligned, each bearing the name of the fallen under an elaborately carved eagle and wreath-encircled swastika. Below all this was the word *HIER* in large capitals, this being the presumed answer of the interred to the summons of the *Führer*. This domed temple of *Ewige Wache*, or Eternal Watch, was continuously guarded by steel-helmeted, strapping S.S. troopers but did not seem to attract many visitors. I then asked whether I might visit Dachau, a concentration camp near Munich where many Jews were said to be confined. That would be impossible without a special pass and 24 hours delay, said Gassner, adding that only Communists, profiteers and other "criminals" were under detention there. "I expect you are going to have racial trouble with your Negroes," he added evasively.

Frau Gassner, blonde, beautiful, petite and lively, joined us for lunch at the famous Hofbräuhaus, and surprised me by telling stories making fun of Hitler. One stuck in memory, about a Muenchener who was arrested for causing a street disturbance. He was charged with repeatedly shouting: "First I come and then comes Hitler." The magistrate asked his name. "Heinrich Heil, your Honor, Heil Hitler!" Many Bavarians would never use that sycophantic greeting, sticking to their traditional *Grüss Gott*. All told, I was in Munich only 12 hours on this trip but it gave opportunity to revisit several of the lovely old places which the bombings would irreparably damage. The Gassners saw me to my train and I sought to balance my thoughts from the tidy and tended countryside, speeding through the long summer evening towards the Alpine barrier and Geneva beyond.

At Zürich a *couchette* was available, but there were no covers and I spent an uncomfortable night, not much relieved by making notes for my article on Nazi Munich. Then, as the train pulled into Cornavin Station in the gray dawn, there was a familiar voice and a broad, smiling face at the window. They belonged to my cheery Swabian friend Fritz Schnable, the German chief of the League of Nation's Publications Division, with whom I had worked closely seven years earlier. Old Fritz had risen at 4:00 A.M. to meet me and take me to the Schnable home for a hot bath and breakfast before the long day started. Respect for the many incorruptible German individualists whom he knew, like Schnable and von Lewinski, kept the reporter from falling into the conventional pattern of indiscriminate hatred. He would think of his friends across the Rhine when Americans asserted, as many came to do, that: "All Huns are uncivilized."

It was a poignant experience to revisit Geneva, outwardly as unchanged as overshadowing Mont Blanc since he had reluctantly left there early in 1931. "Except that Isabel was not with me," he wrote in his journal, it was all "unalloyed pleasure." Yet, in the same entry, this was qualified. ". . . there is something tragic in the tranquility of the place, by contrast with the alarums and excursions for which solutions should be sought at the League H.Q., and are not."

For the editor the return had aspects of Homecoming Day. Many of his old friends were still, somewhat nervously, with the Secretariat and he was lodged at Merimont, the palatial Sweetser residence which Isabel and he had occupied the summer of 1930. Joseph Avenol, who had succeeded Sir Eric Drummond as Secretary-General, gave a big luncheon for him and Mr. Meyer, who was also a Sweetser guest. Together they inspected the new and handsome Palais des Nations, with the many artistic gifts from various governments and the striking Sert murals in the imposing Council Chamber. In the fine library I was shown a shelf with several well-thumbed copies of my book on *The Society of Nations*—a "must" for every serious student of the League, they said graciously. "But over all," I noted, "broods that ominous quiet, though it is clear that the machinery is well-oiled and all ready to function if only the governments will call it into action." I could have stayed a month with pleasure but Meyer now was eager to get back. For those who had shown the travelers attention at Geneva the publisher gave a big dinner at Eaux Vives, the modish lakeside restaurant which the Morleys had come to know well during their residence. Afterwards, at the less pretentious and more familiar Bavaria *Bierstube*, there was time for a couple of steins with magnetic Robert Dell, roving correspondent of the *Guardian*, who before long would be in trouble with the French authorities for alleged pro-Germanism.

Then on to Paris, where Chautemps had now replaced the vacillating Blum as Premier. The French financial situation was desperate; the franc growing weaker daily. With Meyer doing the shrewd questioning an illuminating discussion with the new Prime Minister was obtained. I cabled the essence of this to *The Post* and then hurried to London where a key Parliamentary debate on British policy in the worsening Spanish crisis was scheduled. A Labor Party resolution calling for aid to the collapsing Republican government was up for decision and Prime Minister Chamberlain's insistence on strict neutrality was roundly criticized. The editor had wangled a seat in the crowded press gallery of the House of Commons, where he admired the perfect courtesy with which sharp acrimony was cloaked. When Chamberlain said it was "a time for cool heads" Lloyd George retorted that "any fish can have a cool head. What Britain needs now is a warm heart." But the Prime Minister had the majority solidly behind his pacific course, as later at Munich, and the move to intervene in Spain was defeated, nearly two to one. As I reported, confusion was dominant in France, caution in Britain, indifference in the United States and helplessness in the League of Nations. It was not a combination likely to deter a Nazi takeover in Austria, when Hitler got ready to strike.

This was my last report on a memorable circuit. The next day, June 26, the editor boarded the *Berengaria* at Southampton. At Cherbourg Mr. Meyer rejoined from Paris and they docked in New York on July 2, just 44 days after departure. For me it had been a grueling period. In addition to several cables I had written some twenty careful articles which *The Post* would soon republish in booklet form, titled *Europe Today*. On the whole relations

with my boss had been excellent but judgments were not always uniform. They could not be, in view of Mr. Meyer's very natural refusal to inspect the German scene. In a frank discussion on the return trip the publisher accused his editor of undue resistance to the former's ideas. To this I replied tartly that if a Yes-man had been wanted I was a poor selection. The breeze blew over quickly and probably revealed, more than anything else, the anxieties which both men were bringing back.

It was obvious that the machinery of collective action had completely broken down. The League was moribund. For the first time war now seemed to me a probability. Hitler would force it because his growing megalomania would overstrain the breaking point of British toleration. There would be no resistance to German annexation of Austria, justifiable under the principle of self-determination. There would probably be no war if jerrybuilt Czechoslovakia were dismembered by German pressure. Britain had no treaty commitment there, aside from the general obligations of the distintegrating League Covenant, and France was in no condition to resist. But the third step in Hitler's expansion program would be to recover Danzig and the territorial connection with East Prussia, at Polish expense. Here there would certainly be stern opposition, for different reasons, both from Britain and from Russia. Because of the significance of the Polish vote this would also shake American neutrality.

If war should come, what would be its effect on nations already half-ruined and morally debilitated by the degeneration of the last conflict? What Pandora's box of lasting social evils would be opened by the vengeful emotionalism that renewed hostilities would inevitably produce? The idealized brutalities of Commando training, for instance, would surely have its heritage in a growth of organized gang-sterism, most dangerous in American cities because of racial overtones. Belief in the sanctity of private property, dear to American hearts, would be weakened by countless requisitions, confiscations and authorized destruction. Finally, what would be the effect of total war, with its enormous impetus for centralization, on the structure of a federal republic constitutionally dedicated to the dispersion, division and localization of power? There was more than a chance that such schizophrenia would undermine the basic institutions of the United States, no matter who won or lost on fields of battle.

What then should be the policy of the United States, and what the editorial policy of *The Post*? The answer to the first question should also answer the second, but I was not too confident that this would be the case. It would be no gain for America if Communism should take over in Central Europe, which would be the probable result of a violent Nazi over-throw. The intolerable humiliation and impossible exactions of the Treaty of Versailles were fundamentally responsible for the mass neurosis that had swept Hitler to power. The movement was anathema to countless Germans and, unlike the deeply calculating Communist leadership, was unlikely to last if international stability could be restored. On the other hand Americans were sure to become evermore anti-German if Nazi persecution of the Jews was stepped up, as seemed all too probable. And as a Jew could my publisher be expected to support the difficult policy of neutrality that pure reason suggested as the best American course, more so because the intervention of 1917 had been so barren of good results?

These questions deeply worried me on the voyage home. The sea was calm and the weather glorious. But the editor knew that a hurricane was gathering.

NOTE

[1] In 1941 Miller published a strongly anti-Nazi book: *You Can't Do Business With Hitler*. A more balanced study of the period is found in *Failure of a Mission*, by Sir Nevile Henderson, who in 1937 was the newly-installed British Ambassador to Germany.   [XVIII, Spring 1974, 133–144]

[59]

Albert Speer and the Nazi War Plants

EUGENE DAVIDSON

Eugene (Arthur) Davidson *(1902–   ), educated at Yale (B.A., 1927; postgraduate studies, 1927–1928), is a former head of the Yale University Press and now lives in Santa Barbara, California. President of the Foundation for Foreign Affairs in Washington, D.C., from 1957 to 1970, he was the editor of* Modern Age *from 1960 to 1970. The author of books on* The Death and Life of Germany *(1959),* The Nuremberg Fallacy *(1973), and* The Making of Adolf Hitler *(1977), he has contributed book reviews, articles, and poetry to numerous journals. His article on Albert Speer is condensed from a chapter in Mr. Davidson's book* The Trial of the Germans *(1967), the result of seven years of work in research centers around the world on the documents of the National Socialist period that came to light during and after the Nuremberg trials and on interviews of persons ranging from everyday citizens to members of the German High Command.*

ONE OF THE genuinely gifted men to become part of the Nazi war apparatus was the architect Albert Speer.* Speer became Minister of Arms and Munitions in 1942, when he was thirty-six years old, after Fritz Todt, builder of the West Wall as well as of more durable structures like the Autobahnen, had been killed in an airplane accident. But Speer was far abler than his predecessor, who was mainly an engineer, an efficient organizer of large-scale construction.[1] Speer got rid, as far as he could, of the system of coercion; he put full responsibility for the efficiency of a plant into the hands of the local manager; he improvised, exhorted, parceled out authority among bureaucrats and entrepreneurs, and hundreds of his deputies were "honorary co-workers," borrowed from private industry for the duration of the war and paid only a fraction of what they had been getting as managers or technicians. He resisted anyone when production was threatened—Himmler, Bormann, Goebbels, and finally Hitler himself.

IT WAS OWING to Speer that the biggest year of German manufacture of arms was 1944; only ten months before the end of the war, German production of airplanes and munitions reached an all-time high despite the thousands of bombers attacking German cities around the clock, the closing ring of Allied armies, and the blockade. In 1944 seven times as many weapons were produced as in 1942, five and a half times the number of armored vehicles, and six times the amount of

---

*Albert Speer was released from the Spandau prison in October 1966.

ammunition, but only 30 per cent more workers were employed. Speer made few major miscalculations; he had no part in the decision to put so much material and labor in the costly "V" weapons, expenditures he would have preferred to see devoted to fighter planes so bitterly needed against the Allied bombers. He opposed the diversion of so much labor to the construction of underground factories when other production was vitally needed; nor was it his beltline of factories that failed. The German tanks and planes became sporadically useless after May, 1944, because fuel was lacking following the massed Allied attacks on the synthetic gasoline plants; in these bombings, Speer declared at Nuremberg, 90 per cent of German fuel production was destroyed.

Speer's achievement was of a divided character. He always thought of himself as an artist, and he was certainly a builder and organizer of monumental projects that were intended not only to rescue the Reich from defeat but to help create a resplendent and completely imaginary future Germany in which they would provide a scale of living never before approached in the world; and Speer the builder served with all his talents a nihilistic leader who built only in his own image and who would blow everything up when his luck ran out. In the closing months of the war, when Hitler was at his most deadly in dealing with doubters even when they were old Party comrades—which Speer was not (he had joined the Party only in 1932)—Speer told the Fuehrer bluntly the war was lost. It was the kind of statement that cost the head of many a man who made it to the wrong person, for this was defeatism which immediately became high treason when the Gestapo and the *Volksgericht*, not to mention the Fuehrer himself, heard of it.

Speer in addition disobeyed the direct and unconditional order of Hitler to blow up not only military strongpoints and plants that could be useful to the Allies, but also those that were the sources of German subsistence then and in the future—the factories and bridges, ships, freight cars, locomotives and railroad installations, power stations, and water supplies of the cities lying in the path of the advancing Allied armies. As one device for salvaging everything he possibly could, he quoted to Bormann—who wanted the German people to be forced to converge in the center of the country where they would fight to the last, leaving only scorched earth behind them—Hitler's assurances that the lost territories would soon be recaptured. Despite the Fuehrer's explicit directives, Speer therefore ordered that factories were to be merely "paralyzed," not destroyed, and moreover this was to be done only at the last moment, keeping production and machinery intact as long as possible, and then with luck the Allies would take the factories over without serious damage.[2]

Speer salved his patriotic conscience by telling himself that in any event the Allies would gain little or nothing by capturing the factories, since owing to the deficiencies in transport they at best could not use them for at least nine months. In this way he saved the Minette mines in France from destruction, telling Bormann and the other Party fanatics that a German counterattack would soon restore them to the Reich's uses. No one, he wrote to Hitler, had the right to order the destruction of the means of survival of the nation. And when he finally became convinced that Hitler was identifying with his own lost cause the fate of the people he had professed to love so deeply, Speer planned to kill him. Since everyone who visited the Fuehrer was searched after the July 20 attempt on Hitler's life, Speer wanted to put poison-gas grenades in the ventilating system of Hitler's bunker in Berlin, and he was prevented from carrying out his purpose only because the ingenious idea proved to be technically impracticable. Hitler, with his primitive instinct for danger, had ordered a brick chimney four meters high to be built around the vents so they could not be tampered with.

But despite his furious resistance to Hitler's orders for senseless destruction, Speer was one of the very last among the faithful and unfaithful to take his farewell of the Fuehrer; he flew to the Berlin bunker, which was now the center of the withering, converging Russian attack, only a few days before Hitler committed suicide. In his fashion he remained devoted to the man who had probably wished him as well as Hitler could wish anyone; but Speer would have killed the Fuehrer and the Party leaders with his bare hands rather than accept the senseless loss of the machines that would keep the threadbare survivors of the war alive. He intended to kill Himmler, Goebbels, and Bormann, the chief advocates of scorched earth along with Hitler; he organized the automatic pistols and the cars that would ambush them and he planned to drive one of the cars himself. But the plot failed when Speer found no way to get at Hitler and these others at the same time. He came to the same conclusions as the conspirators of July 20, but in terms of his specialty, which had more to do with the efficient manufacture of goods than of ideas.

Some of the people around Hitler, including Speer, thought Speer enjoyed a special freedom with the Fuehrer because he was an architect—a brilliant practitioner of the profession that Hitler had once chosen for himself and to which the Fuehrer gave his full amateur talents when he set out to rebuild the Reich after he became Chancellor. Speer became Hitler's chief architect in 1934, when he was only twenty-nine years old. He was born in Mannheim on March 19, 1905, the son and grandson of architects. After taking his *Abitur* he studied architecture at Karlsruhe, Munich, and Berlin, where, when Hitler took power, he was an assistant at the Technische Hochschule and practicing his profession at the same time. He deeply impressed the Fuehrer with his new Reichstag, which not only was designed in the heroic style the Fuehrer so doted on, but also was erected in a shorter time than anyone would have thought likely. Speer then, as later, was prodigal with workers and used twice as many as more economical architects might have demanded. Hitler gave him the task of replanning Berlin and along with it the spiritual home of the Party—Nuremberg. Speer told the court that if he had been free to carry out his blueprints, the Reich would have had some of the largest buildings in the world and the whole earthshaking plan would have cost less than two months of war.

Speer thought that if Hitler had permitted himself to have a friend Speer might have been the one chosen because of their common interest. For whatever reason, Speer was able to talk to the Fuehrer in words no one else dared use without incurring any of the penalties inflicted on the generals, for example, who dared to be critical. "Off with their heads" was for doubtful military men and politicians; Speer was neither but he was otherwise everything Hitler had once dreamed of becoming himself. He told the Fuehrer the task given him was nonpolitical; it had to be carried out by technicians and experts of all descriptions, including the 6,000 "honorary co-workers," many of whom took a dim view of the Party. He recalled this pronouncement to Hitler over and over again when the Party, the Gauleiters, and the SS tried to invade his domain where they thought high treason lurked.

Speer began his rearguard action, his one-man resistance movement, late in the war, after the invasion of Germany had started, but once he began to resist he was ready to go just as far as the men of July 20. Although he never joined them, he was highly enough regarded by the conspirators to be their choice for Minister of Economics in the new regime that would succeed Hitler's, and the Fuehrer not only knew about this but was constantly reminded of it by Bormann and the others who never had believed in Speer's loyalty. In his meetings with Hitler, as well as in the memoranda he sent him, Speer became increasingly defeatist, and in mid-March, 1945, he wrote a long report to the Fuehrer, telling him plainly that German industry would collapse within four to eight weeks with certainty and that the war could not be continued after this breakdown.

IT WAS ON March 29, that Speer wrote Hitler a stinging letter summing up their conversation of the day before:

If I write to you again it is because I am not in the position on emotional grounds to share my thoughts with you by word of mouth. First I must tell you how proud and happy I would be if I might continue to work for Germany as your collaborator. To leave my post, even if you ordered me to do so, in this decisive time would seem like desertion to the German people and to my loyal co-workers. Nevertheless I am in duty bound to tell you, without regard to any personal consequences, plainly and unadornedly what my inner feelings are with regard to the situation. I have always told you—as one of the few co-workers—openly and honorably what I think and I shall continue to do so. You distinguished yesterday between the recognition of realities through which one can be convinced that the war no longer may be won and the belief that despite everything it may all come out all right. . . . My belief in a happy turn of

fate for us was unbroken up to March 18. . . . I am an artist and as such was given a job that was completely alien and difficult. I have done much for Germany. Without my work the war might have been lost in 1942–43. I mastered the job not as a specialist but with the characteristics proper to an artist: with the belief in his task and in success, with the instinct for what is right, with a sense for generous solutions, with an inner integrity without which no artist can find proper solutions.

I believe in the future of the German people. . . . I was desolate when I saw in the days of victory in 1940 how we in the broadest circles of our leadership lost our bearing. Here was the time when providence demanded of us decorum and inner modesty. Then victory would have been ours. . . . A precious year was lost for armament and development through easy-going ways and laziness and then, as though providence wanted to warn us, bad luck trailed our military accomplishments. . . . The frost before Moscow, the fog at Stalingrad and the clear sky over the winter offensive of 1944 [Speer is here talking of the German Ardennes offensive, where the weather played a role, but certainly not a decisive one, in bringing the attack to a halt]. . . . When on March 18 I gave you my memorandum I was sure you would approve completely the conclusions I had drawn for the preservation of our people. For you yourself once said that the task of the leadership of a state is to prevent its people at the end of a lost war from coming to an heroic end. Nevertheless you said on that evening, if we have not misunderstood you, clearly and unmistakably: "If the war is lost, the people are lost too. . . . It is not necessary to bother about the fundamentals that the people will need for its most primitive future existence. On the contrary it would be better to destroy these things. For the people have shown themselves weaker and the future belongs entirely to the stronger peoples of the East. Those who survive the war will in any event be only the inferior ones, the best have fallen." Hearing these words, I was most deeply shaken. . . . Up to then I had believed with all my heart in a good end to this war. I hoped that not only our new weapons and planes but above all the fanatical, growing belief in our future would rouse the people and the leadership to the last sacrifices. I was then myself determined to take a glider and fly against the Russian power stations and through my personal involvement to help out, to change fate and at the same time to set an example.

I can, however, no longer believe in the success of our affairs if in these decisive months at the same time, and according to plan, we destroy the substance of our people. That is so great an injustice against our people that fate could never again mean well by us.

Speer then repeated what he had written in a letter of March 15:

> What generations have built up we are not permitted to destroy. If the enemy does so and thus exterminates the German people then the historic guilt is his alone. . . . I can only continue my work with inner probity and with conviction and belief in the future when you, my Fuehrer, acknowledge, as you have before, the necessity for maintaining the substance of our people. . . . Your order of March 19, 1945, takes away the last industrial possibilities and knowledge of it will throw the population into the greatest despair.[3] . . . I ask you therefore not to complete this act of destruction against your people. Should you be able to make this decision in whatever form then I will again have the faith and the courage to be able to work with the greatest energy. . . .

And he closed the letter not with "Heil Hitler" but with "May God Protect Germany."

Speer did succeed in getting Hitler to modify this insane order. He drew up what became the Fuehrer decree of March 30, which declared that since the destruction order was given to prevent the use of the installations by the enemy, demolitions were only to be carried out under immediate threat of capture and were not to weaken the German ability to fight. Bridges and traffic installations were to be destroyed entirely but supply plants need only be paralyzed. Total destruction of especially important plants was only to be carried out with the approval of Speer; and the Party, State, and Armed Forces were to assist him. This document was a remarkable tribute to Speer's influence on Hitler. In addition, Speer was enabled to issue a directive under his own signature on the same date to accompany the Hitler decree, declaring that his previous orders for paralyzing industrial and supply plants were still in effect. Total destruction of the most important plants and of their essential parts was to be carried out only by order of the Fuehrer transmitted through him, and Speer would name such factories with the counsel of the chairman of the armament committees.

Speer's victory was the more astonishing for its taking place at a time when Hitler suspected high treason on every side, when he was ordering death penalties for his closest former collaborators, and when the hopeless battles of the remnants of the German armies were being fought only to give him a few more weeks of life. At this time, when Hitler was identifying the fate of the German people with his own, Speer succeeded in breaking through the impenetrable barriers of fantasy; he forced the Fuehrer to change his mind. Speer was the only man who succeeded in doing this, and Hitler seemingly bore him no ill will.

A radio speech Speer wanted to make early in April, 1945, was canceled by Goebbels, who thought it defeatist, but on April 16, in Hamburg, Speer made a recording of another speech which he planned to have broadcast when the time came—after Hitler's death. In it he said that further destruction or even "paralyzing" operations were not to be carried out, that they were forbidden in Germany and the occupied territories. No bridges were to be blown up and their demolition charges were to be removed; protection was to be provided for factories, railroads, and communication installations. Anyone who resisted the order was to be dealt with by the Army and the Volkssturm (in which only volunteers were henceforth to serve), if necessary by force of arms. Prisoners of war and foreign workers were to remain in their camps, but if they were already on the road toward their homes they should be sent on their way. Political prisoners and Jews in concentration camps were to be separated from the asocial prisoners and be turned over unharmed to the Allies when the occupying troops appeared. Any Werewolf activity was to stop.

Although this speech was never delivered, all Speer's orders were given in its spirit. He made no secret of his implacable opposition to Himmler, Ley, Bormann, Sauckel, Goebbels, and all the other down-the-line Party men who interfered with his job of supplying Germany with weapons and, while hope remained, of obtaining a stalemate or somehow tolerable conditions for Germany's survival.

SPEER'S REMARKABLE SUCCESS in increasing production came from his gift of improvisation and his clear sense of how to organize. He used beltlines and manufactured standardized parts in scattered factories so that if one factory was destroyed, the finished tanks, or whatever, could still be produced. He gave bonuses, threatened punishments, and got rid of as many administrative bureaucrats as he could. The last accomplishment was close to his heart; he was grateful for the fire that destroyed thousands of documents in his ministry, and he used the occasion, he told his co-workers, to drop a long list of officials from their jobs. "We cannot

expect occurrences of this kind will continuously bring new vigor to our work," he told his colleagues. He was opposed to large aggregates, preferring a large number of smaller enterprises; huge factories, he thought, produced huge bureaucracies. He ran his vast production empire with a minimum of manpower; he had twenty-one main committees, which were responsible for the finished products of the armament industry, and twelve so-called "rings" to provide for the delivery of raw materials. The committees and rings had the task of streamlining production and deciding on what the factories should concentrate and on how any improvements in manufacture or use of materials might be made. The committees and rings did the planning, working closely with the over-all Planning Commission, and Speer kept emphasizing that their chairmen must keep in close personal touch with the multifarious web of assignments that had to be carried out according to the directives.

The job of the committees, Speer said, was mainly to back up the factory manager. Exchange of information between plants was constant, and secret material, including patents, was made available to all factories, as were any new discoveries. Speer gave the German plants what they always tended to lack: flexibility and a plant-wide morale, a sense of comradeship and of working for the general cause with enthusiasm without regard to salary and social differences. The main incentives for the workers were provided, to be sure, by the war, but they also knew that only in this, in Speer's fashion, could the previous methods of coercion be kept out of the plants. Always lurking in the background was the Party and its hostility to business and industry and anything it did not directly control. Both the committees and the rings were composed of mixed groups from the Wehrmacht and technical experts from industry. The decision on the development of new weapons was in the hands of the chairmen of the committees, who were company officials, engineers, and construction men, and any decision they made could be overruled only by Speer, or by the Wehrmacht, or by Hitler himself. The plant managers had complete authority in their own plants as far as Speer could give it to them and keep them free from Party interference.

His remarkable record was by no means owing to the underground factories of which so much was later to be heard. They provided but a small fraction of German production; at the end of the war only 300,000 square meters of such plants existed, although there were plans for three million square meters more to come. Both Speer and Field Marshal Milch, who was one of the chief men responsible for the production of fighter planes, for which the underground plants were mainly built, and who sat with Speer on the Central Planning Board as well as on the Jaeger Staff,[4] were against the building of these plants because the idea, they said, had occurred to Goering too late in the war and the time and manpower needed for their building would be better utilized to produce planes in the factories already available.

Speer gladly hired anyone who was able to do the kind of job he needed, and Goebbels, Kaltenbrunner, and Bormann called his ministry a nest of anti-Party sentiment and activity, which it undoubtedly was by their standards in view of the ceaseless attempts of its chief to step up production regardless of the race or political sentiments of his producers and his single-minded efforts to circumvent the destruction orders. Speer was glad to employ Jews or Slavs, Poles, Ukrainians, Czechs, and Russians, all the hated inferior people, if only they could produce. He gratefully put concentration-camp in-

mates and prisoners of war to work for his enterprises. Foreign workers of all nationalities (volunteers, forced laborers, concentration-camp workers, and prisoners of war) made up 40 per cent of the personnel of the German war factories. More than two and a half million Frenchmen worked for Germany—of the more than one million French prisoners of war, only some 48,000 were unemployed. There were over a half million Dutchmen and 150,000 Belgians, and workers came by the millions from the East.[5] Speer wanted them treated well and paid on scales that compared with the Germans, otherwise they would not work properly. He never hesitated either to make use of the SS or to fight it. He elbowed Himmler out of setting up more concentration camp factories, bringing these workers as far as he could under his own authority, and he merely agreed to supply Himmler's Waffen SS divisions with more war material in proportion to the concentration camp workers the Reichsfuehrer SS made available. Speer forbade the Gestapo making arrests in his factories, and protested against their practice of holding prisoners for months because of some minor defect in their papers when they might otherwise be working. His battle was against whatever they or anyone else did that lost workers for the Reich.

In June, 1944, Speer made use of his close relationship with Hitler to protest to him the stupid misuse of Russian prisoners of war by the SS, pointing out that thousands of them had been shipped to SS factories from plants where they had been usefully employed and that most of them were skilled specialists.[6] Speer's protest was a direct attack on Himmler, who was extending his empire as far as it would go. The SS had begun to produce goods on its own account with a woodworking plant in Dachau; this was successful enough from Himmler and Pohl's point of view to warrant extending the SS enterprises to other concentration camps—to Oranienburg, Buchenwald, Neuengamme. In addition, concentration-camp labor was supplied on a rental basis to outside factories that needed it. Himmler wanted to keep all concentration-camp labor available for these SS factories alone, but Speer was able to convince the Fuehrer that war production would be damaged by such a wide-scale diversion of Germany's scarce machine tools. Himmler, in his efforts to recruit labor, ordered that 35,000 Eastern workers who had breached their labor contract be sent "by the quickest means" to one of these concentration camps where he could make use of them.[7] The only ones to be exempt were those in solitary confinement awaiting further interrogation.

Speer stormed against both the attempts of Sauckel to take workers from the protected industries he had set up in the occupied countries and the SS practice of arresting German and foreign workers on some trivial pretext and sending them to concentration camps. Such workers, he said, like the prisoners of war, never came back to the places where they had been employed and their services were lost as they disappeared into the labyrinths of Himmler's domains, for the SS used them in any kind of work. He complained to Hitler that 30,000 to 40,000 workers a month were thus kidnapped out of the economy by Himmler. He told the Fuehrer, too, that the Russians, especially the women workers, if decently treated were usually content with their lot. He wanted humane treatment for the same reasons he wanted coal and oil for his machines, but he loved machines better than people. In one conference he suggested that in order to obtain French specialists who were prisoners of war for German factories the rumor be spread that such men would be freed if they volunteered. The

French would have a list of such experts and once the Germans had it on hand they could simply conscript the specialists. There was no great harm in Speer, but he was a machine man, an efficiency expert, and the human beings were essential counters in his task.

His admiration for the order of the machines that he understood so well even led him at the end of the war to try to stop the manufacture of explosives to prevent their being used to blow up the factories Germany would so desperately need after the fighting was over. Once he recognized the war was lost, he threw in his hand; his factories had to play a role in the future; production for its own sake had no meaning for him. Nor did he have any confidence in the miracle weapons, the V-1s and V-2s. He fought against the manufacture of the new and potent gases Tabun and Sarin, which German chemists had succeeded in producing and against which no gas masks were said to be effective. Tabun and Sarin were five times more powerful than the former war gases, and Goebbels and Bormann and a handful of scorched-earth fanatics wanted to use them to stop the Allied advance. Hitler, however, came to agree with the arguments of Speer and the generals that it would be catastrophic for Germany to use poison gases in view of the Allied control of the air and their almost unhindered ability to hit the German cities with bombs—including gas bombs—in retaliation and Speer was finally able to stop the manufacture of the gases.

With the proclamation by Hitler of total war on July 25, 1944, German men from the ages of sixteen to sixty-five and women from seventeen to fifty had to register for work. At long last Speer's contention that German man and especially woman power was not being adequately employed was acknowledged in the Fuehrer decree. Speer had always wanted the factories manned by German rather than foreign labor, largely because indigenous labor would not increase the demand on the food supplies. But the decree came too late for Speer's purpose; the millions of foreign workers were already in Germany, and it was precisely at this time that the Allied bombardments of the synthetic oil plants made much of the production useless. German cities had long been under heavy bombardment, and no careful canvass of how many women were working and whether their jobs were indispensable could be made. Whole blocks of houses were disappearing at a time; the task of finding living quarters, lining up for food, and getting to and from work if a woman had a job took strength enough; and the "combing-out" squads sent by the Party only increased anxieties without adding much to the labor force. Many women with children were sent to the country, and sometimes whole schools were evacuated. The working mother stayed at her job. But what she did and how long she worked could no longer be efficiently controlled.

Speer acted on behalf of his own technocracy; he gladly took what labor he could from whatever source; he was gratified by the good performance of concentration-camp workers in his factories, and he would have wanted more of them except for the constant threat of Himmler's interference. He estimated at Nuremberg that not more than 33,000 to 36,000 inmates of these camps were at work in the war factories, although they put in much more time than the others—from seventy-two to even a hundred hours a week. Under some of the camp commanders, Obergruppenfuehrer Pohl told his chief, Heinrich Himmler, there were no limits to the hours of concentration-camp labor. The camp commander alone decided how long the prisoners had to work, but in any event work breaks must

be kept to a minimum. "Noon intervals," said Pohl, "only for the taking of meals are forbidden."

Since the concentration-camp laborers Speer had in his factories were for the most part mixed in with other workers, their hours were likely to be limited, and in any event he was against long hours because they were inefficient. But he highly approved of concentration-camp labor for his war industries, as he did prisoners of war, volunteers, and forced laborers. In none of his countless reports, memoranda, or speeches, however, did he write or say anything other than to urge that they be adequately fed and rewarded for their performance. In the environment of hostility and violence in which he operated, he was one of the mildest of the top government officials. His country was, as he saw it, in a life-or-death struggle with its enemies; every German must do his share either at the front or in the factories, and the people in the occupied countries must work too, hopefully in their own plants where they would do their jobs more efficiently. Speer did not think it his concern to decide the legality of what was being done, but his improvised system was based far more on rewards than on punishments, and the typical Nazi exhortations to be ruthless and to take no account of the suffering of foreigners never appear in anything Speer wrote or said. He conceded in his reports that a small majority of his workers, both German and foreign, needed to be disciplined on occasion, to be sent for a period to special camps or even to concentration camps if they deliberately committed major infractions of the work rules or sabotage. But on the whole he used the carrot rather than the stick. He had worked closely with the SS when he took over the Organization Todt, which was then operating in the Crimea, where repairs of all kinds had to be made to roads and bridges and buildings. Speer used Russian conscript labor under SS guards, but no charges were ever made that he was responsible for any mistreatment of the workers.

Speer too turned over all his documents to the Allies while he was still free, in the belief that he had nothing to hide; he had been assigned an important technical task and had carried it out. Thus the Allies had possession of his entire correspondence, and the picture that emerged from it was that of a man for whom nothing was more important than his objectives. He hovered busily over his employees, writing a sharp letter to Ribbentrop when his co-workers were slighted at an official function and the Party brass stepped out in front to take the bows, leaving the Speer contingents who actually did the work in the background. "You know," he wrote Ribbentrop, "that I personally set little store by such things as table order or the distribution of awards; I never attend such occasions if it is not absolutely essential." Nevertheless, Speer commented, those who did the work should have a place next to the chief functionaries at the ceremonies celebrating what they had built. "You know how I dislike discussions of these matters," he wrote, "but I cannot tolerate a situation where my closest associates who have volunteered to work on their own time are pushed to one side."

In the same vein, Speer reprimanded his own co-workers who seemed to him in any way lax in their departmental loyalties. If under the pressure from outside agencies colleagues appeared to be in the slightest degree diverted from the jobs he had assigned them, Speer was immediately on the warpath. Here again he used his reward-and-punishment formula, telling them that they could not serve two masters but if they carried out the assignments he gave them they could call themselves "Deputy Architects of the General Building Inspector of the German Capital." If, however, they did not immediately promise to work for him alone, he pointed out that he had the power and would use it to abrogate their contracts in whole or in part. When one of his assistants, unknown to Speer, wrote a strongly unfavorable letter to Bormann on a man Speer wanted to appoint as a ministerial adviser, Speer demanded that his assistant be sent to a concentration camp and he discharged another member of his staff who was implicated.

Speer had a continual and lively correspondence with the entire Nazi hierarchy, beginning with Goering, who, always concerned with his prerogatives even when he no longer was capable of carrying out a sizable fraction of his assignments, complained bitterly of decisions that had been taken in the economic sphere without consulting him. Since he was head of the Four-Year Plan, no important step, said the Reichsmarschall, could properly be taken without consulting him, and Speer replied that he doubtless had enemies in the Reichsmarschall's entourage who cast a false light on what he was doing but he had to make decisions to perform his job properly, and he reminded Goering that a higher authority was over them both, that they too must work patriotically together for the Fuehrer. Goering was evidently appeased, for the main tenor of his correspondence with Speer was friendly after that and he made no further remonstrances. Speer had to deal with everyone in the higher echelons—with the Reichskommissar Terboven in Norway, with Hans Frank in Poland, with Karl Hermann Frank in Czechoslovakia, with the Army and Navy and Air Force, with Gauleiters and Party leaders of all conditions—and as long as they did not interfere with his task he was equally courteous to them all, even the malodorous Heydrich.

But Speer was quick to sense any encroachment on his territory—whether an attempt on Ley's part to undertake a project Speer thought should be under himself or the actions of any of the other muddle-headed Nazi functionaries out to extend their satrapies. One speech of Sauckel's immediately caused him to protest because, Speer said, Sauckel used the occasion as a platform to state his pretensions to controlling what use was made of the labor he recruited.* More than once Speer complained to Hitler that he thought Sauckel needed to be kept in line by more powerful weapons than he himself had immediately at hand. Sauckel was unwilling Speer said, to use the Hungarian Jews or even to permit them to enter his Gau of Thuringia; and this Speer deplored, for these concentration-camp workers were industrious and other Gauleiters might follow Sauckel's bad precedent and refuse to admit the Jews into a Gau, which would badly hurt German production. The presence of the Jews, Speer said, perhaps for the record, was disturbing to him too, but this was an emergency, and since the Jews were in concentration camps they could not offend the sensibility of the German people or damage them in any way.

Of one transport of 509 Eastern workers Sauckel sent, Speer wrote in indignation on January 25, 1944, 161 were children from one month to fourteen years old; forty-nine men and sixty-nine women were in such a physical state as to be incapable of working, and thus 53 per cent of the entire group, could not be employed. Some months later he denied Sauckel's request for 7,000 workers to be taken temporarily from the armament factories and to be used in manufacturing sugar, telling Sauckel he certainly must be able to round up workers for a short time without disrupting an essential branch of German industry. He could write a

---

*Sauckel was in charge of the procurement of labor.

twelve-page letter to the Fuehrer to buttress his position against Sauckel. Sauckel must regard himself as Speer's assistant, Speer told Hitler; Speer himself must decide how workers were to be employed. And he turned down Field Marshall Keitel's request for his key workers as coolly as Sauckel's, for by 1944 he had convinced Hitler that production was as important as the front.

He was equally sharp with Frank, who planned useless projects for the General Government, and told Frank that only if he was certain he could finish a building (a bank that could be used as temporary sleeping quarters for two hundred people) with local labor that could not be used elsewhere might he proceed with the project. Otherwise the labor was needed in the Reich. On other occasions he reprimanded Frank for his extravagant use of materials. Speer made many visits to the front after which he was accustomed to writing long memoranda recommending improvements in weapons and tanks and on one occasion he noted placards in store windows of the Radom district which he considered extravagant. "I must ask you to see to it that the planning and carrying out of all measures is done with the least expense of work and material," he told the Governor, who took no such parsimonious view of his rights and privileges.

BUT EVEN SPEER'S innumerable jobs, his constant speechmaking and journeys to the front, his conferences with Hitler, department heads, generals and admirals did not wholly fill his time. He continued all during the war to plan for grandiose future cities with green belts, sports facilities, and underground railway stations, and where the occupants of apartment houses would not have to leave their immediate neighborhood to shop for everything they needed; he foresaw vast projects where traffic would be rerouted through congested areas like the Ruhr and through cities. On January 10, 1944, he wrote that a million workers would be needed to rebuild German cities after the war. Apartments in huge barracks would be built for young married people; 400,000, maybe 600,000, would be provided in a year, and in addition two and a half million dwellings would be constructed on conventional lines so that the housing crisis would be solved in three years.

Speer asked Goering to use his influence with Terboven in Norway to make sure the cutting of a natural stone available there would continue, despite the demands of the war, so it could be shipped to the Reich. He paid out large sums (150,000 RM for garden figures, 500,000 RM to a sculptor for the monumental and heroic statues he and Hitler so admired) despite his dedication to channeling German resources into war production. For the training of artisans in Germany, Speer wanted 400 RM a year to be given apprentices; to make sure of the interest of the young workers he asked that they invest 100 RM in their training, in return for which they would get from the State 500 RM a semester.

He could overlook everything that marred his ideal picture of a rationally functioning European economy buttressed with vast building projects and integrated industries. Only a few weeks before the end of the war, on April 9, 1945, he said that Germany had built up in the occupied territories a European economy in the real sense. France, Belgium, and Holland had been permitted to manufacture the kinds of goods for which their factories were best equipped and they had even been enabled to rebuild when rebuilding was possible. It was tragic, Speer thought, that this cooperative work was now being broken down, but he was hopeful that the future would restore this European integration. For he saw clearly,

as he told the court at Nuremberg, that the future would produce intercontinental rockets capable of destroying cities anywhere on the globe and that the nations of the new and old worlds must collaborate or perish. What he failed to notice was the effect of the Pandora's box of hatred he, with his magic enterprises, had helped to open on the world.

WHAT WAS SPEER'S GUILT? At Nuremberg he accepted, he said, the common responsibility of German leaders even in an authoritarian system for what had been done and certainly his own for what had gone on in the area of his authority. Speer was self-confident and composed on the witness stand. He refused, in answer to a prosecution demand, to name the people in Hitler's entourage of whom he was critical—this was no time for professional or personal recriminations—and the Russian prosecutor questioning him had no success against his quiet self-assurance. Soviet prosecutors tended to repeat questions which their Western colleagues had already asked and to which adequate answers had already been given by the defendants—whether because the Russians did not follow the trial closely or, which is more likely, because they wanted their own record of their patriotic role in the court proceedings to be clear when they returned to Moscow. The Soviet prosecutor who cross-examined Speer, Raginsky, at one point told Speer that if he did not wish to he need not answer a question truthfully, but the President of the Court intervened to say that Speer had already and properly answered the question. Speer told Raginsky, when asked how he had come to work so closely with the Fuehrer despite his nefarious character, that the Russians too had read *Mein Kampf* and yet had made their pact with Hitler. The dialogue became lively with implications. Raginsky asked him if it was not true that he had given himself without reservations to his war tasks.

SPEER: "Yes, I believe that was the custom in your State, too."

RAGINSKY: "I am not asking you about our State. We are now talking about your State . . ."

SPEER: "Yes. I only wanted to explain this to you, because apparently you do not appreciate why in time of war one should accept the post of Armament Minister. If the need arises that is a matter of course, and I cannot understand why you do not appreciate that and why you want to reproach me for it."

RAGINSKY: "I understand you perfectly."

SPEER: "Good."

Speer defended the concerns that employed concentration-camp labor; he pointed out that the firms had no control over the camps, which were run by the SS, and the company officers were not even allowed to inspect them. And to this statement he added with true German entrepreneurial grandeur, "The head of a plant could not bother about conditions in such a camp."

Almost the whole of German production by 1944 was in his hands, including the defense plants for the Army, Navy, and Air Force, as well as those manufacturing consumer goods; only the SS plants were outside his authority. In addition, Speer acted as chairman of the Jaeger Staff, with Field Marshal Milch as co-chairman. This committee of three members with equal powers and votes had infringed, as Hitler intended it should, on the last remnants of Goering's former empire, but the Reichsmarschall by 1944, when the Jaeger committee was established, had to parcel out most of the territory over which he had formerly ruled. Speer, though, until June 20, 1944, when Goering finally turned over the plants to

him, had only limited authority over the factories producing for the Luftwaffe, which were manned in part by half-starved Russian workers, because the Reichsmarschall to the end clung to every prerogative as long as he could. Speer tried to improve the Russians' rations, as well as those of the other working prisoners, and he always opposed the barbed wire around the work camps because of its bad effect on morale. From time to time he succeeded in getting supplementary meals for these workers and, after he got those, he tried to have consumer goods made available to them, but any such successes were short-lived. The scarcity of food as a result of the bombardments and the subsequent derangement of transport was genuine enough, although there was always enough for the civilian population, and whatever Speer managed to obtain for his workers, the Russians always got less than the others who labored for the Germans, except for the Jews.

The final malign effect of the Fuehrerprinzip, Speer said at Nuremberg, was that every order, even if it was criminal or insane, was supposed to be carried out unconditionally, without criticism. But obviously he only became aware of this at the very end of the war; up to the scorched-earth order he was concerned solely with his enormous assignment. Secure in his own sense of the correctness of what he was doing, he visited countless factories and talked with the men, including forced laborers, with no escort such as accompanied other Nazi ministers. A wide cross-section of Germans always had confidence in him, from members of the Resistance to Guderian and Jodl, both of whom talked openly to him about Hitler's arbitrary and unreasonable decisions. When they complained to Speer they no longer had much will left to cross Hitler face to face. Speer confessed at Nuremberg that he did not try more than once or twice to approach the Fuehrer directly with criticisms either; the scenes, he said, could be too painful.

German war production, despite Speer's efforts, was always complicated by the incessant battle for power within the State and Party apparatus. Before Speer became Minister of Armaments and instituted his system of self-responsibility for industry, a plant manager faced being sent to a concentration camp if he failed to meet his arbitrarily set norms of production. It had been a coercive system, and Speer tried with success to find a substitute for the rewards and punishments of the competitive, free-enterprise system under the conditions of the war economy. He spent hours talking to meetings of Gauleiters, and the statistics of what he accomplished were so overwhelming that these upholders of the true faith often broke out in loud applause despite their suspicions of him. His speeches were skillfully adapted to the Gauleiters' mentality. Before procurement was coordinated, he told one meeting of Gauleiters at Posen on August 3, 1944, the amount of copper demanded by separate departments was more than the total supply in the world. He gave them astonishing figures on production: in 1941, 75 million shells had been turned out; in 1944, 408 million would be made. Then he gave the figures of fighter-plane production under his Jaeger committee: 3,115 fighter planes and interceptors were constructed despite the Allied bombings in July. He added that new U-boats that had been only sketches in September were being actually put in service in May, with a promise of forty-four a month to come later in the year. These were statistics the most stupid among the Gauleiters could understand. And Speer told them too of the bureaucratic troubles they themselves knew so well, for they often caused them. He related how he had found 180,000

gasoline cans in Breslau lying unused because they had been classified as drinking canteens destined for Rommel's army in Africa and had never been returned to their status as containers for gasoline. He had found trucks immobilized because tires were lacking and had got them on the road within hours; he found other trucks in Army garages—1,000 of them in Vienna—while Panzers could not be shipped to the front for lack of them. Even the Gauleiters were enthusiastic, at least while they were under his spell. But the Party never gave up the battle.

Sauckel, in the chain of command under Speer, tried constantly to expand and strengthen his own organization at Speer's expense. Himmler tried to do the same thing with his SS factories; the Gauleiters under Bormann were always pressing for increased authority over the plant managers and Speer's "honorary co-workers," whom they regarded as well-heeled saboteurs. Goering gave up his authority reluctantly, retreating step by step. On April 22, 1942, he announced that within the framework of the Four-Year Plan, which he directed, the Central Planning Board would be set up with three members, Speer, Milch, and Koerner, as his personal representatives. The board was to have the responsibility of administering the entire economy; allocating raw materials, especially iron, metals, and coal; and deciding on how many workers would be needed for the agreed-on production. These decisions had to be flexible since the Fuehrer's ideas changed on priorities; one month anti-aircraft defense took first place; another, tanks and bombers or fighters had the highest priorities and materials had to be shifted accordingly. The members of the Central Planning Commission theoretically had equal voices in the decisions—the one important exception to the Fuehrerprinzip, it was pointed out at Nuremberg. A unanimous vote was required for a decision and thus any of the three could cast a veto. The committee was dominated, however, by Speer, to whom both Milch and Koerner were entirely ready to turn over the important decisions on production, and as time went on Goering too had been glad to see Speer take charge after he found his own accumulating failures harder and harder to explain.

Speer and the Central Planning Board continually demanded of Sauckel that he conjure up more thousands of workers, and Sauckel, struggling to carry out his part of the patriotic effort, once promised a million fresh workers. He was only able to produce 20,000. But this happened toward the end of the war, when all supplies were failing, including manpower and the means for getting it, and up to 1944 he produced his millions of workers. Furthermore Sauckel had increasingly stiff competition in the battle for obtaining manpower, and Speer was one of his chief competitors. For while Speer demanded the vast contingents of new workers, he at the same time made it impossible for Sauckel to get them from the blocked factories where they were concentrated. Speer insisted that Sauckel keep out of these factories. Sauckel, complaining to the Fuehrer that Speer was hoarding in these enterprises labor that was bitterly needed in Germany, demanded the right to investigate Speer's use of manpower; to send his own men into the blocked factories to determine whether, how, and if what they were producing was really essential to the total war effort. Speer was able on the whole to defend his blocked factories successfully, for when it come to a showdown, Hitler knew that Speer was indispensable and that his methods had worked miracles. Sauckel, on the other hand, was ordered to get hold of so and so many millions of workers, and not only Speer

was a competitor but Himmler, the Army, which needed workers in the rear areas, and the Luftwaffe, which recruited civilian helpers and before 1944 gathered its own labor for aircraft production. Sauckel had other problems as well: he needed millions of workers for agriculture. Here, too, Speer demanded that those qualified be released for factory work between harvest time and spring. But, as Sauckel resentfully pointed out, many of them never returned for the spring planting but stayed on in Speer's factories.

Speer, the court found, had not been guilty of planning or waging aggressive warfare but he was guilty of war crimes and crimes against humanity. He had known, the court said, that his war factories were using slave labor; he had been present at the conference with Hitler where it was agreed that Sauckel was to bring in foreign labor by force and at the meeting where Sauckel had been told to supply at least four million new workers from foreign countries. Speer had also asked for specific nationalities to be provided—Russians for example—and his blocked factories too were illegal, although the tribunal conceded that because of them thousands of foreign workers had been enabled to stay in their own countries. The court also noted that Speer had wanted to use as few concentration-camp workers as possible—because, it said, he mistrusted Heinrich Himmler's ambitions. The judgment declared that he had not been directly concerned with the cruelty of the slave-labor system but he had known of it and knew his demands for labor meant that violence would be used in recruiting manpower. He had also complained about malingering, and the court quoted his saying: "There is nothing to be said against the SS and police taking drastic steps and putting those known as slackers in concentration camps." But again, the judgment pointed out, he had insisted on adequate food and working conditions being provided the labor force so that it could work efficiently. And last of all the tribunal mentioned without comment that he had told Hitler the war was lost and that he had opposed the scorched-earth policy. Then the court sentenced him to twenty years.

NOTES

[1] An article by Alan S. Milward pointed out that many of Speer's organizational reforms had already been introduced by Todt (*Vierteljahrshefte fuer Zeitgeschichte*, Vol. XIV, No. 1, 1966, pp. 40–58).

[2] "Paralysis" meant partial dismantling, removing essential parts from the machinery, shipping them from the plants, hiding them, but not damaging the machinery which must begin as soon as possible to work again for whatever kind of Germany might survive the war.

[3] Hitler's order of March 19 repeated that everything must be done to weaken the enemy and to prevent his further advance. Every possibility of damaging the striking power of the enemy directly or indirectly must be utilized. Industrial installations should not be paralyzed but destroyed:

> It is a mistake to believe that traffic, communications, industrial, and supply centers left undamaged or paralyzed for a short time can be used again when they are recaptured. The enemy in his retreat [this was Hitler's answer to Speer] will leave us scorched earth with no regard for the population. Therefore I order: all military, traffic, information, industrial, and supply centers as well as stocks inside Germany that could be of any use to the enemy . . . are to be destroyed.

The order was to be sent to troop commanders with the greatest possible speed (*N* XLI, p. 430).

[4] Milch, when he started the Jaeger Staff in March, 1944, was given the task of deciding on the new models and at the same time raising the production of German fighter planes from 1000 to 3000 a month, but he immediately called in Speer and thus the two of them sitting both on the Central Planning Board and the Jaeger Staff almost completely replaced Goering in the economic sphere. Milch was always ready to subordinate himself to Speer, whom he regarded with unstinting admiration.

[5] A decree issued by the Chief of Staff of OKH on February 6, 1943, declared it was the duty of everyone—male and female—from the ages of fourteen to sixty-five to work in the operational areas of the East. Special rules were to be established for the Jews, and a work period of fifty-four hours per week was to be standard, with overtime, night and Sunday work a possibility. Regular sickness benefits, however, were to apply. At a later meeting in Rovno on March 10 it was noted that "a million or more workers were to be shipped out within the next four months," largely for agricultural work—the Speer enterprises would get the factory labor from the West. Such was the need for labor that the SD on March 19, 1943, was directed by Sturmbannfuehrer Christensen to relax its most brutal measures in the warfare against the partisans, which resulted in so many of the civilian population joining the bands. The harsh practices Christensen listed were the shooting of the Hungarian Jews, farm workers, and children, and the burning down of villages. He ordered that such measures be curtailed, that "special treatment" be limited. For the time being, Communist Party functionaries, activists, etc. were only to be listed but neither they nor their close relatives were to be arrested. Members of the Comsomols were to be apprehended only if they held leading positions. When villages were burned down the entire population must be put at the disposal of the German authorities, and Christensen added this classical statement on behalf of more humane measures: "As a rule no more children will be shot" (*N* XXXI, 3012-PS, pp. 481–95).

[6] Speer testified at Nuremberg that OKW had opposed using prisoners of war, except for Russians and Italian internees, in the armament industries because the Geneva Convention forbade the use of captured military personnel in such work. The prohibition, however, did not apply to the Soviet Union, which had never signed such international agreements. His reasoning again was entirely pragmatic; he explained that the prisoners of war were mainly producing goods that were not specifically military according to the Geneva Convention; he did not regard the work the French prisoners of war were doing as armament production since in modern war almost any product could have a military use. Some 400,000 prisoners of war, he testified, were used directly in the armament industry, but of these from 200,000 to 300,000 were Italian, the rest Russian (*N* XVI, p. 452).

[7] The contracts the workers signed stated that they agreed not to disclose what they had seen in Germany when they returned home; that they were to report any propaganda or espionage immediately to the German management; and that they covenanted to work conscientiously and well and to be punished, if the necessity should arise, under German law (June, 1943, BDC).

[X, Fall 1966, 383–398]

[VIII]

The Realm of Education

[60]

On Classical Studies

ERIC VOEGELIN

Eric Voegelin (1901–1985) taught law at the University of Vienna, government at Louisiana State University, political theory and philosophy at the University of Munich, and was professor emeritus of political science at the University of Munich and Henry Salvatori Distinguished Scholar at the Hoover Institution, Stanford. Among his many works were the monumental four-volume Order and History *(1956–1974),* The New Science of Politics *(1952),* Anamnesis *(1978),* Science, Politics, and Gnosticism *(Two Essays) (1968), and numerous other publications. He has been called "probably the most influential historian of our century, and certainly the most provocative," and "one of the most distinguished interpreters to Americans of the non-liberal streams of European thought."*

A REFLECTION on classical studies, their purpose and prospects, will properly start from Wolf's definition of classic philology as the study of man's nature as it has become manifest in the Greeks.[1]

The conception sounds strangely anachronistic today, because it has been overtaken by the two closely related processes of the fragmentation of science through specialization and the deculturation of Western society. Philology has become linguistics; and the man who manifested his nature in the Greek language has become the subject matter of specialized histories of politics, literature, art, political ideas, economics, myth, religion, philosophy, and science. Classical studies are reduced to enclaves in vast institutions of higher learning in which the study of man's nature does not rank high in the concerns of man. This fragmentation, as well as the institutional reduction, however, are not sensed as a catastrophe, because the "climate of opinion" has changed in the two hundred years since Wolf's definition. The public interest has shifted from the nature of man to the nature of nature and to the prospects of domination its exploration opened; and the loss of interest even turned to hatred when the nature of man proved to be resistant to the changes dreamed up by intellectuals who want to add the lordship of society and history to the mastery of nature. The alliance of indifference and hatred, both inspired by *libido dominandi*, has created the climate that is not favorable to an institutionalized study of the nature of man, whether in its Greek or any other manifestation. The protagonists of the Western deculturation process are firmly established in our universities.

Still, the end of the world has not come. For "climates of opinion," though they last longer than anyone but their libidinous profiteers would care, do not last

699

forever. The phrase was coined by Joseph Glanvill (1638–1680); it received new currency when Alfred N. Whitehead resumed it in his *Science and the Modern World* (1925); and, following the initiative of Whitehead, the changes of this modern climate ever since the seventeenth century have become the subject of Basil Willey's perceptive and extensive *Background* studies, beginning in 1934. Through Whitehead's, as well as through other initiatives, we know by now what the problem is; Whitehead has stated it flatly: "Modern philosophy has been ruined." More explicitly I would say: The Life of Reason, the ineluctable condition of personal and social order, has been destroyed. However, though these statements are true, one must distinguish between the climate of opinion and the nature of man. The climate of our universities certainly is hostile to the Life of Reason, but not every man is agreeable to have his nature deformed by the "climate" or, as it is sometimes called, the "age." There are always young men with enough spiritual instinct to resist the efforts of "educators" who pressure for "adjustment." Hence, the climate is not static; through the emotionally determined constellation of opinions of the moment there is always at work the resistance of man's nature to the climate. The insight into this dynamics underlies the studies of Willey. As a matter of fact, neither the changes in the climate from indifference to hostility, nor the concomitant waning of institutional support for the Life of Reason, nor the fanatically accelerated destruction of the universities since the Second World War, could prevent the problem of the climate from being recognized, articulated, and explored in the light of our consciousness of human nature. The reflections in which we are engaged here and now are as much a fact in the contemporary situation as the notorious "climate." The freedom of

thought is coming to life again, when the "climate of opinion" is no longer a massive social reality imposing participation in its partisan struggles, but is forced into the position of a pathological deformation of existence, to be explored by the criteria of reason.

This is the setting in which the question of classical studies must be placed. On the one hand, there is a powerful climate of opinion in our universities opposed to accord them any function at all, because classical studies inevitably represent the nature of man as it has become manifest in the Greeks. On the other hand, there are undeniable symptoms of the climate cracking up and the nature of man undeformed reasserting itself. If this movement toward a restoration of reason should gain sufficient momentum to affect the institutional level, classical studies would become an important factor in the process of education. I shall reflect on the two points in this order—though some disorder may creep in as we are dealing not with alternatives belonging to the past but with an ongoing process.

THE EFFORT of the Greeks to arrive at an understanding of their humanity has culminated in the Platonic-Aristotelian creation of philosophy as the science of the nature of man. Even more than with the sophists of their times the results are in conflict with the contemporary climate of opinion. I shall enumerate some principal points of disagreement:

1. *Classic*: There is a nature of man, a definite structure of existence that puts limits on perfectibility.

Modern: The nature of man can be changed, either through historical evolution or through revolutionary action, so that a perfect realm of freedom can be established in history.

2. *Classic*: Philosophy is the endeavor

to advance from opinion (*doxa*) about the order of man and society to science (*epistēmē*); the philosopher is not a philodoxer.

Modern: No science in such matters is possible, only opinion; everybody is entitled to his opinions; we have a pluralist society.

3. *Classic*: Society is man written large.

Modern: Man is society written small.

4. *Classic*: Man exists in erotic tension toward the divine ground of his existence.

Modern: He doesn't; for I don't; and I'm the measure of man.

5. *Classic*: Man is disturbed by the question of the ground; by nature he is a questioner (*aporein*) and seeker (*zetein*) for the whence, the where to, and the why of his existence; he will raise the question: Why is there something, why not nothing?

Modern: Such questions are otiose (Comte); don't ask them, be a socialist man (Marx); questions to which the sciences of world-immanent things can give no answer are senseless, they are *Scheinprobleme* (neopositivism).

6. *Classic*: The feeling of existential unrest, the desire to know, the feeling of being moved to question, the questioning and seeking itself, the direction of the questioning toward the ground that moves to be sought, the recognition of the divine ground as the mover, are the experiential complex, the *pathos*, in which the reality of divine-human participation (*metalepsis*) becomes luminous. The exploration of the metaleptic reality, of the Platonic *metaxy*, as well as the articulation of the exploratory action through language symbols, in Plato's case of his Myths, are the central concern of the philosopher's efforts.

Modern: The modern responses to this central issue change with the "climate of opinion."

In Locke the metaleptic reality and its noetic analysis is transformed into the acceptance of certain "common opinions" which still bear an intelligible relation to the experience from which they derive. The reduction of reality to opinion, however, is not deliberate; Locke is already so deeply involved in the climate of opinion that his awareness for the destruction of philosophy through the transition from *epistēmē* to *doxa* is dulled. Cf. Willey's presentation of the Lockean case.

Hegel, on the contrary, is acutely aware of what he is doing when he replaces the metaleptic reality of Plato and Aristotle by his state of alienation as the experiential basis for the construction of his speculative system. He makes it explicitly his program to overcome philosophy by the dialectics of a self-reflective alienated consciousness.

In the twentieth century, the "climate of opinion" has advanced to the tactics of the "silent treatment." In a case like Sartre's, metaleptic reality is simply ignored. Existence has the character of meaningless *facticité*; its endowment with meaning is left to the free choice of man. The choice of a meaning for existence falls with preference on the opinion of totalitarian regimes who engage in mass-murder, like the Stalinist; the preference has been elaborated with particular care by Merleau-Ponty. The tactics of the "silent treatment," especially employed after the Second World War by the "liberation rabble," however, make it difficult to decide in individual cases whether the counterposition to metaleptic reality is deliberate, or whether the *libido dominandi* is running amok in a climate of opinion that is taken for granted, without questioning, as ultimate reality. On the whole, I have the impression that the consciousness of a counterposition is distinctly less alive than it still was at the time of Hegel. Philosophical illiteracy has progressed so far that the experiential core of philosophizing has disappeared below the horizon and is not even recognized as such when it appears in philosophers like Bergson. The deculturation process has eclipsed it so thoroughly by opinion that sometimes one hesitates to speak even of an indifference toward it.

7. *Classic*: Education is the art of *periagoge*, of turning around (Plato).

Modern: Education is the art of adjusting people so solidly to the climate of opinion prevalent at the time that they feel no "desire to know." Education is the art of preventing people from acquiring the knowledge that would enable them to articulate the questions of existence. Education is the art of pressuring young people into a state of alienation that will result in either quiet despair or aggressive militancy.

8. *Classic*: The process in which metaleptic reality becomes conscious and noetically articulate is the process in which the nature of man becomes luminous to itself as the life of reason. Man is the *zoon noun echon*.

Modern: Reason is instrumental reason. There is no such thing as a noetic rationality of man.

9. *Classic*: Through the life of reason (*bios theōrētikos*) man realizes his freedom.

Modern: Plato and Aristotle were fascists. The life of reason is a fascist enterprise.

The enumeration is not even remotely exhaustive. Everybody can supplement it with juicy items gleaned from opinion literature and the mass media, from conversations with colleagues and students. Still, they make it clear what Whitehead meant when he stated that modern philosophy has been ruined. Moreover, the conflicts have been formulated in such a manner that the character of the grotesque attaching to the deformation of humanity through the climate of opinion becomes visible. The grotesque, however, must not be confused with the comic or the humorous. The seriousness of the matter will be best understood, if one envisions the concentration camps of totalitarian regimes and the gas chambers of Auschwitz in which the grotesqueness of opinion becomes the murderous reality of action.

THE CLIMATE of opinion is unfavorable to classical studies; and the institutional power of its representatives in the universities, the mass media, and the foundations must not be underrated. Nevertheless, cracks in the establishment become noticeable. In particular, the international student revolt has been an eye-opener. Even the spiritually and intellectually underprivileged who live by the bread of opinion alone, have become aware that something is wrong with our institutions of higher learning, though they do not quite know what. Could it be perhaps the professors and not the war in Vietnam? With grim amusement have I watched the discomfiture of assorted leftist professors in Frankfurt and Berlin when their students turned against them, because the professors did not go along when their "critical theory" (a euphemism for irrational, nihilistic opining) was translated by the students into uncritical violence; and the same spectacle is provided in America by the liberal professors who suddenly become conservative, when a lifetime of strenuous effort to ruin the minds of one generation of students after another has at last borne fruit and the minds are really ruined. An incident from my own teaching practice will illuminate the critical point: In the mid-60's I gave a course in classical politics at a major university. All went well as long as the students believed they were offered the customary fare of information on Plato's "opinions." An uproar ensued when they found out that philosophy of politics was to be taken seriously as a science. The idea that some propositions concerning the order of man and society were to be accepted as true, others to be rejected as false, came as a shock; they had never heard of such a thing before. A few actually walked out of the course; but the majority, I am glad to report, stayed on, they became enchanted by Plato, and at the end they profusely expressed their gratitude to have at least learned of an alternative to the drivel of opinions they were routinely fed. But I do not want to go more deeply into this aspect of the matter. It will be sufficient to state that the students have good reasons to revolt; and if the reasons they actually advanced are bad, one should remember that the educational institutions have cut them off from the life of reason so effectively that they cannot even articulate the causes of their legitimate unrest.

By the irrational violence of the attack, the revolt could expose the flabbiness and emptiness of the institutionalized climate and its personnel, but one should not expect the life of reason to emerge from the confrontation of two vacua. More important than the spectacular events is the quiet erosion of the climate through the historical sciences. The nature of man can be deformed by the dominant opinions—the other day I heard a well-intentioned but helpless colleague cry out in anguish: Our world is fragmented!—but it is indestructible and finds ways to reassert itself. The metaleptic reality that is brushed aside as stuff and nonsense, if it claims in public to be the primary concern of man, has deviously crept in again under the respectable cover of comparative religion, comparative literature, the history of art, the science of the myth, the history of philosophy, intellectual history, the exploration of primitive symbolisms in ethnography and anthropology, the study of ancient civilizations, archeology, and pre-history, of Hinduism, Islam, and the Far East, of Hellenistic mystery religions, the Qumram texts, and Gnosticism, of early Christianity and the Christian Middle Ages, and last but not least by classical studies. In the cultural history of Western society, the splendid advance of the historical sciences has become the underground of the great *resistance* to the climate of opinion. In every one of the fields enumerated, we find the men who devote their lives to it, because here they find the spiritual integrity and wholeness of existence which on the dominant level of the universities has been destroyed. No critical attack on the insanity of the "age" can be more devastating than the plain fact that men who respect their own humanity, and want to cultivate it as they should, must become refugees to the Megalithicum, or Siberian shamanism, or Coptic Papyri, to the petroglyphs in the caves of the Ile-de-France, or to the symbolisms of African tribes, in order to find a spiritual home and the life of reason. Moreover, this underground has become the refuge not only for scholars but also for the more sensitive students, as one can ascertain by browsing for an hour in a college book store; the nature of man asserts itself, even if these poor fellows, deprived of proper guidance, grope for support in such exotica as the I-Ching.

Under the historical cover, thus, the substantive knowledge concerning the nature of man is present in our universities. Thanks to the phantasmic enlargement of the historical horizon in time and space that has occurred in the present century, this knowledge has even become more comprehensive and penetrating than at any other time in the history of our universities. At the same time it has become more easily accessible to everybody—I have only to compare the difficulties of access in the 20's, when I was a student, with the present plethora of paperbacks. This formidable presence, however, is slow to develop into a formative force in our institutions of higher learning. One of the reasons for this odd state of things will become apparent from an incident, a few years ago, at a conference on comparative religion: One of the participants broke the great taboo and flatly put it to his *confrères* that the subject matter they were treating was irrelevant by the standards of opinion to which most of them seemed to adhere; sooner or later they would have to make up their minds whether the science of comparative religion was an occupational therapy for persons otherwise unemployable, or whether it was a pursuit of the truth of existence which its subject matter substantively contained; one could not forever explore "religious phenomena," and pretend to their importance, without unreservedly professing that man's search for the divine ground of his existence, as well as the revelatory presence of God in the motivation of the search, constituted his humanity; in brief, he confronted them with the question of truth implied in their admirable achievements as historians. Not everybody present was pleased by such tactlessness. The historical cover, thus, is a sensible device as long as it secures a degree of freedom for the life of reason in institutions which are dominated by an essentially totalitarian climate, but it is in danger of becoming itself a part of the climate, as this incident shows, if the cover is used to sterilize the content and prevent it from becoming effective in our society. The cover will then degenerate into the ideology of historical positivism.

THE ADVANCE of the historical sciences concerning the nature of man in its various manifestations has arrived at a critical juncture: In retrospect from a future historical position, will it be the massive basis for a restoration of the life of reason?

or will it be an interesting last gasp of reason, exhaled by little men who did not have the courage of their convictions, before the totalitarian climate strangled it off for a long time to come?

Assuming the first alternative to be realized, classical studies will have an important function in the process, for in its Greek manifestation man's nature has achieved the luminosity of noetic consciousness and developed the symbols for its self-interpretation. The Greek differentiation of reason in existence has set critical standards for the exploration of consciousness behind which nobody is permitted to fall back. This achievement, however, is not a possession forever, something like a precious heirloom to be handed on to later generations, but a paradigmatic action to be explored in order to be continued under the conditions of our time. But at this point I must stop, for the great question how that is to be done cannot be answered by jotting down a program; concrete action itself would be necessary; and as the Greek manifestation of man's nature covered the range of a civilization, that feat cannot be performed here and now. Hence, I shall conclude these reflections with the designation of two general areas in which no major advance of science beyond its present state seems possible without recourse to, and continuation of, the Greek noetic effort.

1. If anything is characteristic of the present state of the historical sciences, it is the discrepancy between the mountains of material information and the poverty of their theoretical penetration. Whenever I have to touch on problems of the primitive myth or the imperial symbolism of Egypt, of Israelite prophetism, Jewish apocalypse, or Christian gospels, of Plato's historical consciousness compared with that of Deutero-Isaiah, of the Polybian ecumenic consciousness compared with

that of Mani, of magic or hermetism, and so forth, I am impressed by the philosophical and text-critical work done on the sources but feel frustrated because so little work is done to relate the phenomena of this class to the structure of consciousness in the sense of noetic analysis.

2. One of the great achievements of the Greek struggle, both against the older myth and the Sophistic climate of opinion, for insight into the order of man's existence is the exploration of existential deformation and its varieties. Again, very little is done to explore this achievement, to develop it further, and to apply it to the modern phenomena of existential deformation. We do not even have a good study on "alienation," though this very topical subject ought to stir up any classical scholar to voice what he has to say about it on the basis of the sources he knows best.

NOTE

[1] Friedrich August Wolf (1759–1824) created the science of "philology." The work on which his fame still rests is the *Prolegomena ad Homerum* (1795).

[XVII, Winter 1973, 2–8]

[61]

The Educated Man

ELISEO VIVAS

Eliseo Vivas (1901–   ), who has served on the editorial board of Modern Age *since 1957, is a distinguished philosopher, teacher, and man of letters who has written deeply and extensively on value, moral philosophy, aesthetics, and criticism. His many books include* The Moral Life and Ethical Life *(1950),* Creation and Discovery *(1955),* D. H. Lawrence: The Failure and the Triumph of Art *(1960), and* Contra Marcuse *(1971). He is professor emeritus of philosophy at Northwestern University, where he was John Evans Professor of Moral and Intellectual Philosophy from 1951 until his retirement in 1969. Vivas's contributions to the literature of conservatism have been widely read and admired for a generation. Of his world view, Vivas writes: "At the heart of my mature views is the conviction that our urgent need is to slow up the wreckage that our revolutionary age is inflicting on our civilization and to salvage what is still serviceable while there is still time."*

I

If we judge by usage, "education" is one of those terms that obeys Humpty Dumpty's semiotic principle, for it seems to mean what anyone wishes it to mean. For that reason the first part of this paper will be taken up with a bit of dictionary work. But the paper will not be devoted merely to verbal analysis. The verbal distinctions that must be undertaken are ancillary to the substantive elucidations that I hope to accomplish. I would like to begin by distinguishing two different processes that human beings can and that, in a utopia, everyone would undergo: the process of training and that of education.

But before taking up this distinction two prefatory remarks are necessary. The first is that I shall address myself to the problem of the education and training of the intellect, the mind, to the problem, that is, of conceptual or of purely verbal or book education and training, and not to questions that arise from any other kind of education and training. But I do not assume that intellectual education and training are the only kinds there are. Living in a world of books, in an entirely verbal or conceptual world, academic people tend to fall into the fundamental error of believing in the primacy of the concept, as we might call it. This error guides us in the teaching of literature and the arts. But this is not the occasion to dwell on this matter. The second prefatory remark is this: I do not claim that the distinction between training and education that shall occupy us is a novelty discovered by me. If I had discovered it I would be suspicious of it. But old as our awareness of the distinction is, we must dwell on it because many of the fundamental difficulties in education from which we have been suffering for over half a century are fertilized and mulched by the confusion between training and education.

To train is to inculcate a skill, and usually it refers to the inculcation of physical or manipulative skills. A plumber or an automobile mechanic is trained for his work; and if someone says of him that he is an educated man we take the speaker to mean that besides his skill as a plumber or mechanic he is a man who reads in some field or fields and has acquired something besides competence in his trade.

However, a difficulty arises immediately when we ask whether an engineer, an internist, a solid state physicist, or an Elizabethan scholar, is an educated man. A libertarian in matters of language—and I am to some extent one—would merely point out that usage permits the application of the term "education" to these experts. Ordinarily there can be no objection to such usage. Of course a distinguished surgeon or physicist is an educated man in a perfectly legitimate sense of the term.

I imagine that we apply the term "education" to the professions because it is assumed that a higher kind of intelligence is involved in their practice than in the trades, and no one would wish to deny this assumption. In any case, the notion that human activities can be arranged in an order of rank is a true one and not one that can be done away with by an egalitarianism, however intransigent. But we should consider, nevertheless, that our educational institutions are today producing not educated but trained men, although I am perfectly aware of the fact that the successful training required in the professions demands a kind of intellect that the plumber, if he has it, does not use in his trade. We should consider the matter, not in order to derogate from the products of our graduate schools but, again, in order to elucidate the important distinction that I have suggested.

In the pursuit of an education the quarrel between the sciences and the humanities, so much discussed since the publication of Sir Charles Snow's unfortunate Rede lecture, is not one to which we need pay attention. The notion, old hat before the publication of the lecture, that we could solve our educational problems if we could throw a bridge, with two-way traffic, between the two "cultures," is simplistic and false. It must be acknowledged, however, that the abysmal ignorance of the sciences one runs into on the part of people with Ph.D.'s in the humanities is as lamentable as it is appalling. Of course the ignorance of the humanities on the part of scientists is no less abysmal. But lamentable as is this ignorance, the problem of the so-called two cultures is irrelevant to our purposes. For if we forget the labels that we apply to the two distinct uses of the mind in the cultivation of the humanities and the sciences, we are able to see immediately that both kinds of activities are human activities, that both are also humane activities, demanding perhaps different mental talents, but each as profoundly human and humane as the other. In any case, for us at least, the important point is that what our educational institutions impart in either area is training. And if the graduate student, dissatisfied with the training he gets, undertakes to acquire an education, he is soon in trouble with his major professor.

We know that trades admit only of training whereas the professions offer bases from which men may begin to educate themselves. But while it is not improper to speak of an educated Elizabethan scholar, it is simply lazy thinking to assume that he is educated because of the important contributions he has made to his field of competence. Why isn't the specialist an educated man, and what would he have to do to be one? The reason the specialist is not an educated man is that, given the immense amount of knowledge he has to master even in the smallest corner of a discipline, he simply has no time for an education today. There are other complex reasons. But the fact is that for good and bad reasons, specialization dominates our graduate programs.

II

What then would a man have to have to be an educated man? There are several ways of answering this question. Newman puts it in his cadenced prose so well that the temptation to quote him is irresistible: "Our desideratum is," he says in the Preface to *The Idea of a University,* "not the habits and manners of gentlemen . . . but the force, the steadiness, the comprehensiveness and the versatility of intellect, the command over our own powers, the instinctive just estimate of things as they pass before us, which sometimes indeed is a natural gift, but commonly is not gained without much effort and the exercise of years." And less than a page later, in passing, he writes that a properly trained and formed intellect is able to have a connected view or grasp of things. In these statements I would emphasize the term "comprehensive" and the phrase "connected view or grasp of things." It is then not learning alone that makes an educated man. Hobbes said that if he had read as many books as the professors he would know as little as they did. Learning is required, indeed a good deal of it is required today, when the darkness is being rolled back as fast as it is at all the points of the compass. But it is what we do with learning and what learning does to us and for us, that gives it its chief value, and thus distinguishes the educated man from

the merely well-trained specialist: "its chief value," because it would not do to deny that there is value in mere knowledge, even in the essentially sterile knowledge of the quiz-kid type. But the chief value of knowledge consists in our use of it. And, of course, I do not mean the *practical* use of it. I mean the use of knowledge to give us the comprehensiveness and versatility of mind that leads us to a connected view or grasp of things. Let me express it in my own terms: The educated man is a man who has a defensible view of his relations to his fellows and, as a consequence, of his relations to himself, who has a view of the relation of man to the world, including the ultimate mystery on which the world is grounded. Without such a view a man may be most learned. But there is a difference between him and the man who has such a view.

But let us not quarrel about terms. If anyone should prefer to use the term "education" in a broader and less demanding sense there is no reasonable means of preventing him from so doing. But it is no less reasonable, on the other hand, to insist that there is a vast and most important difference in fact between what he calls an educated man and what I suggest we call him.

The difference lies in the lack of breadth of the mere specialist, the narrowness of outlook, and in many defects of intellect and character that flow from this central defect. Not that the specialist lacks opinions on many subjects. But that his opinions are not worth much. We are all acquainted with superb specialists who entertain opinions on subjects on which they are basically ignorant—opinions often held with tenacity, but to which they have no more right than I have to opinions on the nature of quasars and the receding universe. The educated man is able to relate his own expert knowledge to knowledge in other fields. His knowledge of other fields is perforce second-hand, but it can be responsible. And thus he is able to comprehend the totality of human culture within nature and nature itself within the darkness and the mystery of which it is the luminous crest. He may be a specialist in Elizabethan literature, Patristics, or Sumerian archaeology. But his specialized knowledge is placed in a framework of interests that relates it to man's adventure in history and, if he has a ground for believing in it, to his cosmic destiny. I say "if he has a ground for believing in it," because it would be a bigoted man who would assert today that anyone who rejected the problem of human destiny as meaningless would, by that rejection, debar himself from the ranks of the educated. Those who deny the significance of the problem seem to me to condemn themselves to live in a shrivelled world, a world lacking the resonance needed to give it rich value. They are, as I think of them, the lower-case positivists, men who strip themselves of much that is needed to be complete human beings. But if they espouse these shrivelling beliefs as the result of thoughtful facing of what they take to be compelling relevant data, and not as part of the unexamined orthodoxy of their age, it would be sheer dogmatism to assert that they lack an education.

It is thus not difficult to see that the knowledge of the man I have chosen to call "merely trained" is incomplete as well as insulated and that *therefore* the trained man cannot properly raise the question as to the objective or purpose of his own activity. Merely to raise that question he would have to be able to relate his specialized knowledge to other areas of knowledge and to other activities, which is to say that he would have to be able to tear off the insulation that specialization naturally wraps around itself and he would have to make a more or less serious

exploration of activities, interests, disciplines, and concerns beyond his field of specialization. But if he is an educated man, these explorations are made with due diffidence.

A sense of our relation to our fellows and hence to ourselves and to the universe, in order to be adequate, demands a grasp of the temporal perspective and of our place in it. Otherwise stated it demands not only knowledge of our history but of the values of our traditions. History no doubt is today a flourishing discipline. But we are a generation of secular chiliasts: men whose piety is elicited by the glories of the promised land and not by the values of our great traditions. Nor is it paradoxical that our historians fail to deepen our historical sense. Just as we must draw a distinction between the philosophical mind and the philosopher's mind, so we must draw a distinction between the historical mind and the historian's mind. In the great writers, of course, the two are one. But not always in the lesser lights.

III

At this point I can hear some of my readers objecting to this idea of the educated man for the following reason: For you, they say, an educated man is a philosopher. He is a man who has theories about himself and about the world. That means that an alert, well-equipped, finely developed mind, who is not at home in the abstractions so dear to the philosopher, cannot be educated. Your definition excludes too many people who by common consent would be included in the ranks of the educated. To this objection two answers need be made. The first is that I have already pointed out that I was confining my remarks to intellectual or verbal education. But it cannot be held that this is the only means by which our humanity can be brought to flower. The second is that while education, in the sense I have described it, is indeed the acquisition of a conceptual grasp of the sweep of human existence and its place in the universe, a conceptual grasp need not be a "philosophical" grasp, in the sense in which the word "philosophy" is used in our universities. The educated man may have a merely mythic conception of the world or he may have a partly quasi-scientific, partly philosophical or theoretical picture of himself and his world. Otherwise I would be forced to deny that an ancient Egyptian or Mayan or Peruvian priest could have been educated, and that only the fortunate denizens of certain civilizations could be. And such a denial would seem to me to be so narrow that it would open the man who made it to the charge that he lacked the very form of development he was discussing.

A picture of the world, and one which is his own, is the mark of the educated man. And if a man lacks it he is forced to accept the incomplete, incoherent, uncritical notions current in his world about himself and the nature of things. The process of education places a man beyond such a muddle. The educated man holds responsible views, he is aware of their weaknesses and their strengths, he knows which of them are held on trust and which are held on the authority of reason. The mind of the educated man is a broad mind but above all it is his own. His is an *authentic* mind, which is to say that it is a mind whose content is the product of his own effort to arrive at a satisfactory grasp of the nature of things. I use the word "authentic" reluctantly, since it has been kidnapped by the existentialists and I intend it, as indicated, in a sense close to its etymological sense. Again, the educated man is a free man, he is not dogmatic, he is not given to certainties that he does not have a right to have (and

who, in our world, has a right to certainties?) and when he reaches a conclusion, as perforce he must, he accepts it, in Plato's phrase, "with a hesitating trust in human reason."

The educated man is a man capable of growth. Education is not a static condition or state of affairs that, once being achieved, is possessed once and for all, as one possesses a car for which one has paid in full. To achieve an education there are no specifically defined requirements, no mastery of specific disciplines and, above all, no terminal points.

I have assumed, and perhaps it is advisable to make the assumption explicit, that the educated man represents one mode of human excellence. Let me iterate that there are other forms of excellence. But one form to which our civilization from its very beginning has given major recognition is that achieved by the educated man. I do not believe however that this mode of excellence can be pursued for the sake of excellence. Like happiness, the best way to miss it is to pursue it directly. What an educated man pursues is a cognitive mastery of his relation to his fellows and hence to himself and to the universe. Pursuing such mastery seriously he achieves the excellence of education as a by-product. The man who seeks excellence for the sake of excellence is a narcissist and what he achieves is the offensive habit of exhibitionism.

IV

Have I been all along, some of my readers may wonder, disparaging specialization? Not at all. Today we cannot do without it. The world would be better if great physicians were educated. But aside from the fact that they do not have the time to be educated, when I go to my general practitioner I go trusting that he is a competent specialist. And when we trust our generals and our engineers and sanitation experts, the navigator of a ship or plane, no less than a bus driver, we trust them because we take them to be specialists. Today, at any rate, a world of amateurs is inconceivable. Or rather, in the hands of amateurs our world would soon come to a catastrophic end. Nor could such a world ever have existed at the civilized plane. For, as Friedrich Hayek has pointed out, "It might be said that civilization begins when the individual in the·pursuit of his ends can make use of more knowledge than he has himself acquired and when he can transcend the boundaries of his ignorance by profiting from knowledge he does not himself possess." It follows that civilization involves specialization. We tend to think of aristocratic societies as societies of amateurs. And in certain respects they were. But your aristocrat was a specialist in at least three areas: he knew how to use and keep power, he knew how to fight, and he was an expert in the beauty of women and the excellence of horses.

It has been said that education cannot be achieved without a specialized command of one field. This at least is how I understand Whitehead when in one of his essays on education he writes that "the appreciation of the structure of ideas is the side of a cultured mind which can only grow under the influence of a special study." And he continues, "I mean the eye for the whole chessboard, for the bearing of one set of ideas on another." If by the eye for the whole chessboard Whitehead means, as I take him to mean, that the influence of a special study gives one what Newman called comprehensiveness and versatility of intellect, a connected view or grasp of things, I am forced to disagree with Whitehead. However we acquire it, we do not acquire it by the specialized study of Chaucer, the French Revolution, or genetics. Nor does specialized knowledge inculcate humility in the specialist toward disciplines or areas of interest of which he is ignorant. Stop and listen to distinguished specialists settling complex international problems, observe them base their opinions, with which they are well pleased, on tendentious information gathered from newspapers, see them resolve difficult social problems that demand for their elementary understanding a great deal of specialized knowledge of facts that they do not possess, see how they follow the flock together, happy to be with their kind, happy to think with the group, happy to be comforted by the feeling that they belong. Having observed them, having noted with care the push of their unreasoning passion and their tendency to accept opinion and hearsay where facts are called for, ask yourself what is the value of the specialized knowledge these distinguished specialists possess. Ask, does their knowledge make them humble before what they do not know? Press the question: Do these specialists realize that in areas in which they lack the competence they have in their own field, they are opinionated and allow themselves the lazy luxury of entertaining unexamined dogmas which they would not permit an ignorant man to entertain in their own areas of competence? They may be diffident in areas of scientific or humanistic investigation. But on social, on political, and on economic questions—matters as technical as those of which they are masters, whether it be physics or the Eighteenth Century—they talk with the confidence of barbers and the self-assurance of politicians on the hustings.

Whitehead, however, did insist on one trait of the educated mind which is a necessary, although not a sufficient, characteristic of it. The educated man's mind is alive with living and not with dead ideas. It shuns stereotypes, avoids rubberstamps; it thinks freshly, and what it absorbs it animates and transubstantiates. The educated man's view of the world is his own. There was a time in our civilization when such a view could be borrowed from the dominant orthodoxy, which was an orthodoxy because it was dominant. Such a view could be made to fit the personality of the borrower and his circumstances. But where do we go for such a view today? Where, that we can defend our choice? In any case, to be able to defend the choice that he considers the right opinion one must be able to say that what he has borrowed is true. He cannot delegate that responsibility to any authority whatsoever. But to say that a given doctrine is true is to be able to examine it. And the examination, if honest, ends up by transforming and transubstantiating the doctrine. But ideas that are critically assimilated cease to be borrowed. Again, there is no education where there is ignorance. But ignorance has a way of concealing itself under stereotypes and clichés in such a way that those who entertain them do not recognize them for what they are. Unexamined ideas, the soggy mass of stereotypes that make up the mental content of most men, are not ideas—not at any rate ideas in the Leibnizian sense; they are automatic mental responses, solid counters. But an idea is not a cliché, it is a quick, living affair, expanding and contracting as it reaches out to other ideas or is pressed by them.

V

But it is not only what a man does with his learning that makes him an educated man but what that learning does to him and for him. What he does with his learning is to use it to expand, unify, and give precision and coherence to his vision of the world. Thus his learning "places" him in the universe, gives him a proper sense of his own finitude and his own grandeur

and dignity, reveals to him where he stands in the light of knowledge and beyond it, in the encompassing darkness that he cannot penetrate. What his learning does for him is to liberate him, to free him from the superstitious ignorance of the learned, the pedantic and granitic insensibility of the bigoted, the intransigence and blurred myopic vision of the ignorant or the semi-ignorant.

Education is a process by which a man's talents and aptitudes are brought to full flower. It constitutes, therefore, an increase and growth of his humanity in so far as that growth is allowed by his social environment and his physical equipment. But not only his intellectual capacities but his full endowment as a human being— his moral and aesthetic sensibility and his capacity for cosmic piety—should be drawn out by the process of education. And at this point I must briefly observe that our educational institutions, by and large, fail almost entirely in providing education. We train specialists and have lost the vision, which our ancestors once had, of the complete man—a man of formed moral character, aesthetic sensibility, religious capacity, and ample and broad knowledge.

For many reasons we teachers have abdicated almost entirely the responsibility of forming moral character. If a student stays out of the hands of the police and observes a few elementary rules of behavior on campus, we accept him if his intellectual capacities meet our standards. In our large educational factories—our celebrated pluriversities—besides rather elementary demands of scholarly honesty we are not concerned with the kind of person the student is. Cleverness, a verbal, a merely cerebral, talent is all we value. And little else. To keep out of the newspapers in connection with what we think of as unfavorable publicity—any unfavorable publicity, whether the activity that generates it is right, wrong, or neutral in value—is the full extent of the moral demands we make of our students. The development of their aesthetic sensibility we have some concern for. Whether what we undertake along these lines is or is not valuable I shall not consider. But our failure to make moral demands of our students is, when we ponder it, as alarming as it is an eloquent sign of the changes taking place in our society. Grant that moral education cannot be undertaken in college; still, moral demands we could make, thus showing our approval of excellence of character and thereby discouraging traits we recognize as deforming. Nor do we attempt to quicken the cosmic piety of the student. On the contrary, teachers today go out of their way to kill it in him, by the systematic inculcation of a shallow secularistic mentality that leaves the student "enlightened" with quotation marks about the term, and spiritually shrivelled.

But kindly note what I am asserting. I do not maintain that we neglect the moral and religious education of our students. It is a question as to whether, by the time they come to us, they are still susceptible of receiving a moral and a religious education. What I am asserting is that we do not make moral demands of them.

It may be retorted that the training we undertake to impart is difficult enough and urgent enough, and that given the limited facilities and resources of our colleges and universities we cannot in reason be asked to do more than we do. I agree with the retort. But if this is the case, we must acknowledge that in our world education is becoming less and less possible to achieve. It was possible in a world moving more slowly than ours is in which there was less to know, and in which what there was to know required less technical skills and talents than are required to achieve solid knowledge today. To put it

briefly, it would be illusory to expect the proliferation among us, not of polymaths of the stature of Liebniz, but of men who aspired to his range of knowledge and in their measure achieved it. Today, among us, the specialist is king. It should be added that it would take a total revolution in our world before a change could be achieved—and I mean a revolution that would change radically the ethos of our society. The question would arise whether such a revolution would be possible and whether it would be desirable in view of the catastrophic and unforseeable consequences that it would bring in its wake.

In any case, it is generally agreed that the knowledge that our students acquire by the training we provide is necessary, and it must be acknowledged that it is basic to education. Since students have their hands full doing what they are doing, we can hardly ask them to do more. Nor could they do it if they tried. Universities and colleges are institutions staffed by a body of bureaucrats, and education is not a process that can be institutionalized. It is an activity in which the individual must engage by himself. There are no degrees for the educated man; nor, as already noted, are there courses or programs that could achieve the end of education, nor is there a terminal point.

But could it not be urged that while at the graduate level training is what we must continue to aim for, at the undergraduate we should aim to impart a modicum of education? It would be desirable. And many excellent small colleges in the United States aim at the education of their students. But there are factors working against them, four of which we should review hastily. The first is that an ignorant youth cannot be educated, and students who come to college come very poorly trained. During their college years much of their teachers' effort goes into supplying the deficiencies with which the students come to them. We do not fail in this job. But it is a job that colleges should not have to do. Quite obviously, with the present pressures colleges are in a position to make demands—not of the students but of the high schools. Whether we shall make use of the opportunity or not I am in no position to say.

The second reason education does not go on and cannot go on at the undergraduate level is that the undergraduate teacher is of course a product of the graduate schools. After a man has been properly trained, when he begins to teach undergraduates, what he does at the undergraduate level is to train the students. If he is a good scholar he is not likely to be an educated man. The fierce competition for distinguished staffs and the star system puts a premium on productive specialists. The growing specialization in science and technology sets the norm. Men in the humanities seek to imitate the sciences. The drive toward objective evaluation of the student's accomplishment strengthens the processes of specialization. And the rapid increase in knowledge in any field leaves the serious scholar little time for browsing beyond his own field. The rapid enlargement of the staffs demanded today by an increasing college population adds to the drift. Men can be trained fast but education is a slow process that cannot be speeded up. There no doubt are other factors operating to strengthen the processes of specialization, but I have mentioned enough, I trust, to show that it is not a phenomenon that would yield easily to a decision to alter it.

The next reason education does not go on at the undergraduate level I have already mentioned: the process of education cannot be institutionalized, programmed, planned. And what cannot be programmed cannot be undertaken in American colleges and universities. Today matters have gone further. It used to be

that what could not be programmed could not be undertaken. Of late what cannot be punched in a card cannot be undertaken. The number of credit hours and the course name can be punched. But education does not occur when requirements punched in the card have been fulfilled.

The fourth is difficult to broach, but it must be broached in spite of the fact that I am fully aware that there are many people who do not like to hear unpleasant truths. We claim that we value education, but what we really value is training—the professionalism that enables a man to succeed in a career. Education as I have used the term here we do not really value. And we do not value it because it is irrelevant to the activities our society expects its members to undertake. The world in which we live is a world of specialists. For specialists we have great use. But the educated man *qua* educated cannot be employed even by our educational institutions.

VI

We must next ask: Are there not some subjects and disciplines that help lead a man toward the acquisition of an education? I answer that there may be some disciplines and skills that, pursued with a single mind, keep a man from an education; but I do not know any one that is the indispensable road toward an education or a guarantee of one. It is generally assumed that the humanities have this power. But a man merely trained in any one of the humanities is no more of an educated man than a man trained in banking or solid state physics. An expert cryptographer could wonder about the patterns of nature, their wonderful symmetry and harmony; and if he pursues that wonder he will sooner or later be involved in the process of enlarging the range of his interest and the depth of his humanity. On the contrary, a man trained in literature need not ever abandon his trained bias. The assumption that the cultivation of any one of the humanities or any number of them will lead a man to become educated ignores the distinction I am making between training and education. It is not the kind of knowledge a man possesses, as already observed, that makes him an educated man but what that knowledge does to him and what he does with it.

If what I have just said holds, it is desirable to expatiate on it in the light of the claims that are sometimes made for the humanities. I shall make my observations by commenting on a quotation from an article based on a Phi Beta Kappa address entitled "What We Live By," given recently by Professor Franklin B. Krauss at Pennsylvania State University.[1] Professor Krauss writes:

> The humanities are the written repository of the total experience of Western man as stated by writers of superlative literary skill. They are uniquely what they are and therefore cannot be duplicated in any other area of study. To dismiss them as interesting but unessential in contemporary education is to turn one's back completely and indifferently on the explanation of who we are and what we are, as well as on the contemplation of who and what we might become. The multiplication of ingenious machines and of mechanical techniques may improve man's physical condition and surroundings, but the humanities are indispensable to the maintenance of active, moral motivation in all phases of civilized society. This conviction is what we live by.

One could write a longer essay than that of Professor Krauss as a commentary on this short paragraph. I shall take up only some of Professor Krauss's statements. But it is desirable to preface my remarks with a statement of full agreement with Professor Krauss when he tells us that the humanities are unique and therefore cannot be duplicated in any other area of study. I disagree with him about their function, but this is no place in which to reiterate what is to be found under my signature elsewhere.

It is necessary to indicate that the paragraph quoted is the closing paragraph of the essay. Had we heard it as the peroration of the original address we would have had to make allowances for the vague and overblown claims made for the humanities. By means of a peroration an orator seeks to leave the audience in a state of fervid admiration or contempt for that which he admires or despises. But Mr. Krauss's levitated encomium is presented in the last paragraph of an essay and it must be judged, not on its quality as the elevated, closing words of a "speech"—a word that often carries with it an unpleasant redolence—but on the quality of the argument.

Let us turn to some of the assertions. Is the statement that the humanities are the repository of the experience of Western man accurate? It suggests to the hasty reader that they are not the repository of the experience of Eastern man or that the humanities have not been cultivated in the East. I am confident that Mr. Krauss had no such stricture in mind. But of Caesar's wife . . .—the faintest suggestion of unlovely parochialism is unworthy of the breadth we expect of a man who cultivates the humanities. Let us ask, next, whether the humanities are the repository of the total experience of man. I must remind the reader that the claim is similar to one made by Allen Tate in a deservedly well-known essay entitled "The Present Function of Criticism." Mr. Tate asserts: "Literature is the complete knowledge of man's experience, and by knowledge I mean that unique and formed intelligence of the world of which man alone is capable." I do not mention Mr. Tate's essay to suggest a debt on the part of Mr. Krauss to the poet-critic. I mention it to use both claims as bases on which to ground the comment that they bespeak a drastically narrow notion of what makes up the complete or total experience of man. For aren't scientific treatises and papers the repositories of part, and of an important part, of the experience of man? Surely cultures in which science has flourished have provided men with one means of achieving one kind of excellence for which the cultivation of the humanities is no substitute.

The assertion that the humanities are the repositories of the total or complete experience of man may be called scientism in reverse. The statement that the humanities embody an explanation of who we are and what we are is not only another instance of scientism in reverse but a most dubious notion, either involving the misuse of the term "explanation," or making the common but radical error of thinking that they serve as a substitute for science. Mr. Krauss rightly asserts that for the humanities there is no substitute; but he believes that for science there is. To some of us it seems that to use the term "explanation" in connection with the humanities constitutes an unbuttoned use of language that a man who cultivates the humanities should not permit himself. The assertion that the humanities enable us to contemplate who and what we might become calls for qualification. They surely must be included in such a contemplation; and when they are not, the results are the vulgarities and naïvetés of *Walden Two*. But to achieve an adequate idea of who and what we might become we need not only the wisdom that the humanities are supposed to, and sometimes indeed do, provide us with, but we also need knowledge of the sciences, starting from biology if not from physics, and going all the way to the quasi-sciences of man, to those

disciplines that we may call (adapting to my use a term borrowed from the Continent) "philosophical anthropology." And among these we must include psychology, for we cannot exclude it simply because of the vulgar misuse to which it has been put by an enthusiastic would-be novelist, the coarseness of whose superior mind struggles for first place with his naive, pretentiously naive, feeble grasp of the nature of burdened humanity.

In this connection it is not irrelevant to note that it is not only the *soi-disant* "humanists" of our day who ignore science. They have good precedent, for even the Prince of Humanists did also. At a time when the nascent modern science and philosophy were beginning to stir the adventurous minds of Europe, Erasmus, who hated the regnant scholasticism, totally ignored them.

The thesis, finally, that the humanities are indispensable to the maintenance of active, moral motivation in all phases of civilized society is one that cannot be certified as truth by mere assertion. We are confronted with a socio-historical hypothesis, and one therefore that calls for scrupulous examination, a hypothesis that must be tested in the very same manner that empirical hypotheses are tested. Plausible as the hypothesis no doubt appears, I suggest that we consider with care whether it be the expression of generous hope or the statement of sober fact.

It is no doubt true that the multiplication of ingenious machines and of mechanical techniques has so far led ostensibly to the improvement of man's physical condition and surroundings (as it has also led, often, to the worsening of them). But am I rash in pointing out the need for asking ourselves whether the contemptuous reference to machines and techniques does not involve also a touch of what we may call Erewhonian negativism? In Butler the attitude is delightful and its half-truths are not the proper object of serious criticism. Intended seriously, as D. H. Lawrence often intended it, and as our writer seems to intend it, this negativism is—well, it is, to put it kindly, inadmissible. For what would we be today had not machinery and techniques made our civilization possible? How would Mr. Krauss's challenging essay have been circulated before the invention of the printing press? And what would science be without the machinery and techniques employed by such men as the lens grinder of Amsterdam and those of Palomar? The glories of the seventeenth century and the magnificent achievements piled on since then, where would they be? But let that go. What cannot be ignored is that by pitting the humanities against machines and techniques our writer achieves too easy a victory for the superiority of the former. Why did he not contrast them to science?

The failure to select worthy terms of contrast forces me to say, with as much courtesy as I can summon to my aid, that the tactics of such contrast ill befits a free and humane mind. This is not what a "humanist" in our day stands for at his best. But unfortunately "humanists" all too often strike the pose of superior spirituality and in so doing are ingrate and supercilious toward ingenious machines and mechanical techniques. Without machines and techniques there could be no spirituality. Erasmus needed quills and ink and paper, and of course he used the ingenious machine invented by Gutenberg. And we, today, who cultivate the humanities, need a vast industry for the production and propagation of our levitated spirituality.

VII

What is the value of an education? I have already suggested the answer I give this question. But let me make the suggestion fully explicit. Education is one way of achieving human excellence. Not the only way; and a person who does not see there are others can hardly be called an educated man. But there is one kind of human excellence, the excellence of the man who has a defensible grasp of the nature of things and of his place in it, that is particularly valuable, if it is valuable to develop our capacity for understanding and knowledge. This excellence when possessed leads to others, and above all to liberation. Liberation from what? From narrowness, bigotry, dogmatism, the myopia of the provincial. It is repetitious, but it needs to be said again that the educated man has a sense of the dubieties that make up the texture of human living, he sees the certainties at which he has arrived against the background of other certainties that compete with his own and contradict them. Ideally, education leads to the irenic temperament; it loosens the ties with the parish; it makes for a catholic attitude with a small "c."

Because of the high value that education has, it is gratifying to observe that the system—the educational machinery with its efficient bureaucracy, its clerks, its punch cards and the rest of its wonderful equipment—is often defeated by the student and that the number of students who in spite of us teachers seek an education not only tells us something about the inefficiency of our arrangements but also about the depth of man's need to become fully a man. When the student undertakes to become educated few of us refuse in our hearts encouragement and approval to the rebel—although some of us warn him of the risks he is taking while hoping that he will continue to take them. Since what he undertakes is an almost illegal or, at any rate, paralegal operation, we have no statistics about it. We know to the third decimal point how many B.A.'s and M.A.'s and Ph.D.'s are turned out every year in the United States. How many educated men get by in spite of the system we do not know. But more, we may be sure, than the system, if it were totally efficient, would allow.

A professor conveys a sense of a wider horizon and of the wonders beyond the shore of his own restricted field. He knows, because he has visited some of the islands out there. The student somehow glimpses what the older man has seen, and a restlessness takes hold of him, and before long he takes off in his own skiff with little direction but with an impatience that makes the older man smile in admiration and hope, and that possibly awakens deep nostalgia for a happiness he cannot again know. Let me repeat what I have said somewhere else:

> A young man comes into your class on a lovely day in the fall and after the lecture . . . asks an unusually intelligent question. . . . You keep your eye on him and maybe talk with him in the office now and then. Gradually he begins to come in for a chat fairly regularly. As you get to know him you begin to realize that he is not yet quite himself and he knows it. Suddenly, by a miracle—yes, it *is* a miracle— . . . he tips in the womb of nescience and you sense more than see that he has begun to make his painful, groping and wonderfully thrilling way to the light, a light that, after he reaches it, he will call his real world. He has taken his first steps in becoming a fully developed person.

I also said that a teacher who stands by when a student begins to take his first steps toward an education goes through the supreme experience of his teaching life. But while such miracles occur in our educational institutions, the system is not designed to encourage them to happen. And it often penalizes those who undertake such out-of-the-way experiments. Education takes place in our system but it takes place in spite of the system.

It would be unfair not to observe that our institutions of higher learning have good reasons for fearing education and for doing what they decently can to ignore the problem that education poses to them. Ours is a technological society, and not only in the ordinary sense that Jacques Ellul uses the term: a society dedicated to the use of rational means toward clearly defined ends. In such a society the specialist is at a premium and for the educated man the society sees no use. Besides, the educated man is not easily distinguished from the superficial amateur with his unreliable knowledge and his intellectual irresponsibility. One thing we know from the study of anthropology and should know from our study of history is that societies institutionalize diverse values, organizing them in diverse orders of rank. The values and the institutions that anchor them are what we call cultures. In a technological culture there is no use for the mind that is comprehensive and versatile and whose central drive is to gain a connected view or grasp of things.

VIII

I said at the beginning of this paper that I did not claim to have discovered the distinction between education and training. Teachers and educational administrators have been considering it from different points of view for quite some time. The never-ending discussion we teachers seem to be engaged in about the curriculum, our concern that students of the sciences get acquainted with the nature and value of the humanities and that students of the humanities gain some knowledge of the place of science in our world and of its powerful methods, the vague sense we have that what we are doing may not be worth doing—this is all evidence of our radical dissatisfaction with the specialized products of our schools. And I beg to be permitted to say in passing that this paper was already in its final shape when Professor William Arrowsmith's challenging article, "The Shame of the Graduate Schools," in the March 1966 issue of *Harper's* magazine came into my hands. Professor Arrowsmith's attack is on the teaching of the humanities, and I do not believe that it can be re-aimed, by a shift of angle, to the quarter where the sciences are entrenched. In any case, I am in deep sympathy with many of the criticisms of Professor Arrowsmith. The point at which I disagree radically is with Professor Arrowsmith's optimism. Had he placed the graduate schools in their historical and their social perspective he might have gained considerably more understanding of our plight than he seems to have. It bears iteration: the condition of our schools could only be changed by means of a radical revolution—a revolution that would blast the foundations of our society.

When the problem is formulated in historical terms and in terms of the dominant ethos of our society and the existing arrangements of our educational institutions, it does not yet fully disclose its nature. This is disclosed when we express it in terms of our need, as human beings, to achieve the maximum development possible within the enabling frame of our culture. It follows therefore that the problem cannot be solved in the absence of a fully developed philosophical anthropology. And of course the latter, given the present condition in the sciences of man, is nowhere in sight.

It must be acknowledged that for the day-to-day process of living, facing the task of merely staying afloat, education, as I have sketched it, is irrelevant. But it must also be acknowledged that until we devise some sort of solution to the problem of education, our society will be able to continue its triumphant technological development, but it will deprive itself of the possession of as many complete human beings as it might otherwise have.

NOTE

[1] *The Key Reporter*, Vol. XXXI, No. 2, Winter 1965–66, pp. 2–4.   [XI, Winter 1966–67, 45–58]

[62]

The Word and the Rope

W. T. COUCH

W(illiam) T(erry) Couch (1901–   ), the author of The Human Potential: An Essay on Its Cultivation *(1974) and one of the best-known scholarly editors in the country, is now retired and living in Chapel Hill, North Carolina. Before beginning his distinguished career, he served in the United States Army, from October 1920 to March 1923, in the 17th and 19th Field Artillery. An editor of and contributor to* Culture in the South *(1934) and* These Are Our Lives *(1939), as well as editor-in-chief of* Collier's Encyclopedia *(1952– 1959) and its associated works of reference, he was also, successively, director of the University of North Carolina Press (1932–1945) and of the University of Chicago Press (1945–1950). From 1959 to 1966 he was editor-in-chief of the* American Oxford Encyclopedia.

Our social scientists, like most of our teachers and scholars, are in no condition to emulate Socrates.

THERE IS AN ANCIENT STORY—repeated by J. S. Mill in his *Liberty*—of a people, the Locrians, who followed the practice of holding public meetings and allowing anybody who wished to do so to stand up and argue for the abolition of an old law or custom, or the adoption of a new one— provided he met one condition. He had to present himself before the people with a rope tied around his neck. If the people approved what he said, the rope was removed, and he was rewarded. If the people disapproved what he said, he was at once strangled to death.

I believe this story contains an important basic truth about freedom of speech, and I propose here to examine the work of the educator in America today in the light of this story.

The most serious problem of public opinion has been well known for more than two thousand years. This is simply that there are things which need to be said in public, and which the public does not wish to hear. The more such things need to be said, the more certainly the public will not listen. And the more certain it becomes that it will inflict penalties of an extreme sort on anyone who tries to make it listen.

It is tempting to gloss over this problem, to assume that it can always be solved by cleverness and indirect approaches. But while the arts of diplomacy have their uses, it is not difficult to understand why they always have been regarded, even by their most skilled practitioners, with a measure of contempt.

Only recently I saw a perfect illustration of this problem. I was attending a meeting of educators at which a highly controversial subject was being discussed. The issues essential to the subject itself were not stated. Everybody appeared to be in agreement as to what ought to be done. The question discussed was simply this: how could the public be persuaded to do this something that the educators agreed ought to be done? One group said the public can be persuaded to move only step by step. The other said, no, if the proper effort is made, the public can be persuaded to do what needs to be done all at once.

The discussion became warm, and was threatening to become hot. Then a man got up and said, why advocate anything? Why get the people all wrought up—why not help them ask themselves the questions they need to ask? The perfect pattern for handling such matters, he said, is available to all of us. Socrates made it over two thousand years ago, and all we need to do is follow it.

I looked at him, and I could not see him following the pattern that led to the hemlock. He looked to me, and he talked, like the typical American educator—a wiser man than Socrates.

This particular educator was, of course, not the only one present wiser than Socrates. They all knew how to avoid issues and escape the hemlock. The discussion was a fair representation of the present condition of American intellectual life.

If American intellectual life is in a dangerously unhealthy condition, can it truthfully be said that any part of the public is more responsible for this than any other? The answer to this, I believe, is clear. The chief responsibility for the intellectual life of America lies with the educational system. In this system, the most influential, the most responsible people are those in top positions in the leading universities. Are these people doing their duty in American life? What is their duty? I believe this duty has to do with the problem of the rope and the public, and I shall undertake now to make this as clear as I can.

Are there any things that need to be said in America that are not being said?

If I were German or Japanese, I would be interested in the question how far America's present racial policy was a war measure, first a response to the racial policy of the Nazis, later, a mode of competing with the Communists. I would be suspicious of sudden conversions of whole peoples. I would wonder whether there was anything "racistic" in American attitudes toward me and my people. I would be greatly puzzled over how a people could say it believed in the equality of all peoples and at the same time say to me and my people, I will kill you if you do not submit to my will and allow me to make you over in my image. This, I would know only too well, was the real meaning of unconditional surrender and re-education. If someone patiently explained to me that the customs and traditions of my country were not good and needed to be changed, I could not help asking how could it be that some other people, no better than mine, were able to create patterns better than mine had been able to create, patterns so good that mine ought to adopt them.

I might find it in myself to wish that such remarkable people would solve some of the other problems harassing me and the rest of the world. Such as how I could feed and clothe and house myself and my family, take care of bodily needs, and not always have to submit to things to which I did not want to submit. I might not ask for anything so fine as freedom. I might want only to be let alone and allowed to grub my living out of a piece of soil and not have the tax gatherer or someone else constantly threatening to take it away from me. If the people who promised me freedom and peace and justice couldn't give me this, I might ask myself how much their promises were worth.

I would not find it hard to wonder how the conquerors of any country could expect it to join them to fight a former ally of theirs—after telling me and my people that we were the cause of war in the world. I could easily persuade myself that these people did not know much about anything but machines—that they needed sorely to ask themselves some questions and stay with the questions until they learned something about themselves.

If a man who happens to be an American may ask questions for mankind, if Germans and Japanese are members of mankind, then I am not presuming when I imagine these questions. And there are some others that I feel need to be asked.

How many American educators said during World War II that the Communists of Russia were just as untrustworthy as the National Socialists of Germany? How many American educators stood up and said this while saying it had a chance to stop the United States from building up Communist power?

How many books were written and published in the United States during World War II discussing alternatives to the extreme isolationist and extreme interventionist positions? How many stated alternatives to the unconditional surrender policy? How many discussed the deepest and most serious meaning of an unconditional-surrender policy combined with a re-education program?

The Association of American Universities went on record in the year 1953 to the effect that Communism is an "international conspiracy," and that members of a conspiracy have no place in American education. But the Communists had not changed. They have been saying and

doing the same things for many years. Anybody who took the trouble to inform himself knew that they were engaged in mass torture and murder long before World War II, and that they have continued through the years to torture and murder on a scale larger than that of the Nazis. The evidence that Communism was as much an "international conspiracy" before and during World War II as it is now has been plain all along to every man who had eyes to see. Why was the Association of American Universities so late in seeing?

The convinced Communist is not as dangerous as the man who for years sees no danger in Communism, and then suddenly, without any change in Communism, but after a lot of change in public opinion, joins in denouncing Communism as a world-encompassing conspiracy. It would be impossible to give a more perfect demonstration of complete untrustworthiness than conduct of this kind.

Is there any group in American education that has special responsibility for studying such subjects as Communism and Nazism and making its finding available to the public? The answer is the leading social scientists in the leading universities. If any substantial number of the more influential members of this group had discovered the truth and told it during World War II, the experience of America with Communism could have been totally different. The American people do not like torture and murder, whoever engages in them. If the people had been told the truth, I think they would have demanded a policy of balancing Communism against Nazism, stopping the dynamisms of the dictatorships, and giving the people of Germany and Russia a chance to establish decent governments. If the American people had been told the truth about the Chinese agrarians, I believe they would not have permitted a policy of destroying

Japanese power and making China safe for the Communists.

American social scientists generally not only failed to see the truth and tell it. They did the opposite. They were called to Washington for advice, and they went in droves and gave the advice that created the necessity of submission to the Communists or of World War III.

It is true, of course, that President Roosevelt and Congress could have refused to take the advice of the social scientists if they had been so inclined; and if the people generally had wished for their government not to follow the social scientists I think they could have made their wishes effective. But nearly everybody seems to have wanted to be deceived.

Even the maker of the piece of baked and gilded clay seems to have believed that what he was selling was pure gold. If there was any fraud as in the case of the thieves who made and sold imaginary clothes to the emperor, and deceived everybody until a little child saw the truth and said the emperor was naked, it is not clear who was guilty of the fraud. I do not know of any way of stopping the making and selling of gold bricks if everybody, government, people, and wise men, want them to be made and sold.

But how were the people to have any chance to know they were buying gold bricks? The educators, being wiser than Socrates, did not stand up and tell the truth when it most needed to be told. And if they had, they might have found their careers suddenly ended. This is, of course, the dilemma with which we started. I take my chances on the view that there is no real solution of this dilemma. If we think we have a solution, one that leads us to say the dilemma is false and does not represent a permanent and incurable condition, we deceive ourselves and render escape from any of the consequences of the dilemma impossible.

It is, of course, unfair to charge all educators with the responsibility of a part of their number. Most teachers in public schools have had nothing to do with the formation of national or educational policies. The same is true of most teachers in colleges and universities. But we should know by now that bombs fall on the just and unjust alike. To have any chance to stop the bombs, we must find out why they fall. And the teacher, of all persons, should be the most determined to see that this question is asked and answered.

And before condemning the educator, we would do well to ask what we would do under similar circumstances. Our whole case falls to the ground if we do not regard the role of the teacher as the most important in society, and if we do not somehow consider the teacher as one who must, because of the greatness of his calling, transcend the failings of other mortals.

If we know what we are talking about, we know that while we were talking about the rope we were talking about the perennial problem of orthodoxy and heresy and that the rope is the symbol of the means orthodoxies always use to maintain themselves. We know that there is no such thing as a community, a society, that is not governed by an orthodoxy; and we know that a free society is one that while governing itself by its orthodoxy as firmly as any other, at the same time cultivates heresies; and we know it does this because it believes that strong heresies provide the most certain guarantee of freedom. This is the orthodoxy of the free society. And this is the basis for the claim of academic freedom in American universities. The American who believes in freedom, if he understands the problem of the rope and the public, of the mob and the flatterer, will not oppose academic freedom. On the contrary, he will want to know why the social scientists of America on all of the most important questions during the last decade have appeared to the public to be virtually of one mind.

America had thousands of social science teachers during World War II. Very few, so far as I am aware, diagnosed correctly the cases of Communism and Nazism. We expect the bricklayer, the doctor, the lawyer to know more about bricklaying, medicine, law than the rest of us. And we expect, and I think have the right to expect, the teacher to know more about teaching and the subjects he is teaching. We feel that we have the right to judge the teacher by the consequences of his teaching just as we judge the lawyer or doctor or bricklayer by the consequences of his work.

In the field of medicine a man who pretends to knowledge he does not have is called a quack. In law, a shyster. And the professions of medicine and law have long followed the practice of throwing the quacks and shysters out.

What should be done about the quacks and shysters in teaching?

It is not a pleasant thing to think about, but if we face the issue we have to answer, there is no more reason why they should be in teaching than they should be in other professions. But who can be trusted to do the identifying and expelling? If the profession could be trusted, it would never have allowed the quacks and shysters in. But they are in. And their colleagues have not taken, and will not take, initiative against them. They can hardly be expected to take initiative against themselves because this would require a change in spirit, the equivalent of a miracle of this kind is the only really healthy thing that can happen now.

The cure for the quackery and shysterism in the educational system must come from inside, from self-examination and criticism, from public admission of error. It cannot be imposed. But how can the educational world be persuaded to criticize itself and to welcome outside criticism?

Before I try to answer this question, let me say that it is impossible to make a more serious mistake today than to attack American universities for harboring and developing heresies. There is an important sense in which they have done this. It is true that the educators have cultivated heresies, but they are no longer doing so. The heresies they were cultivating have won and now constitute a great, new orthodoxy, and the educators, with the backing of the great foundations, are busy trying to maintain this orthodoxy. One of the basic tenets of this orthodoxy is that the people generally do not have the right to criticize the educators, and the educators have powerful support from press and pulpit and practically all other agencies having to do with public opinion in maintaining this basic tenet.

American education for over two decades now has been governed by this all-powerful orthodoxy. The rule of this orthodoxy has not been checked by any serious criticism. It has been absolute; in the language of the period, totalitarian. The orthodoxy has changed from saying one thing about Communism ten years ago to saying the opposite now. This change has occurred entirely as a consequence of outside pressure. There is no reason for believing that the present orthodoxy is any more honest, any better informed, any more aware of its obligations to society, than the preceding one. If we look for strong heresies, we find none. The social scientists who were going to help remove and destroy the rope that has threatened the freedom of mankind have seen their efforts end in the strangling of millions. Whether they have learned anything from the disasters they have helped to bring about, we do not know; for they have not tried to tell us.

And of all censorship, that of the man who has a story to tell and does not tell it is exceeded only by that of people who need to hear something but will not listen.

Publishers today, with the exception of a few that can be named on the fingers of one hand with fingers to spare, are cooperating with this censorship. Of the thirty-five or more university presses in the United States, none has published anything on this subject that is worth reading. It is certainly true, but it is not enough, to say as one writer does in a recently published book that, during World War II, " . . . we overlooked the need for political thinking. We acted as if we were utterly unaware of the fully advertised objectives of the Communists. . . ." Everybody knows this by now. The important question *is* why we acted this way. And the answer that we feared the Nazis leaves unanswered the question why we did not have at least equal fear of the Communists. If you listen to the voices that the publishers are allowing to get to the public, you will hear very few that try to answer this question.

I cannot banish the feeling that the building up of Communist power was an offense against civilization, and I think Americans need for the good of their souls to consider how this compares with the offenses for which America helped try and condemn and execute Japanese and German leaders after World War II. Of all men in America, the educators are the ones who ought to understand this need most clearly.

It may be that the failure of American education is at least partly a consequence of influences that might be changed. American foundations have for a long time been working in one direction— toward the left. All the rewards in the world of learning during the last two decades have gone to men willing to work in this direction. Such men hold all the key positions. They determine failure and success for others. But America has not yet permitted the leaders to strangle or shoot those who have refused to follow. There are dissenters here and there, some even in universities. I have before me as I write a good example of dissent, one from the University of Pennsylvania, *Social Problems and Scientism,* by A. H. Hobbs. After reading Mr. Hobbs's book, I am sure he will not receive encouragement from any of the large foundations, unless they change their present ways of thinking.

Why? Because Mr. Hobbs asks embarrassing questions. He exposes the orthodoxy and he criticizes it.

But Mr. Hobbs without foundation support has little chance to get a serious hearing as long as others whose interests require that they ignore or discredit him have unlimited support.

I am sorry to say that men can be bought, like sacks of potatoes, even in the scholarly world. And the man who cannot be bought has to eat just like the others. If nobody in the scholarly world is willing to pay such men for honest work, they have to find their work and pay elsewhere.

One foundation with the resources of Carnegie or Rockefeller or Ford that understood the problem would have a chance to restore health to the intellectual world.

It is not beyond the range of possibility that careful and sustained criticism and public pressure could bring the trustees of Carnegie or Rockefeller or Ford to see that there are some things in American tradition worth preserving in American life. It would be unfortunate if all the foundations tumbled in this direction all at once. Scholars are human beings too, and can be demoralized by the power of money. So far, the great foundations have done more harm than good to the social sciences. They dangled the carrot that led the donkey into the bog. Whether they can now do anything to correct the damage they have done is, I believe, extremely doubtful; but this seems to me the best chance.

I do not know of any cure for men who have the answers, who are wiser than Socrates, who know how to fill the great office of the teacher and take no chances with the hemlock. But I will take my chances on the view that the rope and the public are a part of the original scheme of things and cannot be escaped.

[II, Winter 1957–58, 4–9]

[63]

The Circular Travels
of the Professors

JAMES BURNHAM

James Burnham (1905–1987), educated at Princeton and Oxford, was a professor of philosophy at New York University from 1929 to 1953. On the far Left in the 1930s, "inside the beast" of communist unions in Detroit, he worked with A. J. Muste and in 1934 with the Fourth International of Leon Trotsky. Not quite an ideological Marxist, he was editor of the New International *and an active Trotskyite until March 1940. Thereafter, he published* The Managerial Revolution *(1941), condemning liberalism, which he described in* The Machiavellians: Defenders of Freedom *(1943) as a "pigmy ideology" in comparison with the "gigantic ideology of Bolshevism." Emerging as a formidable conservative* engagé *in* The Struggle for the World *(1947)—published, ironically, the same week the Truman Doctrine emerged—he was a consultant to the Central Intelligence Agency, helping to shape global anticommunism and the conservative critique of liberal foreign policies in the cold war. For many years he was a senior editor of* National Review. *A recent study of his thought is Samuel T. Francis's,* Power and History: The Political Thought of James Burnham *(1984).*

IN THE AUTUMN of 1959 professor of history Arthur Schlesinger, Jr., editor Edward Weeks, literary critic Alfred Kazin and playwright Paddy Chayevsky paid a month's visit to the Soviet Union, Poland and Yugoslavia as the first "American writers' delegation" under "the Lacy–Zarubin agreement," which put into effect President Eisenhower's cultural exchange program. The choice of this group—all its members of the far Left and all critics of both American culture and Administration policy—is no doubt a tribute to Mr. Eisenhower's non-partisanship in foreign affairs, or perhaps to his indiffer-ence, though it does seem a rather narrow cross-section for the "people to people" togetherness that the President has long advocated as the solution to Russo-American "misunderstanding." A few months later, Prof. Schlesinger wrote an account of the odyssey for *Harper's* and the English (U.S.-subsidized) magazine *Encounter.*

Our returned traveler promises, at the outset, to stick to "new and concrete impressions," to the "complexities of experience" in place of the "easy abstractions which rule [the] thought" of stay-at-homes. "So superficial an inspection," he disarmingly grants us, "could hardly be expected to yield profound conclusions." However hardly to be expected, though, it does seem to have yielded a good many that are, if not exactly profound, at any rate portentously worded.

As early as his opening paragraph, Prof. Schlesinger has discovered from his officially guided tour of a few cities in three of the two dozen Communist countries that there is a universal "heterogeneity of Communist practise"—which fact, moreover, such is the acuteness of his concrete impressions, he realized to be "the best, if not the only, hope for eventual world peace." And he must have brought in his equipage an outstanding telescope, for half of his second paragraph records his findings on China.

So it goes. "Power, of course, settles heavily on the Sino-Russian side of the spectrum. . . . The heart of Soviet dogmatism is the principle of infallibility. . . . The platonic essence of 'capitalism' does not correspond to the many mutations of a ceaselessly changing economic system. . . . Human nature is too obstinate, various, and elusive to be efficiently mastered by any technique thus far devised short of physical obliteration." Finally, God save the mark: "The one safe generalization about the Soviet Union is that it is in flux." If it were not for Prof. Schlesinger's initial disavowal, one might almost think that these were "easy abstractions." Toward the end of his narrative, our author harks back to his opening candor: "The great value of a few weeks behind the Iron Curtain is to remind oneself of the treachery of abstractions." *Ipse*, that time, surely *dixit*.

It is disappointing, really, that Prof. Schlesinger doesn't tell us a little more about what he saw and heard and smelled. When precisely made and accurately expressed, direct observations of unfamiliar places—"concrete impressions"—can be wonderfully interesting in themselves, as well as occasionally instructive. But even

the rare sentences where Prof. Schlesinger seems merely to be recording observations rather than proclaiming abstractions are suspect on closer notice. "The streets of Moscow are filled with people trickling back from exile and hard labor in Siberia." It may be so, but it is certain that Prof. Schlesinger did *not* observe, and could not have observed, anything of the sort. What percentage of Moscow streets did he see? Among the passersby, how many did he, personally, confirm to be returned exiles? Could he, who does not speak Russian and to whom returned exiles would be most unlikely to pour out their life stories even if he did, have confirmed such a generalization in any case? In similar fashion, most of the assertions about "life and comfort," "consumer goods," Khrushchev's wanting "very much to be liked," about the new Soviet citizens who feel "so free and so affluent" and who "are reaching out for beauty and gaiety, for speed and risk, for autonomy, privacy, and self-expression," dissolve into semantic dust at the lightest touch of a critical finger. True or false, these were not things seen, but conclusions deducted from hearsay or preformed beliefs.

Nor was it from Russia but from his colleague across the Harvard Yard, Prof. John Kenneth Galbraith, that he got the "impressions" out of which, in the rhetoric of the inside-stuff observer, he cast a key paragraph: "It is impressive and scary to see [*sic*—it takes X-ray eyes for this depth of seeing] what energy a great nation can generate when it allocates its talent and resources according to an intelligent [a strangely selected word] system of priorities. . . . The Soviet leadership thinks it important to send a rocket to the moon and not very important to supply tourists with tickets to Odessa, so they apportion their talent and resources accordingly. The able men work on rockets, the dopes on tickets. . . . Our own beloved country meanders along on the opposite theory:

we allow the market to determine our national priorities, which means that we allocate a major share of our talent and resources to consumer services and too often leave the sending of rockets to the moon to men who might be better employed [N.B. Dr. Braun and General Schriever] selling tickets to Odessa. If three-quarters of the national energy now dedicated to creating and satisfying consumer wants were dedicated instead to building national power, we would not have to worry about the Soviet campaign to 'overtake and surpass' the United States." We would not have to worry, it might be added, because if three-quarters of the energy were so allocated, we would all starve to death. But statistics have never been one of Prof. Schlesinger's strong points.

Actually, the only sentences that seem derived from direct, behind-the-Curtain observation are those which describe meetings with Soviet writers (whose words were presumably filtered for Prof. Schlesinger—though this detail is not mentioned—by translators). Curiously, nearly all the facts observed in these meetings contradict the generalities and the abstractions.

In abstractu, Prof. Schlesinger repeatedly informs us that "Soviet citizens talk freely" and "feel free," that "freedom of comment has unquestionably improved since the death of Stalin," that Soviet youth, "as against the bleak and sterile dogmatism of their fathers . . . appear to be reaching out for concreteness, variety, spontaneity," that in sum, "nearly all the changes which have taken place since the death of Stalin have been in what the Western liberal must call the right direction." But whenever Prof. Schlesinger gets down to cases and tells about actual meetings with actual human beings, he invariably finds: "What seem as ascertainable facts to the Westerner are believed in the Soviet Union only when they conform to the official stereotypes"; "Within the elite, manners tend to be pompous and hectoring, and the conception of discussion is hopeless" (if "hopeless," why, then, a cultural exchange program?); "I have never been lied to as casually, contemptuously, and persistently as in the Soviet Union"; "The style in which they discussed such matters [politics, economics, peace] was as discouraging as the substance"; "The hard fact is that the last thing the Soviet Union cares about is a free exchange of ideas." But hard facts make no lasting impression on soft minds.

Prof. Schlesinger is too faithful an ideologue to be able to observe. Like all ideological travelers, he brings back only what he takes with him. What he took on this visit to the other side were his Liberal axioms and values, a theory of Soviet development, and a passionate commitment to a policy of coexistence-at-all-costs—*i.e.,* appeasement.

The theory of Soviet development is a refurbishing of Trotsky's theory of Thermidor—of the inevitable bourgeoisification of revolutions. The rise of Khrushchev—so the theory goes in the Schlesinger adaptation—marks an essential break with the Stalin era. "Since the death of Stalin, [the Soviet Union] has been divesting itself of much of the irrationality which we considered its essence. . . . The implication of the talk about the 'bad times' [of Stalin] is that times are better now. This cannot be gainsaid. . . . It would be a great mistake to suppose that there is no 'real difference' between Stalin's Russia and the Russia of Khrushchev."

On the one hand, Khrushchev has "normalized" the regime and led it in a liberal direction, if not yet all the way to the "liberal Communism [which] Poland and Yugoslavia forced this observer to concede the feasibility of."

On the other hand, and more fundamentally, Khrushchev not merely strengthened the Soviet economy but "took over the Malenkov program . . . and in the last two years has been making a prodigious effort to raise standards of life and comfort. . . . There can be no question [*no* question, mind you, and don't give me any of your statistics on gadgets per capita] that Khrushchev has committed his country to the consumer-goods merry-go-round." The easy-life promises, given time, to crack the hard shell of Communism. "One cannot help feeling that the movement towards a consumer society will in the long run begin to erode the dogmatic monolith. . . . The critical question is whether . . . the consumer-goods passion may not upset the system of priorities and sap the single-minded intensity with which the Soviet economy dedicates itself to the building of national power. One detects already [on sensitive Harvard seismographs, apparently] a new deference to consumer motives."

The consumer-oriented economy and liberalized internal regime promote and indeed demand a peaceful foreign policy. "Stalin *required* international tension: only an overhanging external threat could reconcile his people to his savage interior tyranny. Khrushchev, by diminishing the interior tyranny, diminishes at the same time the need for external crises. . . . I would guess that Khrushchev deeply wants a *détente*."

Now comes the policy payoff. We must "reject the mystique of Either/Or," stop dividing "the world too glibly between the 'democratic' or 'capitalist' and the 'socialist' or 'Communist' camps," and accept a *détente*, so that Khrushchevian Communism can complete its evolution to affluent, liberal and peaceful "de-totalitarianization." The sure way to disaster is for us to try to get tough. "Surely one of the strongest arguments for a *détente* is precisely the fact that relaxation might give the forces of pluralism and tolerance a chance to dissolve the ideological dogmatism of Soviet society. . . . The one thing above all indispensable for the victory of the Polish-Yugoslav [liberalizing] tendency is the relaxation of international tensions. The resumption of the cold war would snuff out the inchoate burgeonings in the Soviet Union."

II

No one will suppose that Prof. Schlesinger could have "observed" all *that* on a month's whirlwind tour. Where, then, did he get in particular this theory of Soviet development that he carried in his knapsack? We have noted that his theory of national power and consumer affluence was borrowed from his campus colleague, Prof. Galbraith. For the theory of development, he had only to drop a couple of miles further down the Charles River to Massachusetts Institute of Technology and the offices of Prof. W. W. Rostow.

In the autumn of 1958 Prof. Rostow delivered a series of lectures at Cambridge University. These were printed by *The Economist* last summer and published this year as *The Stages of Economic Growth.* Therein he "presents an economic historian's way of generalizing the sweep of modern history . . . a theory about economic growth and a more general, if still highly partial, theory about modern history as a whole." The treatise is a neo-Marxian Manifesto, a work of what *Pravda* nowadays calls "revisionism"—that is, watered-down Leninism.

In summary, the Rostow theory identifies "all societies, in their economic dimensions, as lying within one of five categories: the traditional society, the preconditions for the take-off, the drive to maturity, and the age of high mass-consumption." Each society waits around for millennia in the traditional category. In post-Renaissance times one after another has been somehow stirred to set up the preconditions for industrial take-off. From that point on, caught in the gears of compound interest, it mounts more or less inevitably through the successive stages to the high mass-consumption level which the United States and Canada are said to have reached in the 1920's, Britain and Australia in the '30's, and Sweden, Germany, France and Japan a few years ago.

From the point of view of economic history, the Rostow Stages theory seems to be a linguistic device for the arrangement of data, analogous to Toynbee's "challenge and response" terminology or the Hegelian-Marxian "thesis-antithesis-synthesis" triad. As such it is not very elegant—Prof. Rostow not sharing the Schlesinger-Galbraith literary flair—nor does it tell us anything much about the subject matter, other than the rather obvious point that some nations have become industrialized and concomitantly raised their material standard of living. It may have a certain utility in planning the topics for a course of lectures or suggesting the table of contents for a book.

Prof. Rostow, however, is by no means willing to restrict his theory to so modest a role. Though with a running diversionary fire of qualifications, "on the other hands," and "other things being equal," Prof. Rostow is in reality proposing a hypothesis not of linguistics but of substance: a neo-Marxian economic determinism as an inclusive theory of history. If that were not the way in which both he and his readers were understanding it, his book would have little interest for anyone but specialized scholars, instead of the large and still expanding influence that it is in fact having on publicists, chancelleries and Presidential candidates.

Not only are the five stages an economic growth pattern through which every society all but inevitably passes, but the economic transformations are, in turn, all but inevitably correlated with—are the cause of, *tout court*—transformations in customs, politics, beliefs, and so on.

When driving up through the early stages, a nation is terribly aggressive and dangerous to outsiders. But as it enters the affluent stage of automobiles and high mass-consumption, it relaxes. War is no longer in the national interest, no longer "rational." If it is able to do so, the high mass-consumption society prefers to live in peace with others in order to focus on its "inner frontiers" and enjoy its flesh pots, cars, ranch homes, outboards and babies.

So the United States. And Russia now is moving from the stage of maturity to the stage of high mass-consumption: that, at bottom, is the meaning of the change from the Stalin to the Khrushchev era. The Russians want the flesh pots and cars, and Khrushchev wants to give them what they want. Russia's "criteria of national interest" dictate an acceptance of controlled arms limitation, subordination of sovereignty, and a peaceful world of "diffused power." *Our* problem is to carry out "the great act of persuasion" that will get the Russians "to accept the consequences of peace and the age of high consumption, so that they can go forward with the rest of the human race in the great struggle to find new peaceful frontiers* for the human experience." This we can do if we give the newly taking-off nations of Asia, Africa and Latin America lots of help in rushing through *their* stages, and if we "demonstrate to the Russians that there is an interesting and lively alternative . . . to either an arms race or unconditional surrender." (More briefly: foreign aid and appeasement.) Communism in the disagreeable, the aggressive, sense is only—

---

* The appearance of the term "new frontier" as a central concept in Senator John F. Kennedy's speech accepting the Presidential nomination is *not* coincidental.

as a subhead puts it, "A Disease of the Transition." It will fade away as the stages of growth unfold, so long as we don't upset the applecart by challenging it during this "century or so until the age of high mass-consumption becomes universal."

III

Professors Schlesinger, Rostow and Galbraith are leading fellows in the contemporary school of social scientists who write political tracts in the form of history, economics and sociology: a defense of the New Deal in the form of a history of Andrew Jackson; an apology for statism in the guise of an analysis of the new economic equilibrium; a call for recognition of Communist China masked as a scholarly survey of Chinese "prospects."

The essay of Prof. Schlesinger's that I have here examined is insensitive and pedantically abstract if taken as a first-hand account of the experiences of travel; Prof. Rostow's book, taken as a historical theory, is pretentious, dull and almost empty of verifiable content. But it is naive to read them as if travel essay and historical theory. Both are in reality tracts that exploit a respectable, accepted form to propagandize for a political point of view that is unacceptable to most Americans—doubtless even to Messrs. Schlesinger and Rostow—when stated baldly and unadorned: the point of view of unconditional coexistence with Communism; that is, of appeasement.

The Schlesinger-Rostow-Galbraith concept of a Khrushchevian liberalization and *détente*-seeking induced by a growingly consumer-oriented economy falls into place in the long chain of concepts and theories that have served to justify our unwillingness to accept the truth about Communism. The unchanging objective of the Communist world enterprise is and has always been a monopoly of world power, and therefore our destruction. This has been the unchanging objective under all circumstances and in all "stages of growth": in 1903 when the enterprise was founded by a few dozen outcasts with a half-dozen revolvers as armament; in defeat and victory, war and peace, Five Year Plans, War Communism, New Economic Policy or Opening of Virgin Lands; under Lenin, Stalin, Malenkov, Khrushchev, Suslov or Mao.

This truth means that the only thing we can do about Communism, if we are unwilling to surrender, is defeat it. But we of the West have so far declined to face that cheerless conclusion. We therefore invent one theory after another to explain why Communism cannot win, will turn gentle, or will be defeated on our behalf by someone else. In pre-1917 years we explained to ourselves that Communism could not win because Communists were a powerless sect of crackpot fanatics. In 1917 they became patriotic Russian democrats overthrowing reactionary Tsardom. Lenin's New Economic Policy showed them to be reverting to capitalism. Stalin's Socialism in One Country was proof that they had given up world ambitions. With the Popular Front they were transformed into staunch anti-fascist allies. In China there was nothing to worry about, because Chinese Communists were agrarian reformers. After the war, Tito was heavensent as he-who-would-do-our-work-for-us: imperial, international Communism would split into a score of rival national Communisms. The Red Army is really Russian, not Communist, and will restrain Communist adventurism. The Sino-Russian conflict absorbs the energies of the Communist bloc, so that there is no excess for external aggression. At each and every moment there is always a theory, usually a choice of theories, to prove that we don't have to meet the challenge of Communism ourselves, because something internal to Communism or someone else or some great impersonal force of History will do it for us.

The idea of Khrushchev the peace-needing, consumer-oriented liberalizer, risen to power in response to an increasingly affluent Russian economy and comfort-minded citizenry, is a postwar egghead link in this continuous chain of excuse and rationalization.

Then, after the weaving of so much fine ideological cloth by our busy trio, Khrushchev the Liberalizer tore it to pitiful shreds in a single morning in Paris last June. Khrushchev, worse luck, doesn't read Professors Schlesinger or Rostow, or even Professor Galbraith. We might be a good deal better off if he did, and we didn't. [IV, Fall 1960, 380–386]

Intrusion into the Soul of a Child

MAX PICARD

Translated by Henry Regnery

Max Picard (1888–1965) was born in Schopfheim, in the Grand Duchy of Baden. A deeply religious man who converted to Roman Catholicism, he was also a physician (he completed his medical studies in Munich) who displayed a great talent for diagnosis. Growing disgusted with the mechanical methods of therapy, however, he abandoned medicine after practicing only a few years, and undertook the study of philosophy. Settling in the 1920s in the Ticino, Switzerland, because of his wife's health, he lived on Lake Lugano for many years, just a few miles from the Italian frontier, writing such books as The Flight from God *(1951) and* Man and Language *(1963). Branching out as an educational theorist and innovator, he became, above all, a visionary imbued "with a certain majesty."*

I

It is characteristic of our time that educational problems as a rule are considered only in relation to the ungifted or abnormal child; one has the impression that everything starts with the abnormal and that the normal child is considered a special case. This fits the contemporary preoccupation with the exceptional, the out of the ordinary. Almost all phenomena have become formless, so blurred that only the abnormal makes itself evident; it is the abnormal alone that catches the eye.

Only those things seem to matter which are in a state of crisis, are conspicuous; only then do we believe them worthy of discussion. Marriage, for example, is regarded not in its integrity, as something valid in itself which is only secondarily dependent on what happens within it, but as an occasion for crises; marriage is seen solely from the standpoint of crisis. We have developed a special language of crisis, and it is only in this terminology that discussion takes place.

The fact, however, that one considers phenomena purely from the point of view of the abnormal also affects the observer: one perceives only the fragmented, the disturbed aspect, one creates what one looks for. To take an example from classical psychiatry: it is well known that Charcot first described hysteria, and also that many neurotics then formed their neuroses to fit his description. Or take a pupil who is disturbed; under the disruptive eye of the observer he becomes still more disrupted. He may, perhaps, have been only slightly disturbed; then his difficulty is diagnosed, the presence of the observer is sensed, the child unconsciously accommodates the observer by behaving as he is expected to behave.

It is, of course, also true that the disturbed child, because of his difficulty, feels himself isolated, and therefore craves attention; he needs and wishes the company of others, of that one person who searches him out. Mere observation, therefore, can be helpful to him. The experience of being brought out of isolation by the attention of the observer can of itself bring about a cure. Sympathy alone can heal without any special therapy.

It should be mentioned also that many pupils today are not themselves disturbed, but merely reflect the disturbance around them. This has its reasons in the structure of our time: a phenomenon is not only fragmented in itself, it spreads disintegration around it, there is no barrier to halt the disintegration of its surroundings.

II

How does analytical psychology function? (I include under this term the psychoanalysis of Freud, Jung's depth psychology, Adler's individual psychology, existential analysis, etc.)

Analytical psychology attempts to put the child's disorder into relationship with something, with his family surroundings or with some early impression; it sets up a causal relationship between some specific event and the defect in question. Perhaps a pupil has stolen something. The analytical psychologist discovers through his analysis that the pupil has a stepmother who has mistreated him and concludes that the suppressed ego wanted, in compensation, to prove to itself by a daring theft that it could indeed be free. The whole, closed experience which existed in the pupil before the analysis is taken apart, one experience is explained in terms of another, until finally the theft is explained as the end of this long causal relationship. The pupil comes to understand that it is not necessary for him to steal and is, perhaps, freed of the disturbance.

This breaking down of a unified experience into its many successive elements is destructive of the psyche of a child. The psyche of a child lives from its wholeness, it absorbs an experience out of its own wholeness and what it absorbs it retains as a whole. No matter how intense an individual experience may be, it does not remain isolated. It has been observed how little the shock of a bombardment in the war affected the psyches of children. A violent individual experience is dissolved in the wholeness of the psyche, it disappears in the whole, and if it cannot be compensated for, it changes the whole; the whole then has a different orientation than before. In this way a single calamitous event might become the center, and could as a consequence result in a disturbance in the child. But this center then dominates the psyche, becomes the whole, so that the psyche of the child is always, even under such circumstances, a whole.

Obviously psychoses occur in children which are similar in form to the psychoses of adults. In their nature, however, they are entirely different, because their locus is the soul of a child. The child lives from his wholeness out to the elements which come to him. It is not so with adults: here the influence of the whole is constantly less. The adult lives from part to part, he connects a new experience to the chain of existing experiences, and the wholeness of his psyche is hardly more than something which encloses this chain of experiences and gives them a definite quality.

When the analytical psychologist extracts a single experience from the soul of a child's psyche, he takes his own adult psyche as his starting point. But such a procedure is alien to the psyche of a child, from which no single thing can be separated.

I do not say that a child cannot be helped by such methods; I do say that such methods are a trauma for the childish psyche, even if by the use of them the psyche is freed of a defect. The child is forced into the adult state; he is taken out of his own world and brought perhaps into a better one, but in so doing something is lost: the unique world of the child. Consider the psyche of the child in its unity—because of it the child is a child, because of this unity the children of all races belong to each other, because of this unity the soul of the child believes, and because it always has this unity as a whole it can turn itself into a piece of wood, into a doll, a character in a fairy story and yet always remain itself, independent of time and place; a closed, whole world is always present. And it is necessary that man in his childhood should have such a closed, formed, inner world as a pattern for a closed and formed world later on. The world of the child is a distinct, primary phenomenon, a given, that is to say, beyond all human experience, *a priori*, transcendent; man cannot deprive himself of that which was pre-given for him.

The analytical psychologist, by his method, takes the child away from the world of the child into the world of the adult. That is also the danger in present day education, that the educator draws the child too much to himself, that he breaks off the world of youth for the sake of that of the adult. The educator should bring the new to the child in such a way that he protects the psyche of the child. The wholeness of the psyche ought not to be broken, it should only be broadened; the new must be sensed as an increase of the whole—of the whole, not of the individual.

III

I have spoken of the child whose act of stealing the psychologist explained by his family circumstances. What happens as a result of such an explanation? A distinct act against morals, a theft, is represented to be the result of accidental family circumstances, almost as though the family circumstances could be exchanged for the theft. The individual is no longer the cause of a situation, but merely a result; he no longer causes something, he is merely caused. The immediate connection of a person to a given situation is eliminated; the individual is only one of the many possibilities of an external situation. A dishonest act, an error, that which one used to call a sin, through a purely psychological explanation is no longer an act of an individual exercising his freedom. Through such a psychological explanation the individual stands before his act as though in front of something for which he has no responsibility; he stands before it as a stranger. The fact of his being a man has been taken from him together with his freedom to do what he had, indeed, wanted to do. His freedom and his humanity have been thrown into an imaginary room behind him.

Often, to be sure, a psychic or physical cause can be given for a wrong act and further wrong acts prevented by making the wrongdoer aware of the cause, but consider what the individual loses thereby! Where the individual chooses between good and evil or at least stands as one who can choose even if he cannot bring himself to do so, he is in the same situation as the figures of the great tragedies. He does not himself partake of great tragedy, but he is at least in the place where greatness occurs. This place in a great world is taken from him by psychology. Richard III, for the psychologist, did not become a murderer because he had decided to become and remain a king, but because he was a hunchback. But murder and a crooked back are obviously not equivalent. What a man loses by analytical psychology one can see by observing Richard III psychologically: he is deprived of the connection with greatness and the world of values.

IV

Let us return to the pupil who was psychoanalyzed because of a theft. The impulse to steal is taken from him by the treatment; he is not punished either morally or by imprisonment, but he is reduced as a person, because, again, his connection to greatness and the world of values has been severed. Such a pupil has not been healed; all that has happened is that he has been made operational again, he has been repaired. In saying that, however, I do not wish to say that merely to retain his whole human character with its quota of blame and repentance I would not subject a pupil who had gotten into trouble to psychological analysis—to leave him in his state of illness to preserve the whole person would be the most inhumane course of all. This would have been the aesthetic approach. I myself, if I knew of no other therapy, would choose psychological analysis, but in so doing I would, I hope, suffer greatly, because I had been able to heal an individual only by making him into a lesser person. And through *my* suffering, through the recognition of my own insufficiency and my responsibility the suffering and the responsibility which the other could not feel would be replaced—but I would always be certain that my suffering would be insufficient. I do not mean, therefore, that it is better not to free a person from a disorder than to psychoanalyze him, I mean that one must always be aware of the danger in this form of therapy.

A contrast to the psychoanalytical treatment of the erring pupil: In the recently published third volume of Hegel's letters the following is reported: Hegel had an illegitimate son, Ludwig, whom he took into his family when he later married. The illegitimate son, however, felt ill at ease in the family, and became self-centered and crafty. He was sent as a merchant's apprentice to Stuttgart, where he embezzled eight groschen and was no longer permitted to use the name Hegel. This embittered him intensely and he reacted by going as a mercenary to the Dutch East Indies, whether sent by his father or by his own decision to escape his troubles is not known. A contemporary of Hegel's, Professor Leo, reported that Hegel, through this turn of events "suffered deeply, and what he had done, even though convinced of its necessity, was a source of bitter struggle and constant reproach."

In the case of the boy who was treated psychoanalytically, suffering was driven out as a defect: suffering, which belongs to the highest category of human phenomena—for love, goodness, death is there where suffering is—suffering was analyzed away; just as a growth is removed by an operation so was suffering reduced to a manageable degree. The boy was freed of his disturbance, but at the same time lost something of the highest category; he gained something, but probably lost more. In the case of Hegel's son suffering was not taken away. His burden was shared by the father, not only out of love for the son, but also for the sake of the order of the world, to which suffering belongs. Hegel, who understood the human spirit and human history only as idealistic abstractions, here realized concretely and on his own person that the fact of immediate suffering and the remote abstractions of idealistic observation belong together.

The suffering which has been artificially removed perhaps gathers somewhere in secret and then, separated from love, goodness, God, isolated and therefore boundless, breaks loose over humanity in some monstrous way, as in a war more terrible than ever or in some horrible form of cruelty.

Another danger of psychological-ana-

cause it fragments the whole of the psyche
of the child and destroys its unity in order
to reach the cause of the disturbance,
what is the limit to which one may go in
penetrating the psyche of another? Individual means indivisible: at what point
does the investigator reach the indivisible,
where he must stop? In all men, behind
all consciousness and all unconsciousness,
there is an area of silence into which no
one is permitted to speak, into which one
can penetrate only with silence, from
whence only silence comes, and into which
even that One higher than mere man
enters with silence. This area is untouchable, it is so by virtue of itself, it is so *an
sich*. It is untouchable without reason, but
also *with* reason, because from this area
of silence in man emanates the power of
healing and salvation unto man. This area
of silence, however, can be disturbed,
destroyed, by the mere fact of analysis. It
is probable that many cases of disturbance,
without its having been noticed, have been
healed by this area of silence. Perhaps we
should entrust more to this area of silence
and to the wholeness of the psyche than
we do. We should trust to their power
more than to psychotherapy, but who has
the necessary courage? Our time respects
activity above all else, and believes only
in living actively; it is not waiting that
counts, but immediate action. Only what
is done visibly seems real. Quiet, invisible
activity, the activity of non-activity, which
is equivalent to the area of silence, counts
no longer.

A UNESCO official told me that his
organization had sent questionnaires to
various schools. They wished to know how
sixteen to eighteen year old students felt
about death, what they were prepared to
die for. One single answer, he thought,
was significant. It came from a class of
girls: they didn't want to think about
death, and what they were prepared to
die for was a private matter, and should
remain so. I was touched by this, still more
by the fact that the gentleman from
UNESCO told me that he felt ashamed
of himself after receiving this letter,
ashamed that he had tried to violate the
inner privacy of these girls.

The psyche is endangered when one
tries to bore into it by analysis. It is
endangered also because one person, by
such boring in, can dominate another.
One can turn the inner life of another
person not only in a direction with which
that person agrees, but also in a way in
which that person does not wish to go at
all. The method of analytical psychology
penetrates into the other person *before* any
therapy begins; it goes deeper than any
other form of therapy, and its effect depends on such penetration. There is something totalitarian about such a method:
boring into the life of a person belongs
to the totalitarian system, it is akin to the
totalitarianism of politics. Just as in the
totalitarian system a man is no longer
secure in his own house from invasion by
the almighty state, so the inviolability of
the psyche is no longer safe either.

It is true that the therapist must himself
go through analysis before he is permitted
to psychoanalyze others. It is assumed
that he thereby receives the authorization
to enter the psyche of another. But this
is not a genuine authorization. Only he
who is aware that at every moment he
must prove himself before One who stands
higher than man really has such authority.
The analysis which the psychotherapist
goes through is nothing more than the
secularization of the religious act by which
man tests himself before God.

One enters the inner life of another—
that is merely a continuation of the general expansion of our time. In the external
world there is nothing left to conquer, so
now one takes on the inner world. Externally, everything is too bright, one is
blinded by the brightness of the innumerable objects; in the darkness and emp-

tiness of the inner life one is exposed to no such harshness. Emptiness and darkness place no limits on expansion.

Psychoanalysis takes place in time, that is to say, a certain measure of time passes until the state of the psyche has been investigated, but that is not time in which one person shares the fullness of his life with another. Here he lives only in a part of time with another, in that part which involves the symptoms of the disturbance. It can take a long time before the meaning of these symptoms has been determined, but such a time is still only a prolonged moment, for this time has no depth, it is not filled with the fullness of shared life. Time is merely touched on the surface by something with a purpose, and only that is admitted which belongs to the diagnosis. The analyst is with the other only because of the demands of his method. Thus the soul is cheated of time, it is offered only purposeful, clock time. Analytical psychology is a reduction of mutuality to a methodological process without love. It may perhaps happen now and then that an analyst overcomes his method through love, but what person who professionally analyzes one disturbed person after another can trust himself to offer love to each? The analytical method serves as a substitute for love.

V

Analytical psychology concerns itself not only with the disturbed pupil, but with the healthy pupil as well. It subjects him to tests to determine whether, how and to what extent he is gifted. Such tests, however, cannot really determine whether a child is gifted, since the psyche of a child is treated in such testing as nothing more than a psychological apparatus, which registers whatever is brought to it. This psychology proceeds from the entirely false assumption that the psyche of a child simply waits for an opportunity to react,

that it exists only when it reacts. The psyche of a child, however, is not at all prepared to register impressions. It is closed in itself; round, so to speak, turned into itself, not in an egoistical sense, but fulfilling itself, existing in itself, depending on itself. A psyche so organized cannot react at once; it is much too much complete in itself. It is nowhere so incomplete, as is the case with adults, that it can take to itself something coming from outside. The psyche of a child doesn't add, but assimilates; it doesn't adapt itself to a new experience, but encompasses the experience. If it encounters a new experience, however, which it cannot assimilate at once, then it must first go out of itself, leave itself. It must leave much behind before it can approach something new. A whole world is risked in order to take the new experience to itself, so that the movement away from this world is clumsy, slow. The child holds fast to itself.

It is not as with adults, where nothing is risked, where the most recent new experience meets another hardly less recent experience. With a child, as I have said, a world is risked, which is much: a whole world in which every part is really not a part, but represents the whole, so much is everything tied together. The adult later tries consciously to regain this closed world of the child, which is a divine natural gift. But without once having had this world of the child, the adult would not even have the desire to form his inner and outer life as a world to himself. The longing of the human spirit for a world created by itself comes from the memory of the world of the child. This world of the child undergirds the world of the adult, it is necessary to the adult. "Only when infinite variety has been experienced can grace find its way in once more" (Kleist).

A child, enclosed in its round world, cannot react quickly and with clever combinations. Its shyness makes it hesitate to go out of its closed world, and it is essential that a child have such shyness, for shyness is among the most valuable attributes a person can have. In the psychological tests that we have been discussing, however, the child does best that is least shy, the child that is most prepared to react quickly to everything. The world of the child on the one hand, the psychological testing apparatus on the other—these are not equivalent. The testing apparatus has little regard for shyness, it proceeds as though such shyness did not exist, it deprives the adult already present in the child of its shyness. The shyness, however, which a man has from his childhood is an essential part of the man.

One cannot say that the reactions to psychological testing are not true. They are indeed true, but not of the whole person, only of that part of the person that is nothing more than the object of the psychological apparatus. If one wishes through the process of education to obtain not the whole person, but a partial person, then one can indeed operate in accordance with the testing apparatus of psychology. Consider for example how many pathological or neurotic symptoms could have been found in Goethe or Bismarck. They could all have been determined by the testing apparatus of psychology, but that would not have been the whole Goethe or the whole Bismarck. The apparatus of psychology can experience something only in part.

It is indeed a most disturbing thing, one of the many frightening examples of the fact that the knowledge and understanding that have been gained by human association are replaced by quantitative observation, and responsible choice by the counting of points. What a great transformation the meaning of the word test has gone through, from having to do with personal achievement, with accomplishment, therefore with risk and life, to rationalized testing, which measures a person like a robot. (Wilhelm Stählin in *Quatember*.)

Psychoanalysis belongs in its intellectual structure to the positivistic psychologistics of the nineties, as does the individual psychology of Adler and the depth psychology of Jung, the latter being a pseudo-romantic psychologistic. This psychologistic has long been superseded, above all by the phenomenology of Husserl. But it is always true that when a philosophic doctrine has been superseded its practical influence continues. This does not mean that a new pedagogy should be based on Husserl's phenomenology alone; what I mean is that it must again begin with the whole phenomenon, with the whole being of the child, primarily with that, and only secondarily with the reactions of this being.

VI

Man has indeed a psychological structure, but he is not thereby characterized as a man; he is characterized by the act of freedom by which he chooses to live above this structure. A man can be as his structure determines, but he does not have to be. An animal must be as it has been created, a man need not be; man can live above his structure, can live beyond it. A person first begins to be a person when he lives beyond this structure. Perhaps he was given such a structure only as a challenge to live beyond it. I can believe that the psychological structure wishes its owner to live beyond it, presses him to live beyond it. For this reason one can never say that on the basis of his psychological structure a person in a certain situation will react in a predetermined way. When a person is faced with a certain situation he may make a decision which he would never have believed himself capable of, to say nothing of what the apparatus of psychology might have predicted. There is the moment of the psychological reaction, which is a moment of the apparatus of psychology, and there is the moment of eternity, when a person, through the act of free choice, confronts eternity.

It is difficult today to complete the act of freedom, since our whole existence is no longer one of action so much as re-action. No one any longer does anything of his own accord, everyone waits until the other does something so that he can react to it. The whole productive process is based on psychological tests, and the miserable part of it is that the productive apparatus can make use of a person only as a function of a psychological process. The school, however, should help the individual to be a whole person irrespec-tive of the demands of the productive process, which can only use the reduced person delivered by the apparatus of psy-chological evaluation. To be a whole per-son means not to be as determined by the apparatus of psychology, but to live be-yond and above it. If this were done, the productive process would change of itself.

The point, then, is to live beyond the psychological structure. The complete-ness, the closedness, therefore, of the psyche of the child must be protected against the aggressiveness of psychology. The psyche of the child is something original, primary, a given, but it is so only when close to other primary, given phe-nomena.

Such a primary phenomenon, such a given, is represented above all by the parents. It is not enough that the father appears to the child merely as the provider of food and shelter, the primary element of the paternal must become evident to him. (Both Joachim Bodamer and Gabriel Marcel have pointed this out.) The pater-nal as the symbol of the provider existed before the providing father, as did the paternal as the symbol of authority before paternal authority was exercised; the father

must exist as more than merely the older, the more experienced. That, however, is only possible when the actual paternal, fatherly role has a relationship to the Father who is father of all. In the same way the mother must appear as the symbol of care and protectiveness before there is any occasion for actual care and protec-tion. The fact of the existence of the mother is what makes care and protection possible—that is a fact which corresponds to the psyche of a child. For the teacher it is exactly the same: he exists not merely as one who knows more than his pupils, but as one who is a teacher beyond the mere fact of teaching, as one from whom teaching emanates before he actually be-gins to teach. The true physician is one for whom the process of healing begins the moment he enters the sick room, before he examines or prescribes, and just as healing emanates from the true phy-sician so must teaching emanate from the teacher as soon as he opens the door of the school room, before he has explained anything. The concrete act of teaching only catches up to what, through the manner of the teacher, was accomplished in advance. The teacher-pupil relation-ship cannot be created through subject matter, it can only be strengthened, con-firmed by it.

This is how the psyche of the child, this primary given, exists in connection with the other primary, given phenomena with which it is related. These primary, given phenomena are not pure "factualities" (Hölderlin), they go beyond the factual, even beyond the personal, they are an objective quality, and so long as the child stands in a relationship to this objective quality he is safe. The all too subjective is absorbed by the objectivity of these phe-nomena, the dislocations and abnormali-ties of the subjective can be neutralized.

From the following example one will recognize the difference between analytical psychology and a conception which arises from the whole being. A boy rebelled against any task given him by his father or his teacher. Analysis made the boy aware that his father was tyrannical and, in his tyrannical fashion, gave the boy orders unreasonably. As a result of the analysis the boy became more tractable, resistance stopped, and he was able to get along in school. That was much, but soon after he relapsed into a much more serious state—he had not been healed by analysis, only temporarily repaired.

Healing came about when the boy later discovered that his father was more than someone who gave orders, that he was father first of all, and through the discovery of this primary phenomenon the boy on his own found his way to other primary phenomena, to goodness, loyalty, to God. The son no longer stood before his father on the narrow basis of the factual, but in the broad relationship of many primary phenomena which transcend the factual. Father and son now encounter one an-

other from this broad base, no longer in narrow opposition. The boy is given substance and a sense of mutuality in this broad world of primary phenomena. His psyche is absorbed into the wholeness of this world; he is now really healed. Analytical psychology merely repairs, which is often much, but healing is something quite different from repairing.

One should not remove a psychic defect from a person by analysis, one must help him so that he can live with his psychosis, or so that his life and it are shared, without his being aware of it, by others.

It is strange, that the inner life of man has been observed in such a paltry fashion and treated with so little imagination. What we call psychology is one of those masks which have assumed the places in the sanctuary where real images of the gods should stand. (Novalis)

[XVI, Fall 1972, 339–347]. Originally published under the title *Einbruch in die Kinderseele*, Eugen Rentsch Verlag, Erlenbach-Zürich, Switzerland.

[65]

Our Disposable Past: A Protest

RICHARD B. HOVEY

Richard B(ennett) Hovey (1917–   ) is a professor of English and member of the graduate faculty at the University of Maryland, College Park. An advisory editor of Hartford Studies in Literature, *he has contributed numerous articles on literature and education to a variety of journals and books. In his well-received* John Jay Chapman: An American Mind *(1959), Hovey brought to his interpretation a wide knowledge not only of literature but of psychology, sociology, and history as well, resulting in a fascinating portrait of a towering personality and a passionate temperament. From a somewhat different perspective, in his* Hemingway: The Inward Terrain *(1968) Hovey invites us, as Frederick Crews points out in his foreword to the book, "to consider that a writer can be morbid and major at the same time—that a pathetic and at times sinister code of bravado and a desperate moral confusion can go into the making of brilliant art."*

OUR PREOCCUPATION with youth is marked by mixed feelings. Perhaps more than any other people we permissive Americans protect and indulge our children. Surely we provide them with opportunities that would have astounded our own grandparents. So, when the young are ungrateful, we are hurt and angered. And we are baffled, if not outraged, when the most privileged of all, the youngsters in college, erupt into protest highjinks. Newsmen of course focus on the obvious drama, student clashes with police and academic administrators. But the third party remains, somehow, obscure: the faculty. Conservatives sometimes fancy that it is the radicalism of activist professors which does the unsettling. This simplistic search for a scapegoat is understandable but wide, wide of the mark. So seldom do so few such professors have any effect that anxiety about them is a waste. The whole business is far more complicated. Our collegiate young feel alienated for numerous likely reasons. I want to single out one of these because it has been generally ignored and because it does bear directly on the responsibility of us college teachers. In brief, my argument is this: that our campus population is disoriented because it is increasingly cut off from any sense of the past.

Evidently, in the now generation, people concerned about such a subject are just not with it. Bring it up in some circles, and you will be called a square. After all, we are swamped by so many problems calling for immediate attention—taxes, inflation, war, Pentagony, pollution, the pill, population explosion, inner-city decay, suburban sprawl, draining of natural resources, ecological foul-ups, radical

743

feminism, violence, crime, credibility gaps, racism, drug addiction, terrifying medical costs—that for a university creature to prate about past history looks like indulgence in an academic luxury. The past, we say in effect, is not usable, is disposable, dead, and therefore nonsense.

And yet our impatient dismissal of the past is a peculiarly American thing. The attitude is well documented: from, say, our greatest Phi Beta Kappa speaker, Emerson, in some of his moods; to Henry Ford's dictum "History is bunk"; to the sophomore's demand that every quarter hour in the classroom or over his books have immediate relevance; to the haste with which educational leaders take bold, new, innovative approaches to the challenges of our changing campuses—i.e., in the parlance their public relations staffs release to the mass media.

Against this current I paddle my own canoe. The leaky little thing is jammed to the gunwales with my pet prejudices. To itemize the cargo, I admit to this list of partial truisms:

1. History repeats itself—rather, those ignorant of history are condemned to repeat it.

2. We cannot know where we are unless we know where we have been.

3. Much that appears new to us is really not new.

4. All fruitful radicalism, all productive revolutions, were started by persons grounded in some solid tradition.

5. All innovations in art, all gains in thought, have come from those who were masters of what had been achieved before them.

6. Perhaps in science the study of past methods, discoveries, and blunders is small help in tackling some specific problem; but this likelihood has no bearing on the extra-laboratory messiness of most human endeavors in, say, politics, marriage, city-making and city-breaking, education, religion, institutional existence, private life.

7. Without a view of the past we lack perspective; without perspective we can have no common-sense foresight; without foresight we have no vision; and, as the prophet said, "Without vision the people perish."

8. Finally, "Human history," declared one savant after he had survived the First World War, "becomes more and more a race between education and disaster."

So ends my list, but not my prejudices. In honesty, I must admit some more, those of a superfluous academic. For instance, my outmoded notion of what a university should be. It is no longer, in the Latin sense of that word, a university, a one-turning about some center. The up-to-date label is multiversity: a many-turning. Sometimes it looks like a carnival of merry-go-rounds, with every rider snatching for his own brass ring. More kindly viewed, the university today is a huge, intricate and expensive social service station, trying to meet all the multifarious and ever-increasing demands society puts upon it. As to the millions now on our campuses, most students attend to better their lot—which is an item in the American credo—by preparing for some specialized job—which is an item our economy calls for, or used to. Some students come for a liberal education, hopefully, for at least a start on one before they narrow down to the workaday careers life will demand of them. Ideally, such students might become our leaders of opinion. Potentially, they form our "natural aristocracy," the phrase bequeathed on their sort by the equalitarian democrat who founded the University of Virginia. Black or white, rich or poor, personable or otherwise, they are a minority. I intend to speak up in behalf of their minority rights. At least my prejudice about what a university ought to be has some bearing on their predicament. In brief, I am committed to this idea of a university: Whatever else our institutions of higher learning have or will become, the essence of their function in a free society is to foster, in John Jay Chapman's words, "a reverence for intellect and a feeling of unity with the history of mankind." So far as we neglect, cheapen, chip at, or give only commencement rhetoric to this idea, so far do we betray our main reason for existence.

This and other prejudices of mine limit me. One bias I cannot shake is that I am a teacher of the humanities. I work amid the ruins of an antique curriculum. The humanities, since the morning time of Western history, have of course centered on the study of history, letters, philosophy, and the arts. Today we speak of our vast educational enterprises as the Knowledge Industry. By contrast, to acquire and propagate knowledge merely has never been the educational purpose of humanistic study. Rather, it was and is to lead the student into an experience, a disciplined experience stirring the senses and emotions, the conscience and imagination, as well as the intellect. For in the great books and works of art, past and present, lives the compendium of mankind's experience—what the race of man has somehow lived through since civilization has dawned.

Civilization, we are coming to see, is a precarious arrangement. In fact, about one hundred years ago (when mass schooling was in its infancy) a great critic worried about this very precariousness. He argued that if the aim of education is to know ourselves and the world around us, we need culture as a bulwark against the anarchy perennially threatening. And culture, for Matthew Arnold, meant acquainting ourselves with the best that has been known and thought and said. On this humanistic base some of us have found our prescription for liberal education: that we teachers should try to develop the critical-minded yet also well-rounded person, one whose schooling has developed his intellect and character.

Though all this sounds moralistic and Victorian, we cannot dismiss Matthew Arnold. But since his day historical events have shown us that there are two things wrong with his view.

First, to acquire the finest liberal education conceivable is no guarantee that one is civilized. We of the twentieth century know that some of those who perpetrated the horrors of the Nazi concentration camps were, by any ordinary definition of the phrase, devotees of culture. The truth is, such traits of personality and character as sensitivity, conscience, rigor and subtlety of intellect, largeness and warmth of heart cannot be guaranteed by any system of schooling. These gifts a person has, potentially, before he encounters either science or humane letters in a classroom. Without them, though a person may be loaded with degrees, honorary or otherwise, from the world's greatest universities, he remains a barbarian and a potential ally of anarchy. Thus far, I submit, Matthew Arnold has been both right and wrong.

His second error—or was it ours in reading him?—was his emphasis on the best that has been thought and said. By ivory tower dwellers the word *best* can give to culture connotations of the cold, chaste, serene marble of the museums. The truth is, the arts and humanities have never proffered us easy samples of beauty or simple and reassuring models of moral excellence. They have in fact dealt just as fully and freely with the human worst. I do not mean they teach these sorts of things—any more than the Bible does—but the classics are full of crime, violence, treachery, greed, madness, folly, and downright pettiness. This is why they should initiate us into awareness that we human beings are terribly mixed and complicated creatures: and why, for one thing, we have never behaved like specimens in the laboratory—and pray God, never will. One corollary is that, to gain a sense of the past and to profit by a liberal education, is to be moved, not only by mankind's noblest achievements and aspirations, but also by the active presence of evil, all the destructive forces working within us and around us. If a liberal education once meant a preparation for living in this world more than for a livelihood, then to the sweetness and light of culture we need an admixture of this strong and bitter stuff. We are careless readers of, say, the *Iliad* if we glean from it only Homer's wonder at the iron-hearted valor of his epic heroes and his compassion for human suffering. After all, the central squabble among his heroes is over the banalities of money and sex. Jacques Barzun was both wise and witty when he recommended a new label for the humanities: "the misbehavioral sciences."

The sense of the past, as I have been groping for it here, has been described by Herbert J. Muller this way:

It is the story of a "rational animal" who thereby lacks the sureness of instinct, is a prey to irrational desires, and of all animals leads the least sensible life; who alone is free to choose and aspire, and so is forever torn by doubt and discontent, from which spring at once his loftiest values and his ugliest hates and fears; who alone can know truth and virtue, and by the same token is prone to error and evil, capable of folly and brutality. . . . At all times it is the story of the inescapable hazards that man brought upon himself when he took to playing with fire and then, without forethought, set out on the extraordinarily bold adventure of making over his world; while ever since he began to reflect he has been seeking a repose that he can find only in the death he fears.[1]

This historian sees in the past both high tragedy and comedy—and a theme whose spirit is "at once ironic, compassionate, and reverential." To lead our students toward something like this spirit is—or once was—the responsibility of the humanities teacher. This lively, felt, disciplined sense of the past they cannot get for themselves. As we fail our students here we deny them their right to their past. We make them provincials in time. We trap them within their own era. What is dreadful about the protagonist of Orwell's novel *1984* is that the dictator and his establishment have cut Winston Smith off from all but the dimmest, most propagandized impressions of past history. Until by cunning and accident he learns something of the real past, he has no standards, no basis for comparison, no way to judge the totalitarianism that negates his humanity. He endures the unexamined life—which Socrates said was not fit to live. The totalitarian state must impose on its cog-citizens a rigid ideology, demands conditioned reflexes. It wants no critical spirit. It strangles all philosophizing. It cannot tolerate philosophy as the guide to life.

Consider a few symptoms of our indifference to the past. We are lonely, we Americans, a perennial motif in our literature from its colonial beginnings down to Black Humor. In the ever-accelerating pace of these times, no one stays put for long. Americans are most at home when wheels are speeding beneath them. We are too much on the move to form lasting relationships or even to become acquainted with our own selves. We exist and encounter one another in snippets. Coherence is gone, and continuity. Instead of community, we have dehumanized disconnectedness. For community comes out of some bonds with the past, out of common and shared experiences and memories.

Who, for instance, would pretend that any university faculty is a community of scholars? We professors communicate with one another only in bits and fragments. Each has his own little bailiwick. None can count on having with his colleagues anything like a common pursuit, a critical spirit, a shared cultural past. To be sure, specialization is unavoidable and necessary. No denying that. But what troubles me is that I meet so few academicians even brooding over anything to countervail the increasing fragmentation we have all witnessed in the past quarter century. We seem content enough to instruct in our own subject only. We have no comprehensive purpose, hold to no general view of education. Except in the sciences we are unable to agree on anything like standards, requirements, curriculum. We are guided not by our own thinking but by trends and fashions. No longer can an English teacher meet a new class and assume that his students have read certain books, or even one book, in common. As educators we are more alert to followship than committed to leadership, leadership even in our own profession. In the name of freedom and of the watch-words *do-your-thing*—an expression, incidentally, as old as Chaucer—we incline now to let students pick and choose what courses they wish. Does anyone recall that a president of Harvard tried that experiment about a century ago and that it did not work? Or maybe a commercial ethic operates here: students are our customers, meet the market demand, give them what they want—or think they want.

But what exactly do our students want? Who knows? I only know I am sympathetic toward them, because they have reason to feel frustrated and rebellious. Compare them with the college youngsters of the 1950's, the so-called "silent generation," and they look rich in promise. They appear better motivated to study, less taken up with collegiate frivolity, more concerned about social problems, with livelier consciences and quicker hearts.

If their teachers comprise nothing like a community, we might wonder: have the students found one? Some have tried to. There is something which has been named the counterculture of the young—call it Hippiedom, if you prefer. It is a curious, many-faceted development almost unique in history. It is so complex that anything I might say about even a few of its features is sadly inadequate. Yet to glance for a moment, not at the externals—the manners, lingo, beards, hairstyles, blue jeans and such—but at the intellectual furnishings is to agree with the youngsters' most sympathetic historian, Theodore Roszak, that their chief shortcoming is in education. Their bright new ideas are tatters of old ideas.

For the chronicler of thought, Hippiedom provides a rag-bag of tag-ends. Reach in, and out comes a frayed flyer: "Make Love, Not War"; this is crumpled around a plaster-of-paris thingamabob which turns out to be a figurine of Aristophanes, he who gave to war-tormented Athens the glorious bawdy of his sex comedy, *Lysistrata*, the original women's strike for peace. Squeezed against him is a rag-doll: unkempt Diogenes of ancient Corinth, flaunting from his tub of a "pad" his scorn of society's polite frauds. In close proximity are some oddments, facsimile relics of primitive Christianity. Next is a strange-looking, sweat-stained headpiece: it must be what some boy wore when he set off on the Children's Crusade in the Middle Ages. Down in one corner is a notebook, with scribblings garnered from some sort of disquisition on hyper-democracy by one of the more sanguine theorists of the Enlightenment. In another is a biggish bundle, hefted with enthusiasm from the Romantics, quite full of items on self-expression, freedom from constraints, naturalness, and "gut-reaction,"—this last evidently a revised version of Keats' "holiness of the heart's affections." Then appears an odd-shaped container, an import from nineteenth-century European Bohemianism, with the venerable message shock-the-bourgeoisie. (And fastened on this container with a rubber-band is some freakishness from the wonderlands of California.) Alongside it is a neatly crafted leather bag; but no one remembers it is a momento of Victorian William Morris whose heart sickened at the shoddiness of factory-made commodities. The sogginess in the plastic sack just underneath is, almost certainly, a serving portion of John Dewey's pragmatism. And over here, this bulge turns out to be the vague yearnings for the Ineffable All—or is it Nirvana?—of the Orient with, sometimes, impatience to achieve the mystical state by way of drugs.

The catalogue is of course unfair. I may smile a little, but I am not laughing at the young. They have done the best they could, with small help from their teachers, to create out of these patches a past and a tradition which seem to meet their immediate needs. But no wonder their radicalism is naive, their innocence sometimes arrogant, their programs abortive. In sum, their moralism, angry or angelic, has never been shaped into a thought. They are not to blame for their muddle. There is pathos in this clutter, in their search for authority, in their fumblings toward standards.

Is it surprising, then, that our students now ask to participate in such decision-making processes as the hiring and firing and tenuring of professors or that they try to tell their teachers what courses should be offered and how these should be taught? With the cart motorized, why shouldn't the horse trot along behind? So, one finds in a perfectly respectable journal the proposal that, at the end of a semester,

student and teacher should confer to arrive at, *cooperatively,* the mark the student deserves! And the dream of turning a class hour into a rap session, where anyone's opinion is as good as anyone else's and where the nice-guy prof sits in, as needed, only as an informational source on some minutiae. And then those who would reform the grading procedure into either pass-fail or into oblivion, a blessed relief from the pangs of discriminating and judging. As if life beyond the ivied walls does not daily, silently, in one way or another, grade each and every one of us! So I am guilty of another prejudice: whenever I drive across a bridge, consult a lawyer or get a prescription, I fervently pray that the engineers, attorneys, and pharmacists I rely on did not in school earn pass grades only a hairline above failure.

Capers like these do not put me into a fault-finding mood with our young people. Such stuff was not born by miraculous conception of the adolescent brain. It is breathed in from our prevailing climate of opinion. I call it a breakdown in standards. "Whenever the older generation has lost its bearings, the younger generation is lost with it." So remarked Dr. Bruno Bettelheim, a teacher-psychiatrist who has long worked with the young—and who was himself scarred by the Nazis.

Like their professors, the students have found, not a community, but only an aggregation. The generation gap, the don't-trust-anyone-over-thirty attitude, the restiveness of the young, their filial ingratitude—these should be looked into. Something is going wrong. To go no farther than our campuses, too many of us are more frustrated, anxious, and confused than, somehow, we should be. Since this malaise and muddle are tangled up with millions of persons and billions of dollars, the causes and consequences are more serious than the broken windows and broken bones of those newsworthy disturbances which so anger and discomfit Middle America. My private diagnosis is that we are suffering from a nearly tragic failure—at least from a farcical misdirection—in our philosophy of education. In their mushy permissiveness, in their flabby cultural liberalism, too many intellectuals have indulged the appetites of immaturity, including their own. More to the point, I call to account myself and my academic colleagues. We are not facing up to the issues that confront us. Our students storm the administration building—because they have not yet come upon the open secret: that by and large a faculty gets the sort of administrators it deserves, for better or worse. If the house of intellect has become disorderly, we professors are, very considerably, at fault. As to the gap between preachment and practice, we are neither more reprehensible nor admirable than our fellows in other professions. We take our specialties seriously and are afflicted by the occupational disease of nearsightedness.

In this matter of vision I am not at all pretending that professordom is the Mind of America. And yet, on our various campuses we are so many conglomerates of talent and mind-power; enmeshed in our big institutions, we have become, so to speak, the organized brain of society. And all too readily this organized brain has adapted itself to the environment, to external pressures and passing trends. One of its lobes, the scientific-technical, with its useful, humanitarian, and profitable applications, has grown superbly. Another lobe is softening, sickening, maybe dying. In academe the two lobes no longer work together. The first lobe gives us R & D, research and development, and so opens the Pandora's box of all the seeming goods that promise to help us survive with greater ease and wealth on this planet. This is the lobe of knowledge,

and knowledge is power. But power is, merely, power, to be used for good or ill, depending on the motives and enlightenment of the users. The other lobe of the brain—may I call it the wisdom-moral part?—was meant to guide and control us toward using constructively the gifts and curses science has brought us: make it possible not merely to survive but to maintain lives humanly livable and worthwhile. But by and large we academicians no longer put any confidence in this lobe.

And it is we humanities professors who have let it atrophy. We no longer really believe in our work, because we suspect it does not deal with or get at reality. Though our subject is the living past and though we are allegedly keepers of that past, we are without any past ourselves. We have forgotten that, for the Greeks, Memory was the mother of the muses—which is to say, the ground of all inspirations. We humanists lack manly pride because we no longer feel in ourselves any vital and viable link with tradition. We gain no strength from regarding ourselves as, say, buck privates in the company of the great spirits who have marched through history from blind Homer to the lonely, harassed Solzhenitsyn. We no longer struggle to comprehend the human mind and spirit. We have lost our nerve.

Now, I have a partial and prejudiced theory to explain what went wrong. It goes about like this:

Sometime after World War II—the fifties were a crucial decade—all of us professors were oppressed by low salaries in an inflationary economy, discouraged by being of no social consequence, disheartened by the anti-intellectualism long endemic to this nation, then further intimidated and demoralized by the virulent form that anti-intellectualism took in the heyday of Joe McCarthy and the loyalty oaths. Then all at once something happened. Across the night sky we watched the eerie trajectory of Sputnik. America, the leader of the world's technology, shivered down its spine. Crash program: put to work—and train more and more of them—every scientist and technician available lest the Soviets outdistance us and imperil our survival as a nation. Promptly the universities felt the impact of the new terror. Professors whom no one had heard of emerged as national oracles. Washington turned to the campuses; professors made their way to Washington.

As federal funds poured in, the universities began to compete with one another. Now the game was: lure to your campus the Great Man, Nobel Prize winner, if possible. Make the bait ever more tempting as to salaries, grants, benefits, privileges, and with fewer and fewer onerous details—details like, say, teaching. Research was what counted. And because professors were becoming useful and even necessary, their public image metamorphosed from the caricature of absentminded dowdiness to figures of respectability. And since in the public mind the words professor and college teacher were synonyms, a wondrous paradox burgeoned: the greater you were as a teacher, the less teaching you did. (To be sure, I can only sketch my theory here.) But pulled along by the affluence of our colleagues in the sciences, the rest of us professors began in the 1960's to do better financially. That part of it was all to the good.

Yet, in the long run, the consequences of these developments in the American economy as they affected the backwaters of academe have not been wholly beneficial for those who teach and study the liberal arts. In their more modest way and perhaps by accident or even unconsciously, humanities professors took cues from the scientists. Research, with the capital R, was the thing. Get a grant, and

you may be on the way to becoming a made man. (Pun intended.) The rewards were the American dream come true: affluence and status. So we tried to master the techniques of grantsmanship. It was dazzling and flattering to make it. More of us began to feel quite at ease within the system, even to like it. When the game was not grants, we began to learn how to wheel and deal for positions, promotions, and plumes. Opportunism paid off. The operator-type appeared among us in larger numbers. Loyalties became more and more centered, not on teaching, nor on our departments and schools, nor even on our discipline, but on our specialty and, in particular, on the extra-mural acclaim we might win through it. Graduate students whom we trained for the doctorate in the 1960's might have learned from us more about how to maneuver in the corridors of power than to respect real scholarship. Competition within the academic ranks became rougher and trickier for everyone. One breathed an atmosphere of double-talk: lip service to humanistic values; in practice, what's-in-it-for-me?

Research in the humanities often meant publish or perish. The only way to escape that assistant professorship in Mudville's North Central A & M College was to place an article in a so-called reputable journal. So, articles and journals multiplied to deluge proportions. The astonishing busyness and quantity of it all! The scientists spoke of a knowledge explosion. The humanists tried to pretend we had the same thing. In fact, we had only an explosion of printed matter—about eighty percent of it dispensable, stuff for recycling. The worry was to lengthen one's bibliography by measurable inches. Too many adepts mastered the tricks of turning out semi-books, quasi-books, pseudo-books, and non-books. Or if one had small knack at the typewriter, another road to promotion was in being "professionally active": i.e., running off to meetings, serving on committees, and what-not. Here the techniques were politicking toward making connections with whoever had the wherewithal to hand out the prizes.

More and more to emerge as the overriding value in academe was, in one word: prestige. Now, prestige is not genuine fame nor lasting reputation. Prestige is only what other people happen to think of one at a certain time, their quick impression, their rule-of-thumb assessment. To gain prestige is to know how to manipulate mirrors, to make and multiply images and reflected images—and, for those aspiring to celebrity, a public image. All of this is perfectly acceptable in business and advertising. But for an academician to seek prestige rather than what was once a legitimate ambition in which he could take honest professional pride, is to be a lost soul, more or less. As to the heights where the lights and the dollars shine, have we not all, at one time or another, met a dean or department head who, with his elevation to such post, changed even his style of speech and began to make pronouncements in a deanly voice? Listen, and you hear the phony note. It is the sound of pretended authority, authority wangled from an addled system, not authority earned by academic achievement or even administrative accomplishment. Those without genuine dignity need the mask of pompousness. These sorts of foibles, misdemeanors, and sins can, I dare say, be gotten away with more readily among humanists and social scientists than among scientists. But this may be only one more of my prejudices.

Doubtless I am a victim of the schoolmasterish tendency to take too seriously one's role in society. If so, we can be sure that beyond the ivied walls most people are in small danger of exaggerating our importance. Yet these citizens and taxpayers do take seriously what is going on among our students. Exactly here I believe the troubles with our college teachers and the troubles with the students may be closely entangled. I suggest that the alienation, the restiveness, maybe even the riots, of the students have something to do with their disappointment and disillusionment in their college teachers. The students themselves have almost never put this into words. For, given their limited experience, the whole teacher-student relationship is too complex and subliminal for them to articulate fully and precisely. But they do, I suspect, too often sense something pretentious and unreal about their courses and instructors. Sooner or later most of them will intuit such dishonesty. Their feeling comes from the likelihood that seldom does the professor strike them as a real authority.

Emotionally, intellectually, young people want and need authority, are asking for it in the very act of denying it. By authority I do not mean authoritarianism, nor a professor's knowing his field, nor parietal regulations, nor nagging parent-figures. By authority I mean human beings older than themselves whom the young can look up to, or at least look at, with a modicum of unforced respect. Consciously or not, most adolescents are hero-worshippers. Heaven knows I am not recommending any such silliness as students making heroes out of their professors. Yet if some ingredient of this youthful emotion were there, the classroom might be a livelier, more meaningful experience. Somewhere youth needs to find exemplars of conduct. Not finding them among their academic elders, they look elsewhere. For a fruitful learning context, the young need to feel that the professor is not merely a nice guy with competence in his subject; they need also to feel that he has "been there," gone through some human experiences at least a little like their own. They need authority figures, to test their own mettle: someone solid and definite enough that they can count on him and know where he stands, even as they disagree or buck him in the normal process of maturing and becoming independent. Without this sort of thing they feel somehow cheated.

At any rate, my own conviction is that young people—not all but enough of them on our campuses—will respond positively to real and earned authority. And the generation gap, plus our grand muddle over the ends and means of higher education, would have become less costly and anguished had we college teachers, especially humanists, remained true to our better selves. That means true to what was supposed to be our profession, vocation, function, in a free society. Instead, we undermined our authority as we cut ourselves away, willy-nilly, from our common past: the cultural tradition that could have given to our students, yes, even the relevance they call for. We could have conveyed to them at least a little more of reality, hints and clues to the experience of being human. If only we had allowed the great voices of the past to speak through us, as best as we could, however haltingly, so long as we did not distort them hopelessly by careerist self-concern. No, I am not, in my evangelical mood, wishing that we professors had been saints or heroes: only that enough of us had had a touch of the spunk of the broken-down vaudeville performer who stuck to the tradition of his tinsel trade—the show must go on.

What might have been! I have shifted into the past tense. I am elegiac, frankly. I fear that humanistic studies, as part of our American multiversities, are moribund; that, in spite of their numerical expansion, they are fated to go the same way the once powerful professordom of Grecians and Latinists has gone. And go in the same blind way: by default.

No, I am not prescribing that one and all be drilled in Latin paradigms. But I am ending with two quotations, one of which is in that language. *Sunt lacrimae rerum; et mentem mortalia tangunt.* It is a line spoken by Roman Virgil's hero, Aeneas, remembering the fall of a city. His civilization destroyed and himself a displaced person, the hero and his band of war refugees find temporary shelter in ancient Carthage. There in a temple—so fast did bad news travel even in antiquity!—he sees murals depicting the battles and agonies of his compatriots. Stirred and saddened, he muses: "There are tears for these things, and human concerns do touch the soul." The other quotation is from a Sunday supplement item on a course in comic books offered for credit at Indiana University, a course so popular that a hundred students are waiting to enroll. Those admitted are studying Superman and Flash Gordon. Evidently the course is not a sociologist's investigation into contemporary popular culture. An assistant liberal arts dean explains it this way: "In this experiment, we throw away tradition and say that just about everything in the world around us is an appropriate subject for study and scrutiny." No doubt everything is. But I wonder what a Phi Beta Kappa audience prefers.

Maybe we can still make the choice. Maybe it is not too late. For myself, I know where my hopes lie. Still as a prudent fellow I know where I am placing my money. But as a humanities teacher—well, this is one bet I want to lose.

NOTE

[1] Herbert J. Muller, *The Uses of the Past* (New York: Oxford University Press, 1952), Mentor Book reprint, p. 30.   [XVII, Spring 1973, 151–160]

[66]

Paul Goodman
and the Reform of Education

SAMUEL M. THOMPSON

Samuel M(artin) Thompson (1902–   ), professor emeritus of philosophy at Monmouth College, where he has taught since 1926, studied at Tarkio College from 1919 to 1921, received his B.A. from Monmouth College in 1924, and his Ph.D. from Princeton in 1931. The author of A Modern Philosophy of Religion *(1955) and* The Nature of Philosophy *(1961), he has contributed articles to many scholarly journals on such subjects as Locke's theory of ideas, the heritage of Kant, and a modern philosophy of religion.*

I. The Angry Middle-Aged Man

A recent issue of *Harper's Magazine* includes a letter from a young college graduate who describes herself as "a rebel against current trends in business toward management and automation." Twice she has been asked to leave jobs with corporations because of her opposition to the official rules and regulations. "I did not like and still do not like to suppress my individuality and uniqueness," she explains, and adds that the heroes of her college generation are Ayn Rand and Paul Goodman.

A new prophet has indeed come out of the academic wilderness crying his message of judgment and salvation. A first impression may suggest that Goodman is a new H. L. Mencken without the Menckenese. He also lacks Mencken's superb control of his instrument, for Goodman writes carelessly and is without the unfailing sense of the ridiculous which protected Mencken from illusions. Mencken always knew when he was acting the fool and this is a kind of self-knowledge Goodman might use to advantage.

Perhaps Goodman's role, however, is closer to the one played by that contemporary of Mencken most unlike him, Upton Sinclair. To bracket H. L. Mencken and Upton Sinclair is to attain a rather advanced level of absurdity, and yet there is a certain appropriateness in this instance. For Paul Goodman may be said to be attempting to play a Mencken-like role and actually turning out to be another Upton Sinclair.

The line between social satire and muckraking is the distinction between an expression of contempt mixed with sardonic enjoyment of the absurdities of the social scene and exposure for the sake of reform. At one place, in an exceptional moment of realistic self-awareness, Mr.

753

Goodman does indeed see himself in the latter role. Muckraking, he says, "has become the protest of Angry Young Men. My own tone in this book sounds like an Angry Middle-Aged Man, disappointed but not resigned."[1]

This Angry Middle-Aged Man is a disturber of the peace of the Establishment. In the first forty pages of *Growing Up Absurd* we find him to be against the organized system of semimonopolies and their respective rat races, particularly those of government, business, and education; personnel practices; movies, TV, the Book-of-the-Month Club, and the Luce publications; the oneupmanship of the typical junior executive; university faculties who are safe to their businessmen trustees or politically appointed regents; Dr. James Conant; the President of Merck and Company; vocational guidance; the waste of humanity; public officials; built-in obsolescence in automobiles; the "sole prerogative" clause of union contracts; timid school supervisors, bigoted clerics, and ignorant school boards; such spurious educational aims as baby-sitting and the production of physicists; reactionaries, liberals, and demented warriors whose demands mangle the academic curriculum; careers of salesmanship, entertainment, business management, promotion, and advertising; the baboons running the TV networks that put on the phony contests; boondoggling in tail fins; the $64,000 Question; the busy hum of Madison Avenue; tax-dodge Foundations; business lunches, expense accounts, and fringe benefits; comic categories of occupations in the building trades; extra stagehands and musicians in the theater; and sex suppression in the schools.

Mr. Goodman's anger recedes temporarily as he contemplates such positive values as excellence, manliness, and "true human nature." He is for J. K. Galbraith's "social balance"; an environment which meets the needs of the growing boy, youth, and young man until he can better choose and make his own environment. He wants more man's work, honest speech, opportunities to be useful, ingenuous patriotism, and animal ardor. He would have us take people more seriously; he is in favor of uncorrupted fine arts and genuine science; he thinks we need religious convictions of Justification and Vocation and a sense that there is a Creator. He favors racial integration and sexual revolution, with emotional release and sexual expression in children. He wants more useful work which contributes to subsistence, such as the production of food, clothing, and buildings; and he wishes there were more teachers interested in children.

The key to Paul Goodman's occasionally idiosyncratic pattern of likes and dislikes appears to be his profound antipathy to any form of organized power. He is an anarchist of pure essence but he is not, as sometimes described, a syndicalist. The only traces of syndicalism are imaginative rather than active.

There is a good bit of sympathy among right-thinking people for most of the things Paul Goodman approves and rather more resentment perhaps than we realize against many of the things he attacks. He articulates attitudes shared inarticulately by people who have learned to read and are concerned about the current state of our society. In their more human moments most people dislike and distrust organized power, particularly when that power is exercised by other people. Mr. Goodman has a wholesome enthusiasm for the right things and a prophet's zeal and conviction of righteousness in his battles against sin. But the human tragedy, which includes the tragedy of falling short of the Goodman standards, obstructs his view of the human comedy.

II. Moralists, Moralizers, and Reformers

H. L. Mencken was a moralist with a mastery of the moralist's instrument of satire. But what was of greater importance, he understood that a moralist's social criticism must be entirely negative. There is no trace in Mencken of any program for the improvement of society except the one enterprise he so hugely enjoyed, the exposure of boobs and phonies.

Paul Goodman is most effective in his attacks upon organized stupidity and institutional asininities. But he pushes his role as moralist beyond its proper limits and proposes prescriptions for the ills he has exposed. What begins as moral becomes moralistic.

As did Mencken in his day, so today Paul Goodman rejects nearly all that is characteristic of contemporary American society. This makes doubly difficult his attempts to prescribe for its ills; the rejection is so complete there is nothing left upon which to build alternatives. The same would have been true of Mencken had he been interested in proposing remedies, but Mencken wisely refrained from diluting the acid.

What Goodman's proposals really add up to is that we go back and start over. As one reviewer comments, Goodman would cut down to human size "this monster of an industrial-governmental complex" and substitute for it "a self-redeeming initiative on simple neighborhood terms."[2] Here is spelled out the impotency of the anarchist's approach, its lack of realism concerning the necessary conditions of life in society and its utter emptiness of positive content. Goodman simply by-passes the actual problems of our industrial society and proposes to treat the symptoms in terms of personal reactions. Andrew Kopkind calls this "the politics of avoiding politics."[3]

An illustration of Goodman's alienation from reality is his proposal in *The Community of Scholars* for the reform of our colleges and universities. He suggests that the faculties simply walk out of these institutions and withdraw to places where they can teach and study without interference from *"the external control, administration, bureaucratic machinery, and other excrescences that have swamped our communities of scholars."*[4] What the writer fails to realize is that a system of higher education which is driving constantly for its own expansion must have elaborate administrative machinery. Whatever absurdities and abuses this generates, and we all know there are many, the fact is that the alternative today would be the limitation of higher education to a privileged class. However we may regret the fact, it is still the case that bureaucracy and administrative crudities are growing pains of dynamic institutions in a society of mainly quantitative norms. As long as expansion is the prime concern the norms will remain quantitative.

Harold Taylor, who has done as much innovating in college administration as any President, points out that the irony of Goodman's proposal "lies in the fact that as soon as he presents it in his book he becomes involved with administrative detail and must deal with factual things like drawing up a budget, arranging for the use of buildings, and coping with the problem of recruiting a suitable faculty."[5] Harold Taylor should know.

Running through all of Goodman's discussions of education is a concern so strongly biased toward the personal emotional problems of both teachers and students that he misses most of what is central to education itself, the discipline of learning and the growth of knowledge and understanding. He would turn education into therapy; and as one who sets out to remake society, he cannot turn curious people loose to inquire into the objects that intrigue them. Those people have to be processed first so they will not get the wrong answers.

The roles of critic and reformer are incompatible. A critic needs to be skeptical, cynical, always suspicious of appearances, and open to the object. A reformer has to be gullible and capable of a high degree of self-bemusement; he must see facts through special lenses which bend the picture to his demands. If he is to persuade others to support his program he must first be his own devoted convert. The tragedy of Paul Goodman is that he has the skills of a critic but the temperament of a reformer.

By temperament reformers are enemies of order. Although the word itself, *reform,* suggests the re-establishment of an old pattern or the construction of a new one, in either case there is a fatal discontinuity. Reform does not merely expose the ills of the actual but proposes to cure them by destroying the affected parts. Once you destroy the actual, however, you have little left with which to build anything else. A reformer's positive proposals are usually vague and likely to be but disguised negations.

The abolitionists of a century ago, for example, had no program for emancipated Negroes except emancipation itself plus some vague notions of education, vocational training, and the bestowal of political power upon the freed. They grimly imposed their own improvisations upon the remnants of a society wrecked in its economy and maimed in spirit. But the people of that society who had survived were still there and their presence, the brute fact of their presence, still throws its shadows upon the South. The principle that you cannot indict a whole people needs to be broadened into the principle that you cannot absorb individual persons into an abstraction, no matter how worthy and noble are the sentiments

aroused by the words which proclaim the abstraction.

Cynicism concerning reform need not extend to skepticism about change. The great conservative principle is continuity. It is the only position that does not implicitly deny the fact of time. Conservatives may sometimes seem slow to recognize the need for change but this may be because they believe that order, even order with faults, is better than disorder. At least we know what we have. By preserving a present order while changes are introduced a new condition can be obtained in steps susceptible to control.

To say, however, that programs of social change are futile or dangerous is not so much a cynical expression as a realistic recognition of how social changes come about. The roots of all human achievement are in the past and anything new, if it is to succeed, must have an effective continuity with what already exists. To destroy present patterns of life and action is to wipe out the very basis of improvement.

Effective social change has its roots in social criticism, and effective criticism requires sensitivity and response to subtleties and nuances the ordinary person overlooks. It arises out of broadened awareness. Reformers, however, have to wear blinders. A reformer is always exposed to the danger of seeing the other side. His involvement is emotional rather than intellectual and he has to protect his emotions from his intellect. It is this single-minded passion that makes reformers dangerous; they are constantly exposed to the danger of being wrong and have blocked the only equipment they have to recognize the danger signs.

Fruitful change is not so simple as the mere substitution of something new for the old. It requires rather an adaptation, under the guidance of sensitive criticism, of what is already there. Successful reform, except by accident, would require us to see the future all at once. Reformers attempt to accomplish this by creating that future. But no matter what they may think, they are not God and creation *ex nihilo* is not within their power. Existing institutions are products of long growth; they are not *ad hoc* improvisations. And existing institutions are the indispensable means for any fruitful change. There are no panaceas. There is no escape from the particular situation into a land of dreams where we can dispose of contrary facts by forgetting them.

Mr. Goodman welcomes and applauds all signs that young people are rejecting the Great Society and refusing to follow patterns set by the Establishment. His criticism of the cheapness and banalities of those powers is pointed and scathing and much of it is just. But what he overlooks is the fact that the same society which spawns these obscenities also produces reactions against them, including his own. Insofar as he advocates a break with the "system" he strikes at the roots of dissent from it.

Mr. Goodman also overemphasizes the influence of many of the power structures he attacks. The fact is that the "system" does not exist as such, as a monolithic and centralized order. Our society produces out of itself its own resistance against centralization. Its life is one of tensions and conflicts; its genius has been in devising ways to confine these within the limits of a legal structure designed to guarantee the preservation of conflict and rivalry. Its greatest enemy is the drive toward uniformity, a fact which Goodman often seems to recognize. But uniformity is the goal of mass society and this is a relationship he misses.

III. The New Class Structure

Mr. Goodman finds the present class structure of our society to consist of the Organized System, the Poor, and the In-

dependents. Under the Organized System he distinguishes three "statuses": Workers, Organization Men, and Managers. The Poor are the victims of the Organization and the Independents are those who have escaped its snares. Organization Men and Managers are no more free than Workers; all of them are caught in the System.

This provides Mr. Goodman with a foundation for his more detailed sociological analyses and moralisms. It is possible, however, that a different analysis would be more relevant to the problems of education with which he is so occupied. There is a new stratification of our society rapidly developing, a class system based on age groups. The age classes may be identified as the Young, the Active Adults, and the Elderly. The novelty of this emerging social pattern is in the increasingly rigid separation of the three classes.

The principal cause of the separation of the Young from the other age groups is the drive toward uniform universal education, and the Elderly have been isolated as a consequence of the institutionalizing of the economy. Universal education is rapidly eliminating the influence of parents upon their children, and may even eliminate the family itself. The institutional framework of economic production and distribution involves an entirely impersonal management of persons and is removing from the productive life of society more and more of those who are beyond the accepted optimum age range. Our particular concern here, however, is with the isolation of youth and the relation of this to the educational program.

IV. Mass Society vs. The Family

Mr. Goodman fails to reckon with the effects upon the family of our system of public education. The fact is that uniform universal education substitutes the community age-group for the family as the source of values to which children respond. One consequence is a radical discontinuity of value standards of different generations. There is also an intensification of the "natural" friction between those who instruct and those who are instructed. In an adult-oriented society children respect and accept standards they themselves do not understand or appreciate; they are able to do this because they value the approval of adults. In a society in which age groups are relatively separate, control by adults tends to depend mainly upon enforcement. But since no system of order can last long unless those who are subject to its ordinary procedures accept it, the result has been to make the system of education primarily responsive to those to whom the rules apply. This, of course, is the essence of a democratic society, but democratic societies hitherto have been under the control of adults. Whatever may be the limitations and faults of adults, they still are the ones who have the advantages of whatever preparation is available for the exercise of responsibility.

As a social institution the family is essentially authoritarian and so there is a basic tension in our society between family and school. Even a "democratic" family has its democracy imposed upon it. Either it is by the decision of the parents that children are brought into the processes of decision-making, or else the family disintegrates into a scene of conflicts between divergent wills or a collection of individuals whose only relation to each other consists in the fact that they have a common dwelling place.

It would seem quite obvious that if a family is to operate successfully it must have some degree of insulation from the outside world. To the extent that individual members are drawn into close associations outside the family, associations with those of different attitudes and different values, the family itself is weakened. This is the process by which mass societies are created. But individuals who are not in intimate association with each other, living in the same house or apartment, sharing most of their meals, seeing each other in all sorts of situations in which the person is not on guard to present a certain appearance to others, cannot enter into genuinely personal relationships with each other, relationships which involve the whole person. People can know each other as persons and relate to each other as persons only insofar as they are open to each other, express themselves spontaneously and without being on guard, and expose themselves in attitude and emotion. These relations are difficult to preserve in a mass society.

It is interesting to note that many of the attempts in the past to replace the family by some broader kind of association took the form of separated communities. In our own society it is the school which is displacing the family. More and more of a child's time and interest is being absorbed by the school program. The personal contacts which mean the most to him he finds in the school situations. But these are superficial. Those of us who are older can remember among such relationships many which seemed at the time to constitute the very center of our lives. All of our activities revolved about them. But it is instructive to recall how really trivial these were, and how quickly we lost all contact with those with whom we supposed ourselves to be on such close personal terms. A college class reunion becomes a rather pathetic affair after the first moments of greeting and exchange of information about families and jobs. The only things the classmates have in common are their memories of their college days, and there is not much really to be said about those memories any longer.

A consequence of the movement in the

direction of mass society is depersonalization. Individuals become role players, we deal with them and think of them not for themselves but as functions of other things. To talk in general terms about personal relationships between teacher and student, between employer and employee, among the people who live in a neighborhood is simply nonsense.

If people are to live together on a genuinely personal level they must live under conditions in which the outside world does not replace or even color substantially their intimate relations with each other. This means that a family can exist and remain in a healthful state only in a community composed of families of similar cultural, educational, and economic standards.

The family is not an economic unit; the family is not a cultural unit; the family does not provide its own education. For all of these things a family depends upon its community and upon those things which have been transmitted into the present from the past; consequently it needs to be in a community of other families of similar attitudes, values, and aspirations. This is necessary if the external relationships it must maintain are not to be disruptive of its own life and spirit.

V. The Power Structure of Mass Society

Although our society traditionally has considered itself to be family-structured, this has been the case only in part. The growth of cities always creates out of the poor class a mass population. Nor is this true only of modern cities; Republican Rome and Elizabethan London are dramatic examples from the past. The important difference is that today the emergence of democracy has given enormous potential political influence to the masses. Political power is moving from the control by those who have the skills and character to manage the community for the public interest into the hands of those whose main concern is what they can get from the community. It is true that the first group did not always, by any means, live up to their responsibilities. But usually their failures were recognized to be failures and violations of trust. Mass power assumes self-seeking to be the norm rather than a deviation from it.

In a society with a family-structured governing class political power follows economic power; in a mass society, in which human units are interchangeable, economic power follows political power. The masses acquire political power by the extension of the ballot and education. Political leadership and organizational skill emerge with the education of the poor. The individuals who benefit from that education no longer move almost automatically into another class; many of them become the leaders of mass power organizations. The abilities these new leaders develop are not those of production or professional service but rather those of psychological and forensic manipulation.

In a society with a family structure political differences do not ordinarily involve basic issues. Agreements are much more important than differences. Political rivalries are matters of organizational loyalties, family networks, and sectional and economic interests. As class gives way to mass the group structure of a community changes. Persons become members of a public. A man's politics tend to follow the policies adopted by the controlling group of his labor union, his business or professional association, or the city machine. Political power is created by tacit or explicit agreements among groups. The further this goes the more remote are the decision-making acts from individual mass men and the more impersonal is the relation of those men to the governing process.

Our own society has gone far in this

direction, probably beyond the point of no return. Government absorbs a huge proportion of the wealth created by industry and distributes this to those who do not produce it. The primary concern in all this is whether the future will be bread (or cake) and circuses or will belong to a mass society not merely tolerant of differences in skill and ability but one which fosters and encourages individual excellence and originality. The issue will likely be resolved in accordance with the quality of the educational system we develop in the next few years.

The serious weakness of Paul Goodman's educational proposals is his failure to see the inescapable consequences of our actual situation and the need to fit the program to the material. In a sense Mr. Goodman is a reactionary, in the sense that he wants simply to extinguish the present and go back to an earlier world. Like all reactionaries, he is also a romantic, for it is of the essence of romanticism to suppose that the limits of time, and of the time, can be overcome.

VI. Education or Therapy?

Like most educationists Paul Goodman sees the problems of education as problems primarily of method rather than of substance. So method tends to become its own end. But whenever we try to deal with people as persons methodological absolutes are out of place. Method and rule belong to the world of impersonal detail and to apply them to persons is to treat persons as if they were things.

Our educational system does not need primarily to be made over in terms of new methods and organization. It needs rather a more intelligent and flexible use of the methods and organizations which have come out of generations of experience. Adaptation of the present system to

new needs will lead to new methods and to many specific revisions of institutional procedures. But such novelties are not what we start with; they are what we devise as we need them in order to make the institution itself more effective.

Reformers always want to start over, but the trouble is that we always have to begin with what we already have. The supposed new starts which reformers make when they take control are new ways of dealing with the past. But the past is gone and before us lies a future unknown and unexplored except insofar as that future is molded by presently existing institutions and patterns of life. Our only hope lies in the flexibility of our institutional and cultural tools. Reformers make the mistake of turning their reforms into absolutes and thus they open the prospect of always having to reform the reforms. But our society does not have to be treated as a stagnant pool with the only remedy being a continuing round of emptying and refilling with fresh water. If there are stagnant pools in our society they need to be linked again with the living stream of history which is fed from fresh springs and in its continuous movement constantly renews and purifies itself.

The question of educational content Goodman dismisses by waving in our faces an empty abstraction. "There *is* only one curriculum, no matter what the method of education: what is basic and universal in human experience and practice, and the underlying structure of culture."[6] But what is "basic and universal in human experience and practice, the underlying structure of culture," cannot be presented or grasped as such. It has to be got in some one or some few languages, and it has to be got in terms of the tradition of the learner's own community, the face-to-face community in which he knows other people and they know him as persons. Since many of our youth are not in such a community they have no access to what is "basic and universal." The remedy we are trying out in some places is to create a community in the school. But that community is vacuous insofar as its members do not come out of a common background. Today's pressing problems in our schools are the results of the decay of family and of family-centered communities.

Mr. Goodman exposes with dramatic force this pressing educational predicament. Here he is at his best, for here he gets away from empty abstractions and gives us real people. He shows how we are bringing into our school systems an increasing number of youngsters who are emotionally stunted and alienated from the world of the school. They are slum-spawned creatures of the humanoid masses which exist within our urban and rural social ghettos. Those masses contribute little but trouble and the responsible members of the communities which contain them seem utterly incapable of devising means of control, within the limits of a self-governing society, to apply to them. The relationships these masses have to the processes of government are mainly those of passive submission, economic dependence, and rebellion against the forces of order. The human waste of such a way of life is appalling; the individual suffering and hopelessness and the stunting of human potential are enough to make strong men weep. But feeling itself provides no remedies although it may spur intelligence to greater efforts.

Urban mass populations have created problems for education which the system itself seems unable to handle. Its present techniques are inadequate, for they developed in a society of family-structured neighborhoods in which children went to school already prepared for the school program. In mass areas children are not prepared for what the schools ordinarily

offer, and this requires the development of new approaches to teaching. In addition, all the usual and unusual difficulties are intensified by the sheer weight of numbers.

Mr. Goodman properly and effectively reminds us that many children in the elementary and secondary schools of the mass areas and other "deprived" or "underprivileged" sections, to use current jargon, have acute problems of motivation. These children lack the humanizing influences so necessary during the early years, the physical affection and expressions of interest which provide the substance of self-awareness and self-development. We are now coming to recognize this problem, in our "Head Start" programs and in special kindergarten and nursery schools. But these are inadequate in scope and of course such devices will never replace what children are denied in being deprived of family nurture. The best that can be hoped for, perhaps, is some degree of salvage. In the crowded conventional schools of the slums, however, teachers are kept so busy operating the custodial machinery they have little opportunity either to teach or to provide emotional support.

Mr. Goodman's remedy for the dethronement of teaching is not to return it to its proper place but to replace it with therapy. This is his answer to the problem of motivation. He wants student-teacher relations to be in terms of the students' "personal" problems and emotional needs. "At its best . . . teaching-and-learning is erotic," he says, and offers as an explanation of the lack of good teaching that it "always threatens to seem, or to become, sexual; and in America this is a very big deal."[7]

Generalizations about even the culturally deprived are dangerous. We never can be sure about what goes on in human relations behind the doors in even the least prepossessing spots of urban slum or rural blight. Teaching in such areas certainly must be more variable in technique and approach than where children come into school out of backgrounds of personal warmth and love. But one of the variations should be a readiness to abandon therapy with pupils who are ready to learn and to expose them to the intellectual disciplines of the subject matter.

In any event, the solution of our educational problems will not come from general prescriptions, particularly from those which require basic personality reconstruction of teachers and pupils alike. There are not enough people in our population capable of doing the things Mr. Goodman would have teachers do, certainly not enough to staff our schools. Even if there were, the services of such people would be in such demand elsewhere that only a drastic change of our economy could attract them into teaching. What his proposals add up to is a new society of new people; the trouble is that there is no known source of supply of either commodity.

Educational improvement will come as it always has come, from exposure of the bad spots and the attempt to remedy these in terms of the specific situations in which they arise and with the means already at hand. Many such attempts fail, some succeed. The successful devices are imitated in other places and in time there come significant changes of techniques and of emphasis. Uniformity and standardization are the worst enemies of the processes of improvement, for they destroy freedom to experiment at the risk of failure and they impair the flexibility required to adapt to varied local conditions.

Perhaps it is true that in some schools teaching must give way, to some degree, to therapy. But this should always be recognized as a diversion, however necessary, from the main business of the schools. The business of the schools is not to make children for whom basic personality changes are necessary into well-adjusted children but to prepare educable children to become competent adults. Of course they should have satisfactions and enjoyments along the way, but only as adults will they be able to live life in its fulness and depth. On this point Dewey was wrong. School *is* preparation, perhaps not for life as such but for adult life. School is not its own end. Therapy in the school should aim directly at fitting a child for the learning process. Children for whom basic personality changes are necessary need the services not of teachers but of psychiatrists.

How can we evaluate the work of the schools? It is likely that the effectiveness of schooling does not depend nearly so much as some people think on particular devices of organization or methods of instruction. Children grow up and they learn while this growing up goes on. Teaching is important, but more important are the attitudes of families and communities. Children respond to expectations, particularly to the expectations of those who care for them and show an interest in them. The potential of a school program is closely tied to its responsiveness to its pupils' eagerness to grow up and to be accepted and approved. But the very life of our society depends for its future upon the transmission to our youth of intellectual skills and a rational understanding of the physical and human world. Emotional growth comes out of the community of persons, a community to which we should hope the schools will belong but one which they cannot themselves construct and maintain.

To turn the schools into therapeutic institutions is fruitless if the potential for personal development is destroyed before children get to school. If schools must supply what the family supplied in traditional society they will have to begin much earlier. Plato recognized this and so have all communal societies. The recommendation of the Educational Policies Commission, reported recently in the press, would have mandatory schooling for four- and five-year-olds. The Commission notes that "education in this two-year period can affect the character of the child and all his future life more deeply than his education at any later period." The report goes on to say, "Early childhood education, properly conducted, promises significant benefits to American life."[8] But if we are to process children for the benefit of American life the time to start is not when they are four years old. The time to start, as these people well know, is at or before birth. The real challenge will be to get hold of the germ plasm itself. This will transform the Brave New World from dream to reality.

VII. *Frustration in College*

Unfortunately, Mr. Goodman's reforming zeal leads him to universalize his proper concern for the bad spots of our society and to treat the whole scene as just one big sore. With all their advantages the children of the more privileged classes still fail to fit the patterns he prescribes and so they too must be made over. Throughout his discussion is a disturbing absence of evidence that he has either the experience or conception of the intrinsic compelling power upon imagination and intellect of the subject matter of the traditional disciplines. This becomes increasingly troublesome as Mr. Goodman turns his attention to higher education.

Of course young people in college enjoy being objects of personal concern; they should be such objects and most of them are. They have friends and families and usually are in and out of love often

enough to escape monotony. Those among them who are interested in the world of learning, however—and there are many more than one would suppose from reading Goodman—are concerned with the quality of their teachers' interest in the subjects of study rather than in the students' personal affairs. The dramas of ideas and of thought, the mysteries of mathematics and the sciences, the continuities of present and past brought to life in history, the fascination of thinking in other languages, these are some of the things good students get excited about and want from college. They do not see themselves as patients to be cured but as young people looking for enlightenment and understanding. This usually includes understanding themselves but without any strong need to have themselves made over. Many of them sense intuitively that a person who wants to change people just does not like people.

So often in reading Goodman it is hard to suppress the feeling that in some mysterious way there has flowed out and over the paper a stream of those vague, fleeting, uninspected ideas that float about in our minds as we shave or bathe or trim the grass or drive alone in our cars over familiar roads. The question these segments of print prompt is simply, "What is the point?" Soon the answer comes. These are things Mr. Goodman does not like and this is what he is telling us. The frustrations and anxieties of college-student life make him feel sad and forlorn and he wishes it were not so.

It may be fortunate, however, that the experience of youth is not more often entirely satisfying. If it were we would see more of those rather pitiable grown-up college boys and girls still bemused by Greek glamours and football frolics. Much of what Goodman says of the absurdities of the academic system is to the point. The "disposition to teach and grade like a machine, and to try to achieve in a human vacuum,"[9] is something to be resisted by any who want to preserve the human character of a college. But teaching which is on a personal level will be disturbing and frightening to many students just insofar as it is effective. Some cannot take it, and more of our drop-outs than we may realize are of this category. It is always easy to find a respectable reason to quit. But the condition of growth and of any genuinely advanced maturity is repeated failure and frustration and a moderate degree of tentative self-rejection. One suspects that only in primitive societies can childhood and youth be the idyllic states Paul Goodman regrets that our young people do not now enjoy.

Nothing illustrates this point better than some of his comments on the sex life of young people. Of course young people will experiment sexually and will have some sexual satisfactions. They are going to have sex one way or another; they always have and they always will. But the fact is that sex is too important and its fulfillment too exacting to be only a plaything of the moment or even of the season. The way to complete sexual satisfaction is one of fidelity and exclusive intimacy. That way has to be kept open. So long as a society is interested in strengthening the family it is to that society's interest to make sex outside of marriage, particularly for young people, both difficult and frustrating. We need to make it hard for them, not easy.

Mr. Goodman concedes that in the formal business of education the weaknesses of the colleges are not serious. The teachers, he says, "can be respected. Most of them know something and are not bad on their home grounds, in the classroom." The weaknesses are in the personal relationships within the academic community. In this "the colleges have become poor communities. Guidance comes from im-

personal administration; sympathetic clarification of the students' confused ideas comes from nobody; and the teachers brush off attention to themselves."[10]

Here the underlying weaknesses of his proposals become explicit. For one thing, personal relationships cannot be generated or made to order. Such relationships are selective and for most of us they are restricted in scope. Perhaps only in rare marriages are there completely free and open disclosures. Many of those who teach college students do have close relationships with some of their students. There likely is as much or more of this in proportion than between lawyers and their clients, physicians and patients, or between ministers and priests and their parishioners. But such personal rapport is a by-product of the main business and depends upon accidents of temperament and emotional understanding. To set about to create personal relations is to ensure that the relations established will be mostly impersonal.

Furthermore, it is not the business of teachers to provide "sympathetic clarification of the students' confused ideas." College teaching is not a process of telling the students the answers. Rather it is one of exposing the inadequacies of the answers offered and of pushing students, sometimes painfully and even rudely, to grope and grapple beyond the levels which have so far satisfied them. All who are genuine students, and this includes those of their teachers who are still inquiring, are in a state of continuing confusion. For each success raises new problems. The life of the mind is not one maintained by verbal tranquilizers but a life of incessant criticism and frustration and the search for new approaches. Out of this come no systems of pat formulas to be larded over bent heads in the name of learning, but rather a broadened and toughened understanding.

NOTES

[1] Paul Goodman, *Growing Up Absurd* (New York: Random House, 1956), pp. 55–56.

[2] Seymour Krim in *Book Week*, June 20, 1965, p. 3.

[3] *New Republic*, March 20, 1965, p. 20.

[4] Paul Goodman, *The Community of Scholars* (New York: Random House, 1962), p. 168. Italics in original.

[5] "Higher Education and the System," *Commentary*, May 1963, p. 454.

[6] *Growing Up Absurd*, p. 82.

[7] *The Community of Scholars*, p. 102.

[8] Associated Press dispatch, May 31, 1966.

[9] *The Community of Scholars*, p. 120.

[10] *Op. cit.*, pp. 128–29.

[XI, Spring 1967, 183–195]

Solzhenitsyn at Harvard

MARION MONTGOMERY

Marion Montgomery (1925–   ), a member of the editorial advisory board of Modern Age, *is professor of English at the University of Georgia, where he teaches literature and writing. The author of three novels (*The Wandering of Desire, *1962;* Darrell, *1964;* Fugitive, *1974) and three collections of poems (*Dry Lightning, *1960;* Stones from the Rubble, *1965;* The Gull and Other Georgia Scenes, *1969), he has published two critical works on T. S. Eliot (*The American Magus, *1970;* Eliot's Reflective Journey to the Garden, *1979), a brief book on Ezra Pound (*A Critical Essay, *1970), and* The Reflective Journey Toward Order: Essays on Dante, Wordsworth, Eliot and Others *(1973), which he considers a prelude to his acclaimed trilogy* The Prophetic Poet and the Popular Spirit, *the final volume of which (*Why Hawthorne Was Melancholy) *was published in 1984.*

. . . the mistake must be at the root, at the very basis of human thinking in the past centuries. It is the prevailing Western view of the world which was born during the Renaissance and found its political expression starting in . . . the Enlightenment. It became the basis for government and social sciences and could be defined as rationalistic humanism or humanistic autonomy: the proclaimed and enforced autonomy of man from any higher force above him.

—ALEXANDER SOLZHENITSYN
HARVARD UNIVERSITY, JUNE 8, 1978

I think we all have a right to our destiny as individuals. And I have a right to choose mine and everybody else has a right to choose theirs.

—CULTIST CHRISTINE MILLER
AT JONESTOWN, NOVEMBER 1978,
MINUTES BEFORE HER DEATH

A POINT OVERLOOKED in the general (and generally angry) response to Solzhenitsyn's Harvard Commencement Address is that he spoke to a more limited audience than the media's sensational coverage reflects. He spoke to what he must have supposed a responsible intellectual community, and he did so undoubtedly out of what is to us that quaint 19th century European tradition which openly assumes that a nation's intellectual character is established by an intellectual elite. However, the general history of that tradition might well have forewarned him. For the intellectual elite established themselves in such a favored position in large part by fostering egalitarian ideologies, a maneuver of Machiavellian necessity if they were to accumulate and command to their ends the power they recognized as latent in the general body of mankind. It was a maneuver accomplished over a span of time and by a variety of minds, measured variously from the inception of nominalism with William of Occam (Richard

Weaver, *Ideas Have Consequences*) or the dislocations of thought by Machiavelli (Leo Strauss, *Thoughts on Machiavelli*) or by Voltaire and the succeeding philosophies (Eric Voegelin, *From Enlightenment to Revolution*). But whatever the point of inception of the new idolatry examined by Weaver or Strauss or Voegelin, its central requirement for success is to control that power resident in the will of the individual.

That latent power, however, tended to become atomized, following the Renaissance inclination to relocate the primary source of power from its transcendent cause. The medieval understanding had been that man's power in the world was a limited gift from the God of all nature, the Word still active within the world. But that old understanding was progressively abandoned. The origin of power, the post-Renaissance world declared, is man himself; in the new world dawning, man was increasingly celebrated as the maker of his own destiny. That is, in this new beginning is man's word, through which his reason will rule supreme. *Ratio* ceased to function as proconsul with *intellectus* in the kingdom of being; it began to insist upon an absolute authority.[1] Yet a principal danger in this relocation of ultimate power in nature was that such a shift would fracture and divide collective power in the world. The rising spirit of nationalism, the splintering reformations within and outside the Church, become conspicuous signs in our history of a disintegration of community, reaching downward into Western institutions until even the individual family trembles toward collapse in our day.

The ideologist, recognizing the atomizing effect of his own word upon traditional community, recognized as well that he must find a substitute for the Word that had held the old world together—a god larger than the individual, though created in his likeness. Thus one might justify temporal actions performed by the state in the name of such a god. The ideologist must establish a god if he is to control a collective power sufficient to perform the political or social or religious reformations of reality which his newly liberated reason has persuaded his understanding to accept. A symbolic figure of man elevated to god-like stature could be collectively embraced, thus concentrating the lesser atomies of individual man as a reservoir of power. Then only might the ideologist perform the tremendous task of his alchemy, the transformation of reality. For it is most important to control those insistent voices that declare, in the name of liberation, "I think we all have a right to our destiny as individuals. And I have a right to choose mine and everybody else has a right to choose theirs."[2]

Humanity is a term well calculated to serve the ideological sorcerer, appealing as it did (and does) to the individual's vanity. Humanity established as God in nature, through gnosis, easily translates in common language to mean each human a god, particularly in the political marketplace. (Ralph Waldo Emerson was to insist on this translation from a Harvard podium.) Humanity as a vague symbolization of mankind could also appeal to those residual inclinations of charity which lingered as a moral instinct in Western man while the New Testament authority in that matter was being reduced to fiction. Acts committed in the name of humanity become holy acts. In addition, this new myth of humanity could be manipulated through the emerging "science" of historiography, that theology of modernism, which has been devastatingly reviewed for us by Strauss and Voegelin. Through a reconstruction of history, an ultimate reality emerged as a substitute for St. Augustine's City of God; it lay in an imminent world soon to blossom, as might be proved by the juxtaposing of a cloudy version of the past as benighted to the brightening present as expounded by the ideologue. The promise was that a new everyman would emerge, reaching consummation in perfect humanity—at some point just down the road of time. Such was the promise, though its cost was each man's sacrificial journey in the present—under the auspices of the state.

If the new principle is that each man's word is as absolute as his reason can make it, that word will burn as brightly as the power it attracts and controls. Yet with a multitude of contending words born of the multitude of individuals rather than of the Word, where may one locate any center about which the whole consort of being—individuals, families, communities, nations—may revolve in any orderly dance? Shall one join his power to a Jimmy Carter or Ralph Nader? Or, on the darker side of the dilemma, to a Charles Manson or Jim Jones? For the old festive dance of all creation about the Word at creation's heart, which had been the Christian vision, was long ago reduced to a race toward the city of man, now divinized in the name of Humanity. And there exist as many New Jerusalems as unstilled, passionate voices may declare, from Anabaptist Münster in the sixteenth century to Jonestown in the twentieth, from France in the eighteenth century to Russia and China and Iran and Uganda and a multitude in the twentieth.

As Voegelin in particular has shown us, we see in retrospect that ideological reformations of reality, attempted in the intoxicating name of humanity, have proved to be deformations of reality leading into an engulfing chaos. We begin to recognize the spiritual bankruptcy and moral decay of our age as the principal legacy of the Enlightenment's manipulations of Renaissance exuberance. Solzhenitsyn's concern at Harvard was precisely with this dislocation which has been managed by man's aberrant reason. Illusional "reality" brought us to disillusion upon disillusion, and to the threat of a spiritual despair which now infects the general body of Western civilization. In our country, the disturbing symptoms of that despair are visible in our conduct as a nation among nations—for instance, in our new policy toward a murderous regime, Communist China. Our enlightened Eastern policy shadows the high moral stance we assume toward Rhodesia and South Africa. As Solzhenitsyn reminds us, our position on human rights appears strangely ambiguous to the larger world. It is a point shockingly registered on us by the dark spectacle of Jim Jones and the Jonestown massacre, for Jones' was an apocalyptic sacrifice of individuals gathered to him in the name of Humanity. We are confronted by gruesome detail on a cover of *Time*, evidence of the danger of power in the control of ideologists. The horrible deaths of hundreds near at hand arrests us as the deaths of millions in Asia did not.

Our Russian guest at Harvard in 1978 perhaps supposed himself addressing an intelligentsia somewhat different from that with which he was most intimately acquainted. For certainly he is acutely aware of that spiritual strangulation in his own country which we Westerners encounter in its chilling effects as dramatized by Dostoevsky, Tolstoy, Gogol. The insidious tentacles of that European vine springing from the foreheads of *les luminaires* crept into Solzhenitsyn's country and came to flourish there in the nineteenth century with a smothering effect on the Russian spirit like the spectacle of kudzu strangling a Georgia pine. Perhaps, then, Solzhenitsyn supposed himself addressing an intellectual remnant in the West in whom spirit was still alive if apparently dormant. But then Ralph Waldo Emerson had long preceded him at Harvard. In 1837 Emerson called for the emergence of the "American Scholar," by whom he has been generously remembered ever since. What is of ironic significance in the light of Solzhenitsyn's Harvard appearance is that Emerson called for that new scholar to rise out of fundamentally Enlightenment ground, and the degree of his success in conjuring such intellectuals helps account for our continuing veneration of Emerson and our outrage with Solzhenitsyn. The lengthened shadow of Emerson rests more darkly upon our intellectual institutions than our Russian guest could know.[3] (The lengthened shadow of the individual man is history, Emerson confidently asserted, his faith reduced to the temporal and vested in the future.)

That one addresses an "enlightened" audience at Harvard has been the assumption of any speaker there, at least since Charles W. Eliot's inaugural address as president in 1869. The new president appealed to the authority of John Locke, Francis Bacon, and Emerson in arguing that academic power is crucial to the effective operation of the state. In that address one discovers that the state is already becoming the substitute religion which Solzhenitsyn is to attack. "The community," says President Eliot, "does not owe superior education to all children, but only to the *elite*,—to those who, having the capacity, prove by hard work that they have also the necessary perseverance and endurance." Well enough, though Harvard has struggled mightily of late to accommodate itself to state-decreed definitions of *capacity, work, perseverance.* Such a struggle, which has spread throughout the American academy, is an inevitable extension of what President Eliot in his farewell doctrinal epistle in 1909 spoke

of as "The Religion of the Future." In that document he is more explicit about the worship already latent in the inaugural address of 1869, for from the beginning he speaks on behalf of an intellectual priesthood dedicated to the state, rather than to any community in the sense St. Paul means by the term. He calls for Harvard to produce an "aristocracy which excels in manly sports, carries off the honors and prizes of the learned professions, and bears itself with distinction in all fields of intellectual labor and combat." Thus President Eliot's modifications of Emerson's scholar, a shift which moves the American intellectual further from Renaissance humanist toward pragmatist. And the first conspicuous model of Eliot's new man is to be that strong son of Harvard, Theodore Roosevelt.

President Eliot, on the authority of Emerson's assertion that history is but the lengthened shadow of a man (cousin T. S. Eliot will pay devastating respect to Emerson's aphorism in "Sweeney Erect"), sets about establishing a new program of specialization such as will provide the state a complex of long shadows that yet darken our days. Here is President Eliot's understanding of the educated man's proper role in the community: "As tools multiply, each is more ingeniously adapted to its own exclusive purpose. So with men that make the state. For the individual, concentration, and the highest development of his own peculiar faculty, is the only prudence. But for the state, it is variety, not uniformity, of intellectual produce, which is needful." How shallow a conception of the individual is here implied! The individual mind is raw material, to be turned into "produce" serviceable to the "state." The sweetener is that such a "product," turned out through the new elective system in higher education, will compose an aristocracy, specialized in its parts, though as members one of another constituting a whole body of the state. Its central symbol, its "head" as one might say (borrowing from St. Paul), may reflect the complex whole. That is, the president may have written books, stormed up San Juan Hill, explored the West, and so on. In a later day, he may be discovered writing a book on presidents, playing touch football on the White House lawn, and performing other athletic feats not proper to mention short of the daily press.

Thus President Eliot of Harvard College in 1869 called for a new intelligentsia whose principal virtue on the earth would be pragmatic variety, perfected to an efficiency through the practice of intellectual abstractionism upon restricted specializations. And its principal devotion would find focus in the state. The new elite thus nurtured is to replace the older Puritan religious establishment which had governed intellect through Harvard, Yale, and Princeton before the war just over, or had controlled it at least till undermined by such progressive forces as Emerson's unitarianism. That old establishment had not made itself sufficiently powerful to control affairs of state in the days of Southern political ascendancy. It hardly promised to prove dependable to President Eliot's dream of what Solzhenitsyn was to castigate as the "enforced autonomy of man from any higher force above him."

Solzhenitsyn surely did not intend to include two hundred million Americans in his searing indictment of spiritual failures of the American intelligentsia, any more than President Eliot's inaugural address was intended to summon hordes of youth to Boston in an open admissions policy. Or any more than William F. Buckley was to hold Mississippi or Georgia or Oregon culpable for what went wrong between man and God at Yale. Yet a presumption of inclusiveness is reflected in the general response to Solzhenitsyn's

speech in a spectrum ranging from righteous anger to mild regret, from Norman Cousins to William F. Buckley himself. Nor does Solzhenitsyn intend us to think that, by his statement that Russia has been purged by suffering, all Russians have been "born again." "Is it true," asks the *National Review* (July 21, 1978), "that the Russian people have been purged by suffering, and are less materialistic and spiritually stronger than their Western counterparts?" And Buckley, in his syndicated column reprinted in the same issue speaks of "Solzhenitsyn's confusion of his own greatness of spirit with that of most Russians." Not long since, Solzhenitsyn was being praised for that arresting portrait of endurance, Ivan Denisovitch, in whom he shows a purging of one member of a community taken at its fundamental level. It is a more spiritual portrait by far than the one Hemingway gives us of his fisherman in *The Old Man and the Sea*, and it is so precisely because Ivan gains a complexity by being placed in community in such a way as to reveal him a remnant rescued out of the general decay. He is more complex than an allegorical figuring of Everyman such as that Emersonian self-reliant man with a Spanish accent which Hemingway gives us. But the greatness of spirit in Ivan does not encourage one to take him as the author's portrait of most Russians.

II

On another occasion, Solzhenitsyn has remarked that a nation with a great writer has a separate government. That remark should help us set his Harvard address in better perspective—that remark, along with his extended analysis of the decline of the Russian intelligentsia called "The Smatterers" (*From Under the Rubble*). He must have supposed that his Harvard words would be heard against such as these. For he had experienced such an excessive and sudden veneration upon his exile that he might reasonably presume that pieces like his "Smatterers" had been digested with approval by his devouring hosts. Indeed, so generous had been the reception of this man who chose exile rather than abandon his words that he struggled almost helplessly for some privacy, finally settling in New England, a locale known for its close regard for the individual's privacy—so well-known in this respect as to appear in comic portraits of the New Englander as inhospitable. He knew that *From Under the Rubble* had enjoyed a brisk sale in its American edition, surely not through drugstore distribution. He *must* then have been read and pondered. And by whom if not by the American intelligentsia whose capital by popular consent is Harvard University?

Perhaps there was some confusion on Solzhenitsyn's part. Perhaps he assumed too easily that he spoke to a potentially viable community, one fallen on evil days no doubt, yet capable of recall to known but forgotten responsibilities by a prophet scorched in modern fires. The response to his address may well have been a further disappointment to him, exacerbating his sense of homesickness and deepening the disillusionment with Western civilization which was reflected in the speech itself. Perhaps he may even have forgotten for a moment his own portrait of the old Russian intelligentsia, or that it drank at the same waters the West had imbibed much longer than they. Or perhaps there are no longer many surprises possible to him in these matters of which man and his mind are a part. At any rate, he had already presented a portrait of the despiritualized intellectual of his country, only now to discover his double in this Western democracy.

In "The Smatterers" Solzhenitsyn analyzes the failures of the old Russian intel-

ligentsia, failures in consequence of which the "smatterers" emerge as his principal antagonists. The "smatterers" constitute the new intellectual establishment which is now in control of thought and action in his homeland, but they turn out to be (and I suspect to his surprise) very like our own who have emerged from Charles W. Eliot's dream and exercise an analogous control in our own country. (A general control through unreflective "public opinion" is far more subtle than one through brute force, but not necessarily less vicious.) The Russian pilgrim thus discovered himself speaking, for the most part, to American "smatterers" in his address at Harvard. Indeed, his evaluation of that mind in *From Under the Rubble* bears ironic echo of the evaluations President Eliot's dream began to receive at the turn of this century at the hands of such men as Irving Babbitt and George Santayana. For instance, we find him echoing Santayana's portrait of the intellectual of our "genteel tradition" who did not examine President Eliot's position or who would not oppose it. Santayana laments a general effect of Eliot's new Harvard elitism in words that would be at home in Solzhenitsyn's speech: "now analysis and psychology seem to stand alone: there is no spiritual interest, no spiritual need."

The old Russian intelligentsia (so runs the summary in "The Smatterers") became "clannish," with an "unnatural disengagement from the general life of the nation." It became possessed by "Love of egalitarian justice, the social good and material well-being of the people, which paralyzed its love of and interest in the truth; [Dostoevsky's] 'temptation of the Grand Inquisitor': let the truth perish if people will be the happier for it." It was given to "Day-dreaming, a naïve idealism, an inadequate sense of reality." There is still present in the "smatterers" a central inheritance from the old intelligentsia:

"dogmatic idolatry of man and mankind," a "replacement of religion by a faith in scientific progress" such as breeds the new elite, in whom there is a "Lack of sympathetic interest in the history of our homeland, no feeling of blood relationship with its history, insufficient sense of historical reality." Theirs is "The religion of self-deification—the intelligentsia sees its existence as providential for the country." Thus it deified as if in its own image a "people whom it did not know and from whom it was hopelessly estranged." One recognizes here the Russian version of what Allen Tate called a "new provincialism": "that state of mind in which regional men lose their origin in the past and its continuity into the present, and begin every day as if there had been no yesterday." And did Solzhenitsyn or Tate say the following: "the provincial world of the present . . . sees in material welfare and legal justice the whole solution to the human problem. . . . [The provincials] do not live anywhere." Or one might suppose that Solzhenitsyn has been reading Gerhart Niemeyer's *Between Nothingness and Paradise*, or perhaps Voegelin's own Harvard address, recorded in the *Harvard Theological Review* (July 1967), "Immortality: Reality and Symbol," in which Voegelin gives us an analysis of the stages of the deformation of reality in the post-Renaissance world from religious experience through dogma into ideology.

Given the direction taken by the old Russian intelligentsia, the elite "in Russia today is *the whole of the educated stratum*," says Solzhenitsyn, "every person who has been to school above the seventh grade." It is a group having "merely an outward polish," with little intellectual depth, and it includes bureaucrats, party agitators, political instructors. In short, it is made up of those in "the semieducated estate—the 'smatterers.'" Eric Voegelin, in his prefatory chapter (1977) for Niemeyer's

translation of *Anamnesis*, studies our own smatterers. Our intellectual climate, he says, has been established as a result of the academy's absorbing "German intellectuals who emigrated to America" at the outset of World War II, bringing with them neo-Hegelian "ideologies, methodologies, phenomenologies, hermeneutic profundities, and so on." This migration coincided with the "populist expansion of the universities, accompanied by the inevitable inrush of functional illiterates into academic positions in the 1950's and 60's." (When that evaluation gets around, Voegelin will become as popular among academics in the seventies as Jensen and Shockley among undergraduates in the 1960's.) President Eliot in 1869 had promised that "It will be generations before the best of American institutions of education will get growth enough to bear pruning," and we set out on the road to the multiversities, each of them celebrating itself as "the best," usually by claiming kinship with Harvard or Yale or Princeton. The intellectual quality of academic debate as Voegelin witnesses it is still centered on those imported modernist ideas which Voegelin and others have shown to be bankrupt, but it is in considerable decline from the European versions of the same debates that went on at the turn of the century. (Imagine, for instance, the difficulty of showing such academics in a provincial university, bent on imitating Yale, the intellectual poverty of the "Bloomsbury" literary criticism centered at Yale and now widely imitated, the pale afterglow of Husserl's thought clothed in jargony terminology.) "Today," says Voegelin, "the academic world is plagued with figures who could not have gained public attention in the environment of the Weimar Republic," an intellectual milieu for which Voegelin holds scant brief.

In the wider, less provincial context

which I have suggested, Solzhenitsyn's Harvard words carry more force of truth than perhaps even he might have supposed, or than it is comfortable for the Harvard establishment to admit, an establishment with long-lived branches in Washington and in universities across the country, principally the state-supported ones. The loss of courage and will in the new gnostic intellectual, whether he identify himself with the political left or right (and gnosticism has dominated American political thought in both camps since the War Between the States) is surely a conspicuous phenomenon in our time, symbolized by the contending candidates in the last presidential election. It reflects a condition of both spirit and will remarked by traditionalists, those "regionalists" Tate opposes to the "New Provincial," the traditionalist within the classical-Christian world, "based [as Tate says] upon regional consciousness, which held that honor, truth, imagination, human dignity, and limited acquisitiveness, could alone justify a social order however rich and efficient it may be." That condition has also been increasingly under attack from the radical left, one political consequence being the election of a New Southist in populist clothing. The remedy for our national anemia seems fair to finish us off.

Solzhenitsyn said nothing at Harvard that had not been more violently said by word and deed in the 1960's, particularly in that traumatic period when the dominant symbol of our spiritual and intellectual vagaries became the Viet Nam War. But our Russian friend is not speaking primarily of American millions in wandering mazes lost as compared to Russia's spiritual millions. Or at least he probably did not suppose himself speaking of so many. ("I had not thought death had undone so many," says Dante on a similar occasion.) But when he says that his country has now "achieved a spiritual devel-

opment of such intensity that the Western system in its present state of spiritual exhaustion does not look attractive," he might have been Richard Weaver, or Flannery O'Connor, or Donald Davidson or Allen Tate speaking twenty or thirty years ago; in that possibility, the words would have been more internal to America: "Eastern system" to designate the modern gnostic state whose home territory seemed centered in New York City, its business office charged with provincial affairs located in Washington, D.C., and its seminaries for the training of directors of the popular spirit at Harvard and similar institutions. Solzhenitsyn does say "Western *system*" in the translation we have, not "Western *people*," and he has already become aware of individuals here who have made their way up from liberal gnosticism through a "spiritual development." ("I have received letters in America from highly intelligent persons, maybe a teacher in a far-away college who could do much for the renewal and salvation of his country, but his country cannot hear him because the media are not interested in him." *Cannot,* not *will not.*)

III

Solzhenitsyn means by "spiritual development" a return to what Tate speaks of as "regional consciousness" within the classical-Christian tradition. He explains the term in "The Smatterers" and he dramatizes it in Ivan Denisovitch. We are presently stirred by individuals such as he means: Alexander Ginzberg and Anatoly Shcharansky. There have been a number of particular instances called to our attention since the Stalin purge of 1937, fleeting dissidents who blossom in our attention for a moment before fading from our concern, as have literally millions in Cambodia recently, and before that in China, and before that the *Kulaks* of Central Russia and the Ukraine, the proud Estonians, etc., etc. Solzhenitsyn is saying that out of such barbarism, fostered by the old intelligentsia and the new "smatterers," a new intelligentsia is being born. In "The Smatterers" he speaks of a "nucleus" which emerges from the smatterers, to be distinguished from them.[4]

Some Americans on the right, in speaking of that same spiritual phenomenon within our community, are likely to use *remnant* (as I do above) rather than *nucleus* to describe it, the difference in connotation that between a gnawing despair in *remnant* and a generative hope in Solzhenitsyn's *nucleus*. The nucleus, he says, is to be recognized, "not by the academic qualifications of its members, nor the number of books that have been published, nor by the high level of those who 'are accustomed to think and fond of thinking, but not of plowing the land,' nor by the scientific cleverness of a methodology which so easily creates 'professional subcultures,' nor by a sense of alienation from state and people, nor by membership in a spiritual diaspora ('nowhere quite at home'). I would recognize this nucleus by the purity of its aspirations, by its spiritual selflessness in the name of truth, and above all for the sake of *this* country [Russia], in which it lives. This nucleus will have been brought up not so much in the libraries as on spiritual sufferings. . . . I have seen these modest and valiant young people with my own eyes, heard them with my own ears."[5] That is a statement the media ignores, though happy to report Lillian Hellman's full response: "When you're as close to God as Mr. Solzhenitsyn seems to be, then I suppose no world of any kind is good enough." And that of Yale divine William S. Coffin, Jr.: "Nixon used to talk the same language. . . . I suppose Solzhenitsyn would have cheered for the French fighting Ho Chi Minh."

Solzhenitsyn assumed that he spoke to and of a more limited dimension of our complex country than it has been convenient to our intellectual left to admit. Some of the response has been almost at the level of suggesting that jets leave for the East every day, though expressed with more subtlety than our "Southern rabble" used to manage back in the 1950's: "If you don't like it down here, there're buses leaving for the North every hour." Dean Rusk assures us: "we should not roll over and play dead, because [Solzhenitsyn] does not have a strong personal commitment to constitutional democracy or to the notions of individual liberty which are fundamental to us here in the West. . . . we can't take our policy guidance from Mr. Solzhenitsyn." (Fundamental commitment to individual freedom ought to be stronger than a matter of *notions*.) But what is perhaps most shocking to our intellectual left is not Solzhenitsyn's policy guidance, or the absence of an evangelical "strong personal commitment" to an ambiguous abstraction, "constitutional democracy." (Dean Rusk sounds almost strict constructionist here.) The intellectual left finds itself having too easily supposed its own members inhabitants of Solzhenitsyn's country of the mind, only to discover him dissolving those artificial boundaries prescribed by humanism as (in his words) "it made itself increasingly accessible to speculation and manipulation." Thus does one see "the same stones in the foundations of a de-spiritualized humanism and of any type of socialism," including Marxism as practiced by Stalin or National Socialism of Hitler's variety. (Did either Stalin or Hitler commit any act except in the name of mankind?) Solzhenitsyn's country of the spirit must inevitably modify the authority of abstract formality, the letter of the law divorced of spirit and exercised to the limit of pragmatic advantage to the letter itself—the state the highest symbolization in which *person* dissolves to *individual* and thence, by way of *integer,* into insignificance. By his emphasis on spiritual concerns, then, he declares the intellectual left's passport to reality out of order. That emphasis has been increasingly disturbing to the Western establishment since Walter Cronkite's puzzled encounter with Solzhenitsyn in Switzerland in the first days of his exile; in that interview, much more seemed afoot than political issues, but just what Cronkite could not find the handle to. For even then Solzhenitsyn was Russian and intended to remain Russian in ways that could not be reduced to ideological patterns, in ways that neither his nor our smatterers are likely ever to understand.

Little wonder then that in his Harvard sermon he exhibited a most "un-American" antipathy to President Eliot's dream of America. But the intellectual left had itself already prepared the stage for this most shocking episode. It had first made Solzhenitsyn, in a strange deformation of reality (as Eric Voegelin might put it), an expiatory figure, a living sacrifice for its innocent evils of the 1930's. The Stalinist outrages of that decade, being presently reenacted with less physical but more intensely spiritual brutality on such men as Ginzberg and Shcharansky, remain still an embarrassment from which our older left has not yet recovered. (How nice of our Secretary of State to find a few minutes for Shcharansky's "widow" before resuming business with Gromyko.) Because Solzhenitsyn was himself deceived in his youth and yet worked himself beyond deception to an immanence of articulated purgation—from *within* the system—he appeared a welcomed spectacle: mirror or *Doppelgänger.* The system seemed in some degree vindicated. Perhaps the Western Stalinists (Lillian Hellman excluded) were not so simple in their errors. The god worshiped in the 1930's had not

entirely failed, in spite of Arthur Koestler, if it could produce a Solzhenitsyn. But then, just as he is received with open arms, he turns insane; he begins an incessant burning spiritual theme.

Perhaps Solzhenitsyn was an answer to a psychological necessity to the waning left. He certainly found himself immediately elevated as a literary figure, a natural member in our decayed "genteel tradition," being offered naturalized citizenship in that floating country of mind in which one is "nowhere quite at home." He has not only refused that citizenship, but bears witness to a country quite antipathetic to that one offering him asylum, between which countries no detente may be established. We shall no doubt presently find reevaluations of Solzhenitsyn as literary man in the monthly and quarterly left—evaluations closer to the truth of his literary accomplishment than has been afforded him up to his uncouth violation of genteel manners at Harvard. (He at least, so far as I know, does not consider himself of that number that includes Tolstoy and Dostoevsky or—Henry James would wish us to say—Turgenev, though he is comfortable enough with Gorky and Gogol.) Such reconsiderations will have been undertaken, one fears, less to establish the critical truth in the question than to discount the prophet he is. Certainly, judging from the initial response of the dean of the literary left, Norman Cousins, we may expect as much. "He once described Roosevelt and Churchill as cowardly as a result of Yalta," Cousins says, to show what a wild man we have in Solzhenitsyn. "Yet if not for them, it's possible there would be no free world in which Solzhenitsyn could make such pronouncements about the evils of the West." (If not for them, so runs Solzhenitsyn's point, he might perhaps make such pronouncements from home rather than in exile.)

To reduce Solzhenitsyn as literary figure will seem to justify reducing him as prophet, in which office I find him at his greatest. He is a prophet addressing the intelligentsia's responsibility to matters moral and spiritual. As such he has proved as unsettling to the Western left as Jonathan Edwards must have been to Boston society in his surprising enthusiasm for the great awakening of the 1740's, with its loud emotional concern for the spirit lost in gnostic distortions of reality; as unsettling as the frontier evangelists of the great revival proved to Jefferson's dream of an egalitarianism engineered by an elite trained, if not by imported French deistic intellectuals, then by Boston unitarians.

The irony of the *place* at which Solzhenitsyn spoke, in the context of American intellectual history, is worthy of longer thought than has been so far afforded it. The ghosts of Emerson, Charles W. Eliot, F.D.R.'s Brain Trust among many sigh in the wings as he speaks. The late disciples of President Eliot's "Religion of the Future" will understandably be long in recovering from the shock of such violation of sacred ground as that given by this Jacksonian of the spirit, this Soviet misfit. His is a call for a return to the complexities of human existence in Plato's *metaxy*, in Eric Voegelin's In-Between. And by that call he seems to have desecrated the ground upon which the American intellectual left has builded; an intellectual empire trembles. What is called in question is the doctrine (pronounced in President Eliot's farewell words in 1909) that the educated man must reject all "authority, either spiritual or temporal." There must be "no worship, expressed or implied, of dead ancestors, teachers or rulers." Nor may the primary object of the new religion be "the personal welfare or safety of the individual in this world or the other . . . but . . . service to others [for which read

the gnostic deity, 'Humanity'] and . . . contributions to the common good." This religion of the future "will not be propitiatory, sacrificial, or expiatory," nor "perpetuate the Hebrew anthropomorphic representations of God." In such rejections as here prescribed we are nevertheless left with one authority not to be questioned lest one earn the epithet *reactionary* or *regressive*. That authority directs the rejections President Eliot finds necessary, thus purging the popular spirit of its roots in history and of its spiritual relation to the transcendent.

Little wonder that the angry, deracinated spirit of President Eliot stirs against Solzhenitsyn's rites of exorcism, or that it attempts to enlist the populace to remind Solzhenitsyn in a mannerly way that if he doesn't like "the American way" there are planes bound over the polar cap for Siberia (by way of Moscow) every day. This Misfit has attacked the religion our intellectual elite has substituted for our old concern for transcendence, a concern "progressively" lost to us on our way from the Renaissance. It is a loss engineered through the gnostic deification of man as created in the image of the post-Renaissance intelligentsia, "the proclaimed and enforced autonomy of man from any higher force," his own self-sufficiency, that doctrine most central to the thought of Ralph Waldo Emerson. This illusional reconstruction of reality has led us, in Solzhenitsyn's disturbing words, "to the calamity of a despiritualized and irreligious humanistic consciousness." We have become placid subjects to a new authoritarianism in which, as Santayana said long ago, "analysis and psychology seem to stand alone" as the ultimate measures of reality, in a world where "there is no spiritual interest, no spiritual need." Or at least there is scant evidence of that interest and need among the "directors" of the popular spirit, except the emotional alarm sounded in response to Solzhenit-syn's speech. If we admit calamity, there is danger that the popular spirit so long malleable may stir, breaking the bounds of its imprisonment in "humanistic man." The question might well become: what committee of Moseses led us into this entrapping desert? A question to be asked. And it is a question to be answered by a "nucleus" reared on spiritual concerns, but reared not too far from the library. For certain ghosts out of history that still haunt us require being called to account and thus exorcised from the popular spirit of our age so that the person's larger spirit may become generative in the desert.

NOTES

[1] Josef Pieper, in *Leisure: The Basis of Culture*, helps us understand I believe why there was such popular support of the intelligentsia from the lower classes during the eighteenth and nineteenth centuries, when revolutionary movements generally were bent on abolishing cultural hierarchy. In the pursuit of millennial dreams, knowledge as the necessary means to power over nature is elevated over wisdom. A justification is made for it as a species of labor, as "intellectual work." Pieper cites Kant's words (1796): "the law is that reason acquires its possessions through work." Two years later, Wordsworth in "Tintern Abbey" attempts to rescue a larger perspective of mind in nature, to justify that openness to existence which thinkers from Plato and Aristotle to Aquinas had understood as the operation of *intellectus* as complement to *ratio*. In that state of mind, says Wordsworth, one "sees into the life of things." (Pieper cites Heraclitus' description of receptive contemplation as "listening to the essence of things.") But the popular spirit comes to suppose (in Pieper's words) that "if to know is to work, then knowledge is the fruit of our own unaided effort and activity; then knowledge includes nothing which is not due to the effort of man, and there is nothing *gratuitous* about it, nothing 'in-spired' . . . ." Thus we lose the old distinction between *artes liberalis* and *artes serviles,* and educational institutions subsequently receive most general support when they present themselves as species under *artes serviles*. Facts and statistics have become the measure of effective production, whether one is measuring articles or autos. I have in hand a "memo" from the chief academic officer of a large state university which attempts to pattern itself after Harvard and declares its primary commitment as the pursuit of "new knowledge." The "memo" to all "Academic Deans" declares that all instructors are "to adhere to a 2500-teaching-minute requirement" for the 5 hour course. Classes are to meet "the required number of contact minutes," whether in elementary junior-high grammar or graduate-level microbiology.

[2] These words were spoken by cultist Christine Miller to Jim Jones at Jonestown, minutes before the mass suicide, to which he responded, "The best testimony we can make is to leave this goddamn world" (*Time*, March 26, 1979). A little later, in attempting to still the crying and screaming, he rebukes the multitude before him: "This is not the way for people who are socialistic Communists to die. Children it's just something to put you to rest." I cite this modern instance of an ideologist's struggle to maintain power, even if it means annihilation, in order to bracket a period of Western history. The other point to measure from is expounded by Norman Cohn in *The Pursuit of the Millennium*, a study of rising sectarianism in the Middle Ages. In Cohn's pages one experiences a discomforting encounter with our own world, though his treatment of historical materials concludes with 16th century Anabaptist versions of Jonestown. The millenarian sects he studies, says Cohn, have in common a conception of salvation as collective, terrestrial, imminent, total, miraculous. He concludes his 1970 edition as follows: "The old religious idiom has been replaced by a secular one, and this tends to obscure what otherwise would be obvious. For it is the simple truth that, stripped of their original supernatural sanction, revolutionary millenarianism and mystical anarchism are with us still."

[3] See as an example the fourth paragraph of Emerson's address. Here he secularizes St. Paul's crucial metaphor of the Christian Church (Romans 12:4), each person's membership in that body whose head is Christ. Emerson uses an old pagan fable about the gods and by that indirection de-mythologizes Paul. As Mircea Eliade would undoubtedly point out, Emerson's prose reveals that he understands myth as only "fiction." as metaphor very distantly related to man's experience of reality. His own metaphor is revealing in this respect: there is for Emerson "One Man—present to all particular men only partially, namely *society*, of which body the scholar is 'Man Thinking.'" The Enlightenment deification of intramundane man permeates his address to the Harvard scholars.

[4] Recently there has emerged in France the *Nouveaux Philosophes*, accompanied by a general revival

litical left. This growing "nucleus" appears to be flourishing in opposition to the descendants of the Voltairean *philosophes,* as witnessed by the flourishing of periodicals and the appearance of a number of books that have excited debate, such as Bernard-Henri Levy's recent *Barbarism with a Human Face* and (from across the channel) Arianna Stassinopoules' *After Reason.* Thomas Molnar (*National Review,* November 24, 1978) points out that Solzhenitsyn is an important influence on this new spirit stirring in the West. If it has not embraced Solzhenitsyn's spiritual concern as yet, the signs of a movement in that direction are apparent.

[5] In the Spring 1975 issue of *Modern Age,* I called attention to echoes found in *From Under the Rubble* and that Fugitive-Agrarian Work *I'll Take My Stand* (1930) by "Twelve Southerners." "The Smatterers" in particular might have been written by Donald Davidson or Andrew Lytle or Allen Tate, no less than by Richard M. Weaver. It largely was by Davidson: *The Attack on Leviathan.* My "Southern Reflections on Solzhenitsyn" also suggests that the most disturbing aspect of that Russian misplaced person, destined to make him less welcomed among us, is his burning concern for spiritual matters, an aspect played down or ignored altogether in the media, in which it was difficult to find that truth of Solzhenitsyn, that he was then and is a convert to Christianity. I suggested that he confronts the West, at a public level increasingly difficult to ignore, with the dilemma Flannery O'Connor's Misfit in "A Good Man Is Hard To Find" poses to the "good country people" in that story: either Christ was what he said he was, or he was a liar. If liar, then anything goes that pleases.   [XXIII, Fall 1979, 351–361]

[IX]

Art and Criticism

[68]

The Word That Is Spoken

MARTIN BUBER

Translated from the German by Maurice Friedman

Martin Buber *(1878–1965), the Austrian-born Israeli religious thinker and author of* I and Thou *(1937),* The Prophetic Faith *(1949),* Pointing the Way *(1957), and many other religious and philosophical works, needs little in the way of introduction as one of the most eminent thinkers of modern times. Educated at the universities of Vienna, Berlin, Leipzig, and Zurich, he taught for a time, before leaving Germany, at the University of Frankfurt. In 1938 he joined the faculty of the Hebrew University in Jerusalem, retiring from his post after fifteen years to continue his translation of the Bible. In 1954 he received the Goethe Prize in Hamburg. "The Word That Is Spoken," after appearing in the Fall 1961 issue of* Modern Age, *became a chapter in his* Essays in the Knowledge of Man *(1962). The article had originated as the opening lecture in the series "Word and Reality" sponsored by the Bavarian Academy of Fine Arts in Munich in July 1960.*

If we proceed from the human life that each of us lives and the significance of the word for this life, then three modes-of-being of languages are distinguishable. We shall call them present continuance, potential possession, and actual occurrence. By this is meant the continuance, possession, and occurrence at any given time of a certain language.

By present continuance is meant the totality of what can be said in a certain realm of language in a certain segment of time, regarded from the point of view of the person who is able to say what is to be said. The place of this present continuance is, accordingly, the being-with-one-another of all the speakers of this realm of language who again and again make use of its existence in the language which they intend and which they utter, that is, the being-with-one-another of living men in whose personal texture of speech the present continuance becomes actualized. But this place of present continuance would be completely missed if one regarded the continuance as existing outside these men. Every attempt to understand and explain the present continuance of a language as accessible detached from the context of its actual speakers must lead us astray.

By potential possession is meant the totality of what has ever been uttered in a certain realm of language, in so far as it proves itself capable of being included: included in what men intend to utter and do utter. The possession legitimately extends, therefore, from the highest to the most trivial utterance. The place of possession is the sum of what in a language, up to a certain period of time, has been spoken and written in all its forms of preservation, with the decisive limitation, however, that nothing belongs to it except what can still here and today be lifted by a living speaker into the sphere of the living word; what can be brought home in it. No matter how fundamentally the philologist or the historian of literature can objectively apprehend it, even this mode-of-being of language, apparently unfolded in pure objectivity, cannot be detached in its dynamic facticity from the actuality of the word.

The third mode-of-being of language is that of spokenness, or rather being spoken; the word that is spoken. Both of the other two, existence and possession, presuppose a historical acquisition, but here nothing else is to be presupposed other than man's will to communicate as a will capable of being realized. This will originates in men's turning to one another; it wins gesture, vocal sign, the word in the growing fruitfulness of this basic attitude. The elements of continuing language and the forms of possessed language serve it.

The genuine author and genuine dialogue—both draw from the present continuance of language, hence not from the dammed-up basin of possession but from the gushing and streaming waters. The author, however, receives his creative force in fief from his partner in dialogue. Were there no genuine dialogue, there would be no poetry; on the other hand, in the darkness of a world that has become spiritually unproductive, two whose call to one another remains trustworthy can still, drawing from the present continuance of language, help the other to say what they have suffered in common.

What Goethe reports to us in a significant passage about the speech of heaven to earth in its primeval age: *wie das Wort*

so wichtig dort war, weil es ein gesprochenes Wort war (how the word was so important there because it was a spoken word), must also hold true within our human world. We can well believe Goethe. But what then lends this priority to the spoken word? Is not what we take from the present continuance of language in order to think it, or what we take from the possession of language in order to read it, often incalculably superior to the spoken word? The importance of the spoken word, I think, is grounded in the fact that it does not want to remain with the speaker. It reaches out toward a hearer, it lays hold of him, it even makes the hearer into a speaker, if perhaps only a soundless one. But this must not be understood as if the place of the occurrence of language is the sum of the two partners in dialogue or, in the terminology of Jacob Grimm, of the two "fellows in speech"; as though the occurrence of speech were to be understood through the psychophysical comprehension of two individual unities in a given period of time. The word that is spoken is found rather in the oscillating sphere between the persons, the sphere that I call the "between" and that we can never allow to be contained without a remainder in the two participants. If we could take an inventory of all the physical and psychic phenomena to be found within a dialogical event, then there would remain something *sui generis* outside that could not be included—and this is just that which does not allow itself to be understood as the sum of the speech of two or more speakers, together with all the accidental circumstances. This something *sui generis* is their dialogue.

We tend, to be sure, to forget that something can happen not merely "to" us and "in" us but also, in all reality, between us. Let us consider the most elementary of all facts of our intercourse with one another: the word that is spoken is uttered here and heard there, but its spokenness has its place in the between.

II

Against the insight into the dialogical character of speech, it will probably be pointed out that thinking is essentially a man's speaking to himself. A reality is doubtless touched on here, but it is only touched on, not grasped. The so-called dialogue with oneself is only possible because of the basic fact of men's speaking with each other; it is the "internalization" of this capacity. But he who does not shun the difficult task of reflecting on a past hour of his thinking—not according to its outcome but fundamentally, according to its events, beginning with the beginning—may thrust inward to a primal level through which he can now wander without meeting a word. One notices that he has got hold of something without perceiving any conceptuality that wishes to come into being. In such a backward glance the second level allows itself to be seen more clearly, dominated by precisely this wishing to come into being. We may designate it as that of striving toward language. What is within strives over and over again toward becoming language, thought language, comprehensible language. And only now in our work of memory do we enter into the true level of language. Here, indeed, even if it is still soundless, language is already recognizably spoken. But does the thinker speak to himself as to the one thinking? In speaking the inner word he does not want to be heard by himself, for he knows the word already as the person uttering it; rather he wants to be heard by the nameless, unconceived, inconceivable other, by whom he wants to be understood in his having understood. The thinker is originally more sol-itary than the poet, but not in terms of his goal. Like the poet he is turned toward himself without turning himself. Certainly he is a court of his own through which he makes the competent examination of his world of concepts, but this world is not intended for this court, not dedicated to it. Many modern—and that means often de-Socratizing—philosophers have fallen, with the totality of their thought world, into a monologizing hybris, a circumstance which rarely happens to a poet. But this monologism which, to be sure, is well acquainted with the existentialist but not with the existential, brings in all its conjuring force the starkest menace of disintegration.

Every attempt to understand monologue as fully valid conversation, which leaves unclear whether it or dialogue is the more original, must run around on the fact that the ontological basic presupposition of conversation is missing from it, more concretely, the otherness, the moment of surprise. The human person is not in his own mind unpredictable to himself as he is to any one of his partners: therefore, he cannot be a genuine partner to himself, he can be no real questioner and no real answerer; he always "already knows somewhere" the answer to the question, and not, to be sure, in the "unconscious" of modern psychology, but rather in a sphere of conscious existence, a sphere which, although not present at the moment of the question, can in the very next moment flash up into presentness.

In philosophical discussions of language speaking has occasionally been described as " 'monadic' through and through." This interpretation may not validly appeal to Wilhelm von Humboldt's givenness of the Thou in the I; for Humboldt knew exactly through what process the fact of the Thou in the I is established:

through the I becoming a Thou to another I. "From where else could the fundamental possibility of misunderstanding or being misunderstood originate?" asks the philosopher Hönigswald, mistakenly appealing to Humboldt in this connection. But what if precisely this possibility belongs essentially to speaking, because language by its nature is a system of possible tensions—and thinking is for this reason not "speaking with oneself" because it lacks this real tension? It is not true that a dialogue in which two speakers aim at an understanding of the meaning of an event must presuppose, as John Locke thought, an already existing understanding on the meaning of the words employed. When two friends discuss, say, the concept of thought, the two concepts may be very similar in meaning to each other; but we are not to regard them as identical in meaning. This does not cease to be true even when the two of them begin by agreeing on a definition of the concept: the great fact of personal existence will penetrate even into the definition—unless the two "fellows in speech" join in betraying the *logos* for logical analysis. If the tension between what each means by the concept becomes too great, then a misunderstanding arises that can amount to destruction. But below the critical point the tension need by no means remain inoperative; it can become fruitful, it always becomes fruitful where genuine dialogue unfolds out of understanding each other.

From this it follows that it is not the unambiguity of a word but its ambiguity that constitutes living language. The ambiguity creates the problematic of speech and it creates its conquest in an understanding that is not an assimilation but a fruitfulness. The ambiguity of the word, which we may call its aura, must to some extent have already existed whenever men in their multiplicity met each other, ex-

pressing this multiplicity in order not to succumb to it. It is the communal nature of the *logos* as at once "word" and "meaning" which makes man, and it is this which proclaims itself from of old in the communalizing of the spoken word that takes place again and again.

I recall how about forty-five years ago I received from the International Institute for Philosophy in Amsterdam, at the head of which was the mathematician Brouwer, the plan for an academy whose task it should be "to create words of spiritual value for the language of the western peoples," *i.e.*, words freed from ambiguity. I answered that in my judgment one should fight the misuse of the great old words rather than teach the use of new, manufactured ones. For in language, as in general, the *set* community kills the living. Certainly modern science has the right to create for its purposes a medium of thorough understanding that may be employed without a remainder, but science knows that the word that is spoken can never arise in this way.

If, as we have seen, a monological primal character of language cannot be proved from the self-experience of thinking men, still less can it be discovered in the realm of phylogenesis. Certainly, it is an imperatively valid symbol when the biblical narrative shows God as leaving to man the naming of the animals which he leads by him, but this happens to man as a being already standing in a state of adequate communication: it is through God's addressing man—Franz Rosenzweig's *Stern der Erlösung* teaches us—that he establishes man in speech. A precommunicative stage of language is unthinkable. Man did not exist before having a fellow being, before he lived over against him, or toward him, and that means before he had dealings with him. Language never existed before there was address; it could become monologue only after dialogue broke off or broke down. The early speaker was not surrounded by objects on which he imposed names, nor did adventures befall him which he caught with names: the world and destiny became language for him only in partnership. Even when in a solitude, without an answerer, the hearerless word pressed on his throat, this word was connected with the primal possibility, that of being heard.

I will explain what I mean by an ethnological statement of facts: by citing those remarkable word-compounds, only adequately comprehensible to our thinking as a residue of an early stage of language, which are preserved in the language of many societies unrelated to one another—in particular those of the Eskimos and the Algonquins. In these so-called polysynthetic or holophrastic languages, the unit of speech with which one builds is not the word but the sentence. This is a structure that in its fully developed form exhibits components of three different kinds.[1] Two of them, the so-called core element and the formal elements, both the modal as well as the personal, can also emerge as independent. Not so the element of the third kind, which might be designated as preponderantly suffixes: they appear exclusively in their serving function, but it is they that make possible the form of the sentence.

It would, to be sure, be presumptuous to connect our ideas about the origin of language with an attempted reconstruction of the genesis of that particular form of the sentence, but at any rate one is reminded of Hamann's bold statement that at first the word probably "was neither a noun nor a verb but at the least a whole period." We do not find as decisive man confronting things that he undertakes to put into words and only in this way bringing them to their full status as things. As important as this act is, we still find as decisive men-with-one-another who at-

tempt to come to an understanding over situations. Not things but situations are primary. If Stefan George's saying that no things exist for which there is no word may prove true for the things, it is inapplicable to the situations that man must know before he comes to know the things. Out of different situations of different kinds that early man experiences emerge similar, so-to-speak similar-remaining, things and beings, events and states that want to be conceived as such, named as such.

In the early period, which we seek to disclose in this way, language presents itself to us above all as the manifestation and apprehension of an actual situation between two or more men who are bound together through a particular being-directed-to-each-other. This moment may, for example, be grounded in work in which the labor is shared, work in which the participants are often separated from each other, yet not so far that each is unable to hear clearly the articulated utterances of the other. If one man finds himself in a new, unforeseen situation, though not one unknown in its nature— for example, that of a threatening danger the like of which has already existed— then he calls to his comrade something that would be understood by the latter but not by the members of an unfriendly neighboring clan who might possibly be in the vicinity. What I speak of is in no way to be compared with a "cry for help" or a "signal," as they are known to us from the life of animals, the first as improvised, the second as an utterance repeated in unchanged form under similar circumstances. We can derive it from neither of the two, for even the most undifferentiated word designating a primordial situation must, just as a word, have brought to sound that sudden and discovering freedom, alien to the animal, in which one man turns to the other in order to have him take notice of something existing or happening. Every genetic investigation which preserves its disinterestedness confirms for us the old insight which cannot be referred to often enough: that the mystery of the coming-to-be of language and that of the coming-to-be of man are one.

I have already drawn attention to the fact that the solitary category "man" is to be understood as a working together of distance and relations.[2] Unlike all other living beings, man stands over against a world from which he has been set at a distance, and, unlike all other living beings, he can again and again enter into relationship with it. This fundamental double stance nowhere manifests itself so comprehensively as in language. Man—he alone—speaks, for only he can address the other, as the other standing at a distance over against him; but in addressing it, he enters into relationship. The coming-to-be of language also brings with it, however, a new function of distance. For even the earliest speaking does not, like a cry or a signal, have its end in itself: it sets the word outside itself in being, and the word continues, it has continuance. And this continuance wins its life ever anew in the true relation, in the spokenness of the word. Genuine dialogue witnesses to it, and poetry witnesses to it. For the poem is spokenness, spokenness to the Thou, wherever this partner might be.

But—it may be asked—if this is so, if this is not a metaphor but a fact that the poem is a spokenness, then does that not also necessarily mean that not merely the dialogue but also the poem can be regarded according to its content of truth? This question can only be answered with both Yes and No. Every authentic poem is also true, but its truth stands outside all relation to an expressible What. We call poetry the not very frequently appearing form of words that imparts to us a truth which cannot come to words in any other manner than in this one, in the manner of this form. Therefore, every paraphrase of a poem robs it of its truth. I say: the poem speaks; one may also say: the poet speaks, if one does not mean by that the subject of a biography and the author of many works but only the living speaker of this very poem. The speaker is as the poet the speaker of a truth. Nietzsche's jest, "The poets lie too much," misses the depth of this truth, which is submerged in the mystery of the witnessing How. Also bound up with these facts is the problematic of the interpretation of poetry in so far as it seeks anything further than that the word compound be more adequately perceived. The conceptuality that sets as its goal bringing a knowable What to clarity and value, detracts from the genuine understanding of the poem and misses the truth borne by it.

But if the name of truth really belongs to both, the conceptual and the poetic, how can one lay hold of one truth that embraces both? For a first answer to this question about the two truths and the one, an ancient text may help us since it points to the primal phenomenon of language.

A holy scripture of India, the Brahmana of the Hundred Paths, relates that the gods and the demons both sprang from the self-sacrifice of the primal creator and entered into his heritage. Then it says literally: "The heritage, that was the word: truth and falsehood, at once truth and falsehood. Now this and that one spoke the truth, this and that one spoke the falsehood. Since they spoke the same, they were like one another. But now the gods rejected the falsehood and accepted the truth alone; but now the demons rejected the truth and accepted the falsehood alone. Then that truth that was with the demons pondered: 'Well, the gods have rejected the falsehood and have accepted the truth alone. So I shall go thither.' And it came to the gods. But the falsehood that was with the gods pondered: 'Well, the demons have rejected the truth and have accepted the falsehood alone. So I shall go thither.' And it went to the demons. Now the gods spoke the whole truth, the demons spoke the whole falsehood. Since the gods spoke only the truth, they became weaker and poorer; therefore, whoever speaks only the truth always becomes weaker and poorer. But in the end he endures, and in the end the gods endured. And the demons, who only spoke the falsehood, grew and thrived; therefore, whoever speaks only the falsehood grows and thrives. But in the end he cannot endure, and the demons could not endure."

It is worth noticing how here the fate of being is determined through the speaking of the word, and, indeed, through the speaking of the true and of the false word. But what can "true" and "false" mean to us when we transpose the myth into our human reality? Clearly not something that can be grasped only through the relation to a reality existing outside the speaking. The myth knows only the totality of the one, still undivided sphere. When we shift from the myth into our world, therefore, we can turn toward no other sphere commensurate with that one. "One speaks the truth" may, accordingly, be paraphrased by: "One says what he means." But what does "mean" mean in this connection? In our world and in our language it obviously means that just as the speaker, as he who he *is* means what he means, so also as he who he *is* he says what he means. The relation between meaning and saying points us to the relation between the intended unity of meaning and saying, on the one side, and that between meaning and saying and the personal existence itself, on the other side.

In this myth an especially strong accent falls on the establishment of the fact that—expressed in our language—the truth, chemically purified, as it were, of its content of falsehood, is ineffectual in the course of history. Everything depends here on interpreting correctly the words, "But in the end he endures." This is no expression of an optimistic view of history nor is it an eschatological saying. "In the end" means for us: in the pure reckoning of the personal existence. In the language of religion it is expressed thus: "When the books are opened"; that is not there and then, however, but here and now.

The truth that is concerned in this fashion is not the sublime "unconcealment" suitable to Being itself, The *aletheia* of the Greeks; it is the simple conception of truth of the Hebrew Bible, whose *etymon* means "faithfulness," the faithfulness of man or the faithfulness of God. The truth of the word that is genuinely spoken is, in its highest forms—in poetry and incomparably still more so in that message-like saying that descends out of the stillness over a disintegrating human world—indivisible unity. It is a manifestation without a concomitant diversity of aspects. In all its other forms, however, three different elements must be distinguished in it. It is, in the first place, faithful truth in relation to the reality which was once perceived and is now expressed, to which it opens wide the window of language in order that it may become directly perceptible to the hearer. It is, secondly, faithful truth in relation to the person addressed, whom the speaker means as such, no matter whether he bears a name or is anonymous, whether he is familiar or alien. And to mean a man means nothing less than to stand by him and his insight with the elements of the soul that can be sent forth, with the "outer soul," even though at the same time one fundamentally remains and must remain with oneself. And, thirdly, it is the truth of the word that is genuinely spoken, faithful truth in relation to its speaker, *i.e.*, to his factual existence in all its hidden structure. The human truth of which I speak—the truth vouchsafed man—is no pneuma that pours itself out from above on a band of men now become superpersonal: it opens itself to one in one's existence as a person. This concrete person, in the life-space allotted to him, answers with his faithfulness for the word that is spoken by him.

NOTES

[1] I follow here almost throughout the formulation of Edward Sapir, without being able to go along with his general basic view.

[2] "Distance and Relation," trans. by Ronald G. Smith, *Psychiatry*, Vol. XX, No. 2 (May 1957), pp. 97–104.   [V, Fall 1961, 353–360]

[69]

The International Role of Art in Revolutionary Times

William Ernest Hocking (1873–1966) was 86 years old when this essay appeared in the Spring 1960 issue of Modern Age. *Then Alfred Professor of Philosophy Emeritus at Harvard, where he taught from 1914 to 1943, he lived in retirement, but not inactively, on his farm near Madison, New Hampshire. A fellow at the Universities of Göttingen, Berlin, and Heidelberg (1902–1903), he received his Ph.D. from Harvard in 1904. In 1917 he was an observer at the American and British front under British auspices, and he was also an inspector of war-issues courses for the United States War Department (1918). A Gifford lecturer at Glasgow University (1937–1939) and Hibbert lecturer at Oxford and Cambridge (1938), he was a gifted teacher with a "courtly" manner. Among his many books are* The Meaning of God in Human Experience *(1912),* Lasting Elements of Individualism *(1937), and* Freedom of the Press *(1947). This essay was also published as an appendix to Hocking's* Strength of Men and Nations *(1960).*

What is lost in the "modern" is not the Romantic, nor the Classic, but the Eternal.

IN TIMES OF revolutionary change, art has a role of special importance easily overlooked even by the artist himself, a role which calls for a shaking-out of our current views of the nature of art. In broad terms, art is not a copying of the world, nor yet a fantasia on its themes, but a quiet remaking of the world, likely to conceal its proud power under the guise of free fancy.

Art is many things at once: labor and play, the element of aspiration built into utility, of form built into function, of infinitude built into the finite, of the beyond-self built into the living selfhood of things—not as extraneous decor but as the fulfilment of their being. Art is the liveliness of life discerned within the mere factuality of life, lending to those facts the assurance of their meaning. Considering the given situation as the taskmaster we are bound to obey, art is the second mile ("go with him twain") we deliberately add to the mile we are compelled to go— the mile freely added not as a boast, but as a promise of a futurity in command of circumstances, not their servant.

It is the glory of man's spirit that in the midst of misery and confusion and revolt, art lifts its head, not to deny the evil but to share it; and not alone to report the misery, nor yet to denounce or escape it, but to transfigure it. An art that merely reports or re-enacts the human load of footlessness, dismay, or despair—as what we call modern art tends to do—may be a loyal art, refusing romantic honors to the headless powers of the time. But stopping at that point, it risks becoming itself a *headless art,* refusing to enter on the uniquely responsible function of creation—that element of world-shaping purpose which silently pervades even the carefree play of human imagination, by virtue of a "depth-psychology" mistraced by Freud.

For the true artist, the world always begins at the moment of his work. Art is the infinitely recurring rebirth of life through the free man's dream, and of the world, through life.

Art begins in something less than art, perhaps simply in the animal caper that proclaims caprice, the flourish of limb or voice that turns into dance or song—but always the more-than-necessary, and always with a subconscious tribute to life running deeper than the play. From the beginning the steps of civilization have been marked by the signs of joy-in-*form* with which man has lingered over his most compulsory labors, as if to extract from them their tribute to his freedom.

That there is a strand of economic determinism in history no one need doubt: human life is inserted among necessities as tree-roots among stones. But it is the tree, not the stone, that shapes the foliage and the flower: it is humanity, not economy, that dwells on "finishing" its tools and weapons with painstaking ornament, and lends the note of design to its hard-wrought shelters as well as to palace, presidium, temple, and tomb.

Hence it is that the most open book to the soul of a people is the element of "style" in its living quarters, its settlement-planning, its architecture.

Man climbs out of barbarism by way of an accepted dominance signalized in some outstanding structure expressive of "rule" but at the same time of a common desire for unity and joy-in-order. Even underneath the grueling compulsions that built tower and pyramid for the despot, there grew a sense which the despot could neither give nor take away—a sense that "This is ours, not his alone": the finished work became a point of community pride, a tribute not to him but to the human spirit.

When civilization arrives at a nation of free men, the formal centrality in community-planning is not expunged—there is a town hall and a steeple in the New England village. But there is also the homestead. Privacy, as home-right, is built into home-art: not everyone can enter everywhere and always; there is an institution, the "invitation": and this moral factor of controlled association calls on art to embody itself, as in the swinging door, the "yard," the private garden, the hedge or fence, the sidewalk. . . . Leaping forward into new East Asia, free Vietnam, seeking to embody in property its conception of individual dignity, hopes to secure to every family its "basic economy," its own house and lot! The task of art here becomes formidable, as industrialism looms ahead, and with it, the apartment house: can its advent be postponed, or can the apartment be subdued to the needs of the human spirit? Miss Ehrenfest tried it in Russia.

It is precisely the Industrial Revolution which most clearly illustrates the power of the human will-to-form as lying beyond "function." Feudal and post-feudal Europe, inheriting Classical motifs in architecture and city-design, rewove them into a "Western" visual language for the new-built cities. The Industrial Revolution came as a triumph of mechanism and at the same time as a defeat of human solidarity. Nothing more effectively damned its early character than the "satanic mills," the deadening identity of living quarters in the milltowns, and the accompanying murder of landscape beauty in Wales, England, Belgium. The industrial economies of today have profited by the lesson. Industry in America has long since begun to exercise a decent concern for human dignity in the homes of its workers, as well as in its sites and factory-design. Not yet a high achievement (though Joseph Pennell found occasional themes for pictorial art in factory scenes), but a distinct step out of the temper of exploit, a step signalized by a stroke of conscience, as in the ill-fated town of Pullman (1884), intended as an ideal workers' community.

The distinctive spirit of our capitalist civilization, however, expresses (and confesses) itself less in the actual areas of production than in its great office-centers. Something of the dominance of business in America may be gathered from the skyline of New York, not untouched by grace and beauty in its older structures, expressive of a pride-of-power willing at once to outrank and to protect the libraries, churches, colleges, the Town Hall, the Metropolitan Museum . . . which cherish a quieter dignity in the shadow of the skyscrapers.

It is a magnificent skyline; and one wonders what would become of it if the varied peaks of those great towers were replaced by squared-off ends like that of the bleak box-housing of the U.N. Secretariat. The notable thing about present American experiments in architecture under the influence of Functionalism and the *Bauhaus*, is that their "monotonous repetition of cellular façades cloaked with vitreous indifference"—if it expresses any social spirit whatever—is far more symbolic of a *communist* ideal all-alikeness than of a society prizing personality and individual difference!

On the other hand, when the Soviets wish to set up an impressive building, they do not hesitate to borrow architectural themes from classic Europe, as the new university in Moscow may witness. Each pays the other involuntary homage!

The Functionalist commonly forgets the most widely used function of a building. He rightly thinks of the functions of the insiders, the occupants, daily users of the internal spaces. If these are numbered by the hundreds, what of those who daily have to *see* the building, numbered often by the thousands? For them, the structure has a further function which neither it nor they can escape: it must visibly indicate its *raison d'être* in that place and among those surroundings, its role in the community. It must do this by way of the silent speech of form and symbol. It has no right either to the idle luxury of saying nothing (as if, like a movable cracker-box, it could *be*, without being a *member* of any specific environment), or by strident egoism of design crying "Look at me and forget all else."

Hence it is that a competent observer like Sir Albert Richardson, former president of the Royal Academy (whose words I have above quoted), could say that while "fifty years ago America led the world . . . in civic art . . . the present state of architecture in the United States, and indeed throughout the world, reveals soulful despair." Sir Albert believes this guideless period destined to pass.[1]

There are indeed reasons for considering it a temporary phase. Present novelties in skeletal styling and geometrical virtuosity are due in part to developments in engineering and in available materials whose notable capacities have rightly stimulated large-scale experimentation, with natural temptations to extravagance of conception (as in cantilever-projections intended to startle, or spiral ramps expanding skyward). The misfortune is that astonishment is a fading emotion, essentially barren. It is precisely the engineering precocity of these structures, and their admirable durability, that ensures a long toll of public suffering under their defiance of responsible community membership and meaning.

But in this defiance, which is also partly "despair," architecture is not alone. It is but one illustration of a laming common to all contemporary arts, defeating their world-service at a moment of the world's greatest need. We must enlarge our enquiry into the sources of this laming.

I RAISE THE question whether the present phase in all the fine arts inclining to assume the label "modern"—including music, poetry, fiction, and the graphic arts, together with drama and the screen—is not in the main a departure, especially in U.S.A., from the sound instinct of the nation. And at the same time, whether it is not a *natural* departure, whose motive can be understood and thereby put on the way to remedy.

Is it not due essentially to *an impression of failure in the fundamental assumptions of our civilization*, a failure so radical as to require shaking off all prepossessions and conventions in order to *renew one's sense of being*, from which alone the work of art can be initiated? The world-turmoil cannot fail to bring with it so wide a loss of order and predictable circumstance that *no art can today bear to speak simply in terms of beauty or affirmation*. Art must find human experience where it is: in an era of hardness, art must speak for the hard. In sympathy for confusion, modern art must echo confusion. It thus assumes the first half of the artist's task, that of knowing the burden, in order to prepare for the second half—that of lifting the burden. Has "modern" art perhaps simply failed to reach its second half?

As of today, all human life stands in the shadow of the cruel and the meaningless. The quest for sense in the world-process encounters a blank factuality nowhere better expressed than in the work of Sartre and Camus: it is, they report, "The Absurd" in which human existence is set. Man is subjected to the pressure of a faceless universe, silent as to his Whence or Whither. If he feigns to hear voices from within, they can be the voices only of arbitrary powers, tempting him to equally arbitrary treatment of his fellows, whether through exploit, or war. Whereas for those who hear no voices, believe no gods, and yet refuse exploit, revolution promising violent relief proves deceptive, driven as it is to replace tyranny by tyranny. Camus rejects faith, and equally rejects Nihilism: he rejects revolution and equally rejects exploit; for he has a new answer to the exploiter—a personal revolt, which asserts equality with the tyrant and restores the solidarity of mutual respect. But how can the spirit of personal revolt become a world-force able to curb or dominate the "collective passions" driving mankind to desperate action? Here Camus sees the authentic function of art, the sole available curative agency that can reach the minds of men with a speed and on a scale commensurate with that of the ills that menace them. In his great work, *The Rebel*, he asserts the mission of art to be addressed to the present world malady—nothing less.

"When the passions of the time put the fate of the whole world at stake, creation (the function of art) wishes (and is called upon) to dominate the whole of destiny." [2]

This analysis might seem a pure extravagance, were we not witnesses in our own day of the instantaneous uniting force, across the deepest chasms of "collective passion," of a notable musical event in Moscow, or of a ballet, or of a literary masterpiece, or for that matter of the art-element in the near-universal devotion of scientists to the community of truth, as in the Geophysical Year—itself a form of the creative passion invoked by Camus.

To generalize his meaning, let us say that the mission of art is the *Redemption of the Absurd,* overcoming the irrational brute-fact-aspect of existence, not by legality nor by other-worldly hopes, but by the immediate attraction of a vision of human nobility in creating solidarity. The mission of art is to evoke images that universally persuade, and thus create the will to unite.

The power of art in the political arena has never been more highly rated, unless by Plato, who paid the poets of his day the oblique compliment of wishing to exclude them from his ideal Republic, or by Confucius, who declared of the music of his day that there were sounds that dispose men to fair conduct and others that dispose them to disorder: both recognized that there is such a thing as bad art, which can undo the best work of lawmakers. Tolstoi, the artist, would excommunicate art: and the socialists from Saint-Simon onward sought to control art in the interest of social progress. This sense of danger is an admission of its power. But Camus sees clearly that while art, for every reformer, is on trial, it can only exist as free, never as the instrument of a specific polity or diplomacy. As the voice of human hope, art precedes diplomacy, and makes it possible.

It is Friedrich Schiller who most clearly sees art in its historic efficiency. In his *Letters on Aesthetic Education,* he comments on what he considered the failure of the French Revolution.[3] Writing in 1793, all he could see of the outcome of 1789 was that a great attempt to gain Liberty and Fraternity had resulted in a new barbarity and terrorism (as if anticipating Camus' judgment on revolution as fated to beget a new tyranny). Schiller took definite issue with Kant's prescription, namely, to "subordinate the senses," the natural impulses and passions, to reason and law, as an ideal Napoleon might have done, and as the actual Napoleon hoped to do while serving his own ambition. As Schiller saw, "subordination" is not the word. For civilization is not a subduing of impulse: it is a *harmonizing of impulse and reason.* This harmony, he held, is the precise achievement of art: art alone can educate mankind, for only art can act on feelings directly.

Schiller and Camus see art in its most complete scope. To educate is even more than to cure discord; though the curing Camus calls for is perhaps the severer task. For both, the question arises, who or what will educate the artists?

For while this heavy leaning on art for the civilizing and healing movements of history does not rate art too high it does make art *unduly self-sufficient.*

It is wholly right in holding cultural advance to be due to a force of attraction, not solely to compulsion such as economic necessity: the pull and the push commonly act together. But the pull, the prefigured goal of the striving intrinsic to human life, is not a creature of the artist's imagination: it is first of all a trait of reality present in experience to all men, felt by the artist as member of the race, and hence incorporated by him in symbols he could know to be universal.

For the reality we immediately feel is not blank "sensation": it is also *incentive.* Let me venture—as an essay in "depth psychology"—to describe your nuclear awareness of being: there is a life-pulse, a biological directive like Bergson's *élan vital*; but more than that; more, too, than Whitehead's primordial "lure" (so akin to that *ewig Weibliche* of Goethe which "draws us onward"). There is at once a persuasion and a summons, a promise and a task, a sense of destiny and a duty: if you like, a female and a male element, a Yin and a Yang. The Chinese have a remarkable name for it, *Ming*, the "Appointment of Heaven." *Art is a response to the incentive* of this reality as directly felt.

What Schiller and Camus alike neglect is the truth that art is derivative—a response rather than pure origination. It is a creative response, because its proposal is clothed in imagery devised by the artist. Art, let us say, is a creative response to a felt purposive factor in the world-process as always present.

If, as I put the matter many years ago, religion is the "Mother of the arts," [4] we can understand the historical circumstance that the arts are the first language of religion: myth and song, drama and dance, temple and tomb, sculpture and painting, yes, and the primitive laws and sciences as well . . . all appear first as attendants upon the world spirits, and only later fight their way to independence and maturity. And in many ways, the arts remain the most natural, freest, least dogmatic expressions of faith. The poetry of the world not only precedes its philosophy but in many ways remains the most vital expression of our metaphysical sense.

Art must always be free to play, partly because the real demands the widest variety of imagery for its full truth: one might almost venture the paradox that the play of art is too serious for the superficialities of analysis. What Rilke said of his early master, Rodin, touches the essential purport of art: "For him, making a portrait meant seeking eternity in a face, that fragment of the eternal with which that person took part in the great process of eternal things . . . an effort at holding the ultimate court of justice!" And the beginning of *doing* justice, man's creative task adding to the creative work of the world-power.

It may seem at first sight an inversion of the true functions to define the province of art as a type of *justice* ulterior to that of the courts. Yet consider a work like Tolstoi's *Resurrection*, or—to leap into the present moment—like Cozzens' *The Just and the Unjust*. The Greek tragedy was at once play and judgment on the human situation. But come directly to the essential point; consider the words of the ancient story of the woman taken in adultery, "Neither do I condemn thee"—the story itself a work of art, whatever its relation to actual happening: the mind of the race continues to be stirred by it to a deeper justice, because touching a more germinal level of reality-in-the-moral-life. It is, in brief, the region in which art and religion refuse separation: together they carry philosophy nearer to its goal.

And to see this as the great opportunity in our day of fiction, the drama, the screen, is to groan over the waste, whether of the writers or the critics, spending themselves on the trivia of sophisticated psychology. They are misled, no doubt, by the two prevalent learned superstitions of our time—buzzing close to truth—the Freudian unconscious, and the Existentialist being-without-essence. The impact of *Dr. Zhivago* should open their eyes to the fact that art *is* an act of attempted justice, and in its responsible exercise stirs the ultimate issues even when it cannot decide them. Stirs the statesman as well!

It becomes clear that the apparent irrelevance of art to the fateful decisions in public affairs is deceptive. For policy must win response from the faiths of a people; and the faiths rest on what they intuitively trust to, as the ruling powers of history. If Charles Malik, president of the U.N. Assembly, is right in saying that "the Western mind has . . . been softened and undermined from within and without . . . losing faith in itself . . . seeking other gods than those which have so faithfully protected and nurtured it" . . . and that "the deepest thing at stake is its faith in its values and its ability to justify and defend them" . . . the fault is not solely in our thinking: it is in our seeing and our feeling, in the groping incertitude which, shared by the artist, he, the artist, is unable to correct.

But let us be clear that the fault is not in his "modernism," nor the cure in reversion to an earlier era, whether of style, or of faith. What is lost in the "modern" is not the certitudes of yesterday, not the Romantic, nor the Classic, but the Eternal. It is the peculiar advantage of art, that surrendering the exactitudes of science and the fixities of theology for the elastic imagery of metaphor and myth, it is able through its localisms and its periods to *mean* the changeless and universal. It is the undefined identity of all the faiths. It is, as Plotinus says of beauty, "recognized by the soul as something long familiar, arresting and beckoning"—a tie to the timeless, a tie without bonds. It is for this reason that "works of art" never lose their speech. It is not yesterday that is better than today; it is vision and truth that are better than blindness and pretence.

However we define it, the world function of art is momentous, and the more fateful, because its power can only be exercised in responsible freedom. A dictated art loses at once the magic of universality. This does not mean that art has no discipline of its own, and that unbridled frivolity can hold the secret of the artist's sway. That secret is lost the moment the artist identifies his whim with his message; it is lost to any public which—as the U.S.A. now tends to do—allies its arts primarily with holiday-from-sobriety, escape, loose ends.

Play indeed it must be, in the sense of passing beyond necessity, doing what no one could compel it to perform, bearing a fruit of superabundance. Like grace and beauty of body, art is the more-than-required, yielded by the human vital-overflow.

But just on this account, it emerges from the secret places of generic piety: the reverse of Riot, Fling, Drip, Abandon. And to grasp even partially the magnitude of the import of art for the human advance, and for the crux of history today, is to see the abysmal treason of an art which reverses the direction of its function, and instead of redeeming the Absurd in human destiny, steeps the soul in Absurdity, as by a deliberate suicide.

There is valid reason for a wide experimentalism in art, and for an abstraction which—like five-finger exercises—plays among the analytical factors of form. There is valid reason also for a subjectivism which turns the thought of the artist—partly—away from the object to the inner impulse, provided that in expressing his feeling he does not forget that art has to be a language intelligible—without excessive puzzledom—to mankind at large.

There is always valid reason for rebellion against purely conventional limitations of theme and style and symbol, assuming that the rebel is not simply trying to cover, and thus confessing, his own poverty of resource. It has been said, for example, that "in our century, western music has turned to Asia and Africa to save itself from rhythmic and melodic stagnation." [5] When I think of Ravel and Sibelius, yes and even of Elgar and Grieg, I doubt the crisis of impoverishment; but I am sure that there are opening to us wide fields of new resources in the interplay of systems of music long developed in isolation. When Constant Lambert notes the difference between "the modal tunes of European Russia and the chromatic tunes of Eastern Russia," he pays tribute to an Oriental influence which has riches to offer; and such riches are surely more significant than can be found in vacuous tonal drift or non-peaceful competition in cacophony and "barbaric yawp."

A responsible experimentalism has endless promise—responsible to the world-

796

WILLIAM ERNEST HOCKING

function of a deeper justice. An irresponsible experimentalism—tolerable in lighter times as exploration of the sportive end of the wide spectrum—may in the present human pass amount to the potential betrayal of a tacit trust. For the peoples—all of them—must look to their artists—not for policies, programs, doctrines—but for their most immediate rapport with the moving energy of the world, the *feel* of its purposive drive and meaning. Through an art adult to its calling, they may sense that hidden glory, beneath the forbidding mask of Fact, wherein the discords of the nations are, in the "anticipated attainments" of the spirit, already resolved.

NOTES

[1] Letter to *New York Times,* March 1, 1959.
[2] *The Rebel,* tr. Anthony Bower (New York: Vintage Books, 1954), p. 274f.
[3] Cf. Walter Grossmann, "The Idea of Cultural Evolution in Schiller's Aesthetic Education," *The Germanic Review,* Feb. 1959.
[4] *The Meaning of God in Human Experience* (New Haven: Yale University Press, 1912), pp. 13–26.
[5] Fred Grunfeld, in *The Reporter,* April 30, 1959.

[IV, Spring 1960, 129–135]

70

Decorum in the Novel

DONALD DAVIDSON

Donald (Grady) Davidson (1893–1968) was born in Campbellsville, Tennessee. Entering Vanderbilt University in 1909, he was to remain there as a student (B.A., 1917; M.A., 1922) and teacher until his retirement in 1962, except for a four-year stint of teaching before he received his B.A. and the period he served as a lieutenant in the United States Army, 1917–1919. He published five volumes of poetry and two collections of social criticism, The Attack on Leviathan *(1938)—called by Russell Kirk "Southern Agrarianism at its almost-best"—and* Still Rebels, Still Yankees *(1957). He also published a two-volume history,* The Tennessee *(1946, 1948), numerous textbooks, and a libretto for a folk opera (*Singin' Billy, *1952). Considered the most conservative of the Southern Agrarians, he took his stand as a teacher, poet, editor, critic, counselor, and adviser to generations of students as he fought for the preservation of threatened human values.*

THESE ARE THE days when the chickens of liberation are coming home to roost and are turning out to be, not any sort of neat domesticated fowl, but instead, rampaging hawks and buzzards—or even condors. The old empires have been dissolving into what Dryden would have called "the dregs of a democracy." The spectacle has jarred Walter Lippmann—that habitually cheerful prophet—into occasional moments of melancholy apprehension. He has even permitted himself to wonder out loud "how this multitude of governments can be saved from becoming an excited and explosive mob."

For better or worse, we have no Walter Lippmann of the arts to wonder, as well he might, about disorders nearer home, particularly in the literary arts, and above all in the modern novel. These, too, are among the phenomena of liberation. And since the novel is our dominant literary form—important to us as epic and drama were in previous cultures—it would surely be the height of irresponsibility and recklessness not to show some concern when novelists lose all conception of prose fiction as high art and are willing, in the name of freedom, to practice novel-writing as a low art, indeed to claim for this low art a certain eminence and purity, especially when it abandons all the common restraints as to subject matter and language, and crosses the border into what is admittedly the realm of obscenity and debasement.

The liberation of the novel began, in a legal sense, at least as far back as December 6, 1933, in the case of *United States* v. *One Book Entitled Ulysses* (5 Fed. Supp.

182—S.D.N.Y. 1931) when Federal District Judge John M. Woolsey concluded his decision by saying that "whilst in many places the effect of 'Ulysses' on the reader is somewhat emetic, nowhere does it tend to be an aphrodisiac. 'Ulysses' may therefore be admitted into the United States."

Morris L. Ernst, attorney for the publishers in the *Ulysses* case and other important preceding cases, trumpeted his legal victory as "a major event in the history of the struggle for free expression" and lightly ignored the plain judicial indication that the book, in places, was disgusting to the point of nausea. In general, our critics and novelists—when they have bothered to speak on the issue—have monotonously repeated the Ernst motif—"free expression." Indeed, when the matter comes up, they stop being critics and novelists and become crusading liberals, and seldom fail to insinuate that objections to literary obscenity come only from bigots and originate in some hidden inward vileness and impurity. This characteristic emphasis appears in the letter of Archibald MacLeish which Grove Press prefixed to their unexpurgated edition of Lawrence's *Lady Chatterley's Lover*:

> The book as written is forthright and unashamed and honest. Only those to whom words can seem impure per se, or those to whom "certain subjects" cannot be mentioned in print though they are constantly mentioned in life, or those to whom the fundamental and moving facts of human experience are "nasty" could conclude that *Lady Chatterley's Lover*, as Lawrence wrote it, is obscene.
>
> For the test of obscenity in good law and in good sense is Judge Woolsey's test in the *Ulysses* case: dirt for dirt's sake. And in *Lady Chatterley's Lover* there is no dirt for dirt's sake. The purpose of the book is manifestly pure: pure as being the high purpose of a serious artist; pure as being the cleansing purpose of a social reformer who hates the devil himself.[1]

Accepting for the moment Mr. MacLeish's terms, are we being urged to think that while "dirt for dirt's sake" is clearly obscene and deplorable, dirt for art's sake is not obscene, is highly laudable? Here we seem to be on the brink of a formula, or, better, an aesthetic theory that might determine a proper place for obscenity in art, and thereby a principle, if not a rule, of decorum for the novel. But no! A second look reveals that Lawyer MacLeish (LL.B., Harvard, 1919) has tugged the coat-tails of Poet MacLeish and kept him back in the safe and sound territory of *U.S.* v. *One Book Entitled Ulysses*. MacLeish takes his stand upon a *legal*, not an aesthetic, definition of obscenity and as advocate draws from the legal definition the rhetorical fireworks that will dazzle the jury—in this case the American public—and secure a verdict favorable to his client.

This has been the typical strategy of the liberationists, ever since Judge Woolsey handed down his decision in the *Ulysses* case. Publishers, authors, and critics seem content, on the whole, to pass off the legal view of obscenity in literary art as having an aesthetic and moral sovereignty to which all must bow. And indeed, the *Ulysses* case is a landmark. In his thoroughgoing and judicious book, *The Smut Peddlers*, James J. Kilpatrick by no means overstates its far-reaching effect when he writes: "Whenever a publication having the slightest literary merit is brought before the court, the rule of *Ulysses* offers a highly persuasive voice in favor of holding the publication not obscene."[2] That is to say, both author and publisher of many a book may count on a fairly slight simulation of literary merit to give them protection in the Federal courts while a heavy content of fairly obvious pornographic appeal brings in the sales. And who would deny that the confidence of such authors and such publishers has not been justified by the results? From the nineteen-twenties on, the liberationists have steadily forced the issue, without too much damage to the material resources of authors and publishers. With the metropolitan press, in general, on their side, along with most of the literati—who are always pro-freedom and contra-censorship—they have felt assured of ultimate victory in the courts and of overriding all protest, organized or unorganized, in what Mencken used to call the Hinterland.

The legal victory of the Grove Press in the *Lady Chatterley* case a few years ago may seem to clinch the victory for utter liberation.[3] This case, indeed, with the corresponding *Lady Chatterley* case in England, may be a landmark notable as the *Ulysses* case of three decades ago. Undoubtedly the *Lady Chatterley* case inspired confidence in the publisher of the magazine *Eros*, which announced its appearance as "the result of recent court decisions that have realistically interpreted America's obscenity laws and that have given to this country a new breadth of freedom of expression." In a circular as forthright and unashamed as Mr. MacLeish could desire, the expensive new quarterly declared with bland explicitness: "We refer to decisions which have enabled the publication of such heretofore suppressed masterworks as 'Lady Chatterley's Lover.' *Eros* takes full advantage of this new freedom of expression. It is *the* magazine of sexual candor."

People who, for not the best reasons, seek to exploit rulings of the Federal courts are too ready to forget that those who pray the protection of the courts are also at the mercy of the courts. A court ruling does not have the broad prescriptive effect of a statute. A legal complaint against any publication brings up a different case, which may be heard under a less literary-minded judge than Woolsey and may eventuate in a new ruling. We do not have here the kind of "class action"

that, in the school segregation cases, permitted the U.S. Supreme Court to "legislate." Courts exist, after all, for the protection of the community, not for the promotion of literary experiments. Justice Frankfurter, dissenting with Jackson and Burton in the Winters case (1941), chided the permissive majority of the Supreme Court in sharp terms: "The essence of the Court's decision is that it gives publications which have 'nothing of any possible value to society' constitutional protection but denies to the states the power to prevent the grave evils to which, in their rational judgment, such publications give rise."[4] (The publication in this case—*Headquarters Detective*—had been convicted of obscenity in a New York state court.)

Furthermore, despite much "liberalizing" in recent decisions, Justice Brennan of the U. S. Supreme Court, delivering the opinion of the Court in the Roth-Alberts case, made it clear that obscenity is not to be held a kind of "free speech" coming under the protection of the First Amendment to the Constitution. Justice Brennan said:

> All ideas having even the slightest redeeming social importance . . . have the full protection of the guaranties, unless excludable because they encroach upon the limited area of more important interests. But implicit in the history of the First Amendment is the rejection of obscenity as utterly without redeeming social importance. . . . We hold that obscenity is not within the area of constitutionally protected speech of press.[5]

Nevertheless, it is equally clear that the present trend is quite the other way. Our novelists and their publishers are, by and large, assuming that obscenity is protected by the courts—indeed by the Supreme Court; or else—let us allow this as a possibility—they are assuming that there is no longer any such thing as obscenity. A peep into almost any current novel—

whether in the drugstore paperback display or at the regular bookstore counter—is evidence enough.

II

Like the publisher of *Eros*, the novelists of our time have not failed to "take advantage" of the new freedom allowed or invited by the *Ulysses* decision. Or it might be more realistic to say that the decision, combined with other trends, forced, or made it possible to force, a rather wide conformity to the particular kind of freedom practiced by Joyce. This is the familiar cycle in which the non-conformity of one social or artistic phase becomes in its turn a rigid conformity. The eminence of Joyce as artist had already been certified by the most influential critics of the *avant-garde*; T. S. Eliot, for example, writing in the *Dial* of November, 1923, had said: "I hold this book to be the most important expression which the present age has found."

Then why should not the gifted younger authors imitate the master? And why should not the much more numerous less gifted camouflage their deficiencies by an open parade of the Joycean type of dirt? Was it not guaranteed to be Art by both Court and Critic? If their novels were suppressed, as often happened, by the censors of Boston or Gopher Prairie or the Sahara of the Bozart, so much the better! The news, instantly headlined by the metropolitan press, meant sales by the thousands and hundreds of thousands in the uncensored areas. It was "good business." A "trend" was established, which publishers were not only using to advantage in their acceptances, but also, one might suspect, in their editorial advice to aspiring authors, even in their requirements. To be decorous in prose fiction—even to be more free in subject matter and vocabulary than Flaubert and Zola

was, quite possibly, to sign one's own literary death-warrant. It was comparable to parading in aristocratic silks and lace before the mob of righteous *citoyens et citoyennes* in 1793. One must now be *sans-culottes* in the twentieth-century Marxist proletarian or liberal way.

But this is pretty much the normal pattern of liberation—liberation of any sort—when it is imposed by the formula of what we have learned to call "permissiveness." It is actually one of the most drastic and corruptive forms of tyranny. For, because it comes to us first in the mask of liberty, its true nature may not be immediately discerned. When, after long implantation, it is at last discovered to be not liberty but tyranny, the intellectuals do not want to admit how greatly they have been deceived and in turn have deceived others. The vested interests naturally do not want to be disturbed. And others will find it difficult to understand what, after all, is wrong with tyranny. To recover true liberty then will seem hardly worth the pain and effort necessary. But without such recovery, the next phase can only be a tyranny harsher and more sweeping. Such is the affliction brought upon our modern life, in many deeply threatening forms, by "permissiveness," or the loosely sentimental concept of freedom as an unqualified right. And such is the moral and artistic chaos toward which the novel, as a specially privileged art form, for some time has been moving.

What is this special privilege? It is that, though the novel is certainly a public act, and in many ways affects the public interest, the author and his publisher expect, and now to a large extent are conceded, a freedom of language and of subject matter not conceded to other forms of public discourse, and not practiced by educational institutions, churches, legislatures, courts of law (except in certain criminal cases), newspapers, periodicals, and not commonly observed or allowed in either private or public occasions or in the ordinary course of daily life, whether in work or play. Some license of language has invaded the stage, but neither in opera, legitimate drama, movie, television, or radio is there any physically enacted parallel to certain scenes presented and language used by Joyce and Lawrence and their imitators. The only respectable, or at least tolerable, parallels worth mentioning would be found in medical and psychiatric clinics; or perhaps, with less color of legitimacy, those university courses of a clinical nature in which abnormalities and crimes are studied.

Edmund Fuller, in his *Man in Modern Fiction,* is one of the very few writers bold enough to state an issue that for our critics in general seems to be among the unmentionables.

> Because the legal regulations and standards of customary practice, which govern newspapers and periodicals, are more restrictive than those relating to books, there are frequent cases where it would be impossible . . . to quote fully and extensively from passages under debate. The critic may find himself prevented from exhibiting the thing against which he protests (or which he defends). In the same way, common restraints of taste and a due regard for public opinion (without any question of Nice Nellyism) limit and inhibit such textual quotation and discussion on the platform or for any public gathering unless in the relatively clinical tone of some classrooms. . . . *We have a literature today a considerable portion of which could not be read aloud in public without inviting either the police or the lynch rope.* (Italics added.)[6]

Inured though we are to the phenomena of liberation, it is still difficult to imagine a priest reading aloud to his parishioners, either for edification or denunciation, the scatological portions of the writings of Joyce, Lawrence, and numerous other novelists displayed on almost every bookstore counter. Nor does it seem likely that the Methodist Board of Education will soon recommend *Lady Chatterley's Lover* as suitable to be read—aloud or in silence—around the campfires of Methodist youth. In the English obscenity trial of Lawrence's book, Canon T. R. Milford, though testifying for the defense, shrank from any idea of public presentation:

> I think I would make a distinction here about the thing which is done in public—for instance I think it would be indecent to show scenes such as are described in this book on the cinema, still more to do them in public. I think the book is meant to be read by oneself. I should not think it suitable in general to read out in public. Secondly, I think it is incorrect to say we are invited in this book to make a third on any of these occasions. When these two people are together doing things which quite properly are done in private, as I see it and as I felt when I was reading that book, we are invited to identify ourselves with them and not to be a third in the party. I think those scenes would be offensive if someone else was there or someone had been observing from behind a tree.[7]

Here we may do well to notice that Mr. MacLeish, for all his praise of Lawrence's forthrightness and honesty, shows a delicate restraint when he comes to the main issue—that is, when he says that Lawrence, after all, is only using "one of the old familiar four-letter Anglo-Saxon words which we all know about but which the hypocrisy of censorship pretends we do not.[8] But in his approving letter-preface Mr. MacLeish does not quote a single example of Lawrence's use of the old familiar Anglo-Saxon words that he supposes we all know. In this restraint he follows the example of Judge Woolsey in the *Ulysses* decision. The Judge praised Joyce for using "old Saxon words" in "his honest effort to show exactly how the minds of his characters operate."[9] Yet the Judge did not quote a single illustrative passage or so much as mention a single one of these "old Saxon words." Similarly, in the English trial of *Lady Chatterley's Lover,* although the prosecution on occasion read to the jury sensationally lurid passages and did not fail to quote the "old Saxon words," Mr. Justice Byrne, in his charge to the jury, was as puritanical in vocabulary and reference as an Anthony Comstock could have wished. The eminent British critics who paraded as witnesses for the defense—Graham Hough, Helen Gardner, Dame Rebecca West, Kenneth Muir, *et alii*—showed an astounding Victorian capacity for avoiding, themselves, the obscenities that they were so heartily and happily commending in Lawrence.

There is, then, a decorum to be observed in prefaces, in court, in literary criticism at large—a decorum from which the novel is exempted. Apparently so. But we need to examine closely Canon Milford's remark that *Lady Chatterley's Lover,* in its questionable scenes, is not suitable "to read out in public."

In our time the novel is distinguished from poetry and drama by the fact that, whether or not it contains obscenities, it makes not the slightest pretense of being suitable "to read out in public." All contemporary novels, whether noble, trifling, realistic, surrealistic, or downright vile are definitely meant (in Canon Milford's phrase) "to be read by oneself." Who could conceive of a Joyce, a Faulkner, a Hemingway, or any of their ilk going on tour to read from their literary productions as Dickens once did? Prose fiction as a literary medium is now almost entirely dependent upon the printed book or periodical and is heavily conditioned by that circumstance. Novel and story belong to the lone and silent reader, locked in quiet submission to the voiceless page. More than ever before in our history, prose fiction is aimed at that reader, whose name is Multitude and who in abstract mass includes all elements of modern society. The author of this fiction is always distant from his Multitude and, as a person, is invisible to it, except as the meager ritual of the autograph party, the special college lecture, and other such managed appearances may allow. His act of imagination proposes to unroll before the mind's eye— and only before the mind's eye—a "drama" of real life that he hopes to make stronger in its impression than actual life itself, and more lasting. This is a large responsibility for him to undertake. It is *his* responsibility, first of all. But, once his art work is complete, he shares responsibility with his intermediaries who make him known to the Multitude: the publisher above all, the bookseller next, then the educator, and (let us never forget) the librarian. All of these intermediaries are most decidedly public characters.

Are we to hold that an art work of this nature, devised to be read and contemplated in individual privacy, is *not* a public act? And does it for this implied reason acquire some strange immunity from all ordinary taboos and well-established prohibitions, whether of custom, good taste, or law, against indecencies of language and narrative discourse? Canon Milford— whom I find identified as Master of the Temple and author of a Student Christian pamphlet entitled *The Philosophy of Sex*— seems to be saying that the novel does have this immunity.[10] According to the Canon's canon, then, it is all right—and presumably not sinful or corruptive—to accept Lawrence's deliberately sensual invitation to "identify" with Connie and Mellors in their adulterous and lewd conduct, *provided* the identification is achieved through a silent, private reading in a comfortable armchair or leafy nook.

In his shrewd perception of the true nature of the novel as an art medium, Canon Milford seems to have been a little more alert than his fellow-witnesses at the *Lady Chatterley* trial. Still, his moral position is a peculiar one for an eminent cleric to take. He does not think that Lawrence means for the reader to "make a third at the party." He himself would not wish to make such a third—to observe Connie and Mellors from behind a tree, for example. And, in his opinion, to watch a stage or screen representation of their completely ultra-ultra Lawrentian love-making would be to "make a third." But for the thousands of Lawrence's readers-in-seclusion, eyes glued to the seductive pages of *Lady Chatterley* in paperback—for these to "identify" with the adulterous pair is *not* harmful, in the Canon's opinion. He would not ban the book. He would recommend it. He is a mental, not a physical liberationist.

Somehow I cannot think that St. Paul would accept the Canon's critical theory. There is, for example, a text in I Corinthians 8 that reads: "But take heed lest by any means this liberty of yours become a stumblingblock to them that are weak."

Despite the *Ulysses* decision of 1933 and all the liberation that has since taken place, Canon Milford's critical theory is still far from being generally accepted by a great many people outside the select fraternity of literati, publishers, booksellers, and their special friends. To these non-literary outsiders the old rule of Chief Justice Cockburn in *Regina* v. *Hicklin* still is good morals if not current law. "I think the test of obscenity is this," the Chief Justice said, "whether the tendency of the matter charged as obscenity is to deprave and corrupt those whose minds are open to such immoral influences, and into whose hands a publication of this sort may fall."[11] Most deeply concerned are municipal officials in cities and towns throughout the country who must somehow deal with the continuous drive of commercial pornography, sometimes secret, often open, that also seeks the protection of the First Amendment and quite regularly advertises its wares as "Art." The record in Mr. Kilpatrick's *The Smut Peddlers* tells the story. The *Ulysses* case by no means stopped effort, persistent and numerous, to censor at the state or local level, through boycott, protest, or police action. Evidently there are large, relatively inarticulate portions of our society that stand out for a stricter code of behavior in print than our novelists observe. What firm assurance can the literati give such persons that the particular works for which they claim extreme license do *not* tend to "corrupt and deprave?" The literati have no answer to such a question. They have only assertions and opinions in which it is difficult to find any coherent body of principles. They stand on the assumed right of the artist to do as he pleases so long as he produces art. More and more their tendency is to move toward the hooliganism of Henry Miller in his recent manifesto, "I Defy You." That position is:

> One, that no valid definition of "obscenity" has ever been established; two, that no man, no group, no court of law has the right to tell us what we may or may not read; three, that no proof has ever been offered that the reading of so-called obscene books has demoralized its readers; four, that by supposedly protecting the youth of the land through restricting the freedom of adults to read what they please, we are burning down the house to roast the pig.
>
> And last but not least, what is wrong with obscenity, however it be defined? Do we live in a world so pure, so fragile, so delicate, that a little obscenity can wreck it? Does its use, whether in literature or action, endanger our lives?[12]

This is hooliganism in art—the adult parallel to teen-age vandalism, the litterbug's riotous enlistment on the side of all disorder, the house-wrecker's jubilant impulse to pour molasses into the piano and empty garbage on the sofa. We need notice here only one of Mr. Miller's points—his rhetorical question, "What is wrong with obscenity, however it be defined?"

If what is indecorous to society is to be praised as decorous by the artist, indeed made into a principle of art, then the modern alienation of the artist from society, even from civilization itself, becomes disastrous both for society and for art. It is the extreme inversion of value, the journey away from order into chaos, that both art and society must in the end reject. Yet it is this chaos toward which the artist, with a good deal of cynical assistance from the book trade and reviewing media, seems to be leading us in his championship of dirt for art's sake. Dirt for art's sake, the converse of the "dirt for dirt's sake" principle, is held to distinguish art from mere pornography. But the champion of dirt for art's sake wants no court to restrict him, no law to bind him, no critic or preacher to lecture him in the matter of just when, just how, the art of using dirt for art's sake actually is good art, true art. He wants to be sole judge of that issue. But the fact is that he asks to be guaranteed in his irresponsibility and not in his responsibility. There are historical reasons, not often discussed nowadays, for the modern artist's assumption that he, or his book, is not *morally* responsible for the obscene actions or language of his characters.

III

If obscenity is viewed as something merely phenomenal, to be recorded as a facet of human behavior, then indeed the question of "wrong" and "right" may be said not to arise. What is "wrong" with bacteria, rocket fuel, Uranium 235, or switchblade knives, considered merely as phenomena?

Mr. Miller's rhetorical question, "What is wrong with obscenity?" may lead us to the hidden sanction that lurks back of the libertine bravado of dirt for art's sake, or Obscenity as Art. The art involved here is not classic art, or Renaissance art, or romantic art, or the art of any of those pre-Darwinian periods from which the friends and disciples of Joyce and Lawrence like to cite misleading specimens of obscenity that they allege to be analogous to the practice of their own literary idols. It is post-Darwinian modern art that, slowly at first, but with increasing speed and thoroughness, has substituted for the classical sense of order and for Christian ethics its imitation of the skepticism and aloofness held to be proper in natural science. It is not the sanction of art, as known in former times, but the sanction of science that actually rationalizes the famous "objectivity" or assumed neutralism so much praised in modern prose fiction and so often recommended to young writers. This is the hidden factor in Judge Woolsey's decision in the *Ulysses* case. Joyce, said the judge, "sought to make a serious experiment in a new, if not wholly novel, genre"—that is, to represent a day in the life of persons of the lower middle class in Dublin in 1904—and for this purpose developed the technique with which we are familiar.

If Joyce did not attempt to be honest in developing the technique which he has adopted in "Ulysses" [declared Judge Woolsey] the result would be psychologically misleading and thus unfaithful to his chosen technique. Such an attitude would be artistically inexcusable.

It is because Joyce has been loyal to his technique and has not funked its necessary implications, but has honestly attempted to tell what his characters think about, that he has been the subject of so many attacks and that his purpose has been so often misunderstood and misrepresented. For his attempt sincerely and honestly to realize his objective has required him incidentally to use certain words which are generally considered dirty words and has led at times to what many think is a too poignant preoccupation with sex in the thoughts of his characters.[13]

In this passage, as elsewhere in the *Ulysses* decision, the terminology is prevalently scientific rather than literary, although the acquittal of *Ulysses* depended very heavily upon the establishment of the book as an art work of high merit. Hardly a hint of ethical issues enters into the judgment. With almost equal force the terms used might be applied to the publication, for the medical profession, of a psychopathic case study. The novel is, Judge Woolsey says, an example of "a new literary method for the *observation and description of mankind.*" (Italics added.)[14]

Exactly! How familiar the words are! In 1880, the year in which he also published his *Nana*, Emile Zola, in *Le Roman expérimental*, declared "*L'homme métaphysique est mort!*" and confidently predicted the triumph of scientific method in the novel and other art forms. "Doubtless the wrath of Achilles, the love of Dido will endure among our eternally beautiful images," Zola conceded. "But we need to analyze wrath and love, and to see just how those passions function in human beings. . . . The experimental method [i.e., the laboratory method], in literature as in the sciences, is about to define those natural phenomena, both individual and social, for which, up to now, metaphysics has given only irrational and supernatural explanations."[15] The role of the novelist, in short, is that of the detached observer. A modern Dido, if available, is of no more interest to him than a Nana. But since a prostitute is better adapted to clinical observation than a queen, he will generally find it convenient to observe and describe Nana.

It can be argued that Zola's manifesto in *Le Roman expérimental* and his further applications of naturalistic dogma may be taken as a rationalization of his own earlier performance in such works as *L'Assommoir* or, in general, as "showmanship" and self-advertisement. But, like other dubious adventures in advertising, Zola's manifesto has had long-lasting effects. Zola preferred "Naturalism" to "Realism," Mr. F. W. J. Hemmings points out, "mainly because of the connexion immediately established with the natural sciences, and also because 'realism' had associations with an earlier school, that of Champfleury and Duranty. . . ." Mr. Hemmings goes on to say: "It was, of course, the constant reiteration of the word, and its remorseless application to every branch of art and sphere of knowledge, that gave the word its propaganda force. It convinced nobody, for it was not an argument; it impressed thousands."[16]

It impressed, and has continued to impress often in ways hidden or unacknowledged, because the drift of the times has so long favored an uncritical deference toward natural science as authoritarian, indeed as the arbiter of truth in great disputed issues. But a writer would not need to have read Zola to become, in principle, a naturalist. Any urban street corner, the front page of his newspaper, the howl of the police siren, the flicker of the newsreel, the chatter of radio and television, the aimless movement of the faceless crowd, even, alas, the Sunday preachments of his pastor may thrust upon him the unrefuted—though not irrefutable—suspicion that metaphysical man must indeed be dead.

Zola sanctified his own "objective" type of realism by calling it naturalism. The modern novelist no longer thinks of his writing as naturalism. He may be realist, impressionist, expressionist, symbolist, or some variation or combination of these.

All the same he operates under the sanctions of naturalism and makes use of the license that it affords him. In the diagnostic clinic that is his novel he proposes to treat all his patients alike—saint or sinner, prince or pimp. Actually he is rather selective in his choice of patients and almost any day will prefer the unvirtuous woman, even the prostitute, to the virtuous woman. His taste runs to low-grade characters. These submit more readily to clinical examination, and publishers claim that they bring more sales. Heredity as causal determinant no longer gets the emphasis that Zola gave it. For heredity brings up the matter of race, and science (he erroneously thinks) has told him not to think about *that,* lest he entertain "prejudice." Environment still counts heavily—but only if it is ugly, confining, or depressing. Of fear, hunger, and sex—the three instinctive "drives" once used as causal motifs—sex is now most important, indeed has swallowed all. Out of this general pattern, too, comes the license to commit any kind of enormity with language, so long as it is, in Judge Woolsey's words, "frank, honest, and sincere." The low-grade characters of the typical modern novel cannot be expected to talk or behave like Jane Austen's people, or Fenimore Cooper's.

Can we not, then, expect more discretion and taste in the high-grade characters? Not at all. For the high-grade characters, if they appear, must act like low-grade characters. As sophisticates, they must be democratic, for that is the pose of the age—or in the current idiom, its "posture" or "stance." They may be represented, indeed, as more knowledgeable in dirt and eroticism than their ignorant counterparts. Why not? They have read James Joyce, maybe Krafft-Ebing, surely Freud, or at least have had a course in abnormal psychology at Vassar or Harvard. As for the middle-grade characters, they can be ignored, since they probably belong to the John Birch Society or are "segregationists."

If it be argued—in the interest of realism—that high-grade characters do not in actual life use four-letter words, either in public or in private, as freely as is represented, the modern novelist has his answer. "What about their minds?" he queries darkly. "What about their streams-of-consciousness and especially their subconsciousness?" Granted that they will not necessarily be scatological at a formal dinner party and other polite occasions, what are they *thinking* at almost any time?

Thus the Freudian psychology, for the modern novelist, opens every door that Queen Victoria's Darwin, Zola's Claude Bernard, and even our more recent atombusters left discreetly closed. We must have in mind not only the regular doors—which after all open only on bathrooms and bedrooms—but the trapdoors in the cellar where the imprisoned complexes and inhibitions have been locked up. Since Sigmund Freud can pass for some sort of scientist—if psychology is a science—the practicing novelist can make shift to claim for his obscenities a direct sanction that Darwin's biology and Claude Bernard's medicine did not, in truth, extend to Zola's naturalism. If the novelist is *frankly* (not furtively?) scatological, *honestly* (not dishonestly—that is, erroneously? cheatingly?) obscene, and *sincerely* (not commercially?) erotic, then, along with Joyce the Great, he is passing Judge Woolsey's legal-critical test. He is using dirt for art's sake, not "dirt for dirt's sake." He is portraying "objective reality." And "objective," even more than "reality," is one of the principal god-words of the modern regime.

To explore the nature of this objectivity in all its applications would carry this discussion far afield. But at least we can ask whether the objective method affords the novelist any firm principle of selection that will enable him to decide when obscene matter (in language or action) is artistically justifiable and when it is to be excluded as inartistic.

The answer to this question plainly is: No such firm principle has been established by the objective method, and no such principle can be established. For the materials and procedures of the art of fiction do not submit to any laws comparable to the laws of physics, chemistry, biology, and the like. The novelist's "objectivity" is clearly not the laboratory objectivity of the scientist. It is not even a plausible equivalent of that austere mental attitude. It is a rhetorical fiction, a technical device. Thinking of it in favorable terms, we might consider it a mask that the artist puts on in order to reduce his natural partisanship toward his own creations. It helps him to practice a salutary degree of neutralism toward his "observations" and also toward his imaginings and contrivings. From Flaubert and Henry James on down to Conrad, Lawrence, Hemingway, and their successors, this device has brought about an increasingly skillful application of the "limited point of view," with its sharp focus, its intense effects, and its imitation in "discriminated scenes" of the dramatic effects of the stage play. One general result has been a remarkable development of the "form" of the novel, and almost any young first novelist can claim—if he condescends to permit a comparison that to him will be only amusing—that he knows more about *how* to write a novel than Scott, Thackeray, and their contemporaries ever did.

But with this development, unfortunately, has come the notion that the artistic responsibility of the novelist ends when he has given his work the "form" that he thinks it ought to have. For the "content" he is not responsible—not if through right technique he has *discovered*

the "form" belonging to this "content." If the discovered "form" does not automatically screen out certain obscenities in the content, then the novelist's conclusion must be that the obscenities belong to the form and, as art, are not to be impugned, but stubbornly defended.

That is what seems to be implied in Mr. Mark Schorer's notable essay, "Technique As Discovery," though he nowhere takes up the problem of decorum. This essay gives us the ultimate refinement in critical theory of the Flaubertian-Jamesian objective method. "Technique alone," writes Mr. Schorer, "objectifies the materials of art; hence technique alone evaluates those materials. This is the axiom which demonstrates itself so devastatingly whenever a writer declares . . . that he cannot linger with technical refinements."[17]

It seems rather unusual for an axiom to demonstrate itself or to be demonstrated. Nevertheless Mr. Schorer demonstrates this axiom by comparing some novelists who do not "linger with technical refinements" with those who do. For example, the sociological, crusading H. G. Wells of *Tono-Bungay* and the early and decorous, but technically careless Lawrence of *Sons and Lovers* are compared with the James Joyce of *A Portrait of the Artist as a Young Man* and *Ulysses*. The latter novel is, for Mr. Schorer, "the most brilliant technical operation ever made in fiction." He says:

> If we read *Ulysses* with more satisfaction than any other novel of the century, it is because its author held an attitude toward technique and the technical scrutiny of subject matter which enabled him to order, within a single work and with superb coherence, the greatest amount of our experience.[18]

Granting that Joyce's command of the objective method enabled him to "order" in *Ulysses* some fairly sizable chunks of human experience—rather low-grade experience on the whole—are we not enti-tled to ask Mr. Schorer some questions about how the technique works? For ex-ample, what, exactly, is the nature of the "satisfaction" that "we" are supposed to derive from Joyce's continual and indeed tedious "discovery," through his tech-nique, of the fecal, sexual, and certainly often pornographic obsessions of Leo-pold Bloom and certain other characters? How did Joyce's technique "evaluate" this material so that "we" can take it as a good art and not as offensively obscene trash? And—to name some novelists not men-tioned by Mr. Schorer—would Scott's *Bride of Lammermoor,* Balzac's *Cousine Bette,* Dos-toevsky's *The Possessed,* Thackeray's *Vanity Fair* really have been better novels in every way if the secrets of technique known to Joyce could somehow have been revealed to these eminent outmoded authors?

Nothing in Mr. Schorer's brilliant essay answers such questions. Indeed, they are avoided. What Mr. Schorer gives us is his apotheosis of the Flaubertian-Jamesian method, under which the novelist can manage as never before to *organize* his fiction without seeming to reveal himself as the story-teller, and, while so doing, to avoid, or seem to avoid, forcing any sort of moral or metaphysic upon his reader. The more we examine this kind of neu-tralism, the more we are likely to perceive that it is but a thin disguise for the uneasy skepticism or the inner moral uncertainty characteristic of our age. Joyce himself gives the secret away in the sentence, remodeled from Flaubert, that he puts into the mouth of young Stephen Dedalus in *A Portrait of the Artist:* "The artist, like the God of the creation, remains within or behind or above his handiwork, invis-ible, refined out of existence, indifferent, paring his fingernails." This is wonder-fully skillful rhetoric; but the cold Joycean sneer of the final phrase suggests very well the degree of irresponsibility in-

tended. It is a modern novelist's way of saying: "The public be damned!"

The modern critic, defending the ob-jective method, is obliged to be more chaste in his language, since he does not have the privileges of the novelist. But he is fully as irresponsible in those rare in-stances where we find him disposed to face the issue. Mr. Schorer, as author of the Introduction to the Grove Press unex-purgated edition of *Lady Chatterley's Lover,* avoids a direct and explicit defense of obscenity, yet argues in general terms that the novel is realism of a sublimated kind, indeed is "symbolic":

> The progress from the first through the third version of *Lady Chatterley* is the history of an effort to make the events at once maximumly plausible in realistic terms and maximumly meaningful in psychic terms. The result in the third version is a novel in a solid and sustained social context, with a clear and happily developed plot, in which the characters function fully and *the author allows them to speak for themselves;* at the same time it is a novel in which "every bush burns," and which *in itself* finally forms one great symbol. . . ."[19] (Italics added.)

This amounts to a claim that obscenity is to be excused or tolerated both on the ground that it is realistic and on the ground that "symbolism" may sublimate away its viciousness.

But if neither custom nor rule of art can any longer tell the novelist *what* is obscene and what is not, or *when* the obscene may with artistic propriety be used in literature, and if the novelist is also accorded the broad license of the objective method and with it the libertine vagaries of symbolism, then he has little left to guide him but his temperament, and we his readers are at the mercy of that temperament.

Custom, among the literati at least, has offered less and less guidance and control in the thirty years since the *Ulysses* decision. As to rule of art, it is hard to find anything explicit set forth by the masters of modern criticism. A rule of art is perhaps implied in Mr. Schorer's strangely worded appeal to realism as a canon: "maximumly plausible in realistic terms." This is the rule, or argument, of verisimilitude. The four-letter words used by Mellors in *Lady Chatterley* (especially those addressed to Connie in the love scenes and in the repulsive letter with which the book ends) are to be considered "proper" because they are in character; Mellors is the kind of man that would use those words. So the typical argument would run. But the argument of verisimilitude is the feeblest weapon in the modern aesthetic arsenal. The modern movement in all the arts has been steadily directed away from verisimilitude. To claim both the sanction of hard, coarse, matter-of-fact realism (actually naturalism) with its reliance on science, and also the sanction of highly refined symbolism, as Mr. Schorer does, is not convincing. The "reality" of realism (or naturalism) and the "reality" of symbolism are not so easily reconciled.

The British critic, Mr. Graham Hough, more shrewdly says that Mellors' four-letter words "are *meant* to show his frank carnality and vivifying power." (Italics added.)[20] But to discover what Lawrence *meant* to achieve, in this and other particulars, is to discover how fully we are at the mercy of Lawrence's temperament. Lawrence *meant*, this excellent critic says, to convert the public to his own "belief" in sheer sensuality as a purifying force, and the conviction that somehow it can become the regenerating force for society as a whole.[21] From various other sources, including Lawrence's direct pronouncements, we know that Lawrence thought of himself as crusading for the open and general use of the "four-letter words" in the naïve hope that mere frankness would automatically end vileness. Can any art

be truly great that is deeply infected by such folly?

If Lawrence's temperament has its dangerous aspects, Joyce's temperament is still more dangerous—dangerous, that is, to art as well as to society—because the coldness, the dry aloofness, the seeming logicality of his technique conceals, better than Lawrence's, the obsessive predilections of Joyce the man. But the predilections are there, and are hardly less than satanic. His contemporary, John Cowper Powys, though on the whole favorable to Joyce, long ago noted Joyce's abnormal inclination toward the pornographic and obscene:

> Sex, in Joyce's writings, is not invariably accompanied by pleasure, but it is invariably accompanied by the presence of something repulsive and excremental . . . It remains harsh, dry, discordant, erudite, and obsessed by a sort of ice-cold, insane obscenity. . . .
>
> What in English writers—since the eighteenth century—is sentimental, what in French writers is voluptuous and ironical, becomes, the moment Joyce touches it, associated with the school dormitory and the school latrine. . . .[22]

If any confirmation is needed of what Powys wrote, thirty years ago, one has only to read passages of some of Joyce's own letters to his wife Nora in which he indulges himself (to use his words) in "wild filth and obscenity." In a recent critical study, Mary T. Reynolds notes that passages in these exceedingly candid letters "will be found reproduced both in wording and in context in *Ulysses*."[23] Miss Reynolds makes it clear that "erotic stimulation" was the purpose of the letters. But we hardly need such evidence to convince us of this all but psychotic feature of Joyce's temperament. No technique or combination of techniques, no symbolic system, no smooth pretense of objectivity can hide from us that the streams-of-consciousness of Stephen Dedalus and of Leopold and Molly Bloom are portions of that *Cloaca Maxima* which flowed in the mind of James Joyce.

IV

What of the future, with the untrammeled artistic temperament as the judge of decorum, in a time of loose manners and loose morals, sensationalism, vast confusions and equally vast complacencies? Predictions hardly seem worthwhile. The novelists and their ever articulate followers, the critics, show little concern. On the legal side the decisions in the *Ulysses* case, the *Lady Chatterley* case, and subsequent less prominent cases apparently fill the literati and their publishers with blithe assurance. Like the ebullient ex-colonials of the Congo and other liberated regions and tribes, they seem to prefer the shibboleth of freedom to any notion of self-restraint. Will they then allow, even encourage the cult of literary obscenity to proceed without any check other than what may be encountered and (they may suppose) overcome in the courts of law? Certainly no other course, at this writing, is being advocated by notable literary figures, or influential societies of authors or scholars.

It is true that Mr. Wayne Booth in a final brief chapter of *The Rhetoric of Fiction*, expresses some faint qualms about the morality of "impersonal narration." "Is there no limit to what we will praise, provided it is done with skill?" he asks, after commenting on a technically admirable novel about a homicidal maniac.[24] But his answer is evasive. And Graham Hough, after a critical defense of *Lady Chatterley*, adds this: "Lawrence was partly wrong, all the same. There are arcana in nature as well as in religion, and nothing that affects the emotional life as intimately and individually as sex can or ought ever to be fully 'in the open.' "[25] But present

tendencies in our prose fiction threaten to pass all limits and leave no arcana. Deterioration and decline of the novel as an art form must surely be the penalty, in the end, for such indulgence—a license which would be nothing less than art for dirt's sake, as indeed it already is in many obvious instances. But no society can for very long harbor such evil and survive. Censorship, then, would be the deplorable fate toward which the liberationists are hustling us. Much better would be the rise of a new fiction to supplant the now wearisome old, and of writers and publishers wise and bold enough to assert the moral responsibility of the artist to his public and to posterity.

NOTES

[1] D. H. Lawrence, *Lady Chatterley's Lover*. With an Introduction by Mark Schorer, New York: Grove Press, 1959.

[2] James Jackson Kilpatrick, *The Smut Peddlers*. Avon paperback edition, p. 119. In Part II, Chapter 1 of this indispensable book (published originally by Doubleday & Co.), Mr. Kilpatrick reviews not only the entire course of the *Ulysses* case but also several more recent cases.

[3] *Grove Press, Inc.* v. *Christenberry* (175 F. Supp. 488—S.D.N.Y. 1959).

[4] See Kilpatrick, 126–130 for a discussion of the Winters case. (*Winters* v. *New York*, 333 U.S. 507, 1948).

[5] Quoted, Kilpatrick, 105. *See Roth* v. *United States* (354 U.S. 476, 1957).

[6] Edmund Fuller, *Man in Modern Fiction: Some Minority Opinions on Contemporary American Writing*, New York: Random House, 1958, pp. 67–68.

[7] *The Trial of Lady Chatterley: Regina* v. *Penguin Books Ltd.* C. H. Rolph, ed., Penguin Books, 1961, p. 145.

[8] *Lady Chatterley's Lover*, Grove Press edition, p. v.

[9] James Joyce, *Ulysses*, Random House edition, 1934, p. xii.

[10] *The Trial of Lady Chatterley*, p. 145.

[11] Kilpatrick, *op. cit.* p. 107.

[12] Henry Miller, "I Defy You," *Playboy Magazine*, January, 1962, p. 102.

[13] Joyce, *op. cit.* pp. xi–xii.

[14] *Ibid.* p. xiv.

[15] Emile Zola, *Le Roman expérimental*, Paris, 1923, p. 52.

[16] F. W. J. Hemmings, *Emile Zola*, Oxford: The Clarendon Press, 1953, p. 120.

[17] Mark Schorer, "Technique As Discovery," *Hudson Review* I (1948), p. 73.

[18] *Ibid.*, p. 80.

[19] Lawrence, *op. cit.* p. xxvii.

[20] Graham Hough, *The Dark Sun: A Study of D. H. Lawrence*, New York: The Macmillan Co., 1957, p. 161.

[21] *Ibid.* pp. 151–152.

[22] John Cowper Powys, "Modern Fiction," in *Sex in the Arts: A Symposium*. Edited by John Francis McDermott and Kendall B. Taft, New York: Harper & Bros., 1932, pp. 47–48.

[23] Mary T. Reynolds, "Joyce and Nora: The Indispensable Countersign." *Sewanee Review* LXXII (Winter, 1964), pp. 28, 40, 60.

[24] Wayne Booth, *The Rhetoric of Fiction*; Chicago: 1961, p. 196.

[25] Hough, *op. cit.*, 160 f.

[IX, Winter 1964–65, 34–48]

71

Pater Revisited

AUSTIN WARREN

Austin Warren *(1899–1986), an outstanding American scholar–critic and man of letters, resided in Providence, Rhode Island. Professor of English at the University of Michigan, his best-known books included* Richard Crashaw *(1939),* Theory of Literature *(in collaboration with René Wellek; 1942),* Rage for Order *(1948),* New England Saints *(1956), and* Connections *(1970). While studying at Harvard in the early 1920s, he came under the influence of Irving Babbitt, about whom he subsequently wrote with deep insight and sympathy. Warren also taught at the University of Iowa and Boston University, was a senior fellow of the Kenyon School of English and the Indiana School of Letters, and was a member of the editorial boards of* Modern Age, American Literature, *and* The New England Quarterly.

LET ME BEGIN this review with some intellectual autobiography of my own. Young,—when I was 22,—I enrolled in Irving Babbitt's course at Harvard, "Rousseau and Romanticism"; did so knowing nothing of Babbitt's classical and austere "New Humanism." Regarding myself as an idealist, and identifying Romanticism with idealism I was bewildered and shocked to find Babbitt, who so obviously stood for all that was sound and orthodox, attacking Romanticism.

I became a fervent and dogmatic convert to the New Humanism; yet the very next year, when another great teacher, less vigorous but more sensitive than Babbitt, introduced me to Walter Pater's *Marius the Epicurean,* saying, with flattering inaccuracy, that he was sure I already knew and cared for the book, I bought and read it with ardor, unaware, it seems, of any possible dichotomy between Babbitt and the aesthete, Pater. And at about the same time, meeting with the earlier books of George Santayana, I greatly admired his "Life of Reason" series, especially *Reason in Society* and *Reason in Religion,*—books which appeared to me to be stating essentially the same position as Babbitt's, but giving Humanism a more subtle, sophisticated, and civilized form.

In making these identifications I was naive. Babbitt, for whom both men would have been aesthetes, hedonists, and decadents,—and naturalists in the bargain, could have tolerated neither,—would have regarded their views as all the more dangerous because so refined, so gildedly corrupt. For me, however, a young "idealistic" American, all three seemed opponents of the current American world of barbarism, crudeness, and vulgarity; they represented the classics, Greek and Latin (my major in college) and philosophy and religion against the unculture of President Eliot's elective system; they represented the Humanities against the ever ascending sway of the natural and social sciences; they opposed technology and gadgets and industrialism; they were spokesmen for the archaic values which were everywhere being threatened. In making for the three men this broad front of affirmation and rejection I was not wholly misguided or naive.

All three of these generalists I have revisited in my old age, pleased after professional retirement, to return to these writers of life-wisdom, and world-per-spective, and general culture, these writ-ers whom the specialized cares and concerns of middle life force us to neglect. Especially, for the length of a review, I address myself to Walter Pater (1839–1894), who, after long being out of fashion and the attention of readers, scholars, and critics, has recently been receiving heed more expert than my own.

Pater was *the* philosophical teacher of the 1890 generation of young British aesthetes—of Yeats, Lionel Johnson, Ar-thur Symons, A. C. Benson, and Oscar Wilde. It was Wilde who, in his "Decay of Lying" and "The Critic as Artist" (both contained in his book, *Intentions*), with aphoristic brilliance and boldness, pop-ularized Pater's subtle and recondite crit-ical doctrines; it was Wilde who, by his flamboyant postures and the scandal of his life, trial, and condemnation, cast shadows of suspicion on the celibate don and his first book, *The Renaissance.*

Pater's *Renaissance* (1873) is a collection of separately written and published essays, all little masterpieces of what their author calls "aesthetic criticism." Concerned chiefly with Italian painters of fifteenth-century Italy, but also with poetry, and with two essays on scholar-critics, Pico della Mir-andola and Winckelmann, these essays take cognizance of historical scholarship

and art history, yet they centrally aim at rendering in words the impressions of one perceptive observer and his search for a formula which shall express the essence of another man's work. This is literary impressionism of the highest or-der: delicate, subtle, meticulously and beautifully written,—written slowly, and to be read slowly, attending to, bearing down upon, each word. The writing, albeit so sedulous, is yet fresher, less weary, than any of Pater's subsequent work.

What attracted prime interest to the book as it first appeared, however, was the "Conclusion" (1868), a meditative es-say which begins by characterizing the solipsism in which each of us is said to live, our impressions being but those of "the individual in his isolation, each mind keeping as a solitary prisoner its own dream of a world"; and it ends with the hedonistic counsel to seize the moment. Pater is not in general an aphoristic writer, but one aphorism remembered by any who know Pater's name comes from his "Conclusion." It reads, "To burn always with this hard gemlike flame, to maintain this ecstasy, is success in life." (The word *success* is here a jarring note: it did not then have the vulgar commercial sense it now connotes; substitute the word *end*.)

This "Conclusion," said to be immoral and quoted with appended warnings by fellow Oxford dons and ecclesiastics, Pater withdrew from the second edition of his book, not to recant its doctrine but, as he said when he reissued it, to call attention to his next book, *Marius the Epicurean*, in which he had "dealt more fully . . . with the thoughts suggested by the 'Conclu-sion.' "

Marius the Epicurean: His Sensations and Ideas, harder to read than its predecessor, is the central achievement of his life, a masterpiece of a highly specialized sort. It is at once a historical novel, and a novel of ideas. Its titular hero is a young Roman aristocrat who is for a time a secretary to Marcus Aurelius; his purely contemplative life is traced between the ages of (approximately) 18 and 35. In the course of the book, he passes from the pagan country religion of the old Romans to Epicureanism, then considers (but finally rejects) Stoicism, and dies on the verge of the Christian and Catholic religion, indeed, a kind of martyr to the faith he had never overtly accepted. This strange book is almost without action, characters, visual description, or audible speech (the discourse is all reported)—concerned almost exclusively with "sensations" (sensuous impressions) and "ideas" (philosophies). The book is written in Pater's highly mannered style, a style anything but familiar or idiomatic and conversational, a *written style* and furthermore one in which English is written as a "learned language"; a style not matter of factly and rationally lucid but, instead, intuitive and suggestive, one for distinctions, discriminations, qualifications.

II

After a half-century of virtual oblivion, Pater is currently enjoying a revival. One of the first signs of this was an excellent chapter on him in René Wellek's judicious, and judicial, *History of Modern Criticism* (Volume II, 1965); Harold Bloom has a sympathetic essay in *Ringers in the Tower* (1967). Also in 1967 appeared fine monographs on him by Gordon MacKenzie and Gerald Monsman, who made his first appearance with *Pater's Imaginary Portraits*. This is a study of the genre to which most of his work belongs,—the meditative narrative in which the leading character draws his substance from Pater himself, while the description sets it in a past historical period and place. *Marius* is such a portrait; the unfinished *Gaston de*

Latour, set in the France of Montaigne, is another; there is a whole volume of shorter *Imaginary Portraits,* one of them of a young Dutch aristocrat, a disciple of Spinoza's. The chief concern of Monsman's first book, however, is to trace the mythic archetypes which he sees as underlying these portraits. In this work Monsman seems to reflect, sensitive exegete that he is, the influence of Northrop Frye, whose *Anatomy of Criticism* (1957) gave rise to a vogue for mythic and archetypal criticism.

Now in 1980 Monsman has published another, actually his third, book on Pater, Pater's *Art of Autobiography,* a brilliant, subtle (and, I think, partly wrongheaded) treatment of the titular theme. Monsman appears now under the influence of the French Structuralism and Deconstructionism currently vended by the literary departments of Johns Hopkins and Yale: the relevant names among the critics are Barthes, Hillis Miller, Derrida and De Man. For me, an old New Critic, these are not hallowed names; and I have not found their works illuminating, or, for the most part, even intelligible. For me, as for my generation of critics, the center of literary study is the text; but for these others, the text is just what is to be deconstructed in order that one can center on the soul of the author; and the business of the critic is to create his own creation on the pretext of criticizing: "The Critic as Artist" was Wilde's formula for it. Yet, though highly dubious of Monsman's method, I find his use of it the most sensitive and persuasive specimen of its kind with which I have met; and, having followed up his bibliographical leads, which are rather concealed than displayed, I can attest to his mastery of all Pater's writing and the Pater "literature."

Monsman rightly sees Pater's work as a protest against any literature which tries to offer the illusion of life, against Realism and Naturalism, against even Henry

James's attempt to erase the author. Pater's writing flaunts its character of being art and not life: writing and not speech; and emphasizes the presence of the author. The most striking precursor of this kind of work seems to me *Tristram Shandy,* though Sterne appears to be mentioned neither by Pater nor by Monsman. This kind of writing leads to Proust, Joyce, and Virginia Woolf, whose unacknowledged ancestor Monsman sees Pater to be: "these ultra-reflexive writers whose fictional worlds invariably lead back to the generative activity of art itself." And so, Pater's writings, "rather than attempting a veridical illusion of life, . . . affirm the autonomy of their artifice."

Of Monsman's five chapters and Introduction, I recommend especially the Introduction and Chapter I, "Criticism as Creation." And there is certainly a sense in which criticism is, and must be, a form of autobiography: so soon as one goes beyond facts and quotations (and even both of these have to be selected, and by someone, and from some point of view), one must interpret. A sensitive critic writes about his author only what he knows not only from outside but from inside as well, by empathy, by overlap. All we can ask is that objective information and subjective insight be clearly differentiated, that the reader of the criticism can discern on what bases judgments are offered.

What I must totally reject is the attempt, in Chapters 3 and 4, at a post-Freudian explanation of why Pater was never able to complete his second novel, *Gaston de Latour,*—his supposed sense of guilt at having willed, somehow, the death of his father (which occurred when Pater was an infant), of his mother, who died when he was fourteen, and, much later, of his brother (and "sibling rival"), William.

Less fanciful reasons could be offered for the abandonment of *Gaston,* such as the other projects which began to engage and engross Pater—for example, his *Greek Studies* of myth and sculpture, and his *Plato and Platonism* (regarded by Pater as his greatest book). And consider this: Pater had originally planned a trilogy of novels on the same pattern as *Marius,* with the protagonist in each a philosophical or at least contemplative young man, a spectator of life, a figure drawn from its author but set against differing backgrounds of time and place, the latest to be of nineteenth-century England. It is likely that he found himself, when halfway through the second of his series, already weary of the project—already aware of the obvious repetition, the unavoidable monotony.

It is hard to come to final terms with Monsman's 1980 book. I find it difficult to summarize, to state its burden, still more to criticize: it is delicate, subtle, and stimulating, but also hesitant and evasive. Denis Donoghue has called his perceptive review of it (in the *New York Review of Books* for May 14, 1981) "Hide and Seek"—though presumably applying that phrase not only to Monsman but (quite justly) also to Pater. What, finally, does Monsman think of Pater? Does he like him? or admire him? identify with him? I can't say. As for Pater, did his Marius cease being an Epicurean, and become something else, or just (as the central chapter of the novel, "Second Thoughts," suggests) refine upon his hedonism, distinguishing between lower (sensual) and higher (intellectual) pleasure? Did Pater himself, who had been, like Ruskin, one of those boys who play at being priests; who had then a period of mocking disbelief (as one can learn from Thomas Wright's 1908 life of Pater): did he then return to the Church? He did aesthetically, certainly, but did he intellectually, and in faith? What does Monsman think?

Pater's own writings, for which Monsman offers a provocative (as well as elusive) approval, have left me with very mixed and conflicting feelings. I cannot doubt, however, that he is a strangely impressive writer in his low-pitched, slow, languid insistence. For the English-speaking (or reading) world, he remains *the* unique aesthete. His own derivations are almost entirely Continental—Winckelmann, Goethe, Heine, Baudelaire, Gautier, Hugo. Though English, Pater was extraordinarily uncompromising. If, in the latter part of his not long life (he died at 55), he softened the expression of views generally offensive, yet he never recanted. He is a hero of vocal passivity and articulate spectatorship.

[XXV, Fall 1981, 407–410] Review of *Walter Pater's Art of Autobiography*, by Gerald Monsman, New Haven: Yale University Press, 1980.

[72]

Dostoevsky—Our Contemporary

SERGEI LEVITZKY

Sergei Levitzky (1909–1985), a Russian critic and philosopher, was born in Latvia. He received the Ph.D. degree from Charles University, Prague, where he was a pupil of the Russian philosopher Nicolas Lossky. In 1945 he fled to Western Germany, living for four years in displaced persons camps; there he wrote his first book, The First Principles of an Organic Philosophy *(1948). His celebrated book* The Tragedy of Freedom *(1958), written in Russian, enjoys great popularity among Russian dissidents. V. V. Zenkovsky, author of* A History of Russian Philosophy, *describes Levitzky as continuing the philosophical thought of Sergius Bulgakov, Nicolas Berdyaev, and S. L. Frank.*

A WHOLE CENTURY separates us from the date of Dostoevsky's death. Many people perhaps think that Dostoevsky belongs to the eternal stars in our literary horizon, stars which merit great honor but which are out of touch with our modern predicament. No opinion could be more erroneous. Dostoevsky was a reflector of eternal values. Yet, this fact alone would not suffice to call him our contemporary. What makes him our contemporary is the prophetic quality of his genius. Dostoevsky was a prophet of a spiritual malaise that still devours the body of our epoch. It is well known that he predicted with amazing accuracy the Bolshevik revolution. Still more important, however, is the fact that he envisioned in the embryo of Bolshevism the monster which it later turned into. This foresight should not be interpreted as only political. Dostoevsky penetrated deeply into the spiritual roots of evil, which manifested itself in the political domain. He did not find a name for this degeneration, but he discerned that the primary root of evil lies in what may be called humanistic atheism, the denial of God in the name of man. And, because of his artistic intuition, he showed convincingly that the noble and in certain respects humanistic atheism of Ivan Karamazov unavoidably degenerates into the mean and inhumanistic atheism of Smerdyakov, the most repulsive creation of Dostoevsky's prophetic fantasy.

Like most prophets, Dostoevsky was not duly understood in his lifetime. This is especially valid in regard to his nineteenth-century critics, who failed to appreciate the true measure of his genius. Here is what Dostoevsky himself wrote on this subject: "The critics neither like nor cherish me. Only the readers in Russia love me." Indeed, the reading public reacted enthusiastically to Dostoevsky's works. But the critics remained in the dusty rear in this respect. Dostoevsky's contemporary, the philosopher Strakhov, who had

817

no special liking for him, but who some-times paid him due respect, wrote in a letter to Leo Tolstoy—this letter was writ-ten under the fresh impact of the news of the death of Dostoevsky: "He stood quite apart from most of literature, which was inimical to him, and he spoke about what was regarded as temptation or folly. But he alone was worth the whole of literature. It was such a sight that I stood by in amazement." One hastens to add that by "literature" Strakhov meant the critics. And his mention of "temptation and folly" was a paraphrase of Saint Paul.

Literary critics, contemporaries of Dos-toevsky, castigated him for the excessive length of his novels, for the poverty of his natural descriptions, and particularly for the pathological nature of his char-acters. The last accusation continues to be heard in our time. That Dostoevsky's characters do show a certain amount of mental imbalance cannot be disputed. But it is a highly interesting imbalance. What is disturbing is that his critics failed to appreciate his experimental creativity. The outstanding literary critic of the early twentieth century, Dmitri Merejkowski, the author of the first comprehensive study of Dostoevsky, gave, in my opinion, the best reply to these allegations. Merej-kowski compared Dostoevsky's novels to experiments under unusually high tem-peratures. Thus, although iron is nor-mally solid, under great heat it melts and can even evaporate. Now, would it be correct to claim that liquid iron behaves "abnormally"? No, liquid iron behaves quite normally under abnormal condi-tions. Had Merejkowski lived in our time, he would probably change his metaphor and would speak about an atomic reactor, in which the atom splits into mini-particles and releases tremendous energy. Dos-toevsky, as it were, splits the atoms of the psyche, and the result is an atomic explo-sion of soul.

Were it not for laboratory experiments, our knowledge of matter would be much poorer. Analogously, Dostoevsky con-ducts experiments with human souls, placing them under high pressures of suffering and evil, and thus he obtains knowledge about the very depths of the spirit. Yet, experimental as Dostoevsky's novels are, sometimes in them he antici-pates reality. In the mid-sixties of the last century a student, Danilov, murdered an old man from motives somewhat similar to Raskolnikov's. *Crime and Punishment* was published only a few months later. Thus was illustrated Oscar Wilde's paradox that nature sometimes imitates art. Addressing his ideological enemies, the adherents of naturalism in art, Dostoevsky says in this connection: "You, with your short-sighted realism, do not see beyond your noses, whereas we, with our fantasies, predict facts."

What I want to say is basically simple: that Dostoevsky, employing his fantasy, puts his heroes in marginal situations, which may seem bizarre from the stand-point of common sense, but which prompt his heroes to reveal their innermost selves—to the very bottom of their souls. In other words, Dostoevsky was an artist of the subconscious, in an age when the word was not yet coined. Freud was twenty-five years old when Dostoevsky died. Later Freud became an admirer of Dostoevsky and advised his students to read him. If Freud was the Columbus of the subcon-scious in psychology, then Dostoevsky was the Columbus of the subconscious in lit-erature. This fact alone is a strong indi-cation that Dostoevsky is our contempo-rary.

I would like to raise another point, again concerning the alleged "abnormality" of Dostoevsky's characters. Let us take a fresh look at Raskolnikov, Prince Mysh-kin, and Ivan Karamazov. Can they be called "abnormal" in the sense of lacking average intelligence? Of course not. They are "supranormal," rather than subnormal. They have brilliant minds. Their difficulties come "from wit." Even Prince Myshkin, the Idiot, is superior in intelligence when compared with other characters in the novel. And, if he becomes insane at the end, it is because he is emotionally vulnerable.

The enigma of Dostoevsky's characters lies not in their psychopathology, though they are partly pathological, but in their tragic natures. As the Russian poet and critic Vyacheslav Ivanov rightly remarks, Dostoevsky's novels are basically tragedies, and they must be appreciated for this quality. The art of tragedy requires marginal situations. To this unwritten requirement Dostoevsky added a new element: the marginal nature of his characters. Accordingly, not the psychopathology, but the marginal struggle embodied in the moral conflict of his tragic characters, constitutes the essence of Dostoevsky's novels. The interpretation of his novels as tragedies can help us understand their riddle more fully than can a purely psychoanalytical approach to his creativity.

We called Dostoevsky a Columbus of the subconscious in literature. But in order to appreciate Dostoevsky according to his full merit, we must go more deeply into the realm of the human spirit. And this is a crucial point. For the spirit differs from the psyche no less than the psyche from the body. The human spirit is a realm of eternal values, and religion is the highest expression of the spiritual realm. It is the realm in which, in Dostoevsky's words, "The devil struggles with God, and the human heart is their battlefield." Can the meaning of this famous pronouncement be reduced to its purely psychological aspect? Obviously not, insofar as it implies metaphysics, even mysticism. (In the same vein, the music of Beethoven cannot be reduced to his personal psychology, although it is intimately connected with it.)

It is interesting that Dostoevsky himself was not satisfied with a purely psychological interpretation of his creativity. "They call me a psychologist," he writes in a letter to his friend Maikov, "whereas I am only a realist in a higher sense." The expression "realist in a higher sense" means exactly in the realm of the spirit. And if religion is the highest expression of the spiritual realm, then morality and philosophy are also substantial strata of spiritual being. A study of Dostoevsky's aesthetics, of his moral convictions, of his philosophy, leads us more deeply into the mystery of the writer than does a psychoanalytical approach to his creativity. The essence of tragedy is insoluble conflict. And, if the ancient tragedies are tragedies of fate and Shakespeare's, tragedies of human passions, then Dostoevsky's tragedies can be characterized as tragedies of freedom. Dostoevsky's attitude to freedom was ambivalent. On the one hand, he was a defender and even a preacher of freedom. In all world literature we cannot find another such passionate affirmation of freedom as that which he presented in his *Notes from the Underground*. On the other hand, Dostoevsky was against a deification of freedom, against the temptation of superhuman pride, as it may be seen in his presentation of Kirillov with his philosophy of man-godhood.

The spiritual dimension of Dostoevsky's works finds expression in his philosophy. Philosophy does not exhaust, of course, the spiritual dimension, but it constitutes its essential part. "I am somewhat weak in philosophy," Dostoevsky comments modestly, "but not in the love of it. In this love I am even strong." Indeed, the ideas as propounded by such characters as Raskolnikov, Stavrogin, Kirillov, and Ivan Karamazov—apart from their acceptance or repudiation—represent a treasure of philosophic intuitions.

Since the appearance of Lev Shestov's *Dostoevsky and Nietzsche*, we know that Dostoevsky's antiheroes anticipated Nietzsche's superman. The German philosopher himself notes that "Dostoevsky . . . was the only psychologist from whom I had anything to learn. . . ." The scope of Dostoevsky's influence on Nietzsche is still unclear. The difference, of course, is that what constitutes the main part of Nietzsche's teachings is only the negative element in Dostoevsky's integrated worldview.

Moreover, Dostoevsky anticipated modern existentialism—not its rationalistic doctrine, but its spirit. This "philosophy of proud despair" was anticipated by Dostoevsky partly in Kirillov in *The Possessed* and partly in Versilov in *A Raw Youth*. Kirillov says that man must become "mangod" and that man is a "doomed god," a concept that corresponds with the ideas of both Heidegger and Sartre. Heidegger says that man is a "god who has no power over his own existence"; and this, again, corresponds with the spirit of Kirillov's philosophy. Sartre says that man is condemned to his freedom and that fear is a basic human emotion. This idea corresponds with that of Kirillov, who calls his freedom "terrible." The chapter of Heidegger's *Being and Time* entitled "Being to Death" corresponds with Versilov's pronouncement: "Man must die proudly as a god."

Sartre had a special liking for Dostoevsky and often quoted Ivan Karamazov's statement that "If there is no God, then everything is allowed," adding many atheistic commentaries. Again, while Dostoevsky anticipated modern existentialism, he at the same time rejected its atheistic philosophy. If Dostoevsky were miraculously resurrected in our time, he would feel at home in the philosophic atmosphere.

Dostoevsky exerted a tremendous influence on Russian philosophic thought. His influence on Rozanov and Merejkowski is indubitable. Psychologically speaking, Rozanov came, as it were, directly from Dostoevsky's *Notes from the Underground*. Rozanov's book on the Grand Inquisitor, published at the end of the last century, is still one of the best books on Dostoevsky. The author of another excellent book is Merejkowski in his *Tolstoy and Dostoevsky*. Furthermore, Dostoevsky exerted a decisive influence on one of the greatest minds of not only Russian but world philosophy, Nicolas Berdyaev, who wrote one of the very best books on him.

Generally speaking the best books on Dostoevsky have been written by Russian philosophers or philosophizing literary critics: Rozanov, Merejkowski, Berdyaev, Vyacheslav Ivanov, Lossky. Their books represent the cream of Russian critical literature on Dostoevsky. Among the Western books on the Russian genius, those by Eduard Thurneysen, Romano Guardini, and George A. Panichas are the best. One can even say that Dostoevsky has been duly appreciated only in the twentieth century. This is another reason for the title "Dostoevsky—Our Contemporary."

An important point remains. As is well known, Dostoevsky was a fervent Christian. He went through a brief period of atheism in his youth, when he was under the influence of the critic Belinsky and his philosophic inspirer Feuerbach. But even then he could not renounce the "shining image of Christ." When he was condemned to hard labor in Siberia for a minor political offense, his convictions underwent a deep change. Not that Dostoevsky's spirit was broken by penal servitude. He protested against such an interpretation when he became free. But his sufferings in Siberia, as well as his close contact with simple people, convinced him of the indispensability of faith in God. He became a mortal enemy of atheism. He speaks about his newly-acquired faith in the following words: "I believed in God not as a child. My 'Hosannah' went through the furnace of doubt." Elsewhere he says: "These scoundrels [his liberal critics] accuse me of a backward faith in God. But those idiots never even dreamed about the depths of God-denial which I exposed in 'The Grand Inquisitor.' And they want to teach me!"

Dostoevsky struggled with the atheists so passionately precisely because at one time he was nearly one of them. It is humanly difficult to face one's own past errors with equanimity. This explains his wrath in fighting the atheists. His indignation was righteous. Dostoevsky's religious feelings are important not only as far as they concerned him personally. More important is the fact that without taking into account his deep religious feelings, it is impossible to appreciate him fully as a writer. In his *Diary of a Writer* he several times dealt with the idea of "Christian art." His own art was indeed Christian.

Both as an artist and as a thinker, Dostoevsky was saturated with Christian wisdom. This Christian wisdom represents the deepest dimension of his works and of his life. Dostoevsky may be rightly understood only by readers who are themselves religious, even if only potentially. Atheists and agnostics can only scratch the surface of Dostoevsky's creativity; they can never penetrate to its core. For example, the famous French novelist and skeptic André Gide wrote a clever book on Dostoevsky, but this book has a certain superficiality. It helps the reader to appreciate Dostoevsky only if he is somewhat philosophy-minded.

As I said, Dostoevsky's art was basically Christian. Only against the background of his intrinsic Christianity could he create the grandiose images of Raskolnikov or Ivan Karamazov as demonically negative

figures. Dostoevsky did not create an aura of grandeur around these figures, despite their grandiosity. On the contrary, he condemned them not by tendentious moralizing but by demonstrating the spiritual dead-end to which their atheism led them. In the epilogue of *Crime and Punishment* he shows us Raskolnikov on the eve of repentance, and Ivan on the eve of serious mental trouble. Raskolnikov, Stavrogin, and Ivan Karamazov are gigantic dark shadows. It is in the light of Christianity, of the image of Christ, that we perceive these characters as shadows. We can define darkness as an absence of light, but we cannot define light as an absence of darkness.

That Dostoevsky's art was basically Christian may be substantiated by his own commentary on the meaning of *Crime and Punishment*: "Here the whole psychological process of crime is unfolded. The murderer is tormented by insoluble problems and unexpected emotions. Divine and human laws take their toll. And in the end he is forced to give himself up, so that, though he might die in prison, he might once more enjoy the fellowship of other human beings. He is driven to this by the sensation of being isolated from the rest of humanity. The law of truth and human nature triumphed."

It would be instructive at this point to quote Dostoevsky's short comment on Shakespeare: "He was a genius, sent to this sinful earth by God Himself in order to illuminate the human heart with all its passions." These words may also apply to Dostoevsky.

To repeat, Dostoevsky's works are saturated with deep Christian feelings. But these feelings have nothing to do with an Olympic grandeur like Goethe's. Dostoevsky's Christian wisdom was born not from quiet contemplation but rather from a spiritual struggle. He is like an Old Testament prophet rather than an ancient Greek or Hindu sage. His wisdom was

SERGEI LEVITZKY

shaped in a struggle against all the varieties of atheism. Hence its militant character. The motto of his creative path is, as it were, *"per aspera ad astra."*

All this emphasizes once more that Dostoevsky was a tragic genius. However, tragedy is not thinkable without catharsis, a healing effect. By catharsis Aristotle understood the purification and elevation of the soul through fear, hope, and awe. Catharsis is an essential complement of tragedy, without which tragedy would degenerate into a Frankenstein-like accumulation of horrors. Dostoevsky indicates this catharsis in a two-fold way. First, he demonstrates the tendency of all evil toward self-destruction. Since evil contains an inner contradiction, it cannot dominate the world forever. All Dostoevsky's characters treading the evil path either repent and reestablish their spiritual harmony or perish, as do Kirillov, Stavrogin, and Smerdyakov. The self-destruction of evil is exemplified in the New Testament story of the herd of swine hurling itself into an abyss. This is, however, a purely negative catharsis. The second, positive catharsis lies in Dostoevsky's fervent faith in God and in Christ.

Dostoevsky indicates that evil cannot be forgiven if there is no link between God and man, between Creator and creature. There is no "theodicy" if the world, once created by God, is then abandoned by Him. But there exists a link in the person of Christ, Who descended to earth, took human shape, and shared the sufferings of God's creatures. The Christian catharsis is the Redemption.

Dostoevsky did not attain a supreme harmony. His positive characters are somewhat weaker than his embodiments of evil. Besides, as a true artist, Dostoevsky never went in for tendentious moralizing. He kept an "armed neutrality" during conflicts between good and evil. But the disharmony he so forcefully depicted tends toward an invisible harmony, which is, in Heraclitus' words, more beautiful than a visible one. His Hosannah never reached a full, final accord. His creative way ended on a high but interrupted note, like Schubert's *Unfinished Symphony*. Rather than a saint, Dostoevsky was indeed one of the greatest God-seekers. But, in the words of St. Augustine, "Thou would not have sought Me had thou not found Me already." [XXV, Fall 1981, 396–401]

[73]

Irving Babbitt and the Aestheticians

FOLKE LEANDER

Folke Leander (1910–1981) was a Swedish philosopher and teacher whose writings and espousal of the American New Humanism constitute an important interpretative examination of the ideas of that movement. Indeed, all three of his books in English, Humanism and Naturalism *(1937),* The Philosophy of John Dewey *(1939), and* The Inner Check *(1974), reflect his close and lifelong study of Irving Babbitt and Paul Elmer More. In his own philosophy and scholarship and teaching, Leander stressed both the necessity and the acceptance of moral responsibility. His thought and writings ranged widely in the fields of ethics, aesthetics, and logic and across national borders and historical periods. Though his position, rooted in the classical and Judaeo-Christian traditions of humanism, earned him much opposition and made him an outsider in his own country and time, his courage and faith in his mission remained constant.*

WHEN OCCASIONALLY Irving Babbitt's name is mentioned in a book on aesthetics, one can almost tell in advance what is going to be said about him: that, aiming at a moral and cultural reform of his age, he applied to literature a set of standards that have little to do with aesthetic evaluation. However often this may have been repeated, it is hardly a tenable view. It is based upon a separation of aesthetic and ethical values that is increasingly felt to do violence to the facts of artistic experience and to be no more than a polemical, post-Christian and post-Classical oversimplification. Even Benedetto Croce gradually transcended the amoralist position of his early *Estetica*, especially in his practical criticism, and arrived at a point of view that is hardly consistent with it. But the study of aesthetics, as pursued in American and British departments of Phi-losophy, is still largely based on the *Estetica*, whereas Croce's later work has been little studied. The authors of a recent work on the theory of literature are no doubt right in saying that the influence of Croce has been "of a pervasive and atmospheric kind, blending with a generally favorable climate of opinion so as not always to be clearly distinguishable." Nevertheless this influence, direct or indirect, has been exerted only by the *Estetica*, and one may therefore ask whether contemporary aestheticians will not, sooner or later, be forced to undertake a revision of the amoralist postulate, similar to that which Croce himself was unable to avoid, however hard he tried to conceal it. If this should be so, Babbitt's work will be found to have a closer bearing on their problems than has hitherto been assumed.

If one were to summarize the basic

tenets of Crocean aesthetics, the following formulae might be hazarded:

Intuition is a non-intellectual mode of knowing. Knowing what? Knowing life and nature as concretely experienced. Intuition means insight. Insight into what? Into the dynamic development of vital energies.

These definitions form a circuitous way of pointing to something within our experience, namely the artistic imagination as a mode of insight, a kind of knowing. Most modern aestheticians follow Croce with regard to the above doctrines. But let us now raise a question which modern aestheticians do not raise: Can the insight be more or less profound? Are there degrees of poetic truth, degrees of profundity in our imaginative vision of life? This question brings us into the realm of problems, where Babbitt's contribution to aesthetics should be looked for.

In his amoralist phase Croce says there is simply art and non-art; all art is equally true, and there are no degrees of poetic truth. Babbitt's opposition to Croce was directed against this view; and since his was the type of mind that looks for differences rather than agreements, he failed to notice in Croce the presence of another trend of thought, much closer to his own. Babbitt maintained that there is a difference between the poetry which shows us the superficial aspects of life and that which gives us profound insight into life as subjected to a moral world-order. The highest type of art, according to this view, is art which gives us insight into the moral substance of life. There is other art, valuable in its own way, although it does not go beneath the surface of life and therefore does not reach the moral core of reality.

What is the "moral substance of life"? Space does not permit me to go into Babbitt's moral philosophy, nor is this necessary for a comparison with Croce, since the latter's view of the nature of the moral conscience, as expounded in his *Filosofia della pratica*, is in essentials identical with Babbitt's. Moreover, the whole conception of a moral world-order is familiar to anyone who knows his Plato or Aristotle. For the purposes of a comparison we may state that Babbitt and Croce were agreed as to the reality of a "higher will," or moral world-order, and that their disagreement—more partial than Babbitt believed—concerns the relation of art to this world-order. In his amoralist phase Croce thinks that intuition always has the same value, and that no artistically relevant distinctions can be based upon *what* is intuited.

Supreme instances of art penetrating the moral substance of life are, according to Babbitt, the dramas of Aeschylus and Sophocles, the myths of Plato, the poetry of Dante. But Babbitt also taught that this moral substance of life is inexhaustible. It cannot be locked up in a formula. It is infinitely faceted, showing some new aspect from whatever point you approach it. It is primarily through his imagination that man has access to the moral element of life: the insights of the Greek poets preceded the conceptual formulations of the Greek philosophers, just as the parables of Christ preceded the Scholastic elaboration of ethics. If one overlooks the cognitive function of the imagination as such, if one believes that the moral element of poetry is simply an importation into it of intellectual reflections, one falls into the *error of intellectualism*, as did the neo-Classical theorists of "reason" controlling "imagination." Since the imagination *as such* has varying degrees of cognitive insight, works of art may be ranked according to the fullness and clarity of such perception. Babbitt's contribution to aesthetics was a doctrine of the *degrees of poetic truth*, thus liberating Classicism from the error of intellectualism and freeing aesthetics from subservience to Romantic and "Realist" amoralism.

The concept of poetic truth therefore turns out to be much more complex than might be inferred from the over-simplified accounts of it given by recent aestheticians. John Hospers, in his competent book on *Meaning and Truth in the Arts*, takes us no further than to a distinction between *truth-about* and *truth-to*. If you write a book on London, full of facts and statistics, you give *truth-about* London. If you write a poem on London, this poem may be *true-to* your experience of life as lived in that city. Poetry is true-to our feelings as evoked by concrete experience of things and events. It is true-to our emotional reactions to the life in which we participate. Poetic truth, Hospers would agree with the early Croce, is simply adequate expression. This analysis, Babbitt would object, is no doubt correct as far as it goes, but it leaves unexplored an entire dimension of our poetic experience. There is, he would explain, much more to be said in answer to the question: true-to what? Poetry may be true-to moods and states of mind not integrated into a complete personality and hence only conducive to superficial views of reality. Poetry may be true-to the whole personality, including the ethical self; it may be true-to the "human heart," and what is deepest in the human heart, and thus bring us closer to real life. Poetic truth is dependent on *what* is being expressed. To put it in terms of intuition: there is more and more poetic truth, the more our intuition penetrates our experience of life and manages to lay hold of its moral laws—laws that are not created by us for the simple reason that they are the immanent laws of our creative activity, inescapable and not subject to our caprice.

Other philosophers deal with the problem in the same one-sided fashion as does Hospers. Ernst Cassirer, for instance, summarizes his aesthetics as follows:

> In science we try to trace phenomena back to their first causes, and to general laws and principles. In art we are absorbed in their immediate appearance, and we enjoy this appearance to the fullest extent in all its richness and variety. Here we are not concerned with the uniformity of laws but with the multiformity and diversity of intuitions. Even art may be described as knowledge, but art is knowledge of a peculiar and specific kind. We may well subscribe to the observation of Shaftesbury that "all beauty is truth." But the truth of beauty does not consist in a theoretical description and explanation of things; it consists rather in the "sympathetic vision" of things. The two views of truth are in contrast with one another, but not in conflict or contradiction.

Cassirer says that there is such a thing as intuitive insight, but he forgets that this insight may vary in profundity. "Art is not an imitation but a discovery of reality," he goes on to say. A discovery of more or less? He gives no answer to that question. Irwin Edman describes the contrast between intellect and intuition as follows:

> There is a poetic, dramatic, moral truth, truth that is the expression of a fact as humanly encountered or experienced [*What sort of facts?*], not a neutral description of its status in the total uncaring context of things. The arts give the truth of things [*What "things"?*] as they have an impact in the feelings and imaginations of men.

Edman, too, omits the question about the profundity of the level on which the concrete encounter takes place. What encounters what?—that is the problem which he does not raise. Susanne Langer deals adequately with the truth-value of music. It is not just "expression," she says, meaning an immediate outburst of feeling—a theory which she erroneously attributes to Croce. Music, she says, is not as simple as that, for it gives knowledge as well:

> It expresses the composer's knowledge of human feelings.
>
> Music is the formulation and representation of emotions, moods, mental tensions and resolutions—a source of insight.
>
> It makes emotive contents conceivable so that we can envisage and understand them.
>
> A composer articulates subtle complexes of feeling that language cannot even name.
>
> Musicality is often regarded as an essentially unintellectual trait. Perhaps that is why musicians, who know it is the prime source of their mental life and the medium of their clearest insight into humanity, so often feel called upon to despise the more obvious forms of understanding.
>
> Insight is the gift of music; in a very naive phrase, a knowledge of "how feelings go."

She has also an explanation of the truth-value of music. The tones are arranged in dynamic patterns that are isomorphic with the dynamic patterns of vital energies in our practical life. Hence music may serve as a symbolic picture. But she does not mention that the dynamic pattern of musical energies may be that of an ethical soul controlling expansive forces. Irwin Edman has a great deal to say about the truth of works of art:

> One hears more than an arrangement of sounds in Beethoven's Fifth Symphony. One hears the comment of a great spirit on the world in which it lives. In Rembrandt's pictures of old rabbis, or El Greco's of Spanish grandees, they put into canvas a vision of what life essentially meant to them.

But are all interpretations of what life means equally profound? Are imaginative visions of life always equally true? No answer. Edman continues:

> A mood half articulate and half recognized in its confused recurrence becomes,

as it were, clarified forever in a poem or a novel or a drama.

But how far into reality does that mood take us? Edman does not raise the question. Susanne Langer also has a good passage about the truth of literature:

> The "livingness" of a story is really much surer, and often greater, than that of actual experience. Life itself may, at times, be quite mechanical and unperceived by those who live it.

And Edman is perhaps even more lucid when, speaking about a well-known poem, he expresses the same idea as follows:

> Thousands of inarticulate men and women have felt that emotion about their beloved, but in that sonnet of Shakespeare's they find their common emotion rendered with uncommon and vitalizing felicity. A poem of love may teach them by its own instant and luminous reality what the reality of their own love is.

This is excellently said. But, in the name of common sense, cannot poetry give people largely illusory ideas about their own emotions? Emma Bovary was more imaginative than most people, but her imagination hardly reached down to the deeper strata of reality. It is strange that all modern, supposedly scientific, aestheticians should still follow in the wake of the nineteenth century Romantics, thus forgetting the obvious fact that the imagination may also give us superficial notions about life. And it is even more strange that they are perfectly well aware of it in other connections. Susanne Langer is surprised that such an imaginative creature as man should have been able to survive on this earth.

Modern aestheticians, following Croce, interpret the term "catharsis" as referring merely to the act of expression or intuition, quite apart from *what* is expressed or intuited. As Cassirer puts it:

Our passions are no longer dark and impenetrable powers; they become, as it were, transparent ... But the image of a passion is not the passion itself. ... If we accept this view of art we can come to a better understanding of a problem first encountered in the Aristotelian theory of catharsis. ... In this world all our feelings undergo a sort of transubstantiation with respect to their essence and their character.

According to Babbitt, on the other hand, "catharsis" refers to our experience when the imagination penetrates the moral substance of reality. All art does not result in this catharsis, he holds.

As Babbitt pointed out, the notion that all products of the imagination have an equal amount of poetic truth is of fairly recent origin; it goes back to the early Romantics. Before that there had been a distinction between unrestrained imagination (which was at best regarded as idyllic play, at worst as foolish "conceit") and an imagination governed by "reason." The Classical critics, Babbitt held, were right in insisting upon the necessity of a distinction, though wrong in their manner of stating it. And whereas the Classical revival in twentieth-century France remained entangled in the old intellectualist error—you will find it in Maurras, Seillière, Lasserre, Benda—Irving Babbitt avoided it by completely abolishing the old idea of a "reason" controlling the imagination. The truth of art is poetic, and not intellectual. The imagination *as such* lays hold of the moral substance of life. Art is neither intellect nor moral will; art is intuition, nothing else, but intuition *as such* may have varying degrees of depth. Thus Babbitt furnishes a complement to modern aesthetics that will disengage it definitively from the untenable elements of Romanticism, while retaining what is valid in Romantic thought.

The significance of this contribution to aesthetic theory has hardly been fully appreciated, even by those who have best understood Babbitt. Louis J. A. Mercier failed to deal with it adequately in his account of Babbitt's philosophy, and in a recent important essay Austin Warren endorsed Mercier's misinterpretation: "Comparing Babbitt's terms with those of Catholic Scholasticism, Mercier rightly glosses the 'higher imagination' as 'intellect'—that which apprehends universals." Yet Babbitt was very explicit in pointing out that his "imaginative perception of the universal" (i.e., of the Moral Law) is *not* conceptual thought. The imagination is sometimes thought of as a combination of a passive sensuous element and an active rational element which, by being fettered to sense, is not yet reason proper—rather some sort of caterpillar stage in the growth of reason which, when it reaches its full development, will leave its sensuous envelope and soar like a butterfly in the pure air of conceptual thought. This was definitely not Babbitt's view of the imagination. As he pointed out in an important note to *Rousseau and Romanticism*, the error of Greek philosophy was its notion of the imagination as a passive power: "In its failure to bring out with sufficient explicitness this *creative* rôle of the imagination and in the stubborn intellectualism that this failure implies is to be found, if anywhere, the weak point in the cuirass of Greek philosophy." In this context the word "creative" refers to the power of the imagination to disengage essentials from the welter of actualities and thus to attain to a more accurate perception of reality. Babbitt shared Croce's view that the imagination is an active power in its own right, not merely in so far as the intellect is working through it and moving it from the inside like a hand moving a glove. The imagination *as such* "lays hold of," or "has access to," "the universal." It is a non-intellectual mode of cognition in the full sense of the word and not just in a Pickwickian sense.

The harmful effect of foisting on Babbitt an intellectualism that he himself rejected comes to the fore in Warren's essay when, disparaging Babbitt's aesthetic sense and raising the question why he did not become a philosopher instead of a literary critic, he produces the following sentence: "Literature he conceived of as ethics 'touched by emotion.'" This is not true. He conceived of literature as *imagination,* although with varying degrees of moral profundity.

In Gilbert and Kuhn's *A History of Esthetics* there is not a word about Matthew Arnold, which is all the more remarkable since everybody else in the English and American nineteenth century is rather fully treated. Arnold, groping his way towards the idea of various degrees of poetic truth, does not fit into the categories of modern aestheticians, nor does Babbitt when he expands Arnold's somewhat limited attempts into an impressive body of thought. Modern aestheticians do not know what to do with either of them and prefer simply to leave them out.

II

I have said there are two trends in Croce, one towards Romantic Aestheticism, the other towards Babbittian Humanism. The first aspect of Croce's thought has exerted considerable influence on contemporary aesthetic theory; its humanistic side has scarcely been noticed outside Italy, except in certain fields, such as the appreciation of the Baroque. As applied to twentieth century literature, the Humanistic trend in Croce's criticism appears for instance in the following passage of the *Breviario di estetica,* of 1912:

> Contemporary art, sensual, insatiable in the desire for enjoyment, furrowed by turbid

strivings towards a misunderstood aristocracy which turns out to be an ideal of voluptuousness or domination and cruelty; sometimes indulging in a mysticism which is equally egoistic and voluptuous; without faith in God or faith in reason, sceptical and pessimistic—and often powerful in rendering such states of mind—this art, which moralists condemn in vain—when it has been understood in its most profound motives and in its genesis, calls for action, which surely shall not consist in condemning, suppressing or correcting art, but in directing life more energetically towards a saner and profounder morality, which will engender an art more noble in its content. . . .

If the art Croce had in mind was "very powerful in rendering such states of mind," we may ask: Have not all *aesthetically* legitimate demands been satisfied? If "rendering" them means "expressing" them, as seems clearly to be the case, Croce would be in logic bound to answer yes. Yet Croce the Humanist answers no. Again, what is meant by "an art more noble in its content"? Croce's "official" doctrine gives him no right to introduce such a standard of evaluation. Yet Croce the Humanist applies it. In 1917 he wrote an important essay on *"Il carattere di totalità della espressione artistica"* which is rather Babbittian in spirit. Here he says that

> if the moral force is, as it certainly is, a cosmic force and queen of the world [*regina del mondo*], which is a world of liberty, it dominates by its own power; and art is the more perfect, the more clearly it reflects and expresses the development of reality; the more it is art, the better it shows the morality inherent in the nature of things.

This is Humanist aesthetics: art is "the more perfect," the profounder its intuition of reality is. Croce also says that "now, after a century and a half of Romanticism," the tendency, in France and elsewhere, towards a Classical revival is legitimate. He speaks of a Romantic "malady" which can only be overcome in the individual artist by way of a development of his philosophical-ethical-religious character, or *personality*, "the basis of art as of everything else." And if the malady is not overcome, this means prolonged suffering for a *travagliata e travagliante* humanity. True art, he says in this essay, is the expression of the *whole* personality, including the ethical self. Quite so. But what about the art that does not express the whole personality but merely expresses the longings and desires of the non-ethical self? Does Croce want to say it is imperfect as art, because—although *perfect as expression*—it is art *of less noble content?* Or does he want to say it is *imperfect as expression?* If he should choose the former alternative, he would be altogether at one with Babbitt and More. But that would mean an admission that his solution of the form-content problem in the *Estetica* had been over-simplified. If he should choose the latter alternative (imperfect as expression), he would have to maintain that immoral states of mind cannot find perfect expression in art, which seems contrary to the facts of aesthetic experience. Such is the dilemma. And there, I am afraid, Croce leaves the matter.

Croce's point of view grew more and more Classical as time went on, and there is a vast difference between the early *Estetica* and his writings for the forties. Yet, partly perhaps for reasons of personal pride, he clung to his original theory tenaciously, trying to modify it more and more in the Humanist direction but never abandoning it altogether. Babbitt was therefore partly right and partly wrong in attacking him. Croce seems to have read only one of Babbitt's books, *The New Laokoon,* and wrote a very appreciative article on it in 1921; yet it becomes quite clear that he did not understand what Babbitt meant by "inner form," which was

the presence of the ethical imagination, or the dimension of depth. No one can be surprised at this partial incomprehension. Even today, with all of Babbitt's (and More's) books at our disposal, and several interpretative works as well, it is extremely difficult to arrive at something like an adequate understanding of his thought. However, Croce's high estimate of *The New Laokoon,* in so far as he understood it, indicates the direction in which he himself was moving.

Even in the early *Estetica* there was already present a Classical element, viz., Croce's demand for adequate expression, as Vittorio Sainati points out in a recent book—so far the best book written on Croce. For this demand was partly directed against Romantic botchery and obscurity which in Croce's youth had again begun to dominate the literary scene; the Symbolist Movement in France and similar trends elsewhere were just beginning to catch on. And in his essays of the thirties and forties Croce dismisses the poetry of Mallarmé, Valery, and Stefan George as a sign of decadence, related to the works of the Baroque. His earlier evaluations had shown an analogous tendency. To Croce, as to Bernard Berenson, the Baroque and Modern periods represent an artistic decline and fall whose most characteristic symptom is the acceptance of "a kind of ugliness" as the highest artistic standard. A German critic, Gustav René Hocke, has recently devoted a very learned work to the artistic and literary parallels between the twentieth century and the period 1520–1660, a historical context already familiar through T. S. Eliot's favorable criticism of the Metaphysical Poets. Hocke's own perspective, covering both art and literature, is European in general, and he is an ardent admirer of both the Baroque and Modern periods. His evaluations are therefore diametrically opposed to those of Croce. In order to do perfect justice to the Classical element in Croce's writings (which Babbitt never did), one should follow above all the international discussion of the Baroque, where Croce emerges as the staunch upholder of Classical standards.

III

For an elucidation of what has been said we may therefore turn to Croce's studies of the Seicento. There were two tendencies at work in those days, says Croce [in 1911]:

> The first of them is the tendency we would call sensual and which in those days people called "lascivious." . . . The second tendency is the predilection for *ingegnosità*, for "conceit" and wit. . . . Of these two tendencies the first could be artistically fertile, the second not. When in a historical epoch every other sort of sentiment is weak and only sensuality remains vivid—sensuality in the sense of primal and almost animal passion—it is evident that this, and nothing else, constitutes the material for the poetry and art of the period.

But did the Marinist poets express nothing but erotic states of mind?—they did, but without poetic inspiration. Croce quotes a few lines from Marino's *La bruna pastorella*, where two lovers are looking at a volume of poetry and one of them says:

> Here is the table of contents, which accounts for the subjects, listed under headings. Let us skip the serious songs, with which he lauds the heroes, prays to the gods, and bemoans the trophies of death. Let us come to those more suave, in which in a sweet vein he expresses the charming and soft tendernesses and delights of love.

Croce comments: Without willing it or thinking of it, Marino here describes the method by which one should also read all the poets of the Seicento. Their poems are usually divided into amorous, elegiac, heroic, moral, religious and so on, but

only the love songs really count. The rest are written in a mechanical or hypocritical way.

> Strings other than the sensual do not vibrate, or they merely vibrate weakly, in the poets of those days. If, as we have remarked, they write much on religion, there is very little feeling in it. . . . One rarely finds an expression of moral sentiment comparable in energy with the expression of sensual enjoyment.

The Arcadian movement that supplanted Marinism in Italy was equally sterile, Croce goes on to say. And why? Because the sentiments expressed were still the same. "The frivolous habit of mind lived on, the weak religious and political faith, the superficial interest in philosophy." Marinism, Croce concludes, *rappresenta l'assenza del sentimento etico*; it was the absence of moral sentiment; that is what was wrong with it; and that is the reason why its poetry was bad. Croce is very explicit on this point: Marinist poetry was poor and bad, because *what* was expressed was mere sensuality and because moral sentiment was absent. Thus speaks Croce the Humanist, but how does it fit in with his aesthetic theories?

> It is an art and a literature deprived of moral sentiment and therefore, under apparent luxuriance, very restricted and poor. When from the most splendid productions of this art one turns to a picture by Giotto or a terzina by Dante, one is aware of the whole difference.

Let us enjoy this literature for what it is, he continues, and not claim too much for it. Would an Irving Babbitt or a Paul Elmer More have judged otherwise? The divergence between Croce the Humanist and Croce the Romantic aesthete becomes striking, if we now turn to what he says about Pallavicino, an important thinker of the period. Pallavicino wrote an early work on poetry in which he anticipated

Croce's own aestheticism in a most remarkable way. Away with all talk about probability; the imagination must be free! Poetry consists of "primary apprehensions" that have nothing to do with truth or falsehood. The sole aim of poetic tales, says Pallavicino,

> is to adorn our understanding with imagery, that is to say, with sumptuous, novel, marvellous and splendid appearances. . . . See how the world thirsts for beautiful first apprehensions, although these are neither laden with science nor are vehicles of truth.

But later Pallavicino grew dissatisfied with this view of poetry. This is just the lowest function of the imagination, he says, and poetry has the higher and more important task of giving us insight. In his *Estetica* Croce calls this a relapse into the pedagogic, moralist, and intellectualist theory that the young Pallavicino had so happily escaped from. He has not a word about a legitimate motive for Pallavicino's change of mind. Of course Pallavicino could not expound the higher aim of poetry without falling in some degree into the error of intellectualism; that much should be granted to Croce. Yet he was dissatisfied with Marinist poetry for precisely the same reasons as is Croce himself. How, then, can Croce applaud the young Pallavicino and regret his supposed later back-sliding into error?

The Classicism that supplanted Marinism in France was built upon that element of moral insight the absence of which in Italian poetry seems to Croce the cause of its weakness. The conclusions for aesthetic theory should be evident, although Croce—even in his later work—failed to draw them with full clarity. In his definitive work on the period, *Storia della età barocca in Italia* (1929), he came as close to a thorough revision of his youthful amoralism as he would ever come:

> It [i.e., Baroque art] did not lack the force of expanding on the surface, but it lacked that of getting to the depths, because, although born out of a human impulse, it was not referred back to and regenerated in our complete humanity. For this reason it always retained something abstract in its apparent concreteness, something willed in its apparent spontaneity. A narrow poetry; and true poetry is never narrow.

Baroque art, accordingly, is *imperfect as expression*, because it is not the expression of the *whole* man; art that expresses the whole man has moral profundity; narrow art is the expression of only a part of human nature. The difficulty of this view comes to the fore in what is said about "narrow art": it is not "true art," yet it is "art," which is a contradiction in terms according to Crocean aesthetic theory. Croce is left floundering among inconsistencies, because he is unwilling to give up his original monistic theory of beauty (art = expression) and introduce a dual criterion. How much simpler and truer it would be to say, with Babbitt: "narrow art" may be perfect as expression, but *what* is expressed is too superficial. Why did Croce shy away from this obvious conclusion when the facts of aesthetic experience were so obvious to him? He had staked his prestige on a theory that rejected as "moralism" any reference to the varying ethical quality of the "what." It would have been more honest, less misleading, if he had followed Pallavicino's example of openly recanting the superficial aestheticism he had once embraced.

IV

Will contemporary aesthetic theory, which is based on the Romantic Aestheticism that also inspired Croce's *Estetica* and which has indeed developed under the continuous influence of this work, gradually move in the direction of a new Classicism, as did Croce himself? Will it extricate itself from that flirtation with our modern Baroque by which Professors of Philosophy try to give evidence of their aesthetic sensibility? Will they rediscover and re-examine the nexus that unites aesthetic and moral values, both with one another and with the total context of human life? Will aesthetic theory follow the road already taken by the most discerning of modern critics? Some of the representative works in this new vein are Wladimir Weidlé's *Les abeilles d'Aristée*, Roger Caillois' *Babel*, Walter Muschg's *Die Zerstörung der deutschen Literatur*; also a book recently translated into English, Hans Sedlmayr's *Art in Crisis*. To a considerable extent the philosophical aestheticians are lagging behind the critics; their books still read like translations into technical terminology of a somewhat domesticated Oscar Wilde. When they catch up with the critics, the time will have come for a long-delayed discovery of Irving Babbitt in the field of aesthetics similar to that which has already taken place in political theory through the writings of Russell Kirk and Peter Viereck.

NOTES

I. Babbitt, *Rousseau and Romanticism*, 1919, pp. 171–2 (Meridian Books), pp. 307–8.

E. Cassirer, *An Essay on Man*, 1944, pp. 147, 169 f.

B. Croce, *Saggi sulla letteratura italiana del Seicento*, 1911, pp. xxi, 171 f., 382 f., 413, 429. *Nuovi saggi di estetica*, 1920, pp. 70, 132–8. *Aesthetic* (D. Ainslie's transl.), pp. 194, 201 f. *Storia della età barocca in Italia*, Bari 1929, p. 324.

I. Edman, *Arts and the Man* (Mentor Books), pp. 28, 30, 71, 132.

G. R. Hocke, *Die Welt als Labyrinth*, Hamburg 1957 (Rowohlt).

Manierismus in der Literatur, Hamburg 1959 (Rowohlt).

S. Langer, *Philosophy in a New Key* (Mentor Books), pp. 82, 178–198.

Feeling and Form, London 1953, p. 292.

V. Sainati, *L'estetica di Benedetto Croce*, Firenze 1953.

A. Warren, *New England Saints*, Ann Arbor 1956, pp. 154–161.

W. K. Wimsatt, Jr. and C. Brooks, *Literary Criticism*, New York 1957.

See also F. Leander, "Irving Babbitt and Benedetto Croce" in *Göteborgsstudier i litteraturhistoria tillägnade Sverker Ek*, Göteborg 1954.

[IV, Fall 1960, 395–404]

[74]

Henry James and the Sense of the Past

RAYMOND THORBERG

Raymond Thorberg (1914–1987), a university professor and author, contributed to various critical and scholarly journals including Twentieth-Century Literature, Southern Humanities Review, *and* Comparative Literature. *A literary scholar who wrote on Henry James in various issues of* Modern Age, *he also wrote vividly on his experiences as an infantry officer in the Battle of the Bulge during World War II.*

AMONG THE MOST MOVING scenes in all of Henry James' fiction is that of Milly Theale's confronting the Bronzino portrait in *The Wings of the Dove*. It is only the brief "supercession" of "a detached quarter of an hour" yielded to in response to Lord Mark's question, "Have you seen the picture in the house, the beautiful one that is so like you?" Yet its intense rendering of the idea of mortality establishes a tone and a direction for the novel that have been only tentative until this point:

> . . . she found herself, for the first moment, looking at the mysterious portrait through tears. Perhaps it was her tears that made it just then so strange and fair—as wonderful as he had said: the face of a young woman, all magnificently drawn, down to the hands, and magnificently dressed; a face almost livid in hue, yet handsome in sadness and crowned with a mass of hair rolled back and high, that must, before fading with time, have had a family resemblance to her own. The lady in question, at all events, with her slightly Michelangelesque squareness, her

eyes of other days, her full lips, her long neck, her recorded jewels, her brocaded and wasted reds, was a very great personage—only unaccompanied by a joy. And she was dead, dead, dead.

There is here, of course, the kind of one-to-one correlation between a character in a story and the subject of a portrait that we are familiar with in James and elsewhere. Milly is herself a "great personage," if we permit substitution of a modern qualification—her being an immensely rich American girl—for those of the portrait's subject, though in her own view the idea would be simply that of having everything to live for but not being granted life. What the portrait conveys to Milly is not, however, limited to what it was as painted. Her being struck by the thought that the young woman was "dead, dead, dead" undoubtedly owes in part to the strangeness and sadness, to the element of spiritual torment, in Mannerist painting. Yet it owes also in part to Milly's sense of the distance, despite the identification she feels, between herself and the subject of the portrait, of the remoteness caused by the intervening centuries.

The "supercession" of the quarter-hour given to the Bronzino is of "sundry impressions" and of a mood induced by a visit to the country estate of Matcham, where "the great historic house" figures as "the centre of an almost extravagantly grand Watteau-composition." Here, for Milly, the tone is of an "*appointed* felicity"; the total effect of Matcham has been to evoke "all the freshness of her young life, the freshness of the first and only prime." Indeed, the occasion "served to Milly, then and afterward, as a high-water mark of the imagination."

James' purpose in this may be further shown by his comment on the Watteau paintings in the Wallace collection (then at Bethnal Green) in a review article of 1873. "What elegance and innocence combined," he had written of the "scheme of life" presented in these paintings—"a scheme of lounging through endless summer days in grassy glades in a company always select, between ladies who should never lift their fans to hide a yawn, and gentlemen who should never give them a pretext for doing so . . . . Watteau was a genuine poet; he has an irresistible air of believing in these visionary picnics. . . ."

Watteau's world is a world of a continuous present, outside of time, innocent of its ravages, the world of Whitman's bird on Paumanok, "minding no time." Under the spell of the "Watteau-composition" of Matcham, Milly is drawn briefly out of thought of her probable doom. Her newfound friendship with Kate Croy, Lord Mark's interest, Mrs. Lowder's effusive urgings for her to "stay among us" coalesce to further her happiness. The contrast between this suspension and the overwhelming force of the passing of time, which Milly feels before the Bronzino, is obvious; it may be noted too that

James is judging the comparative validity of opposing views of life. Matcham in its "Watteau-composition" present exists only for an illusionary interlude. Lord Mark is waiting to take Milly to see the Bronzino. Mrs. Lowder, pursuing her own idea of using Milly to save Kate from the impecunious Densher, is contributing to a situation in which Milly will ultimately confront the cruelties possible in human relationships.

Besides, as James viewed it in the historical context, the Watteau-world was "impracticable." Watteau's figures are "gentle folks all, but moving in a sphere unshaken by revolutions"—a comment especially charged when made of young aristocrats living in eighteenth-century France. Jonah Raskin (*American Quarterly*, 1965) asserts without qualification that for James "1789 was . . . the most important year in history." As Raskin points out, James shared much of the preoccupation of Europeans, especially those of the conservative classes, with the possibilities of another general collapse, the uprisings of 1848 and the Franco-Prussian War of 1870–71 and the Commune providing sufficient reminders. His shock upon the outbreak of hostilities in 1914 owed less to surprise than to a perception of what he considered parallels between this event and the Revolution.

This criticism, of existing in a consciousness of only the present, is basic to James' view of America and the American experience. For James, America did not possess a past; the point is made most strongly perhaps in his *Hawthorne* (1879):

History, as yet, has left in the United States but so thin and impalpable a deposit that we soon touch the hard substratum of nature; and nature herself, in the Western World, has the peculiarity of seeming rather crude and immature. The very air looks new and young; the light of the sun seems fresh and innocent, as if it knew as yet but few of the secrets of the world and none of the weariness of shining; the vegetation has the appearance of not having reached its majority. A large juvenility is stamped upon the face of things, and in the vividness of the present, the past, which died so young and had time to produce so little, attracts but scanty attention.

It was not simply a matter of quantitative lack of time, of years, decades, or centuries, since the discovery, or the settlement, of North America by English-speaking people; it was, rather, a deliberate rejection of continuity and tradition. "The case against the past," as R. W. B. Lewis observes (*The American Adam*, 1955), had been won by the forces of rationalism, transcendentalism, democracy, and materialism. Lewis quotes Jefferson on the "self-evident" principle of government "*that the earth belongs in usufruct to the living*'; that the dead have neither power nor rights over it." *Walden* had argued against permitting any pathway to become well-worn; and it celebrated various means by which Thoreau sought to establish or to reestablish an "original relation with Nature." Literary independence from Europe, the past, tradition, had been called for by Emerson and Whitman; and James himself comments on the American fondness for local color. Mark Twain, who knew a bandwagon when he saw one, joined in the common effort by valiantly attacking King Arthur's court, church and state in Joan of Arc's fifteenth-century France, and *Ivanhoe*.

The Bostonians, James' chief novel with an American setting, it might be observed, does not concern itself with a Hawthorn-esque or any other New England past but with the very modern issue of feminist movements and women's rights. Nor does *Watch and Ward*. Elsewhere, for example in the story "Four Meetings," Puritanism is treated not so much as a phenomenon of the past as a continuing force against culture, contributing its part to locking Americans in the present by depriving them of contact with the past through culture. When James does treat of a past in America, it is—with some exception made for *Hawthorne*—of one no further back than his own boyhood; in his fiction even this treatment is infrequent, *Washington Square* offering the principal illustration. His choice of names such as Christopher Newman and Prince Amerigo is not to establish historical context; the placing of an Adam Verver in the same novel, *The Golden Bowl*, as Prince Amerigo, indicates, rather, his view of America as a pristine world, associated in the mind with ideas of creation and discovery. Milly Theale is the "heiress of all the ages"— but again the appearance of a linkage with the past is deceptive, and it diminishes upon examination. In *Locksley Hall* Tennyson had applied the phrase (with the masculine form "heir") to a young Englishman, or more broadly, in the context of the poem, to a young European. The idea if not the wording, C. V. Wedgwood notes (*Truth and Opinion*, 1960), appears in Schiller's inaugural lecture at Jena: "Ours are all the treasures which industry and genius, reason and experience have gathered in during the long ages of the world." At any rate, the sufficiently patriotic American would have little difficulty finding the application more appropriate to himself and his own country—the praise for linear progress as opposed to cyclic repetition, the vision of the future enhancing rather than diminishing the measure of present advance, the emphasis upon technology in "the nations' airy navies" and the "ringing grooves of change." The focus is upon the present, the achieved state of the present, material and technological advance; the "ages" are justified insofar as they have helped achieve this fruition. As Miss Wedgwood comments: "This inspiring frame of mind easily degenerated into the smugness which treated the past chiefly as something which could be compared to its disadvantage with the present, so as to demonstrate gratifying human progress." There is also an element of determinism, of an irreversibility of the process, an entrapment in the continually advancing present, felt by Tennyson's young hero as he considers renouncing his heritage, dropping out of history as it were. Milly Theale, upon the edge of a cliff in the Alps, has the same awareness, and she brings sudden fear to her companion, Susan Stringham, that she is contemplating suicide. Mrs. Stringham is mistaken, of course, but Milly is able to draw back only in the literal sense from the height and the precipice.

Unless the American can surmount the disability placed upon him by his heritage, or lack thereof, and by his environment—and James offers numerous examples in which inadequacy of will, or understanding or sympathy, prevent such surmounting—he can make the journey to Europe, but it remains a journey in the physical sense only. He may be a tourist giving up a few weeks or months to an uncomfortable experience, to which he reacts by complaints and by assertions of the superiority of things American to whatever he has seen here. His is the "sacred rage" of disapproval by a Waymarsh, in *The Ambassadors*, or of the view expressed by young Master Randolph, in *Daisy Miller*, that the best of all ships is the one that will take him homeward. Waymarsh, glaring at the centuries-old wall and Rows of Chester, must, it seems, assert his own terms of relationship with the culture of Europe: he darts away from Strether and Maria Gostrey to plunge through the entrance of a shop. What he does in the shop, James does not tell us, but critics who have hypothesized that it is to make a purchase are probably correct. This kind

of American, incapable of experiencing the culture of Europe, of "possessing" it meaningfully, through aesthetic apprehension, is forced back upon the superficial alternative. The central theme of the play *The Outcry* is a protest against the mass sale of art treasures to Americans; and throughout James' fiction the American who uses his money to buy works of art for shipment to America is viewed with disapproval. Even Christopher Newman, though buying only copies of masterpieces from Noémie Nioche, does not altogether escape censure.

A similar failure manifests itself, paradoxically perhaps, in the American who has "gone over," who is more European than the Europeans themselves. Gilbert Osmond, in *The Portrait of a Lady*, is the most notable illustration, holding "an immense esteem for tradition" and the view that "if one was so unfortunate as not to have it one must proceed immediately to make it." Here too is the inability to see Europe except in the present, as end-product. The American "gone over" displaces his own present with the present of Europe. This is another version of refusing the challenge of Europe; such expatriate Americans are static, rigidified, arch-conservative. But sometimes they go successfully under the guise of the genuine, as Gilbert Osmond appears to Isabel Archer, despite the clear and repeated warnings she is given.

The American as Jamesian protagonist, however—a Christopher Newman, an Isabel Archer, a Lambert Strether—begins with a cognizance of the limitations of the American experience and with sufficient force of will to act in terms of that cognizance. He is open to the experience of Europe; he is not already committed in his responses; he has, as Newman is described as having, "that look of being committed to nothing in particular, of standing in an attitude of general hospitality to the chances of life, of being very much at one's own disposal. . . ." The American protagonist begins from his present, and what Europe offers him is a dimension of time, through his responsiveness to its history and to its art and culture as living records of the consciousness which produced them. He begins only with the awareness of a lack—it is something behind the locked door in the "office" at Albany, in *The Portrait of a Lady*; or it is disguised as the desire for a wife, in *The American*; or it is an assignment to bring home an errant young man from the fleshpots of Paris, in *The Ambassadors*.

There is, of course, the view that James was himself a prisoner of his own time. According to T. S. Eliot, James was able to evoke only a "sense of the sense" of the past. For Rebecca West he "possessed an overwhelming sense of the present and almost no sense of the past." It must be admitted that in support of these views considerable evidence would seem to be offered by his own critical writings. For example, he stresses the importance to the writer of being receptive to immediate impressions, of being "one of the people on whom nothing is lost." He says, "A novel is in its broadest definition a personal, a direct impression of life: that, to begin with, constitutes its value, which is greater or less according to the intensity of the impression." He tells the young writer, "All life belongs to you." Then there is the concept of the "germ," the starting point, the basic idea for a novel or a story. A companion on a railway carriage tells him of an "American family, an odd adventurous, extravagant band" with "a small boy, acute and precocious . . . who saw their prowling, precarious life exactly as it was," and he has the origin of "The Pupil." He hears a brief account of an author, recently dead, whose wife had objected to his writings on moral grounds, and "There had come the air-

blown grain which, lodged in a handful of kindly earth, was to produce the story of Mark Ambient" ("The Author of 'Beltraffio' "). The most celebrated is the occasion suggesting *The Spoils of Poynton*. A companion at dinner told him of the conflict between mother and son over a houseful of furniture, and—"I instantly became aware, with my 'sense for the subject,' of the prick of inoculation; the *whole* of the virus . . . being infused by that single touch." He copes with problems of "selection," setting himself against the inclusiveness of the slice of life, of the "saturation" he finds in H. G. Wells and Arnold Bennett.

But now we find that "selection" reaches further, to counter the idea of total openness to impressions, of passive receptivity to whatever "wind-blown germs" may come one's way. Besides the germ itself, there is the necessity that it be "lodged in a handful of kindly earth"; sympathetic reception is not automatic—the germs "accumulate, and we are always picking them over, selecting among them." The "prick of inoculation" for his *Spoils* had required but "ten words"; as his dinner companion kept talking, he thought: "It's the perfect little workable thing, but she'll strangle it in the cradle . . . wherefore I'll stay her hand while there's yet time." He did not stay her hand, of course, but the point is perhaps clear enough that James' creative consciousness was not passive, merely receiving and storing impressions, producing story and novel as the accidents of wind-blown germs determined, but that, rather, it operated very much in terms of *a priori* considerations controlling selection and rejection. Indeed, it might be said that James knew his story before encountering the wind-blown germ, the service of the germ being to provide him the necessary variation of particulars.

For all the quantity of James' works in a career spanning half a century, his characters, his themes, his plots, stripped to their essences, are not numerous—though they compare favorably with those of most other writers claiming a coherent view of life and not merely an urge for novelty. The case can perhaps be made that a single pattern underlies the greater part of the "international" fiction, especially the novels, establishing through an archetypal character the idea of drawing upon the past, of developing a relation between past and present, of—to borrow phrasing Eliot applied to the James Joyce of *Ulysses*—"manipulating a continuous parallel" between the two. *The Portrait of a Lady* offers illustration: Isabel Archer meets the expectation of being, if not the third and last son, then at least the third and last daughter! Mrs. Ludlow is the eldest; Edith, the beauty, is next mentioned, though admittedly James does not specify her as the next eldest. At any rate, these sisters have been disposed of, if not by ogres or dragons then convincingly enough by marriage, the test of which awaits Isabel on the literal and metaphoric levels. She is singled out for her special role, if not by signs or portents accompanying her birth, then by her mystical childhood experiences behind the locked door in the "office" at Albany; and it is here that a fairy godmother, Mrs. Touchett, makes her first appearance, to whisk Isabel off (provided the term is not too strong) to Europe. Mystical also is the ghost at Gardencourt, humorously accounted for by her preconceptions of castles and English manor houses, which, however, allowing adequate interpretation, proves ultimately not a *mis*conception. She has three suitors—Ralph Touchett, it must be remembered, excludes himself—the magic number being maintained. Isabel accepts the third. However much one may be tempted to see a demonic inversion here, it should be remembered that Caspar Goodwood and Lord Warburton would "save" her by marrying her to their own limitations. Add a kindly adviser, and we have a place for Ralph Touchett; add an evil counselor or temptress, and we have Madame Merle.

Chapter 42 is chiefly taken up by what James deemed "the best thing in the book," Isabel's long meditation before the fireplace when she considers the decision she had made in marrying Gilbert Osmond. Here is the night journey, the descent into the underworld, the dark night of the soul. Isabel had made quite explicit, early in the novel, her willingness to accept consequences; it is an aspect of her openness, like Newman's, to experience. "You're not made to suffer," Ralph had told her. "I think people suffer too easily," she replied. Now after her long night of meditation she is spiritually and psychologically prepared for the final act of sacrifice and renunciation, cleansed of the "egoism" with which she began. Against Osmond's prohibition she goes to see the dying Ralph Touchett, knowing that the measure of restraint Osmond had placed upon his cruelty toward her must, upon her return, no longer be maintained.

The religious philosophy of Henry James, Senior, also offers parallels to the novelist's development of his international theme. The limitations placed upon the American by the circumstances of his birth and environment are like those placed upon man by the "original bias to evil in the human heart"—a separation and isolation through "the feeling of life in himself as his own life absolutely, or without respect to other men" (*Society the Redeemed Form of Man*, 1879). The term most frequently employed for this is "selfhood"; others, which may help to clarify the definition, are "self-consciousness" and "the sentiment of personality." It is interesting to note the similarities to the novelist's characterization of Isabel Archer. Isabel "was probably very liable to the sin of self-esteem"; she would be embarrassed to be called an "egoist," yet she "was always planning out her development, desiring her perfection." Henry James, Senior, offers the alternative of man's confronting himself in this aspect and accepting "an experience and conflict through which he is finally led to renounce his cherished personal independence, his diabolic pride of individuality" and work toward the goal of "universal humanity," "the broadest possible fellowship . . . of man and man," a *Divine-Natural* order of human life one day to appear in the earth." Translate the terms sufficiently, and the object of the quest, for the American protagonist in the younger James' novels with an international theme, becomes defined.

Europe, because it possesses a past, which is, further, viable and "visitable," provides the kind of experience constituting both the way and the object of the quest. The experience required is significant experience, mediating between "selfhood" and "universal humanity," or to state it differently, between the "egocentric mode," the isolated individualism, of the American, and the achieved consciousness of European civilization. Despite the increased symbolism of the later novels, this experience continues to derive from a historic past. The same principle of selection dealt with earlier applies also to the historical event; consequently James is able to make use of the past in novels and stories in which the action is of the present time; he does not feel that the past is available only by the placing of his action, or a major part of it, within another epoch. Only in the early "Gabrielle de Bergerac" does he write a conventional "historical" piece, and it is a very minor work.

The past makes itself felt in the international fiction not by isolated, formal recognition of its existence but by the necessary texture of development. For a list of contributions to this texture one might note the famous passage in *Hawthorne* enumerating the "items of high civilization" absent from Hawthorne's America but available in Europe. What these possess in common, besides what already has been predicted, is the dimension of time. Whatever else is involved, time has contributed to making them what they are, sometimes even as the principal agent. Traditions and manners reach back, occasionally to recorded origins, more often not. One's view of the Bellegardes (*The American*), of Prince Amerigo (*The Golden Bowl*), includes their centuries of family history. Madame de Vionnet's apartment, in *The Ambassadors,* conveys the sense of the transmitted, the inherited—in contrast with Maria Gostrey's, which attests to the raiding of boutiques and bazaars. Then there are cathedrals, other centuries-old buildings, such as the Venetian Palazzo Leporelli, in *The Wings of the Dove.*

With such brief mention, I do not deal with these further, partly because they have been adequately dealt with by others, partly because of the indistinctness, the obscurity, of the past they lead us into. Though Ruskin and Henry Adams showed that architecture can be a means of vividly recreating a past epoch, James' efforts in this direction are by comparison quite modest. I have dealt somewhat with painting. As compared with the Bronzino, the "Watteau-composition" reference is more characteristic of James, in that it embraces the entire work of a painter or a major part of it, conveying his particular vision of life and of the society and culture of his time. James, despite his own youthful introduction to brush, palette, and canvas, gives minimum attention to the technical aspects of painting; his concern is primarily with the life rendered there. Thus the Watteau-world, a society locked in its own present, ignorant of the passage of time, nevertheless conveys a sense of this passage to the reader, aware as he is how that world ended with 1789. In the latter chapters of *The Wings of the Dove* Veronese appears to evoke a consciousness of the rich and splendid society of the days of "Venetian glory." Elsewhere in James, other painters are made use of similarly. There is the bridging between past and present, between the painters' partly known, partly created worlds and the partly known, partly created world of James' fiction.

The event recorded in political history provides James with another means of opening corridors into the past; his images and other references range from ancient times to the most recent. Above all, the French Revolution seizes his imagination, but he is less concerned with the political issues than with the dramatic event capable of being captured in figurative language. His political disapproval of the violence which the Revolution engendered is matched by his drawing principally upon this for his images—mobs in the streets, heads fastened upon pikes, victims dragged to execution.

This last, presented in various specific forms, becomes the dominant image of the Revolution in his fiction, as Robert L. Gale's listings in *The Caught Image* (1964) illustrate. Roderick Hudson, in his final crisis of despair, is compared by Rowland Mallet to "some noble young *émigré* of the French Terror, seized before reaching the frontier and showing, while brought back, a white face, indescribable, that anticipated the guillotine." Isabel Archer considers that in a revolution she would be "a high, proud loyalist." To her fancy Mr. Touchett replies, "I'm afraid, after all, you won't have the pleasure of going gracefully to the guillotine just now." Mme. de Vionnet, following the collapse of her liaison with Chad Newsome, receives Strether at her apartment, dressed

"in the simplest, coolest white, of a character so old-fashioned, if he were not mistaken, that Madame Roland must on the scaffold have worn something like it." In the Notebook entries for *The Wings of the Dove* James sees his heroine in a similar image, as he does Mary Theale in the novel. The coalescing, the concentration, of the French Revolution into an image in such fashion could hardly escape the effect of its becoming archetypal; one recognizes it in Strether's likening Mme. de Vionnet's daughter Jeanne to a "small old-time princess of whom nothing was known but that she died young" or in Christina Light's being compared to "some immaculate saint of legend led to martyrdom." In this practice, of course, James was hardly out of step with an age which had produced its Marguerite Gauthiers and Mimis; and his brother William and he had felt—he was to write in his *Autobiography*—the end of their own youth signalized by the death of their cousin Mary Temple.

In only two works of more than minor importance does James concentrate on evoking the past of specific periods and sets of circumstances. In *The Aspern Papers* it is the Italy of Shelley and Byron; in *The Sense of the Past*, the London of 1820. Not accident but artistic principle determined the chronological coincidence—James writes of his delight in a "palpable, imaginable, *visitable* past," a past which is "fragrant of all, or of almost all, the poetry of the thing outlived and lost and gone, and yet in which the precious element of closeness, telling so of connexions but tasting so of differences, remains appreciable." He continues, "With more moves back the element of the appreciable shrinks." (John Balderston, in his play *Berkeley Square*, based upon *The Sense of the Past*, violates the letter at least of James' prescription by removing *his* past action further back, to 1784.)

The Aspern Papers is one of James' finest accomplishments in terms of the "craft of fiction," in structure and development, giving a nearly perfect illustration of organic form. The sense of the past which comes from the given matter of the relationship, long ago, between Jeffrey Aspern and his Juliana, and from descriptions of the Venetian scene, little changed since that time, is sufficient to the artistic purpose. If there is a flaw, it is the emphasizing of the distant and hidden by the too-obvious symbol of the aged Juliana's green eye-shade. The story's real theme, however, is human rapaciousness, displayed in forms more subtle than anything to be found in the jungle but no less ferocious or cruel. The unnamed narrator, Juliana, and in a pathetic way even Tina Bordereau—each pursues a separate intrigue. There is also more than a hint that Jeffrey Aspern had used his mistress for the benefit of his poetry; something about Juliana makes the narrator question, "Was this a sign that her singer had betrayed her, had given her away, as we say nowadays, to posterity?" The narrator's effort to obtain the letters not only attempts to violate a human relationship, but it also subjects him to James' disapproval of seeking an author not in his work but in the details of his private life. Admittedly James is not always consistent in making this disapproval, but when he does make it, it is of something he feels to be particularly modern, owing to popular journalism and its pandering to the most vulgar aspects of popular taste. Thus the past is placed at the service of none but selfish ends—and we find ourselves returning to Henry James, Senior, and the restricting force of selfhood and to the American held fast in his present by the bonds of egocentricity.

James' novel *The Sense of the Past* suggests, on initial encounter, a joining of the international theme with the ghost story. The young American, Ralph Pendrel, comes to London to take possession of a house on Mansfield Square bequeathed to him by a relative who had been impressed by Ralph's book, *An Essay in Aid of the Reading of History*, and had harbored some thought, apparently, of testing and extending Ralph's knowledge in this direction. Ghost-story elements appear at once in the mysteries surrounding the whole business. The international theme is not very much developed by the contacts Ralph makes with the English, which turn out to be minimal; not even the expected "swarm of litigants" gathers to dispute with him over the house; the solicitors handling the transfer of property are strictly professional, incapable of being "corrupted to any human resonance." The only person with whom he has a recorded conversation, in this London of 1910, is the American Ambassador.

But within the house on Mansfield Square he has already been in communication with his alter ego, his double, a Pendrel who had come from America in 1820, whose portrait, the face turned so that Ralph had been unable to see their resemblance, hung in one of the smaller drawing rooms. And when Ralph returns to the house at the beginning of Book IV, after his interview with the Ambassador, he and his double have made an exchange of place in time and of identity, if not altogether of consciousness. (An excellent study of the increasing immersion of Ralph's consciousness in the 1820 world has been made by David W. Beams, in *Criticism*, 1963.) It is as the 1820 Pendrel that he enters the house to meet the Midmore family, including the daughter Molly, who has become his betrothed through transatlantic correspondence. Although he has assumed the 1820 Pendrel's identity, the sum of knowledge concerning the Midmores, details in the development of the relationship between the 1820 Pendrel and Molly Midmore, with which he is of course expected to be familiar, becomes available to him only as needed. "Every question became answerable, in its turn, the moment it was touched"; and "each improvisation, as he might fairly have called them all, gave way without fear to the brightening of further lights." His reference to a miniature, a small portrait of Molly that had been sent to New York, is followed by his ability to bring it out to view, from the "inner left pocket of his coat." When Molly tells him she has kept "his" letters and half-accuses him of having destroyed hers, he hesitates only a moment, then realizes, "Where could they be else than at the bottom of that box at the inn? 'If you can prove one of them missing,' he was thus in twenty seconds ready to answer, 'I'll chew the rest of them up and swallow 'em.' " To prove his intimate knowledge of their contents, he cites instances of Molly's misspelling. Such exercise of his powers aids, and is aided by, his increasing immersion in the 1820 world; but everything does not work out with equal success. Where there should be knowledge of Molly's younger sister Nan, there is only a gap—even to the fact of her existence. Conversely, he displays an ability to discourse on a blue jar at Drydown, the Midmores' country home in Hampshire, in greater detail and accuracy than any source of information through the Midmores could have provided him. As might be expected, he soon discovers that they are watching him in apprehension, with a "slow growth of fear"—as James describes it in the notes. And it seems to him that Perry Midmore, first, then Sir Cantopher Bland, Nan's suitor, are probing him, trying to search him out. He redoubles his own efforts; as the ice gets thinner, he skates all the faster.

James had begun *The Sense of the Past*

at the turn of the century, laid it aside, and then in 1914 dictated notes outlining his plan for completion and took up the novel itself again, only to leave it again unfinished. During the time it lay fallow, he made use of certain of its ideas and devices in "The Beast in the Jungle" and "The Jolly Corner." The notes carry frequent references to *The Turn of the Screw*, which, however, antedated his beginning this novel and are concerned chiefly with technical matters in relation to it, such as the necessity of foreshortening, *Turn* providing a model. Yet these references help confirm the point that he viewed *The Sense of the Past* very much in ghost-story terms.

The similarities between "The Jolly Corner" and "The Beast in the Jungle" on the one hand and *The Sense of the Past* on the other range from details of language to basic thematic elements. The doppelganger device appears in "The Jolly Corner" and in the novel; by interpretation, perhaps, this could be extended to "The Beast in the Jungle," John Marcher's lifelong search culminating in the discovery that it was himself who had prevented its success. More striking is the parallel between *The Sense of the Past* and "The Jolly Corner" of each protagonist's separating himself from an outside, social, rational, ordinary world—the world of daylight in the one story, of the present in the other—to probe into the secrets of a house—his own house, it might be noted. This probing becomes more and more recognizable as a probing of the unconscious self. Both protagonists are struck by fear at the thought of being trapped. Spencer Brydon at one point opens "half a casement" and watches "as for some comforting common fact, some vulgar human note, the passage of a scavenger or a thief, some night-bird however base. He would have blessed that sign of life. . . ." Ralph Pendrel eventually begins to cast about anxiously for means of return to the present. In all three works the *donnée*, the basic situation, is the protagonist's obsession with himself; and the action traces out the consequences in the rejection of experience, an increasing isolation, and a kind of ultimate irrelevance. Only in "The Beast in the Jungle," however, does James stay with his logic to the bitter end; the outcome of *The Sense of the Past* (in the notes for its completion) and that of "The Jolly Corner" are tinged with sentimentality.

Why, then, should James not have solved his problem with *The Sense of the Past* by giving it a different kind of protagonist— a Christopher Newman hospitable to the chances of life, an Isabel Archer willing to affront her destiny? The question is recognized, I hope, as simply rhetorical; an outward-seeking protagonist has no place in a story demanding, essentially, a retreat into the self. It is true that the different paths often lead toward similar discoveries about the nature of man. The difference in the paths, however, is all-important to James—his primary concern is to present life as it is being lived rather than to drive home abstract truths about it or about the universe or whatever. A corollary here is his emphasis upon the particular and individual, "solidity of specification," rather than the high visibility of archetypal patterns. Yet the test of significance is maintained, excluding the simply idiosyncratic from his work; and the typicality and correspondence he seeks as means toward achieving this significance witness the importance to him of the dimension of time. For him the meaningfulness of the present owes in large part to the relations it can establish with the past. Out of these relations comes a sense of distance, of the passage of time, as well as of immediacy from the perception of likeness. James' most successful achievements occur when he can combine the two so as to establish a tension between them. In *The Wings of the Dove* Milly Theale looks through tears at the Bronzino portrait; thus its subject is dimmed and distanced, even more than has already been done by the "fading with time." But were it not for the immediacy, there would have been no tears.

[XVIII, Summer 1974, 272–282]

75

The Crack-Up of American Optimism: Vachel Lindsay, the Dante of the Fundamentalists

PETER VIERECK

Peter (Robert Edwin) Viereck *(1916–   ), a poet who won the Pulitzer Prize in 1949 for his first book of poems,* Terror and Decorum *(1948), is also a university and college teacher.* Metapolitics: From the Romantics to Hitler *(1941),* Conservatism Revisited: The Revolt Against Revolt, 1815–1949 *(1949),* Shame and Glory of the Intellectuals *(1953), and* The Roots of the Nazi Mind *(1961) are the titles of some of his best-known books. He has taught history at Radcliffe, Smith, and Mount Holyoke colleges.*

What is shoddy in the American myth is not affirmation itself; classic tragedy affirms. What is shoddy is not the hard-won affirmation that follows tragic insight but the facile unearned optimism that leads only to disillusionment.

THE END OF an outer material frontier to explore in the West and Midwest has helped cause the increasing inner explorations of the spirit. Vachel Lindsay represents a transition. Apparently still an outer explorer, an evoker of picturesque place-names and loud American noises in the fashion of an older school, yet in reality an inward voyager of the religious imagination and the aesthetic imagination, Lindsay remains the finest religious poet produced by America's most local native roots. He is the Dante of the Fundamentalists.

To call Lindsay a mouthpiece of Fundamentalism is nothing new. What will here be suggested as new (and as fruitful for future application to other writers) is a conservative hypothesis about the threefold interaction between Lindsay's human crack-up, his Ruskin-aesthete mission, and his self-destructive attempt to maintain, against his increasing qualms, his Rousseau-Bryan utopian faith (the faith of his Fundamentalist religion and Populist politics). To explore such non-lyric straitjackets of his lyricism, is, be it stressed, not the same as that totalitarian philistia which judges art by its politics. And what will last of Lindsay is a few dozen lines (to be cited presently) of great lyric art.

The patronizing condescension with which Lindsay is read today is his penalty for having had the courage to be generous, enthusiastic, inelegant. The resultant lyricism is particularly needed by American poetry today to counteract the current taste for fastidious formalism and the current fear of being ridiculous, ultimately a fear of being lyrical. Thus his best poetry, admittedly infrequent, will serve as a corrective to the current unlyrical elegance; while his worst, though more frequent, can no longer do harm, being too unfashionably remote from the current fastidiousness to make the wrong sort—the faddish sort—of converts.

The comparison of Lindsay with Dante is intended not in terms of greatness, whether of poetry or thought, but in terms of voicing one's roots. In their respective religious communities, each was the poet who best voiced his particular heritage. The contrasting views of man in those two heritages will broaden the second part of this discussion from Lindsay to American culture as a whole.

Lindsay is the Dante of the only indigenous American church: Fundamentalist Biblebelt revivalism. For that church he wrote major poetry of mystical vision, as well as the jingley junk (boomlay-boom) for which he is better known. Carrying further, church for church and relic for relic, the analogy with the Florentine poet of Catholicism, we may summarize: Lindsay's Rome was Springfield, Illinois; his Holy Roman Emperor was the specter of Abe Lincoln; his Virgil-guide was Johnny Appleseed. His Beatrice was "A Golden-Haired Girl in a Louisiana Town": "You are my love / If your heart is as kind / As your eyes are now." His martyred Saint Sebastian was Governor Altgeld (persecuted for saving the Haymarket anarchists from lynching). His angel hosts were the Anti-Saloon League and the Salvation Army, lovingly washing in the "blood of the lamb" the stenos and garage mechanics of Chicago.

To continue the analogy: Lindsay's version of the Deadly Sins, as a middle-class Fundamentalist schoolma'am might see

them, was the beguiling depravities of "matching pennies and shooting craps," "playing poker and taking naps." These two lines are from "Simon Legree," a combination of a Negro spiritual with a Calvinistic morality; the result of that combination can only be called intoxicated with sobriety. Dante's medieval heretics partly corresponded to what Lindsay called "the renegade Campbellites," a Fundamentalist splinter-group secession:

> *O prodigal son, O recreant daughter,*
> *When broken by the death of a child,*
> *You called for the graybeard Campbellite elder,*
> *Who spoke as of old in the wild. . . .*
> *An American Millennium. . .*
> *When Campbell arose,*
> *A pillar of fire,*
> *The great high priest of the spring. . . .*

But then, in the same poem, comes the sudden self-mockery of:

> *And millennial trumpets poised, half-lifted,*
> *Millennial trumpets that wait.*

Here the verb "wait," mocking the ever-unfulfilled prophecies of Fundamentalist revivalism, is the kind of slip that occurs accidentally-on-purpose. Such frequent semi-conscious slips represent Lindsay's protest against his self-imposed, self-deceiving role of trying to be more Fundamentalist than any Fundamentalist and more folkish than the real folk.

That self-imposed role, which ultimately became his shirt-of-Nessus, may have resulted from two tacit postulates. First, that poetry readers have no more right to laugh at the homespun Fundamentalist theology of the old American West than at the subtler but perhaps no more pious-hearted theology of Dante's day. Second, that the American small-town carnival deserved as much respect as Dante's medieval pageants; it was as fitting a literary theme; it was no less capable of combining the divine with the humdrum.

Once you concede these two postulates to Lindsay, all the rest seems to follow, including such lofty Lindsay invocations as: "Love-town, Troy-town Kalamazoo" and "Hail, all hail the popcorn stand." It follows that the Fundamentalist prophet, Alexander Campbell, should debate with the devil upon none other than "a picnic ground." It follows that real, tangible angels jostle Lindsay's circus-barkers and salesmen of soda pop. And certainly Lindsay has as much aesthetic right to stage a modern Trojan war, over love, between Osh Kosh and Kalamazoo as Homer between Greeks and Trojans.

SO FAR SO GOOD. But Lindsay often absurdly overstrains this aesthetic right, these old-world analogies. For example, he hails not an easily-hailed American *objet* like, say, Washington's monument, but the popcorn stand.

Lindsay's motive for choosing the popcorn stand is not unconscious crudeness but conscious provocation. In effect he is saying: "By broadening the boundaries of aestheticism to include such hitherto-unacceptable Americana, my poetry is deliberately provoking, and thereby re-educating, all you supercilious eastern-seaboard-conditioned readers or Europe-conditioned readers."

But at the same time there is a suppressed saboteur within Lindsay, as within every exaggerated nationalist. That underground saboteur infiltrates Lindsay's poems via the most awkward-looking, absurdity-connoting letter in our alphabet, the letter "K." For whatever psychological reasons, many Americans go into convulsions of laughter over the names of foreign towns like Omsk, Tomsk, Minsk, Pinsk, and nearer home, Hoboken, Yonkers, Keokuk, Sauk Center, not to mention those two Lindsay favorites, Osh Kosh and Kalamazoo.

The core of each of those place-names

is a throaty, explosive "K." Try to picture each of that same list, from Omsk through Kalamazoo, being spelt with a modest initial "C" or a chic final "que" in place of the "K"; in that case the names would lose half their comic effect on the ordinary American. The letter "K" even *looks* lop-sided, about to topple helplessly forward, an off-balance rube with metaphoric hay-wisps in its hair. More than any other letter, it connotes the awkward yokel. The words "awkward" and "yokel" themselves would not connote half so much awkwardness, were they not so conspicuously spelt with "K."

Aside from place-names and as further evidence for the hitherto unanalyzed role of "K" in American English, here are still other types of "K" usage with contemptuous connotations:

1. Awkward-looking alien animals: auk, aardvark, kangaroo. In each instance, the animal's ridiculousness seems diminished if "c" or "que" are substituted for "K"; no awkward or comic connotation is attached to the Italian word for kangaroo, namely "canguro."

2. Epithets for allegedly crude aliens: yank (from southerners), kike, gook, chink, mick, kraut, bohunk (for Bohemian or Czech), hunky (for Hungarian), spik (for Puerto Rican), smoke (for Negro), snorky (for Swede). These are too many examples to be coincidental, despite the non-K terms of racial contempt that also occur. Since, except for sauerkraut, "K" is lacking in the source-words for these epithets (e.g., Chinese into chink), it seems as if "K" were deliberately added—perhaps as an imitation of throat-clearing—to make a nickname more insulting.

3. Compare the old comic-strip spelling of "Krazy Kat" with the sarcastic spelling of "Kommunist Khrushchev" in a 1960 press release by the New York State Secretary, Caroline K. Simon (self-

hatred of her own middle initial?), and with the 1960 appeal by Admiral Arleigh Burke, Chief of Naval Operations, asking us to spell "Communists" as "Kommunists" in order to make clear their "foreignism" and their "Kremlin bosses."[1] These absurdities (would "Cremlin Communists" evoke a more trustful response?) reflect a very American linguistic bias.

Of course, no such deliberate linguistic analysis determined Lindsay's obsessive use of awkward town-names with "K." Rather, his use was determined by a blind instinct—a shrewdly blind instinct—for catching the very soul of spoken Americana. No one has ever equalled Lindsay's genius for manipulating the unconscious connotations of the colloquial, even though he perversely misused those connotations for the self-torturing purpose of provoking and then staring-down the ridicule of sophisticated audiences.

That willingness to provoke ridicule may produce his worst poems. Yet it is also the root of the moral courage producing his best poems, such as his elegy for the mob-defying Governor Altgeld of Illinois. Political poetry, even courageous political poetry, is by itself merely a rhymed editorial, better written in prose, unless universalized beyond journalism and arid ideologies into the non-political realm of artistic beauty. Lindsay's Altgeld poem remains one of the great American elegies because it does achieve this humanizing process, transfiguring courage into lyric tenderness:

> Sleep softly . . . eagle forgotten . . . under the
>   stone. . . .
> The mocked and the scorned and the wounded,
>   the lame and the poor
> That should have remembered forever . . . remember no more. . . .
> Sleep softly . . . eagle forgotten . . . under the
>   stone,
> Time has its way with you there, and the clay has
>   its own . . .

> To live in mankind is far more than to live in a
>   name,
> To live in mankind, far, far more . . . than to
>   live in a name.

However, more frequently the heroes Lindsay's poetry presents as the American equivalent of old-world Galahads are not exactly Altgelds. For example, the subtitle of his actual poem "Galahad" reads: "Dedicated to all Crusaders against the International and Interstate Traffic in Young Girls." The subtitle of his poem "King Arthur's Men Have Come Again" was equally earnest and uplifting, namely: "Written while a field-worker in the Anti-Saloon League of Illinois." Of course, the moral heritage of rural Fundamentalism particularly objects to alcohol, along with "playing poker and taking naps."

These twin odes to the Anti-Vice Squad and the Anti-Saloon League are bad poems not because the evil they denounce is unserious but because their treatment of that evil sounds like a mock-heroic parody. To explain such bad writing in so good a poet, let us suggest the hypothesis that Lindsay's mentality included a demon of self-destruction, forever turning the preacher into the clown. This compulsion forced Lindsay, again and again in his verse, to strip himself in public of every shred of what he most prized: human dignity. Perhaps this inner demon was related to the compulsion that finally made Lindsay choose not just any method of suicide but the most horribly painful method imaginable: swallowing a bottle of searing acid.

When a poet consistently exalts whatever heroes, place-names, and occupations sound most ludicrous to his modern poetry audience (for example, Lindsay was an avid exalter of college cheerleaders), then it may be either because he has no ear for poetry or because he has an excellent ear knowingly misused. The first explanation is easily ruled out by the beauty of the above Altgeld elegy. Aside from the self-destructive aspect, there is an important messianic-pedagogic aspect making the second explanation the more plausible one. For example, by inserting the pedantic adjective "interstate" in front of "traffic in young girls" and thereby incongruously juxtaposing the prosaic Mann Act law with the poetic word "Galahad," Lindsay says in effect:

"If you accept my hick-Fundamentalist approach to morality, which I happen to consider the only true and autochthonous American religion, then you must also accept the further implications of that approach. You must accept its humorless terminology, its ridicule-provoking bigotries. What is more, you must accept them with a religious spirit exactly as earnest as that with which Homer and Dante accepted their own autochthonous religious traditions."

Thus considered, Lindsay's poetry is not mere clowning, whether intentional or unintentional, but—in his own revealing phrase—"the higher vaudeville." The adjective "higher" makes all the difference; it means a medieval vaudeville, a messianic circus, a homespun midwest equivalent of the medieval fool-in-Christ.

IN REFUSING to be apologetic toward the old world about America's own kind of creativity, Lindsay does have a valid point. In refusing to allow European legends, heroes, place-names a greater claim on glamour than American ones, he again does have a valid point. Likewise when he establishes the American gift for finding loveliness in the exaggerated, the grotesque. But the self-sabotaging demon within him tends to push these valid points to extremes that strain even the most willing "suspension of disbelief."

When Lindsay fails to make us suspend our disbelief, the reason often is this: he is trying to link not two compatibles, such as prosaic object with prosaic rhetoric or fabulous object with fabulous rhetoric, but prosaic object with fabulous rhetoric. Modern university-trained readers of poetry react unsolemnly to: "Hail, all hail the popcorn stand." Why? Because of a gap I would define as the Lindsay disproportion. The Lindsay disproportion is the gap between the heroic tone of the invocation and the smallness of the invoked object.

But Lindsay's aim, rarely understood by modern readers, was to overcome that disproportion between tone and object by conjuring up a mystic grandeur to sanctify the smallness of American trivia. That mystic grandeur derived from his dream of America as a new world free from old-world frailty, free from original sin. His dream-America was infinitely perfectible, whatever its present faults. Even its most trivial objects were sacred, incarnating the old Rousseauistic dream of the natural goodness of man and eternal progress.

Lindsay believed, or felt he ought to believe, in the impossible America invented by the French poet Chateaubriand and other European romantics. Later, much later (nature imitating art) that invented America was sung by Americans themselves, by Emerson and Whitman. In poetry this utopian American myth culminated in Lindsay's "Golden Book of Springfield" and Hart Crane's "The Bridge"; in politics it culminated in the Populist and Progressive movements of the West.

But the laws of history and human nature permit no "new world" to be really new; Americans contain the same very human mixture of aspiration and fallibility as the old world. Europe's romantic expectation of superhuman achievements in democracy or in culture from America, an expectation that duped the Lindsays and the Hart Cranes as well as the European romantic school that invented it, has helped cause the current European disillusionment with America (even entirely aside from the lies of Communist propaganda). Had Europeans not been so exaggeratedly pro-American in their hopes, they would not be so exaggeratedly anti-American in their despair but would see us as ordinary human beings like themselves.

The paradox behind European expectations of the new world appears in a supposed anecdote of the 1800's about Chateaubriand. He had arrived in America to flee European artificiality and to search for the unspoilt noble savage. And sure enough, as Chateaubriand was creeping through the wild jungle then filling northern New York State around Niagara Falls, he glimpsed a tribe of wild Indians between the trees. They were moving in a circle, as if in some primordial folk-ceremony. Bravely defying the dangers primitive America holds for older civilizations, he crept closer and closer through the thicket, to record for his friends in Paris an eye-witness account of unspoilt Americana in the midst of nature's wilderness. Suddenly he recognized what the redskins were dancing. Led by a little mincing French dancing-master, whom they had imported at great expense from Paris for that purpose, the Indians were pirouetting daintily through the latest steps of a formal Parisian ballroom number.

This anecdote is an allegory for European-American literary relations ever since. European critics are forever visiting our American literature to find a mystical, non-existent Noble Primitive. Instead they find some blasé professor, with a tweedy Oxford jacket and Boston accent, dancing with dreadful nimbleness through some complicated *explication de texte* of Proust. . . .

Instead of pouncing with shoddy glee on the absurd aspects of the Lindsay disproportion between tone and object, let us re-examine more rigorously the Chateaubriand-style dream of America behind those absurd aspects. That American myth is part of a romantic, optimistic philosophy seriously maintained, whatever one may think of it, by great or almost-great minds like Rousseau and Emerson. Therefore, it is unjust to dismiss that same philosophy contemptuously in Lindsay merely because his name has less prestige than theirs. What is wrong-headed in him, is wrong-headed in his preceptors also. He and they dreamed of a new world miraculously reborn without the burden of past history. That unhistorical myth of America distinguishes Whitman and Lindsay from Hawthorne and Faulkner in literature. It distinguishes Jefferson from John Adams in political philosophy. It distinguishes Fundamentalist revivalism, with its millennium just around the corner, and also the hope of quick redemption that Lindsay's poetry hailed in the Salvation Army, from Niebuhrian pessimism within the American Protestant religion. While Lindsay is the Dante of the Fundamentalists, he differs from the old-world Catholic Dante by substituting a romantic, optimistic view of man for the tragic view held by traditional Christianity as well as Greek classicism.

ON THIS ISSUE American literature has two conflicting traditions, the first romantic and progressive, the second classical and conservative. The first heartily affirms American folklore, American democratic and material progress. That Whitman-Emerson literary tradition cracked up in Vachel Lindsay and Hart Crane.[2] It cracked up not merely in their personal breakdowns and final suicides—let us not overstress mere biography—but in the aesthetic breakdown of the myth-making part of their poetry. The non-mythic part of their poetry, its pure lyricism, never did break down and in part remains lastingly beautiful.

A second American tradition is that of the literary pessimists, a new-world continuation of the great Christian pessimists of the old world, from Saint Augustine to Kierkegaard and Cardinal Newman. In America the second literary tradition is just as authentically American as the first one but has never received the same popular recognition, being less comforting. The most influential literary voices of our second tradition are Melville, Hawthorne, Henry Adams, William Faulkner. Its greatest political heritage comes from the *Federalist* papers and from the actual anti-Jeffersonian party of the Federalists, with their partly European source not in Rousseau but in Burke. Its most influential theological voices in America today are Paul Tillich and Reinhold Niebuhr. These literary, political, and theological voices are characterized by scepticism about man and mass and by awareness of the deep sadness of history. Therefore, their bulwark against man and mass and against the precariousness of progress is some relatively conservative framework of traditional continuity, whether in culture, literature, politics, or religion.

The necessity of tragedy, the necessity of recognizing human frailty, human limitation, the perpetualness of evil, a chastened scepticism about human nature and progress: such are the tenets of the perhaps primarily philosophical and aesthetic movement (perhaps only secondarily and then often blunderingly political) known as the new conservatism. These tenets seem partly confirmed by the failure of Lindsay's and Hart Crane's attempts to create a new, untragic kind of myth for America. As if original sin stopped west of the Alleghenies! As if the democratic American, like the noble savage of Rousseau, were immune from human frailty and immune from the spiritual price paid for industrial progress.

To be sure, the attitudes of Emerson and of Whitman (often more tragic and ambivalent than realized) were never so naive or unqualified as the above. But such was the over-simplified form their liberal American creed often took in their main literary heirs, including Lindsay and Crane. Note which two are the only American poets Lindsay names in his long "Litany of the Heroes":

Then let us seek out shining Emerson,
Teacher of Whitman, and better priest of man,
The self-reliant granite American.

Emerson, it will be remembered, appealed to what he called "the great optimism self-affirmed in all bosoms." The germ of Lindsay's and Crane's attempts to force themselves to affirm industrial Americana lies in the following optimistic affirmation of material progress that Emerson noted in his journal for 1871: "In my life-time have been wrought five miracles—1. the steamboat; 2. the railroad; 3. the electric telegraph; 4. the application of the spectroscope to astronomy; 5. the photograph—five miracles which have altered the relations of nations to each other." The best rebuttal to this attempt to affirm "miracles" like the railroad, before having made sure whether they were man's master or slave, came from Emerson's friend Thoreau: "We do not ride on the railroad; it rides on us."

Anticipating the attempts of the Emersonian Lindsay to make a "Troytown" out of every Kalamazoo and to find a Helen in every Osh Kosh, Emerson wrote: "Banks and tariffs, the newspaper and caucus," were "dull to dull people but rest on the same foundations of wonder as the town of Troy and the temple of Delphos." There in one sentence stands the whole Lindsay crusade to rebaptize Americana with wonder, a crusade in itself justifiable but lacking, in both Emerson and Lindsay, the criteria for discriminating between which industrial Americana were wonderworthy and which ones, being tied to mean goals, were wonder-destroying. Apropos the mean goals of so much mechanical progress, it was, once again, the profounder Thoreau who punctured in advance the Emerson-Whitman-Lindsay-Crane optimism by warning: "We are now in great haste to construct a magnetic telegraph from Maine to Texas; but Maine and Texas, it may be, have nothing important to communicate."

THE OPTIMISTIC progress-affirming and folklore-affirming voices of Emerson and Whitman cracked up in their disciples Lindsay and Crane when the crushing of the individual in modern mechanization became simply too unbearable to affirm. The modern poet of progress may try to keep up his optimistic grin for his readers while the custard pie of "higher vaudeville" drips down his face. But past a certain point, he can no longer keep up the grin, whether psychologically in his private life or aesthetically in his public poetry. Our overadjusted standardization becomes just one custard pie too many for the unadjusted poet to affirm, no matter how desperately he tries to outshout his inner tragic insight by shouting (in Lindsay's case) "Hail, all hail the popcorn stand" and by hailing (in Crane's case) the Brooklyn Bridge as "the myth whereof I sing." Lindsay and Crane committed suicide in 1931 and 1932 respectively, in both cases in that depression era which seemed temporarily to end the boundless optimism of American material progress.

Lindsay's "Golden Book of Springfield" and Crane's "The Bridge," though so different in other respects, are the two outstanding examples of trying to contrive an untragic myth of affirmation out of our modern industrial progress.

Lindsay and Crane celebrated the American myth more enthusiastically than would the philistine kind of booster because, unlike the philistine, they were boosters not by temperament but by a self-coercion which their temperament was constantly sabotaging. The genuine booster will affirm not all but most Americana; Lindsay and Crane sometimes seemed to try to affirm all. Lindsay's idealizing of the Hollywood cinema, and Hart Crane's romanticizing of what he called the "oil-rinsed ecstasy" of even such gadgets as ball-bearings, were acts of desperation; they were forcing themselves to affirm even those crass aspects of American mechanization that they themselves suffered from most. In both cases the self-coercion proved literally unbearable; neither of our greatest literary optimists could *bear* staying alive on his own yes-saying terms.

Perhaps there is a profound lesson in the fact that both these poets of affirmation led miserable and so-called unsuccessful lives, ending in suicide, while T. S. Eliot, the fastidious no-sayer, who wrote the pessimism of *The Waste Land* instead of glorifying Springfield or the Brooklyn Bridge, has been thriving most successfully. Perhaps the lesson is that our modern industrial age is so unbearable that it drives its own boosters to insanity and self-destruction while acclaiming its knockers with Nobel prizes.

But even aside from our own particular age and the madness that strikes down the muse that would embrace its machines, it is a conservative fact of life that unqualified optimism about human nature results in disaster. Robert Penn Warren showed this in his long poem about Jefferson, *Brother to Dragons*. When events do finally force the excessive optimist to allow for human frailty, he ends up more disillusioned, more inclined to either self-destruction or terrorism than the conservative who was pessimistic from the start.

Lindsay's poems celebrate by specific references every single one of the main voices of American optimism: the Rousseau-Jefferson view of human psychology, the political utopianism of Jacksonian democracy, the economic utopianism of the Populists, the religious utopianism of Fundamentalist chiliasm, and the Emerson-Whitman literary tradition. All five of these often separate voices converge to produce one of Lindsay's most revealing couplets:

> God has great estates just past the line,
> Green farms for all, and meat and corn and wine.

The key line preceding that couplet is "Turn the bolt—how soon we would be free!" That line recalls the radical, anti-traditionalist slogan of that Bible of the French Revolution, Rousseau's *Social Contract* of 1762: "Man is born free and is everywhere in chains." Actually what makes man free is precisely those so-called "chains" of tradition, of established religion, of unbroken historical continuity; they free him from the *hubris* of his own nature, which becomes self-destructive if without traditional "chains." To vary the metaphor, freedom, in the older Christian and Burkean view, depends on a reverent conserving of traffic-lights, not on a Rousseauist-optimist-radical smashing of them.

Despite coercing himself painfully into enjoying progress, Lindsay also had his bitter side about the relationship between the muse and the machine age. Our 1950's, like *his* 1920's, suffered from the pressure of overadjusted public life against the privacy of the free imagination. Resuming the analogy with Dante's *Divine Comedy*, we note that Lindsay's poetry had not only its Paradiso, in his dream of his future Springfield, but its Inferno in the Springfield of his own day. His Inferno was the same as ours: the standardizing side of the America he secretly hated when he affirmed her, secretly loved when he rejected her. "Inferno" is not too strong a word for the soul-destroying commercialism whose symbols, in his poetry, were

broken factory windows. This occasional bitterness about commercialism reflected the same kind of unadjusted poetic imagination as Baudelaire's bitterness about *l'esprit belge*. In Lindsay that anti-cash-nexus reaction produced two of the strongest, leanest lines ever written on the subject:

> Factory windows are always broken. . . .
> End of the factory-window song.

Lindsay hoped a rooted, American Fundamentalist religion from the Midwest would soon, in his own words, be "Building against our blatant, restless time / An unseen, skilful, medieval wall." This neo-medieval wall would overcome, he hoped, the secular materialism he attributed to the midwest of his day. He hoped to regenerate industrialism not by rejecting it pessimistically but by sanctifying it optimistically through a new religious era:

> Think not that incense-smoke, has had its day.
> My friends, the incense-time has but begun. . . .
> And on our old, old plains some muddy stream,
> Dark as the Ganges, shall, like that strange tide—
> (Whispering mystery to half the earth)—
> Gather the praying millions to its side.

Being also an amateur painter, Lindsay distributed on street corners his pictures of censers in the sky, swinging their "incense-time" redeemingly above Springfield, Illinois. To the open-mouthed, dumbfounded burghers of Springfield he distributed, as free messianic tracts, a poem called "The Soul of the City Receiving the Gift of the Holy Ghost":

> Censers are swinging
> Over the town. . .
> Censers are swinging,
> Heaven comes down.
> City, dead city,
> Awake from the dead!

Whenever Lindsay came to believe something, he believed it strongly enough to want to make all his neighbors believe it also. Risking mockery and rebuff, he had the courageous idealism of giving unsolicited home-printed copies of his message to those who least wanted to receive it: "I flooded Springfield with free pamphlets incessantly." For such crusades he might be called either a crank or a genuine American saint. Instead of either of these alternatives, he pictured himself as following the footsteps of his religious and folk hero Johnny Appleseed. Thus in his prose piece, *Adventures Preaching Hieroglyphic Sermons*, Lindsay wrote: "Johnny Appleseed, whom I recommend to all men who love visions, was a man of lonely walking, a literal Swedenborgian all his days, distributing tracts when occasionally he met a settler. . . . I am for Johnny Appleseed's United States."

The more the forces of cash-nexus made Springfield secular, materialistic, overadjusted, the more did Lindsay (in his own words) "hand out to anyone who would take it in the street" the counterforce of his poem "Springfield Magical":

In this, the City of my Discontent,
Sometimes there comes a whisper from the grass,
"Romance, Romance—is here. No Hindu town
Is quite so strange. No Citadel of Brass
By Sinbad found, held half such love and hate". . . .
In this, the City of my Discontent!

How did his good neighbors respond to all this distribution of rhymed broadsides, this revivalist saving of their souls at street corners? Lindsay comments wistfully: "It was at this point that I was dropped from such YMCA work and Anti-Saloon League work as I was doing in the Springfield region."

Such was America's negative response to Lindsay's often valid gospel of beauty. Yet his faith in the American myth prevented him from becoming the type of the irreconcilable martyr-crank. If anything, he was reconciled all too easily to the commercialist society that rejected

him. For example, he tried symbolically to beautify and thereby redeem the industrial revolution by his poem in praise of the electric-light ads on Broadway:

The signs in the street and the signs in the skies
Shall make a new Zodiac, guiding the wise,
And Broadway make one with that marvellous stair
That is climbed by the rainbow-clad spirits of prayer.

These flashing ad-signs of Times Square would indeed be, as Lindsay pretended, the most beautiful thing in the world if only (as Chesterton said) we did not know how to read.

Lindsay could not have continued writing, or even staying alive, in any society to which he could not be reconciled more easily than reality ever permits; he was too steeped in the boundless expectations of the Fundamentalist millennial spirit, the spirit he called "the Resurrection parade."

Thus Lindsay quoted with approval from Alexander Campbell's appropriately named magazine *The Millennial Harbinger*, in which that Fundamentalist prophet wrote in 1865, "the present material universe . . . will be wholly regenerated." Himself a learned man and by no means "crude" in the more popular meaning of Fundamentalist revivalism, Campbell nevertheless fitted into the optimist-Rousseauist tradition by rejecting Original Sin and by rejecting baptism at birth as unnecessary and reactionary—evil allegedly not being present in human nature that early but added by corrupt society later.

What is shoddy in the American myth is not affirmation itself; classic tragedy affirms ("Gaiety transfiguring all that dread"). What is shoddy is not the hard-won affirmation that follows tragic insight but the facile unearned optimism that leads only to disillusionment. Here is a prose example of how Lindsay's valid crusade against the adjective "standard-ized" collapses suddenly into a too-easy optimism:

> I have been looking out of standardized windows of "The Flat-Wheeled Pullman Car." I have been living in standardized hotels, have been eating jazzed meals as impersonal as patent breakfast-food. . . . The unstandardized thing is the overwhelming flame of youth . . . an audience of one thousand different dazzling hieroglyphics of flame. . . . My mystic Springfield is here, also, in its fashion . . . a Springfield torn down and rebuilt from the very foundations, according to visions that might appear to an Egyptian . . . or any one else whose secret movie-soul was a part of the great spiritual movie.

Note the typical Lindsay disproportion by which this moving passage ends with an appalling anticlimax, equating Holly-wood's facile commercialized "visions" with the tragically earned classic ones. Yet his best and worst writing are so intertwined that this "movie soul" gush is immediately followed by one of his finest prose passages about American democracy at its noblest:

> I believe that civic ecstasy can be so splendid, so unutterably afire, continuing and increasing with such apocalyptic zeal, that the whole visible fabric of the world can be changed. . . . And I say: change not the mass, but change the fabric of your own soul and your own visions, and you change all.

In Lindsay's Springfield Paradiso of tomorrow: "civic ecstasy." But in his Springfield Inferno of today: "Factory windows are always broken." Hence his outburst: "I went through the usual Mid-dle West crucifixion of the artist." That outburst, so typical of the Midwest artist of the 1920's and so rarely heard in the more humanistic Midwest of today, was valid enough for his time. It should not be snubbed as sentimental by later and sleeker artists, battening on fellowships

and snob-appeal and producing art more elegant, less anguished than Lindsay's. But let us of the post–Sinclair Lewis gen-eration note also the converse of Lindsay's outburst: namely, the usual verbal cruci-fixion of the Middle West by the artist.

WHEN LINDSAY was a child, an old duck-pond diviner pronounced this Delphic utterance about America's future laureate of Fundamentalism: "A child of destiny and also fond of sweets." This comment, in which the word "also" is particularly important, proved prophetic of Lindsay's combination of a messianic religious mes-sage with a lyrical aestheticism. In his messianic aspect of propagating the un-tragic American myth, he called himself a "cartooning preacher," a half-mocking phrase reminiscent of his phrase "the higher vaudeville." In his aesthetic aspect, preaching what one of his poems called "A Gospel of Beauty," he sometimes saw himself as a log-cabin Pater; it is often overlooked that, in such poems as "The King of Yellow Butterflies," Lindsay was more of a "pure aesthete" than most of the French Parnassians at their most ethe-real.

But Lindsay's aesthetic aspect was more frequently modeled on Ruskin's semi-moralized aestheticism: "One of my crimes was a course of lectures at the YMCA on Ruskin's famous chapters on the nature of Gothic." No wonder "there were days in my home town when the Babbitts . . . were about ready to send me to jail or burn me at the stake for some sort of witchcraft, dimly apprehended, but im-possible for them to define"; that quota-tion reveals Lindsay's admirable coura-geous honesty about making no concessions to the antipoetic clichés of his burgher audiences. But the darker undertone of the quotation also reveals his self-destruc-tive compulsion to state his beliefs, in this case perfectly reasonable beliefs, in the terms most calculated to provoke incomprehension and ridicule.

Lindsay's authentic western Americana were never presented for their own sake, never merely as quaint antiques for the tourist trade. Rather, they were presented for the more serious purposes of either his Whitman-messianic aspect or his Ruskin-aesthetic aspect, depending on whether the given poem happened to be fond of destiny or of sweets. The obsessiveness these two aspects had for him was best summed up in his own words: "Incense and splendor haunt me as I go." In the end the psychological and social meaning of his poems remains secondary to their lyricism; and indeed his poems achieve their occasional social effectiveness only via their lyricism, rather than apart from it. At his best, Lindsay incarnates for America the importance and dignity of spontaneous song: its ennobling and re-humanizing role in a standardized machine age.

Part of Lindsay's aesthetic compulsion, giving him the uniqueness only possessed by major poets, lies in his juxtaposition of the delicate and the grotesque: for example, in his phrase "the flower-fed buffaloes of the spring," subject of one of his purest lyrics. Running through his diversities of titles and subject matter, note also the delicate and the grotesque color-juxtapositions of "the king of yellow butterflies" with "the golden whales of California" and the semantic juxtaposition of "harps in heaven" with "the sins of Kalamazoo." Such gargoyle tenderness is a genre of sensibility explored by few other poets beside Beddoes, Rimbaud, Dylan Thomas, the poets with whom Lindsay's unfulfilled genius, beneath its tough loud disguises, properly belongs. In a situation Beddoes would have cherished, here is a typical example of gargoyle tenderness in Lindsay; "The Song of the Garden-Toad" expresses the agony and hate of worms when the gardener crushes their soil, with unconscious cruelty, in order to plant airy flowers:

> *Down, down beneath the daisy beds,*
> *O hear the cries of pain! . . .*
> *I wonder if that gardener hears*
> *Who made the mold all fine*
> *And packed each gentle seedling down*
> *So carefully in line?*
>
> *I watched the red rose reaching up*
> *To ask him if he heard*
> *Those cries that stung the evening earth*
> *Till all the rose-roots stirred.*
> *She asked him if he felt the hate*
> *That burned beneath them there.*
> *She asked him if he heard the curse*
> *Of worms in black despair.*

Delicacy is not a noun most modern readers associate with Lindsay. Yet his sense of cadence was so very delicate that it disguised itself defensively, his time and place being what they were, beneath ear-splitting auditory signposts. His signposts deliberately pointed in the wrong direction, the loud indelicate direction. Living where he did and believing the myth he believed, he needed to conceal his bitter, introverted sensitivity beneath the extroverted optimism of American folklore—that is, beneath a tone deliberately coarse, chummy, whooping, the whiz-bang clap-trap of poems like "The Kallyope Yell." In such curiosities of our literature, no poet was ever more perversely skilful at sounding embarrassingly unskilful. No poet was ever more dexterous at sounding gauche. What in Whitman was merely a would-be "barbaric yawp," does yawp with an unbearably successful barbarism in Lindsay:

> *I am the Gutter Dream,*
> *Tune-maker born of steam . . .*
> *Music of the mob am I,*
> *Circus-day's tremendous cry:—*
> *Hoot toot, hoot toot, hoot toot, hoot toot,*
> *Willy willy willy wah HOO!*

Followed, as if that were not enough, with the dying fall, the final fading yawp of: "Sizz, fizz."

Consequently Lindsay's poetry is often defined as mere oratory, to be shouted aloud by a mob chorus. Part of him wanted this view to be held. Another part of him lamented: "I have paid too great a penalty for having a few rhymed orations. All I write is assumed to be loose oratory or even jazz, though I have never used the word 'jazz' except in irony." His best work, often his least known work, was produced by the part of him that once confessed: "All my poetry marked to be read aloud should be whispered . . . for the inner ear . . . whispering in solitude."

Admittedly Lindsay is to blame (via the pseudo-tough defense mechanism of his sensitivity) for the fact that his work is generally associated with an extroverted booming voice: for example, with his University of Kansas football cheers, his Salvation Army trumpets. Yet the truest voice of his poetry is its quietness. That quietness produced line after line of imaginative evocation. Line after line of it comes tumbling again and again—at random from a dozen unconnected poems—over that "inner ear" in all of us to which he "whispered." To which his lyricism still whispers today, quietly beautiful, in line after line like this:

"The little lacquered boxes in his hands."

"They shiver by the shallow pools."

"I am a trout in this river of light."

"Stealer of vases of most precious ointment."

"Her ears became the tiniest humorous calf's-ears." (This of the Egyptian bovine deity of love, Hathor.)

"You will go back as men turn to Kentucky,
Land of their fathers, dark and bloody ground."

"Abraham Lincoln Walks At Midnight."

"Sleep softly . . . eagle forgotten . . . under the stone."

"O empty boats, we all refuse, that by our windows wait."

And even when an actual loud "cry" is described, what a dreamy inner cry: "We will sow secret herbs and plant old roses" while "Green monkeys cry in Sanskrit to their souls." Many poets have written of the "sounding sea"; none has made it sound so hushed, so inward as this:

Useful are you. There stands the useless one
Who builds the Haunted Palace in the sun.
Good tailors, can you dress a doll for me
With silks that whisper of the sounding sea?

Here is an entire poem of delicate quietness:

Euclid

Old Euclid drew a circle
On a sand-beach long ago.
He bounded and enclosed it
With angles thus and so.
His set of solemn graybeards
Nodded and argued much
Of arc and of circumference,
Diameter and such.
A silent child stood by them
From morning until noon
Because they drew such charming
Round pictures of the moon.

This Lindsay parable of the two meanings of circles purges the modern reader of arid, abstract rationalism and re-humanizes, re-lyricizes, de-mechanizes him. The poem avoids coyness and cuteness, even if only by a triumphant hair's breadth, and thereby achieves not the facile but the difficult kind of simplicity.

Like Yeats, Lindsay transforms sentimentality into true art by means of the accompanying anti-sentimentality of nervously sinewy rhythms. Note, for example, the craftsmanship with which the lean rhythmic rightness of these two Lindsay quatrains redeems their otherwise sentimental rhetoric:

Why do I faint with love
Till the prairies dip and reel?

My heart is a kicking horse
Shod with Kentucky steel.

No drop of my blood from north
Of Mason and Dixon's line.
And this racer in my breast
Tears my ribs for a sign.

Such poetry is a pure art for art's sake. Yet the same author could also be a poet of urgent social polemic. Here is Lindsay's higher-vaudeville imitation of how a sixteen-year-old Bryanite Populist Democrat in 1896 would have viewed the revolt of western mass egalitarianism against the traditionalism and aristocracy attributed to America's eastern seaboard:

Defeat of western silver.
Defeat of the wheat.
Victory of letterfiles
And plutocrats in miles
With dollar signs upon their coats
And spats on their feet.
Victory of custodians,
Plymouth Rock,
And all that inbred landlord stock.
Victory of the neat. . . .
Defeat of the Pacific and the long Mississippi. . . .
And all these in their helpless days
By the dour East oppressed, . . .
Crucifying half the West,
Till the whole Atlantic coast
Seemed a giant spiders' nest. . . .
And all the way to frightened Maine the old East
*   heard them call. . . .*
Prairie avenger, mountain lion,
Bryan, Bryan, Bryan, Bryan,
Smashing Plymouth Rock with his boulders from
*   the West.*

Let us consider that extraordinary Bryan poem first aesthetically, then politically. Note the sensuous concreteness of imagery. Instead of characterizing Bryan's enemies with the abstract, unlyrical word "the rich," Lindsay says concretely: "Victory of letterfiles/And plutocrats in miles/With dollar signs upon their coats." His self-mocking sense of humor, the subtlety of his pseudo-crudity, explains the sur-

realist fantasy of pretending, with wonderful preposterousness, that plutocrats literally wear dollar signs on their coats.

Taken in its political symbolism, Lindsay's aesthetic image of the Populists "smashing Plymouth Rock" tells more than many prose volumes about the psychology of this recurrent American form of social protest. The invocation "avenger, mountain lion" brings out the motivating importance of revenge in Populism, revenge for having been humiliated and patronized by "that inbred landlord stock" of Plymouth Rock. The same emotion of revenge-for-humiliation is often shared by recent immigrants in Boston and the East as well as by the older American stock in the West, including Wisconsin. Therefore, the emotion portrayed in Lindsay's Bryan poem helps explain the neo-Populist nationalist demagogy of the early 1950's. No wonder the latter was, in part, a demagogy of social inferiority complex that resented primarily not the Communists, whom it denounced, but the social élite (Ivy League colleges, State Department of Groton-Harvard Acheson), whom it implicated.

In Lindsay's day, the midwest dream of messianic mass-ecstasy in politics (really, Fundamentalist revivalism secularized) still had a touching youthful innocence; his Bryan poem, despite its doctrinaire social message, could still succeed in being movingly lyrical; American optimism was cracking but not yet cracked up. In contrast, the neo-Populist demagogy of our own day can find no voice, whether poetic or social-reformist, of Lindsay's cultural or moral stature. For meanwhile American standardization plus Ortega's "revolt of the masses" have transformed salvation-via-mob from innocent dream to sordid nightmare. And from genuine economic needs (such as Populist farmers exploited by railroads) to economic hypochondria.

Even the early Lindsay had not been able to celebrate without tragic qualms (disguised as comic hamming with K's and popcorn stands) this utopian faith in the mass-instinct. After his death, this pure young optimism of the West degenerated into a frustrated and scapegoat-hunting optimism, a soured and hence lynch-mob-minded faith in the avenging People. On the biographical plane: Lindsay himself partly succumbed to this process in the final paranoid[3] fantasies accompanying his suicide. On the plane of social psychology: it is the process whereby soured left-wing radicals, the Populists and La-Follette Progressives of yesteryear, have become right-wing radicals (would-be conservatives) while significantly still retaining their basic Populist-folksy-isolationist resentment against eastern-Anglophile élites.[4] Ponder, for example, the isolationist-Anglophobe career of a Senator Nye or a Senator Wheeler, forever "smashing Plymouth Rock"—first from left, then from right—"with his boulders from the West."

Here are two examples far more extreme. Father Coughlin, starting out as a western free-silver radical of the old Populist left, became a pro-Nazi, Anglophobe, anti-semitic radical of the "right" without ever having to change his (and his mass-movement's) true emotional bias, the bias against fancy eastern city slickers and international bankers. Likewise Ezra Pound's wartime broadcasts for Mussolini, against Jewish and British international bankers, have their true psychological and social origin in the midwestern free-silver Populist background of Pound's earlier tracts on economics and on the "conspiracies" of the Wall Street gold standard.

From this salvation-via-mob dilemma, with its false choice between leftist and rightist mob-hatreds, Lindsay himself pointed the way out. The way out was love: not that philistine-humanitarian love of progress (so aptly refuted by Edmund Burke and Irving Babbitt) whose hug squashes individuals into an impersonal mass; but the creative lyric love that flows healingly from the inner integrity—the holy imagination—of great art. In short, when Lindsay did voice deeply enough the roots of the human condition, he became simply an artist, a fundamental poet, rather than merely the poet of the Fundamentalists. His poem "The Leaden-Eyed" describes perfectly the human price paid for unimaginative standardization and at the same time, through its lyricism, demands the rehumanizing of the machine age:

> Not that they starve, but starve so dreamlessly,
> Not that they sow, but that they seldom reap,
> Not that they serve, but have no gods to serve,
> Not that they die but that they die like sheep.

Such a rehumanizing-through-creativity as Lindsay achieved at his best, seems the only way out from our age of the three impersonal M's: masses, machines, and mediocrity. This great, absurd, and holy poet of America's native religious roots merits the adjective "God-intoxicated" because he found the redeeming religious imagination everywhere, everywhere—in the absurd as well as in the high:

> Once, in the city of Kalamazoo,
> The gods went walking, two and two.

And finally (after boomlay-booms are over) there remains his noble seven-word line that expresses the exhausting yet creative tension between the outer ethical demands of society and the aesthetic demands of inwardness; let us conclude, then, with Vachel Lindsay's quietest line:

> Courage and sleep are the principal things.

NOTES

[1] Burke-Simon quotes are from the *New York Times,* March 20, 1960, p. 43, and the *Paris Herald-Tribune,* editorial page, April 2, 1960.

[2] For a parallel analysis of Crane's machine symbolism, see P. Viereck, "The Poet in the Machine Age," essay in the *Journal of the History of Ideas*, January 1949; also reprinted as appendix of Viereck, *Strike Through the Mask* (New York: Scribner's, 1950).

[3] Lindsay's reputed dying words, after swallowing a bottle of searing Lysol: "They tried to get me; I got them first." Cf. Hart Crane's comparable *cri de coeur*: "I could not pick the arrows from my side"—with his similar frustrated optimism (so much more tragic than Eliotine pessimism) about the mechanized "American dream."

[4] For full documentation (no space here) of this admittedly debatable hypothesis, see the section "Direct Democracy: From Populist Left to Nationalist Right," pp. 129–223, in P. Viereck, *The Unadjusted Man* (Boston: Beacon Press, 1956).

[IV, Summer 1960, 269–284]

76

The Classicism of Robert Frost

GORHAM MUNSON

Gorham (Bert) Munson (1896–1969) was an author and critic who lived in New York. He specialized in American literature of the 1900–1930 era and published many important studies in that field. An authority on Robert Frost, he wrote the article on the poet for the Encyclopaedia Britannica *in 1962, updating his monograph* Robert Frost *of 1929. His book* The Written Word: How To Write Readable Prose *(1949) was based on a course of "unacademic" lectures that was offered beginning in 1931 at the New School for Social Research and was believed to have had the largest registration of any writing course in New York City. Among his posthumous works is the recently published* The Awakening Twenties: A Memoir–History of a Literary Period *(1985).*

ONE NIGHT in the fall of 1926 I found a note in my mailbox that gave me a jump of excitement. I saved that note for many years but cannot reproduce it now, for it vanished, with other literary effects I prized, in an illegal sale of goods I had trustfully stored in a warehouse. It may turn up some day in a pile of rummage, but it is likely, I think, that it was destroyed as worthless at the time of the auction. I was, of course, financially compensated for the loss before the case was brought to trial but what psychological compensation can there be for the destruction of papers that have intense, sentimental, literary significance?

The note on a small sheet of paper—was it torn from a notebook?—was signed "Robert Frost." I do not remember whether it was pencilled or penned, or if it said anything more than to ask me to telephone its signer at Ridgely Torrence's

number in the morning. I was surprised but made an immediate guess. The note had something to do with an interpretative essay on Frost I had published a year and a half earlier in the *Saturday Review of Literature.* I had heard indirectly that Frost had liked this essay. He had been to Dartmouth "barding around," and had told a Wesleyan classmate of mine, George R. Potter, who was teaching there, that he liked my *Saturday Review* piece because "it said something new about me," and Potter had conveyed to me this praise. So I expected some sign of favorable interest when I called the Torrence number from the pay telephone at Charles French Restaurant on Sixth Avenue, where in those days I often went for breakfast.

Frost shyly told me why he had left the note at 144 West Eleventh. John Farrar, the young editor at the George H. Doran Company, a Vermonter, wanted to publish a biography of Robert Frost. He was launching a series—the Murray Hill Biographies—and had commissioned books on Upton Sinclair, Nathaniel Hawthorne, and Edwin Arlington Robinson; now he was looking for someone to write on Frost. Very tactfully Frost sounded me on my willingness to undertake such a commission. He was so tentative in his approach that it would have been easy to decline the flattering suggestion. I said at once that I would like to discuss the suggestion, and Frost invited me to dinner at the Torrence apartment on Morton Street deep in the Village.

I had met Ridgely Torrence several times previously at 107 Waverly Place where he had lived in the top-floor apartment his friend William Vaughn Moody had once occupied. Moody's wealthy widow has retained the apartment and put the Torrences in it, and I had invited myself there in 1918 to look at the amateur paintings of William Vaughn Moody which graced the walls. My memory of these is dim and my notes on them also disappeared in the auction sale disaster, but I believe they were pictures of moors and the sea, bluish in tone and misty in effect. Torrence was the self-effacing poetry editor of *The New Republic*, and was recognized by a few—Colum and Robinson and Frost—as being a fine poet. Frost dedicated a poem to him, "A Passing Glimpse"; the dedication reads: "To Ridgely Torrence on Last Looking into His 'Hesperides.'" This poem concludes with a thought: "Heaven gives its glimpses only to those / Not in a position to look too close"—which seems an appropriate thing to say of the poet who wrote "Light." "I have read it," A. E. Housman said of Torrence's work, "with admiration for its poetic impulse and for the accomplishment of its verse." Yet the anthologists who now rightly remember Trumbull Stickney have already passed over "Light"

and "Adam's Dying" and "The Son" and two or three others of Torrence's best poems.

Thus I came to the Morton Street apartment of the Torrences and was greeted by tall, gentle Ridgely and by Olivia Howard Dunbar, his writing wife who was to write a book after Mrs. Moody's death in 1932 about this shining salon mistress, Harriet Moody, who had encouraged Hart Crane when he was sixteen. I was then presented to the house guest. "Prohibition cocktails" appeared, and we drank them standing up. I noticed that Frost was no sipper but downed his drink like a Vermont farmer, and we proceeded to the table. As was to be expected on this occasion, and as always happened in the company of Frost, Frost led the conversation and contributed the most.

What he told me was certainly flattering, but it was clearly not intended to flatter. He said that when Farrar had asked him to suggest someone to write a Murray Hill biography of him, he had named me because I had said something different about him and he felt I would produce a critical book. He made it clear that he did not want a personal life that invaded the privacy of himself and his family. No, he wanted a biography that would be a critical account of his work, one that would observe the line between the public and the private life and would respect his reticence about his family life. He had never written me about my *Saturday Review* essay because, he said, "I was waiting for a chance to do something to show my appreciation," and that chance had come when John Farrar had asked him to suggest a biographer.

I told Frost that the restrictions he imposed on his biographer were entirely acceptable. I would much rather write a critical biography than a personal, probing, psychological study such as was coming into vogue, and so we parted early that night with the understanding that Farrar would offer me a contract.

IN THE SUMMER of 1924, which I spent at the Woodstock, N.Y., colony, I read all of Frost I could find. I initiated my thorough study of the poet, whose poems I had hitherto read only sporadically, with his most recent book—his fourth—*New Hampshire*. I had been surprised and delighted by the title poem, "New Hampshire," a Horatian satire in a contemporary manner. I had not expected to find a bucolic poet at play in the midst of the sophisticated literary currents of the period, but there Frost was, knowledgeable of the new literary forces, but humorous and satirical about them. "New Hampshire" was different from anything Frost had written before, and I, a modern, responded with an enthusiasm not felt for *A Boy's Will* and the other early volumes of Frost. These I had respected, but "New Hampshire" raised my appreciation of them by providing insight into the poet's direction.

I may as well confess myself the author
Of several books against the world in general.

What did Frost mean by these lines, I asked; for up to then, Frost had been classified by Amy Lowell, Waldo Frank and other champions of the "new poetry" as a votary of the new movement in American literature. But in "New Hampshire" Frost seemed to disassociate himself from the new wave of American writers. He took a stand against their tendencies and revolts.

I was made equally curious by Frost's reply in "New Hampshire" to "a narrow choice the age insists on." According to the poem, Frost had been commanded: "Choose you which you will be—a prude, or puke, / Mewling and puking in the public arms." "Me for the hills where I

don't have to choose" was Frost's first reply, and then he said: "How about being a good Greek, for instance?" In that question I seemed to discover a key to Frost's poetic intentions, but I needed corroboration. That confirmation I received from an accident of reading that same summer at Woodstock.

Edwin and Vera Seaver were living at Zena, near Woodstock, and Edwin was producing a short-lived "little magazine," *1924*—had it survived it would have changed its name with the new year each year—to which I contributed an essay on the negativism of T. S. Eliot. I liked to walk over from "Ma" Russell's boardinghouse to the Seavers' shack for chit-chat about letters and the young generation. One afternoon Seaver told me of the stimulation he had received from Irving Babbitt's famous course at Harvard on Rousseau and romanticism, and he so far overcame my prejudice against Babbitt, which I had acquired from the aspersions of H. L. Mencken and Van Wyck Brooks, that I found myself carrying Seaver's copy of *Rousseau and Romanticism* back to "Ma" Russell's. Soon I was engrossed in this illuminating study of the imagination, its nature, kinds, and function, and the further I read into it, the more light it seemed to throw on the poetics of Robert Frost. Babbitt's study of the imagination gave me an explanation of why Frost went against the general drift of the world and why he wanted to be a good Greek. I saw that Frost was not a romantic poet, as some would have it, but rather a classical poet, as nobody seemed to be remarking.

So I wrote a paper at the end of that summer of '24 that was intended to show that Robert Frost was a poet of humanistic temper. "The purest classical poet of America today is Robert Frost," I declared at the outset of this paper. This was the "something different," the "something new" that I said about Frost that led him to leave a note in my mailbox a couple of years later.

I did not know at the time that Irving Babbitt and Paul Elmer More, the leaders of the New Humanism, as it was to be called in the last years of the twenties, had discovered the humanistic nature of Frost's poetry as early as 1916. In that year Frost was elected to the National Institute of Arts and Letters. "It was over the dead body of Robert Underwood Johnson, and with the backing of Wilbur Cross, Irving Babbitt and Paul Elmer More that I got in," Frost told Elizabeth Shepley Sergeant. "Johnson's resistance had its source in my early refusals by magazines. My backers could only bring me in as a Humanist." "Which means a Platonist," Frost mistakenly added, forgetting that while More was a Platonist, Babbitt might better be termed an Aristotelian.

Nor had I then read any essay on Frost's neighborliness by a follower of Babbitt and More, a young Amherst professor, G. R. Elliott, in which Frost's neighborliness was differentiated from humanitarianism, a romantic cult Frost despised. As Lawrance Thompson was to observe long after Elliott's essay, "the metaphor which represents the key to Frost's social outlook is the metaphor of community relationship: neighborliness." Frost felt, in Thompson's well-chosen words, that "the well-meaning pity of the humanitarians encourages the abandonment of that self-discipline and individual action which is the basic unit of social strength."

A few years later Frost was protesting vigorously against being labelled a New Humanist. He was quite right. His temper was humanistic but his poetry cannot be defined by or confined to intellectual concepts. Lawrance Thompson very sensibly observes that "certain aspects of the Emersonian position in poetic theory proved to be closely akin to the poetic theory and practice of Robert Frost. But Emerson's aesthetic utterances were elucidated and modified into a somewhat extreme aesthetic by the 'new humanist,' whose dogmatic claims were much too rigid to attract Frost." Let it be repeated: the poet Frost will never enlist under the banner of any school of criticism, New Humanist, Neoclassical or Romantic. And a critic who insists on a label for Frost's philosophy and poetry is too much of a schoolmaster in a field where judgments should be flexible.

"There is some truth in Gorham Munson's early judgment," Malcolm Cowley says in his essay, "The Case Against Mr. Frost," referring to the judgment that Frost is "the purest classical poet of America today," and I propose to reassert, more than three decades after my little biography of Frost appeared, the "some truth" in its early judgment that Cowley concedes.

The most classical trait of Frost, I should say, is the high place he gives to form in his *ars poetica*. In his early conversations with me, he several times mentioned form as one of the highest literary qualities. Four years later, at one of his New School for Social Research lectures, I took down verbatim his definition of creation: "Creation has its end implicit in the beginning but not foreknown." Has a better definition of organic form ever been offered? Frost said it again in 1939 in his prose introduction to *Collected Poems*. Of the course of a true poem, he said that "it has an outcome that though unforeseen was predestined from the first image of the original mood—and indeed from the very mood." The principle of the unforeseen but predestined is the very principle of growth or organic form, and in its working exemplifies the classical laws of probability and inevitability.

Frost's classical nature comes out in boldest contrast when we compare him with one of his romantic contemporaries, that rival for whom he had little esteem, Carl Sandburg. Sandburg declared that the past was a bucket of ashes and sought for "new ways to be new," as Frost named the quest for poetic novelty. He practiced the cult of free verse, inspired by the majestic chanting rhythms of Whitman but as someone has observed, producing a banjo version of them. In time, Sandburg became a sentimental humanitarian poet, his credo of "The people, yes" provoking Frost to reply, "The people, yes and no."

In contrast, Frost went back for inspiration to the pastoral poetry of Vergil and the satires of Horace. Except for one poem, "The Lovely Shall Be Choosers," Frost eschewed free verse—"like playing tennis with the net down," he drily remarked—and practiced in the traditional patterns and forms. His triumph was that, in becoming a traditional poet, he escaped being merely conventional and succeeded in being creative. He found, as he put it, "old ways to be new."

How did he achieve newness by working in the old ways? Chiefly, I would say, by experimentation in the "sound of sense." Even as a youthful poet, he would have none of the "musicality of literature" theory advanced by Poe and Lanier, and quite early he was drawn to the study of verbal images, the connotation of tones of voice, the sound of sense. What possibilities of the dramatic there were in the sound of sense! This was the thing, and not any theory of quantitative verse such as Robert Bridges had expounded to him. "The living part of a poem," he had said in refutation of Bridges, "is the intonation entangled somehow in the syntax, idiom and meaning of a sentence."

Frost used a simple illustration that nonetheless gives the whole meaning of his sound of sense creed. Here is a primer version of sense:

I see a dog.
The dog is in the house.
I will put him out.
He will come back.

Now let us put this sense into tones of voice:

There's that dog again.
Get out of here, you brute!
Oh, what's the use! He'll come back.

The sounds bring the words to life. Now they are energetic, dramatic, charged with tone—now they can be taken into poetry.

For a motto, Frost took for himself "common in experience—uncommon in writing." This, too, was a classical approach to material. Not the wild or extravagant or eccentric or peculiar or extreme areas of experience but the central, common, broad areas were to be his material; "uncommonness" was to come from experimentation in the writing of the sound of sense.

By adhering to the traditional forms of poetry and by the use of material common in experience, Frost maintained a common ground with the reader, and in this, too, his poetry has a classical air. He had no truck with self-expression but held to the great norm of communication, the ancient relationship of poet and hearer whereby there was a sharing of the poetic experience. "Only just as much as we can communicate is literature," he said at the New School for Social Research.

I noted above that Frost in applying his principle of growth in the development of organic form observed the humanistic law of probability. Around him the romanticists were indulging in the cult of self-expression. With the encouragement of such critics as J. E. Spingarn, the romanticists of the second and third decades of our century were cultivating spontaneity and originality and genius. They made a cult of wonderful possibilities, and propagated a doctrine of personal expansiveness. This was alien to Frost's conservative temperament. He was drawn to the probable story and away from the improbable though possible story. In *North of Boston* and his other books of the 1914–1930 period, he was the poet of the common in man and nature, not the exploiter of the unique and wonderful. In these books he was an observer of another law of humanistic art—the much misunderstood and misrepresented law of decorum or measure or proportion. His feeling for decorous proportion was yet another classical trait.

The range of Frost's poetry is humanistic. He has written only one poem that could be called naturalistic in the literary sense. That is the terrible "Out, Out—" about the severance of a boy's hand by a buzz saw; the boy dies from the shock. "No more to build on there. And they, since they / Were not the one dead, turned to their affairs." This could well have been an incident in a raw, violent novel of the school of Zola. At the other extreme from naturalism is the religious poem, "The Trial by Existence," which appeared in *A Boy's Will*, the only poem by Frost I would call religious. The point I wish to make is that all the space between the raw naturalism of "Out, Out—" and the religious insight of "Trial by Existence" has been occupied by Frost, and this space may properly be called the humanistic range.

Mark Van Doren has defined the range of Frost better than any other critic, and I have read almost all of the critical writing about Frost. "Mr. Frost's place," Van Doren said in his well-titled essay, "The Permanence of Robert Frost," "is and always has been singularly central. His range has been great enough to carry him close to all the corners, yet he has never quite crossed a line. He has always, in a kind of silence, and with a most remarkable integrity, kept to his center." Frost's

way, Van Doren explained, "consists in occupying or touching both extremes at once, and inhabiting all the space between. [It] consists in finding that golden mean which, far from signifying that the extremes have been avoided, signifies that they have been enclosed and contained."

A poem by Emerson was often used by the New Humanists to epitomize their doctrine of life and letters.

There are two laws discrete
Not reconciled—
Law for man, and law for thing;
The last builds town and fleet,
But it runs wild,
And doth the man unking.

Frost was no systematic philosopher, as Babbitt was, but in "The White-Tailed Hornet or The Revision of Theories" he too wrote an epitome of the dualistic philosophy of the New Humanists, although it is unlikely that he thought he was doing so. The poem is about the fallibility of the instinct of the hornet who cannot recognize the friendly approach of a human being and mistakes nailheads and huckleberries for flies and finally misses the real fly. Turning didactic, the poet writes:

Won't this whole instinct matter bear revision?
Won't almost any theory bear revision?
To err is human, not to, animal.
Or so we pay the compliment to instinct,
Only too liberal of our compliment
That really takes away instead of gives.
Our worship, humor, conscientiousness
Went long since to the dogs under the table.
And served us right for having instituted
Downward comparisons. As long on earth
As our comparisons were stoutly upward
With gods and angels, we were men at least,
But little lower than the gods and angels.
But once comparisons were yielded downward,
Once we began to see our images
Reflected in the mud and even dust,
'Twas disillusion upon disillusion.
We were lost piecemeal to the animals.

Like people thrown out to delay the wolves.
Nothing but fallibility was left to us,
And this day's work made even that seem doubtful.

Here Frost states his resistance to the downward comparisons of Rousseau and Freud and Zola; here he pays tribute to the upward comparisons of Renaissance humanism which inherited them from religion.

Neither Rousseauistic nor Baconian is Frost in his view of nature. "I wouldn't be a prude afraid of nature," Frost declared in "New Hampshire," and again in the same poem he said: "I'd hate to be a runaway from nature." The nature in Frost's poetry is that of a poet who is really deeply versed in country things.

Frost botanized on many a long walk, and on night walks he studied the heavens and Nature. Let the Romanticists attribute human feeling to nature. Let them conceive of nature as impulse and temperament. Let them mean by a return to nature just letting themselves go. Rejecting romanticism, Frost reveals his humanistic temper in his well-known poem, "On the Need of Being Versed in Country Things." This poem tells about a farmhouse that burned down and the barn that was falling down. The birds came through the barn's broken windows and nested inside. For man these ruins were saddening but not for the birds.

For them there was really nothing sad.
But though they rejoiced in the nest they kept
One had to be versed in country things
Not to believe the phoebes wept.

A romantic poet would have sighed over the ruins of human habitation, but Frost, accepting nature as lovely and fair, is aware of her unconcern for man's misfortune and disasters. The birds have taken possession of the old place and the lilac renews its leaf for them, as does the aged elm, but Nature grieves not for man. To be versed in country things is to be

guarded against a serious use of the pathetic fallacy—Frost sometimes jestingly uses it—but it is to observe distinctions, and Frost's sense of demarcation between Man and Nature is humanistic-classical in the Irving Babbitt sense.

The clearest understanding of Frost's attitude toward Nature may be gained from his poem, "The Most of It." One might fairly say that in the first eight lines of this remarkable poem a romantic demand on Nature is made.

He thought he kept the universe alone;
For all the voice in answer he could wake
Was but the mocking echo of his own
From some tree-laden cliff across the lake.
Some morning from the boulder-broken beach
He would cry out on life, that what it wants
Is not its own love back in copy speech,
But counter-love, original response.

The poem then gives the answer to the romanticist's yearning demand.

And nothing ever came of what he cried
Unless it was the embodiment that crashed
In the cliff's talus on the other side,
And then in the far distant water splashed,
But after a time allowed for it to swim,
Instead of proving human when it neared
And someone else additional to him,
As a great buck it powerfully appeared
Pushing the crumpled water up ahead,
And landed pouring like a waterfall,
And stumbled through the rocks with horny tread,
And forced the underbrush—and that was all.

Frost was like an intelligent Greek, New Humanists said, because he was of a positive and critical turn of mind. He came by this turn of mind from the New England culture he had inherited. Born in Mark Twain's America—in San Francisco in 1874—Frost had been brought east in 1885 to be educated in Emerson's New England. (Mark Twain was gone from San Francisco by 1874 and Emerson had died in 1882 but San Francisco and New England retained much of the character they had while these men were on the scene.) Frost's ancestors had come to New England more than two centuries earlier, and one of them had been an Indian fighter. Frost's formative life-experiences took place in a simplified world, the world of the New England farmer from about 1885 to about 1915, and it was in this rural culture that he evolved his classical outlook.

Lawrance Thompson, who is Frost's authorized biographer-apparent, has said that Frost "knows from long experience that strong men and women will work out a life that is good in that stubborn contest with rocky soil and short summers. . . . As a New Hampshire farmer himself in the early years, Frost lived with neighbors of all classes, many of them his superiors in their ability to make a simple but sufficient living out of a little. He has never forgotten his respect and admiration for the courage and self-dependence he saw about him during those years. The rigorous trial by existence in rural communities requires ability and cunning if life is to go on. . . . But the soil has its own peculiar virtue for those who have been hurt and healed by the accidents of choice and circumstances. And Frost has given expression in his poems to that inner strength and satisfaction which comes from living close to the soil."

"Me for the hills where I don't have to choose," Frost said in 1923 when invited to face the complex and tormenting questions of modern urban civilization.

This interpretation of Frost as the most purely classical poet of our times has been dismissed by Yvor Winters in an essay entitled "Robert Frost: or, the Spiritual Drifter as Poet" (1957). "Frost has been praised as a classical poet," Winters noted, "but he is not classical in any sense which I can understand"—a most surprising remark to come from a critic who has conned Babbitt, as Winters has. "Like many of his contemporaries, he is an Emersonian Romantic," Winters continued. "A standard exemplar of irresponsible Romantic Irony," Winters said of Frost as he warmed to his attack; "he believes that impulse is trustworthy and reason contemptible. . . . Frost is at his worst in didactic writing, in spite of his fondness for it: his ideas are impossible and his style is exceptionally shoddy."

Surely this is wrongheaded criticism, and indeed the whole Winters essay ought to be dismissed without rebuttal as a curious example of perverse and arbitrary judgment—just about what one would expect from a critic who is capable of referring to "the Frosts and the Thoreaus, the amateur anarchists and village eccentrics." However, an explanation—or an attempted explanation—of Winters' misreading of certain Frost poems will serve to establish even more firmly the interpretation of Frost as a classical-humanist poet.

As an example of Winters' unfairness, we might start with his reduction of Frost's sound of sense to an endeavor "to make his style approximate as closely as possible the style of conversation. . . . I see no reason why poetry should be called upon to imitate conversation. Conversation is the most careless and formless of human utterance; it is spontaneous and unrevised, and its vocabulary is commonly limited." Now one may speak with approval of a conversational prose style—the style of Laurence Sterne, for example—but Frost never spoke of conversation as imitable by poets. (We are, of course, far beyond the terms of the "advertisement" of the *Lyrical Ballads* that spoke of the Wordsworth-Coleridge experiment to ascertain "how far the language of conversation is adapted for the purposes of poetic pleasure.") Frost called his lyrics "talk-songs," and he had pregnant things to say about speech-rhythms and tones of voice and "the audible page."

Sounds are what he was concerned with—the sound that sense in speech makes—and it is decidedly odd that Winters should so carefully refrain from saying "the style of speech" and insist upon "the style of conversation," as when he says: "the conversational manner will naturally suit a poet who takes all experience so casually, and it is only natural that the conversational manner should often become very conversational indeed." Frost's style is related to utterance, and "conversational manner" dilutes the idea of utterance and substitutes for it the idea of relaxed, informal, and vagrant discourse between persons.

How can we account for Winters' choice of the imprecise word to characterize Frost's manner? Is it because he wishes to show that Frost's poems are imprecise in denotation? But they are not imprecise on the denotative level. Of "The Road Not Taken," Winters says that this poem has for its theme "the whimsical, accidental, and incomprehensible nature of the formative decision." It "is the poem of a man whom one might fairly call a spiritual drifter; and a spiritual drifter is unlikely to have either the intelligence or the energy to become a major poet." "The Road Not Taken" has, according to Winters, a "quality of uncertainty and incomprehension" and a "vague melancholy." This seems plausible enough if one's memory of "The Road Not Taken" has weakened; but turn back for a fresh reading and you will be astounded at what Winters has read into the poem that is simply not there.

The poem is not about a drifter. It is about a traveler in a yellow wood—and one thinks of Thoreau who had said he had traveled much in Concord, Thoreau being an author-naturalist of great appeal to Frost. The traveler comes to diverging roads in a yellow wood and wishes he could "travel both and be one traveler," for they are of nearly equal attraction. He takes a long time to decide which road he will take. One seems a little less traveled by, but only a little less; still this is enough of a consideration to sway the decision of the traveler. He tells himself that on another day he can return and take the first road. But he has enough experience in living to know that a decision of direction puts one on a course that leads on and on, and thus he doubts that he shall ever come back to the fork in the road. It will be a decision that actualizes one potentiality in living while keeping the other potentiality inactual—and that of course, will make a difference.

It may be irrefutably argued that the profound thought of this poem is a dictum of Denis Saurat: "There are two parts in every being: the Actual, which is the expressed, and the Inactual, which is the unexpressed, and they grow together, infinitely, the one out of the other."

What is denoted in this poem is a traveler who makes a deliberate decision based upon a specific consideration to follow a certain course, knowing that in the future he may regret not having followed an almost equally appealing course—but the decision not to take the other course has made "all the difference."

As Saurat has put it, "every existence is infinite; every expression is limited. The expression of any thought or being is necessarily incomplete." Furthermore, "there is in every being the instinct of concentration: of the necessity to choose and reject."

Where in this poem can one read into it a "spiritual drifter"? Or detect the "whimsical, accidental, and incomprehensible nature of the formative decision"? And why should there be objection to the faint melancholy of the last stanza? Do we not all sigh over the inactual part of our lives even while we may be experiencing psychological well-being from the fulfilled potentialities?

> *Ah, when to the heart of man*
> *Was it ever less than a treason*
> *To go with the drift of things. . . .*

Winters performs an even more extraordinary twisting of the meaning of a poem when he discovers romanticism in "The Bear." Let us recall the structure of this fable. It consists of a twelve-line preface, an extended simile, and a two-line conclusion. A poem should begin in delight and end in wisdom, Frost has remarked, and the preface is delightful—a humorous, imagistic picture of the progress cross-country of an uncaged female bear. Frost starts with an animal incident that is entertaining in itself, and he seems unconcerned about where the bear's fall cross-country will lead her. By way of forceful transition to the main body of the poem, the poet remarks that "The world has room to make a bear feel free; / The universe seems cramped to you and me."

Besides being entertaining in itself, the preface has a limited function: it is to set up a contrast between the free bear's behavior and the behavior of the caged bear who is one term in the simile that constitutes most of the poem. Man is the other term.

Man in the simile is not related at all to the preface. The caged bear is related by contrast to the preface, but man is unrelated. "Man acts more like the poor bear in a cage / That all day fights a nervous inward rage, / His mood rejecting all his mind suggests." Modern man, the poet says, lives in a state of conflict between mind and feeling. His science brings him no stability of mind. He is pseudo-religious. He is changeable and fickle in his philosophy. Emotionally restless, in-

tellectually shallow, modern man paces back and forth between metaphysical extremes in his cage, and "never rests the toe-nail click and shuttle of his feet."

The poet sums up his fable in a jest:

> *A baggy figure, equally pathetic*
> *When sedentary and when peripatetic.*

Here is Winters' summary of "The Bear." "The poem compares the wild bear to the bear in a cage; the uncaged bear is a creature of free impulse and is compared by *implication* to man as he would be were he guided by impulse; and the caged bear is compared to *rational* man as he is. . . . Frost tells us in this poem that reasoning man is ridiculous because he appears to labor and to change his mind; and he *implies* that impulsive man would be a wiser and a nobler creature" [Italics mine].

I have searched this poem repeatedly, and there is no implication, such as Winters alleges, to be found. Certainly there is no implication in the prefatory lines that "man as he would be were he guided by impulse" would be like the uncaged bear, and "would be a wiser and nobler creature." "Man," the poem proceeds to say, "acts more like the poor bear in a cage"—can it be that Winters rests his whole case on the word "more"? Does "more" hint at any implication of the sort that Winters asserts? One cannot say that it does. Winters may rest his case on the reading that "more" implies that man is the other term in the unexpressed comparison with the free, impulsive bear; but this comparison is simply not implied by the adverb.

The reader's attention was called to the qualification of the "man" of Frost's poem who becomes in Winters' paraphrase "rational man" (suggesting the eighteenth century man of reason?) and "reasoning man." This again is to alter the satire of Frost. Frost is satirizing man, a pathetic, divided creature, his mind and heart at war, who feels cramped in the universe. He is satirizing not an abstraction called "rational man" but modern man as he is today without a key to the enigmas of the world. How inadequate it is to say that "Frost tells us in this poem that reasoning man is ridiculous because he appears to labor and change his mind." Frost tells us much more, and he regards man as pathetic as well as ridiculous.

Winters, it is plain, tries to get too much out of Frost's metaphors. Disregarding Frost's warning that every metaphor breaks down somewhere, Winters presses and distorts Frost's metaphors to make them yield an extreme romantic attitude.

This business of correcting Winters' forced readings becomes boring. It is untrue to say that "the feeling of the poem ['Tree at My Window'] is one of a melancholy longing to share the dream-like experience more fully." It distorts the meaning of "The Times Table" to say that "the poem deals with a farmer who is given to commenting [sic] on death"; what Frost reproves is the farmer's futile habit of *sighing* over death. But the climax of Winters' almost wilful misunderstanding is reached in his comment on Frost's choice of an epitaph:

I would have written of me on my stone:
I had a lover's quarrel with the world.

Weakly sentimental, says Winters. He then proceeds to over-emphasize the shallowness of the quarrels of lovers, forgetting that it is the depth of love that makes the quarrel shallow. Frost has a fundamental love of the world that subordinates his tragic sense, but it is presumptuous of Winters to read Frost a lesson on the evil of the world and impertinent when he warns Frost that "the evil had better be recognized and taken seriously." "With Frost, however, the sense of the comic in life goes hand in hand with the sense of

the tragic," as Lawrance Thompson has well observed. "Frost's sense of humor," Thompson added, "is able to accept with calmness the sense of tragedy forever present in any inclusive attitude toward life." In short, Frost's optimism should not and indeed cannot be separated "from the underlying obbligato of sadness and tragic realization."

One may recommend to deadly serious critics of the ilk of Winters a couplet written by Frost after many years of suffering from their humorlessness:

It takes all sorts of in and outdoor schooling
To get adapted to my kind of fooling.

That mischievous tone of teasing which one hears in "To a Thinker" and "The Lesson for Today" has diverted Winters from the wisdom of Frost's own thoughts on style.

Winters would have Frost an "Emersonian Romantic"; he would make him an exemplar of that school of romanticism that Irving Babbitt traced back to Rousseau. But this is too systematic for Frost, just as the New Humanism is too systematic for him. Frost does not belong to the schools.

That is not to say, however, that Lawrance Thompson is wrong in asserting that Frost occupies a middle position in life and letters, that he maintains a critical position in the Golden Mean, that he adheres "to the position in the Golden Mean from which these two halves [of human life] may be contemplated." This is one way of saying that Frost's *attitude* toward life is humanistic; it is a way of saying that Frost has the humanistic *temper*; and it is his attitude and temper that made Frost feel in the twenties that he had written several books against the world in general.

When I visited Frost at Amherst in 1927, I found him, to my surprise, quite opposed to the educational policy of Alexander Meiklejohn, who had been president of Amherst College from 1912 to 1924. This was surprising for two reasons. One: I knew that it had been Meiklejohn who had ruled in 1917 that Frost's lack of any academic degree didn't matter and had appointed him an ad interim full professor of English. Two: I knew that Frost had himself been a teacher of marked originality, and I thought that a Meiklejohn-run college would be a congenial environment for him. But I learned that Frost complained of "Meiklejaundice" during the three years (1917–1920) he had served under the experimental educator and had repeatedly wanted to resign. Finally he had gone off to the University of Michigan but had returned to Amherst on Meiklejohn's departure. "Meiklejaundice," I gathered, was romanticism in higher education.

Meiklejohn had been gone four years when I spent my first weekend with Frost, but it was repetitiously evident that his theory and practice still stuck in the poet's craw, for he talked against them persistently and took a lively, hopeful interest in the presidential succession at Amherst (George Daniels Olds was resigning and Arthur Stanley Pease was in the offing). Frost conceded that the English-born Meiklejohn, who had been a professor of philosophy at Brown, was brilliant, but he doubted him as a thinker and an administrator. Meiklejohn had put his liberal-radical views on education into two books: *The Liberal College* (1920) and *Freedom and the College* (1923); but Frost preferred the educational philosophy of Olds and Pease and sided with the faculty conservatives in their resistance to Meiklejohn.

There had been a real rift when Meiklejohn had been dismissed by the trustees and faculty. A number of professors had resigned, too, or had been dropped, and some members of the graduating class of 1923 had publicly declined their diplomas. Frost blamed Meiklejohn for the dissension in the faculty. Elizabeth Shepley Sergeant reports Frost as saying that Meiklejohn was "too high-minded for any *modus vivendi*" with the middle-of-the-road professors.

Frost took pains to see that I met two of his friends on the Amherst faculty. Handsome English professor George F. Whicher came to tea, and at the faculty club I had a long talk with Professor G. R. Elliott, who was then writing *The Cycle of Modern Poetry* and sought advice about a publisher. Elliott revealed to me a strong religious interest, and was later to declare that Irving Babbitt, "a rigorous moral humanist of New England, has indirectly done much for the best interests of religion."

Ezra Pound was even more of a topic than Meiklejohn in my first long session with Frost. I thought that Frost was prompted to reminisce about Pound because I had discussed Pound the night before in a lecture to Amherst students, but I soon found that Frost wanted his biographer to know that he felt deep gratitude to our expatriate poet. I could see that he was ambivalent toward Pound but I noted few signs of hostility whereas he frankly confessed to the state of being fascinated by the young master.

Frost had been writing poetry for twenty years without recognition until Pound wrote his review of *A Boy's Will* for London and Chicago literary magazines. He had been published perhaps a dozen times in American magazines and he had a devoted reader in Mrs. Frost, but he had been pretty often rejected all these years, and he had been deeply hurt in his isolation. (To his dying day he never allowed the later editors of *The Atlantic Monthly* to forget that the *Atlantic* declined his poems in the eighteen-nineties.) Nor had he experienced any literary fellowship until he went to London in 1912. Of a literary milieu—of bookshops for poetry lovers, of cafés for writers, of lectures and readings, of studio teas and summer colonies, of editorial sessions and group-anthologies, of parties and Bohemia—Frost had known nothing. Pound immediately recognized the genuineness of Frost's poetry and introduced him—at the age of thirty-nine—to literary London; Frost, who had been starving for recognition, ate unforgettably of the nourishing food of corroboration of his gift.

Pound's London review of *A Boy's Will* appeared in *The New Freewoman* on September 1, 1913, and his recognition of Frost has the air of being "dashed off."

"Mr. Frost's Book . . . has the tang of the New Hampshire woods, and it has just this utter simplicity. . . . This man has the good sense to speak naturally and to paint the thing, the thing as he sees it. . . . One reads the books for the 'tone,' which is homely, by intent, and pleasing, never doubting that it comes direct from his own life. . . . He is without shame and without affectation."

Thus was the first phase of the criticism of Frost opened, the phase that began with Pound's excited discovery of a new American poet and culminated in Mark Van Doren's fine essay in 1936, "The Permanence of Robert Frost." James M. Cox has noted that "when Richard Thornton in 1937 made the first collection of Frost criticism he wisely entitled the volume *Recognition of Robert Frost*. The collection, essentially a commemorative one honoring Frost's twenty-five years of achievement, was nevertheless fairly representative of the criticism he had received. It showed that during those twenty-five years, though he had been recognized as a poet, his poetry had yet to be appraised." This is a fair description of the criticism of Frost in the 1920's. The critics'

recognition of Frost and the public's recognition of him in buying his books were in step with each other, were truly *pari passu*, in that decade.

Recognition of Frost by the bestowal of honors was also begun in the twenties. The chief of these was the Pulitzer Prize for Poetry awarded him in 1924 for *New Hampshire*, published the previous year. In 1930, as the decade ended in the onset of a vast economic engulfment, a *Collected Poems* was published to signalize the solid reputation of the poet.

One might expect some reaction against this chorus of praise for the poet Frost, and it came as the decade died from the rapidly rising urban critic, Edmund Wilson, who objected to the overrating, as he regarded it, of the poet of rural New England. "Robert Frost," Wilson said with disdain for supporting his judgment, "has a thin but authentic vein of sensibility; but I find him excessively dull, and he certainly writes very poor verse."

I have no doubt that this summary judgment made Frost angry, if it was brought to his attention. Frost was no reader of reviews but somehow unflattering notices did reach him and provoke him to oblique replies in talk with friends. Thus, when Rolfe Humphries called him in *The New Masses* "a counter-revolutionary poet,"—words I am sure Humphries would like to have taken back in later years—Frost was quick to retort privately that Humphries must be a "bargain-counter-revolutionary poet."

I very quickly became acquainted with the angry side of Robert Frost, and at first it astonished me. The new literary generation of the twenties was friendly toward him, but he had no feeling of solidarity with them. He had been one of the advisory editors of *The Seven Arts*; he had been unintelligently touted by Amy Lowell as a figure of the New Poetry;

Waldo Frank had seen him as a precursor of "Our America." But Frost was hostile, as he showed in the satire of "New Hampshire," to the liberal drift of the new generation. One of the journalistic buglers of the liberal writers who were coming to dominate the literary scene was Burton Rascoe, who ran in the *New York Herald Tribune* a diary of his comings and goings in literary society. He had made a remark about Frost that the perhaps hypersensitive poet interpreted as a reflection upon his character. My surprise was great when Frost showed his resentment and told me that he had thought of going to New York to use his fists on the brash journalist.

It was quite noticeable that Frost had no praise for living poets. He never mentioned Edwin Arlington Robinson in all the talks I had with him between 1926 and 1934. He did say that Wallace Stevens, who had been in his class at Harvard but unknown to him at the time, made a formal garden in the wilderness of life, and he once expressed a liking for Thomas Hornsby Ferril. He was impatient with Louis Untermeyer's marital changes and reversals but said never a word about his verse or criticism. That is all I can remember of his references to contemporary poets. I dedicated my modest biography of Frost to Hart Crane "in memory of many enthusiastic conversations about poetry" and in time, in a roundabout way, I heard that Frost had said that the only thing about my book he disliked was the dedication to Crane.

Nor did Frost express any esteem for the new prose writers of the twenties. He derided the novels of Sinclair Lewis— "Sinkler" or "Sink" Lewis, he called him. But he liked detective mystery fiction, and was the first to tell me about the Philo Vance stories of S. S. Van Dine (Willard Huntington Wright).

Frost's jealousy of living poets was understandable although unexpected by his friends, who early came to regard him as a poet without rivals. We must remember that from 1892 to 1912—twenty years— Frost had been denied publication so many times while poets he knew to be his inferiors were being repeatedly published that he contracted a deep-seated jealousy. It required decades of reassurance of his acceptance for jealousy to run its course.

All these—the resentment of criticism, the anger at the new literary liberalism, the jealousy of his contemporaries—were premonitory symptoms of the massively angry Frost who was to emerge fully in the 1930's and to threaten to become a reactionary poet—but never went the distance to reaction.

Had any poet in America achieved by 1930 a more secure position than Frost? He was fifty-six years old and had published five volumes of poems garnered from thirty-five years of mature devotion to his craft. He had extended his range from the early lyrics of *A Boy's Will* through the dramatic narratives of *North of Boston* to the symbolic and philosophic poems of *West-Running Brook*. He was New England's poet in the great line from Longfellow and Emerson—and no one (except Edmund Wilson) doubted his permanence. Would poems like "The Pasture," "The Death of the Hired Hand," "The Road Not Taken," "Stopping by Woods on a Snowy Evening," and "Acquainted with the Night" ever disappear from the anthologies? Surely Frost could face the new decade of change—and in the thirties—with the utmost feeling of security in his place in literary history.

Yet Frost was entering the black decade of his life. His personal life was to be filled with grief and death. The rural culture of 1885 to 1915, the rich soil from which his poems had drawn their nourishment, was to diminish and grow impoverished before his eyes as he drove his old automobile across the depressed New England states. The great passage of America from a rural to an urban civilization went on inexorably while Frost protested and satirized the New Deal and industrial-collective trends. And leadership in poetry appeared to pass to T. S. Eliot. Frost was embittered and despairing—but went on writing and creating some of his finest poems. He called his book in 1936 *A Further Range*, and it indubitably was.

After the dreadful decade was over, it was seen that Frost had grown from a regional poet to a national poet. The forties were to be for Frost a decade of recovery. In the fifties he achieved a status unimaginable by his admirers in the twenties: he became the national bard.

He could well have stopped growing in the 1920's. Not many writers, especially not many poets, surpass after the age of fifty-six the achievements of their middle life—but Frost did. He extended and deepened his achievement. Nothing that we critics wrote of him in the twenties can be stretched enough to encompass the national bardic poet who wrote "A Record Stride," "Neither Out Far Nor In Deep." "The Gift Outright," "Choose Something Like a Star," "A Masque of Reason" and "A Masque of Mercy."

[VIII, Summer 1964, 291–305]

[77]

James Joyce and Aesthetic Gnosticism

THOMAS H. LANDESS

Thomas H. Landess (1931–   ), formerly a professor of English at the University of Dallas, has published a study of Pulitzer Prize-winner Julia Peterkin for the Twayne United States Authors *series, a monograph on contemporary novelist Larry McMurtry, and numerous articles and poems in, among others,* Sewanee Review, Southern Review, *and* Mississippi Quarterly. *He has also written (with M. E. Bradford) a full-length study of Abraham Lincoln's rhetoric and its relation to Lincoln's political thought.*

THE PLIGHT of the artist in the modern world has been the topic of too much fiction, poetry, and commentary to require extensive definition. I would only point out what is already obvious to members of the academy: that the haunting sense of alienation attributed to urban residents of the sixties and seventies was precisely analyzed and rendered by a number of poets and novelists even before the turn of the century; and between 1900 and 1950 virtually every major literary figure addressed himself to this question. Among the most important of these was James Joyce, one of the few genuinely influential figures in the development of twentieth-century fictional technique. His three novels—*A Portrait of the Artist as a Young Man, Ulysses,* and *Finnegan's Wake*—mirror, as well as render, the significant plunge into the pool of self that has been a predominant subject of the novel since the late Victorian period.

Ulysses and *Finnegan's Wake* are undoubtedly the most ambitious of Joyce's works; for in their radical departure from conventional modes of narration they suggest the triumph of individual consciousness over the traditional ordering of action—the subjugation of time and space by the active imagination in league with the will. To a lesser degree *A Portrait of the Artist* suggests the same modernist tendencies, though its meaning is rendered more often in discourse than in the implications of formal complexity; and for this reason *Portrait,* Joyce's first novel, provides us with one of the purest examples in modern literature of the gnostic impulse as it manifests itself in the artistic imagination.

On its most obvious level the central action of the novel is concerned with the intellectual and spiritual growth of Stephen Dedalus, a pattern of development that seems to some critics to include no more than an abnormally painful childhood followed by adolescent rebellion, maturity, and a satisfying sense of true vocation. To such commentators, Stephen

875

is simply Everyboy, his sensibilities heightened by an acute and instinctive awareness of the created order that surrounds him. But he is something more than a Wordsworthian poet, however Romantic his own conception of himself. For Wordsworth conceived of the imagination as responding to some great force from without (call it nature or call it God); and while Joyce's artist has a keen eye for the natural image, he is more interested in the universe of words, for him a realm of existence that transcends the merely given of the created order. In one sense, then, the meaning of *A Portrait of the Artist* can be found in the progression of Stephen Dedalus' soul from the mundane to the supra-mundane, a journey of the spirit that finally culminates in a tenuous flight from the constitution of being itself, a "gnostic" escape in which the author imperfectly believes and which the reader can finally accept only if he is highly credulous or very young. I say "finally accept" because this novel is one of the most carefully wrought in all of English literature, and in the tightly woven texture of the narrative Joyce is able to ensnare even the wariest and most meticulous of readers.

II

Professor Eric Voegelin has told us that the central element in all gnostic experience is that of "the world as an alien place into which man has strayed and from which he must find his way back home to the other world of his origin";[1] and such an attitude is implicit in the first sentence of *A Portrait of the Artist,* for as several critics have noted, through the suggestive use of sounds Joyce has implied an external frame of reference with important meaning:

> Once upon a time and a very good time it was there was a moocow coming down along the road and this moocow that was

coming down along the road met a nicens little boy named baby tuckoo.

> His father told him that story: his father looked at him through a glass: he had a hairy face.

> He was a baby tuckoo.[2]

Although this bit of childish nonsense seems to have been taken from Joyce's own experience, it has additional significance in terms of Stephen Dedalus' evolution; for in the jumble of words one can discern an allusion to the cuckoo which lays its eggs in the nests of other birds.[3] This reference suggests that Stephen's story may be read as a variant of "The Ugly Duckling" in which the young boy, awkward and strange, is raised among an alien brood and suffers painful abuse until he finally matures and then flies away to join his own kind in the community of a finer species. This ancient folk tale in its various versions clearly embodies the potential for a gnostic sense of alienation as defined by Voegelin and others. The implied image of the earth-bound cuckoo or duckling, struggling among inferiors who taunt him for his failure to conform to their communal norm, is a precise analogue to Stephen Dedalus' incipient sense of his own superiority over family, nation, and church. The potential for rebellion against the prison of his world is realized both in the resolution of the ancient tale and in Joyce's development of his central action. The bird flies away, transcending the earth to which he has been confined, and seeks his place in the sky where he sings or soars with a grace and beauty beyond the capabilities of those whom he has left behind.

In *A Portrait of the Artist as a Young Man* Stephen eventually rejects the communal world into which he has been born, a world filled with creatures who are human and hence fallibly annoying to his sensibility. His rejection manifests itself in two ways analogous to the movement of the folk tale. First, he makes a figurative flight into aesthetic gnosis, devising a "theology" of his own which occupies his attention in the latter portions of the novel. Second, he literally abandons Ireland for the freedom of Paris, which was just beginning to serve at this time as the international gathering place for expatriate artists.

It is important to note that the nature of Stephen Dedalus' early alienation is further reinforced by the abundant implications of his name. As "Stephen" he is the counterpart of the first martyr to the Christian faith, stoned to death by Pharisees, the intractable adherents of the old religious order. "Stephen" is the sufferer of corporate abuse, the visionary who preaches a special truth to a world which responds with vindictive hostility. Joyce does little more with this first name than assign it to his character, but Stephen himself recognizes his identification with Daedalus, whom he calls "the old artificer," creator of the labyrinth and escapee from the island prison of Crete. This myth, which, like the cuckoo story, has many potential meanings, may also embody the essentials of gnostic experience. For in Joyce's version the maze which his hero begins to build is his own aesthetic, a private system whose meaning he partially shares with fellow students, lesser intellects incapable of grasping its full significance. The flight of Daedalus, however, is obviously an analogue *in potentia* of the gnostic impulse, particularly when one considers the fact that the mythical artist is accompanied in his ingenious escape by Icarus, whose proud flight too near the sun results in the melting of artificially constructed wings and a consequent fall to his death.

In the initial stages of Joyce's narrative, the folk tale and the Greek myth coalesce into a single action which prefigures the "epiphany" of the hero, that moment when he comes to the realization that he has at last put behind him all of the communal concerns which have bound him to the world:

> Now at the name of the fabulous artificer he seemed to hear the noise of dim waves and to see a winged form flying above the waves and slowly climbing the air. What did it mean? Was it a quaint device opening a page of some medieval book of prophecies and symbols, a hawklike man flying sunward above the sea, a prophecy of the end he had been born to serve and had been following through mists of childhood and boyhood, a symbol of the artist forging anew in his workshop out of the sluggish matter of the earth a new soaring impalpable imperishable being?
>
> His heart trembled; his breath came faster and a wild spirit passed over his limbs as though he were soaring sunward. His heart trembled in an ecstasy of fear and his soul was in flight. His soul was soaring in an air beyond the world and the body he knew was purified in a breath and delivered of incertitude and made radiant and commingled with the element of the spirit.[4]

This passage, which forms a portion of the novel's peripety, renders in unmistakable terms the "religious" nature of this important moment in Stephen Dedalus' life. In the first place, the figure of the flying man is not a creature of this world but is generated in the imagination of the hero/artist as a result of the spoken word, the name "Daedalus." The relationship between the word and the image (word) is immediate, like the leap of an electric spark from pole to pole. The world of concrete things does not seem to intervene, and in the higher order into which his soul has ascended he is transfigured.

The vision of the winged man, whose identification with Horus as well as Daedalus has been noted, is an absurdity that the reader may accept only with a "willing suspension of disbelief," despite the equivocal word, "seemed." Do Stephen's eyes actually participate in a delusion or does the flying form exist only within his imagination? In either case, the moment exemplifies Stephen's rejection of the constitution of being which, as Voegelin has written, "is what it is, and cannot be affected by human fancies." "Hence," he continues, "the metastatic denial of the order of mundane existence is neither a true proposition in philosophy, nor a program of action that could be executed. The will to transform reality into something which by essence it is not is the rebellion against the nature of things as ordained by God."

And indeed both Stephen and Joyce seem to understand this point precisely, when the hero speculates about the origins of his vision as "a quaint device opening a page of some medieval book of prophecies and symbols."[5] He has, after all, been reared by scholastics who recognize magic for what it is—a tool of the devil. The allusion to such sorcery as the alchemical, cabalistic, and hermetic traditions is unmistakable and suggests the degree to which the reader is to understand this scene as the rendition of a desire to transform the given world into something more pleasing to the will, and to do so on a higher level of being.

On the next page the same idea is reintroduced, in even more specific terms: "Yes! Yes! Yes: he would create proudly out of the freedom and power of his soul, as the great artificer whose name he bore, a living thing, new and soaring and beautiful, impalpable, imperishable."[6] Here there can be no mistake about what moves Stephen, if not Joyce. He now believes he has transcended the given world and has become God the Father, able to create *out of himself* a living thing which is to be the beautiful, impalpable, imperishable *logos*. Having been affronted by the alien world into which he has been born, he has successfully escaped into a reality of his own creation where mythological figures can fly above the Irish Sea in response to the implacable urge within him that requires them to do so. And along with the image of Daedalus, his soul also takes leave of its prison, as he sees it, "soaring in an air beyond the world."[7]

But what can he do with the magical powers he has gained? Can he actually control being, reconstitute it? He believes he can, has always coveted such powers. In the first few sentences of the novel, for example, he sings a childish song about a rose, altering its natural color to green in order to suit his fancy. Later, while still a small boy, he acknowledges the impossibility of the green rose in the world as it is constituted; yet he holds out the promise to himself that "perhaps somewhere" such a thing might exist. The union of the rose with the color green is a state of being which the poet, the free soul, has the power to create, just as he is able to make the image of Daedalus fly in order to symbolize his own aspirations.

Having rejected the constitution of being, then, he is ready to exercise the new potential that he has acquired in the course of discovering his true vocation; and in one of the most celebrated passages of modern literature we see him in the process of performing such magical transformations. He is walking along the beach, in the throes of his newly discovered gnosis, feeling that he is about to be introduced to "strange fields and hills and faces," when he sees a girl, "in midstream, alone and still, gazing out to sea." During the course of the novel Stephen has been defined in terms of his changing relationships with women, and thus far his attitudes toward his mother and toward the girls he has known are recognizable as normal developments in the life of a young man. But at this point he looks at the beautiful stranger with a new precocity born of his rejection of the world, and in his eyes she undergoes a miraculous transformation:

> She seemed like one whom magic had changed into the likeness of a strange and beautiful seabird. Her long slender bare legs were delicate as a crane's and pure save where an emerald trail of seaweed had fashioned itself as a sign upon the flesh. Her thighs, fuller and softhued as ivory, were bared almost to the hips where the white fringes of her drawers were like featherings of soft white down. Her slateblue skirts were kilted boldly about her waist and dovetailed behind her. Her bosom was as a bird's soft and slight, slight and soft as the breast of some dark plumaged dove. But her long fair hair was girlish; and girlish and touched with the wonder of mortal beauty her face.[8]

Again, as with the image of the flying man, what *seems* to be is confused with what is; and an alteration of the order of mundane existence takes place. It is possible, of course, to argue that Joyce is merely making use of conventional metaphor here in an effort to render the excitement of Stephen's active imagination. But what follows this extraordinary moment of perception is too charged with abnormal meaning to support such a view, for Joyce makes it explicit that the transformation that Stephen effects is magic and that the girl indeed has been changed (or half-changed) into a winged creature, something like an Egyptian bird god, an analogue to the winged man of the young artist's earlier fancy.

It is important to note that she is no longer herself at all but has become a creature made in the image of her creator. Whatever integrity she has as an object in the real world gives way to the machinations of the artist's will. Therefore the accidental properties she displays are altered in Stephen's perception of her and become a significant contribution to the transformation of her substantial being.

Thus has the gnostic imagination, freed from its prison, captured and subjugated the phenomenal other-than-self and then recreated it on a "higher level" in the image of the ego—Eve reverted to the status of rib, with Stephen, the newest Adam, performing the role of God. The girls whom he has known, desired, failed to win or else paid for in the marketplace: these have coalesced into one image and become the passive instrument of the artist's stricken pride. As he contemplates her standing "in quiet sufferance of his gaze," the passive feminine spirit accepting the form imposed by the active masculine impulse, Stephen is overcome with a fervor which can only be described as that of the religious pagan:

> Heavenly God! cried Stephen's soul in an outburst of profane joy. Her image has passed into his soul forever and no word had broken the holy silence of his ecstasy. Her eyes had called him and his soul had leaped to the call. To live, to err, to fall, to triumph, to recreate life out of life. A wild angel had appeared to him, the angel of mortal youth and beauty, an envoy from the fair courts of life, to throw open before him in an instant of ecstasy the gates of all the ways of error and glory.[9]

The diction in this passage clearly and intentionally suggests the degree to which Stephen's experience is to be understood as the founding of an *Ersatz* religion in which he is both Creator and a portion of the "recreated" order of existence as well. In speaking of the urge to "recreate life out of life" and in designating Stephen's joy as "profane," Joyce gives his reader (and himself) some hint of the mischief that his character is up to. However, the young convert has yet to understand the full implications of his religious zeal, though he is, at this point, thoroughly committed to its authenticity.

Notice that even in the passages quoted above, when Stephen is immersed in the transformations wrought by his own imagination, the reader never quite loses the sense of an old order still surviving and coexistent with the new; for at this stage Stephen still submits partially to the images of color, shape, and motion which in some respects root his experience in the events of a world of particularity.

The awareness of things as they are, however, is increasingly compromised as the novel unfolds; and the latter pages are not dominated by scenes in which Stephen's experience of the concrete is the avenue by which the meaning of the action is explored. Instead, Joyce gives the reader a series of "Platonic dialogues" punctuated by occasional interior monologues, a few fully-rendered moments of dramatic confrontation, and (at the very end) entries in the hero's diary which somewhat ambiguously present his thoughts and feelings as he is about to fly from Ireland. And it is in these passages of argumentation between Stephen and his philosophical adversaries that the author attempts to suggest the final stage of his young rebel's development as an artist—a stage in which the youth uses his scholastic training to forge an aesthetics which will serve him as a credo in lieu of the traditional pieties which he has chosen to reject.

At first glance Joyce's motives in creating a discursive resolution to his action may seem obvious. Stephen wants to be a writer above all else; he must reject other considerations as secondary; and of greatest importance, he needs a well-formulated aesthetic theory in order to undergird his attempts "to recreate life out of life." But, as Walter Sullivan has observed, there are more basic reasons for Joyce's decision to end his narrative

in a flurry of discourse. Mr. Sullivan has suggested the use of the Faustian legend as an analogue to *A Portrait of the Artist*;[10] and though in his discussion he is substantially right, I would merely like to approach the same structural problems with a somewhat different comparison in mind.

In the first place, the desire to be a literary artist is distinctly different from a poet's urge to write poetry; and Stephen's preoccupation with literary theory as a mode of pure speculation is an important indication of what impulse really lies behind his aspirations. In order to write, poets do not need to understand a well-developed literary theory any more than they need to master the discipline of formal grammar, though I suspect the latter would prove more useful than the former, since literary theory of a purely *a priori* nature might tend to lead the would-be artist away from the genuine problems he needs to confront in the act of composition. I would suggest, then, that Stephen the artist does not necessarily benefit from the aesthetics he insists on devising. Certainly the poetry he offers in evidence would tend to refute such a claim.

But Stephen the religious convert absolutely requires this system, because it becomes for him a new theology to replace the old. In lecturing the dean and his friend Lynch on the nature of art and tragedy, Stephen is really satisfying a religious rather than an aesthetic need, and therefore the full implications of this segment of the novel might be better understood after an examination of the faith he has rejected and the manner in which his new religion is defined.

The "old religion," of course, is not merely Roman Catholicism but a more all-encompassing *pietas* which includes a devotion to family, Ireland, and the Church. Stephen's alternative faith is one in which the artist is God the Father, God the Son, and God the Holy Spirit, his own family and community as well as transcendent being. This new vision is born out of the failure of the former orthodoxy, which, as Joyce presents it, has become effete and corrupt, a religion of empty forms and endless hypocrisies. Its priesthood is composed of liars, bullies, drunkards, dullwits, and false rhetoricians. Some of the spokesmen for this moribund establishment speak for Church, some for Ireland, and some for the family; but all are the Pharisees of the *status quo*. Smug or shortsighted, they propagate the cant of a faith which, through Joyce's meticulous rendition, the reader must reject as decadent while applauding the prophet who can proclaim a gospel of regeneration. The moment of that prophet is at hand when Stephen sees (or seems to see) the image of the winged Daedalus and undergoes his ecstatic conversion.

The analogue between the development of Stephen's New Testament and that of first-century Christianity is striking and significant. Forgetting for a moment the idea that Stephen is both creator and incarnate word, let us consider him as a convert become exegete, the St. Paul of his own divine revelation; for in the spiritual journey of Saul of Tarsus is embodied the fullest range of the religious founding that Joyce imitates in this novel, the movement from absolute commitment to the old order to a creative formulation of the theology of the new.

As Stephen becomes in early maturity the chief pride of his Jesuit instructors, so was Paul a brilliant and dedicated Pharisee who held the coats of those who stoned the first Christian martyr. Yet on the road to Damascus Paul was struck blind by the brilliance of Christ's image and immediately submitted without question to a truth he had previously denied with all his considerable intellectual resources. At that moment, drained of theology, he gave himself completely to the all-absorbing other-than-self. As I have already suggested, precisely the same thing happens to Stephen Dedalus.

Yet for Paul and for Stephen, the moment of ecstasy cannot be indefinitely prolonged, but the significance of the truth revealed is followed in both instances by exegesis, a process in which the reason analyzes and then synthesizes the meaning of the irrational revelation. Paul, after regaining his sight, begins to reflect on the life of Jesus and His reported words; and in his Epistles (particularly in *Romans*) he spends much of his time quarreling with the old religion, in order to define the new. Yet as a Jew, trained by "the party of circumcision," his understanding of the new is articulated most often in the terms and rhetoric of the old.

And the same is true of Stephen Dedalus, whose exegesis is grounded in the theology of the faith he has rejected. "McAlister," he says "would call my aesthetic theory applied Aquinas. So far as this side of aesthetic philosophy extends, Aquinas will carry me all along the line. When we come to the phenomena of artistic conception, artistic gestation and artistic reproduction, I require a new terminology and a new personal experience." [11] And so he should, for the two must, of necessity, go hand in hand. Yet the key word in this passage is "personal." Paul's revelation could by no means be termed a pure illumination of self. Indeed his ego was largely submerged in the image of Christ (though there are those who say it surfaces from time to time in a kind of fastidious priggery). But with Stephen the expression of self is the ultimate devotional act. If there is any muse, it is *his* muse rather than *the* muse; and no one else may lay claim to her.

Thus in his arguments with the Pharisees of Ireland he insists on the ultimate supremacy of the so-called "creative act," which he believes must take place outside the community of family, church, and nation. As he puts it in one dogmatic statement to his foil Davin, "The soul is born first in the moments I told you of. It has a slow and dark birth, more mysterious than the birth of the body. When the soul of a man is born in this country there are nets flung at it to hold it back from flight. You talk to me of nationality, language, religion. I shall try to fly by those nets."

Again the image of flight with its echoes of the cuckoo tale, the Daedalus myth, the legend of Horus. But here the mystical experience of flying becomes a trope in discourse, the occasion for a programmatic statement on the creation as defined by the new orthodoxy. And so it goes with Stephen as he contends with adversary after adversary, vanquishing them with an ease that belies the complexity of the positions they advocate. (We might all wish for philosophical opponents so muddle-headed and inarticulate!)

Yet in his last encounter, he meets a formidable peer in his friend Cranly, who is able to teach him the limitations of his own arrogant intellect. The occasion of this final dialogue is initiated by Stephen himself, who, despite his frequent declarations of independence, is deeply troubled by a family quarrel.

—With your people? Cranly asked.
—With my mother.
—About religion?
—Yes, Stephen answered. After a pause Cranly asked:
—What age is your mother?
—Not old, Stephen said. She wishes me to make my easter duty.
—And will you?
—I will not, Stephen said.
—Why not? Cranly said.

—I will not serve, answered Stephen.
—That remark was made before, Cranly said calmly.
—It is made behind now, said Stephen hotly.[12]

Cranly immediately gains the upper hand in this initial segment of the conversation; for not only does he maintain his equanimity, but he also puts his finger precisely on the pressure point of Stephen's rebellious nature: "I will not serve" is the devil's line, and anyone who refuses to live within the constituted limitation of God's autonomy is by definition satanic. Cranly is calm in pointing out the truth because for him it is no shocking discovery: he already knows his friend well. But the interesting thing about the brief exchange is the manner in which Stephen reacts to Cranly's remark. Instead of being amused or coldly contemptuous, he is angered to the point of responding with a silly and ineffectual play on words. Why should the charge of diabolism so disturb him if he has rejected the Church and its dogma? Cranly pursues this question with Jesuitical skill, determining that Stephen neither believes nor disbelieves in the Eucharist and is unwilling to attempt a resolution of this crucial dilemma, largely because in his intellectual pride he is pleased with the new man he has become. The dishonesty of his position is apparent, particularly in light of the pain he causes his mother in refusing to make his communion. Cranly presses him on the issue, first testing him with a statement that Jesus may have been a charlatan, then noting Stephen's manifest shock and asking, "And why were you shocked if you feel sure that our religion is false and that Jesus was not the Son of God?" When Stephen equivocates, Cranly raises essentially the same question in a more sharply focused formulation: "And is that why you will not communicate, because you are not sure of that too, because you feel that the host too may be the body and blood of the son of God and not a wafer of bread? And because you fear that it may be?" "Yes," replied Stephen, "I feel that and I also fear it." "I see," says Cranly.[13]

And so do we. The rebellion, the rejection of the old faith, the mystical revelation, the carefully devised theology—they are all part of a fragile and tenuous system that might well fall to pieces under close and persistent scrutiny. "But does it matter," one is tempted to ask, "if Stephen is skeptical in regard to the Church and credulous in his dedication to the religion of art?" The answer to this question should be clear from Stephen's attitude toward his Easter duty and from his later replies to Cranly: his peculiar commitment to art is born of extravagant pride, pride in his own intellectual integrity; yet it is obviously impossible for any honest thinker to enthrone an ideal and absolute freedom in his heart without first disposing of the other question, the truth or falsity of Christian revelation. For if the eucharist is the body and blood of Jesus Christ, then the artist cannot "recreate life out of life" or "refuse to serve." And an unwillingness to pursue this question is no more or less than a refusal to confront the ultimate lie of his life.

This attitude, of course, is typical of the gnostic, as Voegelin has pointed out:

> The gnostic thinker really does commit an intellectual swindle, and he knows it. One can distinguish three stages in the action of his spirit. On the surface lies the deception itself. It could be self-deception; and very often it is when the speculation of a creative thinker has culturally degenerated and become the dogma of a mass movement. But when the phenomenon is apprehended at its point of origin, deeper than the deception itself will be found the awareness of it. The

thinker does not lose control of himself: the *libido dominandi* turns on its own work and wishes to master the deception as well. This gnostic turning back on itself corresponds spiritually, as we have said, to the philosophical conversion, the *periagoge* in the Platonic sense. However, the gnostic movement of the spirit does not lead to the erotic opening of the soul, but rather to the deepest reach of persistence in the deception, whose revolt against God is revealed to be its motive and purpose.[14]

And, as if to prove Voegelin's thesis some thirty-five years before its publication in *Science, Politics and Gnosticism,* Stephen flees from Cranly back into the narrow and comfortable confines of his gnosis, betraying once again the deceitful nature of his flight: "I will not serve that in which I no longer believe whether it call itself my home, my fatherland, or my church: and I will try to express myself in some mode of life or art as freely as I can and as wholly as I can, using for my defense the only arms I allow myself to use—silence, exile, and cunning." [15]

No more perfect analogue to Satan could exist in a work of realistic fiction, and thus he retreats from the only discursive encounter of the novel in which the question of the constitution of being is placed squarely in the path of his perilous journey. Significantly, this combat is his last. Henceforth he will speak not to others but to himself, in a diary which epitomizes his struggle to sustain the self-illusion. And the last two entries signal his success as a practicing gnostic, whatever his occasional horror at the vision of damnation, an old man with "red-rimmed horny eyes." In his valedictory he tells us that he will persist in worshipping the God of self and to recreate self out of self in order to devise some object for adoration: "Welcome, O life, I go to encounter for the millionth time the reality of experience and to forge in the smithy of my soul the uncreated conscience of my race ... Old father, old artificer, stand me now and forever in good stead." [16]

Who is he at the end of this novel? Is he Daedalus or Icarus? Is this narrative the portrait of the triumphant artist-as-hero or is it the portrait of a damned soul? The critics who have best addressed themselves to this ultimate question, Walter Sullivan and Caroline Gordon, disagree on whether or not the author and the hero are to be equated, though both understand Stephen's story as rooted in impiety. Mr. Sullivan is firm and terse in his conclusion: "Stephen is Joyce." Miss Gordon, on the other hand, seems to say that Joyce's obvious contempt for Stephen continues throughout the narrative beginning with an ironic stance toward the child and ending with the final paragraphs in which the hero's damnation is rendered as deplorable and even tragic.[17] How, then, are we to resolve such an argument in the light of the novel's apparent gnostic implications?

In the first place, I would argue that if Miss Gordon is correct, then Joyce has misapplied his considerable talents as a rhetorician; for those passages which display the full range of his lyric prose are the ones which celebrate Stephen's aesthetic ecstasies, while, with the exception of the Cranly segment, he reserves his keenest irony for scenes in which he renders spokesmen for the old order.

But more importantly, Joyce's structuring of the action makes clear the meaning of his narrative. He spends too many pages of his novel in denigration of the spokesmen for family, Ireland, and church to untie all his intricate knots with one scene featuring Cranly's well-executed attack. However Miss Gordon—all of us—might wish Joyce to be Daedalus, grieving

for his fallen son but himself redeemed, we must finally conclude that at this stage of his career, like Stephen, he has mastered the finer techniques of gnostic self-deception and has been trapped by the artifice of his own creative imagination, the monumental achievement that both tells his life's story and intimates its inherent tragedy.

"Free. Soul free and fancy free. Let the dead bury the dead."[18] This is the new Christ speaking, Stephen/Joyce, the redeemer of self; and we the readers who are allowed into the sanctum sanctorum of his inner soul must listen to his voice in hushed adoration. For it is his spirit that has bridged the gap of years and informed the time in which we live. The rhetoric of freedom so prevalent in our decade is only in part the result of the political revolutions of the eighteenth century. The kind of freedom people speak of today is more likely than not the freedom of Stephen Dedalus and James Joyce, which is something more than emancipation from political tyranny. It is freedom from social custom, freedom from family, freedom from tradition, freedom from church, freedom from the other-than-self, freedom from the created order, freedom from God. And if we as a generation believe passionately and absolutely in this beautiful, impalpable, imperishable illusion, we may in part thank James Joyce for our troubling faith.

NOTES

[1] Eric Voegelin, *Science, Politics and Gnosticism* (Chicago: Henry Regnery Company, 1968), p. 9.
[2] James Joyce, *A Portrait of the Artist as a Young Man* (New York: The Viking Press, 1964), p. 7.
[3] See John Kelleher, "The Perceptions of James Joyce," *The Atlantic Monthly* (March, 1958), 86.
[4] Joyce, p. 169.
[5] *Ibid.*
[6] *Ibid.*, p. 170.

7 *Ibid.*, p. 169.

8 *Ibid.*, p. 171.

9 *Ibid.*, pp. 171–172.

10 Walter Sullivan, *Death by Melancholy: Essays on Modern Southern Fiction* (Baton Rouge: Louisiana State University Press, 1972), pp. 97–113.

11 Joyce, p. 209.

12 *Ibid.*, pp. 238–239.

13 *Ibid.*, p. 243.

14 Voegelin, pp. 32–33.

15 Joyce, pp. 246–247.

16 *Ibid.*, p. 253.

17 Caroline Gordon, *How to Read a Novel* (New York: The Viking Press, 1957), pp. 210–214.

18 Joyce, p. 248.

[XXIII, Spring 1979, 145–153]

Epilogue

[78]

Modern Age
in a Changing World

ANTHONY HARRIGAN

Anthony (Hart) Harrigan (1925–   ), president of the USIC Educational Foundation in Washington, D.C., has been a member of the advisory board of Modern Age *since 1957. Since 1970, he has written a column syndicated in approximately 300 newspapers. A graduate of Bard College, where Bernard Iddings Bell had once been warden and Albert Jay Nock a professor, he is the author of numerous books, including* A Guide to the War in Vietnam *(1965) and* Defense Against Total Attack *(1966), as well as a frequent writer on defense issues for professional military journals in the United States, Germany, France, and the Netherlands. He has lectured at the U.S. National War College and has been the recipient of the Military Review Award given by the U.S. Army Command and General Staff College, Fort Leavenworth.*

THE AMERICA OF 1982 is far removed from the consciousness and mood of 1957, the year *Modern Age* was founded. So much has happened in the United States and the world since that year. It is difficult to recapture the world of the late nineteen-fifties. The necessities and concerns of that period have faded with time. As always, reentering an epoch, to capture its essence, is an arduous task.

From our perspective in the early 1980s, 1957 was a halcyon year. How happy we would be if we could return to the relatively simple problems of that period, if we had the national position, strength and unity that characterized 1957. At the time, of course, we thought that our country and civilization were confronted with the worst of problems and the greatest of

dangers. Everything was simpler then, however. Dwight Eisenhower was President. At the time, we didn't realize that the Eisenhower years would be regarded as a happy, comfortable, mellow interlude in the grim 20th century. Abroad, the United States was in a position of tremendous strength. U.S. superiority in nuclear arms was unquestioned, as was American seapower. John Foster Dulles directed U.S. foreign policy with skill and determination, building a powerful network of alliances. To be sure, however, American policy was not conducted without mistakes. Perhaps the worst was Mr. Eisenhower's failure to support our allies in the Suez crisis, a decision that opened the way to Europe's disastrous retreat from Africa. We had the opportunity to assure a much longer period of European ascendancy in Africa and Asia, which would have been immensely beneficial to the people of what has come to be known as the Third World. In 1959, President Eisenhower would make another fateful error when he allowed a Marxist revolutionary to seize power in Cuba on America's national doorstep. If *Modern Age* had been founded a decade earlier, and, if it had been able to work its influence on our foreign policy, mistakes of this type might have been avoided.

At home, the United States was in the midst of a great social and constitutional upheaval as a result of the termination of legal segregation in schools, public accommodation and employment. Social change was inevitable, but the court decisions involved brought stress and turmoil and were destructive of public education. The Warren Court of the period played havoc with public order in the United States. This havoc has persisted for 25 years, with liberal activism on the bench fueling enormous tensions in American society, promoting lawlessness and social dissidence, and creating a heritage of resentment for the intrusions into matters that are the province of the local community or the family. Over the years, *Modern Age* has addressed these matters in a dignified, scholarly and authoritative way.

Twenty-five years ago America's wealth was unrivaled. Japan was but a puny, struggling industrial power, not the giant it is today. J. M. Reid, editor of the *Glasgow Herald*, writing in the first issue of the review, noted that America was regarded as "a land of colossal wealth and luxury, of millionaires, skyscraping penthouses, and prodigious automobiles." No one in 1957 envisioned an America held hostage to the oil kingdoms of the Middle East, reeling under Japanese competition, with a near-crippled automotive industry, and with depressed cities.

Man's vision always is limited. In 1957,

we could not foresee the massive immigration from Mexico, the Caribbean and Southeast Asia, which is changing the character of the nation. We could not have imagined defeat at arms in Vietnam, the contraction of our fleet, a communist beachhead in Central America, the collapse of African colonies and protectorates into 45 unstable nations.

While we couldn't envision all the things to come in the future, those of us who cheered the emergence of *Modern Age* recognized basic problems that would confront Americans and Europeans in the years ahead. From the beginning, *Modern Age* focused on the dangers of totalitarianism and nihilism—the twin evils of the 20th century. Indeed contributors to *Modern Age*, over a period of a quarter-century, have recognized that there is an enduring cold war between East and West because the Soviet Union is the permanent enemy of liberty. *Modern Age* has never wavered in its analysis of the threat posed by the armed ideology of the Soviet Union. This is a notable achievement when one bears in mind that so great a part of the Western intelligentsia has yielded to the notion that an accommodation with the Soviet empire is possible. And it is well for younger readers of the review to understand that the rich texture of analysis of the Soviet Union, from which we now benefit, existed in only small part when *Modern Age* was established. Much of that texture of analysis and understanding was created by contributions to the new review.

The original list of editorial advisers and contributors to *Modern Age* made up a considerable part of the conservative intellectual community that existed in the mid-1950s. Many of these writers continue to make important scholarly contributions, scholars such as Slobodan M. Draskovich and Erik von Kuehnelt-Leddihn. Others, such as Bernard Iddings Bell, Donald Davidson and David McCord

Wright, are virtually unknown to a new generation of conservatives. B. I. Bell was one of our most brilliant writers on education, a thinker in the vein of Dean W. R. Inge, an exemplar of the Anglican conservative tradition. Donald Davidson, whom I had the pleasure of meeting during the South's turbulent period of social change, was a Southern man of letters, a philosopher of an agrarian society, who combined rare gifts as a historian and literary figure. David McCord Wright was one of my professors at the University of Virginia in 1949. We had friends in common and shared family roots in Charleston, South Carolina. At a time when liberal economics were riding high in American universities, David stressed many of the themes that have been incorporated in Reaganomics. His untimely death deprived the nation of a pioneering free market economist.

One of the happiest features of *Modern Age* over a quarter-century has been the welcome it extends to scholars from all regions of the United States and to those who have come to these shores from Europe. This wasn't customary a generation ago. Many intellectual journals seemed to be the private possession of small coteries; writers from the Middle West and South were treated as provincials. *Modern Age* introduced a wider, more comprehensive intellectual tradition than existed in New York and Boston. Another happy result of the serious, fair and enlightened editorial direction of the review by Russell Kirk and David Collier was that *Modern Age* never became the creature of any intellectual fad or dogma. While economics has received the most informed attention, the review has not been dominated by those who believe that life can be explained in its totality by the influence of economic theory. And while the importance of religion in Western civilization has been a central theme of the review, *Modern Age* has avoided the sec-

tarian spirit. As Russell Kirk noted in his initial statement, "We are not ideologists: we do not believe we have all the remedies for all the ills to which flesh is heir." This wise outlook has colored the review down through the years.

The guidelines established for *Modern Age* in 1957 are as sound today as they were a quarter-century ago. Its current readership undoubtedly shares the view of the founders who declared "We confess to a prejudice against doctrinaire radical alteration, and to a preference for the wisdom of our ancestors." Heaven knows it has been difficult to reconcile this prejudice and preference to a quarter-century of bewildering and hurtful change. After so much buffeting in the 60s and 70s, it is almost a surprise to find that we have a conservative interlude in this country, a time when the liberal ideologists aren't the dominant force. Nevertheless, we must not think that this more conservative period will continue indefinitely. The disorders of the 20th century have not run their course. Internally, the United States is still in a state of considerable disarray. The excessive mobility of our population has destroyed or weakened the sense of community for millions of people. With the decline in community has come a breakdown of civility. There has been a widespread brutalization of society through what can only be referred to as a new paganism, as evidenced in the spread of pornography. These and other developments bode ill for the maintenance, let alone restoration, of civilized values. Indeed, we face a long battle for the mind and soul of the nation. Those who "confess to a prejudice against doctrinaire radical alteration, and to a preference for the wisdom of our ancestors" will not have an easy time in the next 25 years.

Those Americans who recognize the dangers of a statist economy undoubtedly will also confront new threats in the years ahead. The wealth that J. M. Reid cited in 1957 has been severely eroded by indolence, waste of resources through welfarism, unwise disbursements to Third World countries, the excessive growth of government and monopoly unionism. As a result of these practices and developments, America's industrial power has declined. We are less competitive and innovative and consequently are in a poorer overall position to provide for the needs of our people. Moreover, we live in a world of startling change. Our domestic market is the target of countries with subsidized, guided and directed economies. We haven't recognized the economic offensives mounted by Japan and European countries with state-owned or nationalized enterprises. Economic theory in this country must be adjusted to these new international economic realities. If we fail to adjust our thinking, we could become a second-class economic power in the world during the next quarter-century, with ominous results for our security. It is important that *Modern Age* devote considerable attention to the changing economic conditions and practices in the world.

The challenges for the review in the next quarter-century are the challenges facing American life and thought. The Soviet Union and its operations—and its impact upon the thoughts and fears of the Western world—must be an abiding concern. At the same time, readers of this review will need informed discussion of the full range of global possibilities. The world of the 1980s is much more complex than the world of the late 1950s. Much of the globe was inactive a quarter century ago. The so-called emerging nations were still backwaters of history. Even the older, established nations of Latin America were quiet spots. Today, the more than 150 nations are caught up in a variety of economic, political and ideological processes. For one thing, population growth is surging—even as food production declines or is static. The importance of oil has given enormous new strength to countries that were devoid of activity or dynamism. Old ties between nations are being broken and new links are being formed. Greece, for example, is a socialist nation that's pulling away from the West. South Korea has become a formidable industrial power. Japan is deeply involved in the development of Australia's natural resources. Poland has broken away, psychologically at least, from the Soviet Empire. The Soviet Union, for all its military might, is unable to produce food in sufficient quantity to feed its people. It must draw on the agricultural abundance of the United States, Canada and Argentina. It is, truly, a changing world with many new factors to consider in arriving at a strategic estimate of global power.

The United States faces internal and external problems one could not have imagined in 1957. Perhaps the most far-reaching change affecting the United States is the change in the scope and character of immigration. From 1965 to the mid-seventies, immigration to America was around 400,000 a year. Last year, if illegal aliens are counted, it may have totaled 1.25 million a year—substantially greater than the one million entries recorded by 1907. The vast majority of these immigrants are coming from Latin America, with a very substantial number (about 30 per cent) from Southeast Asia. Immigration from Western Europe has slowed to a trickle.

If this level of immigration is continued, our population will rise to 274 million in 2000 and 409 million in 2080. Demographer Leon Bouvier, writing for the Population Reference Bureau, notes that 40 per cent of the 2080 population would be post-1980 immigrants or their descendants. Eighty-five per cent will be from Spanish-speaking lands. Neal R. Peirce, writing in the *Washington Post*, observes that "bilingualism and biculturalism could well tear at the cohesion of America that has been built, at least in part, on the use of a common language, English."

To maintain our established culture under the impact of massive immigration from Latin America, the Caribbean and Southeast Asia will be an enormously difficult task in the next 25 years. This may be our greatest challenge as a nation.

The world will be a disturbed and turbulent place in the next quarter-century. The captive peoples of the Soviet Union will be profoundly restive; Poland is but the first country to experience this. The old Soviet solution of shipping people to Siberia won't work for the Soviets at a time when they will need skilled and mobilized populations to create food and manufactured goods. A decade ago, I heard Richard Helms, then director of the Central Intelligence Agency, warn of the population explosion in Latin America. He was correct in his analysis. Today, we face the spectre of a Bangladesh on our southern border. The Southeast Asian boat people may be only the first of many such peoples who seek to reach us by sea. And who knows what will happen in the Middle East, where the pressures on Israel are intensifying year by year and the country's position becomes more insecure? In the Caribbean, the Haitians may be only the first to attempt a flight to the American mainland.

For a nation of immigrants, it is difficult, even agonizing to close the door to refugees. Nevertheless, it must be done if the United States is not to be trampled, if we are, as Mr. Peirce has said, "to maintain our standard of living and known culture."

The United States approaches this and other problems with serious handicaps, namely a weakened economy, an improving but still weakened defense structure, and all the stresses and strains that result from a society that has lost much of the unity and cultural identity that it had at mid-century. We ought to be consoled, however, by the fact that other nations, including our adversaries, face equally serious handicaps as they struggle for survival and primacy. Moreover, we still enjoy the blessing of liberty and continue to believe that our freedom is more of a strength than what one War of Independence writer referred to as "the sheltered discipline of despots."

The task of intellectual and moral preparation and restoration in which *Modern Age* has been engaged for 25 years is an ongoing task. We must continue to search for ways in which to apply basic principles and tested truths to new situations facing our country and civilization. As a people, we have a continuing task of relating contemporary modes of life to ancient principles. In the midst of the flux of history, we must pursue and uphold the permanent things. Our nation's survival in a threatening world will depend on our ability to understand what is happening elsewhere on this planet and to build on our strengths at every opportunity. No nation arrives at a plateau of security and well-being on which there aren't any threats. We must understand and accept that. The splendid isolation we once enjoyed is gone forever. Our ability to survive, prosper and possess security against foreign attack or a humiliating retreat to a minor status will depend on our will, intelligence, comprehension of the meaning of world events, and principled behavior. Ours has been such a happy lot during our more than 200 years as a nation. We must do everything possible to ensure future generations of Americans an equally blessed existence. If we employ right reason in addressing foreign threats, domestic problems and our inner life as a people, we may achieve our goal in this respect. In this search, study and mission, *Modern Age* has an important role to play.

[XXVI, Summer/Fall 1982, 350–353]

The text of this book is set in Baskerville, a transitional typeface created in the middle of the eighteenth century by John Baskerville (1706–1775), a Birmingham, England, type-founder and printer. Characterized by its vertical stress and crisply defined thick and thin strokes, the typeface influenced the later development of English and European type-forms and has been a popular book face in the United States for more than fifty years.

Editorial services by Harkavy Publishing Service,
New York, New York
Book design by Madelaine Cooke, Athens, Georgia
Typography by Monotype Composition Co., Inc.,
Baltimore, Maryland
Printed and bound by Edwards Brothers Company, Inc.,
Ann Arbor, Michigan